HISTORY OF THE CHRISTIAN CHURCH

HISTORY

OF THE

CHRISTIAN CHURCH

BY

PHILIP SCHAFF

Christianus sum. Christiani nihil a me alienum puto

VOLUME V

THE MIDDLE AGES

FROM GREGORY VII., 1049, TO BONIFACE VIII., 1294

BY

DAVID S. SCHAFF, D.D.

PROFESSOR OF CHURCH HISTORY IN THE WESTERN
THEOLOGICAL SEMINARY, ALLEGHENY

WM. B. EERDMANS PUBLISHING COMPANY

GRAND RAPIDS   MICHIGAN

PHOTOLITHOPRINTED BY EERDMANS PRINTING COMPANY
GRAND RAPIDS, MICHIGAN, UNITED STATES OF AMERICA

PREFACE.

It was the constant hope of Dr. Philip Schaff, the author of the HISTORY OF THE CHRISTIAN CHURCH, that he might live to finish the treatment of the Middle Ages, to which he had devoted one volume, covering the years 600–1050. He frequently said, during the last years of his life, "If I am able to accomplish this, my HISTORY OF THE CHRISTIAN CHURCH will be measurably complete and I will be satisfied then to stop." He entered upon the task and had completed his studies on the pontificates of Gregory VII. and Alexander III., when his pen was laid aside and death overtook him, Oct. 20, 1893. The two volumes found lying open on his study table, as he had left them the day before, Jeremy Taylor's HOLY LIVING AND HOLY DYING and a volume of Hurter's LIFE OF INNOCENT III., showed the nature of his thoughts in his last hours.

Dr. Schaff's distinction as a writer on Church History dated from the year 1851 when his HISTORY OF THE APOSTOLIC CHURCH appeared, first in its original German form, Mercersburg, Pa., pp. xvi, 576, and Leipzig, 1853, and then in English translation, New York and Edinburgh, 1853, 1854. Before that time, he had shown his taste for historical studies in his tract on WHAT IS CHURCH HISTORY? translated by Dr. John W. Nevin, Phila., 1846, pp. 128, and the address on the PRINCIPLE OF PROTESTANTISM, which he delivered at his inauguration as professor in the theological seminary at Mercersburg, 1844. This address was published in its German form and in an English translation by Dr. Nevin, Chambersburg, 1845.

Dr. Schaff continued his publications in this department with the issue of his HISTORY OF THE CHRISTIAN CHURCH, 1–600, in 2 volumes, N.Y., 1858–1867. In the meantime, his attention had been called to the subjects of biblical literature and exegesis, and his labors resulted in the publication of the American edition of Lange's Commentary in 25 volumes and other works. In 1887 he issued his CREEDS OF CHRISTENDOM in 3 volumes. Left free to devote himself to the continuation of his HISTORY, which he was inclined to regard as his chief literary work, he found it necessary, in order to keep abreast of the times and to present a fresh treatment, to begin his studies again at the very beginning and consequently the series, to which this volume belongs, is an independent work written afresh and differing in marked features from its predecessors. For example, the first volume, on the Apostolic age, devotes an extensive treatment to the authorship and dates of the Apostolic writings to which scarcely any space was given in the HISTORY OF THE APOSTOLIC CHURCH of 1851 and the HISTORY OF THE CHRISTIAN CHURCH of 1858–1867. The treatment was demanded by the new attitude of scholarship to the questions presented by the Apostolic age.

Dr. Schaff lived to prepare six volumes of this new work, three on early Christianity, one on mediæval Christianity, and two on the Protestant Reformation. It is of some interest that Dr. Schaff's last writing was a pamphlet on the Reunion of Christendom, pp. 71, a subject which he treated with warm practical sympathy and with materials furnished by the studies of the historian. The substance of the pamphlet had been used as a paper read before the Parliament of Religions at the Columbian Exposition, Chicago. It was a great satisfaction to him to have the Faculty of the Berlin University, — where he had spent part of his student life, 1840–1841, and which had conferred on him the doctorate of divinity in 1854, — bear testimony in their congratulatory letter on the semicentennial of his professorial career that his "HISTORY OF THE CHRISTIAN CHURCH is the most notable monument of universal historical learning produced by the school of Neander" (LIFE OF PHILIP SCHAFF, p. 467).

The further treatment of the Middle Ages, Dr. Schaff left to his son, the author of this volume. It was deemed by him best to begin the work anew, using the materials Dr. Schaff had left as the basis of the first four chapters.

The delay in the issue of the present volume is due chiefly to the requirements of study and in part to the difficulty in getting all the necessary literature. The author has felt unwilling to issue the volume without giving to it as thorough study as it was possible for him to give. This meant that he should familiarize himself not only with the mediæval writings themselves but with the vast amount of research which has been devoted to the Middle Ages during the last quarter of a century and more. As for the literature, not a little of it has been, until recently, inaccessible to the student in this country. At Lane seminary, where the author was a professor, he found in the library an unusually well selected collection of works on the mediæval period made fifty years ago by the wise judgment of two of its professors, Calvin E. Stowe and the late George E. Day, who made tours in Europe for the purpose of making purchases for its shelves. He also owes a debt to the Rev. Dr. Henry Goodwin Smith, for some time professor in the seminary and its librarian, for his liberal use of the library funds in supplementing the works in the mediæval department. In passing, it may be also said that the Cincinnati Public Library, by reason of a large permanent fund given more than a half century ago for the purchase of theological works and by the wise selection of such men as Professor George E. Day, is unusually rich in works for the historical student, some of which may perhaps not be duplicated in this country.

On removing to the Western Theological seminary, the author found
its librarian, Professor James A. Kelso, most ready to fill up the shelves
of the mediæval department so that it now possesses all the more important works both original and secondary.   To the librarians of the
two Roman Catholic libraries of Cincinnati and to other librarians the
author is indebted for the courtesy of the free use of their collections.

An explanation is due for devoting an entire volume to the middle
period of the Middle Ages, 1050–1294, when it was the intention of
Dr. Philip Schaff to embrace it and the third period of the Middle Ages,
1294–1517, in a single volume.   It is doubtful whether Dr. Schaff, after
proceeding with his studies, would have thought it wise to attempt to
execute his original purpose.   However this might have been, to have
confined the treatment of 500 years to the limits of a single volume would
have meant to do a relative injustice and, in the light of recent study, to
have missed a proper proportion.   To the first 600 years, 1–590, the
HISTORY devotes three volumes.   Dr. Schaff intended to devote three
volumes to the Protestant Reformation, two of which he lived to prepare.
The intervening 900 years deserve an equal amount of space.   The period
covered by this volume is of great importance.   Here belong the Crusades, the rejuvenation of monasticism by the mendicant orders, the
development of the canon law, the rise of the universities, the determined
struggles of the papacy with the empire, the development of the Inquisition, the settlement of the sacramental system, and some of the most
notable characters the Christian Church has produced.   No one can fully
understand the spirit and doctrinal system of the Roman communion
without knowing this period.   Nor can any one, without such knowledge, fully understand the meaning of the Protestant Reformation, for
the Reformation was a protest against the mediæval theology and mediæval practices.   The best evidence for the truth of the latter statement is
found in the work of the learned Dominican Denifle, entitled *Luther und
Lutherthum*, and the Protestant rejoinders to its assaults.

A partial list of the more modern works show the amount of study that
has recently been spent upon this period.   Among the great collections
of mediæval documents, besides the older ones by Mabillon, Muratori,
and Migne, are the MONUMENTA GERMANIÆ, intended to give an exhaustive collection of mediæval German writers, the series of collections
of the papal documents called the REGESTA, edited by Jaffé, Potthast,
Auvray, Berger, and others, the CHARTULARIUM UNIVERSITATIS PARI-
SIENSIS, a collection of documents edited by Denifle and Chatelain of the
highest importance for the study of the university system, the RECUEIL
DES HISTORIENS DES CROISADES, the remarkable collection of mediæval
sacred poetry edited by Dreves and Blume filling about 15 volumes, the
Boehmer-Friedberg edition of the Canon Law, and the Rolls Series, containing the writers of mediæval England.   To such works must be
added the new editions of Schoolmen, Albertus Magnus by Borgnet,

Bonaventura by Peltier, Duns Scotus and Thomas Aquinas, and the editions of such writers as Cæsar of Heisterbach, De Voragine, Salimbene, and Etienne de Bourbon. Among the recent students who have made a specialty of this period are Giesebrecht, Gregorovius, Scheffer-Boichorst, Karl Müller, Hauck, Deutsch, Lempp, and other Protestants of Germany, and among German Catholic scholars Döllinger, Father Denifle, Ehrle, Knöpfler, Schwane, Schulte, Funk, and Felder. In France we have Rémusat, Hauréau, Chevalier, Vacandard, Sabatier, Alphandéry. In England and America, we have Dr. Henry Charles Lea, who deserves to be mentioned first, the late Bp. Stubbs, R. L. Poole, Rashdall, Bridges, the editors of the Rolls Series, such as Brewer and Luard, and Prof. D. C. Munro, O. T. Thatcher, and Shailer Mathews.

Except in rare cases, the quotations are taken from the original works, whether they were written in the Middle Ages or are modern discussions. An exception is the *History of the City of Rome* by Gregorovius. It has required severe discipline to check the inclination to extend the notes to a far greater length than they have been carried, especially in such chapters as those on the sacramental system and the Schoolmen. In the tables of literature, the more important modern works have at times been indicated by a star, *.

In the preparation of the volume for the press, efficient aid has been rendered by the Rev. David E. Culley, fellow and tutor in the Western Theological seminary, whose literary and historical tastes and sober judgment have been confirmed by studies abroad.

The second part of this volume, carrying the history from Boniface VIII. to the Reformation, is in an advanced stage of preparation.

In closing, the author indulges the hope that Dr. Philip Schaff's spirit of toleration may be found permeating this volume, and its general historic judgments to be such as Dr. Schaff himself would have expressed.

DAVID S. SCHAFF.

The Western Theological Seminary,
Allegheny, Pa.

CONTENTS.

FROM GREGORY VII. TO BONIFACE VIII. 1049 TO 1294.

		PAGE
§ 1.	GENERAL LITERATURE	1
§ 2.	INTRODUCTORY SURVEY	3

CHAPTER I. THE HILDEBRANDIAN POPES. 1049-1073.

§ 3.	SOURCES AND LITERATURE ON CHAPTERS I. AND II.	7
§ 4.	HILDEBRAND AND HIS TRAINING	9
§ 5.	HILDEBRAND AND LEO IX. 1049-1054	13
§ 6.	VICTOR II. AND STEPHEN IX. (X.) 1055-1058	15
§ 7.	NICOLAS II. AND THE CARDINALS. 1059-1061	16
§ 8.	THE WAR AGAINST CLERICAL MARRIAGE	20
§ 9.	ALEXANDER II. AND THE SCHISM OF CADALUS. 1061-1073	21

CHAPTER II. GREGORY VII. 1073-1085.

§ 10.	HILDEBRAND ELECTED POPE. HIS VIEWS ON THE SITUATION	24
§ 11.	THE GREGORIAN THEOCRACY	27
§ 12.	GREGORY VII. AS A MORAL REFORMER	36
§ 13.	THE ENFORCEMENT OF SACERDOTAL CELIBACY	39
§ 14.	THE WAR OVER INVESTITURE	45
§ 15.	GREGORY VII. AND HENRY IV.	47
§ 16.	CANOSSA. 1077	53
§ 17.	RENEWAL OF THE CONFLICT. TWO KINGS AND TWO POPES	59
§ 18.	DEATH OF GREGORY VII.	64

CHAPTER III. THE PAPACY FROM THE DEATH OF GREGORY VII. TO THE CONCORDAT OF WORMS. 1085-1122.

§ 19.	VICTOR III. AND URBAN II. 1086-1099	70
§ 20.	PASCAL II. AND HENRY V. 1099-1118	73
§ 21.	THE CONCORDAT OF WORMS. 1122	77
§ 22.	THE CONFLICT OF THE HIERARCHY IN ENGLAND	80
§ 23.	WILLIAM RUFUS AND ANSELM	87
§ 24.	ANSELM AND HENRY I.	90

CHAPTER IV. THE PAPACY FROM THE CONCORDAT OF WORMS TO INNOCENT III. 1122-1198.

§ 25.	INNOCENT II. AND EUGENIUS III.	94
§ 26.	ARNOLD OF BRESCIA	96
§ 27.	THE POPES AND THE HOHENSTAUFEN	102
§ 28.	ADRIAN IV. AND FREDERICK BARBAROSSA	105
§ 29.	ALEXANDER III. IN CONFLICT WITH BARBAROSSA	110
§ 30.	THE PEACE OF VENICE. 1177	115
§ 31.	THOMAS BECKET AND HENRY II. OF ENGLAND	120

PAGE

§ 32. THE ARCHBISHOP AND THE KING   128
§ 33. THE MARTYRDOM OF THOMAS BECKET. DEC. 29, 1170   .   . 140
§ 34. THE EFFECTS OF BECKET'S MURDER 144

CHAPTER V. INNOCENT III. AND HIS AGE. 1198–1216.

§ 35. LITERATURE 151
§ 36. INNOCENT'S TRAINING AND ELECTION 152
§ 37. INNOCENT'S THEORY OF THE PAPACY 156
§ 38. INNOCENT AND THE GERMAN EMPIRE 160
§ 39. INNOCENT AND KING JOHN OF ENGLAND   165
§ 40. INNOCENT AND MAGNA CHARTA 171
§ 41. THE FOURTH LATERAN COUNCIL, 1215   174

CHAPTER VI. THE PAPACY FROM THE DEATH OF INNOCENT III.
TO BONIFACE VIII. 1216–1294.

§ 42. THE PAPAL CONFLICT WITH FREDERICK II. BEGUN   .   . 181
§ 43. GREGORY IX. AND FREDERICK II. 1227–1241 .   .   . 184
§ 44. THE CLOSE OF FREDERICK'S CAREER. 1250   .   .   . 190
§ 45. THE LAST OF THE HOHENSTAUFEN   199
§ 46. THE EMPIRE AND PAPACY AT PEACE. 1271–1294   .   . 203

CHAPTER VII. THE CRUSADES.

§ 47. LITERATURE ON THE CRUSADES AS A WHOLE   .   .   . 211
§ 48. CHARACTER AND CAUSES OF THE CRUSADES   .   .   . 214
§ 49. THE CALL TO THE CRUSADES   224
§ 50. THE FIRST CRUSADE AND THE CAPTURE OF JERUSALEM   .   . 231
§ 51. THE LATIN KINGDOM OF JERUSALEM. 1099–1187   .   . 246
§ 52. THE FALL OF EDESSA AND THE SECOND CRUSADE   .   . 252
§ 53. THE THIRD CRUSADE. 1189–1192   256
§ 54. THE CHILDREN'S CRUSADES 266
§ 55. THE FOURTH CRUSADE AND CAPTURE OF CONSTANTINOPLE   . 268
§ 56. FREDERICK II. AND THE FIFTH CRUSADE. 1229   .   . 278
§ 57. ST. LOUIS AND THE LAST CRUSADES. 1248, 1270   .   . 281
§ 58. LAST STRONGHOLD OF THE CRUSADERS IN PALESTINE   .   . 286
§ 59. EFFECTS OF THE CRUSADES 289
§ 60. THE MILITARY ORDERS   295

CHAPTER VIII. THE MONASTIC ORDERS.

§ 61. THE REVIVAL OF MONASTICISM 308
§ 62. MONASTICISM AND THE PAPACY 325
§ 63. THE MONKS OF CLUNY   330
§ 64. THE CISTERCIANS 337
§ 65. ST. BERNARD OF CLAIRVAUX   342
§ 66. THE AUGUSTINIANS, CARTHUSIANS, ETC.   358
§ 67. MONASTIC PROPHETS 370
§ 68. THE MENDICANT ORDERS 379
§ 69. FRANCISCAN LITERATURE 389
§ 70. ST. FRANCIS D'ASSISI 394
§ 71. THE FRANCISCANS 408
§ 72. ST. DOMINIC AND THE DOMINICANS 419

CHAPTER IX. MISSIONS.

PAGE

§ 73. LITERATURE AND GENERAL SURVEY 427
§ 74. MISSIONS IN NORTHEASTERN GERMANY 429
§ 75. MISSIONS AMONG THE MOHAMMEDANS 433
§ 76. MISSIONS AMONG THE MONGOLS 437
§ 77. THE JEWS 442

CHAPTER X. HERESY AND ITS SUPPRESSION.

§ 78. LITERATURE FOR THE ENTIRE CHAPTER 458
§ 79. THE MEDIÆVAL DISSENTERS 461
§ 80. THE CATHARI 470
§ 81. PETER DE BRUYS AND OTHER LEADERS 482
§ 82. THE AMAURIANS AND OTHER SECTS 486
§ 83. THE BEGUINES AND BEGHARDS 489
§ 84. THE WALDENSES 493
§ 85. THE CRUSADES AGAINST THE ALBIGENSES 507
§ 86. THE INQUISITION. ITS ORIGIN AND PURPOSE . . 515
§ 87. THE INQUISITION. ITS MODE OF PROCEDURE . . 525

CHAPTER XI. UNIVERSITIES AND CATHEDRALS.

§ 88. SCHOOLS 534
§ 89. BOOKS AND LIBRARIES 543
§ 90. THE UNIVERSITIES 551
§ 91. THE UNIVERSITY OF BOLOGNA 563
§ 92. THE UNIVERSITY OF PARIS 568
§ 93. OXFORD AND CAMBRIDGE 574
§ 94. THE CATHEDRALS 581

CHAPTER XII. SCHOLASTIC AND MYSTIC THEOLOGY.

§ 95. LITERATURE AND GENERAL INTRODUCTION . . . 587
§ 96. SOURCES AND DEVELOPMENT OF SCHOLASTICISM . . 591
§ 97. REALISM AND NOMINALISM 594
§ 98. ANSELM OF CANTERBURY 597
§ 99. PETER ABÆLARD 609
§ 100. ABÆLARD'S TEACHINGS AND THEOLOGY 620
§ 101. YOUNGER CONTEMPORARIES OF ABÆLARD . . . 627
§ 102. PETER THE LOMBARD AND THE SUMMISTS . . . 631
§ 103. MYSTICISM 636
§ 104. ST. BERNARD AS A MYSTIC 639
§ 105. HUGO AND RICHARD OF ST. VICTOR 643

CHAPTER XIII. SCHOLASTICISM AT ITS HEIGHT.

§ 106. ALEXANDER OF HALES 651
§ 107. ALBERTUS MAGNUS 652
§ 108. THOMAS AQUINAS 659
§ 109. BONAVENTURA 677
§ 110. DUNS SCOTUS 683
§ 111. ROGER BACON 692

CHAPTER XIV. THE SACRAMENTAL SYSTEM.

PAGE

§ 112. LITERATURE ON THE SACRAMENTS 700
§ 113. THE SEVEN SACRAMENTS 701
§ 114. BAPTISM AND CONFIRMATION 708
§ 115. THE EUCHARIST 713
§ 116. EUCHARISTIC PRACTICE AND SUPERSTITION . . . 721
§ 117. PENANCE AND INDULGENCES 729
§ 118. PENANCE AND INDULGENCES 735
§ 119. EXTREME UNCTION, ORDINATION, AND MARRIAGE . . 743
§ 120. SIN AND GRACE 749
§ 121. THE FUTURE STATE 757

CHAPTER XV. POPE AND CLERGY.

§ 122. THE CANON LAW 764
§ 123. THE PAPAL SUPREMACY IN CHURCH AND STATE . . 771
§ 124. THE POPE AND THE CURIA 780
§ 125. THE BISHOPS 792
§ 126. THE LOWER CLERGY 799
§ 127. THE COUNCILS 808
§ 128. THE CHURCH AND CLERGY IN ENGLAND . . . 812
§ 129. TWO ENGLISH BISHOPS 823

CHAPTER XVI. POPULAR WORSHIP AND SUPERSTITION.

§ 130. THE WORSHIP OF MARY 830
§ 131. THE WORSHIP OF RELICS 844
§ 132. THE SERMON 850
§ 133. HYMNS AND SACRED POETRY 859
§ 134. THE RELIGIOUS DRAMA 869
§ 135. THE FLAGELLANTS 875
§ 136. DEMONOLOGY AND THE DARK ARTS 878
§ 137. THE AGE PASSING JUDGMENT UPON ITSELF . . . 889

INDEX 897

THE MIDDLE AGES

FROM GREGORY VII., 1049, TO BONIFACE VIII., 1294

THE MIDDLE AGES.

THE PAPAL THEOCRACY IN CONFLICT WITH THE SECULAR POWER.

FROM GREGORY VII. TO BONIFACE VIII.

A.D. 1049–1294.

THE FIFTH PERIOD OF CHURCH HISTORY.

§ 1. *General Literature.*

SOURCES: J. P. MIGNE: *Patrologiæ cursus completus*, etc. The Latin series containing the writings of the "Fathers, Doctors, and Writers of the Latin Church from Tertullian to Innocent III.," 221 vols. Paris, 1844–1864. Indispensable. The writers of the 11th century begin with vol. 139. — PHILIP LABBÆUS, S.J., d. 1667 : *Sacrosancta concilia ad regiam editionem exacta*, 18 vols. Paris, 1662 sqq. Labbæus lived to see vol. IX. in print. Completed by Gabriel Cossart. This collection has been used in places in this volume. — JOHN D. MANSI, abp. of Lucca, d. 1769 : *Sacrorum conciliorum nova et amplissima collectio*, 31 vols., Florence and Venice, 1759–1798. Extends to the Council of Florence, 1439. New facsimile ed. with continuation. Paris, 1901 sqq. Thus far 38 vols., 0–37, reaching to 1735. — L. A. MURATORI, d. 1750 : *Rerum Italicarum scriptores*, 500–1600, 25 vols. Milan, 1723–1751, with supplemental vols., Florence, 1748, 1770, Venice, 1771, in all 31 parts. Repub. and ed. by G. Carducci et V. Fiorini, Citta di Castello 1902 sqq. — *Monumenta Germaniæ historica*, ed. by G. H. PERTZ, d. 1870, and his coeditors and successors, WATTENBACH, BÖHMER, etc. More than 50 vols. Han., 1826 sqq. They cover the whole history of the empire and papacy. — *Scriptores rerum Germanicarum* for use in schools and drawn from the preceding, ed. by PERTZ, 42 vols. Han., 1840–1894. — *Die Geschichtschreiber der deutschen Vorzeit*, ed. by PERTZ, etc., in German trans, 92 vols. Berlin and Leipzig, 1849–1892. — *The Rolls Series, Rerum Britannicarum medii ævi scriptores*, 97 vols., London, 1858–1891, contains splendid edd. of William of Malmesbury, Roger of Wendover, Ralph of Coggeshall, Richard of Hoveden, Matthew Paris (7 vols.), Grosseteste, and other English mediæval writers. — Bohn's

Antiq. Library, 41 vols. London, 1848–1864 sqq., gives translations of M. Paris, Richard of Hoveden, etc. — J. F. Böhmer : *Regesta imperii*, 1198–1254. New ed. by J. Ficker and Winkelmann, Innsbruck, 1881–1894. — *Regesta pontificum romanorum* from St. Peter to Innocent III., ed. by Jaffé, d. 1878, Berlin, 1851, pp. 951 ; 2d ed. by Wattenbach, Löwenthal, Kaltenbrunner, and Ewald, vol. I. Lips., 1885, from Peter to Innocent II., 64–1143 ; vol. II. Lips., 1888 from Cœlestin II. to Innocent III., 1143–1198. — Continuation by Aug. Potthast, from Innocent III., to Benedict XI., 1198–1304, 2 vols. pp. 2157, Berlin, 1873, 1875. — J. Von Pflugk Harttung : *Acta pontificum rom. inedita*, 3 vols. Tübing. 1881–1888. — Carl Mirbt : *Quellen zur Geschichte des Papsttums und des röm. Katholizismus*, 2d ed. Tübing. 1901, pp. 482. Very convenient and valuable, giving the original Latin documents. — Shailer Mathews: *Select Mediæval Docts. etc., illustr. the Hist. of the Church and Empire, 754–1254*, N. Y. 1892. — Heinrich Denifle, O.P., archivarius of the Vatican Library, d. 1905, and Franz Ehrle, S.J.: *Archiv für Literatur- und Kirchengeschichte des Mittelalters*, Freib. im Br. 1885 sqq. Many important documents were published here for the first time. — *Quellen und Forschungen aus italienischen Archiven und Bibliotheken herausgegeben vom Koenigl-Preussichen Historischen Institut in Rom.*, thus far 8 vols. 1897–1905.

Secondary Works : *Histoire Littéraire de la France*, 1733 sqq. *Dicty. of Natl. Biogr.*, ed. by Leslie Stephen, 63 vols. with Supplem., London, 1885–1903. — Wetzer–Welte : *Kirchen Lexikon*, 2d ed. 12 vols. Freib. im Br. 1882–1901. — Herzog : *Realencyklopaedia für protestantische Theologie und Kirche*, ed. by A. Hauck, 3d ed. 1896 sqq. Thus far 18 vols. — W. Giesebrecht : *Gesch. der deutschen Kaiserzeit*, 3 vols. 5th ed. Leipzig, 1890. — Döllinger–Friedrich : *Das Papstthum*, Munich, 1892. A revision of Döllinger's *The Pope and the Council*, which appeared in 1869 under the pseudonym Janus, as a protest against the doctrine of Papal Infallibility about to be taken up at the Vatican Council. — Ferdinand Gregorovius : *Geschichte der Stadt Rom. im Mittelalter*, Engl. trans. from the 4th German, ed. 1886–1893, Stuttg., by Annie Hamilton, 8 vols. (13 parts), London, 1894–1902. The most valuable general work on the Middle Ages. — James Bryce : *The Holy Roman Empire*, new ed. London, 1904, pp. 575. Thorough and lucid. — Carl J. von Hefele, Bishop of Rottenburg, d. 1893 : *Conciliengeschichte* to 1536, 2d ed. 9 vols. Freib. im Br. 1873–1890. Vols. V.–VII. in 2d ed. by A. Knöpfler. Vols. VIII. IX. were prepared by Cardinal Hergenröther. — A. Hauck : *Kirchengeschichte Deutschlands*, 4 vols. Leipzig, 1887–1903 ; vols. I. II. 4th ed. 1904. — Gibbon : *Decline and Fall of Rome*, ed. by J. B. Bury, 7 vols. London, 1897–1900. — Leopold von Ranke : *Weltgeschichte* to 1453, 9 vols. Leipzig, 1883–1888. — The Church Histories of Neander, Gieseler, Baur, *Die christl. Kirche des Mittelalters*, 1861, Milman, Hagenbach, K. Hase, Rich. C. Trench : *Med. Ch. History*, 1877. The Manuals of Church History of Hefele-Knöpfler, 3d ed. 1902, F. X. Funk, 4th ed. 1902, W. Moeller Engl. trans. 3 vols. 1898–1900, Karl Müller, 2 vols. 1892–1902,

HERGENRÖTHER, rev. by J. P. KIRSCH, 4th ed. 1902 sqq. LOOFS, 1901, HANS VON SCHUBERT, 1904, GEO. P. FISHER, 1887, H. C. SHELDON, 5 vols. N. Y. 1890, A. C. ZENOS, Phil. 1899, A. H. NEWMAN, 2 vols. 1900 sqq. The Histories of Christian Doctrine, of HARNACK Engl. trans. from 3d Ger. ed. 7 vols. Boston, 1897–1900. LOOFS, 3d ed. 1893, GEO. P. FISHER, 1896, SEEBERG, 2 vols. 1895, H. C. SHELDON, 2 vols. 4th ed. 1905. — HALLAM : *Hist. of the Middle Ages.* — GUIZOT : *Hist. of Civilization from the Fall of the Rom. Emp. to the French Revolution.* — LECKY : *Hist. of Rationalism in Europe* and *European Morals.* — H. WEINGARTEN : *Zeittafeln und Ueberblicke zur Kirchengeschichte,* 6th ed. by Arnold, Leipzig, 1905.

FOR LITERATURE : A. POTTHAST : *Bibliotheca Historica medii aevi, Wegweiser durch die Geschichtswerke des europäischen Mittelalters bis 1500,* 2 vols. Berlin, 1864–1868, 2d ed. Berlin, 1896. A work of great industry and value. — U. CHEVALIER : *Répertoire des sources historiques du moyen âge,* Paris, 1877–1886, Supplem. 1888. — W. WATTENBACH : *Deutsche Geschichtsquellen im Mittelalter,* to 1250, 2 vols. Berlin, 1858, 6th ed. 1893 sq.

For other works relating to the whole period of the Middle Ages, see vol. IV. 1-4.

§ 2.   *Introductory Survey.*

THE fifth period of general Church history, or the second period of mediæval Church history, begins with the rise of Hildebrand, 1049, and ends with the elevation of Boniface VIII. to the papal dignity, 1294.

In this period the Church and the papacy ascend from the lowest state of weakness and corruption to the highest power and influence over the nations of Europe. It is the classical age of Latin Christianity : the age of the papal theocracy, aiming to control the German Empire and the kingdoms of France, Spain, and England. It witnessed the rise of the great Mendicant orders and the religious revival which followed. It beheld the full flower of chivalry and the progress of the crusades, with the heroic conquest and loss of the Holy Land. It saw the foundations laid of the great universities of Bologna, Paris, Oxford. It was the age of scholastic philosophy and theology, and their gigantic efforts to solve all conceivable problems and by dialectical skill to prove every article of faith. During its progress Norman and Gothic architecture began to rear the cathedrals. All the arts were made the handmaids of religion ; and legendary poetry and romance flourished. Then the Inquisition was established, involving the theory of the persecution of Jews and heretics as a divine right, and carrying it into execution in awful scenes of torture and blood. It was an age of bright light and deep shadows, of strong faith and stronger superstition, of sublime heroism and wild passions, of ascetic self-denial and sensual indulgence, of Christian devotion and barbarous cruelty.[1] Dante, in his *Divina Commedia*, which "heaven and earth" combined to produce, gives a poetic mirror of Christianity and civilization in the thirteenth and the opening years of the fourteenth century, when the Roman Church was at the summit of its power, and yet, by the abuse of that power and its worldliness, was calling forth loud protests, and demands for a thorough reformation from all parts of Western Christendom.

A striking feature of the Middle Ages is the contrast and co-operation of the forces of extreme self-abnegation as represented in monasticism and extreme ambition for worldly dominion as represented in the papacy.[2] The former gave moral support to the latter, and the latter utilized the former. The monks were the standing army of the pope, and fought his battles against the secular rulers of Western Europe.

The papal theocracy in conflict with the secular powers and at the height of its power is the leading topic. The weak and degenerate popes who ruled from 900–1046 are now succeeded by a line of vigorous minds, men of moral as well as intellectual strength. The world has had few rulers equal to Gregory VII. 1073–1085, Alexander III. 1159–1181, and Innocent III. 1198–1216, not to speak of other pontiffs scarcely second to these masters in the art of government and aspiring aims. The papacy was a necessity and a blessing

[1] Dean Stanley, *Sermons and Addresses in America*, p. 220, speaks of the "grace of the Middle Ages and their hideous atrocities."

[2] The ideas are expressed by the German words *Weltentsagung* and *Weltbeherrschung*.

in a barbarous age, as a check upon brute force, and as a
school of moral discipline.   The popes stood on a much higher
plane than the princes of their time.   The spirit has a right to
rule over the body; the intellectual and moral interests are
superior to the material and political.   But the papal theocracy carried in it the temptation to secularization.   By the
abuse of opportunity it became a hindrance to pure religion
and morals.   Christ gave to Peter the keys of the kingdom
of heaven, but he also said, "My kingdom is not of this
world."   The pope coveted both kingdoms, and he got what
he coveted.   But he was not able to hold the power he
claimed over the State, and aspiring after temporal authority
lost spiritual power.   Boniface VIII. marks the beginning of
the decline and fall of the papal rule ; and the seeds of this
decline and fall were sown in the period when the hierarchy
was in the pride of its worldly might and glory.

In this period also, and chiefly as the result of the crusades,
the schism between the churches of the East and the West
was completed.   All attempts made at reconciliation by pope
and council only ended in wider alienation.

The ruling nations during the Middle Ages were the Latin,
who descended from the old Roman stock, but showed the
mixture of barbaric blood and vigor, and the Teutonic.   The
Italians and French had the most learning and culture.
Politically, the German nation, owing to its possession of the
imperial crown and its connection with the papacy, was the
most powerful, especially under the Hohenstaufen dynasty.
England, favored by her insular isolation, developed the
power of self-government and independent nationality, and
begins to come into prominence in the papal administration.
Western Europe is the scene of intellectual, ecclesiastical,
and political activities of vast import, but its arms and devotion find their most conspicuous arena in Palestine and the
East.

Finally this period of two centuries and a half is a period

of imposing personalities. The names of the greatest of the popes have been mentioned, Gregory VII., Alexander III., and Innocent III. Its more notable sovereigns were William the Conqueror, Frederick Barbarossa, Frederick II., and St. Louis of France. Dante the poet illumines its last years. St. Bernard, Francis d'Assisi, and Dominic, the Spaniard, rise above a long array of famous monks. In the front rank of its Schoolmen were Anselm, Abelard, Albertus Magnus, Thomas Aquinas, Bonaventura, and Duns Scotus. Thomas à Becket and Grosseteste are prominent representatives of the body of episcopal statesmen. This combination of great figures and of great movements gives to this period a variety of interest such as belongs to few periods of Church history or the history of mankind.

CHAPTER I.

THE HILDEBRANDIAN POPES. A.D. 1049–1073.

§ 3. *Sources and Literature on Chapters I. and II.*

See the general literature on the papacy in vol. IV. 202 sqq.; and the list of mediæval popes, 205 sqq.

I. Sources for the Whole Period from 1049 to 1085: —

MIGNE : *Patrol. Lat.*, vols. 140–148. — DAMIANI : *Epistolæ*, in Migne, vol. 144. — BONIZO or BONITHO (Bishop of Sutri, 1091; prisoner of Henry IV., 1082; a great admirer of Gregory VII.): *Liber ad amicum, sive de persecutione ecclesiæ* (in Jaffé's *Monum. Gregor.*, p. 628 sqq., where he is charged with falsehood; but see Giesebrecht and Hefele, IV. 707). — PHIL. JAFFÉ (d. 1870): *Regesta Pontif. Rom.*, pp. 366–443, 2d ed. I. 529–649. — JAFFÉ : *Monumenta Gregoriana* (see below). — K. FRANCKE : *Libelli de lite imperatorum et Pontificum Sæculi XI. et XII. conscripti,* 3 vols. Hannov. 1891–1897, contains the tractarian lit. of the Hildebrandian age. On other sources, see WATTENBACH : *Deutschlands Geschichtsquellen im Mittelalter,* II. 220 sqq. and MIRBT : *Publizistik,* 6–95.

II. Works on the Whole Period from 1049 to 1085: —

HÖFLER: *Deutsche Päpste,* Regensb., 1839 sqq., 3 vols. — C. WILL : *Anfänge der Restauration der Kirche im 11ten Jahrh.*, Marburg, 1859–1862, 2 parts. — THS. GREENWOOD : *Cathedra Petri,* books X. and XI. London, 1861. — GIESEBRECHT : *Gesch. der deutschen Kaizerzeit,* vols. II. and III. (Braunschweig, 5th ed. 1881). — RUD. BAXMANN : *Die Politik der Päpste von Gregor I. bis auf Gregor VII.*, Elberfeld, 1868, 1869. 2 vols. vol. II. 186–434. — WATTENBACH : *Geschichte des röm. Papstthums,* Berlin, 1876 (pp. 97–136). — GREGOROVIUS : *Hist. of the City of Rome.* — HEFELE : *Conciliengeschichte,* IV. 716–900, and V. 1–185. — L. V. RANKE : *Weltgeschichte,* vol. VII. — BRYCE: *Holy Roman Empire. —* FREEMAN : *Hist. of Norman Conq. of England,* vol. IV. Oxford, 1871, and *Hist. of Sicily. —* F. NEUKIRCH: *Das Leben des Petrus Damiani bis 1059,* Gött., 1875. — J. LANGEN: *Geschichte der röm. Kirche von Gregor VII. bis Innocent III.,* Bonn, 1893. — HAUCK : *Kirchengeschichte Deutschlands,* vols. III. IV. — W. F. BARRY : *The Papal Monarchy from 590–1303,* N. Y. 1902.

III. SPECIAL SOURCES AND WORKS ON HILDEBRAND: —

His letters (359), the so-called *Registrum*, in MIGNE, vol. 148, MANSI, XX.
60–391, and best in JAFFÉ, *Monumenta Gregoriana*, Berol., 1865, 712
pp. (in "Bibliotheca Rerum Germanicarum," vol. II.). The first critical
edition. Jaffé gives the *Registrum* in eight books, with fifty-one additional letters collected from MSS., and *Bonithonis episcopi Sutrini
ad amicum.* Gregory's biographies by Cardinal Petrus of Pisa, Bernried,
Amalric, Lambert, etc., in MURATORI : *Rerum Italicarum Scriptores*,
vol. III.; and WATTERICH : *Pontif. Rom. Vitæ*, Lips., 1862, I. 293 sqq.;
Acta Sanct. Maii, die 25, VI. 102–159.

Modern works : JOH. VOIGT (Prof. of Hist. in Königsberg, d. 1863): *Hildebrand als Papst Gregorius VII. und sein Zeitalter*, 1815, 2d ed. Weimar,
1846, pp. 625. The first attempt at an impartial estimate of Gregory
from the Protestant historical standpoint. The first edition was translated into French and Italian, and gave rise to a remarkable Latin correspondence with Clemens Villecourt, bishop of La Rochelle, which is
printed in the preface to the second edition. The bishop tried to
convert Voigt to the Catholic Church, but in vain. — SIR ROGER
GREISLY : *The Life and Pontificate of Gregory VII.*, London, 1832, pp.
372. Impartial, but unimportant. — J. W. BOWDEN : *The Life and Pontificate of Gregory VII.* London, 1840, 2 vols. pp. 374 and 411. — CARD.
NEWMAN : *Hist. Essays, II.* 249–336. — SIR JAMES STEPHEN : *Hildebrand*,
in "Essays on Ecclesiastical Biography," 1849, 4th ed. London, 1860,
pp. 1–58. He calls "Hildebrand the very impersonation of papal arrogance and of spiritual despotism." — SÖLTL : *Gregor VII.*, Leipzig, 1847.
— FLOTO : *Kaiser Heinrich IV. und sein Zeitalter.* Stuttg., 1855, 1856, 2
vols. Sides with Henry IV. — HELFENSTEIN : *Gregor VII. Bestrebungen
nach den Streitschriften seiner Zeit.*, Frankfurt, 1856. — A. F. GFRÖRER
(first a rationalist, then a convert to Rome, 1853 ; d. 1861): *Papst Greg.
VII. und sein Zeitalter.* 7 vols. Schaffhausen, 1859–1861. — GIESEBRECHT :
l.c., vol. III. — A. F. VILLEMAIN: *Hist. de Grégoire VII.* 2 vols. Paris, 1873.
Engl. trans. by *J. B. Brockley*, 2 vols. London, 1874. — S. BARING-GOULD,
in "The Lives of the Saints" for May 25, London, 1873. — W. MARTENS:
*Die Besetzung des päpstlichen Stuhls unter den Kaisern Heinrich III.
und Heinrich IV.* 1887 ; *Gregor VII., sein Leben und Wirken*, 2 vols.
Leipzig, 1894. — W. R. W. STEPHENS: *Hildebrand and his Times*, London,
1888. — O. DELARC : *S. Gregoire VII. et la réforme de l'église au XI.
siècle*, 3 vols. Paris, 1889. — C. MIRBT (Prof. in Marburg) : *Die Stellung
Augustins in der Publizistik des Gregorianischen Kirchenstreits*, Leipzig,
1888. Shows the influence of St. Augustine on both parties in the Gregorian controversy over the relation of Church and State ; *Die Wahl
Gregors VII.*, Marburg, 1892; *Die Publizistik im Zeitalter Gregors
VII.*, Leipzig, 1894, pp. 629. An exhaustive treatment of the copious
tractarian lit. of the Hildebrandian age and its attitude on the various
objects of Gregory's policy ; art. *Gregor VII.*, in Herzog, VII. 96–113. —
MARVIN R. VINCENT : *The Age of Hildebrand*, N. Y. 1896. — Also J.
GREVING : *Paul von Bernried's Vita Gregorii VII.*, Berlin, 1893, pp. 172.

§ 4. *Hildebrand and his Training.*

THE history of the period begins with a survey of the papacy as the controlling power of Western Christendom. It embraces six stages: 1. The Hildebrandian popes, 1049–1073. 2. Gregory VII., 1073–1085, or the assertion of the supreme authority of the papacy in human affairs. 3. From Gregory's death to the Concordat of Worms, 1122, or the settlement of the controversy over investiture. 4. From the Concordat of Worms to Innocent III., 1198. 5. The Pontificate of Innocent III., 1198–1216, or the papacy at its height. 6. From Innocent III. to Boniface VIII., 1216–1294, or the struggle of the papacy with Frederick II. and the restoration of peace between the papacy and the empire.

The papacy had reached its lowest stage of weakness and degeneracy when at Sutri in 1046, under the influence of Henry III., two popes were deposed and a third was forced to abdicate.[1] But the worthless popes, who prostituted their office and outraged the feelings of Christendom during the tenth and the first half of the eleventh century, could not overthrow the papacy any more than idolatrous kings could overthrow the Jewish monarchy, or wicked emperors the Roman Empire.   In the public opinion of Europe, the papacy was still a necessary institution established by Christ in the primacy of Peter for the government and administration of the Church.   There was nothing to take its place.   It needed only a radical reformation in its head, which would be followed by a reformation of the members.   Good men all over Europe anxiously desired and hoped that Providence would intervene and rescue the chair of Peter from the hands of thieves and robbers, and turn it once more into a blessing. The idea of abolishing the papacy did not occur to the mind of the Christians of that age as possible or desirable.

At last the providential man for effecting this necessary

[1] Vol. IV. § 66, pp. 299 sqq.

reformation appeared in the person of Hildebrand, who controlled five successive papal administrations for twenty-four years, 1049–1073, then occupied the papal chair himself for twelve years, 1073–1085, and was followed by like-minded successors.   He is one of the greatest, if not the greatest, of popes, and one of the most remarkable men in history.   He excited in his age the highest admiration and the bitterest hatred.   Opinions about his principles and policy are still divided ; but it is impossible to deny his ability, energy, earnestness, and achievements.

Hildebrand was of humble and obscure origin, but fore-ordained to be a prince of the Church.   He was of small stature, and hence called " Hildebrandellus " by his enemies, but a giant in intellect and character.   His figure was ungainly and his voice feeble; but his eyes were bright and piercing, bespeaking penetration, a fiery spirit, and restless activity. His early life is involved in obscurity.   He only incidentally alludes to it in his later Epistles, and loved to connect it with the supernatural protection of St. Peter and the Holy Virgin.   With a monkish disregard of earthly relations, he never mentions his family.   The year of his birth is unknown.   The veneration of friends and the malice of enemies surrounded his youth with legends and lies.   He was the son of a peasant or goatherd, Bonizo, living near Soana, a village in the marshes of Tuscany, a few miles from Orbitello. The oft-repeated tradition that he was the son of a carpenter seems to have originated in the desire to draw a parallel between him and Jesus of Nazareth.   Of his mother we know nothing.   His name points to Lombard or German origin, and was explained by his contemporaries as hell-brand or fire-brand.[1]   Odilo, the abbot of Cluny, saw sparks of fire issuing from his raiment, and predicted that, like John the Baptist, he would be " great in the sight of the Lord."

[1] The contemporary spellings are: *Yldibrandus, Heldebrandus, Ildebrandus, Oldeprandus.*   William of Malmesbury calls him *homuncio exilis staturæ.*

He entered the Benedictine order in the convent of St. Mary on the Aventine at Rome, of which his maternal uncle was abbot. Here he had a magnificent view of the eternal city.[1] Here he was educated with Romans of the higher families.[2] The convent was under the influence of the reformatory spirit of Cluny, and the home of its abbots on their pilgrimages to Rome. He exercised himself in severe self-discipline, and in austerity and rigor he remained a monk all his life. He cherished an enthusiastic veneration for the Virgin Mary. The personal contemplation of the scandalous contentions of the three rival popes and the fearful immorality in the capital of Christendom must have raised in his earnest soul a deep disgust. He associated himself with the party which prepared for a reformation of the hierarchy.

His sympathies were with his teacher and friend, Gregory VI. This pope had himself bought the papal dignity from the wretched Benedict IX., but he did it for the benefit of the Church, and voluntarily abdicated on the arrival of Henry III. at the Synod of Sutri, 1046. It is strange that Hildebrand, who abhorred simony, should begin his public career in the service of a simonist; but he regarded Gregory as the only legitimate pope among the three rivals, and followed him, as his chaplain, to Germany into exile.

" Victrix causa Deis placuit, sed victa Catoni." [3]

He visited Worms, Spires, Cologne, Aix-la-Chapelle, the old seats of the empire, and spent much time at the court of

[1] Giesebrecht (III. 12 sq.): "*Das Marienkloster auf dem Aventin, jetzt unter dem Namen des Priorats von Malta bekannt, bietet eine entzückende Aussicht . . . Ein hochbegabter Knabe, der hier erwuchs, musste die verschiedensten und mächtigsten Eindrücke erhalten, die sich kaum in einem anderen Gedanken zusammenschliessen konnten, als in dem der unvergleichlichen Hoheit des ewigen Roms.*"

[2] So Martens, etc. Gregory speaks of having been brought up from childhood *a pueritia* by the prince of the apostles and "in the Roman palace."

[3] The German historian, Otto von Freisingen, aptly applies this verse of Lucan to the relation of the two popes, thus comparing Hildebrand to Cato.

Henry III., where he was very kindly treated.   After the death of Gregory at Cologne, 1048, Hildebrand went to Cluny, the nursery of a moral reformation of monasticism. According to some reports, he had been there before.   He zealously gave himself to ascetic exercises and ecclesiastical studies under the excellent abbot Hugo, and became prior of the convent.   He often said afterwards that he wished to spend his life in prayer and contemplation within the walls of this sacred retreat.

But the election of Bishop Bruno of Toul, the cousin of Emperor Henry III., to the papal chair, at the Diet of Worms, brought him on the stage of public action.   " Reluctantly," he said, "I crossed the Alps ; more reluctantly I returned to Rome."   He advised Bruno (either at Cluny or at Besancon) not to accept the triple crown from the hands of the emperor, but to await canonical election by the clergy and people of Rome.   He thus clearly asserted, for the first time, his principle of the supremacy of the Church over the State.

Bruno, accompanied by Hildebrand, travelled to Rome as a pilgrim, entered the city barefoot, was received with acclamations, canonically elected, and ascended the papal chair on Feb. 12, 1049, as Leo IX.

From this time on, Hildebrand was the reigning spirit of the papacy.   He understood the art of ruling through others, and making them feel that they ruled themselves.   He used as his aide-de-camp Peter Damiani, the severe monk and fearless censor of the immoralities of the age, who had conquered the world within and helped him to conquer it without, in the crusade against simony and concubinage, but died, 1072, a year before Hildebrand became pope.[1]

---

[1] See vol. IV. 787 sqq.

§ 5. *Hildebrand and Leo IX.* 1049–1054.

The moral reformation of the papacy began with Hildebrand as leader.[1] He resumed the work of the emperor,
Henry III., and carried it forward in the interest of the
hierarchy. He was appointed cardinal-subdeacon, treasurer
of the Roman Church, and abbot of St. Paul's. He was
repeatedly sent as delegate to foreign countries, where he
acquired an extensive knowledge of affairs. He replenished
the empty treasury and became wealthy himself through the
help of a baptized Jew, Benedictus Christianus, and his son
Leo, who did a prosperous banking business. But money
was to him only a means for exalting the Church. His great
object was to reform the clergy by the destruction of two
well-nigh universal evils : simony (Acts 8 : 18), that is, the
traffic in ecclesiastical dignities, and Nicolaitism (Rev. 2 : 6,
15), or the concubinage of the priests. In both respects he
had the full sympathy of the new pope, and was backed by
the laws of the Church. The reformation was to be effected
in the regular way of synodical legislation under the personal direction of the pope.

Leo, accompanied by Hildebrand, held several synods in
Italy, France, and Germany. He was almost omnipresent
in the Church, and knew how to combine monastic simplicity
with papal dignity and splendor. He was believed to work
miracles wherever he went, and to possess magic powers
over birds and beasts.

In his first synod, held in Rome at Easter, 1049, simony
was prohibited on pain of excommunication, including the
guilty bishops and the priests ordained by them. But it was
found that a strict prosecution would well-nigh deprive the
churches, especially those of Rome, of their shepherds. A penance of forty days was, therefore, substituted for the depo-

---

[1] See E. Martin, *St. Leon IX.*, Paris, 1904, pp. 216 ; Mirbt art. in Herzog,
XI. 379–386.

sition of priests. The same synod renewed the old prohibitions of sexual intercourse of the clergy, and made the concubines of the Roman priests servants of the Lateran palace. The almost forgotten duty of the tithe was enjoined upon all Christians.

The reformatory synods of Pavia, Rheims, and Mainz, held in the same year, legislated against the same vices, as also against usury, marriage in forbidden degrees, the bearing of arms by the clergy. They likewise revealed a frightful amount of simony and clerical immorality. Several bishops were deposed.[1] Archbishop Wido of Rheims narrowly escaped the same fate on a charge of simony. On his return, Leo held synods in lower Italy and in Rome. He made a second tour across the Alps in 1052, visiting Burgundy, Lorraine, and Germany, and his friend the emperor. We find him at Regensburg, Bamberg, Mainz, and Worms. Returning to Rome, he held in April, 1053, his fourth Easter Synod. Besides the reform of the Church, the case of Berengar and the relation to the Greek Church were topics of discussion in several of these synods. Berengar was condemned, 1050, for denying the doctrine of transubstantiation. It is remarkable with what leniency Hildebrand treated Berengar and his eucharistic doctrine, in spite of the papal condemnation; but he was not a learned theologian. The negotiation with the Greek Church only ended in greater separation.[2]

Leo surrounded himself with a council of cardinals who supported him in his reform. Towards the close of his pontificate, he acted inconsistently by taking up arms against the Normans in defence of Church property. He was defeated and taken prisoner at Benevento, but released again

---

[1] In deposing at the Synod of Rheims the abp. of St. Iago, who had assumed the title *apostolicus*, Leo asserted in the strongest terms the primacy of the Roman see, *quod solus Romanæ sedis pontifex universalis, ecclesiæ primas esset et apostolicus*, Mansi, XIX. 738.

[2] The controversy of Berengar is treated in vol. IV. 554 sqq.; the Greek controversy, *ibid.* p. 318 sqq. On the synods during the pontificate of Leo IX., see Jaffé, *Reg.*, 529–549, Hefele, IV. 716–777, and Mirbt, *Quellen*, 95 sq.

by granting them in the name of St. Peter their conquests
in Apulia, Calabria, and Sicily.   The Normans kissed his
toe, and asked his absolution and blessing.   He incurred
the censure of the strict reform party.   Damiani maintained
that a clergyman dare not bear arms even in defence of the
property of the Church, but must oppose invincible patience
to the fury of the world, according to the example of Christ.

Leo spent his remaining days in grief over his defeat.   He
died at Rome, April 19, 1054, in his fifty-third year, after commending his soul to God in a German prayer of humble resignation, and was buried near the tomb of Gregory I.   As he had
begun the reformation of the Church, and miracles were reported, he was enrolled in the Calendar of Saints.   Desiderius,
afterwards Victor III., wrote, "All ecclesiastical interests were
reformed by Leo and in him a new light arose in the world."

§ 6.   *Victor II. and Stephen IX. (X.).*   1055–1058.

Hildebrand was absent in France when Leo died, and hurried to Rome.   He could find no worthy successor in Italy,
and was unwilling to assume the burden of the papacy himself.   He cast his eye upon Gebhard, bishop of Eichstädt,
the ablest, richest, and most influential prelate of Germany,
who was warmly devoted to the emperor.   He proceeded at
the head of a deputation, appointed by the clergy and people, to the German court, and begged the emperor to raise
Gebhard to the papal chair.   After long delay, Gebhard was
elected at a council in Regensburg, March, 1055, and consecrated in St. Peter's at Rome, April 13, as Victor II.   He
continued the synodical war against simony, but died as
early as July 28, 1057, at Arezzo, of a fever.   He was the
last of the German popes.

The cardinal-abbot of Monte Cassino was elected and consecrated as Stephen IX. (X.), Aug. 3, 1057, by the clergy
and people of Rome, without their consulting the German
court; but he died in the following year, March 29, 1058.

In the meantime a great change had taken place in Germany. Henry III. died in the prime of manhood, Oct. 5, 1056, and left a widow as regent and a son of six years, the ill-fated Henry IV. The long minority reign afforded a favorable opportunity for the reform party to make the papacy independent of the imperial power, which Henry III. had wisely exerted for the benefit of the Church, yet at the expense of her freedom.

The Roman nobility, under the lead of the counts of Tusculum, took advantage of Hildebrand's absence in Germany to reassert its former control of the papacy by electing Benedict X. (1058–1060). But this was a brief intermezzo. On his return, Hildebrand, with the help of Duke Godfrey, expelled the usurping pope, and secured, with the consent of the empress, the election of Gerhard, bishop of Florence, a strong reformer, of ample learning and irreproachable character, who assumed the name of Nicolas II. at his consecration, Jan. 25, 1059. Benedict was deposed, submitted, and obtained absolution. He was assigned a lodging in the church of St. Agnes, where he lived for about twenty years.

§ 7. *Nicolas II. and the Cardinals.* 1059–1061.

The pontificate of Nicolas II. was thoroughly under the control of Hildebrand, who became archdeacon and chancellor of the Roman Church in August or September, 1059. His enemies said that he kept Nicolas like an ass in the stable, feeding him to do his work. Peter Damiani calls him the lord of the pope, and said that he would rather obey the lord of the pope than the lord-pope himself.[1] He also grimly

---

[1] His epigrams on Hildebrand (*Opera*, II. 961, 967): —

"*Vivere vis Romæ, clara depromito voce :*
  Plus domino Papæ, quam domino pareo Papæ."

"*Papam rite colo, sed te prostratus adoro :*
  Tu facis hunc Dominum ; te facit iste Deum."

calls Hildebrand his "holy Satan,"[1] because he had sometimes to obey him against his will, as when he desired to lay
down his bishopric at Ostia and retire to a convent, but was
not permitted to do so. He disliked the worldly splendor
which Hildebrand began to assume in dress and mode of living, contrary to his own ascetic principles.

Two important steps were made in the progress of the
hierarchy, — a change in the election of the pope, and an
alliance with the Normans for the temporal protection of the
pope.

Nicolas convened a Lateran Council in April, 1059, the
largest held in Rome down to that time. It consisted of a
hundred and thirteen bishops and a multitude of clergymen;
but more than two-thirds of the prelates were Italians, the
rest Burgundians and Frenchmen. Germany was not represented at all. Berengar was forced at this synod to submit
to a formula of recantation (which he revoked on his return
to France). He calls the bishops "wild beasts," who would
not listen to his idea of a spiritual communion, and insisted
on a Capernaitic manducation of the body of Christ.[2]

A far-reaching act of this council was the transfer of the
election of a pope to the "cardinal-bishops" and "cardinal-
clergy."[3] At the pope's death the initiative was to be taken
by the cardinal-bishops. In case they agreed they were to
call in the cardinal-clergy. In case of agreement between
both these classes of functionaries they were to present the
candidate to the Roman clergy and people for ratification.
The stress thus laid upon the cardinal-bishops is a new
thing, and it is evident that the body of cardinals was accorded a place of importance and authority such as it had

[1] Ep. 1: 16.   [2] See vol. IV. 557 sq.
[3] The canons are given in Mirbt, *Quellen*, 97 sqq. The two classes of
cardinals are called *cardinales episcopi* and *cardinales clerici*. Langen
makes the attempt to identify the latter with "the clergy of Rome," but
without sufficient reason. The clergy, *clerus*, as a special body, are distinctly mentioned in the canons.

c

not enjoyed before. Its corporate history may be said to begin with these canons. The election of the pope was made its prerogative. The synod further prescribed that the pope should be chosen from the body of Roman clergy, provided a suitable candidate could be found among their number. In usual cases, Rome was designated as the place of holding the election. The cardinals, however, were granted liberty to hold it otherwheres. As for the emperor, the language of the canons leaves it uncertain whether any part was accorded to him in the ratification of the elected pope. His name is mentioned with respect, but it would seem that all that was intended was that he should receive due notification of the election of the new pontiff. The matter was, therefore, taken entirely out of the emperor's hands and lodged in the college of cardinals.[1] As Henry was still young and not yet invested with the imperial dignity, it was a favorable opportunity for the papal circle to secure the perpetual control of the papal office for the Romans and the Roman clergy. With rare exceptions, as in the case of the period of the Avignon exile, the election

---

[1] The canons have come down to us in two forms. The second form, falsified in the interest of the emperors, was current at least thirty years after Nicolas's death. The fourth canon bearing on the emperor ran in its original form thus : *salvo debito honore et reverentia dilecti filii nostri Henrici, qui inpresentiarum rex habetur et futurus imperator deo concedente speratur, sicut jam sibi concessimus et successoribus illius qui ab hac apostolica sede personaliter hoc jus impetraverint.* See Scheffer-Boichorst, *Die Neuordnung der Papstwahl durch Nikolas II.*, Strass., 1879, who made a thorough investigation of the subject, Hefele, IV. 800 sqq. ; Hergenröther-Kirsch, *Kirchengesch.*, II. 342 sqq. ; Mirbt, *Nikolas II.*, in Herzog, XIV. 73 sq.; Hauck, *Kirchengesch.* III. 683 sqq. Hergenröther, p. 344 note, interprets the canon as conceding notification and nothing more, in the light of the words of the contemporary Anselm of Lucca (Alexander II.): *ut obeunte Apost. pontifice successor eligeretur et electio ejus regi notificaretur, facta vero electione,* etc., *regi notificata, ita demum pontifex consecraretur.* The imperial bishops of Germany fought against the limitation of the election to clerical circles in Rome. Under Henry III. and IV. the view prevailed among them that no one could be a legitimate pope without the consent of the emperor. See Scheffer-Boichorst, *Zu den Anfängen des Kirchenstreites unter Heinrich IV.*, Innsbruck, 1892, p. 122 sq.

of the pope has remained in the hands of the Romans ever since.

The alliance which Nicolas entered into, 1059, with the Normans of Southern Italy, was the second act in the long and notable part which they played in the history of the papacy. Early in the eleventh century four brothers of the house of Hauteville, starting from Normandy, began their adventurous career in Italy and Sicily. They were welcomed as crusaders liberating the Christian population from the rule of the Saracens and its threatened extension. The kingdom their arms established was confirmed by the apostolic see, and under the original dynasty, and later under the house of Anjou, had a larger influence on the destinies of the papacy for three centuries than did Norman England and the successors of William the Conqueror. Robert Guiscard, who had defeated the army of Leo IX., and held him a prisoner for nine months, was confirmed by Nicolas as duke of Apulia and Calabria. The duchy became a fief of Rome by an obligation to pay yearly twelve dinars for every yoke of oxen and to defend the Holy See against attacks upon its authority. Robert's brother, Roger, d. 1101, began the conquest of Sicily in earnest in 1060 by the seizure of Messina, and followed it up by the capture of Palermo, 1071, and Syracuse, 1085. He was called Prince of Sicily and perpetual legate of the Holy See. One of his successors, Roger II., 1105–1154, was crowned king of Sicily at Palermo by the authority of the anti-pope Anacletus II. A half century later the blood of this house became mingled with the blood of the house of Hohenstaufen in the person of the great Frederick II. In the prominent part they took we shall find these Norman princes now supporting the plans of the papacy, now resisting them.

About the same time the Hautevilles and other freebooting Normans were getting a foothold in Southern Italy, the Normans under William the Conqueror, in 1066, were

conquering England.   To them England owes her introduction into the family of European nations, and her national
isolation ceases.[1]

§ 8.   *The War against Clerical Marriage.*

The same Lateran Council of 1059 passed severe laws
against the two heresies of simony and Nicolaitism.   It
threatened all priests who were unwilling to give up their
wives or concubines with the loss of their benefices and the
right of reading mass, and warned the laity against attending their services.   " No one," says the third of the thirteen
canons, " shall hear mass from a priest who to his certain
knowledge keeps a concubine or a *subintroducta mulier.*"

These severe measures led to serious disturbances in
Northern Italy, especially in the diocese of Milan, where
every ecclesiastical office from the lowest to the highest was
for sale, and where marriage or concubinage was common
among priests of all grades, not excluding the archbishop.[2]
Sacerdotal marriage was regarded as one of the liberties of
the church of St. Ambrose, which maintained a certain independence of Rome, and had a numerous and wealthy clergy.
The Milanese defended such marriage by Scripture texts and
by a fictitious decision of Ambrose, who, on the contrary,
was an enthusiast for celibacy.   Candidates for holy orders,
if unmarried, were asked if they had strength to remain so ;
if not, they could be legally married ; but second marriages
were forbidden, and the Levitical law as to the virginity of
the bride was observed.   Those who remained single were
objects of suspicion, while those who brought up their families in the fear of God were respected and eligible to the

---

[1] Stubbs, ed. of *Rich. de Hoveden*, II. pp. lxxiii. sqq.

[2] Bonizo, a friend of Hildebrand, calls Wido, who was elected bishop of
Milan in 1045, a "*vir illiteratus et concubinarius et absque ulla verecundia
Simoniacus.*"   Migne, Tom. CL. 825; Jaffé, *Mon. Greg.*, 639.   But Hefele,
IV. 793, doubts the charge of concubinage, and also Mirbt, *Publizistik*, 249.

episcopate. Concubinage was regarded as a heinous offence and a bar to promotion.[1]

But the Roman Church and the Hildebrandian party reversed the case, and denounced sacerdotal marriage as unlawful concubinage. The leader of this party in Lombardy was Anselm of Baggio (west of Milan), a zealous and eloquent young priest, who afterwards became bishop of Lucca and then pope (as Alexander II.). He attacked the immorality of the clergy, and was supported by the lowest populace, contemptuously called " Pataria " or " Patarines," *i.e.* " Ragbags."[2] Violent and sanguinary tumults took place in the churches and streets. Peter Damiani, a sincere enthusiast for ascetic holiness, was sent as papal legate to Milan. He defended the Pataria at the risk of his life, proclaimed the supremacy of the Roman see, and exacted a repudiation of all heretical customs.

This victory had great influence throughout Lombardy. But the strife was renewed under the following pope and under Gregory VII., and it was not till 1093 that Urban II. achieved a permanent triumph over Nicolaitism at a great council at Piacenza.

§ 9. *Alexander II. and the Schism of Cadalus.*
1061–1073.

Pope Nicolas II. died July 27, 1061. The cardinals elected, in some unknown place outside of Rome, Anselm, bishop of Lucca, Sept. 30, 1061. He was conducted to Rome in the following night by Norman soldiers, and consecrated, Oct. 1, as Alexander II. His first act was to administer the oath of fealty to Richard, the Norman leader.

---

[1] Lea, *l.c.*, p. 210.

[2] Muratori and Du Cange (sub *Pataria* and *Paterinus*) derive *pataria* from *pate*, which in the Milanese dialect means a huckster or pedler. So also Hefele, IV. 796. Giesebrecht (III. 31) renders Patarina *Lumpengesindel*. The contemporary, Bonizo, interprets the term to mean " ragged," *patarinos id est pannosos vocabant.* See Mirbt, art. *Patara*, in Herzog, XIV. 761 sqq.

The anti-Hildebrandian party of the Roman nobles, headed by Count Girard of Galeria (an excommunicated robber), with the aid of the disaffected Lombard clergy, and the young emperor Henry IV., elected Cadalus (or Cadalous), bishop of Parma, anti-pope. He was consecrated Oct. 28, 1061, as Honorius II., and maintained a schism of ten years. He had been repeatedly charged with simony, and had the sympathy and support of the married or concubinary clergy and the simoniacal laity, who hoped that his success would lead to a modification of discipline and legalization of clerical marriage. The opposition thus became an organized party, and liable to the charge of heresy, which was considered worse than carnal sin. Damiani and Humbert defended the principle that a priest who is guilty of simony or concubinage, and believes himself innocent, is more criminal than he who knows himself to be guilty. Damiani hurled the fiercest denunciation of a Hebrew prophet against the anti-pope. Cadalus entered Rome with an armed force, and maintained himself in the castle of St. Angelo for two years; but at length he sought safety in flight without a single follower, and moved to Parma. He died in 1072. His party was broken up.

Alexander held a council at Mantua, May 31, 1064, and was universally recognized as the legitimate pope; while Cadalus was anathematized and disappeared from history.

During the pontificate of Alexander, the war against simony and Nicolaitism went on under the lead of Hildebrand and Damiani with varying success. The troubles in Lombardy were renewed. Archbishop Wido of Milan sided with Cadalus and was excommunicated; he apologized, did penance, and resumed office. After his death in 1071 the strife broke out again with disgraceful scenes of violence. The Patarine party, supported with gold by the pope, gained the ascendency after the death of Cadalus. The Normans repelled the Mohammedan aggression and won Southern Italy and Sicily for the Church of Rome.

This good service had some weight on the determination of Hildebrand to support the claim of William of Normandy to the crown of England, which was a master-stroke of his policy ; for it brought that island into closer contact with Rome, and strengthened the papal pretension to dispose of temporal thrones.   William fought under a banner blessed by the pope, and founded the Norman dynasty in England, 1066.   The conquest was concluded at Winchester by a solemn coronation through three papal delegates, Easter, 1070.

But in Germany there arose a powerful opposition, not indeed to the papacy, which was the common ground of all parties, but to the Hildebrandian policy.   This led to the conflict between Gregory VII. and Henry IV.   Alexander threatened Henry with excommunication in case he persisted in his purpose to divorce his queen Bertha.

CHAPTER II.

See literature in § 3.

§ 10. *Hildebrand elected Pope.   His Views on the Situation.*

ALEXANDER II. died April 21, 1073, and was buried in the basilica of St. John in Lateran on the following day. The city, usually so turbulent after the death of a pope, was tranquil.   Hildebrand ordered a three days' fast with litanies and prayers for the dead, after which the cardinals were to proceed to an election.   Before the funeral service was closed, the people shouted, "Hildebrand shall be pope!" He attempted to ascend the pulpit and to quiet the crowd, but Cardinal Hugo Candidus anticipated him, and declared: "Men and brethren, ye know how since the days of Leo IX. Hildebrand has exalted the holy Roman Church, and defended the freedom of our city.   And as we cannot find for the papacy a better man, or even one that is his equal, let us elect him, a clergyman of our Church, well known and thoroughly approved amongst us."   The cardinals and clergy exclaimed in the usual formula, "St. Peter elects Gregory (Hildebrand) pope." [1]

This tumultuary election was at once legalized by the cardinals.   He was carried by the people as in triumph to the church of S. Petrus ad Vincula, clothed with the pur-

---

[1] The earliest account is given by Gregory himself in two letters written April 24, 1073, and a third written April 26 to Wibert of Ravenna (*Reg.*, I. 1–3).   It is confirmed by Bonizo.   Gregory frequently referred to his election

ple robe and tiara, and declared elected, as "a man eminent
in piety and learning, a lover of equity and justice, firm in
adversity, temperate in prosperity, according to the apostolic
precept (1 Tim. 3 : 2), 'without reproach . . . temperate, sober-
minded, chaste, given to hospitality, ruling his house well'
. . . already well brought up and educated in the bosom of
this mother Church, for his merits advanced to the office of
archdeacon, whom now and henceforth we will to be called
Gregory, Pope, and Apostolic Primate."[1]

It was eminently proper that the man who for nearly a
quarter of a century had been the power behind the throne,
should at last be pope in name as well as in fact.   He might
have attained the dignity long before, if he had desired it.   He
was then about sixty years old, when busy men begin to long
for rest.   He chose the name Gregory in memory of his
departed friend whom he had accompanied as chaplain into
exile, and as a protest against the interference of the empire
in the affairs of the Church.[2]   He did not ask the previous
confirmation of the emperor, but he informed him of his election, and delayed his consecration long enough to receive the
consent of Henry IV., who in the meantime had become

as having been against his will.   (See Mirbt, *Wahl*, etc., pp. 2, 42.)   The
anti-Gregorian party made the slanderous accusation that he secured his
office by force and bribery, but not till the struggle between him and Henry
IV. had begun.   The subject is thoroughly discussed by Mirbt in his *Wahl
Gregors VII.* p. 56.   In his later work, *Die Publizistik*, p. 582, he again
pronounces Gregory's own account as "the most credible."

[1] The clauses, "the husband of one wife," as well as "having his children
in subjection," are omitted in the quotation from Paul's letter to Timothy.
They would be fatal to the papal theory of clerical celibacy.   See the Latin
text in the *Acta Sanctorum* for May 25, Tom. VI. 117, from the "Acta Romæ
10 Kalend. Maji."   The cardinals concluded the declaration with the questions : "*Placet vobis ?   Placet.   Vultis eum ?   Volumus.   Laudatis eum ?
Laudamus.*"

[2] From Bonizo's account it would seem that the cardinals gave him that
name ; but they probably ascertained his wishes beforehand, or anticipated
them.   Wattenbach (p. 130) regards the assumption of the name Gregory as
an open insult to the empire and the Synod of Sutri, where Henry III. had
deposed three popes, including Gregory VI.

emperor.   This was the last case of an imperial confirmation of a papal election.[1]

Hildebrand was ordained priest, May 22, and consecrated pope, June 29, without any opposition.   Bishop Gregory of Vercelli, the German chancellor of Italy, attended the consecration.   The pope informed his friends, distinguished abbots, bishops, and princes of his election; gave expression to his feelings and views on his responsible position, and begged for their sympathy and prayers.[2]

He was overwhelmed, as he wrote to Duke Godfrey of Lorraine (May 6, 1073), by the prospect of the task before him; he would rather have died than live in the midst of such perils ; nothing but trust in God and the prayers of good men could save him from despair; for the whole world was lying in wickedness; even the high officers of the Church, in their thirst for gain and glory, were the enemies rather than the friends of religion and justice.   In the second year of his pontificate, he assured his friend Hugo of Cluny (Jan. 22, 1075) that he often prayed God either to release him from the present life, or to use him for the good of mother Church, and thus describes the lamentable condition of the times : —

"The Eastern Church fallen from the faith, and attacked by the infidels from without.   In the West, South, or North, scarcely any bishops who have obtained their office regularly, or whose life and conduct correspond to their calling, and who are actuated by the love of Christ instead of worldly ambition.   Nowhere princes who prefer God's honor to their own, and justice to gain.   The Romans, Longobards, and Normans among whom I live, as I often told them, are worse than Jews and heathens.   And when I look to myself, I feel oppressed by such a burden of sin that no other hope of salvation is left me but in the mercy of Christ alone."[3]

---

[1] This is Mirbt's view.   The anti-Gregorian writers, reflecting the policy of Henry IV., insisted that Gregory had not received the royal assent.   The imperial theory was laid down at Brixen, 1080, that any one assuming to be pope without such assent, was an apostate, *si quis sine assensu romani principis papari præsumeret, non papa sed apostata ab omnibus haberetur.*   See Mirbt, *Die Wahl*, etc., pp. 29–38.

[2] Jaffé, *Mon. Greg.* (1885), pp. 9 sqq.

[3] Abridged from *Ep.*, II. 49 ; Jaffé, p. 163 ; Migne, 148, 400.

This picture is true, and we need not wonder that he often longed to retire to the quiet retreat of a convent.   He adds in the same letter that, if it were not for his desire to serve the holy Church, he would not remain in Rome, where he had spent twenty years against his wish.   He was thus suspended between sorrow and hope, seized by a thousand storms, living as a dying man.   He compared himself to a sailor on the high seas surrounded by darkness.   And he wrote to William the Conqueror, that unwillingly he had ascended into the ship which was tossed on a billowy sea, with the violence of the winds and the fury of storms with hidden rocks beneath and other dangers rising high in air in the distance.[1]

The two features which distinguished Gregory's administration were the advocacy of papal absolutism and the promotion of moral reforms.   In both these respects Gregory left an abiding impression upon the thought and practice of Latin Christendom.   Even where we do not share his views we cannot help but admire his moral force and invincible courage.

§ 11.   *The Gregorian Theocracy.*

The Hildebrandian or Gregorian Church ideal is a theocracy based upon the Mosaic model and the canon law.   It is the absolute sovereignty of the Church in this world, commanding respect and obedience by her moral purity and ascetic piety.   By the Church is meant the Roman Catholic organization headed by the pope as the vicar of Christ ; and this hierarchical organization is identified with the Kingdom of God, in which men are saved from sin and death, and outside of which there is no ordinary salvation.   No distinction is made between the Church and the Kingdom, nor between the visible and invisible Church.   The Holy, Catholic, Apostolic, Roman Church has been to popes as visible and tangible as the German Empire, or the Kingdom of France, or the

[1] *Reg.*, I. 70.

Republic of Venice.   Besides this Church no other is recognized, not even the Greek, except as a schismatic branch of
the Roman.

This ideal is the growth of ages.   It was prepared for by
pseudo-Isidor in the ninth, and by St. Augustine in the fifth
century.

St. Augustine, the greatest theological authority of the
Middle Ages, first identified the visible Catholic Church with
the City or Kingdom of God.   In his great apologetic work,
De Civitate Dei, he traced the relation of this Kingdom to the
changing and passing kingdoms of this world, and furnished,
we may say, the programme of the mediæval theocracy which,
in theory, is adhered to by the Roman Church to this day.[1]
But Augustine was not an ecclesiastic like Cyprian and the
popes.   He was more interested in theology than Church
policy; he had little to say about the papacy, and made a
suggestive distinction between " the true body of Christ " and
" the mixed body of Christ," which led the way to the Protestant distinction (first made by Zwingli) between the visible
and invisible Church.[2]   In the Hildebrandian controversy he
is quoted by both parties, and more frequently than any other
father; but neither Gregory nor his most zealous adherents
could quote Augustine in favor of their hierocratic theory of
the apostolic right to depose temporal sovereigns.

The pseudo-Isidorian Decretals went further: they identified the Catholic Church with the dominion of the papal
hierarchy, and by a series of literary fictions carried this

---

[1] Pope Leo XIII., in his encyclical concerning the Christian constitution
of States (*Immortale Dei*, Nov. 1, 1885), defends the mediæval theory of
Church and State, and refers to the authority of St. Augustine, as having in
his *De Civitate Dei* clearly set forth the true principles on this subject for all
time to come. See Schaff's edition of St. Augustine's *Works*, pref. to vol. II.
(New York, 1887). Comp. also Reuter, *Augustinische Studien* (Gotha, 1887),
pp. 106–152, and Mirbt., *l. c.*, who has industriously collected the quotations
from Augustine by the friends and opponents of Gregory VII.

[2] The influence of Augustine's theory upon Wyclif, Hus, and the Reformers is shown in this *Church History*, vol. VI. 522 sqq.

system back to the second century; notwithstanding the
fact that the Oriental Church never recognized the claims
of the bishops of Rome beyond that of a mere primacy of
honor among equal patriarchs.

Gregory VII. actualized this politico-ecclesiastical system
more fully than any previous pope, and as far as human
energy and prudence would admit.   The glory of the Church
was the all-controlling passion of his life.   He held fast to it
in the darkest hours, and he was greatest in adversity.   Of
earlier popes, Nicolas I. and Leo I. came nearest to him in
lofty pretensions.   But in him papal absolutism assumed
flesh and blood.   He was every inch a pope.   He anticipated
the Vatican system of 1870; in one point he fell short of
it, in another point he went beyond it.   He did not claim
infallibility in theory, though he assumed it in fact; but he
did claim and exercise, as far as he could, an absolute authority over the temporal powers of Christendom, which the
popes have long since lost, and can never regain.

Hildebrand was convinced that, however unworthy personally, he was, in his official character, the successor of Peter,
and as such the vicar of Christ in the militant Church.[1]   He
entirely identified himself with Peter as the head of the
apostolic college, and the keeper of the keys of the Kingdom
of Heaven; but he forgot that in temporal affairs Peter was
an humble subject under a hostile government, and exhorted
the Christians to honor the king (1 Pet. 2: 17) at a time
when a Nero sat on the throne.   He constantly appealed to
the famous words of Christ, Matt. 16: 18, 19, as if they
were said to himself.   The pope inherits the lofty position
of Peter.   He is the Rock of the Church.   He is the universal bishop, a title against which the first Gregory protested as an anti-Christian presumption.   He is intrusted

---

[1] Gregory again and again expressed his feeling of personal unworthiness
in such expressions as *cui licet indigni et nolentes præsidemus*, *Reg.*, I. 18,
70, etc. ; Migne, 300, 344, etc.

with the care of all Christendom (including the Greek
Church, which never acknowledged him).   He has absolute
and final jurisdiction, and is responsible only to God, and
to no earthly tribunal.   He alone can depose and reinstate
bishops, and his legates take precedence of all bishops.   He
is the supreme arbiter in questions of right and wrong in
the whole Christian world.   He is above all earthly sovereigns.   He can wear the imperial insignia.   He can depose
kings and emperors, and absolve subjects from their oath of
allegiance to unworthy sovereigns.

These and similar claims are formulated in a document of
twenty-seven brief propositions preserved among Gregory's
letters, which are of doubtful genuineness, but correctly
express his views,[1] and in a famous letter to Hermann, bishop
of Metz.

Among his favorite Scripture quotations, besides the
prophecy about Peter (Matt. 16:18, 19), are two passages
from the Old Testament: the words of the prophet Samuel
to Saul, which suited his attitude to rebellious kings (1 Sam.
15:23): "Rebellion is as the sin of witchcraft, and stubborn-
ness is as idolatry and teraphim; because thou hast rejected
the word of the Lord, he has also rejected thee from being
king"; and the words of the prophet Jeremiah (48:10):
"Cursed be he that doeth the work of the Lord negligently,
and cursed be he that keepeth back his sword from blood."
He meant the spiritual sword chiefly, but also the temporal,
if necessary.   He would have liked to lead an army of soldiers of St. Peter for the conquest of the Holy Land, and
the subjection of all rebellious monarchs.   He projected the
first crusade, which his second successor carried out.

---

[1] *Dictatus Papœ*, Migne, 148, 407 sq.; Mirbt, *Quellen*, p. 113.   Comp: the
note of Gieseler, II. B. 7 (Germ. ed.).   I quote a few: 12. *Quod illi liceat
imperatores deponere.*   22. *Quod Romana Ecclesia numquam erravit, nec in
perpetuum, Scriptura testante, errabit.*   26. *Quod catholicus non habeatur,
qui non concordat Ecclesiæ Romanæ.*   27. *Quod a fidelitate iniquorum
subjectos potest absolvere.*

We must consider more particularly his views on the relation of Church and State.   Public opinion in the Middle
Ages believed neither in co-ordination nor separation of the
two powers, but in the subordination of one to the other
on the basis of union.   Church and State were inseparably
interwoven from the days of Charlemagne and even of Constantine, and both together constituted the Christian commonwealth, *respublica Christiana*.   There was also a general
agreement that the Church was the spiritual, the State, the
temporal power.

But the parties divided on the question of the precise
boundary line.[1]   The papal party maintained the theocratic
superiority of the Church over the State : the imperial party
maintained the cæsaropapistic superiority of the State, or
at least the equality of the two powers.   It was a conflict
between priestcraft and statecraft, between *sacerdotium* and
imperium, the clergy and the laity.   The imperialists emphasized the divine origin and superior antiquity of the civil
government, to which even Christ and the Apostles were
subject; the hierarchical party disparaged the State, and put
the Church above it even in temporal affairs, when they
conflicted with the spiritual.   Emperors like Otto I. and
Henry III. deposed and elected popes; while popes like
Gregory VII. and Innocent III. deposed and elected emperors.

Gregory compares the Church to the sun, the State to the
moon, which borrows her light from the sun.[2]   The episcopal dignity is above the kingly and imperial dignity, as
heaven is above the earth.   He admits the necessity of the
State for the temporal government of men; but in his conflict with the civil power he takes the pessimistic view that

[1] See Mirbt, *Publizistik*, 572–579.
[2] Letter of May 8, 1080, to William of England. Jaffé, 419 sq.; Migne,
148, 569.   Gregory also compared the priesthood to gold and royalty to lead,
Reg., IV. 2.

the State is the product of robbery, murder, and all sorts of crimes, and a disturbance of the original equality, which must be restored by the priestly power. He combined the highest view of the Church and the papacy with the lowest view of the State and the empire.[1]

His theory of the papal power could not have been more explicitly stated than when, writing to Sancho, king of Aragon, he said that Jesus, the king of glory, had made Peter lord over the kingdoms of the world. This principle he consistently acted upon.[2] Henry IV. of Germany he twice deposed and absolved his subjects from allegiance to him. He concluded his second excommunication of Henry IV., at the synod in Lent, March 7, 1080, with this startling peroration: —

"And now, O ye princes and fathers, most holy Apostles Peter and Paul, deal ye with us in such wise that all the world may know and understand that, having the power to bind and to loose in heaven, you have the like power to take away empires, kingdoms, principalities, duchies, marquisates, earldoms, and all manner of human rights and properties. . . . Having such mighty power in spiritual things, what is there on earth that may transcend your authority in temporal things ? And if ye judge the angels, who are high above the proudest of princes, what may ye not do unto those beneath them ? Let the kings and princes of the earth know and feel how great ye are — how exalted your power ! Let them tremble to despise the commands of your Church !

"But upon the said Henry do judgment quickly, that all men may know that it is not by fortune or chance, but by your power, that he has fallen ! May he thus be confounded unto repentance, that his soul may be saved in the day of the Lord ! "

---

[1] In a letter to Bishop Hermann of Metz, March 15, 1081 (*Reg.*, VIII. 21), " *Quis nesciat reges et duces ab illis habuisse principium, qui, Deum ignorantes, superbia, rapinis, perfidia, homicidiis, postremo universis pene sceleribus, mundi principe Diabolo videlicet agitante, super pares scilicet homines, dominari cœca cupidine et intolerabili presumptione affectaverunt,*" St. Augustine likewise combines the two views of the origin of the State, and calls it both a divine ordinance and a " *grande latrocinium,*" an enslavement of men in consequence of sin. See Reuter, *August. Studien, l.c.,* 135 sq. The letter to Hermann is also given in Mirbt, *Quellen,* 105–112.

[2] *Petrum dominus Jesus Christus, rex gloriœ, principem super regna mundi constituit, Reg.,* I. 63 ; Migne, 148, 339.

This is the extreme of hierarchical arrogance and severity. Gregory always assumed the air of supreme authority over kings and nobles as well as bishops and abbots, and expects from them absolute obedience.

Sardinia and Corsica he treated as fiefs.[1] To the Spanish princes, in 1073, he wrote that from of old Spain had belonged to St. Peter, and that it belonged to no mortal man but to the Apostolic see. For had not the Holy See made a grant of Spanish territory to a certain Evulus on condition of his conquering it from pagan hands ?[2] Alfonso of Castile and Sancho of Aragon, he reminded that St. Paul had gone to Spain and that seven bishops, sent by Paul and Peter, had founded the Christian Church in Spain.[3] Philip I., king of France, he coolly told, that every house in his kingdom owed Peter's Pence, and he threatened the king, in case he did not desist from simony, to place his realm under the interdict.[4] A few months later in a letter to Manasses, archbishop of Rheims, he called the king a rapacious wolf, the enemy of God and religion.[5] He summoned the king of Denmark, Sueno, to recognize the dependence of his kingdom upon Rome and to send his son to Rome that he might draw the sword against the enemies of God, promising the son a certain rich province in Italy for his services.[6] Boleslav, duke of Poland, he admonished to pay certain monies to the king of Russia, whose son, as we are informed in another letter, had come to Rome, to secure his throne from the pope.[7] The Hungarian king, Solomon, was reminded that King Stephen had given his kingdom to St. Peter and that it belonged of right to Rome,[8] and he was sharply rebuked for having received his crown from

---

[1] *Reg.*, I. 29, VII. 10 ; Migne, 148, 312, 584.

[2] *Reg.*, I. 7 ; Migne, 289.   [5] *Lupus rapax*, etc.

[3] *Reg.*, I. 64 ; Migne, 339.   [6] *Reg.*, II. 51, 75 ; Migne, 403, 426.

[4] *Reg.*, II. 5, 18, 32.   [7] *Reg.*, II. 73, 74 ; Migne, 423 sq.

[8] *Regnum Hungariæ sanctæ Romanæ ecclesiæ proprium est a rege Stephano beato Petri olim cum omni jure et potestate sua oblatum et devote traditum, Reg.*, II. 13 ; Migne, 373.

D

the king of the Germans as a fief and not having sought it from Rome. On Demetrius, duke of Dalmatia, Gregory conferred the royal title on condition of his rendering a yearly payment of two hundred pieces of silver to himself and his papal successors. To Michael, Byzantine emperor, he wrote, expressing the hope that the Church of Constantinople as a true daughter might be reconciled to its mother, the Church of Rome.[1] In other communications to the emperor, Gregory made propositions concerning a crusade to rescue the Holy Land.

For William the Conqueror, Gregory expressed great affection, addressing him as " best beloved," *carissime*, but solemnly reminded him that he owed his promotion to the throne of England to the favor of the Roman see and bidding him be prompt in the payment of Peter's Pence.[2] The proud Englishman replied that he owed his crown to God and his own sword, not to the pope. He was willing to pay Peter's Pence which his predecessors had paid, but fealty he refused to pay as his predecessors had refused to pay it.[3]

Unbiblical and intolerable as is Hildebrand's scheme of papal absolutism as a theory of abiding validity, for the Middle Ages it was better that the papacy should rule. It was, indeed, a spiritual despotism ; but it checked a military despotism which was the only alternative, and would have been far worse. The Church, after all, represented the moral and intellectual interests over against rude force and pas-

---

[1] *Reg.*, I. 18 ; Migne, 300.

[2] *Reg.*, I. 70, VII. 23 ; Migne, 345, 565 sqq., etc.

[3] " Hubert, your legate in your behalf has bade me to do fealty to you and your successors, and to think better in the matter of the money which my predecessors were wont to send to the Roman Church. The one point I agreed to, the other I did not agree to. Fealty I refused to do, nor will I do it, nor do I find that my predecessors did it to your predecessors." The letter of William the Conqueror to Gregory, written after 1076, the date being uncertain. See Gee and Hardy, *Documents of Eng. Ch. Hist.*, p. 57. The efforts of Gregory to secure William's support in his controversy with Henry IV. failed. *Reg.*, VI. 30, VII. 1 ; Migne, 535, 545.

sions.   She could not discharge her full duty unless she was
free and independent.   The princes of the Middle Ages were
mostly ignorant and licentious despots; while the popes, in
their official character, advocated the cause of learning, the
sanctity of marriage, and the rights of the people.   It was
a conflict of moral with physical power, of intelligence with
ignorance, of religion with vice.

The theocratic system made religion the ruling factor in
mediæval Europe, and gave the Catholic Church an opportunity to do her best.   Her influence was, upon the whole,
beneficial.   The enthusiasm for religion inspired the crusades, carried Christianity to heathen savages, built the
cathedrals and innumerable churches, founded the universities and scholastic theology, multiplied monastic orders and
charitable institutions, checked wild passions, softened
manners, stimulated discoveries and inventions, preserved
ancient classical and Christian literature, and promoted civilization.   The papacy struck its roots deep in the past, even
as far back as the second century.   But it was based in part
on pious frauds, as the pseudo-Isidorian Decretals and the
false Donation of Constantine.

The mediæval theocracy was at best a carnal anticipation
of the millennial reign, when all the kingdoms of this world
shall obey the peaceful sceptre of Christ.   The papacy degenerated more and more into a worldly institution and an
intolerable tyranny over the hearts and minds of men.
Human nature is too noble to be ruled by despotism, and
too weak to resist its temptations.   The State has divine
authority as well as the Church, and the laity have rights
as well as the clergy.   These rights came to the front as
civilization advanced and as the hierarchy abused its power.
It was the abuse of priestly authority for the enslavement
of men, the worldliness of the Church, and the degradation
and profanation of religion in the traffic of indulgences,
which provoked the judgment of the Reformation.

§ 12.   *Gregory VII. as a Moral Reformer.   Simony and Clerical Marriage.*

Gregory VII. must be viewed not only as a papal abso-
lutist, but also as a moral reformer.   It is the close connection of these two characters that gives him such pre-eminence
in history, and it is his zeal for moral reform that entitles
him to real respect; while his pretension to absolute power
he shares with the most worthless popes.

His Church ideal formed a striking contrast to the actual
condition of the Church, ahd he could not actualize it without raising the clergy from the deep slough of demoralization
to a purer and higher plane.

His reforms were directed against simony and Nicolaitism.
What he had done as Hildebrand, by way of advice, he now
carried out by official authority.

In the war on simony he was altogether right from the
standpoint of Protestant as well as Roman Catholic ethics.
The traffic in ecclesiastical dignities was an unmitigated
nuisance and scandal, and doubly criminal if exercised by
bishops and popes.

In his war on Nicolaitism, Gregory was sustained by
ancient laws of the Roman Church, but not by the genuine
spirit of Christianity.   Enforced clerical celibacy has no
foundation in the Bible, and is apt to defeat the sacerdotal
ideal which it was intended to promote.   The real power and
usefulness of the clergy depend upon its moral purity, which
is protected and promoted by lawful matrimony, the oldest
institution of God, dating from the paradise of innocence.

The motives of Gregory in his zeal for sacerdotal celibacy
were partly monkish and partly hierarchical.   Celibacy was
an essential part of his ascetic ideal of a priest of God, who
must be superior to carnal passions and frailties, wholly
devoted to the interests of the Church, distracted by no
earthly cares, separated from his fellow-men, and command-

ing their reverence by angelic purity. Celibacy, moreover, was an indispensable condition of the freedom of the hierarchy. He declared that he could not free the Church from the rule of the laity unless the priests were freed from their wives. A married clergy is connected with the world by social ties, and concerned for the support of the family; an unmarried clergy is independent, has no home and aim but the Church, and protects the pope like a standing army.

Another motive for opposing clerical marriage was to prevent the danger of a hereditary caste which might appropriate ecclesiastical property to private uses and impoverish the Church. The ranks of the hierarchy, even the chair of St. Peter, were to be kept open to self-made men of the humblest classes, but closed against hereditary claimants. This was a practical recognition of the democratic principle in contrast with the aristocratic feudalism of the Middle Ages. Hildebrand himself, who rose from the lowest rank without patronage to the papal throne, was the best illustration of this clerical democracy.

The power of the confessional, which is one of the pillars of the priesthood, came to the aid of celibacy. Women are reluctant to intrust their secrets to a priest who is a husband and father of a family.

The married priests brought forward the example of the priests of the Old Testament. This argument Damiani answered by saying that the Hebrew priest was forbidden to eat before offering sacrifices at the altar. How much more unseemly it would be for a priest of the new order to soil himself carnally before offering the sacraments to God! The new order owed its whole time to the office and had none left for marriage and the family life (1 Cor. 7:32). Only an unmarried man who refuses to gratify carnal lusts can fulfil the injunction to be a temple of God and avoid quenching the Spirit (Eph. 4:30; 1 Thess. 5:19).[1]

<hr>

[1] See Mirbt, p. 278.

These motives controlled also the followers of Gregory and the whole hierarchy, and secured the ultimate triumph of sacerdotal celibacy. The question of abolishing it has from time to time been agitated, and in the exceptional cases of the Maronites and United Greeks the popes have allowed single marriage in deference to old custom and for prudential reasons. Pope Pius II., before he ascended the papal chair (1458–1464), said that good reasons required the prohibition of clerical marriage, but better reasons required its restoration. The hierarchical interest, however, has always overruled these better reasons. Whatever may have been the advantages of clerical celibacy, its evils were much greater. The sexual immorality of the clergy, more than anything else, undermined the respect of the people for their spiritual guides, and was one of the chief causes of the Reformation, which restored honorable clerical marriage, created a pastoral home with its blessings, and established the supremacy of conscience over hierarchical ambition.

From the standpoint of a zealous reformer like Gregory, the morals of the clergy were certainly in a low condition. No practice did he condemn with such burning words as the open marriage of priests or their secret cohabitation with women who were to all intents and purposes their wives. Contemporary writers like Damiani, d. 1072, in his *Gomor-rhianus*, give dark pictures of the lives of the priests. While descriptions of rigid ascetics are to be accepted with caution, the evidence abounds that in all parts of Latin Christendom the law of priestly celibacy was ignored.[1] Modern Catholic historians, like Hefele[2] and Funk,[3] do not hesitate to adduce the proofs of this state of affairs. The pope Benedict IX., according to friendly testimony,

[1] Mirbt, *Publizistik*, 259, says that there was no such thing as a general observance of celibacy in Western Europe.

[2] *Kirchengesch.*, 339.

[3] *Kirchengesch.*, 271.   It will be remembered that in Spain, in the eighth century, King Witiza formally abolished the law of clerical celibacy.

was thinking of taking a wife openly.[1] The legislation, opening with the canons of the Roman synod of 1049 held by Leo IX., and emphasized at the Roman synod of 1059 held under Nicholas II., was given by Gregory VII. such a prominence that one might have supposed the very existence of the Church depended upon the enforcement of clerical celibacy.   There were bishops even in Italy who openly permitted the marriage of priests, as was the case with Kunibert of Turin.[2]   In Germany, Bishop Poppo of Toul did not conceal his quasi-marital relations which Gregory denounced as fornication,[3] and the bishops of Spires and Lausanne had hard work clearing themselves in public synods from a like charge.   Married priests were denominated by synods and by Gregory VII. as "incontinent" or "concubinary priests."[4] Gregory spoke of Germany as afflicted with the "inveterate disease of clerical fornication."[5]   And what was true of Italy and Germany was true of England.

§ 13. *The Enforcement of Sacerdotal Celibacy.*

LITERATURE, special works : HENRY C. LEA : *A Hist. Sketch of Sacerdotal Celibacy in the Christian Church*, Phil. 1867, 2d ed. Boston, 1884. — A. DRESDNER : *Kultur und Sittengeschichte der italienischen Geistlichkeit im 10 und 11 Jahrhundert*, Berlin, 1890. — MIRBT : *Publizistik*, pp. 239–342 ; HEFELE, V. 20 sqq.   The chief contemporary sources are DAMIANI : *de cœlibatu sacerdotum*, addressed to Nicolas II. and *Gomorrhianus*, commended by Leo IX., and other writings, — *Gregory VII.'s Letters.* Mirbt gives a survey of this literature, pp. 274–342.

Gregory completed, with increased energy and the weight of official authority, the moral reform of the clergy as a means for securing the freedom and power of the Church. He held synod after synod, which passed summary laws against simony and Nicolaitism, and denounced all carnal

---

[1] So Bonizo of Sutri *ad amicum*, lib. V.
[2] So Damiani.   See Mirbt, 248.   [3] Gregory, *Reg.*, II. 10.
[4] *Incontinentes sacerdotes et levitæ . . . sacerdotes concubinati.*
[5] *Reg.*, II. 30.

connection of priests with women, however legitimate, as sinful and shameful concubinage.   Not contented with synodical legislation, he sent letters and legates into all countries with instructions to enforce the decrees.   A synod in Rome, March, 1074, opened the war.   It deposed the priests who had bought their dignity or benefices, prohibited all future sacerdotal marriage, required married priests to dismiss their wives or cease to read mass, and commanded the laity not to attend their services.   The same decrees had been passed under Nicolas II. and Alexander II., but were not enforced.   The forbidding of the laity to attend mass said by a married priest, was a most dangerous, despotic measure, which had no precedent in antiquity.   In an encyclical of 1079 addressed to the whole realm of Italy and Germany, Gregory used these violent words, "If there are presbyters, deacons, or sub-deacons who are guilty of the crime of fornication (that is, living with women as their wives), we forbid them, in the name of God Almighty and by the authority of St. Peter, entrance into the churches, *introitum ecclesiæ*, until they repent and rectify their conduct."

These decrees caused a storm of opposition.   Many clergymen in Germany, as Lambert of Hersfeld reports, denounced Gregory as a madman and heretic: he had forgotten the words of Christ, Matt. 19 : 11, and of the Apostle, 1 Cor. 7 : 9 ; he wanted to compel men to live like angels, and, by doing violence to the law of nature, he opened the door to indiscriminate licentiousness.   They would rather give up their calling than their wives, and tauntingly asked him to look out for angels who might take their place.   The bishops were placed in a most embarrassing position.   Some, like Otto of Constance, sympathized with the married clergy ; and he went so far as to bid his clergy marry.[1]   Others, like

---

[1] In a letter to Sicardus, abp. of Aquileja, Jan. 24, 1074, Gregory complained of princes who treated the Church as a servant-maid, *quasi vilem ancillam*, etc. *Reg.*, I. 42 ; Migne, 148, 322.

St. Altmann of Passau, were enthusiasts for sacerdotal celibacy. Others, like Siegfrid of Mainz, took a double attitude.[1] Archbishop Anno of Cologne agreed with the Hildebrandian principle, but deemed it impracticable or inopportune. When the bishops lacked in zeal, Gregory stirred up the laity against the simoniacal and concubinary priests. He exhorted a certain Count Albert (October, 1074) to persist in enforcing the papal orders, and commanded Duke Rudolf of Swabia and Duke Bertolf of Carinthia, January, 1075, to prevent by force, if necessary, the rebellious priests from officiating, no matter what the bishops might say who had taken no steps to punish the guilty. He thus openly encouraged rebellion of the laity against the clergy, contrary to his fundamental principle of the absolute rule of the hierarchy. He acted on the maxim that the end sanctifies the means. Bishop Theodoric of Verdun, who at first sided in the main with Gregory, but was afterwards forced into the ranks of his opponents, openly reproached him for these most extraordinary measures as dangerous to the peace of the Church, to the safety of the clerical order, and even to the Christian faith. Bishop Henry of Spires denounced him as having destroyed the episcopal authority, and subjected the Church to the madness of the people. When the bishops, at the Diet of Worms, deposed him, January, 1076, one of the reasons assigned was his surrender of the Church to the laity.

But the princes who were opposed to Henry IV. and deposed him at Tribur (1076), professed great zeal for the Roman Church and moral reform. They were stigmatized with the Milanese name of Patarini. Even Henry IV., though he tacitly protected the simoniacal and concubinary clergy and received their aid, never ventured openly to defend them ; and the anti-pope Clement III., whom he elected 1080, expressed with almost Hildebrandian severity

---

[1] Gregory, *Reg.*, II. 29, III. 4, commanded him to root out "clerical fornication."

his detestation of clerical concubinage, although he threatened with excommunication the presumptuous laymen who refused to take the sacrament from immoral priests. Bishop Benzo, the most bitter of imperialists, did not wish to be identified with the Nicolaitan heretics.

A contemporary writer, probably a priest of Treves, gives a frightful picture of the immediate results of this reform, with which he sympathized in principle. Slaves betrayed masters and masters betrayed slaves, friends informed against friends, faith and truth were violated, the offices of religion were neglected, society was almost dissolved. The peccant priests were exposed to the scorn and contempt of the laity, reduced to extreme poverty, or even mutilated by the populace, tortured and driven into exile. Their wives, who had been legally married with ring and religious rites, were insulted as harlots, and their children branded as bastards. Many of these unfortunate women died from hunger or grief, or committed suicide in despair, and were buried in unconsecrated earth. Peasants burned the tithes on the field lest they should fall into the hands of disobedient priests, trampled the host under foot, and baptized their own children.[1]

In England, St. Dunstan, archbishop of Canterbury, d. 988, had anticipated the reforms of Hildebrand, but only with temporary success. William the Conqueror made no effort to enforce sacerdotal celibacy, except that the charge of concubinage was freely used as a pretext for removing Anglo-Saxon prelates to make room for Norman rivals. Lanfranc of Canterbury was a Hildebrandian, but could not prevent a reformatory council at Winchester in 1076 from allowing married priests to retain their wives, and it contented itself with the prohibition of future marriages. This prohibition was repeated at a council held in London, 1102, when Anselm occupied the see of Canterbury. Married priests

---

[1] Hauck, III. 780 sq.; Mirbt, *Publizistik*, 269 sqq.; Hefele, V. 30 sqq.

were required to dismiss their wives, and their children were forbidden to inherit their fathers' churches. A profession of chastity was to be exacted at ordination to the sub-diaconate and the higher orders. But no punishment was prescribed for the violation of these canons. Anselm maintained them vigorously before and after his exile. A new council, called by King Henry at London, 1108, a year before Anselm's death, passed severe laws against sacerdotal marriage under penalties of deposition, expulsion from the Church, loss of property, and infamy. The temporal power was pledged to enforce this legislation. But Eadmer, the biographer of Anselm, sorrowfully intimates that the result was an increase of shocking crimes of priests with their relatives, and that few preserved that purity with which Anselm had labored to adorn his clergy.

In Spain, which was as much isolated from the Continent by the Pyrenees as England by the sea, clerical celibacy was never enforced before this period. The Saracenic invasion and subsequent struggles of the Christians were unfavorable to discipline. A canon of Compostella, afterwards bishop of Mondonego, describes the contemporary ecclesiastics at the close of the eleventh century as reckless and violent men, ready for any crime, prompt to quarrel, and occasionally indulging in mutual slaughter. The lower priests were generally married ; but bishops and monks were forbidden by a council of Compostella, in 1056, all intercourse with women, except with mothers, aunts, and sisters wearing the monastic habit. Gregory VII. sent a legate, a certain Bishop Amandus, to Spain to introduce his reforms, 1077. A council at Girona, 1078, forbade the ordination of sons of priests and the hereditary transmission of ecclesiastical benefices. A council at Burgos, 1080, commanded married priests to put away their wives. But this order seems to have been a dead letter until the thirteenth century, when the code of laws drawn up by Alfonso the Wise, known as "Las Siete

Partidas," punished sacerdotal marriage with deprivation of function and benefice, and authorized the prelates to command the assistance of the secular power in enforcing this punishment. " After this we hear little of regular marriage, which was replaced by promiscuous concubinage or by permanent irregular unions."[1]

In France the efforts of reform made by the predecessors of Gregory had little effect. A Paris synod of 1074 declared Gregory's decrees unbearable and unreasonable.[2] At a stormy synod at Poitiers, in 1078, his legate obtained the adoption of a canon which threatened with excommunication all who should listen to mass by a priest whom they knew to be guilty of simony or concubinage. But the bishops were unable to carry out the canon without the aid of the secular arm. The Norman clergy in 1072 drove the archbishop of Rouen from a council with a shower of stones. William the Conqueror came to his aid in 1080 at a synod of Lillebonne, which forbade ordained persons to keep women in their houses. But clerical marriages continued, the nuptials were made public, and male children succeeded to benefices by a recognized right of primogeniture. William the Conqueror, who assisted the hopeless reform in Normandy, prevented it in his subject province of Britanny, where the clergy, as described by Pascal II., in the early part of the twelfth century, were setting the canons at defiance and indulging in enormities hateful to God and man.

At last, the Gregorian enforcement of sacerdotal celibacy triumphed in the whole Roman Church, but at the fearful sacrifice of sacerdotal chastity. The hierarchical aim was attained, but not the angelic purity of the priesthood. The private morals of the priest were sacrificed to hierarchical ambition. Concubinage and licentiousness took the place of holy matrimony. The acts of councils abound in complaints of clerical immorality and the vices of unchastity and drunk-

[1] Lea, p. 309.   [2] *importabilia ideoque irrationabilia.*

enness. "The records of the Middle Ages are full of the evidences that indiscriminate license of the worst kind prevailed throughout every rank of the hierarchy."[1] The corruption again reached the papacy, especially in the fifteenth century.   John XXIII. and Alexander VI. rivalled in wickedness and lewdness the worst popes of the tenth and eleventh centuries.

§ 14.   *The War over Investiture.*

The other great reform-scheme of Gregory aimed at the complete emancipation of the Church from the bondage of the secular power. His conception of the freedom of the Church meant the slavery of the State. The State exercised control over the Church by selling ecclesiastical dignities, or the practice of simony, and by the investiture of bishops and abbots ; that is, by the bestowal of the staff and ring.[2] These were the insignia of ecclesiastical authority; the staff or crosier was the symbol of the spiritual rule of the bishop, the ring the symbol of his mystical marriage with the Church.

The feudal system of the Middle Ages, as it developed itself among the new races of Europe from the time of Charlemagne, rested on land tenure and the mutual obligations of lord and vassal, whereby the lord, from the king down to the lowest landed proprietor, was bound to protect his vassal, and the vassal was bound to serve his lord. The Church in many countries owned nearly or fully one-half of the landed estate, with the right of customs, tolls, coinage of money, etc., and was in justice bound to bear part of the burden attached to land tenure. The secular lords regarded themselves as the patrons of the Church, and claimed the right of appointing and investing its officers, and of bestowing upon them, not only their temporalia, but also the insignia of their spiritual power. This was extremely offensive to churchmen. The bishop, invested by the lord, became

---

[1] Lea, p. 341.   [2] *investitura per baculum et annulum.*

his vassal, and had to swear an oath of obedience, which
implied the duty of serving at court and furnishing troops
for the defence of the country. Sometimes a bishop had
hardly left the altar when his liege-lord commanded him
to gird on the sword. After the death of the bishop, the
king or prince used the income of the see till the election
of a successor, and often unduly postponed the election for
his pecuniary benefit, to the injury of the Church and the
poor. In the appointments, the king was influenced by political, social, or pecuniary considerations, and often sold the
dignity to the highest bidder, without any regard to intellectual or moral qualifications. The right of investiture was
thus closely connected with the crying abuse of simony, and
its chief source.

No wonder that Gregory opposed this investiture by laymen with all his might. Cardinal Humbert had attacked it
in a special book under Victor II. (1057), and declared it an
infamous scandal that lay-hands, above all, female hands,
should bestow the ring and crosier. He insisted that investiture was a purely spiritual function, and that secular princes
have nothing to do with the performance of functions that
have something sacramental about them. They even commit
sacrilege by touching the garments of the priest. By the
exercise of the right of investiture, princes, who are properly
the defenders of the Church, had become its lords and rulers.
Great evils had arisen out of this practice, especially in
Italy, where ambitious priests lingered about the antecham-
bers of courts and practised the vice of adulation, *vitium adu-
lationis*.[1]

The legislation against lay appointments was opened at
the Synod of Rheims, 1049, under the influence of Leo IX.

---

[1] Humbert's work, *adversus simoniacos*, is given in *libelli de lite* and Migne,
vol. 153.   Wido of Arezzo and Damiani expressed the same views.   See
Mirbt, *Publizistik*, 463–471. Of those who received lay investiture it began
to be said "that they entered not in by the door," *non per ostium intra-
verant.*

It declared that no priest should be promoted to office without the election of clergy and people. Ten years later, 1059,
the Synod of Rome pronounced any appointment of cleric
or presbyter to benefice invalid, which was made by a layman.[1] The following year, 1060, the French synods of
Tours and Vienne extended the prohibition to bishops. It
remained for Gregory to stir up all Europe over the question
who had the right of investiture.

By abolishing this custom, Gregory hoped to emancipate
the clergy from the vassalage of the State, and the property
of the Church from the feudal supervision of the prince, as
well as to make the bishops the obedient servants of the
pope.

The contest continued under the following popes, and was
at last settled by the compromise of Worms (1122). The
emperor yielded only in part ; for to surrender the whole
property of the Church to the absolute power of the pope,
would have reduced civil government to a mere shadow. On
the other hand, the partial triumph of the papacy contributed
very much to the secularization of the Church.

§ 15. *Gregory VII. and Henry IV.*

The conflict over investiture began at a Roman synod in
Lent (Feb. 24–28), 1075, and brought on the famous collision
with Henry IV., in which priestcraft and kingcraft strove for
mastery. The pope had the combined advantages of superior age, wisdom, and moral character over this unfortunate
prince, who, when a mere boy of six years (1056), had lost
his worthy father, Henry III., had been removed from the
care of his pious but weak mother, Agnes, and was spoilt in
his education. Henry had a lively mind and noble impulses,
but was despotic and licentious. Prosperity made him proud
and overbearing, while adversity cast him down. His life

---

[1] *ut per laicos nullo modo quilibet clericus aut presbyter obtineat ecclesiam
nec gratis nec pretio,* Mansi, XIX. 898.

presents striking changes of fortune. He ascended and descended twice the scale of exaltation and humiliation. He first insulted the pope, then craved his pardon; he rebelled again against him, triumphed for a while, was twice excommunicated and deposed; at last, forsaken and persecuted by his own son, he died a miserable death, and was buried in unconsecrated earth. The better class of his own subjects sided against him in his controversy with the pope. The Saxons rose in open revolt against his tyranny on the very day that Hildebrand was consecrated (June 29, 1073).

This synod of 1075 forbade the king and all laymen having anything to do with the appointment of bishops or assuming the right of investiture.[1] A synod held in November, 1075, positively forbade bishops, abbots, and other ecclesiastics receiving ecclesiastical appointments from king or any temporal lord whatsoever. At the same synod, Gregory excommunicated five counsellors of Henry for practising simony.[2]

The king, hard pressed by the rebellious Saxons, at first yielded, and dismissed the five counsellors ; but, as soon as he had subdued the rebellion (June 5, 1075), he recalled them, and continued to practise shameful simony. He paid his soldiers from the proceeds of Church property, and adorned his mistresses with the diamonds of sacred vessels. The pope exhorted him by letter and deputation to repent,

---

[1] This statement is based upon the authority of Arnulf of Milan. The decree itself is lost. See Mirbt, *Publizistik*, 492. Arnulf says, *papa . . . palam interdicit regi jus deinde habere aliquod in dandis episcopatibus omnesque laicas personas ab investituris ecclesiarum summovet.*

[2] " *Si quis deinceps episcopatum vel abbatiam de manu alicujus laicæ personæ susceperit, nullatenus inter Episcopos vel Abbates habeatur . . . Si quis Imperatorum, Regum, Ducum, Marchionum, Comitum, vel quilibet sæcularium potestatum aut personarum investituram episcopatus vel alicujus ecclesiasticæ dignitatis dare præsumserit, ejusdem sententiæ vinculo se adstrictum sciat.*" Pagi, *Crit.* ad ann. 1075, No. 2 ; Watterich, I. 365 ; Hefele, V. 47 ; *Reg.*, VI. 5.

and threatened him with excommunication.   The king received his legates most ungraciously, and assumed the tone of open defiance.   Probably with his knowledge, Cencius, a cousin of the imperial prefect in Rome, shamefully maltreated the pope, seized him at the altar the night before Christmas, 1075, and shut him up in a tower ; but the people released him and put Cencius to flight.

Henry called the bishops and abbots of the empire to a council at Worms, under the lead of Archbishop Siegfried of Mainz, Jan. 24, 1076.   This council deposed Gregory without giving him even a hearing, on the ground öf slanderous charges of treason, witchcraft, covenant with the devil, and impurity, which were brought against him by Hugo Blancus (Hugh Leblanc), a deposed cardinal.   It was even asserted that he ruled the Church by a senate of women, Beatrix, Matilda of Tuscany, and Agnes, the emperor's mother. Only two bishops dared to protest against the illegal proceeding.   The Ottos and Henry III. had deposed popes, but not in such a manner.

Henry secured the signatures of the disaffected bishops of Upper Italy at a council in Piacenza.   He informed Gregory of the decree of Worms in an insulting letter: —

" Henry, king, not by usurpation, but by God's holy ordinance, to Hildebrand, not pope, but a false monk.   How darest thou, who hast won thy power through craft, flattery, bribery, and force, stretch forth thy hand against the Lord's anointed, despising the precept of the true pope, St. Peter : ' Fear God, honor the king' ?   Thou who dost not fear God, dishonorest me whom He has appointed.   Condemned by the voice of all our bishops, quit the apostolic chair, and let another take it, who will preach the sound doctrine of St. Peter, and not do violence under the cloak of religion.   I, Henry, by the grace of God, king, with all my bishops, say unto thee, Come down, come down ! " [1]

At the same time Henry wrote to the cardinals and the Roman people to aid him in the election of a new pope.

[1] " *Descende, descende.*"   Bruno, *De bello Saxonico*, in Pertz, VII. 352 sq. There are several variations of the letter of Henry, but the tone of imperious defiance and violence is the same.

E

Roland, a priest of Parma, brought the letter to Rome at the end of February, as Gregory was just holding a synod of a hundred and ten bishops, and concluded his message with the words, " I tell you, brethren, that you must appear at Pentecost before the king to receive from his hands a pope and father; for this man here is not pope, but a ravening wolf." This produced a storm of indignation. The prelates drew swords and were ready to kill him on the spot ; but Gregory remained calm, and protected him against violence.

On the next day (February 22) the pope excommunicated and deposed Henry in the name of St. Peter, and absolved his subjects from their oath of obedience. He published the ban in a letter to all Christians. The sentence of deposition is as follows : —

"Blessed Peter, prince of the Apostles, incline thine ear unto me, and hear me, thy servant, whom from childhood thou didst nurse and protect against the wicked to this day. Thou and my lady, the mother of God, and thy brother, St. Paul, are my witnesses that the holy Roman Church has drawn me to the helm against my will, and that I have not risen up like a robber to thy seat. Rather would I have been a pilgrim my whole life long than have snatched to myself thy chair on account of temporal glory and in a worldly spirit. . . . By thy intercession God has intrusted me with the power to bind and to loose on earth and in heaven.

"Therefore, relying on this trust, for the honor and security of the Church, in the name of the Almighty Father, Son, and Holy Spirit, I do prohibit Henry, king, son of Henry the emperor, from ruling the kingdom of the Teutons and of Italy, because with unheard-of pride he has lifted himself up against thy Church ; and I release all Christians from the oath of allegiance to him which they have taken, or shall take, and I forbid that any shall serve him as king. For it is fitting that he who will touch the dignity of the Church should lose his own. And inasmuch as he has despised obedience by associating with the excommunicate, by many deeds of iniquity, and by spurning the warnings which I have given him for his good, I bind him in the bands of anathema ; that all nations of the earth may know that thou art Peter, and that upon thy rock the Son of the living God hath built His Church, and the gates of hell shall not prevail against it."[1]

The empress-widow was present when the anathema was pronounced on her son. At the same time the pope excom-

[1] Bernried, *Vita Greg.*, c. 68 sq. (in Migne, 148, p. 74) ; Jaffé, 223; Mirbt, *Quellen*, 100; Hefele, V. 70 sqq.

municated all the German and Italian bishops who had deposed him at Worms and Piacenza.

This was a most critical moment, and the signal for a deadly struggle between the two greatest potentates in Christendom.   Never before had such a tremendous sentence been pronounced upon a crowned head.   The deposition of Childeric by Pope Zacharias was only the sanction of the actual rule of Pepin.   Gregory threatened also King Philip of France with deposition, but did not execute it. Now the heir of the crown of Charlemagne was declared an outlaw by the successor of the Galilean fisherman, and Europe accepted the decision.   There were not wanting, indeed, voices of discontent and misgivings about the validity of a sentence which justified the breaking of a solemn oath.   All conceded the papal right of excommunication, but not the right of deposition.   If Henry had commanded the respect and love of his subjects, he might have defied Gregory.   But the religious sentiment of the age sustained the pope, and was far less shocked by the papal excommunication and deposition of the king than by the royal deposition of the pope.   It was never forgotten that the pope had crowned Charlemagne, and it seemed natural that his power to bestow implied his power to withhold or to take away.[1]

Gregory had not a moment's doubt as to the justice of his act.   He invited the faithful to pray, and did not neglect the dictates of worldly prudence.   He strengthened his military force in Rome, and reopened negotiations with Robert Guiscard and Roger.   In Northern Italy he had a powerful ally in Countess Matilda, who, by the recent death of her husband and her mother, had come into full possession of vast dominions, and furnished a bulwark against the discontented

[1] The papal sentence against Henry made a profound impression upon Western Europe.   Bonizo says, *universus noster romanus orbis contremuit, postquam de banno regis ad aures personuit vulgi.*   See Mirbt, 139.

clergy and nobility of Lombardy and an invading army from Germany.[1]

When Henry received the tidings of the sentence of excommunication and deposition, he burst into a furious rage, abused Gregory as a hypocrite, heretic, murderer, perjurer, adulterer, and threatened to fling back the anathema upon his head. William, bishop of Utrecht, had no scruples in complying with the king's wishes, and from the pulpit of his cathedral anathematized Gregory as "a perjured monk who had dared to lift up his head against the Lord's anointed." Henry summoned a national council to Worms on Whitsunday (May 15) to protest against the attempt of Gregory to unite in one hand the two swords which God had separated.[2]

This was the famous figure for the spiritual and temporal power afterwards often employed by the popes, who claimed that God had given both swords to the Church, — the spiritual sword, to be borne by her; the temporal, to be wielded by the State for the Church, that is, in subjection and obedience to the Church.

The council at Worms was attended by few bishops, and proved a failure. A council in Mainz, June 29, turned

---

[1] The excommunication of Henry in 1076 and again in 1080 called forth a controversial literature of some proportions, Mirbt, *Publizistik*, 134–239, as did Gregory's attitude towards simony and clerical celibacy. The anti-Gregorians took the ground that the excommunication was unjust and even called in question the pope's right to excommunicate a king. Gregory's letters make reference to these objections. Writing to Hermann of Metz, *Reg.*, IV. 2, Gregory said that there were some who openly declared that a king should not be excommunicated, *regem non oportet excommunicari*. Gregory justified his act on the ground of the king's companionship with excommunicated persons, his refusal to offer repentance for crimes, and the rupture of the unity of the Church which resulted from the king's course, *Reg.*, IV. 1, etc. The Council of Tribur, Oct. 16, 1076, discussed the questions whether a pope might excommunicate a king and whether Gregory had acted justly in excommunicating Henry. It answered both questions in the affirmative. A hundred years after the event, Otto of Freising, *Gesta Friderici*, I., speaks of the sentence as unheard of before, *quo numquam ante hæc tempora hujusmodi sententiam in principem romanum promulgatam cognoverat*.

[2] *Reg.*, IV. 2 ; Migne, 148, 455.

out no better, and Henry found it necessary to negotiate. Saxony was lost; prelates and nobles deserted him. A diet at Tribur, an imperial castle near Mainz, held Oct. 16, 1076, demanded that he should submit to the pope, seek absolution from him within twelve months from the date of excommunication, at the risk of forfeiting his crown. He should then appear at a diet to be held at Augsburg on Feb. 2, 1077, under the presidency of the pope. Meanwhile he was to abide at Spires in strict privacy, in the sole company of his wife, the bishop of Verdun, and a few servants chosen by the nobles. The legates of Gregory were treated with marked respect, and gave absolution to the excommunicated bishops, including Siegfried of Mainz, who submitted to the pope.

Henry spent two dreary months in seclusion at Spires, shut out from the services of the Church and the affairs of the State. At last he made up his mind to seek absolution, as the only means of saving his crown. There was no time to be lost; only a few weeks remained till the Diet of Augsburg, which would decide his fate.

§ 16. *Canossa.* 1077.

The winter of 1076–1077 was one of the coldest and longest within the memory of men — the Rhine being frozen to a solid mass from November till April — and one of the most memorable in history — being marked by an event of typical significance. The humiliation of the head of the German Empire at the feet of the bishop of Rome at Canossa means the subjection of the State to the Church and the triumph of the Hildebrandian policy.

A few days before Christmas, Henry IV. left Spires on a journey across the Alps as a penitent, seeking absolution from the pope. He was accompanied by his wife with her infant son Conrad (born August, 1071) and one faithful servant. Bertha, daughter of the margrave Odo of Turin and Adelheid of Susa, was betrothed to Henry in 1055 at Zürich, and married to him, July 13, 1066.   She was young, beautiful, virtuous, and amiable; but he preferred to live with mistresses; and three years after the marriage he sought a divorce, with the aid of the unprincipled archbishop Siegfried of Mainz. The pope very properly refused his consent.   The king gave up his wicked intention, and became attached to Bertha. She was born to love and to suffer, and accompanied him as a comforting angel through the bitter calamities of his life.

The royal couple passed through Burgundy and Susa under the protection of Count William and the mother of Bertha, and crossed Mont Cenis.   The queen and her child were carried up and lowered down the icy slopes in rough sledges of oxhide; some horses were killed, but no human lives lost.   When Henry reached the plains of Lombardy, he was received with joy by the anti-Hildebrandian party; but he hurried on to meet the successor of Peter, who alone could give him absolution.

He left his wife and child at Reggio, and, accompanied by his mother-in-law and a few friends, he climbed up the steep hill to Canossa, where Gregory was then stopping on his journey to the Diet at Augsburg, waiting for a safe-conduct across the Alps.

Canossa, now in ruins, was an impregnable fortress of the Countess Matilda, south of Reggio, on the northern slope of the Apennines, surrounded by three walls, and including a castle, a chapel, and a convent.[1]

The pope had already received a number of excommunicated bishops and noblemen, and given or promised them ab-

---

[1] The castle was destroyed by the inhabitants of Reggio in 1255.   The site affords a magnificent view of the Apennines towards the south, and of the plain of the Po towards the north, and the cities of Parma, Reggio, and Modena.   An excursion from Reggio to Canossa and back can be made in eight hours.   For Gregory's own account of the meeting, see *Reg.*, IV. 2, in Migne, 148, 465, and Mirbt, *Quellen*, 101.   See also Hauck, III. 792 sqq.

solution after the case of the chief sinner against the majesty of St. Peter should be decided.

Henry arrived at the foot of the castle-steep, Jan. 21, 1077, when the cold was severe and the ground covered with snow. He had an interview with Matilda and Hugo, abbot of Cluny, his godfather, and declared his willingness to submit to the pope if he was released from the interdict. But Gregory would only absolve him on condition that he would surrender to him his crown and forever resign the royal dignity. The king made the last step to secure the mercy of the pope: he assumed the severest penances which the Church requires from a sinner, as a sure way to absolution. For three days, from the 25th to the 28th of January, he stood in the court between the inner walls as a penitent suppliant, with bare head and feet, in a coarse woollen shirt, shivering in the cold, and knocked in vain for entrance at the gateway, which still perpetuates in its name, " Porta di penitenza," the memory of this event.[1]

The stern old pope, as hard as a rock and as cold as the snow, refused admittance, notwithstanding the earnest entreaties of Matilda and Hugo, till he was satisfied that the cup of humiliation was drained to the dregs, or that further resistance would be impolitic. He first exacted from Henry, as a condition of absolution, the promise to submit to his decision at the approaching meeting of the German nobles under the presidency of the pope as arbiter, and to grant him and his deputies protection on their journey to the north. In the meantime he was to abstain from exercising the functions of royalty.[2]

---

[1] " *Illic*," says Berthold (*Monum. Germ. SS.*, V. 289), "*laneis indutus, nudis pedibus, frigorosus, usque in diem tertium foris extra castellum cum suis hospitabatur.*" During the night the king was under shelter. See Hefele, V. 94 sq.

[2] The last point is omitted by Berthold, but expressly mentioned by Lambert of Hersfeld, and confirmed by Gregory, who says in his account of the Canossa event to the German prelates and princes, that he received Henry

The king made the promise, and two bishops and several nobles, in his behalf, swore upon sacred relics that he would keep it. Hugo, being a monk, could not swear, but pledged his word before the all-seeing God. Hugo, the bishops, nobles, and the Countess Matilda and Adelheid signed the written agreement, which still exists.

After these preliminaries, the inner gate was opened. The king, in the prime of life, the heir of many crowned monarchs, and a man of tall and noble presence, threw himself at the feet of the gray-haired pope, a man of low origin and of small and unimpressive stature, who by his word had disarmed an empire. He burst into tears, and cried " Spare me, holy father, spare me ! " The company were moved to tears ; even the iron pope showed signs of tender compassion. He heard the confession of Henry, raised him up, gave him absolution and his apostolic blessing, conducted him to the chapel, and sealed the reconciliation by the celebration of the sacrifice of the mass.

Some chroniclers add the following incident, which has often been repeated, but is very improbable. Gregory, before partaking of the sacrament, called upon God to strike him dead if he were guilty of the crimes charged on him, and, after eating one-half of the consecrated wafer unharmed, he offered the other half to Henry, requesting him to submit to the same awful ordeal ; but the king declined it, and referred the whole question to the decision of a general council.[1]

only into the communion of the Church, without reinstating him in his reign (*losum ei communionem redidi, non tamen in regno . . . instauravi*), and without binding the faithful to their oath of allegiance, reserving this to future decision. Jaffé, p. 402 ; Hefele, V. 96. The same view he expresses in the sentence of the second excommunication. In view of these facts it is strange that Giesebrecht (III. 403) should discredit the report of Lambert, and hold that Henry regained with the absolution also the royal prerogatives.

[1] This story, first told by Lambert of Hersfeld, who in the main sided with Gregory against Henry, is discredited by Giesebrecht, III. 401 ; Ranke, VII. 284 ; Mirbt, 194–199 ; and the Catholic historians, Döllinger and Hefele

After mass, the pope entertained the king courteously at dinner and dismissed him with some fatherly warnings and counsels, and with his renewed apostolic blessing.

Henry gained his object, but at the sacrifice of his royal dignity. He confessed by his act of humiliation that the pope had a right to depose a king and heir of the imperial crown, and to absolve subjects from the oath of allegiance. The head of the State acknowledged the temporal supremacy of the Church. Canossa marks the deepest humiliation of the State and the highest exaltation of the Church, — we mean the political papal Church of Rome, not the spiritual Church of Christ, who wore a crown of thorns in this world and who prayed on the cross for his murderers.

Gregory acted on the occasion in the sole interest of the hierarchy. His own friends, as we learn from his official account to the Germans, deemed his conduct to be " tyrannical cruelty, rather than apostolic severity." He saw in Henry the embodiment of the secular power in opposition to the ecclesiastical power, and he achieved a signal triumph, but only for a short time. He overshot his mark, and was at last expelled from Rome by the very man against whom he had closed the gate.

His relation to Matilda was political and ecclesiastical. The charge of his enemies that he entertained carnal intimacy with her is monstrous and incredible, considering his advanced age and unrelenting war against priestly concubinage.[1] The countess was the most powerful princess in

(V. 98), reject it as a fable. The pope had no need to protest his innocence, and had referred the charges against the king to a German tribunal ; the king had previously promised him to appear before this tribunal ; his present purpose was simply to get rid of the interdict, so as to be free to act. By declining the ordeal he would have confessed his guilt and justified the pope, and superseded the action of the German tribunal. On the historical value of Lambert's *Annales*, see Giesebrecht, III. 1030–1032, and Wattenbach, *Deutschlands*, *Geschichtsquellen*, II. 87 sqq. Gregorovius repeats the story as authentic.

[1] Lambert refutes this slander (*M. G.*, V. 257), and the best modern historians, Protestant as well as Catholic, reject it. See Neander, Ranke

Northern Italy, and afforded to the pope the best protection
against a possible invasion of a Northern army.   She was
devoted to Hildebrand as the visible head of the Church,
and felt proud and happy to aid him.   In 1077 she made a
reversionary grant of her dominions to the patrimony of
Peter, and thus increased the fatal gift of Constantine, from
which Dante derives the evils of the Church.   She continued the war with Henry, and aided Conrad and Henry V.
in the rebellion against their father.   In the political interest
of the papacy she contracted, in her fifty-fifth year, a second
marriage with Guelph, a youth of eighteen, the son of the
Duke of Bavaria, the most powerful enemy of Henry IV.
(1089); but the marriage, it seems, was never consummated,
and was dissolved a few years afterwards (1095).   She died,
1115.   It is supposed by many that Dante's Matilda, who
carried him over the river Lethe to Beatrice, is the famous
countess ; [1] but Dante never mentions Gregory VII., probably
on account of his quarrel with the emperor.

Canossa has become a proverbial name for the triumph of
priestcraft over kingcraft.[2]   Streams of blood have been shed

(VII. 280), and Hefele (V. 67 sq.).   R'anke says: " *Solche Verhältnisse giebt
es ja zwischen Individuen beiderlei Geschlechtes, die sich nur auf geistigem
Boden entwickeln, in welchen ohne sinnliche Annäherung die tiefste innere
Vereinigung der Gesinnungen und Ueberzeugungen besteht.   Die Markgräfin
glaubte an die Wahrhaftigkeit und den geistigen Beruf des Papstes, und der
Papst andererseits bedurfte ihrer Hülfe.*"

[1] *Purg.*, XXVIII. 40, XXXII. 92 ; XXXII. 28, 82, XXXIII. 119, 121.

[2] Mirbt, *Publizistik*, 181–200, seeks to make out that Henry's act at Canossa
was regarded by his age as an act of humility and not of humiliation.   The
contemporary writers speak of it as an act of unheard of and wonderful
humility, " *mira inaudita humilitas, officium humilitatis.*"   In view of the
profound reverence for the Church which prevailed it may be taken as certain that the people looked upon it as an act of humble piety.   But for
Henry it was a different thing.   As Mirbt agrees, the king was not moved by
deep religious concern but by a desire to hold on to his crown.   For him
Canossa was a humiliation and before the bar of historic judgment the act
wherein the State prostrated itself at the feet of the pope must be regarded as
a humiliation.   For other instances of princely submission to the pope, see
Mirbt, p. 198, note.

to wipe out the disgrace of Henry's humiliation before Hildebrand. The memory of that scene was revived in the *Culturkampf* between the State of Prussia and the Vatican from 1870 to 1887. At the beginning of the conflict, Prince Bismarck declared in the Prussian Chambers that "he would never go to Canossa"; but ten years afterwards he found it politic to move in that direction, and to make a compromise with Leo XIII., who proved his equal as a master of diplomacy. The anti-papal May-laws were repealed, one by one, till nothing is left of them except the technical *Anzeigepflicht*, a modern term for investiture. The Roman Church gained new strength in Prussia and Germany from legal persecution, and enjoys now more freedom and independence than ever, and much more than the Protestant Church, which has innocently suffered from the operation of the May-laws.

§ 17. *Renewal of the Conflict. Two Kings and Two Popes.*

The result of Canossa was civil war in Germany and Italy : king against king, pope against pope, nobles against nobles, bishops against bishops, father against son, and son against father. It lasted several years. Gregory and Henry died in exile. Gregory was defeated by Henry, Henry by his own rebellious son. The long wars of the Guelphs and the Ghibellines originated in that period. The Duke Guelph IV. of Bavaria was present at Forchheim when Henry was deposed, and took up arms against him. The popes sided with the Guelphs against the Hohenstaufen emperors and the Ghibellines.

The friends and supporters of Henry in Lombardy and Germany were dissatisfied, and regarded his humiliation as an act of cowardice, and the pope's conduct as an insult to the German nation and the royal crown. His enemies, a small number of Saxon and Swabian nobles and bishops, assembled at Forchheim, March 13, 1077, and, in the presence of two legates of the pope, but without his express

authority, offered the crown of Germany to Rudolf, Duke
of Swabia, Henry's brother-in-law, but on two important
conditions (which may be traced to the influence of the
pope's legates), namely, that he should denounce a hereditary
claim to the throne, and guarantee the freedom of ecclesiastical appointments. He was crowned March 26, at Mainz,
by Archbishop Siegfried, but under bad omens : the consecrated oil ran short, the Gospel was read by a simoniacal
deacon, the citizens raised a tumult, and Rudolf had to
make his escape by night with Siegfried, who never returned.
He found little support in Southern Germany, and went to
Henry's enemies in Saxony.

Henry demanded from the pope the ban over the robber of
his crown, but in vain. He refused him the promised safe-
conduct to Germany, acted as king, crossed the Alps, and
defeated Rudolf in a battle at Melrichstadt in Franconia,
Aug. 7, 1078, but was defeated by him near Mühlheim in
Thuringia, Jan. 27, 1080, in a decisive battle, which Rudolf
regarded as a divine decision, and which inclined the pope
in his favor.

After long hesitation, Gregory, in a Synod of Rome, March
7, 1080, ventured upon the most extraordinary act even for a
man in the highest position. Invoking the aid of St. Peter
and St. Paul, he fulminated a second and severer ban against
Henry and all his adherents, deprived him again of his kingdoms of Germany and Italy, forbade all the faithful to obey
him, and bestowed the crown of Germany (not of Italy)
on Rudolf. The address was at once a prayer, a narrative,
and a judgment, and combined cool reflection with religious
fervor. It rests on the conviction that the pope, as the
representative of Peter and Paul, was clothed with supreme
authority over the world as well as the Church.[1]

Gregory hazarded a prophecy, which was falsified by his-

[1] See the extract in § 11, p. 32, and Latin text of the address in Mansi,
Harduin, Jaffé, and Shailer Mathews, 51-54.

tory, that before the day of St. Peter and St. Paul (June 29), Henry would either lose his life or his throne.   After the close of the synod, he sent to Rudolf (instead of the iron crown of Charlemagne, which was in possession of Henry) a diadem with the characteristic inscription : —

"*Petra dedit Petro, Petrus diadema Rudolpho.*"[1]

A reconciliation was now impossible.   Henry replied to the papal ban by the election of an anti-pope.   A council of about thirty German and Italian bishops met at Brixen in the Tyrol, June 26, 1080, and deposed Gregory on the frivolous charges of ambition, avarice, simony, sorcery, and the Berengarian heresy.   Cardinal Hugo Candidus and twenty-seven bishops (of Brixen, Bamberg, Coire, Freisingen, Lausanne, etc.) signed the document.   At the same time they elected the excommunicated Archbishop Wibert of Ravenna pope, under the name of Clement III.   He was a man of talent, dignity, and unblemished character, but fell into the hands of simonists and the enemies of reform.   Henry acknowledged him by the usual genuflexion, and promised to visit Rome in the following spring, that he might receive from him the imperial crown.   Wibert returned to Ravenna with the papal insignia and great pomp.

This was the beginning of a double civil war between rival popes and rival kings, with all its horrors.   Gregory counted on the Saxons in Germany, Countess Matilda in Northern Italy, and the Normans in Southern Italy.

Henry was defeated Oct. 15, 1080, on the banks of the Elster, near Naumburg ; but Rudolf was mortally wounded by Godfrey of Bouillon, the hero of Jerusalem,[2] and lost his right hand by another enemy.   He died the same evening, exclaiming, as the story goes: "This is the hand with which I swore fidelity to my lord, King Henry."   But, according

---

[1] The Rock gave the crown to Peter and Peter gives it to Rudolf.

[2] This fact is reported by Albericus of Trois-Fontaines, but doubted by Sybel (*Gesch. des ersten Kreuzzugs*, p. 218) and Hefele (V. 150, note).

to another report, he said, when he heard of the victory of his troops : "Now I suffer willingly what the Lord has decreed for me."   His body with the severed hand was deposited in the cathedral at Merseburg.[1]

Rudolf's death turned his victory into a defeat.   It was regarded in that age as a judgment of God against him and the anti-pope.   His friends could not agree upon a successor till the following summer, when they elected Count Hermann of Luxemburg, who proved incompetent.   In the spring of 1081 Henry crossed the Alps with a small army to depose Gregory, whose absolution he had sought a few years before as a penitent at Canossa.   He was welcomed in Lombardy, defeated the troops of Matilda, and appeared at the gates of Rome before Pentecost, May 21.   Gregory, surrounded by danger, stood firm as a rock and refused every compromise. At his last Lenten synod (end of February, 1081) he had renewed his anathemas, and suspended those bishops who disobeyed the summons.   Nothing else is known of this synod but sentences of punishment.   In his letter of March 15, 1081, to Hermann, bishop of Metz, he justified his conduct towards Henry, and on April 8 he warned the Venetians against any communication with him and his adherents. "I am not afraid," he said, "of the threats of the wicked, and would rather sacrifice my life than consent to evil."

Henry, not being permitted by the Romans to enter their city, as he had hoped, and not being prepared for a siege, spent the summer in Upper Italy, but returned to Rome in Lent, 1082, and again with a larger force at Easter, 1083, and conquered the city and the Church of St. Peter in June. Gregory was intrenched in the Castle of St. Angelo, and fulminated anew his anathema upon Henry and his followers (June 24).   Henry answered by causing Wibert to be enthroned in St. Peter's (June 28), but soon left Rome with Wibert (July 1), promising to return.   He had probably

---

[1] For a good description of the battle, see Giesebrecht, III. 516 sqq.

come to a secret understanding with the Roman nobility to
effect a peaceful compromise with Gregory; but the pope
was inexorable.   In the spring of 1084 Henry returned and
called a synod, which deposed and excommunicated Gregory.
Wibert was consecrated on Palm Sunday as Pope Clement
III., in the Lateran, by two excommunicated bishops of Modena and Arezzo (instead of the bishops of Ostia, Albano,
and Porto).   Henry and his wife, Bertha, received from
him the imperial crown in St. Peter's at Easter, March 31,
1084.   He left Rome with Wibert (May 21), leaving the
defence of the city in the hands of the Romans.   He never
returned.

In the meantime Gregory called to his aid the Norman
chief, Robert Guiscard, or Wiscard.   This bold adventurer
approached from the south with a motley force of Normans,
Lombards, Apulians, and Saracens, amounting to thirty thousand foot and six thousand horse, arrived in Rome, May 27,
1084, liberated the pope, and entered with him the Lateran.
He now began such a pillage and slaughter as even the barbarians had not committed.   Half the city was reduced to
ruins ; many churches were demolished, others turned into
forts ; women and maidens, even nuns, were outraged, and
several thousand citizens sold into slavery.   The survivors
cursed the pope and his deliverer.   In the words of a contemporary, the cruelty of the Normans gained more hearts
for the emperor than a hundred thousand pieces of gold.
Rome was a ghost of her former self.   When Hildebert of
Tours visited her more than ten years later, he saw only
ruins of her greatness.[1]   This was, indeed, a fearful judgment, but very different from the one which Gregory a few
years before had invoked upon Henry.

Many confused reports were circulated about the fate of
Gregory VII.   His faithful friend, the Countess of Tuscany,

---

[1] Hildebert's poem, lamenting the ruins of Rome, is found in Migne, 171,
1441 sq.

assembled troops, sent emissaries in all directions, and stirred up distrust and hatred against Henry in Germany. The following letter remains as evidence of her zeal for Gregory: —

"Matilda, such as she is by the grace of God, if she be anything, to all the faithful residing in the Teutonic kingdom, greeting.

"We would have you know that Henry, the false king, has stolen the seal of the Lord Pope Gregory. Wherefore, if ye are told anything contrary to the words of our envoys, hold it false, and believe not Henry's lies. Further, he has carried away with him the Bishop of Porto, because that man was once familiar with the Lord Pope. If by his help he should attempt anything with you or against you, be sure this bishop is a false witness, and give no credit to those who shall tell you to the contrary. Know that the Lord Pope has already conquered Sutri and Nepi ; Barabbas the robber, that is to say, Henry's pope, has fled like himself. Farewell. Beware of the snares of Henry."

§ 18. *Death of Gregory VII.*

Gregory was again in possession of the Lateran, but he left the scene of melancholy desolation, accompanied by Guiscard and a few cardinals and Roman nobles. He went first to Monte Cassino and then to Salerno. The descent from Canossa to Salerno was truly a *via dolorosa.* But the old pope, broken in body, was unbroken in spirit.

He renewed the ban against Henry and the anti-pope at the close of 1084, and sent a letter to the faithful in Germany, stating that the words of the Psalmist, *Quare fremuerunt gentes* (Ps. 2 : 1, 2), were fulfilled, that the kings of the earth have rebelled against Christ and his apostle Peter to destroy the Christian religion, but could not seduce those who trusted in God. He called upon them to come to the rescue of the Church if they wished to gain the remission of sins and eternal salvation. This is his last written document.

His mind remained clear and firm to the end. He recommended Cardinal Desiderius of Monte Cassino (Victor III.) as his successor, and next to him Otto, bishop of Ostia (Urban II.). He absolved all his enemies, except Henry and Wibert, "the usurper of the apostolic see."[1] He died, May 25, 1085, with the words which best express the meaning of his public life and character: " I have loved righteousness and hated iniquity; therefore I die in exile."[2] " Nay," said one of the bishops, " in exile thou canst not die, who, as the vicar of Christ and his Apostles, hast received all the nations for thine inheritance, and the uttermost parts of the earth for thy possession" (Ps. 2 : 8).

Robert Guiscard, his protector, died a few weeks afterwards (July 17, 1085).

The body of Gregory, clad in the pontifical vestments, was buried in the church of St. Matthew at Salerno, which he had consecrated shortly before. A plain stone marked his grave till John of Procida — although a zealous Ghibelline — erected a sumptuous chapel over it.[3] His name was inserted in the Calendar on the 25th of May, 1584, by Gregory XIII., without a formal canonization; Paul V. ordered a festival, in 1609, for the new saint; and Benedict XIII., in 1728, ordered its general observance. The emperor of Germany, the king of France, and other sovereigns opposed the celebration; but if ever a pope deserved canonization for

---

[1] " *Præter Henricum regem dictum omnes absolvo et benedico, quicumque me hanc habere specialem potestatem in vocem apostolorum Petri et Pauli credunt indubitanter.*" Paulus Bernriedensis, *Vita Greg.*, c. 12 ; Baronius, *Ann.* XVII. 566.

[2] "*Dilexi justitiam et odi iniquitatem; propterea morior in exilio.*" The first two sentences are from Ps. 45 : 8 ; the last is put instead of "*propterea unxit te Deus.*" His enemies spread the false report that he repented of the controversy which he had excited. *Mon. Germ. Script.*, VIII. 470 ; Baxmann, II. 424 sqq.

[3] His monument, erected in 1578 in the cathedral of Salerno, bears the inscription : " *Gregorius VII. Soanensis, P. O. M., Ecclesiæ libertatis vindex acerrimus, assertor constantissimus, qui dum Romani Pontificis auctoritatem adversus Henrici perfidiam strenue tueretur, Salernæ sancte decubuit. Anno Domini 1085, oct. Cal. Jun.*" Hefele, V. 184 ; Gregorovius, *Die Grabmäler der Päpste*, p. 49 ; Giesebrecht, III. 578. Rome, which has so many papal monuments, has none for Gregory VII., except an inscription on a stone in S. Prudentiana, where he is called "*Vir benedictus, moribus ecclesiam renovavit.*" See Gregorovius, IV. 246.

devotion to the papal theocracy, it was Hildebrand.   The eighth centenary of his death was celebrated in the Roman Church, May 25, 1885.

Gregory was, in his own time, and has been since, the subject both of the highest praise and of the severest censure. Modern historians agree in giving him credit for the honesty and courage of his convictions, and concede the purity and loftiness of his motives and aims.   He is the typical representative of papal absolutism in the Middle Ages in conflict with imperial absolutism.   He combined personal integrity, consummate statesmanship, and monastic contempt of the world.   He lived and moved in the idea of the Old Testament theocracy, and had no conception of the free spirit of the gospel.   He was a man of blood and iron, an austere monk, inaccessible to feelings of tenderness, when acting in his official capacity as the head of the Roman hierarchy; yet he showed singular liberality in his treatment of Berengar, and protested against the use of torture.   His piety was absorbed in devotion to the hierarchy, to St. Peter, and to the Virgin Mary.   He was unscrupulous in the choice of means for his end, and approved of civil war for the triumph of the Roman Church.

The lofty principles he espoused he was willing to stake his life upon.   No pope has ever used the term " righteousness " more frequently than he used it.   No pope has ever employed the figure of warfare to describe the conflict he was engaged in more frequently than he employed it.[1]   No man was ever more convinced of the soundness of his cause. He found his authority in the Scriptures and freely used them to convince others, quoting certain passages again and again, such as 1 Sam. 15 : 23, which is found quoted in his writings nineteen times.[2]   He found in Matt. 16 : 18 the

---

[1] Hauck, III. 754 sqq.

[2] In a single letter to Hermann of Metz, *Reg.*, IV. 2, Gregory quotes at least nine passages of Scripture.

certain warrant for the papal supremacy and excepted no
person from the jurisdiction of Peter's successors.[1] As an
advocate of papal absolutism and as a moral reformer he has
left an abiding impress upon the thought and the practice
of Roman Christendom.   Even where we are farthest from
sharing his views, we may admire the man of fearless courage
and moral conviction.

His spirit still moves in the curia, which adheres to the
theocratic theory, without the ability of carrying it into
practice.   The papal Syllabus of 1864 denies that "the
Roman pontiffs have exceeded the limits of their power"
(§ V. 23), and asserts the superiority of the Church over
the State "in litigated questions of jurisdiction" (§ VI. 54).
The politico-ecclesiastical encyclicals of Leo XIII. (*Immortale Dei*, Nov. 1, 1885, and *Libertas præstantissimum naturæ
donum*, June 20, 1888) reasserted substantially, though mod-
erately and cautiously, the Gregorian theory of Church and
State.

Ranke, in his last years, wrote of Gregory:[2] "His hierarchical system rests upon the endeavor to make the cler-
gical order the basis of all human existence.   This makes
intelligible its two characteristic and fundamental principles,
the command of celibacy and the prohibition of lay investiture.   By the first it was intended to build up out of the
lower clergy a body isolated from all the personal and family relationships of human society.   By the second it was
intended to insure the higher clergy against all interference
from the civil power.   The great hierarch thought out well
the platform on which he placed himself.   He met a demand
of the age to see in the priest, as it were, a being belonging
to a higher order.   All that he says betrays dignity, force,

---

[1] *Ubi Deus Petro principaliter dedit potestatem ligandi et solvendi in terra
et in cælo, nullum excepit, nihil ab ejus potestate subtraxit.*   *Reg.*, IV. 2 ;
Migne, 148, 456.

[2] *Weltgesch.* VII. 34 sqq.

and logical connection. . . . His activity, which left nothing untouched, was of a very human sort, while at the same time it embraced religious ideals. The hierarchical principle constituted his real life."

Gregorovius, who carries on a sustained comparison between Gregory and Napoleon, praises Gregory's genius and moral vigor. He says:[1] "Gregory was the heir of the ancient aims of the papacy. But his unexampled genius as ruler and statesman is his own, and no one either in ancient Rome or in modern times has ever reached to his revolutionary daring. . . . His dying words reveal the fundamental basis of his character, which was great and manly. To this grand spirit, a character almost without an equal, belongs a place among the rulers of the earth, men who have moved the world by a violent yet salutary influence. The religious element, however, raises him to a far higher sphere than that to which secular monarchs belong. Beside Gregory, Napoleon sinks to an utter poverty of ideas."

Let us hope that Gregory felt in his heart some of that Christian love and meekness whose commendation closes one of his letters to Hermann, archbishop of Metz,[2] the most drastic expression of papal absolutism he ever made. He

[1] *Hist. of City of Rome*, IV. 256. Of Canossa this author had said, IV. 207 : "The weaponless victory of the monk Gregory has more claim on the admiration of the world than all the victories of an Alexander, a Cæsar, and a Napoleon." Like other Protestant German historians he has no sympathy with Gregory's papal scheme of papal absolutism, but most of the German Church historians, as Mirbt and Hauck, are inclined to magnify the courage and manly vigor of Henry, as well as the justice of his cause, and to underestimate or question the moral quality of Gregory in his conflict with the emperor, and the immediate results of the event at Canossa. Hauck, III. 805, omits a detailed description of that remarkable scene with the remark that it was so well known to Germans as not to need retelling. He pronounces the estimate usually put upon Gregory's intellectual gifts as too high, and declares that the title " Great " is properly associated with the name of the first Gregory and not with the seventh pope of that name. Hildebrand had convictions enough, but lacked in native force, p. 832 sq.

[2] Dated March 15, 1081, *Reg.*, VIII. 21 ; Mirbt, *Quellen*, 105-112 ; Migne, 148, 594-604.

wrote : " If the virtue of love be neglected, no matter what
good any one may do, he will wholly lack the fruit of salvation. To do these things in humility and to love God and
our neighbor as we ought, this presupposes the mercy of him
who said, Learn of me, for I am meek and lowly of heart.
Whosoever humbly follows him shall pass from the kingdom
of submission which passes away, to the kingdom of true
liberty which abides forever."

CHAPTER III.

§ 19. *Victor III. and Urban II.* 1086–1099.

Compare the chapter on the Crusades.

AT the death of Gregory, his imperial enemy was victorious
in Germany, and had recovered part of Saxony; Lombardy
remained loyal to the empire; Matilda was prostrated by
grief and sickness; the anti-pope Wibert (Clement III.,
1080–1100) continued to occupy a part of Rome (the Lateran palace and the castle of St. Angelo); Roger, the new
duke of the Normans, spent his whole force in securing for
himself the sole rule over Calabria and Apulia against his
brother Bohemund. There was a papal interregnum of
twelve months.

At last the excellent Abbot Desiderius of Monte Cassino,
who had raised that convent to the height of its prosperity,
was elected to succeed his friend Gregory, May 24, 1086.
He accepted after long delay, but ruled only eighteen months
as Victor III. He loved monastic solitude, and died Sept. 16,
1087.

He was followed by Otto (Odo), cardinal-bishop of Ostia,
a Frenchman, formerly prior of Cluny, and one of the intimate counsellors of Hildebrand. He assumed the name
Urban II., and ruled from March 12, 1088, to July 29, 1099.
He followed in the steps of Gregory, but with more caution
and adaptation to circumstances. He spent his pontificate
mostly outside of Rome, but with increasing moral influence. He identified himself with the rising enthusiasm for

the holy war of the Cross against the Crescent. This was an immense gain for the papacy, which reaped all the credit and benefit of that extraordinary movement.

He took a noble stand in favor of the sanctity of marriage against the licentious King Philip I. of France, who cast away his legitimate wife, Bertha, 1092, and held adulterous intercourse with Bertrada of Montfort, the runaway wife of the rude Count Fulco of Anjou. This public scandal led to several synods. The king was excommunicated by a synod at Autun in Burgundy, Oct. 16, 1094, and by the Synod of Clermont in 1095. He afterwards dismissed Bertrada, and was absolved by the pope.

Urban continued the war with Henry IV. without scruple as to the means. He encouraged the rebellion of his eldest son, Conrad, a weak and amiable man, who fled for protection to the Countess Matilda, was crowned king of Italy at Monza, and paid the pope the homage of holding his stirrup (the *officium stratoris*) at Cremona (1095). Urban, who had been consecrated pope outside of Rome, was able, 1088, with the aid of the Normans, to enter the city and possess himself of all its parts except the castle of St. Angelo, which remained in the hands of the followers of Wibert. Wibert had been in possession of St. Peter's, which he held as a fortress against Victor III. The streets of the papal city resounded with the war-cries of the two papal armies, while pope and anti-pope anathematized one another. Urban died at Florence in 1101.

The pope arranged an unnatural matrimonial alliance between the widowed countess and the young Guelph of Bavaria, whose father was the most powerful of the emperor's enemies in Germany. It was a purely political match, which made neither party happy, and ended in a divorce (1095). But it gave the papal party a political organization, and opened the long-continued war between the Guelphs and the Ghibellines, which distracted every city in Italy, and is said to have caused seventy-two hundred revolutions and more than seven hundred atrocious murders in that country.[1] Every Italian was born to an inheritance of hatred and revenge, and could not help sharing in the conflict of factions headed by petty tyrants. The Guelphs defended the pope against the emperor, and also the democracy against the aristocracy in the city government. They were strong in pulling down, but were unable to create a new State. The Ghibellines maintained the divine origin and independent authority of the State in all things temporal against the encroachments of the papacy. The party strife continued in Italy long after the German emperor had lost his power. Dante was at first a Guelph, but in mature life joined the Ghibellines and became the most formidable opponent of Pope Boniface VIII.

Urban was able to hold a synod at Piacenza in Lombardy, where Henry IV. had his chief support, during Lent, 1095. It was attended by four thousand priests and monks and over thirty thousand laymen, and the meeting had to be held in the open field. The pope permitted Praxedis (Adelheid), the second wife of Henry IV., to recite the filthy details of acts of impurity to which she had been subjected by her husband, endorsed her shameless story, absolved her from all uncleanness, and remitted every penitential observance, "because she had not blushed to make a public and voluntary confession of her involuntary transgression."[2] After

---

[1] *Guelfi, Welfen*, from *Welf, Wolf*, a family name of the dukes of Bavaria. *Ghibellini, Ghibellinen*, from *Waiblingen*, the patrimonial castle of Conrad of Hohenstaufen in Swabia. Comp. Ferrari, *Histoire des révolutions d'Italie, ou Guelfes et Ghibellins*, Paris, 1858, 4 vols. From the Guelphs descended the house of Brunswick and Hanover, and the royal family of England since George I., 1714.

[2] Praxedis or Eupraxia, or (as the Germans called her) Adelheid was a Russian princess, who married Henry in 1089, two years after Bertha's death. She had preferred the same horrible charges before a synod at Constance in 1094. See Pertz, Tom. VII. 458, XVII. 14 ; Hefele-Knöpfler, V. 211 sq. and 216 ; Greenwood, IV. 561.

thus sealing the damnation of Henry, the synod renewed the laws against simony and Nicolaitism.   Wibert, the anti-pope, was put under anathema, and his consecrations were declared invalid.   The Catholic faith in the true and essential presence of the body and blood of Christ in the eucharist was asserted against the heresy of Berengar.

More important was the Synod of Clermont in France, Nov. 18–28, 1095, which inaugurated the first crusade.   Here Urban preached the most effective sermon on record, and reached the height of his influence.

He passed in triumphal procession, surrounded by princes and prelates, through France and Italy.   He exhorted the people everywhere to repent of their sins and to prove the sincerity of their conversion by killing as many enemies of the cross as they could reach with their swords.   When he reached Rome the anti-pope had been driven away by the Crusaders.   He was enabled to celebrate the Christmas festival of 1096 with unusual magnificence, and held two synods in the Lateran, January, 1097, and April, 1099.   He died, July 29, 1099, a fortnight after the capture of Jerusalem (July 15) by the Crusaders.

§ 20.   *Pascal II. and Henry V.*   1099–1118.

The letters of Paschalis II. in MIGNE, 163. — W. SCHUM: *Die Politik Papst Paschalis II. gegen Kaiser Heinrich V.*   Erfurt, 1877. — G. PEISER: *Der deutsche Investiturstreit unter Heinrich V. bis 1111.*   Berlin, 1883. — GREGOROVIUS IV., HAUCK III., PFLUGK-HARTTUNG: *Die Bullen der Päpste.*   Gotha, 1901, pp. 234–263. — MIRBT, art. *Paschalis II.* in Herzog, XIV. 717–725, and the literature there given.

Pascal II., a monk of Cluny and disciple of Hildebrand, but less firm and consistent, was elected in July, 1099, and reigned till 1118.   Clement III., the anti-pope, died in September, 1100, weary of the world, and left a reputation of integrity, gentleness, and dignity.   The imperialist clergy of Rome elected another anti-pope, Sylvester IV., who soon disappeared noiselessly from the stage.

Pascal gained a complete victory over Henry IV. by supporting the wicked rebellion of his second son, Henry V., the last of the Salic or Franconian line of emperors, 1104–1125.

The unfortunate father died under the anathema in misery at Liège (Lüttich), Aug. 7, 1106. The people of the city which had remained faithful to him, lamented his death; but the papal agents commanded the bishop of Liège to remove his body from consecrated ground to an island in the Maas. Henry V. had not lost all feeling for his father, and complied with his dying request for burial in the imperial sepulchre at Spires. The clergy and the citizens accompanied the funeral procession to the cathedral of St. Mary, which the departed sovereign had himself built and richly endowed. He was buried with all honors. But when Bishop Gebhard, one of his fiercest persecutors, who was absent at the time, heard of it, he caused the body to be forthwith exhumed and removed, and interdicted all services in the church till it should be purified of all pollution. The people, however, could not be deterred from frequent visits to the unconsecrated chapel where the dishonored remains of their monarch and patron were deposited. At last the pope dissolved the ban, on the assurance of Henry V. that his father had professed sincere repentance, and his body was again deposited in the cathedral, Aug. 7, 1111. By his moral defects and his humiliation at Canossa, Henry IV. had promoted the power of the papal hierarchy, and yet, by his continued opposition after that act, he had prevented its complete triumph. Soon after his death an anonymous writer gave eloquent and touching expression to his grief over the imperial lord whom he calls his hope and comfort, the pride of Rome, the ornament of the empire, the lamp of the world, a benefactor of widows and orphans, and a father of the poor.[1]

---

[1] The tract is more eloquent than accurate. It is ascribed by Goldast, Floto, and Gieseler to Bishop Otbert of Lüttich (Liège); by Dr. Jaffé, to an unknown writer in Mainz (see the preface to his German translation, *Das*

Pascal had to suffer for his unscrupulous policy. When Henry V. came into full possession of his power, he demanded the right of investiture over all the churches of the empire, and coronation at Rome. The pope was imprisoned and so hard pressed by Henry, that he resolved to buy the spiritual freedom of the Church by a sacrifice of its temporal possessions (except the patrimony of Peter). A compact to this effect between him and the emperor was signed provisionally, April, 1111. Henry was crowned emperor of the Romans in St. Peter's. But after his return to Germany, a Lateran synod rejected the compact, March, 1112. The pope represented to the synod that, while in the custody of the emperor, with many bishops and cardinals, he had conceded to him the right of investiture to avoid greater evils, and had promised him immunity from excommunication. He confessed that the concession was wrong, and left it with the synod to improve the situation. He made in the sixth session (March 23) a solemn profession of the Catholic faith in the Scriptures of the Old and New Testament, the Canons of the Apostles, the four Œcumenical Synods of Nicæa, Constantinople, Ephesus, and Chalcedon, and the decrees of Gregory VII. and Urban II. against lay-investiture and all other crimes which they had condemned. Then the synod, while the pope kept silent, resolved to annul the treaty which he had been forced to make with King Henry. All exclaimed, "Amen, Amen, *fiat, fiat.*" Twelve archbishops, a hundred and fourteen bishops, fifteen cardinal-priests, and eight cardinal-deacons signed the decree.

The zealous Gregorians wished to go further and to declare lay-investiture a heresy (which would imply that Pope Pascal was a heretic). A French Synod of Vienne, Sept. 16,

Leben Kaiser Heinrich des Vierten, Berlin, 1858); by Druffel and Giesebrecht, to Bishop Erlung of Würzburg, who was chancellor of the emperor from 1103 to 1105. For a good characterization of Henry IV. see Giesebrecht, III. 764–768, and on this biography, pp. 1050 sq.

1112, passed three decrees: 1) Investiture by a layman is a heresy; 2) the enforced compact of Pascal with Henry is null and void; 3) King Henry, who came to Rome under the pretext of peace, and betrayed the pope with a Judas-kiss, is cut off from holy Church until he gives complete satisfaction. The decisions were submitted to the pope, who approved them, October 20 of the same year, to avert a schism. Other provincial synods of France, held by papal legates, launched anathemas against the "tyrant of Germany."

But Henry defied the pope, who had pledged himself never to excommunicate him on account of investiture. After the death of Countess Matilda, July 24, 1115, he hastened for a third time to Italy, and violently seized the rich possessions which she had bequeathed to the chair of St. Peter. Pascal fled to Benevento, and called the Normans to his aid, as Gregory VII. had done. Henry celebrated the Easter festival of 1117 in Rome with great pomp, caused the empress to be crowned, showed himself to the people in his imperial purple, and amused them with shows and processions; but in the summer he returned to Germany, after fruitless negotiations with the pope. He lived to conclude the Concordat of Worms. He was an energetic, but hard, despotic, and unpopular ruler.

Pascal died, Jan. 21, 1118, in the castle of St. Angelo, and was buried in the church of St. John in Lateran. He barely escaped the charge of heresy and schism. He privately condemned, and yet officially supported, lay-investiture, and strove to satisfy both his own conscience and his official duty to the papacy. The extreme party charged him with the sin of Peter, and exhorted him to repent; milder judges, like Ivo of Chartres and Hildebert of Le Mans, while defending the Hildebrandian principle of the freedom of the Church, excused him on the ground that he had yielded for a moment in the hope of better times and from the praiseworthy desire to save the imprisoned cardinals and to avoid bloodshed; and they referred to the example of Paul, who circumcised Timothy, and complied with the wish of James in Jerusalem to please the Jewish Christians.

§ 21. *The Concordat of Worms.* 1122.

EKKEHARDUS URAUGIENSIS: *Chronica* (best ed. by Waiz in *Mon. Germ. Script.,* VI. 260). — UL. ROBERT: *Étude sur les actes du pape Calixte II.* Paris, 1874. — E. BERNHEIM: *Zur Geschichte des Wormser Concordats.* Göttingen, 1878. — M. MAURER: *Papst Calixt II.* München, 1886. — GIESEBRECHT, III. 931–959. — RANKE, VIII. 111–126. — HEFELE-KNÖPFLER, V. 311–384; *Bullaire et histoire de Calixte II.* Paris, 1891. — D. SCHAFER: *Zur Beurtheilung des Wormser Konkordats.* Berlin, 1905.

The Gregorian party elected Gelasius a cardinal-deacon, far advanced in age. His short reign of a year and four days was a series of pitiable misfortunes. He had scarcely been elected when he was grossly insulted by a mob led by Cencius Frangipani and cast into a dungeon. Freed by the fickle Romans, he was thrown into a panic by the sudden appearance of Henry V. at the gates, and fled the city, attempting to escape by sea. The Normans came to his rescue and he was led back to Rome, where he found St. Peter's in the hands of the anti-pope. A wild riot again forced him to flee and when he was found he was sitting in a field near St. Paul's, with no companions but some women as his comforters. He then escaped to Pisa and by way of Genoa to France, where he died at Cluny, 1119. The imperialist party had elected an anti-pope, Gregory VIII., who was consecrated at Rome in the presence of Henry V., and ruled till 1121, but was taken captive by the Normans, mounted on a camel, paraded before Calixtus amid the insults and mockeries of the Roman mob, covered with dust and filth, and consigned to a dungeon. He died in an obscure monastery, in 1125, "still persevering in his rebellion." Such was the state of society in Rome.

Calixtus II., the successor of Gelasius, 1119–1124, was elected at Cluny and consecrated at Vienne. He began his

rule by renewing the sentence of excommunication against
Henry; and in him the emperor found his match.   After holding the Synod of Rheims, which ratified the prohibition of lay-
investiture, he reached Rome, 1120.   Both parties, emperor
and pope, were weary of the long struggle of fifty years,
which had, like the Thirty Years' War five centuries later,
kept Central Europe in a state of turmoil and war.   At the
Diet of Würzburg, 1121, the men of peace were in the majority and demanded a cessation of the conflict and the calling of a council.

Calixtus found it best to comply, however reluctantly, with
the resolution of the German Diet, and instructed his legates
to convoke a general council of all the bishops of France and
Germany at Mainz for the purpose of restoring concord
between the holy see and the empire.   The assembly adjourned from Mainz to Worms, the city which became afterwards so famous for the protest of Luther.   An immense
multitude crowded to the place to witness the restoration of
peace.   The sessions lasted more than a week, and closed
with a solemn mass and the *Te Deum* by the cardinal-bishop
of Ostia, who gave the kiss of peace to the emperor.

The Concordat of Worms was signed, Sept. 23, 1122.   It
was a compromise between the contending parties.   It is the
first of the many concordats which the popes have since that
time concluded with various sovereigns and governments,
and in which they usually make some concession to the civil
power.   If they cannot carry out their principle, they agree
to a *modus vivendi.*

The pope gained the chief point, namely, the right of investiture by delivery of the ring and crosier (the symbols
of the spiritual power) in all the churches of the empire, and
also the restoration of the properties and temporalities of the
blessed Peter which had passed out of the possession of the
holy see during the late civil wars.

On the other hand, the pope granted to the emperor that

the elections to all bishoprics and abbeys of the empire should be made in the emperor's presence, without simony or any kind of corruption; that in cases of dispute the emperor should be at liberty to decide in favor of the person who, in his judgment, had the best claim; and that the candidate thus elected should receive from the emperor the temporalities of his see or abbey by the delivery of a rod or sceptre (the symbol of the temporal power), but without bargain or valuable consideration of any kind, and ever after render unto the sovereign all such duties and services as by law he was bound to render. But the temporalities belonging to the Roman see were exempt from these stipulations.

There are some ambiguities and uncertainties in this treaty which opened the way for future contention. The emperor surrenders the right of investiture (with ring and crosier), and yet takes it back again in a milder form (with the sceptre). The question whether consecration is to precede or to follow investiture was left undecided, except outside of Germany, *i.e.* in Italy and Burgundy, where investiture with the regalia by the sceptre was to take place within six months *after* the consecration. Nothing is said about heirs and successors. Hence the concordat might be understood simply as a treaty between Calixtus and Henry, a temporary expedient, an armistice after half a century of discord between Church and State. After their deaths both the papal tiara and the imperial crown became again apples of discord.

The Concordat of Worms was confirmed by the Ninth Œcumenical Synod (according to the Roman counting), or First Œcumenical Council of the West, held in the Lateran from March 18 to April 6, 1123. It is also called the First Lateran Council. Over three hundred bishops and abbots were present, or, according to other reports, five hundred or even nine hundred and ninety-seven. The documents of Worms were read, approved by all, and deposited in the archives of the Roman Church.

NOTES.

The text of the *Concordatum Wormatiense* or *Pactum Calixtinum* is preserved in the Vatican, and in the Chronicle of Ekkehard (abbot of Aura, near Kissingen, from 1108 to 1125). It has been repeatedly published by Baronius, *Annales;* Goldast, *Constitutiones Imperiales;* Leibnitz, *Corpus juris diplomaticum;* in Gieseler's *Church History;* in German translation, by Hefele-Knöpfler, *Conciliengesch.* V. 373 ; and also by Pertz, in the *Monumenta Germaniæ Legum,* II. 75 sq. (who gives the various readings from seven MSS. of Ekkehard's *Chronica*), and Mirbt, *Quellen,* 115, 116. It is as follows :—

" *In nomine sanctæ et individuæ Trinitatis.*

" *Ego Heinricus Dei gratia Romanorum Imperator Augustus pro amore Dei et s. Romanæ Ecclesiæ et domini P. Calixti, et pro remedio animæ meæ, dimitto Deo et ss. ejus Apostolis Petro et Paulo, sanctæque catholicæ Ecclesiæ omnem investituram per annulum et baculum, et concedo, in omnibus Ecclesiis canonicam fieri electionem et liberam consecrationem. Possessiones et regalia b. Petri, quæ a principio hujus discordiæ usque ad hodiernam diem, sive patris mei tempore, sive etiam meo, ablata sunt, quæ habeo, s. Romanæ Ecclesiæ restituo, quæ autem non habeo, ut, restituantur, fideliter juvabo. Possessiones etiam omnium Ecclesiarum aliarum, et Principum, et aliorum tam clericorum quam laicorum, quæ in guerra ista amissæ sunt, consilio Principum, vel justitia, quas habeo, reddam, quas non habeo, ut reddantur, fideliter juvabo. Et do veram pacem domino Papæ Calixto, sanctæque Romanæ Ecclesiæ, et omnibus, qui in parte ipsius sunt vel fuerunt. Et in quibus s. Romana Ecclesia mihi auxilium postulaverit, fideliter juvabo ; et de quibus mihi fecerit querimoniam, debitam sibi faciam justitiam.*

" *Ego Calixtus Episcopus, servus servorum Dei, tibi dilecto filio Heinrico, Dei gratia Romanorum Imperatori Augusto, concedo, electiones Episcoporum et Abbatum Teutonici regni, qui ad regnum pertinent, in præsentia tua fieri absque simonia et aliqua violentia ; ut si qua inter partes discordia emerserit, Metropolitani et Comprovincialum consilio vel judicio, saniori parti assensum et auxilium præbeas.* Electus *autem regalia per sceptrum a te recipiat, et quæ ex his jure tibi debet, faciat. Ex aliis vero partibus Imperii consecratus infra sex menses regalia per sceptrum a te recipiat, et quæ ex his jure tibi debet, faciat, exceptis omnibus, quæ ad Romanam Ecclesiam pertinere noscuntur. De quibus vero querimoniam mihi feceris, secundum officii mei debitum auxilium tibi præstabo. Do tibi veram pacem et omnibus, qui in parte tua sunt, aut fuerunt tempore hujus discordiæ. Data anno dominicæ Incarnationis MCXXII. IX Kal. Octobr.*"

Then follow the signatures.

§ 22. *The Conflict of the Hierarchy in England. William the Conqueror and Lanfranc.*

The DOMESDAY or DOOMESDAY BOOK (*Liber judicii; Book of judgment; Liber de Wintonia,* because deposited in the cathedral at Winchester, now in the Charter House at Westminster, published in facsimile, 1783 and 1861).

It was prepared between 1080 and 1086 by the "justiciaries" of William the Conqueror for the purpose of ascertaining the taxable wealth and military strength of the conquered country and securing a full and fair assessment. It contains, among other things, a list of the bishops, churches, religious houses, great men, etc. See Freeman's *Norman Conquest*, V. 1–52 and 733–740. He says (Preface, viii.) : "The stores of knowledge in Domesday are boundless " (for secular history, rather than church history). — The *Gesta Wilhelmi* by WILLIAM OF POITIERS, a chaplain and violent partisan of the Conqueror. Also the chronicles of WILLIAM OF JUMIÈGES, ORDERICUS VITALIS, in Migne, 188, Eng. Trans. 4 vols. Bohn's Libr.

LANFRANC (thirty-fourth archbishop of Canterbury, 1005–1089) : *Vita* and (55) *Epistolæ*, in his *Opera*, edited by D'Achery (Paris, 1648), Giles (Oxford, 1844, in 2 vols.), and Migne, 150. — H. BOEHMER, *Die Fälschungen Lanfranks von Cant.* Leipzig, 1902.

* EADMER (monk of Canterbury, pupil and biographer of Anselm) : *Vita Sancti Anselmi*, and *Historia Novorum*, both in Anselm's *Opera* (ed. Migne, 158, 159, and in Rolls Series, 1884). — The biographies of Anselm by FRANK (Tübingen, 1842), HASSE (Leipzig, 1843, vol. I. 235–455), REMUSAT (Paris, 1853 ; German translation by Wurzbach, 1854), DEAN CHURCH (London, 1875), RULE (London, 1883), HOOK (in 2d vol. of *Lives of the Archbishops of Canterbury*, London, 1861–1874), RIGG, 1896, WELCH, 1901.

* WILLIAM OF MALMESBURY (b. a. 1096, d. 1143, son of a Norman father and Saxon mother, monk and librarian in the abbey of Malmesbury) : *De Gestis Regum Anglorum* (a history of England from the Anglo-Saxon Conquest to the end of the reign of Henry I., 1129) ; *Historiæ Novellæ* (a continuation till 1151) ; *De Gestis Pontificum Anglorum* (history of the English Church till 1123). Edited by Savile, in *Rerum Anglicarum Scriptores*, London, 1596 ; best ed. in Rolls Series, English translation by John Sharpe, edited by Giles, in Bohn's "Antiquarian Library," London, 1847.

The Works of HENRY OF HUNTINGDON, WILLIAM OF NEWBURGH, GERVAISE OF CANTERBURY, RALPH OF COGGESHALL, RICHARD OF HOVEDEN, MATTHEW PARIS, etc., as ed. in the *Rerum Britannicarum medii ævi scriptores*, called the Rolls Series, London, 1858 sqq. These works ed. by Stubbs, Luard, and other competent Eng. scholars are indispensable.

J. N. AUG. THIERRY (1795–1856) : *Histoire de la conquête de l'Angleterre par les Normands, de ses causes et de ses suites en Angleterre, en Écosse, et en Irlande et sur le continent.* 5e éd. entièrement revue et augmentée. Paris, 1839, 4 vols. The first edition was published, 1825, in 3 vols., a 6th ed. in 1843, etc. English translation by Hazlitt, 1847.

EDW. A. FREEMAN (Professor of History in Oxford) : *History of the Norman Conquest.* Oxford, 1867–1876 (vols. II., III., IV., and V. See Index, vol. VI.). And his *Reign of William Rufus and the Accession of Henry the First.* Oxford, 1882, 2 vols. (see Index, sub Anselm). An exhaustive treatment of that period by a master in historic research and erudition, with model indexes.

G

BISHOP STUBBS furnishes authentic information in his *Constitutional History
    of England*, 6th ed. 3 vols. 1897 ; *Select Charters and Other Illustrations
    of English Constitutional History to the Reign of Edward I.* (1870) ;
    Memorials of St. Dunstan (1874).
H. GEE and W. J . HARDY : *Documents illustrative of Eng. Ch. Hist.*,
    London, 1896.
W. R. W. STEPHENS: *The Eng. Ch. 1066–1272.*   London, 1891.
    Milman (bk. VIII. ch. VIII.) briefly touches upon this important chapter
of the Church history of England.   Hardwick (*Church History of the Middle
Ages*) ignores it.   Robertson notices the principal facts.   Dean Hook gives
the Lives of Lanfranc and Anselm (II. 73–168 and 169–276).

The conflict between the pope and the emperor for supremacy was repeated, on a smaller scale, in England, between the
archbishop of Canterbury and the king, and was settled
for a season in favor of the hierarchy, several years before the
Concordat of Worms.   The struggle for the freedom of the
Church was indirectly also a struggle for the freedom of
the State and the people from the tyranny of the crown.
Priestcraft prevailed over kingcraft, then aristocracy over
absolute monarchy in the *Magna Charta*, and at last the people over both.

The Anglo-Saxon kings and nobles enriched the Church
of England, their alma mater, by liberal grants of real estate
amounting to about one-third of the land, and thus conferred upon it great political influence.   The bishops ranked
with the nobles, and the archbishops with princes, next
to the king.   The archbishop of Canterbury was usually
intrusted with the regency during the absence of the sovereign on the Continent.

But for this very reason the British sovereigns of the
different dynasties tried to keep the Church in a state of
dependence and subserviency, by the election of bishops and
the exercise of the right of investiture.   They filled the
vacant bishoprics with their chaplains, so that the court
became a nursery of prelates, and they occasionally arro-
gated to themselves such titles as " Shepherd of Shepherds," and even " Vicar of Christ."   In one word, they

aspired to be popes of England long before Henry VIII. blasphemously called himself "Supreme Head of the Church of England."

Under the later kings of the Saxon line the Church had degenerated, and was as much in need of reform as the churches on the Continent. The ascetic reforms of Dunstan took no deep root and soon passed away. Eadward the Confessor (1042–1066) was a monastic saint, but a stranger and shadow in England, with his heart in Normandy, the home of his youth. The old Saxon literature was forgotten, and the clergy was sunk in ignorance.[1]   No ecclesiastical synod broke the slumber. The priests were married or lived in concubinage. Simony was freely exercised.

The Norman Conquest aroused England to new life and activity. It marks the greatest change in English history since the Anglo-Saxon Conquest. It left its impress upon the language, literature, architecture, laws and institutions of the country, without, however, breaking the continuity. The Normans, though a foreign, were yet a kindred race, of Teutonic stock, Romanized and Gallicanized in France. From savage pirates they had been changed into semi-civillized Christians, without losing their bravery and love of adventure, which they showed in the crusades and the conquest of England. They engrafted the French language and manners upon the Anglo-Saxon trunk, and superinduced an aristocratic element on the democratic base. It took a long time for the two nationalities and languages to melt into one.

The amalgamation was an enrichment. The happy combination of Saxon strength and endurance with Norman enterprise and vivacity, in connection with the insular position and the capacity for self-government fostered thereby,

---

[1] It is said of the later Anglo-Saxon clergy that they were scarcely able to stammer out the forms of divine service, and that any one who knew "grammar" was regarded as a prodigy.

prepared the English race for the dominion of the seas and the founding of successful colonies in all continents.[1]

The Norman kings were as jealous of their rights and as much opposed to papal superiority as the German emperors. Their instincts and interests were cæsaropapistic or Erastian. But the Church kept them in check. The Hildebrandian ideas of reform were advocated and carried out in part by two of the most eminent scholars and monks of the age, Lanfranc (1005–1089) and Anselm (1033–1109), who followed each other in the see of Canterbury. They were both of Italian birth, — one from the Lombard city of Pavia, the other from Aosta, — and successively abbots and teachers of the famous convent of Bec in the diocese of Rouen.

William I. of Normandy, surnamed "the Conqueror," the natural son of "Robert the Devil" and the daughter of a tanner, and the first king of the Norman dynasty (1066–1087), enforced his pretension to the English throne under the consecrated banner of Pope Alexander II. by the defeat of Harold in the battle on the hill of Senlac, near Hastings, Oct. 14, 1066. Five years afterwards he made Lanfranc archbishop of Canterbury. He had formerly banished him from Normandy for opposing his marriage with Matilda of Flanders, as being within the forbidden degrees. He overtook the abbot as he was leaving the convent on a lame horse, and hurried him on. The abbot said, "Give me a better horse, and I shall go faster." This cool request turned the duke's wrath into laughter and good-will. He was reconciled, and employed him to obtain the pope's sanction of the marriage, and the removal of the interdict from his territories.

Lanfranc was a moderate Hildebrandian. He had been the chief promoter of the doctrine of transubstantiation in

[1] On the effects of the Norman Conquest, see the fifth volume of Freeman's great work. Comp. also Schaff's essay on the cosmopolitan character and mission of the English language, in his *Literature and Poetry*, New York, 1890, pp. 1–62.

the Berengarian controversy; while Hildebrand protected Berengar as long as he could.[1] He was zealous for clerical celibacy, substituted monks for secular canons in cathedrals, and prohibited, through the Council of Winchester in 1076, the ordination of married priests, but allowed the rural clergy to retain their wives. He did not fully sustain the pope's claim to temporal authority, and disobeyed the frequent summons to appear at Rome. He lived, upon the whole, on good terms with the king, although he could not effect anything against his will. He aided him in his attempt to Normanize the English Church. He was intrusted with the regency when the duke was absent on the Continent. He favored the cause of learning, and rebuilt the cathedral of Canterbury, which had burnt down.

William was a despot in Church and State, and rather grew harder and more reckless of human suffering in his later years. His will was the law of the land. Freeman places him both "among the greatest of men" and "among the worst of men."[2] His military genius and statesmanship are undoubted; but he was utterly unscrupulous in the choice of means. He had a strong sense of religion and reverence for the Church, and was liberal to her ministers; he did not, like his son, keep the benefices vacant and rob her revenues; he did not practise simony, and, so far, he fell in with the Hildebrandian reform.[3] But he firmly insisted on the right of investiture. He declared that he would not allow a single bishop's staff to pass out of his hands. He held his own even against Hildebrand. He felt that he owed his crown only to God and to his own sword. He was will-

---

[1] On Lanfranc's connection with the Berengar controversy, see Schaff, vol. IV. 556 and 567 sq.

[2] *Norman Conquest*, II. 165.

[3] Freeman, V. 169: "He was one of the few princes of that age whose hands were wholly clean from the guilt of simony. His ecclesiastical appointments for the most part do him honor; the patron of Lanfranc and Anselm can never be spoken of without respect."

ing to pay Peter's pence to the pope as alms, but not as tribute, and refused to swear allegiance to Gregory VII.

He made full use of the right of a victor. He subjected the estates of the Church to the same feudal obligations as other lands. He plundered religious houses. He deposed Archbishop Stigand and other Saxon bishops to make room for Norman favorites, who did not even understand the language of the people. These changes were not begun till 1070, when Stigand was tried before the papal legates who had placed the crown on William's head. The main charges were simony and that he had received the pall from the usurping pope, Benedict X. William left only one Englishman, the simple-minded Wulfstan of Worcester, in possession of his see. He gradually extended the same system to abbacies and lower dignities. He allowed no synod to convene and legislate without his previous permission and subsequent confirmation of its decrees, no pope to be acknowledged in England without his will, no papal letters to be received and published without his consent. No ecclesiastic was to leave the kingdom without his permission, and bishops were forbidden to excommunicate a noble for adultery or any capital crime without the previous assent of the king. In these ways the power of the clergy was limited, and a check put upon the supremacy of Rome over the English Church. Lanfranc seems to have fully sympathized with these measures. For after the death of Alexander II., who had been his pupil at Bec, he seems to have treated the popes, especially Gregory VII., coolly. Gregory wrote him several letters threatening him with suspension and for his absence from the synods which were convening in Rome.[1]

On the other hand, the law was passed in William's reign remanding ecclesiastical suits to separate tribunals,[2] a law

---

[1] *Reg. Greg.*, VI. 30, IX. 20; Migne, 148, 621, 643.
[2] Gee and Hardy, 57 sq.

which afterwards gave occasion for much contention. The
bishops' court henceforth used the canon law instead of the
common English law used in the shire courts. Another
important movement in William's reign, sanctioned by synodal authority,[1] was the removal of episcopal seats to larger
towns, the Church conforming itself to the changes of geography. Chichester took the place of Selsey, Salisbury of
Sherborne, Chester of Lichfield, Lincoln of Dorchester, 1085,
Bath of Wells, 1088, and Norwich of Thetford, 1094, which
had taken the place of Elmham, 1078. Osmund, bishop of
Salisbury, nephew of the Conqueror, prepared the liturgical
service called the *Sarum use*, which was adopted in other
dioceses than his own, and later became one of the chief
sources of the Book of Common Prayer.

§ 23. *William Rufus and Anselm.*

William II., commonly called William Rufus or the Red
(for his red hair), the third son and first successor of the
Conqueror, ruled from 1087 to 1100. He bought Normandy
from his brother Robert to enable him to make a crusade.
This is the only good thing he did, besides appointing
Anselm primate of England. He inherited all the vices and
none of the virtues of his father. He despised and hated
the clergy. It was said of him that " he feared God but
little, and man not at all." He was not a sceptic or infidel,
as some represent him, but profane and blasphemous. He
believed in God, like the demons, but did not tremble.
He defied the Almighty. When he recovered from a severe
sickness, he said : " God shall never see me a good man ; I
have suffered too much at his hands." He doubted his
justice, and mocked at the ordeals. He declared publicly
that neither St. Peter nor any other saint had any influence
with God, and that he would not ask them for aid. He used

[1] *The Synod of London*, 1075.   See Wilkins, I. 363 ; Gee and Hardy, 54.

to swear "by the holy face of Lucca."[1] He was not married, but indulged in gross and shameless debaucheries. The people said of him that he rose a worse man every morning, and lay down a worse man every evening.

He had promised Lanfranc at his coronation to exercise justice and mercy and to protect the freedom of the Church, but soon forgot his vow, and began systematically to plunder the Church and to oppress the clergy. He robbed the bishoprics and abbeys of their income by leaving them vacant or selling them to the highest bidders. Within four years he changed thirty cemeteries into royal parks to satisfy his passion for hunting, which at last cost him his life. He used to say : "The bread of Christ is rich ; the kings have given to the Church one-half of its income : why should I not try to win it back ? "

He kept the see of Canterbury vacant for nearly four years (1089–1093). At last he yielded, under the influence of a severe sickness, to the pressure of the better class of bishops and noblemen, and elected Anselm, who was then in England, and well known as a profound theologian and saintly character. A greater contrast can scarcely be imagined. While William Rufus delighted in witnessing the tortures of innocent men and animals, Anselm was singularly tender-hearted : he saved the life of a hare which was chased by the hunters and had sought protection under his horse ; he saw a worthy object for prayer in the sufferings of a bird tortured by a thoughtless child.[2] Yet, with all his gentleness, he could be firm and unyielding in the defence of truth and righteousness.

The primacy was forced upon Anselm in spite of his remonstrance. He foresaw a hard struggle. He compared

---

[1] *Per sanctum vultum de Luca.* A figure of the crucified Saviour in wood which was said to have been carved by Nicodemus, and was preserved in the cathedral at Lucca.

[2] These rare traits of character are mentioned by Eadmer in his *Vita Anselmi.* Freeman, V. 25.

himself to an old and feeble sheep, and the king to a young, wild bull. Thus yoked, he was to draw the plough of the Church of England, with the prospect of being torn to pieces by the ferocity of the bull.[1] He was received with intense enthusiasm at Canterbury by the clergy, the monks, and the people, and was consecrated on the second Sunday of Advent, 1093. He began at once to restore discipline according to the principles of Hildebrand, though with more moderation and gentleness.

A short time elapsed before the relations between the king and the prelate became strained. Anselm supported Urban II.; William leaned to the anti-pope Clement III. The question of investiture with the pallium at once became a matter of dispute. The king at first insisted upon Anselm's receiving it from Clement and then claimed the right to confer it himself. Anselm refused to yield and received it, 1095, from Urban's legate, who brought the sacred vestment to England in a silver casket. The archbishop gave further offence to the king by the mean way, as was said, in which he performed his feudal obligations.[2] William decided to try him in his court. To this indignity Anselm would, of course, not submit. It was the old question whether an English ecclesiastic owed primary allegiance to the pope or to the crown.[3] The archbishop secured the king's reluctant permission, 1097, to go to Rome. But William's petty spirit pursued the departing prel-

[1] Eadmer (*Hist. Nov.*, in Migne's edition of Anselm, II. 368) : "*Indomitum taurum et vetulam ac debilem ovem in aratro conjungere sub uno jugo,*" etc. Ranke, *Weltgesch.*, VIII. 115, makes here a curious mistake by putting into Anselm's mouth the saying that England's plough must be drawn by " two noble and powerful bulls " (*von zwei edlen und kräftigen Stieren, dem König und dem Primas*).

[2] Soon after he was made archbishop, Anselm sent the king £500, a sum far below what the king expected. On another occasion when the king was starting on a campaign against Wales, Anselm sent what the king regarded as a beggarly contingent of ill-trained knights.

[3] The matters in dispute were discussed at Rockingham at a meeting of barons and bishops with Anselm at their head. See Freeman, *W. Rufus*, I. 476 sqq.

ate by ordering Anselm's baggage searched at Dover. He seized the revenues of Canterbury, and Anselm's absence was equivalent to exile. Eadmer reports a remarkable scene before Anselm's departure.[1]   At his last interview with William he refused to leave the king's presence until he had given him his blessing. "As a spiritual father to his son, as Archbishop of Canterbury to the king of England," he said, "I would fain before I go give you God's blessing."   To these words the king made reply that he did not decline the priestly blessing.   It was the last time they met.

Anselm was most honorably received by the pope, who threatened the king with excommunication, and pronounced an anathema on all laymen who exercised the right of investiture and on all clergymen who submitted to lay-investiture.[2]

The Red King was shot dead by an arrow, — nobody knows whether by a hunter or by an assassin, Aug. 2, 1100, while hunting in the New Forest.   " Cut off without shrift, without repentance, he found a tomb in the Old Minster of Winchester; but the voice of clergy and people, like the voice of one man, pronounced, by a common impulse, the sentence which Rome had feared to pronounce.   He received the more unique brand of popular excommunication.   No bell was tolled, no prayer was said, no alms were given for the soul of the one baptized and anointed ruler, whose eternal damnation was taken for granted by all men as a thing about which there could be no doubt." [3]

§ 24. *Anselm and Henry I.*

At the death of the Red King, one archbishopric, four bishoprics, and eleven abbeys were without pastors.   Henry I., his younger brother, surnamed Beauclerc, ascended the

---

[1] *Hist. Nov.*, II., Migne's ed. 159, 402.

[2] According to Eadmer, *Hist. Nov.*, Migne's ed. 159, 414, it was due to Anselm's intercession that Urban withheld from William Rufus the anathema.

[3] Freeman, *Norm. Conq.*, V. 147.

throne (1100–1135). He connected the Norman blood with
the imperial house of Germany by the marriage of his daughter Matilda to Henry V. After the emperor's death, Matilda was privately married to Geoffrey Plantagenet, count
of Anjou (1128), and became the mother of Henry II., the
founder of the Plantagenet dynasty.

King Henry I. is favorably known by his strict administration of justice. He reconciled the clergy by recalling
Anselm from exile, but soon renewed the investiture controversy. He instituted bishops and abbots, and summoned
Anselm to consecrate them, which he steadfastly refused to
do. He sent him into a second exile (1103–1106).[1] The
queen, Maud the Good, who had an extraordinary veneration
for the archbishop, strove to mediate between him and her
husband, and urged Anselm to return, even at the sacrifice
of a little earthly power, reminding him that Paul circumcised Timothy, and went to the temple to conciliate the Jewish brethren.

Pascal II. excommunicated the bishops who had accepted
investiture from Henry. But the king was not inclined to
maintain a hostile attitude to Anselm. They had an interview in Normandy and appealed to the pope, who confirmed
the previous investitures of the king on condition of his surrendering the right of investiture in future to the Church.
This decision was ratified at Bec, Aug. 26, 1106. The king
promised to restore to Anselm the profits of the see during
his absence, to abstain from the revenues of vacant bishoprics
and abbeys, and to remit all fines to the clergy. He retained

---

[1] While in England, Anselm had celebrated the marriage of Henry to Matilda, or Eadgyth (as her English name was), daughter of the Scotch king
Malcolm. Her aunt, a nun at Romsey, had placed the veil upon Eadgyth
when she was a child as a protection against violence. There was a difference
of opinion as to whether this was to be construed as a vow. Anselm pronounced her free. Ladies at the time of the Norman Conquest had temporarily put on the veil as a protection to their virtue. Lanfranc afterwards
declared them free to marry.

the right of sending to vacant sees a *congé d'élire*, or notice to
elect, which carried with it the right of nomination. Anselm
now proceeded to consecrate bishops, among them Roger of
Salisbury, who was first preferred to Henry's notice because
he "began prayers quickly and closed them speedily." [1]

Anselm returned to England in triumph, and was received
by the queen at the head of the monks and the clergy. At
a council held at Westminster in 1107,[2] the king formally re-
linquished the privilege of investiture, while the archbishop
promised to tolerate the ceremony of homage (which Urban
II. had condemned). The synodical canons against clerical
marriage were renewed and made more rigorous (1102, 1107,
1108); but the pope consented for a time that the sons of
priests might be admitted to orders, for the remarkable reason, as Eadmer reports, that "almost the greater and the
better part of the English clergy" were derived from this
class.[3]

During the remaining years of his life, Anselm enjoyed
the friendship and respect of the king, and during the latter's absence on the Continent in 1108, he was intrusted with
the regency and the care of the royal family. He was canonized by the voice of the English people long before the
formal canonization by the pope.[4]

After his death, in April, 1109, the primacy remained vacant till 1114, when it was conferred upon Ralph of Escures,
bishop of Rochester, who had administered its affairs during

---

[1] See Fuller, *Ch. Hist. of Britain*, I. 340.

[2] A previous council had been held at Westminster in 1102. See Freeman,
V. 221, 226, and Gee and Hardy, pp. 63 sq.

[3] Freeman, V. 223: "The newly devised rigor only led to laxity of a
worse kind, which it was intended to stop. But, at any rate, it was now that
the rule of celibacy became for the first time the universal law of the English Church. Anselm's counsel at Westminster [that of 1102] thus marks
an era in our ecclesiastical history."

[4] The canonization by Alexander III. came to nothing, but was renewed
by Alexander VI. Dean Church says that Anselm "suffered the indignity
of a canonization at the hands of Borgia."

the interval.   He is described as a learned, cheerful, affable, good-humored, facetious prelate.   He was called " *nugax*," but his jests and repartees have not been recorded.   He and his two Norman successors, William of Corbeuil, 1123–1136. and Theobald, 1139–1161, lived on good terms with the king and his successor, Stephen.   Thomas Becket, an English man, resumed, in 1162, the controversy between the mitre and the crown with greater energy, but less wisdom, than Anselm.

CHAPTER IV.

THE PAPACY FROM THE CONCORDAT OF WORMS TO INNOCENT III. A.D. 1122–1198.

On the historical sources for this period down to the middle of the thirteenth century, see Wattenbach : *Deutschlands Geschichtsquellen im Mittelalter*, II. 217–442.

§ 25. *Innocent II.*, 1130–1143, *and Eugene III.*, 1145–1153.

Innocent II.: *Epistolæ et Privilegia*, in Migne, *Patrol.*, Tom. 179, fol. 54–636 ; his biographies in Muratori (*Rer. Ital.*, Tom. II. and III.) and Watterich (*Pontif. Rom. Vitæ*, II. 174 sq.). — Anacletus (antipapa): *Epistolæ et Privil.*, in Migne, Tom. 179, fol. 687–732. — Eugenius III. : *Epistolæ*, etc., in Migne, 180, 1013–1614. — The Works of St. Bernard, edited by Mabillon, and reprinted in Migne's *Patrol.* (Tom. 182–185, Paris, 1855) ; Ordericus Vitalis, *Eccl. Hist.*, XII. 11, etc. ; Bohn's Trans. IV.

Jaffé: *Geschichte des deutschen Reichs unter Lothar von Sachsen.* Berlin, 1843.— Mirbt, art. *Innocent II.* in Herzog, IX. 108 sqq. — E. Mühlbacher: *Die streitige Papstwahl d. J. 1130.* Innsbruck, 1876. — W. Bernhardi : *Konrad III.* Leipzig, 1883, 2 vols. — Hefele-Knöpfler, Bd. V. 385–532. — Giesebrecht, Bd. IV. 54 sqq. — Gregorovius, IV. 403 sqq.— Hauck, IV. 130 sqq. — The Biographies of St. Bernard.

Calixtus II. was followed by Honorius II., whose rule of six years, 1124–1130, was an uneventful one. After his death a dangerous schism broke out between Innocent II., 1130–1143, and Anacletus II., 1130–1138, who represented two powerful Roman families, the Frangipani, or Breadmakers,[1] and the Pierleoni.

Innocent, formerly cardinal-legate of Urban II. and mediator of the Concordat of Worms, enjoyed the reputation of

---

[1] The name was derived by legend from the distribution of bread in time of famine by one of the ancestors of the family. Its coat of arms represented two lions rampant, holding a loaf of bread between them. Gregorovius, IV. 404.

superior learning and piety, which even his opponents could not dispute.   He had also the advantage of a prior election, but of doubtful legal validity, since it was effected only by a minority of cardinals, who met in great hurry in an unknown place to anticipate the rival candidate.[1]

Anacletus was a son of Pierleone, Petrus Leonis, and a grandson of Leo, a baptized Jewish banker, who had acquired great financial, social, and political influence under the Hildebrandian popes.   A Jewish community with a few hundred members were tolerated in Trastevere and around the island of the Tiber as a monumental proof of the truth of Christianity, and furnished some of the best physicians and richest bankers, who helped the nobility and the popes in their financial troubles.   Anacletus betrayed his Semitic origin in his physiognomy, and was inferior to Innocent in moral character; but he secured an election by a majority of cardinals and the support of the principal noble families and the Roman community.   With the help of the Normans, he took possession of Rome, banished his opponent, deposed the hostile cardinals, and filled the college with his friends.

Innocent was obliged to flee to France, and received there the powerful support of Peter of Cluny and Bernard of Clairvaux, the greatest monks and oracles of their age.   He was acknowledged as the legitimate pope by all the monastic orders and by the kings of France and England.

Lothaire II. (III.) of Saxony, 1125–1137, to whom both parties appealed, decided for Innocent, led him and St. Bernard to Rome by armed force, and received in turn from the pope the imperial crown, June 4, 1133.

But after Lothaire's departure, Anacletus regained possession of Rome, with the help of the Norman duke, Roger, and

---

[1] The thorough investigation of Mühlbacher is unfavorable to the validity of the election of Gregory (Innocent II.), and Deutsch (note in his edition of Neander's *St. Bernhard*, I. 110 sq.) agrees with him, and bases his claim on purely moral grounds.

the party of the rival emperor, Conrad III. He made Roger II.
king of Sicily, and thus helped to found a kingdom which
lasted seven hundred and thirty years, till it was absorbed
in the kingdom of Italy, 1860.   Innocent retired to Pisa
(1135).   Lothaire made a second expedition to Italy and
defeated Roger II.   Bernard again appeared at Rome and
succeeded in strengthening Innocent's position.   At this
juncture Anacletus died, 1138.   The healing of the schism
was solemnly announced at the Second Lateran Council, 1139.
War soon after broke out between Innocent and Roger, and
Innocent was taken prisoner.   On his release he confirmed
Roger as king of Sicily.   Lothaire had returned to Germany
to die, 1137.   Innocent had granted to him the territories
of Matilda for an annual payment.   On this transaction
later popes based the claim that the emperor was a papal
vassal.

After the short pontificates of Cœlestin II., 1143–1144,
and Lucius II., 1144–1145, Eugene III., a pupil and friend
of St. Bernard, was elected, Feb. 15, 1145, and ruled till
July 8, 1153.   He wore the rough shirt of the monks of
Citeaux under the purple.   He had to flee from Rome, owing
to the disturbances of Arnold of Brescia, and spent most of
his time in exile.   During his pontificate, Edessa was lost
and the second crusade undertaken.   Eugene has his chief
interest from his connection with St. Bernard, his wise and
loyal counsellor, who addressed to him his famous treatise
on the papacy, the *de consideratione*.[1]

§ 26. *Arnold of Brescia.*

OTTO (Bishop of Freising, or Freisingen, d. 1158): *De Gestis Friderici I.*
(lib. II. 20). — GUNTHER (Ligurinus) : *De Gestis Friderici I.*, an epos
written 1187 (lib. III. vers. 262 sqq.). — GERHOH (provost of Reichersberg,
d. 1169): *De investigatione Antichristi*, edited by Scheibelberger. Lincii,
1875. — JOHN OF SALISBURY: *Historia Pontificalis* (written c. 1162,
recently discovered), in *Mon. Germ. Script.*, XX. c. 31, p. 537.— ST. BER-

[1] See the chapters on the Second Crusade and St. Bernard.

NARD: *Epist.*,Migne, 195, 196, 198. —WALTER MAP (archdeacon of Oxford, 1196) : *De Nugis Curialium*, ed. Wright, pp. 41 and 43. The sources are all hostile to Arnold and the Arnoldists.

J. D. KÖLER : *De Arnoldo Brixiensi dissert.* Göttingen, 1742. —GUADA-GNINI : *Apologia di Arnaldo da Brescia.* Pavia, 1790, 2 vols. —K. BECK : *A. v. Brescia.* Basel, 1824. — H. FRANCKE : *Arnold von Brescia und seine Zeit.* Zürich, 1825 (eulogistic). —BENT: *Essay sur A. d. Brescia.* Genève, 1856. —FEDERICO ODORICI : *Arnaldo da Brescia.* 1861. — GEORGES GUIBAL : *Arnauld de Brescia et les Hohenstaufen ou la question du pouvoir temporel de la papauté du moyen age.* Paris, 1868. — *GIESEBRECHT : *Arnold von Brescia.* München, 1873 (in the Reports of the Bavarian Academy of Sciences). Comp. his *Gesch. der d. Kaiserzeit,* IV. 314 sqq. — A. DI GIOVANNI DE CASTRO : *Arnaldo da Brescia e la revoluzione romana dell XII. secolo.* Livorno, 1875.•— A. HAUSRATH : *Arnold von Brescia.* Leipzig, 1891.—DEUTSCH, *A. von Brescia,* in Herzog, II. 117–122 ; GREGOROVIUS, IV. 479 sqq. The Lives of St· Bernard, especially Vacandard and Neander-Deutsch.

During the pontificates of Innocent II., Eugene III., and Adrian IV. occurred the interesting episode of Arnold of Brescia, an unsuccessful ecclesiastical and political agitator, who protested against the secularization of the Church, and tried to restore it to apostolic poverty and apostolic purity. These two ideas were closely connected in his mind. He proclaimed the principle that the Church and the clergy, as well as the monks, should be without any temporal possessions, like Christ and the Apostles, and live from the tithes and the voluntary offerings of the people. Their calling is purely spiritual. All the things of this earth belong to the laity and the civil government.

He practised what he taught, and begged his daily bread from house to house. He was a monk of severe ascetic piety, enthusiastic temper, popular eloquence, well versed in the Scriptures, restless, radical, and fearless.[1] He agreed with the Catholic orthodoxy, except on the doctrines of the eucha-

---

[1] Otto von Freising calls him "*singularitatis amator, novitatis cupidus,*" and ranks him with those characters who are apt to produce heresies and to make schismatic disturbances. St. Bernard denounces him as the author of *a schisma pessimum,* but bears testimony to his ascetic piety, yet with the cruel charge of satanic thirst for the blood of souls : " *Homo est neque manducans neque bibens, solo cum diabolo esuriens et sitiens sanguinem animarum.*"

rist and infant baptism; but his views on these sacraments are not known.[1]

With this ecclesiastical scheme he combined a political one. He identified himself with the movement of the Romans to emancipate themselves from the papal authority, and to restore the ancient republic. By giving all earthly power to the laity, he secured the favor of the laity, but lost the influence of the clergy. It was the political complication which caused his ruin.

Arnold was a native of Brescia in Lombardy, and an ordained reader in the Church. He was a pupil of Abælard, and called armor-bearer to this Goliath.[2] He sympathized with his spirit of independence and hostility to Church authority, and may have been influenced also (as Neander assumes) by the ethical principles of that magnetic teacher. He certainly, at a later period, sided with him against St. Bernard, who became his bitter enemy. But with the exception of the common opposition to the hierarchy, they differed very widely. Abælard was a philosopher, Arnold, a politician; Abælard, a speculative thinker, Arnold, a practical preacher; Abælard, a rationalist, Arnold, an enthusiast. The former undermined the traditional orthodoxy, the latter attacked the morals of the clergy and the temporal power of the Church. Arnold was far below Abælard in intellectual endowment, but far more dangerous in the practical drift of his teaching, which tended to pauperize the Church and to revolutionize society. Baronius calls him " the father of political heresies."

In his ascetic zeal for the moral reform of the clergy,

---

[1] Von Freising: " *Præter hæc* [his views on Church property] *de sacramento altaris, et baptismo parvulorum non sane dicitur sensisse.*" Some Baptists claim him for his supposed rejection of infant baptism. The attempts to bring him into contact with the Waldenses (who are of later date) have no foundation.

[2] Freising: "*Arnaldus iste et Italia, civitate Brixia oriundus, ejusdemque ecclesiæ clericus ac tantum lector ordinatus, Petrum Abailardum olim præceptorem habuerat.*" St. Bernard seems to place the acquaintance at a later period: " *Execratus a Petro apostolo, adhæserat Petro Abailardo.*"

Arnold was in sympathy with the Hildebrandian party, but in his views of the temporal power of the pope, he went to the opposite extreme. Hildebrand aimed at the theocratic supremacy of the Church over the State ; Arnold sought the welfare of the Church in her complete separation from the State and of the clerical office from secular entanglements. Pascal II., we may say, had prepared the way for this theory when he was willing to sacrifice the investiture to the emperor. The Hildebrandian reform had nearly passed away, and the old corruptions reappeared. The temporal power of the Church promoted the worldliness of the clergy. The author of the *Historia Pontificalis* says that Arnold's doctrine agreed with the Gospel, but stood in crying contrast with the actual condition of things. St. Bernard, his opponent, was as much opposed as he to the splendor and luxury of bishops, the secular cares of the popes, and expressed a wish that he might see the day when " the Church, as in olden times, should cast her net for souls, and not for money." [1] All the monastic orders protested against the worldliness of the Church, and realized the principle of apostolic poverty within the wall of convents. But Arnold extended it to the secular clergy as well, and even went so far as to make poverty a condition of salvation for priests and monks. [2]

Arnold's sermons gained great popular applause in Lombardy, and caused bitter disputes between the people and the bishop of Brescia. He was charged before the Lateran Synod of 1139 with inciting the laity against the clergy, was deposed as a schismatic (not as a heretic), commanded to be silent, and was expelled from Italy.

He went again to France and was entangled in the controversy of Abælard with Bernard. Pope Innocent condemned

---

[1] *Epist.*, 238 ad Eugen. III.

[2] Otto v. Freising, *l.c.* : " *Dicebat, nec Clericos proprietatem, nec Episcopos regalia, nec monachos possessiones habentes aliqua ratione salvari posse. Cuncta hæc Principis esse, ab ejusque beneficentia in usum tantum laicorum cedere opportere.* "

both Abælard and Arnold to silence and seclusion in a convent, 1140.   Abælard, weary of strife and life, submitted
and retired to the convent of Cluny, where two years later
he died in peace.[1]   But Arnold began in Paris a course of
public lectures against the worldliness and immorality of the
clergy.   He exposed especially the avarice of the bishops.
He also charged St. Bernard with unholy ambition and envy
against scholars.   Bernard called him a man whose speech
was honey, whose doctrine was poison.   At his request the
king expelled Arnold from France.

Arnold fled to Zürich and was kindly received and protected by the papal legate, Cardinal Guido, his former fellow-
student in Paris.[2]   But Bernard pursued him even there and
denounced him to the bishop of Constance.

After a few years of unknown exile, Arnold appeared in
Rome as the leader of a political movement.   Innocent II.
had allowed him to return to Italy; Eugene III. had pardoned him on condition of his doing penance in the holy
places of Rome.   But after the flight of this pope to France,
Arnold preached again the doctrine of apostolic poverty,
called the popes and cardinals Pharisees and scribes, and
their church a house of merchandise and den of robbers.   He
was protected by the Roman senate, and idolized by the people.   The Romans had renounced the papal authority, expelled
the pope, substituted a purely secular government after the
ancient model, and invited Conrad III. to assume the rôle of
Constantine I. or Justinian.   They lost themselves in dreams

---

[1] Tosti, in his *Storia di Abelardo*, Naples, 1851, says of Abælard that he
had the courage of thought, but not the courage of action (*il coraggio del
pensiero non quello dell' azione*).

[2] This Guido was formerly identified with Guido of Castello who became
Pope Cœlestin II., Sept. 26, 1143, and ruled five months.   But Giesebrecht
and Gregorovius (IV. 455) distinguish the two.   Francke exaggerates Arnold's
influence upon Swiss liberty while at Zürich.   Milman makes him a forerunner of Zwingli, who opposed the hierarchy ; but Zwingli knew little or
nothing of Arnold, and had no idea of pauperizing the Church, or of a separation of Church and State.

of government.   The tradition of the old Roman rule controlled the Middle Ages in various forms : it lived as a
universal monarchy in the German Empire, as a universal
theocracy in the papacy; as a short-lived republic in the
Roman people.   The modern Italians who oppose the temporal power of the pope are more sensible : they simply
claim the natural right of the Italian people to govern themselves, and they confine the dominion of Rome to Italy.

Arnold stepped out of the ecclesiastical into the political
sphere, and surrounded the new republic with the halo of
religion.   He preached in his monastic gown, on the ruins
of the Capitol, to the patres conscripti, and advised them to
rebuild the Capitol, and to restore the old order of senators
and knights.   His emaciated face gave him a ghost-like
appearance and deepened the effect of his eloquence.

But the republican experiment failed.   The people were
at last forced into submission by the interdict of Pope
Adrian IV.   Arnold was banished from Rome, 1154, and
soon afterwards hanged by order of Emperor Frederick I.,
who hated democracy and republicanism.   His body was
burnt and his ashes were thrown into the Tiber, 1155,
lest his admirers should worship his bones.[1]

Arnold's was a voice of protest against the secular aims of
the papacy and the worldliness of the clergy which still has
its hearers. " So obstinate is the ban of the Middle Ages under which Rome is still held, "says Gregorovius," that the soul
of a heretic of the twelfth century has not yet found rest, but
must still haunt Rome." The Catholic Bishop Hefele refused
to class him among " real heretics." [2] In 1883 Brescia raised a
monument to its distinguished son.

The Arnoldists continued for some time to defend the doc-

[1] According to a Brescian poem, Arnold refused to recant and made
only the single request for time for prayer before dying.   Gregorovius, IV.
545.

[2] *Unter die eigentlichen Heretiker.*   Hefele. denies the errors ascribed to
Arnold by Otto of Freising.   *Kirchengesch.* 407.

trines of their master, and were declared heretics by a council of Verona, 1184, after which they disappeared.

But the idea of apostolic poverty and the opposition to the temporal power of the papacy reappeared among the Spirituals of the Franciscan order. Arnold's political scheme of restoring the Roman republic was revived two hundred years later by Cola di Rienzi (1347), but with no better success ; for Rienzi was murdered, his body burnt, and the ashes were scattered to the winds (1354).

§ 27. *The Popes and the Hohenstaufen.*

I. PRINCIPAL SOURCES :

(1) The *Regesta* of the popes from Anastasius IV. to Innocent III. (1153–1198) by JAFFÉ-WATTENBACH (ed. 1886). — The *Opera* of these popes in MIGNE's *Patrol. Lat.* — The *Vitæ* of the popes by PLATINA, WATTERICH, etc.

(2)   OTTO (half-brother of King Conrad III. and uncle of Frederick Barbarossa, and partial to him, bishop of Freising, or Freisingen, in Upper Bavaria, d. 1158) : *De Gestis Friderici I.*, finished by his pupil RAHEWIN or REGUIN. Best ed. by Waitz, 1884. Also his *Chronicle* (*De duabus Civitatibus*, after the model of Augustin's *De Civitate Dei*), continued by OTTO of ST. BLASIEN (in the Black Forest) till 1209. First critical ed. by R. Wilmans in *Mon. Ger. Scr.*, XX. 83–493. — GUNTHER LIGURINUS wrote in 1187 a Latin epic of 6576 verses on the deeds of the Emperor Frederick I. till 1160. See Wattenbach's *Geschichtsquellen*, II. 241 sqq.

II. WORKS ON THE HOHENSTAUFEN PERIOD :

JAFFÉ : *Geschichte des deutschen Reichs unter Konrad III.*, Hanover, 1845.— FR. VON RAUMER : *Geschichte der Hohenstaufen.* Leipzig, 1823. 4th ed. 1871. — W. ZIMMERMANN : *Die Hohenstaufen oder der Kampf der Monarchie gegen den Papst und die republ. Freiheit.* Stuttgart, 1838. 2d ed. 1865, 2 vols. — G. DE CHERRIER : *Histoire de la lutte des papes et des empereurs de la maison de Souabe.* Paris, 1841, 4 vols. — *HERMANN REUTER (Professor of Church History in Göttingen, d. 1888): *Alexander III. und die Kirche seiner Zeit.* 1845. 2d ed. thoroughly rewritten, Leipzig, 1860–1864; 3 vols. (A work of fifteen years' study.) — SCHIRRMACHER : *Kaiser Friedrich II.* Göttingen, 1859–1864, 4 vols.; *Die letzten Hohenstaufen.* Göttingen, 1871. — P. SCHEFFER-BOICHORST : *K. Friedrichs I. letzter Streit mit der Kurie.* Berlin, 1866. — H. PRUTZ : *K. Friedrich I.* Danzig, 1871–1874, 3 vols. — DEL GUIDICE : *Il guidizio e la condanna di Corradino.* Naples, 1876. — RIBBECK : *Friedr. I. und die römische Kurie.* Leipzig, 1881. — UGO BALZANI : *The Popes and the Hohenstaufen.* London and New York, 1888 (pp. 261). — GIESEBRECHT, BRYCE, 167 sqq.; GREGOROVIUS, IV. 424 sqq. ; HAUCK, IV. ; — HEFELE-KNÖPFLER, V. 533 sqq.

With Conrad III. the powerful family of the Hohenstaufen ascended the imperial throne and occupied it from 1138 till 1254. They derive the name from the family castle Hohenstaufen, on a hill in the Rough Alp near Göppingen in Swabia.[1] They were descended from a knight, Friedrich von Büren, in the eleventh century, and his son Friedrich von Staufen, a faithful adherent of Emperor Henry IV., who made him duke of Swabia (1079), and gave him his daughter Agnes in marriage. They were thus connected by blood with the antagonist of Pope Hildebrand, and identified with the cause of the Ghibellines against the Guelphs in their bloody feuds in Germany and Italy. Henry VI., 1190–1197, acquired by marriage the kingdom of Naples and Sicily. His son, Frederick II., raised his house to the top of its prosperity, but was in his culture and taste more an Italian than German prince, and spent most of his time in Italy.

The Hohenstaufen or Swabian emperors maintained the principle of imperialism, that is, the dignity and independence of the monarchy, as a divine institution, against papal sacerdotalism on the one hand, and against popular liberty on the other.

They made common cause with the popes, and served their purposes in the crusades: three of them, Conrad III., Frederick I., and Frederick II., undertook crusades against the Saracens; Conrad III. engaged in the second, which was a failure; Frederick I. perished in Syria; Frederick II. captured Jerusalem. The Hohenstaufen made also common cause with the popes against political and doctrinal dissent: Barbarossa sacrificed and punished by death Arnold of Brescia as a dangerous demagogue; and Frederick II., though probably himself an unbeliever, persecuted heretics.

---

[1] The castle was destroyed in the Peasants' War in 1525. At the foot of the hill is a village and an old church with a fresco picture of Barbarossa, bearing the inscription: "*Hic transibat Cæsar, amor bonorum, terror malorum.*" "Here Cæsar passed away, beloved by the good, dreaded by the bad." Close by is the ancient seat of the Hohenzollern family. On the site of the old castle a splendid castle was erected by William I., the Emperor of Germany.

But on the question of supremacy of power, the Hohenstaufen were always in secret or open war with the popes,
and in the end were defeated.   The conflict broke out under
Frederick Barbarossa, who after long years of contention died
at peace with the Church.   It was continued by his grandson
Frederick II. who died excommunicated and deposed from
his throne by the papacy.   The dynasty went out in tragic
weakness in Conradin, the last male representative, who was
beheaded on the charge of high treason, 1268.   This conflict
of the imperial house of the Hohenstaufen was more imposing
than the conflict waged by Henry IV. with Gregory and his
successors because of the higher plane on which it was fought
and the greater ability of the secular antagonists engaged.
Lasting more than one hundred years, it forms one of the most
august spectacles of the Middle Ages, and furnishes some of
the most dramatic scenes in which kings have ever figured.
The historian Gregorovius has felt justified in saying that
" this Titanic war of the Middle Ages filled and connected
the centuries and formed the greatest spectacle of all ages."

After the fall of the Hohenstaufen, the German Empire
maintained, till its death in 1806, a nominal connection with
the papacy, but ceased to be the central political power of
Europe, except in the period of the Reformation under Charles
V., 1519 – 1558, when it was connected with the crowns of
Austria, the Low Countries, and Spain, and the newly discovered lands of America, and when that mighty monarch,
true to his Austrian and Spanish descent, retarded the Protestant movement for national independence and religious freedom.   The new German Empire, founded on the ruins of the
old and the defeat of France (1870), is ruled by a hereditary
Protestant emperor.

CHRONOLOGICAL TABLE.

A.D.	POPES.	THE HOHENSTAUFEN.	A.D.
1130–1143	Innocent II.	Conrad III.	1138–1152
1143–1144	Cœlestine II.	Crowned emperor at Aix la Chapelle	
1144–1145	Lucius II.	by the papal legates.	
1145–1153	Eugene III.	Frederick I. (Barbarossa).	1152–1190
1153–1154	Anastasius IV.	(Nephew of Conrad.)	
1154–1159	Adrian IV.	Crowned emperor by Adrian IV.	1155
1159–1181	Alexander III.		
1181–1185	Lucius III.		
1185–1187	Urban III.		
1187	Gregory VIII.		
1187–1191	Clement III.	Henry VI.	1190–1197
1191–1198	Cœlestine III.	(Son of Barbarossa.)	
		Crowned emperor by Cœlestine III.	1191
		King of Sicily.	1194
1198–1216	Innocent III.	Otto IV.	1209–1215
		Crowned by Innocent III.	1209
		Deposed by the Lateran Council.	1215
1216–1227	Honorius III.	Frederick II.	
1227–1241	Gregory IX.	(Son of Henry VI. and Constance of	
1241	Cœlestine IV.	Sicily.)	
		Crowned emperor by Honorius III.	1220
1241–1254	Innocent IV.	Conrad IV.	1250–1254
		(Second son of Frederick II.)	
		Crowned king of the Romans.	1237
		Excommunicated, 1252, and again, 1254.	
1254–1261	Alexander IV.	Interregnum.	1254–1273
1261–1264	Urban IV.	Conradin.	
1265–1268	Clement IV.	(Son of Conrad, the last of the Hohenstaufen, b. 1252.)	
		Beheaded.	1268

§ 28. *Adrian IV. and Frederick Barbarossa.*

Lives of Hadrian in MURATORI, *Script. Rer. Ital.* I. III. — MIGNE, vol. 188. —
OTTO OF FREISING. — WILLIAM OF NEWBURGH, 2 vols. London, 1856. —
R. RABY : *Pope Hadrian IV.* London, 1849. — TARLETON : *Nicolas
Breakspear, Englishman and Pope*, 1896. — L. GINNELL : *The Doubtful
Grant of Ireland of Pope Adrian IV. to Henry II.*, 1899. — O. J.
THATCHER : *Studies conc. Adrian IV.* Chicago, 1903. pp. 88. — REU-
TER : *Alex. III.*, vol. I. 1–48, 479–487.

Eugene III. was followed by Anastasius IV., whose rule lasted only sixteen months.

His successor was Nicolas Breakspear, the first and the only Englishman that has (thus far) worn the tiara. He was the son of a poor priest of St. Albans. He went to France in pursuit of bread and learning, became a monk, prior, and abbot of the convent of St. Rufus, between Arles and Avignon. He studied theology and canon law. Eugene III. made him cardinal-bishop of Albano, and sent him as legate to Norway and Sweden, where he organized the Church and brought it into closer contact with Rome.

He occupied the papal chair as Adrian IV., from 1154 to 1159, with great ability and energy. A beggar raised to the highest dignity in Christendom ! The extremes of fortune met in this Englishman. Yet he felt happier in his poverty than in his power. He declared soon after his consecration that " the papal chair was full of thorns and the papal mantle full of holes and so heavy as to load down the strongest man." And after some experience in that high office, he said : " Is there a man in the world so miserable as a pope ? I have found so much trouble in St. Peter's chair that all the bitterness of my former life appears sweet in comparison." [1]

The Romans, under the lead of Arnold, requested him to resign all claim to temporal rule; but he refused, and after a bloody attack made by an Arnoldist upon one of the cardinals in the open street, he laid — for the first time in history — the interdict on the city. By this unbloody, yet awful and most effective, weapon, he enforced the submission of the people. He abolished the republican government, expelled Arnold and his adherents, and took possession of the Lateran.

At this time, Frederick I., called Barbarossa (Redbeard) by the Italians from the color of his beard, one of the bravest, strongest, and most despotic of German emperors, — the

[1] John of Salisbury, *Polycraticus*, VIII. 23 ; Migne, 199, 814.

sleeper in Kyffhäuser,[1] — made, with a powerful army, his
first expedition to Italy to receive the iron crown of royalty
from the Lombards and the golden crown of empire from the
pope (1154).

The pope demanded, as the first condition of his coronation,
the surrender of Arnold. With this Barbarossa willingly
complied and ordered the execution of the popular agitator.
In his first interview with Adrian, he kissed the pope's toe,
but neglected the ceremony of holding the stirrup on descending from his palfrey. Adrian felt indignant and refused to
give him the kiss of peace. When informed that this was an
old custom, Barbarossa on the following day complied with
it, but in an ambiguous way by holding the left stirrup instead of the right. He took forcible possession of Trastevere,
and was solemnly invested, anointed, and crowned, according
to the prescribed ritual, in St. Peter's, amid the acclamations
of the curia, the clergy, and the army (June 13, 1155). An
insurrection of the Roman people was speedily suppressed,
the emperor leading the charge into the rebel ranks. But
on the next morning he retired with the pope to the Tibur-
tine hills. He was reluctantly compelled by the want of supplies and by rumors of rebellion in Lombardy to return with
his army. The pope, shut out from Rome, without foreign
or domestic ally, retired to Benevento, was besieged there
by King William of Sicily (son and successor of Roger II.)
and forced by desertion and famine to submit to the terms of
the conqueror by investing him with the kingdom of Sicily,
the duchy of Apulia, and the principality of Capua. This
involved him in a controversy with the emperor, who regarded

---

[1] See vol. IV. 258, and Rückert's poem there quoted. Em. Geibel also
wrote a beautiful poem on the German dream of sleep and revival of Barbarossa : —

> " Tief im Schoosse des Kyffhäusers
> Bei der Ampel rothem Schein
> Sitzt der alte Kaiser Friedrich
> An dem Tisch von Marmorstein," etc.

Apulia and Capua as parts of the empire. He protested against the divorce from his first, and the marriage to his second, wife, 1156.

To these occasions of offence Adrian added another which Frederick would not bear. It was evoked by the ill-treatment done by robbers to the archbishop of Lund on his way from Rome through Germany to his Scandinavian diocese.[1] Adrian spoke of Frederick's empire as a benefice, *beneficium*, a word which meant either a fief or a gift. In either case the implication was offensive to the Germans, and they chose to interpret it as a claim that the emperor held his empire as a fief of the apostolic see. Two legates, sent by Adrian, attempted to soften down the meaning of the imprudent expression.

The pope was too much of a hierarch and Frederick too much of an emperor to live in peace. In 1158 Frederick led his army across the Alps to reduce Milan and other refractory Lombard cities to submission. Having accomplished this, he assembled a diet on the plain of Roncaglia, near Piacenza, which is memorable for the decision rendered by Bologna jurists, that the emperor held his empire by independent divine right and not by the will of the pope. This was the most decisive triumph the empire had won since the opening of the conflict with Henry IV. But the decision of professors of law did not change the policy of the papacy.

Adrian again gave offence by denying the emperor's right to levy a tax for military purposes, *fodrum*, on estates claimed by the papacy and demanded that he should recognize the papal claim of feudal rights over the Matilda grant, Sardinia, Corsica, Ferrara, and the duchy of Spoleto. Frederick

---

[1] Eskill of Lund seems to have had the loftiest ideas of prelatical prerogative, and boasted that he was accustomed to command kings, not obey them. It is quite possible the emperor took inward satisfaction at his custody. Hauck, IV. 210. Adrian's letter, Mirbt, *Quellen*, 119 sq., speaks of the treatment of the archbishop as "that fearful and execrable deed and sacrilegious crime," *illud horrendum et execrabile facinus et piaculare flagitium.*

proudly retorted that instead of owing fealty to the pope, the popes owed fealty to the emperor, inasmuch as it was by the gift of the emperor Constantine that Pope Sylvester secured possession of Rome. A war of letters followed. Adrian was intending to punish his imperial foe with excommunication when he was struck down by death at Anagni. He was buried in St. Peter's in an antique sarcophagus of red granite which is still shown. So ended the career of a man who by his moral character and personal attractions had lifted himself up from the condition of a child of a poor cleric to the supreme dignity of Christendom, and ventured to face the proudest monarch as his superior and to call the imperial crown a papal *beneficium*.[1]

This English pope, who laid the city of Rome under the interdict, which no Italian or German pope had dared to do, presented Ireland to the crown of England, on the ground that all the islands of the Christian world belong to the pope by virtue of Constantine's donation. The curious bull *Laudabiliter*, encouraging Henry II. to invade and subjugate the land and giving it to him and to his heirs for a possession, may not be genuine, but the authorization was certainly made by Adrian as John of Salisbury, writing about 1159, attests, and it was renewed by Alexander III. and carried out, 1171.[2]

---

[1] Gregorovius, IV. 560, after praising his merits, says of Adrian, "He was shrewd, practical, and unyielding as Anglo-Saxons are wont to be." His "nature was as firm and strong as the granite of his tomb."

[2] The subject has been thoroughly discussed by Professors Thatcher and Scheffer-Boichorst before him. John of Salisbury, *Polycr.* VI. 24 ; Migne, 199, 623, distinctly says that Adrian, "listening to his petitions, conceded and gave" Ireland to Henry and his heirs on the ground that all islands "by ancient law and Constantine's donation, are said to belong to the Church." The pope sent to the king through John a ring of gold set with a precious stone to be a seal of investiture. There is no good reason to doubt this statement. And we know from Roger de Wendover, Rolls Series, I. 11, that an English embassy was sent to Adrian to secure this permission. The bull *Laudabiliter* (Mansi, XXI. 788), which formally confers the island upon the English crown and demands from it the payment of Peter's Pence, is found also in Roger de Wendover (Giles, Trans., I. 529) and Giraldus. Upon internal grounds its genuineness is considered doubtful or flatly denied,

The loyal sons of Ireland will hardly want to have a second trial of an English pope.

§ 29. *Alexander III. in Conflict with Barbarossa.*

See the literature in § 27, especially Reuter's *Alex. III. — Vita Alexandri auctore Bosone Card.*, in Watterich, II. 377 sqq. — Migne, Tom. 200. — The *Regesta* of Alexander III. in Jaffé-Wattenbach's *Reg. Pont. Rom.*, pp. 145–418 ; and of the anti-popes, Victor IV., Pascal III., Calixtus III., and Innocent III., *ibid.*, pp. 418–430. — Milman, bk. VIII. chs. VIII. and IX. — Greenwood, bk. XII. chs. III.-VII. — Gregorovius, IV. 525 sqq. ; Hefele–Knöpfler, V. 570–720. — Moritz Meyer : *Die Wahl Alex. III. und Victors IV.* Göttingen, 1871. — Edw. A. Freeman : *Frederick the First, King of Italy*, in his " Historical Essays," London, 1871, pp. 252–282. — P. Scheffer-Boichorst ; *Friedrich I. letzte Streit mit der Kurie*, 1866. — Wattenbach, 167 sqq. ; Hauck, IV. 227–311. — Gietl : *Die Sentenzen Rolands, nachmals Alexander III.* Freib., 1891.

With Alexander III. (1159–1181) the conflict between Cæsarism and sacerdotalism, which had begun under Adrian, assumed a more serious character. It was not a war for destruction, but for supremacy on the one hand and submission on the other. " Who shall be the greater ? " that was the question. It was the old contention between Church and State under a new phase. Cæsar and pope were alike Catholic Christians as far as they had any religion at all. They were indispensable to each other. The emperor or king needed a pope, as a kind of chief chaplain and father confessor for the control of the consciences of his subjects ; the pope needed the secular arm of an emperor for the protection of the property and rights of the Church and the prosecution of heretics. The emperors elected anti-popes, and the popes supported rival emperors. It was the ambition of the Hohenstaufen to keep Germany and Italy united ; it

as by Thatcher. This author gives, p. 4, a list of review articles on the subject. Scholarship and patriotism have made it possible for Irish writers to use much argument to show that the bull is a forgery and the alleged fact a fancy, whether of a prophetic enemy of Ireland or by a historical bungler is not known. The Protestant has an easier way out of the difficulty in affirming that the pope may make mistakes.

was the interest of the popes to keep them separated, and to foment division in Germany and in Italy, according to the maxim, " *Divide et impera.* "

On the 7th of September, 1159, Cardinal Roland, the chancellor of the Roman curia and a distinguished canonist, ascended the papal chair as Alexander III. He had previously been professor at Bologna, and written the first work on the *Decretum Gratiani.* He had been created cardinal by Eugene III. He had once offended Barbarossa by the question : " From whom does the emperor receive his dignity if not from the pope ? " He had also advised Adrian to excommunicate the emperor. He was a scholar, a statesman, and a vigorous champion of the Hildebrandian theocracy. He had an unusually long pontificate of twenty-one years, and is the most conspicuous pope between Gregory VII. and Innocent III. He had a checkered career of fortune and misfortune in a conflict with the emperor and four anti-popes ; but he consistently adhered to his principles, and at last triumphed over his enemies by moral force and the material aid of the Normans in the south and the Lombards in the north.

The election of Roland by fourteen cardinals was immediately followed by the election of Cardinal Octavian of St. Cecilia, the imperial anti-pope, who called himself Victor IV., and at once took possession of the Vatican. Roland was consecrated at Ninfa, Octavian in the convent of Farfa. They were quartered in the Campagna, a few miles distant from each other, and published contradictory reports with charges of disgraceful violence at the election.[1]

The emperor, who was then besieging the city of Cremona, being appealed to by both parties (though with different

[1] Octavian, according to the report of his enemies, plucked the papal cope from the shoulders of Roland, and invested himself with such indecent haste that the cope was reversed, and the back of it appeared on his breast. The mistake created derisive laughter, and was construed as a divine judgment.

feelings), and using a right exercised by Constantine, Theodosius, Justinian, Charlemagne, and Otto, summoned a council at Pavia to investigate and decide the case, 1160.[1] The rival popes were invited by messengers to appear in person. Octavian, who was always an imperialist, accepted the invitation. Roland distrusted the emperor, and protested against his right to call a council without his permission. He said that he honored him as a special defender of the Church above all other princes, but that God had placed the pope above kings.

The partisan council, which consisted chiefly of bishops from Germany and North Italy, after a grave debate, unanimously decided in favor of Octavian, and excommunicated Roland, Feb. 11, 1160. The emperor paid the customary honors to Victor IV., held his stirrup and kissed his toe. Alexander issued from Anagni a counter-excommunication against the anti-pope and the emperor, March 24, 1160. He thereby encouraged revolt in Lombardy and division in Germany. Another schism rent the Church.

The rival popes despatched legates to all the courts of Europe. France, Spain, and England sided with Alexander. He took refuge in France for three years (1162–1165), and was received with enthusiasm. The kings of France and England, Louis VII. and Henry II., walked on either side of his horse, holding the bridle, and conducting him into the town of Courcy on the Loire. Germany, Hungary, Bohemia, Norway, and Sweden supported Victor. Italy was divided: Rome and Tuscany were under the power of the emperor; Sicily favored the Gregorian pope; the flourishing commercial and manufacturing cities of Lombardy were discontented with the despotic rule of Barbarossa, who was called the destroyer of cities. He put down the revolt with an iron hand; he razed Milan to the ground after a long and atro-

[1] The document is given in Rahewin, *Gesta Frid.* IV. 64, and Mirbt, *Quellen*, 121.

cious siege, scattered the population, and sent the venerated relics of the Magi to the cathedral of Cologne, March, 1162.

Victor IV. died in April, 1164.   Pascal III. was elected his successor without regard to the canonical rules.   At the request of the emperor, he canonized Charles the Great (1165).

Alexander III. put himself at the head of the Lombard league against the emperor; city after city declared itself for him.   In September, 1165, he returned to Italy with the help of Sicily, and French and English gold, and took possession of Rome.

In November, 1166, Frederick crossed the Alps a fourth time, with a strong army, marched to Rome, captured the Leonine city, put Pascal III. in possession of St. Peter's, and was crowned again, with Beatrice, Aug. 1, 1167.   Alexander defended the city on the other side of the Tiber, but soon withdrew to Benevento.   The emperor, victorious over armies, found a more formidable enemy in the Roman fever, which made fearful ravages among his bishops, noblemen, and soldiers.   He lost in a few weeks his bravest knights and two thousand men by the plague.   He broke up his camp in great haste, and marched to Pavia (September, 1167).[1]   He found all Lombardy in league against him, and recrossed the Alps for safety, alone and almost a fugitive, but with unbroken spirit and a determination to return.

The second anti-pope died, Sept. 20, 1168, and with him the power of the schism collapsed.   Calixtus III. was elected his successor, but he was a mere shadow, 1168–1178.[2]

[1] Thomas à Becket, in a letter congratulating Alexander, compared Frederick's discomfiture by pestilence to Sennacherib's defeat at Jerusalem. — 2 Chron. xxxii : 21.

[2] His few acts are recorded in Jaffé-Wattenbach, *Regesta*, pp. 429–430. He submitted to Alexander, and was made archbishop of Benevento.   Of the fourth anti-pope, Lando Sitino, who called himself Innocent III. (1179–1180), nothing is recorded but his election and imprisonment, *ibid.*, p. 431.

I

Barbarossa undertook a fifth campaign to Italy in 1174. He destroyed Susa, and, descending through Piedmont, besieged the new city of Alessandria, which was named in honor of Alexander III., and strongly fortified. Here he found determined resistance. His forces were weakened by a severe winter. He was forsaken by his strongest ally, the Saxon duke, Henry the Lion. He fought a pitched battle against the Lombards, near Legnano, May 29, 1176. He rushed, as usual, into the thickest of the fight, but was defeated after terrible slaughter, and lost his shield, banner, cross, lance, and coffers of silver and gold. He retired with the remnant of his army to Pavia. He was left without a single ally, and threatened in Germany by the dangerous rivalry of Henry the Lion. He now took serious steps towards a reconciliation with Alexander, the spiritual head of his enemies.

The emperor sent Archbishop Christian of Mainz (his chancellor, ablest general, and diplomat), Archbishop Wichmann of Magdeburg, Bishop Conrad of Worms, and Protonotary Wortwin to Anagni, with full powers to treat with the pope (October, 1176). Alexander received the commissioners with marked respect, and in private conferences, lasting over a fortnight, he arranged with them the preliminary terms of peace, which were to be ratified at Venice during a personal interview between him and the emperor.

The pope, provided with a safe-conduct by the emperor, left Anagni on Christmas, 1176, in company with his cardinals and the two commissioners of the kingdom of Sicily, Archbishop Romuald of Salerno and Count Roger of Andria, and arrived at Venice, March 24, 1177. The emperor tarried at Chioggia, near Venice, till July 23. The peace negotiations between the pope and the imperial commissioners began in May and lasted till July. They were conducted on the basis of the previous negotiations in Anagni.

§ 30. *The Peace of Venice.* 1177.

The negotiations resulted in the Peace of Venice, which was embodied in twenty-eight articles.[1] Alexander was acknowledged as legitimate pope. Calixtus, the anti-pope, was remanded to an abbey, while his cardinals were reduced to the positions they had occupied before their appointment to the curia. Beatrice was acknowledged as Frederick's legal wife, and his son Henry as king of the Romans. Rome and the *patrimonium* were restored to the pope, and Spoleto, the Romagna, and Ancona were recognized as a part of the empire.

The peace was ratified by one of the most solemn congresses of the Middle Ages. Absolved from the ban, and after eighteen years of conflict, the emperor met the pope in front of St. Mark's, July 24, 1177. A vast multitude filled the public square. The pope in his pontifical dress sitting upon a throne in front of the portal of the cathedral must have had mingled with his feelings of satisfaction reminiscences of his painful fortunes since the time he was elected to the tiara. Cardinals, archbishops, bishops, and other dignitaries occupied lower seats according to their rank.

The emperor, on arriving in the magnificent gondola of the doge, with a train of prelates and nobles, was received by a procession of priests with banners and crosses, and the shouts of the people. He slowly proceeded to the cathedral. Overcome with feelings of reverence for the venerable pope, he cast off his mantle, bowed, and fell at his feet.[2] Alexander, in tears, raised him up,[3] and gave him the kiss of

[1] For the text see Mirbt, *Quellen*, 121–124. The chief authorities for the Peace of Venice are Alexander's *Letters* to Roger, archbishop of York, in Migne, 200, 1150 sqq. ; and Mansi, XXII. 180 sqq. ; the *Chronicon* of Romuald., archbishop of Salerno and commissioner from Sicily, in Muratori, *Scrip. Rer. Ital.* VII. Mathews, pp. 99–105, also gives the text.

[2] Vita Alex. : "*prostravit se in terram.*" *Chron.* Romualdi (Muratori, VII. 231) : " *totum se extenso corpore prostravit.*"

[3] Romuald. : " *quem Alexander papa cum lacrymis benigne elevans.*"

peace and his benediction.   Thousands of voices responded by singing the *Te Deum*.[1]

Then the emperor, taking the hand of the pope, walked with him and the doge into the church, made rich offerings at the altar, bent his knees, and received again the apostolic benediction.

On the next day (the 25th), being the feast of St. James, the pope, at the emperor's request, celebrated high mass, and preached a sermon which he ordered the patriarch of Aquileia to translate at once into German.   The emperor accompanied him from the altar to the door, and paid him the customary homage of holding the stirrup.[2]   He offered to conduct his palfrey by the bridle across the piazza to the bark ; but the pope dispensed with this menial service of a groom, taking the will for the deed, and gave him again his benediction.

This is the authentic account of contemporary writers and eye-witnesses.   They make no mention of the story that the emperor said to the pope, "I do this homage to Peter, *not* to thee," and that the pope quickly replied, "To Peter *and* to me."

The hierarchical imagination has represented this interview as a second Canossa.   In Venetian pictures the pope is seen seated on a throne, and planting his foot on the neck of the prostrate emperor, with the words of Ps. 91 : 13 : —

[1] Romuald. : "*moxque a Teutonicis Te Deum laudamus est excelsa voce cantatum.*"   Vita Alex. : " *Tunc repleti sunt omnes gaudio et præ nimia lætitia vox conclamantium in Te Deum laudamus insonuit usque ad sidera.*"   Alexander writes to Roger of York : "*innumera multitudine virorum et mulierum præsente, alta voce reddente gratias et laudes Altissimo.*"

[2] Alexander ad Rogerum (Migne, 200, 1131) : " *Cum ascenderemus palafredum nostrum ibi paratum, stapham tenuit, et omnem honorem et reverentiam nobis exhibuit, quam prædecessores ejus nostris consueverunt antecessoribus.*"   It is stated by Godfrey of Viterbo, an attendant of the emperor, that the old pope, through the pressure of the crowd, was thrown from his horse, and that the emperor assisted him to remount.   Pertz, *Archiv*, IV. 363, quoted by Milman, bk. VIII. ch. IX.

" Thou shalt tread upon the lion and the adder :
   The young lion and the serpent shalt thou trample under feet." [1]

There is as much difference between the scenes of Venice and Canossa as there is between the characters of Barbarossa and Henry IV.   Barbarossa was far superior, morally as well as intellectually, to his Salian predecessor, and commanded the respect of his enemies, even in his defeat.   He maintained his dignity and honorably kept his word.

Delegates and letters were sent to all parts of Christendom with the glad tidings of peace.   The emperor left Venice toward the end of September for Germany by a roundabout way, and the pope for Anagni on the 15th of October.   After an exile of ten years, Alexander made a triumphal entry into Rome, March 12, 1178.

He convened, according to previous agreement with the emperor, a synod to ratify the pacification of Christendom, and to remove certain evils which had multiplied during the schism.   The Third Lateran or the Eleventh Œcumenical Council was held in the Constantinian Basilica at Rome during Lent, 1179.   It numbered about three hundred bishops, besides many abbots and other dignitaries,[2] and exhibited the Roman hierarchy in its glory, though it was eclipsed afterwards by the Fourth Lateran Council of 1215.   The details of the transactions are unknown, except twenty-seven chapters which were adopted in the third and last session.

The council, in order to prevent rival elections, placed

---

[1] " *Super aspidem et basiliscum ambulabis*," etc.   This and other stories of the fourteenth century are irreconcilable with contemporary records and are given up by nearly all modern historians.   They may have partly originated in the fresco paintings of Spinello described by Lord Lindsay, *History of Christian Art*, II. 315.   Milman, IV. 435 (Am. ed.), says, " As poetry has so often become, here painting for once became history."   Comp. Reuter, III. 758.

[2] The lists are defective, and the contemporary records vary between 287, 300, 396 bishops, and 1000 members in all.   See Mansi, XXII. 213 sqq.; Hefele, V. 711; Reuter, III. 418 sqq.

the election of popes exclusively in the hands of cardinals,
to be decided by a majority of two-thirds, and threatened with
excommunication and deposition any one who should dare
to accept an election by a smaller number of votes.[1] The
ordinations of the anti-popes (Octavian, Guido, and John of
Struma) were declared invalid.   No one was to be elected
bishop who was not at least thirty years of age and of legitimate birth.   To check the extravagance of prelates on their
visitation journeys, the archbishops were limited to forty or
fifty horses on those occasions, the cardinals to twenty-five,
the bishops to twenty or thirty, the archdeacons to five or
seven.   Ordained clergymen must dismiss their concubines,
or forfeit their benefices.   Unnatural licentiousness was to be
punished by expulsion from the priesthood and confinement
in a convent.   The council prepared the way for a crusade
against the heretics in the South of France, and promised to
those who should engage in it the same plenary indulgence
for two years as had been granted to the crusaders against
the Moslems.

Soon after the synod, Alexander was again driven into
exile by the Roman republic.   He died at Cività Castellana,
Aug. 30, 1181, having reigned longer than any pope before
or after him, except Sylvester I., 314–335, Adrian I., 772–
795, Pius VII., 1800–1823, Pius IX., 1846–1878, and Leo
XIII., 1878–1903.   When Alexander's remains were being
carried to Rome for burial, the populace insulted his memory
by pelting the coffin with stones and mud.[2]   Alexander had
with signal constancy and devotion to the Gregorian prin-

---

[1] " *Ille Romanus Pontifex habeatur, qui a duabus partibus fuerit electus et
receptus.   Si quis autem de tertiœ partis nominatione confisus . . . sibi nomen
Episcopi usurpaverit : tam ipse, quam qui eum recepuerint, excommunicationi
subjaceant et totius sacri ordinis privatione mulctentur,*" etc.   Mansi, XXII.
217.

[2] Reuter, III. 495–499.   A similar insult was offered by the Roman populace to Pius IX. when his coffin was transported in the night from the Vatican
to its last resting-place in the basilica of S. Lorenzo.   He, too, spent some
time in exile after the proclamation of the Roman republic in 1849.

ciples maintained the conflict with Barbarossa. He supported
Thomas à Becket in his memorable conflict with Henry II.
In 1181 he laid the interdict upon Scotland because of the
refusal of its king, William, to acknowledge the canonical
election of John to the see of St. Andrews. Upon Louis
VII. of France he conferred the Red Rose for the support
he had received from that sovereign in the days of his early
exile. He presided over the Third Lateran Council and
prepared the way for the crusade against the Cathari and
Albigenses.

His aged and feeble successor, Lucius III., was elected,
Sept. 1, 1181, by the cardinals alone. The Romans, deprived
of their former share in the election, treated him with barbarous cruelty; they captured twenty or twenty-six of his
partisans at Tusculum, blinded them, except one, crowned
them with paper mitres inscribed with the names of cardinals, mounted them on asses, and forced the priest whom
they had spared to lead them in this condition to "Lucius,
the wicked simoniac." He died in exile at Verona where
he held an important synod.

It is a remarkable fact that some of the greatest popes
— as Gregory VII., Urban II., Innocent II., Eugene III.,
Adrian IV., Alexander III., and three of his successors —
could not secure the loyalty of their own subjects, and were
besieged in Rome or compelled to flee. Adrian IV. said to
his countryman and friend, John of Salisbury, " Rome is not
the mother, but the stepmother of the Churches." The
Romans were always fluctuating between memories of the
old republic and memories of the empire; now setting up
a consul, a senator, a tribune; now welcoming the German
emperor as the true Augustus Cæsar; now loyal to the pope,
now driving him into exile, and ever selling themselves to the
highest bidder. The papal court was very consistent in its
principles and aims, but as to the choice of means for its end
it was subject to the same charge of avarice and venality,

whether at Rome or in exile. Even Thomas Becket, the
stanchest adherent of Alexander III., indignantly rebuked
the cardinals for their love of gold.

Emperor Frederick survived his great rival nearly ten
years, and died by drowning in a little river of Asia Minor,
1190, while marching on the third crusade.

Barbarossa was a man of middle size, bright countenance,
fair complexion, yellow hair and reddish beard, a kind friend
and placable enemy, strictly just, though often too severe,
liberal in almsgiving, attentive to his religious duties, happy
in his second marriage, of the noblest type of mediæval chivalry, the greatest sovereign of the twelfth century, a hero in
fact and a hero in romance.[1] He came into Italy with the
sword of Germany in one hand and the Justinian code in
the other, but failed in subduing the political independence
of the Lombard cities, and in his contest with the spiritual
power of Alexander. The German imagination has cherished
his memory in song and story, placing him next in rank to
Charles the Great among the Roman emperors, exaggerating
his virtues, condoning his faults, which were those of his age,
and hoping for his return to restore the unity and power of
Germany.

§ 31. *Thomas Becket and Henry II. of England.*

For the extensive Becket literature, see ROBERTSON, in "The Contemporary
Review," 1866, I. (Jan.) 270–278, and ULYSSE CHEVALIER, in his *Répertoire
des sources historiques du Moyen Age* (Paris, 1886), s. v. "Thomas," fol.
2207–2209.

I. SOURCES : —

* *Materials for the History of Thomas à Becket, Archbishop of Canterbury.*
  Edited by JAMES CRAIGIE ROBERTSON (Canon of Canterbury, d. 1882)
  and J. BRIGSTOCKE SHEPPARD, LL.D. London, 1875–1885, 7 vols. This
  magnificent work is part of a series of *Rerum Britannic. Medii Aevi
  Scriptores*, or "Chronicles and Memorials of Great Britain and Ire-

---

[1] Rahewin, in his *Gesta Friderici*, IV. 86, gives an animated description of Frederick's appearance, habits, dress, achievements, etc. He calls him
the best of emperors.

land during the Middle Ages," published under direction of the Master of
the Rolls and popularly known as the "Rolls Series." It embraces all
the important contemporary materials for the history of Thomas.
Vols. I.–IV. contain the contemporary *Vitæ* (by William of Canterbury, Benedict of Peterborough, Edward Grim, Roger of Pontigny,
William Fitz-Stephen, John of Salisbury, Alan of Tewkesbury, and Herbert of Bosham, etc.) ; vols. V.–VII., the *Epistolæ, i.e.* the whole
correspondence relating to Thomas.

This collection is much more accurate, complete, and better arranged
(especially in the Epistles) than the older collection of DR. GILES (*Sanctus
Thomas Cantuariensis*, London, 1845–1846, 8 vols., reprinted in Migne's
Patrologia, Tom. 190), and the *Quadrilogus* or *Historia Quadripartita*
(Lives by four contemporary writers, composed by order of Pope Gregory XI., first published, 1495, then by L. Christian Lupus or Wolf, Brussels, 1682, and Venice, 1728).

*Thômas Saga Erkibyskups. A Life of Archb. Th. Becket in Icelandic, with
Engl. transl., notes, and glossary, ed. by Eirikr Magnússon.* London,
1875, and 1883, 2 vols. Part of the "Chronicles and Memorials,"
above quoted.

GARNIER of Pont Sainte-Maxence : *La Vie de St. Thomas le martir.* A
metrical life, in old French, written between 1172 and 1174, published
by Hippeau, and more recently by Professor Bekker, Berlin, 1844, and
Paris, 1859.

The Life and Martyrdom of Thomas Becket by ROBERT OF GLOUCESTER.
Ed. by W. H. Black. London, 1845 (pp. 141). A biography in Alex-
andrine verse, written in the thirteenth century.

II. MODERN WORKS : —

RICHARD HURRELL FROUDE (one of the originators of the Oxford Anglo-
Catholic movement, d. 1836) : *Remains.* London, 1838, 4 vols. The
second vol., part II., contains a history of the contest between Thomas
à Becket and Henry II., in vindication of the former. He was assisted
by J. H. (late Cardinal) Newman.

A. F. OZANAM : *Deux Chanceliers d'Angleterre, Bacon de Verulam et Saint
Thomas de Cantorbéry.* Paris, 1836.

J. A. GILES : *The Life and Letters of Thomas à Becket.* London, 1846,
2 vols.

F. J. BUSS (Rom. Cath.) : *Der heil. Thomas und sein Kampf für die
Freiheit der Kirche.* Mainz, 1856.

JOHN MORRIS (Rom. Cath. Canon of Northampton) : *The Life and Martyrdom of Saint Thomas Becket.* London, 1859.

*JAMES CRAIGIE ROBERTSON : *Becket, Archbishop of Canterbury.* London,
1859. Accurate, but unfavorable to Becket.

*EDW. A. FREEMAN : *St. Thomas of Canterbury and his Biographers.* A
masterly article in the "National Review" for April, 1860, reprinted in

his " Historical Essays," London, 1871, pp. 99–114.   Comp. the summary in his *History of the Norman Conquest*, V. 660 sqq., and his articles against Froude, noticed below.

* JAMES ANTHONY FROUDE : *Life and Times of Thomas Becket*.   First published in "The Nineteenth Century" for 1877, then in book form,
London and New York, 1878 (pp. 150).   Against the Roman and Anglo-
Catholic overestimate of St. Thomas.   This book is written in brilliant
style, but takes a very unfavorable view of Becket (opposite to that of
his elder brother, R. H. Froude), and led to a somewhat personal controversy with PROFESSOR FREEMAN, who charged Froude with habitual
inaccuracy, unfairness, and hostility to the English Church, in " The
Contemporary Review" for 1878 (March, April, June, and September).
Froude defended himself in "The Nineteenth Century" for April, 1879,
pp. 618–637, to which Freeman replied in *Last Words on Mr. Froude*, in
" The Contemporary Review " for May, 1879, pp. 214–236.

* R. A. THOMPSON: *Thomas Becket, Martyr*, London, 1889. — A. S. HUILLIER:
St. Thomas de Cantorbéry, 2 vols., Paris, 1892.

* EDWIN A. ABBOTT : *St. Thomas of Canterbury.   His Death and Miracles*,
2 vols., London, 1888.   This work grew out of studies in preparation of a
critical commentary of the Four Gospels.   It takes the early narratives
of Thomas à Becket, sets them side by side, and seeks to show which are
to be accepted upon the basis of disagreements in regard to event or verbal expression.   It also presents the details in which Dean Stanley and
Tennyson are alleged to have been misled.   The criticism is able, stimulating, and marked by self-confidence in determining what events really
did occur, and how much is to be discarded as unhistoric.   The discussion
has all the merits and demerits of the strict critical method.

III.   Becket is more or less fully treated by MILMAN :   *Latin Christian-
ity*, bk. VIII. ch. VIII. — DEAN STANLEY: *Historical Memorials of Can-
terbury*, Am. ed., 1889. — REUTER : *Alexander III.*, I. 237 sqq., 530 sqq.
DEAN HOOK :   *Lives of the Archbishops of Canterbury*, II. 354–508. —
GREENWOOD : *Cathedra Petri*, bk. XII. ch. VII. — WILLIAM STUBBS : *The
Constitutional Hist. of England*, 6th ed., 3 vols., Oxford, 1897, and
Select Charters and Other Illustrations of the English Constit. Hist.,
8th ed., Oxford, 1900. — GEE and HARDY : *Documents Illustrative of
Engl. Ch. Hist.*, London, 1896. — F. W. MAITLAND : *Rom. Canon
Law in the Ch. of England*, London, 1898, 134–147. — W. R. W.
STEPHENS : *The English Church* (1066–1272), London, 1901, 157–190.
The Histories of LINGARD, GREEN, etc.

LORD TENNYSON has made *Becket* the subject of a historical drama, 1884.

During the pontificate of Alexander III., the papal hierarchy achieved an earlier and greater triumph over the king
of England than over the emperor of Germany.

Thomas Becket, or Thomas à Becket, or St. Thomas of

Canterbury, is, next to Alexander and Barbarossa, the most
prominent historical figure in the twelfth century, and fills
a chapter of thrilling interest in the history of England.
He resumed the conflict of Anselm with the crown, and by
his martyrdom became the most popular saint of the later
Middle Ages.

The materials for his history, from his birth in London to
his murder in his own cathedral by four knights of the royal
household, are abundant.   We have six or seven contemporary biographies, besides fragments, legends, and " Passions,"
state papers, private letters, and a correspondence extending
over the whole Latin Church.   But his life is surrounded
by a mist of romantic legends and theological controversies.
He had extravagant admirers, like Herbert of Bosham, and
fierce opponents, like Gilbert Foliot, in his own day ; and
modern biographers still differ in the estimate of his character, according to their creed and their views on the question of
Church and State, some regarding him as a hero and a saint,
others as a hypocrite and a traitor.   We must judge him
from the standpoint of the twelfth century.

Becket was born in London, Dec. 21, 1118, during the
reign of Henry I.   He was the son of Gilbert Becket, a merchant in Cheapside, originally from Rouen, and of Matilda
or Rose, a native of Caen in Normandy.[1]

In the later legend his father appears as a gallant crusader
and his mother as a Saracen princess, who met in the East
and fell in love with each other.   Matilda helped Gilbert to
escape from captivity, and then followed him alone to England.   Knowing only two English words, " London " and

---

[1] The Norman descent of Becket rests on contemporary testimony, and
is accepted by Giles, Lingard, Robertson, Milman, Hook, Freeman, Reuter,
Hefele.   The commercial advantages of London attracted emigrants from
Normandy.   Lord Lyttleton, Thierry, Campbell, and J. A. Froude make
Becket a Saxon, but without authority.   Becket is a surname, and may be
Norman as well as Saxon.   The prefix à seems to be of later date, and to
have its origin (according to Robertson and Hook) in vulgar colloquial usage.

" Gilbert," she wandered through the streets of the city, till at last she found her beloved in Cheapside as by a miracle, was baptized and married to him in St. Paul's with great splendor.   She had dreams of the future greatness and elevation of her infant son to the see of Canterbury.

Becket was educated at Merton Abbey in Surrey and in the schools of London.   At a later period he attended the universities of Paris, Bologna, and Auxerre, and studied there chiefly civil and canon law, without attaining to special eminence in learning.   He was not a scholar, but a statesman and an ecclesiastic.

He made his mark in the world and the Church by the magnetism of his personality.   He was very handsome, of tall, commanding presence, accomplished, brilliant, affable, cheerful in discourse, ready and eloquent in debate, fond of hunting and hawking, and a proficient in all the sports of a mediæval cavalier.   He could storm the strongest castle and unhorse the stoutest knight.

Archbishop Theobald of Canterbury, 1139–1161, took him into his service, 1142 ; sent him to Bologna, where Gratian then taught canon law; employed him in delicate missions with the papal court; made him archdeacon (1154), and bestowed upon him other profitable benefices, as the provostship of Beverly, a number of churches, and several prebends. When charged, as archbishop, with ingratitude to the king, who had raised him from " poverty," he proudly referred to this accumulation of preferments, and made no attempt to abolish the crying evil of plurality, which continued till the Reformation.   Many a prosperous ecclesiastic regarded his parishes simply as sources of income, and discharged the duties by proxy through ignorant and ill-paid priests.

King Henry II., 1154–1189, in the second year of his reign, raised Becket, then only thirty-seven years of age, at Theobald's instance, to the chancellorship of England.   The chancellor was the highest civil dignitary, and held the cus-

tody of nearly all the royal grants and favors, including vacant bishoprics, abbacies, chaplaincies, and other ecclesiastical
benefices.

Henry, the first of the proud Plantagenets, was an able,
stirring, and energetic monarch. He kept on his feet from
morning till evening, and rarely sat down. He introduced
a reign of law and severe justice after the lawless violence
and anarchy which had disturbed the reign of the unfortunate Stephen.[1] But he was passionate, vindictive, and
licentious. He had frequent fits of rage, during which he
behaved like a madman. He was the most powerful sovereign in Western Europe. His continental dominions were
more extensive than those of the king of France, and embraced Maine and Normandy, Anjou and Aquitaine, reaching
from Flanders to the foot of the Pyrenees. He afterwards
(1171) added Ireland by conquest, with the authority of
Popes Adrian IV. and Alexander III. His marriage to
Queen Eleanor of Aquitaine, who had been divorced for infidelity from King Louis VII. of France, enriched his realm,
but involved him in protracted wars with France and in domestic troubles. Eleanor was jealous of her rivals,[2] incited
her sons, Geoffrey and Richard, to rebel against their father,
was imprisoned in 1173, and released after Henry's death in

[1] Tennyson describes Stephen's reign as —

> " A reign which was no reign, when none could sit
> By his own hearth in peace; when murder common
> As nature's death, like Egypt's plague, had filled
> All things with blood."

[2] The tradition ran that she poisoned his favorite concubine, Rosamund
de Clifford, who, with her labyrinthine bower, figures largely in the literature
of romance, also in Tennyson's *Becket*. On her tomb were inscribed the
lines : —

> " *Hic jacet in tumba* ROSA MUNDI, *non* ROSA MUNDA,
> *Non redolet, sed olet, quœ redolere solet.*"

> " Here Rose the graced, not Rose the chaste, reposes ;
> The smell that rises is no smell of roses."

1189 by his successor, Richard I., Cœur de Lion, who made
her regent on his departure for the Holy Land.   She afterwards retired to the abbey of Fontevrault, and died about
1203.

Becket occupied the chancellorship for seven years (1155–
1162).   He aided the king in the restoration of order and
peace.   He improved the administration of justice.   He was
vigorous and impartial, and preferred the interests of the
crown to those of the clergy, yet without being hostile to the
Church.   He was thoroughly loyal to the king, and served
him as faithfully as he had served Theobald, and as he afterwards served the pope.   Thorough devotion to official duty
characterized him in all the stations of his career

He gave to his high office a prominence and splendor
which it never had before.   He was as magnificent and
omnipotent as Wolsey under Henry VIII.   He was king in
fact, though not in name, and acted as regent during Henry's
frequent absences on the Continent.   He dressed after the
best fashion, surrounded himself with a brilliant retinue of
a hundred and forty knights, exercised a prodigal hospitality,
and spent enormous sums upon his household and public
festivities, using in part the income of his various ecclesiastical benefices, which he retained without a scruple.   He presided at royal banquets in Westminster Hall.   His tables
were adorned with vessels of gold, with the most delicate and
sumptuous food, and with wine of the choicest vintage.   He
superintended the training of English and foreign nobles,
and of the young Prince Henry.   He was the favorite of the
king, the army, the nobility, the clergy, and the people.

The chancellor negotiated in person a matrimonial alliance
(three years before it was consummated) between the heir
of the crown (then a boy of seven years) and a daughter of
the king of France (a little lady of three).   He took with
him on that mission two hundred knights, priests, standard-
bearers, all festively arrayed in new attire, twenty-four

changes of raiment, all kinds of dogs and birds for field sports, eight wagons, each drawn by five horses, each horse in charge of a stout young man dressed in a new tunic. Coffers and chests contained the chancellor's money and presents. One horse, which preceded all the rest, carried the holy vessels of his chapel, the holy books, and the ornaments of the altar. The Frenchmen, seeing this train, exclaimed, "How wonderful must be the king of England, whose chancellor travels in such state!" In Paris he freely distributed his gold and silver plate and changes of raiment, — to one a robe, to another a furred cloak, to a third a pelisse, to a fourth a war-horse. He gained his object and universal popularity.

When, notwithstanding his efforts to maintain peace, war broke out between France and England, the chancellor was the bravest warrior at the head of seven hundred knights, whom he had enlisted at his own expense, and he offered to lead the storming party at the siege of Toulouse, where King Louis was shut up ; but the scruples of Henry prevented him from offering violence to the king of France. He afterwards took three castles which were deemed impregnable, and returned triumphant to England. One of his eulogists, Edward Grim, reports to his credit : "Who can recount the carnage, the desolation, which he made at the head of a strong body of soldiers? He attacked castles, razed towns and cities to the ground, burned down houses and farms without a touch of pity, and never showed the slightest mercy to any one who rose in insurrection against his master's authority." Such cruelty was quite compatible with mediæval conceptions of piety and charity, as the history of the crusades shows.

Becket was made for the court and the camp. Yet, though his life was purely secular, it was not immoral. He joined the king in his diversions, but not in his debaucheries. Being in deacon's orders, he was debarred from marriage, but pre-

served his chastity at a profligate court.   This point is especially mentioned to his credit; for chastity was a rare virtue
in the Middle Ages.

All together, his public life as chancellor was honorable
and brilliant, and secures him a place among the distinguished statesmen of England.   But a still more important
career awaited him.[1]

§ 32. *The Archbishop and the King.*

Compare §§ 22–24 (pp. 80 sqq.).

A year after the death of Theobald, April 18, 1161, Becket
was appointed by the king archbishop of Canterbury.   He
accepted reluctantly, and warned the king, with a smile, that
he would lose a servant and a friend.[2]   The learned and
energetic Bishop Gilbert Foliot of Hereford (afterwards of
London) remarked sarcastically, perhaps from disappointed
ambition, that " the king had wrought a miracle in turning
a layman into an archbishop, and a soldier into a saint."

Becket was ordained priest on the Saturday after Pentecost, and consecrated archbishop on the following day with
great magnificence in Westminster Abbey, June 3, 1162.
His first act was to appoint the Sunday after Whitsunday
as a festival of the Holy Trinity in the Church of England.
He acknowledged Alexander III. as the rightful pope, and
received from him the pallium through his friend, John of
Salisbury.

He was the first native Englishman who occupied the seat
of the primate since the Norman Conquest; for Lanfranc and

---

[1] Freeman, who exalts him as chancellor, thinks that he failed as archbishop; but his martyrdom was his greatest triumph.

[2] Tennyson ingeniously introduces his drama with a game of chess between
Henry and Becket, during which the king informs the chancellor of the fatal
illness of Theobald, and speaks of the need of a mightier successor, who
would punish guilty clerks ; while the chancellor quietly moves his bishop
and checkmates the king ; whereupon Henry kicks over the board, saying : —

" Why, there then — down go bishop and king together."

Anselm were Italians; Ralph of Escures, William of Corbeuil, and Theobald of Bec were Normans or Frenchmen. There is, however, no ground for the misleading theory of Thierry that Becket asserted the cause of the Saxon against the Norman. His contest with the king was not a contest between two nationalities, but between Church and State. He took the same position on this question as his Norman predecessors, only with more zeal and energy. He was a thorough Englishman. The two nations had at that time, by intermarriage, social and commercial intercourse, pretty well coalesced, at least among the middle classes, to which he belonged.[1]

With the change of office, Becket underwent a radical and almost sudden transformation. The foremost champion of kingcraft became the foremost champion of priestcraft; the most devoted friend of the king, his most dangerous rival and enemy; the brilliant chancellor, an austere and squalid monk. He exchanged the showy court dress for haircloth infested with vermin, fed on roots, and drank nauseous water. He daily washed, with proud humility and ostentatious charity, the feet of thirteen dirty beggars, and gave each of them four pieces of silver. He doubled the charities of Theobald, as Theobald had doubled the charities of his predecessor. He wandered alone in his cloister, shedding tears of repentance for past sins, frequently inflicted stripes on his naked back, and spent much time in prayer and reading of the Scriptures. He successfully strove to realize the ideal of a mediæval bishop, which combines the loftiest ecclesiastical pretensions with personal humility, profuse charity, and ascetic self-mortification. He was no hypocrite, but his sanctity, viewed from the biblical and Protestant standpoint, was artificial and unnatural.

[1] "Though of Norman blood, his whole feeling, his whole character is English, and it is clear that no man looked on him as a stranger." Freeman (*l.c.*, pp. 101 sq.).

K

His relation to the king was that of the pope to the emperor. Yea, we may say, as he had outkinged the king as chancellor, so he outpoped the pope as archbishop. He censured the pope for his temporizing policy. He wielded the spiritual sword against Henry with the same gallantry with which he had wielded the temporal sword for him. He took up the cause of Anselm against William Rufus, and of Gregory VII. against Henry IV., but with this great difference, that he was not zealous for a moral reformation of the Church and the clergy, like Hildebrand and Anselm, but only for the temporal power of the Church and the rights and immunities of the clergy. He made no attempt to remove the scandal of pluralities of which he had himself been guilty as archdeacon and chancellor, and did not rebuke Henry for his many sins against God, but only for his sins against the supremacy of the hierarchy.

The new archbishop was summoned by Pope Alexander III. to a council at Tours in France, and was received with unusual distinction (May, 1163). The council consisted of seventeen cardinals, a hundred and twenty-four bishops, four hundred and fourteen abbots; the pope presided in person; Becket sat at his right, Roger of York at his left. Arnolf of Lisieux in Normandy preached the opening sermon on the unity and freedom of the Church, which were the burning questions of the day. The council unanimously acknowledged the claims of Alexander, asserted the rights and privileges of the clergy, and severely condemned all encroachments on the property of the Church.

This was the point which kindled the controversy between the sceptre and the crozier in England. The dignity of the crown was the sole aim of the king; the dignity of the Church was the sole aim of the archbishop. The first rupture occurred over the question of secular taxation.

Henry determined to transfer the customary payment of two shillings on every hide of land to his own exchequer.

Becket opposed the enrolment of the decree on the ground
that the tax was voluntary, not of right.   Henry protested,
in a fit of passion, " By the eyes of God, it shall be enrolled ! "
Becket replied, " By the eyes of God, by which you swear,
it shall never be levied on my lands while I live ! "

Another cause of dispute was the jurisdiction of the ecclesiastical courts.   The king demanded that all clerics accused
of gross misdemeanors be tried by the civil court.   A certain clerk, Philip of Broi, had been acquitted of murder in
the bishop's court.   The king was indignant, but Philip refused to plead in the civil court.   The matter was taken up
by the archbishop, but a light sentence imposed.

The king summoned a Parliament at Westminster, and
demanded in the name of equal justice, and in accordance
with " ancient customs " (of the Norman kings), that all
clerks accused of heinous crimes should be immediately degraded, and be dealt with according to law, instead of being
shielded by their office.   This was contrary to the right of
the priest to be tried only in the court of his bishop, where
flagellation, imprisonment, and degradation might be awarded,
but not capital punishment.

Becket and the bishops agreed that the king's demand was
an infringement of the canon law and argued the case from
Scripture.   Joab, and Abiathar the priest, were guilty of
putting Adonijah to death.   Joab was punished, but the
priest suffered no other punishment than deposition from
office.   Nahum 1: 9 was quoted as against a double tribunal
for clerks.   According to the Septuagint version, this passage declares that God does not give two judgments in the
same case.

The king hastily broke up the Parliament, deprived Becket
of the custody of the royal castles, and of the education of
his son.   The bishops advised the archbishop to yield ; at
first he refused, though an angel from heaven should counsel
such weakness ; but at last he made a concession to the king

at Woodstock, and promised to obey in good faith the customs of the realm.   He yielded at the persuasion of the pope's almoner, Philip de Eleeomosyna, who was bribed by English gold.[1]

The king summoned a great council of the realm to Clarendon, a royal palace a few miles from Salisbury, for the ratification of the concession (Jan. 25, 1164).   The two archbishops, twelve bishops, and thirty-nine lay-barons were present.   Sixteen famous statutes were enacted, under the name of The Clarendon Constitutions, as laws of England. They are as follows : [2]—

THE CONSTITUTIONS OF CLARENDON.

I. Of the advowson and presentation (*de advocatione et presentatione*) to churches : if any dispute shall arise between laics, or between clerks and laics, or between clerks, let it be tried and decided in the court of our lord the king.

II. Churches in the king's fee (*de feudo domini Regis*) shall not be given in perpetuity without his consent and license.

III. Clerks accused of any crime shall be summoned by the king's justiciaries into the king's court to answer there for whatever the king's court shall determine they ought to answer there ; and in the ecclesiastical court, for whatever it shall be determined that they ought to answer there ; yet so that the king's justiciaries shall send into the court of holy Church to see in what way the matter shall there be handled ; and if the clerk shall confess or be convicted, the Church for the future shall not protect him.[3]

---

[1] Tennyson makes Becket say : —

> " This Almoner hath tasted Henry's gold.
> The cardinals have fingered Henry's gold.
> And Rome is venal even to rottenness."

[2] They are found in Matthew Paris, *ad ann.* 1164 ; Mansi, XXI. 1187 ; Wilkins, *Concilia M. Britanniæ*, vol. I. ; Gieseler, II. 89 sqq. (Am. ed. II. 289 sq.) ; Reuter, I. 371–375, 573–577 ; Hefele-Knöpfler, V. 623–628 (in German) ; Stubbs, 135–140 (in Latin) ; Gee and Hardy, 68–73.

[3] Maitland, p. 135 sqq., has thrown light upon this article, and interprets it to mean that a clerk is first to be accused and plead in the temporal court, then to be taken to the ecclesiastical court, and if found guilty and degraded he is to be returned to the temporal court and receive sentence to the layman's punishment.   This procedure was for civil crimes, such as robbery, rape, murder.

IV. No archbishop, bishop, or other exalted person shall leave the kingdom without the king's license ; and if they wish to leave it, the king shall
be empowered, if he pleases, to take security from them, that they will do no
harm to the king or kingdom, either in going or remaining, or in returning.

V. Persons excommunicated are not to give bail, *ad remanentiam*, nor to
make oath, but only to give bail and pledge that they will stand by the judgment of the Church where they are absolved.

VI. Laics shall not be accused, save by certain and legal accusers and
witnesses in presence of the bishop, so that the archdeacon may not lose his
rights, or anything which accrues to him therefrom. And if those who are
arraigned are such that no one is willing or dares to accuse them, the sheriff,
on demand from the bishop, shall cause twelve loyal men of the village to
swear before the bishop that they will declare the truth in that matter according to their conscience.

VII. No one who holds of the king in chief, nor any of his domestic servants, shall be excommunicated, nor his lands be put under an interdict,
until the king shall be consulted, if he is in the kingdom ; or, if he is abroad,
his justiciary, that he may do what is right in that matter, and so that whatever belongs to the king's court may therein be settled, and the same on the
other hand of the ecclesiastical court.

VIII. Appeals, if they arise, must be made from the archdeacon to the
bishop, and from the bishop to the archbishop ; and if the archbishop shall
fail in administering justice, the parties shall come before our lord the king,
that by his precept the controversy may be terminated in the archbishop's
court, so that it may not proceed further without the consent of our lord the
king.

IX. If a dispute shall arise between a clerk and a laic, or between a laic
and a clerk, about a tenement, which the clerk wishes to claim as eleemosynary, but the laic claims as lay fee, it shall be settled by the declaration of
twelve qualified men, through the agency of the king's capital judiciary,
whether the tenement is eleemosynary or lay fee, in presence of the king's
judiciaries. And if it shall be declared that it is eleemosynary, it shall be
pleaded in the ecclesiastical court ; but, if a lay fee, unless both shall claim
the tenement of the same bishop or baron, it shall be pleaded in the king's
court ; but if both shall claim of that fee from the same bishop or baron, it
shall be pleaded in his court, yet so that the same declaration above-named
shall not deprive of seizing him who before was seized, until he shall be
divested by the pleadings.

X. If any man belonging to a city, castle, borough, or king's royal manor
shall be summoned by the archdeacon or bishop to answer for a crime, and
shall not comply with the summons, it shall be lawful to place him under an
interdict, but not to excommunicate him, until the king's principal officer of
that place be informed thereof, that he may justify his appearing to the summons ; and if the king's officer shall fail in that matter, he shall be at the
king's mercy, and the bishop shall forthwith coerce the party accused with
ecclesiastical discipline.

XI. The archbishops, bishops, and all other persons of the kingdom, who hold of the king in chief, shall hold their possessions of the king as barony, and answer for the same to the king's justiciaries and officers, and follow and observe all the king's customs and rectitudes ; and be bound to be present, in the judgment of the king's court with the barons, like other barons, until the judgment proceeds to mutilation or death.

XII. When an archbishopric, bishopric, abbacy, or priory on the king's domain shall be vacant, it shall be in his hand, and he shall receive from it all the revenues and proceeds, as of his domains. And when the time shall come for providing for that church, our lord the king shall recommend the best persons to that church, and the election shall be made in the king's chapel, with the king's consent, and the advice of the persons of the kingdom whom he shall have summoned for that purpose. And the person elected shall there do homage and fealty to our lord the king, as to his liege lord, of life and limb, and of his earthly honors saving his orders, before he is consecrated.

XIII. If any of the king's nobles shall have refused to render justice to an archbishop or bishop or archdeacon, for himself or any of his men, our lord the king shall justice them. And if by chance any one shall have deforced our lord the king of his rights, the archbishops, bishops, and archdeacons shall justice him that he may render satisfaction to the king.

XIV. The chattels of those who are in forfeiture to the king shall not be detained by the Church or the cemetery, in opposition to the king's justice, for they belong to the king, whether they are found in the Church or without.

XV. Pleas for debts which are due, whether with the interposition of a pledge of faith or not, belong to the king's court.

XVI. The sons of rustics shall not be ordained without the consent of the lord, in whose land they are known to have been born.

These Constitutions were drawn up in the spirit and language of feudalism, under the inspiration of the king, by Archbishop Roger of York, Bishop Foliot of London (the chief enemies of Becket), Bishop Joceline of Salisbury, Richard de Luci (the king's chief judiciary), and Joceline of Baliol. They are restrictions on the immunities of the clergy; the last is an invasion of the rights of the people, but is based on the canonical exclusion of slaves from the clerical order without the consent of their masters. They subject the clergy equally with the laity to the crown and the laws of the land. They reduce the Church to an *imperium in imperio*, instead of recognizing her as a distinct and independent *imperium*. They formulate in the shape of legal enactments certain " ancient customs " (*consuetudines*) which date from the time of William the Conqueror, and were conceded by Lanfranc ; but they infringe at many points on the ancient privileges of the Church, and are inconsistent with the hierarchical principle of the exemption of the clergy from temporal jurisdiction.   And this was the chief point of the quarrel between the king and the archbishop.

In the present state of civilization there can be no doubt that the clergy should obey the same laws and be subject to the same penalties as the laity.   But we must not overlook the fact that in the Middle Ages the clerical exemption had a humanitarian as well as a hierarchical feature, and involved a protest against barbarous punishments by mutilation of the human body, man being made in the image of God.   It prepared the way for a mitigation of the criminal code for the benefit of the whole people, the laity as well as the clergy. This explains the large amount of popular sympathy with the cause of Becket.

Becket gave a qualified assent.   On his return to Canterbury he changed his mind and imposed upon himself severe penances, and sought and obtained the pope's absolution from his oath.   But Alexander, hard pressed by Barbarossa and the anti-pope, and anxious to keep the good will of Henry, tried to please both parties.   He granted, at the request of Henry, legatine commission over all England to Archbishop Roger of York, the rival of the primate of Canterbury.   He also afterwards authorized the coronation of Henry's eldest son by the archbishop of York in the Abbey of Westminster (June 18, 1170), although such coronation was the exclusive privilege of the archbishop of Canterbury.   This aggravated the difficulty with the king, and brought on the final crisis.

In the meantime the Clarendon Constitutions were carried out.   Clergymen convicted of crime in the king's court were condemned and punished like laymen.

Becket attempted to flee to the pope, and sailed for the

Continent, but was brought back by the sailors on account
of adverse winds.   This was a violation of the law which
forbade bishops to leave the country without royal permission.

He was summoned before a great council of bishops and
nobles at the royal castle of Northampton in the autumn of
1164, and charged with misconduct in secular affairs while
chancellor and archbishop.   But his courage rose with the
danger.   He refused to answer, and appealed to the pope.
The council ordered him cited to Rome on the charges of
perjury at Clarendon and of commanding his suffragans to
disregard the Constitutions.   The bishops he met with a
haughty refusal when they advised him to resign.   He was
to be arrested, but he threatened the peers with excommunication if they pronounced the sentence.   He took the bold
course of making his escape to the Continent in the disguise
of a monk, at midnight, accompanied by two monks and a
servant, and provided with his episcopal pall and seal.

The king seized the revenues of the archbishop, forbade
public prayers for him, and banished him from the kingdom,
ordered the banishment of all his kinsmen and friends, including four hundred persons of both sexes, and suspended
the payment of Peter's pence to the pope.

Becket spent fully six years in exile, from October, 1164,
to December, 1170.   King Louis of France, an enemy of
Henry and admirer of Becket, received him with distinction
and recommended him to the pope, who, himself in exile,
resided at Sens.   Becket met Alexander, laid before him the
Constitutions of Clarendon, and tendered his resignation.
The pope condemned ten as a violation of ecclesiastical privileges, and tolerated six as less evil than the rest.   He tenderly
rebuked Becket for his weakness in swearing to them, but
consoled him with the assurance that he had atoned for it
by his sufferings.   He restored to him the archiepiscopal
ring, thus ratifying his primacy, promised him his protection,

and committed him to the hospitable care of the abbot of
Pontigny, a Cistercian monastery about twelve leagues distant from Sens.   Here Becket lived till 1166, like a stern
monk, on pulse and gruel, slept on a bed of straw, and submitted at midnight to the flagellation of his chaplain, but
occasionally indulged in better diet, and retained some of his
former magnificence in his surroundings.   His sober friend,
John of Salisbury, remonstrated against the profuse expenditure.

Becket proceeded to the last extremity of pronouncing,
in the church of Vezelay, on Whitsuntide, 1166, the sentence
of excommunication on all the authors and defenders of the
Constitutions of Clarendon.   He spared the king, who then
was dangerously ill, but in a lower tone, half choked with
tears, he threatened him with the vengeance of God, and his
realm with the interdict.   He announced the sentence to
the pope and all the clergy of England, saying to the
latter, " Who presumes to doubt that the priests of God
are the fathers and masters of kings, princes, and all the
faithful ? "

The wrath of Henry knew no bounds.   He closed the
ports of England against the bearers of the instrument of
excommunication, threatening them with shameful mutilation, hanging, and burning.   He procured the expulsion of
Becket from Pontigny, who withdrew to a monastery near
the archiepiscopal city of Sens.   He secured through his
ambassadors several concessions from Alexander, who was
then in exile at Benevento.   The pope was anxious to retain
the support of the king, and yet he wrote soothing letters to
Becket, assuring him that the concessions were to be only
temporary.   Becket answered with indignation, and denounced the papal court for its venality and rapacity.
" Your gold and silver," he wrote to the cardinals, " will
not deliver you in the day of the wrath of the Lord."

The king now determined to use the permission received

from the pope several years before, but afterwards revoked,[1] and have his son crowned by Roger, archbishop of York. This humiliating infringement upon the rights of the primate stirred Becket's blood afresh. He repeated his excommunication. Like Gregory VII., he applied the words, "Cursed is he that refraineth his sword from blood," to the spiritual weapon. He even commanded the bishops of England to lay the whole kingdom under interdict and to suspend the offices of religion (except baptism, penance, and extreme unction), unless the king should give full satisfaction before the feast of purification, Nov. 2, 1170.[2]

These extreme measures were not without effect. Several bishops began to waver and change from the king's cause to that of the archbishop. The king himself was alarmed at the menace of the interdict. The pope pursued his temporizing policy, and counselled concessions by both parties.

The king and the archbishop suddenly made peace in a respectful personal interview at Fretteville (Freteval), a castle between Tours and Chartres, July 22, 1170. Henry said nothing about the Clarendon Constitutions, but made the offer that Becket should crown his daughter-in-law (the daughter of the king of France), and should on that occasion repeat the coronation of his son. Becket laid the blame on the shoulders of Henry's counsellors, and showed moderation and prudence. The king did not offer the kiss of peace, nor did the archbishop demand it.

But while Becket was willing to pardon the king, he

---

[1] See the pope's letter to the archbishop of York in the "Materials," vol. VI. 206 sq., and Robertson's note ; also Reuter, II. 683 sq. The letter is not in the Vatican, but in other MSS., and is admitted as genuine by Jaffé. It was probably written in the beginning of 1170, when Alexander was hard pressed by Barbarossa in the siege of Rome. See the other letters on the subject in "Materials," VII. 257, 305 sqq., 399.

[2] In 1169 Henry proposed to marry one of his daughters to the young king of Sicily, and to give a sum of money to the cities of the Lombard League for the erection of fortifications, provided they would influence Alexander to depose or transfer Becket. See Stubbs, ed. of *Hoveden*, II. xci sq.

meant to exercise his spiritual authority over his evil counsellors, and especially over the archbishop of York and the
bishops of London and Salisbury.   These prelates had recently officiated at the coronation of Henry's son.   And it
was this coronation, even more than the original and more
important dispute about the immunity of the clergy, that led
to the catastrophe.

After prolonged negotiations with the papal court and the
king, Becket returned to his long-neglected flock, Dec. 1,
1170.   On landing at Sandwich (instead of Dover, where
he was expected), he was surprised by enemies, who searched
his baggage, and demanded that he should withdraw his
excommunication of the bishops who were then at Dover.
He refused.   On his way to Canterbury the country clergy
and people met him, cast down their garments, chanting,
"Blessed is he that cometh in the name of the Lord."   He
rode to the cathedral with a vast procession, amid the ringing
of the bells, and preached on the text, "Here we have no
abiding city."

The excommunicated prelates of York, London, and Salisbury sought the protection of the king, who was then at a
castle near Bayeux in Normandy.   He said: "If all are to
be excommunicated who officiated at my son's coronation, by
the eyes of God, I am equally guilty."   One of the prelates
(perhaps Roger of York) remarked, "As long as Thomas
lives, you will never be at peace."   Henry broke out into
one of his constitutional fits of passion, and dropped the fatal
words: "A fellow that has eaten my bread, has lifted up his
heel against me; a fellow that I loaded with benefits, dares
insult the king; a fellow that came to court on a lame horse,
with a cloak for a saddle, sits without hindrance on the
throne itself.   By the eyes of God, is there none of my
thankless and cowardly courtiers who will deliver me from
the insults of this low-born and turbulent priest?"   With
these words he rushed out of the room.

§ 33. *The Martyrdom of Thomas Becket.* Dec. 29, 1170.

On the murder of Becket we have the reports of five eye-witnesses, — Edward Grim (a Saxon monk of Cambridge), William Fitz-Stephen (Becket's chaplain), John of Salisbury (his faithful friend), William of Canterbury, and the anonymous author of a Lambeth MS. Two other biographers, Herbert of Bosham and Roger of Pontigny, though absent from England at that time, were on intimate terms with Becket, and took great pains to ascertain the facts to the minutest details.

Four warlike knights of high birth and large estate, chamberlains to the king,[1] — Sir Reginald Fitz-Urse ("Son of the Bear," whom Becket had originally introduced to the court), Sir William de Tracy (of royal blood), Hugh de Moreville (judiciary of Northumberland and Cumberland), and Sir Richard le Bret or Breton (commonly known as Brito[2]), — eagerly caught at the king's suggestion, and resolved to carry it out in the spirit of passionate loyalty, at their own risk, as best they could, by imprisonment, or exile, or, if necessary, by murder. They seem to have had no premeditated plan except that of signal vengeance. Without waiting for instructions, they at once departed on separate routes for England, and met at the castle of Saltwood, which belonged to the see of Canterbury, but was then occupied by Randulf of Broc. They collected a band of about a dozen armed men, and reached St. Augustine's abbey outside of the walls of Canterbury, early on the 29th of December, which was a Tuesday.

On the morning of that fatal day, Becket had forebodings of his death, and advised the clergy to escape to Sandwich before daylight. He attended mass in the cathedral, confessed to two monks, and received three scourgings, as was his custom. At the banquet he drank more freely than usual, and said to the cupbearer, "He who has much blood to shed, must drink much." After dinner he retired to his

---

[1] *Cubicularii*, gentlemen of the bed-chamber.
[2] The biographers say he was more fit to be called "the Brute."

private room and sat on his bed, talking to his friends, John of Salisbury, William Fitz-Stephen, and Edward Grim. He was then still in full vigor, being in the fifty-third year of his age, retaining his dignified aspect and the lustre of his large eyes.

At about four that afternoon, the knights went to the archbishop's palace, leaving their weapons behind, and concealing their coats of mail by the ordinary cloak and gown. They demanded from him, in the name of the king, the absolution of the excommunicated bishops and courtiers. He refused, and referred them to the pope, who alone could absolve them. He declared: " I will never spare a man who violates the canons of Rome or the rights of the Church. My spirituals I hold from God and the pope; my temporals, from the king. Render unto Cæsar the things that are Cæsar's, and unto God the things that are God's." The knights said, "You speak in peril of your life." Becket replied: "Come ye to murder me in my own house ? You cannot be more ready to kill me than I am to die. You threaten me in vain ; were all the swords in England hanging over my head, you could not terrify me from my obedience to God and my lord the pope. I defy you, and will meet you foot to foot in the battle of the Lord." During the altercation, Becket lost command over his fiery temper. His friend, John of Salisbury, gently censured him for his exasperating tone. The knights quitted the room and called their men to arms.

A few minutes before five the bell tolled for vespers. Urged by his friends, the archbishop, with his cross carried before him, went through the cloisters to the cathedral. The service had begun, the monks were chanting the psalms in the choir, the church was filled with people, when two boys rushed up the nave and created a panic by announcing that armed men were breaking into the cloister. The attendants of Becket, who had entered the church, shut the door and urged him to move into the choir for safety. " Away, you

cowards !" he said, " by virtue of your obedience, I command
you not to shut the door; the church must not be turned
into a fortress." He was evidently prepared and eager for
martyrdom. He himself reopened the door, and dragged the
excluded monks into the building, exclaiming, "Come in, come
in — faster, faster!" The monks and priests were terror-
stricken and fled in every direction, to the recesses and side-
chapels, to the roof above, and the crypt below. Three only
remained faithful, — Canon Robert of Merton, Chaplain
William Fitz-Stephen, and the clerk Edward Grim.[1] One
of the monks confesses that he ran with clasped hands up the
steps as fast as his feet would carry him.

Becket proceeded to the high altar and archiepiscopal
chair, in which he and all his predecessors from time immemorial had been enthroned. There, no doubt, he wished to
gain the crown of martyrdom. It was now about five in the
winter evening; the shades of night were gathering, and the
lamps on the altars shed only a dim light in the dark cathedral. The tragedy which followed was finished in a few
minutes.

In the meantime the knights, clad in mail which covered
their faces up to their eyes, and with drawn swords, followed
by a motley group of ruffians, provided with hatchets, rushed
into the cathedral and shouted: "Where is the traitor?
Where is the archbishop?"[2] Becket replied, descending the
steps of the altar and facing his enemies, "Behold me, no
traitor, but a priest of God!" They again demanded the
absolution of the bishops and his surrender to the king's
justice. "I cannot do otherwise than I have done," he said,
and turning to Fitz-Urse, who was armed with a sword and
an axe, he added; "Reginald, you have received many

---

[1] Modern writers are in the habit of calling him a monk, and so he may
have been. In the contemporary narratives he is called simply " clerk."
Abbott, I. 42 sq.

[2] See Abbott, I. 89 sqq., on the words used, and Becket's reply.

favors at my hands : come you to me and into my church armed ! " The knights tried to drag him out of the sanctuary, not intending to kill him there; but he braced himself against the pillar between the altars of the Virgin, his special patroness, and St. Benedict, whose rule he followed, and said: "I am ready to die. May the Church through my blood obtain peace and liberty ! I charge you in the name of God Almighty that you hurt no one here but me." In the struggle, he grappled with De Tracy and threw him to the pavement. He called Fitz-Urse (who had seized him by the collar of his long cloak) a miserable wretch, and wrenched the cloak from his grasp, saying, "Off, thou pander, thou ! "[1] The soldier, maddened by the foul epithet, waving the sword over his head, struck the first blow, and dashed off his cap. Tracy, rising from the pavement, aimed at his head ; but Edward Grim, standing by, interposed his arm, which was almost severed, and then he sank back against the wall. Becket received blow after blow in an attitude of prayer. As he felt the blood trickling down his face, he bowed his neck for the death-blow, clasped his hands, and said in a low voice: "I commend my cause and the cause of the Church to God, to St. Denis, the martyr of France, to St. Alfege, and to the saints of the Church.[2] In the name of Christ and for the defence of his Church, I am ready to die. Lord, receive my spirit."

These were his last words. The next blow felled him to his knees, the last laid him on the floor at the foot of the altar of St. Benedict. His hands were still joined as if in prayer. Richard the Breton cut off the upper part of his skull, which had received the sacred oil. Hugh of Horsea,

---

[1] "*Lenonem appellans.*" Becket was wont to use violent language. He called Geoffrey Riddell, the archdeacon of Canterbury, "archdevil." Three years after Becket's death, Riddell was made bishop of Ely.

[2] Abbott, I. 147, holds that these words must have been spoken before the blow was struck which dislodged the cap from Becket's head. The blow cut off a piece of the prelate's skull.

the subdeacon, trampled upon his neck, thrust his sword into the ghastly wound, and scattered the blood and the brains over the pavement.[1]   Then he said, "Let us go, let us go : the traitor is dead ; he will rise no more."

The murderers rushed from the church through the cloisters into the palace for plunder ; while a violent thunder-storm broke over the cathedral.   They stole about two thousand marks in gold and silver, and rode off on Becket's fine horses in the thick darkness of the night.

The body of Thomas was buried in the crypt.   The remains of his blood and brains were sacredly kept.   His monkish admirers discovered, to their amazement and delight, that the martyr, who had once been arrayed in purple and fine linen, wore on his skin under his many garments the coarsest haircloth abounding with vermin.   This seemed to betray the perfection of ascetic sanctity according to mediæval notions.[2]   The spot of his "martyrdom" is still shown close to the entrance of the cathedral from the cloister.

§ 34.   *The Effects of Becket's Murder.*

The atrocious murder sent a thrill of horror throughout the Christian world.   The moment of Becket's death was his triumph.   His exalted station, his personal virtues, the sacrilege, — all contributed to deepen the impression.   At first opinion was divided, as he had strong enemies, even at Canterbury.   A monk declared that Becket paid a just penalty for his obstinacy ; others said, "He wished to be king and more than king;" the archbishop of York dared to preach that Becket "perished, like Pharaoh, in his pride."

But the torrent of public admiration soon silenced all opposition.   Miracles took place at his tomb, and sealed his

---

[1] All the authorities relate this brutal sacrilege.

[2] Grim, with whom the other original authorities agree, says that those who saw this haircloth suit, covering the upper and lower parts of Becket's body, put aside all their doubts and acknowledged him as a martyr.

claim to the worship of a saint and martyr. "The blind see, the deaf hear, the dumb speak, the lame walk, the lepers are cleansed, the devils are cast out, even the dead are raised to life." Thus wrote John of Salisbury, his friend.[1] Remarkable cures, no doubt, took place ; credulity and fraud exaggerated and multiplied them. Within a few years after the murder, two collections of his miracles were published, one by Benedict, prior of Canterbury (afterwards abbot of Peterborough), and one by William, monk of Canterbury.[2] According to these reports, the miracles began to occur the very night of the archbishop's death. His blood had miraculous efficacy for those who drank it.[3]

Two years after his death, Feb. 21, 1173, Becket was

---

[1] See his *Vita S. Th.* in the "Materials," etc., II. 322 : *In loco passionis eius . . . paralytici curantur, cœci vident, surdi audiunt, loquuntur muti, claudi ambulant, leprosi mundantur . . . et quod a diebus patrum nostrorum non est auditum, mortui resurgunt.*

[2] William's long *Vita et Passio S. Th.* is printed in the "Materials," vol. I. 173–546. The credulous Alban Butler, in his *Lives of the Saints,* quotes from an old English MS. of a pretended eye-witness, who records two hundred and sixty-three miracles wrought by the intercession of St. Thomas, — many more than are found in the whole Bible.

[3] Dr. Abbott devotes the main part of his work, I : 224 sqq., II. to a detailed description and discussion of the miracles. His closing chapter, II. 307–314, draws a parallel between these miracles and the miraculous works of Christ. He makes a distinction between mighty works wrought on human nature, such as the cure of diseases and the mighty works wrought on "non-human nature," as on bread, water, trees. The reality of the former he accepts, though he denies their supernatural character. The latter "are not to be accepted as historical, but as legends explicable from poetry taken as prose or from linguistic error or from these two combined." He goes on to say the distinction between Christ and Thomas is that "the spirit of St. Thomas had no power to pass into the hearts of men with a permanent vivifying message of its own. The Spirit of him whom we worship has both that power and that message." This is not the place to make an argument for the miracles of the New Testament, but two considerations place them and the miracles of Thomas of Canterbury in different categories. Christ's miracles had the purpose and worth of attesting his mission as the Saviour of the world, and they were original. It was quite easy for the mediæval mind in its fear and love of the wonderful to associate miracles with its saints, Christ's example being before them ; but where it was original, the miracles it believed were for the most part grotesque.

L

solemnly canonized by Alexander III., who had given him only a lukewarm support in his contest with the king. There is scarcely another example of such an early recognition of saintship; but public sentiment had anticipated it. At a council in Westminster the papal letters of canonization were read. All the bishops who had opposed Becket were present, begged pardon for their offence, and acquiesced in the pope's decision. The 29th of December was set apart as the feast of " St. Thomas of Canterbury."

King Henry II., as the supposed author of the monstrous crime, was branded with a popular excommunication. On the first news, he shut himself up for three days in his chamber, rolled himself in sackcloth and ashes, and obstinately refused food and comfort. He lived secluded for five weeks, exclaiming again and again, " Alas, alas that it ever happened ! " He issued orders for the apprehension of the murderers, and despatched envoys to the pope to exculpate himself and to avert the calamity of excommunication and an interdict. After long delay a reconciliation took place in the cathedral of Avranches in Normandy, before the papal legates, the archbishop of Rouen, and many bishops and noblemen, May 22, 1172.[1] Henry swore on the holy Gospels that he had neither commanded nor desired the death of Becket, that it caused him more grief than the death of his father or his mother, and that he was ready to make full satisfaction. He pledged himself to abrogate the Statutes of Clarendon; to restore the church of Canterbury to all its rights and possessions ; to undertake, if the pope should require it, a three years' crusade to Jerusalem or Spain, and to support two hundred knights in the Holy Land. After these pledges he said aloud : " Behold, my lord legates, my body is in your hands ; be assured that whatever you order, whether to go to Jerusalem or to Rome or to St. James

[1] A granite pillar in the Norman cathedral at Avranches bears an inscription in memory of the event. It is given by Stanley, p. 136.

[at Compostella in Spain], I am ready to obey." He was led by the bishops into the church and reconciled. His son, who was present, promised Cardinal Albert to make good his father's pledges. This penance was followed by a deepest humiliation at Canterbury.

Two years later, July 12, 1174, the king, depressed by disasters and the rebellion of his wife and his sons, even made a pilgrimage to the tomb of Becket. He dismounted from his horse as he came in sight of the towers of Canterbury, walked as a penitent pilgrim in a woollen shirt, with bare and bleeding feet, through the streets, knelt in the porch of the cathedral, kissed the sacred stone on which the archbishop had fallen, threw himself prostrate before the tomb in the crypt, and confessed to the bishops with groans and tears his deep remorse for the hasty words which had led to the murder.   Gilbert Foliot, bishop of London, once Becket's rival and enemy, announced to the monks and bystanders the king's penitence and intention to restore the rights and property of the Church, and to bestow forty marks yearly on the monastery to keep lamps burning at the martyr's tomb. The king, placing his head and shoulders on the tomb, submitted to the degrading punishment of scourging, and received five stripes from each bishop and abbot, and three stripes from each of the eighty monks.   Fully absolved, he spent the whole night on the bare ground of the crypt in tears and prayers, imploring the forgiveness of the canonized saint in heaven whom he had persecuted on earth.

No deeper humiliation of king before priest is recorded in history. It throws into the shade the submission of Theodosius to Ambrose, of Edgar to Dunstan, of Barbarossa to Alexander, and even the scene at Canossa.

Fifty years after the martyrdom, Becket's relics were translated with extraordinary solemnity from the tomb in the crypt to the costly shrine of Becket, which blazed with gold and jewels, in the reconstructed Canterbury cathedral (1220).

And now began on the largest scale that long succession of
pilgrimages, which for more than three hundred years made
Canterbury the greatest sacred resort of Western Christendom, next to Jerusalem and Rome.   It was more frequented
than Loreto in Italy and Einsiedeln in Switzerland.   No less
than a hundred thousand pilgrims were registered at Canterbury in 1420.   From all parts of England, Scotland, Wales,
and Ireland, from France and the far north, men and women
flocked to the shrine: priests, monks, princes, knights, scholars, lawyers, merchants, mechanics, peasants.   There was
scarcely an English king, from Henry II. to Henry VIII.,
who did not from motives of piety or policy pay homage
to the memory of the saint.   Among the last distinguished
visitors were John Colet, dean of St. Paul's, and Erasmus,
who visited the shrine together between the years 1511 and
1513, and King Henry VIII. and Emperor Charles V., who
attended the last jubilee in 1520.   Plenary indulgences were
granted to the pilgrims.   Some went in December, the month
of his martyrdom ; a larger number in July, the month of
the translation of his relics.   Every fiftieth year a jubilee
lasting fifteen days was celebrated in his honor.   Six such
jubilees were celebrated, — 1270, 1320, 1370, 1420, 1470, 1520.
The offerings to St. Thomas exceeded those given to any
other saint, even to the holy Virgin.

Geoffrey Chaucer, the father of English poetry, who lived
two centuries after Becket's martyrdom, has immortalized
these pilgrimages in his Canterbury Tales, and given us
the best description of English society at that time.

The pilgrimages promoted piety, social intercourse, superstition, idleness, levity, and immorality, and aroused moral
indignation among many serious and spiritually minded men.

The superstitious idolatry of St. Thomas was continued
down to the time of the Reformation, when it was rudely
but forever crushed out.   Henry VIII. cited Becket to
appear in court to answer to the charges of treason and re-

bellion. The case was formally argued at Westminster. His guilt was proved, and on the 10th of June, 1538, St. Thomas was condemned as a "rebel and a traitor to his prince." The rich shrine at Canterbury was pillaged ; the gold and jewels were carried off in two strong coffers, and the rest of the treasure in twenty-six carts. The jewels went into the hands of Henry VIII., who wore the most precious of them, a diamond, the "Regale of France," in the ring on his thumb ; afterwards it glittered in the golden "collar" of his daughter, the bigoted Queen Mary. A royal proclamation explained the cause and mode of Becket's death, and the reasons for his degradation. All festivals, offices, and prayers in his name were forbidden. The site of his shrine has remained vacant to this day.

The Reformation prepared the way for a more spiritual worship of God and a more just appreciation of the virtues and faults of Thomas Becket than was possible in the age in which he lived and died, — a hero and a martyr of the papal hierarchy, but not of pure Christianity, as recorded in the New Testament. To the most of his countrymen, as to the English-speaking people at large, his name has remained the synonym for priestly pride and pretension, for an arrogant invasion of the rights of the civil estate. To a certain class of English High Churchmen he remains, like Laud of a later age, the martyr of sacerdotal privilege, the unselfish champion of the dowered rights of the Church. The atrocity of his taking-off no one will choose to deny. But the haughty assumption of the high prelate had afforded pretext enough for vehement indignation and severe treatment. Priestly robes may for a time conceal and even protect pride from violence, but sooner or later it meets its just reward. The prelate's superiority involved in Becket's favorite expression, "saving the honor of my order," was more than a king of free blood could be expected to bear.

This dramatic chapter of English history may be fitly

closed with a scene from Lord Tennyson's tragedy which
presents the personal quality that brought about Thomas à
Becket's fall.[1]

JOHN OF SALISBURY.

Thomas, I would thou hadst returned to England
Like some wise prince of this world from his wars,
With more of olive-branch and amnesty
For foes at home — thou hast raised the world against thee.

BECKET.

Why, John, my kingdom is not of this world.

JOHN OF SALISBURY.

If it were more of this world it might be
More of the next.   A policy of wise pardon
Wins here as well as there.   To bless thine enemies —

BECKET.

Ay, mine, not Heaven's.

JOHN OF SALISBURY.

And may there not be something
Of this world's leaven in thee too, when crying
On Holy Church to thunder out her rights
And thine own wrong so piteously.   Ah, Thomas,
The lightnings that we think are only Heaven's
Flash sometimes out of earth against the heavens.
The soldier, when he lets his whole self go
Lost in the common good, the common wrong,
Strikes truest ev'n for his own self.   I crave
Thy pardon — I have still thy leave to speak.
Thou hast waged God's war against the King; and yet
We are self-uncertain creatures, and we may,
Yea, even when we know not, mix our spites
And private hates with our defence of Heaven.

---

[1] Sir Henry Irving, the distinguished English actor, died Oct. 20, 1905,
seven days after a performance of this drama, the last time he appeared on
the stage.

CHAPTER V.

INNOCENT III. AND HIS AGE. A.D. 1198–1216.

§ 35. *Literature.*

Sources: *Innocentii III. Opp. omnia*, in Migne, 4 vols. 214–217; three vols. contain Innocent's official letters; a 4th, his sermons, the *de contemptu mundi*, and other works. — S. Baluzius : *Epistolarum Inn. III. libri undecim*, 2 vols. Paris, 1682. — Böhmer : *Regesta imperii 1198–1254*, new ed. by J. Ficker, Innsbruck, 1881. — Potthast : *Regesta*, pp. 1–467, 2041–2056 — *Gesta Innoc. III. auctore anonymo sed coævo* (a contemporary Life, about 1220), in Migne, 214, pp. xvii–ccxxviii, and Baluzius. — Mansi, XXII. — Mirbt : *Quellen*, 125–136, gives some of the characteristic passages. For the older edd. of Inn.'s letters and other works, see Potthast, *Bibliotheca med. ævi*, I. 520, 650.

Modern Works: Friedrich von Hurter (1787–1866) : *Geschichte Papst Innocenz des Dritten und seiner Zeitgenossen*, 2 vols. Hamburg, 1833–1835; 3d ed. 4 vols. 1841–1844 (trans. into French and Italian). The last two volumes are devoted to the monastic orders and the eccles. and social conditions of the thirteenth century. An exhaustive work full of enthusiastic admiration for Innocent and his age. Hurter wrote it while antistes or pastor of the Reformed Church in Schaffhausen, Switzerland, and was led by his studies to enter, with his family, the Roman Catholic communion in 1844 and became imperial counsellor and historiographer of Austria. Gfrörer, likewise a Protestant, dazzled by the splendor of the Gregorian papacy in the preparation of his *Life of Gregory VII.*, was also led to join the Roman communion. — Jorry : *Hist. du pape Inn. III.* ; Paris, 1853. — F. F. Reinlein : *Papst Inn. III. und seine Schrift de contemptu mundi*, Erlangen, 1871 ; also *Inn. III. nach s. Beziehung zur Unfehlbarkeitsfrage*, Erlangen, 1872. — H. Elkan : *Die Gesta Inn. III. im Verhältniss zu d. Regesten desselben Papstes*, Heidelberg, 1876. — Fr. Deutsch : *Papst Inn. III. und s. Einfluss auf d. Kirche*, Bresl., 1876. — Leop. Delisle : *Mémoire sur les actes d'Inn. III, suivi de l'itinéraire de ce pontife*, Paris, 1877. — J. N. Brischar, Roman Catholic : *Papst Inn. III. und s. Zeit*, Freib. im Br. 1883. — J. Langen : *Gesch. d. röm. Kirche von Gregor. VII. bis Inn. III.*, Bonn, 1893 ; also Hefele-Knöpfler, vol. V. — the Works on the Hohenstaufen and the Crusades. — Ranke : *Weltgesch.*, VIII. 274 sqq. — the Histories of Rome by Reumont, Bryce, and Gregorovius. — Hauck : *Kirchengeschichte Deutschlands*, IV. 658–745. — T. F. Tout : *The Empire and the Papacy*, 918–1272, N.Y. 1898. — H. Fisher : *The Med. Empire*, 2 vols. London, 1898. — For fuller lit., see Chevalier ; *Répertoire*, pp. 1114 sq. and Suppl. 2659, and art. *Inn. III.*, by Zöpffel-Mirbt, in Herzog, IX. 112–122.

§ 36. *Innocent's Training and Election.*

THE brilliant pontificate of Innocent III., 1198–1216, lasted as long as the combined and uneventful reigns of his five predecessors: Lucius III., 1181–1185; Urban III., 1185–1187; Gregory VIII. less than two months, 1187; Clement III., 1187–1191; Cœlestin III., 1191–1198. It marks the golden age of the mediæval papacy and one of the most important eras in the history of the Catholic Church. No other mortal has before or since wielded such extensive power. As the spiritual sovereign of Latin Christendom, he had no rival. At the same time he was the acknowledged arbiter of the political destinies of Europe from Constantinople to Scotland. He successfully carried into execution the highest theory of the papal theocracy and anticipated the Vatican dogmas of papal absolutism and infallibility. To the papal title "vicar of Christ," Innocent added for the first time the title "vicar of God." He set aside the decisions of bishops and provincial councils, and lifted up and cast down kings. He summoned and guided one of the most important of the councils of the Western Church, the Fourth Lateran, 1215, whose acts established the Inquisition and fixed transubstantiation as a dogma. He set on foot the Fourth Crusade, and died making preparation for another. On the other hand he set Christian against Christian, and by undertaking to extirpate religious dissent by force drenched parts of Europe in Christian blood.

Lothario, Innocent's baptismal name, was born about 1160 at Anagni, a favorite summer resort of the popes. He was the son of Count Trasmondo of the house of the Conti de Segni, one of the ruling families of the Latium.[1] It furnished nine popes, of whom Innocent XIII. was the last.

---

[1] Like Hildebrand, Innocent may have combined Germanic with Italian blood. Upon the basis of such family names among the Conti as Lothaire and Richard, Gregorovius finds evidence of Lombard origin.

He studied theology and canon law at Paris and Bologna, and became proficient in scholastic learning. Through the influence of three uncles, who were cardinals, he was rapidly promoted, and in 1190, at the age of twenty-nine, was appointed cardinal-deacon by one of them, Pope Clement III. Though the youngest member of the curia, he was at once assigned a place of responsibility.

During the pontificate of Cœlestin III., a member of the house of the Orsini which was unfriendly to the Conti, Lothario withdrew into retirement and devoted himself to literature. The chief fruit of this seclusion is the work entitled *The Contempt of the World* or the *Misery of the Mortal Estate*.[1] It might well have been followed, as the author says in the prologue, by a second treatise on the dignity of man's estate. To this time belongs also a work on the sacrifice of the mass.[2] After his elevation to the papal throne, Innocent composed an Exposition of the Seven Penitential Psalms. While pope he preached often both in Rome and on his journeys. His sermons abound in mystical and allegorical figures. Of his letters more than five hundred are preserved.

The *Contempt of the World* is an ascetic plaint over the sinfulness and woes of this present life. It proceeds upon the basis of Augustine's theory of total depravity. The misery of man is described from the helplessness of infancy to the decrepitude of age and the sufferings of the future estate. Pessimistic passages are quoted from Jeremiah, Ecclesiastes, and Job, and also from Horace, Ovid, and Juvenal. Three master passions are constantly tormenting man, — avarice, lust, and ambition, — to which are added the innumerable ailments of the body and troubles of the soul. The author deplores the fate of masters and servants, of the

---

[1] The *de contemptu mundi sive de miseria conditionis humanæ* was first printed at Ulm, 1448, then at Lyons, 1473, Nürnberg, 1477, etc. See Migne's ed. 217, 701–746.

[2] *Mysterium evangelicæ legis et sacramentum eucharistiæ* or *de missarum mysteriis*.

married and the unmarried, of the good and the bad, the
rich and the poor.   " It is just and natural that the wicked
should suffer; but are the righteous one whit better off ?
Here below is their prison, not their home or their final
destiny.   As soon as a man rises to a station of dignity,
cares and trouble increase, fasting is abridged, night
watches are prolonged, nature's constitution is undermined,
sleep and appetite flee, the vigor of the body gives way
to weakness, and a sorrowful end is the close of a sorrowful life." [1]   In the case of the impenitent, eternal
damnation perpetuates the woes of time.   With a description of these woes the work closes, reminding the reader
of the solemn cadences of the *Dies Iræ* of Thomas of Celano
and Dante's *Inferno*.[2]

Called forth from retirement to the chief office in Christendom, Innocent had an opportunity to show his contempt
of the world by ruling it with a strong and iron hand.   The
careers of the best of the popes of the Middle Ages, as well
as of ecclesiastics like Bernard of Clairvaux and Thomas of
Canterbury, reveal the intimate connection between the hierarchical and ascetic tendencies.   Innocent likewise displayed
these two tendencies.   In his treatise on the mass he anticipated the haughty assumption of the papacy, based on the
rock-foundation of Peter's primacy, which as pope he afterwards displayed.

On the very day of Cœlestin's burial, the college of cardinals unanimously chose Lothario pope.   Like Gregory I.,
Gregory VII., Alexander III., and other popes, he made a

---

[1] II. 29.

[2] The *Dies Iræ* has been ascribed to Innocent.   Here are the concluding
words of this famous treatise.   " *Ibi erit fletus et stridor dentium* (Matthew
xiii.), *gemitus et ululatus, luctus et cruciatus, stridor et clamor, timor et tre-
mor, dolor et labor, ardor et fœtor, obscuritas et anxietas, acerbitas et asperi-
tas, calamitas et egestas, angustia et tristitia, oblivio et confusio, torsiones et
punctiones, amaritudines et terrores, fames et sitis, frigus et cauma, sulphur
et ignis-ardens in sæcula sæculorum.   Unde liberet nos Deus, qui est benedictus in sæcula sæculorum.   Amen.*"   III. 17 ; Migne, 217, 746.

show of yielding reluctantly to the election. He was ordained priest, and the next day, February 22, was consecrated bishop and formally ascended the throne in St. Peter's.

The coronation ceremonies were on a splendid scale. But the size of Rome, whose population at this time may not have exceeded thirty-five thousand, must be taken into account when we compare them with the pageants of the ancient city.[1] At the enthronization in St. Peter's, the tiara was used which Constantine is said to have presented to Sylvester, and the words were said, "Take the tiara and know that thou art the father of princes and kings, the ruler of the world, the vicar on earth of our Saviour Jesus Christ, whose honor and glory shall endure throughout all eternity." Then followed the procession through the city to the Lateran. The pope sat on a white palfrey and was accompanied by the prefect of the city, the senators and other municipal officials, the nobility, the cardinals, archbishops, and other church dignitaries, the lesser clergy and the popular throng — all amidst the ringing of bells, the chanting of psalms, and the acclamations of the people. Along the route a singular scene was presented at the Ghetto by a group of Jews, the rabbi at their head carrying a roll of the Pentateuch, who bowed low as they saluted their new ruler upon whose favor or frown depended their protection from the populace, yea, their very life. Arrived at the Lateran, the pope threw out handfuls of copper coins among the people with the words, " Silver and gold have I none, but such as I have give I thee." The silver key of the palace and the golden key of the basilica were then put into his hands, and the senate did him homage. A banquet followed, the pope sitting at a table alone.[2] Upon such pomp and show of worldly power the Apostles, whose lot was poverty, would have looked with wonder, if they had been

[1] See Gregorovius, V. 7.

[2] Elaborate descriptions of the ceremonies are given by Hurter, I. 92 sqq., and Gregorovius, V. 7–15.

told that the central figure of it all was the chief personality
in the Christian world.

When he ascended the fisherman's throne, Innocent was
only thirty-seven years old, the youngest in the line of popes
up to that time.   Walter von der Vogelweide gave expression
to the fear which his youth awakened when he wrote, *O wê der
bâbest ist ze junc, hilf hêrre dîner kristenheit.*   "Alas ! the
pope is so young.   Help, Lord, thy Christian world."   The
new pontiff was well formed, medium in stature,[1] temperate in his habits, clear in perception, resolute in will, and
fearless in action.   He was a born ruler of men, a keen judge
of human nature, demanding unconditional submission to
his will, yet considerate in the use of power after submission
was once given,— an imperial personality towering high above
the contemporary sovereigns in moral force and in magnificent
aims of world-wide dominion.

§ 37.   *Innocent's Theory of the Papacy.*

The pope with whom Innocent is naturally brought into
comparison is Hildebrand.   They were equally distinguished
for moral force, intellectual energy, and proud assertion of
prelatic prerogative.   Innocent was Hildebrand's superior in
learning, diplomatic tact, and success of administration, but
in creative genius and heroic character he was below his
predecessor.   He stands related to his great predecessor as
Augustus to Julius.   He was heir to the astounding programme of Hildebrand's scheme and enjoyed the fruits of his
struggles.   Their personal fortunes were widely different.
Gregory was driven from Rome and died in exile.   To Innocent's good fortune there seemed to be no end, and he closed
his pontificate in undisputed possession of authority.

Innocent no sooner ascended the papal chair than he began

[1] *Statura mediocris*, etc.   See *Gesta*, Migne, 214, XVII.   The portrait
prefixed in Hurter has no historic value.   For Innocent's personal habits
and methods of conducting business, see Hurter, II. 743 sqq.

to give expression to his conception of the papal dignity.
Throughout his pontificate he forcibly and clearly expounded
it in a tone of mingled official pride and personal humility.   At his coronation he preached on the faithful and wise
servant.   " Ye see," he said, " what manner of servant it is
whom the Lord hath set over his people, no other than the
vicegerent of Christ, the successor of Peter.   He stands in
the midst between God and man ; below God, above man;
less than God, more than man.   He judges all and is judged
by none.   But he, whom the pre-eminence of dignity exalts,
is humbled by his vocation as a servant, that so humility
may be exalted and pride be cast down ; for God is against
the high-minded, and to the lowly He shows mercy ; and
whoso exalteth himself shall be abased."

Indeed, the papal theocracy was Innocent's all-absorbing
idea.   He was fully convinced that it was established of God
for the good of the Church and the salvation of the world.
As God gave to Christ all power in heaven and on earth,
so Christ delegated to Peter and his successors the same
authority.   Not man but God founded the Apostolic see.[1]   In
his famous letter to the patriarch of Constantinople, Nov. 12,
1199,[2] he gave an elaborate exposition of the commission to
Peter.   To him alone the command had been given, " Feed
my sheep."   On him alone it had been declared, " I will build
my church."   The pope is the vicar of Christ, yea of God
himself.[3]   Not only is he intrusted with the dominion of the
Church, but also with the rule of the whole world.   Like
Melchizedek, he is at once king and priest.   All things in
heaven and earth and in hell are subject to Christ.   So are
they also to his vicar.   He can depose princes and absolve

[1] *Apostolicæ sedis primatus quem non homo sed Deus, imo verius Deus
homo constituit.*

[2] *Reg.* II. 209 ; Migne, 214, 758–765.

[3] *Cum non humana sed divina fiat auctoritate quod in hac parte per sum-
mum pontificem adimpletur, qui non hominis puri sed veri Dei vere vicarius appellatur.*   I. 326 ; Migne, 214, 292.

subjects from the oath of allegiance.   He may enforce submission by placing whole nations under the interdict.   Peter
alone went to Jesus on the water and by so doing he gave
illustration of the unique privilege of the papacy to govern
the whole earth.   For the other disciples stayed in the ship
and so to them was given rule only over single provinces.
And as the waters were many on which Peter walked, so over
the many congregations and nations, which the waters represent, was Peter given authority — yea over all nations whatsoever (*universos populos*).[1]   In this letter he also clearly
teaches papal infallibility and declares that Peter's successor
can never in any way depart from the Catholic faith.

Gregory VII.'s illustration, likening the priestly estate
(*sacerdotium*) to the sun, and the civil estate (*regnum* or
imperium) to the moon, Innocent amplified and emphasized.   Two great lights, Innocent said, were placed by
God in the firmament of heaven, and to these correspond the
" pontifical authority and the regal authority," the one to
rule over souls as the sun rules over the day, the other to rule
over the bodies of men as the moon rules over the night.   And
as the moon gets its light from the sun, and as it is also less
than the sun both in quality and in size, and in the effect
produced, so the regal power gets its dignity and splendor
from the pontifical authority which has in it more inherent
virtue.[2]   The priest anoints the king, not the king the priest,
and superior is he that anoints to the anointed.[3]   Princes

---

[1] *Nam cum aquæ multæ sint, populi multi, congregationesque aquarum
sunt maria, per hoc quod Petrus super aquas maris incessit, super universos
populos se potestatem accepisse monstravit.*   II. 209 ; Migne, 214, 760 ; Potthast, 82.   In this letter Innocent quotes no less than twenty-five passages of
Scripture.

[2] *Sicut luna lumen suum a sole sortitur, quæ re vera minor est isto quan-
titate simul et qualitate, situ pariter et effectu, sic regalis potestas ab auctoritate pontificali suæ sortitur dignitatis splendorem,* etc.   See Mirbt,
Quellen, 130.

[3] *Minor est qui unguitur quam qui ungit, et dignior est unguens quam
unctus.*   Migne, 216, 1012, 1179 ; Potthast, 98.

have authority in separate lands ; the pontiff over all lands. The priesthood came by divine creation ; the kingly power by man's manipulation and violence.[1] "As in the ark of God," so he wrote to John of England, "the rod and the manna lay beside the tables of the law, so at the side of the knowledge of the law, in the breast of the pope, are lodged the terrible power of destruction and the genial mildness of grace." Innocent reminded John that if he did not lift his foot from off the Church, nothing would check his punishment and fall.[2] Monarchs throughout Europe listened to Innocent's exposition and obeyed. His correspondence abounds with letters to the emperor, the kings of Hungary, Bohemia, Sicily, France, England, the Danes, Aragon, and to other princes, teaching them their duty and demanding their submission.

Under Innocent's rule, the subjection of the entire Christian world to the Roman pontiff seemed to be near realization. But the measures of force which were employed in the Latin conquest of Constantinople, 1204, had the opposite effect from what was intended. The overthrow of the Byzantine empire and the establishment of a Latin empire in its stead and the creation of a new hierarchy of Constantinople only completed the final alienation of the Greek and Latin churches. To Innocent III. may not be denied deep concern in the extension of Christendom. But the rigorous system of the Inquisition which he set on foot begat bitterness and war of churchman against Christian dissenter and of Christian against Mohammedan. More blood was shed at the hand of the Church during the pontificate of Innocent, and under his immediate successors carrying out his policy, than in any

---

[1] *Sacerdotium per ordinationem divinam, regnum autem per extorsionem humanam.* He also speaks of the unity of the Church as the product of grace and the divisions of the empire as the product of or judgment of sin. *Ecclesia per Dei gratiam in unitate consistit, et imperium peccatis exigentibus est divisum.* Migne, 216, 1179 ; Potthast, 98.

[2] Migne, 217, 922. Gregorovius pronounces this "probably the most imperious document of the papal power." V. 104.

other age except during the papal counter-Reformation in the
sixteenth and seventeenth centuries. The audacious papal
claim to imperialism corrected itself by the policy employed
by Innocent and his successors to establish the claim over the
souls and bodies of men and the governments of the earth.[1]

§ 38. *Innocent and the German Empire.*

ADDITIONAL LITERATURE. — Ed. WINKELMANN: *Philip von Schwaben und
Otto IV. von Braunschweig*, 2 vols. Leipzig, 1873–1878. — R. SCHWEMER:
*Innocent III. und d. deutsche Kirche während des Thronstreites von
1198–1208*, Strassburg, 1882.

The political condition of Europe was favorable to Innocent's assertion of power. With the sudden death of
Henry VI., Sept. 28, 1197, at the early age of thirty-two, the
German empire was left without a ruler. Frederick, the
Emperor's only son, was a helpless child. Throughout Italy
a reaction set in against Henry's hard and oppressive rule.
The spirit of national freedom was showing itself, and a
general effort was begun to expel the German princes and
counts from Italian soil.

Innocent III. has been called by Ranke Henry's real successor.[2] Taking advantage of the rising feeling of Italian
nationality, the pope made it his policy to separate middle
and lower Italy from the empire, and, in fact, he became the
deliverer of the peninsula from foreign agents and mercenaries.
He began his reign by abolishing the last vestiges of the
authority of the empire in the city of Rome. The city prefect, who had represented the emperor, took the oath of
allegiance to the pope, and Innocent invested him with a

---

[1] Hauck, IV. 743, acknowledging the genius of Innocent, expresses the
somewhat disparaging judgment that "he was more of a rhetorician than
a theologian, and more of a jurist and administrator than a statesman."
Many Protestant writers of Germany show their national feeling by a disposition to disparage Gregory VII. and Innocent III.

[2] *Weltgeschichte*, VIII. 274. Matthews, 105 sq. gives Henry VI.'s Testament.

mantle and silver cup.   The senator likewise acknowledged Innocent's authority and swore to protect the Roman see and the regalia of St. Peter.

The pope quickly pushed his authority beyond the walls of Rome.   Spoleto, which for six centuries had been ruled by a line of German dukes, Assisi, Perugia, and other cities, submitted.   Mark of Anweiler, the fierce soldier of Henry VI., could not withstand the fortunate diplomacy and arms of Innocent, and the Romagna, with Ravenna as its centre, yielded.   A Tuscan league was formed which was favorably disposed to the papal authority.   Florence, Siena, Pisa, and other cities, while refusing to renounce their civic freedom, granted privileges to the pope.   Everywhere Innocent had his legates.   Such full exercise of papal power over the State of the Church had not before been known.

To confirm her son Frederick's title to the crown of Sicily, his mother delivered the kingdom over to the pope as a papal fief.   She survived her imperial consort only a year, and left a will appointing Innocent the guardian of her child. The intellectual training and political destinies of the heir of the Hohenstaufen were thus intrusted to the hereditary foe of that august house.   Innocent was left a free hand to prosecute his trust as he chose.[1]

In Germany, Innocent became the umpire of the imperial election.   The electors were divided between two aspirants to the throne, Philip of Swabia, the brother of Henry VI., who was crowned at Mainz, and Otto, the son of Henry the Lion, who was crowned at Aachen by Adolf, archbishop of Cologne.   Otto was the nephew of Richard Cœur de Lion and John of England, who supported his claims with their gold and diplomacy.   Both parties made their appeal to Rome, and it is not a matter of surprise that Innocent's sympathies

---

[1] One of Frederick's first acts was to release a portion of his patrimony to the pope's brother, Count Richard.   At a later period, under Honorius, Frederick recalled his gift.

M

were with the Guelf, Otto, rather than with the Hohenstaufen.   Moreover, Philip had given offence by occupying,
as duke of Tuscany, the estates of Matilda.

Innocent made the high claim that the German throne
depended for its occupant "from the beginning and ultimately" upon the decision of the papal see.   Had not the
Church transferred the empire from the East to the West?
And had not the Church itself conferred the imperial crown,[1]
passing by the claims of Frederick and pronouncing Philip
"unworthy of empire"?   Innocent decided in 1201 in favor of
Otto, "his dearest son in Christ who was himself devoted to
the Church and on both sides was descended from devout
stock."   The decision inured to Rome's advantage.   By the
stipulation of Neuss, subsequently repeated at Spires, 1209,
Otto promised obedience to the pope and renounced all claim
to dominion in the State of the Church and also to Naples
and Sicily.   This written document was a dangerous ratification of the real or pretended territorial rights and privileges of the papacy from Constantine and Pepin down.

Civil war broke out, and when the tide of success turned
in Philip's favor, the pope released him from the sentence
of excommunication and was about to acknowledge him as
emperor[2] when the murderous sword of Otto of Wittelsbach,
in 1208, brought Philip's career to a tragic end.   The year
following Otto was crowned in St. Peter's, but he forgot
his promises and proceeded to act out the independent policy
of the rival house of the Hohenstaufen.[3]   He laid heavy hand
upon Central Italy, distributing rich estates and provinces

---

[1] *Imperium principaliter et finaliter dignoscitur pertinere, principaliter
quia ipsa transtulit imperium ab Oriente ad Occidentem; finaliter quia ipsa
concedit coronam imperii.*   Migne, 216, 1182 ; Potthast, 98 ; also Migne, 216,
1048; Potthast, 119.

[2] The very archbishop of Cologne who had crowned Otto now put the
crown on Philip's head.

[3] Otto had sought to join the fortunes of the two houses by marrying
Philip's daughter, Beatrice, who died soon after the nuptials.

among his vassals and sequestrating the revenues of the clergy. He then marched to Southern Italy, the territory of Frederick, and received the surrender of Naples.

All that Innocent had gained seemed in danger of being lost. Prompt measures showed him equal to the emergency. He wrote that the stone he had erected to be the head of the corner had become a rock of offence. Like Rachel he mourned over his son whom he lamented to have made king. Otto was excommunicated and a meeting of magnates at Nürnberg, 1211, declared him deposed, and, pronouncing in favor of Frederick, sent envoys to Palermo to convey to him the intelligence. Otto crossed the Alps to reclaim his power, but it was too late. Frederick started north, stopping at Rome, where Innocent saw him for the first and last time, April, 1212. He was elected and crowned king at Frankfurt, December, 1212, and was recognized by nearly all the princes at Eger the year following. Before setting out from Italy he had again recognized Sicily as a fief of Rome. At Eger he disavowed all imperial right to the State of the Church.[1]

Otto joined in league with John of England and the Flemish princes against Philip Augustus of France; but his hopes were dashed to the ground on the battlefield of Bouvines, Belgium, 1415. His authority was thenceforth confined to his ancestral estate. He died 1218. Innocent had gained the day. His successors were to be defied by the young king, Frederick, for nearly half a century.

With equal spirit and decision, Innocent mingled in the affairs of the other states of Europe. In France, the controversy was over the sanctity of the marriage vow. Philip Augustus put away his second wife,[2] a Danish princess, a

---

[1] This was the so-called Golden Bull of Eger, July 12, 1213. Frederick calls himself in it, "King of the Romans and of Sicily." He promised to defend Sicily for the Roman Church as a "devoted son and Catholic prince," *devotus filius et Catholicus princeps.* Mirbt, *Quellen,* 131 sqq.; Matthews, 115 sqq.

[2] Migne, 215, 1493, etc.

few months after their marriage, and took the fair Agnes
of Meran in her stead.   The French bishops, on the plea of
remote consanguinity, justified the divorce.   But Innocent,
listening to the appeals of Ingeborg, and placing France
under the interdict, forced the king to take her back.[1]

The Christian states of the Spanish peninsula felt the
pontiff's strong hand.   The kingdom of Leon was kept under
the interdict five years till Alfonso IX. consented to dismiss
his wife on account of blood relationship.   Pedro, king of
Aragon, a model of Spanish chivalry, received his crown
at Rome in 1204 and made his realm a fief of the Apostolic
see.   Sancho, king of the newly risen kingdom of Portugal,
was defeated in his effort to break away from the pope's
suzerainty.

In the North, Sweden accepted Innocent's decision in favor
of the house of Schwerker, and the Danish king, who was
attempting to reduce the tribes along the Baltic to Christianity, was protected by the pope's threat of interdict upon
all molesting his realm.   The king of England was humbled
to the dust by Innocent's word.   To the king of Scotland a
legate was sent and a valuable sword.   Even Iceland is said
to have been the subject of Innocent's thought and action.

In the Southeast, Johannitius of Bulgaria received from
Innocent his crown after bowing before his rebuke for having
ventured to accept it from Philip of Swabia.   Ottoker, prince
of Bohemia, was anointed by the papal legate, and Emmeric
of Hungary made a vow to lead a crusade, which his brother
Andrew executed.   Thus all the states of Europe west of
Russia were made to feel the supremacy of the papal power.
The conquest of Constantinople and the Holy Land, as we
shall see, occupied an equal share of attention from this tireless and masterful ruler, and the establishment of the Latin
Empire of Constantinople, 1205, was regarded as a signal
triumph for the papal policy.

[1] The pope legitimatized the children of Agnes, who died in 1201.

§ 39. *Innocent and King John of England.*

" This royal throne of kings, this sceptr'd isle,
This earth of majesty, this seat of Mars,
This other Eden, demi-paradise ;
This fortress, built by nature for herself,
Against infection, and the hand of war ;
This happy breed of men, this little world,
This precious stone set in the silver sea,
Which serves it in the office of a wall,
Or as a moat defensive to a house,
Against the envy of less happier lands ;
This blessed plot, this earth, this realm, this England,
This nurse, this teeming womb of royal kings,
Fear'd by their breed, and famous by their birth."
                    —Shakespeare, *Richard II.*, Act II. Sc. 1.

ADDITIONAL LITERATURE. — The *Chronicle* of ROGER OF WENDOVER (the first of the St. Alban annalists) and the revision and continuation of the same by MATTHEW PARIS (a monk of St. Alban's, the last and greatest of the monastic historians of England), ed. by H. R. LUARD in Rolls Series, 7 vols. London, 1872–1883, vol. II. Engl. trans. of Wendover by J. A. GILES, Bohn's Lib. 2 vols. London, 1849 ; of M. Paris by GILES, 3 vols. London, 1852–1854.—*Memorials* of WALTER OF COVENTRY, ed. by STUBBS, 2 vols. 1872 sq. — RADULPH OF COGGESHALL : *Chronicon Anglicanum*, ed. by J. STEVENSON, 1875. *The Annals of Waverley, Dunstable, and Burton*, all in the Rolls Series. — W. STUBBS : *The Constitutional Hist. of England*, 6th ed. 3 vols. Oxford, 1897, and *Select Charters*, etc., 8th ed. Oxford, 1900, pp. 270–306. — GEE and HARDY : *Documents*, London, 1896. —R. GNEIST : *Hist. of the Engl. Court*, Engl. trans. 2 vols. London, 1886, vol. I. 294–332. — E. GÜTSCHOW : *Innocent III. und England*, Munich, 1904, pp. 198. — The Histories of LINGARD (R. C.), GREEN, MILMAN, FREEMAN (*Norman Conquest*, vol. V.). — For Stephen Langton, DEAN HOOK : *Lives of the Abp. of Canterbury*, and art. *Langton*, in *Dict. of Natl. Biog.* — Also W. HUNT, art. *John*, in *Dict. of Natl. Biog.* XXIX. 402–417. — Sir JAMES H. RAMSEY : *The Angevin Empire, 1154–1216*, London, 1903. He calls John a brutal tyrant, hopelessly depraved, without ability in war or politics.

Under Innocent, England comes, if possible, into greater prominence in the history of the papacy than during the controversy in the reign of Alexander III., a generation before. Then the English actors were Henry II. and Thomas à Becket. Now they are Henry's son John and Becket's successor Stephen Langton. The pope was victorious, inflicting the deepest humiliation upon the English king; but he afterwards lost the advantage he had gained by supporting John against his barons and denouncing the Magna Charta of English popular rights. The controversy forms one of the most interesting episodes of English history.

John, surnamed Sansterre or Lackland, 1167–1216, succeeded his brother Richard I. on the throne, 1199. A man of decided ability and rapid in action but of ignoble spirit, low morals, and despotic temper, he brought upon his realm such disgrace as England before or since has not suffered. His reign was a succession of wrongs and insults to the English people and the English church.

John had joined Richard in a revolt against their father, sought to displace his brother on the throne during his captivity after the Third Crusade, and was generally believed by contemporaries to have put to death his brother Geoffrey's son, Arthur of Brittany, who would have been Richard's successor if the law of primogeniture had been followed. He lost Normandy, Anjou, Maine, and Aquitaine to the English. Perjury was no barrier to the accomplishment of his plans. He set aside one wife and was faithless to another. No woman was too well born to be safe against his advances. He plundered churches and convents to pay his debts and satisfy his avarice, and yet he never undertook a journey without hanging charms around his neck.[1]

Innocent came into collision with John over the selection of a successor to Archbishop Hubert of Canterbury, who

[1] The contemporary annalists know no words too black to describe John's character. Lingard says, "John stands before us polluted with meanness, cruelty, perjury, murder, and unbridled licentiousness." Green, after quoting the words "foul as hell is, hell itself is defiled with the foul presence of John," says, "In his inner soul John was the worst outcome of the Angevins. . . . But with the wickedness of his race he inherited its profound abilities." III. chap. I. Hunt, in *Dict. of Natl. Biog.*, XXIX. 406, uses these words, "He was mean, false, vindictive, abominably cruel, and scandalously immoral."

died 1205.[1] The monks of Canterbury, exercising an ancient privilege, chose Reginald one of their number. With the king's support, a minority proceeded to another election and chose the king's nominee, John de Grey, bishop of Norwich. John was recognized by the suffragan-bishops and put into possession by the king.

An appeal was made by both parties to Rome, Reginald appearing there in person. After a delay of a year, Innocent set aside both elections and ordered the Canterbury monks, present in Rome, to proceed to the choice of another candidate. The choice fell upon Stephen Langton, cardinal of Chrysogonus. Born on English soil, Stephen was a man of indisputable learning and moral worth. He had studied in Paris and won by his merits prebends in the cathedral churches of Paris and York. The metropolitan dignity could have been intrusted to no shoulders more worthy of wearing it.[2] While he has no title to saintship like à Becket, or to theological genius like Anselm, Langton will always occupy a place among the foremost of England's primates as a faithful administrator and the advocate of English popular liberties.

The new archbishop received consecration at the pope's own hand, June 17, 1207, and held his office till his death, 1228.[3] The English king met the notification with fierce resistance, confiscated the property of the Canterbury chapter, and expelled the monks as guilty of treason. Innocent replied with the threat of the interdict. The king swore by

[1] He had before come into collision with John over the harsh treatment of the archbishop of Dublin. Works of Innocent III., *Reg.*, VI. 63 ; Migne, 215, 61 ; Potthast, 167.

[2] His scholarly tastes are attested by his sermons, poems, and comments on books of the Bible which still exist in manuscript in the libraries of Oxford, Cambridge, Lambeth, and of France. He is falsely credited by some with having been the first to divide the entire Bible into chapters. See Hook, *Archbishops of Canterbury*, II. 678.

[3] Innocent, in his letter to John of May 26, 1207, declared he would turn neither to the right nor to the left in confirming the election. Potthast, 264.

God's teeth[1] to follow the censure, if pronounced, with the mutilation of every Italian in the realm appointed by Innocent, and the expulsion of all the prelates and clergy.   The sentence was published by the bishops of London, Ely, and Worcester, March 22, 1208.[2]   They then fled the kingdom.

The interdict at once took effect, casting a deep gloom over the nation.   The church bells remained unrung. The church buildings were closed.   The usual ministrations of the priesthood remained unperformed.   The great doors of the monasteries were left unopened, and worshippers were only admitted by secret passages.   Penance was inflicted upon the innocent as well as the erring.   Women, after childbirth, presented themselves for purification outside the church walls.   The dead were refused burial in consecrated ground, and the service of the priest was withheld.

John, although he had seen Philip Augustus bend under a similar censure, affected unconcern, and retaliated by confiscating the property of the higher clergy and convents and turning the inmates out of doors with little more than the clothes on their backs.   The concubines of the priests were forcibly removed and purchased their ransom at heavy expense.   A Welshman accused of murdering a priest was ordered by the king dismissed with the words, " Let him go, he has killed my enemy."   The relatives of the fugitive bishops were thrown into prison.

In 1209 Innocent added to the interdict the solemn sentence of the personal anathema against the king.[3]   The bishops who remained in England did not dare publish it, "becoming like dumb dogs not daring to bark."[4]   John persisted in his defiant mood, continued to eke out his vengeance upon the innocent, and sought to divert the attention of his subjects

---

[1] This and the expression "by God's feet" were John's favorite forms of objurgation.

[2] See Migne, 217, 190; Potthast, 286.

[3] Potthast, 316.

[4] A favorite expression of Matthew Paris.

by negotiations and wars with Scotland, Ireland, and Wales. Geoffrey, archdeacon of Norwich, who had been in his service and now felt he could no longer so remain, was thrown into prison and there allowed to languish to death, covered from shoulders to feet with a cope of lead.[1]

One more weapon lay in the pope's power.   In 1212 John was declared unworthy of his throne, and deposed.   His subjects were absolved from the obligation of allegiance, and Christian princes were summoned to execute the sentence and take the crown.   Gregory VII. had resorted to the same precarious measure with Henry IV. and been defeated.   The bull was published at Soissons by Langton and the exiled bishops.   Philip of France was quick to respond to the summons and collected an army.   But the success of the English fleet checked the fear of an immediate invasion of the realm.

The nation's suspense, however, was taxed almost beyond the point of endurance.   The king's arbitrary taxes and his amours with the wives and daughters of the barons aroused their determined hatred.   Pressed from different sides, John suddenly had a meeting at Dover with the pope's special envoy, the subdeacon Pandulf.[2]   The hermit, Peter of Wakefield, had predicted that within three days of Ascension Day the king would cease to reign.   Perhaps not without dread of the prediction, and not without irony to checkmate the plans of the French monarch, John gave in his submis-

---

[1] Another example of John's unspeakable cruelty was his treatment of a rich Jew of Bristol upon whom he had made a demand for 10,000 marks. On his refusing, John ordered ten teeth to be taken out, one each day.   The executioner dentist began with the molars.   The sufferer held out till he had been served this way seven times.   He then yielded, giving up the money, which, as Matthew Paris says, he might have done seven days before, thus saving himself all his agony.   Luard's ed., II. 528.

[2] Shakespeare is responsible for the popular mistake which makes Pandulf a cardinal. *King John*, Act III. Sc. 1.   He served as legate in England, 1217–1221.   The official documents call him "subdeacon and familiar to our lord the pope Innocent."

sion, and on May 15, 1213, on bended knee, delivered up to Pandulf his kingdom and consented to receive it back again as a papal fief.   Five months later the act was renewed in the presence of Nicolas, cardinal-archbishop of Tusculum, who had been sent to England with legatine authority.   In the document which John signed and swore to keep, he blasphemously represented himself as imitating him "who humbled himself for us even unto death."   This notorious paper ran as follows: —

"We do freely offer and grant to God and the holy Apostles Peter and Paul and the holy Roman Church, our mother, and to our Lord the pope Innocent and his Catholic successors, the whole realm of England and the whole realm of Ireland with all their rights and appurtenances for the remission of our sins and those of all our race, as well quick as dead; and from now receiving back and holding these, as a feudal dependant, from God and the Roman Church, do and swear fealty for them to our Lord the pope Innocent and his Catholic successors and the Roman Church." [1]

John bound himself and England for all time to pay, in addition to the usual Peter's pence, 1000 marks annually to the Apostolic see, 700 for England and 300 for Ireland. The king's signature was witnessed by the archbishop of Dublin, the bishop of Norwich, and eleven noblemen.   John also promised to reimburse the outlawed bishops, the amount finally settled upon being 40,000 marks.

Rightly does Matthew Paris call this the "detestable and lamentable charter." [2]   But although national abasement could scarcely further go, it is probable that the sense of shame with which after generations have regarded John's act was only imperfectly felt by that generation of Englishmen.[3]   As a political measure it succeeded, bringing as it

[1] Potthast, 416.   The Latin in Matthew Paris, Luard's ed. II. 541-546; a translation is given by Gee and Hardy, 75-79.

[2] IV. 479, *carta detestabilis quam lacrimabilis memoriæ Johannes infeliciter confecit.*

[3] Henry II. had become the feudatory of Alexander III., and Richard I., after resigning his crown to the emperor, had held it for the payment of a yearly rent.   Lingard offers extenuating considerations for John's surrender, which, however, he denominates "certainly a disgraceful act."

did keen disappointment to the warlike king of France. The interdict was revoked in 1214, after having been in force more than six years.

The victory of Innocent was complete. But in after years the remembrance of the dishonorable transaction encouraged steadfast resistance to the papal rule in England. The voice of Robert Grosseteste was lifted up against it, and Wyclif became champion of the king who refused to be bound by John's pledge. Writing to one of John's successors, the emperor Frederick II. called upon him to remember the humiliation of his predecessor John and with other Christian princes resist the intolerable encroachments of the Apostolic see.

§ 40. *Innocent and Magna Charta.*

An original manuscript of the Magna Charta, shrivelled with age and fire, but still showing the royal seal, is preserved in the British Museum. A facsimile is given in the official edition of the Statutes of the Realm. Stubbs gives the Latin text in Select Charters, etc., 296–306.

In his treatment of the Great Charter, the venerable instrument of English popular rights, Innocent, with monarchical instinct, turned to the side of John and against the cause of popular liberty. Stephen Langton, who had released John from the ban of excommunication, espoused the popular cause, thereby incurring the condemnation of the pope. The agreement into which the barons entered to resist the king's despotism was treated by him with delay and subterfuge. Rebellion and civil war followed. As he had before been unscrupulous in his treatment of the Church, so now to win support he made fulsome religious promises he probably had no intention of keeping. To the clergy he granted freedom of election in the case of all prelates, greater and less. He also made a vow to lead a crusade. After the battle of Bouvines, John found himself forced to return to England,

and was compelled by the organized strength of the barons to meet them at Runnymede, an island in the Thames near Windsor, where he signed and swore to keep the Magna Charta, June 15, 1215.

This document, with the Declaration of Independence, the most important contract in the civil history of the English-speaking peoples, meant defined law as against uncertain tradition and the arbitrary will of the monarch. It was the first act of the people, nobles, and Church in combination, a compact of Englishmen with the king. By it the sovereign agreed that justice should be denied or delayed to no one, and that trial should be by the peers of the accused. No taxes were to be levied without the vote of the common council of the realm, whose meetings were fixed by rule. The single clause bearing directly upon the Church confirmed the freedom of ecclesiastical elections.

After his first paroxysms of rage, when he gnawed sticks and straw like a madman,[1] John called to his aid Innocent, on the ground that he had attached his seal under compulsion. In fact, he had yielded to the barons with no intention of keeping his oath. The pope made the fatal mistake of taking sides with perjured royalty against the reasonable demands of the nation. In two bulls[2] he solemnly released John from his oath, declaring that "the enemy of the human race had, by his crafty arts, excited the barons against him." He asserted that the "wicked audacity of the barons tended to the contempt of the Apostolic see, the detriment of kingly prerogative, the disgrace of the English nation, and the endangering of the cross." He praised John for his Christian submission to the will of the supreme head of Christendom, and the pledge of annual tribute, and for his vow to lead a crusade. As for the document itself, he "utterly reprobated and condemned it" as "a low and base instrument, yea, truly wicked and deserving to be reprobated by all, especially

---

[1] M. Paris, Luard's ed. II. 611.   [2] Aug. 24, 1215, Potthast, 435.

because the king's assent was secured by force."[1] Upon
pain of excommunication he forbade its observance by the
king, and pronounced it "null and void for all time."[2]

The sentence of excommunication which Innocent fulminated against the refractory barons, Langton refused to publish. For his disobedience the pope suspended him from his
office, Nov. 4, 1215, and he was not allowed to resume
it till 1219, when Innocent had been in his grave three years.
London, which supported the popular cause, was placed
under the interdict, and the prelates of England who took
the popular side Innocent denounced "as worse than Saracens, worse than those open enemies of the cross."[3]

The barons, in self-defence, called upon the Dauphin of
France to accept the crown. He landed in England,
but was met by the papal ban.[4] During the struggle
Innocent died, but his policy was continued by his successor.
Three months later, Oct. 19, 1216, John died at Newark,

[1] *Compositionen hujusmodi reprobamus penitus et damnamus . . . com-
positio non solum sit vilis et turpis, verum etiam illicita et iniqua ut
merito sit ab omnibus reprobanda.* M. Paris, Luard's ed., II. 619 sq. Another
ground given by Innocent for annulling the document was that he as England's overlord had not been consulted before the king's signature was
attached.

[2] The language is the strongest: *tam cartam quam obligationes . . . irri-
tantes penitus et cassantes, ut nullo unquam tempore aliquam habeant firmi-
tatem.* M. Paris, Luard's ed. II. 619. See Hurter, II. 656 sq. Some excuse
has been found by advocates of papal infallibility for this fierce sentence upon
the ground that Innocent was condemning the mode by which the king's consent was obtained. Innocent adduces three considerations, the conspiracy of
the barons to force the king, their disregard of his Crusading vow, and the neglect of all parties to consult the pope as overlord. He condemns, it is true, the
document as a document, and it has been said the contents were not aimed at.
Innocent's mistake and official offence were that, passing by entirely, the
merits of the Charter, he should have espoused the despotism of the iniquitous
king.

[3] Potthast, 437 ; M. Paris, in Luard, II. 627. About the same time at
John's request, Innocent annulled the election of Simon Langton, Stephen's
brother, to the see of York.

[4] Thomas Fuller remarks that "the commonness of these curses caused
them to be contemned, so that they were a fright to few, a mock to many,
and a hurt to none."

after suffering the loss of his goods in crossing the Wash.
He was thrown into a fever, but the probable cause of his
death was excess in eating and drinking.[1] He was buried at his
own request in Worcester cathedral.   In his last moments
he received the sacrament and commended his children to
the protection of the pope, who had stood by him in his
last conflict.

§ 41. *The Fourth Lateran Council*, 1215.

LITERATURE. — Works of Innocent, Migne, 217. — MANSI, xxii. — LABBÆUS,
xi. — POTTHAST, *Regesta*, I. 437 sqq., gives a summary of the canons
of the council. — HEFELE-KNÖPFLER, V. 872 sqq. — HURTER, II. 538
sqq. — LEA : *Hist. of the Inquisition, passim.*

The Fourth Lateran, otherwise known as the Twelfth
Œcumenical Council, was the closing act of Innocent's pontificate, and marks the zenith of the papal theocracy.   In his
letter of convocation,[2] the pope announced its object to be
the reconquest of Palestine and the betterment of the
Church.   The council was held in the Lateran and had three
sittings, Nov. 11, 20, 30, 1215.   It was the most largely
attended of the synods held up to that time in the West.
The attendance included 412 bishops, 800 abbots and priors,
and a large number of delegates representing absent prelates.
There were also present representatives of the emperor
Frederick II., the emperor Henry of Constantinople, and the

---

[1] Roger of Wendover says he surfeited himself with peaches and new
cider. M. Paris, Luard's ed., II. 667. Shakespeare, following a later tradition, represents him as dying of poison administered by a monk: —
  "The king, I fear is poisoned by a monk,

              *   *   *   *   *   *   *

  It is too late; the life of all his blood
  Is touched corruptibly ; and his pure brain
  (Which some suppose the soul's frail dwelling-house)
  Doth, by the idle comments that it makes,
  Foretell the ending of mortality."
                                   — *King John*, Act V. Sc. 6 sq.
[2] April 19, 1213.

kings of England, France, Aragon, Hungary, Jerusalem, and other crowned heads.[1]

The sessions were opened with a sermon by the pope on Luke 22 : 15, " With desire have I desired to eat this passover with you before I suffer." It was a fanciful interpretation of the word "passover," to which a threefold sense was given : a physical sense referring to the passage of Jerusalem from a state of captivity to a state of liberty, a spiritual sense referring to the passage of the Church from one state to a better one, and a heavenly sense referring to the transition from the present life to the eternal glory. The deliverances are grouped under seventy heads, and a special decree bearing upon the recovery of Jerusalem. The headings concern matters of doctrine and ecclesiastical and moral practice. The council's two most notable acts were the definition of the dogma of transubstantiation and the establishment of the institution of the Inquisition against heretics.

The doctrinal decisions, contained in the first two chapters, give a comprehensive statement of the orthodox faith as it concerns the nature of God, the Incarnation, the unity of the Church, and the two greater sacraments. Here transubstantiation is defined as the doctrine of the eucharist in the universal Church, " outside of which there is no possibility of salvation."[2]

The council expressly condemned the doctrine of Joachim of Flore, that the substance of the Father, Son, and Spirit is not a real entity, but a collective entity in the sense that a collection of men is called one people, and a collection of

---

[1] The invitation included the prelates of the East and West, Christian emperors and kings, the grand-masters of the Military Orders, and the heads of monastic establishments.

[2] *In qua idem ipse sacerdos et sacrificium Jesus Christus, cujus corpus et sanguis in sacramento altaris sub speciebus panis et vini veraciter continentur, transubstantiatis pane in corpus, et vino in sanguinem*, etc. Mansi, XXII. 982; Mirbt, *Quellen*, 133.

believers one Church. It approved the view of Peter the
Lombard whom Joachim had opposed on the ground that his
definition would substitute a quaternity for the trinity in
the Godhead.[1]

Amaury of Bena, a teacher in Paris accused of pantheistic teachings, was also condemned by name. He had
been accused and appeared before the pope at Rome in 1204,
and recalled his alleged heresy.[2] He or his scholars taught
that every one in whom the Spirit of God is, becomes united
with the body of Christ and cannot sin.

The treatment of heretics received elaborate consideration in the important third decree.[3] The ecclesiastical and
moral regulations were the subject of sixty-seven decrees.
The rank of the patriarchal sees is fixed, Rome having the
first place.[4] It was an opportune moment for an array of
these dignitaries, as Innocent had established a Latin succession in the Eastern patriarchates which had not already been
filled by his predecessors. To avoid the confusion arising
from the diversity of monastic rules, the establishment of
monastic orders was thenceforth forbidden.[5]

The clergy are warned against intemperance and incon-
tinence and forbidden the chase, hunting dogs and falcons,
attendance upon theatrical entertainments, and executions,
duelling, and frequenting inns. Prescriptions are given
for their dress. Confession is made compulsory at least
once a year, and imprisonment fixed as the punishment
of priests revealing the secrets of the confessional. The
tenure of more than one benefice is forbidden except by the

---

[1] The Lombard had defined the substance of the three persons as a real
entity, *quædam summa res.*

[2] See Hauck, art. *Amalrich,* in Herzog, I. 432 sq.

[3] See chapters on the Inquisition and the Cathari.

[4] The patriarchs of Jerusalem and Constantinople, of the Latin succession,
were conspicuous at the council, and also Antioch by a representative, the
Melchisite patriarch of Alexandria, and the Maronite patriarch.

[5] Chapter XIII.

pope's dispensation.   New relics are forbidden as objects of
worship, except as they might receive the approbation of the
pope.   Physicians are bidden, upon threat of excommunication, to urge their patients first of all to summon a priest, as
the well-being of the soul is of more value than the health
of the body.   Jews and Saracens are enjoined to wear a different dress from the Christians, lest unawares carnal intercourse be had between them.   The Jews are bidden to keep
within doors during passion week and excluded from holding civil office.[1]

The appointment of a new crusade was the council's last
act, and it was set to start in 1217.   Christians were commanded to refrain from all commercial dealings with the
Saracens for four years.   To all contributing to the crusade,
as well as to those participating in it, full indulgence was
promised, and added eternal bliss.[2]   Another important
matter which was settled, as it were in a committee room of
the council, was the appeal of Raymund VI., count of Toulouse, for redress from the rapacity of Simon de Montfort,
the fierce leader of the crusade against the Albigenses in
Southern France.

The doctrinal statements and ecclesiastical rules bear
witness to the new conditions upon which the Church had
entered, the Latin patriarchs being in possession in the East,
and heresy threatening its unity in Southern France and
other parts of the West.

Innocent III. survived the great council only a few months
and died scarcely fifty-six years old, without having outlived
his authority or his fame.   He had been fortunate in all his
undertakings.   The acts of statecraft, which brought Europe
to his feet, were crowned in the last scene at the Lateran

---

[1] A repetition of the decrees of the synod of Toledo, 581.

[2] *Plenam suorum peccaminum de quibus fuerint corde contriti et ore confessi veniam indulgemus et in retributione justorum salutis eternæ polli-
cemur augmentum.*

N

Council by the pious concern of the priest. To his succes-
sors he bequeathed a continent united in allegiance to the
Holy See and a Church strengthened in its doctrinal unity.
Notwithstanding his great achievements combining mental
force and moral purpose, the Church has found no place for
Innocent among its canonized saints.

The following are a few testimonies to his greatness : —

Gregorovius declares[1] that, although he was

"Not a creative genius like Gregory I. and Gregory VII., he was one of the
most important figures of the Middle Ages, a man of earnest, sterling, austere
intellect, a consummate ruler, a statesman of penetrating judgment, a high-
minded priest filled with religious fervor, and at the same time with an
unbounded ambition and appalling force of will, a true idealist on the papal
throne, yet an entirely practical monarch and a cool-headed lawyer. . . . No
pope has ever had so lofty and yet so real consciousness of his power as Innocent III., the creator and destroyer of emperors and kings."

Ranke says :[2] —

"A superstitious reverence such as Friedrich Hurter renders to him in his
remarkable book I am not at all able to accord. Thus much, however, is certain. He stands in the foremost rank of popes, having world-wide significance.
The task which he placed before himself he was thoroughly equal to. Leaving out a few dialectic subtleties, one will not find in him anything that is
really small. In him was fulfilled the transition of the times."

Baur gives this opinion :[3] —

"With Innocent III. the papacy reached its height and in no other period
of its long history did it enjoy such an undisturbed peace and such a glorious
development of its power and splendor. He was distinguished as no other in
this high place not only by all the qualities of the ruler but by personal virtues, by high birth and also by mind, culture, and learning."[4]

---

[1] V : 102 sq. Gibbon, ch. LIX, after acknowledging Innocent's talents
and virtues, has this criticism of two of the most far-reaching acts of his
reign : "Innocent may boast of the two most signal triumphs over sense and
humanity, the establishment of transubstantiation, and the origin of the Inquisition."

[2] *Weltgeschichte*, viii : 334.

[3] *Geschichte des Mittelalters*, p. 220.

[4] For judgments of mediæval authors, see Potthast, *Regesta*, 461. The
contemporaneous author of the *Gesta Innocentii*, Migne, 214, p. xviii., thus
describes Innocent: "Fuit vir perspicacis ingenii et tenacis memoriæ, in divinis
et humanis litteris eruditus, sermone tam vulgari quam litterali disertus, ex-
ercitatus in cantilena et psalmodia, statura mediocris et decorus aspectu,

Hagenbach:[1] —

" Measured by the standard of the papacy, Innocent is beyond controversy the greatest of all the popes. Measured by the eternal law of the Gospel of Jesus Christ, that which here seems great and mighty in the eyes of the world, seems little in the kingdom of heaven, and amongst those things which call forth wonder and admiration, only that will stand which the Spirit of God, who never wholly withdraws from the Church, wrought in his soul. How far such operation went on, and with what result, who but God can know? He alone is judge."

---

medius inter prodigalitatem et avaritiam, sed in eleemosynis et victualibus magis largus, et in aliis magis parcus, nisi cum necessitatis articulus exigebat severus contra rebelles et contumaces, sed benignus erga humiles et devotos; fortis et stabilis, magnanimus et astutus; fidei defensor, et hæresis expugnator; in justitia rigidus, sed in misericordia pius; humilis in prosperis, et patiens in adversis; naturæ tamen aliquantulum indignantis, sed facile ignoscentis."

[1] *Kirchengeschichte des Mittelalters*, ch. **XIX.**

CHAPTER VI.

THE PAPACY FROM THE DEATH OF INNOCENT III. TO BONIFACE VIII. 1216–1294.

LITERATURE: The *Chronicles* of this period, *e.g.* M. PARIS, ed. by LUARD—the Franciscan SALIMBENE, ed. by A. BERTANI, Parma, 1857; Engl. trans. by COULTON, Lond., 1906. — RICHARD A ST. GERMANO: *chronicon rerum per orbem gestarum, 1189–1243;* the chronicon *Placentinum* and chron. *de rebus in Italia gestis,* ed. by HUILLARD-BRÉHOLLES, Paris, 1856. For Honorius III., *Opera omnia,* ed. by HORAY in *Medii œvi bibliotheca patristica,* I.-V., Paris, 1879–1883, and *Regesta,* ed. by the order of Leo XIII., by P. PRESUTTI, Rome, 1888, 1 vol. For Gregory IX., *Opera omnia,* Antwerp, 1572. Fifteen volumes of Gregory's letters are in MS. in the Vatican: *Les Registres de Grégoire IX., 1227–1235, Recueil des bulles publiées d'après les MSS. originaux du Vatican par* L. AUVRAY, Paris, 1896. For Innocent IV., *Registres d'Innocent IV.,* ed. by E. BERGER, 3 vols. Paris, 1884-1897. — The *Regesta* of POTTHAST and BÖHMER.—*Lives of the Popes,* in Muratori (two), and by PLATINA. — MANSI: *Councils,* XXIII.

C. HÖFLER: *Kaiser Friedrich II.,* Munich, 1844.—ED. WINKELMANN: *Gesch. Kaisers Friedrichs II.,* etc., 2 vols., Berlin and Reval, 1863–1865. — T. L. KINGTON: *Hist. of Fred. II., Emp. of the Romans,* 2 vols., London, 1862.—F. W. SCHIRRMACHER: *Kaiser Fried. II.,* 3 vols. Götting., 1859–1865. — HUILLARD-BRÉHOLLES: *Historia diplomatica Friderici II.,* etc., 6 vols., two parts each, Paris, 1852–1861. A great work. Vol. I. gives the life of Frederick, the other volumes documents. — HUILLARD-BRÉHOLLES: *Vie et correspondance de la Vigne, ministre de l'empéreur Fred. II.,*Paris, 1866. — E. WINKELMANN: *Kaiser Friedrich II.,* 2 vols. Leipzig, 1896 sq. — P. BALAN: *Storia di Gregorio IX. e di suoi tempi,* 3 vols., Modena, 1872 sq. —CHAMBRIER: *Die letzten Hohenstaufen u.das Papstthum,* Basel, 1876. — RAUMER: *Gesch. der Hohenstaufen,* 5th ed., Leipzig, 1878. Vol. V.—J. ZELLER: *L'emp. Fred. II. et la chute de l'emp. Germ. du moyen âge,* Paris, 1885.—J. FELTEN: *Papst Gregor IX.,* Freib. im Br., 1886. — UGO BALZANI: *The Popes and the Hohenstaufen,* London, 1888.—C. KÖHLER: *D. Verhältniss Fried. II. zu den Päpsten seiner Zeit.,* Breslau, 1888. — J. CLAUSEN: *Papst Honorius III.,* Bonn, 1895. — H. FISHER: *The Mediæval Empire,* 2 vols. London, 1898. — F. FEHLING: *Fried. II. und die römischen Kardinäle,* Berlin, 1901. — H. KRABBO: *Die Besetzung der deutschen Bisthümer unter der Regierung Kaiser Fried. II., 1212–1250,* Berlin, 1901. — TH. FRANZ: *Der grosse*

Kampf zwischen Kaiserthum und Papstthum zur Zeit des Hohenstaufen, Fried. II., Berlin, 1903. Not important. — W. KNEBEL : *Kaiser Fried. II. und Papst Honorius III.*, *1220–1227*, Münster, 1905, pp. 151. — HEFELE, V. — WATTENBACH, 196–211. — GREGOROVIUS, V. — RANKE, VIII. — FREEMAN : *The Emp. Fred. II.* in his *Hist. Essays*, 1st series, pp. 283–313, London, 1871. — Art. *Fred. II.*, by FUNK, in Wetzer-Welte, IV. 2029–2035, and arts. in Herzog, *Gregory IX.*, by MIRBT, and *Honorius III.*, and *Innocent IV.*, by SCHULZ, with the copious lit. there given. Also, *Das Briefbuch des Thomas von Gasta, Justitiars Fried. II.* in *Quellen u. Forschungen aus italienischen Archiven und Bibliotheken,* Rome, 1895.

§ 42.   *The Papal Conflict with Frederick II. Begun.*

BETWEEN the death of Innocent III. and the election of Boniface VIII., a period of eighty years, sixteen popes sat on the throne, several of whom were worthy successors of the greatest of the pontiffs.   The earlier half of the period, 1216–1250, was filled with the gigantic struggle between the papacy and Frederick II., emperor of Germany and king of Sicily.   The latter half, 1250–1294, was marked by the establishment of peace between the papacy and empire, and the dominance of the French, or Norman, influence over the papacy.

Scarcely was Innocent in his grave when Frederick II. began to play his distinguished rôle, and to engage the papacy in its last great struggle with the empire — a desperate struggle, as it proved to be, in which the empire was at last completely humbled.   The struggle kept Europe in turmoil for nearly forty years, and was waged with three popes, — Honorius III., Gregory IX., and Innocent IV., the last two, men of notable ability.   During all this time Frederick was the most conspicuous figure in Christendom.   The struggle was carried on not only in the usual ways of diplomacy and arms, but by written appeals to the court of European opinion.

Frederick II., the grandson of Frederick Barbarossa, was born near Ancona, 1194.   His father, Henry VI., had joined Sicily to the empire by his marriage with the Norman prin-

cess Constance, through whom Frederick inherited the
warm blood of the South. By preference and training, as
well as birth, he was a thorough Italian. He tarried on
German soil only long enough to insure his crown and to
put down the rebellion of his son.[1] He preferred to hold his
court at Palermo, which in his letters he called "the Happy
City." The Romans elected him king in 1196, and at his
father's death a year later he became king of Sicily. The
mother soon followed, and by her will "the child of Apulia,"
as Frederick was called, a boy then in his fourth year, passed
under the guardian care of Innocent III. After Otto's star
had set, he was crowned king at Frankfurt, 1212, and at
Aachen, 1215. Frederick was not twenty when Innocent's
career came to an end.

Honorius III., 1216–1227, was without the ambition or
genius of his predecessor Innocent III. He confirmed the
rules and witnessed the extraordinary growth of the two great
mendicant orders of St. Francis and St. Dominic. He
crowned Peter of Courtenay, emperor of Byzantium, the
only Byzantine emperor to receive his crown in Rome.[2] The
pope's one passion was the deliverance of Jerusalem. To
accomplish this, he was forced to look to Frederick. To induce him to fulfil the vow made at his coronation, in 1215,
to lead a crusade, was the main effort of his pontificate.
The year 1217, the date set for the crusade to start, passed
by. Honorius fixed date after date with Frederick, but the
emperor had other plans and found excuses for delay. In
1220 he and his wife Constantia received the imperial crown
at the hands of the pope in Rome.[3] For the second time

---

[1] Ranke, VIII. 337, calls him a foreigner on German soil.

[2] The coronation took place outside the walls of the city. Peter died in
prison on his way to Constantinople.

[3] The coronation ceremonies passed off amidst the general good will of the
Roman populace and were interrupted by a single disturbance, a dispute over
a dog between the ambassadors of Florence and Pisa which ultimately involved
the cities in war. Villani, VI. 2.

Frederick took the cross. He also seemed to give proof of piety by ratifying the privileges of the Church, announcing his determination to suppress heresy, and exempting all churches and clerics from taxation. In the meantime his son Henry had been elected king of the Romans, and by that act and the pope's subsequent ratification the very thing was accomplished which it had been Innocent's shrewd policy to prevent; namely, the renewal of the union of the empire and the kingdom of Sicily in one hand. Frederick was pursuing his own course, but to appease Honorius he renewed the pledge whereby Sicily was to remain a fief of the papal see.

The fall of Damietta,[1] in 1221, was adapted to fire a sincere crusader's zeal; but Frederick was too much engaged in pleasure and absorbed in his scheme for extending his power in Italy to give much attention to the rescue of the holy places. In hope of inflaming his zeal and hastening the departure of the crusade, Honorius encouraged the emperor's marriage with Iolanthe, daughter of John of Brienne, king of Jerusalem, and heiress of the crown.[2] The nuptials were no sooner celebrated than Frederick assumed the title of king of Jerusalem; but he continued to show no sign of making haste. His aggravating delays were enough to wear out a more amiable disposition than even Honorius possessed. A final agreement was made between them in 1225, which gave the emperor a respite of two years more, and he swore upon penalty of excommunication to set forth October, 1227. Four months before the date appointed for the crusade Honorius died.

The last year of Honorius's reign, Frederick entered openly upon the policy which involved him in repeated wars with the papacy and the towns of Northern Italy. He renewed the imperial claims to the Lombard cities. Upon these claims

[1] Damietta, an important harbor in Egypt, had been chosen by the crusaders as their base of operations against Jerusalem and the point from which Jerusalem was to be reached.

[2] On the ground that Iolanthe was immediate heir to the crown through her mother.

the Apostolic see could not look with complacency, for, if realized, they would have made Frederick the sovereign of Italy
and cramped the temporal power of the papacy within a limited and at best an uncertain area.

§ 43. *Gregory IX. and Frederick II.* 1227–1241.

An antagonist of different metal was Gregory IX., 1227–
1241. Innocent III., whose nephew he was, seemed to have
risen again from the grave in him. Although in years he was
more than twice as old as the emperor,[1] Gregory was clearly
his match in vigor of mind and dauntless bravery, and greatly
his superior in moral purpose. In asserting the exorbitant
claims of the papacy he was not excelled by any of the popes.
He was famed for eloquence and was an expert in the canon law.

Setting aside Frederick's spurious pretexts for delaying
the crusade, Gregory in the first days of his pontificate insisted upon his fulfilling his double pledge made at his coronation in 1215 and his coronation as emperor in Rome, 1220.[2]
Frederick at last seemed ready to comply. The crusaders
assembled at Brindisi, and Frederick actually set off to sea
accompanied by the pope's prayers. Within three days of
leaving port the expedition returned, driven back by an
epidemic, as Frederick asserted, or by Frederick's love of
pleasure, as Gregory maintained.

The pope's disappointment knew no bounds. He pronounced against Frederick the excommunication threatened
by Honorius.[3] As the sentence was being read in the church
at Anagni, the clergy dashed their lighted tapers to the

---

[1] His exact age is not known. M. Paris, Luard's ed., IV. 162; Giles's
trans., I. 383, says that at the time of his death he was almost a centenarian
(*fere centenarius*).

[2] Frederick had received the cross at his coronation in Rome from the hand
of Gregory, then Cardinal Ugolino.

[3] "The English chronicler," speaking of the pope's act, uses his favorite
expression, "that he might not be like a dog unable to bark" (*ne canis
videretur non valens latrare*). Luard's ed., M. Paris, III. 145; Giles's trans.
of Roger of Wendover, II. 499.

floor to indicate the emperor's going out into darkness. Gregory justified his action in a letter to the Christian princes, and spoke of Frederick as "one whom the Holy See had educated with much care, suckled at its breast, carried on its shoulders, and whom it has frequently rescued from the hands of those seeking his life, whom it has brought up to perfect manhood at much trouble and expense, exalted to the honors of kingly dignity, and finally advanced to the summit of the imperial station, trusting to have him as a wand of defence and the staff of our old age." He declared the plea of the epidemic a frivolous pretence and charged Frederick with evading his promises, casting aside all fear of God, having no respect for Jesus Christ. Heedless of the censures of the Church, and enticed away to the usual pleasures of his kingdom, he had abandoned the Christian army and left the Holy Land exposed to the infidels.[1]

In a vigorous counter appeal to Christendom, Frederick made a bold protest against the unbearable assumption of the papacy, and pointed to the case of John of England as a warning to princes of what they might expect. "She who calls herself my mother," he wrote, "treats me like a stepmother." He denounced the secularization of the Church, and called upon the bishops and clergy to cultivate the self-denial of the Apostles.

In 1228 the excommunication was repeated and places put under the interdict where the emperor might be. Gregory was not without his own troubles at Rome, from which he was compelled to flee and seek refuge at Perugia.

The same year, as if to show his independence of papal dictation and at the same time the sincerity of his crusading purpose, the emperor actually started upon a crusade, usually called the Fifth Crusade. On being informed of the expedition, the pope excommunicated him for the third time and inhibited the patriarch of Jerusalem and the Military Orders

---

[1] Luard's ed., M. Paris, III. 145 sq. See *Registres*, p. 107.

from giving him aid. The expedition was successful in spite
of the papal malediction, and entering Jerusalem Frederick
crowned himself king in the church of the Holy Sepulchre.
Thus we have the singular spectacle of the chief monarch of
Christendom conducting a crusade in fulfilment of a vow to
two popes while resting under the solemn ban of a third.
Yea, the second crusader who entered the Holy City as a
conqueror, and the last one to do so, was at the time not only
resting under a triple ban, but was excommunicated a fourth
time on his return from his expedition to Europe.   He was
excommunicated for not going, he was excommunicated for
going, and he was excommunicated on coming back, though
it was not in disgrace but in triumph.

The emperor's troops bearing the cross were met on their
return to Europe by the papal army whose banners were inscribed with the keys. Frederick's army was victorious.
Diplomacy, however, prevailed, and emperor and pope dined
together at Anagni (Sept. 1, 1230) and arranged a treaty.

The truce lasted four years, Gregory in the meantime
composing, with the emperor's help, his difficulties with the
municipality of Rome.   Again he addressed Frederick as
"his beloved son in Christ."   But formal terms of endear-
ment did not prevent the renewal of the conflict, this time
over Frederick's resolution to force his authority upon the
Lombard cities.   This struggle engaged him in war with the
papacy from this time forward to his death, 1235–1250. After
crushing the rebellion of his son Henry in the North, and
seeing his second son Conrad crowned, the emperor hastened
south to subdue Lombardy.[1]   " Italy," he wrote in answer to
the pope's protests, 1236, " Italy is my heritage, as all the
world well knows."   His arms seemed to be completely suc-

---

[1] Henry died in an Italian prison.   Conrad, whose mother was Iolanthe,
was nine years old at the time of his coronation.   In 1235 Frederick married
for the third time Isabella, sister of Henry III. of England.   This marriage
explains Frederick's repeated appeals to the clergy and people of England.

cessful by the battle of Cortenuova, 1237.   But Gregory
abated none of his opposition.   " Priests are fathers and
masters of kings and princes," he wrote, "and to them is
given authority over men's bodies as well as over their souls."
It was his policy to thwart at all hazards Frederick's designs
upon upper Italy, which he wanted to keep independent of
Sicily as a protection to the papal state.   The accession of
the emperor's favorite son Enzio to the throne of Sardinia,
through his marriage with the princess Adelasia, was a new
cause of offence to Gregory.[1]   For Sardinia was regarded as
a papal fief, and the pope had not been consulted in the
arrangements leading to the marriage.   And so for the fifth
time, in 1239, Gregory pronounced upon the emperor the
anathema.[2]   The sentence charged him with stirring up
sedition against the Church in Rome from which Gregory had
been forced to flee in the conflicts between the Ghibelline and
Guelf parties, with seizing territory belonging to the Holy
See, and with violence towards prelates and benefices.[3]

A conflict with the pen followed which has a unique place
in the history of the papacy.   Both parties made appeal to public opinion, a thing which was novel up to that time.   The pope
compared [4] the emperor to the beast in the Book of Revelation which "rose out of the sea full of words of blasphemy
and had the feet of a bear and the mouth of a lion, and like
a leopard in its other parts, opens its mouth in blasphemies
against God's name, his dwelling place, and the saints in
heaven.   This beast strives to grind everything to pieces
with his claws and teeth of iron and to trample with his feet
on the universal world."   He accused Frederick of lies and

[1] Potthast, p. 952 ; Huillard-Bréholles, VI. 1, 136.

[2] In view of these repeated fulminations it is no wonder that the papal
legate, Albert of Bohemia, wrote from Bavaria that the clergy did not care
a bean (*faba*) for the sentence of excommunication.   Huillard-Bréholles,
V. 1032 ; Potthast, 908.

[3] The document is given in full in M. Paris, Luard's ed., III. 553 sq.

[4] Bréholles, V. 327–340 ; Paris, III. 590–608.

perjuries, and called him " the son of lies, heaping falsehood
on falsehood, robber, blasphemer, a wolf in sheep's clothing,
the dragon emitting waters of persecution from his mouth like
a river." He made the famous declaration that " as the king
of pestilence, Frederick had openly asserted that the world
had been deceived by three impostors,[1] — Jesus, Moses, and
Mohammed, two of these having died in glory and Jesus having been suspended on the cross. Moreover, he had denied
the possibility of God's becoming incarnate of a virgin."[2]

This extensive document is, no doubt, one of the most
vehement personal fulminations which has ever proceeded
from Rome. Epithets could go no further. It is a proof of
the great influence of Frederick's personality and the growing spirit of democracy in the Italian cities that the emperor
was not wholly shunned by all men and crushed under the
dead weight of such fearful condemnations.

In his retort,[3] not to be behind his antagonist in Scripture
quotations, Frederick compared Gregory to the rider on the
red horse who destroyed peace on the earth. As the pope
had called him a beast, *bestia*, so he would call him a wild
beast, *belua*, antichrist, a second Balaam, who used the prerogative of blessing and cursing for money. He declared
that, as God had placed the greater and lesser lights in the
heavens, so he had placed the priesthood, *sacerdotium*, and
the empire, *imperium*, on the earth. But the pope had
sought to put the second light into eclipse by denying the
purity of Frederick's faith and comparing him to the beast
rising out of the sea. Indignantly denying the accusation
of the three impostors, he declared his faith in the " only

[1] The charge is made in an encyclical of Gregory sent forth between
May 21 and July 1, 1239.

[2] *Iste rex pestilentiæ a tribus barotoribus, ut ejus verbis utamur, scilicet
Christo Jesu, Moyse et Mohameto totum mundum fuisse deceptum, et duobus
eorum in gloria mortuis, ipsum Jesum in ligno suspensum manifeste propo-
nens, etc.*

[3] Bréholles, V. 348 sqq.

Son of God as coequal with the Father and the Holy Spirit, begotten from the beginning of all worlds. Mohammed's body is suspended in the air, but his soul is given over to the torments of hell."

Gregory went further than words and offered to the count of Artois the imperial crown, which at the instance of his brother, Louis IX. of France, the count declined. The German bishops espoused Frederick's cause. On the other hand, the mendicant friars proved true allies of the pope. The emperor drove the papal army behind the walls of Rome. In spite of enemies within the city, the aged pontiff went forth from the Lateran in solemn procession, supplicating deliverance and accompanied by all the clergy, carrying the heads of the Apostles Peter and Paul.[1] When Frederick retreated, it seemed as if the city had been delivered by a miracle. However untenable we may regard the assumptions of the Apostolic see, we cannot withhold admiration from the brave old pope.

Only one source of possible relief was left to Gregory, a council of the whole Church, and this he summoned to meet in Rome in 1241. Frederick was equal to the emergency, and with the aid of his son Enzio checkmated the pope by a manœuvre which, serious as it was for Gregory, cannot fail to appeal to the sense of the ludicrous. The Genoese fleet conveying the prelates to Rome, most of them from France, Northern Italy, and Spain, was captured by Enzio, and the would-be councillors, numbering nearly one hundred and including Cardinal Otto, a papal legate, were taken to Naples and held in prison.[2] In his letter of condolence to the imprisoned dignitaries the pope represents them as awaiting their sentence from the new Pharaoh.[3] Brilliant as was the

---

[1] Bréholles, V. 777 sqq.

[2] M. Paris with his usual vivacity says, " They were heaped together like pigs."

[3] Bréholles, V. 1120–1138 ; G. C. Macaulay gives a lively account of the proceeding in art. *Capture of a General Council*, Engl. Hist. Rev., 1891, pp. 1–17.

coup de main, it was destined to return to trouble the inventor. And the indignity heaped by Frederick upon the prelates was at a later time made a chief charge against him.

Gregory died in the summer of 1241, at an age greater than the age of Leo XIII. at that pope's death. But he died, as it were, with his armor on and with his face turned towards his imperial antagonist, whose army at the time lay within a few hours of the city. He had fought one of the most strenuous conflicts of the Middle Ages. To the last moment his intrepid courage remained unabated. A few weeks before his death he wrote, in sublime confidence in the papal prerogative: " Ye faithful, have trust in God and hear his dispensations with patience. The ship of Peter will for a while be driven through storms and between rocks, but soon, and at a time unexpected, it will rise again above the foaming billows and sail on unharmed, over the placid surface."

The Roman communion owes to Gregory IX. the collection of decretals which became a part of its statute book.[1] He made the Inquisition a permanent institution and saw it enforced in the city of Rome. He accorded the honors of canonization to the founders of the mendicant orders, St. Francis of Assisi and Dominic of Spain.

§ 44. *The First Council of Lyons and the Close of Frederick's Career.* 1241–1250.

ADDITIONAL LITERATURE. — MANSI, XXIII. 605 sqq.; HEFELE, V. 105 sqq. — C. RODENBERG : *Inn. IV. und das Königreich Sicilien,* Halle, 1892.— H. WEBER: *Der Kampf zwischen Inn. IV. und Fried. II.* Berlin, 1900. — P. ALDINGER : *Die Neubesetzung der deutschen Bisthümer unter Papst Inn. IV.*, Leipzig, 1900. — J. MAULBACH : *Die Kardinäle und ihre Politik um die Mitte des XIII. Jahrhunderts, 1243–1268,* Bonn, 1902.

Gregory's successor, Cœlestin IV., survived his election less than three weeks. A papal vacancy followed, lasting the unprecedented period of twenty months. The next pope, Innocent IV., a Genoese, was an expert in the canon

---

[1] See section on The Canon Law.

law and proved himself to be more than the equal of Frederick in shrewdness and quickness of action. At his election
the emperor is reported to have exclaimed that among
the cardinals he had lost a friend and in the pope gained
an enemy. Frederick refused to enter into negotiations
looking to an agreement of peace until he should be released
from the ban. Innocent was prepared to take up Gregory's
conflict with great energy. All the weapons at the command
of the papacy were brought into requisition: excommunication, the decree of a general council, deposition, the election of a rival emperor, and the active fomenting of rebellion
in Frederick's dominions. Under this accumulation of burdens Frederick, like a giant, attempted to bear up, but in
vain.[1] All Western Christendom was about to be disturbed
by the conflict. Innocent's first move was to out-general
his antagonist by secretly leaving Rome. Alexander III.
had set the precedent of delivering himself by flight. In the
garb of a knight he reached Civita Vecchia, and there met
by a Genoese galley proceeded to Genoa, where he was received with the ringing of bells and the acclamation, " Our
soul is escaped like a bird out of the snare of the fowler."
Joined by cardinals, he continued his journey to Lyons,
which, though nominally a city of the empire, was by reason
of its proximity to France a place of safe retreat.

The pope's policy proved to be a master stroke. A
deep impression in his favor was made upon the Christian
world by the sight of the supreme pontiff in exile.[2] The division of European sentiment is shown by the method which
a priest of Paris resorted to in publishing Innocent's
sentence of excommunication against the emperor. " I am
not ignorant," he said, " of the serious controversy and un-

---

[1] M. Paris says he had never heard of such bitter hatred as the hatred
between Innocent IV. and Frederick. Luard's ed., V. 193.

[2] M. Paris, heretofore inclining to the side of Frederick, at this point distinctly changes his tone. See, for example, Luard's ed., IV. 478.

quenchable hatred that has arisen between the emperor and the pope. I also know that one has done harm to the other, but which is the offender I do not know. Him, however, as far as my authority goes, I denounce and excommunicate, that is, the one who harms the other, whichever of the two it be, and I absolve the one which suffers under the injury which is so hurtful to the cause of Christendom."

Innocent was now free to convoke again the council which Frederick's forcible measures had prevented from assembling in Rome. It is known as the First Council of Lyons, or the Thirteenth Œcumenical Council, and met in Lyons, 1245. The measures the papal letter mentioned as calling for action were the provision of relief for the Holy Land and of resistance to the Mongols whose ravages had extended to Hungary, and the settlement of matters in dispute between the Apostolic see and the emperor. One hundred and forty prelates were present. With the exception of a few representatives from England and one or two bishops from Germany, the attendance was confined to ecclesiastics from Southern Europe.[1] Baldwin, emperor of Constantinople, was there to plead his dismal cause. Frederick was represented by his able counsellor, Thaddeus of Suessa.

Thaddeus promised for his master to restore Greece to the Roman communion and proceed to the Holy Land in person. Innocent rejected the promises as intended to deceive and to break up the council. The axe, he said, was laid at the root, and the stroke was not to be delayed. When Thaddeus offered the kings of England and France as sureties that the emperor would keep his promise, the pope sagaciously replied that in that case he would be in danger of having three princes to antagonize. Innocent was plainly master of the

---

[1] Two German bishops seem to have been present. Hefele, V. 982 sq. Catholic historians have been concerned to increase the number of attending prelates from the north.

situation. The council was in sympathy with him. Many
of its members had a grudge against Frederick for having
been subjected to the outrage of capture and imprisonment
by him.

At one of the first sessions the pope delivered a sermon
from the text, " See, ye who pass this way, was ever sorrow
like unto my sorrow? " He dwelt upon five sorrows of
the Church corresponding to the five wounds of Christ: the
savage cruelty of the Mongols or Tartars, the schism of the
Greeks, the growth of heresy, the desolation of Jerusalem,
and the active persecution of the Church by the emperor.
The charges against Frederick were sacrilege and heresy.
As for the charge of heresy, Thaddeus maintained that it
could be answered only by Frederick in person, and a delay
of two weeks was granted that he might have time to appear.
When he failed to appear, Innocent pronounced upon him
the ban and declared him deposed from his throne. The
deliverance set forth four grave offences; namely, the violation of his oath to keep peace with the Church, sacrilege
in seizing the prelates on their way to the council, heresy,
and withholding the tribute due from Sicily, a papal fief.
Among the grounds for the charge of heresy were Frederick's contempt of the pope's prerogative of the keys, his treaty
with the Sultan on his crusade, allowing the name of Mohammed to be publicly proclaimed day and night in the temple,
having intercourse with Saracens, keeping eunuchs over his
women, and giving his daughter in marriage to Battacius,
an excommunicated prince. The words of the fell sentence
ran as follows: —

" Seeing that we, unworthy as we are, hold on earth the authority of
our Lord Jesus Christ, who said to us in the person of St. Peter, ' whatsoever ye shall bind on earth,' etc., do hereby declare Frederick, who has
rendered himself unworthy of the honors of sovereignty and for his crimes
has been deposed from his throne by God, to be bound by his sins and cast
off by the Lord and we do hereby sentence and depose him ; and all who are
in any way bound to him by an oath of allegiance we forever release and

o

absolve from that oath ; and by our apostolic authority, we strictly forbid
any one obeying him. We decree that any who gives aid to him as emperor or king shall be excommunicated ; and those in the empire on whom
the selection of an emperor devolves, have full liberty to elect a successor in
his place." [1]

Thaddeus appealed from the decision to another council.[2]
His master Frederick, on hearing what was done, is said to
have asked for his crown and to have placed it more firmly
on his head.   In vain did the king of France, meeting Innocent at Cluny, make a plea for the emperor, finding, as the
English chronicler said, "but very little of that humility
which he had hoped for in that servant of the servants of
God."   Frederick's manifesto in reply to the council's act
was addressed to the king of England and other princes, and
reminded them of the low birth of the prelates who set
themselves up against lawful sovereigns, and denied the
pope's temporal authority.   He warned them that his fate
was likely to be theirs and announced it as his purpose to
fight against his oppressors.   It had been his aim to recall the
clergy from lives of luxury and the use of arms to apostolic
simplicity of manners.   When this summons was heeded,
the world might expect again to see miracles as of old.
True as these principles were, and bold and powerful as was
their advocate, the time had not yet come for Europe to
espouse them, and the character of Frederick was altogether
too vulnerable to give moral weight to his words.[3]

The council's discussions of measures looking to a new
crusade did not have any immediate result.   The clergy,
besides being called upon to give a twentieth for three years,
were instructed to see to it that wills contained bequests for
the holy enterprise.

[1] Mansi, XXIII. 612 sqq., 638; Luard's ed. of M. Paris, IV. 445–456.
Gregorovius calls this decree "one of the most ominous events in universal
history," V. 244.   [2] Bréholles, VI. 318.

[3] Too much credit must not be given to Frederick for a far-seeing policy
based upon a love of truth or a perception of permanent principles. The
rights of conscience he nowhere hints at, and probably did not dream of.

One of the interesting figures at the council was Robert Grosseteste, bishop of Lincoln, who protested against ecclesiastical abuses in England, such as the appointment of unworthy foreigners to benefices, and the exorbitant exactions for the papal exchequer. The pope gave no relief, and the English bishops were commanded to affix their seals confirming King John's charter of tribute.[1] The only notable achievement of the council of Lyons was the defeat of Frederick. Innocent followed it up with vigorous measures. Frederick's manifesto he answered with the reassertion of the most extravagant claims. The bishop of Rome was intrusted with authority to judge kings. If, in the Old Testament, priests deposed unworthy monarchs, how much more right had the vicar of Christ so to do. Innocent stirred up the flames of rebellion in Sicily and through the mendicant orders fanned the fires of discontent in Germany. Papal legates practically usurped the government of the German Church from 1246 to 1254. In the conflict over the election of bishops to German dioceses, Innocent usually gained his point, and in the year 1247–1248 thirteen of his nominees were elected.[2] At the pope's instigation Henry Raspe, landgrave of Thuringia, was chosen emperor, 1246, to replace Frederick, and at his death, a year later, William of Holland.

In Italy civil war broke out. Here the mendicant orders were also against him. He met the elements of revolt in the South and subdued them. Turning to the North, success was at first on his side but soon left him. One fatality followed another. Thaddeus of Suessa fell, 1248. Peter de Vinea, another shrewd counsellor, had abandoned his master. Enzio, the emperor's favorite son, was in prison.[3] Utter defeat fell upon him before Parma and forced him to abandon all Lombardy. As if there had not been curs-

---

[1] M. Paris, Luard's ed., IV. 478.   [2] See Aldinger.

[3] The tragic career of this gifted man and consummate flower of chivalry is deeply engraven in the romance and architecture of Bologna.

ings enough, Innocent, in 1247, had once more launched the anathema against him. Frederick's career was at an end. He retired to Southern Italy, a broken man, and died near Lucera, an old Samnite town, Dec. 13, 1250. His tomb is at the side of the tomb of his parents in the cathedral of Palermo. He died absolved by the archbishop of Palermo and clothed in the garb of the Cistercians.[1]

Stupor mundi, the Wonder of the World — this is the title which Matthew Paris applies to Frederick II.[2] Europe had not seen his equal as a ruler since the days of Charlemagne. For his wide outlook, the diversity of his gifts, and the vigor and versatility of his statecraft he is justly compared to the great rulers.[3] Morally the inferior of his grandfather, Barbarossa, Frederick surpassed him in intellectual breadth and culture. He is the most conspicuous political figure of his own age and the most cosmopolitan of the Middle Ages. He was warrior, legislator, statesman, man of letters. He won concessions in the East and was the last Christian king of Jerusalem to enter his realm. He brought order out of confusion in Sicily and Southern Italy and substituted the uniform legislation of the Sicilian Constitutions for the irresponsible jurisdiction of ecclesiastical court and baron. It has been said he founded the system of centralized government[4] and prepared the way for the monarchies of later times. He struck out a new path

---

[1] This is the more credible narrative. Villani, an. 1250, tells the story that Manfred bribed Frederick's chamberlain, and stifled the dying man with a wet cloth.

[2] *Principum mundi maximus, stupor quoque mundi et immutator mirabilis*, "greatest of the princes of the earth, the wonder of the world and the marvellous regulating genius [innovator] in its affairs." Luard's M. Paris, V. 190, 196. In his letters Frederick styled himself *Fredericus Dei gratia Romanorum imperator et semper augustus, Jerusalem et Siciliæ rex.*

[3] Kington, I. 475 sqq.

[4] Gregorovius, V. 271. This view is not discredited by the decentralizing charters Frederick gave to German cities on which Fisher, *Mediæval Empire*, lays so much stress. See his good chapter on "Imperial Legislation in Italy" (XI).

by appealing to the judgment of Christendom. With an
enlightenment above his age, he gave toleration to Jew and
Mohammedan.

In his conflict with the pope, he was governed, not by
animosity to the spiritual power, but by the determination to
keep it within its own realm.   In genuine ideal opposition to
the hierarchy he went farther than any of his predecessors.[1]
Döllinger pronounced him the greatest and most dangerous
foe the papacy ever had.[2]   Gregory and Innocent IV. called
him "the great dragon" and declared he deserved the fate
of Absalom.   And yet he did not resort to his grandfather's
measures and set up an anti-pope.[3]   Perhaps he refrained
from so doing in sheer disdain.

It has been surmised that Frederick was not a Christian.
Gregory charged him specifically with blasphemy.   But
Frederick as specifically disavowed the charge of making
Christ an impostor, and swore fealty to the orthodox faith.[4]
If he actually threw off the statement of the three impostors
as charged, it must be regarded as the intemperate expression
of a mood.[5]   Neander expresses the judgment that Frederick
denied revealed religion.   Schlosser withholds from him all
religious and moral faith.   Ranke and Freeman leave the

[1] Ranke, VIII. 369 sqq.   [2] *Akademische Vorträge*, III. 213.
[3] Cardinal Rainer's letter as given by M. Paris, Luard's ed., V. 61–67 ;
Giles's trans., II. 298 sqq.   Peter the Lombard, writing to one of his presbyters, says *ecclesia Romana totis viribus contra imperatorem et ad ejus
destructionem*, Bréholles, V. 1226.
[4] For the charge, that he denied the incarnation by the Virgin Mary and
other charges, see above and Bréholles, V. 459 sq. ; M. Paris, Luard's ed., III.
521.
[5] The statement was floating about in the air.   It is traced to Simon
Tornacensis, a professor of theology in Paris, d. 1201, as well as to Frederick.   A book under the title *De tribus impostoribus* can be traced into the
sixteenth century.   It produced the extermination of the Canaanites and
other arguments against the revealed character of the Bible and relegated
the incarnation to the category of the myths of the gods.   See Herzog, *Enc.*
IX. 72–75 ; and F. W. Genthe, *De impostura religionum*, etc., Leipzig, 1833 ;
Benrath's art. in Herzog, IX. 72–75 ; Reuter, *Gesch. der Aufklärung im M.A.*,
II. 275 sqq.

question of his religious faith an open one. Hergenröther
makes the distinction that as a man he was an unbeliever, as
a monarch a strict Catholic.   Gregorovius holds that he
cherished convictions as sincerely catholic as those professed
by the Ghibelline Dante.   Fisher emphasizes his singular
detachment from the current superstitions of his day.[1]
Huillard-Bréholles advances the novel theory that his movement was an attempt to usurp the sovereign pontificate and
found a lay papacy and to combine in himself royalty and
papal functions.

Frederick was highly educated, a friend of art and learning.
He was familiar with Greek, Latin, German, French, and
Arabic, as well as Italian.   He founded the University of Naples.   He was a precursor of the Renaissance and was himself
given to rhyming.   He wrote a book on falconry.[2]   It was
characteristic of the man that while he was besieging Milan
in 1239, he was sending orders back to Sicily concerning his
forests and household concerns, thus reminding us of Napoleon and his care for his capital while on his Russian and
other campaigns.   Like other men of the age, he cultivated
astrology.   Michael Scott was his favorite astrologer.   To
these worthy traits, Frederick added the luxurious habits
and apparently the cruelty of an Oriental despot.   Inherit-
ing the island of which the Saracens had once been masters,
he showed them favor and did not hesitate to appropriate
some of their customs.   He surrounded himself with a
Saracenic bodyguard[3] and kept a harem.[4]

[1] *Med. Emp.*, II. 163.

[2] Ranke calls it one of the best treatments of the Middle Ages on the subject. For Frederick's influence on culture and literature, see Bréholles,
I. ch. 9. Also Fisher's *Med. Emp.*, II. ch. 14, "The Empire and Culture."

[3] This bodyguard was with him on his last campaign and before Parma.

[4] Of his cruelty and unrestrained morals, priestly chroniclers could not say
enough. See Kington, II. 474. sqq. He was legally married four times;
Amari, in his *History of the Mohammedans in Sicily*, calls him a "baptized
sultan." For Frederick's relation to the Mohammedans, see Bréholles, I.
325–375.

Freeman's judgment must be regarded as extravagant when he says that "in mere genius, in mere accomplishments, Frederick was surely the greatest prince that ever wore a crown." [1] Bryce pronounces him "one of the greatest personages in history." [2] Gregorovius declares that "with all his faults he was the most complete and gifted character of his century." Dante, a half-century after his death, puts the great emperor among the heresiarchs in hell. When the news of his death reached Innocent IV., that pontiff wrote to the Sicilians that heaven and hell rejoiced at it. A juster feeling was expressed by the Freiburger Chronicle when it said, "If he had loved his soul, who would have been his equal?" [3]

§ 45.   *The Last of the Hohenstaufen.*

ADDITIONAL LITERATURE. — *Letters* of Urban IV. in Mansi, vol. XXIII. — POTTHAST: *Regesta*, 1161–1650. — *Les Registres of Alexander IV.*, *Recueil des bulles de ce pape d'après les MSS. originaux des archives du Vatican*, Paris, 1886, *of Urban IV.*, Paris, 1892, *of Clement IV.*, Paris, 1893–1904. — * DÖLLINGER : *Der Uebergang des Papstthums an die Franzosen*, in *Akademische Vorträge*, III. pp. 212–222, Munich, 1891. Lives of the popes in Muratori and Platina.

The death of Frederick did not satisfy the papacy. It had decreed the ruin of the house of the Hohenstaufen. The popes denounced its surviving representatives as "the viperous brood" and "the poisonous brood of a dragon of poisonous race."

In his will, Frederick bade his son Conrad accord to the

---

[1] *Hist. Essays*, I. 286. He says again, p. 283, "It is probable there never lived a human being endowed with greater natural gifts." We may agree with Freeman's statement that in Frederick's career "are found some of the most wonderful chapters in European history," p. 313.

[2] *Holy Rom. Emp.*, ch. XIII.

[3] Herbert Fisher says, "Of all the mediæval emperors, Frederick II. alone seems to have the true temper of the legislator." *Med. Emp.*, II. 167. Equal to his best generalizations is Gibbon's characterization of Frederick's career, as "successively the pupil, the enemy, and the victim of the Church," ch. LIX.

Church her just rights and to restore any he himself might have unjustly seized but on condition that she, as a merciful and pious mother, acknowledge the rights of the empire. His illegitimate son, the brilliant and princely Manfred, he appointed his representative in Italy during Conrad's absence.

Innocent broke up from Lyons in 1251, little dreaming that, a half century later, the papacy would remove there to pass an exile of seventy years.[1] After an absence of six years, he entered Rome, 1253.   The war against Frederick he continued by offering the crown of Sicily to Edmund, son of the English Henry III.   Conrad descended to Italy and entered Naples, making good his claim to his ancestral crown.   But the pope met him with the sentence of excommunication. Death, which seemed to be in league with the papacy against the ill-fated German house, claimed Conrad in 1254 at the age of 26.   He left an only son, Conradin, then two years old.[2]

Conrad was soon followed by Innocent to the grave, 1254. Innocent lies buried in Naples.   He was the last of the great popes of an era that was hastening to its end.   During the reign, perhaps, of no other pope had the exactions of Rome upon England been so exorbitant and brazen.   Matthew Paris charged him with making the Church a slave and turning the papal court into a money changer's table.   To his relatives, weeping around his death-bed, he is reported to have exclaimed: "Why do you weep, wretched creatures? Do I not leave you all rich?"

Under the mild reign of Alexander IV., 1254-1261, Manfred made himself master of Sicily and was crowned king at Palermo, 1258.

---

[1] M. Paris reports that a cardinal, after delivering a farewell sermon in Innocent's name, said, "Since our arrival in the city, we have done much good and bestowed alms.   On our arrival we found three or four brothels, but now, at our departure, we leave only one behind, but that extends from the eastern to the western gate of the city."   Luard's ed., V. 237.

[2] A few months before, Henry, Frederick's son by Isabella of England, had died.   His son Enzio languished to his death in a Bologna prison, 1272.

Urban IV., 1261–1264, was consecrated at Viterbo and did not enter Rome during his pontificate. He was a shoemaker's son and the first Frenchman for one hundred and sixty years to occupy the papal throne. With him the papacy came under French control, where it remained, with brief intervals, for more than a century. Urban displayed his strong national partisanship by his appointment of seven French cardinals in a conclave of seventeen. The French influence was greatly strengthened by his invitation to Charles of Anjou, youngest brother of Louis IX. of France, to occupy the Sicilian throne, claiming the right to do so on the basis of the inherent authority of the papacy and on the ground that Sicily was a papal fief. For centuries the house of Anjou, with Naples as its capital, was destined to be a disturbing element in the affairs, not only of Italy, but of all Europe.[1] It stood for a new alliance in the history of the papacy as their ancestors, the Normans, had done in the age of Hildebrand. Called as supporter and ward of the papacy, Charles of Anjou became dictator of its policy and master of the political situation in Italy.

Clement IV., 1265–1268, one of the French cardinals appointed by Urban, had a family before he entered a Carthusian convent and upon a clerical career. He preached a crusade against Manfred, who had dared to usurp the Sicilian throne, and crowned Charles of Anjou in Rome, 1266. Charles promised to pay yearly tribute to the Apostolic see. A month later, Feb. 26, 1266, the possession of the crown of Sicily·was decided by the arbitrament of arms on the battlefield of Benevento, where Manfred fell.

On the youthful Conradin, grandson of Frederick II., the hopes of the proud German house now hung. His title to the imperial throne was contested from the first. William of Holland had been succeeded by the rival emperors, the

---

[1] See the pages on the last popes of this period and of the last period of the Middle Ages, especially under Alexander VI. and Julius II.

rich Duke Richard of Cornwall, brother of Henry III., elected in 1257 by four of the electors, and Alfonso of Castile, elected by the remaining three.[1]   Conradin marched to Italy to assert his rights, 1267, was met by the papal ban, and, although received by popular enthusiasm even in Rome, he was no match for the tried skill of Charles of Anjou.   His fortunes were shattered on the battlefield of Tagliacozzo, Aug. 23, 1268.   Taken prisoner, he was given a mock trial. The Bolognese lawyer, Guido of Suzarra, made an ineffective plea that the young prince had come to Italy, not as a robber but to claim his inheritance.   The majority of the judges were against the death penalty, but the spirit of Charles knew no clemency, and at his instance Conradin was executed at Naples, Oct. 29, 1268.   The last words that fell from his lips, as he kneeled for the fatal stroke, were words of attachment to his mother, " O mother, what pain of heart do I make for you ! "

With Conradin the male line of the Hohenstaufen became extinct.   Its tragic end was enacted on the soil which had always been so fatal to the German rulers.   Barbarossa again and again met defeat there ; and in Southern Italy Henry VI., Frederick II., Conrad, Manfred, and Conradin were all laid in premature graves.

At Conradin's burial Charles accorded military honors, but not religious rites.   The Roman crozier had triumphed over the German eagle.   The Swabian hill, on which the proud castle of the Hohenstaufen once stood, looks down in solemn silence upon the peaceful fields of Württemberg and preaches the eloquent sermon that " all flesh is as grass and all the glory of man is as the flower of grass."   The colossal claims of the papacy survived the blows struck again and again by

---

[1] Alfonso never visited Germany.   Richard spent part of his time there, but was destitute of political power.   The threat of excommunication deterred the electors from electing Conradin.   For the imperial electoral college, see Fisher, *Med. Emp.*, I. 225 sq., and for Richard, see *Richard v. Cornwall seit sr. Wahl z. deutschen König.*, 1905.

this imperial family, through a century. Italy had been
exposed for three generations and more to the sword, rapine,
and urban strife. Europe was weary of the conflict. The
German minnesingers and the chroniclers of England and
the Continent were giving expression to the deep unrest.
Partly as a result of the distraction bordering on anarchy,
the Mongols were threatening to burst through the gates of
Eastern Germany. It was an eventful time. Antioch, one
of the last relics of the Crusaders in Asia Minor, fell back to
the Mohammedans in 1268. Seven years earlier the Latin
empire of Constantinople finally reverted to its rightful
owners, the Greeks.

In the mighty duel which has been called by the last great
Roman historian [1] the grandest spectacle of the ages, the empire had been humbled to the dust. But ideas survive, and
the principle of the sovereign right of the civil power within
its own sphere has won its way in one form or another among
European peoples and their descendants. And the fate of
young Conradin was not forgotten. Three centuries later
it played its part in the memories of the German nation, and
through the pictures of his execution distributed in Martin
Luther's writings contributed to strengthen the hand of the
Protestant Reformer in his struggle with the papacy, which
did not fail.

§ 46.   *The Empire and Papacy at Peace.*   1271-1294.

POPES.—Gregory X., 1271-1276 ; Innocent V., Jan. 21–June 22, 1276; Adrian
    V., July 12–Aug. 16, 1276 ; John XXI., 1276-1277 ; Nicolas III., 1277–
    1280 ; Martin IV., 1281-1285 ; Honorius IV., 1285-1287 ; Nicolas IV.,
    1288-1292 ; Cœlestin V., July 5–Dec. 13, 1294.
LITERATURE.—POTTHAST : *Regest.*, pp. 1651-1922. *Les Registres de Grégoire
    X. et Jean XXI.*, 3 vols., Paris, 1892-1898, *de Nicolas III.*, Paris, 1904,
    d'Honorius IV., Paris, 1886, *de Nicolas IV.*, Paris, 1880. Lives of the
    above popes in MURATORI : *Rer. Ital. scr.*, vol. III. — MANSI : *Councils*,
    XXIV. — HEFELE, VI. 125 sqq. — TURINAAZ, *La patrie et la famille de
    Pierre de Tarantaise, pape sous le nom d'Innocent V.*, Nancy,

---

[1] Gregorovius.

1882. — H. Otto : *Die Beziehungen Rudolfs von Hapsburg zu Papst Gregor X.*, Innsbruck, 1895. — A. Demski : *Papst Nicolas III.*, Münster, 1903, pp. 364. — R. Sternfeld : *Der Kardinal Johann Gaëtan Orsini, Papst Nic. III., 1244-1277*, Berlin, 1905, pp. 376. Reviewed at length by Haller in "Theol. Literaturzeitung," 1906, pp. 173-178. — H. Finke : *Concilienstudien zur Gesch. des 13ten Jahrhunderts*, Münster, 1891. — For Cœlestin V., Finke : *Aus den Tagen Bonifaz VIII.*, Münster, 1902 ; H. Schulz, *Peter von Murrhone*, 1894 ; and Celidonio, *Vita di S. Pietro del Morrone*, 1896. — The articles on the above popes in Wetzer-Welte and Herzog (*Gregory X.*, by Mirbt, *Cœlestin V., Innocent V., Honorius IV.*, etc., by Hans Schulz). — The Histories of Gregorovius, Ranke, etc.

The death of Clement IV. was followed by the longest interregnum the papacy has known, lasting thirty-three months, Nov. 29, 1268, to Sept. 1, 1271. It was due largely to the conflict between the French and Italian parties in the conclave and was prolonged in spite of the stern measures taken by the municipality of Viterbo, where the election occurred. Cardinals were even imprisoned. The new pope, Gregory X., archdeacon of Liège, was not an ordained priest. The news reached him at Acre while he was engaged in a pilgrimage. A man of peaceful and conciliatory spirit, he is one of the two popes of the thirteenth century who have received canonization. Pursuing the policy of keeping the empire and the kingdom of Southern Italy apart, and setting aside the pretensions of Alfonso of Castile,[1] he actively furthered the election of Rudolf of Hapsburg to the imperial throne.

The elevation of Rudolf inaugurated a period of peace in the relations of the papacy and the empire. Gregory X. had gained a brilliant victory. The emperor was crowned at Aachen, Oct. 24, 1273. The place of the Hohenstaufen was thus taken by the Austrian house of Hapsburg, which has continued to this day to be a reigning dynasty and loyal to the Catholic hierarchy. In the present century its power has been eclipsed by the Hohenzollern, whose original birth seat in Württemberg is a short distance from that of

[1] Richard, duke of Cornwall, had died April 2, 1272.

the Hohenstaufen.[1] The establishment of peace by Rudolf's election is celebrated by Schiller in the famous lines : [2]—

> " Then was ended the long, the direful strife,
>   That time of terror, with no imperial lord."

Rudolf was a man of decided religious temper, was not ambitious to extend his power, and became a just and safe ruler. He satisfied the claims of the papacy by granting freedom to the chapters in the choice of bishops, by promising to protect the Church in her rights, and by renouncing all claim to Sicily and the State of the Church. In a tone of moderation Gregory wrote: " It is incumbent on princes to protect the liberties and rights of the Church and not to deprive her of her temporal property. It is also the duty of the spiritual ruler to maintain kings in the full integrity of their authority."

The emperor remained on good terms with Gregory's successors, Innocent V., a Frenchman, Adrian V., a Genoese, who did not live to be consecrated, and John XXI., the only priest from Portugal who has worn the tiara. Their combined reigns lasted only eighteen months. John died from the falling of a ceiling in his palace in Viterbo.

The second Council of Lyons, known also as the Fourteenth Œcumenical Council, was called by Gregory and opened by him with a sermon. It is famous for the attempt made to unite the Greek and Western Churches and the presence of Greek delegates, among them Germanus, formerly patriarch of Constantinople. His successor had temporarily been placed in confinement for expressing himself as opposed to ecclesiastical union. A termination of the schism seemed to be at hand. The delegates announced the Greek emperor's

---

[1] The ancient seat of the Hapsburgs was in Aargau, Switzerland, scarcely one hundred miles away from Zollern.

[2] " *Dann geendigt nach langem verderblichen Streit,*
    War die kaiserlose, die schreckliche Zeit."
                                            — *Der Graf von Hapsburg.*

full acceptance of the Latin creed, including the procession of the Holy Spirit from the Son and the primacy of the bishop of Rome. The Apostles' Creed was sung in Greek and Latin. Papal delegates were sent to Constantinople to consummate the union; but the agreement was rejected by the Greek clergy. It is more than surmised that the Greek emperor, Michael Palæologus, was more concerned for the permanency of the Greek occupation of Constantinople than for the ecclesiastical union of the East and the West upon which the hearts of popes had been set so long.

Other important matters before the council were the rule for electing a pope, and the reception of a delegation of Mongols who sought to effect a union against the Mohammedans. Several members of the delegation received baptism. The decree of the Fourth Lateran, prohibiting new religious orders, was reaffirmed.

The firm and statesmanlike administration of Nicolas III. checked the ambition of Charles of Anjou, who was plotting for the Greek crown. He was obliged to abjure the senatorship of Rome, which he had held for ten years, and to renounce the vicariate of Tuscany. Bologna for the first time acknowledged the papal supremacy. Nicolas has been called the father of papal nepotism,[1] and it is partly for his generosity to his relatives that, before the generation had passed away, Dante put him in hell : [2] —

> " To enrich my whelps, I laid my schemes aside,
>   My wealth I've stowed, — my person here."

Again, in 1281, the tiara passed to a Frenchman, a man of humble birth, Martin IV. Charles was present at Viterbo when the election took place and was active in securing it.[3]

---

[1] See the elaborate art. *Nepotismus* in Wetzer-Welte, IX. 109 sqq.; and Haller in *Literaturzeitung*, see above.

[2] *Inferno*, XIX. 72 sqq. The term " whelps " refers to the Orsini or *bear* clan, to which Nicolas belonged.

[3] See the art. *Martin* by Knöpfler in Wetzer-Welte, VIII. 919 sq.

Martin showed himself completely complaisant to the designs of the Angevin house and Charles was once more elected to the Roman senatorship. Seldom had a pope been so fully the tool of a monarch.[1] In Southern Italy Frenchmen were everywhere in the ruling positions. But this national insult was soon to receive a memorable rebuke.

In resentment at the hated French régime, the Sicilians rose up, during Easter week, 1282, and enacted the bloody massacre known as the Sicilian Vespers. All the Normans on the island, together with the Sicilian wives of Normans, were victims of the merciless vengeance. The number that fell is estimated at from eight to twenty thousand. The tragedy gets its name from the tradition that the Sicilians fell to their work at the ringing of the vesper bell.[2] Charles's rule was thenceforward at an end on the Panormic isle. Peter of Aragon, who married Constance, the daughter of Manfred and the granddaughter of Frederick II., was crowned king. For nearly two hundred years thereafter the crowns of Sicily and Naples were kept distinct.

Not to be untrue to Charles, Martin hurled the anathema at the rebels, placed Aragon and Sicily under the interdict, and laid Christendom under a tribute of one-tenth for a crusade against Peter. The measures were in vain, and Charles's galleys met with defeat off the coast of Calabria. Charles and Martin died the same year, 1285, the latter, like Gregory X., at Perugia.

After an interregnum of ten months, Nicolas IV. ascended the papal throne, the first Franciscan to be elevated to the office. His reign witnessed the evacuation of Ptolemais or Acre, the last possession of the Crusaders in Syria. Nicolas died in the midst of futile plans to recover the Holy Places.

---

[1] "He was led about by the nose by Charles," Muratori, XI. 492. So Hergenröther, *Kirchengesch.*, II. 310.

[2] See Ranke, VIII. 531 sqq.

Another interregnum of twenty-seven months followed, April 4, 1292 to July 5, 1294, when the hermit Peter de Murrhone, Cœlestin V., was raised to the papal throne, largely at the dictation of Charles II. of Naples.   His short reign forms a curious episode in the annals of the papacy.   His career shows the extremes of station from the solitude of the mountain cell to the chief dignity of Europe.   He enjoyed the fame of sanctity and founded the order of St. Damian, which subsequently honored him by taking the name of Cœlestines. The story ran that he had accomplished the unprecedented feat of hanging his cowl on a sunbeam.   At the time of his elevation to the papal throne Cœlestin was seventy-nine.

An eye-witness, Stefaneschi, has described the journey to the hermit's retreat by three bishops who were appointed to notify him of his election.   They found him in a rude hut in the mountains, furnished with a single barred window, his hair unkempt, his face pale, and his body infirm.   After announcing their errand they bent low and kissed his sandals.   Had Peter been able to go forth from his anchoret solitude, like Anthony of old, on his visits to Alexandria, and preach repentance and humility, he would have presented an exhilarating spectacle to after generations.   As it is, his career arouses pity for his frail and unsophisticated incompetency to meet the demands which his high office involved.

Clad in his monkish habit and riding on an ass, the bridle held by Charles II. and his son, Peter proceeded to Aquila, where he was crowned, only three cardinals being present. Completely under the dominance of the king, Cœlestin took up his residence in Naples.   Little was he able to battle with the world, to cope with the intrigues of factions, and to resist the greedy scramble for office which besets the path of those high in position.   In simple confidence Cœlestin gave his ear to this counsellor and to that, and yielded easily to all applicants for favors.   His complaisancy to Charles is seen in his appointment of cardinals. Out of twelve whom he created, seven were Frenchmen, and three Neapolitans. It would seem as if he fell into despair at the self-seeking and worldliness of the papal court, and he exclaimed, "O God, while I rule over other men's souls, I am losing the salvation of my own." He was clearly not equal to the duties of the tiara. In vain did the Neapolitans seek by processions to dissuade him from resigning. Clement I. had abjured his office, as had also Gregory VI. though at the mandate of an emperor. Peter issued a bull declaring it to be the pope's right to abdicate. His own abdication he placed on the ground "of his humbleness, the quest of a better life and an easy conscience, on account of his frailty of body and want of knowledge, the badness of men, and a desire to return to the quietness of his former state." The real reason for his resigning is obscure. The story went that the ambitious Cardinal Gaëtani, soon to become Cœlestin's successor, was responsible for it. He played upon the hermit's credulity by speaking through a reed, inserted through the wall of the hermit's chamber, and declared it to be heaven's will that his reign should come to an end.[1] As

[1] The author of the suggestion that Cœlestin should abdicate has given rise to a good deal of controversy in recent years. Was Benedict Gaëtani (Boniface VIII.) the author, or did the suggestion come from the senile old pope himself. Hans Schulz, a Protestant, has recently called in question the old view that laid the blame on Benedict, and regards it as probable that Cœlestin was the first to propose abdication, and that Benedict being called in gave the plan his sanction. He says, however, that in the whole matter "Benedict's eye was directed to the papal crown as his own prize." See Herzog's *Enc.*, IV. 203. Hergenröther-Kirsch, *Kirchengesch.*, II. 312, and Finke, *Aus den Tagen Bonifaz VIII.*, p. 39 sqq., both Roman Catholic historians, have adopted the same position, as does also Scholz, *Publizistik zur Zeit Philipp IV. und Bonifaz VIII.*, p. 3. The contemporary historians differ about the matter, but upon the whole are against the cardinal. The charge that he was at the bottom of the abdication and the main promoter of it was one of the chief charges brought against him by his enemy, Philip the Fair of France. One of the measures for humiliating Boniface proposed by the king was the canonization of Cœlestin as one whom Boniface had abused. See Document of the year 1305, printed for the first time by Finke, p, xcviii. A tract

P

the Italians say, the story, if not true, was well invented,
si non è vero è ben trovato.

In abandoning the papacy the departing pontiff forfeited
all freedom of movement. He attempted to flee across the
Adriatic, but in vain. He was kept in confinement by Boniface VIII. in the castle of Fumone, near Anagni, until his
death, May 19, 1296. What a world-wide contrast the simplicity of the hermit's reign presents to the violent assertion
and ambitious designs of Boniface, the first pope of a new
period !

Cœlestin's sixth centenary was observed by pious admirers
in Italy.[1] Opinions have differed about him. Petrarch
praised his humility. Dante, with relentless severity held
him up as an example of moral cowardice, the one who made
the great renunciation.

> " Behold ! that abject one appeared in view
>   Who, mean of soul, the great refusal made." [2]
>
> *Vidi e cenobbi la ombra di colui*
> *Che fece per viltate il gran rifuto.*

A new era for the papacy was at hand.

issued by one of Boniface's party attempted to parry this suggestion by declaring that Boniface, who was then dead, had merits which entitled him to canonization above Cœlestin. The author said, " *si canonizatio Celestini petitur,
multo magis canonizacio sanctissimi patris domini Bonifacii, postulari
debet et approbari.*" He continues, " Cœlestin's canonization is asked because
he profited himself and died in *sua simplicitate ;* Boniface's ought to be asked
for because he profited others and died for the freedom of the Church." See
the document printed for the first time in Finke, p. lxxxv, and which
Finke puts in 1308. Cœlestin was canonized 1313 by Clement V.

[1] A memorial volume was published under the title *Celestin V ed il vi
Centenario della sua incoronazione*, Aquila, 1894.

[2] *Inferno, III.* 58 sq.

CHAPTER VII.

THE CRUSADES.

"No idle fancy was it when of yore
  Pilgrims in countless numbers braved the seas,
  And legions battled on the farthest shore,

  Only to pray at Thy sepulchral bed,
  Only in pious gratitude to kiss
  The sacred earth on which Thy feet did tread."
                        — UHLAND, *An den Unsichtbaren.*

§ 47. *Literature on the Crusades as a Whole.*

SOURCES. — First printed collection of writers on the Crusades by JAC. BON-
GARS : *Gesta Dei* (and it might be added, *et diaboli*) *per Francos, sive
orientalium expeditionum,* etc., 2 vols. Hanover, 1611. Mostly reports
of the First Crusade and superseded. — The most complete collection,
edited at great expense and in magnificent style, *Recueil des Historiens
des Croisades publié par l'Académie des Inscriptions et Belles-Lettres,* viz.
Historiens Occidentaux, 5 vols. Paris, 1841–1895 ; *Histt. Orientaux,* 4 vols.
1872–1898 ; *Histt. Grecs,* 2 vols. 1875–1881 ; *Documents Arméniens,* 1869.
The first series contains, in vols. I., II., the *Historia rerum in partibus
transmarinis gestarum* of William of Tyre and the free reproduction in
French entitled *L'Estoire de Eracles Empéreur et la Conqueste de la terre
d'Outremer.* Vol. III. contains the *Gesta Francorum ;* the *Historia de
Hierolosymitano itinere* of PETER TUDEBODUS, *Hist. Francorum qui
ceperunt Jherusalem* of RAYMUND OF AGUILERS or Argiles ; *Hist. Jheru-
solymitana* or *Gesta Francorum Jherusalem perigrinantium 1095–1127,*
of FULCHER OF CHARTRES ; *Hist. Jherusol.* of ROBERT THE MONK, etc.
Vol. IV. contains *Hist. Jherusolem.* of BALDRIC OF DOL (Ranke, VIII.
82, speaks highly of Baldric as an authority) ; *Gesta Dei per Francos*
of GUIBERT OF NOGENT ;* *Hist. Hier.* of ALBERT OF AACHEN, etc. Vol. V.
contains *Ekkehardi Hierosolymita* and a number of other documents. —
Migne's *Latin Patrology* gives a number of these authors, *e.g.,* Fulcher
and Petrus Tudebodus, vol. 155 ; Guibert, vol. 156 ; Albert of Aachen
and Baldric, vol. 166 ; William of Tyre, vol. 201. — Contemporary
Chronicles of ORDERICUS VITALIS, ROGER OF HOVEDEN, ROGER OF
WENDOVER, M. PARIS, etc. — Reports of Pilgrimages, *e.g.,* COUNT RIANT :

Expéditions et pèlerinages des Scandinaves en Terre Sainte au temps des Croisades, Paris, 1865, 1867 ; R. Röhricht: *Die Pilgerfahrten nach d. heil. Lande vor den Kreuzzügen*, 1875 ; *Deutsche Pilgerreisen nach dem heil. Lande*, new ed. Innsbruck, 1900 ; H. Schrader : *D. Pilgerfahrten nach. d. heil. Lande im Zeitalter vor den Kreuzzügen*, Merzig, 1897. — Jaffé : *Regesta.* — Mansi : *Concilia.* — For criticism of the contemporary writers see Sybel, *Gesch. des ersten Kreuzzugs*, 2d ed. 1881, pp. 1–143. — H. Prutz (Prof. in Nancy, France) : *Quellenbeiträge zur Gesch. der Kreuzzüge*, Danzig, 1876. — R. Röhricht: *Regesta regni Hierosolymitani 1097–1291*, Innsbruck, 1904, an analysis of 900 documents.

Modern Works. — *Friedrich Wilken (Libr. and Prof. in Berlin, d. 1840) : *Gesch. der Kreuzzüge*, 7 vols. Leipzig, 1807–1832. — J. F. Michaud : *Hist. des croisades*, 3 vols. Paris, 1812, 7th ed. 4 vols. 1862. Engl. trans. by W. Robson, 3 vols., London, 1854, New York, 1880. — *Röhricht (teacher in one of the Gymnasia of Berlin, d. 1905; he published eight larger works on the Crusades): *Beiträge zur Gesch. der Kreuzzüge*, 2 vols. Berlin, 1874–1878; *D. Deutschen im heil. Lande, Innsbruck*, 1894 ; *Gesch. d. Kreuzzüge*, Innsbruck, 1898. — B. Kugler (Prof. in Tübingen): *Gesch. der Kreuzzüge*, illustrated, Berlin, 1880, 2d ed. 1891. — A. de Laporte : *Les croisades et le pays latin de Jérusalem*, Paris, 1881. — *Prutz : *Kulturgesch. der Kreuzzüge*, Berlin, 1883. — Ed. Heyck: *Die Kreuzzüge und das heilige Land*, Leipzig, 1900. — Histories in English by Mills, London, 1822, 4th ed. 2 vols. 1828 ; Keightley, London. 1847 ; Proctor, London, 1858 ; Edgar, London, 1860 ; W. E. Dutton, London, 1877 ; G. W. Cox, London, 1878 ; J. I. Mombert, New York, 1891 ; *Archer and Kingsford: *Story of the Crus.*, New York, 1895 ; J. M. Ludlow : *Age of the Crusades*, New York, 1896 ; Art. *Kreuzzüge* by Funk in Wetzer-Welte, VII. 1142–1177. — Ph. Schaff in "Ref. Quarterly Rev.," 1893, pp. 438–459. — J. L. Hahn : *Ursachen und Folgen der Kreuzzüge*, Greifswald, 1859. — Chalandon : *Essai sur le règne d'Alexis Comnène*, Paris, 1900. — *A. Gottlob : *D. päpstlichen Kreuzzugs-Steuren des 13. Jahrhunderts*, Heiligenstadt, 1892, pp. 278 ; *Kreuzablass und Almosenablass*, Stuttgart, 1906, pp. 314. — *Essays on the Crusades* by Munro, Prutz, Diehl, Burlington, 1903. — H. C. Lea : *Hist. of Auric. Confession and Indulgences*, vol. III. — See also *Gibbon, LVIII–LIX ; Milman ; Giesebrecht : *Gesch. d. deutschen Kaiserzeit ;* Ranke : *Weltgesch.*, VIII. pp. 88–111, 150–161, 223–262, 280–307 ; IX. 93–98 ; Finlay : *Hist. of the Byznt. and Gr. Empires, 1057–1453 ;* Hopf : *Gesch. Griechenlands vom Beginn des Mittelalters*, etc., Leipzig, 1868 ; Besant and Palmer: *Hist. of Jerusalem*, London, 1890 ; Guy Le Strange : *Palestine under the Moslems*, London, 1890.

The Poetry of the Crusades is represented chiefly by Raoul de Caen in *Gestes de Tancrède ;* Torquato Tasso, the Homer of the Crusades, in *La Jerusalemme liberata ;* Walter Scott: *Tales of the Crusades, Talisman, Quentin Durward*, etc. The older literature is given in full by Michaud ; *Bibliographie des Croisades*, 2 vols. Paris, 1822, which form vols. VI., VII. of his *Histoire des Croisades.*

THE FIRST CRUSADE.

SOURCES. — See Literature above. *Gesta Francorum et aliorum Hierosolymitorum* by an anonymous writer who took part in the First Crusade, in Bongars and *Recueil des Croisades*. See above. Also Hagenmeyer's critical edition, *Anonymi Gesta Francorum*, Heidelberg, 1890. — ROBERTUS, a monk of Rheims: *Hist. Hierosolymitana*, in Bongars, *Rec.*, and Migne, vol. 155. — BALDRICH, abp. of Dol: *Hist. Hierosol.*, in Bongars, and *Rec.* — RAYMUND DE AGUILERS, chaplain to the count of Toulouse: *Hist. Francorum*, 1095–1099, in Bongars, *Rec.*, and Migne, vol. 155. See CLEM. KLEIN: *Raimund von Aguilers*, Berlin, 1892. — FULCHER, chaplain to the count of Chartres and then to Baldwin, second king of Jerusalem: *Gesta Francorum Jerusalem perigrinantium* to 1125, in Bongars, *Rec.*, and Migne, vol. 155. — GUIBERT, abbot of Nogent: *Gesta Dei per Francos*, to 1110, in Bongars, *Rec.*, Migne, vol. 156. — ALBERTUS OF AACHEN (AQUENSIS): *Hist. Hierosol. expeditionis*, to 1121, in Bongars, *Rec.*, Migne, vol. 166. See B. KUGLER: *Albert von Aachen*, Stuttgart, 1885. — WILLIAM OF TYRE, abp. of Tyre, d. after 1184: *Hist. rerum in partibus transmarinis gestarum*, Basel, 1549, under the title of *belli sacri historia*, in Bongars, *Rec.*, Migne, vol. 201, Engl. trans. by WM. CAXTON, ed. by MARY N. COLVIN, London, 1893. — ANNA COMNENA (1083–1148): *Alexias*, a biogr. of her father, the Greek emperor, Alexis I., in *Rec.*, Migne, *Pat. Graeca*, vol. 131; also 2 vols. Leipzig, 1884, ed. by REIFFERSCHEID; also in part in HAGENMEYER, *Peter der Eremite*, pp. 303–314. — EKKEHARD OF URACH: *Hierosolymita seu libellus de oppressione, liberatione ac restauratione sanctae Hierosol.*, 1095–1187, in *Rec.*, and Migne, vol. 154, and HAGENMEYER: *Ekkehard's Hierosolymita*, Tübingen, 1877, also *Das Verhältniss der Gesta Francorum zu der Hiersol. Ekkehards* in "Forschungen zur deutschen Gesch.," Göttingen, 1875, pp. 21–42. — PETRUS TUDEBODUS, of the diocese of Poitiers: *Hist. de Hierosolymitano itinere*, 1095–1099, largely copied from the *Gesta Francorum*, in Migne, vol. 155, and *Recueil.* — RADULPHUS CADOMENSIS (Raoul of Caen): *Gesta Tancredi*, 1099–1108, Migne, vol. 155, and *Recueil.* — RIANT: *Inventaire critique des lettres hist. des croisades*, I., II., Paris, 1880. — H. HAGENMEYER: *Epistulæ et chartæ ad historiam primi belli sacri spectantes quæ supersunt*, etc., 1088–1100, Innsbruck, 1901. See the translation of contemporary documents in *Trans. and Reprints*, etc., published by Department of History of Univ. of Penn., 1894.

The Poetry of the First Crusade: *La Chanson d'Antioche*, ed. by PAULIN PARIS, 2 vols. Paris, 1848. He dates the poem 1125–1138, and *Nouvelle Étude sur la Chanson d'Antioche*, Paris, 1878. — *La Conquête de Jérusalem*, ed. by C. HIPPEAU, Paris, 1868. — *Roman du Chevalier au Cygne et Godefroi de Bouillon*.

MODERN WORKS. — *H. VON SYBEL: *Gesch. des ersten Kreuzzugs*, Düsseldorf, 1841, 3d ed. Leipzig, 1900. The Introduction contains a valuable critical estimate of the contemporary accounts. Engl. trans. of the Introd. and four lectures by Sybel in 1858, under the title, *The Hist. and Lit. of* *the Crusades*, by LADY DUFF GORDON, London, 1861. — J. F. A. PEYRE: *Hist. de la première croisade*, Paris, 1859. — *HAGENMEYER: *Peter der Eremite*, Leipzig, 1879; *Chron. de la première croisade*, 1094–1100, Paris, 1901. — RÖHRICHT: *Gesch. des ersten Kreuzzuges*, Innsbruck, 1901. — F. CHALANDON: *Essai sur le règne d'Alexis I. Comnène*, 1081–1118, Paris, 1900. — PAULOT: *Un pape Français, Urbain II.*, Paris, 1902. — D. C. MUNRO: *The Speech of Urban at Clermont*, "Am. Hist. Rev." 1906, pp. 231–242. — Art. in Wetzer-Welte, by FUNK, *Petrus von Amiens*, vol. IX.

§ 48. *Character and Causes of the Crusades.*

> " 'O, holy Palmer!' she began,—
> For sure he must be sainted man
> Whose blessed feet have trod the ground
> Where the Redeemer's tomb is found."
> — *Marmion*, V. 21.

THE Crusades were armed pilgrimages to Jerusalem under the banner of the cross. They form one of the most characteristic chapters of the Middle Ages and have a romantic and sentimental, as well as a religious and military, interest. They were a sublime product of the Christian imagination, and constitute a chapter of rare interest in the history of humanity. They exhibit the muscular Christianity of the new nations of the West which were just emerging from barbarism and heathenism. They made religion subservient to war and war subservient to religion. They were a succession of tournaments between two continents and two religions, struggling for supremacy, — Europe and Asia, Christianity and Mohammedanism. Such a spectacle the world has never seen before nor since, and may never see again.[1]

These expeditions occupied the attention of Europe for more than two centuries, beginning with 1095. Yea, they continued to be the concern of the popes until the beginning of the sixteenth century. Columbus signed an agreement April 17, 1492, to devote the proceeds of his undertaking

[1] Gibbon, who treats with scorn the Crusades as a useless exhibition of religious fanaticism, calls them the " world's debate," Ch. LIX.

beyond the Western seas to the recovery of the holy sepulchre.   Before his fourth and last journey to America he
wrote to Alexander VI., renewing his vow to furnish troops
for the rescue of that sacred locality.[1]   There were seven
greater Crusades, the first beginning in 1095, the last ter-
minating with the death of St. Louis, 1270.   Between
these dates and after 1270 there were other minor expeditions, and of these not the least worthy of attention were
the tragic Crusades of the children.

The most famous men of their age were identified with
these movements.   Emperors and kings went at the head of
the armies, — Konrad III., Frederick Barbarossa, Frederick
II., Richard I. of England, Louis VII., Philip Augustus and
Louis IX. of France, Andrew of Hungary.   Fair women of
high station accompanied their husbands or went alone to
the seats of war, such as Alice of Antioch, Queen Eleanor of
France, Ida of Austria, Berengaria, wife of Richard, and
Margaret, queen of Louis IX.   Kings' sons shared the same
risks, as Frederick of Swabia, Sigurd, and Edward, son of
Henry III., accompanied by Eleanor, his wife.   Priests,
abbots, and higher ecclesiastics fought manfully in the ranks
and at the head of troops.[2]   The popes stayed at home, but
were tireless in their appeals to advance the holy project.
With many of the best popes, as Honorius III. and
Gregory X., the Crusades were their chief passion.   Monks,
like Peter the Hermit, St. Bernard, and Fulke of Neuilly,
stirred the flames of enthusiasm by their eloquence.   But if

---

[1] John Fiske, *Discovery of America*, I. 318, 419, 505.

[2] The *Itinerary of Richard I.*, giving an account of the Third Crusade,
lays stress upon the good fighting qualities of the prelates and clergy.   It
speaks of one priest who was incessantly active against the enemy, hurling
darts from a sling with indefatigable toil, I. 42.   The archbishop of Besançon
superintended the construction of a great machine for battering down the
walls of Acre and met its expense, I. 60.   Two hundred knights and
three hundred followers served under archbishop Baldwin of Canterbury,
old man as he was, and "abbots and bishops led their own troops, fighting
manfully for the faith," I. 62.

some of the best men of Europe and those most eminent in station went on the Crusades, so also did the lowest elements of European society, — thieves, murderers, perjurers, vagabonds, and scoundrels of all sorts, as Bernard bears witness.[1] So it has been in all wars.

The crusading armies were designated by such titles as the army "of the cross," "of Christ," "of the Lord," "of the faith."[2] The cross was the badge of the Crusaders and gave to them their favorite name. The Crusaders were called the soldiers of Christ,[3] pilgrims, *peregrini*, and "those signed with the cross," *crucisignati* or *signatores*. Determining to go on a crusade was called "taking the cross" or "taking the sign of the cross."[4]

Contemporaries had no doubt of the Crusades being a holy undertaking, and Guibert's account of the First Crusade is called "The Deeds of God, accomplished through the Franks," *Gesta Dei per Francos*.

Those who fell under Eastern skies or on their way to the East received the benefits of special indulgence for sins committed and were esteemed in the popular judgment as martyrs. John VIII., 872–882, pressed by the Saracens who were devastating Italy, had promised to soldiers fighting bravely against the pagans the rest of eternal life and, as far as it belonged to him to give it, absolution from sins.[5] This precedent was followed by Urban II., who promised the first

---

[1] *De militibus templi*, V., Migne, 182, 928.

[2] Roger of Wendover, Luard's ed., M. Paris, III : 35.

[3] *Milites Christi*, Robert the Monk, VII., *Rec.*, III. 867 ; *Christi militia*, Guibert, VII., II., *Rec.*, IV. 229. The army was also called *crucifer exercitus*, Ekkehard, *Rec.* V. 16.

[4] The French terms were *se croiser*, *prendre la croix*, *prendre le signe de la croix*. See, for example, Villehardouin, 2, 8, 18, Wailly's ed. pp. 3, 7, 13. This historian of the Fourth Crusade also calls the Crusaders *les croisés*, 38, Wailly's ed. p. 24.

[5] *Quoniam illi, qui cum pietate catholicæ religionis in belli certamine cadunt, requies eos æternæ vitæ suscipiet contra paganos atque infideles strenue dimicantes*, etc., Gottlob, *Kreuzablass*, 25.

Crusaders marching to Jerusalem that the journey should be counted as a substitute for penance.[1] Eugenius, 1146, went farther, in distinctly promising the reward of eternal life. The virtue of the reward was extended to the parents of those taking part in Crusades. Innocent III. included in the plenary indulgence those who built ships and contributed in any way, and promised to them "increase of eternal life." God, said the abbot Guibert, chronicler of the First Crusade, invented the Crusades as a new way for the laity to atone for their sins, and to merit salvation.[2]

The rewards were not confined to spiritual privileges. Eugenius III., in his exhortations to the Second Crusade, placed the Crusaders in the same category with clerics before the courts in the case of most offences.[3] The kings of France, from 1188 to 1270 joined with the Holy See in granting to them temporal advantages, exemption from debt, freedom from taxation and the payment of interest. Complaint was frequently made by the kings of France that the Crusaders committed the most offensive crimes under cover of ecclesiastical protection. These complaints called forth from Innocent IV., 1246, and Alexander IV., 1260, instructions to the bishops not to protect such offenders. William of Tyre, in his account of the First Crusade, and probably reading into it some of the experiences of a later date, says (Bk. I. 16), "Many took the cross to elude their creditors."[4]

If it is hard for us to unite the idea of war and bloodshed with the achievement of a purely religious purpose, it must

---

[1] *Quicumque pro sola devotione . . . ad liberandam ecclesiam Dei Jerusalem profectus fuerit, iter illud pro omni pœnitentia reputetur*, Gottlob, 72 sqq.; Mirbt. *Quellen*, 114.

[2] *Gesta*, I. 1; *Rec.*, IV. 124.

[3] Lea, *Hist. of Inquis.*, I. 44, says, " Crusaders were released from earthly as well as heavenly justice by being classed with clerks and subjected only to spiritual justice."

[4] See *Origin of the Temporal Privileges of Crusaders*, by Edith C. Bramhall, " Am Jour. of Theol." 1901, pp. 279–292, and Gottlob, *Kreuzablass*, pp. 140 sqq.

be remembered that no such feeling prevailed in the Middle
Ages.   The wars of the period of Joshua and the Judges still
formed a stimulating example.   Chrysostom, Augustine, and
other Church Fathers of the fifth century lifted up their voices
against the violent destruction of heathen temples which went
on in Egypt and Gaul ; but whatever compunction might have
been felt for the wanton slaying of Saracens by Christian
armies in an attitude of aggression, the compunction was
not felt when the Saracens placed themselves in the position
of holding the sacred sites of Palestine.

Bernard of Clairvaux said, pagans must not be slain if they
may by other means be prevented from oppressing the faithful.   However, it is better they should be put to death than
that the rod of the wicked should rest on the lot of the
righteous.   The righteous fear no sin in killing the enemy
of Christ.   Christ's soldier can securely kill and more safely
die.   When he dies, it profits him ; when he slays, it profits
Christ.   The Christian exults in the death of the pagan because Christ is glorified thereby.   But when he himself is
killed, he has reached his goal.[1]   The conquest of Palestine
by the destruction of the Saracens was considered a legal act
justified by the claim which the pope had by reason of the
preaching of the Apostles in that country and its conquest
by the Roman empire.[2]

In answer to the question whether clerics might go to war,
Thomas Aquinas replied in the affirmative when the prize
was not worldly gain, but the defence of the Church or the
poor and oppressed.[3]

[1] *De militibus templi*, II., III., Migne, 182, 923 sq.

[2] This is what Fulcher meant, *Rec.*, III. 323, when he put into Urban's
mouth the words *nunc jure contra barbaros pugnent qui olim fratres dimica-
bant.*   Two hundred years later Alvarus Pelagius made the same argument:
quamvis Saraceni Palestinam possident, juste tamen exinde depelluntur, etc.
See Schwab, *Joh. Gerson*, 26.

[3] *Summa*, II. (2), 188, 3 ; Migne, III., 1366 sq.: *militare propter aliquid
mundanum est omni religioni contrarium, non autem militare propter obse-
quium Dei*, etc.   He adds that clerics going to war must act under the command of princes or of the Church, and not at their own suggestion.

To other testimonies to the esteem in which the Crusaders
were held may be added the testimony of Matthew Paris.
Summing up the events of the half-century ending with
1250, he says : [1] " A great multitude of nobles left their
country to fight faithfully for Christ. All of these were
manifest martyrs, and their names are inscribed in indelible
characters in the book of life." Women forced their husbands to take the cross.[2] And women who attempted to
hold their husbands back suffered evil consequences for it.[3]
Kings who did not go across the seas had a passion for the
holy sepulchre. Edward I. commanded his son to take his
heart and deposit it there, setting apart £2000 for the expedition. Robert Bruce also wanted his heart to find its
last earthly resting-place in Jerusalem.

The Crusades began and ended in France. The French
element was the ruling factor, from Urban II., who was a
native of Châtillon, near Rheims, and Peter of Amiens, to
St. Louis.[4] The contemporary accounts of the Crusades are
for the most part written by Frenchmen. Guibert of Nogent
and other chroniclers regard them as especially the work of
their countrymen. The French expression, *outre-mer*, was
used for the goal of the Crusades.[5] The movement spread
through all Europe from Hungary to Scotland. Spain alone
forms an exception. She was engaged in a crusade of her own
against the Moors ; and the crusades against the Saracens in

[1] Luard's ed., V. 196.

[2] Baldric of Dol, *Hist. Jerus.*, I. 8 ; *Rec.*, IV. 17 : *gaudebant uxores
abeuntibus maritis dilectissimis*, etc.

[3] Cæsar of Heisterbach, *Dial.*, X. 22, speaks of a woman suffering with
severe pains in childbirth who was delivered with ease, so soon as she consented to her husband's going on a crusade.

[4] The name Franks became the current designation for Europeans in the
East, and remains so to this day. The crusading enthusiasm did not fully
take hold of Germany till the twelfth century. Hauck, *Kirchengesch.
Deutschlands*, IV. 80.

[5] The expression was a translation of the Latin *ultra mare*, used for the
East, and, so far as I know, for the first time by Gregory VII., *Reg.* II. 37 ;
Migne, 148, 390.

the Holy Land and the Moors in Spain were equally commended by an œcumenical council, the First Lateran
(*can.* 13).   The Moors were finally expelled from Granada
under Ferdinand and Isabella, and then, unwearied, Spain
entered upon a new crusade against Jews and heretics at
home and the pagan Indians of Mexico and Peru.   In Italy
and Rome, where might have been expected the most zeal
in the holy cause, there was but little enthusiasm.[1]

The aim of the Crusades was the conquest of the Holy
Land and the defeat of Islam.   Enthusiasm for Christ was
the moving impulse, with which, however, were joined the
lower motives of ambition, avarice, love of adventure, hope
of earthly and heavenly reward.   The whole chivalry of
Europe, aroused by a pale-faced monk and encouraged by a
Hildebrandian pope, threw itself steel-clad upon the Orient
to execute the vengeance of heaven upon the insults and barbarities of Moslems heaped upon Christian pilgrims, and to
rescue the grave of the Redeemer of mankind from the grasp
of the followers of the False Prophet.   The miraculous aid
of heaven frequently intervened to help the Christians and
confound the Saracens.[2]

The Crusaders sought the living among the dead.   They
mistook the visible for the invisible, confused the terrestrial
and the celestial Jerusalem, and returned disillusioned.[3]
They learned in Jerusalem, or after ages have learned through

---

[1] Gregorovius, IV. 288, says no traces of enthusiasm can be found in
Rome. "Senate and people would probably have laughed in derision had
Urban summoned them to rise in religious enthusiasm to forsake the ruins of
Rome and advance to the rescue of Jerusalem." The Crusades were a finan-
cial detriment to Rome by diverting pilgrimages from the tombs of the
Apostles to the tomb of the Saviour.

[2] Here is one such miracle. At the battle of Ramleh, 1177, there was a
miraculous extension of the cross borne by the bishop of Bethlehem. It
reached to heaven and extended its arms across the whole horizon. The
pagans saw it, were confused, and fled. Hoveden, II. 133 sq.

[3] Hegel, *Philosophie der Gesch.*, 3d ed. 1848, p. 476, brings out this idea
most impressively.

them, that Christ is not there, that He is risen, and ascended into heaven, where He sits at the head of a spiritual kingdom.　They conquered Jerusalem, 1099, and lost it, 1187; they reconquered, 1229, and lost again, 1244, the city in which Christ was crucified.　False religions are not to be converted by violence, they can only be converted by the slow but sure process of moral persuasion.　Hatred kindles hatred, and those who take the sword shall perish by the sword.　St. Bernard learned from the failure of the Second Crusade that the struggle is a better one which is waged against the sinful lusts of the heart than was the struggle to conquer Jerusalem.

The immediate causes of the Crusades were the ill treatment of pilgrims visiting Jerusalem and the appeal of the Greek emperor, who was hard pressed by the Turks.　Nor may we forget the feeling of revenge for the Mohammedans begotten in the resistance offered to their invasions of Italy and Gaul.[1]　In 841 they sacked St. Peter's, and in 846 threatened Rome for the second time, and a third time under John VIII.　The Normans wrested a part of Sicily from the Saracens at the battle of Cerame, 1063, took Palermo, 1072, Syracuse, 1085, and the rest of Sicily ten years later.　A burning desire took hold of the Christian world to be in possession of —

> " those holy fields
> Over whose acres walked those blessed feet
> Which fourteen hundred years ago were nail'd
> For our advantage on the bitter cross."
>
> — SHAKESPEARE.

From an early day Jerusalem was the goal of Christian pilgrimage.　The mother of Constantine, Helena, according to the legend, found the cross and certainly built the church over the supposed site of the tomb in which the Lord lay. Jerome spent the last period of his life in Bethlehem, trans-

---

[1] Röhricht, *Gesch. d. ersten Kreuzzuges*, p. 6, says that in these struggles " the crusading enthusiasm was born."

lating the Scriptures and preparing for eternity.   The effect
of such examples was equal to the station and fame of the
pious empress and the Christian scholar.   In vain did such
Fathers as Gregory of Nyssa,[1] Augustine, and even Jerome
himself, emphasize the nearness of God to believers wherever
they may be and the failure of those whose hearts are not
imbued with His spirit to find Him even at Jerusalem.

The movement steadily grew.   The Holy Land became
to the imagination a land of wonders, filled with the divine
presence of Christ.   To have visited it, to have seen Jerusalem, to have bathed in the Jordan, was for a man to have
about him a halo of sanctity.   The accounts of returning
pilgrims were listened to in convent and on the street with
open-mouthed curiosity.   To surmount the dangers of such
a journey in a pious frame of mind was a means of expiation
for sins.[2]   Special laws were enacted in the pilgrim's behalf.
Hospitals and other beneficent institutions were erected for
their comfort along the main route and in Jerusalem.

Other circumstances gave additional impulse to the movement, such as the hope of securing relics of which Palestine
and Constantinople were the chief storehouses ; and the opportunity of starting a profitable trade in silk, paper, spices,
and other products of the East.

These pilgrimages were not seriously interrupted by the
Mohammedans after their conquest of Jerusalem by Omar in

---

[1] See the beautiful testimony of Gregory, who advised a Cappadocian abbot
against going with his monks to Jerusalem, Schaff, *Ch. Hist.* III. 906.

[2] Fulke the Black, count of Anjou (987–1040), made three journeys to
Jerusalem in penance for sacrilege and other crimes.   He had burned his
young wife at the stake dressed in her gayest attire, and caused his son to
crouch at his feet harnessed as an ass.   At Jerusalem he showed his devotion by going about with a halter about his neck.   He bit off a piece of the
Lord's tombstone with his teeth and carried back to Europe objects most
sacred and priceless, such as the fingers of Apostles and the lamp in which
the holy fire was lit.   Odolric, bishop of Orleans, gave a pound of gold for
the lamp and hung it up in the church at Orleans, where its virtue cured multitudes of sick people.

637, until Syria and Palestine passed into the hands of the sultans of Egypt three centuries later.   Under Hakim, 1010, a fierce persecution broke out against the Christian residents of Palestine and the pilgrims.   It was, however, of short duration and was followed by a larger stream of pilgrims than before.   The favorite route was through Rome and by the sea, a dangerous avenue, as it was infested by Saracen pirates.   The conversion of the Hungarians in the tenth century opened up the route along the Danube.   Barons, princes, bishops, monks followed one after the other, some of them leading large bodies of pious tourists.   In 1035 Robert of Normandy went at the head of a great company of nobles. He found many waiting at the gates of Jerusalem, unable to pay the gold bezant demanded for admission, and paid it for them.   In 1054 Luitbert, bishop of Cambray, is said to have led three thousand pilgrims.   In 1064 Siegfried, archbishop of Mainz, was accompanied by the bishops of Utrecht, Bamberg, and Regensburg and twelve thousand pilgrims.[1]   In 1092 Eric, king of the Danes, made the long journey.   A sudden check was put upon the pilgrimages by the Seljukian Turks, who conquered the Holy Land in 1076.   A rude and savage tribe, they heaped, with the intense fanaticism of new converts, all manner of insults and injuries upon the Christians.   Many were imprisoned or sold into slavery.   Those who returned to Europe carried with them a tale of woe which aroused the religious feelings of all classes.

The other appeal, coming from the Greek emperors, was of less weight.[2]   The Eastern empire had been fast losing its hold on its Asiatic possessions.   Romanus Diogenes was

---

[1] Hauck, IV. 79.

[2] Ekkehard, 5, *Rec.*, V. 14, may exaggerate when he speaks of very frequent letters and embassies from the Greek emperors to the West, *per legationes frequentissimas et epistolas etiam a nobis visas . . . lugubriter inclamanter*, etc.   The letter of Alexius to Robert of Flanders, 1088, has been the subject of much inquiry.   Hagenmeyer pronounces it genuine, after a most careful investigation, *Epistulæ*, etc., 10–44.

defeated in battle with the Turks and taken prisoner, 1071. During the rule of his successor, an emir established himself in Nicæa, the seat of the council called by the first Constantine, and extended his rule as far as the shores of the sea of Marmora.   Alexius Comnenus, coming to the throne 1081, was less able to resist the advance of Islam and lost Antioch and Edessa in 1086.   Thus pressed by his Asiatic foes, and seeing the very existence of his throne threatened, he applied for help to the West.   He dwelt, it is true, on the desolations of Jerusalem; but it is in accordance with his imperial character to surmise that he was more concerned for the defence of his own empire than for the honor of religion.

This dual appeal met a response, not only in the religious spirit of Europe, but in the warlike instincts of chivalry; and when the time came for the chief figure in Christendom, Urban II., to lift up his voice, his words acted upon the sensitive emotions as sparks upon dry leaves. [1]

Three routes were chosen by the Crusaders to reach the Holy Land.   The first was the overland route by way of the Danube, Constantinople, and Asia Minor.   The second, adopted by Philip and Richard in the Third Crusade, was by the Mediterranean to Acre.   The route of the last two Crusades, under Louis IX., was across the Mediterranean to Egypt, which was to be made the base of operations from which to reach Jerusalem.

§ 49.   *The Call to the Crusades.*

> " the romance
> Of many colored Life that Fortune pours
> Round the Crusaders."
> — WORDSWORTH, *Ecclesiastical Sonnets.*

The call which resulted in the first expedition for the recovery of Jerusalem was made by Pope Urban II. at the

[1] Diehl, in *Essays on the Crusades*, 92, seems even to deny that an appeal was ever made by the Byzantine emperor Alexius for aid to the West, and

Council of Clermont, 1095. Its chief popular advocate was Peter the Hermit.

The idea of such a movement was not born at the close of the eleventh century. Gregory VII., appealed to by Michael VII. of Constantinople, had, in two encyclicals, 1074,[1] urged the cause upon all Christians, and summoned them to go to the rescue of the Byzantine capital. He reminded them that the pagans had forced their way almost up to the walls of the city and killed many thousands of their brethren like cattle.[2] He also repeatedly called attention to the project in letters to the counts of Burgundy and Poitiers and to Henry IV. His ulterior hope was the subjection of the Eastern churches to the dominion of the Apostolic see. In the year 1074 he was able to announce to Henry IV. that fifty thousand Christian soldiers stood ready to take up arms and follow him to the East, but Gregory was prevented from executing his design by his quarrel with the emperor.

There is some evidence that more than half a century earlier Sergius IV., d. 1012, suggested the idea of an armed expedition against the Mohammedans who had "defiled Jerusalem and destroyed the church of the Holy Sepulchre." Earlier still, Sylvester II., d. 1003, may have urged the same project.[3]

Peter the Hermit, an otherwise unknown monk of Amiens, France, on returning from a pilgrimage to Jerusalem, spread

speaks of it as an invention of a later time.   Certainly no criticism could be more unwarranted unless all the testimonies of the contemporary writers are to be ruthlessly set aside.

[1] *Reg.*, I. 49 ; II. 37, Migne, 148, 329, 390.

[2] *multa millia Christianorum quasi pecudes occidisse*, *Reg.*, I. 49.

[3] See Jules Lair, *Études crit. sur divers textes des Xe et XIe siècles. Bulle du pape Sergius IV.*, etc., Paris, 1899. Lair, in opposition to Riant, Pflugk-Harttung, etc., gives reasons for accepting as genuine Sergius's letter, found 1857.   For Sylvester's letter see Havet, *Lettres de Gerbert*, Paris, 1889. Röhricht, *Gesch. d. ersten Kreuzzuges*, 8, pronounces Sylvester's letter a forgery, dating from 1095.   Lair tries to prove it was written by Sergius IV.

its tale of woes and horrors.[1]   In Jerusalem he had seen the
archbishop, Simeon, who urged him to carry to Europe an
appeal for help against the indignities to which the Christians
were subjected.   While asleep in the church of the Holy
Sepulchre and after prayer and fasting, Peter had a dream in
which Christ appeared to him and bade him go and quickly
spread the appeal that the holy place might be purged.[2]   He
hurried westward, carrying a letter from Simeon, and secured the ear of Urban at Rome.   This is the story as told
by William of Tyre and by Albert of Aachen before him.
Alleged dreams and visions were potent forces during the
First Crusade, and it is altogether likely that many a pilgrim,
looking upon the desolation of Jerusalem, heard within himself the same call which Peter in imagination or in a real
dream heard the Lord making to him.

Urban listened to Peter's account as he had listened to the
accounts of other returning pilgrims.   He had seen citizens
of Jerusalem itself with his own eyes, and exiles from Antioch,
bewailing the plight of those places and begging for alms.[3]

---

[1] The date of the pilgrimage is not given, but may be accepted as having
fallen between 1092–1094.   Peter is called "the Hermit" by all the accounts,
beginning with the earliest, the *Gesta Francorum*.   There is no good ground
for doubting that he was from Amiens, as Albert of Aachen distinctly states.
William of Tyre says from the "bishopric of Amiens."   Hagenmeyer, p. 39,
accepts the latter as within the truth.

[2] William of Tyre, Bk. I. 12, *Rec.*, I. 35, gives only a few lines to the
visions and the words spoken by the Lord.   His account of the meeting
with Urban is equally simple and scarcely less brief.   Peter found, so he
writes, "the Lord Pope Urban in the vicinity of Rome and presented the letters from the patriarch and Christians of Jerusalem and showed their misery
and the abominations which the unclean races wrought in the holy places.
Thus prudently and faithfully he performed the commission intrusted to
him."

[3] At the Council of Clermont Urban made reference to the "very many
reports" which had come of the desolation of Jerusalem, Fulcher, *Rec.*, III.
324.   Robert the Monk, I. 1, *Rec.*, III. 727, says *relatio gravis sæpissime
jam ad aures nostras pervenit*.   According to Baldric he appealed to the
many among his hearers who could vouch for the desolate condition of
the holy places from their own experience, *Rec.*, IV. 14.   See Hagenmeyer,
74–77.

Peter, as he journeyed through Italy and across the Alps,[1] proclaimed the same message. The time for action had come.

At the Council of Piacenza, in the spring of 1095, envoys were present from the emperor Alexius Comnenus and made addresses, invoking aid against the advancing Turks.[2] In the following November the famous Council of Clermont, Southern France, was held, which decreed the First Crusade.[3]

The council comprised a vast number of ecclesiastics and laymen, especially from France. Urban II. was present in person. On the day of the opening there were counted fourteen archbishops, two hundred and fifty bishops, and four hundred abbots. Thousands of tents were pitched outside the walls. On the ninth day, the pope addressed the multitude from a platform erected in the open air. It was a fortunate moment for Urban, and has been compared to Christmas Day, 800, when Charlemagne was crowned.[4] The address was the most effective sermon ever preached by a pope or any other mortal. It stirred the deepest feelings of the hearers and was repeated throughout all Europe.[5]

At Clermont, Urban was on his native soil and probably spoke in the Provençal tongue, though we have only Latin reports. When we recall the general character of the age and the listening throng, with its mingled feelings of love of

---

[1] So William of Tyre, Bk. I. 13. Later writers extend the journey of Peter inordinately.

[2] William of Tyre does not mention this embassy. It may be because of the low opinion he had of Alexius, whom (II. 5) he pronounces scheming and perfidious.

[3] There is no statement that the council formally decreed the Crusade. For the acts we are dependent upon scattered statements of chroniclers and several other unofficial documents.

[4] Ranke, *Weltgeschichte.* According to William of Tyre, Peter the Hermit was present at Clermont. The contemporary writers do not mention his presence.

[5] Gregorovius, IV. 287, is right when he says, "the importance of Urban's speech in universal history outweighs the orations of Demosthenes and Cicero."

adventure and credulous faith, we cannot wonder at the response made to the impassioned appeals of the head of Christendom. Urban reminded his hearers that they, as the elect of God, must carry to their brethren in the East the succor for which they had so often cried out. The Turks, a "Persian people, an accursed race,"[1] had devastated the kingdom of God by fire, pillage, and sword and advanced as far as the Arm of St. George (the Hellespont). Jerusalem was laid waste. Antioch, once the city of Peter, was under their yoke. As the knights loved their souls, so they should fight against the barbarians who had fought against their brothers and kindred.[2] Christ himself would lead the advancing warriors across sea and mountains. Jerusalem, "the navel of the world," and the land fruitful above all others, a paradise of delights, awaited them.[3] "The way is short, the toil will be followed by an incorruptible crown."[4]

A Frenchman himself, Urban appealed to his hearers as

[1] Robert the Monk, I. 1, *Rec.*, III. 727. The contemporary writers, giving an account of Urban's speech, are Baldric, Guibert, Fulcher, and Robert the Monk. All of them were present at Clermont. William of Tyre greatly elaborates the address, and Röhricht calls William's account an invention which is a masterpiece of its kind, — *eine Erdichtung die ein Meisterstück seiner Art*, etc., *Gesch. des ersten Kreuzzuges*, p. 20. Röhricht, pp. 235–239, and Munro, "Am. Hist. Rev.," 1906, pp. 231–243, make interesting attempts to reconstruct Urban's address. The different accounts are not to be regarded as contradictory, but as supplementary one of the other. Röhricht, p. 20, expresses the opinion that none of the accounts of the address is "accurate." No doubt the spirit and essential contents are preserved. Urban made prominent the appeals for aid from the East, the desolations of Jerusalem, and the sufferings of Christians in the East. See Munro.

[2] Fulcher, *Rec.*, III. 324. I follow chiefly the accounts of Fulcher and Robert. Robert represents the appeals for aid as coming from Jerusalem and Constantinople.

[3] Robert the Monk, I. 2, *Rec.*, III. 729. The expression "navel of the earth," *umbilicus terrarum*, used here by Robert, was a common one for Jerusalem.

[4] Baldric, *Rec.*, IV. 15, *via brevis est, labor permodicus est qui tamen immarcescibilem vobis rependet coronam.* Gregory VII., *Reg.*, II. 37, Migne, 148, 390, had made the same promise, quoting 2 Cor. iv. 17, that for the toils of a moment the Crusaders would secure an eternal reward.

Frenchmen, distinguished above all other nations by remarkable glory in arms, courage, and bodily prowess. He appealed to the deeds of Charlemagne and his son Lewis, who had destroyed pagan kingdoms and extended the territory of the Church.

To this moving appeal the answer came back from the whole throng, "God wills it, God wills it." [1] "It is," added the pope, "it is the will of God. Let these words be your war-cry when you unsheathe the sword. You are soldiers of the cross. Wear on your breasts or shoulders the blood-red sign of the cross. Wear it as a token that His help will never fail you, as the pledge of a vow never to be recalled." [2]

Thousands at once took the vow and sewed the cross on their garments or branded it upon their bare flesh. Adhemar, bishop of Puy, knelt at Urban's feet, asking permission to go, and was appointed papal legate. The next day envoys came announcing that Raymund of Toulouse had taken the vow. The spring of 1096 was set for the expedition to start. Urban discreetly declined to lead the army in person.[3]

The example set at Clermont was followed by thousands throughout Europe. Fiery preachers carried Urban's message. The foremost among them, Peter the Hermit, traversed Southern France to the confines of Spain and Lorraine and went along the Rhine. Judged by results, he was one of the most successful of evangelists. His appearance was well suited to strike the popular imagination. He rode on an ass, his face emaciated and haggard, his feet bare, a slouched

---

[1] *Deus vult, Deos lo volt, Diex el volt.* These are the different forms in which the response is reported. For this response in its Latin form, Robert the Monk is our earliest authority, I. 2, *Rec.*, III. 729. He says *una vociferatio* "*Deus vult, Deus vult.*"

[2] In the First Crusade all the crosses were red. Afterwards green and white colors came into use. Urban himself distributed crosses. Guibert, II. 5, *Rec.*, IV. 140, and Fulcher, I. 4, state that Urban had the Crusaders wear the cross as a badge.

[3] Urban's letters, following up his speech at Clermont, are given by Hagenmeyer, *Epistulæ*, p. 136 sqq.

cowl on his head,[1] and a long mantle reaching to his ankles, and carrying a great cross. In stature he was short.[2] His keen wit,[3] his fervid and ready, but rude and unpolished, eloquence,[4] made a profound impression upon the throngs which gathered to hear him.[5] His messages seemed to them divine.[6] They plucked the very hairs from his ass' tail to be preserved as relics. A more potent effect was wrought than mere temporary wonder. Reconciliations between husbands and wives and persons living out of wedlock were effected, and peace and concord established where there were feud and litigation. Large gifts were made to the preacher. None of the other preachers of the Crusade, Volkmar, Gottschalk, and Emich,[7] could compare with Peter the Hermit for eloquence and the spell he exercised upon the masses. He was held in higher esteem than prelates and abbots.[8] And Guibert of Nogent says that he could recall no one who was held in like honor.[9]

In a few months large companies were ready to march against the enemies of the cross.

---

[1] *Petrum more heremi vilissima cappa tegebat,* Radulf of Caen. The above description is taken from strictly contemporary accounts.

[2] The *statura brevis* of Radulf becomes in William of Tyre's account *pusillus, persona contemptibilis.*

[3] I have thus translated Radulf's *spiritus acer.*

[4] Albert of Aachen : *neminem invenerunt qui tam ferocissimo et superbo loqui auderet quousque Petrus.*

[5] So Guibert speaks of the crowds listening to him as *tanta populorum multitudo.* Hagenmeyer, p. 114, accepting Guibert's statement, refers to immense throngs, *ungeheure Zahl.*

[6] Guibert: *quidquid agebat namque seu loquebatur quasi quiddam subdivinum videbatur.*

[7] So Ekkehard, XII., *Rec.,* V. 20 sq. who has something derogatory to say of all of these preachers and also of Peter's subsequent career. *Quem postea multi hypocritam esse dicebant.*

[8] Robert the Monk, I. 5, *Rec.,* III. 731. *Super ipsos præsules et abbates apice religionis efferebatur.*

[9] Guibert : *neminem meminerim similem honore haberi.* Baldric speaks of him as *Petrus quidam magnus heremita,* or as we would say, "that great hermit, Peter."

A new era in European history was begun.[1] A new passion had taken hold of its people. A new arena of conquest was opened for the warlike feudal lord, a tempting field of adventure and release for knight and debtor, an opportunity of freedom for serf and villein. All classes, lay and clerical, saw in the expedition to the cradle of their faith a solace for sin, a satisfaction of Christian fancy, a heaven-appointed mission. The struggle of states with the papacy was for the moment at an end. All Europe was suddenly united in a common and holy cause, of which the supreme pontiff was beyond dispute the appointed leader.

§ 50. *The First Crusade and the Capture of Jerusalem.*

> " And what if my feet may not tread where He stood,
> Nor my ears hear the dashing of Galilee's flood,
> Nor my eyes see the cross which He bowed Him to bear,
> Nor my knees press Gethsemane's garden of prayer,
>
> Yet, Loved of the Father, Thy Spirit is near
> To the meek and the lowly and penitent here ;
> And the voice of Thy Love is the same even now,
> As at Bethany's tomb or on Olivet's brow."
> — WHITTIER.

The 15th of August, 1096, the Feast of the Assumption, fixed by the Council of Clermont for the departure of the Crusaders, was slow in coming. The excitement was too intense for the people to wait. As early as March throngs of both sexes and all ages began to gather in Lorraine and at Treves, and to demand of Peter the Hermit and other leaders to lead them immediately to Jerusalem.[2] It was a hetero-

---

[1] Hegel, *Philosophie der Gesch.*, p. 444, calls the Crusades " the culminating point of the Middle Ages." Contemporaries like Guibert of Nogent, 123, could think of no movement equal in glory with the Crusades. Ordericus Vitalis, III. 458, praised the union of peoples of different tongues in a project so praiseworthy.

[2] For the account of these early expeditions, we are chiefly dependent upon Albert of Aachen. Guibert makes no distinction of sections, and has only a cursory notice of the expeditions before the arrival of Peter in Constantinople.

geneous multitude of devout enthusiasts and idle adventurers, without proper preparation of any kind. The priest forsook his cell, the peasant left his plough and placed his wife and children on carts drawn by oxen, and thus went forth to make the journey and to fight the Turk. At the villages along the route the children cried out, "Is this Jerusalem, is this Jerusalem?" William of Malmesbury wrote (IV. 2) "The Welshman left his hunting, the Scot his fellowship with lice, the Dane his drinking party, the Norwegian his raw fish. Fields were deserted of their husbandmen; whole cities migrated. . . . God alone was placed before their eyes."

The unwieldy bands, or swarms, were held together loosely under enthusiastic but incompetent leaders. The first swarm, comprising from twelve thousand to twenty thousand under Walter the Penniless,[1] marched safely through Hungary, but was cut to pieces at the storming of Belgrade or destroyed in the Bulgarian forests. The leader and a few stragglers were all that reached Constantinople.

The second swarm, comprising more than forty thousand, was led by the Hermit himself. There were knights not a few, and among the ecclesiastics were the archbishop of Salzburg and the bishops of Chur and Strassburg. On their march through Hungary they were protected by the Hungarian king; but when they reached the Bulgarian frontier, they found one continuous track of blood and fire, robbery and massacre, marking the route of their predecessors. Only a remnant of seven thousand reached Constantinople, and they in the most pitiful condition, July, 1096. Here they were well treated by the Emperor Alexius, who transported them across the Bosphorus to Asia, where they were to await the arrival of the regular army. But they pre-

---

[1] Sine Pecunia, Sansavoir, Habenichts. These preliminary expeditions, Röhricht and other historians call *Die Züge der Bauern*, the campaigns of the peasants.

ferred to rove, marauding and plundering, through the rich provinces. Finally, a false rumor that the vanguard had captured Nicæa, the capital of the Turks in Asia Minor, allured the main body into the plain of Nicæa, where large numbers were surrounded and massacred by the Turkish cavalry. Their bones were piled into a ghastly pyramid, the first monument of the Crusade. Walter fell in the battle; Peter the Hermit had fled back to Constantinople before the battle began, unable to control his followers. The defeat of Nicæa no doubt largely destroyed Peter's reputation.[1]

A third swarm, comprising fifteen thousand, mostly Germans under the lead of the monk Gottschalk, was massacred by the Hungarians.

Another band, under count Emich of Leiningen, began its career, May, 1096, by massacring and robbing the Jews in Mainz and other cities along the Rhine. Albert of Aachen,[2] who describes these scenes, does not sympathize with this lawlessness, but saw a divine judgment in its almost complete annihilation in Hungary. This band was probably a part of the swarm, estimated at the incredible number of two hundred thousand,[3] led by banners bearing the likeness of a goose and a goat, which were considered as bearers of the divine Spirit.[4] Three thousand horsemen, headed by some noblemen, attended them, and shared the spoils taken

[1] See Hagenmeyer, 204 sq. Peter apologized to the emperor for the defeat on the ground of his inability to control his followers, who, he declared, were unworthy to see Jerusalem. Anna Comnena calls Peter the "inflated Latin."

[2] I. 26.

[3] Anna Comnena says the Crusaders flowed together from all directions like rivers. She gives the number of Peter's army as eighty thousand foot and one hundred thousand horse. Fulcher speaks of the numbers setting out from the West as "an immense assemblage. The islands of the sea and the whole earth were moved by God to make contribution to the host. The sadness was for those who remained behind, the joy for those who departed."

[4] This is upon the testimony of Albert of Aachen and Guibert. See Röhricht, *Erster Kreuzzug*, 240 sq., and references there given.

from the Jews.[1] When they arrived at the Hungarian frontier they had to encounter a regular army. A panic seized them, and a frightful carnage took place.

These preliminary expeditions of the first Crusade may have cost three hundred thousand lives.

The regular army consisted, according to the lowest statements, of more than three hundred thousand. It proceeded through Europe in sections which met at Constantinople and Nicæa. Godfrey, starting from lower Lorraine, had under him thirty thousand men on foot and ten thousand horse. He proceeded along the Danube and by way of Sofia and Philipoppolis. Hugh of Vermandois went by way of Rome, where he received the golden banner, and then, taking ship from Bari to Durazzo, made a junction with Godfrey in November, 1096, under the walls of Constantinople. Bohemund, with a splendid following of one hundred thousand horse and thirty thousand on foot,[2] took the same route from Bari across the Adriatic. Raymund of Toulouse, accompanied by his countess, Elvira, and the papal legate, bishop Adhemar,[3] traversed Northern Italy on his way eastward. The last of the main armies to start was led by Robert, duke of Normandy, and Stephen of Blois, who crossed the Alps, received the pope's blessing at Lucca, and, passing through Rome, transported their men across the Adriatic from Bari and Brindisi.

Godfrey of Bouillon[4] was accompanied by his brothers,

[1] Mannheimer, *Die Judenverfolgungen in Speier, Worms und Mainz im Jahre 1096, während des ersten Kreuzzuges*, Darmstadt, 1877. Hagenmeyer, p. 139, clears Peter of Amiens of the shameful glory of initiating this *racial massacre*, and properly claims it for count Emich and his mob. See also Röhricht, *Gesch. d. ersten Kreuzzuges*, 41–46.

[2] Albert of Aachen, II. 18.

[3] Gibbon calls him "a respectable prelate alike qualified for this world and the next."

[4] Bouillon, not to be confounded with Boulogne-sur-mer, on the English Channel, is a town in Belgian Luxemburg, and was formerly the capital of the lordship of Bouillon, which Godfrey mortgaged to the bishop of Liège in 1095. It has belonged to Belgium since 1831.

Baldwin and Eustace. Hugh, count of Vermandois, was a brother of Philip I. of France. Robert of Normandy was the eldest son of William the Conqueror, and had made provision for his expedition by pledging Normandy to his brother, William Rufus, for ten thousand marks silver. Raymund, count of Toulouse, was a veteran warrior, who had a hundred thousand horse and foot at his command, and enjoyed a mingled reputation for wealth, wisdom, pride, and greed. Bohemund, prince of Tarentum, was the son of Robert Guiscard. His cousin, Tancred, was the model cavalier. Robert, count of Flanders, was surnamed " the Sword and Lance of the Christians." Stephen, count of Chartres, Troyes, and Blois, was the owner of three hundred and sixty-five castles. These and many other noblemen constituted the flower of the French, Norman, and Italian nobility.

The moral hero of the First Crusade is Godfrey of Bouillon, a descendant of Charlemagne in the female line, but he had no definite command. He had fought in the war of emperor Henry IV. against the rebel king, Rudolf of Swabia, whom he slew in the battle of Mölsen, 1080. He had prodigious physical strength. With one blow of his sword he clove asunder a horseman from head to saddle. He was as pious as he was brave, and took the cross for the single purpose of rescuing Jerusalem from the hands of the infidel. He used his prowess and bent his ancestral pride to the general aim. Contemporary historians call him a holy monk in military armor and ducal ornament. His purity and disinterestedness were acknowledged by his rivals.

Tancred, his intimate friend, likewise engaged in the enterprise from pure motives. He is the poetic hero of the First Crusade, and nearly approached the standard of "the parfite gentil knyght" of Chaucer. He distinguished himself at Nicæa, Dorylæum, Antioch, and was one of the first to climb the walls of Jerusalem. He died in Antioch, 1112.

His deeds were celebrated by Raoul de Caen and Torquato Tasso.[1]

The emperor Alexius, who had so urgently solicited the aid of Western Europe, became alarmed when he saw the hosts arriving in his city. They threatened to bring famine into the land and to disturb the order of his realm. He had wished to reap the benefit of the Crusade, but now was alarmed lest he should be overwhelmed by it. His subtle policy and precautions were felt as an insult by the Western chieftains. In diplomacy he was more than their match. They expected fair dealing and they were met by duplicity. He held Hugh of Vermandois in easy custody till he promised him fealty. Even Godfrey and Tancred, the latter after delay, made the same pledge. Godfrey declined to receive the emperor's presents for fear of receiving poison with his munificence.

The Crusaders had their successes. Nicæa was taken June 19, 1097, and the Turks were routed a few weeks later in a disastrous action at Dorylæum in Phrygia, which turned into a more disastrous flight. But a long year elapsed till they could master Antioch, and still another year came to an end before Jerusalem yielded to their arms. The success of the enterprise was retarded and its glory diminished by the selfish jealousies and alienation of the leaders which culminated in disgraceful conflicts at Antioch. The hardships and privations of the way were terrible, almost beyond description. The Crusaders were forced to eat horse flesh, camels, dogs, and mice, and even worse.[2] The sufferings from thirst exceeded, if possible, the sufferings from hunger. To these discouragements was added the manifest treachery of the Greek emperor at the capture of Nicæa.[3]

---

[1] Gibbon : "In the accomplished character of Tancred we discover all the virtues of a perfect knight, the true spirit of chivalry, which inspired the generous sentiments and social offices of man far better than the base philosophy, or the baser religion, of the times."　[2] Fulcher, I. 13, *Rec.*, III. 336.

[3] Raymund of Agiles says Alexius treated the crusading army in such wise that so "long as ever he lives, the people will curse him and call him a traitor."

During the siege of Antioch, which had fallen to the Seljuks, 1084, the ranks were decimated by famine, pestilence, and desertion, among the deserters being Stephen of Chartres and his followers. Peter the Hermit and William of Carpentarius were among those who attempted flight, but were caught in the act of fleeing and severely reprimanded by Bohemund.[1] Immediately after the first recapture of the city, through the treachery of Phirouz, an Armenian, the Crusaders were themselves besieged by an army of two hundred thousand under Kerboga of Mosul. Their languishing energies were revived by the miraculous discovery of the holy lance, which pierced the Saviour's side. This famous instrument was hidden under the altar of St. Peter's church. The hiding place was revealed in a dream to Peter Barthelemy, the chaplain of Raymund of Toulouse.[2] The sacred weapon was carried in front of the ranks by Raymund of Agiles, one of the historians of the Crusade, and it aroused great enthusiasm. Kerboga withdrew and the city fell into the Crusaders' hands, June 28, 1098.[3] Bohemund appropriated it to himself as his prize. Baldwin, after the fall of Nicæa, had done the same with Edessa, which became the easternmost citadel of the Crusaders. Others followed the examples of these leaders and went on independent expeditions of conquest. Of those who died at Antioch was Adhemar.

[1] The contemporary authorities represent the reprimand as given to Carpentarius. As Hagenmeyer suggests, Peter was included and Carpentarius' name alone mentioned because he was of royal blood.

[2] Among those who helped to dig for the weapon was Raymund of Agiles. Its authenticity was a matter of dispute, Adhemar being one of those who doubted. Barthelemy went through the ordeal of fire to prove the truth of his statements, but died in consequence of the injuries he suffered.

[3] According to Robert the Monk, IV., *Rec.*, III. 824, a heavenly sign was granted on the eve of the final attack, a flame burning in the western sky, *ignis de cœlo veniens ab occidente*. One of the interesting remains of the crusadal period are two letters written by Stephen, count of Chartres, to his wife Adele, the one before Nicæa and the other during the siege of Antioch. They are given in Hagenmeyer, *Epistulæ*, pp. 138, 149.

The culmination of the First Crusade was the fall of Jerusalem, July 15, 1099. It was not till the spring following the capture of Antioch, that the leaders were able to compose their quarrels and the main army was able again to begin the march. The route was along the coast to Cæsarea and thence southeastward to Ramleh. Jerusalem was reached early in June. The army was then reduced to twenty thousand fighting men.[1] In one of his frescos in the museum at Berlin, representing the six chief epochs in human history, Kaulbach has depicted with great effect the moment when the Crusaders first caught sight of the Holy City from the western hills. For the religious imagination it was among the most picturesque moments in history as it was indeed one of the most solemn in the history of the Middle Ages. The later narratives may well have the essence of truth in them, which represent the warriors falling upon their knees and kissing the sacred earth. Laying aside their armor, in bare feet and amid tears, penitential prayers, and chants, they approached the sacred precincts.[2]

A desperate but futile assault was made on the fifth day. Boiling pitch and oil were used, with showers of stones and other missiles, to keep the Crusaders at bay. The siege then took the usual course in such cases. Ladders, scaling towers, and other engines of war were constructed, but the wood had to be procured at a distance, from Shechem. The trees around Jerusalem, cut down by Titus twelve centuries before, had never been replaced. The city was invested on three sides by Raymund of Toulouse, Godfrey, Tancred, Robert of Normandy, and other chiefs. The suffering due

---

[1] The figures are differently given. See Sybel, 412, and Röhricht, *Gesch. des ersten Kreuzzuges*, 183. William of Tyre gives the number as twenty-one thousand, and the army defending Jerusalem as forty thousand.

[2] Raymund of Agiles reports that the Crusaders forgot the exhortation of Peter Barthelemy to make the last part of the journey barefoot. "They remembered their weariness no more, and hastening their steps reached the walls amidst tears and praises."

to the summer heat and the lack of water was intense. The valley and the hills were strewn with dead horses, whose putrefying carcasses made life in the camp almost unbearable. In vain did the Crusaders with bare feet, the priests at their head, march in procession around the walls, hoping to see them fall as the walls of Jericho had fallen before Joshua.[1] Help at last came with the arrival of a Genoese fleet in the harbor of Joppa, which brought workmen and supplies of tools and food.

Friday, the day of the crucifixion, was chosen for the final assault. A great tower surmounted by a golden cross was dragged alongside of the walls and the drawbridge let down. At a critical moment, as the later story went, a soldier of brilliant aspect[2] was seen on the Mount of Olives, and Godfrey, encouraging the besiegers, exclaimed: "It is St. George the martyr. He has come to our help." According to most of the accounts, Letold of Tournay[3] was the first to scale the walls. It was noticed that the moment of this crowning feat was three o'clock, the hour of the Saviour's death.

The scenes of carnage which followed belong to the many dark pages of Jerusalem's history and showed how, in the quality of mercy, the crusading knight was far below the ideal of Christian perfection. The streets were choked with the bodies of the slain. The Jews were burnt with their synagogues. The greatest slaughter was in the temple enclosure. With an exaggeration which can hardly be credited, but without a twinge of regret or a syllable of

[1] On this occasion Peter the Hermit and Arnulf, afterwards archbishop of Jerusalem, made addresses on the Mount of Olives to restore unity among the crusading leaders, especially Tancred and Raymund. Albert of Aachen, VI. 8, *Rec.*, IV. 471, says, *ad populos sermones . . . plurimam discordiam quæ inter Peregrinos de diversis causis excreverat exstinxerunt.* Tancred had stirred up much jealousy by raising his banner over Bethlehem. Hagenmeyer, p. 259, accepts Albert's account as genuine against Sybel.

[2] *Miles splendidus et refulgens.*

[3] Guibert, VII. 7, *Rec.*, IV. 226 ; Robert the Monk, VII., *Rec.*, III. 867.

excuse, it is related that the blood of the massacred in the temple area reached to the very knees and bridles of the horses.[1] "Such a slaughter of the pagans had never been seen or heard of. The number none but God knew."[2]

Penitential devotions followed easily upon the gory butchery of the sword. Headed by Godfrey, clad in a suit of white linen, the Crusaders proceeded to the church of the Holy Sepulchre and offered up prayers and thanksgivings. William of Tyre relates that Adhemar and others, who had fallen by the way, were seen showing the path to the holy places. The devotions over, the work of massacre was renewed. Neither the tears of women, nor the cries of children, nor the protests of Tancred, who for the honor of chivalry was concerned to save three hundred, to whom he had promised protection — none of these availed to soften the ferocity of the conquerors.

As if to enhance the spectacle of pitiless barbarity, Saracen prisoners were forced to clear the streets of the dead bodies and blood to save the city from pestilence. "They wept and transported the dead bodies out of Jerusalem," is the heartless statement of Robert the Monk.[3]

Such was the piety of the Crusaders. The religion of the Middle Ages combined self-denying asceticism with heartless cruelty to infidels, Jews, and heretics. "They cut down with the sword," said William of Tyre, "every one whom they found in Jerusalem, and spared no one. The

---

[1] So Raymund of Agiles, an eyewitness, *usque ad genua et usque ad frenos equorum*, XX., *Rec.*, III. 300. This he calls "the righteous judgment of God."

[2] So the *Gesta: tales occisiones de paganorum gente nullus unquam audivit nec vidit . . . nemo scit numerum eorum nisi solus deus.* The slain are variously estimated from forty thousand to one hundred thousand. Guibert, *Gesta*, VII. 7, *Rec.*, IV. 227, further says that in the temple area there was such a sea of blood, *sanguinis unda*, as almost to submerge the pedestrian.

[3] IX., *Rec.*, III. 869. Robert gives an awful picture of the streets filled with dismembered bodies and running with gore.

victors were covered with blood from head to foot." In the next breath, speaking of the devotion of the Crusaders, the archbishop adds, " It was a most affecting sight which filled the heart with holy joy to see the people tread the holy places in the fervor of an excellent devotion." The Crusaders had won the tomb of the Saviour and gazed upon a fragment of the true cross, which some of the inhabitants were fortunate enough to have kept concealed during the siege.

Before returning to Europe, Peter the Hermit received the homage of the Christian inhabitants of Jerusalem, who remembered his visit as a pilgrim and his services in their behalf. This was the closing scene of his connection with the Crusades.[1] Returning to Europe, he founded the monastery at Huy, in the diocese Liège, and died, 1115. A statue was dedicated to his memory at Amiens, June 29, 1854. He is represented in the garb of a monk, a rosary at his waist, a cross in his right hand, preaching the First Crusade.

Urban II. died two weeks after the fall of Jerusalem and before the tidings of the event had time to reach his ears.

No more favorable moment could have been chosen for the Crusade. The Seljukian power, which was at its height in the eleventh century, was broken up into rival dynasties and factions by the death of Molik Shah, 1092. The Crusaders entered as a wedge before the new era of Moslem conquest and union opened.

NOTE ON THE RELATION OF PETER THE HERMIT TO THE FIRST CRUSADE.

The view of Peter the Hermit, presented in this work, does not accord with the position taken by most of the modern writers on the Crusades. It is based on the testimony of Albert of Aachen and William of Tyre, historians of the First Crusade, and is, that Peter visited Jerusalem as a pilgrim, conversed with the patriarch Simeon over the desolations of the city, had a dream in the church of the Holy Sepulchre, returned to Europe with letters from Simeon which he presented to the pope, and then

---

[1] William of Tyre is the earliest witness to this scene. Leaving out embellishments, it does not seem to be at all unnatural. Hagenmeyer, pp. 265–269, calls it the " sheer invention of William's fancy."

preached through Italy and beyond the Alps, and perhaps attended the Council of Clermont, where, however, he took no prominent part.

The new view is that these occurrences were fictions. It was first set forth by von Sybel in his work on the First Crusade, in 1841. Sybel's work, which marks an epoch in the treatment of the Crusades, was suggested by the lectures of Ranke, 1837.[1] Its author, after a careful comparison of the earliest accounts, announced that there is no reliable evidence that Peter was the immediate instigator of the First Crusade, and that not to him but to Urban II. alone belongs the honor of having originated the movement. Peter did not make a pilgrimage to Jerusalem, meet Urban, or preach about the woes of the Holy City prior to the assembling of the Synod of Clermont.

These views, with some modification, have been advocated by Hagenmeyer in his careful and scholarly work on Peter the Hermit and in other writings on the First Crusade.[2] In our own country the same view has been set forth by eminent scholars. Professor Oliver J. Thatcher, in an article on the *Latin Sources of the First Crusade*,[3] says, "The stories about Peter the Hermit, his pilgrimage to Jerusalem, his visions there, his journey to the pope at Rome, his successful appeals to Urban to preach a crusade, and Peter's commanding position as one of the great preachers and leaders of the Crusade, all are found to be without the least foundation in fact." Dr. Dana C. Munro has recently declared that the belief that Peter was the instigator of the First Crusade has long since been abandoned.[4]

It is proper that the reasons should be given in brief which have led to the retention of the old view in this volume. The author's view agrees with the judgment expressed by Archer, *Story of the Crusades*, p. 27, that the account of Albert of Aachen "is no doubt true in the main."

Albert of Aachen wrote his History of Jerusalem about 1120-1125,[5] that is, while many of the Crusaders were still alive who took part in the siege of Jerusalem, 1099. William, archbishop of Tyre, was born probably in Jerusalem about 1130. He was a man of learning, acquainted with Hebrew, Greek, Latin, and Arabic; well read in the Bible, as his quotations show, and travelled in Europe. He is one of the ablest of the mediæval historians, and his work is the monumental history of the Latin Kingdom of Jerusalem. He was by his residence thoroughly acquainted with Palestine. It is not unworthy of mention that William's History represents the "office of the historian to be not to write what pleases him, but the material which the

---

[1] Sybel, *Gesch. des ersten Kreuzzugs*, p. ii.

[2] Hagenmeyer, *Peter der Eremite*, p. 102, says, Dem Papste allein ist der Ruhm zu erhalten den ihm der Einsiedler von Amiens bis auf unsere Tage zur grösseren Hälfte streitig gemacht hat. Also Sybel, p. 243.

[3] *Report of the Am. Hist. Association*, 1900, p. 504 sq. See also the very emphatic statements of G. L. Burr in art. *The year 1000 and the Antecedents of the Crusades* in the "Am. Hist. Rev.," April, 1901, pp. 429-439, and Trans. and Reprints of the Univ. of Pa., 1894, pp. 19 sqq.

[4] The Speech of Urban II. etc., in "Am. Hist. Rev.," 1906, p. 232.

[5] He says he reports what he heard, *ex auditu et relatione*.

time offers," bk. XXIII. From the sixteenth to the twenty-third book he writes from personal observation. William stands between the credulous enthusiasm of the first writers on the Crusades and the cold scepticism of some modern historians.

The new view, setting aside these two witnesses, bases its conclusion on the strictly contemporary accounts. These are silent about any part Peter took in the movement leading to the First Crusade prior to the Council of Clermont. They are: (1) the *Gesta Francorum*, written by an unknown writer, who reached Jerusalem with the Crusaders, wrote his account about 1099, and left the original, or a copy of it, in Jerusalem. (2) Robert the Monk, who was in Jerusalem, saw a copy of the *Gesta*, and copied from it. His work extends to 1099. He was present at the Council of Clermont. (3) Raymund, canon of Agiles, who accompanied the Crusaders to Jerusalem. (4) Fulcher of Chartres, who was present at Clermont, continued the history to 1125, accompanied the Crusaders to Jerusalem, and had much to do with the discovery of the holy lance. (5) The priest Tudebodus, who copied from the *Gesta* before 1111 and added very little of importance. (6) Ekkehard of Urach, who made a pilgrimage to Jerusalem, 1101. (7) Radulph of Caen, who in 1107 joined Tancred and related what he heard from him. (8) Guibert of Nogent, who was present at Clermont and wrote about 1110. (9) Baldric of Dol, who was at Clermont and copied from the *Gesta* in Jerusalem.

Another contemporary, Anna Comnena, b. 1083, is an exception and reports the activity of Peter prior to the Council of Clermont, and says he made a pilgrimage to Jerusalem, but was not permitted by the Turks to enter. He then hastened to Europe and preached about the woes of the city in order to provide a way to visit it again. Hagenmeyer is constrained by Anna's testimony to concede that Peter actually set forth on a pilgrimage to Jerusalem, but did not reach the city.

The silence of nine contemporary writers is certainly very noticeable. They had the means of knowing the facts. Why, then, do we accept the later statements of Albert of Aachen and William of Tyre? These are the considerations.

1. The silence of contemporary writers is not a final argument against events. Eusebius, the chief historian of the ancient Church, utterly ignores the Catacombs. Silence, said Dr. Philip Schaff, referring to the Crusades, "is certainly not conclusive," "Reformed Ch. Rev.," 1893, p. 449. There is nothing in the earlier accounts contradictory to Peter's activity prior to the Clermont synod. One and another of the writers omit important events of the First Crusade, but that is not a sufficient reason for our setting those events aside as fictitious. The *Gesta* has no account of Urban's speech at Clermont or reference to it. Guibert and Fulcher leave out in their reports of Urban's speech all reference to the appeal from Constantinople. Why does the *Gesta* pass over with the slightest notice Peter's breaking away from Germany on his march to Constantinople? This author's example is followed by Baldric, Tudebod, Fulcher, and Raymund of Agiles. These writers have not a word to say about Gottschalk, Volkmar, and Emich. As Hagenmeyer says, pp. 129, 157, no reason can be assigned for these silences,

and yet the fact of these expeditions and the calamities in Hungary are not doubted.

2. The accounts of Albert of Aachen and of William of Tyre are simply told and not at all unreasonable in their essential content. William definitely makes Peter the precursor of Urban. He was, he said, "of essential service to our lord the pope, who determined to follow him without delay across the mountains. He did him the service of a forerunner and prepared the minds of men in advance so that he might easily win them for himself." There is no indication in the archbishop's words of any purpose to disparage Urban's part in preparing for the Crusade. Urban followed after John the Baptist. William makes Urban the centre of the assemblage at Clermont and gives to his address great space, many times the space given to the experiences of Peter, and all honor is accorded to the pope for the way in which he did his part, bk. I. 16.

3. Serious difficulties are presented in the theory of the growth of the legend of Peter's activity. They are these : (1) Albert of Aachen lived close to the events, and at the most twenty-five years elapsed between the capture of Jerusalem and his writing. (2) There is nothing in Peter's conduct during the progress of the Crusade to justify the growth of an heroic legend around him. The very contrary was the case. Moreover, neither Albert nor William know anything about Peter before his pilgrimage. Hagenmeyer has put the case in the proper light when he says, "Not a single authority suggests that Peter enjoyed any extraordinary repute before his connection with the Crusade. On the contrary, every one that mentions his name connects it with the Crusade," p. 120. (3) It is difficult to understand how the disposition could arise on the part of any narrator to transfer the credit of being the author of the Crusade from a pope to a monk, especially such a monk as Peter turned out to be. In reference to this consideration, Archer, p. 26, has well said, "There is little in the legend of Peter the Hermit which may not very well be true, and the story, as it stands, is more plausible than if we had to assume that tradition had transferred the credit from a pope to a simple hermit." (4) We may very well account for Anna Comnena's story of Peter's being turned back by the Turks by her desire to parry the force of his conversation with the Greek patriarch Simeon. It was her purpose to disparage the Crusade. Had she admitted the message of Simeon through Peter to the pope, she would have conceded a strong argument for the divine approval upon the movement. As for Anna, she makes mistakes, confusing Peter once with Adhemar and once with Peter Barthelemy.

(5) All the accounts mention Peter. He is altogether the most prominent man in stirring up interest in the Crusade subsequent to the council. Hagenmeyer goes even so far as to account for his success by the assumption that Peter made telling use of his abortive pilgrimage, *missglückte Pilgerfahrt*. As already stated, Peter was listened to by "immense throngs"; no one in the memory of the abbot of Nogent had enjoyed so much honor. "He was held in higher esteem than prelates and abbots," says Robert the Monk. As if to counteract the impression upon the reader, these writers emphasize that Peter's influence was over the rude and lawless masses, and, as Guibert says,

that the bands which followed him were the dregs of France. Now it is difficult to understand how a monk, before unknown, who had never been in Jerusalem, and was not at the Council of Clermont, could at once work into his imagination such vivid pictures of the woe and wails of the Christians of the East as to attain a foremost pre-eminence as a preacher of the Crusade.

(6) Good reasons can be given for the omission of Peter's conduct prior to the Council of Clermont by the earliest writers. The Crusade was a holy and heroic movement. The writers were interested in magnifying the part taken by the chivalry of Europe. Some of them were with Peter in the camp, and they found him heady, fanatical, impracticable, and worse. He probably was spurned by the counts and princes. Many of the writers were chaplains of these chieftains, — Raymund, Baldwin, Tancred, Bohemund. The lawlessness of Peter's bands has been referred to. The defeat at Nicæa robbed Peter of all glory and position he might otherwise have had with the main army when it reached Asia.[1] In Antioch he brought upon himself disgrace for attempting flight, being caught in the act by Tancred and Bohemund. The *Gesta* gives a detailed account of this treachery, and Guibert[2] compares his flight to an angel falling from heaven. It is probably with reference to it that Ekkehard says, "Many call him hypocrite."[3] Strange to say, Albert of Aachen and William of Tyre omit all reference to his treacherous flight.[4] It is not improbable that, after the experiences they had of the Hermit in the camp, and the disregard and perhaps the contempt in which he was held by the princes, after his inglorious campaign to Constantinople and Nicæa, the early writers had not the heart to mention his services prior to the council. Far better for the glory of the cause that those experiences should pass into eternal forgetfulness.

Why should legend then come to be attached to his memory ? Why should not Adhemar have been chosen for the honor which was put upon this unknown monk who made so many mistakes and occupied so subordinate a position in the main crusading army ? Why stain the origin of so glorious a movement by making Peter with his infirmities and ignoble birth responsible for the inception of the Crusade ? It would seem as if the theory were more probable that the things which led the great Crusaders to disparage, if not to ridicule, Peter induced the earlier writers to ignore his meritorious activity prior to the Council of Clermont. After the lapse of time, when the memory of his follies was not so fresh, the real services of Peter were again recognized. For these reasons the older portrait of Peter has been regarded as the true one in all its essential features.

---

[1] *Nach einer solchen Katastrophe war offenbar auch bei diesen alles Ansehen für ihn dabei*, Hagenmeyer, p. 204.

[2] *Ut stellæ quoque juxta Apocalypsim de cœlo cadere viderentur, Petrus ille*, etc.

[3] Ekkehard XIII., *Rec.*, V. 21, says that Peter's cohorts became the object of derision to the Turks as soon as they reached Asia Minor, *cohortes . . . paganis fuerant jam ludibrio factæ.*

[4] Hagenmeyer, pp. 220 sqq., 243, suggests that at the time of William's writing such things were no longer told.

§ 51. *The Latin Kingdom of Jerusalem.*
1099–1187.

LITERATURE. — G. T. DE THAUMASSIÈRE : *Assises et bons usages du royaume de Jérusalem*, etc., Paris, 1690, 1712; *Assises de Jérusalem*, in *Recueil des Historiens des croisades*, 2 vols., Paris, 1841–1843. — HODY : *Gode-froy de Bouillon et les rois Latins de Jérus.*, 2d ed., Paris, 1859. — RÖHRICHT : *Regesta Regni Hierosolymitani*, Innsbruck, 1893; *Gesch. des Königreichs Jerus. 1100–1291*, Innsbruck, 1898. — LANE-POOLE : *Saladin and the Fall of the Kingdom of Jerus.*, N.Y., 1898.   The first biography of Saladin in English, written largely from the standpoint of the Arab historians. — C. R. CONDER : *The Latin Kingd. of Jerus.*, London, 1899. — F. KÜHN : *Gesch. der ersten Patriarchen von Jerus.*, Leipzig, 1886. — FUNK : art. *Jerusalem, Christl. Königreich*, in " Wetzer-Welte," VI. p. 1335 sqq.

Eight days after the capture of the Holy City a permanent government was established, known as the Latin kingdom of Jerusalem. Godfrey was elected king, but declined the title of royalty, unwilling to wear a crown of gold where the Saviour had worn a crown of thorns.[1] He adopted the title Baron and Defender of the Holy Sepulchre. The kingdom from its birth was in need of help, and less than a year after the capture of the city the patriarch Dagobert made an appeal to the "rich" German nation for reënforcements.[2] It had a perturbed existence of less than a century, and in that time witnessed a succession of nine sovereigns.

[1] The official title of the kings was *rex Latinorum in Hierusalem*. In rejecting the crown, says William of Tyre, " Godfrey did so as a believing prince. He was the best of kings, the light and mirror of all others," *lumen et speculum*, IX. 9, *Rec.*, I. 377. The clergy had dreamed of the complete subjection of the civil government of Jerusalem to the spiritual government under the patriarch. The first patriarch not only secured for his jurisdiction one-fourth of Jerusalem and Jaffa, but the promise from Godfrey of the whole of both cities, provided Godfrey was successful in taking Cairo or some other large hostile city, or should die without male heirs. See Röhricht, *Gesch. des ersten Kreuzzuges*, p. 218.

[2] See Dagobert's appeal in Hagenmeyer, *Epistulæ*, 176 sq., 412 sqq. He speaks of " Jerusalem as the most excellent of all places for sanctity, " and says that " for this reason it was oppressed by the pagans and infidels." Fulcher, writing of the year 1100, declares that there were only three hundred knights and as many footmen left for the defence of Jerusalem, Jaffa, and Ramleh. See quotation in Hagenmeyer, 415.

Godfrey extended his realm, but survived the capture of Jerusalem only a year, dying July 18, 1100. He was honored and lamented as the most disinterested and devout among the chieftains of the First Crusade. His body was laid away in the church of the Holy Sepulchre, where his reputed sword and spurs are still shown. On his tomb was the inscription : "Here lies Godfrey of Bouillon, who conquered all this territory for the Christian religion. May his soul be at rest with Christ." [1]

With the Latin kingdom was established the Latin patriarchate of Jerusalem. The election of Arnulf, chaplain to Robert of Normandy, was declared irregular, and Dagobert, or Daimbert, archbishop of Pisa, was elected in his place Christmas Day, 1099. [2] Latin sees were erected throughout the land and also a Latin patriarchate of Antioch. Dagobert secured large concessions from Godfrey, including the acknowledgment of his kingdom as a fief of the patriarch. After the fall of Jerusalem, in 1187, the patriarchs lived in Acre. [3]

The constitution and judicial procedure of the new realm were fixed by the Assizes of Jerusalem. These were deposited under seal in the church of the Holy Sepulchre and are also called the Letters of the Holy Sepulchre. [4] They were afterwards lost, and our knowledge of their contents is derived from the codes of Cyprus and the Latin kingdom of Constantinople, which were founded upon the Jerusalem code.

These statutes reproduced the feudal system of Europe. The conquered territory was distributed among the barons,

---

[1] *Hic jacet inclitus dux Godefridus de Bouillon qui totam sitam terram acquisivit cultui christiano, cujus anima regnet cum Christo.*

[2] According to Raymund of Agiles, Arnulf was a man of loose life and his amours subjects of camp songs.

[3] From the fall of Acre, 1291 to 1848, the patriarchs, with two exceptions, lived in Rome. In 1848 Valerga, appointed patriarch by Pius IX., took up his residence in Jerusalem.

[4] Wilken devotes a long treatment to the subject, I. pp. 307–424.

who held their possessions under the king of Jerusalem as
overlord.   The four chief fiefs were Jaffa and Ascalon,
Kerat, east of the Jordan, Galilee, and Sidon.   The counts
of Tripoli and Edessa and the prince of Antioch were independent of the kingdom of Jerusalem.   A system of courts
was provided, the highest being presided over by the king.
Trial by combat of arms was recognized.   A second court
provided for justice among the burgesses.   A third gave it to
the natives.   Villeins or slaves were treated as property according to the discretion of the master, but are also mentioned
as being subject to the courts of law.   The slave and the
falcon were estimated as equal in value.   Two slaves were
held at the price of a horse and three slaves at the price of
twelve oxen.   The man became of age at twenty-five, the
woman at twelve.   The feudal system in Europe was a
natural product.   In Palestine it was an exotic.

The Christian occupation of Palestine did not bring with
it a reign of peace.   The kingdom was torn by the bitter
intrigues of barons and ecclesiastics, while it was being
constantly threatened from without.   The inner strife was
the chief source of weakness.   The monks settled down in
swarms over the country, and the Franciscans became the
guardians of the holy places.   The illegitimate offspring of
the Crusaders by Moslem women, called *pullani*, were a
degenerate race, marked by avarice, faithlessness, and debauchery.[1]

Godfrey was succeeded by his brother Baldwin, count of
Edessa, who was crowned at Bethlehem.   He was a man of
intelligence and the most vigorous of the kings of Jerusalem.
He died of a fever in Egypt, and his body was laid at the
side of his brother's in Jerusalem.

During Baldwin's reign, 1100–1118, the limits of the

---

[1] *Fulani*, "anybodies."   The designation *fulan ibn fulan*, "so and so,
the son of so and so," is a most opprobrious mode of address among the
Arabs.

kingdom were greatly extended.[1]   Cæsarea fell in 1101, St. Jean d'Acre, otherwise known as Ptolemais, in 1104, and Berytus, or Beyrut, in 1110.   Sidon capitulated to Sigurd, son of the king of Norway, who had with him ten thousand Crusaders.   One-third of Asia Minor was reduced, a part of the territory reverting to the Greek empire.   Damascus never fell into European hands.   With the progress of their arms, the Crusaders reared strong castles from Petra to the far North as well as on the eastern side of the Jordan.   Their ruins attest the firm purpose of their builders to make their occupation permanent.   " We who were Westerners," said Fulcher of Chartres, " are now Easterners.   We have forgotten our native land."   It is proof of the attractiveness of the cause, if not also of the country, that so many Crusaders sought to establish themselves there permanently.   Many who went to Europe returned a second time, and kings spent protracted periods in the East.

During Baldwin's reign most of the leaders of the First Crusade died or returned to Europe.   But the ranks were being continually recruited by fresh expeditions.   Pascal II., the successor of Urban II., sent forth a call for recruits. The Italian cities furnished fleets, and did important service in conjunction with the land forces.   The Venetians, Pisans, and Genoese established quarters of their own in Jerusalem, Acre, and other cities.   Thousands took the cross in Lombardy, France, and Germany, and were led by Anselm, archbishop of Milan, Stephen, duke of Burgundy, William, duke of Aquitaine, Ida of Austria, and others.   Hugh of

---

[1] The following mode of reducing a tribe of robbers is characteristic.   The robbers took refuge in a cave.   Baldwin resorted to smoking them out.   Two emerged ; Baldwin spoke kindly to them, dressed one up and sent him back with fair promises, while he put the other to death.   Ten others emerged. One was sent back and the other nine put to death.   The same method was employed till two hundred and thirty had been induced to come forth and were put to death.   The fires were then started again till all came forth and met the same fate.

Vermandois, who had gone to Europe, returned. Bohemund likewise returned with thirty-four thousand men, and opposed the Greek emperor. At least two Christian armies attempted to attack Islam in its stronghold at Bagdad.

Under Baldwin II., 1118–1131, the nephew of Baldwin I., Tyre was taken, 1124. This event marks the apogee of the Crusaders' possessions and power.

In the reign of Fulke of Anjou, 1131–1143, the husband of Millicent, Baldwin II.'s daughter, Zengi, surnamed Imaded-din, the Pillar of the Faith, threatened the very existence of the Frankish kingdom.

Baldwin III., 1143–1162, came to the throne in his youth.[1] His reign witnessed the fall of Edessa into Zengi's hands, 1144, and the progress of the Second Crusade, as also the rise of Zengi's son, Nureddin, the uncle of Saladin, who conquered Damascus, 1154.

Amalric, or Amaury, 1162–1173, carried his arms and diplomacy into Egypt, and saw the fall of the Fatimite dynasty which had been in power for two centuries. The power in the South now became identified with the splendid and warlike abilities of Saladin, who, with Nureddin, healed the divisions of the Mohammedans, and compacted their power from Bagdad to Cairo. Henceforth the kingdom of Jerusalem stood on the defensive. The schism between the Abassidæ and the Fatimites had made the conquest of Jerusalem in 1099 possible.

Baldwin IV., 1173–1184, a boy of thirteen at his accession, was, like Uzziah, a leper. Among the regents who conducted the affairs of the kingdom during his reign was the duke of Montferrat, who married Sybilla, the king's sister. In 1174 Saladin, by the death of Nureddin, became caliph of the whole realm from Damascus to the Nile, and started on the *path of God*, the conquest of Jerusalem.

Baldwin V., 1184–1186, a child of five, and son of Sybilla,

[1] From this point William of Tyre writes as an eye-witness, XVI. sqq.

was succeeded by Guy of Lusignan, Sybilla's second husband.   Saladin met Guy and the Crusaders at the village
of Hattin, on the hill above Tiberius, where tradition has
placed the delivery of the Sermon on the Mount.   The Templars and Hospitallers were there in force, and the true cross
was carried by the bishop of Acre, clad in armor.   On
July 5, 1187, the decisive battle was fought.   The Crusaders
were completely routed, and thirty thousand are said to have
perished.   Guy of Lusignan, the masters of the Temple [1]
and the Hospital, and Reginald of Châtillon, lord of Kerak,
were taken prisoners by the enemy.   Reginald was struck to
death in Saladin's tent, but the king and the other captives
were treated with clemency. [2]   The true cross was a part of
the enemy's booty.   The fate of the Holy Land was decided.

On Oct. 2, 1187, Saladin entered Jerusalem after it had
made a brave resistance.   The conditions of surrender were
most creditable to the chivalry of the great commander.
There were no scenes of savage butchery such as followed
the entry of the Crusaders ninety years before.   The inhabitants were given their liberty for the payment of money, and
for forty days the procession of the departing continued.
The relics stored away in the church of the Holy Sepulchre
were delivered up by the conqueror for the sum of fifty
thousand bezants, paid by Richard I. [3]

Thus ended the Latin kingdom of Jerusalem.   Since then
the worship of Islam has continued on Mount Moriah

---

[1] According to the letter of Terricius, Master of the Temple, two hundred
and ninety Templars perished, and the Saracens covered the whole land
from Tyre to Gaza like swarms of ants.   Richard of Hoveden, *an.* 1187,
says the Templars fought like lions.

[2] Saladin offered a glass of water to Guy.   When Guy handed it to Reginald, Saladin exclaimed, "I did not order that.   You gave it," and at once
despatched Reginald by his own hand, or through a servant.   Reginald had
plundered a caravan in which Saladin's sister was travelling.   Lane-Poole,
Saladin, p. 215.

[3] The bezant was worth three dollars.

without interruption. The Christian conquests were in constant danger through the interminable feuds of the Crusaders
themselves, and, in spite of the constant flow of recruits and
treasure from Europe, they fell easily before the unifying
leadership of Saladin.

After 1187 a line of nominal kings of Jerusalem presented a romantic picture in European affairs. The last
real king, Guy of Lusignan, was released, and resumed his
kingly pretension without a capital city.   Conrad of Montferrat, who had married Isabella, daughter of Amalric, was
granted the right of succession.   He was murdered before
reaching the throne, and Henry of Champagne became king
of Jerusalem on Guy's accession to the crown of Cyprus.
In 1197 the two crowns of Cyprus and Jerusalem were
united in Amalric II.   At his death the crown passed to
Mary, daughter of Conrad of Montferrat.   Mary's husband
was John of Brienne.   At the marriage of their daughter,
Iolanthe, to the emperor Frederick II., that sovereign assumed the title, King of Jerusalem.

§ 52.   *The Fall of Edessa and the Second Crusade.*

LITERATURE. — ODO OF DEUIL (near Paris), chaplain of Louis VII. : *De pro-
fectione Ludovici VII. in Orientem 1147–1149* in Migne, 185, translated
by GUIZOT : *Collection*, XXIV. pp. 279–384. — OTTO OF FREISING, d.
1158, half brother of Konrad III. and uncle of Fred. Barbarossa : *Chronicon*, bk. VII., translated in Pertz-Wattenbach, *Geschichtschreiber der
Deutschen Vorzeit*, Leipzig, 1881. Otto accompanied the Crusade. —
KUGLER : *Gesch. des 2ten Kreuzzuges*, Stuttgart, 1866. — The *De consideratione* and *De militibus Christi* of Bernard and the *Biographies* of
Bernard by NEANDER, ed. by DEUTSCH, II. 81–116 ; MORISON, pp.
366–400 ; STORRS, p. 416 sqq. ; VACANDARD, II. 270–318, 431 sqq. —
F. MARION CRAWFORD has written a novel on this Crusade : *Via Crucis,
a Story of the Second Crusade*, N.Y., 1899.

The Second Crusade was led by two sovereigns, the
emperor Konrad III. and Louis VII. of France, and owed its
origin to the profound impression made in Europe by the
fall of Edessa and the zealous eloquence of St. Bernard.

Edessa, the outer citadel of the Crusader's conquests, fell, December, 1144.   Jocelyn II., whose father, Jocelyn I., succeeded Baldwin as proprietor of Edessa, was a weak and pleasure-loving prince.   The besiegers built a fire in a breach in the wall, a piece of which, a hundred yards long, cracked with the flames and fell.   An appalling massacre followed the inrush of the Turks, under Zengi, whom the Christians called the Sanguinary.[1]

Eugenius III. rightly regarded Zengi's victory as a threat to the continuance of the Franks in Palestine, and called upon the king of France to march to their relief.   The forgiveness of all sins and life eternal were promised to all embarking on the enterprise who should die confessing their sins.[2]   The pope also summoned Bernard to leave his convent, and preach the crusade.   Bernard, the most conspicuous personage of his age, was in the zenith of his fame.   He regarded the summons as a call from God,[3] and proved to be a leader worthy of the cause.

At Easter tide, 1146, Louis, who had before, in remorse for his burning the church at Vitry with thirteen hundred persons, promised to go on a crusade, assembled a great council at Vézelai.   Bernard was present and made such an overpowering impression by his address that the hearers pressed forward to receive crosses.   He himself was obliged to cut his robe to pieces to meet the demand.[4]   Writing to Eugenius, he was able to say that the enthusiasm was so great that " castles and towns were emptied of their inmates.   One man could hardly be found for seven women, and the women were

[1] See Otto of Freising, VII. 30.

[2] Gottlob, *Kreuzablass*, 106 sqq.   Eugenius quoted Urban II.'s decree of indulgence at Clermont.

[3] *De consideratione*, II. 1, Reinkens' translation, pp. 31–37.   In this chapter of his famous tract, Bernard explains and justifies his course in the Crusade.

[4] Odo, I. 1, *cœperunt undique conclamando cruces expetere . . . coactus est vestes suas in cruces scindere et seminare.*

being everywhere widowed while their husbands were still
alive."

From France Bernard proceeded to Basel and Constance
and the cities along the Rhine, as far as Cologne. As in the
case of the First Crusade, a persecution was started against
the Jews on the Rhine by a monk, Radulph. Bernard firmly
set himself against the fanaticism and wrote that the Church
should attempt to gain the Jews by discussion, and not
destroy them by the sword.

Thousands flocked to hear the fervent preacher, who added
miraculous healings to the impression of his eloquence.
The emperor Konrad himself was deeply moved and won.
During Christmas week at Spires, Bernard preached before
him an impassionate discourse. "What is there, O man,"
he represented Christ as saying, seated in judgment upon
the imperial hearer at the last day, — "What is there which
I ought to have done for thee and have not done?" He
contrasted the physical prowess,[1] the riches, and the honors
of the emperor with the favor of the supreme judge of
human actions. Bursting into tears, the emperor exclaimed:
"I shall henceforth not be found ungrateful to God's mercy.
I am ready to serve Him, seeing I am admonished by Him."
Of all his miracles Bernard esteemed the emperor's decision
the chief one.

Konrad at once prepared for the expedition. Seventy
thousand armed men, seven thousand of whom were
knights, assembled at Regensburg, and proceeded through
Hungary to the Bosphorus, meeting with a poor reception
along the route. The Greek emperor Manuel and Konrad
were brothers-in-law, having married sisters, but this tie
was no protection to the Germans. Guides, provided by
Manuel, "children of Belial" as William of Tyre calls

[1] As a proof of Konrad's strength, William of Tyre, XVII. 4, relates that
at the siege of Damascus he hewed a man clad in armor through head, neck,
and shoulder to the armpit with one stroke of his blade.

them, treacherously led them astray in the Cappadocian
mountains.[1] Famine, fever, and the attacks of the enemy
were so disastrous that when the army fell back upon Nicæa,
not more than one-tenth of its original number remained.

Louis received the oriflamme from Eugenius's own hands
at St. Denis, Easter, 1147, and followed the same route taken
by Konrad. His queen, Eleanor, famed for her beauty, and
many ladies of the court accompanied the army. The two
sovereigns met at Nicæa and proceeded together to Ephesus.
Konrad returned to Constantinople by ship, and Louis, after
reaching Attalia, left the body of his army to proceed by
land, and sailed to Antioch.

At Antioch, Eleanor laid herself open to the serious charge
of levity, if not to infidelity to her marriage vow. She and
the king afterward publicly separated at Jerusalem, and
later were divorced by the pope. Eleanor was then joined
to Henry of Anjou, and later became the queen of Henry II.
of England. Konrad, who reached Acre by ship from Constantinople, met Louis at Jerusalem, and in company with
Baldwin III. the two sovereigns from the West offered their
devotions in the church of the Holy Sepulchre. At a council
of the three held under the walls of Acre,[2] they decided to
direct their arms against Damascus before proceeding to the
more distant Edessa. The route was by way of Lake
Tiberias and over the Hermon. The siege ended in complete
failure, owing to the disgraceful quarrels between the camps
and the leaders, and the claim of Thierry, count of Flanders,
who had been in the East twice before, to the city as his own.
Konrad started back for Germany, September, 1148. Louis,

---

[1] Bk. XVI. 20. William suggests that Manuel's jealousy was aroused
because Konrad asserted the title, king of the Romans. Diehl, *Essays on
the Crusades*, p. 107, doubts the statement that Manuel's guides intentionally
misled and betrayed the Germans. He, however, acknowledges that Greek
inhabitants of Asia Minor "fleeced or starved the Latins."

[2] William of Tyre, XVII., gives a list of the distinguished personages
present, Bishop Otto of Freising, the emperor's brother, being among them.

after spending the winter in Jerusalem, broke away the following spring. Bernard felt the humiliation of the failure keenly, and apologized for it by ascribing it to the judgment of God for the sins of the Crusaders and of the Christian world. " The judgments of the Lord are just," he wrote, " but this one is an abyss so deep that I dare to pronounce him blessed who is not scandalized by it."[1] As for the charge that he was responsible for the expedition, Bernard exclaimed, " Was Moses to blame, in the wilderness, who promised to lead the children of Israel to the Promised Land ? Was it not rather the sins of the people which interrupted the progress of their journey ? "

Edessa remained lost to the Crusaders, and Damascus never fell into their power.

§ 53.   *The Third Crusade.*   1189–1192.

For Richard I.: *Itinerarium perigrinorum et gesta regis Ricardi*, ed. by Stubbs, London, 1864, Rolls Series, formerly ascribed to Geoffrey de Vinsauf, but, since Stubbs, to Richard de Templo or left anonymous. Trans. in *Chronicles of the Crusades*, Bohn's Libr., 1870. The author accompanied the Crusade. — DE HOVEDEN, ed. by Stubbs, 4 vols., London, 1868–1871 ; Engl. trans. by Riley, vol. II. pp. 63–270. — GIRALDUS CAMBRENSIS : *Itinerarium Cambriæ*, ed. by Brewer and Dimock, London, 7 vols. 1861–1877, vol. VI., trans. by R. C. HOARE, London, 1806. — RICHARD DE DEVIZES : *Chronicon de rebus gestis Ricardi*, etc., London, 1838, trans. in Bohn's *Chron. of the Crusades*. — ROGER WENDOVER. — DE JOINVILLE : *Crusade of St. Louis*, trans. in *Chron. of the Crus.*

For full list of authorities on Richard see art. *Richard* by ARCHER in *Dict. of Nat. Biog.* — G. P. R. JAMES : *Hist. of the Life of R. Cœur de Lion*, new ed. 2 vols. London, 1854. — T. A. ARCHER : *The Crusade of Richard I.*, being a collation of Richard de Devizes, etc., London, 1868. — GRUHN : *Der Kreuzzug Richard I.*, Berlin, 1892.

For Frederick Barbarossa : ANSBERT, an eye-witness : *Hist. de expeditione Frid., 1187–1196*, ed. by Jos. Dobrowsky, Prague, 1827. — For other sources, see WATTENBACH : *Deutsche Geschichtsquellen*, II. 303 sqq., and POTTHAST : *Bibl. Hist.*, II. 1014, 1045, etc. — KARL FISCHER : *Gesch. des Kreuzzugs Fried. I.*, Leipzig, 1870. — H. PRUTZ : *Kaiser Fried. I.*, 3 vols. Dantzig, 1871–1873. — VON RAUMER : *Gesch. der Hohenstaufen*, vol. II. 5th ed. Leipzig, 1878. — GIESEBRECHT : *Deutsche Kaiserzeit*, vol. V.

[1] *De consideratione*, II. 1.

For Saladin: BAHA-ED-DIN, a member of Saladin's court, 1145–1234, the
best Arabic Life, in the *Recueil, Histt. Orientaux*, etc., III., 1884, and
in Palestine, Pilgrim's Text Soc., ed. by Sir C. W. Wilson, London,
1897.— MARIN: *Hist. de Saladin, sulthan d'Égypte et de Syrie*, Paris,
1758. — LANE-POOLE: *Saladin and the Fall of Jerusalem*, New York,
1898, a full list and an estimate of Arab authorities are given, pp. iii–xvi.
   See also the general Histories of the Crusades and RANKE : *Weltgesch.*,
VIII.

The Third Crusade was undertaken to regain Jerusalem,
which had been lost to Saladin, 1187.   It enjoys the distinction of having had for its leaders the three most powerful
princes of Western Europe, the emperor Frederick Barbarossa, Philip Augustus, king of France, and the English king
Richard I., surnamed Cœur de Lion, or the Lion-hearted.[1]   It
brought together the chivalry of the East and the West at
the time of its highest development and called forth the
heroism of two of the bravest soldiers of any age, Saladin
and Richard.   It has been more widely celebrated in romance
than any of the other Crusades, from the songs of the mediæval minstrels to Lessing in his *Nathan the Wise* and Walter
Scott in *Talisman*.   But in spite of the splendid armaments,
the expedition was almost a complete failure.

On the news of Saladin's victories, Urban III. is alleged
to have died of grief.[2]   An official summons was hardly necessary to stir the crusading ardor of Europe from one end to
the other.   Danes, Swedes, and Frisians joined with Welsh-
men, Englishmen, Frenchmen, and Germans in readiness
for a new expedition.   A hundred years had elapsed since
the First Crusade, and its leaders were already invested with

---

[1] The story of Richard's seizing a lion and tearing out its throbbing heart
was a subject of English romance in the fourteenth century and probably of
French romance in the thirteenth century.

[2] It required at least fifteen days for a ship to go from Acre to Marseilles,
and about the same time for news to reach Rome from Jerusalem.   The
indulgences offered to Crusaders by Alexander III., on the news of Saladin's
conquests in Egypt and his defeat of the Christians at Banias, 1181, are
quoted by Gottlob, 119 sq.   Alexander appealed to the examples of Urban II.
and Eugenius III.

a halo of romance and glory. The aged Gregory VIII., whose reign lasted less than two months, 1187, spent his expiring breath in an appeal to the princes to desist from their feuds. Under the influence of William, archbishop of Tyre, and the archbishop of Rouen, Philip Augustus of France and Henry II. of England laid aside their quarrels and took the cross. At Henry's death his son Richard, then thirty-two years of age, set about with impassioned zeal to make preparations for the Crusade. The treasure which Henry had left, Richard augmented by sums secured from the sale of castles and bishoprics.[1] For ten thousand marks he released William of Scotland from homage, and he would have sold London itself, so he said, if a purchaser rich enough had offered himself.[2] Baldwin, archbishop of Canterbury, supported his sovereign, preaching the Crusade in England and Wales, and accompanied the expedition.[3] The famous Saladin tax was levied in England, and perhaps also in France, requiring the payment of a tithe by all not joining the Crusade.

Richard and Philip met at Vézelai. Among the great lords who joined them were Hugh, duke of Burgundy, Henry II., count of Champagne, and Philip of Flanders. As a badge for himself and his men, the French king chose a red cross, Richard a white cross, and the duke of Flanders a green cross.

In the meantime Frederick Barbarossa, who was on the verge of seventy, had reached the Bosphorus. Mindful of his experiences with Konrad III., whom he accompanied on the Second Crusade, he avoided the mixed character of Konrad's army by admitting to the ranks only those who were physically strong and had at least three marks. The army

---

[1] He sold the archbishopric of York for 3,000 pounds. Henry is reported to have left 900,000 pounds in gold and silver. Rog. of Wendover, *an.* 1180.

[2] Richard of Devizes, X.

[3] Giraldus Cambrensis accompanied the archbishop and gathered the materials for his Itinerary on the way.

numbered one hundred thousand, of whom fifty thousand sat in the saddle.   Frederick of Swabia accompanied his father, the emperor.

Setting forth from Ratisbon in May, 1189, the German army had proceeded by way of Hungary to Constantinople. The Greek emperor, Isaac Angelus, far from regarding the Crusaders' approach with favor, threw Barbarossa's commissioners into prison and made a treaty with Saladin.[1]   He coolly addressed the western emperor as "the first prince of Germany."   The opportunity was afforded Frederick of uniting the East and West once more under a single sceptre. Wallachians and Servians promised him their support if he would dethrone Isaac and take the crown.   But though there was provocation enough, Frederick refused to turn aside from his purpose, the reconquest of Jerusalem,[2] and in March, 1190, his troops were transferred across the Bosphorus.   He took Iconium, and reached Cilicia.   There his career was brought to a sudden termination on June 10 in the waters of the Kalycadnus river into which he had plunged to cool himself.[3]   His flesh was buried at Antioch, and his bones, intended for the crypts of the church of the Holy Sepulchre, were deposited in the church of St. Peter, Tyre. A lonely place, indeed, for the ashes of the mighty monarch, and far removed from those of his great predecessor, Charlemagne at Aachen!   Scarcely ever has a life so eminent had such a tragic and deplored ending.   In right imperial fashion, Frederick had sent messengers ahead, calling upon

[1] Frederick announced his expedition in a letter to Saladin, in which he enumerated the tribes that were to take part in it, from the "tall Bavarian" to the sailors of Venice and Pisa.   See *Itin. reg. Ricardi de Hoveden*, etc.

[2] Ranke, VIII. 246 sqq., spicily speculates upon the possible consequences of Isaac's dethronement, and, as a German, regrets that Frederick did not take the prize, *Es war ein Moment das nicht so leicht wieder kommen konnte.*

[3] Another account by one who accompanied the expedition was that in his impatience to proceed, Barbarossa strove to swim the river and was drowned. Ranke, VIII. 249, regards the view taken in the text as the better one.

Saladin to abandon Jerusalem and deliver up the true cross. With a demoralized contingent, Frederick of Swabia reached the walls of Acre, where he soon after became a victim of the plague, October, 1190.

Philip and Richard reached the Holy Land by the Mediterranean. They sailed for Sicily, 1190, Philip from Genoa, Richard from Marseilles. Richard found employment on the island in asserting the rights of his sister Joan, widow of William II. of Sicily, who had been robbed of her dower by William's illegitimate son, Tancred. " Quicker than priest can chant matins did King Richard take Messina." [1] In spite of armed disputes between Richard and Philip, the two kings came to an agreement to defend each other on the Crusades. Among the curious stipulations of this agreement was one that only knights and the clergy were to be allowed to play games for money, and the amount staked on any one day was not to exceed twenty shillings.

Leaving Sicily,[2] whence Philip had sailed eleven days before, Richard proceeded to Cyprus, and as a punishment for the ill treatment of pilgrims and the stranding of his vessels, he wrested the kingdom in a three weeks' campaign from Isaac Comnenus. The English at their occupation of Cyprus, 1878, might well have recalled Richard's conquest. On the island, Richard's nuptials were consummated with Berengaria of Navarre, whom he preferred to Philip's sister Alice, to whom he had been betrothed. In June he reached Acre. " For joy at his coming," says Baha-ed-din, the Arab historian, " the Franks broke forth in rejoicing, and lit fires in their camps all night through. The hosts of the Mussulmans were filled with fear and dread." [3]

---

[1] *Itinerary*, III. 16.

[2] Richard's fleet, when he sailed from Messina, consisted of one hundred and fifty large ships and fifty-three galleys.

[3] The *Itinerary*, III. 2, says Richard's arrival was welcomed with transports of joy, shoutings, and blowing of trumpets. He was taken ashore as if the desired of all nations had come, and the night was made so bright with

Acre, or Ptolemais, under Mount Carmel, had become the metropolis of the Crusaders, as it was the key to the Holy Land. Christendom had few capitals so gay in its fashions and thronged with such diverse types of nationality. Merchants were there from the great commercial marts of Europe. The houses, placed among gardens, were rich with painted glass. The Hospitallers and Templars had extensive establishments.

Against Acre, Guy of Lusignan had been laying siege for two years. Released by Saladin upon condition of renouncing all claim to his crown and going beyond the seas, he had secured easy absolution from the priest from this solemn oath. Baldwin of Canterbury, Hubert Walter, bishop of Salisbury, and the justiciar Ranulf of Glanvill had arrived on the scene before Richard. "We found our army," wrote the archbishop's chaplain,[1] "given up to shameful practices, and yielding to ease and lust, rather than encouraging virtue. The Lord is not in the camp. Neither chastity, solemnity, faith, nor charity are there — a state of things which, I call God to witness, I would not have believed if I had not seen it with my own eyes."

Saladin was watching the besiegers and protecting the garrison. The horrors of the siege made it one of the memorable sieges of the Middle Ages.[2] It was carried on from

wax torches and flaming lights "that it seemed to be usurped by the brightness of the day, and the Turks thought the whole valley was on fire." Richard of Devizes, LXIII., says, "The besiegers received Richard with as much joy as if it had been Christ who had come again."

[1] The *Itinerary*, I., 66, says Baldwin was made sick unto death when he saw "the army altogether dissolute and given up to drinking, women, and dice."

[2] The loss before Acre was very heavy. The *Itinerary* gives a list of 6 archbishops, 12 bishops, 40 counts, and 500 knights who lost their lives. IV. 6. De Hoveden also gives a formidable list, in which are included the names of the dukes of Swabia, Flanders, and Burgundy, the archbishops of Besançon, Arles, Montreal, etc. Baldwin died Nov. 19, 1190. The *Itinerary* compares the siege of Acre to the siege of Troy, and says (I. 32) "it would certainly obtain eternal fame as a city for which the whole world contended."

the sea as well as on the land.   Greek fire was used with
great effect by the Turks.[1]   The struggle was participated
in by women as well as the men.   Some Crusaders apos-
tatized to get the means for prolonging life.[2]   With the aid
of the huge machine Check Greek, and other engines constructed by Richard in Sicily, and by Philip, the city was made
to surrender, July, 1191.   By the terms of the capitulation
the city's stores, two hundred thousand pieces of gold,
fifteen hundred prisoners, and the true cross were to pass
into the hands of the Crusaders.

The advance upon Jerusalem was delayed by rivalries
between the armies and their leaders.   Richard's prowess,
large means, and personal popularity threw Philip into the
shade, and he was soon on his way back to France, leaving
the duke of Burgundy as leader of the French.   The French
and Germans also quarrelled.[3]   A fruitful source of friction
was the quarrel between Guy of Lusignan and Conrad of
Montferrat over the crown of Jerusalem, until the matter
was finally settled by Conrad's murder and the recognition
of Guy as king of Cyprus, and Henry of Champagne, the
nephew of both Richard and Philip Augustus, as king of
Jerusalem.

A dark blot rests upon Richard's memory for the murder
in cold blood of twenty-seven hundred prisoners in the full
sight of Saladin's troops and as a punishment for the non-

---

[1] The *Itinerary* and other documents make frequent reference to its
deadly use.   Among the machines used on both sides were the *petrariæ*,
which hurled stones, and mangonels used for hurling stones and other missiles.   *Itinerary*, III. 7, etc.   One of the grappling machines was called a
" cat."   The battering ram was also used, and the *sow*, a covering under
which the assailants made their approach to the walls.   King Richard was an
expert in the use of the *arbalest*, or cross-bow.

[2] The price of a loaf of bread rose from a penny to 40 shillings, and a horse-
load of corn was sold for 60 marks.   De Hoveden, etc.   Horse flesh was
greedily eaten, even to the intestines, which were sold for 10 sols.   Even
grass was sought after to appease hunger.   A vivid description of the pitiful
sufferings from famine is given in the *Itinerary*, I. 67–83.

[3] *Itinerary*, I. 44.

payment of the ransom money.   The massacre, a few days
before, of Christian captives, if it really occurred, in part
explains but cannot condone the crime.[1]

Jaffa and Ascalon became the next points of the Crusaders' attack, the operations being drawn out to a wearisome length.   Richard's feats of physical strength and
martial skill are vouched for by eye-witnesses, who speak
of him as cutting swathes through the enemy with his
sword and mowing them down "as the reapers mow down
the corn with their sickles."   So mighty was his strength
that, when a Turkish admiral rode at him in full charge,
Richard severed his neck and one shoulder by a single blow.
But the king's dauntless though coarse courage was not
joined to the gifts of a leader fit for such a campaign.[2]   His
savage war shout, "God and the Holy Sepulchre aid us,"
failed to unite the troops cloven by jealousies and to

---

[1] This pretext is upon the sole authority of de Hoveden, *an.* 1191.   He
says, however, that Saladin did not execute the Christian captives until
Richard had declined to withdraw his threat and to give more time for the
payment of the ransom money and the delivery of the true cross.   Archer,
Hist. of the Crusades, p. 331, thinks that Baha-ed-din's account implies
Saladin's massacre ; but Lane-Poole, *Life of Saladin*, p. 307, is of the contrary opinion.   The *Itinerary*, IV. 4, states that Richard's followers "leapt
forward to fulfil his commands, thankful to the divine grace for the permission to take such vengeance for the Christians whom the captives had slain
with bolts and arrows."   It has nothing to say of a massacre by Saladin.
Lane-Poole, carried away by admiration for Saladin, takes occasion at this
point to say that "in the struggle of the Crusades the virtues of civilization,
magnanimity, toleration, real chivalry, and gentle culture were all on the
side of the Saracens."   The duke of Burgundy was party to the massacre
of the Turkish captives.

[2] *Itinerary*, VI. 23.   Here is a description of one of Richard's frequent frays
as given in the *Itinerary*, VI. 4 : "Richard was conspicuous above all the rest
by his royal bearing.   He was mounted on a tall charger and charged the
enemy singly.   His ashen lance was shivered by his repeated blows ; but
instantly drawing his sword, he pressed upon the fugitive Turks and mowed
them down, sweeping away the hindmost and subduing the foremost.   Thus
he thundered on, cutting and hewing.   No kind of armor could resist his
blows, for the edge of his sword cut open the heads from the top to the teeth.
Thus waving his sword to and fro, he scared away the routed Turks as a
wolf when he pursues the flying sheep."

establish military discipline. The camps were a scene of confusion. Women left behind by Richard's order at Acre came up to corrupt the army, while day after day "its manifold sins, drunkenness, and luxury increased." Once and perhaps twice Richard came so near the Holy City that he might have looked down into it had he so chosen.[1] But, like Philip Augustus, he never passed through its gates, and after a signal victory at Joppa he closed his military achievements in Palestine. A treaty, concluded with Saladin, assured to the Christians for three years the coast from Tyre to Joppa, and protection to pilgrims in Jerusalem and on their way to the city. In October, 1192, the king, called back by the perfidy of his brother John, set sail from Acre amid the laments of those who remained behind, but not until he had sent word to Saladin that he intended to return to renew the contest.

The exploits of the English king won even the admiration of the Arabs, whose historian reports how he rode up and down in front of the Saracen army defying them, and not a man dared to touch him. Presents passed between him and Saladin.[2] One who accompanied the Third Crusade

[1] De Joinville, *Life of St. Louis*, an. 1253, says no doubt with truth that Richard would have taken Jerusalem but for the envy and treachery of the duke of Burgundy. He repeats the saying of Richard, which is almost too good not to be true. When an officer said, "Sire, come here and I will show you Jerusalem," the king throwing down his arms and looking up to heaven exclaimed, "I pray thee, O Lord God, that I may never look on the Holy City until I can deliver it from thy enemies." The *Itinerary* has nothing to say on the subject. Richard of Devizes, XC., states that Hubert, bishop of Salisbury, after his pilgrimage to Jerusalem, urged the king to go in as a pilgrim, but that "the worthy indignation of his noble mind would not consent to receive from the courtesy of the Gentiles what he could not obtain by the gift of God."

[2] Baha-ed-din, as quoted by Lane-Poole, p. 354. De Hoveden speaks of fruits, the *Itinerary* of horses. Later story ascribes to Saladin a yearly grant of one thousand bezants of gold to the Knights of St. John at Acre. In order to test the charity of the knights, the sultan had gone to the hospital in disguise and found the reports of their merciful treatment well founded. Of this and of the story of his knighthood at the hands of Humphrey of Toron, and vouched for by the contemporary *Itinerary* of King Richard, the Arab authorities know nothing. See Lane-Poole, *Life of Saladin*, 387 sqq.

ascribes to him the valor of Hector, the magnanimity of Achilles, the prudence of Odysseus, the eloquence of Nestor, and equality with Alexander. French writers of the thirteenth century tell how Saracen mothers, long after Richard had returned to England, used to frighten their children into obedience or silence by the spell of his name, so great was the dread he had inspired. Destitute of the pious traits of Godfrey and Louis IX., Richard nevertheless stands, by his valor, muscular strength, and generous mind, in the very front rank of conspicuous Crusaders.

On his way back to England he was seized by Leopold, duke of Austria, whose enmity he had incurred before Joppa. The duke turned his captive over to the emperor, Henry VI., who had a grudge to settle growing out of Sicilian matters. Richard was released only on the humiliating terms of paying an enormous ransom and consenting to hold his kingdom as a fief of the empire. Saladin died March 4, 1193, by far the most famous of the foes of the Crusaders. Christendom has joined with Arab writers in praise of his chivalric courage, culture, and magnanimity.[1] What could be more courteous than his granting the request of Hubert Walter for the station of two Latin priests in the three churches of the Holy Sepulchre, Nazareth, and Bethlehem?[2]

The recapture of Acre and the grant of protection to the pilgrims on their way to Jerusalem were paltry achievements

[1] A western legend given by Vincent de Beauvais relates that as Saladin was dying he called to him his standard-bearer and bade him carry through the streets of Damascus the banner of his death as he had carried the banner of his wars ; namely, a rag attached to a lance, and cry out, " Lo, at his death, the king of the East can take nothing with him but this cloth only."

[2] The *Itinerary* gives a story of Saladin and the notorious miracle of the holy fire until recently shown in the church of the Holy Sepulchre. It may well be true. When Saladin, on one occasion, saw the holy flame descend and light a lamp, he ordered the lamp blown out to show it was a fraud. But it was immediately rekindled as if by a miracle. Extinguished a second and a third time, it was again and again rekindled. " Oh, what use is it to resist the invisible Power ! " exclaims the author of the *Itinerary*, V. 16.

in view of the loss of life, the long months spent in making ready for the Crusade, the expenditure of money, and the combination of the great nations of Europe.   In this case, as in the other Crusades, it was not so much the Saracens, or even the splendid abilities of Saladin, which defeated the Crusaders, but their feuds among themselves.   Never again did so large an army from the West contend for the cross on Syrian soil.

§ 54.   *The Children's Crusades.*

> " The rich East blooms fragrant before us ;
>   All Fairy-land beckons us forth,
>   We must follow the crane in her flight o'er the main,
>   From the posts and the moors of the North."
>   — CHARLES KINGSLEY, *The Saint's Tragedy.*

LITERATURE. — For the sources, see WILKEN: *Gesch. der Kreuzzüge,* VI. 71–83. — DES ESSARDS: *La Croisade des enfants,* Paris, 1875. — RÖHRICHT, *Die Kinderkreuzzüge,* in Sybel, *Hist. Zeitschrift,* vol. XXXVI., 1876. — G. Z. GRAY: *The Children's Crusade,* N.Y., 1872, new ed. 1896. — ISABEL S. STONE: *The Little Crusaders,* N.Y., 1901. — HURTER: *Innocent III.,* II. 482–489.

The most tragic of the Crusader tragedies were the crusades of the children.   They were a slaughter of the innocents on a large scale, and belong to those mysteries of Providence which the future only will solve.

The crusading epidemic broke out among the children of France and Germany in 1212.   Begotten in enthusiasm, which was fanned by priestly zeal, the movement ended in pitiful disaster.

The French expedition was led by Stephen, a shepherd lad of twelve, living at Cloyes near Chartres.   He had a vision, so the rumor went, in which Christ appeared to him as a pilgrim and made an appeal for the rescue of the holy places. Journeying to St. Denis, the boy retailed the account of what he had seen.   Other children gathered around him. The enthusiasm spread from Brittany to the Pyrenees.   In vain did the king of France attempt to check the movement. The army increased to thirty thousand, girls as well as boys, adults as well as children.[1] Questioned as to where they were going, they replied, " We go to God, and seek for the holy cross beyond the sea." They reached Marseilles, but the waves did not part and let them go through dryshod as they expected.[2]

The centres of the movement in Germany were Nicholas, a child of ten, and a second leader whose name has been lost. Cologne was the rallying point. Children of noble families enlisted. Along with the boys and girls went men and women, good and bad.

The army under the anonymous leader passed through Eastern Switzerland and across the Alps to Brindisi, whence some of the children sailed, never to be heard from again. The army of Nicholas reached Genoa in August, 1212. The children sang songs on the way, and with them has been wrongly associated the tender old German hymn : —

> " Fairest Lord Jesus,
>   Ruler of all nature,
> O Thou of man and God, the son,
>   Thee will I cherish,
>   Thee will I honor,
> Thou, my soul's glory, joy, and crown."

The numbers had been reduced by hardship, death, and moral shipwreck from twenty to seven thousand. At Genoa the waters were as pitiless as they were at Marseilles. Some of the children remained in the city and became, it is said, the ancestors of distinguished families.[3] The rest marched on

---

[1] Hurter regards the numbers handed down as greatly exaggerated.

[2] An epigram, dwelling upon the folly of the movement, ran : —
> " *Ad mare stultorum*
>   *Tendebat iter puerorum.*"
> " To the sea of the fools
>   Led the path of the children."

[3] Wilken for this assertion quotes the *History of the Genoese Senate and People*, by Peter Bizari, Antwerp, 1679.   One of the families was the house of the Vivaldi.

through Italy to Brindisi, where the bishop of Brindisi refused to let them proceed farther. An uncertain report declares Innocent III. declined to grant their appeal to be released from their vow.

The fate of the French children was, if possible, still more pitiable. At Marseilles they fell a prey to two slave dealers, who for " the sake of God and without price " offered to convey them across the Mediterranean. Their names are preserved, — Hugo Ferreus and William Porcus. Seven vessels set sail. Two were shipwrecked on the little island of San Pietro off the northwestern coast of Sardinia. The rest reached the African shore, where the children were sold into slavery.

The shipwreck of the little Crusaders was commemorated by Gregory IX., in the chapel of the New Innocents, *ecclesia novorum innocentium*, which he built on San Pietro. Innocent III. in summoning Europe to a new crusade included in his appeal the spectacle of their sacrifice. " They put us to shame. While they rush to the recovery of the Holy Land, we sleep." [1]   Impossible as such a movement might seem in our calculating age, it is attested by too many good witnesses to permit its being relegated to the realm of legend,[2] and the trials and death of the children of the thirteenth century will continue to be associated with the slaughter of the children of Bethlehem at the hand of Herod.

§ 55. *The Fourth Crusade and the Capture of Constantinople.* 1200–1204.

LITERATURE. — NICETAS ACOMINATUS, Byzantine patrician and grand logothete. During the Crusaders' investment of Constantinople his palace was burnt, and with his wife and daughter he fled to Nicæa : *Byzan-*

---

[1] See Wilken, VI. 83.

[2] So Wilken, *Sie ist durch die Zeugnisse glaubwürdiger Geschichtschreiber so fest begründet, dass ihre Wahrheit nicht bezweifelt werden kann*, p. 72. Röhricht, *Hist. Zeitschrift*, XXXVI. 5, also insists upon the historical genuineness of the reports.

tina Historia, 1118–1206, in *Recueil des historiens des Croisades, histor. Grecs*, vol. I., and in Migne, *Patr. Gr.*, vols. 139, 140. — GEOFFROI DE VILLEHARDOUIN, a prominent participant in the Crusade, d. 1213 ? : *Hist. de la Conquête de Constantinople avec la continuation de Henri de Valenciennes*, earliest ed., Paris, 1585, ed. by DU CANGE, Paris, 1857, and N. DE WAILLY, Paris, 1871, 3d ed. 1882, and E. BOUCHET, with new trans., Paris, 1891. For other editions, see POTTHAST, II. 1094. Engl. trans. by T. SMITH, London, 1829. — ROBERT DE CLARY, d. after 1216, a participant in the Crusade : *La Prise de Constant.*, 1st ed. by P. RIANT, Paris, 1868. — GUNTHERUS ALEMANNUS, a Cistercian, d. 1220 ? : *Historia Constantinopolitana*, in Migne, *Patr. Lat.*, vol. 212, 221–255, and ed. by RIANT, Geneva, 1875, and repeated in his *Exuviæ Sacræ*, a valuable description, based upon the relation of his abbot, Martin, a participant in the Crusade. — *Innocent III. Letters*, in Migne, vols. 214–217. — CHARLES HOPF : *Chroniques Græco-Romanes inédites ou peu connues*, Berlin, 1873. Contains DE CLARY, the *Devastatio Constantinopolitana*, etc. — C. KLIMKE : *D. Quellen zur Gesch. des 4ten Kreuzzuges*, Breslau, 1875. — Short extracts from VILLEHARDOUIN and DE CLARY are given in *Trans. and Reprints*, published by University of Pennsylvania, vol. III., Philadelphia, 1896.

PAUL DE RIANT : *Exuviæ sacræ Constantinopolitanæ*, Geneva, 1877–1878, 2 vols. — TESSIER : *Quatrième Croisade, la diversion sur Zara et Constantinople*, Paris, 1884. — E. PEARS : *The Fall of Constantinople, being the Story of the Fourth Crusade*, N.Y., 1886. — W. NORDAU : *Der vierte Kreuzzug*, 1898. — A. CHARASSON : *Un curé plébéien au XIIe Siècle, Foulques, Prédicateur de la IVe Croisade*, Paris, 1905. — GIBBON, LX., LXI. — HURTER : *Life of Innocent III.*, vol. I. —RANKE : *Weltgesch.*, VIII. 280–298. — C. W. C. OMAN : *The Byzantine Empire*, 1895, pp. 274–306. — F. C. HODGSON : *The Early History of Venice, from the Foundation to the Conquest of Constantinople, 1204*, 1901. An appendix contains an excursus on the historical sources of the Fourth Crusade.

It would be difficult to find in history a more notable diversion of a scheme from its original purpose than the Fourth Crusade. Inaugurated to strike a blow at the power which held the Holy Land, it destroyed the Christian city of Zara and overthrew the Greek empire of Constantinople. Its goals were determined by the blind doge, Henry Dandolo of Venice. As the First Crusade resulted in the establishment of the Latin kingdom of Jerusalem, so the Fourth Crusade resulted in the establishment of the Latin empire of Constantinople.

Innocent III., on ascending the papal throne, threw

himself with all the energy of his nature into the effort of reviving the crusading spirit.   He issued letter after letter [1] to the sovereigns of England, France, Hungary, and Sicily. [2] He also wrote to the Byzantine emperor, urging him to resist the Saracens and subject the Greek church to its mother, Rome. [3]   The failure of preceding crusades was ascribed to the sins of the Crusaders.   But for them, one Christian would have chased a thousand, or even ten thousand, and the enemies of the cross would have disappeared like smoke or melting wax.

For the expense of a new expedition the pope set apart one-tenth of his revenue, and he directed the cardinals to do the same.   The clergy and all Christians were urged to give liberally.   The goods and lands of Crusaders were to enjoy the special protection of the Holy See.   Princes were in- structed to compel Jewish money-lenders to remit interest due from those going on the expedition.   Legates were de- spatched to Genoa, Pisa, and Venice to stir up zeal for the project; and these cities were forbidden to furnish to the Saracens supplies of arms, food, or other material.   A cardi- nal was appointed to make special prayers for the Crusade, as Moses had prayed for Israel against the Amalekites.

The Cistercian abbot, Martin, preached in Germany; [4] and the eloquent Fulke of Neuilly, receiving his commission from Innocent III., [5] distinguished himself by winning thou- sands of recruits from the nobility and populace of Burgundy, Flanders, and Normandy.   Under his preaching, in 1199, Count Thibaut of Champagne, [6] Louis of Blois, Baldwin of

---

[1] See the ample description of Hurter, I. pp. 221–230, etc.

[2] *Epp. of Innocent*, I. 353, 354, etc., Migne, 214, 329 sqq.

[3] *Ep.* I. 353, Migne, 214, 325 sqq.

[4] Guntherus, Migne, 212, 225.

[5] A French translation of Innocent's letter commissioning Fulke to preach the Crusade is given by Charasson, p. 99.

[6] Thibaut, then twenty-two, and Louis, then twenty-seven, were nephews of the king of France, Villehardouin, 3 ; Wailly's ed., p. 5.   Thibaut died before the Crusaders started from France.

Flanders, and Simon de Montfort took the vow.   So also did Villehardouin, marshal of Champagne, who accompanied the expedition, and became its spicy historian.   As in the case of the First Crusade, the armament was led by nobles, and not by sovereigns.

The leaders, meeting at Soissons in 1200, sent a deputation to Venice to secure transportation for the army.   Egypt was chosen as the point of landing and attack, it being held that a movement would be most apt to be successful which cut off the Saracens' supplies at their base in the land of the Nile.[1]

The Venetian Grand Council agreed to provide ships for 9000 esquires, 4500 knights, 20,000 foot-soldiers, and 4500 horses, and to furnish provisions for nine months for the sum of 85,000 marks, or about $1,000,000 in present money.[2] The agreement stated the design of the enterprise to be " the deliverance of the Holy Land."   The doge, Henry Dandolo, who had already passed the limit of ninety years, was in spite of his age and blindness full of vigor and decision.[3]

The crusading forces mustered at Venice.   The fleet was ready, but the Crusaders were short of funds, and able to pay only 50,000 marks of the stipulated sum.   Dandolo took advantage of these straits to advance the selfish aims of Venice, and proposed, as an equivalent for the balance of the passage

---

[1] Villehardouin, who was one of the six members of the commission (Wailly's ed., p. 11), says, "The Turks could be more easily destroyed there than in any other country."   Egypt was often called by the Crusaders "the land of Babylon."

[2] Wailly's edition of Villehardouin, p. 452, makes the sum 4,420,000 francs.   It reckons a mark as the equivalent of 52 francs.   The Grand Council added fifty armed galleys "for the love of God," on condition that during the continuance of the alliance Venice should have one-half the spoils of conquest.

[3] Villehardouin describes him as a man *de bien grand cœur*.   He died at ninety-seven, in 1205, and was buried in the Church of St. Sophia.   In his reply to the deputation, the doge recognized the high birth of the Crusaders in the words, " we perceive that the lords are in the highest rank of those who do not wear a crown " (Villehardouin, 16 ; Wailly's ed., 13).

money, that the Crusaders aid in capturing Zara.[1]   The
offer was accepted.   Zara, the capital of Dalmatia and the
chief market on the eastern coast of the Adriatic, belonged
to the Christian king of Hungary.   Its predatory attacks
upon Venetian vessels formed the pretext for its reduction.[2]
The threat of papal excommunication, presented by the
papal legate, did not check the preparations; and after the
solemn celebration of the mass, the fleet set sail, with
Dandolo as virtual commander.

The departure of four hundred and eighty gayly rigged
vessels is described by several eye-witnesses [3] and constitutes
one of the most important scenes in the naval enterprise of
the queen of the Adriatic.

Zara was taken Nov. 24, 1202, given over to plunder,
and razed to the ground.   No wonder Innocent wrote that
Satan had been the instigator of this destructive raid upon
a Christian people and excommunicated the participants in
it.[4]

Organized to dislodge the Saracens and reduced to a fili-
bustering expedition, the Crusade was now to be directed
against Constantinople.   The rightful emperor, Isaac Angelus, was languishing in prison with his eyes put out by the
hand of the usurper, Alexius III., his own brother.   Isaac's
son, Alexius, had visited Innocent III. and Philip of Swabia,

---

[1] Villehardouin, 56 sqq.; Wailly's ed., 33 sq.

[2] Villehardouin mentions only the proposition to go against Zara. Robert
of Clary and other writers state that Dandolo made a previous proposition that
the fleet should proceed to Mohammedan territory and that the first booty
should be used to pay the Crusaders' debt.   He then substituted the proposition to go against Zara, and the Crusaders were forced by their circumstances to accept.   There is some ground for the charge that in May, 1202,
Dandolo made a secret treaty with the sultan of Egypt.   See Pears, 271 sqq.

[3] Villehardouin and Robert de Clary.   Clary's account is very vivacious
and much the more detailed of the two.

[4] A deputation afterwards visited Innocent and secured his absolution,
Villehardouin, 107; Wailly's ed., 61.   The news of the death of Fulke of
Neuilly reached the Crusaders on the eve of their breaking away from
Venice.   Villehardouin, 73; Wailly's ed., 43, calls him *le bon, le saint homme.*

appealing for aid in behalf of his father.   Philip, claimant
to the German throne, had married the prince's sister.   Greek
messengers appeared at Zara to appeal to Dandolo and the
Crusaders to take up Isaac's cause.   The proposal suited
the ambition of Venice, which could not have wished for a
more favorable opportunity to confirm her superiority over
the Pisans and Genoans, which had been threatened, if not
impaired, on the Bosphorus.

As a compensation, Alexius made the tempting offer of
200,000 marks silver, the maintenance for a year of an
army of 10,000 against the Mohammedans, and of 500
knights for life as a guard for the Holy Land, and the submission of the Eastern Church to the pope.   The doge fell
in at once with the proposition, but it was met by strong
voices of dissent in the ranks of the Crusaders.   Innocent's
threat of continued excommunication, if the expedition was
turned against Constantinople, was ignored.   A few of the
Crusaders, like Simon de Montfort, refused to be used for
private ends and withdrew from the expedition.[1]

Before reaching Corfu, the fleet was joined by Alexius in
person.   By the end of June, 1203, it had passed through the
Dardanelles and was anchored opposite the Golden Horn.
After prayers and exhortations by the bishops and clergy,
the Galata tower was taken.   Alexius III. fled, and Isaac
was restored to the throne.

The agreements made with the Venetians, the Greeks
found it impossible to fulfil.   Confusion reigned among
them.   Two disastrous conflagrations devoured large portions of the city.   One started in a mosque which evoked

[1] Villehardouin, 109.   Pears, p. 268, speaks pathetically of the Crusaders
as "about to commit the great crime of the Middle Ages, by the destruction
of the citadel against which the hitherto irresistible wave of Moslem invasion
had beaten and been broken."   Not praiseworthy, it is true, was the
motive of the Crusaders, yet there is no occasion for bemoaning the fate of
Constantinople and the Greeks.   The conquest of the Latins prolonged
the successful resistance to the Turks.

the wrath of the Crusaders.[1]   The discontent with the hard
terms of the agreement and the presence of the Occidentals
gave Alexius Dukas, surnamed Murzuphlos from his shaggy
eyebrows, opportunity to dethrone Isaac and his son and to
seize the reins of government.   The prince was put to death,
and Isaac soon followed him to the grave.

The confusion within the palace and the failure to pay the
promised reward were a sufficient excuse for the invaders to
assault the city, which fell April 12, 1204.[2]   Unrestrained
pillage and riot followed.   Even the occupants of convents
were not exempted from the orgies of unbridled lust.
Churches and altars were despoiled as well as palaces.
Chalices were turned into drinking cups.   A prostitute
placed in the chair of the patriarchs in St. Sophia, sang
ribald songs and danced for the amusement of the soldiery.[3]

Innocent III., writing of the conquest of the city, says : —

"You have spared nothing that is sacred, neither age nor sex.   You
have given yourselves up to prostitution, to adultery, and to debauchery
in the face of all the world.   You have glutted your guilty passions, not
only on married women, but upon women and virgins dedicated to the
Saviour.   You have not been content with the imperial treasures and
the goods of rich and poor, but you have seized even the wealth of the
Church and what belongs to it.   You have pillaged the silver tables of
the altars, you have broken into the sacristies and stolen the vessels."[4]

To the revolt at these orgies succeeding ages have added regret for the irreparable loss which literature and art suffered

[1] Arabs were allowed to live in the city and granted the privileges of their
religious rites.   Gibbon with characteristic irony says, "The Flemish pilgrims
were scandalized by the aspect of a mosque or a synagogue in which one God
was worshipped without a partner or a son."

[2] Villehardouin, 233, Wailly's ed. p. 137, pronounces the capture of Constantinople one of the most difficult feats ever undertaken, *une des plus
redoutables choses à faire qui jamais fut*.   A city of such strong fortifications
the Franks had not seen before.

[3] Hurter (I. p. 685), comparing the conquest of Constantinople with the
capture of Jerusalem, exalts the piety of Godfrey and the first Crusaders
over against the Venetians and their greed for booty.   He forgot the awful
massacre in Jerusalem.

[4] *Reg.*, VIII.   *Ep.*, 133.

in the wild and protracted sack.   For the first time in eight
hundred years its accumulated treasures were exposed to
the ravages of the spoiler, who broke up the altars in its
churches, as in St. Sophia, or melted priceless pieces of bronze
statuary on the streets and highways.[1]

Constantinople proved to be the richest of sacred storehouses, full of relics, which excited the cupidity and satisfied the superstition of the Crusaders, who found nothing
inconsistent in joining devout worship and the violation of
the eighth commandment in getting possession of the objects
of worship.[2]   With a credulity which seems to have asked
no questions, skulls and bones of saints, pieces of wearing
apparel, and other sacred objects were easily discovered and
eagerly sent to Western Europe, from the stone on which
Jacob slept and Moses' rod which was turned into a serpent,
to the true cross and fragments of Mary's garments.[3]   What
California was to the world's supply of gold in 1849 and the
mines of the Transvaal have been to its supply of diamonds
— that the capture of Constantinople was to the supply of
relics for Latin Christendom.   Towns and cities welcomed
these relics, and convents were made famous by their possession.   In 1205 bishop Nivelon of Soissons sent to Soissons
the head of St. Stephen, the finger that Thomas thrust into
the Saviour's side, a thorn from the crown of thorns, a portion
of the sleeveless shirt of the Virgin Mary and her girdle, a
portion of the towel with which the Lord girded himself at
the Last Supper, one of John the Baptist's arms, and other
antiquities scarcely less venerable.   The city of Halberstadt
and its bishop, Konrad, were fortunate enough to secure

---

[1] Nicetas gives a list of these losses.   See Gibbon, LX., and Hurter.

[2] Villehardouin, 191; Wailly's ed., 111, says *des reliques il n'en faut
point parler, car en ce jour il y en avait autant dans la ville que dans le reste
du monde.*   The account of Guntherus, Migne, 212, 253 sqq., is the most elaborate.   His informant the Abbot Martin, was an insatiable relic hunter.

[3] See Riant; Hurter, I. 694–702; Pears, 365–370.   A volume would scarce
contain the history, real and legendary, of these objects of veneration.

some of the blood shed on the cross, parts of the sponge and reed and the purple robe, the head of James the Just, and many other trophies. Sens received the crown of thorns. A tear of Christ was conveyed to Seligencourt and led to a change of its name to the Convent of the Sacred Tear.[1] Amiens received John the Baptist's head; St. Albans, England, two of St. Margaret's fingers. The true cross was divided by the grace of the bishops among the barons. A piece was sent by Baldwin to Innocent III.

Perhaps no sacred relics were received with more outward demonstrations of honor than the true crown of thorns, which Baldwin II. transferred to the king of France for ten thousand marks of silver.[2] It was given free passage by the emperor Frederick II. and was carried through Paris by the French king barefoot and in his shirt. A part of the true cross and the swaddling clothes of Bethlehem were additional acquisitions of Paris.

The Latin Empire of Constantinople, which followed the capture of the city, lasted from 1204 to 1261. Six electors representing the Venetians and six representing the Crusaders met in council and elected Baldwin of Flanders, emperor.[3] He was crowned by the papal legate in St.

---

[1] A curious account is given by Dalmatius of Sergy, of his discovery of the head of St. Clement in answer to prayer, and the deception he practised in making away with it. The relic went to Cluny and was greatly prized. See Hurter. The successful stealth of Abbot Martin is told at length by the German Guntherus, Migne, 212, 251 sq.

[2] Matthew Paris, in his account, says, "It was precious beyond gold or topaz, and to the credit of the French kingdom, and indeed, of all the Latins, it was solemnly and devoutly received in grand procession amidst the ringing of bells and the devout prayers of the faithful followers of Christ, and was placed in the king's chapel in Paris." Luard's ed., IV. 75; Giles's trans., I. 311.

[3] The mode of election was fixed before the capture of the city, Villehardouin, 234, 256-261; Wailly's ed., 137, 152 sqq. The election took place in a chamber of the palace. The leader of the French forces, Boniface of Montferrat, married the widow of the emperor Isaac and was made king of Salonica. Innocent III. (VIII. 134, Migne, 215, 714) congratulated Isaac's widow upon her conversion to the Latin Church.

Sophia and at once set about to introduce Latin priests and subdue the Greek Church to the pope.

The attitude of Innocent III. to this remarkable transaction of Christian soldiery exhibited at once his righteous indignation and his politic acquiescence in the new responsibility thrust upon the Apostolic see.[1] He appointed the Venetian, Thomas Morosini, archbishop; and the Latin patriarchate, established with him, has been perpetuated to this day, and is an almost unbearable offence to the Greeks.[2] If Innocent had followed Baldwin's suggestions, he would have convoked an œcumenical council in Constantinople.

The last of the Latin emperors, Baldwin III., 1237–1261, spent most of his time in Western Europe making vain appeals for money. After his dethronement, in 1261, by Michael Palæologus he presents a pitiable spectacle, seeking to gain the ear of princes and ecclesiastics. For two hundred years more the Greeks had an uncertain tenure on the Bosphorus. The loss of Constantinople was bound to come sooner or later in the absence of a moral and muscular revival of the Greek people. The Latin conquest of the city was a romantic episode, and not a stage in the progress of civilization in the East ; nor did it hasten the coming of the new era of letters in Western Europe. It widened the schism of the Greek and the Latin churches. The only party to reap substantial gain from the Fourth Crusade was the Venetians.[3]

[1] He wrote to Baldwin that, while it was desirable the Eastern Church should be subdued, he was more concerned that the Holy Land should be rescued. He urged him and the Venetians to eat the bread of repentance that they might fight the battle of the Lord with a pure heart.

[2] The Greek patriarch had left the city reduced to a state of apostolic poverty, of which Gibbon, LXI, says that "had it been voluntary it might perhaps have been meritorious."

[3] Pears concludes his work, *The Fall of Constantinople*, by the false judgment that the effects of the Fourth Crusade were altogether disastrous for civilization. He surmises that, but for it, the city would never have fallen into the hands of the Turks, and the Sea of Marmora and the Black Sea would now be surrounded by "prosperous and civilized nations," pp. 412 sqq. There was no movement of progress in the Byzantine empire for the Crusaders to check.

§ 56.   *Frederick II. and the Fifth Crusade.* 1229.

Röhricht : *Studien zur Gesch. d. V. Kreuzzuges*, Innsbruck, 1891. —
    Hauck, IV. 752–764, and the lit., §§ 42, 49.

Innocent III.'s ardor for the reconquest of Palestine continued unabated till his death.   A fresh crusade constituted
one of the main objects for which the Fourth Lateran Council was called.   The date set for it to start was June 1,
1217, and it is known as the Fifth Crusade.   The pope
promised £30,000 from his private funds, and a ship to
convey the Crusaders going from Rome and its vicinity.
The cardinals joined him in promising to contribute one-
tenth of their incomes and the clergy were called upon
to set apart one-twentieth of their revenues for three
years for the holy cause.   To the penitent contributing
money to the crusade, as well as to those participating in it,
full indulgence for sins was offered.[1]   A brief, forbidding
the sale of all merchandise and munitions of war to the
Saracens for four years, was ordered read every Sabbath
and fast day in Christian ports.

Innocent died without seeing the expedition start.   For
his successor Honorius III., its promotion was a ruling passion, but he also died without seeing it realized.

In 1217 Andreas of Hungary led an army to Syria, but
accomplished nothing.   In 1219 William of Holland with
his Germans, Norwegians, and Danes helped John of
Brienne, titular king of Jerusalem, to take Damietta.   This
city, situated on one of the mouths of the Nile, was a
place of prime commercial importance and regarded as the
key of Egypt.   Egypt had come to be regarded as the
proper way of military approach to Palestine.   Malik-al-
Kameel, who in 1218 had succeeded to power in Egypt,
offered the Christians Jerusalem and all Palestine, except

---

[1] *Plenam suorum peccaminum veniam indulgemus.*   See Mansi, XXII.
1067 ; Mirbt, *Quellen*, 126, Gottlob, 137 sq.

Kerak, together with the release of all Christian prisoners, on condition of the surrender of Damietta. It was a grand opportunity of securing the objects for which the Crusaders had been fighting, but, elated by victory and looking for help from the emperor, Frederick II., they rejected the offer. In 1221 Damietta fell back into the hands of Mohammedans.[1]

The Fifth Crusade reached its results by diplomacy more than by the sword. Its leader, Frederick II., had little of the crusading spirit, and certainly the experiences of his ancestors Konrad and Barbarossa were not adapted to encourage him. His vow, made at his coronation in Aachen and repeated at his coronation in Rome, seems to have had little binding force for him. His marriage with Iolanthe, granddaughter of Conrad of Montferrat and heiress of the crown of Jerusalem, did not accelerate his preparations to which he was urged by Honorius III. In 1227 he sailed from Brindisi; but, as has already been said, he returned to port after three days on account of sickness among his men.[2]

At last the emperor set forth with forty galleys and six hundred knights, and arrived in Acre, Sept. 7, 1228. The sultans of Egypt and Damascus were at the time in bitter conflict. Taking advantage of the situation, Frederick concluded with Malik-al-Kameel a treaty which was to remain in force ten years and delivered up to the Christians

---

[1] For the text of Frederick's summons to his crusade of 1221, see Mathews, *Select Med. Documents*, 120 sq.

[2] Funk, in Wetzer-Welte, VII. 1166, says that in view of contemporary testimony, Frederick's sickness cannot be doubted. Roger Wendover, *an.* 1227, however, doubted it. Funk is wrong in saying that it was not till 1239 that Gregory, aggravated by the emperor's conduct, impeached Frederick's plea of sickness. In his sentence of excommunication of 1228, Gregory asserted that Frederick "was enticed away to the usual pleasures of his kingdom and made a frivolous pretext of bodily infirmity." In 1235, at a time when emperor and pope were reconciled, Gregory spoke of Jerusalem "as being restored to our well-beloved son in Christ, Frederick."

Jerusalem with the exception of the mosque of Omar and the Temple area, Bethlehem, Nazareth, and the pilgrim route from Acre to Jerusalem.[1]   On March 19, 1229, the emperor crowned himself with his own hand in the church of the Holy Sepulchre.   The same day the archbishop of Cæsarea pronounced, in the name of the patriarch of Jerusalem, the interdict over the city.[2]

Recalled probably by the dangers threatening his kingdom, Frederick arrived in Europe in the spring of 1229, but only to find himself for the fourth time put under the ban by his implacable antagonist, Gregory.   In 1235 Gregory was again appealing to Christendom to make preparations for another expedition, and in his letter of 1239, excommunicating the emperor for the fifth time, he pronounced him the chief impediment in the way of a crusade.[3]

It was certainly a singular spectacle that the Holy City should be gained by a diplomatic compact and not by hardship, heroic struggle, and the intervention of miracle, whether real or imagined.   It was still more singular that the sacred goal should be reached without the aid of ecclesiastical sanction, nay in the face of solemn papal denunciation.

Frederick II. has been called by Freeman an unwilling Crusader and the conquest of Jerusalem a grotesque episode in his life.[4]   Frederick certainly had no compunction about living on terms of amity with Mohammedans in his kingdom, and he probably saw no wisdom in endangering his relations with them at home by unsheathing the sword against them abroad.[5]   Much to the disgust of Gregory IX. he visited the mosque of Omar in Jerusalem without making any protest

---

[1] See Röhricht, *Regesta regni Hier.*, 262, and Bréholles, III. 86–90.

[2] Geroldus was patriarch of Jerusalem and notified Gregory IX. of Frederick's "fraudulent pact with the Egyptian sultan."   Röhricht, 263.

[3] In 1240 a petition signed by German bishops and princes and addressed to Gregory urged him to cease from strife with Frederick as it interfered with a crusade.   Bréholles, V. 985.

[4] *Hist. Essays*, I. 283–313.   [5] Bréholles, V. 327–340.

against its ritual.   Perhaps, with his freedom of thought, he did not regard the possession of Palestine after all as of much value.   In any case, Frederick's religion—whatever he had of religion—was not of a kind to flame forth in enthusiasm for a pious scheme in which sentiment formed a prevailing element.

Gregory's continued appeals in 1235 and the succeeding years called for some minor expeditions, one of them led by Richard of Cornwall, afterwards German emperor-elect.   The condition of the Christians in Palestine grew more and more deplorable and, in a battle with the Chorasmians, Oct. 14, 1244, they met with a disastrous defeat, and thenceforth Jerusalem was closed to them.

§ 57.   *St. Louis and the Last Crusades.*   1248, 1270.

LITERATURE. — JEHAN DE JOINVILLE, d. 1319, the next great historical writer in old French after Villehardouin, companion of St. Louis on his first Crusade: *Hist. de St. Louis*, 1st ed. Poitiers, 1547 ; by Du Cange, 1668 ; by Michaud in *Mémoires à l'hist. de France*, Paris, 1857, I. 161–329, and by de Wailly, Paris, 1868.   For other edd. see Potthast, *Bibl.*, I. 679–681. Engl. trans., M. TH. JOHNES, Haford, 1807, included in *Chronicles of the Crusades*, Bohn's Libr. 340–556, and J. HUTTON, London, 1868. — TILLEMONT : *Vie de St. Louis*, publ. for the first time, Paris, 1847–1851, 6 vols. — SCHOLTEN : *Gesch. Ludwigs des Heiligen*, ed. by Junkemann and Janssen, 2 vols. Münster, 1850–1855. — GUIZOT : *St. Louis and Calvin*, Paris, 1868. — MRS. BRAY : *Good St. Louis and his Times*, London, 1870. — WALLON : *St. Louis et son Temps*, 3d ed. Tours, 1879. — ST. PATHUS : *Vie de St. Louis*, publiée par F. Delaborde, Paris, 1899. — F. PERRY: *St. Louis, Most Christian King*, London, 1901. — LANE-POOLE: *Hist. of Egypt in the M. A.*, N.Y., 1901.

One more great Crusader, one in whom genuine piety was a leading trait, was yet to set his face towards the East and, by the abrupt termination of his career through sickness, to furnish one of the most memorable scenes in the long drama of the Crusades.   The Sixth and Seventh Crusades owe their origin to the devotion of Louis IX., king of France, usually known as St. Louis.   Louis combined the piety of the monk with the chivalry of the knight, and stands in

the front rank of Christian sovereigns of all times.[1] His
religious zeal showed itself not only in devotion to the confessional and the mass, but in steadfast refusal, in the face
of threatened torture, to deviate from his faith and in patient
resignation under the most trying adversity.   A considerate
regard for the poor and the just treatment of his subjects
were among his traits.   He washed the feet of beggars and,
when a Dominican warned him against carrying his humility too far, he replied, " If I spent twice as much time in
gaming and at the chase as in such services, no man would
rise up to find fault with me."

On one occasion, when he asked Joinville if he were called
upon to choose between being a leper and committing mortal
sin, which his choice would be, the seneschal replied, " he
would rather commit thirty mortal sins than be a leper."
The next day the king said to him, " How could you say what
you did ?   There is no leper so hideous as he who is in a state
of mortal sin.   The leprosy of the body will pass away at
death, but the leprosy of the soul may cling to it forever."

The sack of Jerusalem by the Chorasmians,[2] who were
being pushed on from behind by the Mongols, was followed by the fall of Gaza and Ascalon.   It was just one hundred years since the news of the fall of Edessa had stirred
Europe, but the temper of men's minds was no longer the
same.   The news of disasters in Palestine was a familiar
thing.   There was now no Bernard to arouse the conscience
and give directions to the feelings of princes and people.
The Council of Lyons in 1245 had for one of its four objects
the relief of the holy places.   A summons was sent forth

[1] " Piety was his ruling passion."   Guizot, p. 117.   De Joinville frequently calls him "the good king " and Matthew Paris " that most Christian
king."

[2] See the account in a letter from the prelates of the Holy Land in
Matthew Paris, *an.* 1244.   The invaders were called Tartars by Robert,
patriarch of Jerusalem, in his letter to Innocent IV.   Röhricht, *Reg. regni
Hier.*, p. 290.

by pope and council for a new expedition, and the usual
gracious offers were made to those who should participate in
the movement. St. Louis responded. During a sickness in
1245 and at the moment when the attendants were about to
put a cloth on his face thinking he was dead, the king had
the cross bound upon his breast.

On June 12, 1248, Louis received at St. Denis from the
hand of the papal legate the oriflamme, and the pilgrim's
wallet and staff. He was joined by his three brothers,
Robert, count of Artois, Alphonso, count of Poitiers, and
Charles of Anjou. Among others to accompany the king
were Jean de Joinville, seneschal of Champagne, whose
graphic chronicle has preserved the annals of the Crusade.[1]
The number of the troops is given at thirty-two thousand.
Venetian and Genoese fleets carried them to Cyprus, where
preparations had been made on a large scale for their maintenance. Thence they sailed to Egypt. Damietta fell, but after
this first success, the campaign was a dismal disaster. Louis'
benevolence and ingenuousness were not combined with the
force of the leader. He was ready to share suffering with
his troops but had not the ability to organize them.[2] His
piety could not prevent the usual vices from being practised
in the camps.[3]

[1] Joinville, accompanied by twenty knights, joined the king at Cyprus.
He was a man of religious fervor, made pilgrimages to all the shrines in the
vicinity of his castle before his departure, and never failed in his long absence
to confine himself to bread and water on Fridays (*History, an.* 1250). One
of his paragraphs gives a graphic insight into the grief which must have been
felt by thousands of Crusaders as they left their homes for the long and uncertain journey to the East. It runs: "In passing near the castle of Joinville,
I dared never turn my eyes that way for fear of feeling too great regret
and lest my courage should fail on leaving my children and my fair castle of
Joinville, which I loved in my heart."

[2] Joinville speaks of Louis having "as much trouble in keeping his own
people together in time of peace as in the time of his ill fortunes." *an.* 1249.

[3] Within a stone's throw of the king's tent were several brothels. A
curious punishment was prescribed by the king for a knight caught with
a harlot at Acre. Joinville, pt. II. *an.* 1250, Bohn's trans. 484.

Leaving Alexandria to one side, and following the advice
of the count of Artois, who argued that whoso wanted to kill
a snake should first strike its head, Louis marched in the
direction of the capital, Cairo, or Babylon, as it was called.
The army was harassed by a sleepless foe, and reduced by
fevers and dysentery.   The Nile became polluted with the
bodies of the dead.[1]   At Mansourah the Turks dealt a
crushing defeat.   On the retreat which followed, the king
and the count of Poitiers were taken prisoners.   The count
of Artois had been killed.   The humiliation of the Crusaders
had never been so deep.

The king's patient fortitude shone brightly in these misfortunes.   Threatened with torture and death, he declined
to deviate from his faith or to yield up any of the places in
Palestine.   For the ransom of his troops, he agreed to
pay 500,000 livres, and for his own freedom to give up
Damietta and abandon Egypt.   The sultan remitted a
fifth part of the ransom money on hearing of the readiness
with which the king had accepted the terms.

Clad in garments which were a gift from the sultan, and
in a ship meagrely furnished with comforts, the king sailed
for Acre.   On board ship, hearing that his brother, the
count of Anjou, and Walter de Nemours were playing for
money, he staggered from his bed of sickness and throwing
the dice, tables, and money into the sea, reprimanded the
count that he should be so soon forgetful of his brother's
death and the other disasters in Egypt, as to game.[2]   At
Acre, Louis remained three years, spending large sums upon
the fortifications of Jaffa, Sidon, and other places.   The
death of Blanche, his mother, who had been acting as queen-
regent during his absence, induced him to return to his
realm.

Like Richard the Lion-hearted, Louis did not look upon

[1] See the appalling description of Joinville, *an.* 1249.
[2] Joinville, *an.* 1250.

Jerusalem. The sultan of Damascus offered him the opportunity and Louis would have accepted it but for the advice
of his councillors,[1] who argued that his separation from the
army would endanger it, and pointing to the example of
Richard, persuaded the king that it would be beneath his
dignity to enter a city he could not conquer. He set sail
from Acre in the spring of 1254. His queen, Margaret, and
the three children born to them in the East, were with him.
It was a pitiful conclusion to an expedition which once had
given promise of a splendid consummation.

So complete a failure might have been expected to destroy
all hope of ever recovering Palestine. But the hold of the
crusading idea upon the mind of Europe was still great.
Urban IV. and Clement III. made renewed appeals to
Christendom, and Louis did not forget the Holy Land.
In 1267, with his hand upon the crown of thorns, he announced to his assembled prelates and barons his purpose
to go forth a second time in holy crusade.

In the meantime the news from the East had been of continuous disaster at the hand of the enemy and of discord
among the Christians themselves. In 1258 forty Venetian
vessels engaged in conflict with a Genoese fleet of fifty ships
off Acre with a loss of seventeen hundred men. A year
later the Templars and Hospitallers had a pitched battle. In
1263 Bibars, the founder of the Mameluke rule in Egypt,
appeared before Acre. In 1268 Antioch fell.

In spite of bodily weakness and the protest of his nobles,
Louis sailed in 1270.[2] The fleet steered for Tunis,[3] proba-
bly out of deference to Charles of Anjou, now king of
Naples, who was bent upon forcing the sultan to meet his

[1] Joinville, *an.* 1253.

[2] Joinville declined the king's appeal to accompany him, and advised
against the expedition on the ground of the peaceable state of France with
the king at home, and of the king's physical weakness which prevented him
from wearing armor or sitting on horseback long at a time.

[3] Since 1881 a dependency of France.

tributary obligations to Sicily.[1] Sixty thousand men constituted the expedition, but disaster was its predestined portion.
The camp was scarcely pitched on the site of Carthage when
the plague broke out. Among the victims was the king's
son, John Tristan, born at Damietta, and the king himself.
Louis died with a resignation accordant with the piety
which had marked his life. He ordered his body placed on
a bed of ashes; and again and again repeated the prayer,
" Make us, we beseech thee, O Lord, to despise the prosperity of this world and not to fear any of its adversities."
The night of August 24 his mind was upon Jerusalem, and
starting up from his fevered sleep, he exclaimed, " Jerusalem !
Jerusalem ! we will go." His last words, according to the
report of an attendant, were, " I will enter into thy house,
O Lord, I will worship in thy holy sanctuary, I will glorify
Thy name, O Lord."[2] The next day the royal sufferer passed
to the Jerusalem above. His body was taken to France and
laid away in St. Denis.[3] In 1297 the good king was canon-
ized, the only one of the prominent participants in the
Crusades to attain to that distinction, unless we except
St. Bernard.

§ 58. *The Last Stronghold of the Crusaders in Palestine.*

With Louis the last hope of Christian tenure of any part
of Palestine was gone. At his death the French army dis-
banded.

In 1271 Edward, son and heir of Henry III. of England,

[1] The sultan had agreed to pay yearly tribute to Roger II. In the treaty
made at the close of the expedition, he agreed to make up the arrearages of
tribute to Charles.

[2] M. Paris, *an.* 1271.

[3] The question whether the king's heart was deposited in the Sainte
Chapelle at Paris or not, led to a spirited discussion in 1843. See Letronne,
*Examen critique de la découverte du pretendu cœur de St. Louis faite a la
Sainte Chapelle le 15 Mai 1843,* Paris, 1844 ; Lenormant, *Preuves de la
découverte du cœur de St. Louis,* Paris, 1846.

reached Acre by way of Tunis. His expedition was but a wing of Louis's army. A loan of 30,000 marks from the French king enabled him to prepare the armament. His consort Eleanor was with him, and a daughter born on the Syrian coast was called Joan of Acre. Before returning to England to assume the crown, he concluded an empty treaty of peace for ten years.

Attempts were made to again fan the embers of the once fervid enthusiasm into a flame, but in vain. Gregory X., who was in the Holy Land at the time of his election to the papal chair, carried with him westward a passionate purpose to help the struggling Latin colonies in Palestine. Before leaving Acre, 1272, he preached from Ps. 137:5, "If I forget thee, O Jerusalem, let my tongue cleave to the roof of my mouth." His appeals, issued a day or two after his coronation, met with little response. The Council of Lyons, 1274, which he convened, had for its chief object the arrangements for a Crusade. Two years later Gregory died, and the enterprise was abandoned.

In 1289 Tripoli was lost, and the bitter rivalry between the Military Orders hastened the surrender of Acre, 1291,[1] and with it all Christian rule in Syria was brought to an end. The Templars and Hospitallers escaped. The population of sixty thousand was reduced to slavery or put to the sword. For one hundred and fifty years Acre had been the metropolis of Latin life in the East. It had furnished a camp for army after army, and witnessed the entry and departure of kings and queens from the chief states of Europe. But the city was also a byword for turbulence and vice. Nicolas IV. had sent ships to aid the besieged, and again called upon the princes of Europe for help ; but his call fell on closed ears.

As the Crusades progressed, a voice was lifted here and there calling in question the religious propriety of such

[1] For a contemporary description of Acre, see *Itin. regis Ricardi*, I. 32.

movements and their ultimate value. At the close of the
twelfth century, the abbot Joachim complained that the
popes were making them a pretext for their own aggrandizement, and upon the basis of Joshua 6 : 26 ; 1 Kings 16 : 24,
he predicted a curse upon an attempt to rebuild the walls of
Jerusalem. " Let the popes," he said, "mourn over their
own Jerusalem — that is, the universal Church not built with
hands and purchased by divine blood, and not over the
fallen Jerusalem." [1] Humbert de Romanis, general of the
Dominicans, in making out a list of matters to be handled at
the Council of Lyons, 1274, felt obliged to refute no less than
seven objections to the Crusades. They were such as these.
It was contrary to the precepts of the New Testament to
advance religion by the sword ; Christians may defend themselves, but have no right to invade the lands of another; it is
wrong to shed the blood of unbelievers and Saracens ; and
the disasters of the Crusades proved they were contrary to
the will of God. [2]

Raymundus Lullus, after returning from his mission to
North Africa, in 1308, declared [3] " that the conquest of the
Holy Land should be attempted in no other way than as
Christ and the Apostles undertook to accomplish it — by
prayers, tears, and the offering up of our own lives. Many
are the princes and knights that have gone to the Promised
Land with a view to conquer it, but if this mode had been
pleasing to the Lord, they would assuredly have wrested it
from the Saracens before this. Thus it is manifest to pious
monks that Thou art daily waiting for them to do for love
to Thee what Thou hast done from love to them."

The successors of Nicolas IV., however, continued to cling
to the idea of conquering the Holy Land by arms. During
the fourteenth and fifteenth centuries they made repeated

---

[1] *Com. in Jerem.*, see Neander, *Ch. Hist.*, IV. 189 sqq., Engl. trans.

[2] Mansi, XXIV. 111-120.

[3] *Contemplations of God.* See Zwemer, *Life of Raymund Lull*, 52, 149.

appeals to the piety and chivalry of Western Europe, but these were voices as from another age.   The deliverance of Palestine by the sword was a dead issue.   New problems were engaging men's minds.   The authority of the popes — now in exile in Avignon, now given to a luxurious life at Rome, or engaged in wars over papal territory — was incompetent to unite and direct the energies of Europe as it had once done.   They did not discern the signs of the times. More important tasks there were for Christendom to accomplish than to rescue the holy places of the East.

Erasmus struck the right note and expressed the view of a later age.   Writing at the very close of the Middle Ages making an appeal[1] for the proclamation of the Gospel by preaching and speaking of wars against the Turks, he said, "Truly, it is not meet to declare ourselves Christian men by killing very many but by saving very many, not if we send thousands of heathen people to hell, but if we make many infidels Christian; not if we cruelly curse and excommunicate, but if we with devout prayers and with our hearts desire their health, and pray unto God, to send them better minds."[2]

§ 59.   *Effects of the Crusades.*

> ". . . The knights' bones are dust
> And their good swords are rust ;
> Their souls are with the saints, we trust."
>   — COLERIDGE.

LITERATURE. — A. H. L. HEEREN : *Versuch einer Entwickelung der Folgen der Kreuzzüge für Europa,* Göttingen, 1808 ; French trans., Paris, 1808. — MAXIME DE CHOISEUL-DAILLECOURT: *De l'influence des croisades sur l'état des peuples de l'Europe,* Paris, 1809.   Crowned by the French

---

[1] *Enchiridion militis christiani,* Methuen's ed. 1905, p. 8 sq.

[2] No appellation was too degrading to give to the enemies of the cross. The most common one was dogs.   The biographers of Richard I. have no compunction in relating in one line gifts made by Saracens and in the next calling them dogs.   See *Itin. Ricardi,* etc.   So Walter Map says *sepulchrum et crux Domini præda sunt* canum *quorum fames in tantum lassata fuit et sanguine martyrorum,* etc., Wright's ed., I. 15, p. 229.

U

Institute, it presents the Crusades as upon the whole favorable to civil liberty, commerce, etc. — J. L. HAHN: *Ursachen und Folgen der Kreuzzüge*, Greifsw., 1859. — G. B. ADAMS: *Civilization during the M. A.*, N.Y., 1894, 258–311. See the general treatments of the Crusades by GIBBON, WILKEN, MICHAUD, ARCHER-KINGSFORD, 425–451, etc., and especially PRUTZ (*Kulturgeschichte der Kreuzzüge* and *The Economic Development of Western Europe under the Influence of the Crusades* in Essays on the Crusades, Burlington, 1903), who in presenting the social, political, commercial, and literary aspects and effects of the Crusades lays relatively too much stress upon them.

The Crusades failed in three respects. The Holy Land was not won. The advance of Islam was not permanently checked. The schism between the East and the West was not healed. These were the primary objects of the Crusades.

They were the cause of great evils. As a school of practical religion and morals, they were no doubt disastrous for most of the Crusaders. They were attended by all the usual demoralizing influences of war and the sojourn of armies in an enemy's country. The vices of the Crusading camps were a source of deep shame in Europe. Popes lamented them. Bernard exposed them. Writers set forth the fatal mistake of those who were eager to make conquest of the earthly Jerusalem and were forgetful of the heavenly city. "Many wended their way to the holy city, unmindful that our Jerusalem is not here." So wrote the Englishman, Walter Map, after Saladin's victories in 1187.

The schism between the East and the West was widened by the insolent action of the popes in establishing Latin patriarchates in the East and their consent to the establishment of the Latin empire of Constantinople. The memory of the indignities heaped upon Greek emperors and ecclesiastics has not yet been forgotten.

Another evil was the deepening of the contempt and hatred in the minds of the Mohammedans for the doctrines of Christianity. The savagery of the Christian soldiery, their unscrupulous treatment of property, and the bitter rancors in the Crusading camps were a disgraceful spectacle

which could have but one effect upon the peoples of the
East.   While the Crusades were still in progress, the objection was made in Western Europe, that they were not followed by spiritual fruits, but that on the contrary the
Saracens were converted to blasphemy rather than to the
faith.   Being killed, they were sent to hell.[1]

Again, the Crusades gave occasion for the rapid development of the system of papal indulgences, which became a
dogma of the mediæval theologians.   The practice, once
begun by Urbán II. at the very outset of the movement, was
extended further and further until indulgence for sins was
promised not only for the warrior who took up arms against
the Saracens in the East, but for those who were willing to
fight against Christian heretics in Western Europe.   Indulgences became a part of the very heart of the sacrament of
penance, and did incalculable damage to the moral sense of
Christendom.   To this evil was added the exorbitant taxations levied by the popes and their emissaries.   Matthew
Paris complains of this extortion for the expenses of Crusades
as a stain upon that holy cause.[2]

And yet the Crusades were not in vain.   It is not possible
to suppose that Providence did not carry out some important, immediate and ultimate purpose for the advancement
of mankind through this long war, extending over two hundred years, and involving some of the best vital forces of
two continents.   It may not always be easy to distinguish
between the effects of the Crusades and the effects of other
forces active in this period, or to draw an even balance between them.   But it may be regarded as certain that they
made far-reaching contributions to the great moral, reli-

---

[1] So Humbert de Romanis, 1274; Mansi, XXIV. 116.   A sixth objection against the Crusades as stated and answered by him ran as follows:
*quod ex ista pugna non sequitur fructus spiritualis quia Saraceni magis
convertuntur ad blasphemiam quam ad fidem; occisi autem ad infernum
mittuntur*, etc.

[2] II. 338, etc.

gious, and social change which the institutions of Europe underwent in the latter half of the Middle Ages.

First, the Crusades engaged the minds of men in the contemplation of a high and unselfish aim. The rescue of the Holy Sepulchre was a religious passion, drawing attention away from the petty struggles of ecclesiastics in the assertion of priestly prerogative, from the violent conflict of papacy and empire, and from the humdrum casuistry of scholastic and conventual dispute.[1] Even Gibbon[2] admits that "the controlling emotion with the most of the Crusaders was, beyond question, a lofty ideal of enthusiasm."

Considered in their effects upon the papacy, they offered it an unexampled opportunity for the extension of its authority. But on the other hand, by educating the laity and developing secular interests, they also aided in undermining the power of the hierarchy.

As for the political institutions of Europe, they called forth and developed that spirit of nationality which resulted in the consolidation of the states of Europe in the form which they have since retained with little change. When the Crusades began, feudalism flourished. When the Crusades closed, feudalism was decadent throughout Europe, and had largely disappeared from parts of it. The need petty knights and great nobles had to furnish themselves with adequate equipments, led to the pawn or sale of their estates and their prolonged absence gave sovereigns a rare opportunity to extend their authority. And in the adjoining camps of armies on Syrian soil, the customs and pride of independent national life were fostered.

Upon the literature and individual intelligence of Western Europe, the Crusades, no doubt, exerted a powerful influence,

---

[1] Archer, p. 447, well says: "They raised mankind above the ignoble sphere of petty ambitions to seek after an ideal that was neither sordid nor selfish. They called forth all that was heroic in human nature, and filled the world with the inspiration of noble thoughts and deeds."

[2] *Decline and Fall*, LVIII.

although it may not be possible to weigh that influence in exact balances. It was a matter of great importance that men of all classes, from the emperor to the poorest serf, came into personal contact on the march and in the camp. They were equals in a common cause, and learned that they possessed the traits of a common humanity, of which the isolation of the baronial hall kept them ignorant. The emancipating effect which travel may always be expected to exert, was deeply felt.[1] The knowledge of human customs and geography was enlarged. Richard of Hoveden is able to give the distances from place to place from England to the Holy Land. A respectable collection of historical works grew out of the expeditions, from the earliest annalists of the First Crusade, who wrote in Latin, to Villehardouin and John de Joinville who wrote in French. The fountains of story and romance were struck, and to posterity were contributed the inspiring figures of Godfrey, Tancred, and St. Louis—soldiers who realized the ideal of Christian chivalry.

As for commerce, it would be hazardous to say that the enterprise of the Italian ports would not, in time, have developed by the usual incentives of Eastern trade and the impulse of marine enterprise then astir. It cannot be doubted, however, that the Crusades gave to commerce an immense impetus. The fleets of Marseilles and the Italian ports were greatly enlarged through the demands for the transportation of tens of thousands of Crusaders ; and the Pisans, Genoese, and Venetians were busy in traffic at Acre, Damietta, and other ports.[2]

[1] This is clearly apparent from the English and other mediæval chronicles, such as the Chronicles of M. Paris, Hoveden, etc.

[2] The ships of the two great Military Orders alone carried great numbers of pilgrims. In 1182 one of their ships was wrecked on the Egyptian coast with 1500 pilgrims. In 1180 several vessels met the same fate, 2500 pilgrims were drowned and 1500 sold into slavery. In 1246 their ships carried from the port of Marseilles alone 6000 pilgrims. See Prutz in *Essays*, p. 54. This author, in laying weight upon the economic influences of the Crusades, says properly, that they "had only in part to do with religion, and particu-

In these various ways the spell of ignorance and narrow-
ing prejudice was broken, and to the mind of Western
Europe a new horizon of thought and acquisition was
opened, and remotely within that horizon lay the institutions
and ambitions of our modern civilization.

After the lapse of six centuries and more, the Crusades
still have their stirring lessons of wisdom and warning, and
these are not the least important of their results. The
elevating spectacle of devotion to an unselfish aim has seldom been repeated in the history of religion on so grand a
scale. This spectacle continues to be an inspiration. The
very word " crusade " is synonymous with a lofty moral or
religious movement, as the word " gospel " has come to be used
to signify every message of good.

The Crusades also furnish the perpetual reminder that
not in localities is the Church to seek its holiest satisfaction
and not by the sword is the Church to win its way; but by
the message of peace, by appeals to the heart and conscience,
and by teaching the ministries of prayer and devout worship
is she to accomplish her mission. The Crusader kneeling
in the church of the Holy Sepulchre learned the meaning
of the words, " Why seek ye the living among the dead? He
is not here, He is risen." And all succeeding generations
know the meaning of these words better for his pilgrimage
and his mistake.

Approaching the Crusades in enthusiasm, but differing
from them as widely as the East is from the West in
methods and also in results, has been the movement of
modern Protestant missions to the heathen world which
has witnessed no shedding of blood, save the blood of its
own Christian emissaries, men and women, whose aims have

larly with the church," p. 77.   Arabic words, such as damask, tarif, and
bazar, were introduced into the vocabularies of European nations, and products, such as saffron, maize, melons, and little onions, were carried back by
the Crusaders.   The transfer of money made necessary the development of
the system of letters of credit.

been not the conquest of territory, but the redemption of the race.[1]

§ 60. *The Military Orders.*

LITERATURE. — The sources are the Rules of the orders and the scattered notices of contemporary chroniclers. No attempt is made to give an exhaustive list of the literature. — P. H. HELYOT: *Histoire des ordres monastiques, religieux et militaires,* 8 vols. Paris, 1719. — PERROT: *Coll. hist. des ordres de chivalrie,* etc., 4 vols. Paris, 1819. Supplementary vol. by Fayolle, 1846. — BIELENFELD: *Gesch. und Verfassung aller geistlichen und weltlichen Ritterorden,* 2 vols. Weimar, 1841. — F. C. WOODHOUSE: *The Military Religious Orders of the Middle Ages,* London, 1879. — G. UHLHORN: *Die christliche Liebesthätigkeit im Mittelalter,* Stuttgart, 1884. — HURTER: *Life of Innocent III.,* vol. IV. 313 sqq. — The general Histories of the Crusades. — STUBBS: *Const. Hist. of England.*
For the Knights of St. John: ABBE VERTOT: *Hist. des chevaliers hospitaliers de S. Jean de Jérusalem,* etc., 4 vols. Paris, 1726, and since. — TAAFE: *History of the Knights of Malta,* 4 vols. London, 1852. — L. B. LARKING: *The Knights Hospitallers in England,* London, 1857. — A. WINTERFELD: *Gesch. des Ordens St. Johannis vom Spital zu Jerusalem,* Berlin, 1859. — H. VON ORTENBURG: *Der Ritterorden des hl. Johannis zu Jerusalem,* 2 vols. Regensb. 1866. — GENL. PORTER: *Hist. of the Knights of Malta of the Order of St. John of Jerusalem,* London, 1883. — VON FINCK: *Uebersicht über die Gesch. des ritterlichen Ordens St. Johannis,* Berlin, 1890. — G. HÖNNICKE: *Studien zur Gesch. des Hospitalordens, 1099–1162,* 1897. — *J. D. LE ROULX: *De prima origine Hospitaliorum Hierosol.,* Paris, 1885 ; *Cartulaire général de l'Ordre des Hospitaliers St. Jean de Jérusalem,* 3 vols., Paris, 1894 ; *Les Hospitaliers en Terre Sainte et à Chypre, 1100–1310,* Paris, 1904, pp. 440. — J. VON PFLUGK-HARTTUNG: *Die Anfänge des Johanniterordens in Deutschland,* Berlin, 1899, and *Der Johanniter- und der Deutsche Orden im Kampfe Ludwigs des Baiern mit der Kirche,* Leipzig, 1900. — KNPÖFLER: *Johanniter* in Weltzer-Welte, VI. 1719–1803. For other lit. see LE ROULX: *Les Hospitaliers,* pp. v–xiii.
For the Knights Templars: The literature is very abundant. BERNARD OF CLAIRVAUX: *De laude novæ militiæ, ad milites templi,* Migne, 182, pp. 921–940. — DUPUY: *Hist. des Templiers,* Paris, 1650. — F. WILCKE: *Gesch. des Tempelherren Ordens,* 2 vols. Leipzig, 1827, 2d ed. Halle, 1860.

---

[1] The Crusades, said the eloquent Dr. Richard S. Storrs, *Bernard of Clairvaux,* p. 558, furnished " as truly an ideal enthusiasm as that of any one who has sought to perform his missionary work in distant lands or has wrought into permanent laws and institutions the principles of equity and the temper of love. And they must forever remain an example resplendent and shining of what an enthusiasm that is careless of obstacles and fearless of danger can accomplish."

—*C. H. Maillard de Chambure : *Règle et Statuts secrets des Templiers*, Paris, 1840 (from three old French MSS.).— W. Havemann : *Gesch. des Ausgangs des Tempelherren Ordens*, Stuttgart, 1846. — Michelet : *Procès des Templiers*, 2 vols. Paris, 1841–1851. — Boutaric : *Clement V.* *Philippe le Bel et les Templiers*, Paris, 1874, and *Documents inédites de Philippe le Bel*, Paris, 1861.—*Henri de Curzon : *La Règle du Temple*, Paris, 1886. —*H. Prutz : *Geheimlehre und Geheimstatuten des Tempelherren Ordens*, Berlin, 1879, *Entwicklung und Untergang des Tempelherrenordens*, Berlin, 1888. — K. Schottmüller : *D. Untergang des Templer-Ordens*, 2 vols. Berlin, 1887. — W. Cunningham : *Growth of English Industry*, London, 1890.— J. Gmelin : *Schuld oder Unschuld des Templerordens*, Stuttgart, 1893. — *Döllinger : *Der Untergang des Tempelordens* in his " Akadem. Vorträge," Munich, 1891, III. 245–274, the last public address the author delivered before the Academy of Sciences of Munich. — A. Grange : *Fall of the Knights Templars*, " Dublin Review," 1895, pp. 329 sqq. — G. Schnürer : *D. ursprüngliche Templerregel*, Freib. 1903. — Mansi, XXI. 359–372, also gives the Rule of the Templars as set forth at the Synod of Troyes, 1128. — J. A. Froude : *The Knights Templars* in Short Essays. — Hefele-Knöpfler, VI. — *Funk: *Templer* in Wetzer-Welte, XI. pp. 1311–1345. — H. C. Lea : *Hist. of the Inquisition*, III. and *Absolution Formula of the Templars*, Amer. Soc. of Ch. Hist. Papers, V. 37–58.

For the Teutonic Knights : Strehlke : *Tabulæ ordinis teutonicæ.* — Hennes : *Codex diplomaticus ordinis S. Mariæ Theutonicorum*, 2 vols. Mainz, 1845–1861. — E. Hennig : *Die Statuten des deutschen Ordens*, Würzburg, 1866. — M. Perlbach : *Die Statuten des Deutschordens*, Halle, 1890. — Joh. Voigt : *Geschichte des Deutschen Ritter-Ordens*, 2 vols. Berlin, 1857–1859. — H. Prutz : *Die Besitzungen des deutschen Ordens im heiligen Lande*, Leipzig, 1877. — C. Herrlich : *Die Balley Brandenburg*, etc., Berlin, 1886. — C. Lempens: *Geschichte d. Deutschen Ordens u. sr. Ordensländer Preussen u. Livland*, 1904. — Ranke : *Univ. Hist.*, VIII. 455–480. — Uhlhorn : *Deutschorden*, in Herzog, IV.

> " And by the Holy Sepulchre
> I've pledged my knightly sword
> To Christ, His blessed church, and her,
> The mother of our Lord."
>
> — Whittier, *Knights of St. John.*

A product of the Crusades and their most important adjunct were the three great Military Orders, the Knights of St. John, the Knight Templars, and the Teutonic Knights. They combined monastic vows with the profession of arms. Their members were fighting monks and armed almoners. They constituted a standing army of Crusaders and were

the vigilant guardians of Latin institutions in Palestine for
nearly two centuries.   The Templars and the Knights of
St. John did valiant service on many a battle-field in
Palestine and Asia Minor.[1]   In 1187 they shared in the
disastrous defeat of the Christian forces at Tiberias.   From
that time their strength was concentrated at Acre.[2]   After
the fall of Acre, 1291, the three orders retired to Europe,
holding the Turks in check for two centuries longer in the
South and extending civilization to the provinces on the
Baltic in the North.   They combined the element of romance,
corresponding to the chivalric spirit of the age, with the
element of philanthropy corresponding to its religious
spirit.

These orders speedily attained to great popularity, wealth,
and power.   Kings did them honor.   Pope after pope
extended their authority and privileges.   Their grand masters were recognized as among the chief personages of Christendom.   But with wealth and popularity came pride and
decay.   The strength of the Knights of St. John and the
Templars was also reduced by their rivalry which became
the scandal of Europe, and broke out into open feuds and
pitched battles as before Acre, 1241 to 1243 and in 1259.[3]
After the fall of Acre, which was ascribed in large part to
their jealousy, Nicholas IV. sought to combine them.[4]   The
Knights of St. John were predominantly a French order,
the Teutonic Knights exclusively a German order.   The
Templars were œcumenical in their constituency.

---

[1] At the battle of Gaza with the Chorasmians, 1244, of two hundred and sixteen Knights of St. John who entered the battle, two hundred remained
dead on the field.

[2] After the battle of Tiberias, the Knights of St. John, for a few years,
made their strong fortress, Margat, the base of their operations.

[3] See M. Paris, *an.* 1259.   The famous antithesis of Gibbon (chap. LVIII.)
pleases the ear and contains some truth, but makes a wrong impression.
"The Knights of the Temple and St. John neglected to live, but they prepared to die in the service of Christ."

[4] The synod of Salzburg, 1292, decided in favor of the union.

I. The order of the Knights of St. John, or the Hospitallers,[1] derived its name from the church of St. John the Baptist in Jerusalem.[2] It seems to have grown out of a hospital in the city erected for the care of sick and destitute pilgrims. As early as the time of Charlemagne a hospital existed there. Before the year 1000 a cloister seems to have been founded by the Normans close by the church of the Holy Sepulchre known as St. Maria de Latina, with accommodations for the sick.[3] About 1065 or 1070 a hospital was built by a merchant from Amalfi, Maurus.[4] At the time of the capture of Jerusalem, Gerard stood at the head of one of these institutions. Gerard seems to have come from Southern France.[5] He prescribed for his brotherhood a mantle of black with a white cross. Godfrey of Bouillon liberally endowed it and Baldwin further enriched it with one-tenth of the booty taken at the siege of Joppa. Gerard died in 1120 and was succeeded by Raymund du Puy, who gave the order great fame and presided over it for forty years.[6]

The order increased with astonishing rapidity in numbers, influence, and wealth. Gifts were received from all parts of Europe, the givers being remembered in prayers offered

[1] *Fratres hospitalis S. Johannis, Hospitalarii, Johannitæ, milites hospitalis S. Johannis.* From the fourteenth century they were also known as the Knights of Rhodes and from the sixteenth as the Knights of Malta. For a list of the houses of the female members of this order, Le Roulx, *Les Hospitaliers*, 300 sq.

[2] The bull of Pascal, II. 1113, speaks of the hospital in Jerusalem adjoining the church of the Baptist, *xenodochium . . . juxta Beati Johannis Baptistæ ecclesiam.*

[3] William of Tyre, XVIII. 5 ; de Vitry, *Hist. Jerus.*, 64. The Mary, whose name the convent bore, was Mary Magdalene.

[4] Le Roulx, *Les Hospitaliers*, 33, connects the order with the hospital founded by Maurus, *nous croyons pouvoir persister à penser que les Amalfitans furent les précurseurs des Hospitaliers.*

[5] William of Tyre, VII. 23, states that he was held in chains during the siege of Jerusalem.

[6] See Le Roulx, pp. 44 sqq. Gerard is called in an old chronicle " Guardian of the hospital of the poor in Jerusalem," *guardianus hospitalis pauperum,* etc., Hurter, IV. 315, note.

up in Jerusalem.   Raymund systematized the rules of the
brotherhood and gave it a compact organization and in 1113
it gained papal sanction through Pascal II.   At that time
there were affiliated houses at St. Giles, Asti, Pisa, Otranto,
and Tarentum.[1]   In 1122 Calixtus II. made the important
announcement that those giving protection to pilgrims were
entitled to the same reward as the pilgrims themselves and
all who gave to the Hospital in the earthly Jerusalem, should
receive the joys of the heavenly.   Bull followed bull, granting the order privileges.   Innocent III. exempted the members from excommunication at the hand of bishops and made
the order amenable solely to the pope.   Anastasius IV., 1154,
gave them the right to build churches, chapels, and grave-
yards in any locality.[2]

The military feature of the organization was developed
after the philanthropic feature of nursing and caring for
unfortunate pilgrims and it quickly became the dominant
feature.   Raymund du Puy makes a clear distinction in the
order between cleric and lay brethren.   Innocent II., 1130,
speaks of its members as priests, knights, and lay brethren,
the last taking no vows.   In its perfected organization the
order was divided into three classes, knights, chaplains, and
serving brethren.   The knights and chaplains were bound
by the threefold pledge of charity, poverty, and obedience.[3]
The military brothers or knights formed the majority of the

---

[1] Woodhouse, p. 20, gives a list of no less than fifty-four houses belonging
to the Hospital in England.

[2] The bull in Mansi, XXI. 780.

[3] They were monks.   The order had no priests until the time of Alexander III., who gave it the right to receive priests and clerics.   Priests became
necessary in order that the new custom might be followed which gave to
priests alone the right of absolution.   During the first century of their
existence, the members of military orders made confession of their sins
in the open chapters and were punished at the order of the Master by
public scourging or otherwise.   The strict church law of confession and of
absolution by the priest was not defined till later by the Fourth Lateran
Council, and Thomas Aquinas.   See Lea, *The Absolution Formula of the
Templars.*

order and from them the officials were elected.[1]   The hospital work was not abandoned.   In 1160 John of Wizburg states from personal observation that more than two thousand sick were cared for in the hospital of Jerusalem, and that in a single day forty deaths occurred.   After the transfer of the order to Rhodes, the knights continued to carry on hospital work.

After Clement IV., 1267, the title of the chief official was " Grand master of the Hospital of Jerusalem and Guardian of the Poor of Jesus Christ:"   The distinctive dress of the order was, after 1259, a red mantle with a white Maltese cross worn on the left breast that " God through this emblem might give faith and obedience and protect us and all our Christian benefactors from the power of the devil."   Its motto was *pro fide*, " for the faith." [2]   The whole body was divided about 1320 into seven *langues* or provinces, Provence, France, Auvergne, Italy, Germany, Aragon, England. Castile was added in 1464.   Affiliated houses in Europe and the East sent two-thirds of their income to Jerusalem.[3]   One of the interesting rules of the order was that the knights always went two and two and carried their own light with them.

After the fall of Acre, the Hospitallers established themselves on the island of Cyprus and in 1310 removed to the island of Rhodes, where massive walls and foundations continue to attest the labor expended upon their fortifications and other buildings.   From Rhodes, as a base, they did honorable service.

Under the grand master La Valette, the Knights bravely defended Malta against the fleet of Suleymon the Mag-

---

[1] Le Roulx, 290 sq.

[2] For the formula of admission, see Le Roulx, 288 sq.

[3] See Uhlhorn for the amount of linen and other goods expected from the various houses in Europe.   There was a female branch of the order of which, however, very little is known.   In 1188 Sancha, queen of Aragon, founded a rich convent for it at Sixena near Saragossa.

nificent until Europe felt the thrill of relief caused by the
memorable defeat of the Turkish fleet by Don John at
Lepanto, 1571. From that time the order continued to
decay.[1]

II. The Knight Templars[2] before the fall of Acre had, if
possible, a more splendid fame than the Knights of St. John;
but the order had a singularly tragic ending in 1312, and was
dissolved under moral charges of the most serious nature.
From the beginning they were a military body. The order
owes its origin to Hugo de Payens (or Payns) and Godfrey
St. Omer, who entered Jerusalem riding on one horse, 1119.
They were joined by six others who united with them in making a vow to the patriarch of Jerusalem to defend by force of
arms pilgrims on their way from the coast to Jerusalem.

Baldwin II. gave the brotherhood quarters in his palace
on Mount Moriah, near the site of Solomon's temple, whence
the name Templars is derived. Hugo appeared at the
council of Troyes in 1128,[3] and made such persuasive appeals at the courts of France, England, and Germany, that
three hundred knights joined the order. St. Bernard wrote
a famous tract in praise of the " new soldiery." [4] He says :
" Never is an idle word, or useless deed, or immoderate
laughter or murmur, if it be but in a whisper, among the
Templars allowed to go unpunished. They take no pleasure
in the absurd pastime of hawking. Draughts and dice they
abhor. Ribald songs and stage plays they eschew as insane
follies. They cut their hair close ; they are begrimed

---

[1] *On October 31, 1898, the emperor William II. of Germany, while on a
visit to Jerusalem, dedicated the Protestant church of the Redeemer, built on
the ancient site of the hospital of the Knights of St. John, opposite the
church of the Holy Sepulchre.*

[2] *Templarii, fratres militiæ templi, equites templarii, pauperes commili-
tiones Christi templique Salamonis,* are some of the titles by which they
were known. There was not nearly as much resemblance between the Hospitallers and Templars as between the Templars and Teutonic knights.
Curzon, p. xi.

[3] William of Tyre. See Hefele, V. 401 sq.   [4] *De laude novæ militiæ.*

with dirt and swarthy from the weight of their armor and the heat of the sun. They never dress gayly, and wash seldom. They strive to secure swift and strong horses, but not garnished with ornaments or decked with trappings, thinking of battle and victory, not of pomp and show. Such has God chosen to vigilantly guard the Holy Sepulchre." [1]

The order spread with great rapidity.[2] Matthew Paris, no doubt, greatly exaggerates when he gives the number of their houses in the middle of the thirteenth century as nine thousand.[3] Their annual revenues have been estimated as high as 54,000,000 francs.[4] The order was divided into provinces, five of them in the east — Jerusalem, Tripolis, Antioch, Cyprus, and the Morea ; and eleven in the west — France, Aquitaine, Provence, Aragon, Portugal, Lombardy, Hungary, England, Upper and Lower Germany, Sicily, and perhaps a twelfth, Bohemia. Popes, beginning with Honorius II., heaped favors upon them. They were relieved from paying taxes of all sorts. They might hold services twice a year in churches where the interdict was in force. Their goods were placed under the special protection of the Holy See. In 1163 Alexander III. granted them permission to have their own priests.[5]

Like the Hospitallers, the Templars took the triple vow and, in addition, the vow of military service and were di-

---

[1] On St. Bernard's services to the order, see the biographies by Morison, 141 sqq., and Storrs, 567–574.

[2] In England they settled at the old Temple outside of Holborn, whence they removed to the new Temple on the Thames, 1185. The Temple church was completed in 1240. M. Paris gives an account of the dedication and the banquet which was provided by the Hospitallers. Stephen and his queen gave the Templars several places about 1150. Woodhouse, p. 260, gives a list of twenty-seven English houses.   [3] *An.* 1244.

[4] At the end of the thirteenth century. This is the estimate of de Chambure. Schottmüller estimates them at 40,000,000 francs. William of Tyre, XII. 7, speaks of their possessions as "immense." Their wealth and greed were proverbial.

[5] Funk calls Alexander's bull the *Magna Charta* of the order. Wetzer-Welte, XI. 1315.

vided into three classes: the knights who were of noble birth, the men at arms or serving brethren (*fratres servientes, armigeri*), and chaplains who were directly amenable to the pope. The dress of the knights was a white mantle with a red cross, of the serving brethren a dark habit with a red cross. The knights cropped their hair short and allowed their beards to grow. They were limited to three horses, except the grand master who was allowed four, and were forbidden to hunt except the lion, the symbol of the devil, who goes about seeking whom he may devour.[1] The order had for its motto "not unto us, not unto us, but unto Thy name, O Lord, give the glory."[2] The members in cloister observed the regular conventual hours for prayer, and ate at a common table. If money was found in the effects of a deceased brother, his body was denied all prayer and funeral services and placed in unconsecrated ground like a slave.[3] They were bidden to flee from the kisses of women and never to kiss a widow, virgin, mother, sister, or any other female.[4] On acount of their poverty, two ate from the same dish, but each had his own portion of wine to himself.[5]

The head of the order was called Grand Master, was granted the rank of a prince, and included in the invitations to the œcumenical councils, as, for example, the Fourth Lateran and the second council of Lyons. The Master of the Temple in England was a baron with seat in Parliament.

The Templars took part in all the Crusades except the first and the crusade of Frederick II., from which they held aloof on account of the papal prohibition. Their discipline was conspicuous on the disastrous march of the French from

---

[1] With reference to 1 Pet. 5:8, Curzon, 58.

[2] *Non nobis, Domine, non nobis sed tuo nomini da gloriam.*

[3] Curzon, XXVII.

[4] *Fugiat feminæ oscula Christi militia,* Mansi, XXI. 72; also Schnürer, 153.

[5] Schnürer, Rule XI. p. 138.

Laodicea to Attalia and their valor at the battle of Hattim, before Gaza[1] and on many other fields.[2]   The order degenerated with riches and success.[3]   To drink like a Templar, *bibere templariter*, became proverbial for fast living.   Their seal, representing the two founders entering Jerusalem in poverty on one horse, early came to misrepresent their real possessions.

A famous passage in the history of Richard of England set forth the reputation the Templars had for pride.   When Fulke of Neuilly was preaching the Third Crusade, he told Richard he had three daughters and called upon him to provide for them in marriage.   The king exclaimed, " Liar, I have no daughters."   " Nay, thou hast three evil daughters, Pride, Lust, and Luxury," was the priest's reply.   Turning to his courtiers, Richard retorted, " He bids me marry my three daughters.   Well, so be it.   To the Templars, I give my first-born, Pride, to the Cistercians my second-born, Lust, and to the prelates the third, Luxury."[4]

---

[1] M. Paris, Luard's ed., IV. 337 sqq., gives the letters from the patriarch of Jerusalem and the vice-master of the Temple, 1244.   This chronicler is very severe upon the Templars for their arrogant pride and their jealous rivalry of the Hospitallers.   An example of this jealousy was their refusal to accompany King Amalric to Egypt because to the Hospitallers had been assigned first place.

[2] Among their fortresses was the castle Pilgrim near Acre, built 1218, whose great size and splendor are described by James de Vitry.

[3] The houses of the order became important money centres in France and England in the thirteenth century, and furnished to kings, bishops, and nobles a safety-deposit for funds and treasures of plate, jewels, and important records.   Henry III. and other English kings borrowed from them, as did also French kings.   The Templars also acted as disbursers for monies loaned by Italian bankers or as trustees for other monies, as, for example, the annual grant of one thousand marks promised by John to his sister-in-law, Berengaria. John frequently stopped at the house of the Templars in London.   See Cunningham, *Growth of English Industries and Commerce*, 3d ed.   Leopold Delisle, *Les operations financières des Templiers*, Paris, 1889.   Eleanor Ferris, *Financial Relations of the Knights Templars to the English Crown*, in " Am. Hist. Rev.," October, 1902.

[4] Charasson, quoting Richard de Hoveden, *Vie de Foulques de Neuilly*, 89 sq.

The order survived the fall of Acre less than twenty
years.   After finding a brief refuge in Cyprus the knights
concentrated their strength in France, where the once famous organization was suppressed by the violent measures
of Philip the Fair and Clement V.   The story of the suppression belongs to the next period.

III. The order of the Teutonic Knights[1] never gained
the prominence in Palestine of the two older orders.
During the first century of its existence, its members devoted themselves to the maintenance and care of hospitals
on the field of battle.   They seldom appeared until the
historic mission of the order opened in the provinces of
what is now northeastern Germany which were reduced to
subjection and to a degree of civilization by its arms and
humanizing efforts.

The order dates from 1190, when a hospital was erected
in a tent under the walls of Acre by pilgrims from Bremen
and Lübeck.   Frederick of Swabia commended it, and
Clement III. sanctioned it, 1191.[2]   It was made a military
order in 1198 by a bull of Innocent III.[3] and in 1221
Honorious III. conferred upon it the privileges enjoyed by
the Hospitallers and Templars.   The order was made up
almost exclusively of German elements.[4]   The members
took the triple vow.   Their dress was a white mantle with
a black cross.   Women were affiliated with some of the
hospitals, as at Bremen.   The first possession of the order
in Europe was a convent at Palermo, the gift of Henry VI.,
1197.   Its first hospital in Germany was St. Kunigunde,

---

[1] *Deutscher Orden, Ordo S. Mariæ Theutonicorum.*

[2] Under the name *domus hospitalis S. Mariæ Theutonicorum in Jerusalem.*   A German hospital was dedicated in Jerusalem to St. Mary, 1128.

[3] At the council of Constance, 1415, the king of Poland protested against
their right to convert by the sword.

[4] In the conflict of Lewis the Bavarian with the papacy, the Teutonic
order espoused the emperor's cause and received from him important gifts
and privileges

x

at Halle. Subsequently its hospitals extended from Bremen and Lübeck to Nürnberg and further south. Its territory was divided into bailiwicks, *balleyen*, of which there were twelve in Germany. The chief officer, called Grand Master, had the dignity of a prince of the empire.

Under Hermann von Salza (1210-1239), the fourth grand master, the order grew with great rapidity. Von Salza was a trusted adviser of Frederick II., and received the privilege of using the black eagle in the order's banner. Following the invitation of the monk Christian and of Konrad of Morovia, 1226, to come to their relief against the Prussians, he diverted the attention and activity of the order from the Orient to this new sphere. The order had the promise of Culmland and half of its conquests for its assistance.

After the fall of Acre, the headquarters were transferred to Venice and in 1309 to Marienburg on the Vistula, where a splendid castle was erected. Henceforth the knights were occupied with the wild territories along the Baltic and southwards, whose populations were still in a semibarbaric state. In the hour when the Templars were being suppressed, this order was enjoying its greatest prosperity. In 1237 it absorbed the Brothers of the Sword.[1]

At one time the possessions of the Teutonic knights included fifty cities such as Culm, Marienburg, Thorn, and Königsberg, and lands with a population of two million. Its missionary labors are recorded in another chapter. With the rise of Poland began the shrinkage of the order, and in the battle of Tannenberg, 1410, its power was greatly shaken. In 1466 it gave up large blocks of territory to Poland, including Marienburg, and the grand master swore fealty to the Polish king. The order continued to hold Prussia and Sameland as fiefs. But the discipline had become loose, as was indicated by the popular saying, "Dressing and undressing, eating and drinking, and going

---

[1] *Fratres militiæ Christi, gladiferi*, a military order founded in 1202.

to bed are the work the German knights do." [1] In 1511 the margrave, Albrecht of Brandenburg, was made grand master and refused to be a vassal of Poland. Following the counsel of Luther, he laid down the mantle and cross of the order, married 1523, and laid the foundation of the greatness of the duchy of Prussia, which he made hereditary in his family, the Hohenzollern. [2] The black eagle passed to the Prussian coat of arms. [3]

---

[1] *Kleider aus, Kleider an, Essen, Trinken, Schlafengehen, ist die Arbeit so die Deutsche Herren han.*

[2] Luther in 1523 wrote a tract calling upon the Teutonic knights to abandon their false rule of celibacy and to practise the true chastity of marriage. *Ermahnung an die Herren Deutschen Ordens falsche Keuschheit zu meiden und zur rechten ehelichen Keuschheit zu greifen.* Albrecht introduced the Lutheran reformation into Brandenburg. He married the Danish princess Dorothea.

[3] Several orders combining military and religious vows existed in Spain and Portugal and did service against the Moors. The order of Iago of Campostella received the papal sanction in 1175 and protected pilgrims to the shrine of Campostella. The order of Calatrava received papal approval 1164, and took an active part in the struggle against the Moors. The order of Alcantara was recognized by Lucius III., 1183. The headship of the last two bodies was transferred to the crown under Ferdinand the Catholic.

CHAPTER VIII.

THE MONASTIC ORDERS.

§ 61. *The Revival of Monasticism.*

LITERATURE. — The *Letters* of ANSELM, BERNARD, PETER THE VENERABLE, WILLIAM OF THIERRY, HILDEGARD, etc. — ABÆLARD : *Hist. calamitatum*, his autobiography, Migne, 178. — HONORIUS OF AUTUN : *De vita claustrali*, Migne, 172, 1247 sqq. — BERNARD : *De conversione ad clericos sermo*, in Migne, 182, 853–59, and *De præcepto et dispensatione*, 851–953. — The Treatments of THOMAS AQUINAS, DUNS SCOTUS, etc., in their *Summas*. — PETRUS VENERABLIS : *De miraculis*, in Migne, 189. — CÆSAR OF HEISTERBACH (ab. 1240) : *Dialogus Miraculorum*, ed. by J. Strange, 2 vols. Col. 1851. Excerpts in German trans. by A. KAUFMANN, 2 parts, Col. 1888 sq. — THOS. À CHANTIMPRÉ (d. about 1270) : *Bonum universale de apibus*, a comparison of a convent to a beehive. Excerpts in German by A. KAUFMANN, Col. 1899 ; *Annales monastici*, ed. by LUARD, 5 vols. London, 1865–69. — JACOBUS DE VORAGINE : *Legenda aurea*, English by W. CAXTON (about 1470), Temple classics ed. 7 vols. London, 1890. — WILLIAM OF ST. AMOUR (d. 1272) : *De periculis novissorum temporum in Denifle Chartularium Univ.*, Paris, vol. I.

The *Lives* of ANSELM, BERNARD, WILLIAM OF THIERRY, FRANCIS, DOMINIC, NORBERT, etc. — H. HELYOT (Franciscan, d. 1716) : *Hist. des ordres monastiques, religieux et militaires et des congrégations séculières de l'une et de l'autre sexe qui ont été établies jusqu' à présent*, 8 vols. Paris, 1714–19 ; Germ. trans., 8 vols. Leip. 1753–56. He gives a long list of the older authorities. — MRS. JAMIESON : *Legends of the Monastic Orders*, London, 1850. — A. BUTLER : *Lives of the Fathers, Martyrs, and Other Principal Saints*, 12 vols. Dublin, 1868 sqq. — SIR WILLIAM DUGDALE: *Monasticon anglicanum*, ed. by J. CALEY, etc., 8 vols. London, 1846. Based on the ed. of 1817. — T. D. FOSBROKE : *Brit. Monasticism, or Manners and Customs of the Monks and Nuns of England*, London, 1803, 3d ed. 1845. — MONTALEMBERT: *Les moins d'occident depuis St. Benoit jusqu' à St. Bernard*, Paris, 1860–77 ; Engl. trans., 7 vols. London, 1861 sqq. — O. T. HILL : *Engl. Monasticism, Its Rise and Influence*, London, 1867. — S. R. MAITLAND : *The Dark Ages*, ed. by FRED. STOKES, 5th ed., London, 1890. — WISHART : *Short Hist. of Monks and Monasticism*, Trenton, 1900. — E. L. TAUNTON : *The Engl. Black Monks of St. Benedict*, 2 vols. London, 1897. — A. GASQUET : *Engl. Monastic Life*, London, 1904, and since. — HURTER : *Innocent III.*, vol.

IV. 84–311.— J. C. ROBERTSON : *View of Europe during the Middle Ages*, in introd. to his *Life of Chas. V.* — H. VON EICKEN : *Gesch. und System der mittelalterlichen Weltanschauung*, Stuttgart, 1887. — A. JESSOPP : *The Coming of the Friars*, London, no date, 7th ed., chap. *Daily Life in a Med. Monastery*, 113–166. — HARNACK : *Monasticism*, Giessen, 1882, 5th ed. 1901, trans. by C. R. GILLETT, N.Y., 1895. — STEPHENS : *Hist. of the Engl. Church*, chap. XIV. (*Monastic Orders*).—HAUCK, III. 441–516, IV. 311–409. — LITTLEDALE : *Monachism*, in *Enc. Brit.* — DENIFLE : *Luther und Lutherthum*, Mainz, 1904 sq., draws in his treatment of monasticism, upon his great resources of mediæval scholarship.

THE glorious period of monasticism fell in the Middle Ages, and more especially in the period that is engaging our attention. The convent was the chief centre of true religion as well as of dark superstition. With all the imposing movements of the age, the absolute papacy, the Crusades, the universities, the cathedrals and scholasticism, the monk was efficiently associated. He was, with the popes, the chief promoter of the Crusades. He was among the great builders. He furnished the chief teachers to the universities and numbered in his order the profoundest of the Schoolmen. The mediæval monks were the Puritans, the Pietists, the Methodists, the Evangelicals of their age.[1] All these classes of Christians have this in common, that they make earnest with their religion, and put it into zealous practice.

If it be compared with the monachism of the earlier period of the Church, the mediæval institution will be found to equal it in the number of its great monks and to exceed it in useful activity. Among the distinguished Fathers of the Post-Nicene period who advocated monasticism were St. Anthony of Egypt, Athanasius, Basil, Gregory of Nyssa, Ambrose, Augustine, Jerome, and Benedict of Nursia. In

[1] Thomas Aquinas, *Summa*, II. (2), 188, 6 sqq., Migne, III. 1372 sqq., combines the active and contemplative features of the monastic life, as did Benedict of Nursia, but laying more stress than the latter upon the active feature. It must be remembered that Thomas was a Dominican, and had had full experience of the practical activity of the two great mendicant orders.

the Middle Ages the list is certainly as imposing. There we have Anselm, Albertus Magnus, Bonaventura, Thomas Aquinas, and Duns Scotus among the Schoolmen, St. Bernard and Hugo de St. Victor, Eckart, and Tauler among the mystics, Hildegard and Joachim of Flore among the seers, the authors of the *Dies iræ* and *Stabat mater* and Adam de St. Victor among the hymnists, Anthony of Padua, Bernardino of Siena, Berthold of Regensburg and Savonarola among the preachers, and in a class by himself, Francis d'Assisi.

Of the five epochs in the history of monasticism two belong to the Middle Ages proper.[1] The appearance of the hermit and the development of the eremite mode of life belong to the fourth century. Benedict of Nursia of the sixth century, and his well-systematized rule, mark the second epoch. The development of the Society of Jesus in the sixteenth century marks the last epoch. The two between are represented by the monastic revival, starting from the convent of Cluny as a centre in the tenth and eleventh centuries, and the rise and spread of the mendicant orders in the thirteenth century. Cluny was for a century almost the only reforming force in Western Europe till the appearance of Hildebrand on the stage, and he himself was probably trained in the mother convent. Through its offshoots and allied orders Cluny continued to be a burning centre of religious zeal for a century longer. Then, at a time of monastic declension, the mendicant orders, brought into existence by St. Francis d'Assisi and Dominic of Spain, became the chief promoters of one of the most notable religious revivals that has ever swept over Europe.

The work done by men like William of Hirschau, Bruno and Norbert in Germany, Bernard and Peter the Venerable

---

[1] This is the classification of Harnack, *Monasticism*, 44 sqq. Denifle, *Luther und Lutherthum*, I. 199 sqq., who fiercely combats Harnack, says "it is the height of misunderstanding, *Unverstand*, to speak of Jesuitism as monastic."

in France, and St. Francis in Italy, cannot be ignored in any true account of the onward progress of mankind. However much we may decline to believe that monasticism is a higher form of Christian life, we must give due credit to these men, or deny to a series of centuries all progress and good whatsoever.

The times were favorable for the development of monastic communities. If our own is the age of the laic, the mediæval period was the age of the monk. Society was unsettled and turbulent. The convent offered an asylum of rest and of meditation. Bernard calls his monks " the order of the Peaceful." Feud and war ruled without. Every baronial residence was a fortress. The convent was the scene of brotherhood and co-operation. It furnished to the age the ideal of a religious household on earth. The epitaphs of monks betray the feeling of the time, *pacificus*, "the peaceful "; *tranquilla pace serenus*, " in quiet and undisturbed repose " ; *fraternæ pacis amicus*, " friend of brotherly peace."

The circumstances are presented by Cæsar of Heisterbach under which a number of monks abandoned the world, and were " converted " — that is, determined to enter a convent. Now the decision was made at a burial.[1] Now it was due to the impression made by the relation of the wonderful things which occurred in convents. This was the case with a young knight, Gerlach,[2] who listened to an abbot who was then visiting a castle, as he told his experiences within cloistral walls. Gerlach went to Paris to study, but could not get rid of the seed which had been sown in his heart, and entered upon the monastic novitiate. Sometimes the decision was made in consequence of a sermon.[3] Cæsar of Heisterbach himself was " converted " by a description given by Gerard of Walberberg, abbot of Heisterbach, while they were on the way to Cologne during the troublous times of Philip of Swabia and Otto IV. Gerard described

---

[1] *Dial.*, I. 21 ; Strange ed. I. 28.   [2] *Dial.*, I. 18.   [3] *Dial.*, I. 24.

the appearance of the Virgin, her mother Anna, and St. Mary Magdalene, who descended from the mountain and revealed themselves to the monks of Clairvaux while they were engaged in the harvest, dried the perspiration from their foreheads, and cooled them by fanning.   Within three months Cæsar entered the convent of Heisterbach.[1]

There were in reality only two careers in the Middle Ages, the career of the knight and the career of the monk.   It would be difficult to say which held out the most attractions and rewards, even for the present life.   The monk himself was a soldier.   The well-ordered convent offered a daily drill, exercise following exercise with the regularity of clockwork; and though the enemy was not drawn up in visible array on open field, he was a constant reality.[2]   Barons, counts, princes joined the colonies of the spiritual militia, hoping thereby to work out more efficiently the problem of their salvation and fight their conflict with the devil.   The Third Lateran, 1179, bears witness to the popularity of the conventual life among the higher classes, and the tendency to restrict it to them, when it forbade the practice of receiving money as a price of admission to the vow.[3]   The monk proved to be stronger than the knight and the institution of chivalry decayed before the institution of monasticism which still survives.

By drawing to themselves the best spirits of the time, the convents became in their good days, from the tenth well into the thirteenth century, hearthstones of piety, and the chief

[1] *Dial.*, I. 17 ; Strange ed. I. 24.

[2] See Church, *Life of St. Anselm*, chap. III., The Discipline of a Norman Monastery.

[3] In England the gentry class was especially drawn upon. See Jessopp, p. 161.   At Morimond, Otto son of the margrave of Austria stopped overnight with fifteen young nobles.   The sound of the bells and the devotions of the monks made such an impression that they prayed to be received into the brotherhood.   Henry, son of Louis VI., was so moved by what he saw on a visit to Clairvaux that he determined to take the vow.   See Morison, *Life of St. Bernard*, p. 195.

centres of missionary and civilizing agencies.   When there was little preaching, the monastic community preached the most powerful sermon, calling men's thoughts away from riot and bloodshed to the state of brotherhood and religious reflection.[1]   The motto *aratro et cruce*, "by the cross and the plough," stood in their case for a reality.   The monk was a pioneer in the cultivation of the ground, and, after the most scientific fashion then known, taught agriculture, the culture of the vine and fish, the breeding of cattle, and the culture of wool.   He built roads and the best buildings.   In intellectual and artistic concerns the convent was the chief school of the times.   It trained architects, painters, and sculptors.   There the deep problems of theology and philosophy were studied ;   there manuscripts were copied, and when the universities arose, the convent furnished them with their first and their most renowned teachers.   In northeastern Germany and other parts of Europe and in Asia it was the outer citadel of church profession and church activity.

So popular was the monastic life that religion seemed to be in danger of running out into monkery and society of being transformed into an aggregation of convents.   The Fourth Lateran sought to counteract this tendency by forbidding the establishment of new orders.[2]   But no council was ever more ignorant of the immediate future.   Innocent III. was scarcely in his grave before the Dominicans and Franciscans received full papal sanction.

During the eleventh and twelfth centuries the important change was accomplished whereby all monks received priestly ordination.   Before that time it was the exception for a monk to be a priest.   Extreme unction and absolution had been administered in the convent by unordained

---

[1] Montalembert lays stress upon intercessory prayer as the chief service rendered by the monastery of the West.   " They prayed much, they prayed always for those whose prayers were evil or who prayed not at all."   *Monks of the West*, Engl. trans., I. 42 sq.   [2] Canon 13.

monks.[1]   With the development of the strict theory of
sacerdotalism, these functions were forbidden to them, as by
the ninth œcumenical council, 1123.   The synod of Nismes,
thirty years earlier, 1096, thought it answered objections to
the new custom sufficiently by pointing to Gregory the Great,
Gregory of Tours, and Augustine as cases of monks who had
priestly ordination.   On the other hand the active movement within the convents to take a larger part in the affairs
of society was resisted by œcumenical councils, as, for example, the Second Lateran, 1139, which forbade monks
practising as physicians or lawyers.

The monastic life was praised as the highest form of
earthly existence.   The convent was compared to Canaan[2]
and treated as the shortest and surest road to heaven.   The
secular life, even the life of the secular priest, was compared
to Egypt.   The passage to the cloister was called conversion,
and the monks converts, *conversi*, or the religious.[3]   They
reached the Christian ideal.   Renouncing the vow was pronounced turning to the company of the lost, to the lion's
mouth, and to the realm of blackness and death.[4]

---

[1] This has been sufficiently shown by Lea, *Absolution Formula of the
Templars*, in Papers of Am. Soc. of Ch. Hist., vol. V.; also Hefele, V. 381.
As late, however, as the thirteenth century there were monks in England
who had not received priestly ordination.   See Stevenson, *Life of Grosseteste*, 158.   In the fifth century the consecration of the monk was treated
in some quarters as a distinct sacrament.

[2] It would be difficult to find more attractive pictures of earthly happiness
than are given in the descriptions of mediæval convents by eye-witnesses, as
of the convent of Clairvaux by William of St. Thierry, Migne, 185, 248, and
Peter de Roya, Migne, 182, 710.

[3] It was even compared to the conversion of St. Paul.   See Eicken, 324.
Cæsar of Heisterbach devotes a chapter of his *Dialogus* to *conversion*, that is,
the assumption of the monastic vow.   Canon 13 of the Fourth Lateran,
Mansi, XXII. 1002, speaks of monastics as "the religious," of the orders as
"religions," and of entering a convent as "being converted to religion."   So
Martin V. at the Council of Constance, 1418, charges Wyclif with declaring
that "all religions owe their origin to the devil," that is, all orders.   Mirbt,
Quellen, 158.

[4] St. Bernard, *Ep.*, 112 ; Migne, 182, 255 sq.

Bishop Otto of Freising speaks of the monks as "spending their lives like angels in heavenly purity and holiness.
They live together one in heart and soul, give themselves
at one signal to sleep, lift up as by one impulse their lips in
prayer and their voices in reading. . . .   They go so far, that
while they are refreshing the body at table, they listen to the
reading of the Scriptures. . . .   They give up their own wills,
their earthly possessions, and their parents, and, following the
command of the Gospel and Christ, constantly bear their
cross by mortifying the flesh, being all the while full of heavenly homesickness."[1]

The enthusiastic advocacy of the monastic life can only
be explained by a desire to get relief from the turbulence of the social world and a sincere search after holiness.
There is scarcely a letter of Anselm in which he does not advocate its superior advantages.   It was not essential to become a monk to reach salvation, but who, he writes, "can
attain to it in a safer or nobler way, he who seeks to love God
alone or he who joins the love of the world with the love of
God?"[2]   He loses no opportunity to urge laymen to take the
vow.   He appeals to his kinsmen according to the flesh to
become his kinsmen in the Spirit.[3]

Bernard was not at peace till he had all his brothers and
his married sister within cloistral walls.

---

[1] *Chronicle*, VII. 35, where he passes a lengthy panegyric upon monks.
For another pleasing description of a convent and its appointments, see the
account which Ingulph, abbot of Croyland, gives of the burning of his abbey
in 1091.   He does not forget to mention that "the very casks full of beer in
the cellar were destroyed." See Maitland, 286–292.

[2] *Ep.*, II. 29 ; Migne, 158, 1182.

[3] *Ep.*, II. 28 ; Migne, 1180, *conspirituales* as well as *consanguinei*. A similar
exhortation he directs to his two uncles. *Ep.*, I. 45.   See Hasse, *Life of Anselm*, I. 93 sqq.   Anselm, however, knew how to make an exception where a
layman was devoting himself entirely to religious works.   Visiting the
Countess Matilda, shortly before her death, he recommended her not to take
the veil, as she was doing more good in administering her estates than she
might be able to do behind convent walls.   Nevertheless he recommended her
to have a nun's dress within reach so that she might put it on when dying.

Honorius of Autun, in his tract on the cloistral life,[1] after declaring that it was instituted by the Lord himself, calls the convent a shore for those tired on the sea, a refuge for the traveller from the cold and anxieties of the world, a bed for the weary to rest on, an asylum for those fleeing from the turmoils of the state, a school for infants learning the rule of Christ, a gymnasium for those who would fight against vices, a prison career for the criminal from the broad way till he goes into the wide hall of heaven, a paradise with different trees full of fruits and the delights of Scripture.

The monastic life was the angelic life. "Are ye not already like the angels of God, having abstained from marriage," exclaimed St. Bernard, in preaching to his monks,[2] and this was the almost universal representation of the age.

Kings and princes desired to be clad in the monastic habit as they passed into the untried scenes of the future. So Frederick II., foe of the temporal claims of the papacy as he was, is said to have died in the garb of the Cistercians. So did Roger II. of Sicily, 1163, and Roger III., 1265. William of Nevers was clad in the garb of the Carthusian order before he expired. Louis VI. of France passed away stretched on ashes sprinkled in the form of a cross. So did Henry, son of Henry II. of England, expire, laid on a bed of ashes, 1184. William the Conqueror died in a priory with a bishop and abbot standing by.[3]

It was the custom in some convents, if not in all, to lay out the monks about to die on the floor, which was sometimes covered with matting. First they rapped on the death table. Waiting the approach of death, the dying often had wonderful visions of Christ, the Virgin, and the saints. The imagination at such times was very vivid, and the reports which

---

[1] *De vita claustrali*, Migne, 172, 1247.

[2] *Sermo de diversis* 37, *quomodo non jam nunc estis sicut angeli Dei in cœlo, a nuptiis penitus abstinentes*, etc.   Migne, 183, 641.   Comp. 184, 703 sq.

[3] *Ordericus Vitalis*, VII. 14.   For the case of Hugh of Grantmesnil, see *Order. Vit.*, VII. 28.

the dying gave on returning for a moment to consciousness seem to have been generally accepted.[1]

The miraculous belonged to the monk's daily food. He was surrounded by spirits. Visions and revelations occurred by day and by night.[2] Single devils and devils in bands were roaming about at all hours in the cloistral spaces, in the air and on foot, to deceive the unwary and to shake the faith of the vigilant. The most elaborate and respectable accounts of monks, so beset, are given by Peter the Venerable in his work on Miracles, by Cæsar of Heisterbach, and Jacobus de Voragine. Cæsar's *Dialogue of Miracles* and Voragine's *Golden Legend* are among the most entertaining storybooks ever written. They teem with legends which are accepted as true. They simply reflect the feeling of the age, which did not for a moment doubt the constant manifestation of the supernatural, especially the pranks and misdemeanors of the evil one and his emissaries.

Peter the Venerable gives a graphic picture of how these restless foes pulled the bedclothes off from sleeping monks and, chuckling, carried them to a distance, how they impudently stood by, making fun while the modest monastic attended to the necessities of nature,[3] and how they threw the faithful to the ground, as at night they went about through convent precincts making "holy thefts of prayer."[4]

Peter tells a good story of a poor monk who suddenly saw before him an immense demon standing at his bedside, who with difficulty bore his weight with his wings. Two others

---

[1] See Cæsar of Heisterbach, *Dial.*, XI. 6,19, etc.; *pulsata est tabula defunctorum pro eo.* Strange ed. II. 274, also Hodges, *Fountains Abbey*, p. 115.

[2] Guido said of his brother St. Bernard, "One thing I know and am assured of by experience that many things have been revealed to him in prayer." Migne, 185, 262.

[3] *Eos sibi derisiorie astitisse.*

[4] *Præterea quosdam nocturnis horis, aliis quiescentibus sancta orationum furta quærentes et eadem causa claustrum et ecclesiam peragrantes, multis aliquando terroribus appetebant ita ut in eorum aliquos visibiliter, irruerent et ad terram verberando prosternerent.* De miraculis, I. 17 ; Migne, 189, 883.

appeared at once and exclaimed to the first, "What are you doing here?" "I can do nothing," was the reply, "on account of the protection which is given by the cross and the holy water and the singing of psalms. I have labored all night and can do nothing." The two replied, "We have come from forcing a certain Gaufrid to commit adultery and the head of a monastery to fornicate with a boy, and you, idle rogue, do something, too, and cut off the foot of this monk which is hanging outside his bed." Seizing a pickaxe which was lying under the bed, the demon struck with all his might, but the monk with equal celerity drew in his foot and turned to the back side of the bed and so escaped the blow. Thereupon the demons took their departure.[1]

It is fair to suppose that many of these experiences were mere fancies of the brain growing out of attacks of indigestion or of headache, which was a common malady of convents.[2]

The assaults of the devil were especially directed to induce the monk to abandon his sacred vow. Writing to a certain Helinand, Anselm mentions the four kinds of assault he was wont to make. The first was the assault through lust of the pleasures of the world, when the novice, having recently entered the convent, began to feel the monotony of its retired life. In the second, he pushed the question why the monk had chosen that form of life rather than the life of the parish priest. In the third, he pestered him with the question why he had not put off till late in life the assumption of the vow, in the meantime having a good time, and yet in the end getting all the benefits and the reward of monkery. And last of all, the devil argued why the monk had bound himself at all by a vow, seeing it was possible to serve God just as acceptably without a vow. Anselm an-

---

[1] *De mirac.*, I. 14 ; Migne, 189, 877.
[2] Cæsar of Heisterbach, *Dial.*, IV. 30, VII. 24. See Kaufmann's ed., II. 87, note.

swered the last objection by quoting Ps. 76 : 11, and declaring the vow to be in itself well pleasing to God.[1]

It is unfair to any institution to base our judgment of its merits and utility upon its perversions. The ideal Benedictine and Franciscan monk, we should be glad to believe, was a man who divided his time between religious exercises and some useful work, whether it was manual labor or teaching or practical toil of some other kind. There were, no doubt, multitudes of worthy men who corresponded to this ideal. But there was another ideal, and that ideal was one from which this modern age turns away with unalloyed repugnance. The pages of Voragine and the other retailers of the conventual life are full of repulsive descriptions which were believed in their day, and presented not only a morbid view of life but a view utterly repulsive to sound morality and to the ideal. A single instance will suffice. In the curious legend of St. Brandon the Irish saint, whose wanderings on the ocean have been connected with America, we have it reported that he found an island whereon was an abbey in which twenty-four monks lived. They had come from Ireland and had been living on the island eighty years when they welcomed St. Brandon and his twelve companions. In all this time they had been served from above every week day with twelve loaves of bread, and on Sabbaths with double that number, and they had the same monotonous fare each day, bread and herbs. None of them had ever been sick. They had royal copes of cloth of gold and went in processions. They celebrated mass with lighted tapers, and they said evensong. And in all those eighty years they had never spoken to one another a single word ! What an ideal that was to set up for a mortal man ! Saying mass, keeping silence, going in processions with golden copes day in and day out for eighty long years, every proper instinct of nature thus buried, the gifts of God despised, and life turned into an

[1] *Ep.*, II. 12 ; Migne, 158, 1161 sqq.

indolent, selfish seclusion ! And yet Voragine, himself an archbishop, relates that " Brandon wept for joy of their holy conversation." [1]

Gifts of lands to monastic institutions were common, especially during the Crusades. He who built a convent was looked upon as setting up a ladder to heaven. [2] Battle Abbey, or the Abbey of St. Martin of the Place of Battle, as the full name is, was built by William the Conqueror on the battle-field of Hastings and finally dedicated by Anselm, 1094. The Vale Royal in Cheshire, the last Cistercian home founded in England, was established by Edward I. in fulfilment of a vow made in time of danger by sea on his return from Palestine. He laid the first stone, 1277, and presented the home with a fragment of the true cross and other relics.

Most of the monastic houses which became famous, began with humble beginnings and a severe discipline, as Clairvaux, Citeaux, Hirschau, and the Chartreuse. The colonies were planted for the most part in lonely regions, places difficult of access, in valley or on mountain or in swamp. The Franciscans and Dominicans set a different example by going into the cities and to the haunts of population, howbeit also choosing the worst quarters. The beautiful names often assumed show the change which was expected to take place in the surroundings, such as Bright Valley or *Clairvaux*, Good Place or *Bon Lieu*, the Delights or *Les Delices* (near Bourges), Happy Meadow or *Felix Pré*, Crown of Heaven or *Himmelskrone*, Path to Heaven or *Voie du Ciel*. [3] Walter Map, writing in the last part of the twelfth century, lingers on the fair names of the Cistercian convents, which,

---

[1] Temple Classics ed., vol. VII.

[2] *Qui claustra construit vel delapsa reparat cœlum ascensurus scalam sibi facit*, quoted by Hurter, IV. 450. The Norman convent Les deux Amoureux got its name and foundation from the disappointed love of a poor knight and a young lady whose father refused her to the lover except on condition of his carrying her to the top of a distant hill. The knight made the attempt and fell dead on accomplishing the task, she quickly following him.

[3] See Montalembert, I. 66.

he says, "contain in themselves a divine and prophetic element, such as House of God, Gate of Salvation," etc.[1]

With wealth came the great abbeys of stone, exhibiting the highest architecture of the day.   The establishments of Citeaux, Cluny, the Grande Chartreuse, and the great houses of Great Britain were on an elaborate scale.   No pains or money were spared in their erection and equipment.   Stained glass, sculpture, embroidery, rich vestments, were freely used.[2]   A well-ordered house had many parts,— chapel, refectory, calefactory, scriptorium for writing, locutorium for conversation, dormitory, infirmary, hospital.[3]   Not a single structure, but an aggregation of buildings, was required by the larger establishments.   Cluny, in 1245, was able to accommodate, at the same time, the pope, the king of France, and the emperor of Constantinople, together with their retinues. Matthew Paris says Dunfermline Abbey, Scotland, was ample enough to entertain, at the same time, three sovereigns without inconvenience the one to the other.   The latest conveniences were introduced into these houses, the latest news there retailed.   A convent was, upon the whole, a pretty good place to be in, from the standpoint of worldly well-being.   What the modern club house is to the city, that the mediæval convent was apt to be, so far as material appointments went.   In its vaults the rich deposited their valuables. To its protection the oppressed fled for refuge.   There, as at Westminster, St. Denis, and Dunfermline, kings and princes chose to be buried.   And there, while living, they were often glad to sojourn, as the most notable place of comfort and ease they could find on their journeys.

[1] *Casa .Dei*, House of God ; *Vallis Domini*, the Lord's Valley, *Portus Salutis*, Gate of Salvation ; *Ascende Cœlum*, Ascent of Heaven ; *Lucerna; Claravallis*, etc.   Map, I. 24 ; Wright's ed., p. 40.

[2] The luxury and pomp of Cluny called forth the well-known protest of St. Bernard.

[3] See art. *Abbey*, in "Enc. Brit.," by Dr. Venable, and also Jessopp, and especially Gasquet, pp. 13-37.

Y

The conventual establishment was intended to be a self-sufficient corporation, a sort of socialistic community doing all its own work and supplying all its own stuffs and food.[1] The altruistic principle was supposed to rule. They had their orchards and fields, and owned their own cattle. Some of them gathered honey from their own hives, had the fattest fish ponds, sheared and spun their own wool, made their own wine, and brewed their own beer. In their best days the monks set a good example of thrift. The list of minor officials in a convent was complete, from the cellarer to look after the cooking and the chamberlain to look after the dress of the brethren, to the cantor to direct the singing and the sacristan to care for the church ornaments. In the eleventh century the custom was introduced of associating lay brethren with the monasteries, so that in all particulars these institutions might be completely independent. Nor was the convent always indifferent to the poor.[2] But the tendency was for it to centre attention upon itself, rather than to seek the regeneration and prosperity of those outside its walls.

Like many other earthly ideals, the ideal of peace, virtue, and happy contentment aimed at by the convent was not reached, or, if approached in the first moments of overflowing ardor, was soon forfeited. For the method of monasticism is radically wrong. Here and there the cloister was the "audience chamber of God." But it was well understood that convent walls did not of themselves make holy. As, before, Jerome, Gregory of Nyssa, and Augustine had borne

---

[1] The term " convent " primarily means a society of persons. In legal instruments the usual form in England in the Middle Ages was " the prior and convent of. " See Jessopp, p. 119, who calls attention to the endless bickerings and lawsuits in which the mediæval convents of England were engaged. For the monk in his monastery, see Taunton, I. 65–96.

[2] At one time Cluny cared for 17,000 poor. In the famine of 1117 the convent of Heisterbach, near Cologne, fed 1500 a day. In a time of scarcity Bernard supported 2000 peasants till the time of harvest.

testimony to that effect, so now also did different voices. Ivo of Chartres (d. 1116) condemns the monks who were filled with the leaven of pride and boast of their ascetic practices and refers to such passages as 1 Tim. 4 : 8 and Rom. 14 : 17. The solitudes of the mountains and forests, he says, will not make men holy, who do not carry with them rest of soul, the Sabbath of the heart, and elevation of mind. Peter of Cluny wrote to a hermit that his separation from the world would not profit unless he built a strong wall against evil in his own heart, and that wall was Christ the Saviour. Without this protection, retirement to solitude, mortifications of the body, and journeyings in distant lands, instead of availing, would bring temptations yet more violent. Every mode of life, lay and clerical, monastic and eremitic, has its own temptations.

But prosperity was invariably followed by rivalry, arrogance, idleness, and low morals. If Otto of Freising gives unstinted praise to the cloistral communities, his contemporary, Anselm of Havelberg,[1] condemns the laziness and gossip of the monks within and without the convent walls. Elizabeth of Schönau and Hildegard of Bingen, while they looked upon the monastic life as the highest form of earthly existence, saw much that was far from ideal in the lives of monks and nuns.[2] There is a *chronique scandaleuse* of the convents as dark and repulsive as the *chronique scandaleuse* of the papacy during the pornocracy, and under the last popes of the Middle Ages. In a letter to Alexander III., asking him to dissolve the abbey of Grestian, the bishop of the diocese, Arnulf, spoke of all kinds of abuses, avarice, quarrelling,

---

[1] Hauck, IV. 312.

[2] Hauck, IV. 401 sqq., says that there were not many abbesses in Germany like Hildegard and Elizabeth of Schönau. The complaints of corrupt monks and nuns came from Saxony, Swabia, Lorraine, the Rhine land, and Switzerland. See quotations in Hauck.

murder, profligacy.   William of Malmesbury,[1] writing in
1125, gives a bad picture of the monks of Canterbury.   The
convent of Brittany, of which Abælard was abbot, revealed,
as he reports in his autobiography, a rude and shocking
state of affairs.   Things got rapidly worse after the first
fervor of the orders of St. Francis and Dominic was cooled.
Teachers at the universities, like William of St. Amour of
Paris (d. 1270), had scathing words for the monkish insolence and profligacy of his day, as will appear when we consider the mendicant orders.   Did not a bishop during the
Avignon captivity of the papacy declare that from personal
examination he knew a convent where all the nuns had carnal intercourse with demons ?   The revelations of St. Bridget
of Sweden (d. 1375), approved at the councils of Constance
and Basel, reveal the same low condition of monastic virtue.
Nicolas of Clemanges (d. 1440) wrote vigorous protests
against the decay of the orders, and describes in darkest
colors their waste, gluttony, idleness, and profligacy.   He
says a girl going into a convent might as well be regarded
as an abandoned woman at once.   It was true, as Cæsar of
Heisterbach had said in a homily several centuries before,
" Religion brought riches and riches destroyed religion." [2]

The institution of monasticism, which had included the
warmest piety and the highest intelligence of the Middle
Ages in their period of glory, came to be, in the period of
their decline, the synonym for superstition and the irreconcilable foe of human progress.   And this was because there is
something pernicious in the monastic method of attempting

---

[1] *Gesta pontificum*, Rolls Series, p. 70, as quoted by Taunton, I. 22.
William says, " The monks of Canterbury, like all then in England, amused
themselves with hunting, falconry, and horse racing.   They loved the rattle
of dice, drink, and fine clothes, and had such a retinue of servants that they
were more like seculars than monks."

[2] *Religio peperit divitias, divitiæ religionem destruxerunt*, Hom. III. 96.
Jessopp, *Coming of the Friars*, says that in England the monks of the thirteenth century were better than their age, which is not difficult of belief.

to secure holiness, and something false in its ideal of holiness.   The monks crushed out the heretical sects and resented the Renaissance.   Their example in the period of early fervor, adapted to encourage thrift, later promoted laziness and insolence.   Once praiseworthy as educators, they became champions of obscurantism and ignorance. Chaucer's prior, who went on the pilgrimage to the tomb of Thomas à Becket, is a familiar illustration of the popular opinion of the monks in England in the fourteenth century: —

> " He was a lord full fat and in good point ;
>   His eyen stepe and rolling in his head
>   That stemed as a fornice of a led ;
>   His botes souple, his hors in gret estat,
>   Now certainly he was a sayre prelat.
>   He was not pale as a forpined gost ;
>   A fat swan loved he best of any rost ;
>   His palfrey was as broune as is a bery."

And yet it would be most unjust to forget the services which the monastery performed at certain periods in the history of mediæval Europe, or to deny the holy purpose of their founders.   The hymns, the rituals, and the manuscripts prepared by mediæval monks continue to make contribution to our body of literature and our Church services.   An age like our own may congratulate itself upon its methods of Church activity, and yet acknowledge the utility of the different methods practised by the Church in another age.   We study the movements of the past, not to find fault with methods which the best men of their time advocated and which are not our own, but to learn, and become, if possible, better fitted for grappling with the problems of our own time.

§ 62.   *Monasticism and the Papacy.*

Monasticism and the papacy, representing the opposite extremes of abandonment of the world and lordship over the world, strange to say, entered into the closest alliance. The monks came to be the standing army of the popes,

and were their obedient and valorous champions in the
battles the popes waged with secular rulers.   Some of the
best popes were monastic in their training, or their habits, or both.   Gregory VII. was trained in the Benedictine
convent on the Aventine, Victor III. proceeded from Monte
Cassino, Urban II. and Pascal II. from Cluny, Adrian IV. from
St. Albans.   Eugenius III., the pupil of St. Bernard, continued after he was made pope to wear the shirt of the
monks of Citeaux next to his body.   Innocent III. wrote
the ascetic work, *Contempt of the World.*[1]

One monastic order after the other was founded from
the eleventh to the thirteenth century.   The organizing
instinct and a pious impulse dotted Christendom with new
convents or rebuilt old ones from Mt. Carmel to northern
Scotland.[2]   Innocent III., after the manner in which the
modern Protestant justifies the denominational distinctions
of Protestantism, likened these various orders to troops clad
in different kinds of armor and belonging to the same army.
"Such variety," he said, "does not imply any division of allegiance to Christ, but rather one mind under a diversity of
form."[3]   So Peter of Blois writing to the abbot of Eversham
said, that as out of the various strings of the harp, harmony
comes forth, so out of the variety of religious orders comes
unity of service.   One should no less expect to find unity
among a number of orders than among the angels or heavenly bodies.   A vineyard bears grapes both black and white.
A Christian is described in Holy Writ as a cedar, a cypress,
a rose, an olive tree, a palm, a terebinth, yet they form one
group in the Lord's garden.[4]

---

[1] Monks were declared by the synod of Nismes, 1096, to be better qualified
for ruling than the secular clergy.   Hefele, V. 244.

[2] For lists, see Helyot and Dr. Littledale's art. *Monachism,* "Enc. Brit."

[3] *Ep.,* III. 38 ; Migne, 214, 921.

[4] *Ep.,* 97 ; Migne, 207, 304 sq. Speaking of the variety of expression which
Christ allows, he says in a way worthy of a modern advocate of the Evangelical Alliance, *ipsa varietas est uniformitatis causa.*

It was the shrewd wisdom of the popes to encourage the orders, and to use them to further the centralization of the ecclesiastical power in Rome. Each order had its own monastic code, its own distinctive customs. These codes, as well as the orders, were authorized and confirmed by the pope, and made, immediately or more loosely, subject to his sovereign jurisdiction. The mendicant orders of Sts. Francis and Dominic were directly amenable to the Holy See. The Fourth Lateran, in forbidding the creation of new orders, was moved to do so by the desire to avoid confusion in the Church by the multiplication of different rules. It commanded all who wished to be monks to join one of the orders already existing. The orders of St. Francis and St. Dominic, founded in the face of this rule, became the most faithful adherents the papacy ever had, until the Society of Jesus arose three centuries later.

The papal favor, shown to the monastic orders, tended to weaken the authority of the bishops, and to make the papacy independent of the episcopal system. Duns Scotus went so far as to declare that, as faith is more necessary for the world than sacramental ablution in water, so the body of monks is more important than the order of prelates. The monks constitute the heart, the substance of the Church. By preaching they start new life, and they preach without money and without price. The prelates are paid.[1]

Papal privileges and exemptions were freely poured out upon the orders, especially upon the Mendicants. They were the pets of the popes. They were practically given freedom to preach and dispense the sacrament in all places and at all times, irrespective of the bishops and their jurisdiction. The constant complaints and clashing which resulted, led to endless appeals of monasteries against the decisions of bishops, which flowed in a constant stream to Rome, and gave the members of the curia a rare chance to

[1] See the remarkable passage quoted by Seeberg, *Duns Scotus*, 478 sq.

ply their trade.[1] The convents, by their organization and
wealth, and by the number of their constituents, who were
free to go to Rome and spend an indefinite time there, were
able to harass and to wear out the patience of their opponents, the bishops, or prolong the cases till their death.[2]

The riches, luxury,[3] and power of the great convents became proverbial.   In Lorraine and other parts of Europe
they were the leading influence.[4] Abbots often took precedence of bishops, just as the general chapters of the orders,[5]
made up of representatives from the farthest East to the
Atlantic, were more imposing than the diocesan and even
the provincial councils.

A little earlier than our period the abbot of Weissenburg
was able to muster as many men as his diocesan bishop of
Spires, and the three abbots of Reichenau, St. Gall, and
Kempten, three times as many as the bishop of the extensive
diocese of Constance.[6] In the twelfth century the abbot

---

[1] Matthew Paris gives one case after the other, as do the other English
chroniclers.   Jessopp, *Coming of the Friars*, says that the history of mediæval English monasticism is made up of stories of everlasting litigation.   The
convents were always in trouble with their bishops.

[2] Bishop Stubbs, *Const. Hist.*, III. 329, says of the English monasteries
that they were the stronghold of papal influence which the pope supported
as a counterpoise to that of the diocesan bishops.   For this reason the popes
never made appointments of English abbots, and seldom, if ever, interfered
with the elections by the monks.

[3] Dr. Jessopp, p. 155, says of the English monks: "After all, it must be
confessed that the greatest of all delights to the thirteenth-century monks was
eating and drinking.   The dinner in a great abbey was clearly a very important event of the day.   It must strike any one who knows much of the
literature of this age, that the weak point in the monastic life of the thirteenth century was the gormandizing." He says, however, that little is heard
of drunkenness.   The ale brewed in the convents was an important item in
the year's menu.   Richard of Marisco, bishop of Durham, gave the Abbey of
St. Albans the tithes of Eglingham, Northumberland, to help the monks
make a better ale, "taking compassion upon the weakness of the convent's
drink."

[4] See Hauck, III. 493.   "*Das Mönchthum*," he says, "*war in Lothringen
die führende Macht.*"

[5] The Fourth Lateran instructed them to meet every three years.

[6] Hauck, III. 442.

of Fulda claimed precedence over the great archbishop of Cologne. Beginning with John XVIII. (1004–1009) the abbots were not seldom vested with the insignia of the episcopal office. The English abbots of St. Albans, Bardney, Westminster, and the heads of other English abbeys were mitred.[1] They were great personages ; they sat in œcumenical councils ; the bells were rung as they passed ; they engaged in the hunt, had their horses and armed retinues, and entertained on an elaborate scale. The abbot of St. Albans ate from a silver plate, and even ladies of rank were invited to share the pleasures of repasts at English abbeys.

Thus, by wealth and organization and by papal favor, the monastic orders were in a position to overshadow the episcopate. Backed by the pope they bade defiance to bishops, and in turn they enabled the papacy most effectually to exercise lordship over the episcopate.

In the struggle with the heretical sects the orders were the uncompromising champions of orthodoxy, and rendered the most effective assistance to the popes in carrying out their policy of repression. In the Inquisition they were the chief agents which the papacy had. They preached crusades against the Albigenses and were prominent in the ranks of the crusaders. In the work of bloody destruction, they were often in the lead, as was Arnold of Citeaux. Everywhere from Germany to Spain the leading Inquisitors were monks.

Again, in the relentless struggle of the papacy with princes and kings, they were always to be relied upon. Here they did valiant service for the papacy, as notably in the struggle against the emperor, Frederick II., when they sowed sedition and organized revolt in Germany and other parts of his empire.

---

[1] So also were the abbots of Bury St. Edmunds, St. Augustine at Canterbury, Croyland, Peterborough, Evesham, Glastonbury, and Gloucester ; but the abbot of Glastonbury had the precedence, till Adrian IV. gave it to the abbot of St. Albans.

Once more, as agents to fill the papal treasury, they did efficient and welcome service to the Holy See. In this interest they were active all over Europe. The pages of English chroniclers are filled with protests against them on the score of their exactions from the people.[1] The pope treated the orders well, and in turn was well served by them. They received high favors, and they had the rare grace of showing gratitude.

The orders of this period may be grouped in five main families: the family which followed the Benedictine rule, the family which followed the so-called Augustinian rule, the Carmelites, the hermit orders of which the Carthusians were the chief, and the original mendicant orders,[2] the Franciscans and Dominicans.

§ 63.   *The Monks of Cluny.*

LITERATURE.—See lit. vol. IV. pp. 367 and 861; MABILLON: *Ann. ord. S. Bened.*, III.–V., Paris, 1706–1708; *Statuta Cluniacensia*, Migne, 189, 1023–47.— BERNARD ET BRUEL: *Recueil des chartes de l'abbaye de Cluni*, to 1300, 6 vols. Paris, 1876–93; *Consuetudines monasticæ*, vol. I.; *Consuet. Farfenses*, ed. by ALBERS, Stuttgart, 1900. The *consuetudines* are statutes and customs which convents adopted supplementary to the Rules of their orders. These of Farfa, a convent in Italy, were taken down from Odilo of Cluny and enforced at Farfa. THE *Lives* OF ST. BERNARD. — C. A. WILKENS: *Petrus der Ehrwürdige*, Leipzig, 1857, 277 pp. — M. KERKER: *Wilhelm der Selige, Abt zu Hirschau*, Tübingen, 1863. — WITTEN: *Der Selige Wilhelm, Abt von Hirschau*, Bonn, 1890. — CHAMPLY: *Hist. de l'abbaye de Cluny*, Mâcon, 1866. — L'HUILLIER: *Vie de Hugo*, Solesmes, 1887. — K. SACKUR: *Die Cluniacenser bis zur Mitte des 11ten Jahrhunderts*, 2 vols. Halle, 1892–94. — H. KUTTER: *Wilhelm von St. Thierry, ein Representant der mittelalterlichen Frömmigkeit*, Giessen, 1898. — MAITLAND: *The Dark Ages*, 1890, pp. 350–491. — HAUCK, vol. III. — Art. *Hirschau*, in Herzog, VIII. 138 sqq.

[1] M. Paris and other English chroniclers are continually damning these Mendicant tax gatherers for their extortion. They were raising money for the pope in England as early as 1234.

[2] Hurter, *Innocent III.*, IV. 238. Gasquet gives an elaborate list of the monastic houses of England, pp. 251–318, and an account of the religious orders represented in England, together with instructive engravings, 211 sqq. According to Gasquet's list there were more than fifteen hundred conventual houses in England alone.

The convent of Cluny,[1] located twelve miles northwest of Mâcon, France, stood at the height of its influence in the eleventh and twelfth centuries. Founded in 910 by Duke William of Aquitaine, and directed by a succession of wise abbots, it gained an eminence, second only to that of Monte Cassino among the monasteries of the West, and became the nursery of a monastic revival which spread over Europe from the Adriatic to Scotland.

No religious locality in the Latin church enjoyed a purer fame than Cluny. Four of its abbots, Odo, Majolus, Odilo, and Hugh, attained the dignity of canonized saints. Three popes were among its monks, Gregory VII.,[2] Urban II., and Pascal II., and the antipope Anacletus II. Gelasius II., driven from Rome, 1118, took refuge within its walls and died there lying on ashes and there was buried. The cardinals who elected Calixtus II., his successor, met at Cluny. Kings joined with popes in doing it honor.

The Cluniacs re-enforced the rule of St. Benedict in the direction of greater austerity. In Lorraine and Germany the Cluny influence began to be felt after the monastic reform, led by such men as Abbot Gerhard of Brogne in the tenth century, had run its course.[3] Such monastic leaders as William, abbot of St. Benignus at Dijon, Poppo, abbot of Stablo and Limburg, and William of Hirschau represented the Benedictine rule and were in full sympathy with Cluny. Hirschau in the Black Forest became a centre of Cluniac influence in Southern Germany and one of the chief centres of intelligence of the age.[4] Its abbot William, 1069–91, a vigorous disciplinarian and reformer, had received a thorough scholastic training at the convent of St. Emmeram, Regensburg. He was in correspondence with Anselm and

[1] The town now has four thousand inhabitants.
[2] Hauck, III. 596, thinks there is no doubt Gregory was a Cluniac.
[3] Hauck, III. 345 sqq.
[4] A list of the German convents adopting the rule of Cluny, or a modified form of it, is given by Hauck, III. 863.

visited Gregory VII. in Rome about the year 1075. The convent became a Gregorian stronghold in the controversy over the right of investiture. With the rule of Cluny before him William, in 1077, drew up a similar code for Hirschau, known as the *Constitutiones Hirsaugienses*, and introduced the white dress of the Cluniacs which gave rise to the sneer that the monks were cleansing their garments instead of their hearts.[1] Under William the Conqueror the Cluniacs established themselves in England at Barnstaple. William thought so well of them that he offered to one of their number, Hugh, the supervision of the religious affairs of the realm. The second house in England was the important establishment, St. Pancras at Lewes, set up by Gundrada and the Earl of Warren, the Conqueror's son-in-law, 1077.[2] Bermondsey, Wenlock, and Thetford were other important houses. The Cluniac houses in England were called priories and their heads priors or deans.[3] Hugo, who held the position of abbot of Cluny for sixty years, 1048–1109, was the friend of Gregory VII. and during his administration Cluny was visited by Urban II., one of Hugo's disciples, after the adjournment of the synod of Clermont. Hugo began the erection of the great basilica in 1089, which was dedicated by Innocent II. in 1131. It was the next greatest church after St. Peter's in the West.

Under Pontius, the seventh abbot, 1109–22, the current of

[1] William erected new buildings at Hirschau to accommodate the large accessions of monks and founded a *scriptorium* and a library. Among his writings was a work on music, *de musica et tonis.* Hirschau was turned into a Protestant school by Duke Christoph, 1556. Its buildings were destroyed by the army of Louis XIV. The ruins are among the most venerable monuments of Württemberg.

[2] Gundrada had visited Cluny. On her tombstone was placed the inscription *Intulit ecclesiis Anglorum balsama morum,* "She brought the balm of good manners to the churches of England." See Stephens, p. 254.

[3] When the monasteries were repressed by Henry VIII., there were thirty-two Cluniac houses in England. Gasquet, 218. Taunton, I. 27, speaks of thirty-eight houses and three hospitals in London belonging to the Cluniacs.

decay ran deep and strong. The convent had become rich
in lands and goods. The plain furnishings had been discarded for rich appointments, and austerity of habits gave
way to self-indulgence. Papal favors were heaped upon
Pontius, and Pascal, his godfather, sent him the dalmatic.[1]
Calixtus II. put his own ring on Pontius' finger, gave him
the right to exercise the prerogatives of cardinal, and the
monks of Cluny the right to celebrate service with closed
doors, while the interdict was in force in the diocese.

Pontius gave way completely to worldly ambition, and
assumed the title of archabbot, which was the exclusive
prerogative of the head of the convent of Monte Cassino.
Charges were made against him by the bishop of Macon and,
forced to resign, he set his face towards Jerusalem as a
pilgrim.   The pilgrimage did not arouse any feelings of submission, and on his return the deposed abbot made an effort
to seize his former charge. He forced the convent gates and
compelled the monks to swear him fealty. The sacred vessels of gold and silver were melted down and divided among
the wild intruders. The devastation was then carried beyond the convent walls to the neighboring estates. The
anathema was laid upon Pontius by Honorius II., and, summoned to Rome, he was thrown into prison, where he died,
impenitent, 1126. This was one of the most notorious cases
of monastic malversation of office in the Middle Ages.

Peter the Venerable had been elected abbot of Cluny
during Pontius' absence in the East and filled the office for
nearly forty years, 1122–57. He was the friend of St. Bernard, one of the most eminent of the mediæval monks and one
of the most attractive ecclesiastical personages of his age.
Born in Auvergne and trained in a Cistercian convent, he was

[1] The wide-sleeved over-garment stretching to the feet. The mitre, the
distinctive cap of the bishop, was also frequently sent to abbots. One of the
first instances was its presentation by Alexander II. to the abbot of St.
Augustine of Canterbury. The abbot of Fulda received it and also the ring
from Innocent II., 1137.

only twenty-eight when he was made abbot. Under his administration Cluny regained its renown. In addition to the study of the Bible, Peter also encouraged the study of the classics, a course which drew upon him bitter attacks. He visited the Cluniac houses abroad in England and Spain.

On the tenth anniversary of his official primacy, Peter welcomed two hundred priors and twelve hundred and twelve members of the order at Cluny. Four hundred and sixty monks constituted the family of the mother house. No less than two thousand convents are said to have acknowledged the Cluniac rule, two of which were at Jerusalem and Mt. Tabor. In 1246 Peter introduced through a General Chapter seventy six new rules, re-enforcing and elaborating the Benedictine code already in force.[1] The use of meat was entirely forbidden except to the weak and infirm, and also the use of all confections made with honey, spices, and wine.

To the labors of abbot Peter added the activity of an author. He wrote famous tracts to persuade the Jews and Mohammedans, and against the heretic Peter de Bruys. His last work was on miracles,[2] in which many most incredible stories of the supernatural are told as having occurred in convents.

It was while this mild and wise man held office, that Abæ-lard knocked at Cluny for admission and by his hearty permission spent within its walls the last weary hours of his life.

During Peter's incumbency St. Bernard made his famous attack against the self-indulgence of the Cluniacs. Robert, a young kinsman of Bernard, had transferred his allegiance from the Cistercian order to Cluny. Bernard's request that he be given up Pontius declined to grant. What his predecessor had declined to do, Peter did. Perhaps it was

---

[1] See Migne, 189, 1026 sqq. The volume contains Peter's works.

[2] *Liber duo illustrium miraculorum.* A translation of the Koran was made under Peter's patronage. A revised edition by Bibliander was published at Basel, 1543. These works are contained in Migne, vol. 189, 507-903, which also prints Peter's letters and sermons, and the hymns which are ascribed to him.

not without feeling over the memory of Pontius' action that
Bernard wrote, comparing[1] the simple life at Citeaux with
the laxity and luxury prevailing at Cluny.

This tract, famous in the annals of monastic controversial
literature, Bernard opened by condemning the lack of
spirituality among his own brethren, the Cistercians. "How
can we," he exclaims, " with our bellies full of beans and our
minds full of pride, condemn those who are full of meat, as
if it were not better to eat on occasion a little fat, than be
gorged even to belching with windy vegetables! " He then
passed to an arraignment of the Cluniacs for self-indulgence
in diet, small talk, and jocularity. At meals, he said, dish
was added to dish and eggs were served, cooked in many
forms, and more than one kind of wine was drunk at a
sitting. The monks preferred to look on marble rather
than to read the Scriptures. Candelabra and altar cloths
were elaborate. The art and architecture were excessive.
The outward ornamentations were the proof of avarice and
love of show, not of a contrite and penitent heart. He had
seen one of them followed by a retinue of sixty horsemen
and having none of the appearance of a pastor of souls. He
charged them with taking gifts of castles, villas, peasants,
and slaves, and holding them against just complainants.[2] In
spite of these sharp criticisms Peter remained on terms of
intimacy with Bernard. He replied without recrimina-
tion, and called Bernard the shining pillar of the Church.
A modification of the rule of St. Benedict, when it was
prompted by love, he pronounced proper. But he and
Bernard, he wrote, belonged to one Master, were the soldiers
of one King, confessors of one faith. As different paths
lead to the same land, so different customs and costumes,
with one inspiring love, lead to the Jerusalem above,

---

[1] *Apologia ad Guillelmum.* Migne, 182, 895–918.

[2] To this charge Peter replied that such property was much better in the
hands of the monks than of wild laymen.

the mother of us all. Cluniacs and Cistercians should ad-
monish one another if they discerned errors one in the other,
for they were pursuing after one inheritance and following
one command. He called upon himself and Bernard to
remember the fine words of Augustine, "have charity, and
then do what you will," *habe charitatem et fac quicquid vis.*[1]
What could be more admirable? Where shall we go for a
finer example of Christian polemics?

After Peter's death the glory of Cluny declined.[2] Six
hundred years later, 1790, the order was dissolved by the
French Government. The Hotel de Cluny, the Cluniac house
in Paris, once occupied by the abbot, now serves as a museum
of Mediæval Art and Industry under the charge of the
French government.[3]

The piety of Western Christendom owes a lasting debt to
Cluny for the hymn "Jerusalem the Golden," taken from the
de contemptu mundi written by Bernard of Cluny, a contemporary of Peter the Venerable and St. Bernard of Clairvaux.[4]

> Jerusalem the Golden,
> With milk and honey blest,
> Beneath thy contemplation
> Sink heart and voice opprest.
> I know not, oh, I know not
> What social joys are there,
> What radiancy of glory,
> What light beyond compare.

[1] *Ep.*, I. 28 ; Migne, 189, 156. A number of Peter's letters to Bernard
are preserved, all of them laying stress upon the exercise of brotherly affection. In strange contrast to his usual gentleness, stands his sharp arraignment of the Jews. See § 77 on Missions to the Jews.

[2] The election of the abbot was taken out of the hands of the monks. During the Avignon captivity the popes, and later the French king, claimed the
right to appoint that official. The Guises had the patronage of the abbey for
nearly a hundred years. In 1627 Richelieu was appointed abbot.

[3] The Hotel de Cluny was a stopping place for distinguished people.
There Mary, sister of Henry VIII. of England, resided during her widowhood
and there James V. of Scotland was married, 1537, to Madeleine, daughter of
Francis I. The municipality of Cluny purchased the abbey buildings and in
part dismantled them.

[4] See Schaff, *Christ in Song*, and Julian, *Hymnology*.

§ 64. *The Cistercians.*

LITERATURE. — *Exordium parvum ordinis Cisterciensiæ*, Migne, 166. *Exordium magnum ord. Cisterc.*, by CONRAD OF EBERBACH, d. 1220; Migne, 185. — MANRIQUEZ : *Ann. ord. Cisterc.*, 4 vols. Lyons, 1642. — MABILLON : *Ann. ord. St. Benedict*, Paris, 1706–1708. — P. GUIGNARD : *Les monuments primitifs de la règle Cistercienne, publiés d'après les manuscripts de l'abbaye de Citeaux*, Dijon, 1878, pp. cxii. 656. — PIERRE LE NAIN: *Essai de l'hist. de l'ordre de Citeaux*, Paris, 1696.— J. H. NEWMAN : *The Cistercian Saints of England*, London, 1844.— FRANZ WINTER : *Die Cistercienser des nord-östlichen Deutschlands bis zum Auftreten der Bettelorden*, 3 vols. Gotha, 1868–1871.— L. JANAUSCHEK: *Origines Cisterciensium*, Vienna, 1877. — B. ALBERS : *Untersuchungen zu den ältesten Mönchsgewohnheiten. Ein Beitrag zur Benedictinerordensregel der X–XIlten Jahrhunderte*, Munich, 1905. — SHARPE : *Architecture of the Cisterc.*, London, 1874. — *Cisterc. Abbeys of Yorkshire*, in " Fraser's Mag.," September, 1876.— DEAN HODGES: *Fountains Abbey, The Story of a Mediæval Monastery*, London, 1904. — DEUTSCH : art. *Cistercienser*, in Herzog, IV. 116–127 ; art. *Harding*, in " Dict. Natl. Biogr.," XXIV. 333–335 ; the *Biographies of St. Bernard*. For extended lit. see the work of JANAUSCHEK.

With the Cluniac monks the Cistercians divide the distinction of being the most numerous and most useful monastic order of the Middle Ages,[1] until the Mendicant Friars arose and distanced them both.   They are Benedictines and claim the great name of St. Bernard, and for that reason are often called Bernardins in France. Two popes, Eugenius III. and Benedict XII., proceeded from the order.   Europe owes it a large debt for its service among the half-barbarian peasants of Eastern France, Southern Germany, and especially in the provinces of Northeastern Germany.   Its convents set an example of skilled industry in field and garden, in the training of the vine, the culture of fish, the cultivation of orchards, and in the care of cattle.[2]

[1] Cardinal Hergenröther says, " The Cistercians reached a much higher distinction than the order of Cluny." *Kirchengesch.*, II. 351.

[2] In England they were careful breeders of horses (Giraldus Cambrensis, *Speculum ecclesiæ*, IV. 130, and Brewer's Preface, IV. 24) and were noted for their sheep and wool. Their wool was a popular article of royal taxation. John seized a year's product to meet the payment of Richard's ransom. M. Paris, Luard's ed., II. 399. Henry III. forbade the monks to sell their

The founder, Robert Molêsme, was born in Champagne, 1024, and after attempting in vain to introduce a more rigorous discipline in several Benedictine convents, retired to the woods of Molêsme and in 1098 settled with twenty companions on some swampy ground near Citeaux,[1] twelve miles from Dijon.   Here Eudes, duke of Burgundy,[2] erected a building, which went at first by the name of the New Monastery, *novum monasterium.*

Alberic, Robert's successor, received for the new establishment the sanction of Pascal II., and placed it under the special care of the Virgin.   She is said to have appeared to him in the white dress of the order.[3]

Under the third abbot, Stephen Harding, an Englishman, known as St. Stephen, who filled the office twenty-five years (1110–1134),[4] the period of prosperity set in.   In 1113 Bernard with thirty companions entered the convent, and the foundation of four houses followed, 1113–1115, — La Ferté, Potigny, Clairvaux, and Morimond, — which continued to have a rank above all the other Cistercian houses subsequently founded.

New houses followed rapidly.   In 1130 there were 30 Cistercian convents, in 1168, 288.   A rule was framed forbidding the erection of new establishments, but without avail, and their number in the fourteenth century had risen

wool.   Henry II., 1257, taxed it heavily, etc.   M. Paris, IV. 324, V. 610.   See Stubbs, *Const. Hist.*, I. 541, II. 181, 200.

[1] The name comes from the stagnant pools in the neighborhood.

[2] He died on a Crusade.   At his request his bones were taken back and buried at Citeaux, which became the burial place of his successors.

[3] See Helyot, V. 404.   According to Hauck, IV. 337, the Cistercians were the first to introduce into Germany the exaggerated cult of the Virgin.

[4] He was a man of much administrative ability.   William of Malmesbury, IV. 1, speaks of Stephen as "the original contriver of the whole scheme, the especial and celebrated ornament of our times."   It is related that on a journey to Rome, and before entering Citeaux, he repeated the whole Psalter.   Basil had enjoined the memorizing of the Psalter.   According to the biographer of abbot Odo of Cluny, the monks of Cluny daily repeated 138 Psalms.   Maitland, p. 375.

to 738.[1] The order, though never the recipient of such privileges as were dispensed to Cluny, was highly honored by
some of the popes. Innocent III. showed them special favor,
and promised them the precedence in audiences at Rome.[2]

The *carta charitatis*, the Rule of Love, the code of the
Cistercians, dates from Harding's administration and was
confirmed by Calixtus II. — 1119. It commanded the strict
observance of the Benedictine Rule, but introduced a new
method of organization for the whole body. In contrast to
the relaxed habits of the Cluniacs, the mode of life was made
austerely simple. The rule of silence was emphasized and flesh
forbidden, except in the case of severe illness. The conventual menu was confined to two dishes. All unnecessary adornment of the churches was avoided, so that nothing should remain in the house of God which savored of pride or superfluity.
The crosses were of wood till the statutes of 1157 allowed
them to be of gold. Emphasis was placed upon manual
labor as an essential part of monastic life. A novice at
Clairvaux writes enthusiastically of the employment of the
monks, whom he found with hoes in the gardens, forks and
rakes in the meadows, sickles in the fields, and axes in the
forest.[3] In some parts they became large landowners and
crowded out the owners of small plats.[4] At a later period
they gave themselves to copying manuscripts.[5] Their
schools in Paris, Montpellier (1252), Toulouse (1281), Oxford
(1282), Metz, and other places were noted, but with the exception of Bernard they developed no distinguished Schoolmen or writers as did the mendicant orders.[6] They were not

---

[1] Janauschek has shown that 1800, the number formerly given, is an
exaggeration.   [2] Hurter, IV. 184 sqq.

[3] Peter de Roya, *Ep*. St. Bernard, 492; Migne, 182, 711.

[4] Hauck, IV. 336.

[5] One of the regulations of the chapter of 1134 enjoined silence in the
scriptorium. *In omnibus scriptoriis ubicunque ex consuetudine monachi
scribunt silentium teneatur sicut in claustro.* Maitland, p. 450.

[6] The Cistercians are said to have produced the first Swedish translation of
the Bible. Hurter, IV. 180.

given to the practice of preaching or other spiritual service among the people.[1]   The general chapter, 1191, forbade preaching in the parish churches and also the administration of baptism.   The order became zealous servants of the pope and foes of heresy.   The abbot Arnold was a fierce leader of the Crusades against the Albigenses.

Following the practice introduced at the convent of Hirschau, the Cistercians constituted an adjunct body of laymen, or conversi.[2]   They were denied the tonsure and were debarred from ever becoming monks.   The Cistercian dress was at first brown and then white, whence the name Gray Monks, *grisei*.   The brethren slept on straw in cowl and their usual day dress.

The administration of the Cistercians was an oligarchy as compared with that of the Cluniacs.   The abbot of Cluny was supreme in his order, and the subordinate houses received their priors by his appointment.   Among the Cistercians each convent chose its own head.   At the same time the community of all the houses was insured by the observance of the Rule of 1119, and by yearly chapters, which were the ultimate arbiters of questions in dispute.   The five earliest houses exercised the right of annual visitation, which was performed by their abbots over five respective groups.   A General Council of twenty-five consisted of these five abbots and of four others from each of the five groups.   The General Chapters were held yearly and were attended by all the abbots within a certain district.   Those at remote distances attended less frequently: the abbots from Spain, every two years; from Sweden and Norway, every three

---

[1] St. Bernard declared that the office of the monk is 'not to preach, but to be an ascetic, and that the town should be to him as a prison, and solitude as paradise, *quod monachus non habet docentis sed plangentis officium, quippe cui oppidum carcer esse debet et solitudo paradisus*.   A monk who goes out into the world, he said, turns things round and makes his solitude a prison and the town paradise.   *Ep.*, 365 ; Migne, 182, 570.

[2] Called at Hirschau also *barbati*, the bearded.

years; from Scotland, Ireland, Hungary, and Greece, every
four years; and from the Orient, every seven years.   It
became a proverb that "The gray monks were always on
their feet."

The Cistercians spread over all Western Europe.   The
Spanish orders of Alcantara and Calatrava adopted their rule.
The first Cistercian house in Italy was founded 1120 at Tigl-
ieto, Liguria, and in Germany at Altenkamp about 1123.[1]
In England the order got a foothold in 1128, when William
Gifford, bishop of Winchester, founded the house of Waverley
in Surrey.[2]   Among the prominent English houses were,
Netley near Southampton, founded by Henry III., Rivaulx,
and Fountains,[3] the greatest abbey in Northern England.   In
1152 there were fifty Cistercian houses in England.[4]   Melrose
Abbey, Scotland, also belonged to this order.

Of all the Cistercian convents, Port Royal has the most
romantic history.   Founded in 1204 by Mathilda de Gar-
lande in commemoration of the safe return of her husband
from the Fourth Crusade, it became in the seventeenth century a famous centre of piety and scholarship.   Its association
with the tenets of the Jansenists, and the attacks of Pascal
upon the Jesuits, brought on its tragic downfall.   The
famous hospice, among the snows of St. Gotthard, is under
the care of St. Bernard monks.

In the thirteenth century the power of the Cistercians
yielded to the energy of the orders of St. Francis and St.

[1] See Hauck, IV. 325 sqq., for the names of the German houses.

[2] Shortly after Harding's death, William of Malmesbury, IV. I, Rolls ed.,
II. 385, describes the order "as a model for all monks, a mirror to the studious, and a goad to the slothful."   Gasquet, p. 221, says that three-fourths
of the hundred Cistercian houses suppressed by Henry VIII. were founded in
the 12th century.

[3] The ruins of Fountains Abbey in Yorkshire is described by Motley
(correspondence, I. 359) as "most picturesque, and the most exquisite, and
by far the most impressive ruins I have ever seen, and much more beautiful
than Melrose Abbey."   For the ground plan, see Dr. Venables, art. *Abbey*, in
"Enc. Brit.," I. 19, and photographs of the walls (as they are).   Hodges.

[4] Stephens, *Hist. of Engl. Church*, p. 261.

Dominic. It was not a rare thing for them to pass over to
the newer monastic organizations.[1] In 1335 Benedict XIII.
enacted regulations in the interest of a severe discipline,
and in 1444 Eugenius IV. felt called upon to summon the
General Chapter to institute a rigid reform. With the
Reformation many of the houses were lost to the order in
England and Germany. The Trappists started a new
movement towards severity within the order. The French
Revolution suppressed the venerable organization in 1790.
The buildings at Citeaux, presided over by a succession of
sixty-two abbots, are now used as a reformatory institution.

§ 65. *St. Bernard of Clairvaux.*

Virtus in pace acquiritur, in pressura probatur, approbatur in victoria,
St. Bernard.[2]

LITERATURE. — The Works of St. Bernard, ed. by MABILLON, 2 vols. Paris,
1667, reprinted with additions in Migne, 182–185, Engl. trans. by SAML.
J. EALES, London, 1889, 2 vols. — *Xenia Bernardina*, a Memorial ed.
by Cistercian convents of Austro-Hungary, 6 vols. Vienna, 1891. —
LEOP. JANAUSCHEK : *Bibliographia Bernardina*, Vienna, 1891. The
tract *De consideratione*, trans. by Bp. J. H. REINKENS, Münster, 1870.

BIOGRAPHIES. — Contemporary, in Migne, vol. 185 : I. the so-called *Vita prima*,
in six parts, by WILLIAM OF THIERRY (while Bernard was still living),
GAUFRID OF CLAIRVAUX, and ERNALD, abbot of Bona Vallis ; II. the *Vita
secunda*, by ALANUS OF AUXERRE ; III. Fragments collected by GAUFRID ;
IV. a *Life*, by JOHN THE HERMIT, full of legendary materials.—Modern,
by NEANDER, Berlin, 1813, 1848, 1868, new ed. with Introd. and Notes,
by * S. M. DEUTSCH, 2 vols. Gotha, 1889. Engl. trans. London, 1843.
— ELLENDORF, Essen, 1837. — ABBÉ T. RATISBONNE, 2 vols. Paris,
1841, etc. Full of enthusiasm for Bernard as a saint. — * J. C. MORI-
SON, London, 1863 ; rev. ed. 1868, 1884. Cool and impartial. — CAPE-
FIGUE, Paris, 1866. — CHEVALLIER, 2 vols. Lille, 1888. — HOFMEISTER,
Berlin, 1891. — EALES (Rom. Cath.), London, 1891.— * RICHARD S.
STORRS, 1892, stimulating and eloquent.—*L'ABBÉ E. VACANDARD, 2 vols.
Paris, 1895, 2d ed. 1897. A thorough study following a number of

---

[1] As early as 1223 such Cistercians are called *fugitives* by the General
Chapter. Contrasting the Cistercians with the Dominicans, Matthew Paris,
an. 1255, Luard's ed., V. 529, says of them, " They do not wander through the
cities and towns, but they remain quietly shut up within the walls of their
domiciles, obeying their superiors."

[2] *Ep.*, 126 ; Migne, 182, 271.

previous presentations in magazines and brochures. — J. LAGARDÈRE, Besançon, 1900. — DEUTSCH, art. *Bernhard*, in Herzog, II. 623–639. Also H. KUTTER : *Wilhelm von St. Thierry, ein Representant der mittelalterlichen Frömmigkeit*, Giessen, 1898. For other literature see chapters, Mystical Theology and Hymns.

St. Bernard, 1090–1153, founder and abbot of the convent of Clairvaux, was the model monk of the Middle Ages, the most imposing figure of his time, and one of the best men of all the Christian centuries. He possessed a magnetic personality, a lively imagination, a rich culture, and a heart glowing with love for God and man. Although not free from what might now be called ecclesiastical rigor, he was not equalled by any of his contemporaries in services for the Church and man. " In his countenance," according to the contemporary biographer who knew him well, "there shone forth a pureness not of earth but of heaven, and his eyes had the clearness of an angel's and the mildness of a dove's eyes." [1] There is no spotless saint in this world, and Bernard was furthest from claiming perfection, but he came as near the mediæval ideal of ascetic holiness as any man of his century. [2]

In the twelfth century there were at least two other ecclesiastics of the first order of genius, Anselm and Innocent III. The former passed away a few years after the century opened. Innocent began his papal reign two years before it went out. Anselm has pre-eminence as a profound theological thinker and dialectician. Innocent ruled the world, as pope never ruled it before or since. Between the two fall the intellectual genius and activity of Bernard,

---

[1] *Vita prima*, III. 1 ; Migne, 185, 303. Gaufrid, the biographer, presents an elaborate description of his qualities. He says, Bernard was *magnanimus in fide, longanimis in spe, profusus in charitate, summus in humilitate, præcipuus in pietate*. Alanus *in Vita secunda*, XVII. 47, Migne, 185, 497, gives this high praise, *humanissimus in affectione, magis tamen forte in fide*.

[2] This was the judgment of Philip Schaff, *Literature and Poetry*, p. 282. Bernard not seldom used in his letters such expressions as this, *Nonne ego puer parvulus*, Am I not as a little child ? *Ep.*, 365 ; Migne, 182, 570.

combining some of the qualities of Anselm and Innocent. As a mystical theologian he is allied to Anselm, whose *Meditations* give him a high place in the annals of devotional literature.   And Bernard was also a statesman, although he did not attain the eminence of Innocent and shrank from participation in public affairs which were so much to the taste of the great pope.   Contemporary with himself was Peter Abælard, whose brilliant mind won for him enviable fame as a teacher and thinker.   But Abælard never won the confidence of his own age, and is not to be compared with Bernard in moral dignity.

By preference a monk, Bernard figured, with almost equal prominence, in the history of the papacy, the Crusades, mysticism, monasticism, and hymnology.   In the annals of monasticism, the pulpit, and devotional literature he easily occupies a place in the front rank.   He was called the "honey-flowing doctor," *doctor mellifluus*.   Twenty years after his death he was canonized by Alexander III. as "shining pre-eminently in his own person by virtue of sanctity and religion, and in the whole Church by the light of his doctrine and faith."[1]   Pius VIII., in 1830, admitted him to the select company of the *doctors* of the Church.   Both Calvin and Luther, who ridiculed the Schoolmen as a body, held him in high regard.[2]

[1] The document is given in Migne, 185, 622 sq.

[2] Calvin says, *Instt.* IV. 2, 11, "in his *de consideratione* Bernard speaks as though the very truth itself were speaking."   Luther, directed to Bernard by Staupitz, studied his works, and often appealed to his words.   Köstlin, *Life of Luther*, I. 81.   He praised Bernard for not having depended upon his monk's vow, but upon the free grace of Christ for salvation.   Denifle, *Luther und Lutherthum*, I. 56–64, tries to make out that Luther falsified when he represented Bernard as putting aside, as it were, his monastic profession as a thing meritorious.   Luther, in an animated passage, declared that at the close of his life Bernard had exclaimed, *tempus meum perdidi quia perdite vixi*, "I have lost my time because I have lived badly, but there is one thing that consoles me, a contrite and broken heart Thou dost not despise."   You see, said Luther, how Bernard hung his cowl on the hook and returned to Christ.   It seems, according to Denifle, that the two clauses

Bernard was descended from a noble family of Burgundy, and was born at Fontaines near Dijon.   He was one of seven children, six of whom were sons.   His mother, Aletha, like Nonna and Monica, was a deeply pious woman and planted in the son the seeds of religious faith.[1]   Carried away for a time with enthusiasm for scholastic learning, the son was overwhelmed, while on a lonely journey, with religious impressions, and, entering a chapel, resolved to dedicate himself wholly to God.   He entered the convent of Citeaux, two of his brothers following him at once, and the rest later into the monastic life.

This was in 1113 that Bernard cast in his lot with the Cistercians, and the event proved to be an epoch in the history of that new community.   His diet was bread and milk or a decoction of herbs.[2]   He devoted himself to the severest asceticism till he was reduced almost to a shadow, and his feet became so swollen from standing at devotions as almost to refuse to sustain his body.   In after years, Bernard reproached himself for this intemperate self-mortification which unfitted his body for the proper service of the Lord.   But his spirit triumphed over his, physical infirmities.[3]   While he was engaged in work in the fields, it soared aloft to heavenly things.   He studied the Scriptures and the Fathers.

were not uttered at the same time by Bernard.   The exclamation, "I have lost my life," was made in a sermon on the Canticles, Migne, 183, 867, and the other part was said by Bernard in a time of severe sickness.   This is not the place to take up Denifle's charge that Luther was playing fast and loose with Bernard's utterances to make out a case, but it is sufficient to say that Luther was intending to emphasize that Bernard depended solely upon grace for salvation, and this position is justified by expressions enough in Bernard's writings.

[1] Her piety is greatly praised by contemporaries.   The abbot of St. Benignus at Dijon begged her body for his convent.   William of St. Thierry said of her that "she ruled her household in the fear of God, was urgent in works of mercy, and brought up her sons in all obedience," *enutriens filios in omni disciplina.   Vita prima*, I. 1.

[2] Migne, 185, 250.

[3] *Virtus vehementius in infirmitate ejus refulgens*, etc.   *Vita prima*, VIII. 41; Migne, 185, 251.

His writings betray acquaintance with the classics and he
quotes Seneca, Ovid, Horace, and other classical writers.
The works of nature also furnished him with lessons, and he
seems to have approached the modern estimate of nature as
an aid to spiritual attainment. " Thou wilt find," he wrote,[1]
" something greater in the woods than in books. The trees
and rocks will teach thee what thou canst not hear from
human teachers. And dost thou not think thou canst suck
honey from the rocks and oil from the hardest stones ! "
This seems to lose its weight in view of what one of
Bernard's biographers relates. Bernard travelled the whole
day alongside the Lake of Geneva, and was so oblivious to
the scenery that in the evening, at Lausanne, he was obliged
to inquire what they had seen on the journey. We are
probably justified in this case in ascribing an ascetic purpose
to the monkish writer.[2]

In 1115, in company with twelve companions, Bernard
founded Clairvaux — *Claravallis*, Clear Valley — in a locality
which before had been called Wormwood, and been the seat
of robbers. William of St. Thierry, Bernard's close friend
and biographer, is in doubt whether the name *vallis absinthialis* came from the amount of wormwood which grew there
or from the bitter sufferings sustained by the victims of the
robbers.[3] But he does not fail to draw the contrast between

[1] To an Englishman, Henry Murdoch, *Ep.*, 106; Migne, 182, 242. *Aliquid
amplius invenies in silvis quam in libris. Ligna et lapides docebunt te, quod
a magistris audire non possis. An non putas posse te sugere mel de petra
oleumque de saxo durissimo ?* etc. The words remind us of Shakespeare's
oft-quoted lines :

books in the running brooks,
Sermons in stones, and good in everything.

[2] *Vita prima*, III. 2 ; Migne, 185, 306. A mediæval description of the
beauties of nature is a rare thing. The Canticle of the Sun, by Francis
d'Assisi, is an exception. Otto of Freising accompanied Frederick Barbarossa
on his journey to Rome to receive the imperial crown, and speaks with much
enthusiasm about the military display of the Germans, but had not a word
to say about the glories of Rome or its monuments. See Fisher, *Med. Empire*,
II. 229.   [3] *Vita prima*, I. 5.

the acts of violence for which the place was once notorious, and the peace which reigned in it after Bernard and his companions set up their simple house.   Then he says, "the hills began to distil sweetness, and fields, before sterile, blossomed and became fat under the divine benediction."[1]

In this new cloistral retreat Bernard preached, wrought miracles, wrote innumerable letters,[2] received princes and high ecclesiastics.   From there he went forth on errands of high import to his age.   The convent soon had wide fame, and sent off many shoots.[3]

William of St. Thierry[4] draws an attractive picture of Clairvaux, which at this long distance compels a feeling of rest.   William says: —

I tarried with him a few days, unworthy though I was, and whichever way I turned my eyes, I marvelled and thought I saw a new heaven and a new earth, and also the old pathways of the Egyptian monks, our fathers, marked with the recent footsteps of the men of our time left in them.   The golden ages seemed to have returned and revisited the world there at Clairvaux. . . .   At the first glance, as you entered, after descending the hill, you could feel that God was in the place ; and the silent valley bespoke, in the simplicity of its buildings, the genuine humility of the poor of Christ dwelling there.   The silence of the noon was as the silence of the midnight, broken only by the chants of the choral service, and the sound of garden and field implements.   No one was idle.   In the hours not devoted to sleep or prayer, the brethren kept busy with hoe, scythe, and axe, taming the wild land and clearing the forest.   And although there was such a number in the valley, yet each seemed to be a solitary.[5]

[1] *Apud vallem quæ prius dicebatur vallis absinthialis et amara, cœperunt montes stillare dulcedinem*, etc.   *Vita prima*, XIII. 61 ; Migne, 185, 260.   See also Alanus, *Vita secunda*, VI. 18.

[2] His letters include long compositions abounding in allegory and moralizations and brief pithy statements, which approach the subject in hand with modern directness.   Alanus gives a list of churchmen high in position going forth from Clairvaux.   *Vita secunda*, XX. 54 ; Migne, 185, 154.

[3] Vacandard, vol. II., Appendix, gives a list of sixty-eight convents founded by Bernard.

[4] William was born at Liège about 1085, and died about 1149.   In 1119 he was made abbot of the Cistercian convent of Thierry near Rheims.   We meet him frequently in the company of Bernard, and in the controversies over Abælard and Gilbert of Poitiers.

[5] *Vita prima*, I. 7 ; Migne, 182, 268.

Here is another description by the novice, Peter de Roya, writing from Clairvaux : [1] —

"Its monks have found a Jacob's ladder with angels upon it, descending to provide help to the bodies of the monks that they fail not in the way, and also ascending, and so controlling the monks' minds that their bodies may be glorified. Their song seems to be little less than angelic, but much more than human. . . .   It seems to me I am hardly looking upon men when I see them in the gardens with hoe, in the fields with forks and rakes and sickles, in the woods with axe, clad in disordered garments — but that I am looking on a race of fools without speech and sense, the reproach of mankind. However, my reason assures me that their life is with Christ in the heavens."

Bernard, to whom monastic seclusion was the highest ideal of the Christian life, bent his energies to induce his friends to take the vow.   Its vigils and mortifications were the best means for developing the two cardinal virtues of love and humility.[2]   His persistent effort to persuade his sister Humblina shocks our sense of what is due to the sacred ties of nature, but was fully justified by the examples of St. Anthony and Benedict of Nursia.   Humblina was married to a husband of rank and had a family.   When she appeared one day at Clairvaux, Bernard refused to go down to see her, for he had insisted before on her taking the veil and she had declined.   Now she finally communicated to him the bitter cry, " If my brother despises my body, let not the servant of God despise my soul." [3]   Bernard then heeded and again called upon her to renounce the vanities of the world and lay aside the luxuries of dress and ornaments.   Returning to her household, Humblina, after two years, and with her husband's consent, retired to the convent of Juilly, where she spent the remainder of her days.

---

[1] The genuineness of the letter is questionable. *Ep.*, 492; Migne, 182, 706–713.

[2] *Ep.*, 142; Migne, 182, 297.

[3] *Si despicit frater meus carnem meam, ne despiciat servus Dei animam meam. Veniat, præcipiat, quicquid præceperit, facere parata sum.   Vita secunda*, VII. 22; Migne, 185, 482.   Was ever sister's appeal more tender ?

Bernard's attack upon the conventual establishment of Cluny was born of mistaken zeal.   If of the two men Peter the Venerable appears to much better advantage in that controversy, it was different when it came to the treatment of the Jews.   Here Peter seems to have completely laid aside his mild spirit, while Bernard displays a spirit of humaneness and Christian charity far beyond his age.   In the controversy with Abælard, a subject which belongs to another chapter, the abbot of Clairvaux stands forth as the churchman who saw only evil in views which did not conform strictly to the doctrinal system of the Church.

Bernard was a man of his age as well as a monastic.   He fully shared the feelings of his time about the Crusades.   In 1128, at the Synod of Troyes, his voice secured recognition for the Knight Templars, "the new soldiery."   The ignoble failure of the Second Crusade, which he had preached with such warmth, 1146, called forth from him a passionate lament over the sins of the Crusaders, and he has given us a glimpse into the keen pangs he felt over the detractions that undertaking called forth.[1]   The ill issue was not his fault. He himself was like Moses, who led the people towards the Holy Land and not into it.   The Hebrews were stiff-necked. Were not the Crusaders stiff-necked also and unbelieving, who in their hearts looked back and hankered after Europe? Is it any wonder that those who were equally guilty should suffer a like punishment with the Israelites?   To the taunt that he had falsely represented himself as having delivered a message from God in preaching the Crusade, he declared the testimony of his conscience was his best reply.   Eugenius, too, could answer that taunt by what he had seen and heard.   But, after all was said, it was a great honor to have the same lot with Christ and suffer being unjustly condemned (Ps. 69 : 9).

When, at a later time, Bernard was chosen at Chartres to

[1] *De consideratione*, II. 1; Migne, 182, 743.

lead another Crusade, the choice was confirmed by the pope, but the Cistercians refused to give their consent.[1]

In the reigns of Innocent II. and Eugenius III. Bernard stood very near the papacy.   He did more than any other single individual to secure the general recognition of Innocent II. as the rightful pope over his rival, Anacletus II. He induced the king of France to pronounce in favor of Innocent.   Bent on the same mission, he had interviews with Henry I. of England at Chartres, and the German emperor at Liège.   He entertained Innocent at Clairvaux, and accompanied him to Italy.   It was on this journey that so profound were the impressions of Bernard's personality and miracles that the people of Milan fell at his feet and would fain have compelled him to ascend the chair of St. Ambrose. On his third journey to Rome, in 1138,[2] Bernard witnessed the termination of the papal schism.   In a famous debate with Peter of Pisa, the representative of Anacletus, he used with skill the figure of the ark for the Church, in which Innocent, all the religious orders, and all Europe were found except Anacletus and his two supporters, Roger of Sicily and Peter of Pisa.   But an attempt, he said, was being made to build another ark by Peter of Pisa.   If the ark of Innocent was not the true ark, it would be lost and all in it. Then would the Church of the East and the Church of the West perish.   France and Germany would perish, the Spaniards and the English would perish, for they were with Innocent.   Then Roger, alone of all the princes of the earth, would be saved and no other.[3]

---

[1] Bernard refers to this election in a letter to Eugenius, *Ep.*, 256.   " Who am I," he writes, "to establish camps and march at the head of armed men ?"

[2] It was on this journey that St. Bernard performed the miracle which has a humorous side.   While he was crossing the Alps, the devil broke one of his carriage wheels.   Bernard repaired the damage by commanding the devil to take the place of the broken wheel, which he did, and the wagon moved on again to the traveller's comfort.

[3] *Vita prima*, II. 7, 45; Migne, 185, 294 sq.

Eugenius III. had been an inmate of Clairvaux and one of Bernard's special wards. The tract *de consideratione*[1] which, at this pope's request, Bernard prepared on the papal office and functions is unique in literature, and, upon the whole, one of the most interesting treatises of the Middle Ages. Vacandard calls it "an examination, as it were, of the pope's conscience."[2] Here Bernard exhorts his spiritual son, whom he must address as "most holy father," and whom he loves so warmly, that he would follow him into the heavens or to the depths, whom he received in poverty and now beholds surrounded with pomp and riches. Here he pours out his concern for the welfare of Eugenius's soul and the welfare of the Church under his administration. He adduces the distractions of the papal court, its endless din of business and legal arbitrament, and calls upon Eugenius to remember that prayer, meditation, and the edification of the Church are the important matters for him to devote himself to. Was not Gregory piously writing upon Ezekiel while Rome was exposed to siege from the barbarians! Teacher never had opportunity to impress lessons upon a scholar more elevated in dignity, and Bernard approached it with a high sense of his responsibility.[3]

As a preacher, Bernard excels in the glow of his imagination and the fervor of his passion. Luther said, " Bernard is superior to all the doctors in his sermons, even to Augustine himself, because he preaches Christ most excellently."[4] In common with his other writings, his sermons abound in quotations from the Scriptures.[5] They are not pieces of careful logical statement nor are they keen analyses of the

[1] Migne, 182, 727–808.

[2] "Une sorte d'examen de conscience d'un pape." *Vie de S. Bernard*, II. 454.

[3] Bernard's view of the functions of the papacy is given in the chapter on the Papacy.

[4] Bindseil, *Colloquia*, III. 134.

[5] Deutsch, Herzog, II.634, says *Er besass eine Bibelerkenntniss wie wenige.*

states of conscience, but appeals to the highest impulses of the
religious nature.   His discourse on the death of his brother
Gerard is a model of tender treatment [1] as his address before
Konrad was of impassioned fervor.[2]   The sermons on the
Canticles preached within convent walls abound in tropical
allegory, but also in burning love to the Saviour.   One of
the most brilliant of modern pulpit orators has said, "the
constant shadow of things eternal is over all Bernard's sermons." [3]   His discourses, so speaks his biographer Gaufrid,
were congruous to the conditions of his hearers.   To rustic
people he preached as though he had always been living
in the country and to all other classes as though he were
most carefully studying their occupations.   To the erudite
he was scholarly; to the uneducated, simple.   To the spiritually minded he was rich in wise counsels.   He adapted
himself to all, desiring to bring to all the light of Christ.[4]

The miraculous power of Bernard is so well attested by
contemporary accounts that it is not easy to deny it except
on the assumption that all the miraculous of the Middle
Ages is to be ascribed to mediæval credulity.   Miracles
meet us in almost every religious biographer of the Middle
Ages.   The biographer of Boniface, the apostle of Germany,
found it necessary to apologize for not having miracles to
relate of him.   But the miracles of Bernard seem to be
vouched for as are no other mediæval works of power.   The
cases given are very numerous.   They occurred on Bernard's
journeys in Toulouse and Italy, nearer home in France, and
along the Rhine from Basel northward.   William of St.
Thierry, Gaufrid, and other contemporaries relate them in
detail.   His brothers, the monks Gerard and Guido, agree
that he had more than human power.   Walter Map, the

---

[1] For translation see Morison, p. 227 sqq., who calls it, "among funeral sermons assuredly one of the most remarkable on record."

[2] See Dr. Storrs's description, p. 461 sqq.

[3] Storrs, p. 388.   [4] *Vita prima*, III. 13; Migne, 185, 306.

Englishman who flourished in the latter years of Bernard's life and later, speaks in the same breath of Bernard's miracles and his eloquence.[1]   But what, to say the least, is equally important, Bernard himself makes reference to them and marvelled at his power.   Miracles, he said, had been wrought of old by saintly men and also by deceivers, but he was conscious neither of saintliness nor of fraud.[2]   He is reported as recognizing his power, but as being reluctant to speak of it.[3]   In a letter to the Toulousans, after his visit in their city, he reminded them that the truth had been made manifest in their midst through him, not only in speech but in power.[4]   And appealing to the signs which had accompanied his preaching the Second Crusade, he speaks of his religious shrinking which forbade his describing them.[5]

These miracles were performed at different periods of Bernard's life and, as has been said, in different localities. The bishop of Langres, a near relative, says that the first miracle he saw Bernard perform was upon a boy with an ulcer on his foot.   In answer to the boy's appeal, Bernard made the sign of the cross and the child was healed.   A mother met him carrying her child which had a withered hand and crooked arm.   The useless members were restored and the child embraced its mother before the bystanders.[6] A boy in Charletre, ten years old, unable to move his head and carried on a pillow, was healed and shown to Bernard four years afterwards.

Sometimes Bernard placed his hand upon the patient, sometimes made the sign of the cross, sometimes offered

---

[1] I. 24, Wright's ed., p. 20.

[2] *Ego mihi nec perfectionis conscius sum nec fictionis.   Vita prima*, III. 7 ; Migne, 185, 314 sq.

[3] *Vita prima*, I. 13 ; Migne, 185, 262.

[4] *Ep.*, 242 ; Migne, 182, 436.

[5] *Verecundia, de consid.* II. 1 ; Migne, 185, 744.   The word used here is *signa.*   See also *Vita prima*, I. 9 ; Migne, 185, 252.

[6] William of St. Thierry, in *Vita prima*, I. 9 ; Migne, 185, 253.

2 A

prayer, sometimes used the consecrated wafer or holy water.[1] In Milan many persons possessed with evil spirits were healed.[2] As for the miracles performed on his tour along the Rhine from Constance and Basel to Cologne, when he was engaged in preaching the Second Crusade, Hermann, bishop of Constance, with nine others kept a record of them, declaring the very stones would cry out if they were not recorded.[3] After a sermon at Basel, says Gaufrid, a woman, who was mute, approached Bernard and after he had uttered a prayer, she spoke. A lame man walked and a blind man received his sight.[4] Thirty men, moved by the sight of Bernard's healing power, accompanied him back from Germany to France to take the monastic vow.[5]

Abælard and his pupil, Berengar, were exceptions to their age in expressing doubts about the genuineness of contemporary miracles, but they do not charge Bernard by name with being self-deceived or deceiving others. Morison, a writer of little enthusiasm, no credulity, and a large amount of cool, critical common sense, says that Bernard's "miracles are neither to be accepted with credulity nor denied with fury."[6] Neander recognized the superior excellence of the testimony,[7] refused to pronounce a sentence

---

[1] *Febricitantibus multis sanctus manus imponens et aquam benedictam porrigens ad bibendum, sanitatem obtinuit*, etc., Migne, 185, 278.

[2] The only case I have found which was not a case of healing in Bernard's miracles occurred at the dedication of the church of Foigny, where the congregation was pestered by swarms of flies. Bernard pronounced the words of excommunication against them and the next morning they were found dead and people shovelled them out with spades.

[3] *Vita prima*, VI.; Migne, 185, 374 sqq.

[4] *Vita prima*, IV. 5 sqq.; Migne, 185, 338-359. See Morison's remarks, 372 sqq.

[5] A strange story is told of Bernard's throwing dice with a gambler. The stake was Bernard's horse or the gambler's soul. Bernard entered into the proposition heartily and won. The gambler is said to have led a saintly life thereafter. *Gesta Romanorum*, Engl. trans. by Swan, p. 317.

[6] *Life of Bernard*, p. 66. Dr. Morison died 1905.

[7] *Der Heilige Bernhard*, I. 135-141; II. 92-95. See also Neander's *Ch. Hist*, Engl. trans. IV. 256 sq.

denying their genuineness, and seeks to explain them by the conditions of the age and the imposing personality of Bernard as in the case of those possessed with evil spirits.[1] A presumption against the miracles of Bernard, which can hardly be put aside, is the commonness of miracles in the mediæval convent and in the lives of eminent men like Norbert, not to speak of the miracles wrought at shrines, as at the shrine of Thomas à Becket and by contact with relics. On the other hand, there are few mortal men whom miracles would so befit as Bernard.

Bernard's activity was marked, all through, by a practical consideration for the needs of life, and his writings are full of useful suggestions adapted to help and ameliorate human conditions. He was a student by preference, but there were men in his day of more scholastic attainments than he. And yet in the department of speculative and controversial theology his writings also have their value. In his work on the Freedom of the Will[2] he advocated the position that the power to do good was lost by sin, and prevenient grace is required to incline the will to holiness. In his controversy with Abælard he developed his views on the Trinity and the atonement. In some of his positions he was out of accord with the theology and practice of the Roman Communion. He denied the immaculate conception of Mary[3] and accepted foot washing as one of the sacraments. In his views on baptism he was as liberal as the most liberal of his age in declaring that baptism was not indispensable to salvation when the opportunity is not afforded.[4]

[1] " When such works," Neander says in his history, " appear in connection with a governing Christian temper actuated by the spirit of love, they may perhaps be properly regarded as solitary workings of that higher power of life which Christ introduced into human nature." These words are adopted by Dr. Storrs, who says " it cannot be doubted that a most extraordinary force operated through Bernard on those who sought his assistance." *Life of Bernard*, p. 199 sq.　[3] *Ep.*, 174; Migne, 182, 332.

[2] *De gratia et libero arbitrio.*　　[4] *De baptismo aliisque questionibus.*

Severe at times as Bernard, the Churchman, from the standpoint of this tolerant age seems to be, the testimonies to his exalted moral eminence are too weighty to be set aside. Bernard's own writings give the final and abundant proof of his ethical quality. It shines through his works on personal religion, all those treatises and sermons which give him a place in the front rank of the mystics of all ages.[1]

William of St. Thierry, himself no mean theological writer, felt that in visiting Bernard's cell he had been "at the very altar of God." Joachim of Flore praised him in enthusiastic language and evidently regarded him as the model monk.[3] The impression upon Hildegard, the prophetess of the Rhine, was the same.[4] In his Memoir of St. Malachy, Bernard, as has been said, put "an image of his own beautiful and ardent soul."[5] No one but a deeply religious character could have written such a life. Malachy, the Irish archbishop, visited Clairvaux twice and on the second visit he remained to die, 1148. Bernard wrote: —

"Though he came from the West, he was truly the dayspring on high to us. With psalms and hymns and spiritual songs we followed our friend on his heavenward journey. He was taken by angels out of our hands. Truly he fell asleep. All eyes were fixed upon him, yet none could say when the spirit took its flight. When he was dead, we thought him to be alive; while yet alive, we thought him to be dead.[6] The same brightness and serenity were ever visible. Sorrow was changed into joy, faith had triumphed. He has entered into the joy of the Lord, and who am I to make lamentation over him? We pray, O Lord, that he who was our guest may be our leader, that we may reign with Thee and him for evermore. Amen."

[1] See chapter on Mysticism.

[2] *Domus ipsa incutiebat reverentiam sui ac si ingrederer ad altare Dei*, *Vita prima*, VII. 33; Migne, 185, 246.

[3] *Concordia*, V. 38. See Schott, *Die Gedanken des Abtes Joachim*, Brieger's Zeitschrift, 1902, 171.

[4] Hildegard's Works, *Ep.*, 29 ; Migne, 197, 189.

[5] Morison, p. 242.

[6] *Mortuus vivere et vivens mortuus putabatur*, *Vita St. Malachy*, XXXI. 74 ; Migne, 185, 1116. Tender as he is to his Irish friend, Bernard described the Irish people as utter barbarians in that age.

Bernard's sense of personal unworthiness was a controlling element in his religious experience.   In this regard he forms a striking contrast to the self-confidence and swagger of Abælard.   He relied with childlike trust upon the divine grace.   In one of his very last letters he begged his friend the abbot of Bonneval to be solicitous in prayer to the Saviour of sinners in his behalf.   His last days were not without sorrow.   His trusted secretary was found to have betrayed his confidence, and used his seal for his own purposes.   William of St. Thierry and other friends had been passing away.   Bernard's last journey was to Metz to compose a dispute between bishop Stephen and the duke of Lorraine.   Deutsch, perhaps the chief living authority on Bernard, says: " Religious warmth, *Genialität*, is the chief thing in his character and among his gifts." [1]   Harnack pays this tribute to him, that " he was the religious genius of the twelfth century, the leader of his age in religion." [2]   " Bernard," said Luther, — and he was not easily deceived by monkish pretension, — " Bernard loved Jesus as much as any one can." [3]   Ray Palmer has imparted to his version of Bernard's hymn its original religious fervor, —

> " Jesus, Thou Joy of loving hearts,
> Thou Fount of life, Thou Light of men,
> From the best bliss which earth imparts
> We turn unfilled to Thee again."

The encomium of Bernard's early biographer Alanus is high praise, but probably no man since the Apostles has deserved it more: " The majesty of his name was surpassed by his lowliness of heart," [4]

vincebat tamen sublimitatem nominis humilitas cordis.

[1] Herzog, II. 634

[2] *Dogmengeschichte*, III. 301.

[3] Bindseil, *Colloquia*, III. 152.   *Bernhardus hat den Jesus so lieb als einer sein mag.*

[4] *Vita secunda*, XVII.; Migne, 185, 498.

§ 66. *The Augustinians, Carthusians, Carmelites, and other Orders.*

Among the greater orders which came into existence before 1200 are the Augustinians, the Premonstrants, the Carthusians, and the Carmelites.

1. The Augustinians were a distinct family from the Benedictines, followed the so-called rule of St. Augustine, and were divided into the canons regular of St. Augustine and the mendicant friars of St. Augustine.

The bodies of canons regular were numerous, but their organization was not compact like that of the stricter monastic orders,[1] They were originally communities of secular clerics, and not conventual associations. They occupied a position between the strict monastic existence and an independent clerical life. Their origin can be assigned to no exact date. As early as the eleventh century a rule, ascribed to St. Augustine, appeared in several forms. It was professed by the clerical groups forming the cathedral chapters, and by bodies of priests associated with other churches of prominence.[2] The various church services, as, for example, the service of song, and the enforced rule of celibacy, encouraged or demanded a plurality of clergymen for a church.

Moved by the strong impulse in the direction of conventual communities, these groups inclined to the communal life and sought some common rule of discipline. For it they looked back to Augustine of Hippo, and took his household

[1] See art. *Augustiner*, in Herzog, II. 254 sqq., and in Wetzer-Welte, I. 1655 sqq.   Theod. Kolde, *D. deutsche Augustiner Congregation und Joh. von Staupitz*, Gotha, 1879.

[2] At Campell, near Paris, there were not less than fifty priests, whose number was reduced by Innocent III. to twenty-two.   See Hurter, III. 375. The terms *canonicus sæcularis* and *regularis* do not occur before the twelfth century.   Up to that time they were known as *clerici religiosi, clerici regulares, clerici professi, clerici communiter viventes*, etc.   So Denifle, *Archiv für Lit. und Kirchengeschichte* for 1885, p. 174.   He quotes Amort, *Vetus disciplina canonicorum regul. et sæcul.*, Venice, 1747, I. 333.

as their model. We know that Augustine had living with him a group of clerics. We also know that he commended his sister for associating herself with other women and withdrawing from the world, and gave her some advice. But so far as is known Augustine prescribed no definite code such as Benedict afterwards drew up, either for his own household or for any other community.

About 750 Chrodegang, bishop of Metz, drew up a code for his cathedral chapter, whom he enjoined to live together in common,[1] and here and there in Germany isolated communities of this kind were formed.

In the twelfth century we find many groups of clerics who adopted what began to be known as the rule of St. Augustine.[2] Under Innocent III. organizations were formed by William Langlois of the Paris University, and others under the name canons regular to live distinctly under this code.   Innocent IV.[3] and Alexander IV., 1256, definitely recognized the rule.

The Augustinian rule established a community of goods. Even gifts went into the common fund. The clerics ate together and slept in one dormitory. They wore a common dress, and no one on returning his suit to the clothing room retained any peculiar right to it. The papal attempts to unite these groups into a close organization proved to be in vain.[4] In England the Augustinian canons had charge of Carlisle cathedral.

---

[1] Chrodegang provided a common table for the clergy of his chapter, and a common dormitory. The Roman synods of 1059, 1063, recommended priests to have their revenues in common.

[2] The tradition runs that this rule was prescribed by Innocent II., 1139, for all canons regular. Helyot, II. 21.

[3] In a bull, Dec. 16, 1243, Innocent speaks of the *regula S. Augustini et ordo.* See Potthast, p. 954. The most distinguished convent of regular canons in France was the convent of St. Victor.

[4] The cathedral of Bristol is built up from the old abbey of St. Augustine. The Augustinian, or Austin, canons were also called the Black Canons in England. They were very popular there. St. Botolph's, Colchester, their first English house, was established about 1100. At the suppression of the mon-

The Augustinian hermits, or Austin friars, as they were called in England, were monastics in the true sense. They arose after the canons regular,[1] adopted the rule of St. Augustine, and were mendicants. In the closing period of the Middle Ages they were addicted to preaching. To this order John of Staupitz and Luther belonged.[2]

The rule of St. Augustine was also adopted with modification by the Premonstrants, the Gilbertines of England,[3] and other orders, and was made the basis by Dominic of his first rule.

2. The Premonstrants adopted the Augustinian rule, were called from their dress White Canons, and grew with great rapidity.[4] They had houses from Livland to Palestine, and from Great Britain to Spain. Their founder, Norbert, born about 1080 in Xantes, on the Lower Rhine, was a great preacher and one of the most influential men of his age. Thrown from his horse during a storm, he determined to devote himself in earnest to religion. He gave up his position in the Cologne Cathedral and entered the Benedictine Convent of Sigeberg. Norbert then travelled about in Germany and France as a preacher of repentance,[5] calling the people

asteries there were one hundred and seventy houses in England, and a much larger number in Ireland. Gasquet, p. 225. See W. G. D. Fletcher, *The Blackfriars in Oxford.*   [1] See Hurter, III. 238.

[2] In England they had thirty-two friaries at the time of the dissolution. Gasquet, 241.

[3] The Gilbertines, founded by St. Gilbert, rector of Sandringham, about 1140, were confined to England. There were twenty-six houses at the time of the suppression of the monasteries. The convents for men and women used a common church.

[4] Norbert's *Works and Life* are given in Migne, vol. 170, and his *Life* in *Mon. Ger.* XII., 670 sqq.; Germ. trans. by Hertel, in *Geschichtschreiber der deutschen Vorzeit*, Leipzig, 1881. See also Hauck, IV. 350–66; J. von Walter, *Die ersten Wanderprediger Frankreichs*, vol. II. Leipzig, 1906, pp. 119–129, and the art. *Prœmonstratenser*, X. 267 sqq., and Norbert, IX. 448 sqq., in Wetzer-Welte, and *Prœmonstratenser*, in Herzog, XV. 606 sqq., and the literature there given; and Gasquet, *The Engl. Prœmonstratensians*, in transactions of the Royal Hist. Soc., vol. XVII. London, 1903.

[5] Walter puts Norbert in the group of the itinerant preachers of the age.

together by a sheep's bell. With others like-minded with himself he settled, 1119, in the woods at Coucy, near Laon, France, giving the spot the name of Præmonstratum, or Prémontré, the designated field,[1] with reference to his having been directed to it by a higher power. The order secured papal sanction 1126, and received, like other orders, special papal privileges. Innocent III. bespoke the special intercession of the Premonstrants as he did that of the Cistercians. The first rule forbade meat and eggs, cheese and milk. As in the case of the Cistercians, their meals were limited to two dishes. At a later date the rule against meat was modified. Lay brethren were introduced and expected to do the work of the kitchen and other manual services. The theological instruction was confined to a few prayers, and the members were not allowed to read books.[2]

Norbert in 1126 was made archbishop of Magdeburg and welcomed the opportunity to introduce the order in Northeastern Germany. He joined Bernard in supporting Innocent II. against the antipope Anacletus II. He died 1134, at Magdeburg, and was canonized in 1582. Peter the Venerable and Bernard of Clairvaux praised the order and Norbert himself as a man who stood near to God.[3] Miracles were ascribed to him, but Abælard ridiculed the claim.

The almost incredible number of one thousand houses is claimed for this order in its flourishing period. There was also an order of Premonstrant nuns, which is said to have numbered ten thousand women during Norbert's lifetime.[4] Their earliest settlement in England was at Newhouse, Lincolnshire, 1143. Norbert and Bruno, the Carthusian, were the only Germans who established monastic orders in this period.[5]

[1] *Pratum monstratum.*
[2] Hurter, IV. 206.
[3] Bernard, *Sermon*, XXII.; *Ep.*, 56.
[4] See Hurter, IV. 208.
[5] In England there were more than thirty Premonstrant convents at the suppression of the monasteries. Bayham and Easley are their best preserved abbeys.

3. More original and strict were the Carthusians,[1] who
got their name from the seat of their first convent, Chartreuse, *Cartusium*, fourteen miles from Grenoble, southeast of
Lyons. They were hermits, and practised an asceticism
excelling in severity any of the other orders of the time.[2]
The founder, St. Bruno, was born in Cologne, and became
chancellor of the cathedral of Rheims. Disgusted with the
vanities of the world,[3] he retired with some of his pupils to
a solitary place, Saisse Fontaine, in the diocese of Langres,
which he subsequently exchanged for Chartreuse.[4] The
location was a wild spot in the mountains, difficult of access,
and for a large part of the year buried in snow. Bruno was
called by Urban II. to Rome, and after acting as papal adviser, retired to the Calabrian Mountains and established
a house. There he died, 1101. He was canonized 1514. In
1151 the number of Carthusian houses was fourteen, and

---

[1] *Consuetudines Carthusienses*, printed among Bruno's Works in Migne,
153, 651-759. Peter Dorland, *Chronicon Carthusianæ*, Col. 1608. For
literature see Wetzer-Welte, art. *Karthäuser*, VII. 203, and the art. Bruno,
vol. II. 1356-63. Bruno's Works in Migne, 152, 153. In his Com. on the
Romans he anticipates Luther by inserting *sola*, "*alone*" in Rom. 3 : 28,
"a man is justified by faith *alone*, without the works of the law." See Dr.
Fr. Duesterdieck, *Studien u. Kritiken*, 1903, p. 506.

[2] The device of the order is a globe surmounted by a lion with the motto
Stat crux dum volvitur orbis, "The cross stands while the globe turns."

[3] The following legend was invented to account for Bruno's decision. In
1082 he was present at the mortuary services over Raymond, canon of Notre
Dame, Paris. When the words were said, " *Quantas habes iniquitates et
peccata ?* " " how many sins and iniquities hast thou ? " the dead man rose up
and replied, " *justo dei judicio accusatus sum*," " I am accused by the just
judgment of God." The next day at the repetition of the words, the dead rose
again and exclaimed, " *justo dei judicio judicatus sum*," " I am judged by the
just judgment of God." The third day the dead man rose for the third time
and cried out, " *justo dei judicio condemnatus sum*," " I am condemned by
the just judgment of God." This incident was inserted into the Roman
Breviary, but removed by order of Urban VIII., 1631. Hergenröther says
the legend is still defended by the Carthusians. *Kirchengesch.*, II. 353.

[4] Peter the Venerable says of a visit to Chartreuse, *Ep.*, VI. 24, *inaccessi-
biles pene nivibus et glacie altissimas rupes non abhorrui*, "I shrank not
back from the high rocks made inaccessible by snow and ice." Hurter's
description, IV. 150, makes the location attractive.

they gradually increased to one hundred and sixty-eight. The order was formally recognized by Alexander III., 1170.

The first Carthusian statutes were committed to writing by the fifth prior Guigo, d. 1137. The rule now in force was fixed in 1578, and reconfirmed by Innocent XI., 1682.[1] The monks lived in cells around a central church, at first two and two, and then singly.[2] They divided their time between prayer, silence, and work, which originally consisted chiefly in copying books. The services celebrated in common in the church were confined to vespers and matins. The other devotions were performed by each in seclusion. The prayers were made in a whisper so as to avoid interfering with others. They sought to imitate the Thebaid anchorites in rigid self-mortification. Peter the Venerable has left a description of their severe austerities. Their dress was thin and coarse above the dress of all other monks.[3] Meat, fat, and oil were forbidden; wine allowed, but diluted with water. They ate only bean-bread. They flagellated themselves once each day during the fifty days before Easter, and the thirty days before Christmas. When one of their number died, each of the survivors said two psalms, and the whole community met and took two meals together to console one another for the loss.[4] No woman was allowed to cross the threshold. For hygienic purposes, the monks bled themselves five times a year, and were shaved six times a year.[5] They avoided adornment in their

---

[1] *Nova collectio statutorum Ord. Carthusiensis*, Paris, 1682.

[2] For the plan of a Carthusian monastery, see Dr. Venables' art. *Abbey*, in "Enc. Brit.," I. 20 sq.

[3] *Vestes vilissimas ac super omne religionis propositum abjectissimas ipsoque visu horrendas assumpserunt.* Pet. Ven., *De miraculis*, II. 28.

[4] A movement among the Carthusians to pass over into other orders, where the discipline was less rigid, was severely rebuked by Innocent III. Hurter, IV. 161.

[5] *Medicinis, excepto cauterio et sanguinis minutione perraro utimur*, quoted by Hurter, IV. 154, from the Constitutions of Guigo. Bleeding for medicinal purposes seems to have been common in convents. It was

churches and church dignities.[1]   They borrowed books from Cluny and other convents for the purpose of copying them.[2] The heads of the Carthusian convents are called priors, not abbots.   In its earlier history the order received highest praise from Innocent III. and Peter the Venerable, Bernard, and Peter of Celle.   Bernard shrank from interrupting their holy quiet by letters, and lauded their devotion to God.   So at a later time Petrarch, after a visit to their convent in Paris, penned a panegyric of the order.

In England the Carthusians were not popular.[3]   They never had more than eleven houses.   The first establishment was founded by Henry II., at Witham, 1180.   The famous Charterhouse in London (a corruption of the French Chartreuse), founded in 1371, was turned into a public school, 1611.   In Italy the more elaborate houses of the order were the Certosa di San Casciano near Florence, the Certosa at Pisa, and the Certosa Maria degli Angeli in Rome.[4]

In recent times the monks of the Chartreuse became famous for the Chartreuse liqueur which they distilled.   In its preparation the young buds of pine trees were used.

practised in the convent of Heisterbach, Cæsar of Heisterbach, *Dial.*, XI. 2. According to the life of Bernard of Thiron, it was the custom in some convents for monks suffering from headache or other physical ailments to have the abbot place his hands on their bodies, trusting to his miraculous power for healing.   See Walter, *Die ersten Wanderprediger Frankreichs*, Leipzig, 1906, II. p. 50.

[1] And yet they have furnished at least four cardinals, seventy archbishops and bishops, and have had rich churches noted for their works of art like the one in Naples, or the church at Pavia, where lapis lazuli is freely used.   See Hurter, IV. 158.

[2] Pet. Ven., *Epp.*, I. 24, IV. 38.   Peter gives a list of the books he sent.

[3] " The discipline was too rigid, the loneliness too dreadful for our tastes and climate."   Jessopp, *The Coming of the Friars*, p. 125.

[4] The order was suppressed in France at the time of the Revolution.   The monks, however, were permitted to return to Grand Chartreuse in 1816, paying a rental of 3000 francs to the government.   The mother convent has again been broken up by the Associations Law of 1903.   There were at that time one hundred and fifty monks in the house.   Some of them went to Piedmont, and others to Tarragona, Spain, where they have set up a distillery for their precious liqueur.

4. The Carmelites, or the Order of the Blessed Mary the Virgin of Mt. Carmel, had their origin during the Crusades, 1156.[1] The legend carries their origin back to Elijah, whose first disciples were Jonah, Micah, and Obadiah. Obadiah's wife became the first abbess of the female community. Their history has been marked by much division within the order and bitter controversies with other orders.

Our first trustworthy notice is derived from Phocas, a Greek monk, who visited Mt. Carmel in 1185. Berthold of Calabria, a Crusader, made a vow under the walls of Antioch that in case the Christians were victorious over Zenki, he would devote himself to the monastic life. The prayer was answered, and Berthold with ten companions established himself on Mt. Carmel.[2] The origin of the order became the subject of a violent dispute between the Carmelites and the Jesuits. The Jesuit Papebroch precipitated it in 1668 by declaring that Berthold was the founder. He was answered by the Carmelite Daniel[3] and others who carried the origin back to Elijah. Appeal was made to Innocent XII., who, in 1698, in the bull *redemptoris*, commanded the two orders to maintain silence till the papal chair should render a decision. This has not yet been done.[4]

The community received its rule about 1208 from Albert, afterwards patriarch of Constantinople. It was confirmed

---

[1] *Ordo B. M. V. de Monte Carmelo* is the name given by Innocent IV. The brethren are called *fratres eremiti de monte Carmelo*, by Honorius III., in his sanction of the order, 1226. The art. *Carmelite*, in Wetzer-Welte, II. 1966–1976, and *Karmeliter*, in Herzog, X. 84–88, give a good account and contain lists of literature. Potthast, I. No. 7524.

[2] The convent on Mt. Carmel is a conspicuous object as you approach the coast from the Mediterranean, and from the hills round about Nazareth. The present building was erected in 1828, and is an hour's walk from Haifa. Napoleon used the former buildings for a hospital during his Syrian campaign.

[3] *Speculum Carmelitarum seu historia Eliani ordinis*, 4 vols. Antwerp, 1680.

[4] Benedict XIII., in 1725, gave quasi-sanction to the order's claim by permitting it to erect a statue to Elijah in St. Peter's. It bears the inscription *Universus ordo Carmelitarum fundatori suo St. Eliœ prophetœ erexit.*

by Honorius III., 1226. Its original sixteen articles gave
the usual regulations against eating meat, enjoined daily
silence, from vespers to tierce (6 P.M. to 9 A.M.), and provided that the monks live the hermit's life in cells like the
Carthusians. The dress was at first a striped garment,
white and black, which was afterwards changed for brown.

With the Christian losses in Palestine, the Carmelites began to migrate westwards. In 1238 they were in Cyprus,
and before the middle of the thirteenth century they were
settled in far Western Europe. The first English house was
at Alnwick, and a general chapter was held at Aylesford,
1246.·

From the general of the order, Simon Stock, an Englishman (1245–65), dates the veneration of the scapulary,[1] a
jacket which he received from the Virgin Mary. It exempts,
so the story runs, those who die with it on, from the fires of
purgatory. Mary promised to go down to purgatory every
Saturday, and release those who have worn it. The story is
included in the Breviary,[2] and was pronounced true and to
be believed by all, by Benedict XIV. In 1322 John XXII.,
in obedience to a vision, issued the famous bull *Sabbatina*,
which promised to all entering the order, deliverance from
purgatory by Mary, the first Saturday after their decease.[3]

---

[1] The Carmelites are often called the Brotherhood of the Scapulary. The
scapulary is a sleeveless jacket covering the breast and back, and was
originally worn over the other garments when the monk was at work. The
garment has been the frequent subject of papal decree down to Leo XIII.,
1892. July 16 has been set apart since 1587 as a special festival of the scapulary, and is one of the feasts of the Virgin. A work has been written on
the proper use of the scapulary, by Brocard: *Recueil des instructions sur la
devotion au St. Scapulaire de Notre Dame de Monte Carmelo*, Gand, 4th
ed. 1875. Simon Stock was one hundred when he died.

[2] Hergenröther-Kirsch, *Kirchengesch.*, II. 362, says it is introduced as a
matter of "pious opinion," *fromme Meinung.*

[3] The original bull has not been found, and its authenticity has been a subject of warm dispute in the Catholic church. The pertinent words of Mary
are *Ego mater gratiose descendam sabbato post eorum mortem et, quot inve-
niam in purgatorio, liberabo.* "I, mother, will graciously descend on the

After the success of the Franciscans and Dominicans, the Carmelites, with the sanction of Innocent IV., adopted the practice of mendicancy, 1245, and the cœnobite life was substituted for life in solitary cells. The rules concerning clothing and food were relaxed to meet the climatic conditions of Europe.

A division took place in the order in 1378. The wing, holding to the stricter rule as confirmed by Innocent IV., is known as the Carmelites of the Ancient Observance. Both wings have their respective generals. The Carmelite name most famous in the annals of piety is that of St. Theresa, the Spanish saint who joined herself to the Carmelites, 1533. She aided in founding seventeen convents for women and fourteen for monks. This new branch, the Barefoot Carmelites, spread to different parts of Europe, Mt. Carmel, Africa, Mexico, and other countries. The monks wear leathern sandals, and the nuns a light shoe.[1]

Of the other numerous monastic orders, the following may be mentioned. The Antonites, or Brothers of the Hospital of St. Antonius[2] are named after the Egyptian hermit, St. Anthony. The founder, Gaston, prayed to St. Anthony for the deliverance of his son from a disease, then widely prevalent, and called St. Anthony's fire, *morbus sacer*. The prayer was answered, and the father and his son devoted themselves to a religious life. The order was sanctioned by

Sabbath after their death, and whomever I find in purgatory I will free." One ground for doubting the authenticity of the bull is that Mary promises to forgive sins. Paul V., in 1613, decreed that this "pious faith" should be preached. See art. *Sabbatina*, in Wetzer-Welte, X. 1444-1447.

[1] By the decision of Clement VIII., 1593, the Barefoot monks became an independent order, and elect their own general superior. Hurter, IV. 213, concludes his short account of the Carmelites by saying, that among other things which they used to exaggerate to a ridiculous extent was the number of their houses, which they gave at 7500, and of their monks, which they gave as 180,000.

[2] Falco, *Antonianæ hist. compendium*, Lyons, 1534. Uhlhorn, *D. christl. Liebesthätigkeit d. Mittelalters*, Stuttg. 1884, 178-186, 343 sqq.

Urban II., 1095, and was intended to care for the sick and poor. In 1118 it received from Calixtus II. the church of St. Didier de Mothe, containing St. Anthony's bones. In 1218 Honorius III. gave the members permission to take monastic vows, and in 1296 Boniface VIII. imposed on them the Augustinian rule. They had houses in France, Germany, Hungary, and Italy. It used to be the custom on St. Anthony's day to lead horses and cattle in front of their convent in Rome to receive a form of blessing.[1]

The Trinitarians, *ordo sanctissima Trinitatis de redemptione captivorum*, had for their mission the redemption of Christian captives out of the hands of the Saracens and Moors. Their founder was John of Matha (1160–1213). The order was also called the *ordo asinorum*, Order of the Asses, from the fact that its members rode on asses and never on horseback.[2]

The order of Font Evraud (*Fontis Ebraldi in Poitiers*) had the peculiarity that monks and nuns were conjoined in associated cloisters, and that the monks were under the supervision of an abbess. The abbess was regarded as the representative of the Virgin Mary, and the arrangement as in conformity with the word of Christ, placing John under the care of Mary. A church built between the male and female cloisters was used in common. The order was founded by Robert d' Abrissel (d. 1117), whom Urban II. heard preach, and commissioned as a preacher, 1096. Robert was born in Brittany, and founded, 1095, a convent at Craon. He was a preacher of great popular power. The

---

[1] The Antonites regarded St. Anthony as the patron of stable animals, a view popularly held in Italy. An example of this belief is given in the *Life of Philip Schaff*, 56 sq.

[2] The Trinitarians were also called Maturines, from their house in Paris near St. Mathurine's chapel. They had a few houses in England. A Spanish order with the same design, the *Ordo B. V. M. de Mercede redemptionis captivorum*, was founded by Peter Nolasco and Raymond of Pennaforte. See Hurter, IV. 219.

nuns devoted themselves especially to the reclamation of fallen women.[1] A special rule forbade the nuns to care for their hair, and another rule commanded them to shave their heads three times a year.[2]

The Order of Grammont, founded by Stephen of Auvergne, deserves mention for the high rank it once held in France. It enjoyed the special patronage of Louis VII. and other French sovereigns, and had sixty houses in France. It was an order of hermits. Arrested while on a pilgrimage, by sickness, Stephen was led by the example of the hermits of Calabria to devote himself to the hermit life. These monks went as far in denying themselves the necessities of life as it is possible to do and yet survive,[3] but monks and nuns became notorious for licentiousness and prostitution.[4]

The Brothers of the Sack[5] wore a dress of rough material cut in the shape of a bag. They had convents in different countries, including England, where they continued to have houses till the suppression of the monasteries. They abstained entirely from meat, and drank only water. The Franciscans derisively called them *Bushmen* (Boscarioli). They were indefatigable beggars. The Franciscan chronicler, Salimbene,[6] is sure Gregory X. was divinely inspired in abolishing the order, for " Christian folk were wearied and burdened with the multitude of beggars."

---

[1] The last abbess died 1799. Since 1804 the abbey of Font Evraud has been used as a house for the detention of convicts. Henry II. of England and Richard Cœur de Lion were buried at Font Evraud. For the literature of the order, see Herzog, VI. 125, and J. von Walter, *Die ersten Wanderprediger Frankreichs, Studien zur Gesch. des Mönchthums, Robert von Abrissel*, I. Leipzig, 1903.

[2] *Ut capillos non nutriant suós.* Walter, *Wanderprediger*, II. 112.

[3] Hurter, IV. 140. See art. *Grammont*, in Wetzer-Welte, VI. 990 sqq.

[4] Walter, II. 143.

[5] *Fratres saccati, fratres de sacco, saccophori*, etc. See art. *Sackbrüder*, in Herzog, XVII. 327. Gasquet, 241 sq.

[6] See Coulton, p. 301.

§ 67.   *Monastic Prophets.*

St. Hildegard and Joachim of Flore.

Literature. — Hildegard's works in Migne, vol. 197, and some not there given in Pitra : *Analecta sacra.* For a list see Preger: *Geschichte der deutschen Mystik*, I. 13–36. — *Lives* by Godefrid and Theodorich, contemporaries in Migne. — Dahl, Mainz, 1832. — Clarius, with translation of Hildegard's letters, 2 vols. Regensburg, 1854. — Richaud, Aix, 1876. — J. P. Schmelzeis, Freiburg, 1897. — P. Franche, Paris, 1903. — Benrath, in Herzog, VIII. 71 sq. — Hildegard's *Causæ et curæ*, ed. by Kaiser, Leipzig, 1903, is a sort of mediæval manual of medicine.

Joachim's published works, *Liber concordiæ novi et veteris Testamenti*, Venice, 1519 ; *Expositio in Apocalypsin and Psalterium decem chordarum*, Venice, 1527. The errors of Joachim are given in Mansi, xxii. 981 and Denifle: *Chartularium Univ., Par I.* 272–275. — Salimbene : *Chronicon*, Parma, 1857 ; Coulton's trans., London, 1906. — Luna Consentinus, d. 1224, perhaps an amanuensis : *Synopsis virtutum b. Joach.* in *Ughelli, Italia sacra*, IX. 205 sqq. — Gervaise : *Hist. de l'abbé Joachim*, 2 vols. Paris, 1745. — Reuter : *Gesch. der Aufklärung*, 1877, pp. 191–218. — Renan in *Nouvelles études d'hist. rel.*, Paris, 1884, pp. 217–323. — *Denifle : *Das Evangelium æternum und die Commission zu Anagni*, in *Archiv für Lit.- und Kirchengesch.*, 1885, pp. 49–142. *Döllinger : *Die Papstfabeln des Mittelalters*, 2d ed. by J. Friedrich, Stuttgart, 1890 ; Engl. trans. of 1st ed. by H. B. Smith, N.Y., 1872, pp. 364–391. — *Artt : *Joachim*, in Wetzer-Welte by Ehrle, VI. 1471–1480, and in Herzog by Deutsch, IX. 227–232. — *E. Schott: *Die Gedanken Joachims* in *Brieger's Zeitschrift*, 1902, pp. 157–187.

The monasteries also had their prophets. Men's minds, stirred by the disasters in Palestine, and by the spread of heresy in Europe, here and there saw beyond the prevailing ritual of church and convent to a new era in which, however, neither hierarchy nor convent would be given up. In the twelfth century the spirit of prophecy broke out almost simultaneously in convents on the Rhine and in Southern Italy. Its chief exponents were Hildegard of Bingen, Elizabeth of Schönau, and Joachim, the abbot of Flore.[1] They rebuked the clerical corruption of

---

[1] Among others who were expecting the millennium soon to dawn, was Norbert, who wrote to St. Bernard that the age in which he lived was the age of antichrist. Bernard, *Ep.*, 56 ; Migne, 182, 50, wrote back taking a contrary view.

their time, saw visions, and Joachim was the seer of a new age.

Hildegard (1098–1179), abbess of the Benedictine convent of Disebodenberg, near Bingen on the Rhine, was the most prominent woman in the church of her day.[1] What Bernard of Clairvaux was to France, that, though in a lesser degree, she was to Germany. She received letters from four popes, Eugenius, Anastasius, Adrian, and Alexander III., from the emperors Konrad III. and Frederick Barbarossa, from Bernard and many ecclesiastics in high office as well as from persons of humble position. Her intercessions were invoked by Frederick, by Konrad for his son,[2] and by Bernard. Persons from afar were moved to seek her aid, as for example the patriarch of Jerusalem who had heard that a "divine force operated in and through her."[3] Her convent was moved from Disebodenberg to Rupertsberg and she finally became abbess of the convent of Eibingen.

Infirm of body, Hildegard was, by her own statement, the recipient of visions from her childhood. As she wrote to St. Bernard, she saw them "not with the external eye of sense but with the inner eye." The deeper meanings of Scripture "touched her breast and burnt into her soul like a flame."[4] Again she said that, when she was forty-two years old, a fiery light of great brightness, coming from the open heavens, transfused her brain and inflamed her whole heart and breast like a flame as the sun lightens everything upon which his

---

[1] The name of Héloïse was perhaps as widely known, but it was for her connection with Abelard, not for her works in the Church. The Latin form of Hildegard is Hildegardis. M. Paris, Luard's Ed., V. 195, in his summary of the events of 1200–1250, mentions Hildegard and Elizabeth of Thuringia as the prominent religious female characters of the period, but Hildegard died 1177.   [2] *Ep.*, XXVI. sq. ; Migne, 197, 185 sq.

[3] *Ep.*, XXII.   On the other hand, Hildegard asked Bernard to pray for her.

[4] *animam meam sicut flammam comburens*, Migne, 197, 190. St. Bernard, writing to Hildegard, spoke of the "sweetness of her holy love," and Hildegard compares the abbot of Clairvaux to the eagle and addresses him as the most mild of fathers, *mitissime pater*.

rays fall.[1]   What she saw, she saw not in dreams nor in
sleep nor in a frenzied state nor in hidden places but while
she was awake and in pure consciousness, using the eyes and
ears of her inner man according to the will of God.[2]   Eugenius III., on a visit to Treves, 1148, investigated her revelations, recognized the genuineness of her miracles, and
encouraged her to continue in her course.[3]   Bernard spoke
of her fame of making known heavenly secrets through the
illumination of the Holy Ghost.

It is reported by contemporaries of this godly woman that
scarcely a sick person came to her without being healed.[4]
Her power was exerted in the convent and outside of it and
upon persons of both sexes.   People from localities as distant as Sweden sought her healing power.   Sometimes the
medium used was a prayer, sometimes a simple word of command, sometimes water which, as in one case, healed paralysis
of the tongue.

As a censor of the Church, Hildegard lamented the low
condition of the clergy, announced that the Cathari would
be used to stir up christendom to self-purification, called
attention to the Scriptures and the Catholic faith as the
supreme fonts of authority, and bade men look for salvation
not to priests but to Christ.

She was also an enthusiastic student of nature.   Her
treatises on herbs, trees, and fishes are among the most
elaborate on natural objects of the Middle Ages.   She gives
the properties of no less than two hundred and thirteen
herbs or their products, and regarded heat and cold as
very important qualities of plant life.   They are treated
with an eye to their medicinal virtue.   Butter, she says, is

---

[1] *non visiones in somnis, nec dormiens, nec in phrenesi, nec corporeis oculis
aut auribus exterioris, nec in abditis locis percepi, sed eas vigilans, circum-
spiciens in pura mente oculis et auribus interioris hominis*, etc.   Scivias, I.
Præfatio, Migne, 197, 384.

[2] Scivias. See Migne, 197, 93. This is the chief collection of her visions.
Migne, 197, 383–739.   [3] *Ep.*, I.; Migne, 197, 146.   [4] Migne, 197, 117.

good for persons in ill health and suffering from feverish
blood and the butter of cows is more wholesome than the
butter of sheep and goats. Licorice,[1] which is mildly heat-
ing, gives a clear voice and a suave mind, clarifies the eyes,
and prepares the stomach for the process of digestion. The
" basilisca," which is cold, if placed under the tongue, restores
the power of speech to the palsied and, when cooked in
wine with honey added, will cure fevers provided it is drunk
frequently during the night.[2]

A kindred spirit to Hildegard was Elizabeth of Schönau,
who died 1165 at the age of thirty-six.[3] She was an inmate of
the convent of Schönau, not far from Bingen, and also had visions which were connected with epileptic conditions. In her
visions she saw Stephen, Laurentius, and many of the other
saints. In the midst of them usually stood "the virgin of virgins, the most glorious mother of God, Mary."[4] When she
saw St. Benedict, he was in the midst of his monkish host,
monachalis turba. Elizabeth represented herself as being
"rapt out of the body into an ecstasy." [5] In the interest of
purity of life she did not shrink from rebuking even the archbishop of Treves and from pronouncing the Apostolic chair
possessed with pride and filled with iniquity and impiety.
On one occasion she saw Christ sitting at the judgment with
Pilate, Judas, and those who crucified him on his left hand
and also, alas! a great company of men and women whom
she recognized as being of her order.[6] Hildegard and Elizabeth have a place in the annals of German mysticism.

Joachim of Flore,[7] d. 1202, the monastic prophet of South-

---

[1] *de plantis*, Migne, 197, 1139.   [2] Migne, 197, 1210.

[3] Her writings are given in Migne, 195, 119–196. First complete edition
by F. W. C. Roth : *Die Visionen der heiligen Elizabeth*, Brünn, 1884.
See Preger: *Gesch. d. deutschen Mystik*, 1, 37–43.   [4] Migne, 195, 146.

[5] a *corpore rapta sum in exstasim*, p. 135, or *eram in exstasi et vidi*, p. 145.

[6] Migne, 195, 146.

[7] After the convent St. Johannes in Flore, which he founded. The members of Joachim's order are called in the papal bull, *Florentii fratres*, Potthast, No. 2092, vol. I. 182.

ern Europe, exercised a wide influence by his writings, especially through the adoption of his views by the Spiritual wing
of the Franciscan order.   He was first abbot of the Cistercian convent of Corazza in Calabria, and then became the
founder and abbot of St. John in Flore.   Into this convent
he introduced a stricter rule than the rule of the Cistercians.
It became the centre of a new order which was sanctioned
by Cœlestin III., 1196.

Joachim enjoyed the reputation of a prophet during his
lifetime.[1]   He had the esteem of Henry VI., and was encouraged in his exegetical studies by Lucius III. and other
popes.   After his death his views became the subject of conciliar and papal examination.   The Fourth Lateran condemned his treatment of the Trinity as defined by Peter the
Lombard.   Peter had declared that the Father, Son, and
Holy Spirit constitute a certain supreme essence, *quœdam
summa res*, and this, according to Joachim, involved a substitution of a quaternity for the Trinity.   Those who adopted
Joachim's view were condemned as heretics, but Joachim and
the convent of Flore were distinctly excepted from condemnation.[2]

Joachim's views on the doctrine of the Trinity are of slight
importance.   The abbot has a place in history by his theory
of historical development and his eschatology.   His opinions
are set forth in three writings of whose genuineness there is
no question, an exposition of the Psalms, an exposition of the
Apocalypse, and a Concord of the Old and New Testaments.[3]

---

[1] When Richard Cœur de Lion was in Sicily on his way to Palestine in
1190, he was moved by Joachim's fame to send for him.   The abbot interpreted to him John's prophecy of antichrist, whom he declared was already
born, and would in time be elevated to the Apostolic chair and strive against
everything called of God.   De Hoveden, Engl. trans., II. pp. 177 sqq.

[2] Joachim had set forth his views against the Lombard in a tract to which
the council referred.   See Mansi, xxii., and Hefele-Knöpfler, V. 880 sq.

[3] Joachim, in a list, 1200, gives these three writings and also mentions
works against the Jews and on the articles of the Christian faith.   Schott, p. 170,

Interwoven with his prophecies is Joachim's theory of historical development. There are three ages in history. The Old Testament age has its time of beginning and bloom. So has that of the New Testament. But a third age is to follow. The basis for this theory of three periods is found in a comparison of the Old and New Testaments, a comparison which reveals a parallelism between the leading periods of the history of Israel and the periods of Christian history. This parallelism was disclosed to Joachim on an Easter night, and made as clear as day.

The first of the three ages was the age of the Father, the second the age of the Son, of the Gospel, and the sacraments, the third, the age of the Holy Spirit which was yet to come. The three were represented by Peter, Paul, and John. The first was an age of law, the second of grace, the third of more grace. The first was characterized by fear, the second by faith, the third was to be marked by charity. The first was the age of servants, the second of freedmen, the third of friends. The first brought forth water, the second wine, the third was to bring forth oil. The first was as the light of the stars, the second of the dawn, the third of the perfect day. The first was the age of the married, and corresponded to the flesh; the second of priests, with the elements of the flesh and the Spirit mixed; the third of monks, and was to be wholly spiritual. Each of these ages had a beginning, a maturity, and an end.[1] The first began with Adam, and entered upon its maturity with Abraham. The second began in the

---

counts twenty-four works, genuine and ungenuine, which are ascribed to him. Among those pronounced ungenuine are the commentaries on Jeremiah and Isaiah which were much used by the Franciscans from the middle of the thirteenth century on. They call Rome, Babylon and show a bitter hostility to the pope, representations which are in conflict with Joachim's genuine writings. They also abound in detailed prophecies of events which actually occurred. "If these books were genuine," says Döllinger, p. 369, "the exact fulfilment of the many predictions would present the most wonderful phenomenon in the history of prophecy."

[1] *principium, fructificatio, finis.*

days of Elijah, and entered upon its maturity with Christ.
The third began in the days of St. Benedict in the sixth century. Its maturity had already begun in the days of Joachim
himself. The consummation was to begin in 1260.

The Gospel of the letter is temporal not eternal, and
gives way in the third period to the Eternal Gospel, Rev.
14 : 6. Then the spiritual meaning of the Gospel will
be fully known. Joachim did not mean to deny the permanent authority of the two Testaments, when he put into
his third period the full understanding of them, in the spiritual sense, and the complete embodiment of their teachings
in life and conduct. The Eternal Gospel he described, not
as a newly written revelation, but as the spiritual and permanent message of Christ's Gospel, which is hidden under
the surface of the letter. This Gospel he also called the
Spiritual Gospel, and the Gospel of the Kingdom.[1] It was
to be preached in the whole earth and the Jews, Greeks, and
the larger part of mankind, were to be converted. A spiritual Church would result,[2] by which was meant, not a church
separate from the papacy, but a church purified. The
Eternal Gospel was to be proclaimed by a new order, the
" little ones of Christ."[3] In his *Apocalypse*, Joachim speaks
of two prophets of this new order.[4] This prediction was
subsequently applied to Francis and Dominic.

It was in the conception of the maturition of the periods as
much as in the succession of the periods that the theory of
development is brought out.[5] In the development of the
parallels between the history of Israel and the Christian
Church, Joachim discovered a time in each to correspond to
the seven seals of the Apocalypse. The first seal is indicated

[1] See Denifle, pp. 53 sqq.

[2] *spiritualis ecclesia*, also called *ecclesia contemplativa*, Denifle, pp. 56 sqq.

[3] *Parvuli Christi* or *parvuli de latina ecclesia*, a name for monks.

[4] In some passages Joachim also speaks of two orders. See Döllinger, 376.

[5] So Schott, p. 180, *Die Fructification ist nichts anders als ein neuer Ausdruck für den Entwicklungsgedanken.*

in the Old Testament by the deliverance from Egypt, in the New by the resurrection of Christ ; the second seal respectively by the experiences in the wilderness and the persecutions of the ante-Nicene Church ; the third by the wars against the Canaanites and the conflict with heresy from Constantine to Justinian; the fourth by the peril from the Assyrians and the age lasting to Gregory III., d. 741 ; the fifth by the Babylonian oppression and the troubles under the German emperors ; and the sixth by the exile, and the twelfth Christian century with all the miseries of that age, including the violence of the Saracens, and the rise of heretics. The opening of the seventh seal was near at hand, and was to be followed by the Sabbatic rest.

Joachim was no sectary. He was not even a reformer. Like many of his contemporaries he was severe upon the vices of the clergy of his day. " Where is quarrelling," he exclaims, " where fraud, except among the sons of Juda, except among the clergy of the Lord ? Where is crime, where ambition, except among the clergy of the Lord ? " [1] His only remedy was the dawning of the third age which he announced. He waged no polemic against the papacy,[2] submitted himself and his writings dutifully to the Church,[3] and called the church of Peter the throne of Christ. He was a mystical seer who made patient biblical studies,[4] and saw in the future a more perfect realization of the spiritual Church, founded by Christ, exempt from empty formalism and bitter disputes.

An ecclesiastical judgment upon Joachim's views was precipitated by the Franciscan Gerardus of Borgo San Donnino, who wrote a tract called the *Introduction to the Eternal Gospel*, [5] expounding what he considered to be

[1] See Schott, 175. [2] Döllinger, 379 ; Schott, 178, etc.
[3] The Fourth Lateran Council, Canon II.
[4] He also quotes freely from Jerome, Ambrose, Gregory the Great, and other Fathers.
[5] *Introductorius in Evangelium æternum.*

Joachim's teachings. He declared that Joachim's writings were themselves the written code of the Eternal Gospel,[1] which was to be authoritative for the third age, as the Old and New Testaments were authoritative for the ages of the Father and the Son. Of this last age the abbot of Flore was the evangelist.

When Gerard's work appeared, in 1254, it created a great stir and was condemned by professors at Paris, the enemies of the Franciscans, William of St. Amour among the number. The strict wing of the Franciscans, the Spirituals, adopted some of Joachim's views and looked upon him as the prophet of their order. Articles of accusation were brought before Innocent IV. His successor, Alexander IV., in 1255 condemned Gerardo and his book without, however, passing judgment upon Joachim.[2] Gerardo and other Spirituals were thrown into prison, where Gerardo died eighteen years after. John of Parma was deposed from his office as head of the Franciscans for his Joachimism. The Franciscan chronicler Salimbene was also for a while a disciple of Joachim, and reports that the prophet predicted that the order of the Friars Minor should endure to the end while the order of Preachers should pass away.[3] In 1263 a synod of Arles condemned the writings of Joachim. A century after Joachim's death, the Franciscan Spirituals, John Peter Olivi and Ubertino da Casale, were identified with his views. The traces of Joachimism are found throughout the Middle Ages to their close. Joachim was the millenarian prophet of the Middle Ages.

[1] Or the " Gospel of the Holy Spirit."   See Denifle, p. 60.
[2] The practical English monk, M. Paris, speaks of Joachim's doctrines as "new and absurd."   III. p. 206.
[3] Coulton's *Reproduction*, pp. 105, 163.

§ 68.   *The Mendicant Orders.*

For literature, see §§ 69, 72.

A powerful impulse was imported into monasticism and the life of the mediæval Church by the two great mendicant orders,[1] the Dominicans and the Franciscans, who received papal sanction respectively in 1216 and 1223. In their first period they gained equally the esteem of scholars, princes, and popes, and also the regard of the masses, though not without a struggle.[2] Dante praised them; great ecclesiastics like Grosseteste welcomed their coming to England as the dawn of a new era.   Louis IX. would have divided his body between them.   But it has been questioned whether the good services which they rendered in the first years of their career are not more than counterbalanced by their evil activity in later periods when their convents became a synonym for idleness, insolence, and ignorance.

The appearance of these two organizations was without question one of the most momentous events of the Middle Ages,[3] and marks one of the notable revivals in the history of the Christian Church.   They were the Salvation Army of the thirteenth century, and continue to be powerful organizations to this day.   At the time when the spirit of the Crusades was waning and heresies were threatening to sweep away the authority, if not the very existence of the hierarchy, Francis d'Assisi and Dominic de Guzman, an Italian and a Spaniard, united in reviving the religious energies and

---

[1] *Ordines mendicantium.*

[2] The practice of mendicancy was subsequently adopted by the Carmelites, 1245, the Augustinian friars, 1256, and several other orders.   In 1274 Gregory X. abolished all mendicant orders except the Franciscans, Dominicans, Augustinian friars, and Carmelites.

[3] Wilhelm Kothe: *Kirchliche Zustände Strassburgs im 14ten Jahrhundert*, Freib. im Br., 1903, says the mendicant monks were distrusted in Strassburg from the beginning and the Dominicans had to remain outside of the walls till 1250, and their attempt at that time to build a chapel stirred up a warm conflict.

strengthening the religious organization of the Western
Church. As is usually the case in human affairs, the personalities of these great leaders were more powerful than solemnly enacted codes of rules. They started monasticism on a
new career. They embodied Christian philanthropy so that
it had a novel aspect. They were the sociological reformers
of their age. They supplied the universities and scholastic
theology with some of their most brilliant lights. The
prophecies of Joachim of Flore were regarded as fulfilled in
Francis and Dominic, who were the two trumpets of Moses
to arouse the world from its slumber, the two pillars appointed to support the Church. The two orders received papal recognition in the face of the recent decree of the Fourth
Lateran against new monastic orders.

Two temperaments could scarcely have differed more
widely than the temperaments of Francis and Dominic.
Dante has described Francis as an Ardor, inflaming the world
with love; Dominic as a Brightness, filling it with light.

> The one was all seraphical in Ardor,
> The other by his wisdom upon earth
> A Splendor was of light cherubical.[1]

Neither touched life on so many sides as did Bernard.
They were not involved in the external policies of states.
They were not called upon to heal papal schisms, nor were
they brought into a position to influence the papal policy.
But each excelled the monk of Clairvaux as the fathers of
well-disciplined and permanent organizations.

Francis is the most unpretentious, gentle, and lovable of all
monastic saints.[2] Dominic was cold, systematic, austere.
Francis is greater than his order, and moves through his personality. Dominic was a master disciplinarian, and has exerted his influence through the rules of his order. Francis

---

[1] *Paradiso*, canto XI. Longfellow's trans.
[2] Harnack says: "If ever man practised what he preached, that man
was Francis." *Monachism*, p. 68.

has more the elements of a Christian apostle, Dominic of an ecclesiastical statesman. Francis we can only think of as mingling with the people and breathing the free air of the fields; Dominic we think of easily as lingering in courts and serving in the papal household. Francis' lifework was to save the souls of men; Dominic's lifework was to increase the power of the Church. The one sought to carry the ministries of the Gospel to the masses; the other to perpetuate the integrity of Catholic doctrine. Francis has been celebrated for the humbleness of his mind and walk; Dominic was called the hammer of the heretics.

It is probable that on at least three occasions the two leaders met.[1]   In 1217 they were both at Rome, and the curia proposed the union of the two brotherhoods in one organization. Dominic asked Francis for his cord, and bound himself with it, saying he desired the two orders to be one. Again, 1218, they met at the Portiuncula, Francis' beloved church in Assisi, and on the basis of what he saw, Dominic decided to embrace mendicancy, which his order adopted in 1220. Again in 1221 they met at Rome, when Cardinal Ugolino sought to manipulate the orders in the interest of the hierarchy. This Francis resented, but in vain.

It was the purpose neither of Francis nor Dominic to reform existing orders, or to revive the rigor of rules half-obeyed. It may be doubted whether Francis, at the outset, had any intention of founding an organization. His object was rather to start a movement to transform the world as with leaven. They both sought to revive Apostolic practice.

The Franciscan and Dominican orders differed from the older orders in five important particulars.

The first characteristic feature was absolute poverty. Mendicancy was a primal principle of their platforms. The rules of both orders, the Franciscans leading the way, for-

---

[1] Karl Müller accepts the evidence which Sabatier gives. See *Literatur-Zeitung*, 1895, p. 181.

bade the possession of property. The corporation, as well
as the individual monk, was pledged to poverty. The intention of Francis was to prohibit forever the holding of
corporate property as well as individual property among his
followers. [1]

The practice of absolute poverty had been emphasized by
preachers and sects in the century before Francis and Dominic began their careers, and sects, such as the Humiliati, the
Poor Men of Lombardy, and the Poor Men of Lyons, were
advocating it in their time. Robert d'Abrissel, d. 1117,
had for his ideal to follow "the bare Christ on the cross,
without any goods of his own." [2] One of the biographers
of Bernard of Thiron, d. 1117, calls him "Christ's poor
man," *pauper Christi*, and says that this "man, poor in spirit,
followed unto death the Poor Lord." [3] Likewise the followers of Norbert, the founder of the Premonstrant order, were
called the "poor men of Christ," *pauperes Christi*. Of another itinerant preacher, Vitalis of Savigny, who lived about
the same time, his biographer said that he decided to bear
Christ's light yoke by walking in the steps of the Apostles. [4]
The minds of select men and classes of men were deeply
moved in the thirteenth century to follow closely the example of the Apostles, and they regarded Christ as having
taught and practised absolute poverty. Arnold of Brescia's
mind worked in the same direction, as did also the heretical
sects of Southern France and Northern Italy. The imitation of Christ lay near to their hearts, and it remained for
Francis of Assisi to realize most fully this pious ideal of the
thirteenth century. [5]

---

[1] This does not mean that the Franciscans in their early period were idlers.
They were expected to work. Sabatier, *S. François*, VIII. p. 138.

[2] *nudus nudum Christum in cruce sequi*, Walter, *Wanderprediger*.

[3] *Pauperem dominum ad mortem pauper spiritu pauper sequebatur*, Walter, II. 44.

[4] *Leve jugum Christi per apostolorum vestigia ferre decrevit*, Walter, II. 83.

[5] Walter, *Wanderprediger Frankreichs*, p. 168, has brought this out well.

The second feature was their devotion to practical activities in society. The monk had fled into solitude from the
day when St. Anthony retired to the Thebaid desert. The
Black and Gray Friars, as the Dominicans and Franciscans
were called from the colors of their dress, threw themselves
into the currents of the busy world. To lonely contemplation they joined itinerancy in the marts and on the thorough-
fares.[1] They were not satisfied with warring against their
own flesh. They made open warfare upon the world. They
preached to the common people. They relieved poverty.
They listened to the complaints of the oppressed.[2]

A third characteristic of the orders was the lay brotherhoods which they developed, the third order, called Tertiaries, or the penitential brothers, *fratres de pœnitentia*.[3]
Convents, like Hirschau, had before initiated laymen into
monastic service. But the third order of the Franciscans
and Dominicans were lay folk who, while continuing at their
usual avocations, were bound by oath to practise the chief
virtues of the Gospel. There was thus opened to laymen
the opportunity of realizing some of that higher merit belonging theretofore only to the monastic profession. Religion was given back to common life.

A fourth feature was their activity as teachers in the
universities. They recognized that these new centres of
education were centres of powerful influence, and they
adapted themselves to the situation. Twenty years had
scarcely elapsed before the Franciscans and Dominicans
entered upon a career of great distinction at these universities. Francis, it is true, had set his face against learning,

---

[1] Hergenröther says, "Chivalry reappeared in them in a new form. In happy
unison were blended peace and battle, contemplation and active life, faith and
love, prudent moderation and flaming enthusiasm." *Kirchengeschichte*, II. 369.

[2] "Of one thing," says Trevelyan, "the friar was never accused. He is
never taunted with living at home in his cloister and allowing souls to perish
for want of food." *England in the Age of Wycliffe*, p. 144.

[3] So called in the bull of Gregory IX., 1228 ; Potthast, I. p. 703.

and said that demons had more knowledge of the stars than
men could have.   Knowledge puffeth up, but charity edi-
fieth.   To a novice he said, " If you have a psaltery, you will
want a breviary ; and if you have a breviary, you will sit on
a high chair like a prelate, and say to your brother, ' Bring
me a breviary.'"   To another he said, "The time of tribulation will come when books will be useless and be thrown
away."[1]   But from Alexander IV. and his successors the
Franciscans received special privileges for establishing
schools, and, in spite of vigorous opposition, both orders
gained entrance to the University of Paris.   The Dominicans
led the way, and established themselves very early at the seats
of the two great continental universities, Paris and Bologna.[2]
Their convent at Paris, St. Jacques, established in 1217, they
turned into a theological school.   Carrying letters of recommendation from Honorius III., they were at first well received
by the authorities of the university.   The Franciscans established their convent in Paris, 1230.   Both orders received from
the chancellor of Paris license to confer degrees, but their arrogance and refusal to submit to the university regulations soon
brought on bitter opposition.   The popes took their part, and
Alexander IV.[3] commanded the authorities to receive them
to the faculty.   Compliance with this bull was exceedingly
distasteful, for the friars acknowledged the supreme authority
of a foreign body.   The populace of Paris and the students
hooted them on the streets and pelted them with missiles.   It
seemed to Humbert, the general of the Dominicans, as if
Satan, Leviathan, and Belial had broken loose and agreed to
beset the friars round about and destroy, if possible, the fruit-

---

[1] See the quotations from the *Speculum* and *Vita secunda* of Celano, in
Seppelt, pp. 234 sqq.   Also Sabatier, *S. François*, ch. XVI.

[2] For the relations of the mendicant orders with the University of Paris,
see Denifle, *Chartularium Univ. Parisiensis*, I. ; Seppelt, *Der Kampf der
Bettelorden an der Univ. Paris in der Mitte des 13ten Jahrh.* ; Felder,
Gesch. der wissenschaftlichen Studien im Franziskanerorden bis c. 1250.

[3] *Chartul.*, I. 285.

ful olive which Dominic, of most glorious memory, had planted in the field of the Church.[1]   In 1257 Alexander IV. could congratulate all parties that tranquillity had been established.[2]

At Paris and Oxford, Cologne, and other universities, they furnished the greatest of the Schoolmen.   Thomas Aquinas, Albertus Magnus, Durandus, were Dominicans ; John of St. Giles, Alexander Hales, Adam Marsh, Bonaventura, Duns Scotus, Ockham, and Roger Bacon were of the order of St. Francis.   Among other distinguished Franciscans of the Middle Ages were the exegete Nicolas of Lyra, the preachers Anthony of Padua, David of Augsburg, Bernardino of Siena, and Bertholdt of Regensburg (d. 1272) ; the missionaries, Rubruquis and John of Monte Corvino ; the hymn-writers, Thomas of Celano and Jacopone da Todi. Among Dominicans were the mystics, Eckhart and Tauler, Las Casas, the missionary of Mexico, and Savonarola.

The fifth notable feature was the immediate subjection of the two orders to the Apostolic see.   The Franciscans and Dominicans were the first monastic bodies to vow allegiance directly to the pope.   No bishop, abbot, or general chapter intervened between them and him.   The two orders became his bodyguard and proved themselves to be the bulwark of the papacy.   Such organized support the papacy had never had before.   The legend represents Innocent III. as having seen in a vision the structure of the Lateran supported by two monks.[3]   These were Francis and Dominic, and the facts of history justified the invention.   They helped the pope to establish his authority over the bishops.[4]   And wherever

[1] *Chartul.*, I. 309–313, gives Humbert's long letter.

[2] *Chartul.*, I. 381.   See chapter on Universities.

[3] Villani, V. 25, says, " This vision was true, for it was evident the Church of God was falling through licentiousness and many errors, not fearing God."

[4] Bishop Creighton, *Hist. Lectures*, p. 112, says, "The friars were far more destructive to ecclesiastical jurisdiction than any Nonconformist body could be, at the present day, to the influence of any sensible clergyman." He is speaking of the Anglican Church.

2 c

they went, and they were omnipresent in Europe, they made
it their business to propound the principle of the supremacy
of the Holy See over princes and nations and were active in
strengthening this supremacy.   In the struggle of the empire with the papacy, they became the persistent enemies of
Frederick II. who, as early as 1229, banished the Franciscans
from Naples.   When Gregory IX. excommunicated Frederick in 1239, he confided to the Franciscans the duty of
publishing the decree amidst the ringing of bells on every
Sunday and festival day.   And when, in 1245, Innocent IV.
issued his decree against Frederick, its announcement to the
public ear was confided to the Dominicans.

Favor followed favor from the Roman court.   In 1222 Honorius III. granted, first to the Dominicans and then to the
Franciscans, the notable privilege of conducting services in
their churches in localities where the interdict was in force.[1]
Francis' will, exhorting his followers not to seek favors from
the pope, was set aside.   In 1227 Gregory IX. granted his
order the right of general burial in their churches [2] and a
year later repeated the privilege conceded by Honorius [3]
granting them the right of celebrating mass in all their
oratories and churches.[4]   They were exempted from episcopal authority and might hear confessions at any place.
The powerful Gregory IX. from the very beginning of his
pontificate, showed the orders great favor.[5]

Orthodoxy had no more zealous champions than the Franciscans and Dominicans.   They excelled all other orders
as promoters of religious persecution and hunters of heretics.
In Southern France they wiped out the stain of heresy with
the streams of blood which flowed from the victims of their
crusading fanaticism.   They were the leading instruments

---

[1] The bulls are dated March 7 and 29.   See Potthast, I. 590.   The same
privilege was conceded to the Carmelites, April 9, 1229.

[2] Potthast, I. 697, 721.   [4] June 10, 1228, Potthast, I. 707.

[3] Potthast, I. 701, 706.   [5] See Potthast, Nos. 6508, 6542, 6654, etc.

of the Inquisition. Torquemada was a Dominican, and so
was Konrad of Marburg. As early as 1232 Gregory IX.
confided the execution of the Inquisition to the Dominicans,
but the order of Francis demanded and secured a share in
the gruesome work. Under the lead of Duns Scotus the
Franciscans became the unflagging champions of the doctrine
of the immaculate conception of Mary which was pronounced
a dogma in 1854, as later the Jesuits became the unflagging
champions of the dogma of papal infallibility.

The rapid growth of the two orders in number and influence was accompanied by bitter rivalry. The disputes
between them were so violent that in 1255 their respective
generals had to call upon their monks to avoid strife. The
papal privileges were a bone of contention, one order being
constantly suspicious lest the other should enjoy more favor
at the hand of the pope than itself.

Their abuse of power called forth papal briefs restricting
their privileges. Innocent IV. in 1254, in what is known
among the orders as the " terrible bull," [1] revoked the permission allowing them to admit others than members of the
orders to their services on festivals and Sundays and also the
privilege of hearing confession except as the parochial priest
gave his consent. Innocent, however, was no sooner in his
grave than his successor, Alexander IV., announced himself
as the friend of the orders, and the old privileges were
renewed.

The pretensions of the mendicant friars soon became unbearable to the church at large. They intruded themselves into every parish and incurred the bitter hostility of
the secular clergy whose rights they usurped, exercising
with free hand the privilege of hearing confessions and

---

[1] Potthast, II. 1280. Innocent died a few weeks after issuing this bull
and, as is said, in answer to the prayers of the mendicants. Hence came
the saying, " from the prayers of the Preachers, good Lord, deliver us."
A litanis prædicatorum libera nos, Domine.

granting absolution.   It was not praise that Chaucer intended when he said of the Franciscan in his Canterbury
Tales, — He was an easy man to give penance.

These monks also delayed a thorough reformation of the
Church.   They were at first reformers themselves and
offered an offset to the Cathari and the Poor Men of Lyons
by their Apostolic self-denial and popular sympathies.   But
they degenerated into obstinate obstructors of progress in
theology and civilization.   From being the advocates of
learning, they became the props of popular ignorance.   The
virtue of poverty was made the cloak for vulgar idleness and
mendicancy for insolence.

These changes set in long before the century closed in
which the two orders had their birth.   Bishops opposed
them.   The secular clergy complained of them.   The universities ridiculed and denounced them for their mock piety
and vices.   William of St. Amour took the lead in the
opposition in Paris.   His sharp pen compared the mendicants to the Pharisees and Scribes and declared that Christ
and his Apostles did not go around begging.   To work was
more scriptural than to beg.[1]   They were hypocrites and it
remained for the bishops to purge their dioceses of them.
Again and again, in after years, did clergy, bishops, and
princes appeal to the popes against their intrusive insolence,
but, as a rule, the popes were on their side.

The time came in the early part of the fifteenth century

---

[1] In his treatise *de periculis novissorum temporum*, " The Perils of the
Last Times," Basel, 1555, William has been held up as a precursor of Rabelais
and Pascal on account of his keen satire.   He was answered by Bonaventura
and by Thomas Aquinas in his *contra impugnantes religionem*.   Alexander IV.
ordered William's treatise burnt, and in the bull, dated Oct. 5, 1256,
declared it to be "most dangerous and detestable," *valde perniciosum et
detestabilem*.   See Potthast, II. 1357.   When an edition of William's treatise
appeared at Paris, 1632, the Mendicants secured an order from Louis XIII.
suppressing it.   William was inhibited from preaching and teaching and
retired to Franche-Comte, where he died.   See *Chartularium Univ. Parisiensis*, I. Nos. 295, 296, 314, 318, 321, 332, 339, 343, 315, etc.

when the great teacher Gerson, in a public sermon, enumerated as the four persecutors of the Church, tyrants, heretics, antichrist, and the Mendicants.[1]

§ 69. *Franciscan Literature.*

I. St. Francis: Works in Latin text, ed. by Wadding, Antwerp, 1623, by de la Haye, Paris, 1841, Col., 1849, Paris, 1880–Quaracchi, 1904. — Bernardo da Fivizzano: *Oposcoli di S. Fr. d'Assise*, Florence, 1880. Gives the Latin text and Ital. trans., the Rule of 1223, St. Francis' will, letters, etc. — French trans. by Ed. d'Alençon: *Les Opuscules de S. François*, Paris, 1905. — H. Boehmer: *Analekten zur Gesch. des Franc. von Assisi, Francisci opuscula, regula pœnitentium*, etc., *mit einer Einleitung*, Tübingen, 1904. — *Writings of St. Francis of Assisi*, trans. by Father Paschal Robinson, Phil., 1906.

Lives. — 1. Thomas of Celano: *Vita prima*, written 1228 at the command of Gregory IX., to justify the canonization of Francis, Rome, 1880. — 2. Th. of Celano: *Vita secunda*, written about 1247 and revealing the struggles within the Franciscan order, ed. by Fivizzano, Rome, 1880. Both lives ed. by H. G. Rosedale: *Thomas de Celano, St. F. d'Assisi with a crit. Introd. containing a description with every extant version in the original Latin*, N.Y., 1904. Also Ed. d'Alençon: *Th. a Celano, S. Franc. Assisiensis vita et miracula*, etc., pp. lxxxvii, 481, Rome, 1906. — *Fr. of Assisi according to Th. of Celano. His descriptions of the Seraphic Father*, 1229–1257, Introd. by H. G. Rosedale, Lond., 1904. — 3. *Legenda trium sociorum*, the Legend of the Three Companions, Leo, Angelo, and Rufino, intimate associates of Francis. Written in 1246 and first publ. in full by the Bollandists as an appendix to Celano's *Lives*, Louvaine, 1768, Rome, 1880. It has been preserved in a mutilated condition. The disputes within the order account for the expurgation of parts to suit the lax or papal wing. — 4. *Speculum perfectionis seu S. Francesci Assisiensis legenda antiquissima, auctore fratre Leone, nunc primum edidit*, Paul Sabatier, Paris, 1898; also ed. by Ed. Lemmens, Quaracchi, 1901. Sabatier dates it 1227. Eng. trans. by Constance, *Countess de la Warr*, Lond., 1902. See note below. — 5. *Legenda major*, or *Aurea legenda major*, by Bonaventura, in Peltier's ed., and Quaracchi, 1898, Engl. trans., Douai, 1610, and by Miss Lockhart with Pref. by Card. Manning, Lond., 3d ed., 1889.

---

[1] Matthew Paris in his résumé of the chief events of 1200–1250 has this to say of the decay of the orders, "These Preachers and Minorites at first led the life of poverty and greatest sanctity and devoted themselves assiduously to preaching, confessions, divine duties in the church, reading and study, and abandoned many revenues, embracing voluntary poverty in the service of God and reserving nothing in the way of food for themselves for the morrow, but within a few years, they got themselves into excellent condition and constructed most costly houses, etc." Luard's ed., V. 194.

Written in obedience to the order of the Franciscan Chapter and approved by it at Pisa, 1263. Here the legendary element is greatly enlarged. Once treated as the chief authority, it is now relegated to a subordinate place, as it suppresses the distinctive element represented by Francis' will. — 6. *Liber conformitatum*, by BARTHOLOMEW ALBERICUS of Pisa, d. 1401. Institutes forty comparisons between Francis and Christ. Luther called it *der Barfussmönche Eulenspiegel und Alkoran*, The owls' looking-glass and Koran of the Barefoot monks. — 7. *Actus B. Francesci et sociorum ejus*, ed. SABATIER, Paris, 1902. A collection of sayings and acts of Francis, handed down from eye-witnesses and others, hitherto unpubl. and to be dated not later than 1328. — 8. *Legenda* of JULIAN OF SPIRES. About 1230. — 9. *Legenda* of BERNARD OF BESS, publ. in the *Analecta Franciscana* III., Quaracchi, near Florence. A compilation. — 10. *Francisci beati sacrum commercium cum domina paupertate*, with an Ital. trans. by ED. D'ALENÇON, Rome, 1900. Engl. trans., *The Lady Poverty*, by MONTGOMERY CARMICHAEL, N.Y., 1902. Goes back, at least, to the 13th century, as Ubertino da Casale was acquainted with it. — 11. The *Fioretti, or Little Flowers of St. Francis*, first publ., 1476, ed. SABATIER, Paris, 1902, pp. xvi., 250. Engl. trans. by ABBY L. ALGER, Boston, 1887, and WOODROFFE, London, 1905. Belongs to the 14th century. A collection of legends very popular in Italy. Sabatier says none of them are genuine, but that they perfectly reveal the soul of St. Francis. — 12. *Fratris Fr. Bartholi de Assisio Tractatus de indulgentia S. Mariæ de Portiuncula*, ed. SABATIER, Paris, 1900. Belongs to the 14th century. See *Lit.-zeitung*, 1901, 110 sqq. — 13. *Regula antiqua fratrum et sororum de pœnitentia seu tertii ordinis S. Francisci, nunc primum ed.*, SABATIER, Paris, 1901. See S. MINOCCHI : *La Leggenda antica. Nuova fonte biogr. di S. Francesco d'Assisi tratto da un codice Vaticana*, Florence, 1905, pp. 184. Unfavorably noticed by LEMPP, in *Lit.-zeitung*, 1906, p. 509, who says that the contents of the MS. were for the most part drawn from the *Speculum perfectionis*.

MODERN BIOGRAPHIES. — By CHAVIN DE MALAN, Paris, 1841, 2d ed., 1845. — K. HASE, Leip. 1856, 2d ed., 1892. First crit. biog. — MRS. OLIPHANT, Lond., 1870. — MAGLIANO, 2 vols., Rome, 1874, Eng. trans., N.Y., 1887. — L. DE CHÉRANCÉ, Paris, 1892, Engl. trans., 1901. — HENRY THODE, Berlin, 1885, 1904. — * PAUL SABATIER, a Protestant pastor : *Vie de S. François d'Assise*, Paris, 1894. 33d ed., 1906. Crowned by the French Academy. Engl. trans. by L. S. HOUGHTON, N.Y., 1894. I use the 27th ed. — W. J. KNOX-LITTLE, Lond., 1896. — P. DOREAU, Paris, 1903, p. 648. — A. BARINE : *S. Fr. d'Assisi et le légende des trois Compagnons*, Paris, 1901. — J. HERKLESS : *Francis and Dominic*, N.Y., 1904. — H. v. REDERN, Schwerin, 1905. — * G. SCHNÜRER : *Franz von Assisi. Die Vertiefung des religiösen Lebens im Abendlande zur Zeit der Kreuzzüge*, Munich, 1905. — NINO TAMASSIA : *S. Francesco d'Assisi e la sua leggenda*, Padua, 1906, p. 216. — F. VAN ORTROY : *Julien de Spire, biographe de St. François*,

Brussels, 1890. — J. E. WEIS : *Julian von Speier*, d. 1285, Munich, 1900.
— ED. LEMPP : *Frère Elie de Cortona*, Paris, 1901. — H. TILEMANN :
*Speculum perfectionis und Legenda trium sociorum, Ein Beitrag zur
Quellenkritik der Gesch. des hl. Franz. von Assisi*, Leip. 1902. — POTT-
HAST : *Bibl. Hist.*, II. 1319 sqq. gives a list of ninety biographies. For
further lit. see ZÖCKLER in Herzog, VI. 197–222, and "Engl. Hist.
Rev." 1903, 155 sqq., for a list and critical estimate of the lit., W.
GOETZ : *Die Quellen zur Gesch. des hl. Franz von Assisi*, Gotha, 1904.
First published in Brieger's *Zeitschrift* and reviewed in *Lit.-zeitung*,
1905, pp. 8–10.

II. THE FRANCISCANS : Earliest Chronicles. — JORDANUS DA GIANO : *de
primitivorum fratrum in Teutoniam missorum conversatione et vita
memorabilia*, for the years 1207–1238, in *Analecta Franciscana*, pp. 1–19.
— THOMAS OF ECCLESTON, a Franciscan : *de adventu Minorum in An-
gliam*, 1224–1250 in the *Analecta Franciscana* and best in *Monumenta
Franciscana*, ed. by J. S. BREWER, with valuable Preface, London, 1858,
Engl. trans. by Cuthbert, London, 1903. The volume also contains the
Letters of Adam de Marisco, etc.; vol. II., ed. by RICHARD HOWLETT,
with Preface, contains fragments of Eccleston and other English docu-
ments bearing on the Franciscans. — *Analecta Franciscana sive chronica
aliaque documenta ad historiam Minorum spectantia*, Quaracchi, 1885.
— *Bullarium Franciscanum sive Romanqrum pontificum constitutiones,
epistolæ, diplomata*, etc., vols. I.–IV., Rome, 1759, ed. by J. H. SBARA-
GLEA and ROSSI, vols. V., VII., Rome, 1898–1904, ed. by CONRAD EUBEL ;
the collection extends to 1378. — *Seraphicæ legationis textus originales*,
Quaracchi, 1897, containing the Rule of 1223 and other documents. —
LUKE WADDING : *Annales Minorum*, 7 vols., Lyons, 1625–1648, the
most valuable history of the order. — DENIFLE and EHRLE give valuable
materials and criticisms in *Archiv für Lit. und Kirchengeschichte d.
Mittelalters*, vol. I. 145 sqq. ; 509–569, III. 553 sqq. ; VI. 1 sqq., Berlin,
1885–1891. — KARL MÜLLER : *Die Anfänge des Minoriten-ordens und
der Bussbruderschaften*, Freib., 1885. — A. G. LITTLE : *The Grey-
friars in Oxford*, Oxford, 1891. — EUBEL : *Die avignonesische Obedienz
der Mendikanten-Orden*, etc., *zur Zeit des grossen Schismas beleuchtet
durch die von Clement VII. und Benedict XIII. an dieselben gerichteten
Schreiben*, Paderborn, 1900. — PIERRE MADONNET : *Les origines de
l'ordre de pœnitentia*, Freib., 1898; also *Les règles et le gouvernement de
l'ordre de pœnitentia au XIIIe siècle* (1212–1234), Paris, 1902. — F. X.
SEPPELT : *Der Kampf der Bettelorden an der Universität Paris in der Mitte
des 13ten Jahrh.* Heiligenstadt, 1892. — F. GLASER : *Die franziskanische
Bewegung. Ein Beitrag zur Gesch. sozialer Reformideen im Mittelalter*, Stuttg., 1903. — H. FELDER : *Gesch. der wissenschaftlichen Studien
im Franziskanerorden bis c. 1250*, Freib., 1904, pp. 557. RICARD ST.
CLARA : *St. Claire d'Assise*, Paris, 1895. — E. WAUER : *Entstehung und
Ausbreitung des Klarissenordens besonders in deutschen Minoritenpro-
vinzen*, Leip., 1906. — E. KNOTH : *Ubertino da Casale*, Marburg, 1903.
— E. JACOB : *Johannes von Capistrano, Die auf der kgl. und Univ.*

Bibliothek zu Breslau befindlichen handschriftlichen Aufzeichnungen von Reden und Tractaten Capistrans, etc., 2 Parts, Breslau, 1903–1905. — L. DE CHÉRANCÉ: *St. Antoine de Padoue*, Paris, 1906. — HELYOT: *Relig. Orders*, VII. 1–421. — LEA: *Hist. of the Inquisition*, I. 242–304. — M. CREIGHTON: *The Coming of the Friars*, in Lectures and Addresses, pp. 69–84. — A. JESSOPP : *The Coming of the Friars.* — STEVENSON: *Life of Grosseteste*, London, 1899, pp. 59–87. — HAUCK, IV. 366–483.

Note on the recent literature on St. Francis. — A phenomenal impulse was given to the study of the life of St. Francis by the publication of Sabatier's biography in 1894. This biography, Karl Müller placed " at the summit of modern historical workmanship." *Lit.-zeitung*, 1895, pp. 179–186. It showed a mastery of the literature before unknown and a profound sympathy with the spirit of the Italian saint. It has revolutionized the opinion of Protestants in regard to him, and has given to the world a correct picture of the real Francis. Strange that a Protestant pastor should have proved himself the leading modern student of Francis and one of his most devoted admirers ! Sabatier has followed up his first work with tireless investigations into the early literature and history of St. Francis and the Franciscans, giving up his pastorate, making tour after tour to Italy, and spending much time in Assisi, where he is held in high esteem, and is pointed out as one of the chief sights of the place. He has been fortunate in his discoveries of documents and, as an editor, he has created a new Franciscan literature. His enthusiasm and labors have stimulated a number of scholars in Germany, Italy, and Switzerland to make a specialty of the early Franciscan literature such as Minocchi, Madonnet, Müller, Lempp, and Schnürer. His Life of St. Francis has been put on the Index because it is said to misrepresent Catholic customs.

While Sabatier's presentation of Francis' career and character may be said to have gained general acceptance, except among Franciscans, there is a large difference of opinion in regard to the dates of the early documents and their original contents. This literary aspect of the subject has become greatly complicated by the publication of manuscripts which differ widely from one another and the divergent criticisms of scholars. This confusion has been likened by Müller, *Lit.-zeitung*, 1902, p. 593, and Lempp, *Lit.-zeitung*, 1906, p. 509, to a thicket through which it is almost impossible to see a path. The confusion grows out of the determined policy of Gregory IX. and the conventual wing of the early Franciscans to destroy all materials which show that Francis was opposed to a strict discipline within the order and insisted upon the rule of absolute poverty. The Franciscan chapter of 1264 ordered all biographies of Francis, written up to that time, destroyed, except the biography by Bonaventura. St. Francis' insistence upon the rule of absolute poverty, the original Rule, and his will, were to be utterly effaced. The new study, introduced by the clear eye of Sabatier, has gone back of this date, 1264, and rescued the portrait of the real Francis.

The attention of scholars is chiefly concentrated on the *Speculum perfectionis* published by Sabatier, 1898, and the original Rule of the Franciscan

Tertiaries. The *Speculum perfectionis* is a life of Francis and, according to Sabatier (*Introd.* li.), is the first biography, dating back to 1227. The discovery of the document is one of the most interesting and remarkable of recent historical discoveries. The way it came to be found was this: —

Materials for the Life of Francis are contained in a volume entitled *Speculum vitæ St. Francisci et sociorum ejus*, published first at Venice, 1504, and next at Paris, 1509. In studying the Paris edition of 1509, Sabatier discovered 118 chapters ascribed to no author and differing in spirit and style from the other parts. He used the document in the construction of his biography and was inclined to ascribe it to the three companions of Francis, — Leo, Angelo, and Rufino. See *Vie de S. François*, pp. lxxii. sq. At a later time he found that in several MSS. these chapters were marked as a distinct document. In the MS. in the Mazarin library he found 124 distinctive chapters. In these are included the 16 of the Paris edition of 1509. These chapters Sabatier regards as a distinct volume, the *Speculum perfectionis*, written by Leo, the primary composition bearing on Francis' career and teachings. The date for its composition is derived from the Mazarin MS. which gives the date as MCCXXVIII. This date Sabatier finds confirmed by indications in the document itself, p. xxii. etc.

This sympathetic, lucid, and frank narrative puts Francis in a new light, as a martyr to the ambitious designs of Gregory IX. who set aside the rule of absolute poverty which was most dear to Francis' heart and placed over him a representative of his own papal views. Leo, so Sabatier contends (*Introd.* p. li.), wrote his work immediately after the announcement by Elias of Cortona of the intention to erect an imposing cathedral over the "Little Poor Man." Leo was unable to suppress his indignation and so uttered his protest against the violent manipulation of Francis' plan and memory.

Serious objection has been raised to Sabatier's date of the *Speculum perfectionis*. In agreement with Minocchi, — Tilemann, Goetz, and others have adopted the date given in the Ognissanti (a convent in Florence) MS. namely MCCCXVII, and by a careful study of the other lives of Francis conclude that the *Speculum* is a compilation. Some of its contents, however, they agree, antedate Thomas à Celano's *Vita secunda* or second Life of Francis or are still older. Müller, *Lit.-zeitung*, 1899, 49–52, 1902, p. 598, and Lempp, while not accepting the early date of 1227, place the document in the first half of the 13th century and regard it as an authority of the first rank, *eine Quelle ersten Ranges*. It shows a deep penetration into the real mind ˙and soul of Francis, says Lempp, *Lit.-zeitung*, 1905, pp. 9 sq. Tilemann also ascribes to the document the highest value. For the numerous articles in Reviews, by Minocchi, van Ortroy, etc., see Tilemann, *Speculum perfectionis*, p. 4.

If Sabatier has given us the real Francis of history, as there is reason to believe he has, then the spectacle of Francis' loss of authority by the skilled hand of Cardinal Ugolino, Gregory IX., is one of the most pathetic spectacles in history and Francis stands out as one of the most unselfish and pure-minded men of the Christian centuries.

§ 70.   *St. Francis d'Assisi.*

"Not long the period from his glorious birth,
　　When, with extraordinary virtue blest,
　　This wondrous sun began to comfort earth,
Bearing, while yet a child, his father's ire,
　　For sake of her whom all as death detest,
　　And banish from the gate of their desire,
Before the court of heaven, before
　　His father, too, he took her for his own ;
　　From day to day, then loved her more and more,
Twelve hundred years had she remained, deprived
　　Of her first spouse, deserted and unknown,
　　And unsolicited till he arrived.

*　　*　　*　　*　　*　　*　　*　　*　　*

But lest my language be not clearly seen,
　　Know, that in speaking of these lovers twain,
　　Francis and Poverty henceforth, I mean."

— DANTE, *Paradiso* XI., Wright's trans.

High up in the list of hagiography stands the name of
Francis of Assisi, the founder of the order of the Francis-
cans.   Of all the Italian saints, he is the most popular in
Italy and beyond it.[1]

Francesco, — Francis, — Bernardone, 1182–1226, was born
and died in Assisi.   His baptismal name was Giovanni, John,
and the name Francis seems to have been given him by his
father, Pietro Bernardone, a rich dealer in textile fabrics,

---

[1] The former unfavorable view of most Protestant historians concerning
Francis is no longer held. Hallam, *Middle Ages*, II. 197, called him "a
harmless enthusiast, pious and sincere, but hardly of sane mind." Lea, representing the present tendency, goes far, when he says, " No human creature
since Christ has more fully incarnated the ideal of Christianity than Francis." *Hist. of Inquis.*, I. 260. Harnack says, " If ever a man practised what
he preached, it was St. Francis." An anonymous writer, reviewing some of
the Franciscan literature in the *Independent*, 1901, p. 2044, seriously pronounced the judgment that " Since the Apostles, Francis received into his being the love of Christ toward men and the lower creatures more fully than
any other man, and his appearance has been an epoch of spiritual history
only less significant than that of the original Good Tidings." More judicious is Sabatier's verdict, *Vie de S. Franc.*, p. viii., "that Francis is pre-eminently the saint of the Middle Ages. Owing nothing to the Church, he was
truly theodidact."

with reference to France, to which he made business journeys. Francis studied Latin and was imperfectly acquainted
with the art of writing. He had money to spend, and spent
it in gayeties. In a war between Assisi and Perugia he joined
the ranks, and was taken prisoner. When released, he was
twenty-two. During an illness which ensued, his religious
nature began to be stirred. He arose from his bed disgusted
with himself and unsatisfied with the world. Again he enlisted, and, starting to join Walter of Brienne in Southern
Italy, he proceeded as far as Spoleto. But he was destined
for another than a soldier's career. Turning back, and
moved by serious convictions, he retired to a grotto near Assisi for seclusion. He made a pilgrimage to Rome, whether
to do penance or not, is not known. His sympathies began
to go out to the poor. He met a leper and shrank back in
horror at first, but, turning about, kissed the leper's hand,
and left in it all the money he had. He frequented the
chapels in the suburbs of his native city, but lingered most
at St. Damian, an humble chapel, rudely furnished, and
served by a single priest. This became to his soul a Bethel.
At the rude altar he seemed to hear the voice of Christ. In
his zeal he took goods from his father and gave them to the
priest. So far as we know, Francis never felt called upon to
repent of this act. Here we have an instance of a different
moral standard from our own. How different, for example,
was the feeling of Dr. Samuel Johnson, when, for an act of
disobedience to his father, he stood, as a full-grown man, a
penitent in the rain in the open square of Litchfield, his head
uncovered!

The change which had overcome the gay votary of pleasure brought upon Francis the ridicule of the city and his
father's relentless indignation. He was cast out of his father's house. Without any of those expressions of regret
which we would expect from a son under similar circumstances, he renounced his filial obligation in public in these
words: "Up to this time I have called Pietro Bernardone
father, but now I desire to serve God and to say nothing
else than 'Our Father which art in heaven.'" Henceforth

Francis was devoted to the religious life. He dressed scantily, took up his abode among the lepers, washing their sores, and restored St. Damian, begging the stones on the squares and streets of the city.   This was in 1208.

Francis now received from the Benedictine abbot of Mt. Subasio the gift of the little chapel, Santa Maria degli Angeli.[1] Under the name of the Portiuncula — Little Portion — it became the favorite shrine of the saint and his early companions.   There Francis had most of his visions, and there he died.[2] In later years he secured from Honorius III. the remarkable concession of plenary indulgence for every one visiting the chapel between vespers of Aug. 1 to vespers of Aug. 2 each year.   This made the Portiuncula a shrine of the first rank.

In 1209 Francis heard the words, "Preach, the kingdom of heaven is at hand, heal the sick, cleanse the lepers, cast out devils.   Provide neither silver nor gold, nor brass in your purses."   Throwing away his staff, purse, and shoes, he made these Apostolic injunctions the rule of his life.   He preached repentance and gathered about him Bernardo di Quintavallo, Egidio, and other companions.   The three passages commanding poverty and taking up the cross, Matt. xvi : 24–26 ; xix : 21 ; Luke ix : 1–6, were made their Rule.[3] The Rule meant nothing less than full obedience to the Gospel.   The Lesser Brethren, *fratres minores*, for such came to be their name, begged from door to door, where they could not earn their bread, went barefoot[4] and slept in hay lofts, leper hospitals, and wherever else they could find lodgment.

[1] The *Speculum perfectionis*, pp. 94 sqq., leaves no room for doubting the gift of the church to Francis.   The gift was made on condition that the chapel should always remain the centre of the brotherhood.

[2] That is, in the cell a few yards from Portiuncula. Both Portiuncula and the cell, which has been turned into a chapel, are now under the roof of the basilica.

[3] Sabatier limits the Rule to these passages of Scripture.   Thomas of Celano, *Vita sec.*, II. 10, says that Francis "used chiefly the words of the Holy Gospel" but says further that "he added a few other things which were necessary for a holy life *pauca tamen inseruit alia.*"

[4] In case of necessity the wearing of sandals was permitted. *Speculum*, p. 8.

They were to preach, but especially were they to exemplify the precepts of the Gospel in their lives. Living was the most important concern, more important than sermons and than learning. Learning, Francis feared, would destroy humility. To a woman who came to him for alms he gave a copy of the New Testament, which they read at matins, the only book in the convent at the time. The convent did not even possess a breviary.[1] A life of good works and sympathies was what Francis was seeking to emphasize. In his will, Francis calls himself an illiterate, *idiota*. Thomas à Celano also speaks of him in the same way. The word seems to have had the double sense of a man without education and a man with little more than a primary education. It was also used of laymen in contrast to clerics. Francis' education was confined to elemental studies, and his biographers are persistent in emphasizing that he was taught directly of God.[2] Two writings in Francis' handwriting are in existence, one in Assisi and one in Spoleto.[3]

In 1210 Francis and some of his companions went to Rome, and were received by Innocent III.[4] The English chronicler reports that the pope, in order to test his sincerity, said " Go, brother, go to the pigs, to whom you are more fit to be compared than to men, and roll with them, and to them preach the rules you have so ably set forth." Francis obeyed, and returning said, "My Lord, I have done so."[5] The pope then gave his blessing to the brotherhood and informally sanc-

---

[1] *Speculum*, 38 ; 2 *Cel.* 3, 35. The woman was expected to sell the book.

[2] On the meaning of *idiota*, see Felder, p. 61, and Boehmer, p. xi. Felder, pp. 59 sqq., makes an effort to parry the charges that Francis lacked education and disparaged education for his order. Celano calls him *vir idiota* and says *nullis fuit scientiae studiis innutritus.* He also speaks of him as singing in French as he walked through a forest. See the notes in Felder.

[3] See Boehmer, pp. xiii. sq., 69 sq.

[4] Giotto has made the meeting with Innocent seated on his throne the subject of one of his frescoes. A splendid contrast indeed, the sovereign of kings and potentates and yet the successor of Peter, recognizing the humble devotee, whose fame was destined to equal his own! The date usually given is 1209. Sabatier gives reasons for the change to 1210. *St. François*, p. 100.

[5] M. Paris, Luard's ed., III. 132. Sabatier remarks that the incident has a real Franciscan color and is to be regarded as having some historic basis.

tioned their rule, granted them the tonsure, and bade them
go and preach repentance.

The brotherhood increased rapidly. The members were
expected to work. In his will Francis urged the brethren
to work at some trade as he had done. He compared an idle
monk to a drone.[1] The brethren visited the sick, especially
lepers, preached in ever extending circles, and went abroad
on missionary journeys. Francis was ready to sell the very
ornaments of the altar rather than refuse an appeal for aid.
He felt ashamed when he saw any one poorer than himself.[2]

At this time occurred one of the most remarkable episodes
of Francis' career. He entered into marriage with Poverty.
He called Poverty his bride, mother, sister, and remained
devoted to her with the devotion of a knight.[3] The story
runs thus. Francis, with some companions, went out in
search of Poverty. Two old men pointed out her abode on
a high mountain. There Poverty, seated "on the throne
of her neediness," received them and Francis praised her as
the inseparable companion of the Lord, and "the mistress
and queen of the virtues." Poverty replied that she had
been with Adam in paradise, but had become a homeless
wanderer after the fall until the Lord came and made her
over to his elect. By her agency the number of believers
was greatly increased, but after a while her sister Lady
Persecution withdrew from her. Believers lost their fortitude. Then monks came and joined her, but her enemy
Avarice, under the name of Discretion, made the monks rich.
Finally monasticism yielded completely to worldliness, and
Poverty removed wholly from it. Francis now joined himself to Poverty, who gave him and his companions the kiss

---

[1] *Speculum*, p. 49. See also *Cel.* 10; 2 *Cel.* 97. Sabatier insists that
Francis had "no intention of creating a mendicant order, but a working
order." *S. François*, p. 138. Denifle also called attention to this feature,
Archiv, 1885, p. 482.

[2] *Speculum*, xvii.

[3] Celano in his first *Life* speaks of the sacred intercourse between Francis
and holy Poverty, *commercium cum sancta paupertate*. The work entitled
Sacrum commercium, etc., relates in full the story accounting for Francis'
espousal of Poverty.

of peace and descended the mountain with them. A new era was begun. Henceforth the pillow of the friends was a stone, their diet bread and water, and their convent the world.[1]

In 1212 Clara of Sciffi entered into the horizon of Francis' life. She was twelve years his junior and sixteen when she first heard him preach at the Cathedral of Assisi. The sermon entered her soul. With Francis' aid she escaped from her father's house, and was admitted to vows by him.[2] He conducted her to a house of Benedictine nuns. A younger sister, Agnes, followed Clara. The Chapel of St. Damian was set apart for them, and there the order of Clarisses was inaugurated. Clara outlived Francis, and in 1253 expired in the presence of brothers Leo, Angelo, and Ginefro.

In 1217 Francis was presented to Honorius III. and the curia. At the advice of Cardinal Ugolino, later Gregory IX., he prepared himself and memorized the sermon. Arrived in the pontiff's presence, he forgot what he had prepared and delivered an impromptu discourse, which won the assembly.

Francis made evangelistic tours through Italy which were extended to Egypt and Syria 1219. Returning from the East the little Poor Man, *il poverello*, found a new element had been introduced into the brotherhood through the influence of the stern disciplinarian Ugolino. This violent

---

[1] Jacopone da Todi took up the idea and represented Poverty going through the earth and knocking at the door of convent after convent, and being turned away. Hase, with reference to Francis' apotheosis of Poverty, says, that Diogenes was called a mad Socrates, and so Francis was a mad Christ, *ein verrückter Christus*. *Kirchengesch.* II. 382. In its opening chapter the *Commercium* explains the beatitude, "Blessed are the poor in spirit," to refer to the renunciation of worldly goods, and puts into the hands of Poverty the keys of the kingdom of heaven.

[2] Francis was a deacon and never a priest. According to Thomas à Celano, Francis was austere in his relations to women, and knew only two women by sight. Sabatier, pp. 169 sq., pronounces this portraiture false and speaks of "the love of St. Francis and St. Clara." Here, as in other places, the biographer allows himself the license of the idealist. Francis' last message to Clara is given in the *Speculum Perfectionis*, pp. 180 sqq. The Franciscan Rule of 1223 forbids "suspicious conferences with women," but allows the friars to enter monastaries of nuns by permission of the Holy See. See Robinson, p. 73.

change made the rest of the years a time of bitter, though
scarcely expressed, sorrow for him. Passing through Bologna
in 1220, he was pained to the depths at seeing a house being
erected for the brothers.   Cardinal Ugolino had determined
to manipulate the society in the interest of the curia.   He
had offered Francis his help, and Francis had accepted the
offer.   Under the cardinal's influence, a new code was adopted
in 1221, and still a third in 1223 in which Francis' distinctive wishes were set aside.   The original Rule of poverty
was modified, the old ideas of monastic discipline introduced,
and a new element of absolute submission to the pope added.
The mind of Francis was too simple and unsophisticated for
the shrewd rulers of the church.   The policy of the ecclesiastic henceforth had control of the order.[1]   Francis was set
aside and a minister-general, Pietro di Catana, a doctor of
laws and a member of the nobility was put at the head of the
society.   This was the condition of affairs Francis found on
his return from Syria.   He accepted it and said to his
brethren, "From henceforth I am dead for you. Here is
brother Peter di Catana whom you and I will obey," and
prostrating himself, he promised the man who had superseded
him obedience and submission.[2]

This forced self-subordination of Francis offers one of the
most touching spectacles of mediæval biography.   Francis

---

[1] According to the *Speculum*, pp. 1-4, 76, Francis made three Rules.
Sabatier defines them as the Rule of 1210, confirmed by Innocent III., the
Rule of 1221, confirmed by Honorius III., which in part misrepresented
Francis' views.   The Rule of 1223 went further in this direction and completely overthrew Francis' original intention.   The first clause of the Rule of
1223 runs, "Brother Francis promises obedience and reverence to the lord
pope, Honorius, and his successors."   This rule is still in force in the
first Franciscan order.   Madonnet substantially agrees with Sabatier as does
Karl Müller.   Father Robinson, himself a Franciscan friar, pp. 25-31, 182,
following the Quaracchi editors, who are Franciscans also, denies the genuineness of the Rule of 1221, and holds that there were only two Rules, and that
there is no conflict between them.   This conclusion is in the face of Francis'
will and the plain statement of Leo's *Legenda* which, however, Robinson
pays little attention to.

[2] See Sabatier, *S. François*, p. 23.   Peter of Catana died March 10, 1221,
a year after his elevation.

had withheld himself from papal privileges. He had favored freedom of movement. The skilled hand of Ugolino
substituted strict monastic obedience. Organization was to
take the place of spontaneous devotion. Ugolino was, no
doubt, Francis' real as well as professed friend. He laid
the foundation of the cathedral in Assisi to his honor, and
canonized him two years after his death. But Francis'
spirit he did not appreciate. Francis was henceforth helpless to carry out his original ideas,[1] and yet, without making
any outward sign of insubordination, he held tenaciously to
them to the end.

These ideas are reaffirmed in Francis' famous will. This
document is one of the most affecting pieces in Christian
literature. Here Francis calls himself "little brother," *frater parvulus*. All he had to leave the brothers was his benediction, the memory of the early days of the brotherhood,
and counsels to abide by the first Rule. This Rule he had
received from no human teacher. The Almighty God himself had revealed it unto him, that he ought to live according
to the mode of the Holy Gospel. He reminded them how
the first members loved to live in poor and abandoned
churches. He bade them not accept churches or houses,
except as it might be in accordance with the rule of holy
poverty they had professed. He forbade their receiving
bulls from the papal court, even for their personal protection. At the same time, he pledged his obedience to the
minister-general and expressed his purpose to go nowhere
and do nothing against his will "for he is my lord."
Through the whole of the document there runs a chord of
anguish.[2]

Francis' heart was broken. Never strong, his last years
were full of infirmities. Change of locality brought only
temporary relief. The remedial measures of the physician,

---

[1] Almost everything done in the order after 1221 was done either "without Francis' knowledge or against his will and mind," are the words of
Sabatier. *S. François,* p. 316.

[2] For the Latin text of this remarkable writing see *Speculum*, 309–313.
Sabatier gives a French trans., in his *S. Francois*, 389 sqq.

such as the age knew, were employed.   An iron, heated to
white heat, was applied to Francis' forehead.   Francis shrank
at first, but submitted to the treatment, saying, "Brother
Fire, you are beautiful above all creatures, be favorable to
me in this hour."   He jocosely called his body, Brother Ass.[1]
The devotion of the people went beyond all bounds.   They
fought for fragments of his clothing, hairs from his head, and
even the parings of his nails.

Two years before his death Francis composed the Canticle
to the Sun, which Renan has called the most perfect expression of modern religious feeling.[2]   It was written at a time
when he was beset by temptations, and blindness had begun
to set in.   The hymn is a pious outburst of passionate love
for nature.   It soars above any other pastorals of the Middle
Ages.   Indeed Francis' love for nature is rare in the records
of his age, and puts him into companionship with that large
modern company who see poems in the clouds and hear sym-
phonies in flowers.   He loved the trees, the stones, birds,
and the plants of the field.   Above all things he loved the
sun, created to illuminate our eyes by day, and the fire which
gives us light in the night time, for "God has illuminated
our eyes by these two, our brothers."

Francis had a message for the brute creation and preached
to the birds.   "Brother birds," he said on one occasion,
"you ought to love and praise your Creator very much.   He
has given you feathers for clothing, wings for flying, and all
things that can be of use to you.   You have neither to sow,
nor to reap, and yet He takes care of you."   And the birds
curved their necks and looked at him as if to thank him.
He would have had the emperor make a special law against
killing or doing any injury to "our sisters, the birds." [3]

[1] This designation was not original with Francis.   In the fourth century
Hilarion called his body the ass which ought to have chaff and not bar-
ley.   Schaff, *Ch. Hist.* III., 190.

[2] *Nouvelles Etudes d'hist. rel.*, 2d ed., Paris, 1844, pp. 333–351.   No
reasonable doubt is possible that Francis was the author of the *Canticle*, now
that the *Speculum* has been published (pp. 234 sqq., and Sabatier's remarks,
278–283).

[3] *Speculum*, 223–226.   See Longfellow's poem, *The Sermon of St. Francis.*

Later tradition narrated very wonderful things about his power over nature,[1] as for example the taming of the fierce wolf of Gubbio.   He was the terror of the neighborhood. He ran at Francis with open mouth, but laid himself down at Francis' feet like a lamb at his words, "Brother Wolf, in the name of Jesus Christ, I command you to do no evil to me or to any man."   Francis promised him forgiveness for all past offences on condition of his never doing harm again to human being.   The beast assented to the compact by lowering his head and kneeling before him.   He became the pet of Gubbio.

The last week of his life, the saint had repeated to him again and again the 142d Psalm, beginning with the words, "I cry with my voice unto Jehovah," and also his Canticle to the Sun.   He called in brothers Angelo and Leo to sing to him about sister Death.[2]   Elias of Cortona, who had aided the Roman curia in setting aside Francis' original Rule, remonstrated on the plea that the people would regard such hilarity in the hour of death as inconsistent with saintship.   But Francis replied that he had been thinking of death for two years, and now he was so united with the Lord, that he might well be joyful in Him.[3]   And so, as Thomas à Celano says, "he met death singing."[4]   At his request they carried him to the Portiuncula chapel.   On his way he asked that his bed be turned so that once more his face might be towards Assisi.   He could no longer see, but he could pray, and so he made a supplication to heaven for the city.[5]   At the church he broke bread

---

[1] *Little Flowers of Francis*, 93–99.   Anthony of Padua, also a Franciscan, according to the same authority, pp. 165 sqq., preached to the fishes at Rimini and called upon them to praise God, seeing they had been preserved in the flood and saved Jonah.   The fishes ascended above the water and opened their mouths and bowed their heads.   The people of the city were attracted and Anthony used the occasion to preach a powerful sermon. In the legend of St. Brandon, it is narrated that when St. Brandon sang, the fishes lay as though they slept.   *Aurea Legenda*, Temple Classics, vol. V.

[2] *Speculum*, p. 241.

[3] *Quoniam, gratia Spiritus sancti cooperante, ita sum unitus et conjunctus cum Domino meo quod per misericordiam suam bene possum in ipso altissimo jocundari.   Speculum*, p. 237.

[4] *Mortem cantando suscepit.*   2 Cel., 3, 139.   [5] *Speculum*, 244 sq.

with the brethren, performing the priestly service with his own lips. On Oct. 3, 1226, to use Brother Leo's words, he " migrated to the Lord Jesus Christ whom he had loved with his whole heart, and followed most perfectly."

Before the coffin was closed, great honors began to be heaped upon the saintly man. The citizens of Assisi took possession of the body, and Francis' name has become the chief attraction of the picturesque and somnolent old town. He was canonized two years later.[1] The services were held in Assisi, July 26, 1228, Gregory IX. being present. The following day, the pontiff laid the corner stone of the new cathedral to Francis' memory. It was dedicated by Innocent IV. in 1243, and Francis' body was laid under the main altar.[2] The art of Cimabue and Giotto has adorned the sanctuary within. The statuary of the modern sculptor, Dupré, in front, represents the great mendicant in the garb of his order with arms crossed over his chest, and his head bowed. Francis was scarcely dead when Elias of Cortona made the astounding announcement of the *stigmata.* These were the marks which Francis is reported to have borne on his body, corresponding to the five wounds on Christ's crucified body. In Francis' case they were fleshy, but not bloody excrescences. The account is as follows. During a period of fasting and the most absorbed devotion, Christ appeared to Francis on the morning of the festival of the Holy Cross, in the rising sun in the form of a seraph with outstretched wings, nailed to the cross. The vision gone, Francis felt pains in his hands and side. He had received the *stigmata.* This occurred in 1224 on the Verna,[3] a mountain on the Upper Arno three thousand feet above the sea.

The historical evidence for the reality of these marks is as follows. It was the day after Francis' death that Elias of Cortona, as vicar of the order, sent letters in all directions

---

[1] Potthast, 8236, 8240, vol. I. 709–710.

[2] There, after much searching, it is said to have been found, 1818. Pius VII., in 1822, declared it to be the genuine body of Francis.

[3] Sabatier gives a charming description of the region, showing his own intense sympathy with nature.

to the Franciscans, announcing the fact that he had seen the *stigmata* on Francis' body. His letter contained these words: " Never has the world seen such a sign except on the Son of God. For a long time before his death, our brother had in his body five wounds which were truly the *stigmata* of Christ, for his hands and feet have marks as of nails, without and within, a kind of scars, while from his side, as if pierced by a lance, a little blood oozed." The *Speculum Perfectionis*, perhaps the first biography of Francis, refers to them incidentally, but distinctly, in the course of a description of the severe temptations by which Francis was beset.[1] Thomas à Celano, not later than 1230, describes them more at length, and declares that a few saw them while Francis was still alive. Gregory IX. in 1237 called upon the whole Church to accept them, and condemned the Dominicans for calling their reality in question.[2] The first portrait of Francis, dating from 1236, exhibits the marks.

On the other hand, a very strong argument against their genuineness is the omission of all reference to them by Gregory IX. in his bull canonizing Francis, 1228. Francis' claim to saintship, we would think, could have had no better authentication, and the omission is inexplicable.[3]

---

[1] p. 194. It is at first sight striking that the author does not give a detailed description of this wonderful event. From another standpoint the passing reference may be regarded as a stronger testimony to its reality. See Sabatier's observations, *Speculum*, pp. lxvi. sqq. It will be remembered that Sabatier places this document in 1227, only seven months after Francis' death.

[2] In three bulls, Potthast, 10307, 10308, 10309, vol. I. 875.

[3] The evidence for the genuineness is accepted by Sabatier, *S. François*, 401 sqq. Among other testimonies he adduces a Benediction upon Leo ostensibly written by Francis' own hand, and found among the archives of Assisi. See *Speculum*, p. lxvii. sq. On the margin of this document Leo has written his authentication. He vouches for the scene on the Verna and the stigmata. If this document be genuine, as Sabatier insists, it is the most weighty of all the testimonies. Hase stated, as strongly as it can be stated, the view that the whole tale was a fraud, invented by Elias, *Francis of Assisi*, 143–202, and *Kirchengeschichte*, II. 385 sqq. Elias was the only eye-witness, and it is contrary to all laws that he should have denied the people the privilege of looking at the marks, after the saint was dead, if they had really been there. On the contrary, he hurried the body to the grave.

Three explanations have been given of the stigmata on the supposition that Francis' body really bore the scars. 1. They were due to supernatural miracle. This is the Catholic view. In 1304 Benedict XI. established a festival of the stigmata. 2. They were the product of a highly wrought mental state proceeding from the contemplation of Christ on the cross. This is the view of Sabatier.[1] 3. The third explanation treats them as a pious fraud practised by Francis himself, who from a desire to feel all the pains Christ felt, picked the marks with his own fingers.[2] Such a course seems incredible. In the absence of a sufficient moral reason for the impression of the stigmata, it is difficult for the critical mind to accept them. On the other hand, the historical attestation is such that an effort is required to deny them. So far as we know, Francis never used the stigmata to attest his mission.[3]

The study of the career of Francis d'Assisi, as told by his contemporaries, and as his spirit is revealed in his own last testament, makes the impression of purity of purpose and humility of spirit, — of genuine saintliness. He sought not positions of honor nor a place with the great. With simple mind, he sought to serve his fellow-men by republishing the precepts of the Gospel, and living them out in his own example. He sought once more to give the Gospel to the common people, and the common people heard him gladly.

Hase makes a strong case, but it must be remembered that he wrote without having before him the later evidence brought to light by Sabatier.

[1] *S. François*, 401 sqq. Sabatier does not regard them as miraculous but as unusual, as, for example, are the mathematical powers and musical genius of youthful prodigies. According to Hase, this was also Tholuck's explanation. See art. *Stigmatization*, in Herzog, XIV. 728–734, which takes the same view and compares the scars to the effects of parental states before childbirth.

[2] So Hausrath. The first Franciscan chronicler, Salimbene, d. 1287, no doubt expressed the feeling of his age when he said, "Never man on earth but Francis has had the five wounds of Christ." The Dominicans claimed the stigmata for St. Catherine of Siena, but Sixtus IV., in 1475, prohibited her being represented with them.

[3] Bonaventura's legendary *Life* makes Francis a witness to the *stigmata*, but he evidently is seeking to establish the fact against doubts.

He may not have possessed great strength of intellect. He lacked the gifts of the ecclesiastical diplomat, but he certainly possessed glowing fervor of heart and a magnetic personality, due to consuming love for men.   He was not a theological thinker, but he was a man of practical religious sympathies to which his deeds corresponded.   He spoke and acted as one who feels full confidence in his divinely appointed mission.[1]   He spoke to the Church as no one after him did till Luther came.

Few men of history have made so profound an impression as did Francis.   His personality shed light far and near in his own time.   But his mission extends to all the centuries. He was not a foreigner in his own age by any protest in matters of ritual or dogma, but he is at home in all ages by reason of his Apostolic simplicity and his artless gentleness. Our admiration for him turns not to devotion as for a perfect model of the ideal life.   Francis' piety, after all, has a mediæval glow.   But, so far as we can know, he stands well among those of all time who have discerned the meaning of Christ's words and breathed His spirit.   So Harnack can call him the "wonderful saint of Assisi," and Sabatier utter the lofty praise "that it was given to him to divine the superiority of the spiritual priesthood." [2]

The Canticle of the Sun

O most high, almighty, good Lord God, to Thee belong praise, glory, honor, and all blessing !

Praised be my Lord God with all His creatures, and specially our brother the sun, who brings us the day and who brings us the light ; fair is he and shines with a very great splendor : O Lord he signifies to us Thee !

Praised be my Lord for our sister the moon, and for the stars, the which He has set clear and lovely in heaven.

Praised be my Lord for our brother the wind and for air and cloud, calms and all weather by the which Thou upholdest life in all creatures.

Praised be my Lord for our sister water, who is very serviceable unto us and humble and precious and clean.

---

[1] In his will he refers again and again to his divine appointment. *Deus mihi dedit,* "God has given to me."

[2] *Monasticism,* Engl. trans., p. 67, and *S. François,* p. viii.

Praised be my Lord for our brother fire, through whom Thou givest us light in the darkness; and he is bright and pleasant and very mighty and strong.

Praised be my Lord for our mother the earth, the which doth sustain us and keep us, and bringeth forth divers fruits and flowers of many colors, and grass.

Praised be my Lord for all those who pardon one another for His love's sake, and who endure weakness and tribulation; blessed are they who peaceably shall endure, for Thou, O most Highest, shalt give them a crown.

Praised be my Lord for our sister, the death of the body, from which no man escapeth. Woe to him who dieth in mortal sin! Blessed are they who are found walking by the most holy will, for the second death shall have no power to do them harm.

Praise ye and bless the Lord, and give thanks unto Him and serve Him with great humility.[1]

§ 71. *The Franciscans.*

"Sweet Francis of Assisi, would that he were here again!"
—TENNYSON.

The Brethren Minor —*fratres minores*, or Minorites, the official title of the Franciscans— got their name from the democratic faction in Assisi, the Minores, whom Francis at a time of feud reconciled to the party of the aristocrats. Before the curia at Rome, Francis insisted upon the application of the name as a warning to the members not to aspire after positions of distinction.[2] They spread rapidly in Italy and beyond; but before the generation had passed away to which Francis belonged, the order was torn by internal strife, growing out of the attempt to conserve the principles originally laid down by Francis. The history of no other order has anything to show like this protracted conflict within its own membership over a question of principle. The protracted dispute has an almost unique place in the polemic theology of the Middle Ages.

According to the Rule of 1210 and Francis' last will they

---

[1] The version of Matthew Arnold, *Essays in Criticism*, 1st series. A recent translation is given in Robinson; the *Writings of St. Francis*, pp. 150 sqq., by the Franciscan, Stephen Donovan. Boehmer, p. 65, gives the Latin text.

[2] *Speculum*, p. 76. *Domine*, said Francis, *minores ideo vocati sunt fratres mei ut majores fieri non præsumant.*

were to be a free brotherhood devoted to evangelical poverty and Apostolic practice, rather than a close organization
bound by precise rules.[1] Innocent III. counselled him to take
for his model the rule of the older orders, but Francis
declined and went his own path. He builded upon a few
texts of Scripture. From 1216, when Cardinal Ugolino became associated with the order as patron and counsellor, a
new influence was felt, and rigid discipline was substituted
for the freer organization of Francis.

At the chapter of 1217, the decision was made to send
missionaries beyond the confines of Italy. Elias of Cortona,
once a mattress-maker in Assisi and destined to be notorious
for setting aside Francis' original plan, led a band of missionaries to Syria. Others went to Germany, Hungary, France,
Spain and England. As foreign missionaries, the Franciscans showed dauntless enterprise, going south to Morocco
and east as far as Pekin. They enjoy the distinction of having accompanied Columbus on his second journey to the New
World and were subsequently most active in the early
American missions from Florida to California and from
Quebec along the St. Lawrence and the Great Lakes and
southward to the Gulf of Mexico.

The Rule of 1221, by its lack of unity and decision, betrays two influences at work, one proceeding from Ugolino
and one from Francis. There are signs of the struggle
which had already begun several years before. The Rule
placed a general at the head of the order and a governing
body was constituted, consisting of the heads of the different
houses. Poverty, however, is still enjoined and the duty of
labor is emphasized that the members might be saved from
becoming idlers. The sale of the products of their labor
was forbidden except as it might benefit the sick.

The Rule of 1223, which is briefer and consists of twelve
chapters, repeats the preceding code and was solemnly
approved by the pope November 29 of the same year. This

---

[1] See Sabatier, *S. François*, pp. 80 sqq. Also Madonnet, *Les Origines
de l'ordo de Pœnitentia*, pp. 4, 21 sq. etc., who presents this feature of
Francis' society in its early days in a clear light.

code goes still further in setting aside the distinguished will
of Francis.   The mendicant character of the order is strongly
emphasized.   But obedience to the pope is introduced and
a cardinal is made its protector and guardian.   The Roman
Breviary is ordered to be used as the book of daily worship.
Monastic discipline has taken the place of biblical liberty.
The strong hand of the hierarchy is evident.   The freedom
of the Rule of 1210 has disappeared.[1]   Peter di Catana
was made superior of the order, who, a few months later,
was followed by Elias of Cortona.   Francis' appeal in his
last testament to the original freedom of his brotherhood
and against the new order of things, the papal party did all
in its power to suppress altogether.

The Clarisses, the Minorite nuns, getting their name from
Clara of Sciffi who was canonized in 1255, were also called
Sisters of St. Damian from the Church of St. Damian.
Francis wrote a Rule for them which enforced poverty [2]
and made a will for Clara which is lost.   The sisters
seem at first to have supported themselves by the toil
of their hands, but by Francis' advice soon came to depend
upon alms.[3]   The rule was modified in 1219 and the order
was afterwards compelled to adopt the Benedictine rule.[4]

The Tertiaries, or Brothers and Sisters of Penitence, [5] were
the third order of St. Francis, the Clarisses being reckoned
as the second, and received papal recognition for the first time
in the bull of Nicolas IV., 1289.[6]   It is doubtful whether
Francis ever prescribed for them a definite rule.   Of the
existence of the Tertiaries during his life there is no doubt.
They are called by Gregory IX. in 1228 the Brothers of the
Third Order of St. Francis.[7]   The Rule of 1289 is made for

[1] See Sabatier, *Vie de S. François*, pp. 273 sqq.

[2] This Rule has only recently been found and published in the *Seraphicæ
legislationis textus originales*, Quaracchi, 1897.   See Robinson, pp. 75 sqq.

[3] See *Speculum*, p. 181 and note.

[4] Finally by Urban IV., 1263.   See Potthast, II. 1515.   Affiliated houses
were erected at Burgos, Spain, 1219; Rheims, France, 1220; Prague, 1235,
etc.

[5] *Frates et sorores de pœnitentia.*   [6] See Potthast, II. 1856.

[7] Potthast, I. 703.   Nicolas IV., however, speaks of a rule given by Francis.

a lay corporation, and also for a conventual association from which latter, married persons are excluded. The purpose of Francis included all classes of laics, men and women, married and unmarried. His object was to put within the reach of laymen the higher practice of virtue and order of merit associated with the monastic life. It is quite probable that Francis took his idea from the Humiliati, known as the Poor Men of Lombardy, *Pauperes Lombardici*, or perhaps from the Waldenses, known as the Poor Men of Lyons and also well known in Northern Italy in Francis' day. The Humiliati had groups of laymen in the twelfth century living according to semi-conventual rules. In 1184 they were condemned by Lucius III. There seem to have been three grades, the lay Humiliati, who in the ordinary avenues of life observed specific ascetic practices; second, those who were living in convents as monks or nuns ; and third, canons, who were priests and lived together in common. These three grades were sanctioned by Innocent III. in 1201 and were protected by later popes, as for example Innocent IV.[1]

It is possible that Francis' first plan was for an organization of laymen, and that the idea of an organization of monks developed later in his mind. The division of the Franciscans into three grades was permanently established by the chapter of 1221.[2] The earliest rule of the Tertiaries in thirteen chapters sets forth the required style of dress, the asceticisms they were to practise, and the other regulations they were to observe. They were to abstain from all oaths except in exceptional cases, provided for by the pope, to make confession three times a year, have if possible the advice of

[1] See the art. *Humiliaten* in Herzog, VIII. 447–449, by Zöckler who quotes H. Tiraboschi, *Memorie degli Humiliati*, 3 vols. Modena, 1766. Sabatier, *Regula antiqua*, p. 15, upon the basis of Jacques de Vitry and other authorities, says the Humiliati were at the height of their zeal and activity in 1220. He confesses that the Tertiary Rule, the *Regula Antiqua*, is probably in part a copy of the Rule of the Humiliati sanctioned by Innocent III. and says, " Perhaps we have heretofore ascribed an undue originality to the Franciscan movement."

[2] See Walter Goetz, *Die Regel des Tertiarierordens*, in Brieger's *Zeitschrift*, 1902, pp. 97 sqq.

the diocesan in making their wills, receive to their number no one accused of heresy, and were neither to use deadly weapons nor to carry them.[1] Women, if married, were not to be admitted without the consent of their husbands, and all who had families were enjoined to care for them as a part of the service of God (VI. 6).[2] The Tertiaries still exist in the Roman Catholic Church.

To follow the history of the Franciscans from 1223, the stricter party, who sought to carry out Francis' practice of strict Apostolic poverty and his views as set forth in his last will, were known as the Observants, or Spirituals, or Zealots. The party, favoring a relaxation of Francis' Rule and supported by Gregory IX., were often called the Conventuals from occupying convents of their own, especially more pretentious buildings in cities.[3] Now the one party, now

[1] VI. 3, *arma mortalia contra quempiam non recipiant vel secum ferant.* This most interesting statement was changed by Nicolas IV. in 1289 so that it read, "The brethren shall not carry arms of attack except for the defence of the Roman Church, the Christian faith, or their country, or unless they have authority from their superiors." The Humiliati received papal exemption from Honorius III. against going to war. See Sabatier, *Regula antiq.*, p. 22, Note.

[2] The development of the Tertiary order is a matter of dispute. Sabatier has recently made known two rules of the Tertiary order; the first, found in Florence, the second which he himself discovered in the convent of Capistrano in the Abruzzi. To compare them with the Rule contained in Nicolas IV.'s bull, *supra montem*, 1289, the Rule of Nicolas has 20 chapters, the Florentine 19, that of Capistrano 13. See the table given by Walter Goetz, p. 100. Sabatier in his edition of the Capistrano Rule, *Regula Antiqua*, p. 12, puts it very close to the death of Francis, between 1228 and 1234. *Les Règles*, etc., p. 153, goes further and puts it back to 1221, thus making it the second Rule of St. Francis. At any rate, it must for the present be regarded as the oldest form of the Rule. Goetz, p. 105, while dating the *Regula Antiqua* much earlier than 1289, is inclined to regard it as a compilation. In 1517 Leo X. perfected the regulations concerning Tertiary orders and divided the members into two classes, those taking no vows and living in the ordinary walks of life and those who live in convents. The best general treatment of the subject is furnished by Karl Müller, *Die Anfänge des Minoritenordens.*, pp. 115–171, and Madonnet who gives a convenient list of the papal utterances on the Tertiaries, *Les Règles*, etc., pp. 146 sq.

[3] The Observants looked to Portiuncula as the centre of the order, the Conventuals to the cathedral of Assisi.

the other was in the ascendant. The popes were against the Observants. The inward discord lasted throughout the thirteenth century and far into the fourteenth[1] and was suppressed, rather than allayed, for the first time by Leo X., who separated the Franciscans into two orders. In the meantime Observants continued to agitate the scheme of St. Francis, and some of them laid down their lives as martyrs for their principles.

The matter in dispute among the Franciscans was the right of the order as a corporation to hold property in fee simple. The papal decisions in favor of such tenure began with the bull of Gregory IX., 1230. It allowed the order to collect money through "faithful men" appointed for districts, these monies to be applied to the rearing of conventual buildings, to missions, and other objects, and to be held in trust for the givers. This privilege was elaborated by Innocent IV., 1245, and was made to include the possession of books, tools, houses, and lands. Innocent made the clear distinction between tenure in fee simple and tenure for use and granted the right of tenure for use. By this was meant that the order might receive gifts and bequests and hold them indefinitely as for the donors. This was equivalent to perpetual ownership, and might be compared to modern thousand-year leases. Innocent also made the tenure of all property within the order subject to the immediate supervision of the pope.

Determined resistance was offered by the Observants to these papal decrees, and they were persecuted by Elias of Cortona, who vigorously pushed the papal policy. But they were strong and Elias was deposed from the headship of the order by the chapter of 1227. He was reinstated in 1232, but again deposed in 1239. He espoused the cause of Frederick II., and died 1253.

One of the leading men of the wing true to Francis was Brother Leo, the author of what is probably the first biography of Francis, the *Speculum Perfectionis*, the Mirror of

[1] Ubertino da Casale's interpretation of Francis' purpose is given by Knoth, pp. 99 sq.

Perfection.   When the project was bruited of erecting the great church at Assisi over Francis' remains and Elias placed a marble vessel on the site to receive contributions, Leo, who regarded the project as a profanation of the memory of the saint, dashed the vessel to pieces.   For this act he was banished, amidst tumult, from Assisi.[1]

It seemed for a while doubtful which party would gain the upper hand.   The Observants were in power under John of Parma, general of the order for ten years, 1247–1257, when he was obliged to resign and retire into strict monastic seclusion.   John was followed by Bonaventura, 1257–1274, the great Schoolman, who, in the main, cast his influence on the side of the Conventuals.   The Observants became identified with the dreams of Joachim of Flore and applied his prophecy of a new religious order to themselves.   These views became a new source of discord and strife lasting for more than a century.   Bonaventura pronounced against the adoption of Joachim's views by condemning Gerardo Borgo's *Introduction* to Joachim's writings.   The Life of St. Francis, written by Bonaventura at the mandate of the General Chapter of Narbonne, 1260, and declared the authoritative biography of the saint by the Chapter of 1263, suppressed Francis' will and other materials favorable to the contention of the Observants, and emphasized the churchly and disciplinary elements of the order.   The Observants, from this time on, fought a brave but hopeless battle.   They could not successfully wage war against the policy pushed by the papal court.

The report that Gregory X., through the acts of the council of Lyons, 1274, intended to force the order to hold property, stirred opposition into a flame and a number of the Observants were thrown into prison, including Angelo Clareno, an influential author.   Nicholas III., in the bull *Exiit qui seminat*,[2] 1279, again made a clear distinction between owning property in fee simple and its tenure for use, and confirmed the latter right.   He insisted upon the principle that the pope is the ultimate owner of the property of the order.

---

[1] Sabatier, *Speculum*, pp. li sq.   [2] Potthast, II. 1746.

The bull expressly annulled St. Francis' prohibition forbidding the order to seek privileges from the pope. The Franciscan general, Bonagratia, and his two successors, accepted the bull, but Peter Olivi, d. 1298, who had acquired wide influence through his writings, violently opposed it. Cœlestin V. sought to heal the division by inviting the Observants to join the order of the Cœlestin hermits which he had founded, and Angelo Clareno, who had been released from prison, took this course. It was opposed by Olivi and the Observant preacher Ubertino da Casale,[1] d. after 1330, who remained through much persecution true to the original principles of Francis.

And so the century in which Francis was born went out with the controversy still going on with unabated warmth. A somewhat new aspect was given to the controversy in the fourteenth century. The dogmatic question was then put into the foreground, whether Christ and his Apostles practised absolute poverty or not. In 1323 John XXII. sought to put a final stop to the dissension by giving papal authority to the statement that they did not practise absolute poverty. Thus the underlying foundation of the strict Franciscan Rule was taken away.

In another respect the Franciscans departed from the mind of their founder. Francis disparaged learning. In 1220 he reprimanded and then cursed Pietro Staccia, a doctor of laws, for establishing a Franciscan school at Bologna. On hearing of a famous doctor, who had entered the order, he is reported to have said, " I am afraid such doctors will be the destruction of my vineyard. True doctors are they who with the meekness of wisdom exhibit good works for the betterment of their neighbors." To Anthony of Padua, Francis wrote — and the genuineness of the letter is not disputed — " I am agreed that you continue reading lectures on theology to the brethren provided that kind of study does not extinguish in them the spirit of humility and prayer."[2] But Francis'

---

[1] Ubertino, during seven days of rigid seclusion on the Verna, wrote the ascetic work *Arbor vitæ crucifixæ.* See Knoth, 9–14.

[2] Lempp, *Anthony of Padua*, p. 439.

followers departed from his teachings and adapted themselves to the current of that wonderful thirteenth century,
established schools in their convents aud were well settled,
before the century was half gone, at the chief centres of university culture.   In 1255 an order called upon Franciscans,
going out as missionaries, to study Greek, Arabic, Hebrew,
and other languages.

The order spread rapidly from Palestine to Ireland.[1]   It
was introduced into France by Pacifico and Guichard of
Beaujolais, a brother-in-law of the French king.   The first
successful attempt to establish branches in Germany was
made, 1221, by Cæsar of Spires, who had been converted by
Elias of Cortona on his journey to Syria.   He was accompanied
by twelve priests and thirteen laymen, among them, Thomas
of Celano and Jordan of Giano upon whose account we depend
for the facts.   The company separated at Trent, met again
at Augsburg, and then separated once more, carrying their
propaganda along the Rhine aud to other parts of the country.   Houses were established at Mainz, Worms, Spires, and
Cologne which in 1522 were united into a custody.   The
year following four German custodies were added.[2]   Cæsar
of Spires, the flaming apostle of the order in Germany, belonged to the Observant wing, and had to suffer severe persecution and was put to death in prison.

As for England, nine Franciscans, four of them clerics,
only one of whom was in priest's orders, landed at Dover,
1224, and went to Canterbury, and then to London.   The
account of their early labors on English soil, by Thomas of
Eccleston, a contemporary,[3] is one of the freshest and most

---

[1] The Franciscans became guardians of the holy places in Palestine.   In
answer to my question put to a Franciscan in Nazareth, whether the Church
of the Annunciation there was the veritable place where Mary had received the
message of the angel, he replied, " Most certainly !   We Franciscans have
been in this land 600 years and have thoroughly investigated all these
matters."   [2] See Hauck, IV. pp. 378 sq.

[3] All that we know about his life is gotten from his account of the Franciscans in England.   He died about 1260.   Eccleston gives the names of the
nine first missionaries.   *Mon. Franc.*, pp. 5 sqq.   Agnellus of Pisa stood at
their head.   Three of the clerics were Englishmen.

absorbing relations of English affairs in the Middle Ages.
At Canterbury they were entertained by the monks of Fes-
kamp, and at London by the Black Friars. At Oxford they
received a warm welcome. Grosseteste announced their advent with a sermon from the words, " They that sat in darkness have seen a great light." It was as if the door to a
new religious era had been opened. Of their settlement in
St. Ebbe's parish, Oxford, it was said that " there was sown a
grain of mustard seed which grew to be greater than all the
trees." They were quickly settled at Cambridge, Norwich,
Northampton, Yarmouth, and other centres. They were
the first popular preachers that England had seen, and the
first to embody a practical philanthropy.[1] The condition of
English villages and towns at that day was very wretched.
Skin diseases were fearfully prevalent, including leprosy..
Destructive epidemics spread with great rapidity. Sanitary
precautions were unknown. Stagnant pools and piles of
refuse abounded.[2]

Partly from necessity and partly from pure choice these
ardent religionists made choice of quarters in the poorest
and most neglected parts of the towns. In Norwich they
settled in a swamp through which the city sewerage passed.
At Newgate, now a part of London, they betook themselves
to Stinking Lane. At Cambridge they occupied the decayed
gaol.

No wonder that such zeal received recognition. The
people soon learned to respect the new apostles. Adam
Marsh joined them, and he and Grosseteste, the most influential English ecclesiastic of his day, lectured in the Franciscan school at Oxford. The burgesses of London and
other towns gave them lands, as did also the king, at Shrews-
bury. In 1256 the number of English friars had increased
to 1242, settled in forty-nine different localities.[3] The Franciscans also gave an impetus to learning ; they set up schools,

---

[1] Creighton, p. 107.

[2] See the descriptions of Jessopp, *Coming of the Friars*, pp. 21 sqq., and
Brewer's *Mon. Franc.*, pp. xv. sq.

[3] *Mon. Franc.*, p. xli.

2 E

as at Oxford, where Robert Grosseteste delivered lectures
for them. Most of the great English Schoolmen belonged
to the Franciscan order. Eccleston describes the godly
lives of the early English Franciscans, their abstinence, and
their light-heartedness.[1] Less than fifty years after their
advent, one of their number, Robert Kilwarby, was sitting
in the archepiscopal chair of Canterbury ; to another Franciscan, Bonaventura, was offered the see of York, which he
declined.

In time, the history of the Franciscans followed the usual
course of human prosperity.[2] They fell from their first
estate. With honors and lands came demoralization. They
gained an unsavory reputation as collectors of papal revenues. Matthew Paris' rebukes of their arrogance date
back as far as 1235, and he said that Innocent IV. turned
them from fishers of men into fishers of pennies. At the
sequestration of the religious houses by Henry VIII., the
Franciscan convent of Christ's Church, London, was the first
to fall, 1532.[3]

[1] He tells a comic story of William de Madeley, at Oxford, who, finding a
pair of shoes, put them on and went to matins. Going to sleep he dreamt he
was attacked by thieves, and thrust out his feet to show that he was a friar.
But lo ! the shoes were still on, and starting up he flung them out of the window. Another poor friar, Gilbert de Vyz, so he relates, was badly treated by
the devil. It happened at Cornhill. The devil at his final visit exclaimed,
" Sir, do you think you have escaped me ? " De Vyz picked up a handful
of lice and threw it at the devil, and he vanished. p. 13.

[2] John L'Estrange says that, at the time they were falling out of favor,
one English will out of every three conveyed property to the Franciscans.
Quoted by Howlett in his Preface to *Mon. Franc.*, II. p. xxvii.

[3] According to Gasquet, p. 237, there were sixty-six Franciscan houses.
Addis and Scannell's *Catholic Dict.*, p. 388, gives a list of sixty-four. The
first house of the Franciscan nuns, or Poor Clares, was founded outside of
Aldgate, London, 1293, and was known as " the Minories," a name the
locality still retains. At the time of the dissolution of the monasteries they
had three houses in England.

§ 72.   *St. Dominic and the Dominicans.*

LITERATURE. — The earliest *Life* by JORDANUS, Dominic's successor as head of
the order: *de principiis ordinis prædicatorum* in QUÉTIF-ECHARD, who
gives five other early biographies (Bartholomew of Trent, 1244–1251,
Humbert de Romanis, 1250, etc.), and ed. by J. J. BERTHIER, Freib., i.
Schw., 1892. — H. D. LACORDAIRE, d. 1861 : *Vie de S. Dominique*, Paris,
1840, 8th ed. 1882.   Also *Hist. Studies of the Order of S. Dom. 1170–
1221*, Engl. trans., N.Y., 1869. — E. CARO : *S. Dom. et les Dominicains*,
Paris, 1853. — A. T. DRANE : *Hist. of St. Dom.*, *Founder of the Friar
Preachers*, London, 1891. — BALME ET LELAIDIER : *Cartulaire ou hist.
diplomatique de S. Dom.*, Paris, 1892. — J. GUIRAUD : *S. Dom.*, Paris,
2d ed., 1899. — For titles of about thirty lives, see Potthast, II. 1272.
— QUÉTIF-ECHARD : *Script. ord. Prædicatorum*, 2 vols. Paris, 1719–
1721. — RIPOLL AND BERMOND : *Bullarium ord. Præd.*, 8 vols. Rome,
1737 sqq. — MAMACHI : *Annal. ord. Præd.*, Rome, 1756. — *Monumenta ord. fratrum Præd. hist.*, ed. by B. M. REICHERT, Louvaine
and Rome, 10 vols., 1897–1901.   Vol. III. gives the acts of the general
chapters of the order, 1220–1303. — A. DANZAS : *Etudes sur les temps
primitifs de l'ordre de S. Dom.*, Paris, 1873–1885. — *DENIFLE : *Die Constitutionen des Predigerordens vom Jahre 1228*, and *Die Constitutionen
des Raymunds von Peñaforte 1238–1241* in *Archiv für Lit. und Kirchengesch.*, 1885, pp. 165–227 and 1889, 530–565. — HELYOT : *Rel. Orders.* —
LEA : *Hist. of Inquisition*, I. 242–304, etc.   Wetzer-Welte, art. *Dominicus*, III. 1931–1945. — W. LESCHER : *St. Dominic and the Rosary*, London, 1902. — H. HOLZAPFEL : *S. Dom. und der Rosenkranz*, Munich, 1903.

The Spaniard, Dominic, founder of the order of preachers,
usually called the Dominicans,[1] lacks the genial personal
element of the saint of Assisi, and his career has little to
correspond to the romantic features of his contemporary's
career.   Dominic was of resolute purpose, zealous for propa-
gating the orthodox faith, and devoted to the Church and
hierarchy.   His influence has been through the organization
he created, and not through his personal experiences and contact with the people of his age.   This accounts for the small
number of biographies of him as compared with the large
number of Francis.

Domingo, or Dominic, was born 1170 at Calaroga, Spain,
and died Aug. 6, 1121, in Bologna.[2]   His mother, Juana of

---

[1] *Ordo prædicatorum*, *fratres prædicatores*, or simply *prædicatores*, as in
the papal bulls and the constitutions of the order.

[2] His descent from the noble family of Guzman has been disputed by the
Bollandists.

Aza, is worshipped as a saint in the Dominican ritual. At
seven the son passed under the priestly instruction of an
uncle.   Ten years were subsequently spent at Palencia in the
study of philosophy and theology, and he is said to have
excelled as a student.   About 1195, he was made canon at
Osma, which gives its name to the episcopal diocese, within
whose bounds he was born.   In 1203 he accompanied his
bishop, Diego d'Azeveda, to France [1] on a mission to secure
a bride for the son of Alfonzo VIII. of Castile.   This and
subsequent journeys across the Pyrenees brought him into
contact with the Albigenses and the legates despatched by
Innocent III. to take measures to suppress heresy in Southern
France.   Dominic threw himself into the movement for suppressing heresy and started upon a tour of preaching.   At
Prouille in the diocese of Toulouse, he erected an asylum
for girls to offset the schools established by the Albigenses,
for the training of the daughters of impoverished noblemen.
He was on intimate terms with Simon de Montfort, but, so
far as is known, he took no active part in the Albigensian
crusade except as a spiritual adviser.[2]   His attempt to establish a mission for the conversion of heretics received the support of Fulke, bishop of Toulouse, who in 1215 granted him
one-sixth of the tithes of his diocese.   Among the first to
ally themselves to Dominic was Peter Cellani, a citizen of
Toulouse, who gave him a house.

An epoch in Dominic's career was his visit in Rome during
the sessions of the Fourth Lateran Council, when he received
encouragement from Innocent III. who declined to assent to
the proposal of a new order and bade him adopt one of the
existing monastic constitutions.[3]   Dominic chose the rule of
the canons regular of St. Augustine,[4] adopted the black dress

[1] Jordanus says, they went *ad Marchias*, which probably refers to the
domain of Hugo of Lusignan, Count de la Marche, and not to Denmark, as
often represented.

[2] The bull canonizing Dominic says, *hæreticos caritative ad pœnitentiam
et conversionem fidei hortabatur*, he affectionately exhorted heretics to return
to the faith.   [3] Potthast, I. 436.

[4] See Denifle, *Archiv*, 1885, p. 169, who says that Dominic took as the
basis of his rule the rule of the Premonstrants and insists that his followers

of the Augustinians, and built the convent of St. Romanus at Toulouse.   He was again in Rome from September, 1216, to Easter, 1217.   Honorius III. in 1216 approved the organization, and confirmed it in the possession of goods and houses.   An unreliable tradition states that Honorius also conferred upon Dominic the important office of Master of the Palace, *magister palatii.*   The office cannot be traced far beyond Gregory IX.[1]

The legendary accounts of his life represent the saint at this time as engaged in endless scourgings and other most rigorous asceticisms.   Miracles, even to the raising of the dead, were ascribed to him.

In 1217 Dominic sent out monks to start colonies.   The order took quick root in large cities, — Paris, Bologna, and Rome, — the famous professor of canon law at Paris, Reginald, taking its vows.   Dominic himself in 1218 established two convents in Spain, one for women in Madrid and one for men at Seville.   The first Dominican house in Paris, the convent of St. Jacques, gave the name Jacobins to the Dominicans in France and Jacobites to the party in the French Revolution which held its meetings there.   In 1224 St. Jacques had one hundred and twenty inmates.   The order had a strong French element and included in its prayers a prayer for the French king.   From France, the Dominicans went into Germany.   Jordanus and other inmates of St. Jacques were Germans.   They quickly established themselves, in spite of episcopal prohibitions and opposition from other orders, in Cologne, Worms, Strassburg, Basel, and other German cities.[2]   In 1221 the order

were canons regular.   Denifle was a Dominican, and in his able article gives too much credit to Dominic for originality.

[1] This important office according to Echard at first gave to the incumbent the right to fix the meaning of Scripture at the Pontifical court.   It has since come to have the duty of comparing all matters with the catholic doctrine before they are presented to the pope, selecting preachers for certain occasions, conferring the doctors' degree, etc.   Wetzer-Welte avoids giving offence to the Dominicans by making the ambiguous statement, III. 1934, that Dominic *gewissermassen der erste Mag. palatii wurde.*

[2] Hauck, IV. 391–394.

was introduced into England, and at once settled in Oxford.[1] The Blackfriars Bridge, London, carries in its name
the memory of their great friary in that city.

The first General Chapter was held 1220 in Bologna.
Dominic preached with much zeal in Northern Italy. He
died, lying on ashes, at Bologna, Aug. 6, 1221, and lies buried
there in the convent of St. Nicholas, which has been adorned
by the art of Nicholas of Pisa and Michael Angelo. As compared with the speedy papal recognition of Francis and
Anthony of Padua, the canonization of the Spanish saint
followed tardily, thirteen years after his death, July 13, 1234.[2]

At the time of Dominic's death, the preaching friars had
sixty convents scattered in the provinces of Provence, Northern France, Spain, Lombardy, Italy, England, Germany,
and Hungary, each of which held its own chapter yearly. To
these eight provinces, by 1228, four others had been added,
Poland, Denmark, Greece, and Jerusalem.[3] Combined they
made up the General Chapter. Each of the provinces was
presided over by a provincial or provincial prior, and the
convents by a prior or sub prior. The title and dignity
of abbot were not assumed. At the head of the whole
body stands a grand-master.[4] Privilege after privilege was
conferred by the Holy See, including the important right
to preach anywhere and everywhere.[5] The constitutions
of 1228 are the earliest we possess, but they are not the
oldest. They were revised under Raymund de Peñaforte,
the third general.[6]

Mendicancy was made the rule of the order at the first

---

[1] At the suppression of the monasteries under Henry VIII., the Dominicans had 58 houses in England (Gasquet, p. 237), or 57 according to Addis
and Scannell, *Dict.*, p. 301.

[2] Potthast, I. 810.

[3] See the Constitution of 1228, Denifle, pp. 212, 215.

[4] *Magister generalis.* In 1862 Pius IX. limited his tenure of office to
twelve years. Since 1272 he has lived at St. Maria sopra Minerva in
Rome.

[5] May 16, 1227. See Potthast, I. 684. Denifle makes much of this point,
pp. 176-180.

[6] Denifle gives the best edition in *Archiv* for 1885, pp. 193-227.

General Chapter, 1220.[1]   The example of St. Francis was
followed, and the order, as well as the individual monk,
renounced all right to possess property.   The mendicant
feature was, however, never emphasized as among the Franciscans.   It was not a matter of conscience with the Dominicans, and the order was never involved in divisions over the
question of holding property.   The obligation of corporate
poverty was wholly removed by Sixtus IV., 1477.   Dominic's
last exhortation to his followers was that "they should have
love, do humble service, and live in voluntary poverty."[2]
But the precept never seems to have been taken much to
heart by them.

Unlike the man of Assisi, Dominic did not combine
manual labor with the other employments of his monks.
For work with their hands he substituted study and preaching.   The Dominicans were the first monastics to adopt
definite rules of study.   When Dominic founded St. Jacques
in Paris, and sent seventeen of his order to man that convent,
he instructed them to "study and preach."   Cells were
constructed at Toulouse for study.[3]   A theological course
of four years in philosophy and theology was required before a license was given to preach,[4] and three years more of
theological study followed it.

Preaching and the saving of souls were defined as the
chief aim of the order.[5]   Humbert de Romanis, its fifth

---

[1] Denifle, pp. 181 sqq., states that the idea of poverty was in Dominic's mind
before Honorius sanctioned the order, and that it was thoroughly as original
with him as it was with Francis.   This view seems to be contradicted by the bull
of Honorius, 1216, which confirms Dominic and his followers in the possession
of goods.   Jordanus, c. 27, states that the principle of poverty was adopted that
the preachers might be freed from the care of earthly goods, *ne predicationis
impediretur officium sollicitudine terrenorum.*   Francis adopted this principle
as a means of personal sanctification ; Dominic, in order that he and his
followers might give themselves up unreservedly to the work of saving souls.

[2] *Caritatem habete, humilitatem servite, pauperitatem voluntariam possi-
dete.*   [3] Denifle, pp. 185 sqq.

[4] *Nullus fiat publicus doctor, nisi per 4 annos ad minus theologiam
audierit.*   Const., 1228, II. 30.

[5] *Ordo noster specialiter ob prædicationem et animarum salutem ab initio
institutus.*   Prol. to Constitution of 1228.

general, declared that the end of the order was not study, but that study was most necessary for preaching and the salvation of souls.   Study, said another, is ordained for preaching, and preaching for the salvation of men, and this is the final end.[1] No one was permitted to preach outside the cloister until he was twenty-five.[2] And for preaching they were not to receive money or other gifts, except food.   As Vincent Ferrer and Savonarola were the most renowned of the Dominican preachers of the Middle Ages, so Lacordaire was their most renowned orator in the nineteenth century. The mission of the Dominicans was predominantly with the upper classes.   They represented the patrician element among the orders.

The annals of the Inquisition give to the Dominican order large space.   The Dominicans were the most prominent and zealous "inquisitors of heretical depravity." Dante had this in mind when he characterized Dominic as " Good to his friends, dreadful to his enemies," "*Benigno ai suoi ed ai nimici crudo.*"[3]

In 1232 the conduct of the Inquisition was largely committed to their care.   Northern France, Spain, and Germany fell to their lot.[4] The stern Torquemada was a Dominican, and the atrocious measures which were afterwards employed to spy out and punish ecclesiastical dissent, have left an indelible blot upon the name of the order.   The student of history must regard those efforts to maintain the orthodox faith as heartless, even though it may not have occurred to the participants to so consider them.   The order's device, given by Honorius, was a dog bearing a lighted torch in his mouth, the dog to watch, the torch to illuminate the world.   The picture in their convent S. Maria Novella, at Florence, represents the place the order came to occupy as hunters of heretics.   It portrays dogs dressed in the Dominican colors, black and white, chasing away foxes, which stand for

---

[1] Quoted by Denifle, p. 190.   [2] Const. II. 31–33.   [3] *Paradiso*, XII.
[4] See Potthast, II. 9386, 9388 (Gregory IX., 1234), etc.   The Franciscans were made inquisitors in Italy and Southern France.   See chapter on the Inquisition.

heretics, while pope and emperor, enthroned and surrounded by counsellors, look on with satisfaction at the scene.   It was in connection with his effort to exterminate heresy that Dominic founded, in 1220, the " soldiery of Christ," composed of men and women, married and unmarried.   Later, the order called itself the Brothers and Sisters of Penitence, or the Third Order, or Tertiaries of St. Dominic.   As was the case with the Franciscan Tertiaries, some of them lived a conventual life.

The rosary also had a prominent place in the history of the Dominicans.   An untrustworthy tradition assigns to Dominic its first use.   During the crusades against the Albigenses, Mary, so the story runs, appeared to Dominic, and bade him use the rosary as a means for the conversion of the heretics.   It consists of fifteen *pater nosters* and one hundred and fifty *ave Marias*, told off in beads.   The Dominicans early became devotees of the rosary, but soon had rivals in the Carmelites for the honor of being the first to introduce it.   The notorious Dominican inquisitor and hunter of witches, Jacob Sprenger, founded the first confraternity of the rosary.   Pius V. ascribed the victory of Lepanto, 1571, to its use.   In recent times Pius IX. and Leo XIII. have been ardent devotees of the rosary.   Leo, in his encyclical of Sept. 1, 1883, ascribed its introduction to " the great Dominic, as a balm for the wounds of his contemporaries."   This encyclical represents Mary as " placed on the highest summit of power and glory in heaven . . . who is to be besought that, by her intercession, her devout Son may be appeased and softened as to the evils which afflict us."[1]

[1] Leo commended the rosary in repeated encyclicals, Aug. 30, 1884, 1891, etc., coupling plenary indulgence for sin with its use.   He also ordered the title *regina sanctissimi rosarii*, "queen of the most holy rosary," inserted into the liturgy of Loreto.   On the history of the rosary, see Lea, *Hist. of Auric. Conf.*, III. 484 sqq., and especially the dissertation *St. Dominikus und der Rosenkranz*, by the Franciscan, Heribert Holzapfel.   This writer declares, point blank, that the rosary was not invented nor propagated by Dominic. There is no reference to it in the original Constitution of 1228, which contains detailed prescriptions concerning prayer and the worship of the Virgin, nor

Leo XIII. paid highest honor to the Dominicans when he pronounced Thomas Aquinas the authoritative teacher of Catholic theology and morals, and the patron of Catholic schools.

in any of the eighteen biographical notices of the thirteenth century. Holzapfel makes the statement, p. 12, that the entire thirteenth and fourteenth centuries know nothing of any association whatsoever of St. Dominic with the rosary. Sixtus IV., 1478, was the first pope to commend the rosary; but Sixtus does not associate it with the name of Dominic. Such association began with Leo X. What has become of the author of this bold denial of the distinct statement of Leo XIII. in his encyclical of ten years before, September, 1883, I do not know. Holzapfel distinctly asserts his opposition to the papal deliverances on the rosary, when he says, p. 37, " High as the regard is in which the Catholic holds the authority of Peter's successors in religious things, he must be equally on his guard against extending that authority to every possible question." Perhaps Father Holzapfel's pamphlet points to the existence of a remainder of the hot feeling which used to exist between the Thomists and Scotists.

CHAPTER IX.

MISSIONS.

§ 73. *Literature and General Survey.*

LITERATURE: I. FOR NORTHEASTERN GERMANY.—H. HAHN: *Gesch. d. kathol. Mission,* 5 vols., Col., 1857–1865.— G. F. MACLEAR: *Hist. of Christ. Missions during the M. A.,* London, 1863.— C. A. H. KALKAR: *Gesch. d. röm.-kathol. Mission,* German trans., Erlang., 1867.— TH. SMITH: *Med. Missions,* Edinburg, 1880.— P. TSCHACKERT: *Einführung d. Christenthums in Preussen,* in Herzog, IX. 25 sqq.— *Lives of Otto of Bamberg* by EBO and HERBORD (contemporaries) in Jaffé; *Bibl. Rerum Germanic.,* Berlin, 1869, vol. V. trans. in *Geschichtschreiber der deutschen Vorzeit,* Leipzig, 1869.— Otto's *Letters* in Migne, vol. 173.— Mod. Lives by F. X. SULZBECK, Regensb., 1865, and J. A. ZIMMERMANN, Freib. im Br., 1875.— For copious lit. see POTTHAST: *Bibl. Hist.,* II. 1504 sq.— For VICELINUS, see *Chronica Slavorum Helmodi* (a friend of Vicelinus), ed. by PERTZ, Hann., 1868. Trans. by WATTENBACH in *Geschichtschreiber der deutschen Vorzeit,* Leipzig, 1888.— WINTER: *Die Prämonstratenser d. 12ten Jahrhunderts und ihre Bedeutung für das nordöstl. Deutschland. Ein Beitrag zur Gesch. der Christianisirung und Germanisirung des Wendenlandes,* Leipzig, 1865. Also *Die Cisterzienser des nordöstl. Deutschlands,* 3 vols., Gotha, 1868.— E. O. SCHULZE: *D. Kolonisierung und Germanisirung der Gebiete zw. Saale und Elbe,* Leipzig, 1896.— EDMUND KRAUSCH: *Kirchengesch. der Wendenlande,* Paderb., 1902.— HAUCK: III. 69–150,623–655.— RANKE: *Weltgesch.,* VIII. 455–480.— The arts. ALBERT OF RIGA, OTTO VON BAMBERG, VICELINUS, and WENDEN in Wetzer-Welte and Herzog. See Lit. under *Teutonic Knights,* p. 296.

II. FOR THE MOHAMMEDANS.— Works on FRANCIS D'ASSISI, see § 69.— For RAYMUNDUS LULLUS: *Beati Raymundi Lulli doctoris illuminati et martyris opera,* ed. by JOHN SALZINGER, Mainz, 1721–1742, 10 vols. (VII., X. wanting). His *Ars magna* (*opera quæ ad artem universalem pertinent*), Strassburg, 1598. Last ed., 1651. Recent ed. of his Poems *Obras rimadas,* Palma, 1859. For the ed., of Raymund's works publ. at Palma but not completed see Wetzer-Welte, *Raim. Lullus,* X. 747–749.— Lives by PERROQUET,Vendome, 1667; Löw, Halle, 1830.—*A. HELFFERICH: *R. Lull und die Anfänge der Catalonischen Literatur,* Berlin, 1858; W. BRAMBACH, Karlsr., 1893; ANDRÉ, Paris, 1900.—*S. M. ZWEMER: *Raymund Lull, First Missionary to the Moslems,* New York, 1902.— LEA: *Hist. of the Inquis.,* III. 563–590.— REUSCH: *Der Index,* etc., I. 26–33.—ZÖCKLER, in Herzog, XI. 706–716.

III. For the Mongols. — D'Ohson : *Hist. des Mongols*, Paris, 1824. — H. H.
Howorth : *Hist. of the Mongols*, 3 vols., London, 1876–1880. — Abbé
Huc: *Le Christianisme en Chine, en Tartare et en Thibet*, Paris, 1857. —
Külb: *Gesch. der Missionsreisen nach der Mongolei während des 13ten
und 14ten Jahrhunderts*, 3 vols., Regensb., 1860. — Col. Henry Yule :
Travels and Life of Marco Polo, London, 1871 ; Rev. ed. by H. Cordier,
New York, 1903. — R. K. Douglas (Prof. of Chinese in King's Col.,
London): *Life of Jenghiz Khan.* — Gibbon, chaps. XLVII., LXIV. ;
Ranke, VIII. 417–455 ; and arts. Rubruquis, *Mongolen*, etc., in Herzog,
Wetzer-Welte.

The missionary operations of this period display little of
the zeal of the great missionary age of Augustine, Columba,
and Boniface, and less of achievement. The explanation is
to be found in the ambitions which controlled the mediæval
church and in the dangers by which Europe was threatened
from without. In the conquest of sacred localities, the Crusades offered a substitute for the conversion of non-Christian
peoples. The effort of the papacy to gain supreme control
over all mundane affairs in Western Christendom, also filled
the eye of the Church. These two movements almost drained
her religious energies to the full. On the other hand the
Mongols, or Tartars, breaking forth from Central Asia with
the fierceness of evening wolves, filled all Europe with dread,
and one of the chief concerns of the thirteenth century was to
check their advance into the central part of the continent.
The heretical sects in Southern France threatened the unity
of the Church and also demanded a share of attention which
might otherwise have been given to efforts for the conversion
of the heathen.

Two new agencies come into view, the commercial trader
and the colonist, corresponding in this century to the ships
and trains of modern commerce and the labors of the geo-
graphical explorer in Africa and other countries. Along the
shores of the Baltic, at times, and in Asia the tradesman and
the explorer went in advance of the missionary or along the
same routes. And in the effort to subdue the barbarous
tribes of Northeastern Germany to the rules of Christendom, the sword and colonization played as large a part as
spiritual measures.

The missionary history of the age has three chapters,— among the pagan peoples of Northeastern Germany and along the Baltic as far as Riga, among the Mohammedans of Northern Africa, and among the Mongols in Central and Eastern Asia. The chief missionaries whose names have survived are Otto of Bamberg and Vicelinus who labored in Northeastern Europe, Rubruquis, and John of Monte Corvino who travelled through Asia, Francis d'Assisi and Raymundus Lullus who preached in Africa.

The treatment which the Jews received at the hand of the Church also properly belongs here.

§ 74. *Missions in Northeastern Germany.*

At the beginning of this period the Wends,[1] who were of Slavic origin, were the ruling population in the provinces along the Baltic from Lübeck to Riga with elements in the territory now covered by Pommerania, Brandenburg intermingled, and parts of Saxony, which were neither German nor Slavic but Lithuanian.[2] Charlemagne did not attempt conquest beyond the river Elbe. The bishoprics of Würzburg, Mainz, Halberstadt, Verden, and Bremen-Hamburg, bordering on the territories of these tribes, had done little or nothing for their conversion. Under Otto I. Havelberg, Meissen, Merseburg, and other dioceses were established to prosecute this work. At the synod of Ravenna, 967, Otto made the premature boast that the Wends had been converted.

The only personality that looms out above the monotonous level of Wendish history is Gottschalk, who was converted in England and bound together a number of tribes in an extensive empire. He was interested in the conversion

---

[1] See § 60. Tacitus calls the Wends *Venedi*, a name which seems to come from the Slavonic *voda*, or the Lithuanian *wandu*, meaning "water," and referring to the low and often marshy lands they occupied.

[2] The two translations of Luther's catechism, 1545, 1561, into the language of this people seem to point to their Lithuanian origin, Tschackert in Herzog, XVI. 26.

of his people, and churches and convents were built at Mecklenburg, Lübeck, Oldenburg, and other centres. But with Gottschalk's murder, in 1066, the realm fell to pieces and the Wend tribes from that time on became the object of conquest to the dukes of Poland and Saxony. Attempts to Christianize them were met with violent resistance. Wends and Germans hated one another.[1] These barbarous tribes practised polygamy, infanticide,[2] burned the bodies of their dead, had their sacred springs, graves, and idols.

Two centuries were required to bring the territories occupied by these peoples, and now for the most part inhabited by Germans, under the sway of the Church. The measures employed were the instructions of the missionary, the sword as wielded by the Teutonic Knights, and the colonization of the lands with German colonists. The sacraments and ritual of the Church were put in the forefront as conditions of union with the Church. The abolition of barbarous customs was also insisted upon. The bishopric and the convent were made the spiritual citadels of the newly evangelized districts.

The first to labor among the Wends, who was actuated by true missionary zeal, was the Spanish Cistercian, Bernard. He was without any knowledge of the language and his bare feet and rude monastic garb were little adapted to give him an entrance to the people whose priests were well clad.

Bernard was followed by Otto, bishop of Bamberg, 1102–1139, who made his first tour at Bernard's instance. He won the title of Apostle of Pommerania. In 1124 he set his face towards the country, furnished with the blessing of Honorius II. and well supplied with clerical helpers. He won the good-will of the Pommeranian duke, Wratislaw, who, in his youth, as a prisoner of war, had received baptism. The bap-

---

[1] Hauck gives illustrations of the cruelties of the two peoples in time of war, III. 90 sqq.

[2] They thought nothing of strangling girls when there were a number born to the same mother. *Si plures filias aliqua genuisset, ut cetera facilius providerent, aliquas ex eis jugulabant, pro nihilo ducentes parricidium.* Herbord, II. 16

tism of seven thousand at Pyritz has a special interest from its bearing on the practice of immersion followed at that time. Tanks were sunk into the earth, the rims rising knee high above the ground.   Into these, as the chronicler reports,[1] it was easy to descend.   Tent-coverings were drawn over each of them.   Otto instructed the people in the seven sacraments [2] and insisted upon the abandonment of polygamy and infanticide.

At Stettin he destroyed the temple of the god Triglar, and sent the triple head of the idol to Rome as a sign of the triumph of the cross.

In 1128 Otto made a second tour to Pommerania. He spoke through an interpreter. His instructions were followed by the destruction of temples and the erection of churches. He showed his interest in the material as well as spiritual well-being of the people and introduced the vine into the country.[3] His work was continued by Norbert of Magdeburg and the Premonstrants.

Vicelinus, d. 1154, the next most important name in the history of missions among the Wends, preached in the territory now covered by Holstein and the adjoining districts. He had spent three years in study at Paris and was commissioned to his work by Adalbert, archbishop of Bremen-Hamburg.   The fierce wars of Albert the Bear, of North Saxony, 1133–1170, and Henry the Lion, 1142–1163, against the Wagrians and Abotrites, the native tribes, were little adapted to prepare the way for Christianity.   Vicelinus founded the important convent of Segeberg which became a centre of training for missionaries.   Lübeck accepted Christianity, and in 1148 Vicelinus was ordained bishop of Oldenburg.

The German missionaries went as far as Riga. The sword played a prominent part in the reduction of the local tribes.

---

[1] *Facilis erat in aquam descendere*, Herbord, II. 16. The detailed description of the baptismal scenes leaves not a particle of doubt that immersion was practised.

[2] This is the earliest notice of the seven sacraments, provided Herbord's report is not interpolated.

[3] Herbord, II. 41.

Under papal sanction, crusade followed crusade. The Livo-
nians received their first knowledge of Christianity through
Meinhard, d. 1196,[1] who had been trained at Segeberg. He
had been preceded by Bremen merchants and set forth on
his mission in a Bremen merchant vessel. He was ordained
bishop of the new diocese of Uexkull whose name was
changed in 1202 to the diocese of Riga.

Meinhard's successor, the Cistercian Berthold, sought at
first to win his way by instruction and works of charity, but
was driven away by violence. He returned in 1198, at the
head of a crusade which Cœlestin had ordered. After his
death on the field of battle his successor, bishop Albert of
Apeldern, entered the country in 1199 at the head of another
army. The lands were then thrown open to colonists.
With the sanction of Innocent III., Albert founded the order
of the Brothers of the Sword. Their campaigns opened the
way for the church in Esthaonia and Senegallen. In 1224
the see of Dorpat was erected, which has given its name to
the university of Dorpat.

Eastern Prussia, lying along the Weichsel, was visited in
1207 by the German abbot, Gottfried. Two of the native
princes were converted by Christian, a monk from Pommerania, donated their lands to the Church, and travelled to
Rome, where they received baptism. Christian was made
bishop of Prussia between 1212 and 1215. An invitation sent
to the Teutonic Knights to aid in the conversion of the tribes
was accepted by their grand-master, Hermann of Salza, in
1228. In 1217 Honorius III. had ordered a crusade, and
in 1230 Gregory IX. renewed the order. The Teutonic
Knights were ready enough to further religious encroachment
by the sword, promised, as they were, a large share in the
conquered lands. From 1230 to 1283 they carried on continual wars. They established themselves securely by building fortified towns such as Kulm and Thorn, 1231, and
Königsberg, 1255. A stream of German colonists followed

---

[1] Gregory IX., as late as 1237, calls this people pagans, *pagani Livoniæ*.
Potthast, 10383.

where they conquered.   In 1243 Innocent IV. divided Prussia into four sees, Kulm, Pomesania, Sameland, and Ermeland.   It was arranged that the bishops were to have one-third of the conquered territory.   In 1308 the German Knights seized Danzig at the mouth of the Weichsel and a year later established their headquarters at Marienburg.[1] By the battle of Tannenberg, 1410, and the Peace of Thorn, 1466, they lost Prussia west of the Weichsel, and thereafter their possessions were confined to Eastern Prussia.   The history of the order closed when the grand-master, Albrecht of Brandenburg, accepted the Reformation and made the duchy hereditary in his family.

§ 75.   *Missions among the Mohammedans.*

Two important names are associated with the missions among the Mohammedans, Francis of Assisi and Raymundus Lullus, and with their labors, which were without any permanent results, the subject is exhausted.   The Crusades were adapted to widen the gulf between the Christians and the Mohammedans, and to close more tightly the ear of the followers of the False Prophet to the appeals of the Christian emissary.

Franciscan friars went in 1213 to Morocco and received the martyr's crown, but left no impression upon the Mohammedans.[2]   St. Francis made his tour to Syria and Egypt in 1219, accompanied by eleven companions.   The accounts are meagre and uncertain.[3]   Francis landed at Acre and proceeded to the crusading camp under the walls of Damietta, where he is represented as preaching before the sultan and to the Mohammedan troops.   The story is told that the

[1] Ranke, VIII. 469, regards the fabric of the Teutonic Knights as having offered the only effective check against the invasion of Central Europe by the Mongols.

[2] Müller, *Anfänge des Minoritenordens*, 207 sqq., has set this mission beyond doubt.

[3] Jacob of Vitry, *Hist. Occ.*, 32, and Giordano di Giano are our chief authorities.   Sabatier, in his *Life of Francis*, accepts the testimony, but dismisses the tour in a few lines.

sultan was so much touched by Francis' preaching that he gave the Franciscan friars admission to the Holy Sepulchre, without payment of tribute.

Raymundus Lullus, 1235?–1315, devoted his life to the conversion of Mohammedans and attested his zeal by a martyr's death. He was one of the most noteworthy figures produced during the Middle Ages in Southwestern Europe. He made three missionary tours to Africa and originated the scheme for establishing chairs at the universities to teach the Oriental languages and train missionaries. He also wrote many tracts with the aim of convincing unbelievers of the truth of Christianity.

Lullus was born in Palma on the island of Majorca. His father had gained distinction by helping to wrest the Balearic islands from the Saracens. The son married and had children, but led a gay and licentious life at court and devoted his poetic gifts to erotic sonnets. At the age of thirty-one he was arrested in his wild career by the sight of a cancer on the breast of a woman, one of the objects of his passion, whom he pursued into a church, and who suddenly exposed her disease. He made a pilgrimage to Campostella, and retired to Mt. Randa on his native island. Here he spent five years in seclusion, and in 1272 entered the third order of St. Francis. He became interested in the conversion of Mohammedans and other infidels and studied Arabic under a Moor whom he had redeemed from slavery. A system of knowledge was revealed to him which he called "the Universal Science," *ars magna* or *ars generalis*. With the aid of the king of Aragon he founded, in 1276 on Majorca, a college under the control of the Franciscans for the training of missionaries in the Arabic and Syriac tongues.

Lullus went to Paris to study and to develop his Universal Science. At a later period he returned and delivered lectures there. In 1286 he went to Rome to press his missionary plans, but failed to gain the pope's favor. In 1292 he set sail on a missionary tour to Africa from Genoa. In Tunis he endeavored in vain to engage the Mohammedan scholars in a public disputation. A tumult arose and Lullus narrowly escaped with his life. Returning to Europe, he again sought to win the favor of the pope, but in vain. In 1309 he sailed the second time for Tunis, and again he sought to engage the Mohammedans in disputation. Offered honors if he would turn Mohammedan, he said, "And I promise you, if you will turn and believe on Jesus Christ, abundant riches and eternal life."

Again violently forced to leave Africa, Lullus laid his plans before Clement V. and the council of Vienne, 1311. Here he presented a refutation of the philosophy of Averrhoes and pressed the creation of academic chairs for the Oriental languages. Such chairs were ordered erected at Avignon, Paris, Oxford, Salamanca, and Bologna to teach Greek, Hebrew, Chaldee, and Arabic.[1]

Although nearly eighty years old the indefatigable missionary again set out for Tunis. His preaching at Bougia led, as before, to tumults, and Lullus was dragged outside of the city and stoned. Left half dead, he was rescued by Christian seamen, put on board a ship, and died at sea. His bones are preserved at Palma.

For a period of nearly fifty years this remarkable man had advocated measures for carrying the Gospel to the Mohammedans. No impression, so far as we know, was made by his preaching or by his apologetic writings upon unbelievers, Jew or Mohammedan, but with his name will always be associated the new idea of missionary institutes where men, proposing to dedicate themselves to a missionary career, might be trained in foreign languages. But Lullus was more than a glowing advocate of missions. He was a poet and an expert scholastic thinker.[2] Spain has produced

---

[1] The object of the chairs was declared to be to further the exposition of the Scriptures and the conversion of unbelievers. See Hefele, VI. 545. A little earlier the pamphleteer Peter Dubois had urged it as the pope's duty to establish institutes for the study of the Oriental languages as it was his duty to see that the Gospel was preached to all peoples. See Scholz, *Die Publizistik zur Zeit Philipps des Schönen*, 427–431.

[2] According to the catalogue in the Escurial prepared by D. Arias de Loyola, Lullus wrote 410 tracts, most of which exist only in MS., and are distributed among the libraries of Europe. Of these, 46 are controversial

no Schoolman so famous. He was a prolific author, and
in his application of thought to the physical sciences, he
has been compared to his fellow Franciscan, Roger
Bacon.[1]

His Universal Science he applied to medicine and law,
astrology and geography, grammar and rhetoric, as well as
to the solution of theological problems.[2] It was a key to
all the departments of thought, celestial and terrestrial.
Ideas he represented by letters of the alphabet which were
placed in circles and other mathematical diagrams. By
the turning of the circles and shifting of lines these ideas
fall into relations which display a system of truth. The
word "God," for example, was thus brought into relation
with nine letters, B–K, which represented nine qualities:
goodness, greatness, eternity, power, wisdom, volition, virtue,
truth, and glory. Or the letters B–K represented nine questions, such as, what, *quid;* from what, *de quo;* why, *quare;*
how much, *quantum.* Being applied to God, they afford
valid definitions, such as " God's existence is a necessity."
This kaleidoscopic method, it is not improbable, Lullus
drew from Jewish and Arabic sources, and he himself called
it Cabalistic.

The philosophy of Lullus found a number of adherents
who were called Lullists. It was taught at the universities
of Valencia and Aragon. Giordano Bruno drew from it.
Eymericus, the inquisitor, became the bitter foe of the
Lullists, arraigned their leader's teachings before the Roman
court, and exhibited a bull of Gregory XI. (1372) condemn-

works against the Mohammedans, Jews, and Averrhoists. Lea speaks of
Lullus " as perhaps the most voluminous author on record." III. 581.

[1] Reuter, *Gesch. der Aufklärung*, II. 95 sq.

[2] In his work on the miracles of heaven and earth, *de miraculis cœli et
mundi*, he represents a father leading his son through woods and across
fields, over deserts and through cities, among plants and animals, into
heaven and hell, and pointing out the wonders they saw. In his *Blan-
querna magister christianæ perfectionis* he presents an ethical drama in
which the hero is introduced to all stations of religious life, monk, abbot,
bishop, cardinal, and pope, and at last gives up the tiara to retire to the
seclusion of a convent.

ing them as heretical.[1]   Philip II. read some of the Major-
can's writings and left annotated copies in the Escurial
library.   Lullus' works were included in the *Index* of
Paul IV., 1559, but ordered removed from the list by the
council of Trent.   A papal decision of 1619 forbade Lullus'
doctrine as dangerous.   In 1847 Pius IX. approved an
office for the "holy Raymundus Lullus" in Majorca,
where he is looked upon as a saint.   The Franciscans have,
since the time of Leo X., commemorated the Spaniard's
memory in their Breviary.

§ 76.   *Missions among the Mongols.*

Central Asia and what is now the Chinese Empire were
almost as unknown to Western Europe in the twelfth century as the lake region of Central Africa was before the
journeys of Speke, Livingstone, and Stanley.   To the Nestorians, with their schools at Edessa and Nisibis, naturally
belonged the task of spreading the Gospel in Central and
Eastern Asia.   They went as far as China, but after the
ninth century their schools declined and a period of stagnation set in.   Individual Nestorians reached positions of influence in Asiatic courts as councillors or physicians and
Nestorian women became mothers of Mongol chiefs.   But
no Asiatic tribe adopted their creed.

In the twelfth century the brilliant delusion gained cur-
rency throughout Europe of the existence in Central Asia of
a powerful Christian theocracy, ruled over by the Presbyter
John, usually called Prester-John.[2]   The wildest rumors were

---

[1] The genuineness of this bull has been a subject of much controversy.
Commissions were even appointed by later popes to investigate the matter,
and the bull, with other documents originating with Gregory, was not found.
Hergenröther pronounces for its genuineness, *Kirchengesch.*, II. 540.   Eymericus ascribed Lullus' teachings to the suggestion of the devil, and declared
that Lullus maintained the erroneous proposition that "all points of faith
and the sacraments, and the power of the pope may be proved by reasoning,
necessary, demonstrative, and evident."

[2] G. Oppert, *D. Presbyter Johannes in Sage u. Gesch.*, Berlin, 1864, 2d
ed. 1870.   Brunet, *La légende du Prêtre-Jean*, Bordeaux, 1877.   Zarncke,
D. Priester-Johannes, Leipzig, 1879.

spread concerning this mysterious personage who was said to combine the offices of king and priest. According to Otto of Freisingen, a certain bishop of Gabala in 1145 had brought Eugenius III. the information that he was a Nestorian Christian, was descended from one of the three Wise Men, and had defeated the Mohammedans in a great battle.[1] A letter, purporting to come from this ruler and addressed to the Emperor Manuel of Constantinople, related that John received tribute from seventy kings, and had among his subjects the ten tribes of Israel, entertained at his table daily twelve archbishops and twenty bishops, and that his kingdom was overflowing with milk and honey.[2] Gradually his dominions were reported to extend to Abyssinia and India.

To put themselves into communication with this wonderful personage and bring him into subjection to Rome engaged the serious attention of several popes. Alexander III., in 1177, sent his physician Philip with commission to inform the king of the faith of Western Christendom. He also addressed him in a letter as his "most dear son in Christ, John, king of the Indies and most holy of priests." The illusion abated as serious efforts to find the kingdom were made. Rubruquis wrote back to Europe from the region where John was reported to have ruled that few could be found who knew anything about Prester-John and that the stories which had been told were greatly exaggerated. He added that a certain ruler, Coirchan, had been followed by a Nestorian shepherd, called John. It has been conjectured by Oppert that the word " Coirchan," through the Syrian Juchanan, became known as John in Europe. A prince of that name whom the Chinese call Tuliu Tasha fled from China westwards, and established a kingdom in Central Asia. Nestorians were among his subjects. Chinese tradition has it that

---

[1] *Chronicon*, VII. 33.   Otto also reports the bishop of Gabala as declaring that out of respect for his ancestors, the Magians, who had worshipped at the cradle of the Redeemer, John had started with an army to relieve Jerusalem, but for want of boats got no further than the Tigris.

[2] The letter must have had an extensive circulation, as it exists in more than 100 MSS., 13 in Paris, 15 in Munich, 8 in the British Museum, etc.

the prince was a Buddhist. Thus dwindles away a legend which, to use Gibbon's language, "long amused the credulity of Europe."

In the twelfth and thirteenth centuries Asia witnessed the establishment of the vast Mongol empire. Scarcely ever has military genius among uncivilized peoples had more wonderful display than in its founders, Zenghis Khan and his successors, especially Kublai and Mangu.[1] The empire stretched from the Chinese Sea to the Dnieper, and from Bagdad to the Arctic. Their armies were the terror of Europe. What the Mohammedans had accomplished in Spain it was feared the Mongols would do for the whole continent. They destroyed Moscow and advanced as far as Cracow in Poland, and Buda Pesth in Hungary, 1241. The empire rapidly disintegrated, and was divided into four main sections : the empire of the Great Khan, including China and Thibet; the empire of Central Asia ; Persia, extending to the Caucasus, and the loose kingdom of the Golden Horde in Russia and Siberia.[2] The first council of Lyons, in 1245, had as one of its objects to provide a defence against the imminent menace of these Tartars,[3] as they were called, and a delegation of sixteen of them appeared at the second council of Lyons, 1274, in the hope of forming an alliance against the Saracens.

The Church sent forth several deputations of missionaries to these tribes, some of whom were received at the court of the Great Khan. The most fearless and adventuresome of

[1] It was at Kublai's court that Marco Polo (about 1324) spent many years. The origin of the Mongols is lost in legend. The Mongol historian Sanang Setzen traces it back to a blue wolf. Zenghis Khan, 1162–1227, is known among the Chinese as Ching-sze, perfect warrior. The word "Mongol" comes from *mong*, meaning brave.

[2] Hulagu, one of Mangu's brothers, overthrew the Caliphate of Bagdad, 1258, and established the Mongol empire of Persia. He took in marriage a daughter of the Byzantine emperor, Michael Palæologus.

[3] See Hefele, V. 1096, 1114. A provincial synod at Erfurt, a few years before, 1241, had considered measures for defence against the Tartars. Hefele, V. 1084. For some of the papal bulls bearing on missions among the Mongols, see Potthast, 7429, 7490, 7537, 7550, 9130, 9139, 9141, 10350, 10421.

their number was William Rubruquis, or Ruysbroeck, the
Livingstone of his age, who committed to writing a vivid
account of his experiences.   John of Monte Corvino ventured as far as Pekin, then known in Europe as Cambaluc
and among the Mongols as Khanbaligh, " the city of the
Khan."

Merciless as they were in battle, the Mongols were tolerant in religion.   This was due in part to the absence among
them of any well-defined system of worship.   Mangu Khan,
in answer to the appeals of Rubruquis, said, " We Mongols
believe that there is only one God, in whom we live and die.
But as God has given to the hand different fingers, so He
has given to men different ways to Himself.   To you
Christians he has given the Holy Scriptures ; to us, sooth-
sayers and diviners."

Kublai showed the same spirit when he said to Marco Polo,
" There are four prophets who are worshipped by the four
different tribes on the earth.   Christians look upon Christ
as their God, the Saracens upon Mohammed, the Jews upon
Moses, and the heathen upon Sogomombar-Khan (Buddha).
I esteem and honor all four and pray that He who is supreme
amongst them may lend me His help."   Alexander Severus perhaps did no better when he placed side by side statues
of Abraham, Christ, and Orpheus and other pagan gods.
It was not till after the contact of the missionaries with the
Mongols that the khans of the East adopted Buddhism, while
the tribes of Persia and the West chose the rites of Islam.

In 1245 Innocent IV. despatched four Dominicans to the
Mongol chief in Persia and three Franciscans to the Great
Khan himself.   The next effort was due to Louis IX., then
engaged in his first Crusade.   Ambassadors from the Mongol chief of Tartary visited the French king at Cyprus.[1]
Louis returned the compliment by sending back two Dominicans in 1248, and, two years later, two Franciscans, and,
in the pious hope of seeing the Tartars converted, he also
sent a present of a tent embroidered with representations of

---

[1] Joinville, *Chronicle of the Crusades*, Engl. trans., pp. 384 sqq., 476 sqq.

Scriptural scenes and so constructed as to have the shape, when put up, of a chapel. It is from one of these two Franciscans, Rubruquis, that our first reliable information of the Mongols is drawn. He found Nestorian priests using the Syriac liturgy, which they did not understand, and joining with the Mohammedans and Buddhists in offering a blessing over the khan's cups. Rubruquis reached Karkorum and had a hospitable reception at the court of Mangu Khan. One of Mangu's secretaries was a Christian, another a Mohammedan, the third a Buddhist. A religious disputation was held in the khan's presence. After Rubruquis had asserted that all God's commandments are contained in the Scriptures, he was asked whether he thought Mangu kept them. The missionary adroitly replied that "it was his desire to lay before the khan all God's commandments and then the khan would be able to judge for himself whether he kept them or not."

The Mongolian chiefs in Persia and the Christians were joint enemies of the Caliph of Egypt, and after the Mongolian conquest of the caliphate of Bagdad, embassies were sent by the pope to Persia, and Dominican and Franciscan convents established in that land; but after their adoption of Islam in the fourteenth century, the Mongols persecuted the Christians and the convents were destroyed.

In Central Asia among the Jagatai Mongols events took the same course. At first, 1340, permission was granted to the missionaries to prosecute their work. John of Marignola preached and baptized converts. These Mongols afterwards also adopted Mohammedanism and persecuted the Christians.

In the Mongol empire of China the efforts gave larger promise of fruitfulness. Nicolo and Maffei Polo[1] carried a request from Kublai Khan to Gregory X. for missionaries

[1] Nicolo was the father of Marco Polo, Maffei was Marco's uncle. Marco was born in 1254 and went on his first journey to Asia when he was seventeen, 1271. The party went first to the island of Ormus on the Persian Gulf, at that time an important market for the exchange of goods. Of it Milton speaks : —

High on a throne of royal state, which far
Outshone the wealth of Ormus and of Ind.

to instruct his people in Christianity and European habits.
Two Dominicans accompanied the Polos on their return
journey, Marco Polo being of the party. The missionaries
did not reach their destination. Three years later Franciscans were sent. John of Monte Corvino, a Franciscan sent
out by Nicholas IV., reached the court of the Great Khan at
Cambaluc, and in 1303 was joined by Arnold, a Franciscan
from Cologne. They translated the New Testament and the
Psalms into the Tartar language, bought and trained one
hundred and fifty boys, built two churches, one of them close
to the palace and overtopping it, and baptized six thousand
converts. In 1307 John was made archbishop of Pekin,
archiepiscopus Cambalensis, and died 1330. The khans
passed over to the Buddhist faith and in 1368 the Ming
dynasty which raised itself to power abolished Christianity.
It remained for the Jesuits three hundred years later to
renew missionary operations in China.

§ 77. *The Jews.*

LITERATURE : The Works of PETER THE VENERABLE, and BERNARD, in
    MIGNE, and the English Chroniclers, WILLIAM OF NEWBURGH,
    WALTER OF COVENTRY, MATTHEW PARIS, etc., in the Rolls Series. —
    T. BASNAGE : *Hist. des Juifs depuis Jésus Christ*, 5 vols. Rotterdam,
    1706. — D. BLOSSIUS TOVEY : *Anglia Judaica or Hist. Antiquities of the
    Jews in Engl.*, Oxford, 1738. — DEPPING : *Les Juifs dans le moyen âge*,
    Paris, 1834. — E. H. LINDO : *Hist. of the Jews of Spain and Portugal*,
    London, 1848. — TH. HALLEY : *Les Juifs en France*, etc., Paris,
    1845. — M. MARGOLIOUTH : *Hist. of the Jews in Great Britain*, 3 vols.
    London, 1851. — H. H. MILMAN : *Hist. of the Jews*, 3 vols. London,
    1863. — JOSÉ AMADOR DE LOS RIOS : *Historia social, politica, y religiosa
    de los Judios de Espana y Portugal*, 3 vols. Madrid, 1875, 1876. —
    H. GRAETZ (Prof. at Breslau, d. 1891) : *Gesch. der Juden von den
    ältesten Zeiten bis auf die Gegenwart*, 3d ed., Leipzig, 1888-1894,
    11 vols. ; Engl. trans. by BELLA LÖWY, London, 5 vols. 1891-1892. —
    J. JACOBS : *The Jews of Angevin England.* Documents and Records
    from Latin and Hebrew Sources, London, 1893. — I. ABRAHAMS : *Jewish
    Life in the M. A.*, London, 1896. — E. RODOCANACHI : *Le Saint Siège
    et les Juifs*, Paris, 1891. — DÖLLINGER : *Die Juden in Europa in
    Akad. Vorträge*, I. 208-241. — LEA : *Chapters from the Relig. Hist. of
    Spain*, Phil., 1890, pp. 437-469 — HEFELE : IV.-VI. — LECKY : *Hist.
    of Europ. Morals.* — JANSSEN : *Hist. of the German People*, II. 73 sqq.
    The *Lives* of ST. BERNARD. — D. S. SCHAFF : *The Treatment of the
    Jews in the Middle Ages*, Bibliotheca Sacra, 1903, pp. 547-571.

Would that it might be said of the mediæval church that it felt in the well-being of the Jews, the children of Abraham according to the flesh, a tithe of the interest it manifested in the recovery of the holy places of their ancient land. But this cannot be said. Though popes, bishops, and princes, here and there, were inclined to treat them in the spirit of humanity, the predominant sentiment of Europe was the sentiment of hatred and disdain. The very nations which were draining their energies to send forth armaments to reconquer the Holy Sepulchre joined in persecuting the Jews.

Some explanation is afforded by the conduct of the Jews themselves. Their successful and often unscrupulous money dealings, the flaunting of their wealth, their exclusive social tendencies, their racial haughtiness, and their secretiveness, strained the forbearance of the Christian public to the utmost.[1] The edicts of councils and civil edicts put it beyond reasonable question that, in an offensive way, they showed contempt for the rites and symbols of the Christian faith. The provocation was great, but it does not justify a treatment of the Jewish people in all parts from Bohemia to the Atlantic which lacked the elements of common humanity. The active efforts that were made for their conversion seem to betray fully as much of the spirit of churchly arrogance as of the spirit of Christian charity. Peter the Venerable, in the prologue to his tract addressed to the Jews, said, "Out of the whole ancient world, you alone were not ignorant of Christ ; yea, all peoples have listened, and you alone do not hear. Every language has confessed him, and you alone deny. Others see him, hear him, apprehend him, and you alone remain blind, and deaf, and stony of heart."

The grounds upon which the Jews were persecuted were three : 1. Their fathers had crucified Christ, and the race,

---

[1] William of Newburgh, Hamilton's ed., I. 282, says the tendency of the royal protection in England was to make them proud and stiffnecked against Christians.   Green pronounces the attitude of the Jew in England one " of proud and even insolent defiance."   *Hist. of Engl. People*, bk. III. ch. IV.

predestined to bear the guilt and the punishment of the deed, was receiving its merited portion; 2. They perpetrated horrible atrocities upon Christian children, and mocked the host and the cross; 3. They imposed upon the Christians by exacting exorbitant rates of interest. In no Christian state were they safe. They were aliens in all, and had the rights of citizenship in none. The "enemies of Christ" and " the perfidious" were common names for them, and canonists and theologians use the latter expression. The ritual of Good Friday contained the words, "Let us pray also for the perfidious Jews."[1] The Decretals of Gratian, the Third and Fourth Lateran and other councils class together under one and the same canon the Jews and the Saracens.[2] Such eminent men as Peter the Venerable have more good to say of the Saracen than of the Jew.

Three classes are to be taken into account in following the treatment of the Jews, — the popes, including the prelates, the princes, and the mass of the people with their priests.

Taking the popes one by one, their utterances were, upon the whole, opposed to inhumane measures and uniformly against the forced baptism of the Jews. Gregory the Great protected them against frenzied persecution in Southern Italy. Innocent IV., 1247, denied the charge of child murder brought against them, and threatened with excommunication Christians oppressing them.[3] Martin IV., in 1419, issued a bull in which he declared that he was following his predecessors in commanding that they be not interrupted in their synagogal worship, or compelled to accept baptism, or persecuted for commercial transactions with Christians. On the other hand, the example of Innocent III. gave countenance to the severest measures, and Eugenius IV. quickly annulled the injunctions of his predecessor, Martin IV.

---

[1] *Oremus et pro perfidis Judaeis.* Döllinger, p. 216.

[2] The caption of Gratian's *Decretals*, ch. XV. 6, is *de Judaeis et Saracenis et eorum servis.*

[3] Graetz, VII. 106.

As for the princes, the Jews were regarded as being under their peculiar jurisdiction. At will, they levied taxes upon them, confiscated their goods, and expelled them from their realms. It was to the interest of princes to retain them as sources of revenue, and for this reason they were inclined to protect them against the violence of blind popular prejudice and rage. Frederick II. imposed upon them perpetual slavery as a vengeance upon them for the crucifixion.[1]

The inception of the Crusades was accompanied by violent outbursts against the Jews. Innocent III., in 1216, established the permanent legal basis of their persecution. Their expulsion from Spain, in 1492, represents the culminating act in the mediæval drama of their sufferings. England, Germany, France, Spain, Portugal, and Hungary joined in their persecution. In Italy they suffered least. Tens of thousands were burned or otherwise put to death. They were driven, at one time or another, from almost every country. The alternative of baptism or death was often presented to them. The number of those who submitted to death was probably larger than the number who accepted baptism. Most of those, however, who accepted baptism afterwards openly returned to the faith of their fathers or practised its rites in secret.[2]

It is an interesting fact that, during these centuries of persecution, the Jews, especially in Spain and France, developed an energetic literary activity. Gerschom, Raschi, and the Kimchis belong to France. The names of Maimonides and Benjamin of Tudela head a long list of scholarly Spanish Jews. The pages of Graetz are filled with the names and achievements of distinguished students in medicine and other departments of study.[3]

---

[1] *Perpetuam servitutem ad perpetuam Judaici sceleris ultionem*, Bréholles, I. 57.

[2] Döllinger's statement, p. 235, that the number who submitted to compulsory baptism was very insignificant compared to the number who accepted death is not justified by the statistics given by Graetz.

[3] Jacobs, *Jews in Angevin England*, tries to prove that the English Jews also developed a culture of their own. Graetz positively denies this, VI. 225.

The path of anti-Semitism was early struck by Church and Christian state. The mediæval legislation followed closely the precedent of earlier enactments.[1] The synod of Elvira, 306, forbade Christians to eat with Jews and intermarry with them. Theodosius II., 439, excluded them from holding public office. The civil edicts, offering the alternative of baptism or death, were inaugurated by King Sisibut of Spain. When princes, as in Lyons, protected Jewish merchants, prelates violently protested, as did Agobard, archbishop of Lyons, apostle as he was in some particulars of modern enlightenment.[2] Among the enactments of this period are the following: The Jews were forbidden to employ Christian nurses, servants, or laborers, to publicly sell meat, to work on Sundays or feast days, to employ Christian physicians,[3] or to practise usury, and were commanded to make a money payment to the priest at Easter, and to wear a distinguishing patch or other object on their garments. On the other hand, Christians were forbidden to attend Jewish funerals and marriages, and were punished for borrowing from Jews.

None of the regulations was so humiliating as the one requiring the Jew to wear a distinguishing costume or a distinguishing patch upon his garments. This patch was ordered placed on the chest, or on both chest and back, so that the wearer might be distinguished from afar, as of old the leper was known by his cry " unclean," and that Christians might be prevented from ignorantly having carnal connection with the despised people. At the instance of Stephen Langton the synod of Oxford, 1222, prescribed a woollen patch, and Edward I., 1275, ordered the yellow patch worn by all over seven. Louis IX. ordered that the color of the

---

[1] See art. *The Treatment of the Jews*, in Bibl. Sac., 1903, 552 sqq. and the authorities there cited.

[2] Agobard wrote five tracts against the Jews. See Wiegand's instructive brochure, *Agobard von Lyon und die Judenfrage*, Erl., 1901. Agobard asserted that Judaism and Christianity were as far apart as Ebal and Gerizim.

[3] The reason given by the synod of Salamanca, 1335, against the employment of Jewish physicians was that they were bent upon the extermination of the Christians.

patch should be red or saffron, the king of England that it should be yellow. Its size and shape were matters of minute enactment. The Fourth Lateran gave the weight of its great authority to this regulation about dress, and decreed that it should be enforced everywhere. Dr. Graetz pronounces this law the culminating blow in the humiliation of his kinsmen. He declares that Innocent III. brought more misery upon the Jews than all their enemies had done before, and charges him with being the first pope who turned the inhuman severity of the Church against them.[1]

The position Innocent took was that God intended the Jews to be kept, like Cain, the murderer, to wander about on the earth designed by their guilt for slavery till the time should come in the last days for their conversion.[2]

With this view, the theologians coincided. Peter the Venerable, a half-century before Innocent, presented the case in the same aspect as did the great pope, and launched a fearful denunciation against the Jews. In a letter to Louis VII. of France, he exclaimed, "What would it profit to fight against enemies of the cross in remote lands, while the wicked Jews, who blaspheme Christ, and who are much worse than the Saracens, go free and unpunished. Much more are the Jews to be execrated and hated than the Saracens ; for the latter accept the birth from the Virgin, but the Jews deny it, and blaspheme that doctrine and all Christian mysteries. God does not want them to be wholly exterminated, but to be kept, like the fratricide Cain, for still more severe torment and disgrace. In this way God's most just severity has dealt with the Jews from the time of Christ's passion, and will continue to deal with them to the end of the world, for they are accursed, and deserve to be."[3] He counselled that they be spoiled of their ill-gotten gains and the money derived from their spoliation be applied to wrest the holy places from the Saracens.

[1] VII. 4, 16.

[2] In letters to Alfonso of Castile, 1205, and to the count of Nevers, 1208.

[3] *ad majus tormentum et ad majorem ignominiam . . . sic de damnatis damnandisque Judaeis*, lib. IV. ep. 36 ; Migne's ed., vol. 189, 365–367.

Of a different mind was Bernard. When the preparations were being made for the Second Crusade, and the
monk Radulf went up and down the Rhine, inflaming the
people against the Jews, the abbot of Clairvaux set himself against the "demagogue," as Neander called Radulf.[1]
He wrote a burning epistle to the archbishop of Mainz, reminding him that the Lord is gracious towards him who
returns good for evil. "Does not the Church," he exclaimed,
"triumph more fully over the Jews by convincing and con-
verting them from day to day than if she once and for all
should slay them by the edge of the sword!" How bitter
the prejudice was is seen in the fact that when Bernard met
Radulf face to face, it required all his reputation for sanctity
to allay the turbulence at Mainz.[2]

Turning to England we find William of Newburgh, Roger
de Hoveden, and other chroniclers approving the Jewish persecutions. Richard of Devizes[3] speaks of "sacrificing the
Jews to their father, the devil," and of sending "the bloodsuckers with blood to hell." Matthew Paris, in some of his
references, seems not to have been in full sympathy with the
popular animosity.

Among great English ecclesiastics the Jews had at least two
friendly advocates in Hugh of Lincoln and Robert Grosseteste.
Grosseteste laid down the principle that the Jews were not
to be exterminated, on the grounds that the law had been
given through them, and that, after passing through their
second captivity, they would ultimately, in accordance with
the eleventh chapter of Romans, embrace Christianity. He,
however, declared that Cain was the type of the Jews, as
Abel was the type of Christ. For the sake of God's mercy,
they should be preserved, that Christ might be glorified;
but for the sake of God's justice, they were to be held in
captivity by the princes, that they might fulfil the predic-

---

[1] Otto of Freising says that "very many were killed in Mainz, Worms,
Spires, and other places." *De gestis Frid.* I. 37-39.

[2] Graetz, VI. 148, 151, pronounces Bernard "a truly holy man, a man of
apostolic simplicity of heart."

[3] Howlett's ed., p. 383.

tion concerning Cain, and be vagabonds and wanderers on the earth. They should be forcibly prevented from pursuing the occupation of usurers.[1] The bishop was writing to the dowager countess of Winchester, who had offered a refuge on her lands to the Jews expelled by Simon de Montfort from Leicester. That he was not altogether above the prejudices of his age is vouched for by a letter, also written in 1244, in which he calls upon his archdeacons to prevent Jews and Christians living side by side. Grosseteste's predecessor, Hugh of Lincoln, protected the Jews when they were being plundered and massacred in 1190, and Jews showed their respect by attending his funeral.[2]

No charge was too serious to be laid at the door of the Jews. When the Black Death swept through Europe in 1348, it did not occur to any one to think of the Saracens as the authors of that pestilence. The Jew was guilty. In Southern France and Spain, so the wild rumor ran, he had concocted poisons which were sent out wholesale and used for contaminating fountains. From Barcelona and Seville to the cities in Switzerland and Germany the unfortunate people had to suffer persecution for the alleged crime. In Strassburg, 1349, the entire Hebrew population of two thousand was seized, and as many as did not consent to baptism, were burnt in their own graveyard and their goods confiscated. In Erfurt and other places the entire Jewish population was removed by fire or expulsion.

The canonical regulations against usury gave easy excuse for declaring debts to the Jews not binding. Condemned by Tertullian and Cyprian, usury was at first forbidden to laymen as well as clerics, as by the synod of Elvira; but at the council of Nice, 325, the prohibition was restricted to the clergy. Later Jerome, Augustine, and Leo I. again applied the prohibition to all Christians. Gratian received it into the canon law. Few subjects claimed so generally the

---

[1] Grosseteste's Letters, Luard's ed., 33–39. Stevenson, *Life of Grosseteste*, 97–101, holds that he had no intention of discouraging the countess in her humane effort.

[2] Thurston, *Life of St. Hugh of Lincoln*, 277 sqq., 547.

2 G

attention of the mediæval synods as usury.[1] Alexander
III., at the Third Lateran, 1179, went so far as to declare
usury forbidden by the Old Testament as well as by the New
Testament. Clement V. put the capstone on this sort of
legislation by declaring, at the council of Vienne, 1311, null
and void all state and municipal laws allowing usury and
pronouncing it heresy to deny that usury is sin. No distinction was made between rates of interest. All interest
was usurious. The wonder is that, with such legislation on
the Church's statute-books, any borrower should have felt
bound by a debt to a Jew.

Eugenius III. offered all enlisting in the Second Crusade
exemption from interest due Jewish creditors. Gregory IX.
made the same offer to later Crusaders.

The charge was frequently repeated against the Jews that
they were guilty of the murder of Christian children for
ritualistic purposes, especially at the time of the Passover.
This almost incredible crime again and again stirred the
Christian population into a frenzy of excitement which issued
in some of the direst miseries the Jewish people were called
upon to endure.[2]

In France, Philip Augustus, using as a pretext the alleged
crucifixion of a Christian child, in 1182, expelled the Jews
from his realm and confiscated their goods. The decree of
expulsion was repeated by Louis IX. in the year before he
set out on his last crusade, by Philip the Fair in 1306 and
1311, and by other French monarchs, but it was never so
strictly enforced as in Spain. Louis IX. also ordered all
copies of the Targum destroyed. In 1239 Gregory IX. issued
a letter to the archbishops of France, Castile, Aragon, Portugal, and England, commanding the same thing.[3]

[1] See index in Hefele under *Wucher*. On the whole subject of Usury see
Jacobson, art. *Wucher*, in Herzog, 2d ed., XVII. 341-349. In 1228 the king of
Spain restricted Jewish money lenders to the rate of 20%. Hefele, V. 986.
In 1368 the city of Frankfurt paid Jewish brokers 52% on a loan of 1000
florins. In Augsburg, Vienna, and other cities the interest was often as
high as 86⅔%. See Janssen, II. 74.

[2] Lea, in his *Hist. of Spain*, 437-469, cites a large number of cases down
to recent times.   [3] Graetz, VII. 401-406.

In Germany, from the First Crusade on, the Jews were subjected to constant outbreaks, but usually enjoyed the protection of the emperors against popular fury. In the fifteenth century, they were expelled from Saxony 1432, Spires and Zürich 1435, Mainz 1438, and other localities.

In England the so-called Jewries of London, Lincoln, Oxford, and three or four other cities represented special tribunals and modes of organization, with which the usual courts of the land had nothing to do.[1] From the reign of Henry II., 1133–1189, when the detailed statements of Jewish life in England begin, bishops, priests, and convents were ready to borrow from the Jews. Nine Cistercian convents were mortgaged to the famous Aaron of Lincoln, who died 1187. He boasted that his money had built St. Albans, a boast which Freeman uses to prove the intolerable arrogance of the Jews. The arm of St. Oswald of Peterboro was held by a Jew in pawn. The usual interest charged was two pence a week on the pound, or forty-three per cent a year. And it went as high as eighty per cent. The promissory note is preserved which Herbert, pastor of Wissenden, gave to Aaron of Lincoln for 120 marks at two pence a week.[2] The Jews were tallaged by the king at pleasure. They belonged to him, as did the forests.[3] The frequency and exorbitance of the exactions under John and Henry III. are notorious. At the time of the levy of 1210 many left the kingdom. It was at that time that the famous case occurred of the Jew of Bristol, already referred to, whose teeth John ordered pulled out, one each day, till he should make over to the royal treasury ten thousand marks. The description that Matthew Paris gives is highly

[1] It is possible the first Jews came to England with William the Conqueror. Jacobs, p. 3. A law of Edward the Confessor, however, has a reference to Jews.

[2] Jacobs, p. 67, 308. The mortgages were called *cartæ debitorum*, M. Paris, Luard's ed., II. 358, etc. Jacobs, p. 381, estimates the number of Jews in England in 1200 at 2000. London had 100 families, Lincoln 82, Norwich 42, etc. Peter the Venerable also bears witness to the money dealings of convents with Jews, *de mirac.*, II. 15; Migne, 189, 927.

[3] Stubbs, *Const. Hist.*, II. 530 sqq.

interesting, but it was not till four centuries had elapsed, that another historian, Thomas Fuller, commenting upon this piece of mediæval dentistry, had the hardihood to say, this Jew "yielding sooner, had saved his teeth, or, stubborn longer, had spared his money; now having both his purse and his jaw empty by the bargain. Condemn we here man's cruelty, and admire Heaven's justice; for all these sums extorted from the Jews by temporal kings are but paying their arrearages to God for a debt they can never satisfy; namely, the crucifying of Christ." Old prejudices die hard.

Henry III.'s exactions became so intolerable that in 1255 the Jews begged to be allowed to leave the realm. This request, to rely again upon Matthew Paris, the king refused, and then, like "another Titus or Vespasian," farmed them out to his rich brother Richard, Earl of Cornwall, that, "as he himself had excoriated them, so Richard might eviscerate them."[1]

The English Crusaders, starting on the Third Crusade, freely pillaged the Jews, indignant, as the chroniclers relate, that they should have abundance and to spare while they, who were hurrying on the long journey to Jerusalem, had not enough for their barest wants.[2] It was at this time, on the evening of the coronation of Richard I., that the horrible massacre occurred in which neither sex nor age was spared. At York, five hundred were shut up in the castle, and the men, in despair, after putting to death their own wives and daughters, were many of them burned to death.[3]

English communities were roused to a lamentable pitch of excitement by the alleged crucifixion of Christian boys. Among the more notorious cases were William of

---

[1] *Ut quos excoriaverat, comes eviscerat.*   Luard's ed., V. 487 sq.

[2] M. Paris, II. 358 sq.

[3] See M. Paris and especially William of Newburgh, Hamilton's ed., II. 24–28, and de Hoveden.   Matthew and de Hoveden are careful to say that the mortgage papers the Jews held were burnt with them.   See Graetz's description, VI. 219 sqq.

Norwich 1144, Harold of Gloucester 1168, Robert of
Edmonsbury 1181, and Hugh of Lincoln 1255. Although
these children were popularly known as saints, none of
them have been canonized by the Church. The alleged
enormities perpetrated upon Hugh of Lincoln, as given by
Matthew Paris, are too shocking to be enumerated at
length. The same chronicler interjects the statement
that the deed was "said often to have occurred." In the
excitement over little Hugh, eighteen Jews were gibbeted.[1]
The marvel is that the atrocious charge was believed, and
that no protest against the belief has come down to us
from those days.

Some English Jews, under pressure of fear, submitted
to baptism, and some also of their free will. The first
case of the latter kind, so far as I know, is given by
Anselm.[2] The convert became a monk. An isolated case
occurred here and there of a Christian turning Jew. A
deacon was hanged for this offence.[3]

The last act in the history of the Jews in mediæval England was their banishment by Edward I. in 1290. From
that time until the Caroline age, England was free from
Jewish inhabitants. Cromwell added to his fame by giving them protection in London.

The treatment the Jews received in Spain is justly regarded as the most merciless the race received in the
Middle Ages. Edward I. protected against plunder the
sixteen thousand Jews whom he banished from England.
But Ferdinand of Spain, when he issued the fell decree
for his Jewish subjects to leave Spain, apparently looked
on without a sign of pity. Spain, through its Church

---

[1] M. Paris, Luard's ed., III. 543, IV. 30, 377, V. 516. As usual, the
guilty parties were the richest Jews in the place. The chroniclers are not
agreed in regard to the exact motives actuating the Jews in these murders.

[2] Jacobs, p. 8. Hermann, a monk of Cologne, gives an account of his conversion from Judaism, Migne, 170, 806 sqq. A most singular attempt by
the devil to blot out the baptism of a German Jewish girl is given by Cæsar
of Heisterbach, *Dial.*, II. 26. She was to be drawn three times through the
hole in the outhouse, the effects of baptism being left behind.

[3] M. Paris, III. 71.

councils, had been the leader in restrictive legislation. The
introduction of the Inquisition made the life of this people
more and more severe, although primarily its pitiless regulations had no application to them. Persecutions filled
the land with ungenuine proselytes, the *conversos*, and these
became subject to the inquisitorial court.

The final blow given by Ferdinand and Isabella fell in
1492, the year of the discovery of the New World, in a part
of which was to be put into practice religious toleration as it
was never before practised on the earth. The edict expelled
all unbaptized Jews from Spain. Religious motives were behind it, and religious agents executed it. The immediate
occasion was the panic aroused by the alleged crucifixion of
the child of La Guardia — *el santo niño de la Guardia* — one
of the most notorious cases of alleged child murder by the
Jews.[1] Lope de Vega and other Spanish writers have made
the case famous in Spanish literature. Ferdinand, according
to Llorente, moved by the appeals of a Jewish embassy and
Spanish grandees, was about to modify his sentence, when
Torquemada, hastening into the presence of the king and his
consort, presented the crucifix, exclaiming, " Judas Iscariot
sold Christ for thirty pieces of silver. Your majesties are
about to sell him for three thousand ducats. Here he is, take
him and sell him."

The number of Jews who emigrated from Spain, in the
summer of 1492, is estimated at 170,000 to 400,000.[2] They
went to Italy, Morocco, and the East, and, invited by king
Manuel, 100,000 passed into Portugal. But here their tarrying was destined to be short. In 1495 an edict offered them
the old alternative of baptism or death, and children under
fourteen were taken forcibly from their parents, and the
sacred Christian rite was administered to them. Ten years
later two thousand of the alleged ungenuine converts were
massacred in cold blood.

[1] See Lea's elaborate account in *Rel. Hist. of Spain*, 437–468; also Graetz,
VIII. 466–472. The child's body could not be found, but the Inquisitors
easily accounted for this by the report that it had been carried to heaven on
the third day after the murder.   [2] Graetz, VIII. 349, puts it at 300,000.

Such was the drama of sufferings through which the Jews
were made to pass during the mediæval period in Western
Europe. As against this treatment, what efforts were made to
win the Jews by appeals to the gospel? But the question might
well be asked whether any appeals could be expected to win
them when such a spirit of persecution prevailed. How
could love and such hostility go together? The attempts
to convince them were made chiefly through tracts and
disputations. Anselm, while he did not direct his treatise
on the atonement, *cur deus homo*, to the Jews, says, that his
argument was sufficient to persuade both Jew and pagan.
Grosseteste sought to show the fulfilment of the old law and
to prove the divinity of Christ in his *de cessatione legalium*,
written in 1231.[1] The most famous of these tracts was written
by Peter the Venerable. In Migne's edition it fills more
than one hundred and forty columns, and would make a
modern book of more than three hundred pages of the ordinary size. Its heading, little adapted to win the favor of
the people to whom it was addressed, ran "A Tract against
the Inveterate Hardness of the Jews" (*inveteratam duritiem*).
The author proceeded to show from the Hebrew Scriptures
the divinity of Christ, at the same time declaring that "to
the blind even the light is as night and the sun as the shades
of darkness."

Some idea can be gotten of the nature of some of Peter's
arguments from one of the many Scripture texts adduced
to prove that Christ is the Son of God, Isa. lxvi. 9: "Shall
I bring to the birth, and not cause to bring forth? saith Jehovah. Shall I that caused to bring forth shut the womb?
saith thy God." "What could be more clear, O Jews," adds
the author, "in proving the generation of the Son of God?
For if God begat, so far as He begat, He is necessarily Father,
and the Son of God, so far as He is begotten, is necessarily

[1] For the use made of it by Sir John Eliot and John Selden, see Stevenson, p. 104. Among other tracts on the Jewish question were those of Rupert
of Deutz; *Dial. inter Christum et Judæum*, Migne, 170, 559–610; Richard of
St. Victor, *de Emmanuele*, Migne, 196, 601–666; Alanus ab Insulis, *Contra
Judæos*, Migne, 210, 400–422.

Son." In taking up the proof that the Messiah has already come, Peter naïvely says that "if the Jew shall presume to think when the argument is finished that he lives, Peter holds the sword of Goliath, and, standing over the Jew's prostrate form, will use the weapon for his destruction, and ' with its edge' cleave his blasphemous head in twain." [1]

If the mild abbot of Cluny, Peter the Venerable, approached the Jews in such an arrogant tone, what was to be expected from other writers, like Peter of Blois who wrote upon the *Perfidy of the Jews*?

Public disputations were resorted to in Southwestern Europe. Not a few Jews, "learned men, physicians, authors, and poets," to use the language of Graetz,[2] adopted the Christian faith from conviction, and "became as eager in proselyting as though they had been born Dominicans." At the public disputations, representative rabbis and chosen Christian controversialists disputed. Jewish proselytes often represented the Christian side. The most famous of these disputations, the disputation of Tortosa, extended through a year and nine months, 1413–1414, and held sixty-eight sittings. Many baptisms are reported to have followed this trial of argumentative strength, and Benedict XIII. announced his conclusions in a bull forbidding forced baptism, as opposed to the canons of the church, but insisting on the Jews wearing the distinctive patch, and enacting that they should listen to three Christian sermons every year, — on Easter, in Advent, and in midsummer. Raymundus Lullus appealed for the establishment of chairs in Hebrew with an eye to the conversion of the Jews, as did also the Dominican Raymundus of Peñaforte. At the beginning of the fifteenth century the propaganda of the eloquent preacher Vincent Ferrer was crowned with success, and the lowest estimates place the number who received baptism under his influence at twenty thousand. The most distinguished of the Spanish converts was Rabbi Solomon Helevi, 1353–1435, who occupied the archiepiscopal chair of Burgos. The Christian

---

[1] Migne's ed., 189, 553.   [2] viii. 83.

scholar Nicolas of Cusa, if not born a Jew, was of Jewish descent.

In London there was an attempt to reach the Jews by a sort of university settlement, the *domus conversorum*, intended for the protection of Jewish proselytes.   It was established in 1233, and an annual grant of seven hundred marks from the royal exchequer promised for its maintenance; but no reports have come down to us of its usefulness.

These efforts relieve, it is true, the dark picture, but relieve it only a little.   The racial exclusiveness of the Jew, and the defiant pride which Christendom associates with him when he attains to prosperity, still render it difficult to make any impression upon him by the presentation of the arguments for Christianity.   There have been converts.   Neander was a Jew born.   So were Paulus Cassel and Adolf Saphir.   Delitzsch had a Jew for one of his parents.   Döllinger is authority for the statement that thirty years ago there were two thousand Christians in Berlin of Jewish descent.   There is fortunately no feeling to-day, at least in the church of the West, that it should come to the aid of Providence in executing vengeance for the crucifixion of Christ, a thought which ruled the Christian mind in the Middle Ages.   In view of the experience of the mediæval church, if for no other reason, the mode of treatment suggested to the modern church is by the spirit of brotherly confidence and Christian love.

CHAPTER X.

HERESY AND ITS SUPPRESSION.

§ 78. Literature for the Entire Chapter.

GENERAL WORKS: FLACIUS ILLYRICUS : *Catalogus testium veritatis qui ante nostram ætatem reclamarunt papæ*, Basel, 1556. — DU PLESSIS D'ARGEN-TRÉ : *Coll. judiciorum de novis erroribus qui ab initio XII. sæc. usque ad 1632 in ecclesia postscripti sunt et notati*, 3 vols. Paris, 1728. — * DÖLLINGER : *Beiträge zur Sektengesch. des Mittelalters*, Munich, 1890. A most valuable work. Part II., pp. 736, contains original documents, in the collection of which DÖLLINGER spent many years and made many journeys. — PAUL FREDERICQ : *Corpus documentorum hær. pravitatis Neerlandicæ*, 5 vols. Ghent, 1889 sqq. — CÆSAR OF HEISTERBACH : *Dialogus*. — ETIENNE DE BOURBON : *Anecdotes Historiques*, ed. by LECOY DE LA MARCHE, Paris, 1877. — MAP : *De nugis curialium*, Wright's ed. — *Epp. Innocentii III.*, Migne, 214–216. — JACQUES DE VITRY : *Hist. orientalis*, Douai, 1572, and in MARTÈNE and DURAND, *Thes. anecd.*, 5 vols. Paris, 1717. — ARNOLD : *Unpartheiische Kirchen- und Ketzerhistorie*, Frankf., 1729. — FÜSSLIN : *Kirchen- und Ketzergesch. der mittleren Zeit*, 3 vols. Leipzig, 1770–1774. — MOSHEIM : *Versuch einer unparthei. Ketzergesch.*, Helmstädt, 1746. — HAHN : *Gesch. der Ketzer im Mittelalter*, 3 vols. Stuttg., 1845–1847. — * A. JUNDT : *Hist. du panthéisme pop. au moyen âge*, Paris, 1875. — * LEA : *Hist. of the Inquisition*, 3 vols. N.Y., 1888. On the sects, I. 57–208. — M. F. TOCCO : *L'eresia nel medio evo*, Florence, 1884. — P. ALPHANDÉRY : *Les idées morales chez les Hetérédoxes Latins au début du XIII siècle*, Paris, 1903. — HEFELE-KNÖPFLER, . vol. V. — A. H. NEWMAN : *Recent Researches concerning Med. Sects* in Papers of Amer. Soc. of Ch. Hist. 1892, IV. 167–221.

FOR THE CATHARI, § 80 : BONACURSUS (at first a Catharań teacher) : *Vita hæreticorum seu contra Catharos* (1190 ?), Migne, 204. 775–792. — ECBERTUS (canon of Cologne about 1150) : *Sermones XIII. adv. Catharorum errores*, Migne, 195. — ERMENGAUDUS : *Contra hæret.*, Migne, 204, 1235–1275. — MONETA CREMONENSIS (1240) : *Adv. Catharos et Valdenses*, Rome, 1763. — RAINERIUS SACCHONE (d. about 1263, was a leader among the Cathari for seventeen years, then became a Dominican and an active inquisitor): *De Catharibus et Leonistis seu pauperibus de Lugduno* in Martène-Durand, *Thes. Anecd.*, V. 1759–1776. — BERNARDUS GUIDONIS : *Practica inquisitionis hereticæ pravitatis*, ed. by

C. DOUAIS, Paris, 1886. — C. DOUAIS, bp. of Beauvais: *Documents pour servir à l'hist. de l'inquis. dans le Languedoc*, 2 vols. Paris, 1900. *Trans. and Reprints*, by Univ. of Phila., III. No. 6. — *C. SCHMIDT: *Hist. et Doctr. de la secte des Cathares ou Albigeois*, 2 vols. Paris, 1849.

FOR THE PETROBRUSIANS, ETC., § 81 : DÖLLINGER : I. 75–110. — PETER VENE-RABILIS : *Adv. Petrobrusianos*, Migne, 189. 719–850 ; *Acta episc. Ceno-mannensium*, in Mabillon, *Veter. Analecta*, p. 315, Paris, 1723. — For Henry of Lausanne, GAUFRID : *Vita Bernardi*, Migne, 185. 312 sqq. ; *Epp. Bernardi*, 241, Migne, 182, 434 sqq. — *Lives* of St. Bernard. — HAUCK ; art. in Herzog Ency., VII. 606 sq. — J. VON WALTER : *Die ersten Wanderprediger Frankreichs*, II. 130–141, Leipzig, 1906. — For Tanchelm, *Vita Norberti*, cap. 16. — OTTO OF FREISING: *De gestis Frid.*, cap. 54. — HAUCK : IV. 88–92.

FOR THE BEGUINES AND BEGHARDS, § 83 : BERNARDUS GUY : pp. 141 sqq., 264–268. — FREDERICQ, II. 9 sqq., 72 sqq. — DÖLLINGER, II. 378–416, 702 sqq. —*J. L. MOSHEIM : *De Beghardis et Beguinabus*, Leipzig, 1790. — G. UHLHORN: *D. christl. Liebesthätigkeit im Mittelalter*, pp. 376–394. — H. DELACROIX : *Le Mysticisme speculatif en Allemagne au 14e siècle*, Paris, 1900, pp. 52–134. — ULLMANN: *Reformers before the Reformation.* — LEA: II. 350 sqq. — *HAUPT, art. *Beguinen und Begharden* in Herzog, II. 516–526, and art. *Beguinen* in Wetzer-Welte, II. 204 sqq.

FOR THE WALDENSES, § 84, the works of RAINERIUS, MONETA, BERNARDUS GUY. — DÖLLINGER : *Beiträge.* — BERNARDUS, ABBAS FONTIS CALIDI (d. about 1193) : *Adv. Waldensium sectam*, Migne, 204. 793–840. — ALANUS AB INSULIS (d. about 1202) : *Adv. hæret. Waldenses, Judæos et Paganos*, Migne, 210. 377–399 ; — *Rescriptum hæresiarcharum Lombardiæ ad Leonistas in Alemannia*, by the so-called "ANONYMOUS OF PASSAU" (about 1315), ed. by PREGER in *Beiträge zur Gesch. der Waldesier im Mittelalter*, Munich, 1875. GIESELER, in his *De Rainerii Sacchone*, Götting., 1834, recognized this as a distinct work. — *Etienne de Bourbon*, pp. 290–296, etc. — DAVID OF AUGSBURG : *Tractatus de inquis. hæreticorum*, ed. by PREGER, Munich, 1878. Döllinger gives parts of Bernard Guy's *Practica*, II. 6–17, etc., the *Rescriptum*, II. 42–52, and DAVID OF AUGSBURG, II. 315–319. — Also FREDERICQ, vols. I., II.

MOD. WORKS, § 84 : PERRIN : *Hist. des Vaudois*, Geneva, 1619, in three parts, —the Waldenses, the Albigenses, and the Ten Persecutions of the Vaudois. The Phila. ed. (1847) contains an Introd. by PROFESSOR SAMUEL MILLER of Princeton. — GILLES : *Hist. eccles. des églises réf. en quelques vallées de Piémont*, Geneva, 1648. — MORLAND : *Hist. of the evang. Churches of the Valleys of Piedmont*, London, 1658. — LEGER : *Hist. générale des églises evang. des Vallées, etc.*, Leyden, 1669, with large maps of the three Waldensian valleys and pictures of the martyrdoms. Leger, a leading Waldensian pastor, took refuge in Leyden from persecution. — PEYRAN : *Hist. Defence of the Waldenses*, London, 1826. — GILLY (canon of Durham): *Waldensian Researches*, London, 1831. — MUSTON : *Hist. des Vaudois*,

Paris, 1834 ; *L'Israel des Alpes*, Paris, 1851, Engl. trans., 2 vols. London, 1857.—BLAIR : *Hist. of the Waldenses*, 2 vols. Edinb., 1833.—MONAS-TIER : *Hist. de l'église vaudoise*, 2 vols. Lausanne, 1847. — * A. W. DIECKHOFF : *Die Waldenser im Mittelalter*, Götting. 1851.—* J. J. HER-ZOG : *Die romanischen Waldenser*, Halle, 1853. —MAITLAND : *Facts and Documents of the Waldenses*, London, 1862.—F. PALACKY : *Die Beziehun-gen der Waldenser zu den ehemaligen Sekten in Böhmen*, Prague, 1869. —* JAROSLAV GOLL : *Quellen und Untersuchungen zur Gesch. der Böh-mischen Brüder*, Prague, 1878–1882.—* H. HAUPT : *Die relig. Sekten in Franken vor der Reformation*, Würzb. 1882 ; *Die deutsche Bibelüberset-zung der mittelalterlichen Waldenser in dem Codex Teplensis*, Würzb., 1885; *Waldenserthum und Inquisition im südöstlichen Deutschland*, Freib., 1890; *Der Waldensische Ursprung d. Codex Teplensis*, Würzb., 1886. — MONTET : *Hist. litt. des Vaudois du Piémont*, Paris, 1885.—*L. KELLER : *Die Waldenser und die deutschen Bibelübersetzungen*, Leipzig, 1886.— * F. JOSTES : *Die Waldenser und die vorluth. deutsche Bibelübersetzung*, Munich, 1885 ; *Die Tepler Bibelübersetzung*, Münster, 1886. —*PREGER : *Das Verhältniss der Taboriten zu den Waldesiern des 14ten Jahrhunderts*, Munich, 1887 ; *Die Verfassung der französ. Waldesier, etc.*, Munich, 1890. —*K. MÜLLER : *Die Waldenser und ihre einzelnen Gruppen bis zum Anfang des 14ten Jahrhunderts*, Gotha, 1886.—* E. COMBA: *Hist. des Vaudois d'Italie avant la Réforme*, Paris, 1887, new ed. 1901, Engl. trans., London, 1889. — SOFIA BOMPIANI : *A Short Hist. of the Ital. Waldenses*, N.Y. 1897. See also LEA : *Inquis.*, vol. II. — E. E. HALE : *In his Name*, Boston, 1887, a chaste tale of the early Waldenses in Lyons. — H. C. VEDDER : *Origin and Early Teachings of the Waldenses* in "Am. Jour. of Theol.," 1900, pp. 465–489.

FOR THE CRUSADES AGAINST THE ALBIGENSES, § 85 : Innocent III.'s *Letters*, Migne, 214–216. The Abbot PIERRE DE VAUX DE CERNAY in *Rec. Hist. de France*, XXI. 7 sqq. — HURTER : *Inn. III.* vol. II. 257–349, 379–389, 413–432. — HEFELE-KNÖPFLER : V. 827–861, etc. — LEA : I. 114–209. — A. LUCHAIRE : *Inn. III. et la croisade des Albigeois*, Paris, 1905. — MANDELL CREIGHTON : *Simon de Montfort*, in *Hist. Biog.*

FOR THE INQUISITION, §§ 86, 87, see DOUAIS, BERNARD GUY, and other sources and the works of DÖLLINGER, SCHMIDT, LEA, HURTER (II. 257–269), HEFELE, etc., as cited above. — MIRBT : *Quellen zur Gesch. des Papstthums*, 2d ed., pp. 125–146 ; — *Doct. de modo proced. c. hœret.*, in MARTÈNE-DURAND, *Thes. anecd.*, V. 1795–1822.—NIC. EYMERICUS (inquis.-general of Spain, d. 1399) : *Directorium inquisitorum*, ed. F. PEGNA, Rome, 1578. For MSS. of Eymericus, see DENIFLE : *Archiv*, 1885, pp. 143 sqq. — P. FREDERICQ : *Corpus documentorum inquis. hœr. prav. Neer-landicœ*, 5 vols. Ghent, 1889–1902. Vol. I. opens with the year 1025. — LUD. A PARAMO (a Sicilian inquisitor) : *De orig. et progressu officii s. inquis.*, Madrid, 1598. — P. LIMBORCH : *Hist. inquis.*, Amster., 1692, includes the important *liber sententiarum inquis. Tolosonœ*, Engl. trans., 2 vols. London, 1731. — J. A. LLORENTE (secretary of the Ma-drid Inquis. 1789–1791) : *Hist. critique de l'inquis. d'Espagne* (to Ferdi-

nand VII.), 4 vols. Paris, 1817.   Condens. Engl. trans., Phil. 1843. —
RULE: *Hist. of the Inquis.*, 2 vols. London, 1874.—F. HOFFMANN:
Gesch. der Inquis. (down to the last cent.), 2 vols. Bonn, 1878. —
C. MOLINIER: *L'Inquis. dans le midi de la France au 13ᵉ et 14ᵉ siècle*,
Paris, 1881. — FICKER : *Die gesetzl. Einführung der Todesstrafe für
Ketzerei* in *Mittheilungen für Oester. Geschichtsforschung*, 1880, pp.
188 sqq. — J. HAVET: *L'hérésie et le bras séculier au moyen âge*, Paris,
1881. — TAMBURINI : *Storia generale dell' Inquisizione*, 4 vols. — L.
TANON : *L'hist. des tribunaux de l'inquis. en France*, Paris, 1893. —
HENNER : *Beiträge zur Organization und Kompetenz der päpstlichen
Ketzergerichte*, Leipzig, 1893. — GRAF VON HOENSBROECH : *Das Papst-
thum, etc.*, Leipzig, 1900 ; 4th ed., 1901.   Chap. on the Papacy and the
Inquis., I. 1–206. — P. FLADE : *Das römische Inquisitionsverfahren in
Deutschland bis zu den Hexenprocessen*, Leipzig, 1902. — HURTER : art.
Inquisition in Wetzer-Welte, VI. 765 sqq., and Herzog, IX. 152–167. —
E. L. TH. HENKE : *Konrad von Marburg*, Marb., 1861. — B. KALTNER :
Konrad v. Marburg u. d. Inquis. in Deutschland, Prague, 1882. — R.
SCHMIDT : *Die Herkunft des Inquisitionsprocesses*, Freib. i. Breis. 1902. —
C. H. HASKINS : *Robert le Bougre and the Beginnings of the Inquis. in
Northern France* in "Amer. Hist. Rev.," 1902, pp. 421–437, 631–653.
—The works on canon law by HINSCHIUS, FRIEDBERG, and PH. HERGEN-
RÖTHER (R.C.), pp. 126, 601–610. — E. VACANDARD : *L'inquisition, Etude
hist. et crit. sur le pouvoir coercitif de l'église*, Paris, 1907, pp. 340.

§ 79.   *The Mediæval Dissenters.*

THE centralization of ecclesiastical authority in the papacy
was met by a widespread counter-movement of religious in-
dividualism and dissent.   It was when the theocratic programme of Gregory VII. and Innocent III. was being
pressed most vigorously that an ominous spiritual revolt
showed itself in communities of dissenters.   While the crusading armaments were battling against the infidel abroad,
heretical depravity, to use the official term, arose in the
Church at home to disturb its peace.

For nearly five hundred years heresy had been unknown
in Western Europe.   When Gregory the Great converted
the Arians of Spain and Lombardy in the latter part of the
sixth century, it was supposed that the last sparks of heresy
were extinguished.   In the second half of the eleventh century here and there, in Milan, Orleans, Strassburg, Cologne,
and Mainz, little flames of heresy shot forth; but they were
quickly put out and the Church went on its way again in

peace. In the twelfth century, heresy again broke out simultaneously in different parts of Europe, from Hungary to the
Pyrenees and northwards to Bremen.   The two burning
centres of the infection were Milan in Northern Italy and
Toulouse in Southern France.   The Church authorities
looked on with alarm, and, led by the pope, proceeded to
employ vigorous measures to stamp out the threatening
evil.   Jacques of Vitry, after visiting Milan, called it a pit
of heretics, *fovea hæreticorum*, and declared that there was
hardly a person left to resist the spiritual rebels, so numerous
were they in that city.[1]   At different points in Lombardy
the clergy were actually driven out and Piacenza remained
three years without a priest.   In Viterbo, in the very vicinity
of Rome, the Patarenes were in the majority in 1205, as
Innocent III. testified.   But it was in Languedoc that the
situation was most alarming, and there papal armies were
marshalled to crush out the contagion.

The dissenting movement started with the people and
not with the schools or princes, much provocation as the
princes had for showing their resentment at the avarice and
worldliness of the clergy and their invasion of the realm of
civil authority.   The vast majority of those who suffered
punishment as heretics were of the common people.   Their
ignorance was a constant subject of gibe and derision as
they stood for trial before the ecclesiastical tribunals.   The
heresy of a later period, the fifteenth century, differs in this
regard, having scholars among its advocates.

Our knowledge of the mediæval sectaries and their practices is drawn almost wholly from the testimonies of those
who were arrayed against them.   These testimonies are found
in tracts, manuals for the treatment of heresy, occasional
notices of ecclesiastical writers like Salimbene, Vitry, Etienne
de Bourbon, Cæsar of Heisterbach, or Matthew Paris, in the
decrees of synods and in the records of the heresy trials themselves.   These last records, written down by Catholic hands,
have come down to us in large numbers.   Interesting as they

---

[1] See the quotation at length in Alphandéry, p. 29.

[2] Migne, 214. 537; 215. 654.

are, they must be accepted with caution as the statements of enemies. As for Catharan literature, a single piece has survived [1] and it is a painful recollection that, where so many suffered the loss of goods, imprisonments, and death for their religious convictions, only a few lines remain in their own handwriting to depict their faith and hopes.

The exciting cause of this religious revolt is to be looked for in the worldliness and arrogance of the clergy, the formalism of the Church's ritual, and the worldly ambitions of the papal policy. In their depositions before the Church inquisitors, the accused called attention to the pride, cupidity, and immorality of the priests. Tanchelm, Henry of Lausanne, and other leaders directed their invectives against the priests and bishops who sought power and ease rather than the good of the people.

Underneath all this discontent was the spiritual hunger of the masses. The Bible was not an altogether forgotten book. The people remembered it. Popular preachers like Bernard of Thiron, Robert of Abrissel and Vitalis of Savigny quoted its precepts and relied upon its authority. There was a hankering after the Gospel which the Church did not set forth. The people wanted to get behind the clergy and the ritual of the sacraments to Christ himself, and, in doing so, a large body of the sectaries went to the extreme of abandoning the outward celebration of the sacraments, and withdrew themselves altogether from priestly offices. The aim of all the sects was moral and religious reformation. The Cathari, it is true, differed in a philosophical question and were Manichæans, but it was not a question of philosophy they were concerned about. Their chief purpose was to get away from the worldly aims of the established church, and this explains their rapid diffusion in Lombardy and Southern France.[2]

A prominent charge made against the dissenters was that they put their own interpretations upon the Gospels and Epistles and employed these interpretations to establish their

---

[1] Published by Cunitz in *Beiträge zu den theol. Wissenschaften*, 1854, IV.

[2] See Lempp's criticism of Alphandéry's work, *Theol. Lit.-zeitung*, 1905, p. 601 sq.

own systems and rebuke the Catholic hierarchy.   Special
honor was given by the Cathari to the Gospel of John, and
the Waldensian movement started with an attempt to make
known the Scriptures through the vulgar tongue.   The
humbler classes knew enough about clerical abuses from their
own observation; but the complaints of the best men of the
times were in the air, and these must also have reached their
ears and increased the general restlessness.   St. Bernard
rebuked the clergy for ambition, pride, and lust.   Grosseteste
called clerics antichrists and devils.   Walter von der Vogelweide, among the poets, spoke of priests as those —

> " Who make a traffic of each sacrament
> The mass' holy sacrifice included."

These men did not mean to condemn the priestly office, but
it should occasion no surprise that the people made no distinction between the office and the priest who abused the
office.

The voices of the prophets were also heard beyond the walls
of the convent, — Joachim of Flore and Hildegard.   Of an
independent ecclesiastical movement they had no thought.
But they cried out for clerical reform, and the people, after
long waiting, seeing no signs of a reform, found hope of relief
only in separatistic societies and groups of believers.   The
prophetess on the Rhine, having in mind the Cathari, called
upon all kings and Christians to put down the Sadducees and
heretics who indulged in lust, and, in the face of the early
command to the race to go forth and multiply, rejected
marriage.   But to her credit, it is to be said, that at a time
when heretics were being burnt at Bonn and Cologne, she
remonstrated against the death penalty for the heretic on
the ground that in spite of his heresy he bore the image of
God.[1]   She would have limited the punishment to the sequestration of goods.

It is also most probable that the elements of heresy were
introduced into Central and Western Europe from the East.
In the Byzantine empire the germs of early heresies continued

[1] For quotation see Döllinger, I. 111.

to sprout, and from there they seem to have been carried to the West, where they were adopted by the Manichæan Cathari and Albigenses. Travelling merchants and mercenaries from Germany, Denmark, France, and Flanders, who had travelled in the East or served in the Byzantine armies, may have brought them with them on their return to their homes.

The matters in which the heretical sects differed from the Catholic Church concerned doctrine, ritual, and the organization of the Church. Among the dogmas repudiated were transubstantiation and the sacerdotal theory of the priesthood. The validity of infant baptism was also quite widely denied, and the Cathari abandoned water baptism altogether. The worship of the cross and other images was regarded as idolatry. Oaths and even military service were renounced. Bernard Guy, inquisitor-general of Toulouse and our chief authority for the heretical beliefs current in Southern France in the fourteenth century, says [1] that the doctrine of transubstantiation was denied on the ground that, if Christ's body had been as large as the largest mountain, it would have been consumed long before that time. As for adoring the cross, thorns and spears might with· equal propriety be worshipped, for Christ's body was wounded by a crown of thorns and a lance. The depositions of the victims of the Inquisition are the simple statements of unlettered men. In the thousands of reports of judicial cases, which are preserved, charges of immoral conduct are rare.

A heretic, that is, one who dissented from the dogmatic belief of the Catholic Church, was regarded as worse than a Saracen and worse than a person of depraved morals. In a sermon, issued by Werner of St. Blasius about 1125, the statement is made that the " holy Catholic Church patiently tolerates those who live ill, *male viventes*, but casts out from

---

[1] So also Peter the Venerable in his *c. Petrobrus*, Migne, 189. 1185. Bernard Guy was born in Southern France, 1261. He entered the Dominican order and administered the office of inquisitor-general for sixteen years, prosecuting Cathari and other heretics. He was made bishop of Tuy, 1323. His *Practica inquisitionis*, a manual to be used by inquisitors, is a most interesting and valuable document.

2 H

itself those who believe erroneously, *male credentes*."[1]   The
mediæval Church, following the Fathers, did not hesitate to
apply the most opprobrious epithets to heretics. The synod of
Toulouse, 1163, refering to the heretics in Gascony, compared
them to serpents which, just for the very reason that they
conceal themselves, are all the more destructive to the simple-
minded in the Lord's vineyard. Perhaps the most frequent
comparison was that which likened them to Solomon's little
foxes which destroy the vines.[2]   Peter Damiani[3] and others
liken them to the foxes whose tails Samson bound together and
drove forth on their destructive mission. Innocent III. showed
a preference for the comparison to foxes, but also called heretics scorpions, wounding with the sting of damnation, locusts
like the locusts of Joel hid in the dust with vermin and countless in numbers, demons who offer the poison of serpents in
the golden chalice of Babylon, and he called heresy the black
horse of the Apocalypse on which the devil rides, holding the
balances.   Heresy is a cancer which moves like a serpent.[4]

The Fourth Lateran also used the figure of Samson's foxes,
whose faces had different aspects, but whose tails were bound
together for one and the same fell purpose.[5]   Gregory IX.,[6]
speaking of France, declared that it was filled with a multitude of venomous reptiles and the poison of the heresies.
Etienne de Bourbon, writing in the last years of the twelfth
century, said that "heretics are dregs and depravity, and for
that reason cannot return to their former faith except by
a divine miracle, even as cinders, which cannot be made into
silver, or dregs into wine."[7]   St. Bernard likened heretics to

---

[1] *Deflorationes SS. Patrum*, Migne, 157. 1050.

[2] *Vulpeculœ sunt heretici, quœ demoliuntur vineas*, Honorius of Autun,
Migne, 172. 503 ; *Etienne de Bourbon*, p. 278, etc.

[3] Migne, 145 : 419.

[4] *Epp: I.* 94 ; *II.* 99 ; *IX.* 208, etc., Migne, 214. 81, etc., *Morbus iste qui
serpit ut cancer, Ep. II. 1.*

[5] *Facies quidem habentes diversas sed caudas ad invicem collegatas quia
de varietate conveniunt in id ipsum*, Mirbt, p. 133. The same expression in
De Bourbon, p. 278.

[6] *Venenatorum multitudo reptilium et hœresum sanies scaturire dicitur.*
Gregory's bull, 1235, bearing on the inquisitor, Robert le Bougre, in Auvray,
2736, and Fredericq, I. 100.   [7] p. 289.

dogs that bite and foxes that deceive.[1]   Free use was made
of the withered branch of John 15. 6, which was to be cast
out and burnt, and of the historical examples of the destruction of the Canaanites and of Korah, Dothan, and Abiram.
Thomas Aquinas put heretics in the same category with coin
clippers who were felons before the civil tribunal.   Earth-
quakes, like the great earthquake in Lombardy of 1222, and
other natural calamities were ascribed by the orthodox to
God's anger against heresy.[2]

The principle of toleration was unknown, or at best only
here and there a voice was raised against the death penalty,
as in the case of Hildegard, Rupert of Deutz,[3] and Peter
Cantor, bishop of Paris.[4]   Bernard went farther and admonished Eugenius III. against the use of force in the treatment
of heretics [5] and in commenting upon Cant. II. 15, " take me
the foxes that spoil the vines," he said, that they should be
caught not by arms but by arguments, and be reconciled to
the Church in accordance with the purpose of Him who wills
all men to be saved.   He added that a false Catholic does
more harm than an open heretic.[6]   The opinion came to prevail, that what disease is to the body that heresy is to the
Church, and the most merciful procedure was to cut off
the heretic.   No distinction was made between the man and
the error.   The popes were chiefly responsible for the policy
which acted upon this view.   The civil codes adopted and pronounced death as the heretic's " merited reward," *poena
debita*.[7]   Thomas Aquinas and the theologians established it by
arguments.   Bernard Guy expressed the opinion of his age
when he declared that heresy can be destroyed only when its
advocates are converted or burnt.   To extirpate religious dissent, the fierce tribunal of the Inquisition was established.

---

[1] *De consid.* III. 1.   [2] Coulton's *Salimbene*, p. 13.

[3] See Döllinger, *Akad. Vorträge*, III. 280.

[4] Gutjahr, *Petrus Cantor Paris. sein Leben u. Schriften*, Grätz, 1899.

[5] *De consid.* III. 1.

[6] *Serm. in Cant.*, 64, 65, Migne, 183. 1086, 1091, *plus nocet falsus catholicus quam verus hereticus.*

[7] This was the usual expression used by the Church and in legal documents.
Flade, p. 114.

The last measure to be resorted to was an organized crusade, waged under the banner of the pope, which shed the blood of the mediæval dissenters without pity and with as little compunction as the blood of Saracens in the East.

The confusion, which reigned among the Church authorities concerning the sectaries, and also the differences which existed among the sectaries themselves, appear from the many names by which they were known. The most elaborate list is given in the code of Frederick II. 1238,[1] and enumerates nineteen different sects, among which the most familiar are Cathari, Patarenes, Beguines, Arnoldists, and Waldenses. But the code did not regard this enumeration as exhaustive, and adds to the names " all heretics of both sexes, whatever be the term used to designate them."   And in fact the list is not exhaustive, for it does not include the respectable group of Northern Italy known as the Humiliati, or the Ortlibenses of Strassburg, or the Apostolicals of Belgium.   One document speaks of no less than seventy-two, and Salimbene of one hundred and thirty different sects.[2] The council of Verona, 1183, condemned " first of all the Cathari and Patarenes and those who falsely called themselves Humiliati or Poor Men of Lyons, also the Passagini, Josephini, and Arnoldists, whom we put under perpetual ånathema."   The lack of compact organization explains in part the number of these names, some of which were taken from localities or towns and did not indicate any differences of belief or practice from other sectaries. The numbers of the heretics must be largely a matter of conjecture. A panic took hold of the Church authorities, and some of the statements, like those of Innocent III., must be regarded as exaggerations, as are often the rumors about a hostile army in a panic-stricken country, awaiting its arrival.   Innocent pronounced the number of heretics in Southern France in-

[1] *Catharos, Patarenos, Speronistas, Leonistas, Arnaldistas, Circumcisos, Passaginos, Josephinos, Garatenses, Albanenses, Franziscos, Bagnarolos, Commixtos, Waldenses, Roncarolos, Communellos, Warinos et Ortolinos cum illis de Aqua Nigra et omnes hæreticos utriusque sexus, quocumque nomine censeantur.* Bréholles, V. 280.

[2] Döllinger, II. 300 ; Coulton's *Salimbene*, p. 13.

numerable.[1]   According to the statement of Neumeister, a heretical bishop who was burnt, the number of Waldensian heretics in Austria about 1300 was eighty thousand.[2]   The writer, usually designated "the Passau Anonymous," writing about 1315, said there was scarcely a land in which the Waldenses had not spread.   The Cathari in Southern France mustered large armies and were massacred by the thousands. Of all these sects, the only one which has survived is the very honorable body, still known as the Waldenses.

The mediæval dissenters have sometimes been classed with the Protestants.   The classification is true only on the broad ground of their common refusal to be bound by the yoke of the Catholic hierarchy.   Some of the tenets of the dissenters and some of their practices the Protestant Reformation repudiated, fully as much as did the established Church of the Middle Ages.   Interesting as they are in themselves and by reason of the terrible ordeals they were forced to undergo, the sects were side currents compared with the great stream of the Catholic Church, to which, with all its abuses and persecuting enormities, the credit belongs of Christianizing the barbarians, developing learning, building cathedrals, cultivating art, furnishing hymns, constructing theological systems, and in other ways contributing to the progress of mankind.   That which makes them most interesting to us is their revolt against the priesthood, in which they all agreed, and the emphasis they laid upon purity of speech and purity of life.   Their history shows many good men, but no great personality.   Peter Waldo is the most notable among their leaders.

A clear classification of the mediæval heretics is made difficult if not impossible by the uncertainty concerning the opinions held by some of them and also by the apparent confusion of one sect with another by mediæval writers.

The Cathari, or Manichæan heretics, form a class by themselves.   The Waldenses, Humiliati, and probably the Arnoldists, represent the group of evangelical dissenters.   The Amauricians and probably the Ortlibenses were pantheistic.

[1] *Ep.* I. 94, Migne, 214. 81.   [2] Flade, p. 17.

The isolated leaders, Peter de Bruys, Henry of Lausanne, Eudo, and Tanchelm, were preachers and iconoclasts — using the term in a good sense — rather than founders of sects. The Beguines and Beghards represented a reform movement within the Church, one wing going off into paths of doctrinal heresy and lawlessness, and incurring thereby the anathemas of the ecclesiastical authorities.

§ 80. *The Cathari.*

The most widely distributed of the heretical sects were the Cathari. The term comes from the Greek *katharos*, meaning pure, and has given to the German its word for heretic, *Ketzer*. It was first used by the Cathari themselves.[1] A grotesque derivation, invented by their enemies, associated the sect with the cat, whose form it was the pleasure of the devil to assume.[2] From their dualistic tenets they were called New Manichæans. From the quarter they inhabited in Milan, called Pataria, or the abode of the junk dealers, they received the name Patarenes.[3]

[1] Schmidt. II. 276; Döllinger, I. 127. The term " Cathari " occurs in the twelfth century in Ecbertus and the acts of the Third Lateran Council, 1179, which speak of the heretics in Southern France as Cathari, Patrini, Publicani, or as known by some other name. *Quos alii Catharos, alii Patrinos, alii Publicanos*, etc., *alii aliis nominibus vocant.* Innocent III. called them Cathari and Patarenes, *Epp.* I. 94 ; II. 228 ; VIII. 85, 105, etc.

[2] Alanus de Insulis, Migne, 210. 266, says, " The Cathari are so called from the cat, whose posterior parts they are said to kiss and in whose form, as they say, Lucifer appears to them." Jacob de Voragine, in his *Legenda aurea*, refers to the use made of the cat by Satan in connection with heresy. He relates that on one occasion some ladies, who had been heretics, were kneeling at St. Dominic's feet and suddenly cried out : " 'Servant of God, help us.' 'Tarry awhile,' Dominic said, 'and ye shall see what ye have been serving.' Suddenly a black cat sprang up in their midst, right horrible, with long tail standing upright and emitting from the after end a terrible stench. After a while the cat climbed up the bell rope to the steeple, and the ladies were converted."

[3] Schmidt, who discusses the names in an elaborate note (II. 275–284), says that a portion of Milan was still called Contrada de' Patari in the eighteenth century. Frederick II., in his Sicilian code, derived the name Patarenes from *patior*, to suffer. *Patarenos se nominant velut expositos passioni*, Huillard-Bréholles, IV. 6. So also Walter Map, *De nugis*, Wright's ed., p. 61, who says the devil persuaded the Patarenes that they would become perfect by suffering and doing what he commanded.

In Southern France they were called Albigenses, from the town of Albi, one of the centres of their strength. From the territory in Eastern Europe, whence their theological tenets were drawn, they were known as Bulgari, Bugares, or Bugres.[1] Other titles were given to them in France, such as Tessarants, Textores, from their strength among the weavers and industrial classes, or Publicani and Poplicani, a corruption of Paulicians.[2]

It was the general belief of the age that the Cathari derived their doctrinal views from heretical sects of Eastern Europe and the Orient, such as the Paulicians and Bogomili. This was brought out in the testimony of members of the sect at their trials, and it has in its favor the official recognition which leaders from Eastern Europe, Bosnia, and Constantinople gave to the Western heretics. The Paulicians had existed since the fifth century in Asia Minor, and had pushed their way to Constantinople.[3] The Bogomili, who were of later origin, had a position of some prominence in Constantinople in the early part of the twelfth century.[4] It is also possible that seeds of Manichæan and Arian heresy were left in Italy and Southern France after these systems were supposed to be stamped out in those regions.

The Paulicians rejected the Old Testament and taught a strict dualism. The Bogomili held to the Sabellian Trinity, rejected the eucharist, and substituted for baptism with water a ritual of prayer and the imposition of hands. Mar-

[1] M. Paris, Luard's ed., III. 520, speaks of "Bugares" as a common appellation for the "Paterini, Jovinians, Albigenses, and those stained with other heresies," and associates with them Robert Bugre, who from being a heretic became a Dominican and noted Inquisitor. The modern word "bugger" is derived from his name.

[2] Döllinger, I. 129 sq.

[3] Ibid., I. 1–51, gives an elaborate description of the Paulicians and the Bogomili. He regards the Paulicians as the bridge between the Gnostics of the ancient Church and the sectaries of the Middle Ages, p. 3.

[4] Ibid., p. 114, says that the teachings of the Cathari and the Bogomili are so much alike that the "direct descent of the former from the latter must be regarded as beyond doubt." Our knowledge of the Bogomili is derived from Euthymus, whose *Narratio de Bogomilis* was edited by Gieseler, Göttingen, 1842.

riage they pronounced an unclean relationship. The worship of images and the use of the cross were discarded.

It was in the early years of the eleventh century, that the first reports of the appearance of heresy were bruited about here and there in Italy and Southern France. About the year 1000 a certain Leuthard, claiming to be inspired, appeared in the diocese of Châlons, destroying crosses and denouncing tithes. In 1012 Manichæan separatists appeared for the first time in Germany, at Mainz,[1] and in 1022 at Orleans, where King Robert and his consort Constance were present at their trial. Fifteen were tried, and thirteen remained steadfast and perished in the flames. Constance is said to have struck one of them, her former confessor, with a staff and to have put out one of his eyes.[2] Heretics appeared at Liège in 1025. About the same time a group was discovered in Treves who denied transubstantiation and rejected infant baptism.[3] The castle of Monteforte near Turin became a stronghold for them, and in 1034 Heribert, archbishop of Milan, seized some of their number, including their leader Gerard. They all accepted death in the flames rather than adore a cross. In 1052 they appeared at Goslar, where the guilty were discerned by their refusal to kill a chicken. With these notices, and a few more like them, the rumor of heresy is exhausted for nearly a century.

About the middle of the twelfth century, heresy suddenly appeared again at Liége, and prosecutions were begun. In 1145 eight men and three women were burnt at Cologne. The firmness of the victims was exemplified in the case of a young woman, who was held back for a time with the promise of marriage, but, on seeing her coreligionists burnt, broke from her keepers and, hiding her face in her dress, threw herself into the flames. And so, Cæsar of Heisterbach goes on to say, she descended with her fellow-heretics to hell.[4] At Rheims, 1157, and again at Cologne in 1163 we hear of trials and burnings, but thereafter the Cathari are no more heard of in Germany.

[1] Hauck, *Kirchengesch.*, III. 431.   [3] Hauck, IV. 88.
[2] Schmidt, I. 31; Hefele, IV. 674 sqq.   [4] *Dial.*, V. 19.

Their only appearance in England was at Oxford, 1161, when more than thirty illiterate Germans, men and women, strove to propagate their errors. They were reported as "detesting" marriage, the eucharist, baptism, and the Catholic Church, and as having quoted Matt. 5: 10, "Blessed are they which are persecuted for righteousness' sake, for theirs is the kingdom of heaven." A council of bishops ordered them branded on the forehead and flogged.[1] Henry II. would not allow heretics to be burnt to death, though offences in his reign against the forest laws were punished with blinding and castration.[2]

In France the Cathari were strong enough in 1167 to hold a council at St. Felix de Caraman near Toulouse. It was attended by Nicetas of Constantinople, to whom the title of pope was given. He was accompanied by a Catharan bishop, Marcus of Lombardy.[3] Contemporary reports represent the number of heretics as very large. They were compared by William of Newburgh to the sand of the sea, and were said by Walter Map to be infinite in number in Aquitaine and Burgundy.[4] By the end of the twelfth century they were reported to have followers in nearly 1000 cities.[5] The Dominican Rainerius gave 4,000,000 as a safe estimate of their number and declared this was according to a census made by the Cathari themselves.[6] Joachim of Flore stated that they were sending out their emissaries like locusts.[7] Such statements are not to be taken too seriously, but they indicate a widespread religious unrest. Men did not know whereunto heresy might grow. In Southern France the priests were the objects of ridicule. In that region, as well as in many of the cities of Lombardy, the Cathari had schools for girls and boys.

[1] William of Newburgh, Hamilton's ed., pp. 121–123. Walter Map, *De Nugis*, p. 62, reduces the number to sixteen. They were called Publicani by the Oxford council, 1260.

[2] Stubbs, ed. of De Hoveden, II. p. liv. sq.

[3] Döllinger, I. 121 sq., has no hesitation in declaring him a bishop of the Paulicians.

[4] *Superabundant jam ad omnem infinitatem.*

[5] Cæsar of Heisterbach, quoted by Döllinger, I. 124.

[6] p. 1768.   [7] Döllinger, I. 125.

Agreed as the Cathari were in opposing many customs and doctrines of the established Church, they were divided among themselves and broken up into sects, — seventy-two, according to one document.[1] Chief among them were the Albanenses and Concorrezzi, deriving their names from two Lombard towns, Alba and Concorreggio, near Monza.[2] A position intermediate between them was occupied by the Bagnolenses, so called from the Italian town of Bagnolo, near Lodi. This third party had a bishop whose authority was acknowledged by the Cathari in Mantua, Brescia, and Bergamo.[3]

The differences between the Albanenses and Concorrezzi were of a theological character and concerned the nature of God and the origin of matter. The Albanenses were strict dualists. Matter is eternal and the product of the evil god. Paul speaks of the things, which are seen, as dung. The Concorrezzi seem to have rejected dualism and to have regarded evil as the creation of Lucifer, the highest of the angels.

In matters of ritual and practical conduct, and in antagonism to the Church establishment, all groups of the Cathari were agreed. Since Schmidt wrote his *History of the Cathari*, it has been common to represent Catharism as a philosophical system,[4] but it is difficult to understand the movement from this standpoint. How could an unlettered folk, as they were, be concerned primarily or chiefly with a metaphysical construction? Theirs was not a philosophy, but a daily faith and practice. This view alone makes it possible

[1] Döllinger, II. 300.

[2] Ibid., I. 117 ; II. 82. Schmidt derived them from Albania and from Coriza in Dalmatia.

[3] Rainerius is our chief authority for these statements. He makes the above threefold classification (Martène, V. 1761), and then proceeds to give the doctrinal and practical errors the sects had in common, and those which separated them. He also gives a list of the Catharan centres in Lombardy and other parts. See also the important document, the *Supra stella*, by Salvus Burce, 1235, published by Döllinger, II. 52–84. The title was chosen to distinguish it from a Catharan treatise entitled *Stella*, the Star.

[4] See also Alphandéry, p. 35. Lempp, in a criticism of Alphandéry's work, *Lit.-zeitung*, 1905, p. 601, takes the view which is presented in the text.

to understand how the movement gained such rapid and widespread acceptance in the well-ordered and prosperous territory of Southern France, a territory in which Cluny had exercised its influence and was located.

The Cathari agreed — to use the expression of their opponents — in vituperating the established Church and in calling its adherents Romanists.   There are two Churches, they held, — one of the wicked and one of the righteous.   They themselves constituted the Church of the righteous, outside of which there is no salvation,[1] having received the imposition of hands and done penance according to the teaching of Christ and the Apostles.   Its fruits proved that the established Church was not the true Church.   The true Church endures persecution, does not prescribe it.   The Roman Church sits in the place of rule and is clothed in purple and fine linen.   The true Church teaches first.   The Roman Church baptizes first.   The true Church has no dignitaries, prelates, cardinals, archdeacons, or monks.   The Roman Church is the woman of the Apocalypse, a harlot, and the pope anti-Christ.

The depositions at their trials indicate that the Cathari made much use of the Scriptures.   The treatises of Bonacursus, Ermengaudus, and other writers in refutation of Catharan teachings abound in quotations of Scripture, a fact indicating the regard the heretics had for them.   They put spiritual interpretations upon the miracles and freely allegorized parables.   In the parable of the Good Samaritan, the man who fell among the thieves was Adam, whose spirit, at God's command, descended from heaven to earth and fell among thieves in this lower world.[2]   The priest and the Levite were Melchizedek and Aaron, who went the "same way," that is, could not help him.   The Old Testament they discredited, pronouncing it the work of the devil.   Its God is an evil god.[3]

---

[1] Döllinger, II. 322, etc.; Douais, II. 105, etc.; Bonacursus, Migne, 204. 777.

[2] Bonacursus, p. 775.

[3] Döllinger, II. 294, etc. ; Ermengaudus, 1237.   Lea, I. 563–567, gives a document, apparently dating from about 1300, in which a Catharan uses

The Catharan doctrine seems to have highly exalted Christ, though it denied the full reality of his human nature. He was created in heaven and was not born on the earth, but passed through Mary as through a pipe. He neither ate material food nor drank material drink. As for John the Baptist, he was one of the major demons and was damned for doubting when he sent to Christ the question, "Art thou he that should come or do we look for another?"[1]

A strange account of the fall of the angels was current in Southern France. Satan ascended to heaven and waited in vain thirty-two years for admittance. He was then noticed and admitted by the porter. Hidden from the Father, he remained among the angels a year before he began to use his art to deceive. He asked them whether they had no other glory or pleasure besides what he saw. When they replied they had not, he asked whether they would not like to descend to his world and kingdom, promising to give them gifts, fields, vineyards, springs, meadows, fruits, gold, silver, and women. Then he began to praise woman and the pleasures of the flesh. When they inquired more particularly about the women, the devil said he would descend and bring one back with him. This he did. The woman was decked in jewels and gold and beautiful of form. The angels were inflamed with passion, and Satan seeing this, took her and left heaven. The angels followed. The exodus continued for nine days and nights, when God closed up the fissure which had been made.[2]

The Cathari divided themselves into two classes, the *Per-*

Scripture to prove that the God of the Old Testament is not the God of the New. He deposed, " God says in Genesis, ' Ye shall not eat the tree of life.' But the God of the New Testament says in the Apocalypse ' to him that overcometh I will give to eat of the tree of life.' That one prohibits, this one promises. Therefore they are antagonistic, one to the other." Again he deposed, " Genesis says I will place enmity between thee and the woman. The God of the Old Testament is thus the sower of discord and enmity. But the God of the New Testament is the giver of peace and the reconciler of all things. Hence they are antagonistic."

[1] Bonacursus, p. 777 ; Ermengaud, p. 1234 sq. ; Douais, II. 93, 96, 103, etc.
[2] Döllinger, II. 149-153.

fecti and the *Credentes*, or Believers. The Perfect were
those who had received the rite of the *consolamentum*, and
were also called *bons hommes*,[1] good men, or good Chris
tians, or the Girded, *vestiti*,[2] from the fact that after receiving the consolamentum they bound themselves with a cord.
The number of the Good Men, Rainerius, about 1250, gave
as four thousand. The Credentes corresponded, in a general
way, to the catechumens of the early Church, and placed
all their hope in the consolamentum, which they looked forward to receiving. By a contract, called the *convenenza*, the
Catharan officials pledged themselves to administer the consolamentum to the Credentes in their last hours.

The consolamentum took the place of baptism and meant
more. Its administration was treated by the Catholic authorities as equivalent to an initiation into heresy — *hæreticatio*,
as it was called. The usual form in which the court stated
the charge of heresy was, "He has submitted to heretica-
tion."[3] The rite, which women also were allowed to administer, was performed with the laying on of hands and the
use of the Gospel of John, which was imposed upon the head
or placed at the candidate's breast.[4] The candidate made a
confession of all his sins of thought, word, work, and vision,
and placed his faith and hope in God and the consolamentum
which he was about to receive. The kiss of peace followed.[5]

The Perfect had a monopoly of salvation. Those not receiving the consolamentum were considered lost or passed
at death into another body and returned to the earth. The
rite involved not only the absolution of all previous sins
but of sins that might be committed thereafter. However,

---

[1] *Boni homines*, Döllinger, II. 22, 27, etc.; *Boni Christiani*, II. 4, 17, 25,
etc. In Southern France one of the oft-repeated charges was that the accused
called the Cathari *bons hommes*, Douais, II. 9, 11, 14, 25, etc. The Credentes
are so called by French synods, by Innocent III., in letters written by papal
legates, etc. See Hefele, V. 846, 850, etc.; Döllinger and Douais under
Credentes in Index.

[2] Synod of Toulouse, 1229, etc. See Schmidt, II. 127.

[3] *Hæreticationi interfuit*, Douais, II. 17, 19, 22, etc.

[4] *Ante pectus*, Rainerius, p. 1764. An elaborate description is given in an
Appendix to Rainerius, Martène, V. 1776.

[5] Ermengaud, Migne, 204. 1302; Rainerius, p. 1764; Döllinger, II. 41.

relapse was possible and sometimes occurred.[1] At death, the
spirit was reunited with the soul, which had been left behind
in heaven. There is no resurrection of the body. The
administration of the consolamentum seems to have been
confined to adults until the fourteenth century, when it was
administered to sick children. Those who submitted to it
were said to have "made a good ending."[2]

The consolamentum involved the renunciation of the seven
sacraments. Baptism with water was pronounced a material
and corruptible thing, the work of the evil god. Even little
children were not saved who received absolution and imposition of hands.[3] The baptism of the established Church was
the baptism of John the Baptist, and John's baptism was
an invention of the devil.[4] Christ made a clear distinction
between baptism with water and the baptism of power,
Acts 1 : 5. The latter he promised to the Church.

As for the eucharist, the Cathari held that God would
not appoint the consecrated host as a medium of grace, nor
can God be in the host, for it passes through the belly, and
the vilest part of the body.[5] For the mass was substituted
consecrated bread before the common meal. This bread was
often kept for months. There was also, in some quarters, a
more solemn celebration twelve times a year, called the *ap-
parellamentum*, and the charge was very frequently made
that the accused had attended this feast.[6] Some deposed
that they were eating Christ's body and drinking his blood
while they were listening to the words of Scripture. Among
the requirements made of those who received the consolamentum were that they should not touch women, eat animal

---

[1] Among those who recanted was the rich citizen Morand of Toulouse,
who did penance by standing naked to the waist at the altar of St. Saturninus
and allowing himself to be scourged in the presence of the papal legate.   He
went on a pilgrimage to Jerusalem, but on his return went back to the Cathari
and died as one of the Perfect.   Schmidt, I. 77 sqq.

[2] Döllinger, II. 30.   [3] Ibid., II. 5, 322.

[4] Ibid., II. 21, 34, 65, 90, 283, etc.

[5] *In latrinam ventris et per turpissimum locum, quœ non possunt fieri, si
esset ibi deus.*   Döllinger, II. 5.

[6] Douais, II. 17, 22, 27, 45, etc.

food, kill animals, take oaths, or favor war and capital punishment.

The marriage bed was renounced as contrary to God's
law, and some went so far as to say openly that the human
body was made by the devil. The love of husband and wife
should be like the love of Christ for the Church, without
carnal desire. The command to avoid looking on a woman,
Matt. 5: 27, 28, was taken literally, and the command to
leave husband and wife was interpreted to mean the renunciation of sexual cohabitation. Witnesses condemned marriage absolutely,[1] and no man or woman living in sexual
relations could be saved. The opinion prevailed, at least
among some Catharan groups, that the eating of the forbidden fruit in Eden meant carnal cohabitation.[2]

As for animal nourishment, not only were all meats forbidden, but also eggs and cheese. The reason given was
that these were the product of carnal intercourse.[3] The
words of Peter on the housetop, Acts 10: 14, were also
quoted. The Cathari, however, allowed themselves fish, in
view of Christ's example in feeding the multitude and his
example after his resurrection, when he gave fish to his
disciples. The killing of animals, birds, and insects, except
frogs and serpents, was also forbidden.[4] The ultimate ground
for this refusal to kill animal life was stated by one of the
Inquisitorial manuals to be a belief in metempsychosis, the
return of the souls of the dead in the bodies of animals.

The condemnation of capital punishment was based on
such passages as : " Give place unto wrath, vengeance is
mine, I will repay, saith the Lord," Rom. 12: 19 ; and the
judicial execution of heretics and criminals was pronounced
homicide, a survival from the Old Testament and the influence of its evil god. The Cathari quoted Christ's words,

---

[1] Moneta, p. 315 ; *jacere cum uxore sua sicut cum meretrice*, Döllinger, II.
30 ; *matrimonium est meretricium*, Douais, II. 93 ; Döllinger, II. 18, 21, 23,
25, 28, 40, 156, 300, etc. ; *omnem carnalem concubitum dampnabilem dicunt*,
Douais, II. 93, 96, etc.

[2] Bonacursus, p. 776 ; Douais, II. 93, 103, etc.

[3] Ibid., p. 777 ; Rainerius, p. 1762 ; Döllinger, II. 294, 300.

[4] Döllinger, II. 5, 152, 181, 248, 294.

" Ye have heard how it hath been said an eye for an eye and a tooth for a tooth." [1] One of the charges made against the established Church was that it countenanced war and marshalled armies.

The interdiction of oaths was in obedience to the words of Christ, and was in the interest of strict integrity of speech.[2]

The Cathari also renounced priestly vestments, altars, and crosses as idolatrous. They called the cross the mark of the beast, and declared it had no more virtue than a ribbon for binding the hair. It was the instrument of Christ's shame and death, and therefore not to be used.[3] Thorns or a spear would be as appropriate for religious symbols as the cross.

They also rejected, as might have been expected, the doctrines of purgatory and indulgences.[4]

In addition to the consolamentum, the Cathari practised two rites called the *melioramentum* and the *endura*.[5] The melioramentum, which is adduced again and again in the judicial sentences, was a veneration of the officials administering the consolamentum, and consisted of a threefold salutation. The Catholics regarded it as a travesty of the adoration of the host.[6]

The endura, which has been called the most cruel practice the history of asceticism has to show, was a voluntary starvation unto death by those who had received the consolamentum. Sometimes these rigorous religionists waited for thirteen days for the end to come,[7] and parents are said even to have left their sick children without food, and mothers to have withdrawn the breast from nursing infants in executing the rite. The reports of such voluntary suicide are quite numerous.

---

[1] Salve Burce, in Döllinger, II. 71, a remarkable passage ; Douais, II. 94 ; Rainerius, p. 1762.

[2] Bonacursus, p. 777 ; Ermengaud, p. 1269. See Alphandéry, p. 83 sq.

[3] Döllinger, under *Kreuz* in Index II. 730 ; Bonacursus, p. 777 ; Douais, II. 94.

[4] Rainerius, 1762. See Alphandéry, p. 44.

[5] See Döllinger in Index under these two words and Schmidt, II. 71–103.

[6] Döllinger, I. 193, 210 ; II. 4, 25, 30, etc.; Douais, II. 23, etc.

[7] Alphandéry, p. 51 ; Döllinger, II. 205.

Our knowledge of the form of Church government practised by the Cathari is scant. Some of the groups of Italy
and Languedoc had bishops. The bishop had as assistants
a "major" and a "minor" son and a deacon, the two former
taking the bishop's place in his absence.[1] Assemblies were
held, as in 1241, on the banks of the Larneta, under the
presidency of the heretical bishop of Albi, Aymeri de Collet.
A more compact organization would probably have been
adopted but for the measures of repression everywhere put
in force against the sect.

The steadfast endurance of the Catharan dissenters before
hostile tribunals and in the face of death belong to the annals
of heroism and must call forth our admiration as it called
forth the wonder of contemporaries like Bernard.[2] We
live, said Everwin of Steinfeld,[3] —

"A hard and wandering life. We flee from city to city like sheep in
the midst of wolves. We suffer persecution like the Apostles and the
martyrs because our life is holy and austere. It is passed amidst prayers,
abstinences, and labors, but everything is easy for us because we are not of
this world."

Dr. Lea, the eminent authority on the Inquisition, has said
(I. 104) that no religion can show a more unbroken roll of
victims who unshrinkingly and joyfully sought death in
its most abhorrent form in preference to apostasy than the
Cathari. Serious as some of the errors were which they
held, nevertheless their effort to cultivate piety by other
methods than the Church was offering calls for sympathy.
Their rupture with the established organization can be to a
Protestant no reason for condemnation; and their dependence
upon the Scriptures and their moral tendencies must awaken
within him a feeling of kinship. He cannot follow them in their
rejection of baptism and the eucharist. In the repudiation
of judicial oaths and war, they anticipated some of the later
Christian bodies, such as the Quakers and Mennonites.

[1] Rainerius, p. 1766 ; Döllinger, II. 82, 278, 295, 324. At the time of
Nicetas' visit, Bernard Raymund was ordained bishop of Toulouse, Guiraud
Mercier, bishop of Carcassonne, and Raymund of Casalis, bishop of Val d'Aran.
[2] *Sermon*, 65, Migne, 183. 1091.   [3] Quoted by Schmidt, II. 94.

§ 81. *Peter de Bruys and Other Independent Leaders.*

Independent of the Cathari and yet sharing some of their
views and uniting with them in protest against the abuses of the
established Church, were Peter de Bruys, Henry of Lausanne,
and other leaders.   Peter and Henry exercised their influence
in Southern France.   Tanchelm and Eudo preached in Flanders
and Brittany.   At least three of them died in prison or otherwise suffered death by violence.   Bernard of Clairvaux, Peter
the Venerable, Otto of Freising, and other contemporary
Catholic writers are very severe upon them and speak contemptuously of their followers as drawn from the ignorant
classes.

Tanchelm, a layman, preached in the diocese of Cologne
and westwards to Antwerp and Utrecht.   There was at the
time only a single priest in Antwerp, and he living in concubinage.   Tanchelm pronounced the sacraments of no avail
when performed by a priest of immoral life and is said to
have turned "very many from the faith and the sacraments." [1]   He surrounded himself with an armed retinue
and went through the country carrying a sword and preceded
by a flag.   Success turned his head.   According to his contemporary, Abælard, he gave himself out to be the Son of
God. [2]   He went through the public ceremony of marrying
the Virgin Mary, with her portrait before him.   The people
are said by Norbert's biographer to have drunk the water
Tanchelm washed in.   He was imprisoned by the archbishop
of Cologne, made his escape, and was killed by a priest,
1115.   His preaching provoked the settlement of twelve
Premonstrants in Antwerp, and Norbert himself preached in
the Netherlands, 1124.

The movement in Brittany was led by Eudo de l'Etoile,
who also pretended to be the Son of God.   He was one of the
sect of the Apostolicals, a name given to heretical groups in
France and Belgium whose members refused flesh and repu-

[1] Fredericq, *Corpus Inq.*, I. 6.   For Tanchelm, see Fredericq, vols. I. and
II., and *Life of Norbert* in *Mon. Germ.*, ch. 16.

[2] *Introd. ad Theol.*, in Migne, 178. 1056, and Fredericq, I. 26.

diated marriage and other sacraments [1] Eudo died in prison
about 1148.

The movement led by Peter de Bruys and Henry of Lausanne was far more substantial. Both leaders were men of
sound sense and ability. Of the personal fortunes of Peter,
nothing more is known than that he was a priest, appeared
as a reformer about 1105 in Southern France, and was burnt
to death, 1126. Peter the Venerable has given us a tolerably satisfactory account of his teachings and their effect.[2]

Of Henry of Lausanne, Peter's successor, we know more.[3] He
was a Benedictine monk, endowed with an unusual gift of eloquence. His name is associated with Lausanne because, as Bernard tells us, he at one time lived there. The place of his birth
is not known. Abandoning the convent, he preached in the
diocese of Le Mans during the absence of its bishop, Hildebert,
in Rome, and by his permission. Henry won the people, but
drew upon himself the hostility of the clergy whose vices
he denounced. The bishop, on his return, expelled Henry
from his diocese. The evangelist then went to Lausanne and
from there to Southern France, joining in the spiritual crusade
opened by Peter de Bruys. He practised poverty and preached
it to the laity. One of the results of his preaching was that
women of loose morals repented and young men were persuaded to marry them. Cardinal Alberic, sent to stamp out
the Henrician heresy, called to his aid St. Bernard, the bishop
of Chartres and other prelates. According to Bernard's
biographer, miracles attended Bernard's activity.[4] Henry

---

[1] Döllinger, I. 98–104. Otto of Freising, *De gestis Frid.*, 54, says he called
himself Eudo or Eon, from the liturgical formula, *per eum qui venturus est
judicare*, etc. He is also mentioned by Abælard in his *Introd. ad Theol.*

[2] *Adv. Petrobrusianos*, Migne, 189. 719–850. Abælard gives a few lines to
him. Migne, 178. 1056. Peter speaks of Peter de Bruys and Henry of
Lausanne as *duo homuncios*, p. 728. See Döllinger, I. 75–98.

[3] See Peter the Venerable, *Adv. Petrobrus.*, Bernard, *Ep.*, 241, in Migne,
182. 435. Döllinger, I. 79 sqq.; J. von Walter, *Die ersten Wanderprediger
Frankreichs*, II. 130–140; Hauck, in Herzog, VIII. 606 sqq.

[4] *Vita S. Bernardi*, Migne, 185, 312 sqq. See the *Lives* of Bernard by
Neander-Deutsch, II. 191–231; Vacandard, II. 200 sqq.; Morison, p. 302
sqq., 404 sq.

was seized and imprisoned. What his end was, is not known.

Peter the Venerable, at the outset of his treatise, laid down five errors of the Petrobrusians which he proposed to show the falseness and wickedness of. (1) The baptism of persons before they have reached the years of discretion is invalid. Believers' baptism was based upon Mark 16 : 16, and children, growing up, were rebaptized. (2) Church edifices and consecrated altars are useless. (3) Crosses should be broken up and burnt. (4) The mass is nothing in the world. (5) Prayers, alms, and other good works are unavailing for the dead. These heresies the good abbot of Cluny called the five poisonous bushes, *quinque vigulta venenata*, which Peter de Bruys had planted. He gives half of his space to the refutation of the heresy about baptism.

Peter and Henry revived the Donatistic view that piety is essential to a legitimate priesthood. The word " Church" signifies the congregation of the faithful and consists in the unity of the assembled believers and not in the stones of the building.[1] God may be worshipped as acceptably in the market-place or a stable as in a consecrated edifice. They preached on the streets and in the open places. As for the cross, as well might a halter or a sword be adored. Peter is said to have cooked meat in the fire made by the crosses he piled up and burnt at St. Gilles, near the mouth of the Rhone. Song, they said, was fit for the tavern, but not for the worship of God. God is to be worshipped with the affections of the heart and cannot be moved by vocal notes or wooed by musical modulations.[2]

The doctrine of transubstantiation was distinctly renounced, and perhaps the Lord's Supper, on the ground that Christ gave up his body on the night of the betrayal once for all.[3] Peter not only called upon the priests to marry, but according to Peter the Venerable, he forced unwilling monks to take wives.

[1] *Nomen ecclesiæ congregationem fidelium signat*, etc., *Pet. Ven.*, p. 762. Peter goes back as far as Noah's altar to prove the sacredness of localities.

[2] *Pet. Ven.*, pp. 765, 847 sq.

[3] Peter of Cluny's meaning is not clear at this point, pp. 722, 765, 787.

St. Bernard and Peter the Venerable,[1] opposing the heretical view about infant baptism, laid stress upon Christ's invitation to little children and his desire to have them with him in heaven. Peter argued that for nearly five hundred years Europe had had no Christian not baptized in infancy, and hence according to the sectaries had no Christians at all. If it had no Christians, then it had no Church; if no Church, then no Christ. And if this were the case, then all our fathers perished; for, being baptized in infancy, they were not baptized at all. Peter and Henry laid chief stress upon the four Gospels, but it does not appear that they set aside any part of the Scriptures.[2]

The synod of Toulouse, 1119, in condemning as heretics those who rejected the Lord's Supper, infant baptism, and priestly ordination, condemned the Petrobrusians, though Peter de Bruys is not mentioned by name. Those who hung upon the preaching of Peter de Bruys and Henry of Lausanne were soon lost among the Cathari and other sects.[3] Bernard's description of the religious conditions in Southern France is no doubt rhetorical, but shows the widespread disaffection which prevailed at that time against the Church. He says that churches were without worshippers, the people without priests, and Christians without Christ. The sanctuary of the Lord was no longer regarded as sacred or the sacraments as holy. The festival days were deprived of their solemnities. The children were debarred from life by the

---

[1] Bernard, Migne, 182. 434 ; Peter, pp. 729, 761 sq.

[2] Döllinger, I. 83, makes the charge that they renounced the Old Testament. But Peter of Cluny does not say so and, had it been so, he certainly would have emphasized that heresy.

[3] Döllinger, I. 75 sqq., makes an elaborate attempt to prove that Peter and Henry were Cathari, but the differences in their teachings and practices seem to make this impossible. So Newman (Papers of Am. Soc. of Ch. Hist., IV. 184–189), Hauck, and Walter, p. 130. Peter and Henry are nowhere called Manichæans or dualists by Peter the Venerable and Bernard, who would scarcely have omitted this charge had there been just ground for it. They commended marriage ; the Cathari rejected it. They insisted upon adult baptism ; the Cathari repudiated all baptism. None of the rites peculiar to the Cathari were associated with Peter and Henry.

denial of baptism, and souls were hurried to the last tribunal, unreconciled by penance and unfortified by the communion.

§ 82.   *The Amaurians and Other Isolated Sects.*

Occupying a distinct place of their own were the pantheistic coteries of dissenters, the Amaurians and Ortlibenses, and perhaps other groups, like the Passagians and Speronistæ, of which we know scarcely more than the names.

The Amaurians, or Amauricians,[1] derived their origin from the speculations of the Paris professor, Amaury of Bena, a town,in the diocese of Chartres.   Innocent III. cited him to appear at Rome and condemned his views.   On his return to Paris, the university obliged him to publicly confess his errors.   He died about 1204.   His followers were condemned by a synod, held in Paris, 1209.

From the detailed account given by Cæsar of Heisterbach, we learn that a number of Amaury's followers were seized and examined by the bishops.   Eight priests and William the Goldsmith, called also one of the seven apostles, were burnt.   Four other priests were condemned to lifelong imprisonment.   Amaury's bones were exhumed and thrown into a field.[2]

The Amaurians seem to have relied for their pantheistic views upon John Scotus Erigena, whose work, *De divisione naturæ*, was also condemned at the synod of Paris, 1209. Amaury's system was also condemned by the Fourth Lateran, which represented him as holding that God was all things, *deus erat omnia*.   To this he added the two doctrines: that every Christian must believe that he is a member of Christ's body, this faith being as necessary to salvation as the faith

---

[1] Mansi, XXII. 801–809; Denifle, *Chartul. Un. Paris*, I. 70, 71, 72, 79, 107, etc. ; Cæsar of Heisterbach, Strange ed., II., 304 sqq.; Martène-Durand, *Thes. anec.*, IV. 165 sq. ; Jundt, *Hist. du pantheisme*, etc., p. 20 sq. ; Preger, *Gesch. der deutschen Mystik*, I. 173–184 ; Delacroix, *Le mysticisme speculatif*, etc., 32–51 ; Alphandéry, pp. 141–154.   For other sources, see Delacroix, p. 39 sq.

[2] *Chartularium*, p. 70.   Here, also, are given the names of the priests who were burnt or imprisoned.

in Christ's birth and death; and that to him who abides in love, sin is not reckoned. God becomes incarnate in believers who are members of Christ's body, as He became incarnate in the body of Jesus. God was as much in the body of Ovid as He was in the body of Augustine. Christ is no more in the consecrated bread than in any other bread or object. The Amaurians denied the resurrection of the body, and said that heaven and hell are states of the soul. The sinner carries hell in himself, even as a mouth holds a bad tooth.[1] The believer can no more sin than can the Holy Spirit who dwells in him. The pope is antichrist and the Roman Church, Babylon. The relics of the martyrs are nothing but dust.

From these statements the conclusion is to be drawn that Amaury and his followers insisted upon the liberty of the Spirit working independently of outer rites and dwelling in the heart. The Fourth Lateran, in its second canon, declared that the father of lies had so blinded Amaury's mind that his doctrine was the raving of an insane man rather than a heresy. Amaury absorbed Joachism, for he speaks of three ages, the ages of the Father and the Son, and the age of the Spirit, which was the last age, had begun in Amaury's time, and would continue to the consummation of all things. Amaury's followers seem to have become merged with the Brethren of the Free Spirit.[2]

The synod of Paris, which condemned the Amaurians, also condemned David of Dinant, and ordered one of his works, the *Quarternuli*, burnt. His writings were also forbidden by the statutes of the University of Paris of 1215, which forbade the reading of some of the works of Aristotle, Amaury the heretic, and Maurice of Spain.[3] David seems to have been a professor at Paris and died after 1215. He shared the pantheism of Amaury, was quoted by Albertus

---

[1] *Putridus dens in ore*, synod of Paris, 1209.

[2] So Preger, I. 212, on the basis of the "Anonymous of Passau." For the ninety-seven errors ascribed to the Brethren of the Free Spirit, see Preger, I. 461–469, and Hauck, in Herzog, I. 431.

[3] *Chartul.*, pp. 70, 79.

Magnus, and his speculations have been compared with the system of Spinoza.[1]

Belonging to the same class were the followers of Ortlieb of Strassburg, called Ortlibenses, Ortilibarii, Oriliwenses, Ortoleni,[2] and by other similar names. Some of their number were probably among the many heretics burnt in Strassburg, 1212. They were charged with holding that the world is eternal and God is immanent in all things. He did not have a Son, till Jesus was born of Joseph and Mary. They denied the resurrection of the body. The death and resurrection of Christ had only a symbolic import. The body of Christ is no more in the eucharistic bread than in any other bread. The established Church was the courtesan of the Apocalypse. The four Gospels are the chief parts of the Scriptures. They allowed marriage but condemned carnal cohabitation. The Ortlibenses were, like the Amaurians, spiritualists, and said that a man must follow the guidance of the Spirit who dwells in him.[3] They were a part of that extensive group designated by the general name of the Brethren of the Free Spirit, who fill so large a place as late as the fifteenth century.

The Passagii, or Passageni, a sect whose name is first mentioned in the acts of the synod of Verona, seem to have been unique in that they required the literal observance of the Mosaic law, including the Jewish Sabbath and circumcision. It is possible they are identical with the *Circumcisi* spoken of in the code of Frederick II. As late as 1267 and 1274 papal bulls call for the punishment of heretics who had gone back to Jewish rites, and the Passagii[4] may be referred to.

---

[1] Preger, I. 184–191.

[2] This name, given in the code of Frederick II., would seem to refer to the same sect. The "Anonymous of Passau," writing about 1316, is our chief authority. See Müller, *Die Waldenser*, pp. 147 sqq. ; Döllinger, *Beiträge*, II. 301, 703, etc.; Preger, II. 191–196 ; Delacroix, 52–76 ; Alphandéry, 154–167 ; Deutsch, art. *Ortlieb*, in Herzog, XIV. 499–501. Alphandéry urges the affiliation of the Ortlibenses with the Vaudois, chiefly because of their frequent juxtaposition in mediæval writings.

[3] Delacroix, p. 73, insists upon the identity of the Amaurians and Ortlibenses in all essential matters.   [4] See Döllinger, II. 327 ; Alphandéry, 168 sqq.

The Luciferans [1] were so called on account of the prominence they gave Lucifer as the prince of the lost angels and the maker of the material world and the body, and not because they worshipped Lucifer. It is doubtful whether they were a distinct sect. The name was applied without precision to Cathari and others who held that Lucifer was unjustly cast out of heaven. Heretics of this name were burnt in Passau and Saltzburg, 1312–1315 and 1338, and as late as 1395 in other parts of Austria.

As for the Warini, Speronistæ, and Josephini, who are also mentioned in the Frederican code, we know nothing more than the names. [2]

§ 83. *The Beguines and Beghards.*

While the Cathari and Waldenses were engaging the attention of the Church authorities in Southern Europe, communities, called Beguines and Beghards, were being formed along the lower Rhine and in the territories adjacent to it. They were lay associations intended at first to foster a warmer type of piety than they found in the Church. [3] Their aims were closely allied to the aims of the Tertiaries of St. Francis, and at a later period they were merged with them. Long before the close of the thirteenth century, some of these communities developed immoral practices and heretical tenets, which called forth the condemnation of pope and synods.

The Beguines, who were chiefly women, seem to have derived their origin and their name from Lambert le Bègue, a priest

---

[1] The notices are scattered. See under *diabolus* and *Lucifer* in Döllinger and Alphandéry, pp. 174 sqq. M. Paris, writing of 1226 and Frederick's march through Northern Italy, speaks of Milan being a refuge and receptacle of all sorts of heretics, Patarines, Luciferi, Publicani, Albigenses, and usurers.

[2] The Josephini are mentioned by the synod of Verona, 1184, and the bull of Gregory IX., June 25, 1231, and the Speronistæ by Salve Burce, Döllinger, II. 62, and in the bulls of Gregory IX., Aug. 20, 1229, June 25, 1231. See Fredericq, I. 75 sq.

[3] Hase, Karl Müller, *Kirchengesch.* I. 570, Alphandéry, p. 2 sqq., and others treat the subject under the head of lay-activity.

of Liége, who died about 1177.[1] In a document of that year
he is said to have preached to women and girls the value of
chastity by word and example.[2] It was a time when priestly
concubinage in Holland was general. Like Peter Valdez,
Lambert gave up his goods, sought to make known the Scriptures to the people, and founded in Liége the hospital of St.
Christopher and a house for women which in derision was
called the *beguinage*. The women renounced their goods and
lived a semi-conventual life, but took no vows and followed
none of the approved monastic Rules. Houses were established in Flanders, France, and especially in Germany, as for
example at Valenciennes, 1212, Douai, 1219, Antwerp, 1230,
Ghent, 1233, Frankfurt, 1242.   In 1264 St. Louis built a
beguinage in Paris which he remembered in his will. The
beguinage of Ghent was a small town in itself, with walls,
infirmary, church, cemetery, and conventual dwellings.
According to Matthew Paris, writing of the year 1250, their
number in Germany, especially in the vicinity of Cologne,
was countless.[3] Their houses were often named after their
founders, as the Schelenhaus in Cologne, after Herman
Schele, the Burgenhaus in Strassburg (1292), after a widow
by the name of Burga.   Other secular names were given,
such as the Golden Frog, *zum goldenen Frosch*, the Wolf, *zum
Wolf*, the Eagle, *zum Adler*.[4]

The communities supported themselves by spinning, weav-
ing, caring for the sick, and other occupations. Some of the
houses forbade begging. Some of them, as those in Cologne,
were afterwards turned into hospitals. As a rule they
practised mendicancy and went about in the streets crying

---

[1] The Beguines are called a sect, *secta Bequinarum*, in Guy's *Practica*,
p. 264, etc. The term Beguines, or Bequini, is also derived from *beggan*, to beg,
as by Jundt, or from *bègue*, to stammer. See Haupt, in Herzog, II. 517.
Lea, p. 351, seems inclined to advocate the old opinion which derived the
name from St. Begga, d. 694, the mother of Pepin of Heristal and the reputed
founder of a convent.

[2] *Premium castitatis verbo et exemplo predicavit*, Fredericq, II. 33.

[3] *Multitudo innumerabilis*, Luard's ed., V. 194. In another place, IV. 278,
he gives the number as 2,000. He also states that they were governed by
no Church Rule, *nullius sancti regula coarctatæ*.   [4] Uhlhorn, p. 380.

Brod durch Gott, "Bread for the sake of God." They wore a distinctive dress.[1]

The earliest community of Beghards known to us is the community of Löwen, 1220. The Beghards practised mendicancy and they spread as far as Poland and Switzerland. It was not long till they were charged with loose tendencies, a disregard of the hierarchy, and heresy. Neither the Beguines as a body nor the Beghards ever received distinct papal sanction.[2]

Both associations were the objects of synodal enactment as early as the middle of the thirteenth century. The synod of Mainz, 1259, warned the Beghards against going through the streets, crying, "Bread for God's sake," and admonished them to put aside offensive peculiarities and not to mingle with Beguines. Another synod of Mainz, 1261, referred to scandals among the Beguines. A synod of Cologne, a year later, condemned their unchurchly independence and bade them confess to priests on pain of excommunication. In 1310 synods, held at Treves and Mainz, forbade clerics entering beguinages on any pretext whatever and forbade Beghards explaining the Bible to the ignorant.[3]

The communities became more and more the objects of suspicion, and a sharp blow was struck at them in 1312 by Clement V. and the council of Vienne. The council forbade their communal mode of life, and accused them of heresies.[4] They were accused of refusing to adore the host and of holding that it is possible to reach a state of perfection in this world. A person reaching this state is under no obligation to fast and pray, but may yield himself without sin to all the appetites of the body.[5]

[1] The brief of Boniface IX. mentions "gray and other colors," Döllinger, *Beiträge*, II. 383.

[2] A synod of Béziers, p. 299, forbade both male and female societies on the ground that there was no papal sanction. Wetzer-Welte, II. 204, calls them *ordensähnliche Gesellschaften*, and Alphandéry, p. 2, *extra-ecclésiastiques*.

[3] Hefele, VI. 490, 500.   [4] Hefele, VI. 543, 544.

[5] The *actus carnis* is no sin, for it is an impulse of nature. Döllinger, II. 384–407, 702 sqq. They were also accused with denying a hell.

Clement's bull erred by its failure to discriminate between heretical and orthodox communities, a defect which was corrected by John XXII.   This pope expressly gave protection to the orthodox communities.   In the fourteenth century, the number of houses increased very rapidly in Germany and by 1400 there was scarcely a German town which had not its beguinage.   Up to that date, fifty-seven had been organized in Frankfurt, and in the middle of the fifteenth century there were one hundred and six such houses in Cologne and sixty in Strassburg.   In 1368 Erfurt had four hundred Beguines and Beghards.[1]

In the earlier part of the fourteenth century, the Beguines appeared in Southern France, where the Inquisition associated them closely with the Tertiaries of St. Francis and accused them of adopting the views of John Peter Olivi.[2]

In the latter part of the fourteenth century, the Inquisition broke up many of the houses in Germany, their effects being equally divided between itself, the poor, and the municipality. Gregory XI., 1377, recognized that many of the Beghards were leading good lives.   Boniface IX., 1394, made a sharp distinction between the communities and classed the heterodox Beghards with Lollards and Swestriones.[3]   But to other "Beghards and Beguines, who practised voluntary poverty"[4] and devoted themselves to the good of the people, he gave papal recognition.   To avoid persecution, many of them took refuge with the Franciscans and enrolled themselves as Tertiaries of the Franciscan order.   With the Reformation the Beghards and Beguines for the most part disappear as separate communities.[5]

[1] Haupt, in Herzog, II. 519.

[2] Bernard Guy, 264 sqq.   See also the letter of the bishop of Utrecht, Oct. 6, 1318, in Fredericq, II. 74.

[3] "Sisters," a popular name for the Beguines.

[4] *Willige Armen*, see Döllinger, II. 381–383.   Gregory XII., Eugene IV., and Sixtus IV. also commended the orthodox societies.

[5] There are still religious houses in Belgium and Holland called beguinages. In 1896 there were fifteen in Belgium and in Holland, one in Breda, and one in Amsterdam.   For the Brethren of the Free Spirit, who are often associated with the Beghards but had a different origin, see part II. of this volume.

These sectaries were in part forerunners and contemporaries of other communities with a pious and benevolent design developed in Holland in the fourteenth and fifteenth centuries, and with which German mysticism is closely associated.

§ 84.   *The Waldenses.*

" O lady fair, I have yet a gem which a purer lustre flings
  Than the diamond flash of the jewelled crown on the lofty brow of kings ;
  A wonderful pearl of exceeding price, whose virtue shall not decay,
  Whose light shall be as a spell to thee and a blessing on thy way ! ''
                              —WHITTIER, *The Vaudois Teacher.*

Distinct from the Cathari and other sects in origin and doctrine, but sharing with them the condemnation of the established Church, were the Waldenses.   The Cathari lived completely apart from the Catholic Church.   The Waldenses, leaning upon the Scriptures, sought to revive the simple precepts of the Apostolic age.   They were the strictly biblical sect of the Middle Ages.   This fact, and the pitiless and protracted persecutions to which they were subjected, long ago won the sympathies of the Protestant churches.   They present a rare spectacle of the survival of a body of believers which has come up out of great tribulation.

Southern France was their first home, but they were a small party as compared with the Albigenses in those parts. From France they spread into Piedmont, and also into Austria and Germany, as recent investigations have clearly brought out.   In Italy, they continue to this day in their ancestral valleys and, since 1870, endowed with full rights of citizenship.   In Austria, they kept their light burning as in a dark place for centuries, had a close historic connection with the Hussites and Bohemian Brethren, and prepared, in some measure, the way for the Anabaptists in the time of the Reformation.

The Waldenses derive their origin and name from Peter Waldus or Valdez,[1] who died before 1218, as all the con-

---

[1] Valdesius, Valdensius, or Waldunus.   The name is given in these and other forms by writers of the thirteenth century.   De Bourbon, p. 290 ; Guy, p. 244 ; Döllinger, II. 6, 300, etc.   Bernard, abbot of Fontis Calidi, Migne,

temporary writers agree. They were also called Poor Men
of Lyons, from the city on the Rhone where they originated,
and the *Sandalati* or Sandalled, from the *coarse shoes* they
wore.[1]

The name by which they were known among themselves
was Brethren or the Poor of Christ,[2] based probably upon
Matt. 5 : 3, " Blessed are the poor in spirit."   According to
the Anonymous writer of Passau, writing in the early years
of the fourteenth century, some already in his day carried
the origin of the sect back to the Apostles.   Until recently
all Waldensian writers have claimed for it Apostolic origin
or gone at least as far back as the seventh century.   Professor Comba, of the Waldensian school in Florence, has
definitely given up this theory in deference to the investigations of Dieckhoff, Herzog, and other German scholars.

Of Waldo's life little is known.   A prosperous merchant
of Lyons, he was aroused to religious zeal by the sudden
death of a leading citizen of the city, of which he was a
witness, and by a ballad he heard sung by a minstrel on the
public square.   The song was about St. Alexis, the son of
wealthy parents who no sooner returned from the marriage
altar than, impressed by the claims of celibacy, he left his bride,
to start on a pilgrimage to the East.   On his return he called
on his relatives and begged them to give him shelter, but
they did not recognize who he was till they found him dead.
The moral drawn from the tale was : life is short, the times
are evil, prepare for heaven.

204. 793, allegorizes when he says they were called " Valdenses, as though
they came from a dense valley and are involved in its deep thick darkness of
errors."   Alanus de Insulis, Migne, 210, p. 377 sqq., says the " Waldenses
are so called from their heresiarch Waldus, the founder of the new sect who
presumed to preach without authority of prelate, without divine inspiration,
knowledge, or letters.   A philosopher without head, a prophet without
vision, an apostle without mission, a teacher without instructor, whose
disciples, or rather *musciples* (*discipuli imo muscipuli*), seduce the unwary
in different parts of the world."

[1] Pauperes de Lugduno, Leonistæ, etc.   Zabatati, or Insobbalati, because
the shoe was cut in the shape of a shield.   Guy, 245 ; Döllinger, II. 92,
233, etc.

[2] *Inter se vocant Fratres seu Pauperes Christi.*   Guy, p. 256.

Waldo sought counsel from a priest, who told him there were many ways to heaven, but if he would be perfect, he must obey Christ's precepts, and go and sell all that he had and give to the poor, and follow him.   It was the text that had moved Anthony of Egypt to flee from society.   Waldo renounced his property, sent his two daughters to the convent of Fontevrault, gave his wife a portion of his goods, and distributed the remainder to the poor.   This was about 1170.

His rule of life, Waldo drew from the plain precepts of the Bible.   He employed Bernard Ydros and Stephen of Ansa to translate into the vernacular the Gospels and other parts of the Scriptures, together with sayings of the Fathers.   He preached, and his followers, imitating his example, preached in the streets and villages, going about two by two.[1]   When the archbishop of Lyons attempted to stop them, they replied that "they ought to obey God, rather than men."

Very unexpectedly the Waldenses made their appearance at the Third Lateran council, 1179, at least two of their number being present.   They besought Alexander III. to give his sanction to their mode of life and to allow them to go on preaching.   They presented him with a copy of their Bible translation.   The pope appointed a commission to examine them.   Its chairman, Walter Map, an Englishman of Welsh descent and the representative of the English king, has left us a curious account of the examination.   He ridicules their manners and lack of learning.[2]   They fell an easy prey to his questionings, like birds, as he says, who do not see the trap or net, but think they have a safe path.   He commenced with the simplest of questions, being well aware, as he said, that a donkey which can eat much oats does not disdain milk diet.   On asking them whether they believed

---

[1] *Per vicos et plateas evangelium prœdicare et Valdesius multos homines utriusque sexus viros et mulieres complices sibi fecit ad similem prœsumptionem*, etc.   Guy, p. 244.

[2] *de nugis*, Wright's ed., p. 64 sq.   Map, who felt highly honored by his appointment, called them simple and illiterate, *idiotœ et illiterati*, terms used also by de Bourbon, p. 292, and Guy, p. 244.

in the persons of the Trinity they answered, "Yes." And
"*in* the Mother of Christ?" To this they also replied
"Yes." At that the committee burst out laughing at their
ignorance, for it was not proper to believe *in*, but to believe
on, Mary. "Being poor themselves, they follow Christ
who was poor, — *nudi nudum Christum sequentes.* Certainly
it is not possible for them to take a more humble place,
for they have scarcely learned to walk. If we admit them,
we ourselves ought to be turned out." This vivacious
committee-man, who delighted so much in chit-chat, as the
title of his book indicates, further says that the Waldenses
went about barefooted, clad in sheep-skins, and had all things
common like the Apostles.

Without calling the Waldenses by name, the council
forbade them to preach. The synod of Verona, 1184, designated them as "Humiliati, or Poor Men of Lyons," and
anathematized them, putting them into the same category
with the Cathari and Patarines. Their offence was preaching
without the consent of the bishops.

Although they were expelled from Lyons and excommunicated by the highest authority of the Church, the Waldenses
ceased not to teach and preach. They were called to take
part in disputations at Narbonne (1190) and other places.
They were charged with being in rebellion against the
ecclesiastical authorities and with daring to preach, though
they were only laymen. Durandus of Huesca, who had
belonged to their company, withdrew in 1207 and took
up a propaganda against them. He went to Rome and
secured the pope's sanction for a new order under the
name of the "Catholic Poor" who were bound to poverty;
the name, as is probable, being derived from the sect he had
abandoned.

Spreading into Lombardy, they met a party already organized and like-minded. This party was known as the Humiliati. Its adherents were plain in dress and abstained from
oaths and falsehood and from lawsuits. The language, used
by the Third Œcumenical council and the synod of Verona,

identified them with the Poor Men of Lyons.[1]   Originally,
as we know from other sources, the two groups were closely
affiliated.   It is probable that Waldo and his followers
on their visits in Lombardy won so much favor with the
older sect that it accepted Waldo's leadership.   At a
later date, a portion of the Humiliati associated themselves
in convents, and received the sanction of Innocent III.   It
seems probable that they furnished the model for the third
order of St. Francis.[2]   One portion of the Humiliati early
became known as the Poor Men of Lombardy and had among
their leaders, John of Roncho.   A portion of them, if not all,
were treated by contemporaries as his followers and called
Runcarii.[3]   Contemporary writers treat the two groups as
parts of the same body and distinguish them as the Ultramontane and the Lombard Poor Men or as the Ultramontane
and Italic Brethren.[4]

A dispute arose between the Humiliati and the Poor Men
of Lyons as to their relation to one another and to Peter
Waldo, which led to a conference, in 1218, at Bergamo.   Each
party had six representatives.[5]   The two points of discord

---

[1] The exact relation of the Poor Men of Lyons to the Humiliati is still
a matter of discussion.   Müller, in his *Anfänge des Minoritenordens*,
etc., has done much to change our knowledge of the Humiliati.   The view
taken above may account for the language of the Verona council, *Humiliati
vel Pauperes de Lugduno*, which was probably chosen for the very purpose
of indicating that the resemblance between the two parties was so close as to
make it uncertain whether there were two sects or only one.   This view
seems to be borne out by the two statements of Salve Burce.   Döllinger, II.
64, 74.

[2] See p. 411.   Sabatier, *Regula Antiqua*, p. 15, expresses the opinion that
Francis may have been more indebted to them than we have supposed.

[3] Salve Burce, who was acquainted with Roncho, called him "a simple man,
without education," *idiota absque literis*.   Döllinger, II. 64.

[4] Rainerius, Martène, p. 1775, *Rescriptum*, p. 57; Guy, p. 247; Döllinger,
II. 320, etc.   Rainerius is in substantial agreement with Burce who says that
the Poor Men of Lombardy derived their existence from the Ultramontane
Poor.

[5] The account is given in the *Rescriptum*.   See Preger, Döllinger, II. 42–
52, and Müller, *Die Waldenser*, p. 22.   The separation between the Lombard
and the Lyonnese parties is referred to in the list of inquisitorial questions
to be put to them.   Döllinger, II. 320 sq.

2 K

were the eucharist and whether Waldo was then in paradise. The Lombards contended that the validity of the sacrament depended upon the good character of the celebrant. The question about Waldo and a certain Vivetus was, whether they had gone to heaven without having made satisfaction before their deaths for all their sins.[1] The Lyonnese claimed that Waldo was in paradise and made the recognition of this fact a condition of union with the Lombard party. The controversy at Bergamo points to a definite rejection of Waldo's leadership by the Lombard Waldenses. Salve Burce, 1235, who ridiculed the Waldensians on the ground of their recent origin, small number, and lack of learning, compared the Poor Men of Lombardy and the Poor Men of Lyons with the two Catharan sects, the Albanenses and the Concorrezzi, and declared the four were as hostile, one to the other, as fire and water.[2] This is an isolated testimony and not to be accepted. But it is the charge, so often repeated since by the Catholic Church, that Protestantism means division and strife.

In the crusades against heretics, in Southern France, the Waldenses were included, but their sufferings were small compared with those endured by the Albigenses. Nor do they seem to have furnished many victims to the Inquisition in the fourteenth century. Although Bernard Guy opened his trials in 1308, it was not till 1316 that a Waldensian was sentenced to perpetual imprisonment and another to death by burning. Three years later, twenty-six were condemned to perpetual imprisonment, and three to death in the flames.[3] In 1498, Louis XII. granted them limited toleration. During the Reformation period, in 1545, twenty-two villages inhabited by the French Waldenses were pillaged and burnt by order of the parliament of Provence.

It was in Italy and Austria that the Waldenses furnished their glorious spectacle of unyielding martyrdom. From

---

[1] *Rescriptum*, Döllinger, II. 46.

[2] Döllinger, II. 73.

[3] Summing up all the cases under Guy, Lea, II. 149, says that there was no very active persecution against the Lyonnese Waldenses.

France they overflowed into Piedmont, partly to find a refuge in its high valleys, seamed by the mountain streams of the Perouse, the Luserne, and the Angrogne.   There, in the Cottian Alps, they dwelt for some time without molestation. They had colonies as far south as Calabria, and the emigration continued in that direction till the fifteenth century.[1] But the time of persecution came.   In 1209, Otto IV. issued an edict of banishment and in 1220 Thomas, count of Savoy, threatened with fines all showing them hospitality.   But their hardy industry made them valuable subjects and for a hundred years there was no persecution in the valleys unto death.   The first victim at the stake perished, 1312.

Innocent VIII., notorious for his official recognition of witchcraft, was the first papal persecutor to resort to rigorous measures.   In 1487, he announced a crusade, and called upon Charles VIII. of France and the duke of Savoy to execute the decree.   Everything the Waldenses had endured before, as Leger says, was as "roses and flowers" compared with what they were now called upon to suffer.   Innocent furnished an army of eighteen-thousand.   The Piedmontese Waldenses were forced to crouch up higher into the valleys, and were subject to almost incredible hardship.   The most bitter sufferings of this Israel of the Alps were reserved for the sixteenth and seventeenth centuries, after they had accepted the Reformation.[2]   It was of the atrocious massacres perpetrated at that time that Milton exclaimed,

"Avenge, O Lord, thy slaughtered saints,
     Whose bones lie scattered on the Alpine mountains cold."

The history of the Waldensian movement in different parts of Germany and Austria has scarcely less interest than the Franco-Italian movement.   It had a more extensive influence by preparing the way for other separatist and evan-

[1] Comba, p. 103 sq.; Lea, II. 259 sqq.

[2] In 1530 the mediæval period of their history closes.   At that date two of their number, Morel and Peter Masson, were sent to consult with Bucer, Œcolampadius, and other Reformers.   Morel was beheaded on his return journey.   His letter to Œcolampadius and the Reformer's reply are given by Dieckhoff, pp. 364–373.   The Waldenses adopted the Reformation, 1532.

gelical movements. It is supposed that a translation of parts of the Scriptures belonging to the Waldenses was in circulation in Metz at the end of the twelfth century. Copies were committed to the flames. It is also supposed that Waldenses were among the heretics ferreted out in Strassburg in 1212, eighty of whom were burnt, twelve priests and twenty-three women being of the number. The Waldenses spread as far north as Königsberg and Stettin and were found in Swabia, Poland, Bavaria, and especially in Bohemia and the Austrian diocese of Passau.[1]

They were subjected to persecution as early as in 1260. Fifty years later there were at least forty-two Waldensian communities in Austria and a number of Waldensian schools. Neumeister, a bishop of the Austrian heretics, who suffered death with many others in 1315, testified that in the diocese of Passau alone the sect had over eighty thousand adherents.[2] In 1318 Dominican and Franciscan inquisitors were despatched to Bohemia and Poland to help the authorities in putting the heresy down. Bohemia had become the most important centre of Waldensianism. With these Austrian heretics the Poor Men of Lombardy kept up a correspondence[3] and they received from them contributions.

In spite of persecutions, the German Waldenses continued to maintain themselves to the fifteenth century.

The Austrian dissenters were active in the distribution of the Scriptures. And Whittier has based his poem of the Vaudois Teacher upon the account of the so-called Anonymous writer of Passau of the fourteenth century. He speaks of the Waldenses as going about as pedlers to the houses of the noble families and offering first gems and other goods

---

[1] See Comba, 74 sqq. A number of the documents given by Döllinger are interrogatories for use against the Waldenses of Germany and Austria, or accounts of their trials. One of them, in German, belongs as late as the sixteenth century, Döllinger, II. 701 sq. Haupt, Keller, Preger, and Goll have extended our knowledge of the Austrian Waldenses.

[2] Haupt, *Waldenserthum*, p. 21.

[3] Comba, in the French trans. of his work, and Müller, *Die Waldenser*, p. 103, print a consolatory letter from them to their suffering Bohemian friends.

and then the richest gem of all, the Word of God. This writer praised their honesty, industry, and sobriety. Their speech, he said, was free from oaths and falsehoods.

We have thus three types of Waldenses: the Poor Men of Lyons, the Poor Men of Lombardy, and the Austrian Waldensians.[1] As for their dissent from the established Church, it underwent in some particulars, in their later periods, a development, and on the other hand there was developed a tendency to again approach closer to the Church.[2]

In their earliest period the Waldenses were not heretics, although the charge was made against them that they claimed to be "the only imitators of Christ." Closely as they and the Cathari were associated geographically and by the acts of councils, papal decrees, and in literary refutations of heresy, the Waldenses differ radically from the Cathari. They never adopted Manichæan elements. Nor did they repudiate the sacramental system of the established Church and invent strange rites of their own. They were also far removed from mysticism and have no connection with the German mystics as some of the other sectaries had. They were likewise not Protestants, for we seek in vain among them for a statement of the doctrine of justification by faith. It is possible, they held to the universal priesthood of believers. According to de Bourbon and others, they declared all good men to be priests. They placed the stress upon following the practice of the Apostles and obeying the teachings of the Sermon on the Mount, and they did not know the definition

---

[1] The earliest writers, as the abbot Bernard and Alanus, make no distinctions. Rainerius, 1260, does, as do also the *Rescriptum* which has an eye to the Waldenses of Passau and Salve Burce in his *Supra Stella*, 1235, who refers more particularly to the Poor Men of Lombardy. David of Augsburg, 1256, an inquisitor of high repute, has in mind the Waldensians, as a body. Bernard Guy, 1320, treats of the Lyonnese Waldensians. The documents given by Döllinger extend to the sixteenth century, many of them bearing upon the Waldenses of Austria.

[2] At the time of the Reformation, according to Morel, dancing and all sports were forbidden, except the practice of the bow and other arms. Comba, p. 263, recognizes this opposite tendency, the Waldenses approaching closer to the established Church in their practice of the sacraments.

which Luther put on the word "justification." They approached more closely to an opinion now current among Protestants when they said, righteousness is found only in good men and good women.[1]

The first distinguishing principle of the Waldenses bore on daily conduct and was summed up in the words of the Apostles, "we ought to obey God rather than men." This the Catholics interpreted to mean a refusal to submit to the authority of the pope and prelates. All the early attacks against them contain this charge.[2] Alanus sought to refute the principle by adducing Christ's submission to the authority of Pilate, John 19 : 11, and by arguing that the powers that be are ordained of God. This was, perhaps, the first positive affirmation of a Scriptural ground for religious independence made by the dissenting sects of the Middle Ages. It contains in it, as in a germ, the principle of full liberty of conscience as it was avowed by Luther at Worms.

The second distinguishing principle was the authority and popular use of the Scriptures. Here again the Waldenses anticipated the Protestant Reformation without realizing, as is probable, the full meaning of their demand. The reading of the Bible, it is true, had not yet been forbidden, but Waldo made it a living book and the vernacular translation was diligently taught. The Anonymous writer of Passau said he had seen laymen who knew almost the entire Gospels of Matthew and Luke by heart, so that it was hardly possible to quote a word without their being able to continue the text from memory.

The third principle was the importance of preaching and the right of laymen to exercise that function. Peter Waldo and his associates were lay evangelists. All the early documents refer to their practice of preaching as one of the worst heresies of the Waldenses and an evident proof of their arrogance and insubordination. Alanus calls them false preachers, *pseudo-prædicatores*. Innocent III., writing, in 1199, of

---

[1] De Bourbon, p. 297.

[2] The abbot Bernard, Migne, 204. 796, sqq., 817 sqq.; Alanus, Migne, 210. 380 sqq. ; de Bourbon, p. 292 ; Döllinger, II. 6, 51.

the heretics of Metz, declared their desire to understand
the Scriptures a laudable one but their meeting in secret
and usurping the function of the priesthood in preaching
as only evil. Alanus, in a long passage, brought against the
Waldenses that Christ was sent by the Father and that
Jonah, Jeremiah, and others received authority from above
before they undertook to preach, for " how shall they
preach unless they be sent." The Waldenses were without
commission. To this charge, the Waldenses, as at the disputation of Narbonne, answered that all Christians are in
duty bound to spread the Gospel in obedience to Christ's
last command and to James 4 : 17, " to him that knoweth to
do good and doeth it not, to him it is sin." [1] The denial
of their request by Alexander III., 1179, did not discourage
them from continuing to preach in the highway and house
and, as they had opportunity, in the churches. [2]

The Waldenses went still further in shocking old-time
custom and claimed the right to preach for women as well as
for men, and when Paul's words enjoining silence upon the
women were quoted, they replied that it was with them more
a question of teaching than of formal preaching and quoted
back Titus 2 : 3, " the aged women should be teachers of
good things." The abbot Bernard of Fontis Calidi, in con-
testing the right of laics of both sexes to preach, quoted the
Lord's words commanding the evil spirit to hold his peace
who had said " Thou art the Holy One of God," Mark 1 : 25.
If Christ did not allow the devil to use his mouth, how
could he intend to preach through a Waldensian ? [3] In one
of the lists of errors, ascribed to the Waldenses, is their rejection of the universities of Paris, Prague, and Vienna and of
all university study as a waste of time. [4]

It was an equally far-reaching principle when the Waldenses declared that it was spiritual endowment, or merit,

[1] Comba, pp. 47–52, gives a translation of the disputation at Narbonne.
The abbot Bernard, Migne, 204. 805, also quotes James 4 as a passage upon
which the Waldenses relied.

[2] De Bourbon, p. 291; Guy, p. 292, etc.

[3] Migne, 204. 806 sq., 825; Döllinger, II. 300, etc.   [4] Döllinger, II. 340.

and not the Church's ordination which gave the right to bind and loose, to consecrate and bless.[1] This was recognized by their opponents as striking at the very root of the sacerdotal system. They charged against them the definite affirmation of the right of laymen to baptize and to administer the Lord's Supper. No priest, continuing in sin, could administer the eucharist, but any good layman might.[2] The charge was likewise made that women were allowed the function also, and Rainerius says that no one rose up to deny the charge. It was also charged that the Waldenses allowed laymen to receive confessions and absolve.[3] Differences on this point among the Waldenses were brought out at the conference at Bergamo.

As for the administration of baptism, there were also differences of view between the Waldenses of Italy and those of France. There was a disposition, in some quarters at least, to deny infant baptism and to some extent the opinion seems to have prevailed that infants were saved without baptism.[4] Whatever the views of the early Waldenses were at the time of the Reformation, according to the statement of Morel, they left the administration of the sacraments to the priests. The early documents speak of the secrecy observed by the Waldenses, and it is possible more was charged against them than they would have openly acknowledged.

To the affirmation of these fundamental principles the Waldenses, on the basis of the Sermon on the Mount, added the rejection of oaths,[5] the condemnation of the death penalty,[6]

---

[1] *Magis operatur meritum ad consecrandum vel benedictionem, ligandum vel solvendum, quam ordo vel officium*, Alanus, Migne, 204, 385. Alphandéry, p. 129, justly lays stress upon this charge.

[2] *Consecratio corporis et sanguinis Christi potest fieri a quolibet justo, quamvis sit laycus*, Guy, p. 246. Also Rainerius, p. 1775, David of Augsburg, and Döllinger, II. 7.   [3] Alanus, Migne, 210, 386.

[4] Rainerius declares without qualification that the Poor Men of Lombardy held to the salvation of infants not baptized, but the *Rescriptum* declares that baptism was regarded as necessary for all. So also David of Augsburg. See Döllinger, II. 45.

[5] Alanus, 210, 392 ; de Bourbon, pp. 292, 296 ; Guy, p. 246 ; Döllinger, II. 85 (Salve Burce), 107, 126, etc.

[6] Alanus, 210, 394 ; Guy, p. 246 ; Döllinger, II. 76, 107, 143, etc.

and some of them purgatory and prayers for the dead.[1] There
are but two ways after death, the Waldenses declared, the
way to heaven and the way to hell.[2]

The Waldenses regarded themselves, as Professor Comba
has said, as a church within the Church, a select circle. They
probably went no further, though they were charged with
pronouncing the Roman Church the Babylonian harlot, and
calling it a house of lies.[3] As early as the thirteenth century,
the Waldenses were said, as by de Bourbon, to be divided
like the Cathari into the Perfect and Believers, but this may
be a mistake. In the beginning of the fourteenth century,
in Southern France they elected a superintendent, called
Majoralis omnium, whom, according to Bernard Guy, they
obeyed as the Catholics did the pope, and they also had
presbyters and deacons. In other parts they had a
threefold ministry, under the name of priests, teachers, and
rectors.[4]

From the first, the Lyonnese branch had a literature of
its own and in this again a marked contrast is presented
to the Cathari. Of the early Waldensian translation of the
Bible in Romaunt, there are extant the New Testament

[1] The abbot Bernard, Migne, 204, 828, 833; De Bourbon, p. 295; Döllinger,
II. 93, 107, 143, etc. The story of creation ascribed to the négro, according to which God, in making man, made an image of clay and set it up
against the fence to dry, is as old as Etienne de Bourbon (d. 1261) and the
earliest Waldenses. Bourbon says, p. 294, that he had heard of a Waldensian who, in his testimony, had stated that God made a form of soft clay as
boys do in their play, and set it up under the sun to dry, and that the cracks
made by the sun were veins through which the blood began to run, and then
God breathed His spirit upon the face of the image.

[2] The Waldensian teaching 'of the two ways has been regarded by Harnack
and Keller as a reminiscence of the *Teaching of the Twelve Apostles*. Comba,
p. 341, with more probability refers it to the Sermon on the Mount. The
reference was, not so·much to the two ways in this life, but to the denial
of purgatory, Döllinger, II. 252, 287, 300, etc.

[3] Rainerius, p. 1775 ; Guy, p. 247. Also, the abbot Bernard, Migne, 204,
795 sqq., and Alanus, Migne, 210, 379 sqq.

[4] Döllinger, II. 92. At a later date the minister among the Italian Waldenses was called *barba*, uncle. Comba, p. 147. Morel, in his letter to Œcolampadius, declared that these distinctions were not maintained by the Waldenses. See Dieckhoff, p. 259 sq.

complete and the Psalms, Proverbs, Song of Solomon, and
Ecclesiastes. A translation in French had preceded this
Waldensian version.[1] The German translation of the Bible
found at Tepl, Bohemia, may have been of Waldensian
origin.[2]

The *Nobla Leyczon*,[3] dating from the early part of the thirteenth century and the oldest extant piece of Waldensian literature next to the version of the Bible, is a religious poem
of four hundred and seventy-nine lines. It has a strictly
practical purpose. The end of the world is near, man fell,
Noah was spared, Abraham left his own country, Israel went
down to Egypt and was delivered by Moses. Christ preached
a better law, he trod the path of poverty, was crucified, and
rose again. The first line ran "O brothers, listen to a noble
teaching." The poem closes with the scene of the Last Judgment and an exhortation to repent.

Through one channel the Waldenses exercised an influence
over the Catholic Church. It was through the Waldensian
choice of poverty. They made the "profession of poverty,"
as Etienne de Bourbon calls it, or "the false profession of
poverty," as Bernard Guy pronounced it. By preaching and
by poverty they strove after evangelical perfection, as was
distinctly charged by these and other writers. Francis d'Assisi took up with this ideal and was perhaps more immediately
the disciple of the obscure Waldensians of Northern Italy
than can be proved in so many words. The ideal of Apostolic poverty and practice was in the air and it would not de-
tract from the services of St. Francis, if his followers would
recognize that these dissenters of Lyons and Italy were actu-

---

[1] Berger, *La Bible française au moyen âge*, Paris, 1884. There are marked
differences in the MSS. of the Romaunt version, in language, etc. Comba,
pp. 182–185, gives paragraphs from different MSS.

[2] So Haupt and Keller, *Die Reform. und die älteren Reformparteien*, Leipzig, 1886, pp. 257–260. Jostes ascribed the Version to Catholic sources, an
opinion Dr. Philip Schaff was inclined to adopt. *Independent*, Oct. 8, 1885.
Nestle, art. "German Versions," in Herzog, III. 66, pronounces the question
an open one.

[3] The title is from *lectio*, reading. The text is given by Herzog, pp. 445–457,
and an English translation by Perrin, pp. 263–271.

ated by his spirit, and thus antedated his propaganda by nearly half a century.[1]

NOTE. Lit. bearing on the early Waldenses. For the titles, see § 79. — A new era in the study of the history and tenets of the Waldenses was opened by Dieckhoff, 1851, who was followed by Herzog, 1853. More recently, Preger, Karl Müller, Haupt, and Keller have added much to our knowledge in details, and in clearing up disputed points. Comba, professor in the Waldensian college at Florence, accepts the conclusions of modern research and gives up the claim of ancient origin, even Apostolic origin being claimed by the older Waldensian writers. — The chief sources for the early history of the sect are the abbot Bernard of Fontis Calidi, d. 1193; the theologian Alanus de Insulis, d. about 1200; Salve Burce (whose work is given by Döllinger), 1235; Etienne de Bourbon, d. 1261, whose work is of an encyclopædic character, a kind of ready-reference book; the *Rescriptum hæresiarcharum* written by an unknown priest, about 1316, called the Anonymous of Passau; an Austrian divine, David of Augsburg, d. 1271; and the Inquisitor in Southern France, Bernard Guy, d. 1331. Other valuable documents are given by Döllinger, in his *Beiträge*, vol. II. These writers represent a period of more than a hundred years. In most of their characterizations they agree, and upon the main heresies of the Waldenses the earliest writers are as insistent as the later.

The Waldensian MSS., some of which date back to the thirteenth century, are found chiefly in the libraries of Cambridge, Dublin (Trinity College), Paris, Geneva, Grenoble, and Lyons. The Dublin Collection was made by Abp. Ussher who purchased in 1634 a number of valuable volumes from a French layman for five hundred and fifty francs. The Cambridge MSS. were procured by Sir Samuel Morland, Cromwell's special envoy sent to Turin to check the persecutions of the Waldenses.

§ 85. *The Crusades against the Albigenses.*

The mediæval measures against heretics assumed an organized form in the crusades against the Albigenses, before the institution of the Inquisition received its full development. To the papacy belongs the whole responsibility of these merciless wars. Toulouse paid a bitter penalty for being the head

---

[1] Felder, the Roman Catholic author of the able *Gesch. der wissenschaftlichen Studien im Franziskanerorden*, 1904, approaches this view very closely, recognizes the effort of the Waldenses to realize the ideal of Apostolic poverty, and says, p. 1 sq., that Francis of Assisi in his work was moved by "the idea deeply rooted in his age, *eine tief gewurzelte Zeitidee.*"

centre of heresy.[1] According to Innocent III., the larger part
of its nobility was infected with heretical depravity, so that
heresy was entrenched in castles as well as professed in the
villages.[2] The count of Toulouse, the first lay peer of
France, — owing fealty to it for Provence and Languedoc, —
brought upon himself the full wrath and punishments of the
Apostolic see for his unwillingness to join in the wars against
his own subjects. A member of the house led one of the most
splendid of the armies of the first Crusade to Jerusalem.
At the opening of the Albigensian crusades the court of
Toulouse was one of the gayest in Europe. At their close it
was a spectacle of desolation.

Councils, beginning with the synod of Toulouse, 1119,
issued articles against heresy and called upon the secular
power to punish it. Mild measures were tried and proved
ineffectual, whether they were the preaching and miracles of
St. Bernard, 1147, or the diplomatic address of papal legates.
Sixty years after Bernard, St. Dominic entered upon a tour
of evangelism in the vicinity of Toulouse, and some heretics
were won; but in spite of Dominic, and synodal decrees,
heresy spread and continued to defy the Church authorities.

It remained for Innocent III. to direct the full force of his
native vigor against the spreading contagion and to execute
the principles already solemnly announced by œcumenical and
local councils. To him heretics were worse than the infidel
who had never made profession of Christianity. While
Christendom was sending armaments against the Saracens,
why should it not send an armament to crush the spiritual
treason at home ? In response to papal appeals, at least four
distinct crusades were set on foot against the sectaries in
Southern France. These religious wars continued thirty
years. Priests and abbots went at the head of the armies
and, in the name of religion, commanded or justified the
most atrocious barbarities. One of the fairest portions of

---

[1] The Fourth Lateran spoke of the city as *quæ magis hæretica labes
corrupta.*   [2] Ep. II. 99 ; Migne, 214, 647.

Europe was laid waste and the counts of Toulouse were stripped by the pope of their authority and territory.

The long conflict was fully opened when Innocent called upon Louis VII. to take the field, that "it might be shown that the Lord had not given him the sword in vain," and promised him the lands of nobles shielding heresy.[1] Raymund VI., who was averse to a policy of repression against his Catharan subjects, was excommunicated by Innocent's legate, Peter of Castelnau, and his lands put under interdict. Innocent called him a noxious man, *vir pestilens*,[2] and threatened him with all the punishments of the future world. He threatened to call upon the princes to proceed against him with arms and take his lands. "The hand of the Lord will descend upon thee more severely, and show thee that it is hard for one who seeks to flee from the face of His wrath which thou hast provoked."

A crisis was precipitated in 1208 by the murder of Peter of Castelnau by two unknown assassins.[3] Again, the supreme pontiff fulminated the sentence of excommunication against the Tolosan count, and made the expulsion of all heretics from his dominions the condition of withdrawing suspicion against him as the possible murderer of Peter.[4] Nowhere else was the intrepid energy of Innocent more signally displayed! A crusade was announced. The connections of Raymund with France through his uncle, Louis VII., and with Aragon through Pedro, whose sister he had married, interposed difficulties. And the crusade went on. The Cistercians, at their General Chapter, decided to preach it. Princes and people from France, Flanders, and even Germany swelled the ranks. The same reward was promised to those who took the cross against the Cathari and Waldenses, as to those who went across the seas to fight the intruder upon the Holy Sepulchre.

---

[1] *Epp.*, VII. 186, 212; Migne, 215, pp. 503, 527. In the second letter Innocent compares heretics to Samson's foxes and to beasts, *belluas*.

[2] *Ep.*, X. 69; Migne, 215. 1165 sqq.

[3] For another version of the murder, see Lea, I. 145. It has been compared to Becket's taking-off. [4] *Ep.*, XI. 26, 32; Migne, 215. 1354, 1361.

In a general epistle to the faithful, Innocent wrote : —

"O most mighty soldiers of Christ, most brave warriors; Ye oppose the agents of anti-Christ, and ye fight against the servants of the old serpent. Perchance up to this time ye have fought for transitory glory, now fight for the glory which is everlasting. Ye have fought for the body, fight now for the soul. Ye have fought for the world, now do ye fight for God. For we have not exhorted you to the service of God for a worldly prize, but for the heavenly kingdom, which for this reason we promise to you with all confidence." [1]

Awed by the sound of the coming storm, Raymund offered his submission and promised to crush out heresy. The humiliating spectacle of Raymund's penance was then enacted in the convent church of St. Gilles. In the vestibule, naked to the waist, he professed compliance with all the papal conditions. Sixteen of the count's vassals took oath to see the hard vow was kept and pledged themselves to renew the oath every year, upon pain of being classed with heretics. Then holding the ends of a stole, wrapped around the penitent's neck like a halter, the papal legate led Raymund before the altar, the count being flagellated as he proceeded. [2]

Raymund's submission, however, did not check the muster of troops which were gathering in large numbers at Lyons. [3] In the ranks were seen the archbishops of Rheims, Sens, and Rouen; the bishops of Autun, Clermont, Nevers, Baseur, Lisieux, and Chartres; with many abbots and other clergy. At their side were the duke of Burgundy, the counts of Nevers, St. Pol, Auxerre, Geneva, and Poitiers, and other princes. The soldier, chosen to be the leader, was Simon de Montfort. Simon had been one of the prominent leaders of the Fourth Crusade, and was a zealous supporter of the papacy. He neglected not to hear mass every day, even after the most bloody massacres in the campaigns in South-

---

[1] *Ep.*, XI. 230 ; Migne, 215. 1546. Innocent wrote repeatedly and at length, encouraging the enterprise. *Epp.*, XI. 33, 229, etc. ; Migne, 215. 1361, etc.   [2] See full description in Hurter, II. 317 sq., and Lea, I. 150 sq.

[3] Hurter, II. 322, always careful, speaks of the army as a *zahllose Menge*, and then of 50,000. Lea, I. 152, is inclined to accept a much larger number, 20,000 knights and 200,000 footmen.

ern France. His contemporaries hailed him as another
Judas Maccabæus and even compared him to Charlemagne.[1]

In spite of the remonstrance of Raymund, who had joined
the army, the papal legate, Arnold of Citeaux, refused to
check its march. Béziers was stormed and horrible scenes
followed. The wild soldiery heeded well the legate's command, "Fell all to the ground. The Lord knows His own."[2]
Neither age nor sex was spared. Church walls interposed
no protection and seven thousand were put to death in St.
Magdalen's church alone. Nearly twenty thousand were
put to the sword. According to the reports of the papal
legates, Milo and Arnold, the "divine vengeance raged wonderfully against the city.[3] . . . Ours spared neither sex nor
condition. The whole city was sacked, and the slaughter
was very great."

At Carcassonne the inhabitants were allowed to depart,
the men in their shirts, the women in their chemises, carrying
with them, as the chronicler writes, nothing else except
their sins, *nihil secum præter peccata portantes.* Dread had
taken hold of the country, and village after village was
abandoned by the fleeing inhabitants. Raymund was again

---

[1] Hurter, II. 325 sqq., dwells upon his virtues, including the virtues of
humanity and fidelity. Hefele, also a Roman Catholic, V. 843, calls him
cruel, *grausam.* The council of Lavaur pronounced him the "brave soldier
of Christ and the invincible warrior of the Lord's battles," *intrepidum,
Christi athletam et invictum dominici prælii bellatorem,* Mansi, xxii. 887. The
Fourth Lateran honored his services as having exceeded those of all others in
fidelity and courage. By his mother, Alice, he inherited the earldom of
Leicester which passed to his son Simon. See Stephen, *Dict. Nat. Biogr.*

[2] *Cædite eos, novit enim dominus qui sunt ejus,* Cæsar of Heisterbach,
V. 21; Strange ed., I. 302. And so Cæsar adds, "an innumerable multitude
were killed in that city." Hurter speaks of the "unbridled frenzy" of the
troops, *zügellose Wuth,* II. 331. Describing other scenes of carnage during
the crusade he uses such expressions as "horrible butchery," *furchtbarer
Gemetzel,* "heartrending barbarities," *empörende Gräuel,* pp. 420, 423, 427,
etc. He expresses the charitable hope that the abbot of Citeaux did not
say what was ascribed to him by so good and churchly a witness as Cæsar of
Heisterbach. Brischar, in Wetzer-Welte, I. 434, speaks with horror of the
barbarities of Simon's troops.

[3] *Epp. Inn.,* XII. 108, 109 ; Migne, 216. 137–142. *Ultione divina in eam
mirabiliter sæviente.*

put under excommunication at a council held at Avignon.[1] The conquered lands were given to Montfort. The war continued, and its atrocities, if possible, increased. New recruits appeared in response to fresh papal appeals, among them six thousand Germans.[2] At the stronghold of Minerve, one hundred and forty of the Albigensian Perfect were put to death in the flames. The ears, noses, and lips of prisoners were cut off.

Again, in 1211, the count of Toulouse sought to come to an agreement with the legates. But the terms, which included the razing to the ground of all his castles, were too humiliating. The crusade was preached again. All the territory of Toulouse had been overrun and it only remained for the crusaders to capture the city itself.

Pedro of Aragon, fresh from his crushing victory over the Moors at Novas de Tolosa, now interceded with the pope for his brother-in-law. The synod of Lavaur, 1213, appointed referee by Innocent, rejected the king's propositions. Pedro then joined Raymund, but fell at the disastrous defeat of Muret the same year, 1213. It was a strange combination whereby the king of Aragon, who had won the highest distinction a year before as a hero of the Catholic faith, was killed in the ranks of those who were rebels to the papal authority.[3] The day after, the victor, Montfort, barefoot, went to church, and ordered Pedro's battle-horse and armorial trappings sold and the proceeds distributed to the poor.[4] By the council of Montpellier, 1215, the whole land, including Toulouse, was granted to Montfort, and the titles conferred on him of count of Toulouse, viscount of Béziers and Carcassonne, and duke of Narbonne.[5]

---

[1] Hefele, V. 846 sqq.   [2] Hurter, II. 383, 416.

[3] Pedro's son, Jayme, ascribed his father's defeat to his moral laxity. The Albigensian nobles had placed their wives and daughters at his disposal and, it is reported, he was so weakened the morning of the engagement that he could not stand at the celebration of the mass. Lea, I. 177.   [4] Hurter, II. 567.

[5] As an illustration of how the best of friends may fall out, Montfort's right to the title, duke of Narbonne, was vehemently contested by Arnold of Citeaux, who claimed it as archbishop of Narbonne, an office to which he had been appointed.

The complications in Southern France were one of the chief questions brought before the Fourth Lateran Council, 1215. Raymund was present and demanded back his lands, inasmuch as he had submitted to the Church ; but by an overwhelming majority, the synod voted against him and Montfort was confirmed in the possession of his conquests.[1] When Raymund's son made a personal appeal to Innocent for his father, the pope bade him "love God above all things and serve Him faithfully, and not stretch forth his hand against others' territory " and gave him the cold promise that his complaints against Montfort would be heard at a future council.[2]

The further progress of the Albigensian campaigns requires only brief notice here, for they were converted into a war of territorial plunder. In 1218, Montfort fell dead under the walls of Toulouse, his head crushed by a stone. In the reign of Honorius, whose supreme concern was a crusade in the East, the sectaries reasserted themselves, and Raymund regained most of his territory. But the pope was relentless, and again the sentence of excommunication was launched against the house of Toulouse.

In 1226, Louis VIII. took the cross, supported by the French parliament as well as by the Church. Thus the final chapter in the crusades was begun, a war of the king of France for the possession of Toulouse. Louis died a few months later. Arnold of Citeaux, for nearly twenty years their energetic and iron-hearted promoter, had preceded him to the grave. Louis IX. took up the plans of his royal predecessor, and in 1229 the hostilities were brought to a close by Raymund's accepting the conditions proposed by the papal legate.

[1] Hurter, II. 567 sqq. ; Hefele, V. 881 sq., 902 sq. ; Potthast, *Regesta*, I. 439.

[2] In a passage recapitulating Innocent's relations to the war, Hurter, II. 709–711, says that, although it was in part carried on without regard to the principles of humanity and right, and beginning as a religious war, it was turned into a war of aggrandizement, yet Innocent was guiltless, his sole purpose being to purify the land of heresy.

Raymund renounced two-thirds of his paternal lands in favor of France. The other third was to go at his death to his daughter who subsequently married Louis IX.'s brother, and, in case there was no issue to the marriage, it was to pass to the French crown, and so it did at the death of Jeanne, the last heir of the house of Toulouse. Thus the domain of France was extended to the Pyrenees.

Further measures of repression were directed against the remnants of the Albigensian heresy, for Raymund VII. had promised to cleanse the land of it. The machinery of the Inquisition was put into full action as it was perfected by the great inquisitorial council of Toulouse, 1229. The University of Toulouse received papal sanction, and one of its chief objects was announced to be "to bring the Catholic faith in those regions into a flourishing state."[1] In 1244, the stronghold of Montségur was taken, the last refuge of the Albigenses. Two hundred of the Perfect were burned.

The papal policy had met with complete but blighting success and, after the thirteenth century, heresy in Southern France was almost like a noiseless underground stream. Languedoc at the opening of the wars had been one of the most prosperous and cultured parts of Europe. At their close, its villages and vineyards were in ruins, its industries shattered, its population impoverished and decimated. The country that had given promise of leading Europe in a renaissance of intellectual culture fell behind her neighbors in the race of progress. Protestant generations, that have been since sitting in judgment upon the barbarous measures, conceived and pushed by the papacy, have wondered whether another movement, stirred by the power of the Gospel, will not yet arise in the old domain that responded to the religious dissent and received the warm blood of the Albigenses, the Waldenses, and of Peter de Bruys and his followers.

THE STEDINGER. While the wars against the Albigenses were going on, another people, the Stedinger, living in the vicinity of Bremen and Oldenburg, were also being reduced by a papal crusade. They represented the spirit of national independence rather than doctrinal dissent

[1] Potthast, 9173.

and had shown an unwillingness to pay tithes to the archbishop of Bremen. When a husband put a priest to death for an indignity to his wife, the archbishop Hartwig II. announced penalty after penalty but in vain. Under his successor, Gerhard (1219–1258), the refractory peasants were reduced to submission. A synod of Bremen, in 1230, pronounced them heretics, and Gregory IX., accepting the decision, called upon a number of German bishops to join in preaching and prosecuting a crusade. The same indulgence was offered to the crusaders in the North as to those who went on the Church's business to Palestine. The first campaign in 1233 was unsuccessful, but a second carried all the horrors of war into the eastern section of the Stedingers' territory. In 1234 another army led by a number of princes completely defeated this brave people at Altenesch. Their lands were divided between the archbishop of Bremen and the count of Oldenburg.

§ 86. *The Inquisition. Its Origin and Purpose.*

The measures for the repression and extermination of heresy culminated in the organized system, known as the Inquisition. Its history presents what is probably the most revolting spectacle in the annals of civilized Europe.[1] The representatives of the Church appear, sitting as arbiters over human destiny in this world, and in the name of religion applying torture to countless helpless victims, heretics, and reputed witches, and pronouncing upon them a sentence which, they knew, involved perpetual imprisonment or death in the flames. The cold heartlessness, with which the fate of the heretic was regarded, finds some excuse in the pitiless penalties which the civil tribunals of the Middle Ages meted out for civil crimes, such as the breaking of the victim on the wheel, burning in caldrons of oil, quartering with horses, and flaying alive, or the merciless treatment of princes upon refractory subjects, as when William the Conqueror at Alençon punished the rebels by chopping off the hands and feet of thirty-two of the citizens and throwing them over the walls. It is nevertheless an astounding fact that for the mercy of

[1] Such a calm Church historian as Karl Müller, an expert in mediæval history, pronounces a similar judgment, " *Die Thätigkeit der Inquisition ist vielleicht das entsetzlichste was die Geschichte der Menschheit kennt.*" *Kirchengesch.*, I. 590.

Christ the Church authorities, who should have represented
him, substituted relentless cruelties.   In this respect the dissenting sectaries were infinitely more Christian than they.

It has been argued in extenuation of the Church that she
stopped with the decree of excommunication and the sentence to lifelong imprisonment and did not pronounce the
sentence of death.   And the old maxim is quoted as true of
her in all times, that the Church abhors blood — *ecclesia non
sitit sanguinem.*   The argument is based upon a pure techni-
cality.   The Church, after sitting in judgment, turned the
heretics over to the civil authorities, knowing full well that,
as night follows day, the sentence of death would follow her
sentence of excommunication.[1] Yea, the Church, through
popes and synodal decrees, again and again threatened, with
her disfavor and fell spiritual punishments, princes and municipalities not punishing heresy.   The Fourth Lateran forbade priests pronouncing judgments of blood and being
present at executions, but at the very same moment, and at the
pope's persistent instigation, crusading armies were drench-
ing the soil of Southern France with the blood of the Albigenses.   A writer of the thirteenth century says in part
truly, in part speciously, "our pope does not kill nor condemn any one to death, but the law puts to death those
whom the pope allows to be put to death, and they kill themselves who do those things which make them guilty of
death."[2]

The official designation of the Inquisitorial process was
the Inquisition of heretical depravity.[3]   Its history during
the Middle Ages has three main chapters: the persecution
of doctrinal heretics down to 1480, the persecution of

[1] The usual expression for turning heretics over to the civil tribunal was
sæculari judicio relinquere, and for perpetual imprisonment, *in perpetuum
carcerem retrudi* or *perpetuo commorari.*

[2] Martène, *Thes.,* V. 1741.

[3] *Inquis. hæreticæ pravitatis.* The first case, so far as I know, of the
use of the expression "inquisition of heretics," *inquis. hæreticorum,* was by
the synod of Toulouse, 1229.   Heretical depravity was the usual expression
for heresy, *Inn. Ep.,* II., 142, etc.; Migne, 214. 698.   The term "*inquirare*"
was a judicial term in use before.   See Schmidt.

witches in the fourteenth and fifteenth centuries, and the Spanish Inquisition organized in 1480.[1] The Inquisition with its penalties had among its ardent advocates the best and most enlightened men of their times, Innocent III., Frederick II., Louis IX., Bonaventura, Thomas Aquinas. A parallel is found in the best Roman emperors, who lent themselves to the bloody repression of the early Church. The good king, St. Louis, declared that when a layman heard the faith spoken against, he should draw his sword and thrust it into the offender's body up to the hilt.[2]

The Inquisition was a thoroughly papal institution, wrought out in all its details by the popes of the thirteenth century, beginning with Innocent III. and not ending with Boniface VIII. In his famous manual for the treatment of heresy the Inquisitor, Bernard Guy, a man who in spite of his office elicits our respect,[3] declares that the " office of the Inquisition has its dignity from its origin for it is derived, commissioned, and known to have been instituted by the Apostolic see itself." This was the feeling of the age.

Precedent enough there was for severe temporal measures. Constantine banished the Arians and burned their books. Theodosius the Great fixed death as the punishment for heresy. The Priscillianists were executed in 385. The great authority of Augustine was appealed to and his fatal interpretation of the words of the parable " Compel them to come in," [4] justifying force in the treatment of the Donatists, was made to do service far beyond what that father probably ever intended. From the latter part of the twelfth century, councils advocated the death penalty, popes insisted upon it, and Thomas Aquinas elaborately defended it. Heresy, so the theory and the definitions ran, was a crime

---

[1] This is the date given by Lea, *Span. Inq.*, I. 161. Sixtus IV. authorized the Spanish Inquisition, Nov. 1, 1478.

[2] De Joinville, Bohn's ed., p. 362.

[3] *Practica*, p. 176, *habet excellentiam altitudinis ex sua origine, quia immediate a sede apostolica dirivatur, committitur et noscitur institutum.*

[4] *Cogite intrare. Ep.*, 93, *ad Vincent, contra Gaudent.*, I. 1. On the other hand he expressed himself against putting upon them the sufferings they deserved. *Ep.*, 100, *ad Donat.*, etc.; Migne, 33. 360.

the Church could not tolerate.   It was Satan's worst blow.

Innocent III. wrote that as treason was punished with death and confiscation of goods, how much more should these punishments be meted out to those who blaspheme God and God's Son.   A crime against God, so he reasoned, is surely a much graver misdemeanor than a crime against the secular power.[1]

The calm discussion, to which the eminent theologian, Thomas Aquinas, subjects the treatment due heretics, was made at least a quarter of a century after the Inquisition was put into full force.   Leaning back upon Augustine and his interpretation of "compel them to come in," he declared in clearest terms that heretics deserved not only to be separated from the Church by excommunication, but to be excluded from the earth by judicial death.[2]   Errors in geometry do not constitute mortal guilt, but errors in matters of faith do.   As falsifiers of coin are put to death, much more may they justly be put to death who perform the more wicked act of corrupting the faith.   The heretic of whose reclamation the Church despairs, it delivers over to the secular tribunal to be executed out of the world.   The principle was that those who were baptized were under the immediate jurisdiction of the Church and the Church might deal with them as it saw fit.   It was not till the fourteenth century, that the jurisdiction of the Church and the pope was extended to the heathen by Augustinus Triumphus, d. 1328,[3] and other papal writers.   Sovereigns were forbidden

---

[1] *Ep.*, II. 1.   Hurter, II. 264, thus describes Innocent's attitude to incorrigible heretics.   They are fallen under the power of Satan, should be deprived of all their possessions, and the bodies of the dead dug up from consecrated ground.   Secular princes were to draw the sword against them, for the Lord has confided it to the mighty for the protection of the pious and the dismay of evil-doers and nowhere could it be put to better use than upon those who were seeking to lure others away from the true faith and rob them of eternal life.

[2] *Meruerunt non solum ab ecclesia per excommunicationem separari sed etiam per mortem a mundo excludi.   Summa*, II. Pt. II. 11; Migne's ed., III. 109.

[3] This is the interpretation Hefele puts upon the passage, V. 716.

by the council of Vienne, 1312, to allow their Mohammedan subjects to practise the rites of their religion.[1]

The legislation, fixing the Inquisition as a Church institution and elaborating its powers, began with the synod of Tours in 1163 and the œcumenical council of 1179. A large step in advance was made by the council of Verona, 1184. The Fourth Lateran, 1215, and the council of Toulouse, 1229, formally established the Inquisition and perfected the organization. Gregory IX., Innocent IV., and Alexander IV. enforced its regulations and added to them. From first to last the popes were its chief promoters.

The synod of Tours, 1163, called upon the bishops and clergy to forbid the Catholics from mingling with the Albigenses and from having commercial dealings with them and giving them refuge. Princes were instructed to imprison them and confiscate their goods. The Third Lateran, 1179, extended the punishments to the defenders of heretics and their friends. It gave permission to princes to reduce heretics to slavery and shortened the time of penance by two years for those taking up arms against them. At the council of Verona, 1184, pope Lucius III. and the emperor, Frederick Barbarossa, joined in making common cause in the sacred undertaking and announced their attitude in the cathedral. Frederick had the law of the empire against heretics recited and threw his glove down upon the floor as a token that he would enforce it. Then Lucius announced the decree of the council, which enjoined bishops to visit, at least once a year, all parts of their sees, to try all suspects, and to turn them, if guilty, over to the civil authorities. Princes were ordered to take an oath to support the Church against heresy upon pain of forfeiting their dignities. Cities, refusing to punish offenders, were to be cut off from other cities and, if episcopal seats, were to be deprived of that honor.

Innocent III., the most vigorous of persecutors, was no sooner on the throne than he began to wage war against

[1] *Pagani jure sunt sub papœ obedientia*, 23, art. I.

heretical infection.   In one letter after another, he struck at
it and commended military armaments for its destruction.
The Fourth Lateran gave formal and final expression to
Innocent's views.   The third canon opens with an anathe-
matization of heretics of all names. It again enjoined princes
to swear to protect the faith on pain of losing their lands.
To all taking part in the extermination of heretics — *ad hæreticorum exterminium* — was offered the indulgence extended
to the Crusaders in Palestine.   All " believers " and also
the entertainers, defenders, and friends of heretics were to be
excommunicated and excluded from receiving their natural
inheritance.[1]   Bishops were instructed to go through their
dioceses once or twice a year in person or through representatives for the purpose of detecting heresy, and in case
of neglect, they were to be deposed.

For more than a century after Innocent, the enforcement of
the rules for the detection and punishment of heretics form the
continual subject of bulls issued by the Apostolic see and of
synodal action especially in Southern France and Spain.
Innocent IV. and Alexander IV. alone issued more than one
hundred such bulls.[2]

The regulations for the episcopal supervision of the Inquisition were completed at the synod of Toulouse, 1229.
Bishops were commanded to appoint a priest and laymen to ferret out heretics — *inquirant hæreticos* — in houses and rooms.
They were authorized to go outside their sees and princes
outside of their realms to do this work.   But no heretic
was to be punished till he had been tried before the bishop's
tribunal.   Princes were ordered to destroy the domiciles
and refuges of heretics, even if they were underground.   If
heretics were found to reside on their lands without their

---

[1] *Credentes, præterea receptores, defensores et fautores hæreticorum.*
Frederick II., in his Constitution of 1220, uses these terms, and they became
the accepted, legal form of statement.   See Bernard Guy, pp. 176, 194, etc.
The term "*fautor*" became the usual term, in the subsequent history of the
Inquisition, for the abettors of heresy.   The term " believers " is the technical
term used for the Cathari, etc.

[2] Between 1255–1258, Alexander IV., according to Flade, p. 1, issued no
less than thirty-eight bulls against heretics.

knowledge, such princes were to be punished. Men above fourteen and women above twelve were obliged to swear to inform on heretics. And all, wishing to avoid the charge of heresy, were bound to present themselves at the confessional at least once a year. As a protection against heretical infection, boys above the age of seven were obliged to go to church every Sabbath and on festival days that they might learn the *credo*, the *pater noster*, and the *ave Maria*.

The legislation of the state showed its full sympathy with the rules of the Church. Peter of Aragon, 1197, banished heretics from his dominions or threatened them with death by fire. In 1226, Don Jayme I. of Aragon forbade all heretics entering his kingdom. He was the first prince to prohibit the Bible in the vernacular *Romancia*, 1234. From another source, whence we might have expected better things, came a series of severe edicts. At his coronation, 1220, Frederick II. spoke of heretics as the viperous sons of perfidy, and placed them under the ban of the empire.[1] This law was renewed at Ravenna, 1232, and later in 1238, 1239. The goods of heretics were to be confiscated and to be diverted from their children, on the ground that it was a far graver thing to offend against the spiritual realm than to offend a temporal prince. Four years later, 1224, the emperor condemned them to the penalty of being burned, or having their tongues torn out at the discretion of the judge.[2] The Sicilian Constitutions of 1231 made burning alive in the sight of the people the punishment for heretics previously condemned by the Church.[3]

---

[1] *Vipereos perfidiœ filios.* Frederick's oath ran *Catharos, Patarenos, Speronistas, Leonistias, Arnaldistas, Circumcisos et omnes hœreticos utriusque sexus quocumque nomine censeantur perpetua damnamus infamia, diffidamus atque bannimus.* See Bréholles, II. 6, 7, and Mirbt, p. 137. Hefele says Torquemada himself could not have used more vigorous language than Frederick used on this occasion. V. 993.

[2] *Ignis judicio concremandus, ut vel ultricibus flammis pereat aut eum linguœ plectro deprivent.* Bréholles, II. 422; Mirbt, 138. Flade, p. 9, is wrong in saying that the first express mention of burning as the punishment for heretics in Frederick's laws was in 1238.

[3] The terms Frederick used at this time drew heavily upon the dictionary. He calls heretics fierce wolves, most wicked angels, children of depravity,

The princes and cities of Italy followed Frederick's example. In Rome, after 1231, and at the demand of Gregory
IX., the senator took oath to seize heretics pointed out by
the Inquisition, and to put them to death within eight days of
the ecclesiastical sentence. In Venice, beginning with 1249,
the doge included in his oath the pledge to burn heretics. In
France, the rules of the Inquisition were fully recognized in
Louis IX.'s laws of 1228. The two great codes of Germany,
the Sachsenspiegel and the Schwabenspiegel, ordered heretics
burned to death.[1] A prince not burning heretics was himself
to be treated as a heretic. In England, the act for the burning
of heretics — *de comburendo hæretico* — was not passed till a
century later, 1401.

That the Church fully accepted Frederick's severe legislation, is attested by the action of Honorius III. who sent the
emperor's edict of 1220 to Bologna with instructions that it
be taught as part of the canon law. Frederick's subsequent
legislation was commended by popes and bishops,[2] and ordered
to be inscribed in municipal statute books.

To more efficiently carry out the purpose of the Inquisition, the trial and punishment of heresy were taken out of
the hands of the bishops and put into the hands of the monastic orders by Gregory IX. As early as 1227, this pope
appointed a Dominican of Florence to proceed against the
heretical bishop, Philip Paternon. In 1232, the first Dominicans were appointed inquisitors in Germany and Aragon.[3]

serpents deceiving the doves, serpents vomiting out poison. Bréholles, IV. 5.
Gregorovius, V. 162, says Frederick issued decrees against heretics every
time he made peace with the pope. "His laws against heresy form the
harshest contrast to his otherwise enlightened legislation."

[1] For the Sachsenspiegel, see Mirbt, 139. The act of the Schwabenspiegel
runs "where persons are believed to be heretics, they shall be accused
before the spiritual court. When convicted, they shall be taken in hand by
the secular court, which shall sentence them as is right, that is, they shall be
burnt at the stake." Wackernagel's ed., p. 241, sqq.

[2] Thus the Archbishop of Milan reënforced it at a provincial council, 1287.
Hefele, VI. 253, and Lea, I. 322 sq. The synod of Mainz, 1233, instructed bishops to scrupulously observe the imperial and papal edicts. Hefele, V. 1027.

[3] Frederick II. united in appointing the Dominicans inquisitors of Germany. Bréholles, IV. 298-301.

In 1233, Gregory took the decisive step of substituting the Dominicans for the bishops as agents of the Inquisition, giving as his reason, the multitude of cares by which the bishops were burdened.[1] The Inquisitors were thus made a distinct clan, disassociated from the pastoral care of souls. The friars were empowered to deprive suspected priests of their benefices, and to call to their aid the secular arm in suppressing heresy. From their judgment there was no appeal except to the papal court. The Franciscans were afterwards joined with the Dominicans in this work in parts of Italy, in France, and later in Sardinia and Syria and Palestine. Complaint was made by bishops of this interference with their prerogatives,[2] and, in 1254, Innocent IV. listened to the complaint so far as to decree that no death penalty should be pronounced without consulting with them. The council of Vienne ordered the prisons containing heretics to be guarded by two gaolers, one appointed by the Inquisitor and one by the bishop.

One more step remained to be taken. By the famous bull *ad exstirpanda*, of 1252, Innocent IV. authorized torture as a measure for extorting confessions. The merciless use of this weapon was one of the most atrocious features of the whole procedure.

The Inquisitors, in spite of papal authority, synodal action, and state legislation, did not always have an easy path. In 1235, the citizens of Narbonne drove them out of their city. In 1242, a number were murdered in Avignon, whom Pius IX., in 1866, sought to recompense by giving them the honor of canonization as he had done the year before to the bloodiest of Inquisitors, the Spaniard Arbues, d. 1485. Parma, according to Salimbene,[3] was placed, in 1279, under interdict

---

[1] Potthast, 8932, 9126, 9143, 9152, 9153, 9235. From the appointment of the Dominicans grew up the false notion that Dominic was the founder of the Inquisition. So Limborch (I. ch. X.) who calls him a "cruel and bloody man." Lacordaire, I. 197 sqq. shows Limborch's authorities to be unreliable. But the eloquent French Dominican, in his zeal, goes too far when he declares Philip II. the author of the Inquisition. Philip II. had enough sins to bear without this one being added to the heap.

[2] See Lea, I. 348 sq.   [3] Coulton, p. 203.

for three years, the punishment for the act of " certain fools "
who broke into the convent of the Dominicans and killed
one or two friars in retribution for their having burned for
heresy a certain noble lady and her maid.   The distinguished
Inquisitor, Peter of Verona, otherwise known as Peter
Martyr, was murdered at Como, 1252.   In Germany the
resistance of the Inquisition was a frequent occurrence and
more than one of its agents atoned for his activity by a
violent death.   Of these, Konrad of Marburg was the most
notorious.

Down to the very close of the Middle Ages, the pages of
history were disfigured by the decrees of popes and synods,
confirming death as the penalty for heresy, and for persons
supposed to be possessed with witchcraft.   The great council
of Constance, 1415, did not get away from this atmosphere,
and ordered heretics punished even by the flames, — *puni-
antur ad ignem.*   And the bull of Leo X., 1520, condemning
Luther, cursed as heresy the Reformer's liberal statement
that the burning of heretics is contrary to the will of the
Spirit.

To the great humiliation of the Protestant churches, religious intolerance and even persecution unto death were
continued long after the Reformation.   In Geneva, the pernicious theory was put into practice by state and church,
even to the use of torture and the admission of the testimony
of children against their parents, and with the sanction
of Calvin.   Bullinger, in the second Helvetic Confession,
announced the principle that heresy should be punished
like murder or treason.   The treatment of the Anabaptists is
a great blot on the page of the Reformation, Strassburg
being the only centre that tolerated them.   Cranmer persuaded Edward VI. to burn women.   Elizabeth saw the death
penalty executed upon Puritans.   The spirit of intolerance
was carried across the seas, and was as strong in the seventeenth and eighteenth centuries in the American colonies,
with some exceptions, as it was in Europe.   The execution
of Quakers in Boston, and of persons accused of witchcraft

in Salem, together with the laws of Virginia and other colonies, were the unfortunate survivals of the vicious history of the Middle Ages, which forgot Christ's example as he wept over Jerusalem, and the Apostle's words, " vengeance is mine, I will repay," saith the Lord.

So far as we know, the Roman Catholic Church has never officially revoked the theory and practice of the mediæval popes and councils, but on the contrary the utterances of Piux IX. and Leo XIII. show the same spirit of vicious reprobation for Protestants and their agencies.

§ 87. *The Inquisition. Its Mode of Procedure and Penalties.*

The Inquisition was called the Holy Office — *sanctum officium* — from the praiseworthy work it was regarded as being engaged in. Its chief officials, the Inquisitors, were exempted by Alexander IV., 1259, and Urban IV., 1262, from all ecclesiastical jurisdiction, whether bishops, archbishops, or papal legates, except the jurisdiction of the Apostolic [1] see, and from all interference by the secular power. They also enjoyed the right to excommunicate, lay the interdict, and to absolve their agents for acts of violence.[2] The methods of procedure offend against all our modern ideas of civil justice. The testimony of wives and children was valid or required [3] and also of persons known to be criminals. Suspicion and public rumor were sufficient grounds of complaint, seizure, and formal proceedings, a principle clearly stated by the council of Toulouse, 1229, in its eighteenth canon, and recognized by the state. The Sicilian Constitutions of 1231, ordered that heretics be diligently hunted out and, when there " was only the slightest suspicion of guilt," they were to be taken before the bishop.[4] The intention, as opposed to the outward commission, was made a sufficient

---

[1] See the presentation of Bernard Guy, pp. 209–211.

[2] *Ad exstirpanda*, 1252, two bulls of Alexander IV., 1257, 1260, council of Vienne, 1312, etc.

[3] Eymericus II., 110, 199, etc., as quoted by Flade, p. 54.

[4] Bréholles, IV. 5 sqq.

ground of accusation. The Inquisitor might at the same time be police, prosecutor, and judge.

It is due to Innocent III. to say that he did not invent the inquisitorial mode of procedure, but drew it from the practice already in vogue in the state.[1]

A party, not answering a citation within a year, was declared a heretic even when no proofs were advanced. Likewise, one who harbored a heretic forty days after a warning was served was treated as a heretic.[2] At the trials, the utmost secrecy was observed and names of the accusers were not divulged. In commending this measure of secrecy, Paramo declared that the example was set by God himself in carrying out the first inquisition, in the garden of Eden, to defeat the subtlety of Satan who otherwise might have communicated with Adam and Eve.

Penitent heretics, if there was any doubt of their sincerity, were obliged to change their places of abode and, according to the synod of Toulouse, if they belonged to the Perfect, had to do so in all cases. The penances imposed were fines, which were allowed by papal decree as early as 1237 and 1245, pilgrimages, and wearing of two crosses on the left and right side of the body called the *poena confusibilis*.

The pilgrimage to Jerusalem was forbidden by a synod of Narbonne, 1243, which referred to a recent papal deliverance prohibiting it, that the sacred places might be protected against the infection of heresy. Young women were often ex-

---

[1] Schmidt, in his *Herkunft d. Inquisitionsprocesses*, finds the beginnings of the inquisitorial mode of procedure in the legislation of Charlemagne. The element of *inquisitio* came to dominate in the legal procedure of all Western Europe, except England. Its leading feature was that public fame or suspicion — *publica fama, mala fama, clamor publicus, infamia*, etc., — justifies magistrates in seizing the suspect and instituting trial. The Normans attempted in vain to introduce it into England, where the Magna Charta established a different principle. The Normans, however, carried the inquisition with them to Southern Italy, where Frederick II. found it in vogue. Innocent, a student of canon law, found it exactly to his purpose to adopt the inquisitorial mode of procedure.

[2] Physicians were forbidden to practise medicine on persons suspected of heresy and were forced to take oath not to defend it. Synods of Toulouse, 1229; Béziers, 1246; Albi, 1254.

cused from wearing the crosses, as it might interfere with their prospects of marriage. According to French law, pregnant women condemned to death, were not executed till after the birth of the child.

Local synods in Southern France ordered heretics and their defenders excommunicated every Sunday and that sentence should be pronounced amidst the ringing of bells and with candles extinguished. And as a protection against heresy, the bells were to be rung every evening.

Imprisonment for life was ordered by Gregory IX., 1229, for all induced to return to the faith through fear of punishment.[1] The prisons in France were composed of small cells. The expenditures for their erection and enlargement were shared by the bishop and the Inquisitors. French synods spoke of the number sentenced to life-imprisonment as so great that hardly stones enough could be found for the prison buildings.[2] The secular authorities destroyed the heretic's domicile, confiscated his goods,[3] and pronounced the death penalty.

The rules for the division of confiscated property differed in different localities. In Venice, after prolonged negotiations with the pope, it was decided that they should pass to the state.[4] In the rest of Italy they became, in equal parts, the property of the state, the Inquisition, and the curia; and in Southern France, of the state, the Inquisitors, and the bishop. Provision was made for the expenses of the Inquisition out of the spoils of confiscated property. The temptation to plunder became a fruitful ground for spying out alleged heretics. Once accused, they were all but helpless. Synods encouraged arrests by offering a fixed reward to diligent spies.

[1] Potthast, 8445. The council of Toulouse, Canon XI., prescribed that the expense of incarceration be met by the bishop, provided the culprit had no goods of his own.

[2] Synod of Narbonne, 1243, etc.; Hefele, V. 1104. There were two forms of imprisonment, the *murus largus*, giving the freedom of the prison and the *murus strictus*, or solitary imprisonment.

[3] Synods of Toulouse, 1229; Albi, 1254.

[4] Lea, I. 512.

Not satisfied with seeing the death penalty executed upon the living, the Inquisition made war upon the dead, and exhumed the bodies of those found to have died in heresy and burned them.[1] This relentless barbarity reminds us of the words, perhaps improperly ascribed to Charles V. who, standing at Luther's grave, is reported to have refused to touch the Reformer's bones, saying, " I war with the living, not with the dead." The council of Verona, 1184, ordered relapsed heretics to be turned over forthwith to the secular authorities.[2]

In the period before 1480 the Inquisition claimed most of its victims in Southern France. Douais has given us a list of seventeen Inquisitors-general who served from 1229 to 1329.[3] The sentences pronounced by Bernard de Caux, called the Hammer of the Heretics, 1244–1248 give the names of hundreds who were adjudged to the loss of goods or perpetual imprisonment, or both.[4]

During the administration of Bernard Guy, as inquisitor of Toulouse, 1306–1323, forty-two persons were burnt to death, sixty-nine bodies were exhumed and burnt, three hundred and seven were imprisoned, and one hundred and forty-three were condemned to wear crosses.[5] A single instance may suffice of a day's doings by the Inquisition.

[1] This was often done. The most famous case was that of Wyclif whose bones were exhumed and burnt by the order of the council of Constance. One of the notable instances of prosecution after death was that of Roger, count of Foix, surnamed the Good. His wife and a sister were Waldenses, and another sister a Catharan. In 1263, years after the count's death, proceedings were begun against him. See Lea, II. 53 sqq.

[2] Lea, I. 533, in closing a long treatment says, " We are perfectly safe in asserting that but for the gains to be made out of fines and confiscations, the work of the Inquisition would have been much less thorough, and it would have sunk into comparative insignificance as soon as the first frantic zeal of bigotry had exhausted itself." The synods of Béziers, 1233 ; Albi, 1254, etc., made a silver mark the reward of ferreting heretics out. Hefele, V. 1035; VI. 50.

[3] Documents, etc., I. CXXIX–CCVI.

[4] Douais, II. 1–89. Molinier, as quoted by Lea, II. 45, estimates the number of persons tried under this Inquisitor in two years at 8000 to 10,000.

[5] Douais, I. CCV, where a table is given of the sentences passed under Guy.

On May 12, 1234, six young men, twelve men, and eleven women were burnt at Toulouse.

In the other parts of France, the Inquisition was not so vigorously prosecuted. It included, as we have seen, the order of the Templars. In 1253 the Dominican provincial of Paris was made the supreme Inquisitor. Among the more grim Inquisitors of France was the Dominican Robert le Petit, known as Le Bougre from his having been a Patarene.[1] Gregory IX. appointed him inquisitor-general, 1233, and declared God had " given him such special grace that every hunter feared his horn." [2] The French king gave him his special aid and a royal bodyguard to attend him. He had hundreds of victims in Western Burgundy and the adjoining regions. In one term of two or three months, he burnt fifty of both sexes.[3] At Cambrai he burnt twenty, at Douai ten. His last deed was to burn at Mt. Aimé in 1239, twenty-seven, or according to another account more than one hundred and eighty — "a holocaust very great and pleasing to God " as the old chronicler put it.[4] In 1239 he was himself consigned to perpetual imprisonment for his misdeeds.

In the Spanish kingdom of Aragon, the number of heretics does not seem to have been large. In 1232 the archbishop of Tarragona was ordered by Gregory IX. to proceed against heretics in conjunction with the Dominicans.[5] One of the most famous of all Inquisitors, the Spanish Dominican, Eymericus, was appointed Inquisitor-general 1357, was deposed 1360, and reappointed 1366. He died in exile. His *Directorium inquisitorum*, written 1376, is the most famous treatise on the mode of treating heresy. Heretics, in his judgment, were justly offered the alternative of submission or the stake. The small number of the victims under the

---

[1] Lea, II. 115 sqq., and especially Haskins.

[2] Bull, Aug. 22, 1235, Portland, 9994.

[3] According to M. Paris he also buried victims alive. Luard's ed., iii. 361.

[4] Haskins, p. 635, adopts the larger number. "And so," said Albericus, " as the story runs, that dogs once came from all directions and tore themselves to pieces in battle at this same place, as a sort of prophecy of what was to be, so these Bugres, worse than dogs, were exterminated in one day to the triumph of Holy Church." Quoted by Haskins.   [5] Potthast, 8932.

2 M

earlier Inquisition in Spain was fully made up in the series of holocausts begun under Ferdinand in 1480.

In Northern and Central Italy, the Inquisition was fully developed, the first papal commissioners being the bishops of Brescia and Modena, 1224. The cases of heresy in Southern Italy were few and isolated. In Rome, the first pyres were lighted in 1231, in front of St. Maria Maggiore. From that year on, and at the demand of Gregory IX., the Roman senator took an oath to execute heretics within eight days of their conviction by the ecclesiastical court. The houses sheltering them were to be pulled down. The sentence condemning heretics was read by the Inquisitor on the steps of the Capitol in the presence of the senator.[1] At a later period the special order of San Giovanni Decollato — John, the Beheaded — was formed in Rome, whose members accompanied the condemned to the place of death.

In Germany, the Inquisition did not take full hold till the crusade against witchcraft was started. The Dominicans were formally appointed to take charge of the business in 1248. Of sixty-three papal Inquisitors, known by name, ten were Franciscans, two Augustinians, one of the order of Coelestin, and the rest Dominicans.[2] The laws of Frederick II. were renewed or elaborated by Rudolf, 1292, and other emperors,[3] and the laws of the Church by many provincial councils.[4] The bishops of Treves, Mainz, and Cologne interfered at times with the persecution of the Beghards and Beguines, and appealed, as against the papal Inquisitors, to

---

[1] Gregorovius, V. 156–161. The assertion has often been made, by the Spaniard Balmes in 1842, the Abbé Cœur, 1846, a writer in the *Dublin Review*, 1850, and others, that Rome never witnessed an execution for heresy. Döllinger and Reusch in their edition of Bellarmin, Bonn, 1887, p. 233, have paid their respects to this mistake and give a list of more than twenty persons, Waldenses, Lutherans, and Jews, burnt in the papal city as late as 1553–1635.   [2] Flade, p. 37 sq.

[3] Henry VII., 1312 and Charles IV., 1369, 1371, 1373, etc. ; Flade, p. 10. According to Charles' law the confiscated property of heretics was divided into three parts which went respectively for alms, to the Inquisitors, and to municipalities for the repair of streets and walls.

[4] Flade, p. 24, gives a list of seventy-one between 1227–1452.

their rights, as recognized in the papal bulls of 1259 and 1320. After the murder of Konrad of Marburg, Gregory IX. called upon them in vain to prosecute heretics with vigor. In fact the Germans again and again showed their resentment and put Inquisitors to death.[1]

The centres of heresy in Germany were Strassburg, as early as 1212, Cologne, and Erfurt. The number of victims is said to have been very large and at least five hundred can be accounted for definitely in reported burnings.[2] Banishment, hanging, and drowning were other forms of punishment practised. In 1368 the Inquisitor, Walter Kerlinger, banished two hundred families from Erfurt alone. The prisons to which the condemned were consigned were wretched places, the abode of filth, vermin, and snakes.[3]

As Torquemada stands out as the incorporation of all that is inhuman in the Spanish Inquisition, so in the German does Konrad of Marburg.

This Dominican ecclesiastic, whom Gregory IX. called the "Lord's watch-dog," first came into prominence at the court of Louis IV. of Thuringia on the Wartburg, the old castle which was the scene of the contests of the Minnesingers, and was destined to be made famous by Luther's confinement after the diet of Worms, 1521. Konrad became confessor of Louis' wife, the young and saintly Elizabeth. The daughter of King Andreas II. of Hungary, she was married to the Landgrave of Thuringia in 1221, at the age of fourteen. At his death at Brindisi, on his way to the Holy Land, in 1227, she came more completely under the power of Konrad. Scarcely any scene in Christian history exhibits such wanton and pitiless cruelty to a spiritual ward as he displayed to the tender woman who yielded him obedience. From the Wartburg, where she was adored for her charities and

---

[1] For names see Flade, pp. 6, 7.

[2] Flade, p. 116. The pages of this author must be read to gain any adequate idea of the horrors of the Inquisition in Germany. He pronounces it even more bloody than the Inquisition in Southern France.

[3] Flade, p. 87.

good works, she removed to Marburg. There Konrad subjected her to daily castigations and menial services, deprived
her gradually of all her maids of honor, and separated her
from her three children. On one occasion when she visited
a convent of nuns at Oldenburg, a thing which was against
their rigid rule, Konrad made Elizabeth and her attendant lie
prostrate and receive a severe scourging from friar Gerhard
while he himself looked on and repeated the Miserere. This,
the most honored woman of mediæval Germany, died of her
castigations in 1231. Four years later she was canonized,
and the St. Elizabeth church was begun which still stands
to her memory in Marburg.

The year of Elizabeth's death, Gregory IX. invested Konrad
with a general inquisitorial authority and right to appoint
his own assistants and call upon the secular power for aid.
Luciferans, so called, and other heretics were freely burned.
It was Konrad's custom to burn the offenders the very
day their sentences were pronounced.[1] A reign of terror
broke out wherever he went. He was murdered in 1233, on
his way back to Marburg from the diet of Mainz. After
his death Gregory declared him to be a man of consummate
virtue, a herald of the Christian faith. Konrad was buried
at the side of Elizabeth, but the papal inquisition in Germany
did not recover for many a year from the blow given to it by
his merciless hardness of heart. And so, as the Annals of
Worms remarked, "Germany was freed from the abominable
and unheard-of tribunal of that man."[2]

In the Lowlands, Antwerp, Brussels, and other cities were
lively centres of heresy and afforded a fine opportunity for
the Inquisitor. The lists of the accused and of those executed in the flames and by other means include Waldenses,
Beguines, Beghards, Apostolicals, Lollards, and other sectaries. Their sufferings have been given a splendid memorial
in the volumes of Fredericq. Holland's baptism of blood on

---

[1] Roman Catholic writers have recently tried to remove the impression
that Konrad's victims were numerous. See Benrath's reply, art. Konrad of
Marburg, Herzog, X. 749 sqq.

[2] Quoted by Wagenmann, Herzog, 2d, VIII. 192.

a grand scale was reserved for the days of Philip II. and the Duke of Alva in the sixteenth century.

In England, the methods of the Inquisition never had any foothold.   When the papal agents arrived to prosecute the Templars, King Edward forbade the use of torture as contrary to the common law of the realm.   The flogging of the Publicani, who are said to have made a single English convert, has already been referred to.   In 1222 a deacon, who had turned Jew, was hanged.[1]   The parliamentary act for burning heretics, passed in 1401, was directed against the followers of Wyclif and the Lollards.   It was not till the days of Henry VIII. that the period of prosecutions and burnings in England for heresy fully began.

[1] See Stubbs, *Const. Hist.*, II. 353 (note) sqq., who says that if there was any persecution for heresy before 1382, it must have taken the ordinary form of prosecution in the spiritual court.   See Prof. Maitland, *Can. Law in the Church of England*, p. 158 sq.

CHAPTER XI.

UNIVERSITIES AND CATHEDRALS.

§ 88. *Schools.*

Literature : John of Salisbury : *Metalogicus*, Migne, 199. 823–946.— Guibert of Nogent: *De vita sua*, I. 4–7 ; Migne, 153. 843–850. — A. H. L. Heeren : *Gesch. d. class. Lit. im MlA.*, 2 vols. Götting., 1822. — S. R. Maitland : *The Dark Ages, Essays on the State of Rel. and Lit.*, 800–1200 a.d., Lond., 1845, 5th ed. 1890. — H. Heppe : *D. Schulwesen d. MlA.*, etc., Marb., 1860. — Schaarschmidt : *J. Saresberiensis* (John of Salisbury), Leip., 1862. — Léon Maître : *Les écoles épiscopales et monastiques de l'occident*, 768–1180 a.d., Paris, 1866. — E. Michaud : *G. de Champeaux et les écoles de Paris au 12e siècle*, Paris, 1867. — J. B. Mullinger: *The Schools of Chas. the Great*, Lond., 1877 ; *Hist. of the Univ. of Cambr. to 1535*, Cambr., 1873. — *R. L. Poole : *The School of Chartres*, being chap. IV of his *Illustr. of the Hist. of Med. Thought*. — *F. A. Specht: *Gesch. d. Unterrichtswesens in Deutschland von d. ältesten Zeiten bis zur Mitte des 13ten Jahrh.*, Stuttg., 1885. — *A. and G. Schmid: *Gesch. d. Erziehung bis auf unsere Zeit*, pp. 94–333, Stuttg., 1892. — Miss Drane : *Christ. Schools and Scholars*, Lond., 2d ed. 1881. —*J. E. Sandys : *A Hist. of Class. Scholarship from 600 b.c. to the end of the M. A.*, Cambr., 1903. — Mirbt : *Publizistik im Zeitalter Greg. VII.*, pp. 104 sqq.— Rashdall : *Universities*, vol. I.

Education and the advance of true religion are inseparable. The history of literary culture in this period is marked by the remarkable awakening which started in Western Europe in the latter part of the eleventh century and the rise of the universities in the twelfth century. The latter was one of the most important events in the progress of the intellectual development of the race. The renaissance of the eleventh century showed itself in a notable revival of interest in schools, in the appearance of eminent teachers, in a renewed study of the classics, and in an enlarged sweep of the human mind.

The municipal schools of the Roman Empire were swept away by the barbarian invasions of the fourth and fifth centuries, and few vestiges of them were left. The weight of opinion in the Church had been hostile to Pagan learning from the time of Tertullian and Jerome and culminated in Justinian's act, closing the university of Athens. But it is doubtful whether the old Roman schools would have withstood the shock from the assaults of Goth, Vandal, and Hun, even had Church teachers been friendly to classical literature.

The schools of the earlier Middle Ages were associated with the convents and cathedrals, and it was not till the thirteenth century that the municipal school appeared again, and then it was in the far North, in Germany, and the Lowlands. The first name in the history of the new education is Cassian who founded the convent school of St. Victor, Marseilles, 404. But it was to Benedict of Nursia that Western Europe owed the permanent impulse to maintain schools. The Benedictine Rule made education an adjunct of religion, provided for the training of children by members of the order, and for the transcription of manuscripts. To the Benedictines, especially to the Cistercians, are our libraries indebted for the preservation of the works of classical and patristic writers.

The wise policy of Charlemagne in establishing the Palace school, a sort of normal school for the German Empire, and in issuing his Capitularies bearing on education, and the policy of Alfred in England, gave a fresh impulse to learning by the patronage of royalty. Alcuin at the court of Charlemagne, Asser in England, and John Scotus Erigena at the court of Charles the Bold, were some of the more eminent teachers. It is possible the education was not confined to clerics, for convents had two kinds of schools, the one, the interior, for oblates intended for the monastery, and the exterior school which seems to have had a more general character. The cathedral schools had for their primary, if not for their sole purpose, the training of youth for cathedral positions — *canonici puri*. The main, if not the exclusive, purpose of education was to prepare men for the priesthood and the convent.[1] In the eleventh century all

---

[1] See Mullinger, *Schools of Chas. the Great*, pp. 31 sqq.; Rashdall, p. 28; Hauck, IV. 450, etc.

the convents and cathedrals in Germany had schools,[1]—
Corvey on the Weser and Hildesheim being noted; and,
in Italy, the schools of Milan and Parma were well known.

But in that century the centre of education shifted to
France. The schools at Bec, Rheims, Orleans, Laon, and
Paris had no rivals and their fame attracted students, even
monks, priests, and bishops, from England and Germany.[2]
The fame of Rheims, where Gerbert, afterwards Sylvester II.,
d. 1003, had won the title of " restorer of studies," gave
way to the greater fame of Bec, under Lanfranc and Anselm.
Students were drawn from afar and, in the judgment of the
glowing panegyrist, Ordericus Vitalis, Athens, in its most
flourishing period, would have honored Lanfranc in every
branch of learning.[3]   These two priors were followed by a
succession of teachers whom Ordericus calls " careful pilots
and skilful charioteers."   Seldom has so splendid a compliment been paid a teacher by a man risen to eminence as was
paid by Alexander II. to Lanfranc,[4] on Lanfranc's visit to
Rome, after he was made archbishop of Canterbury.   Rising
to welcome him with open arms, the pope remarked to the
bystanders that he received Lanfranc as his teacher, at whose
feet he had sat, rather than as archbishop.   Guibert of
Nogent, who died about 1120, is authority for the statement that teachers were very rare in France in his early
years, but, at the time when he was writing, every considerable town in France had a teacher.[5]   That mothers were
anxious to have their sons educated is evident from the
example of Guibert's statement concerning his own mother.

As in the earlier period of the Middle Ages, so in this

---

[1] Mirbt, pp. 105 sq.

[2] Schmid, pp. 250 sq. ; Mirbt, pp. 106 sq.   Hauck, IV. 452–456, gives reasons for disparaging the schools of Germany.

[3] *Ord. Vit.*, IV. 7, 11 ; Bohn's ed., II. 40, 68. He speaks of the seed of
learning sown by Lanfranc — *liberalium artium et sac. lectionis sedimen
per Lanfr. coepit.*

[4] *Vita Lanf.*, Migne, 150. 49.   *Maître*, p. 122, calls Bec, *la sœur aînée de
l'univ. de Paris*, and Schmid, p. 248, *die erste Hochschule der Wissenschaft.*
Church, in his *Life of Anselm*, pp. 53 sqq., has remarks on mediæval education.

[5] *De vita sua*, Migne, 156. 844.

middle period, the idea of universal education was not thought of. Nor was there anything such as we call belles lettres and general literature.[1] All literature had an immediate bearing on religious subjects.[2] Such men as Walter Map and John of Salisbury, who approach nearest our modern idea of men of letters, were clerics. The founders of convents, like Herlouin, founder of Bec, were often men who could neither read nor write. Ordericus says that during the reigns of six dukes, before Lanfranc went to Bec, scarce a single Norman devoted himself to studies. Duke William of Aquitaine, d. 1030, however, was educated from childhood and was said to have spent his nights in reading till sleep overcame him, and to have had a collection of books.[3]

The most brilliant teachers of this era were Anselm of Laon, William of Champeaux, Bernard of Chartres, William of Conches, and, above all, Abælard. They all belonged to France. In their cases, the school followed the teacher and students went not so much to a locality as to an educator. More and more, however, the interest centred in Paris, which had a number of schools, — the Cathedral school, St. Genevieve, St. Victor, St. Denis.[4] Our knowledge of these men is derived chiefly from Abælard and John of Salisbury. John studied in France for twelve years, 1137–1149, and sat under them all. His descriptions of the studies of the age, and the methods and rivalries of teachers, are given in the *Metalogicus.*

William of Champeaux, d. 1121, the pupil of Anselm of Laon, won fame at the Cathedral school of Paris, but lost his position by clash with the brilliant abilities of Abælard. He retired to St. Victor and spent the last eight years of his life in the administration of the see of Chalons. He was an extreme realist.

---

[1] Guizot, *Hist. of Civilization,* Bohn's ed., II. 22 sqq. Cardinal Newman in his *Hist. Essays,* through his admiration of monastic institutions, allowed himself to speak of the state of learning in Europe in the first half of the M. A. in terms which will not bear a moment's investigation. See Laurie, p. 36.

[2] Hauck, III. 342. [3] Wattenbach, p. 592. [4] See Poole, p. 110.

The teaching of Anselm of Laon and his brother Ralph drew students from as far south as Milan and from Bremen in the North. The brothers were called by John of Salisbury the "splendid luminaries of Gaul," [1] and "doctor of doctors" was an accepted appellation of Anselm. This teacher, d. 1117, perhaps the pupil of Anselm of Bec, had Abælard among his hearers and won his contumely. But John of Salisbury's praise, and not Abælard's contempt, must determine our judgment of the man. His *glossa interlinearis*, a periphrastic commentary on the Vulgate, was held in high esteem for several centuries.[2]

Bernard of Chartres, about 1140, was celebrated by John of Salisbury as the "most overflowing spring of letters in Gaul in recent times" and "the most perfect Platonist of our age." [3] He acknowledged his indebtedness to the ancient writers in these words, " We are as dwarfs mounted on the shoulders of giants, so that we are able to see more and further than they; but this is not on account of any keenness of sight on our part or height of our bodies, but because we are lifted up upon those giant forms. Our age enjoys the gifts of preceding ages, and we know more, not because we excel in talent, but because we use the products of others who have gone before." [4]

William of Conches, d. 1152 (?), got his name from the Norman hamlet in which he was born. Like his teacher, Bernard of Chartres, he laid stress upon a thorough acquaintance with grammar as the foundation of all learning, and John of Salisbury seems to have written the *Metalogicus* to vindicate the claims his teachers made for the fundamental importance of this study as opposed to dialectics. But he was advocating a losing cause. Scholasticism was crushing out the fresh sprouts of humanism.[5] William of Conches

---

[1] *Splendidissima lumina Galliarum.   Metal.*, Migne, 199. 832.

[2] He also wrote allegorical notes on the Canticles, Matthew, and Revelation. Migne, vol. 162.

[3] *Metal.*, Migne, 199. 854.

[4] *Metal.*, III. 4 ; Migne, 199. 900.

[5] See Rashdall, I. 67.

took liberties with received opinions and denied that Eve was literally created from Adam's rib.   The root of his teachings Poole finds in William's own words, " through knowledge of the creature we attain to the knowledge of the Creator." [1]

The studies continued, at least theoretically, to follow the scheme of the old *trivium*, including grammar, rhetoric, and dialectic; and the *quadrivium*, including arithmetic, geometry, astronomy, and music.   These branches had a wider scope than we associate with some of the titles.   Grammar, for example, with Bernard of Chartres, included much more than technical rules and the fundamental distinctions of words.   It took in the tropes and figures of speech, analyzed the author's body of thought, and brought out the allusions to nature, science, and ethical questions.   The teaching extended far beyond the teaching of the Capitularies of Charlemagne.   Nevertheless, all these studies were the vestibule of theology and valuable only as an introduction to it. Jacob of Vitry, d. 1244, comparing the seven liberal arts with theology,[2] said, " Logic is good for it teaches us to distinguish truth from falsehood, grammar is good for it teaches how to speak and write correctly ; rhetoric is good for it teaches how to speak elegantly and to persuade.   Good too are geometry which teaches us how to measure the earth, arithmetic or the art of computing which enables us to estimate the brevity of our days, music which reminds us of the sweet chant of the blessed, astronomy which leads us to consider the heavenly bodies shining resplendently before God.   But far better is theology which alone can be called a liberal art, since it alone delivers the human soul from its woes."

Innocent III., through the canons of the Fourth Lateran, ordered all cathedrals to have teachers of grammar and lectors in theology, and offered the rewards of high office only to those who pursued hard study with the sweat of the brow.[3]   He had in mind only candidates of theology.

---

[1] See Poole's art. in Herzog, 2d ed., XVIII. 132 sqq.

[2] Quoted by Compayré, p. 200.

[3] *Qui diutius sudavit in scholis et laudabiliter proferit in eis.*   Hurter, III. 244.

The text-books in use for centuries were still popular, such
as Cassiodorus, the *Isagoge* of Porphyry, Aristotle on the *Categories*, and his *De interpretatione*, Boethius on *Music* and the
Consolations of Philosophy, Martianus Capella and the gram-
mars of Priscian and Donatus.[1] A new movement, however,
was distinctly perceptible, and nothing is more sure proof of it
than the open use of the classics by some of the leading educators in their lectures and their use in the writings of the time.

The condemnation, passed by Jerome on the ancient
classics, was adopted by Cassian and handed down to the
later generations. The obscurantists had the field with little
or few exceptions for centuries. It is not to Alcuin's credit
that, in his latter years, he turned away from Virgil as a collection of "lying fables" and, in a letter to a novice, advised
him not to assoil his mind with that poet's rank luxuriance.[2]
It was argued by Leo, in his reply to Arnulf of Orleans, 991,
that the Apostle Peter was not acquainted with such writers
as Plato, Virgil, and Terence, or any of the pseudo-philosophers, and God had from the beginning not chosen orators
and philosophers but ignorant and rustic men as His agents.[3]
Peter the Venerable raised his voice against them. But such
warnings[4] were not sufficient to induce all men to hold
themselves aloof from the fascinations of the Latin writers.

Gerbert taught Virgil, Statius, Terence, Juvenal, Persius,
Horace, and Lucan.[5] From these he passed on to the department of philosophy. Peter Damiani compared the study of
the poets and philosophers to the spoiling of the Egyptians.
They served to sharpen the understanding ; the study of
the writers of the Church to build a tabernacle to God.
Anselm of Bec recommended the study of Virgil and other
classics, counselling the exclusion of such treatises as contained suggestions of evil.[6] John of Salisbury's teachers

---

[1] See Laurie, pp. 62 sq.; Mullinger, pp. 63 sq., etc.

[2] Quoted by Mullinger, p. 110.

[3] Migne, 139. 337 sq., quoted by Schmid, p. 243.

[4] Migne, 189. 77. For other warnings, see Wattenbach, pp. 324 sqq., and
Sandys, pp. 595 sq.

[5] Richer, *Historiæ*, III. 45, quoted by Schmid, p. 241.

[6] *Ep.*, I. 55, *exceptis his in quibus aliqua turpitudo sonat.*

were zealous in reading such writings. John, who in the small compass of the *Metalogicus* quotes no less than seven classical poets, Statius, Martian, Virgil, Horace, Ovid, Catullus, and Persius, and some of these a number of times, says that if you search in Virgil and Lucan, you will be sure to find the essence of philosophy, no matter what philosophy you may profess.[1] He complained of the old school who compared the student of the classic poets and historians to the slow-going ass, and laughed at him as duller than a stone.[2] Abælard gave to Virgil the esteem due a prophet. Peter of Blois, d. 1204, the English archdeacon, quotes Cicero, Sallust, Livy, Curtius, Tacitus, Suetonius, Seneca (Letters), and other writers. Grosseteste was familiar with Ovid, Seneca, Horace, and other classics. But the time for the full Renaissance had not yet come. In the earliest statutes of the University of Paris the classics were excluded from the curriculum of studies. The subtle processes of the Schoolmen, although they did not altogether ignore the classic compositions, could construct the great theological systems without their aid, though they drew largely and confidently upon Aristotle.

The *Discipline* of the schools was severe. A good flogging was considered a wholesome means of educational advancement. It drove out the evil spirits of intellectual dulness and heaviness. *Degere sub virga*, to pass under the rod, was another expression for getting an education. At a later date, the ceremony of inducting a schoolmaster included the presentation of a rod and required him, at least in England, to show his prowess by flogging a boy publicly.[3] If the case of Guibert of Nogent was a typical one, then the

---

[1] Migne, 199. 854. The quotations from the poets in the *Polycraticus* are even more numerous. John also quoted the historians Sallust, Suetonius, Valerius Maximus, etc., but does nothing more than to refer by name to Livy, Cæsar, and Tacitus. See Sandys, 521.

[2] *Metal.*, I. 3; Migne, 199. 830. See Sandys, pp. 504 sqq., for Latin quotations from 1100 on.

[3] "Then shall the Bedell purvay for every master in Gramer a shrewde boy whom the master in Gramer shall bete openlye in the Scolys," etc. Mullinger, *Univ. of Cambridge*, I, 345.

process of getting an education was indeed a painful piece of physical experience.

Guibert's account of his experiences is the most elaborate description we have of mediæval school life, and one of the most interesting pieces of schoolboys' experience in literature.[1] The child, early sent to school by his widowed mother, was unmercifully beaten with fist and rod by his teacher, a man who had learned grammar in his advanced years. Though the teacher was an indifferent grammarian, Guibert testifies to the vigor of his moral purpose and the wholesome moral impression he made upon his pupils. The whipping came every day. But the child's ardor for learning did not grow cold. On returning to his home one evening and loosening his shirt, his mother saw the welts and bruises on his shoulders, for he had been beaten black and blue that day;[2] she suggested, in indignation and pity, that her boy give up preparation for the priesthood, and offered to give him the equipment for the career of a knight. But Guibert, greatly excited, resented any such suggestion.

At Cluny the pupils slept near the masters, and if they were obliged to get up at night, it was not till they had the permission of a master. If they committed any offence in singing the Psalms or other songs, in going to bed, or in any other way, they were punished in their shirts, by the prior or other master, with switches prepared beforehand.[3]

But there were not wanting teachers who protested against this method. Anselm urged the way of affection and confidence and urged that a skilful artificer never fashioned his image out of gold plate by blows alone. With wise and gentle hand he pressed it into shape. Ceaseless beating only

---

[1] De vita sua, I. 4-6 ; Migne, 156. 843-848 ; Guizot, in his Hist. of Civilization, Bohn's ed., II. 94 sqq. ; Schmid, p. 249, and Laurie, pp. 80 sqq., consider the account of so much importance that they give it at length in the original, or in translation.

[2] Ipsa liventes attendit ulnulas dorsicula ex viminum illisione cutem ubique prominulam. De vita sua, Migne, 156. 847.

[3] Quoted by Schmid, p. 246, note.

brutalizes. To an abbot who said " day and night we do not
cease to chastise the children confided to our care and yet
they grow worse and worse," Anselm replied : " Indeed! And
when they are grown up, what will they become ? Stupid
dolts. A fine education that, which makes brutes of men! . . .
If you were to plant a tree in your garden and were to enclose
it on all sides, so that it could not extend its branches, what
would you find when, at the end of several years, you set it
free from its bounds ? A tree whose branches were bent and
scraggy, and would it not be your fault for having so
unreasonably confined it ? " [1]

The principle ruled that an education was free to all whose
circumstances did not enable them to pay for it. Others
paid their way. Fulbert of Chartres took a fee from the
rapidly increasing number of students, regarding philosophy as worth what was paid for it. But this practice
was regarded as exceptional and met with opposition. [2]
The words of Alcuin, " If you desire to study, you will
have what you seek without money," were inscribed on the
convent of St. Peter at Salzburg. [3] It was the boast that
the care given to the humblest scholar at Cluny was as
diligent as the care given to children in the palace. [4]

§ 89. *Books and Libraries.*

LITERATURE :   E. EDWARDS : *Libraries and Founders of Libraries,* Lond.,
1865. — T. GOTTLIEB: *Mittelalt. Bibliotheken,* Leip., 1890. — F. A. GAS-
QUET: *Notes on Med. Libraries,* Lond., 1891. — E. M. THOMPSON: *Hd.-
book of Gr. and Lat. Palæography,* Lond., 1893. Contains excellent fac-
similes of med. MSS., etc. — J. W. CLARK : *Libraries in the Med. and
Renaiss. Periods,* Cambr., 1894. — G. H. PUTNAM : *Books and their Mak-
ers, 476–1709,* 2 vols. N.Y., 1896 sq. See his elaborate list of books on
monastic education, libraries, etc., I. xviii. sqq. — MIRBT: *Publizistik im
Zeitalter Greg. VII.,* pp. 96 sqq. and 119 sqq. — *MAITLAND : The Dark
Ages.* — *W. WATTENBACH : D. Schriftwesen im Mittelalter,* 3d ed.,
Leip., 1896. — Art. *Bibliothek* in Wetzer-Welte, II. 783 sqq. *Transl. and
Reprints* of Univ. of Pa. II. 3.

---

[1] Quoted by Compayré, p. 303.   [2] Hauck, IV. 452.   See Schmid, p. 250.
[3] *Discere si cupias gratis quod quæris habebis.* Migne, 101. 757.
[4] Schmid, p. 246.

Books and schools go together and both are essential to progress of thought in the Church. The mediæval catalogue of the convent of Muri asserts strongly the close union of the intellectual and religious life. It becomes us, so it ran, always to copy, adorn, improve, and annotate books, because the life of the spiritual man is nothing without books.[1]

Happy was the convent that possessed a few volumes.[2] The convent and the cathedral were almost the sole receptacles for books. Here they were most safe from the vandalism of invaders and the ravages of fire, so frequent in the Middle Ages; and here they were accessible to the constituency which could read. It was a current saying, first traced to Gottfried, canon of St. Barbe-en-Auge, that a convent without a library is like a fortress without arms.[3] During the early Middle Ages, there were small collections of books at York, Fulda, Monte Cassino, and other monasteries. They were greatly prized, and ecclesiastics made journeys to get them, as did Biscop, abbot of Wearmouth, who made five trips to Italy for that purpose. During the two centuries and more after Gregory VII., the use and the number of books increased; but it remained for the zeal of Petrarch in the fourteenth century to open a new era in the history of libraries. The period of the Renaissance which followed witnessed an unexampled avidity for old manuscripts which the transition of scholars from Constantinople made it possible to satisfy.

To the convents of Western Europe, letters and religion owe a lasting debt, not only for the preservation of books, but for their multiplication. The monks of St. Benedict have the first place as the founders of libraries and guardians of patristic and classical literature. Their Rules required them to do a certain amount of reading each day, and at the begin-

---

[1] *Quia vita omnium spiritualium hominum sine libris nihil est*, quoted by Wetzer-Welte, II. 792.

[2] Hurter, *Innocent III.* IV. 179.

[3] *Claustrum sine armario quasi est castrum sine armamentario.* See Maitland, p. 230 ; Wattenbach, p. 570.

ning of Lent each received a book from the cloistral collection and was expected to read it " straight through." This direction shines as a light down through the history of the monastic institutions, though many a convent probably possessed no books and some of them had little appreciation of their value.

A collection of several hundred books was relatively as large a library as a collection of hundreds of thousands of volumes would be now. Fleury, in the twelfth century, had 238 volumes, St. Riquier 258.[1] The destruction of the English monastery of Croyland in the eleventh century involved the loss of " 300 original and more than 400 smaller volumes." The conventual buildings were destroyed in the night by fire. The interesting letter of the abbot Ingulph, relating the calamity, speaks of beautiful manuscripts, illuminated with pictures and adorned with crosses of gold. The good abbot, after describing the loss of the chapel, infirmary, and other parts of the buildings, went on to say " our cellar and the very casks, full of beer, were also burnt up." [2]

Catalogues are preserved from this period. Edwards gives a list of thirty-three mediæval catalogues of English libraries.[3] The catalogue of Prüfening in Salzburg, 1158, prepared by " one who was a born librarian," [4] arranged the volumes in three classes : copies of the Scriptures, the Fathers, and modern writers. The books, most frequently found, were the Bible, or parts of it, the liturgical books, — Augustine, Gregory the Great, Jerome, and Ambrose, — and among the writers of the Carlovingian age, Bede and Alcuin. The catalogue of Corbie, Picardy, dating from the twelfth century, gives 39 copies of Augustine, 16 of Jerome, 13 of Bede, 15 of Boethius, and 5 of Cicero, as well as copies of Terence, Livy, Pliny, and Seneca.[5] Of later mediæval writers, the works of Anselm, Bernard, Hugo, and Abælard are found most often, but many collections were without a single recent writer. The otherwise rich collection of St.

---

[1] Clark, p. 25. [2] Maitland, pp. 286 sqq.
[3] Edwards, pp. 448–454. [4] Hauck, IV. 448. [5] Edwards, p. 52.

Michelsberg, in Bamberg, had only a single recent work, the *Meditations* of Anselm. The Prüfening library had a copy each, of Anselm, Hugo, Abælard, the Lombard and Gratian. Classical authors were common. The library at Durham had copies of Cicero, Terence, Virgil, Horace, Claudian, Statius, Sallust, Suetonius, Quintilian and other Latin authors.[1] Sometimes the classics were catalogued by themselves as at Neumünster.

Gifts of books were regarded as worthy benefactions. Peter, bishop of Paris, before starting out for the Holy Land, gave 300 works over to the care of the convent of St. Victor.[2] Grosseteste willed his collection to the Oxford Franciscans.[3] Gerbert, afterwards Sylvester II., says that the liberality of friends enabled him to buy a number of books in Rome, Italy, and Flanders.[4] The admiring chronicler treats it as a claim to fame, that Theodoric secured, for his abbey of St. Evroult, the books of the Old and New Testaments and an entire set of Gregory the Great. Others followed his good example and secured the works of Jerome, Augustine, Ambrose, and other Fathers.[5] Peter the Venerable declared that at Cluny books, notably the works of Augustine, were held more precious than gold.[6]

Libraries were sometimes given with the stipulation that the books should be loaned out. This was the case with Jacob of Carnarius who, in 1234, gave his library to the Dominicans of Vercelli on this condition. In 1270, Stephen, at one time archdeacon of Canterbury, donated his books to Notre Dame, Paris, on condition of their being loaned to poor theological students, and Peter of Joigny, 1297, bequeathed his collection directly to poor students.[7] In the following century Petrarch left his books to St. Marks, Venice, and

[1] Edwards, p. 56. See also Sandys, pp. 500 sqq.

[2] Hurter, III. 314. A list of books is preserved which the archbishop of far Northern Lund gave to the cathedral.

[3] Stevenson, *Life of Gross.*, p. 86.   [4] *Ep.*, 44; Migne, 139. 214.

[5] *Order. Vit.*, III. 3.

[6] *Libri maxime Augustiniani, ut nosti, apud nos auro pretiosiores. sunt.*

[7] *Chart. Univ. Paris.*, I. 493. Translated in the Univ. of Penn. *Translations and Reprints.*

Boccaccio willed his possessions of this kind to the Augustinian friars of Florence.

Manuscripts were sometimes offered at the altar or at the shrines of saints as offerings for the healing of the giver's soul, — *pro remedio animœ suœ.*[1]   On the other hand, in cases of emergency, books were put in pawn or sold.   William of Longchamps, bishop of Ely, 1190, pawned 13 copies of the Gospels for the redemption of Richard I.[2]   The abbot Diemo of Lorsch, 1139, needing money to pay for military equipments, sold three books ornamented with gold and precious stones.[3] Here and there, a tax was levied for the benefit of a library, as in the case of Evesham, 1215, and the synod of Lyons the same year adopted a like expedient.[4]   Prince Borwin of Rostock, in 1240, gave the monastery of Dargun a hide of land, the proceeds of which were to be used for the needs of the library.[5]

Of all books, copies of the Scriptures were held in highest esteem.   They were often bound in covers, inlaid with gold and silver, and sometimes ornamented with precious stones and richly illuminated.   Paul, abbot of St. Albans, placed in the abbey-library eight Psalters and two Gospels highly ornamented with gold and gems, as well as a copy of the Collects, a copy of the Epistles, and 28 other books.   In 1295, the dean of St. Paul's found in the cathedral 12 copies of the Gospels adorned with jewels, and a thirteenth copy kept in a case with relics.[6]

Books were kept first in *armaria* or horizontal presses and the librarian was called *armarius.*   About the fourteenth century shelves were introduced along the cloistral walls.[7] As early as the thirteenth century books were fastened by chains to protect them from being stolen by eager readers.[8] The statutes of Trinity College, Cambridge, 1350, required

---

[1] Maitland, pp. 98 sq., 238 sqq.   [4] Wattenbach, p. 582.
[2] Maitland, p. 250.   [5] Putnam, I. 159.
[3] Wattenbach, p. 546.   [6] Maitland, p. 242.
[7] Clark, p. 24, and Gasquet, pp. 20–28.

[8] Such chained books were, in the Sorbonne from 1289 on, "for the common use of the brethren" — *in communem sociorum utilitatem.*

that certain books remain continually in the library, chained to
their places, for the use of the fellows.   This custom was still
in vogue in England in the sixteenth century, when copies of
the English Bible were kept chained to the reading desks in
the churches.   The old Benedictine rule was still enforced
for the distribution of books.   Lanfranc's statutes for the
English Benedictines, 1070, required the return of the books
by the monks the first Sunday in Lent.   They were then
to be laid out on the floor and distributed for the ensuing
year, one book to each monk.   Any one failing to read his
book was obliged to fall on his face and confess his neglect.[1]
The loan of books was not uncommon.   Bernard borrowed
and lent as did Peter the Venerable.[2]   The Cistercians provided for such loans to outside parties and the synod
of Paris, 1212, insisted that convents should not recede
from this good practice which it pronounced a work of
mercy.

The book-room, or *scriptorium*, was part of a complete
conventual building.   It served as a place of writing and
of transcribing manuscripts.   Sometimes a monk had his own
little book-room, called *scriptoriolum*, or kept books in his
cell.   Nicholas, Bernard's secretary, described his little room
as next to the infirmary and "filled with choice and divine
books."[3]   Peter of Celle, successor to John of Salisbury in
the see of Chartres, spoke of his *scriptoriolum* as filled with
books, where he could be free from the vanity and vexations
of the world.   The place had been assigned to him, he said,
for reading, writing, meditating, praying, and adoring the
Lord.[4]

Abbots themselves joined to their other labors the work
of the copyist.   So it was with Theodoric of St. Evroult,
1050–1057, a skilful scribe who, according to Ordericus

---

[1] Putnam, I. 152.   The statutes of Oriel College, Oxford, 1329, ordered the
books taken out once a year, Nov. 2, each person, according to age, taking
out a single volume.   Clark, p. 34.

[2] *Ep.*, 88 ; Migne, 182. 219.   See Coulton's *Salimbene*, p. 167.

[3] *Ep.*, 35 ; Migne, 196. 1626.

[4] Maitland, p. 442.

Vitalis,[1] left "splendid monuments of his calligraphic skill," in copies of the Collects, Graduale, and Antiphonary which were deposited in the convent collection. Theodoric also secured the services of others to copy commentaries and the heptateuch.[2] Convents were concerned to secure expert transcribers. Copying was made a special feature of St. Albans by the abbot Paul, 1077–1093. He secured money for a *scriptorium* and brought scribes from a distance. In the latter part of the eleventh century, Hirschau in Southern Germany was noted for this kind of activity, through its abbot William, who saw that twelve good copyists were trained for his house. These men made many copies and William is said to have presented books to every convent he reformed. The scribe, Othlo of Emmeram, of the same century, has left us a list of the books he gave away.[3]

Diligence as a copyist sometimes stood monks in good stead when they came to face the realities of the future world. Of such an one, Ordericus makes mention.[4] This monk had copied with his own hand a bulky volume of Scripture, but he was a man of many moral offences. When the evil spirits laid claim to his soul, the angels produced the holy volume which the monk had transcribed. Every letter was counted and balanced against a sin. At last, it was found the letters had a majority of one. The devils tried to scrape up another sin, but in vain, and the Lord permitted the fortunate monk to return to the body and do proper penance.

Copying was sometimes prescribed as a punishment for cloistral offences and the Carthusian rules withheld wine from the monk who was able to copy and would not ply his art. It seems at times to have been a most confining and wearisome task. Lewis, a monk of Wessobrunn in Bavaria, had some of this feeling when he appended to a transcription

---

[1] III. 3 ; Engl. trans., I. 406.   Ordericus frequently refers to copyists. III. 5, IV. 19, etc.

[2] The heptateuch included the first seven books of the Old Testament.

[3] See his own description, Maitland, pp. 454 sqq.

[4] III. 3 ; Engl. trans., I. 407.

of Jerome's commentary on Daniel the following words and claimed the prayers of the reader: —

Dum scripsit friguit, et quod cum lumine solis
Scribere non potuit, perfecit lumine noctis.

"When he wrote he froze, and what he could not complete by the light of day, he finished by the light of the night." [1]

The price of books continued to be high till the invention of the printing-press. A count of Anjou paid for a copy of the homilies of Haimo of Halberstadt 200 sheep and a large quantity of provisions. In 1274, a finely written Bible sold for 50 marks, about $170, when labor cost a shilling a day. Maitland computed that it would take a monk ten months to transcribe the Bible and that the labor would be worth to-day £60 or £70.[2] The prices, however, were often greatly reduced, and Richard of Bury, in his *Philobiblion*, says that he purchased from the convent of St. Albans 32 volumes for £50.

The copyists, like the builders of the cathedrals, usually concealed their names. It was a custom with them to close their task by appending some pious or, at times, some witty sentiment. A line, frequently appended, ran, *finito libro, sit laus et gloria Christo.* "The book is finished. Praise and honor be to Christ." The joy authors often feel at the completion of their writings was felt by a scribe when he wrote, *libro completo, saltat scriptor pede leto.* "Now the book is done, the scribe dances with glad foot." Another piously expressed his feelings when he wrote, *dentur pro penna scriptori cœlica regna.* "May the heavenly reward be given to the scribe for his work with the quill." [3]

The pleasures of converse with books in the quiet of a library are thus attractively set forth by a mediæval theologian, left alone in the convent when the other monks had gone off for recreation: —

"Our house is empty save only myself and the rats and mice who nibble in solitary hunger. There is no voice in the hall, no footstep on the stairs. . . . I sit here with no company but books, dipping into dainty

---

[1] Maitland, p. 444.   [2] p. 232.
[3] Wattenbach., pp. 471-534, gives a number of subscriptions.

honeycombs of literature.   All minds in the world's literature are concentrated in a library.   This is the pinnacle of the temple from which we may see all the kingdoms of the world and the glory of them.   I keep Egypt and the Holy Land in the closet next to the window.   On the side of them are Athens and the empire of Rome.   Never was such an army mustered as I have here.   No general ever had such soldiers as I have. No kingdom ever had half such illustrious subjects as mine or subjects half as well disciplined.   I can put my haughtiest subjects up or down as it pleases me. . . .   I call Plato and he answers " here," — a noble and sturdy soldier ;   " Aristotle," " here," — a host in himself.   Demosthenes, Pliny, Cicero, Tacitus, Cæsar.   " Here," they answer, and they smile at me in their immortality of youth.   Modest all, they never speak unless spoken to.   Bountiful all, they never refuse to answer.   And they are all at peace together. . . .   All the world is around me, all that ever stirred human hearts or fired the imagination is harmlessly here.   My library cases are the avenues of time.   Ages have wrought, generations grown, and all their blossoms are cast down here.   It is the garden of immortal fruits without dog or dragon."

§ 90.   *The Universities.*

Literature : *Chartularium Universitatis Parisiensis*, ed. by H. Denifle, O. P. and A. Chatelain, adjunct librarian of the Sorbonne, 4 vols. Paris, 1889-1897.   This magnificent work gives the documents bearing on the origin, organization, customs, and rules of the University of Paris from 1200-1452 ; and forms one of the most valuable recent contributions to the study of the Middle Ages. — *Auctarium Chartularii Univ. Paris.*, ed. by Denifle and Chatelain, 2 vols. Paris, 1893-1897.   It gives the documents bearing on the hist. of the English "nation" in Paris from 1393-1466. — Denifle : *Urkunden zur Gesch. der mittelalt. Universitäten*, in *Archiv für Lit.- und Kirchengesch.*, V. 167 sqq., 1889. — Engl. trans. of the charter of Fred. Barbarossa, 1158 ; the Privilege of Philip Augustus, 1200 ; the charter of Frederick II. founding the Univ. of Naples ; the Regulations of Robert de Courçon, 1215, etc., are given in the *Trans. and Reprints of the Dep. of Hist., Univ. of Penn.* — C. E. Bulæus (Du Boulay) : *Hist. univ. Paris., etc., a Carolo Magno ad nostra tempora* (1600), 6 vols. Paris, 1665-1673.   A splendid work, but wrong in its description of the origin of the university and some matters of its organization. — F. C. von Savigny, Prof. in Berlin, d. 1861 : *Gesch. des röm. Rechts im M. A.*, Heidel., 2d ed., 1834, vol. III. — J. H. Newman : Office and Work of Universities, London, 1856, vol. III of his *Hist. Sketches.*   An exaggerated estimate of mediæval culture. — I. Döllinger : *D. Universitäten sonst und jetzt*, in his *Akad. Vorträge*, Nordl., 1889. — *Denifle : *D. Entstehung d. Universitäten d. Mittelalters bis* 1400, Berlin, 1885, pp. 814.   Marks an epoch in the treatment of the subject; is full of learning and original research, but repetitious and contentious. Denifle intended to write three more volumes. — * S. S. LAURIE : *The Rise and Constit. of Universities*, etc., Camb., 1892. — G. COMPAYRÉ : *Abelard and Origin and Early Hist. of Universities*, N. Y., 1893. — * H. RASHDALL : *The Universities of Europe in the M. A.*, 2 vols., Oxford, 1895. — P. SCHAFF : *The Univ. Past, Present and Future*, in *Lit. and Poetry*, pp. 256–278.

The university appears in Europe as an established institution in the twelfth century. It quickly became the restless centre of intellectual and literary life, the workshop of learning and scientific progress. Democratic in its constitution, it received men from every rank and sent them forth with new ideas and equipped to be the leaders of their age.

Origin. — The universities were a product of the mediæval mind, to which nothing in the ancient world, in any adequate way, corresponded. They grew up on the soil of the cathedral and conventual studies, but there was no organic continuity between them and the earlier schools. They were of independent growth, coming into being in response to a demand, awakened by the changed circumstances of life and the revival of thought in Europe. No clatter and noise announced their coming, but they were developed gradually from imperfect beginnings into thoroughly organized literary corporations.

Nor were the universities the immediate creation of the Church. Church authority did not bring them into being as it did the Crusades. All that can be said is that the men who wrought at their foundations and the lower superstructures were ecclesiastics and that popes were wise enough early to become their patrons and, as in the case of Paris, to take the reins of their general administration into their own hands. The time had come for a specialization of studies in the departments of human knowledge, the arts, law, medicine, and theology, which last, according to Jacob of Vitry, "alone can be called a liberal art, since it alone delivers the human soul from its woes."

The universities owed their rise to the enthusiasm of

single teachers[1] whose dialectic skill and magnetism attracted students wherever they happened to be. Bologna
through Irnerius and other teachers, and Paris through a
group of men, of whom Abælard was the most prominent
figure, were the centres where the university idea had its
earliest and most substantial realization. These teachers
satisfied and created a demand for specialization in education.

Due credit must not be withheld from the guilds whose
organization furnished a pattern for the university, especially in the case of Bologna. The university was the
literary guild, representing a like-minded community of
intellectual interests and workers. It is also possible that
some credit must be given to Arabic influences, as in the
case of the school of medicine at Salerno.

The first universities arose in Italy, the earliest of all
being Salerno and Bologna. These were followed by Paris
and other French universities. England came next, and
then Spain. Prague was the first to embody the idea in
Central Europe. The distinctively German universities do
not date beyond the second half of the fourteenth century,
Vienna, 1365, Erfurt, 1379, Heidelberg, 1385, Cologne, 1388.
The three Scotch universities, St. Andrews, Glasgow, and
Aberdeen, were established in the fifteenth century. That
century also witnessed the birth of the far northern Universities of Copenhagen and Upsala. By the end of the fifteenth century there were nearly eighty of these academic
institutions. Some of these passed out of existence and
some never attained to more than a local celebrity.

Salerno, Bologna, Paris, Padua, Oxford, Cambridge, and
other universities owed their existence to no papal or royal
charter. Toulouse, 1229 and Rome, 1244 were the first to
be founded by papal bulls. The University of Naples was
founded by the emperor, Frederick II., 1224. The Spanish

[1] " A teacher inspired by a love of teaching gathered around him a circle
of scholars eager to learn. Other teachers followed, the circle of listeners
increased, and thus, by a kind of inward necessity, an enduring school was
founded." Savigny, XX. 58.

Universities of Palencia, 1212, Salamanca, 1230, and Seville, 1254, were established by the kings of Castile. Prague, 1347, was founded by a double charter from the pope and Charles IV. Some universities had their origin in disaffection prevailing in universities already established: Padua started in a defection of students from Bologna; Cambridge, in 1209, in a defection of students from Oxford, and Leipzig, in 1409, grew out of the dissatisfaction of the German "nation" with its treatment at Prague. Heidelberg is the earliest institution of papal creation which went over to the Reformation.[1]

Organization. — A university originally signified not a body of studies or a place where studies were prosecuted, but an aggregation of teachers and students—*universitas magistrorum et scholarium.* The term "university" was used of any group of persons and was a common expression for "your body" or "all of you"—*universitas vestra.*[2] In the twelfth and thirteenth centuries it was frequently applied to guilds. The literary guild, or university, denoted the group of persons carrying on studies. The equivalent in the Middle Ages for the term "university," as we use it, was *studium* and *studium generale,* "study" or "general study." Thus the University of Bologna was called *studium Bononie* or *Bononiense,* — as it is still called *studio Bolognese* in Italy, — Paris, *studium Parisiense,* Oxford, *studium Oxoniense.* The addition "general" had reference to students, not to a variety of branches of knowledge, and denoted that the *studium*

---

[1] According to Denifle, after the middle of the thirteenth century, no university came into existence without a papal bull. I. 777. But Kaufmann disputes this view and, as it would seem, with reason. See Laurie, p. 137; Rashdall, I. 13. The mediæval custom of giving a university legal existence by a papal bull was renewed for the United States when Leo XIII. chartered the University of Washington City, 1888.

[2] Innocent III., 1205, addressed the professors of Paris in this way, *universitatem vestram rogamus, Chart.,* I. 63. In this letter Innocent also addresses the corporation as *universis magistris et scholaribus.* So also Gregory IX., 1251, Alex. IV., 1256, etc., *Chart.,* I. 136, 342, but the expression "university of masters and scholars," *universitas magistrorum et scholarium,* seems to have been used first in 1221. *Chart.,* I. ix, 98, 99.

was open to students from every quarter.[1] By the fifteenth
century the term " university " had come to have its present
meaning.   The designation of a seat of learning as *alma* or
alma mater dates from the thirteenth century.

A full university requires at least four faculties, the arts
— now known at the German universities as the faculty of
philosophy,— law, medicine, and theology. This idea was
not embodied in the earliest foundations and some of the
universities remained incomplete during their entire existence.   Salerno was a medical school.   Bologna was for
more than a century only a school of law.   Salamanca, the
most venerable of existing Spanish educational institutions,
did not have a faculty of theology till the end of the fourteenth century.[2]   Paris, which began as a seat of theological
culture, had no formal provision for the study of civil law till
the seventeenth century, although civil law was taught there
before 1219.[3]   Nearly one half of the universities did not
include theology in the list of studies.   The Italian universities were, almost without an exception, at first confined to the
study of jurisprudence and medicine.   The reason for this
may have been a purpose not to come into collision with the
episcopal and conventual schools, which existed for the training of priests.   The faculty of the arts, the lowest of the
faculties, included the seven studies covered by the *trivium*
and *quadrivium*, but was at a later period expanded so as to
include metaphysical, linguistic, historic, and other studies
not covered by the study of law, medicine, and theology.
Theology was known as the highest and master study.
Alexander IV., writing to Paris, 1256, said that theology
ruled over the other studies like a mistress, and they followed her as servants.[4]

[1] Rashdall, I. 8, a " general study " might be founded for each separate
faculty as the *studium generale in theologica facultate*.   Denifle, I. 5.

[2] The term " faculty " at first seems to have been synonymous with
"science," or branch of knowledge.   Thus Frederick II., in chartering the
University of Naples, spoke of those who teach the science of surgery,
chirurgiæ facultatem instruunt.

[3] Honorius III., 1219, forbade the teaching of civil law in Paris. *Chart.*, I.
p. xxviii, 92.   [4] *Præest reliquis sicut superior*, etc., *Chart.*, I. 343.

The university had its own government, endowments, and privileges. These privileges, or bills of rights, were of great value, giving the body of teachers and students protection from the usual police surveillance exercised by municipalities and included their exemption from taxation, from military service except in cases of exigency, and from the usual modes of trial before the municipal authorities. Suits brought against members of the University of Paris were tried before the bishop of Paris. In Bologna, such suits were tried before the professor of the accused student or the bishop. By the privilege of Philip Augustus, 1200, the chattels of students at Paris were exempt from seizure by the civil officer. The university was a state within the state, a free republic of letters.[1] The master and students formed, as it were, a separate class. When they felt that their rights were abused, they resorted to what was called cessation, *cessatio*, a suspension of the functions of the university or even removal to some other locality. In 1229 the University of Paris suspended for two years on account of the delay of Queen Blanche to give redress for the violent death of two students during the carnival. Many professors left Paris till not a single one of fame remained. The bishop of Paris launched excommunications against the chief offenders; but the university was victorious and the king made apology for the injuries inflicted and the pope revoked the ecclesiastical censures. Gregory IX., 1231, confirmed this privilege of suspending lectures.[2] This feature survives in the German universities which cling to Lehrfreiheit, the professor's liberty to teach, as conscience dictates, without fear of interference from the state.

The Model Universities. — In the administration of their affairs the universities followed Bologna and Paris as models. In Bologna the students were in control, in Paris the masters in conjunction with the students. As for their relation

[1] The University of Cambridge in its calendar is still styled "a literary republic." Laurie, p. 186.

[2] *Chart.*, I. 138, *liceat vobis usque ad satisfactionem condignam suspendere lectiones.*

to the pope and the authority of the Church, Bologna was always free, antipapal and anticlerical, as compared with her younger sister in France. The democratic principle had large recognition. The first element to be noticed is the part played by the different faculties. In Paris the faculties were fully organized by the middle of the thirteenth century. In 1281, the university as a body promised to defend each of its faculties.[1] Long before that time each faculty passed upon its own degrees, regulated its own lectures, and performed other special acts.

The second element was the part which the so-called nations had in the administration. In Bologna there were four nations, the Italians, English,[2] Provençals, and Germans. The students of Paris were likewise divided into four groups, representing France, Picardy (including the Netherlands), Normandy, and England, the last giving place, in 1430, to Germany. The distinctive organization at Paris goes back to the early years of the thirteenth century.[3] At first floating colonies brought together by national and linguistic affinities, the nations were developed into corporate organizations, each with a code of its own. They were in turn divided into provinces. An elective official, known as the rector, stood at the head of the whole corporation. At Bologna he was called, as early as 1194, "rector of the associations," *rector societatum.* He directed the affairs of the university in conjunction with a board of counsellors representing the provinces.

The first record calling the head of the University of Paris

---

[1] *Chart.*, I. 590. The term "faculty" was first used of the university of Paris by Honorius III., 1219. *Chart.*, I. x, 87.

[2] English archdeacons were expected, after their election, to go to Bologna to study canon law. See Capes, *Hist. of the Eng. Church*, p. 240.

[3] *Chart.*, I. 215, Honorius III., 1222, speaks of "nations," but does not definitely give the number. *Chart.*, I. 103, Du Boulay, following a spurious document, dates their organization as far back as 1206. Denifle puts the existence of the four nations in Paris as far back as 1215-1222. See *Chart.*, I. xxi. The first clear trace of the division into nations seems to be in a bull of Honorius III., 1217, and concerns Bologna. It is addressed to the *scolaribus universitatis de urbe, de campania et de Tuscia, Bononie commorantibus.*

rector[1] occurs in a bull of Alexander IV., 1259, but the
office, no doubt, existed long before. He was chosen by
the proctors or presidents of the four nations. The rector
had to be a master of arts and might be a layman, but must
be a celibate. He performed on great occasions, and wore
a striking costume. He was responsible to the body whose
agent he was. The Paris rector was addressed as "your
amplitude," *vestra amplitudo.*

At Paris there was also a chancellor, and he was the older
officer. He stood at the head of the chapter of Notre Dame
and was called interchangeably chancellor of the cathedral
and chancellor of Paris. To him belonged the prerogative
of giving the license to teach and confer degrees. His
authority was recognized, time and again, by the popes, and
also restricted by papal decree, so that what he lost the
rector gained.[2] In Bologna, by the decree of Honorius III.,
1219, the archdeacon of the diocese conferred the degrees.[3]

Degrees. — By 1264, at latest, each faculty at Paris had
its own dean[4] and exercised the right to grant the license
to teach in its own department. Such license, — *jus docendi,*
or *legendi,* — when conferred by Bologna or Paris, carried
with it the right to teach everywhere, — *jus ubique docendi.*
Gregory IX., 1233, and other popes conferred the same prerogative upon the masters of Toulouse and other universities
but it seems doubtful whether their degrees were respected.
Even a degree from Oxford did not carry the right of lecturing at Paris without a reëxamination. When Alexander
IV. granted to the masters of Salamanca the right of teaching
everywhere, Bologna and Paris were expressly excepted.[5]

The question of mediæval degrees offers much difficulty.
There seem to have been three stages: bachelor, or *baccalau-
reus,* licentiate, and doctor or master. They corresponded
to the three grades in the guilds: apprentice, assistant, and
master. The bachelors were received. after examination
and did subordinate lecturing. The degree was not merely

---

[1] *Rector univ. magistrorum et scolarium, Chart.,* I. ·pp. xxiii, 379.

[2] *Chart.,* I. p. xix.   [4] *Chart.,* I. pp. xi, 441.

[3] *Chart.,* I. 90 sqq.   [5] Rashdall, I. 16.

a testimonial of work done, but a certificate entitling the holder to ply the trade of reading or teaching. The titles, master, *magister*, doctor, *dominus*, and professor, *scholasticus*, were synonymous. "Doctor" was the usual title at Bologna, and "master" at Paris, but gradually "doctor" came to be used chiefly of the graduates in canon law at Paris, and "master" of graduates in theology.[1] In his charter of 1224, Frederick spoke of the "doctors and masters in each faculty," no doubt using the words as synonyms. The test for the degrees was called the "determination," *determinance*, the main part of which was the presentation of a thesis and its defence against all comers.

Eight years was fixed by Robert de Courcon, 1215, as the period of preparation for the theological doctorate, but in the beginning of the fourteenth century it was extended to fourteen years. In the department of jurisprudence a course of eight years, — in medicine a course of six years, — was required.

Teachers and Studies. — The teaching was done at first in convents and in private quarters. In 1253 there were twelve professors of theology in Paris, nine of them teaching in convents and belonging to the orders. University buildings were of slow growth, and the phenomenon presented by such great universities as Johns Hopkins, Cornell, and the University of Chicago, starting out fully equipped with large endowments and buildings, was unknown in the Middle Ages. Professors and students had to make their own way and at first no provision was made by king or municipality for salaries. The professor lived by lecture fees and the gifts of rich students. Later, endowments were provided, and cities provided funds for the payment of salaries.[2] Col-

---

[1] By the fifteenth century the title "doctor" had come to be the usual one for theologians in Germany, as Dr. Luther, Dr. Eck. Rashdall, I. 22. It was also applied to all the superior faculties. The title "master" was gradually restricted to the faculty of arts, and has gone out of use in Germany.

[2] By the fourteenth century most of the professors in Bologna were paid by the municipality. Savigny, quoted by Compayré, p. 283.

leges were at first bursaries, or nostels, where students lived together, gratuitous provision being made for their support.[1] The earliest endowment of this kind, which still exists, is the college of the Sorbonne at Paris, founded by Robert of Sorbon, 1257, for sixteen secular students, four from each nation. The term " secular " was used in distinction from conventual. Another famous college was the college of Navarre on St. Genevieve, founded by the queen of Philip the Fair, Jeanne of Navarre, 1304. Rashdall, I. 478-517, gives a list of more than sixty colleges, or bursaries, founded in Paris before 1500. From being places of residence for needy students, the colleges came to include masters, as at Oxford and Cambridge. At Bologna the college system was never developed to the same extent as at Paris and in England.

With rare exceptions, the teachers in all the faculties were ecclesiastics, or, if laymen, unmarried. John XXII., in 1331, granted a dispensation to a married man to teach medicine in Paris, but it was an exception. Not till 1452 was the requirement of celibacy modified for the faculty of medicine in Paris, and till 1479 for Heidelberg; and not till a later date were the legal professors of Paris and Bologna exempted from this restriction. The Reformation at once effected a change in the universities under Protestant influence.[2]

The lectures were given in Latin and students as well as masters were required to use Latin in conversation. Learning of any kind was regarded as too sacred a thing to be conveyed in the vulgar dialects of Europe.[3] The studies at

[1] A bursa at the University of Paris was the sum of money paid each week in board. Auctar., I. pp. xlv, xlix; Chart., II. 673 sqq., etc.

[2] See Rashdall, II. 647 sqq. Compayré, p. 286, commenting upon the marital prohibition, observes that the rod would not have been retained so long in the universities if the teachers had had families.

[3] A good illustration of the use of Latin by students is given in the most interesting dialogue of two students on their way to Wittenberg, the MS. of which was discovered by Prof. Haussleiter, 1898, in the library of Jena, and published. Leipzig, 1903, D. Univ. Wittenb. n. d. Schilderung d. Mag. Andreas Meinhardi, 1507.

the University of Paris were authoritatively prescribed by the papal legate, Robert de Courcon, 1215.[1] Gregory IX., 1231, also took part in stating what the text-books should be. The classics had no place. Certain works of Aristotle were forbidden, as were also, at a later date, the writings of Amauri of Bena, David of Dinant, and other supposed or real heretics. Gregory IX. warned the divinity students against affecting philosophy, and to be satisfied with becoming "theodocts."[2]

Attendance and Discipline. — The attendance at the mediæval universities has been a matter of much dispute. Some of the figures seem to be incredibly large.[3] No matriculation books exist for the earliest periods, and not till the end of the fourteenth century do we have actual records of the number of graduations in Paris. Odefridus, a writer of the thirteenth century, gives the number of students at Bologna two generations before, as 10,000. Paris was reported to have had 25,000 students, and Oxford as many as 30,000,[4] or at one time, to follow Wyclif, 60,000. Speaking of his own times Wyclif, however, gives the more reasonable figure, 3000. In his days of unobscured fame, Abælard lectured to 3000 hearers, and this figure does not seem to be exaggerated when we consider the great attraction of his personality. In any estimate, it must be remembered that the student body included boys and also men well up in years. Rashdall makes 1500 to 3000 the maximum number for Oxford.[5]

There was no such thing as university discipline in the thirteenth century, as we understand discipline. The testimonies are unanimous that the students led a wild life.[6] Many of them were mere boys, studying in the department of arts. There were no dormitories, and the means of com-

---

[1] *Chart.*, I. 78.

[2] *satagant fieri theodocti, Chart.*, I. 138. Students were obliged to swear they had "heard" the required books. *Chart.*, I., 227 sqq., for the year 1252; II. 673, for the year 1347, etc.   [3] Denifle, p. 248.

[4] Richard Fitz-Ralph, archbishop of Armagh, writing about 1330, sets the number of students in his own day at six thousand.

[5] See Rashdall, II. 584 sqq.   [6] *Chart.*, I. Nos. 60, 197, 425, etc.

munication then at hand did not make it possible for parents to exercise the checks upon absent sons such as they may exercise to-day. Felix Platter, d. 1614, states in his autobiography that, as late as the middle of the sixteenth century, it required twenty days to make the journey from Basel to the school of Montpellier. At Paris students were excused from the payment of fees on account of the long distances from which they had come, the journeys often requiring several months and involving perils from robbers.[1] Complaint was made in Paris, 1218, of scholars who broke into houses, carrying off girls and women; and in 1269 a public proclamation denounced gangs of students who broke into houses, ravished women, and committed robberies and "many other enormities hateful to God."[2] In Paris the inns—*tabernæ*— were numerous. English students were noted for their drinking, and "to drink like an Englishman and to sing like a Norman" became proverbial.[3] The duel was a common way of settling disputes, and Gregory IX., 1231, forbade students going through the streets carrying arms.[4]

The rescript given by Frederick Barbarossa to Bologna, 1158, presented a picture of students as those "who exile themselves through love of learning and wear themselves out in poverty." The facts do not support any rosy picture of social equality, such as we would expect in an ideal democracy. The number who were drawn to the universities from love of adventure and novelty must have been large. The nobleman had his special quarters and his servants, while the poor student begged his bread. It was the custom of the chancellor of Oxford to issue licenses for the needy to beg.[5]

---

[1] *Auctar.*, I. p. xlvi. [2] *Chart.*, I. 426 ; Compayré, p. 276.

[3] *Cantat ut Normannus, bibit ut Anglicanus, Auctar.*, I. p. lvi. For the fighting abilities of the English nation see *Auctar.*, I. p. lx. Rashdall, II. 678 sqq., gives a number of cases of fights between town and gown in Paris. The cases of 1278 and 1304 were the most notorious. [4] *Chart.*, I. 138.

[5] Rashdall, II. 656 sqq. Rashdall gives the following estimate of living in Oxford in the fifteenth century. Meat was $\frac{1}{4}$ *d.* a pound ; butter and cheese, $\frac{1}{2}$ *d.* a pound, while six pounds of wheat cost 4 *d.* Thus, $1\frac{1}{2}$ pounds of bread, 1 pound of meat, and $\frac{1}{4}$ pound of butter and cheese made up about 1 *d.* a day, or 7 *d.* a week, "a tolerably substantial basis for a student's diet."

At Bologna the rich occupied the first seats.[1]   Robert of
Courçon commended the gift of garments and other articles
to needy scholars.

The mediæval universities were the centres of the ideals
and hopes of the younger generation.   There, the seeds were
sown of the ecclesiastical and intellectual movements of
after times and of the revolutions which the conservative
groups pronounced scientific novelties and doctrinal heresies.

A mediæval writer pronounced the three chief forces for
the maintenance of the Catholic faith to be the priesthood,
the empire, and the university.   This was not always the
case.   From Paris went forth some of the severest attacks
on the theory of papal absolutism, and from there, a century later, the reformers, Gerson and D'Ailly, proceeded.
Hussitism was begotten at Prague.   Wyclif's teachings
made Oxford a seat of heresy.   Wittenberg, the last of
the mediæval universities to open its doors, protected and
followed Luther.   Basel, Pius II.'s creation, Heidelberg,
Oxford, Cambridge, St. Andrews, and other universities
became the bulwarks of the new ideas.   On the other hand,
the Sorbonne, Louvaine, and Cologne ordered Luther's works
burnt.   As an agent of culture and the onward progress of
mankind, the Middle Ages made no contribution to modern
times comparable in usefulness to the university.

§ 91.   *The University of Bologna.*

LITERATURE : MURATORI: *Antiqq. Ital.*, III. 884 sqq.   Important documents
bearing on the state of learning in Italy. — *Acta nationis Germanicæ univ.
Bononiensis*, ed. E. FRIEDLÄNDER et C. MALAGOLA, Berl., 1887. — CARLO
MALAGOLA : *Statuti della università e dei collegi dello studio Bolognese*,
p. 524, Bologna, 1888. — DENIFLE : *D. Statutem d. Juristen Univ. Bologna, 1317–1347*, in *Archiv. für Lit.- und Kirchengesch.*, III. 196–409,
1887.   Superseded by MALAGOLA. — GIACOMO CASSANI (Prof. of Canon
Law, Bologna) : *Dell' antico Studio di Bologna e sua origine*, Bologna,
1888. — H. FITTING : *Die Anfänge der Rechtsschule zu Bologna*, Berl.,
1888. — SAVIGNY (see above) gives a full account with special reference
to the study of Roman law, but must be supplemented and corrected by
DENIFLE : *Universitäten*, etc. — For publications called forth by the

---

[1] Compayré, p. 271.

eighth centenary, 1888, see P. Schaff : *Lit. and Poetry*, p. 278.   For full Lit., see Rashdall, I. 89-91.

Bologna is the most venerable of European universities. Salerno, which preceded it in time, became sufficiently famous as a medical school to call forth from Petrarch the praise of being the fountain-head of medicine, — *fons medicinæ*, — but its career was limited to two centuries.[1] The origin of Salerno is lost in obscurity. There seems to be no sufficient evidence to show that the school owed its origin to the convent of Monte Cassino which was eighty miles away. It was the outgrowth of the awakened interest in medicine in Southern Italy in which Greek and Arabic influences had a part.

In 1888, Bologna celebrated its eight hundredth anniversary and continues to be one of the most flourishing schools of Southern Europe. As early as the thirteenth century, the tradition was current that Theodosius II., in 433, had granted to it a charter. But its beginnings go no further back than the latter part of the eleventh or the earlier years of the twelfth century. At that period Irnerius, d. about 1130, was teaching the code of Justinian[2] and a little later the Camaldulensian monk, Gratian, taught canon law in the convent of St. Felix. These two masters of jurisprudence, civil and ecclesiastical, are looked upon as the fathers of the university.

Bologna became the chief school for the study of both laws in Europe. The schools of arts added 1221, of medicine 1260, and theology 1360 — by a bull of Innocent VI. — never obtained the importance of the school of law.

On a visit to the city in 1155 Frederick Barbarossa granted the university recognition and in 1158, on the field of Roncaglia, gave it its first charter.[3] This is the oldest piece of university

[1] See Laurie, p. 123 sqq.; Rashdall, I. 80 sqq.

[2] Rashdall, I. 120, associates an " epoch in the study of law " with Irnerius, but insists upon the activity of law teachers before his day. When Laurie, p. 128, still calls Irnerius the " rediscoverer " of the Roman law, the title is only relatively true.

[3] The document of 1155 is known as the *Authentica Habita.* A historical poem discovered and published by Giesebrecht, 1879, describes Frederick's visit of 1155. The document of 1158 is addressed to " all scholars and especially the professors of divine and sacred law." Denifle, p. 49 sqq.

legislation.   Thenceforth Bologna was a second and better
Berytus, the nurse of jurisprudence, *legum nutrix*, and adopted
the proud device, *Bononia docet* — "Bologna teaches."   To
papal patronage she owed little or nothing, and in this respect
as in others her history did not run parallel with the University
of Paris.[1]   Students flocked to her by hundreds and thousands
from all parts of Western Europe.

The student body, which was in control, was at first divided
into four "universities" or guilds.   The statutes of the German "nation " have been preserved and declare as its object
fraternal charity, mutual association, the care of the sick
and support of the needy, the conduct of funerals, the termination of quarrels, and the proper escort of students about
to take the examination for the degree of doctor.[2]   By the
fourteenth century, the four "universities" had given place
to the two groups called the Ultramontanes and the Cismon-
tanes, each of which was subdivided into smaller groups presided over by counsellors, *conciliarii*.

The rectors of the faculties were elected for two years and
were required to be secular clerics, unmarried, and wearing
the clerical habit.   The ceremonies of installation included
the placing of a hood on their heads.   The two rectors of the
two jurist " universities " gave place to a single rector after
the middle of the fourteenth century.

The professors took oaths to the student bodies, to follow
their codes.   If they wished to be absent from their duties,
they were obliged to get leave of absence from the rectors.
They were required to begin and close their lectures promptly
at the ringing of the bell under penalty of a fine and were
forbidden to skip any part of the text-books or postpone
the answer to questions to the end of the lecture hour.   Another rule required them to cover a certain amount of ground

---

[1] The first papal bull was that of Clement III., 1189, forbidding masters
and scholars making a bid for a house already occupied by students.

[2] Denifle, p. 130, makes the scholastic guilds to have originated with the
Germans. As a mercantile organization the guild was in existence in Bologna
before studies began to flourish there. Foreign merchants residing there had
their own societies. Also Rashdall, I. 160.

in a given period.[1]   The professors were kept in awe by the
threat which the student body held over them of migrating
when there was cause for dissatisfaction.   This sort of boycott
was exercised a number of times as when Bolognese students
decamped and departed to Vicenza 1204, Padua 1222, and
for the last time to Siena 1321.

The professors, at first, were dependent upon fees and at
times stopped their lectures because of the failure of the students to pay up.   The jurist, Odefridus of Bologna, announced
on one occasion that he would not lecture in the afternoons of
the ensuing term because "the scholars want to profit but not
to pay."   Professorial appointments were at first in the hands
of the student body but afterwards became the prerogative of
the municipality.   This change was due in part to the obligation undertaken by the city government to pay fixed salaries.[2]   Strange to say, about the middle of the thirteenth
century, the professorships at Bologna became largely hereditary.

A noticeable, though not exceptional, feature of Bologna
was the admission of learned women to its teaching chairs.
Novella d'Andrea, 1312–1366, the daughter of the celebrated
jurist Giovanni d'Andrea, lectured on philosophy and law, but
behind a curtain, lest her face should attract the attention of
the students from their studies.   Among other female professors have been Laura Bassi, d. 1778, doctor and professor
of philosophy and mathematics; Chlotilda Tambroni, who expounded the Greek classics, 1794–1817; and Giuseppina
Cattani, who, until a few years ago, lectured on pathology.
In Salerno, also, women practised medicine and lectured, as
did Trotula, about 1059, who wrote on the diseases of women.
In Paris, as we have been reminded by Denifle, the daughters

---

[1] This was called reaching a certain " point," *punctum*, which was a division
in the civil text-book and in Gratian's *Decretum*.   Rashdall, I. 199.

[2] The first instance of a lecturer with a fixed salary was Garsias, the canonist,
to whom £150 were promised.   In 1289 two chairs were endowed at £150 and
£100.   In 1838 there were at Bologna 27 professors of civil law, 12 of canon
law, 14 of medicine, and 15 of the arts.   Laurie, p. 140.   In 1381 there were 23
salaried professors of the law and the city grant amounted to £63,670.   Rashdall, I. 212 sq.

of one Mangold taught theology in the latter part of the eleventh century.[1]

On the other hand, due care was taken to protect the students of Bologna against the wiles of women. The statutes of its college, founded by Cardinal Albornoz, 1367, for Spanish students, forbade them dancing because " the devil easily tempts men to evil through this amusement," and also forbade women to " enter the premises because a woman was the head of sin, the right hand of the devil, and the cause of the expulsion from paradise." [2]

A graduate of civil law was required at Bologna to have studied seven years, and of canon law six years. To become a doctor of both laws, *utriusque juris*, a term of ten years was prescribed. In 1292, Nicholas IV. formally granted the Bolognese doctors the right to lecture everywhere, a right they had exercised before. The promotion to the doctorate was accompanied with much pageantry and involved the candidate in large outlay for gifts and banquets.[3]

The class rooms in canon and civil jurisprudence at Bologna became synonymous with traditional opinions. There was no encouragement of originality. With the interpretation of the text-books, which had been handed down, the work of the professor was at an end. This conservatism Dante may have had in mind when he made the complaint that in Bologna only the Decretals were studied. And Roger Bacon exclaimed that " the study of jurisprudence has for forty years destroyed the study of wisdom [that is philosophy, the sciences, and theology], yes, the church itself and all departments." [4] When the Renaissance came, it did not start with Bologna or any of the other Italian univer-

---

[1] Denifle, I. 233, Ordericus Vitalis speaks of women practitioners and mentions one by name who had studied at Palermo. Engl. trans. I. 433. There were female physicians in Paris in the fourteenth century, one of whom, Jacoba, healed a royal chancellor. *Chart.*, II. 263 sqq. The statutes of the medical faculty of Paris forbade a physician attending a patient who had not paid his bill to another physician and prohibited his practising with Jews or women practitioners. Rashdall, II. 430.

[2] Rashdall, I. 204.   [3] For these expenses see Rashdall, I. 229 sqq.

[4] Brewer's ed., p. 418. Bridges, *Opus Majus of Rog. Bacon*, I. p. lxxxiii sq.

sities but in the courts of princes and popes and especially
in the city of Florence. The universities produced no
Savonarola and encouraged no religious or doctrinal reform.

NOTE. — An account of the brilliant celebration of the eighth centenary of Bologna, 1888, is given by Philip Schaff : The University, etc.,
in *Lit. and Poetry*, pp. 265–278. On that occasion Dr. Schaff represented
the University of New York. The exercises were honored by the
presence of Humbert and the queen of Italy. The ill-fated Frederick
III. of Germany sent from his sick-room a letter of congratulation, as in
some sense the heir of Frederick Barbarossa. The clergy were conspicuous by their absence from the celebration, although among the
visitors was Father Gavazzi, the ex-Barnabite friar, who in 1848 fired
the hearts of his fellow-citizens, the Bolognese, for the cause of Italian
liberty and unity and afterwards became the eloquent advocate of a new
evangelical movement for his native land, abroad as well as at home. A
contrast was presented at the five hundredth anniversary of the University of Heidelberg, 1886, which Dr. Schaff also attended, and which
was inaugurated by a solemn religious service and sermon.

§ 92. *The University of Paris.*

LITERATURE : The works of BULÆUS, DENIFLE, RASHDALL, etc., as given
in § 90. Vol. I. of the *Chartularium* gives the official documents bearing
on the history of the Univ. from 1200–1286 with an *Introd.* by Denifle. —
CREVIER : *Hist. de l' Univ. de Paris*, 7 vols. Paris, 1761, based on Bulæus.
— P. FERET : *La Faculté de theol. de Paris et ses docteurs les plus célèbres
au moyen âge*, 5 vols. Paris, 1894 sqq. — A. LUCHAIRE : *L'univ. de Paris
sous Phil. Auguste*, Paris, 1899. — C. GROSS : *The Polit. Infl. of the Univ.
of Paris in the M.A.*, in *Am. Hist. Rev.*, 1901, pp. 440–446. — H. FELDER :
Gesch. der wissenschaftl. Studien im Franziskanerorden bis c. 1250, Freib.,
1904. — F. X. SEPPELT : *D. Kampf d. Bettelorden an d. Univ. zu Paris in d.
Mitte d. 13ten Jahrh.*, Breslau, 1905. — RASHDALL : *Universities*, I. 270–557,
and the table of Lit. there given.

The lustre of the University of Paris filled all Western
Europe as early as the first years of the thirteenth century.
It continued to be the chief seat of theological and general
learning till the Reformation. In 1231 Gregory IX. called
Paris " the parent of the sciences, another Kerieth Sepher, a
city of letters, in which, as in a factory of wisdom, the precious stones and gold of wisdom are wrought and polished
for the Church of Christ." [1] In the same strain Alexander

[1] *Chart.*, I. 137.

IV., 1256, eulogized the university[1] as "that most excellent state of letters, a famous city of the arts, a notable school of erudition, the highest factory of wisdom, — *officina sapientiæ*, —and the most efficient gymnasium of study. There, a clear spring of the sciences breaks forth at which the peoples of all nations drink." Three hundred years later, in 1518, Luther, in his protest to Cajetan, expressed his willingness to have his case go before the University of Paris to which he referred "as the parent of studies and from antiquity ever the most Christian University and that in which theology has been particularly cultivated."

The old tradition, which traced the origin of the university back to Charlemagne, the pride of the French has been slow to abandon. Du Boulay devoted an entire volume to its assumed history before the year 1000. Not even was Abælard its founder. The most that can be said is, that that brilliant teacher prepared the way for the new institution,[2] whose beginnings belong to the period 1150–1170.

From its earliest era of development, the university received the recognition of royalty and the favor of popes who were quick to discern its future importance. In the year 1200 Philip Augustus, king of France, conferred upon it a valuable privilege, granting the students and teaching body independent rights over against the municipal government. Among its venerable documents are communications from Innocent III., his legate, Robert of Courçon, Honorius III. and Gregory IX., 1231. From that time on, the archives abound in papal letters and communications addressed to the pope by the university authorities.

In Paris, as has already been said, the masters were the controlling body. The first use of the expression "university of masters and scholars" occurs in 1221.[3] The earliest example of statutes is found in a bull of Innocent III., written about 1209.[4] Later, Innocent recognized the corporate rights of the body when he permitted it to have a represen-

---

[1] *Chart.*, I. 343. [2] Denifle, p. 677. [3] *Chart.*, I. 98 sq.
[4] Denifle gives the date as 1208 or 1209, *Chart.*, I. 67. Rashdall, I. 301, puts it in 1210.

tative at Rome and ordered an expelled master to be read-
mitted. The statutes of Robert of Courçon, 1215, prescribed
text-books and other regulations. A university seal was
used as early as 1221.[1] Disputes between the university
and the chancellor of the cathedral and other church authorities of Paris date back as far as 1213.

There has been much difference of opinion as to what was
the original norm of the organization of the university.
Denifle, the leading modern authority, insists against Du
Boulay that it was the four faculties and not the "nations,"
and he finds the faculties developed in the earliest years of
the thirteenth century.[2] Some association of masters existed
as early as 1170, about which time, John of Celle, abbot of
St. Albans, 1195–1214, was admitted into its membership.[3]
In 1207, Innocent III. spoke of the " body of masters," and
in 1213 he recognized the right of the masters to insist upon
the conferring of the license to teach upon the candidates
whom they presented. The chancellor was left no option
in the matter.[4] In the middle of the thirteenth century, his
authority was still more curtailed by the withdrawal of some
of the masters to the hill of St. Genevieve on the western
bank of the Seine. The abbot of St. Genevieve, who began
to be styled "Chancellor of St. Genevieve" in 1255, assumed
the right to confer licensures or degrees and the right was
recognized by papal decree.[5]

The four nations seem to have been developed out of
the demand for discipline among the students of cognate
regions and for mutual protection against the civil authorities. It is quite possible the example set in Bologna
had some influence in Paris.

---

[1] *Chart.*, I. 100. The seal was broken 1225. The seal of 1292 is preserved
in Paris, *Chart.*, I. p. ix sq.

[2] *Universitäten*, pp. 64 sqq., 655 sqq. Du Boulay was followed by Savigny.
Seppelt, p. 221, agrees with Denifle.

[3] John's biographer, Thomas of Walsingham, says John was a diligent
student in Paris " in his youth " and was taken into "the association of the
elect masters."   [4] *Chart.*, I. 73, 75, 85.

[5] *Chart.*, I. 75, 85. The formula used by the chancellor of St. Genevieve
is given in the *Chart.*, I. 299.

The bull of Gregory IX., 1231, *parens scientiarum*, called by Denifle the "magna charta of the university," recognized and sealed its liberties.   It was called forth by the suspension of lectures which had lasted two years.   The trouble originated in a brawl in an inn, which developed into a fight between gown and town.   The police of the city, with the assent of Queen Blanche, interfered, and killed several of the students.   The professors ordered a "cessation" and, when they found that justice was not done, adjourned the university for six years.   Some of them emigrated to England and were employed at Oxford and Cambridge.[1]   Others settled down at other schools in France.   The trouble was brought to an end by Gregory IX., who ratified the right of the masters to secede, and called upon Blanche to punish the offending officials, forbade the chancellor to have any prisons, and the bishop from imposing mulcts or imprisoning students.

It is possible that the office of rector goes back as far as 1200, when an official was called "the head of the Paris scholars."[2]   As early as 1245 the title appears distinctly and the rector is distinguished from the proctors.[3]   At a later time it was the proper custom, in communicating with the university, to address the "rector and the masters."   The question of precedence as between the rector and other high dignitaries, such as the bishop and chancellor of Paris, was one which led to much dispute and elbowing.   Du Boulay, himself an ex-rector, takes pride in giving instances of the rector's outranking archbishops, cardinals, papal

---

[1] See Henry III.'s letter, *Chart.*, I. 119.

[2] *Capitale Parisiensium scolarium*, *Chart.*, I. 60.   This, the view of Du Boulay, is adopted by Savigny.   Rashdall, I. 297, gives the expression an entirely different signification, and says it does not refer to persons at all but to chattels.   Denifle, p. 119, takes an entirely different view, and denies that the university had a rector in the full sense till the middle of the fourteenth century.   His view is that the rector of the faculty of the Arts gradually came to be recognized as the rector of the whole university.   Rashdall gives good grounds for holding that he was the recognized head of the university, certainly as far back as the middle of the thirteenth century.

[3] *Chart.*, I. 179, 379.

nuncios, peers of France, and other lesser noteworthies at public functions.[1]

The faculties came to be presided over by deans, the nations by proctors.   In the management of the general affairs of the university, the vote was taken by faculties.

The liberties, which the university enjoyed in its earlier history, were greatly curtailed by Louis XI. and by his successors in the latter half of the fifteenth century.   The university was treated to sharp rebukes for attempting to interfere with matters that did not belong to it.   The right of cessation was withdrawn and the free election of the rectors denied.[2]   The police of the city were invested with larger jurisdiction, and the sovereign's will was made a controlling element.

The fame of the University of Paris came from its schools of arts and theology.   The college of the Sorbonne, originally a bursary for poor students of theology, afterwards gave its name to the theological department.   It was founded by Robert of Sorbon, the chaplain of St. Louis, the king himself giving part of the site for its building.   In the course of time, its halls came to be used for disputations, and the decisions of the faculty obtained a European reputation. Theological students of twenty-five years of age, who had studied six years, and passed an examination, were eligible for licensure as bachelors.   For the first three years they read on the Bible and then on the *Sentences* of the Lombard.   These readers were distinguished as *Biblici* and *Sententiarii*.   The age limit for the *doctorate* was thirty-five.

One of the most interesting chapters in the history of the university is the struggle over the admission of the mendicant friars in the middle of the thirteenth century.   The papacy secured victory for the friars.   And the unwilling university was obliged to recognize them as a part of its teaching force.

The struggle broke out first at the time of the " cessation," 1229, when, as it would seem, the Dominicans secretly

[1] Bulæus, V. 359.   [2] *Amer. Hist. Rev.*, 1901, p. 442.

favored the side of the civil magistrates against the university authorities, and poisoned the court against them.   The Dominicans were established in Paris, 1217 and the Franciscans, 1220, and both orders, furnished with letters of commendation by Honorius III., were at first well received, so the masters themselves declared in a document dated 1254.[1] But they soon began to show arrogance and to demand the right to degrees for their students without promising submission to the statutes of the university.   One of the first two Dominican masters to teach at the university was the Englishman, John of Giles.   After preaching on poverty in St. Jacques, John descended from the pulpit and put on the Dominican robes.

At the "cessation" of 1251 the two Dominicans and one Franciscan, who were recognized as masters by the university, refused to join with the other authorities, and, after the settlement of the difficulty, the two Dominicans were refused readmittance.   A statute was passed forbidding admission to the fellowship, *consortium*, of the university for those who refused to take the oath to obey its rules.   The friars refused to obey the statute and secured from Alexander IV. an order requiring the university to receive them, and setting aside all sentences passed against them.[2]

The friction continued, and the seculars sought to break the influence of the Franciscans by pointing out the heresies of Joachim of Flore.   The friars retorted by attacking William of St. Amour whose work, *The Perils of the Last Times*, was a vigorous onslaught upon mendicancy as contrary to Apostolic teaching.   William's book, which called out refutations from Thomas Aquinas and Bonaventura, was burnt, and refusing to recant, the author was suspended from teaching and banished from France.[3]   The friars were hooted on the streets and beaten.   By 1257 tranquillity was

---

[1] *Chart.*, I. 253.   Felder, pp. 159 sqq., strange to say, entirely passes over this conflict so that the reader would never dream there had been one.

[2] *Chart.*, I. 285, *omnes sententias privationis seu separationis a consortio . . . penitus revocamus.*

[3] *Chart.*, I. 362, 363, 367, 404, etc.

restored, as we are assured by Alexander IV. Thus the
papacy made repayment to the university for its readiness
from of old to accept its guidance by depriving the institution of its liberties.[1]

From the middle of the fourteenth century, the University of Paris played no mean part in the political affairs of
France. More than once she spoke before the court and
before the peers of the realm, and more than once was she
rebuked for her unsolicited zeal.[2] French kings themselves
styled her "the daughter of the king." She was actively
zealous in the persecution of Joan of Arc.[3]

As a factor in the religious history of Europe, the university figured most prominently during the Western schism —
1378-1418. She suggested the three ways of healing the rupture and, to accomplish this result, sent her agents through
Western Europe to confer with the kings and other powers.
Under the guidance of her chancellors, Gerson and D'Ailly,
the discussions of the Reformatory councils of Pisa and Constance were directed, which brought the papal schism to an
end. The voting by nations at Constance was her triumph.

As for disputes on distinctly doctrinal questions, the university antagonized John XXII. and his heresy, denying the
beatific vision at death. In 1497 she exacted from all candidates for degrees an oath accepting the dogma of the immaculate conception. When the Protestant Reformation came,
she decided against that movement and ordered the books of
Luther burnt.

§ 93. *Oxford and Cambridge.*

LITERATURE: ANTHONY WOOD (1632-1695) : *Hist. et Antiquitates Univ.
  Oxoniensis*, 2 vols. Oxford, 1674. A trans. from MS. by Wase and
  Peers, under the supervision of Dr. Fell from Wood's English MS.
  Wood was dissatisfied with the translation and rewrote his work, which

---

[1] See Rashdall, I. 391. The account given above differs from the account
of Seppelt who justifies the friars at every step and finds in the good reception they at first received from the university masters a proof that they
conducted themselves properly all the way through.

[2] See *Amer. Hist. Rev.*, 1901, p. 442 sq.   [3] *Chart.*, IV. Nos. 510-528.

was published a hundred years after his death with a continuation by
JOHN GUTSCH : *The Hist. and Antiquities of the Colleges and Halls in
the Univ. of Oxf.*, 2 vols. Oxford, 1786–1790. Also : *The Hist. and Antiquities of Oxf., now first published in English from the original MS. in
the Bodleian Library*, 2 vols. Oxford, 1792-1796. By the same : *Athenæ
Oxonienses*, 2 vols. London, 1691–1692, 3d ed., by Ph. Bliss, 1813-1820,
4 vols. The last work is biographical, and gives an account of the
Oxonian writers and bishops from 1500–1690.

Oxford Historical Society's Publications, 45 vols. CONTENTS : *University
Register*, 1449–1463, 1505–1671, ed. by W. C. BOASE, 5 vols.; Hearne's
Collectanea, 1705-1719, 6 vols.; *Early History of Oxford* (727–
1100); *Memorials of Merton College*, etc. — V. A. HUBER : *D. engl.
Universitäten*, 2 vols. Cassel, 1839. Engl. trans. by F. W. NEWMAN,
a brother of the cardinal, 3 vols. London, 1843. — C. JEAFFERSON :
Annals of Oxford, 2 vols. 2d ed. London, 1871. — H. C. M. LYTE :
Hist. of the Univ. of Oxf. from the Earliest Times to 1530, Oxford,
1886. — H. C. BRODRICK : *Hist. of the Univ. of Oxf.*, London, 1887. —
RASHDALL : *Universities*, II. 319–542. — JESSOPP : *The Coming of the
Friars*, pp. 262–302. — THOMAS FULLER : *Hist. of the Univ. of Cambr.*
ed. by PRITCHARD and WRIGHT, Cambridge, 1840. — C. H. COOPER :
Annals of Cambr., 4 vols. 1842–1852 ; *Memorials of Cambr.*, 3 vols. 1884.
— MULLINGER : *Hist. of the Univ. of Cambr. from the earliest times to
the accession of Charles I.*, 2 vols. Cambridge, 1873–1883 ; *Hist. of the
Univ. of Cambr.*, London, 1887, an abridgment of the preceding work.
For extensive Lit., see Rashdall, II. 319 sqq., 543 sq.

Next to Paris in age and importance, as a school of philosophy and theology, is the University of Oxford, whose
foundation tradition falsely traces to King Alfred. The
first historical notice of Oxenford, or Oxford, occurs in 912.
Three religious institutions were founded in the town, from
any one of which or all of which the school may have had its
inception : the priory of St. Frideswyde, Osseney abbey, and
the church of the canons regular of St. George's in the Castle.
The usually accepted view connects it with the first. But it
is possible the university had its real beginning in a migration from Paris in 1167. This view is based upon a statement
of John of Salisbury, that France had expelled her alien
scholars and an order of Henry II. forbidding clerks to
go to the Continent or to return from it without a license
from the justiciar.[1] Before that time, however, there was
teaching in Oxford.

---

[1] Rashdall, II. 331–345, argues the point with much force.

The first of the teachers, Thibaut d'Estampes, Theobaldus Stampensis, moved from St. Stephen's abbey, Caen, and taught in Oxford between 1117 and 1121. He had a school of from sixty to a hundred pupils, and called himself an Oxford master, *magister oxenfordiœ*. He was ridiculed by a monk as a " petty clerk " *tantillus clericellus*, one of those " wandering chaplains, with pointed beards, curled hair, and effeminate dress, who are ashamed of the proper ecclesiastical habit and the tonsure," and was also accused of being " occupied with secular literature."

The University of Cambridge, which first appears clearly in 1209,[1] did not gain a position of much rank till the fifteenth century and can show no eminent teacher before that time. The first papal recognition dates from the bull of Gregory IX., 1233, which mentions a chancellor.[2]

During the Reformation period, Cambridge occupied a position of note and influence equal to Oxford. Fisher, bishop of Rochester, martyred by Henry VIII. and one of the freest patrons of learning, was instrumental in the foundation of two colleges, Christs, 1505, and St. John, 1511. Among its teachers were Erasmus, and later Bucer and Fagius, the Continental Reformers. Tyndale, the translator of the first printed English New Testament, and Thomas Bilney, both of them martyrs, were its scholars. So were the three martyrs, Cranmer, Latimer, and Ridley, though they were burnt at Oxford. During the Elizabethan period, the university was a stronghold of Puritanism with Cartwright and Travers occupying chairs. Cudworth and the Neo-Platonists flourished there. And in recent years its chairs have been filled by such representatives of the historical and exegetical schools

[1] Mullinger and others find that the priory of Barnwell furnished the germ of the university in the early years of the twelfth century. Rashdall, II. 545, denies this origin. Legend ascribed the foundation of the university to a Spanish prince, Cantaber, of uncertain date, or to King Arthur or to the Saxon king Sigebert of the seventh century.

[2] Gregory IX.'s bull, addressed to the *cancellarius et universitas scholarium Cantabrigiensium*, is preserved in the Vatican Archives and printed by Denifle, *Universitäten*, pp. 370 sq. The university archives were burned by townsmen during riots, 1261 and 1322.

as Bishop Lightfoot, Westcott, his successor at Durham, Ellicott, bishop of Gloucester and Bristol, and John Anthony Hort.

Oxford and Cambridge differ from the Continental universities in giving prominence to undergraduate studies and in the system of colleges and halls, and also in the closer vital relations they sustain to the Church.

In 1149 the Italian, Vacarius, introduced the study of civil law in Oxford, if we are to follow the doubtful testimony of Gervaise of Canterbury, though it is more probable that he delivered his lectures in the household of the archbishop of Canterbury, Theobald.[1] He wrote, it is said, a digest of laws "sufficient for deciding all legal problems which are wont to be discussed in the schools."

One of the very earliest notices of Oxford as a seat of study is found in a description by Giraldus Cambrensis, the Welsh traveller and historian. About the year 1185 he visited the town and read " before the faculties, doctors, and students " his work on the *Topography of Ireland*.[2] The school was evidently of some importance to attract such a man. Walter Map, archdeacon of Oxford, is called by Giraldus " an Oxford master." The first degree known to have been conferred was given to Edmund Rich, afterwards archbishop of Canterbury. From Geraldus it is evident that the masters were grouped in faculties. As early as 1209 and in consequence of the hanging of three students by the mayor, there was a migration of masters and students, said to have been three thousand in number, from which the University of Cambridge had its beginning.[3]

The University of Oxford was less bound by ecclesiastical

---

[1] For the quotation from Gervaise see Rashdall, II. 336. John of Salisbury puts the teaching in the archbishop's household.

[2] Quoted by Rashdall, II. 341.

[3] Roger of Wendover, *anno* 1290, says that Oxford was completely forsaken of all masters and students who went, some to Cambridge and some to Reading. These students had lived together with a fourth who killed a woman and then fled. For other cessations see Rashdall, II. 395, etc. For other attempts to form universities at Northampton, Stamford, and Durham (by Cromwell), see Rashdall, II. 396 sqq.

2 P

authority than Paris.   An unsuccessful attempt was made
by the bishop of Lincoln, in whose diocese it was located, to
assert supervisory authority.   The bull of Innocent IV., issued
1254, was the nearest approach to a papal charter and confirmed the university in its "immunities and ancient customs."   In 1201 a chancellor is mentioned for the first time.
From the beginning this official seems to have been elected
by the university.   He originally held his office for a term of
two years.   At the present time the chancellor is an honorary
dignitary who does not pretend to reside in Oxford.

In 1395, the university was exempted by papal bull from all
control of bishops or *legati nati*.   This decree was revoked
in 1411 in consequence of the disturbances with Wyclif and
his followers, but, in 1490, Sixtus IV. again renewed the exemption from ecclesiastical authority.

The university was constantly having conflicts with the
town and its authorities.   The most notable one occurred in
1354.   As usual, it originated in a tavern brawl, the keeper
of the place being supported not only by his fellow-townsmen
but by thousands from the neighboring country.[1]   The chancellor fled.   The friars brought out the host and placed it
between the combatants, but it was crushed to the earth and
a scholar put to death while he was clinging to the friar who
held it.   Much blood was shed.   The townsmen, bent upon
paying off old scores, broke into twenty college inns and halls
and pillaged them.   Even the sanctity of the churches was not
respected, and the scholars were hunted down who sought
shelter in them.   The students left the city.   The chancellor
appealed the case to the king, and through his authority and
the spiritual authority of the bishop the town corporation
was forced to make reparation.   The place was put under interdict for a year.   Officials were punished and restitution of
goods to the students was made.   The interdict was withdrawn only on condition that the mayor, bailiffs, and sixty
burghers should appear in St. Mary's church on the anniversary of the breaking out of the riot, St. Scholastica's day, and

---

[1] Two thousand entered the city gates. See Rashdall's account, II. 403 sqq.

do penance for the slaughtered students, each burgher laying
down a penny on the high altar, the sum to be divided equally
between poor students and the curate.   It was not till 1825,
that the university agreed to forego the spectacle of this
annual penance which had been kept up for nearly five centuries.   Not for several years did the university assume its
former aspect.[1]   Among the students themselves peace did
not always reign.   The Irish contingent was banished, 1413,
by act of parliament for turbulence.[2]

The arrival of the Dominicans and Franciscans, as has been
said in other places, was an event of very great interest at
Oxford, but they never attained to the independent power
they reached in Paris.   They were followed by the Carmelites, the Augustinians, and other orders.

The next important event was the controversy over Wyclif
and the doctrines and persons of the Lollards, which filled the
years of the last quarter of the fourteenth century and beyond.

At the English universities the college system received a
permanent development.   Endowments, established by the
liberality of bishops, kings, and other personalities, furnished
the nucleus for corporations and halls consisting of masters and
students, each with a more or less distinct life of its own.   These
college bodies and their buildings continue to impart to Oxford
and Cambridge a mediæval aspect and to recall on every hand
the venerable memories of past centuries.   Twenty-one of
these colleges and five halls remain in Oxford.   The oldest
are University College founded by a bequest of William of
Durham at his death, 1249; Merton, 1264; Balliol founded by
the father of the Scotch king, 1266; Exeter, 1314; Oriel, 1324;
Queen's College, 1340; the famous New College, 1379, founded
by William of Wykenham, bishop of Winchester; All Souls,

[1] Rashdall, II. 411, says, that by the middle of the fifteenth century the "town
was almost entirely subjugated to the authority of the university."   He also
says, II. 416, that "few things are more calculated to make us realize the enormous extent to which civilization has succeeded in curbing the natural passions,
even of the lowest strata of modern society, than the annals of the mediæval
university."   [2] Rashdall, II. 416

1438; Magdalen, 1448, where Wolsey was fellow. Among the illustrious men who taught at Oxford, in the earlier periods, were Edmund Rich, Roger Bacon, Grosseteste, Adam Marsh, Duns Scotus, Ockam, Bradwardine, Richard of Armagh, Wyclif.

As a centre of theological training, Oxford has been closely identified with some of the most important movements in the religious history of England. There Wyclif preached his doctrine and practical reforms. There the Humanists, Grocyn, Colet, and Linacre taught. The school was an important religious centre in the time of the Reformation, in the Commonwealth period, and the period of the Restoration. Within its precincts the Wesleys and Whitefield studied and the Methodist movement had its birth, and there, in the first half of the last century, Pusey, Keble, and Newman exerted the spell of their influence, and the Tractarian movement was started and fostered. Since the year 1854 Oxford and Cambridge have been open to Dissenters. All religious tests were abolished 1871. In 1885 the spiritual descendants of the Puritans, the Independents, established Mansfield College, in Oxford, for the training of ministers.

Note. — List of Mediæval Universities.[1]

Before 1100, Salerno.

1100-1200. — Bologna, 1150?; Paris, 1160?; Oxford, 1170?; Reggio and Modena.

1200-1300. — Vicenza, 1204; Cambridge, 1209; Palencia, Spain, 1212, by Alfonzo VIII. of Castile, abandoned; Arezzo, 1215; Padua, 1222; Naples, 1224; Vercelli, 1228; Toulouse, 1229, by Gregory IX.; Salamanca, 1230, by Ferdinand III. of Castile and confirmed by Alexander IV., 1254; Curia Romana, 1244, by Pope Innocent IV.; Piacenza, Italy, 1248; Seville, 1254, by Alfonso X. of Castile; Montpellier, 1289, by Nicolas IV.; Alcala, 1293, by Sancho of Aragon, transferred 1837 to Madrid; Pamiers, France, 1295, by Boniface VIII.

1300-1400. — Lerida, 1300, by James II. of Aragon and Sicily; Rome, 1303, by Boniface VIII.; Angérs, 1305; Orleans, 1306, by Philip the Fair and Clement V.; Perugia, 1308, by Clement V.; Lisbon, 1309, by King Diniz, transferred to Coimbra; Dublin, 1312, chartered by Clement V.

[1] Comp. the tables of Denifle, 807–810, Compayré, 50–52, and Rashdall in Table of Contents, vol. II.

but not organized; Treviso, 1318; Cahors, 1332, by John XXII.; Grenoble, 1339, by Benedict XII.; Verona, 1339, by Benedict XII.; Pisa, 1343,
by Clement VI.; Valladolid, 1346, by Clement VI.; Prague, 1347, by
Clement VI. and Charles IV.; Perpignan, 1349, by Peter IV. of Aragon,
confirmed by Clement VII., 1379; Florence, 1349, by Charles IV.; Siena,
1357, by Charles IV.; Huesca, 1359; Pavia, 1361, by Charles IV. and
by Boniface VIII., 1389; Vienna, 1365, by Rudolf IV. and Urban V.;
Orange, 1365; Cracow, 1364, by Casimir III. of Poland and Urban V.;
Fünfkirchen, Hungary, 1365, by Urban V.; Orvieto, 1377; Erfurt, 1379,
by Clement VII.; Cologne, 1385, Urban VI.; Heidelberg, 1386, by the
Elector Ruprecht of the Palatinate and Urban VI.; Lucca, 1387; Ferrara, 1391; Fermo, 1398.

1400–1500. — Würzburg, 1402; Turin, 1405; Aix, in Provence, 1409;
Leipzig, 1409; St. Andrews, 1411; Rostock, 1419; Dôle, 1423; Louvain,
Belgium, 1425; Poictiers, 1431; Caen, 1437; Catana, Sicily, 1444; Bar-
celona, 1450; Valence, France, 1452; Glasgow, 1453; Greifswald, 1455;
Freiburg im Breisgau, 1455; Basel, 1459; Nantes, 1460; Pressburg, 1465;
Ingolstadt, 1472; Saragossa, 1474; Copenhagen, 1475; Mainz, 1476;
Upsala, 1477; Tübingen, 1477; Parma, 1482; Besançon, 1485; Aber-
deen, 1494; Wittenberg, 1502, by Frederick the Wise, Elector of Saxony.

§ 94.   *The Cathedrals.*

LITERATURE: J. FERGUSSON: *Hist. of Architecture in All Countries*, 2 vols.
1865–1867, and since. — SIR G. G. SCOTT: *The Rise and Devel. of Med.
Arch.*, London, 1879. — VIOLLET-LE DUC: *Lectures on Arch.*, Engl. trans.,
2 vols. London, 1877. — T. R. SMITH: *Arch. Gothic and Renaissance*,
N.Y., 1880. — B. FERREE: *Christ. Thought in Arch.*, in *Papers of
Am. Soc. of Ch. Hist.*, 1892, pp. 113–140. — F. X. KRAUS: *Gesch. der
christl. Kunst*, 2 vols. Freib., 1896–1900. — F. BOND: *Engl. Cathedrals*,
London, 1899. — R. STURGIS: *Dict. of Arch. and Building*, 3 vols. N.Y.,
1901 sq. — Art. *Kirchenbau* by HAUCK, in Herzog, X. 774–793. —
P. LACROIX: *The Arts of the Middle Ages*, Engl. trans., London. —
RUSKIN: *Stones of Venice, Seven Lamps of Arch.*, and other writings.
This enthusiastic admirer of architecture, especially the Gothic, judged
art from the higher standpoint of morality and religion.

The cathedrals of the Middle Ages were the expression of
religious praise and devotion and entirely the product of the
Church.   No other element entered into their construction.
They were hymns in stone, and next to the universities are
the most imposing and beneficent contribution the mediæval
period made to later generations.   The soldiery of the Crusades failed in its attempt at conquest.   The builders at
home wrought out structures which have fed the piety and

excited the admiration of all ages since. They were not due
to the papacy but to the devotion of cities, nobles, and
people.

It was a marked progress from the *triclinia*, or rooms in
private houses, and crypts, in which the early Christians
worshipped, to the cathedral of St. Sophia, at the completion
of which Justinian is said to have exclaimed, " O Solomon, I
have excelled thee."   And what a change it was from the
huts and rude temples of worship of Central and Northern
Europe to the splendid structures dedicated to Christian
worship, — the worship which Augustine of Canterbury, and
Boniface, and St. Ansgar had introduced among the barbarous Northern tribes!

It is also characteristic that the great mediæval structures
were not palaces or buildings devoted to commerce, although
the Gothic palace of the doges, in Venice, and the town halls
of Brussels, Louvaine, and other cities of Belgium and Holland are extensive and imposing.   They were buildings
devoted to religion, whether cathedral or conventual structures.   They were often, as in France, placed on an elevation
or in the centre of the city, and around them the dwellings
clustered as if for protection.

The great cathedrals became a daily sermon, bearing testimony to the presence of God and the resurrection of Christ.
They served the people as a Bible whose essential teachings
they beheld with the eye.   Through the spectacle of their
walls and soaring spires, their thoughts were uplifted to
spiritual things.   Their ample spaces, filled or dimly lit
with the sunlight piercing through stained-glass windows,
reminded them of the glory of the life beyond, which makes
itself known through varied revelations to the lonely and
mysterious existence of the earth.   The strong foundations
and massive columns and buttresses typified the stability of
God's throne, and that He hath made all things through the
word of His power.

Their construction occupied years and, in cases, centuries
were necessary to complete them.   Who càn estimate the
prayers and pious devotion which the laying of the first

stones called forth, and which continued to be poured out till the last layer of stones was laid on the towers or fitted into the finial? Their sculpture and stained-glass windows, frescoes, and paintings presented scenes from Scripture and the history of the Church. There, kings and queens, warriors, and the men whom the age pronounced godly were laid away in sepulture, a custom continued after the modern period had begun, as in the case of Luther and Melanchthon, whose ashes rest in the Castle Church of Wittenberg. In spite of frequent fires consuming parts of the great churches or the entire buildings, they were restored or reconstructed, often several times, as in the case of the cathedrals of Chartres, Canterbury, and Norwich. Central towers collapsed, as in the case of Winchester, Peterborough, Lincoln, and other English cathedrals, but they were rebuilt. In the erection of these churches princes and people joined, and to further this object they gave their contributions of material and labor. The women of Ulm gave up all their ornaments to advance the work upon the cathedral of that city, and to the construction of the cathedral in Cologne Germans in all lands contributed.

The eleventh century is the beginning of one of the most notable periods of architecture in the world's history, lasting for nearly three centuries. It has a distinct character of its own and in its service high talent was consecrated. The monks may be said to have led the way by their zeal to erect strong, ample, and beautiful cloistral establishments. These called forth in France the ambition of the bishops to surpass them. Two styles of architecture are usually distinguished in this period, the Romanesque, called in England also the Norman, and the Gothic. Writers on architecture make a number of subdivisions and some have included all the architecture of the twelfth to the fifteenth centuries under the title Gothic, or Christian Pointed. During these centuries Europe, from the South to far Northern Scotland and Sweden, was dotted with imposing structures which on the one hand vied with St. Sophia of Constantinople, and on the other have been imitated but not equalled since.

In Rome as late as the thirteenth century, when Honorius
III. began the construction of San Lorenzo, the old basilica
style continued to rule. The Romanesque style started from
Northern Italy and, in the beginning of the eleventh century,
crossed the Alps, where it had its most glorious triumphs.
In Italy, the cathedral of Pisa represents the blending of the
old and the new, the cruciform shape and the dome. In
Germany, the cathedrals of Spires, Worms, and Mainz belong
to this period, and in England its earlier cathedrals, or portions of them, like Winchester, begun about 1070, Worcester
about 1084, Peterborough about 1120, Norwich about 1096,
Ely about 1083, Durham about 1099.

For the fundamental ground plan of the basilica was substituted the form of the cross. The size of the choir was
increased and the choir was elevated. It was the age of the
priesthood, and sacerdotalism was represented in the enlargement of the altar, in increased and rich stalls for the clergy,
and spaces at the rear of the altar. These features also
belong to the preceding period, but now receive greater
emphasis. The large end of the cross, or nave, especially in
the English cathedrals, was greatly extended so that the
altar and its furniture were seen from afar, for the chief doors
were in that end, which faced the west. In England, the
transepts, or arms of the cross, became long and spacious.
The tower became a prominent feature, and buttresses were
added to the walls. In Italy, the tower took the shape of a
campanile, which was built in addition to the dome, and was
sometimes a separate building and never an essential part of
it. The vaulted and groined roof took the place of the flat
roof.

The Gothic style, so called in Italy from its reputed
barbaric features, found altogether its highest development
in the North, and started in Northern France. It is the
grandest style of church architecture ever wrought out. It
was shown in the height of the church walls and in spires
struggling to reach to the very throne of God itself. The
vault of the cathedral of Amiens is 147 feet above the floor,
of Beauvais 157 feet, of Cologne 155 feet. This style devel-

oped the pointed arch, perpendicular lines, the lancet window. It had some of the features of the Lombardy poplars, soaring, stern, solemn. In its strong, ramparted buttresses, its towers, and its massive columns, it represented the hardihood and strength of the northern forest. Its pointed roofs were adapted to receive the storms of snow common to the North. Its flying buttresses and elaborate carvings within, and its splendid entrances, especially in the French cathedrals, typified the richness of Christian promise and hope.

The Gothic style started in France in the thirteenth century. Notable examples are found in Rheims, begun 1211, Amiens, Laon, and in Notre Dame, Paris, begun in 1163. The arches are less pointed than in England and the portals are on a much grander scale and more highly ornamented. At Notre Dame we have one of the finest specimens of flying buttresses. In its case and most cases of French Gothic there are towers. The cathedrals of Paris, Amiens, and Rheims have unfinished towers. The Sainte Chapelle in Paris is a splendid piece of pure Gothic.

In Germany, fine examples of Gothic are found in the church at Marburg dedicated to St. Elizabeth, in Nürnberg, Bamberg, Freiburg, Strassburg, and other cities. The cathedral of Cologne is said to be the most perfect specimen of Gothic in existence. Its choir was begun in 1248, Konrad of Hochsteden laying the corner-stone in the presence of the newly elected emperor, William of Holland, and many princes. The choir was dedicated in 1322. By 1437 one of the towers was finished up to one-third of its present height. At the time of the Reformation the roof was covered with boards. In the nineteenth century the original plans were discovered and the completion of the edifice, including the two spires, was made a national undertaking. The work was finished in 1880.

England is rich in memorials of mediæval architecture which began with the arrival of the Normans. The nation's life is interwoven with them, and Westminster Abbey is perhaps the most august place of sepulture in the world. In addition to the cathedrals already mentioned, Lincoln, Canterbury, York, Salisbury, and other great churches were begun in this period. Addition after addition was made till the noble churches of England got their final shape. The tower is one of the prominent features of the English cathedral, Lichfield being probably the most important with spires. The finest outside impression is made by Salisbury and Lincoln minsters. Many of these cathedrals were built by Benedictine monks, such as Canterbury, Durham, Ely, and Norwich, and by the canons regular of St. Augustine, as Carlisle and Bristol. Lincoln, Chichester, Salisbury, York, St. David's, and others were served by secular priests.

The architects of Scotland seem to have come from England and to have built after English models. The noblest of her mediæval churches are Glasgow, St. Andrews, Dumblane, and Elgin, and among her convents, Kelso, Dryburgh, Holyrood, and Melrose.

In Spain, great minsters at Toledo, Burgos, and other cities were built in Gothic style in the thirteenth century, and Seville, which offers the largest floor surface of all the Christian churches, and is also of the same type, was begun in 1401 and completed 1520.

In Italy, Gothic was never fully at home. The cathedrals of Milan, Florence, and Siena are regarded as its finer specimens. Siena was begun in 1243. The minster of Milan was not begun till 1385. It is the largest Christian church after Seville and St. Peter's. Its west façade is out of accord with the rest of the structure, which is pure Gothic. It is built of white marble and soars up to the clouds in hundreds of spires. Within full sight of the Milan cathedral are the Alps, crowned with snow and elevated far above the din of human traffic and voices; and in comparison with those mightier cathedrals of God, the creations of man seem small even as man himself seems small in comparison with his Maker.

CHAPTER XII.

SCHOLASTIC AND MYSTIC THEOLOGY.

§ 95. *Literature and General Introduction.*

LITERATURE: I. — The works of ANSELM, ABÆLARD, PETER THE LOMBARD, HUGO OF ST. VICTOR, ALBERTUS MAGNUS, THOMAS AQUINAS, BONAVENTURA, DUNS SCOTUS, and other Schoolmen.

II. — R. D. HAMPDEN (bishop of Hereford, d. 1868): *The Scholastic Philos. considered in its Relation to Christ. Theol.*, Bampton Lectures, Oxf., 1832, 3d ed. 1848. — B. HAUREAU: *De la philos. scholast.*, 2 vols. Paris, 1850. — W. KAULICH: *Gesch. d. scholast. Philos.*, Prag, 1863. — C. PRANTL: *Gesch. d. Logik im Abendlande*, 4 vols. Leip., 1861-1870. — F. D. MAURICE (d. 1872): *Med. Philos.*, London, 1870. — *A. STÖCKL (Rom. Cath.): *Gesch. d. Philos. d. Mittelalters*, Mainz, 3 vols. 1864-1866. Vol. I. covers the beginnings of Scholasticism from Isidore of Seville to Peter the Lombard; Vol. II., the period of its supremacy; Vol. III., the period of its decline down to Jesuitism and Jansenism. — H. REUTER (Prof. of Ch. Hist. at Göttingen, d. 1889): *Gesch. d. rel. Aufklärung im Mittelalter*, 2 vols. Berlin, 1875-1877. Important for the sceptical and rationalistic tendencies of the M. A. — TH. HARPER: *The Metaphysics of the School*, London, 1880. — K. WERNER (Rom. Cath.): *D. Scholastik des späteren Mittelalters*, 4 vols. Wien, 1881-1887. Begins with DUNS SCOTUS. — The relevant chapters in the *Histories of Doctrine*, by HARNACK, LOOFS, FISHER, SEEBERG, SHELDON, and the Rom. Cath. divines, and J. BACH: *Dogmengesch. d. Mittelalters*, 2 vols. 1873-1875, and *J. SCHWANE: *Dogmengesch. d. mittleren Zeit*, 1882. — The *Histories of Philos.* by RITTER, ERDMANN, UEBERWEG-HEINZE, and *Scholasticism*, by PROF. SETH, in *Enc. Brit.* XXI. 417-431.

SCHOLASTICISM is the term given to the theology of the Middle Ages. It forms a distinct body of speculation, as do the works of the Fathers and the writings of the Reformers. The Fathers worked in the quarries of Scripture and, in conflict with heresy, wrought out, one by one, its teachings into dogmatic statements. The Schoolmen collected, analyzed and systematized these dogmas and argued their reasonableness against all conceivable objections. The Reformers, throwing off the yoke of human authority, and disparaging

the Schoolmen, returned to the fountain of Scripture, and
restated its truths.

The leading peculiarities of Scholasticism are that it subjected the reason to Church authority and sought to prove
the dogmas of the Church independently by dialectics. As for
the Scriptures, the Schoolmen accepted their authority and
show an extensive acquaintance with their pages from Genesis
to Revelation. With a rare exception, like Abælard, they
also accepted implicitly the teaching of the Fathers as
accurately reflecting the Scriptures. A distinction was
made by Alexander of Hales and others between the Scriptures which were treated as truth, *veritas*, and the teaching of the Fathers, which was treated as authority,
auctoritas.

It was not their concern to search in the Scriptures for
new truth or in any sense to reopen the investigation of the
Scriptures. The task they undertook was to confirm
what they had inherited. For this reason they made no
original contributions to exegesis and biblical theology.
They did not pretend to have discovered any new dogmas.
They were purveyors of the dogma they had inherited from
the Fathers.

It was the aim of the Schoolmen to accomplish two things, —
to reconcile dogma and reason, and to arrange the doctrines
of the Church in an orderly system called *summa theologiæ*.
These systems, like our modern encyclopædias, were intended
to be exhaustive. It is to the credit of the human mind that
every serious problem in the domains of religion and ethics
was thus brought under the inspection of the intellect. The
Schoolmen, however, went to the extreme of introducing into
their discussions every imaginable question, — questions
which, if answered, would do no good except to satisfy a
prurient curiosity. Anselm gives the best example of treatises on distinct subjects, such as the existence of God, the
necessity of the Incarnation, and the fall of the devil. Peter
the Lombard produced the most clear, and Thomas Aquinas
the most complete and finished systematic bodies of divinity.

With intrepid confidence these busy thinkers ventured

upon the loftiest speculations, raised and answered all sorts
of doubts and ran every accepted dogma through a fiery ordeal to show its invulnerable nature.   They were the knights
of theology, its Godfreys and Tancreds.   Philosophy with
them was their handmaid, — *ancilla*, — dialectics their sword
and lance.

In a rigid dialectical treatment, the doctrines of Christianity are in danger of losing their freshness and vital power,
and of being turned into a theological corpse.   This result
was avoided in the case of the greatest of the mediæval
theologians by their religious fervor. Anselm, Thomas Aquinas, and Bonaventura were men of warm piety and, like
Augustine, they combined with the metaphysical element a
mystical element, with the temper of speculation the habit of
meditation and prayer.

He is far from the truth who imagines the mediæval
speculations to be mere spectacular balloonings, feats of intellectual acrobatism.   They were, on the contrary, serious
studies pursued with a solemn purpose.   The Schoolmen
were moved with a profound sense of the presence of God
and the sacrifice of the cross, and such treatments as the
ethical portions of Thomas Aquinas' writings show deep interest in the sphere of human conduct.   For this reason, as
well as for the reason that they stand for the theological
literature of more than two centuries, these writings live,
and no doubt will continue to live.[1]

Following Augustine, the Schoolmen started with the
principle that faith precedes knowledge — *fides præcedit intellectum*.   Or, as Anselm also put it, " I believe that I may
understand ; I do not understand that I may believe " *credo
ut intelligam, non intelligo ut credam*.   They quoted as proof
text, Isa. 7: 9.   " If ye will not believe, surely ye shall

---

[1] 1. Milman, *Hist. of Lat. Christianity*, VIII. 257, is certainly unjust when
he says : " With all their search into the unfathomable, the Schoolmen have
fathomed nothing ; with all their vast logical apparatus, they have proved
nothing to the satisfaction of the inquisitive mind."   One has only to think of
the ontological argument of Anselm and the cosmological arguments of
Thomas Aquinas and the statements wrought out on the satisfaction of Christ
to feel that the statement is not true.

not be established." Abælard was an exception, and reversed
the order, making knowledge precede faith ; but all
arrived at the same result. Revelation and reason, faith and
science, theology and philosophy agree, for they proceed
from the one God who cannot contradict himself.

In addition to the interest which attaches to Scholasticism
as a distinct body of intellectual effort, is its importance as
the ruling theology in the Roman Catholic Church to this
day.   Such dogmas as the treatment of heresy, the supremacy of the Church over the State, the immaculate conception,
and the seven sacraments, as stated by the Schoolmen, are
still binding, or at any rate, they have not been formally
renounced.   Leo XIII. bore fresh witness to this when, in his
encyclical of Aug. 4, 1879, he pronounced the theology of
Thomas Aquinas the standard of Catholic orthodoxy, and the
safest guide of Christian philosophy in the battle of faith
with the scepticism of the nineteenth century.

The Scholastic systems, like all the distinctive institutions
and movements of the Middle Ages, were on an imposing
scale.   The industry of their authors cannot fail to excite
amazement.   Statement follows statement with tedious but
consequential necessity and precision until chapter is added
to chapter and tome is piled upon tome, and the subject
has been looked at in every possible aspect and been exhausted.   Duns Scotus produced thirteen folio volumes, and
perhaps died when he was only thirty-four.   The volumes
of Albertus Magnus are still more extensive.   These theological systems are justly compared with the institution of
the mediæval papacy, and the creations of Gothic architecture, imposing, massive, and strongly buttressed.   The
papacy subjected all kingdoms to its divine authority.
Architecture made all materials and known mechanical arts
tributary to worship.   The Schoolmen used all the forces of
logic and philosophy to vindicate the orthodox system of
theology, but they used much wood and straw in their
constructions, as the sounder exegesis and more scriptural
theology of the Reformers and these later days have
shown.

§ 96. *Sources and Development of Scholasticism.*

The chief feeders of Scholasticism were the writings of Augustine and Aristotle. The former furnished the matter, the latter the form ; the one the dogmatic principles, the other the dialectic method.

The Augustine, who ruled the thought of the Middle Ages, was the churchly, sacramentarian, anti-Manichæan, and anti-Donatist theologian. It was the same Augustine, and yet another, to whom Luther and Calvin appealed for their doctrines of sin and grace. How strange that the same mighty intellect who helped to rear the structure of Scholastic divinity should have aided the Reformers in pulling it down and rearing another structure, at once more Scriptural and better adapted to the practical needs of life!

Aristotle was, in the estimation of the Middle Ages, the master philosophical thinker. The Schoolmen show their surpassing esteem for him in calling him again and again "the philosopher." Dante excluded both him and Virgil as pagans from paradise and purgatory and placed them in the vestibule of the inferno, where, however, they are exempt from actual suffering. Aristotle was regarded as a forerunner of Christian truth, a John the Baptist in method and knowledge of natural things — *precursor Christi in naturalibus.* Until the thirteenth century, his works were only imperfectly known. The *Categories* and the *de interpretatione* were known to Abælard and other Schoolmen in the Latin version of Boethius, and three books of the *Organon* to John of Salisbury. His *Physics* and *Metaphysics* became known about 1200, and all his works were made accessible early in the thirteenth century through the mediation of the Arab philosophers, Avicenna, d. 1037, Averrhoes, d. 1198, and Abuacer, d. 1185, and through Jewish sources. Roger Bacon laments the mistakes of translations made from the Arabic, by Michael Scot, Gerard of Cremona, and others.[1]

---

[1] See Roger Bacon : *Opus Majus*, Bridges' ed. I. 54–56 ; Sandys, *Class. Scholarship*, pp. 507, 540–546, 568–sqq., and Seth, *Enc. Brit.*, XXI. 419.

At first the Stagyrite was looked upon with suspicion or even prohibited by the popes and synods as adapted to breed heresy and spiritual pride.[1]   But, from 1250 on, his authority continued supreme.   The saying of Gottfried of St. Victor became current in Paris.

> Every one is excluded and banned
> Who does not come clad in Aristotle's armor.[2]

The Reformers shook off his yoke and Luther, in a moment of temper at the degenerate Schoolmen of his day, denounced him as "the accursed pagan Aristotle" and in his *Babylonish Captivity* called the mediæval Church "the Thomistic or Aristotelian Church."

The line of the Schoolmen begins in the last year of the eleventh century with Roscellinus and Anselm.   Two centuries before, John Scotus Erigena had anticipated some of their discussions of fundamental themes, and laid down the principle that true philosophy and true religion are one. But he does not seem to have had any perceptible influence on Scholastic thought.   The history divides itself into three periods: the rise of Scholasticism, its full bloom, and its decline.[3]   To the first period belong Anselm, d. 1109, Roscellinus, d. about 1125, Abælard, d. 1142, Bernard, d. 1153, Hugo de St. Victor, d. 1161, Richard of St. Victor, d. 1173, and Gilbert of Poictiers, d. 1154,   The chief names of the second period are Peter the Lombard, d. 1160, Alexander of Hales, d. 1243, Albertus Magnus, d. 1280, Thomas Aquinas, d. 1274, Bonaventura, d. 1274, Roger Bacon, d. 1294, and Duns Scotus, d. 1308.   To the period of decline belong, among others, Durandus, d. 1334, Bradwardine,

---

[1] The council of Paris, 1209, forbade the use of his *Natural Philosophy*. Gregory IX., 1231, condemned the *Physics*, but in 1254 the University of Paris prescribed the number of hours to be devoted to the explanation of Aristotle's works.

[2] *Omnis hic excluditur, omnis est abjectus.*
Qui non Aristotelis venit armis tectus.   Chart., I. p. xviii.

[3] Cousin made three periods, the first when philosophy was in subjection to theology, the second when they were in union, and the third when they were separated.

d. 1349, and Ockam, d. 1367.   England, France, Germany, Italy, and Spain made contributions to this galaxy of men. Gabriel Biel, professor at Tübingen, who died 1495, is usually called the last of the Schoolmen.   Almost all the great Schoolmen were monks.

The two centuries included between the careers of Anselm and Duns Scotus show decided modifications of opinion on important questions such as the immaculate conception, and in regard to the possibility of proving from pure reason such doctrines as the incarnation and the Trinity.   These two doctrines Thomas Aquinas, as well as Duns Scotus and Ockam, declared to be outside the domain of pure ratiocination.   Even the existence of God and the immortality of the soul came to be regarded by Duns Scotus and the later Schoolmen as mysteries which were to be received solely upon the authority of the Church.   The argument from probability was emphasized in the last stages of Scholastic thought as it had not been before.

In their effort to express the minutest distinctions of thought, the Schoolmen invented a new vocabulary unknown to classical Latin, including such words as *ens, absolutum identitas, quidditas, hœcceitas, aliquiditas, aleitas*.[1]   The sophistical speculations which they allowed themselves were, for the most part, concerned with the angels, the Virgin Mary, the devil, the creation, and the body of the resurrection.   Such questions as the following were asked and most solemnly discussed by the leading Schoolmen.   Albertus Magnus asked whether it was harder for God to create the universe than to create man and whether the understandings of angels are brighter in the morning or in the evening.   " Who sinned most, Adam or Eve ? " was a favorite question with Anselm, Hugo de St. Victor,[2] and others.   Alexander of Hales attempted to settle the hour of the day at which Adam sinned and, after a long discussion, concluded it was at the ninth hour, the hour at which Christ expired.   Bonaventura debated whether several angels can be in one place

---

[1] " Otherness," applied by Rich. de St. Victor to the Trinitarian distinctions.

[2] *de sacram.*, I. 7 ; Migne's ed., 176, 290.

2 Q

at the same time, whether one angel can be in several places at the same time, and whether God loved the human race more than He loved Christ.[1] Anselm, in his work on the Trinity, asked whether God could have taken on the female sex and why the Holy Spirit did not become incarnate. Of the former question, Walter of St. Victor, speaking of Peter the Lombard, very sensibly said that it would have been more rational for him to have asked why the Lombard did not appear on earth as an ass than for the Lombard to ask whether God could have become incarnate in female form. The famous discussion over the effect the eating of the host would have upon a mouse will be taken up in connection with the Lord's Supper. Albertus Magnus, Bonaventura, Thomas Aquinas, and others pondered over the problem. It was asked by Robert Pullen whether man in the resurrection will receive back the rib he lost in Eden, and whether a man will recover all the clippings of his finger nails.

Such endless discussions have been ridiculed as puerile and frivolous, though, as has already been said, they grew out of the desire to be exhaustive. At last and justly, they brought Scholasticism into disrepute. While it was losing itself in the clouds and mists of things transcendental, it neglected the earth at its feet. As the papacy passed sentence upon itself by intolerable ambition, so Scholasticism undermined its authority by intellectual sophistries and was set aside by the practical interests of the Renaissance and Humanism and by simple faith, searching through the Scriptures, to reach the living sympathy of Christ.[2]

§ 97. *Realism and Nominalism.*

The underlying philosophical problem of the Scholastic speculations was the real and independent existence of general or generic concepts, called *universalia* or universals. Do they necessarily involve substantial being? On this ques-

[1] Peltier's ed., V. 38.

[2] Thomas Fuller quaintly compared the Schoolmen to those who built their houses in London on small patches of ground " improving their small bottom with towering speculations."

tion the Schoolmen were divided into two camps, the Realists
and the Nominalists.[1] The question, which receives little
attention now, was regarded as most important in the Middle Ages.

Realism taught that the universals are not mere generalizations of the mind but have a real existence. Following
Plato, as he is represented by Aristotle, one class of Realists
held that the universals are creative types, exemplars in the
divine mind. Their view was stated in the expression — *universalia ante rem* — that is, the universals exist before the individual, concrete object. The Aristotelian Realists held that
the universals possess a real existence, but exist only in individual things. This was the doctrine of *universalia in re.*
Humanity, for example, is a universal having a real existence.
Socrates partakes of it, and he is an individual man, distinct
from other men. Anselm, representing the Platonic school,
treated the universal humanity as having independent existence by itself. Duns Scotus, representing the second theory,
found in the universal the basis of all classification and gives
to it only in this sense a real existence.

The Nominalists taught that universals or general conceptions have no antecedent existence. They are mere names —
nomina, flatus vocis, voces — and are derived from a comparison
of individual things and their qualities. Thus beauty is a
conception of the mind gotten from the observation of objects which are beautiful. The individual things are first
observed and the universal, or abstract conception, is derived
from it. This doctrine found statement in the expression
universalia post rem, the universal becomes known after the
individual. A modification of this view went by the name
of Conceptualism, or the doctrine that universals have existence as conceptions in the mind, but not in real being.[2]

[1] H. Doergens, *Lehre von d. Universalien*, Heidelb., 1867 ; J. H. Löwe,
D. Kampf zwischen d. Realismus und Nominalismus im Mittelalter, Prag,
1876. Art. "Universalien," in Wetzer-Welte, XII. 305 sqq. *The Histt. of
Philosophy.*

[2] According to John of Salisbury there were no less than thirteen different
shades of opinion on the subject. See Prantl, *Gesch. der Logik*, II. 118.

The starting-point for this dialectical distinction may have
been a passage in Porphyry's *Isagoge*, as transmitted by
Boethius. Declining to enter into a discussion of the question, Porphyry asks whether the universals are to be regarded
as having distinct substantial existence apart from tangible
things or whether they were only conceptions of the mind,
having substantial existence only in tangible things.[1] The
distinction assumed practical importance when it was applied
to such theological doctrines as the Trinity, the atonement,
and original sin.

The theory of Realism was called in question in the eleventh
century by Roscellinus, a contemporary of Anselm and the
teacher of Abælard, who, as it would seem, advocated Nominalism.[2] Our knowledge of his views is derived almost exclusively from the statements of his two opponents, Anselm
and Abælard. He was serving as canon of Compiegne in the
diocese of Soissons, 1092, when he was obliged to recant his
alleged tritheism, which he substituted for the doctrine of
the Trinity.

The views of this theologian called forth Anselm's treatise
on the Trinity, and Abælard despised him as a quack dialectician.[3] Anselm affirmed that Roscellinus' heretical views
on the Trinity were the immediate product of his false philosophical principle, the denial that universals have real existence. Roscellinus called the three persons of the Godhead
three substances, as Scotus Erigena had done before. These
persons were three distinct beings equal in power and will,

---

[1] The passage from Porphyry runs — *mox de generibus et speciebus illud
quidem sive subsistant, sive in solis nudis intellectibus posita sint, sive subsis-
tentia corporalia sint an incorporalia, et utrum separata a sensibilibus, an in-
sensibilibus posita et circa hæc consistentia, dicere recusabo. Altissimum
enim negotium est hujusmodi et majoris egens inquisitionis.* See Gieseler,
Ch. Hist., Germ. ed., III. 384.

[2] Otto of Freising, *de gest. Frid.*, I. 47, spoke of him as the originator of
Nominalism in that age, *qui primus nostris temporibus in logica sententiam
vocum instituit.* According to John of Salisbury, nominalism almost wholly
vanished with Roscellinus, *Metalog.*, II. 17.

[3] *Pseudo-Dialecticus. Ep.*, 21. *De fide trin.* 3. *tres personæ sunt tres res
sicut tres angeli aut tres animæ, ita tamen ut voluntas et potestas omnino sunt
idem.* Also *Ep.*, II. 41.

but each separate from the other and complete in himself, like three men or angels.   These three could not be one God in the sense of being of the same essence, for then the Father and the Holy Spirit would have had to become incarnate as well as the Son.

Defending the orthodox doctrine of the Trinity, Anselm proceeded on the basis of strict realism and declared that the three persons represented three relations and not three substances.   Fountain, brook, and pond are three ; yet the same water is in each one and we could not say the brook is the fountain or the fountain is the pond.   The water of the brook may be carried through a pipe, but in that case it would not be the fountain which was carried through, nor the pond.   So in the same way, the Godhead became incarnate without involving the incarnation of the Father and Holy Spirit.

The decision of the synod of Soissons and Anselm's argument drove Nominalism from the field and it was not again publicly avowed till the fourteenth century when it was revived by the energetic and practical mind of Ockam, by Durandus and others.   It was for a time fiercely combated by councils and King Louis XI., but was then adopted by many of the great teachers of the fourteenth and fifteenth centuries.

§ 98. *Anselm of Canterbury.*

LITERATURE : The *Works* of Anselm.   First complete ed. by GERBERON, Paris, 1675, reprinted in Migne, vols. 158, 159. — Anselm's *opuscula*, trans. Chicago, 1903, pp. 288. — Anselm's *Devotions*, trans. by Pusey, Oxf., 1856, London, 1872, and by C. C. J. Webb., London, 1903. — Trans. of *Cur Deus homo* in *Anc. and Mod. Library*, London. — The *Life* of Anselm by his secretary and devoted friend EADMER : *de vita Anselmi* and *Historia novorum* in Migne, and ed. by RULE in Rolls series, London, 1884. — JOHN OF SALISBURY'S *Life*, written to further Anselm's canonization by Alexander III., Migne, 199 : 1009–1040, is based upon Eadmer.— WILLIAM OF MALMESBURY in *Gesta Pontificum* adds some materials. — *Modern Lives*, by * F. R. HASSE, 2 vols. Leip., 1843–1852, Abrdg. trans. by * W .TURNER, London, 1850.   One of the best of hist. monographs. — *C. DE REMUSAT : Paris, 1853, last ed., 1868. — *DEAN R. W. CHURCH (d. 1890) : London, new ed., 1877 (good account of Anselm's career, but pays little attention to his philosophy and theology). — M. RULE : 2 vols. London, 1883,

eulogistic and ultramontane. — P. RAGEY: 2 vols. Paris, 1890. — J. M.
RIGG : London, 1896. — A. C. WELCH, Edinburgh, 1901. — *W. R. W.
STEPHENS in *Dict. Natl. Biog.*, II. 10–31. — P. SCHAFF, in *Presb. and
Ref'd Review*, Jan., 1894. — *ED. A. FREEMAN: *The Reign of William
Rufus*, 2 vols. London, 1882. — H. BÖHMER: *Kirche u. Staat in England
u. in der Normandie im XI. u. XIIten Jahrh.*, Leip., 1899. — Anselm's
philosophy is discussed by RITTER, ERDMANN, and UEBERWEG-HEINZE in
their Histories of Philos.; his theology is treated by BAUR: *Gesch. d.
Christl. Lehre. von d. Versöhnung, Tübingen*, 1838, 142–189. — RITSCHL :
Rechtfertigung u. Versöhnung, and in the Histories of Doctrine. —
KÖLLING: *D. satisfactio vicaria*, 2 vols., Gütersloh, 1897–1899. A vigorous presentation of the Anselmic view. — LEIPOLDT : *D. Begriff
meritum in Anselm*, in *Theol. Studien u. Kritiken*, 1904. — LE CHAN-
OINE PORÉE : *Hist. de l'Abbaye du Bec*, Paris, 1901.

Anselm of Canterbury, 1033–1109, the first of the great
Schoolmen, was one of the ablest and purest men of the
mediæval Church. He touched the history of his age at
many points. He was an enthusiastic advocate of monasticism. He was archbishop of Canterbury and fought the battle of the Hildebrandian hierarchy against the State in England. His Christian meditations give him a high rank in
its annals of piety. His profound speculation marks one
of the leading epochs in the history of theology and won for
him a place among the doctors of the Church. While
Bernard was greatest as a monk, Anselm was greatest as a
theologian. He was the most original thinker the Church
had seen since the days of Augustine.[1]

Life. — Anselm was born at Aosta, in Piedmont, at the
foot of the great St. Bernard, which divides Italy from
western Switzerland.[2] He had a pious mother, Ermenberga.
His father, Gundulf, a worldly and rude nobleman, set himself violently against his son's religious aspirations, but on
his death-bed himself assumed the monastic garb to escape
perdition.

In his childish imagination, Anselm conceived God Al-

---

[1] Loofs, p. 271, says, " He is perhaps the most important of all the mediæval
theologians."

[2] Church gives a graphic picture of " wild Aosta lulled by Alpine rills."
Aosta was a Roman settlement bearing the name Augusta Prætoria, and was
made a bishopric about the fifth century.

mighty as seated on a throne at the top of the Alps, and in a dream, he climbed up the mountain to meet Him. Seeing, on his way, the king's maidens engaged in the harvest field, for it was Autumn, neglecting their work he determined to report their negligence to the king. The lad was most graciously received and asked whence he came and what he desired. The king's kindness made him forget all about the charges he was intending to make. Then, refreshed with the whitest of bread, he descended again to the valley. The following day he firmly believed he had actually been in heaven and eaten at the Lord's table. This was the story he told after he had ascended the chair of Canterbury.

A quarrel with his father led to Anselm's leaving his home. He set his face toward the West and finally settled in the Norman abbey of Le Bec, then under the care of his illustrious countryman Lanfranc. Here he studied, took orders, and, on Lanfranc's transfer to the convent of St. Stephen at Caen, 1063, became prior, and, in 1078, abbot. At Bec he wrote most of his works. His warm devotion to the monastic life appears in his repeated references to it in his letters and in his longing to get back to the convent after he had been made archbishop.

In 1093, he succeeded Lanfranc as archbishop of Canterbury. His struggle with William Rufus and Henry I. over investiture has already been described (pp. 88–93). During his exile on the Continent he attended a synod at Bari, where he defended the Latin doctrine of the procession of the Holy Spirit against the Greek bishops who were present.[1]

The archbishop's last years in England were years of quiet, and he had a peaceful end. They lifted him from the bed and placed him on ashes on the floor. There, "as morning was breaking, on the Wednesday before Easter," April 21, 1109, the sixteenth year of his pontificate and the seventy-sixth of his life, he slept in peace, as his biographer Eadmer says, "having given up his spirit into the hands of

---

[1] His views were set forth in the *de processione Spiritus Sancti.* He argued that the Spirit proceeded from the Father not as father but as God. He must therefore also proceed from the Son as God.

his Creator." He lies buried in Canterbury Cathedral at the side of Lanfranc.

Anselm was a man of spotless integrity, single devotion to truth and righteousness, patient in suffering, and revered as a saint before his official canonization in 1494.[1] Dante associates him in Paradise with Nathan, the seer, and Chrysostom, both famous for rebuking vice in high places, and with the Calabrian prophet, Joachim.[2]

Writings. — Anselm's chief works in the departments of theology are his *Monologium* and *Proslogium*, which present proofs for God's existence, and the *Cur Deus homo*, "Why God became Man," a treatise on the atonement. He also wrote on the Trinity against Roscellinus ; on original sin, free will, the harmony of foreknowledge and foreordination, and the fall of the devil. To these theological treatises are to be added a number of writings of a more practical nature, homilies, meditations, and four hundred and twelve letters in which we see him in different relations, as a prelate of the Church, a pastor, as a teacher giving advice to pupils, and as a friend.[3] His correspondence shows him in his human relations. His meditations and prayers reveal the depth of his piety. His theological treatises betray the genius of his intellect. In extent they are far less voluminous than the works of Thomas Aquinas and other Schoolmen of the later period.

Theology. — Anselm was one of those rare characters in whom lofty reason and childlike faith work together in perfect harmony. Love to God was the soul of his daily life and love to God is the burning centre of his theology. It was not doubt that led him to speculation, but enthusiasm for truth and devotion to God. His famous proposition, which Schleiermacher adopted as a motto for his own theology, is that faith precedes knowledge — *fides præcedit intellectum.* Things divine must be a matter of experience

---

[1] See quotations in Freeman, *W. Rufus*, II. 661.

[2] *Paradiso*, XII. 137.

[3] Freeman has an excursus on Anselm's letters in his *W. Rufus*, II. 570-588.

before they can be comprehended by the intellect.   " He
who does not believe," Anselm said, " has not felt, and he
who has not felt, does not understand." [1]   Christ must come
to the intellect through the avenue of faith and not to faith
through the avenue of intellect.[2]   On the other hand, Anselm
declared himself against blind belief, and calls it a sin of
neglect when he who has faith, does not strive after knowledge.[3]

These views, in which supernaturalism and rationalism
are harmonized, form the working principle of the Anselmic
theology.   The two sources of knowledge are the Bible and
the teaching of the Church which are in complete agreement
with one another and are one with true philosophy.[4]   Anselm
had a profound veneration for the great African teacher,
Augustine, and his agreement with him in spirit and method
secured for him the titles " the second Augustine " and the
" Tongue of Augustine."

Anselm made two permanent contributions to theology,
his argument for the existence of God and his theory of the
atonement.

The ontological argument, which he stated, constitutes
an epoch in the history of the proofs for God's existence.
It was first laid down in the *Monologium* or *Soliloquy*, which
he called the example of meditation on the reasonableness
of faith, but mixed with cosmological elements.   Starting
from the idea that goodness and truth must have an existence independent of concrete things, Anselm ascends from
the conception of what is relatively good and great, to Him
who is absolutely good and great.

In the *Proslogium*, or *Allocution*, the ontological argument
is presented in its purest form.   Anselm was led to its
construction by the desire to find out a single argument,

---

[1] *Qui non crediderit, non experietur, et qui expertus non fuerit non in-
telliget, de fide trin.*, 2; Migne, 158, 264.

[2] *Ep.*, II. 41 ; Migne, 158. 1193, *Christianus per fidem debet ad intellectum
proficere non per intellectum ad fidem.*

[3] *Cur Deus homo*, I. 2 ; Migne, 158. 364.

[4] Eadmer: *nihil asserere nisi quod aut canonicis aut Augustini dictis
posse defendi videret.*

sufficient in itself, to prove the divine existence. The
argument was the result of long reflection and rooted in
piety and prayer. Day and night the author was haunted
with the idea that God's existence could be so proved.
He was troubled over it to such a degree that at times he
could not sleep or take his meals. Finally, one night, during vigils, the argument stood clearly before his mind in
complete outline. The notes were written down while the
impression was still fresh in Anselm's mind. The first copy
was lost; the second was inadvertently broken to pieces.

Anselm's argument, which is the highest example of
religious meditation and scholastic reasoning, is prefaced
with an exhortation and the words, "I do not seek to
understand in order that I may believe, but I believe in
order that I may understand, for of this I feel sure, that,
if I did not believe, I would not understand."

The reasoning starts from the idea the mind has of God,
and proceeds to the affirmation of the necessity of God's objective existence. The mind has a concept of something
than which nothing greater can be conceived.[1] This even
the fool has, when he says in his heart, "there is no God,"
Ps. 14 : 1. He grasps the conception when he listens, and
what he grasps is in his mind. This something, than which
nothing greater can be conceived, cannot exist solely in the
mind. For, if it existed solely in the mind, then it would
be possible to think of it as existing also in reality (objec-
tively), and that would be something greater.[2] This is
impossible. This thing, therefore, than which nothing
greater can be conceived, exists both in the mind and in
reality. This is God. "So truly," exclaims Anselm, "dost
Thou exist, O Lord God, that it is not possible to conceive
of Thee as not existing. For, if any mind could conceive
of anything better than Thou art, then the creature would
ascend above the Creator and become His judge, which is
supremely absurd. Everything else besides Thyself can
be conceived of as not existing."

[1] .aliquid quo majus nihil cogitari potest.

[2] si vel in solo intellectu est, potest cogitari esse et in re, quod majus est.

The syllogism, compact as its presentation is and precise as its language seems to be, is nevertheless defective, as a logical statement. It begs the question. It offends against the principle that deductions from a definition are valid only on the supposition that the thing defined exists. The definition and the statement of God's existence are in the major premise, "there is something than which nothing greater can be conceived." And yet it was the objective existence of this being, Anselm wanted to prove. Setting this objection aside, there is the other fatal objection that objective existence is not a predicate. Objective being is implied when we affirm anything. This objection was stated by Kant.[1] Again, Anselm confused, as synonymous, understanding a thing and having a conception in the understanding.[2]

The reasoning of the *Proslogium* was attacked by the monk Gaunilo of Marmontier, near Bec, in his *Liber pro insipiente*. He protested against the inference from the subjective conception to objective reality on the ground that by the same method we might argue from any of our conceptions to the reality of the thing conceived, as for example for the existence of a lost island, the Atlantis. "That, than which nothing greater can be thought," does not exist in the mind in any other way than does the perfection of such an island. The real existence of a thing must be known before we can predicate anything of it. Gaunilo's objection Anselm answered by declaring that the idea of the lost island was not a necessary conception while that of the highest

---

[1] Thomas Aquinas said that, even if the name of God means *illud quo majus cogitari non potest*, yet it would not be possible to proceed to the affirmation of God's real existence, because the atheist denies that there is *aliquid quo majus cogitari non potest*, *Summa*, I. ii. 2. Hegel replied to Kant that the *Begriff an und für sich selbst enthält das Sein also eine Bestimmtheit*. Professor E. Caird, in an article, *Anselm's Argument for the Being of God* (*Journal of Theolog. Studies*, 1900, pp. 23–39), sums up his objection to Anselm's argument by saying, "It is the scholastic distortion of an idea which was first presented in the Platonic philosophy," etc. Ritschl, *Justification and Reconciliation*, p. 217, makes the same objection when he says Anselm confuses reality and thought.

[2] *intelligere* and *in intellectu esse*.

being was, and that it was to it alone his argument
applied.

Untenable as Anselm's argument is logically, it possesses
a strong fascination, and contains a great truth. The being
of God is an intuition of the mind, which can only be explained by God's objective existence. The modern theory of
correlation lends its aid to corroborate what was, after all,
fundamental in the Anselmic presentation, namely, that the
idea of God in the mind must have corresponding to it a
God who really exists. Otherwise, we are left to the mystery
which is perhaps still greater, how such an idea could ever
have taken firm and general hold of the human mind.[1]

The doctrine of the atonement.—With the *Cur Deus homo*,
" Why God became Man," a new chapter opens in the development of the doctrine of the atonement. The treatise,
which is in the form of a dialogue, is the author's most elaborate work, and he thought the argument sufficient to break
down the objections of Jew and Pagan to the Christian system.

Anselm was the first to attempt to prove the necessity of
the incarnation and death of the Son of God by the processes
of pure reason. He argued that the world cannot be redeemed by an arbitrary decree of God, nor through man or
angel. Man is under the domination of the devil, deserves
punishment, and is justly punished; but the devil torments
him without right,[2] for he does not do it by the authority of
God, but from malice. The handwriting of ordinances against
the sinner (Col. 2 : 14) is not a note due the devil, but the sentence of God that he who sinned should be the servant of sin.

---

[1] A careful statement of the history of the ontological argument was
given by Köstlin, *D. Beweise fürs Dasein Gottes*, in *Studien u. Kritiken*, 1875,
1876.   Also Ruze, *D. ontol. Gottesbeweis seit Anselm*, Halle, 1882.

[2] *Quamvis homo juste a diabolo torqueretur, ipse tamen illum injuste
torquebat*, etc., I. 7 ; Migne, 158. 367 sq.   Again Anselm takes up this point,
II. 20; p. 427 sq., and says it was not necessary for God to descend to conquer
the devil or to proceed judicially against him in order to liberate man.
Nothing else did God owe the devil but punishment, and nothing else did
man owe the devil but to treat him as he had been treated, that is, to
conquer him as man himself had been conquered.   All that was demanded by
the devil, man owed to God and not to the devil.

God cannot allow his original purpose to be thwarted. Sin must be forgiven, but how ? Man owes subjection to God's will.   Sin is denying to God the honor due him.[1] Satisfaction must be rendered to justice before there can be forgiveness.   Bare restitution, however, is not a sufficient satisfaction.   For his "contumely," man must give back more than he has taken. He must compensate God's honor.[2] Just as he who has inflicted a wound must not only heal the wound, but pay damages to satisfy the demands of violated honor.

All sin, then, must either receive punishment or be covered by satisfaction.   Can man make this satisfaction?   No. Were it possible for him to lead a perfectly holy life, from the moment he became conscious of his debt, he would be simply doing his duty for that period.   The debt of the past would remain unsettled. But sin, having struck at the roots of man's being, he is not able to lead a perfect life.

God's justice, then, man is not able to satisfy.   Man ought, but cannot.   God need not, but does.   For, most foreign to God would it be to allow man, the most precious of his creatures, to perish.   But as God himself must make the satisfaction, and man ought to make it, the satisfaction must be made by one who is both God and man, that is, the God-man.[3]

To make satisfaction, the God-man must give back to God something he is not under obligation to render.   A life of perfect obedience he owes.   Death he does not owe, for death is the wages of sin, and he had no sin.   By submitting to death, he acquired merit.   Because this merit is infinite in value, being connected with the person of the infinite Son of God, it covers the infinite guilt of the sinner and constitutes the satisfaction required.

[1] *Non aliud est peccare quam Deo non reddere debitum* I. 11; Migne, p. 376.

[2] *pro contumelia illata plus reddere quam abstulit. . . . Debet omnis qui peccat, honorem quem rapuit, Deo solvere et hæc est satisfactio quam omnis peccator Deo debet facere.*

[3] *Satisfactio quam nec potest facere nisi Deus nec debet nisi homo, necesse est ut eam faciat Deus-homo,* II. 6; Migne, p. 404.

Anselm concludes his treatise with the inquiry why the
devil and his angels are not saved by Christ. His answer is
that they did not derive their guilt and sinful estate through
a single individual as men do from Adam. Each sinned for
himself. For this reason each would have to be saved for
himself by a God-angel. In declaring the salvation of fallen
angels to be impossible, Anselm closes with the words, "I do
not say that this is impossible as though the value of Christ's
death were not great enough to be sufficient for all the sins
of men and fallen angels, but because of a reason in the un-
changeable nature of things which stands in the way of the
salvation of the lost angels." [1]

It is the merit of Anselm's argument that, while Athanasius
and Augustine had laid stress upon the article that through
Christ's sufferings atonement was made, Anselm explained
the necessity of those sufferings. He also did the most valuable service of setting aside the view, which had been handed
down from the Fathers, that Christ's death was a ransom-price
paid to Satan. Even Augustine had asserted the rights
of the devil. Again, Anselm laid proper stress upon the guilt
of sin. He made earnest with it, not as a mistake, but as a
violation of law, a derogation from the honor due to God.

The subject of the atonement was not exhausted by the
argument of the *Cur Deus homo*. No one theory can com-
prehend its whole meaning. Certain biblical features have
been made prominent since his day which Anselm did not
emphasize. Each creative age has its own statement of theology, and now one aspect and now another aspect of the un-
changeable biblical truth is made prominent. The different
theories must be put into their proper places as fragments of
the full statement of truth. Anselm regarded the atonement

---

[1] II. 22; Migne, 158. 431. It is a matter of dispute how far Anselm drew
upon the doctrine of penance which had been handed down from the Fathers
or from the German law with its *Wehrgeld*, or debt of honor ; or whether he
drew upon them at all. It is probable that the Church's penitential system
had affected the chivalric idea of honor. Harnack, *Dogmengesch.*, III. 252
sq., and Ritschl, *Justification*, etc., p. 263, make the objection against Anselm's argument that it was based upon an "idea of God's justice which implies an equality in private rights between God and man."

from the legal rather than from the moral side of the divine
nature.   The attribute of justice is given a disproportionate
emphasis.   Man's relation to God is construed wholly as the relation of a subordinate to a superior.   The fatherhood of God
has no adequate recognition.   The actor in human redemption
is God, the sovereign and the judge.   Anselm left out John
3 : 16 and the Parable of the Prodigal Son.[1]

Anselm as a mystic. — In Anselm, mysticism was combined with scholasticism, pious devotion with lofty speculation, prayer with logical analysis.   His deeply spiritual
nature manifests itself in all his writings, but especially in
his strictly devotional works, his *Meditations and Prayers.*[2]
They are in danger of suffering neglect in the attention
given to Anselm's theological discussions.

The Schoolman's spiritual reflections abound in glowing
utterances from the inner tabernacle of his heart.   Now he
loses himself in the contemplation of the divine attributes,
now he laments over the deadness and waywardness of man.
Now he soars aloft in strains of praise and adoration, now
he whispers low the pleadings for mercy and pardon.   At
one moment he surveys the tragedy of the cross or the joys
of the redeemed ; at another the terrors of the judgment
and hopeless estate of the lost.   Such a blending of mellow
sentiment with high speculations is seldom found.   No one
of the greater personages of the Middle Ages, except Bernard, excels him in the mystical element ; and he often reminds us of Bernard, as when he exclaims, " O good Jesus,
how sweet thou art to the heart of him who thinks of thee

---

[1] Harnack gives prolonged attention to Anselm's argument (*Dogmengesch.,*
III. 341–358) and, in specifying its merits and defects, declares that the defects
largely outweigh the merits.   Anselm's theory is not at all to be adopted, *die
Theorie ist völlig unannehmbar.*   It would not be necessary, Harnack says,
to waste many words over the defects if it were not that the theology of the
present day is stuck in traditionalism and neglects all the canons of Gospel, —
ethics, logic, and culture.   He declares it to be a fearful thought that God may
not forgive from pure love, but had to have his honor appeased by sacrifice.
Anselm's argument taken by itself does not justify such severe criticism, and,
if his other writings and his own character be taken into account, he will be
absolved from the implied charges.

[2] *Meditationes seu Orationes,* Migne, 158. 709–1014.   See Hasse, I. 176–232.

and loves thee."[1]   Or again, when he exclaims in his tenth
meditation, " O benign Jesus, condescending Lord, holy Master, sweet in mouth, sweet in heart, sweet in ear, inscrutably,
unutterably gentle, self-sacrificing, merciful, wise, mighty,
most sweet and lovely "— *valde dulcis et suavis.* The soaring grandeur of Anselm's thoughts may be likened to the
mountains of the land of his birth, and the pure abundance
of his spiritual feeling to the brooks and meadows of its
valleys.   He quotes again and again from Scripture, and its
language constitutes the chief vehicle of his thoughts.

In the first meditation, Anselm makes the famous comparison of human life to the passage over a slender bridge,
spanning a deep, dark abyss whose bed is full of all kinds of
foul and ghastly things.[2]   The bridge is a single foot in
width.   What anguish would not take hold of one obliged
to cross over it, with eyes bandaged and arms tied, so as not
to be able even to use a staff to feel one's way !   And how
greatly would not the anguish be increased, if great birds
were flying in the air, intent on swooping down and defeating
the purpose of the traveller !   And how much more anguish
would be added if at every step a tile should fall away from
behind him !   The ravine is hell, measureless in its depth,
horribly dark with black, dismal vapors ![3]   And the perilous
bridge is the present life.   Whosoever lives ill falls into
the abyss.   The tiles are the single days of a man's existence
here below.   The birds are malign spirits.   We, the trav-
ellers, are blinded with ignorance and bound with the iron
difficulty of doing well.   Shall we not turn our eyes unto
the Lord " who is our light and our salvation, of whom shall
we be afraid"? Ps. 27. 1.

The Prayers are addressed to the Son and Spirit as well
as to the Father.   To these are added petitions to the Vir-

---

[1] *Jesu bone, quam dulcis es in corde cogitantis de te et diligentis te*, Migne,
158. 770.

[2] Rule, 1. 48, describes from personal observation the ancient and dizzy
bridge, le Pont de l'Aël, over a torrent near Aosta, which, as he says, Anselm
in making his description may have had in mind.

[3] *Sine mensura profundum, et tenebrosa caligine horribiliter obscurum*,
Migne, 158. 719.

gin, on whom Anselm bestows the most fulsome titles, and to the saints. In this Anselm was fully the child of his age. These devotional exercises, the liturgy of Anselm's soul, are a storehouse of pious thought to which due appreciation has not been accorded. The mystical element gives him a higher place than his theological treatises, elevated and important as they are.[1]

§ 99. Peter Abælard.

LITERATURE : *Works* of ABÆLARD : ed. first by DUCHESNE, Paris, 1616. — COUSIN: *Ouvrages inédites d'Abélard*, Paris, 1836, containing the *Dialectica* and *Sic et Non ;* also the *Opera omnia*, 2 vols. Paris, 1849–1859. Reprod. in Migne, vol. 178. — R. STÖLZLE : *De unitate et trinitate divina*, first ed., Freib. im Br., 1891. — Ed. of his *Letters* by R. RAWLINSON, Lond., 1718. — Engl. trans. of *Letters of Abælard and Heloise*, in Temple Classics. BIOGRAPHICAL: Abælard's Autobiography: *Hist. calamitatum*, in Migne, 178. 113–180. — BERENGAR: *Apologeticus contra Bernardum*, etc., in Migne, 178. 1856–1870. — Bernard's letters as quoted below. — OTTO OF FREISING : *De Gestis Frid.*, 47 sqq. — JOHN OF SALISBURY: *Metalog.* and *Hist. Pontificalis.* — Modern Lives by A. F. GERVAISE, Paris, 1728 ; COUSIN, in the *Ouvrages*, 1836 ; WILKINS, Göttingen, 1855 ; CH. DE RÉMUSAT, Paris, 1845, 2 vols., new ed., 1855 ; O. I. DE ROCHELY (*Abél. et le rationalisme moderne*), Paris, 1867 ; BONNIER (*Abél. et S. Bernard*), Paris, 1862 ; VACANDARD (*P. Abél. et sa lutte avec S. Bernard*), Paris, 1881 ; *S. M. DEUTSCH (*P. Abœl., ein kritischer Theologe des 12ten Jahrh.*, the best exposition of Abælard's system, Leip., 1883; A. HAUSRATH, Leip., 1893; JOSEPH MCCABE, London, 1901. — E. KAISER : *P. Abél. Critique*, Freib., 1901. — The story of Abælard and Heloise has been specially told by MAD. GUIZOT, 2 vols., Paris, 1839 ; JACOBI, Berl., 1850; WRIGHT, New York, 1853 ; KAHNIS, Leip., 1865, etc. — COMPAYRÉ, *Abél. and the Orig. and Early His. of Universities.* — R. L. POOLE : *P. Abailard* in *Illustrations of Med. Thought*, Lond., 1884, pp. 136–167. — STÖCKL : *Phil. des Mittelalters*, I. 218–272. — DENIFLE : *D. Sentenzen d. Abael. und die Bearbeitungen seiner Theologie vor Mitte des 12ten Jahrh.* in *Archiv für Lit. und Kirchengesch.*, etc., 1885, pp. 402–470, 584–624 ; HEFELE, *Councils*, V. 451–488. — The Histories of Philos. of UEBERWEG-HEINZE and RITTER. — The Lives of St. Bernard by NEANDER, I. 207–297 ; II. 1–44 ; MORISON, 254–322 ; VACANDARD, II. 120–181. — The Histories of Doctrine of SCHWANE, HARNACK, LOOFS, FISHER, SEEBERG, SHELDON.

---

[1] The later Schoolmen did not lean back upon Anselm's theology as we might have expected them to do. He was, however, often quoted, as by Thomas Aquinas and Albertus Magnus, *e.g.*, *Summa*, I. 3, 13, etc., Borgnet's ed., XXXI. 60, 69, 326.

2 R

During the first half of the twelfth century, Peter Abælard, 1079–1142, was one of the most conspicuous characters
of Europe. His fame was derived from the brilliance of his
intellect. He differed widely from Anselm. The latter was
a constructive theologian ; Abælard, a critic. Anselm was
deliberate, Abælard, impulsive and rash. Anselm preferred
seclusion ; Abælard sought publicity. Among teachers exercising the spell of magnetism over their hearers, Abælard stands in the front rank and probably has not been
excelled in France. In some of his theological speculations
he was in advance of his age. His personal misfortunes
give to his biography a flavor of romance which belongs to
no other Schoolman. A man of daring thought and
restless disposition, he was unstable in his mental beliefs
and morally unreliable. Our main authority for his
career is the *Story of Misfortunes, Historia calamitatum*,
written by his own hand, (Migne, 178. 113–180,) in the
form of a letter.

The eldest son of a knight, Abælard was born at the
village of Palais or le Pallet, a few miles from Nantes. His
original name was Pierre de Palais. Both his parents entered
convents. Abælard had for his first teacher Roscellinus.
He listened to William of Champeaux, then at the head of
the cathedral school at Paris, and soon began with confidence to refute William's positions.[1] He then established
independent schools at Melun and Corbeil. After a period
of sickness, spent under his father's roof, he returned to Paris.
He again listened to William on rhetoric, but openly announced himself as an antagonist of his views, and taught on
Mt. Genevieve, then covered with vineyards. Abælard represents himself as having drawn almost the last scholar away
from the cathedral school to Genevieve. We next find him
under Anselm of Laon, who, with his brother Radulf, had
made the school of Laon famous. Again Abælard set him-

---

[1] From this point and the enmity of William, he dates his misfortunes.
*Hinc calamitatum mearum quæ nunc perseverant coeperunt exordia et quo
amplius fama extendebatur nostra, aliena in me succensa est invidia,* Migne,
p. 116.

self up against his teacher, describing him as having a wonderful flow of words, but no thoughts.   When he lit a fire, he
filled the whole house with smoke.[1]   He was like the barren
fig tree with the promise of leaves and nothing more.
Abælard started at Laon counter lectures on Ezekiel.

Now the opportunity of his life came and he was called
to preside over the cathedral school at Paris.   William of
Champeaux had retired to St. Victor and then had been
made bishop.   The years that immediately followed were
the most brilliant in Abælard's career.   All the world seemed
about to do him homage.   Scholars from all parts thronged
to hear him.   He lectured on philosophy and theology.   He
was well read in classical and widely read in sacred literature.   His dialectic powers were ripe and, where arguments
failed, the teacher's imagination and rhetoric came to the
rescue.   His books were read not only in the schools and
convents, but in castles and guildhouses.   William of Thierry
said[2] they crossed the seas and overleaped the Alps.   When
he visited towns, the people crowded the streets and strained
their necks to catch a glimpse of him.   His remarkable influence over men and women must be explained not by his
intellectual depth so much as by a certain daring and literary art and brilliance.   He was attractive of person, and
Bernard may have had this in mind when he says, Abælard was outwardly a John though he had the heart of a
Herod.[3]   His statements were clear.   He used apt analogies
and quoted frequently from Horace, Ovid, and other Latin
poets.   To these qualities he added a gay cheerfulness which
expressed itself in compositions of song and in singing, which
made him acceptable to women, as in later years Heloise reminded him.[4]

In the midst of this popularity came the fell tragedy of his
life, his connection with Heloise, whom Remusat has called

---

[1] *Verborum usum habebat mirabilem, sed sensu contemptibilem et ratione
vacuum*, Migne, p. 123.

[2] *Ep.*, 326; St. Bernard's Works, Migne, 182. 531.

[3] Remusat gives an attractive picture of his appearance, I. 43 sq.

[4] *Ep.*, II. ; Migne, 178. 188.

"the first of women."[1] This, the leading French woman of
the Middle Ages, stands forth invested with a halo as of
queenly dignity, while her seducer forfeits by his treatment
of her the esteem of all who prefer manly strength and fidelity
to gifts of mind, however brilliant.

Heloise was probably the daughter of a canon and had her
home in Paris with her uncle, Fulbert, also a canon.   When
Abælard came to know. her, she was seventeen, attractive in
person and richly endowed in mind.   Abælard prevailed
upon Fulbert to admit him to his house as Heloise's teacher.
Heloise had before been at the convent of Argenteuil.   The
meetings between pupil and tutor became meetings of lovers.
Over open books, as Abælard wrote, more words of love
were passed than of discussion and more kisses than instruction.   The matter was whispered about in Paris.   Fulbert
was in rage.   Abælard removed Heloise to his sister's in
Brittany, where she bore a son, called Astralabius.[2] Abælard
expressed readiness to have the nuptial ceremony performed,
though in secret, in order to placate Fulbert.   Open marriage
was eschewed lest he should himself suffer loss to his fame, as
he himself distinctly says.[3]

The *Story of Misfortunes* leaves no doubt that what he was
willing to do proceeded from fear and that he was not actuated by any sense of honor toward Heloise or proper view of
woman or of marriage.   What accord, he wrote, "has study
with nurses, writing materials with cradles, books and desks
with spinning wheels, reeds and ink with spindles !   Who,
intent upon sacred and philosophical reflections could endure
the squalling of children, the lullabies of nurses and the
noisy crowd of men and women !   Who would stand the dis-
agreeable and constant dirt of little children! "

[1] See his description, I. 47 sqq.

[2] A letter is preserved written by Abælard to his son. It indicates affection. The father urges him to study the Scriptures. An Astralabius is
mentioned as belonging to the chapter of Nantes in 1150. Hausrath, p. 173,
conjectures he was Abælard's son.

[3] *Ut amplius mitagarem, obtuli me ei satisfacere eam scilicet quam corru-
peram mihi matrimonio copulando, dummodo id secreto fieret, ne famæ
detrimentum incurrerem.* Migne, p. 130.

Abælard declared a secret marriage was performed in obedience to the demands of Heloise's relatives.   At best it was a mock ceremony, for Heloise persisted in denying she was Abælard's wife.   With mistaken but splendid devotion, she declined to marry him, believing that marriage would interrupt his career.   In one of her letters to him she wrote: "If to you, the name of wife seems more proper, to me always was more dear the little word friend, or if you do not deem that name proper, then the name of concubine or harlot, *concubina vel scortum*.   I invoke God as my witness that, if Augustus had wished to give me the rule over the whole world by asking me in marriage, I would rather be your mistress, *meretrix*, than his empress, *imperatrix*.   Thy passion drew thee to me rather than thy friendship, and the heat of desire rather than love." [1]

Abælard removed Heloise to Argenteuil and she assumed the veil.   He visited her in secret and now Fulbert took revenge.   Entering into collusion with Abælard's servant, he fell upon him at night and mutilated him.   Thus humiliated, Abælard entered the convent of St. Denis, 1118, — not from any impulse of piety but from expediency. [2]   He became indifferent to Heloise.

New trials fell upon his chequered career — charges of heresy.   He was arraigned for Sabellian views on the Trinity at Soissons, 1121, before the papal legate.   Roscellinus, his old teacher, opened the accusations.   Abælard complains that two enemies were responsible for the actual trial and its issue, Alberic and Lotulf, teachers at Rheims.   He was obliged to commit his book to the flames [3] and to read publicly a copy of the Athanasian Creed.

Again he got himself into difficulty by opposing the current belief, based upon Bede's statement, that Dionysius or

---

[1] *Concupiscentia te mihi potius quam amicitia sociavit, libidinis ardor potius quam amor.*   *Ep.*, II. ; Migne, p. 186.

[2] Deutsch, p. 35.   *So war Abælard Mönch geworden, nicht von innerem Verlangen getrieben*, etc.   His relations with Heloise made freedom in his position as a public teacher in the open for the time impossible.

[3] *Introductio in theologiam.*   Abælard is our chief authority for the trial. *Hist. Calam.*, Migne, pp. 141–150.   See Otto of Freising.

St. Denis, the patron of France, was the Dionysius converted by Paul at Athens.   The monks of St. Denis would not tolerate him.   He fled, retracted his utterance, and with the permission of Suger, the new abbot of St. Denis, settled in a waste tract in Champagne and built an oratory which he called after the third person of the Trinity, the Paraclete.   Students again gathered around him, and the original structure of reeds and straw was replaced by a substantial building of stone. But old rivals, as he says, again began to pursue him just as the heretics pursued Athanasius of old, and "certain ecclesiastics" — presumably Norbert, the founder of the Premonstrants, and Bernard of Clairvaux — were stirred up against him.   Abælard, perhaps with not too much self-disparagement, says of himself that, in comparison to them, he seemed to be as an ant before a lion.   It was under these circumstances that he received the notice of his election as abbot of the monastery of St. Gildas on the sea, in his native Brittany.   He went, declaring that "the envy of the Francians drove him to the West, as the envy of the Romans drove Jerome to the East."

The monks of St. Gildas are portrayed by Abælard as a band of unmitigated ruffians.   They had their wives and children settled upon the convent's domains.   They treated their new abbot with contempt and violence, twice, at least, attempting his life.   On one occasion it was by drugging the chalice.   He complained of the barrenness of the surroundings.   Bernard described him as an abbot without discipline. In sheer despair, Abælard fled and in "striving to escape one sword I threw myself upon another," he said.   At this point the autobiography breaks off and we know little of its author till 1136.[1]

In the meantime the nuns of Argentueil were driven out of their quarters.   In 1127, Abælard placed Heloise in charge of the Paraclete, and under her management it became pros-

[1] Abælard closes his autobiography by declaring that like another Cain he was dragged about the earth, a fugitive and vagabond, but also by quoting passages upon the providence of God as that all things work together for good to them that love Him.

perous. He had observed a cold silence for a protracted period, but now and again visited the Paraclete and delivered sermons to the nuns. Heloise received the *Story of Misfortunes*, and, in receiving it, wrote, addressing him as "her lord or rather father, her husband or rather brother, from his handmaid or rather daughter, his consort or rather sister." Her first two letters have scarcely, if ever, been equalled in the annals of correspondence in complete abandonment of heart and glowing expressions of devotion. She appealed to him to send her communications. Had she not offered her very being on the altar for his sake! Had she not obeyed him in everything, and in nothing would she offend him!

Abælard replied to Heloise as the superior of the nuns of the Paraclete. She was to him nothing more. He preached to her sermons on prayer, asked for the intercession of the nuns on his behalf, and directed that his body be laid away in the Paraclete. He rejoiced that Heloise's connection with himself prevented her from entering into marriage and giving birth to children. She had thereby been forced into a higher life and to be the mother of many spiritual daughters. Heloise plied him with questions about hard passages in the Scriptures and about practical matters of daily living and monastic dress, — a device to secure the continuance of the correspondence. Abælard replied by giving rules for the nuns which were long and severe. He enjoined upon them, above all else, the study of the Scriptures, and called upon them to imitate Jerome who took up Hebrew late in life. He sent them sermons, seven of which had been delivered in the Paraclete. He proposed that there should be a convent for monks close by the Paraclete. The monks and nuns were to help each other. An abbot was to stand at the head of both institutions. The nuns were to do the monks' washing and cooking, milk the cows, feed the chickens and geese.

In 1137 and again in 1139, we find Abælard suddenly installed at St. Genevieve and enjoying, for a while, meteoric popularity. John of Salisbury was one of his pupils. How the change was brought about does not fully appear.

But Abælard was not destined to have peace. The final
period of his restless career now opens. Bernard was at
that time the most imposing religious personality of Europe,
Abælard was its keenest philosophical thinker. The one
was the representative of churchmanship and church authority, the other of freedom of inquiry. A clash between
these two personalities was at hand. It cannot be regarded
as an historical misfortune that these two men met on the
open field of controversy and on the floor of ecclesiastical
synods. History is most true to herself when she represents
men just as they were. She is a poor teacher, when she
does not take opportunity to reveal their infirmities as well
as their virtues.

Abælard was as much to blame for bringing on the conflict by his self-assertive manner as Bernard was to blame
by unnecessarily trespassing upon Abælard's territory.
William, abbot of St. Thierry, addressed a letter to Bernard
and Geoffrey, bishop of Chalons, announcing that Abælard
was again teaching and writing doctrinal novelties. These
were not matters of mean import, but concerned the doctrine
of the Trinity, the person of Christ, the Holy Spirit, and
God's grace. They were even receiving favor in the curia
at Rome. William adduced no less than thirteen errors.[1]

The first open sign of antagonism was a letter written by
Abælard, brimming over with self-conceit. On a visit to
Heloise at the Paraclete, Bernard had taken exception to the
use of the phrase "supersubstantial bread" in the Lord's
Prayer, instead of "daily bread" as given by Luke. Abælard heard of the objection from Heloise, and, as if eager to
break a lance with Bernard, wrote to him, showing he was
in error. He became sarcastic, pointing out that, at Clairvaux, novelties were being practised which were otherwise

---

[1] *Ep. Bernardi*, 326 ; Migne, 132. 531 sqq. William sent to Bernard
Abælard's *Theologia* and other works to make good his charges. He feared
Abælard would become "a dragon" whom no one could destroy. Kutter,
in his *Wilhelm von St. Thierry*, pp. 34, 36, 43, 48, insists, as against Deutsch,
that William was the exciting originator of the trial of Abælard, which was
soon to follow, and that Bernard preferred silence and peace to conflict, and
was aroused to action by William's appeal.

unknown to the Church.   New hymns were sung and certain intercessory prayers left out as if the Cistercian monks
did not stand in need of intercession also.[1]

So far as we know, Bernard did not answer this letter.
After some delay, he acted upon the request of William of
Thierry.   He visited Abælard in Paris and sought to secure
from him a promise that he would retract his errors.[2]

The difference was brought to open conflict at the synod
of Sens, 1141, where Abælard asked that his case might be
presented, and that he might meet Bernard in argument.
Arnold of Brescia seems to have been among those present.[3]
Bernard was among friends and admirers.   Abælard had
few friends, and was from the first looked upon with suspicion.   Bernard had come to the synod to lay the whole
weight of his influence against Abælard.   He had summoned the bishops as friends of Christ, whose bride called
to them out of the thicket of heresies.   He wrote to the
cardinals and to Innocent II., characterizing Abælard as a
ravenous lion, and a dragon.   With Arnold as his armor-
bearer at his side, Abælard stood like another Goliath
calling out against the ranks of Israel, while Bernard felt
himself a youth in dialectical skill.

At a preliminary meeting with the bishops, Bernard went
over the case and it seems to have been decided, at least in
an informal way, that Abælard should be condemned.[4]   The

[1] *Ep. Abœl.*, X.; Migne, 178. 335.

[2] Bernard's biographer, Gaufrid, states that Abælard promised amend-
ment.   No reference was made to such a promise in the charges at Sens, an
omission difficult to understand if the promise was really made.   See
Remusat, I. 172, and Poole, p. 163.

[3] *Ep. Bernardi*, 189; Migne, 182. 355.   Bernard describes the meeting
and sets forth the danger from Abælard's influence, *Epp.* 187–194, 330–338.
For an account of this trial, see my art., "St. Bernard the Churchman" in
Princeton Rev., 1903, pp. 180 sqq.

[4] This preliminary meeting rests upon the testimony of Berengar and
upon a passage in John of Salisbury, *Hist. Pontif.*, chap. VIII. 9.   John,
in describing the trial of Gilbert of Poictiers, says Bernard wanted to have
Gilbert's case prejudged in a preliminary sitting and by the same method he
had resorted to in the case of Abælard, — *arte simili magistrum Petrum
agressus erat.*   Berengar's defence of Abælard descends to passionate invec-

next day Bernard publicly presented the charges, but, to the
great surprise of all, Abælard declined to argue his case and
appealed it to the pope. Passing by Gilbert of Poictiers,
Abælard is said to have whispered Horace's line,

"Look well to your affairs now that your neighbor's house is burning."

Nam tua res agitur, paries cum proximus ardet.

To Rome the case must go. Abælard no doubt felt that
he had nothing to hope for from the prelates.[1] From Innocent II., whose side he had espoused against the antipope,
Anacletus, he might expect some favor and he had friends
in the curia. The synod called upon the supreme pontiff
to brand Abælard's heresies with perpetual condemnation —
perpetua damnatione — and to punish their defenders. The
charges, fourteen in number, concerned the Trinity, the
nature of faith, the power and work of Christ, and the nature of sin.[2] Bernard followed up the synodal letter with a
communication to the pope, filling forty columns in Migne,
and letters to cardinals, which are full of vehement charges
against the accused man. Abælard and Arnold of Brescia
were in collusion. Abælard had joined himself with Arius
in ascribing degrees within the Trinity, with Pelagius in
putting free will before grace, and with Nestorius in sepa-
rating the person of Christ. In name and exterior a monk,
he was at heart a heretic. He had emerged from Brittany
as a tortuous snake from its hole and, as in the case of the
hydra, seven heads appeared where before there had been
but one.[3] In his letter to the pope, he declared the only

---

tive. Migne, 178. 1858 sqq. Berengar represents the bishops and Bernard
as being heated with wine at this preliminary conference, when they decided
against Abælard. The details of his account and his charges against Bernard
are altogether out of accord with his character as it is otherwise known to us.
Deutsch (Neander's *St. Bernard*, II. 1 sqq.) cannot free Bernard from unfairness in the part he took at this conference, as Vacandard does.

[1] The statement is not inconsistent with the representation of Otto of
Freising, a disinterested reporter, who gives as reason for refusing to make
an argument that he feared a popular tumult.

[2] Migne, 182. 1049-1051. Also Hefele, V. 463 sqq.

[3] *Ep.*, 331 ; Migne, 182. 537. There are nine of these letters to the cardinals, 188, 192, 193, 331-335, 338. The longest letter was the one addressed

thing Abælard did not know was the word *nescio*, " I do not know."

The judgment was swift in coming and crushing when it came.   Ten days were sufficient.   The fourteen articles were burned by the pope's own hand in front of St. Peter's in the presence of the cardinals.   Abælard himself was declared to be a heretic and the penalty of perpetual silence and confinement was imposed upon him.   The unfortunate man had set out for Rome and was hardly well started on his journey, when the sentence reached him.   He stopped at Cluny, where he met the most useful friend of his life, Peter the Venerable.   At Peter's intercession, Innocent allowed the homeless scholar to remain in Cluny whence the pope himself had gone forth.

Following Peter's counsel, Abælard again met Bernard face to face.   In a defence of his orthodoxy, addressed to Heloise, he affirmed his acceptance of all the articles of the Church from the article on the Trinity to the resurrection of the dead.   As it was with Jerome, so no one could write much without being misunderstood.

But his turbulent career was at an end.   He was sent by Peter to St. Marcellus near Chalons for his health, and there he died April 21, 1142, sixty-three years old.   His last days in Cluny are described by Peter in a letter written to Heloise, full of true Christian sympathy.   He called Abælard a true philosopher of Christ.   One so humble in manner he had not

to the pope, 190 ; Migne, 182. 1051-1071.   The great vehemence of these letters have exposed Bernard in some quarters to unmitigated condemnation. From the standpoint of Christian moderation and charity they are difficult to understand and cannot be justified.   Hausrath, p. 248, etc., represents him as *der werltkluge Abt von Clairvaux*, resorting to all the arts of diplomacy to secure a verdict against Abælard.   M'Cabe, in a very readable chapter, pp. 322-354, takes the same view.   Without excusing him, it must be remembered in passing judgment that heresy was regarded with horror in that age. Bernard, no doubt, also shrank from Abælard as a man who sought applause rather than the advancement of the Church.   Morison, p. 302, speaks " of a horror of great darkness falling upon Bernard," when he recognized the dangers of a new era.   Neander, *St. Bernard*, II. 3, says that no one can question that Bernard's zeal proceeded from a pure Christian purpose, but that he used the weapons of hatred under the mask of holy love.

seen.   He was abstinent in meat and drink.   He read continually and prayed fervently.   Faithfully he had committed
his body and soul to his Lord Redeemer for time and eternity.
"So Master Peter finished his days and he who was known
in almost the whole world for his great erudition and ability
as a teacher died peacefully in Him who said 'Learn of me,
for I am meek and lowly of heart,' and he is, as we must believe, gone to Him."

Abælard's body was carried to the Paraclete and there
given rest.   Twenty-two years later, Heloise was laid at his
side.   The inscription placed over the tomb ran, "The
Socrates of the Gauls, the great Plato of the Occidentals, our
Aristotle, who was greater or equal to him among the logicians!   Abælard was the prince of the world's scholars,
varied in talent, subtle and keen, conquering all things by
his mental force.   And then he became a conqueror indeed,
when, entering Cluny, he passed over to the true philosophy
of Christ."[1]   At a later time the following inscription was
placed over the united dust of these remarkable and unfortunate personages, "Under this marble lie the founder of
this convent, P. Abælard and the first abbess Heloise, once
joined by studies, mind, love, forbidden marriage, — *infaustis
nuptiis,* — and penitence and now, as we hope, in eternal
felicity."

At the destruction of the Paraclete during the French
Revolution, 1792, the marble sarcophagus was removed to
Paris and in 1816 it was transferred to the cemetery of Père
la Chaise.   There it remains, the chief object of interest in
that solemn place of the dead, attracting Frenchmen and
visitors from distant lands who commemorate, with tears of
sympathy and a prayer over the mistakes of mortals, the unfortunate lovers.

§ 100.   *Abælard's Teachings and Theology.*

Furnished with brilliant talents, Abælard stands in the
front rank of French public teachers.   But he was a creature
of impulse and offensively conscious of his own gifts and

[1] Migne, 178. 103.

acquirements.   He lacked the reverent modesty and equilib-
rium which become greatness.   He was deficient in moral
force to lift him above the whips and stings of fortune, or
rather the calamities of his own making.   He seems to
have discerned no goal beyond his own selfish ambition.   As
Neander has said, if he had been a man of pure moral character, he would have accomplished more than he did in the
domain of scholarly study.   A man of the highest type could
not have written his *Story of Misfortunes* in the tone that
Abælard wrote.   He shows not a sign of repentance towards
God for his treatment of Heloise.   When he recalls that episode, it is not to find fault with himself, and it is not to do
her any reparation.

His readiness to put himself in opposition to his teachers
and to speak contemptuously of them and to find the motive
for such opposition in envy, indicates also a lack of the higher
moral sentiment.   It is his own loss of fame and position
that he is continually thinking of, and lamenting.   Instead
of ascribing his misfortunes to his own mistakes and mis-
temper, he ascribes them to the rivalry and jealousy of
others.[1]   His one aim in his troubles seems to have been
to regain his popularity.

Abælard's writings are dialectic, ethical, and theological
treatises, poems and letters to Heloise, and his autobiography.
His chief theological works are a *Commentary on the Romans*,
the *Introduction to Theology*, and a *Christian Theology*, the
last two being mainly concerned with the Trinity, a colloquy
between a philosopher, a Jew, and a Christian and the *Sic et
Non*, Yes and No.   In the last work the author puts side
by side in one hundred and fifty-eight chapters a collection
of quotations from the Fathers which seem to be or really

[1] The *Story of Misfortunes* was written while he was abbot of St.
Gildas.   It has been compared to the Confessions of Augustine.   But no
comparison could more sadly offend against truth.   Abælard revealed his
inward states to gain a worldly end.   He wanted to draw attention to himself and prepare the way for a new career.   His letters to Heloise are not so
much to assure her of his orthodoxy as to make that impression upon the
Church authorities.   This is the position taken by Deutsch, pp. 43 sqq.,
Hausrath, 275 sqq., and Nitzsch, art. *Abælard*, in Herzog.

are contradictory. The compiler does not offer a reconciliation. The subjects on which the divergent opinions are collated range from the abstruse problem of the Trinity and the person of Christ to the questions whether Eve alone was seduced or Adam with her, whether Adam was buried on Calvary (the view taken by Ambrose and Jerome) or not (Isidore of Seville), and whether Adam was saved or not. His chief writing on Ethics was the *Scito te ipsum*, " Know thyself."

In some of his theological conceptions Abælard was in advance of his age. The new seeds of thought which he let fall have germinated in recent times. His writings show that, in the twelfth century also, the critical sense had a representative.

1. In the conflict over Realism and Nominalism Abælard occupied an intermediate position. On the one hand he ridiculed the nominalism of Roscellinus, and on the other he controverted the severe realism of William of Champeaux. He taught that the universal is more than a word, *vox*. It is an affirmation, *sermo*.[1] That which our thinking finds to be common, he declared to be real, and the forms of things existed in the divine mind before the creation.

2. Of much more interest are Abælard's views of the ultimate seat of religious authority and of inspiration. Although his statements at times seem to be contradictory, the conclusion is justified that he was an advocate of a certain freedom of criticism and inquiry, even though its results contradicted the authority of the Church. He recognized the principle of inspiration, but by this he did not mean what Gregory the Great taught, that the biblical authors were altogether passive. They exercised a measure of independence, and they were kept from all mistakes.

---

[1] The French writers designate Abælard's theory Conceptualism, and hold that he substituted *conceptus* for *voces*. Deutsch, p. 105. Walter Map, writing in the second half of the twelfth century, speaks of Abælard as " the leader of the Nominalists, *princeps nominalismi*, who sinned more in dialectics than he did in his treatment of Scripture." Wright's ed., I. 24, p. 41.

The rule upon which he treated the Fathers and the Scriptures is set forth in the Prologue of the *Sic et Non*.[1] In presenting the contradictory opinions of the Fathers he shows his intellectual freedom, for the accredited belief was that their statements were invariably consistent. Abælard pronounced this a mistake. Did not Augustine retract some of his statements? Their mistakes, however, and the supposed mistakes of the Scriptures may be only imaginary, due to our failure to understand what they say. Paul, in saying that Melchisedek has neither father nor mother, only meant that the names of his parents were not given in the Old Testament. The appearance of Samuel to Saul at the interview with the witch of Endor was only a fancy, not a reality. Prophets did not always speak with the Spirit of God, and Peter made mistakes. Why should not the Fathers also have made mistakes? The authority of Scripture and the Fathers does not preclude critical investigation. On the contrary, the critical spirit is the proper spirit in which to approach them. "In the spirit of doubt we approach inquiry, and by inquiry we find out the truth, as He, who was the Truth said, 'Seek and ye shall find, knock and it shall be opened unto you.'"[2]

The mystical and the philosophical elements, united in Anselm, were separated in Abælard. But Abælard followed the philosophical principle further than Anselm. He was a born critic, restless of mind, and anxious to make an innovation. In him the inquisitive temper was in the ascendant over the fiducial. Some writers even treat him as the forerunner of modern rationalism. In appearance, at least, he started from a principle the opposite of Anselm's, namely, "nothing is to be believed, until it has been understood."[3] His definition of faith as a presumption of

[1] See also *Introd. ad Theol.*, Migne, 178. 980.

[2] *Dubitando ad inquisitionem venimus, inquirendo veritatem percipimus. Sic et Non*, Migne, p. 1349. Deutsch, pp. 159 sq., speaks of this spirit of free inquiry, *Die Freiheit der Forschung*, as the note running through all Abælard's writings.

[3] *Hist. Calam.*, Migne, 178. 142. *Nec credi posse aliquid nisi primitus intellectus*, etc.

things not seen[1] was interpreted by Bernard and other contemporaries to mean that faith was an uncertain opinion.
What Abælard probably meant was, that faith does not rest
upon authority, but upon inquiry and experience.   There
are times, however, when he seems to contradict himself and
to set forth the opposite principle.   He says, " We believe in
order to know, and unless ye believe, ye cannot know."[2]
His contemporaries felt that he was unsound and that his
position would overthrow the authority of the Church.[3]

The greater doctrines of the Trinity and the existence of
God, Abælard held, could not be proved as necessary, but
only as probable.   In opposition to the pruriency of Scolas-
ticism, he set up the principle that many things pertaining
to God need neither to be believed, nor denied, for no danger is involved in the belief or denial of them.[4]   He gives
as examples, whether God will send rain on the morrow or
not, and whether God will grant pity to a certain most
wicked man or not.   On the other hand he declared that to
affirm that we cannot understand what has been taught
about the Trinity is to say that the sacred writers themselves did not understand what they taught.[5]   As for the
Catholic faith, it is necessary for all, and no one of sound
mind can be saved without it.[6]

3. In his statement of the doctrine of the Trinity,
Abælard laid himself open to the charge both of modalism

---

[1] *Introd. ad Theol.*, Migne, p. 1051, also p. 959. *Fides quippe dicitur
existimatio non apparentium, cognitio vero ipsarum rerum experientia per
ipsam earam præsentiam.*

[2] *Credimus ut cognoscamus; nisi credideritis, non intelligetis.*   See
other quotations in Hefele, V. 463–469 ; also Deutsch, in his chapter on Faith
and Knowledge, pp. 168 sqq.

[3] So the charges of Bernard and the Synod of Sens, and Otto of Freising.
De gestis Frid., 48.

[4] *Introd. ad Theol.*, Migne, p. 986.

[5] *Introd. ad Theol.*, Migne, p. 1052.

[6] *Catholica quippe est fides, id est universalis quæ ita omnibus necessaria
est ut nemo discretus absque ea salvari possit*, Migne, p. 986. In view of
such a statement, Poole's remark has much in its favor, " it was not really
Abælard's results that formed the strength of the indictment against him,
but the method by which he reached them," p. 153.

and Arianism. It called forth Bernard's severest charges. Abælard made no contribution to the subject. The idea of the Trinity he derived from God's absolute perfections. God, as power, is the Father; as wisdom, He is the Son; as love, the Spirit. The Scriptures are appealed to for this view. The Father has put all things in His power, Acts 1:7. The Son, as Logos, is wisdom. The Holy Spirit is called good, Ps. 143:10, and imparts spiritual gifts. The figure gave much umbrage, by which he compared the three persons of the Trinity to the brass of which a seal is made, the form of the seal, and the seal itself proceeding from, or combining the brass and the form. "The brass itself which is the substance of the brazen seal, and the seal itself of which the brass is the substance, are essentially one; yet the brass and the seal are so distinct in their properties, that the property of the brass is one, and the property of the brazen seal another." These are ultimately three things: the brass, *aes*, the brass capable of sealing, *sigillabile*, and the brass in the act of sealing, *sigillans*.

4. In his treatment of the atonement, Abælard has valuable original elements.[1] Strange to say, he makes no reference to Anselm's great treatise. Man, Abælard said, is in the power of the devil, but the devil has no right to this power. What rights does a slave have over another slave whom he leads astray? Christ not only did not pay any price to the devil for man's redemption, he also did not make satisfaction to divine justice and appease God's wrath. If the fall of Adam needed satisfaction by the death of some one, who then would be able to satisfy for the death of Christ? In the life and death of the Redeemer, God's purpose was to manifest. His love and thus to stir up love in the breast of man, and to draw man by love back to Himself. God might have redeemed man by a word, but He chose to set before man an exhibition of His love in Christ. Christ's love constitutes the merit of Christ. The theory anticipates the modern moral influence theory of the atonement, so called.

[1] They are found in his *Com. on Romans*, as well as in his *Introd. ad Theol.* and his *Sermons*, V., X., XII.

2 s

5. Abælard's doctrine of sin likewise presents features of difference from the view current in his time.[1] The fall occurred when Eve resolved to eat the forbidden fruit, that is, after her desire was aroused and before the actual partaking of the fruit.[2]

The seat of sin is the intention, which is the root, bearing good and bad fruit.[3] Desire or concupiscence is not sin. This intention, *intentio*, is not the simple purpose, say, to kill a man in opposition to killing one without premeditation, but it is the underlying purpose to do right or wrong. In this consciousness of right or wrong lies the guilt. Those who put Christ to death from a feeling that they were doing right, did not sin, or, if they sinned, sinned much less grievously than if they had resisted their conscience and not put him to death. How then was it that Christ prayed that those who crucified him might be forgiven? Abælard answers by saying that the punishment for which forgiveness was asked was temporal in its nature.

The logical deduction from Abælard's premises would have been that no one incurs penalty but those who voluntarily consent to sin. But from this he shrank back. The godless condition of the heathen he painted in darkest colors. He, however, praised the philosophers and ascribed to them a knowledge through the Sibylline books, or otherwise, of the divine unity and even of the Trinity.[4] Bernard wrote to Innocent II. that, while Abælard labored to prove Plato a Christian, he proved himself to be a pagan. Liberal as he was in some of his doctrinal views, he was wholly at one with the Church in its insistence upon the efficiency of the sacraments, especially baptism and the Lord's Supper.

Because Abælard stands outside of the theological circle

[1] They are set forth more particularly in the ethical treatise *Scito te ipsum* and the *Com. on Romans*, especially in an excursus on original sin, appended to chap. V., Migne, pp. 866–874.

[2] He thinks the tree whose fruit excited the sexual passions was the vine. *Hexaemeron*, Migne, p. 777.

[3] *Com. on Romans*, chap. II. 6.   Deutsch, pp. 344 sqq., deals at length with Abælard's views on sin.

[4] *Introd. ad Theol.*, Migne, p. 1008.

of his day, he will always be one of the most interesting
figures of the Middle Ages.   His defect was in the lack of
moral power.   The student often finds himself asking the
question, whether his statements were always the genuine
expression of convictions.   But for this lack of moral force,·
he might have been the Tertullian of the Middle Ages,
whom he is not unlike in dash and original freshness of
thought.   The African Father, so vigorous in moral power,
the Latin Church excludes from the number of the saints on
account of his ecclesiastical dissent.   Abælard she cannot
include on account of moral weakness.[1]   Had he been willing
to suffer and had he not retracted all the errors charged
against him, he might have been given a place among the
martyrs of thought.[2]   As it is, his misfortunes arouse our
sympathy for human frailties which are common ; his theology and character do not awaken our admiration.

§ 101.   *Younger Contemporaries of Abælard.*

LITERATURE : For Gilbert (Gislebertus) of Poictiers.   His *Commentaries* on
   Boethius' *De trinitate* are in Migne, 64. 1255 sqq.   The *De sex principiis*,
   Migne, 188. 1250–1270.   For his life: GAUFRID OF AUXERRE, Migne, 185.
   595 sqq. — OTTO OF FREISING, *De gestis Frid.*, 50–57. — J. OF SALISBURY,
   Hist. pontif., VIII. — POOLE, in *Illustr. of the Hist. of Med. Thought*,
   pp. 167–200.   HEFELE, V. 503–508, 520–524. — NEANDER-DEUTSCH, *St.
   Bernard*, II. 130–144.
For John of Salisbury, *Works* in Migne, vols. 190, 199, and J. A. Giles,
   Oxford, 1848, 5 vols. — *Hist. pontificalis romanus*, in *Mon. German.*,
   vol. XX. — *Lives* by REUTER, Berlin, 1842. — * C. SCHAARSCHMIDT, *Joh.
   Saresbriensis nach Leben und Studien, Schriften und Philosophie*,
   Leip., 1862, and art. in Herzog, IX. 313–319. — Denimuid, Paris, 1873. —
   SCHUBERT: *Staatslehre J. von Sal.*, Berlin, 1897. — STUBBS, in *Study of
   Med. and Mod. Hist.*, Lectt. VI., VII. — POOLE, in *Illustr. etc.*, pp. 201–
   226, and *Dict. of Natl. Biogr.*, XXIX. 439–446.

   [1] Hausrath, pp. 293 sqq., assigns to Abælard a place in the front rank of
such martyrs.   He justifies him for declining to stand by his conclusions in
these words : " It would be unfair to demand that a scholar, who was under
the pressure of such circumstances (that is mediæval ecclesiasticism), should
have the courage of a farm hand, or carry his views to their logical conclusion like a statesman."

   [2] Abælard left admiring pupils, some of whom, like Omnibene, wrote
books of *Sentences* based upon their teacher's *Theology*, and followed his threefold division of faith, the sacraments, and love.   See Denifle, *Archiv*, pp.
613 sqq.

Among Abælard's younger contemporaries and pupils were Gilbert of Poictiers, John of Salisbury, and Robert Pullen, theologians who were more or less influenced by Abælard's spirit of free inquiry. Peter the Lombard, d. 1164, also shows strong traces of Abælard's teaching, especially in his Christology.[1]

Gilbert of Poictiers, 1070–1154, is better known by his public trial than by his writings, or any permanent contributions to theology.   Born at Poictiers, he studied under Bernard of Chartres, William of Champeaux, Anselm of Laon, and Abælard.   He stood at the head of the cathedral school in Chartres for ten years, and in 1137 began teaching in Paris.   In 1142 he was made bishop of Poictiers. His two principal works are *De sex principiis*, an exposition of Aristotle's last six categories, which Aristotle himself left unexplained, and a commentary on the work on the Trinity, ascribed to Boethius.   They occupy only a few pages in print.

Gilbert's work on the Trinity involved him in a trial for heresy, in which Bernard was again a leading actor.[2]   The case was brought before the synods of Paris, 1147, and Rheims, 1148.   According to Otto of Freising, Gilbert was a man of earnest purpose.   It was his dark and abstruse mode of statement and intense realism that exposed him to the accusation of unorthodoxy.

Some of Gilbert's pupils were ready to testify against him, but sufficient evidence of tritheism were not forthcoming at Paris and the pope, who presided, adjourned the case to Rheims. At Rheims, Bernard who had been appointed prosecutor offended some of the cardinals by his methods of conducting the prosecution.   Both Otto of Freising and John of Salisbury [3]

---

[1] Denifle includes the Lombard in the theological school of Abælard. See his *Abælard's Sentenzen und d. Bearbeitungen seiner Theologie*, Archiv, 1885, pp. 613–624.

[2] Neander-Deutsch, *St. Bernard*, II. 131.   Poole, p. 181, calls Gilbert's exposition of the Trinity " one of the subtlest and most elaborate contributions to theological metaphysics the Middle Ages produced."

[3] *Hist. pontif.*, VIII.; Migne, pp. 522 sqq.   One of the accusers was Adam du Petit Pont, an Englishman, afterwards bishop of St. Asaph.   He got

state that a schism was threatened and only averted by the good sense of pope Eugenius.

To the pope's question whether Gilbert believed that the highest essence, by virtue of which, as he asserted, each of the three persons of the Trinity was God, was itself God, Gilbert replied in the negative.[1] Gilbert won the assembly by his thorough acquaintance with the Fathers. The charge was declared unproven and Gilbert was enjoined to correct the questionable statements in the light of the fourth proposition brought in by Bernard. The accused continued to administer his see till his death. Otto of Freising concludes his account by saying, that either Bernard was deceived as to the nature of Gilbert's teaching as David was deceived by Mephibosheth, 2 Sam. 9 : 19 sqq., or that Gilbert covered up his real meaning by an adroit use of words to escape the judgment of the Church. With reference to his habit of confusing wisdom with words Walter of St. Victor called Gilbert one of the four labyrinths of France.

John of Salisbury, about 1115–1180, was the chief literary figure and scholar among the Englishmen of the twelfth century, and exhibits in his works the practical tendency of the later English philosophy.[2] He was born at Salisbury and of plebeian origin. He spent ten or twelve years in "divers studies" on the Continent, sat at the feet of Abælard on Mt. Genevieve, 1136, and heard Gilbert of Poictiers, William of Conches, Robert Pullen, and other renowned teachers. A full account of the years spent in study is given in his *Metalogicus*. Returning to England, he stood in a confidential relation to archbishop Theobald. At a later time he espoused Becket's cause and was present in the cathedral when the

his name from the school he set up on a little bridge connecting Paris with the Latin quarter. Schaarschmidt, p. 13.

[1] Otto of Freising states the four detailed charges as follows: 1. *divina essentia non est Deus*. 2. *proprietates personarum non sunt ipsae personæ*. 3. *theolog. personæ in nulla prædicantur propositione*. 4. *divina natura non est incarnata*. Gaufried, Migne, 185. 617, states the first three a little differently.

[2] Stephens calls him "by far the most distinguished English scholar of his century." *Hist. of the Engl. Ch.*, pp. 320 sqq.

archbishop was murdered.   He had urged the archbishop not
to enter his church.   In 1176 he was made bishop of Chartres.
He says he crossed the Alps no less than ten times on ecclesiastical business.

By his reminiscences and miscellanies, John contributed,
as few men did, to our knowledge of the age in which he
lived.   He had the instincts of a Humanist, and, had he lived
several centuries later, would probably have been in full sympathy with the Renaissance.   His chief works are the *Metalogicus*, the *Polycraticus*, and the *Historia pontificalis*.   The
Polycraticus is a treatise on the principles of government and
philosophy, written for the purpose of drawing attention
away from the trifling disputes and occupations of the world
to a consideration of the Church and the proper uses of life.[1]
He fortified his positions by quotations from the Scriptures
and classical writers, and shows that the Church is the true
conservator of morality and the defender of justice in the
State.   He was one of the best-read men of his age in the
classics.[2]

In the *Metalogicus*, John calls a halt to the casuistry of
Scholasticism and declares that the reason is apt to err as
well as the senses.   Dialectics had come to be used as an exhibition of mental acumen, and men, like Adam du Petit
Pont, made their lectures as intricate and obscure as possible,
so as to attract students by the appearance of profundity.
John declared that logic was a vain thing except as an instrument, and by itself as useless as the "sword of Hercules in a
pygmy's hand."   He emphasized the importance of knowledge that can be put to use, and gave a long list of things
about which a wise man may have doubts, such as providence
and human fortune, the origin of the soul, the origin of

---

[1] Schaarschmidt calls it "the first great theory of the state in the literature
of the Middle Ages."   In view of the variety of its contents, Poole, p. 218,
says that "it is to some extent an encyclopædia of the cultivated thought of
the middle of the twelfth century."

[2] Poole says, "No writer of his age can be placed beside him in the extent
and depth of his classical reading."   *Dict. of Natl. Biog.*, XXIX. 441.   Schaarschmidt speaks of his marvellous acquaintance with the classics — *eine staun-
enswerthe Vertrautheit.*

motion, whether all sins are equal and equally to be punished.
God, he affirmed, is exalted above all that the mind can conceive, and surpasses our power of ratiocination.[1]

The *Historia pontificalis* is an account of ecclesiastical matters falling under John's own observation, extending from the
council at Rheims, 1148, to the year 1152.

§ 102. *Peter the Lombard and the Summists.*

LITERATURE: *Works* of P. Lombard, Migne, vols. 191, 192. — PROTOIS,
P. *Lomb. son épôque, sa vie, ses écrits et son influence*, Paris, 1881.
Contains sermons not found in Migne. — KÖGEL: *P. Lomb. in s. Stellung
zur Philos. des Mittelalters*, Leip., 1897. — *O. BALTZER: *D. Sentenzen
d. P. Lomb., ihre Quellen und ihre dogmengeschichtl. Bedeutung*, Leip.,
1902. — *DENIFLE: *D. Sentenzen Abœlards*, etc., in *Archiv*, 1885, pp. 404
sqq. — Arts. *Lombardus*, in Wetzer-Welte, IX. 1916–1923, and * Herzog,
by Seeberg, XI. 630–642. — STÖCKL, *Philos. des Mittelalters*, I. 390–411.
The Histories of Doctrine of SCHWANE, pp. 160 sqq., BACH, HARNACK,
FISHER, etc.

Peter the Lombard is the father of systematic theology in
the Catholic Church. He produced the most useful and
popular theological text-book of the Middle Ages, as Thomas
Aquinas produced the most complete theological system.
In method, he belongs to the age of the great theologians
of the thirteenth century, when Scholasticism was at its
height. In point of time, he has his place in the twelfth
century, with whose theologians, Bernard, Abælard, Gilbert,
Hugo of St. Victor, and others, he was personally acquainted.

Peter was born at Novara, in Northern Italy, and died
in Paris about 1164.[2] After studying in Bologna, he went
to France and attended the school of St. Victor and the
cathedral school in Paris, and came under the influence of
Abælard. He afterwards taught in Paris. Walter Map,
describing his experiences in France, calls him "the famous
theologian." In 1159 he was made bishop of Paris.

[1] *Metalog.*, VII. 2.

[2] This is the date given on an ancient epitaph in Paris, but the date is
made uncertain by the appointment of a bishop of Paris as the Lombard's
successor, 1160. This would seem to indicate his death occurred at that time
unless he was deposed on the charge of simony, of which, as Walter of St.
Victor says, he was guilty. Migne, 199. 1140.

His monumental work, the Four Books of Sentences, *libri quatuor sententiarum*, covers, in a systematic way, the whole field of dogmatic theology, as John of Damascus had done four hundred years before in his summary of the Orthodox Faith.   It won for its author the title, the Master of Sentences, *magister sententiarum*.   Other systems of theology under the name of *sentences* had preceded the Lombard's treatise.   Such a work was ascribed to Abælard by St. Bernard.[1] This was probably a mistake.   It is certain, however, that Abælard's scholars — Roland (afterwards Alexander III.), while he was professor at Bologna, 1142, and Omnebene — produced such works and followed Abælard's threefold division of faith, charity, and the sacraments.[2] Of more importance were the treatises of Anselm of Laon, Robert Pullen,[3] and Hugo of St. Victor, who wrote before the Lombard prepared his work.   Robert Pullen, who died about 1147, was an Englishman and one of the first teachers at Oxford, then went to Paris, where he had John of Salisbury for one of his hearers about 1142, enjoyed the friendship of St. Bernard, came into favor at Rome, and was appointed cardinal by Cœlestin II.

The Lombard's work is clear, compact, and sententious, moderate and judicial in spirit, and little given to the treatment of useless questions of casuistry.   In spite of some attacks upon its orthodoxy, it received wide recognition and was used for several centuries as a text-book, as Calvin's *Institutes*, at a later period, was used in the Protestant churches.   Down to the sixteenth century, every candidate for the degree of B.A. at Paris was obliged to pass an examination in it.   Few books have enjoyed the distinction of

---

[1] *Liber quem dicunt sententiarum*, *Ep.*, 188 ; Migne, 182. 553.   Walter of St. Victor declares it to have been by Abælard's hand or taken from his works, *aut ex libris ejus excerptus.*   See Deutsch, *P. Abælard excursus.*

[2] Denifle, *Archiv*, 1885, learnedly establishes the relation of these works to Abælard.   They exist in MSS. at Nürnberg, Munich, etc.   Omnebene expressly declared his work to be a compilation taken from different sources.

[3] *Sententiarum theologicarum libri*, VII. ; Migne, vol. 186.   His name is spelt Pullein, Pullan, etc.   See Rashdall's art. in *Dict. of Nat'l Biogr.*, XLVII. 19.

having had so many commentaries written upon them. One hundred and sixty are said to be by Englishmen, and one hundred and fifty-two by members of the order of St. Dominic. The greatest of the Schoolmen lectured and wrote commentaries upon it, as Alexander Hales, Albertus Magnus, Bonaventura, Thomas Aquinas, Durandus, and Ockam.[1]

Not uninfluenced by the method pursued by Abælard in the *Sic et Non*, the Lombard collated statements from the Fathers and he set about making his compilation to relieve the student from the task and toil of searching for himself in the Fathers.[2] Augustine furnished more than twice as many quotations as all the other Fathers together.[3] The Lombard went further than Abælard and proposed to show the harmony existing between the patristic statements. In the arrangement of his material and for the material itself he drew largely upon Abælard, Gratian, and Hugo of St. Victor,[4] without, however, quoting them by name. Upon Hugo he drew for entire paragraphs.

The *Sentences* are divided into four parts, treating of the triune God, created beings and sin, the incarnation, the Christian virtues and the decalogue, and the sacraments with some questions in eschatology. The author's method is to state the doctrine taught by the Church, to confirm it from Scripture, then to adduce the opinions of the Fathers and, if they seemed to be in conflict, to reconcile them. His ulti-

---

[1] The Jesuit Possevin gives a list of 246 commentaries in print. See Wetzer-Welte, IX. 1921, which speaks of the number of commentaries as *unzählig*, "without number." Hergenröther (*Gesch.* II. 516) speaks of them in the same way as *zahllos*. The first commentary, according to Werner (*Thom. von Aquino*, I. 314), was by William of Seignelay, teacher in Paris and later bishop of Paris.

[2] *Prolog.* to the *Sentences, brevi volumine complicans patrum sententias appositis eorum testimoniis*, etc.

[3] Baltzer, pp. 2–5, gives the results of a careful study. Augustine furnishes 1000 quotations. Hilary comes next, being quoted 85 times. Baltzer's book is a laborious comparison of every paragraph of the Lombard with the Fathers and his predecessors among the Schoolmen, especially Abælard and Hugo of St. Victor.

[4] Denifle (*Archiv*, pp. 621 sqq.) is authority for the statement that he also quotes from Gandulf's *Sentences* which still remain in MS. at Turin.

mate design was to lift up the light of truth in its candle-
stick, and he assures us his labor had cost him much toil and
sweat of the brow.[1]

The Lombard's arguments for the divine existence are
chiefly cosmological. God's predestination of the elect is
the cause of good in them and is not based upon any foreseen
goodness they may have. Their number cannot be increased or
diminished. On the other hand, God does not take the initiative in the condemnation of the lost. Their reprobation follows
as a consequence upon the evil in them which is foreseen.[2]

In the second book, the Lombard makes the famous statement which he quotes from Augustine, and which has often
been falsely ascribed as original to Matthew Henry, that the
woman was not taken from Adam's head, as if she were to
rule over him or from his feet as if she were to be his slave,
but from his side that she might be his consort. By the
Fall man suffered injury as from a wound, *vulneratio*, not
deprivation of all virtue. Original sin is handed down
through the medium of the body and becomes operative
upon the soul by the soul's contact with the body. The root
of sin is concupiscence, *concupiscentia*. The Lombard was a
creationist.[3] God knew man would fall. Why He did not
prevent it, is not known.

In his treatment of the atonement, Peter denied that
Christ's death was a price paid to the devil. It is the manifestation of God's love, and by Christ's love on the cross, love
is enkindled within us. Here the Lombard approaches the
view of Abælard. He has nothing to say in favor of Anselm's view that the death of Christ was a payment to
the divine honor.[4]

[1] Migne, 192. 522.

[2] *Reprobatio Dei est præscientia malitiæ in quibusdam non finiendæ, et
præparatio poenæ non terminandæ.*   [3] II. 31 ; Migne, p. 211.

[4] *Mors nos justificat, dum per eam caritas excitatur in cordibus nostris,*
III. 19 ; Migne, p. 285. John of Cornwall, his pupil, expressly says that the
Lombard learned his view of the atonement from Abælard and often had
Abælard's *Theologia* in his hands, Migne, 199. 1052. See Denifle, pp. 616 sqq.
Baltzer, pp. 96 sqq., goes so far as to say that his silence is to be interpreted
as a denial of the Anselmic theory.

In his treatment of the sacraments, the Lombard commends immersion as the proper form of baptism, triune or single.[1] Baptism destroys the guilt of original sin. The Lord's Supper is a sacrifice, and the elements are transmuted into the body and blood of Christ. Water is to be mixed with the wine, the water signifying the people redeemed by Christ's passion.

It is remarkable that a work which came into such general esteem, and whose statements are so carefully guarded by references to Augustine, should have been attacked again and again as heretical, as at the synod of Tours, 1163, and at the Third Lateran, 1179; but at neither was any action taken. Again at the Fourth Lateran, 1215, Peter's statement of the Trinity was attacked. Peter had said that the Father, Son, and Spirit were "a certain highest being," and that the substance neither begets nor is begotten, nor does it proceed from anything.[2] Joachim charged that he substituted a quaternity for the Trinity and called him a heretic, but the council took another view and pronounced in favor of Peter's orthodoxy. Walter of St. Victor went so far as to accuse the author of the *Sentences* with Sabellianism, Arianism, and "novel heresies."[3] In spite of such charges no one can get as clear an idea of mediæval theology in a succinct form as in Peter Lombard unless it be in the *Breviloquium* of Bonaventura.

The last and one of the clearest of the Summists of the twelfth century was Alanus de Insulis, Alain of Lille, who was born at Lille, Flanders, and died about 1202.[4] His works were much read, especially his allegorical poems, *Anticlaudianus* and *De planctu naturæ*.

[1] IV. 3; Migne, p. 335.

[2] *Quædam summa res est Pater et Filius et Spiritus et illa non est generans neque genita nec procedens.*

[3] From time to time questionable articles continued to be cited from the Lombard. In the middle of the thirteenth century the number of such articles at variance with the doctrine of the Church was given as eight. The doctors of Paris increased the number. Eymeric wrote a treatise on twenty-two such heretical statements. A list of fifteen are given at the close of Peter's *Sentences.* Migne, 451–454.

[4] He is probably a different man from Alanus, archbishop of Auxerre, with whom he has often been identified, and who spent the last twenty years

In the *Rules of Sacred Theology* Alanus gives one hundred and
twenty-five brief expositions of theological propositions.   In the five
books on the *Catholic Faith*,[1] he considers the doctrine of God, creation
and redemption, the sacraments, and the last things.   The Church is
defined as the congregation of the faithful confessing Christ and the
arsenal of the sacraments.[2]   Alanus' work, *Against Heretics*, has already
been used in the chapters on the Cathari and Waldenses.

Another name which may be introduced here is Walter of St. Victor,
who is chiefly known by his characterization of Abælard, Gilbert of
Poictiers, Peter the Lombard, and the Lombard's pupil, Peter of Poictiers,
afterwards chancellor of the University of Paris, as the four labyrinths of
France.   He likened their reasoning to the garrulity of frogs, — *ranarum
garrulitas*, — and declared that, as sophists, they had unsettled the faith
by their questions and counterquestions.   Walter's work has never been
printed.   He succeeded Richard as prior of the convent of St. Victor.
He died about 1180.[3]

§ 103. *Mysticism.*

LITERATURE : The *Works* of St. Bernard, Hugo and Richard of St. Victor,
    Rupert of Deutz, and also of Anselm, Bonaventura, Thomas Aquinas, all
    in Migne's *Patrology.* — G. ARNOLD : *Historie und Beschreibung d. myst.
    Theologie*, Frankf., 1703. — H. SCHMID : *D. Mysticismus des Mittelalters*,
    Jena, 1824. — J. GÖRRES (Prof. of Hist. in Munich, founder of Ger-
    man ultramontanism, d. 1848) : *D. christl. Mystik*, 4 vols. Regensb.,
    1836-1842.   A product of the fancy rather than of sober historical in-
    vestigation. — A. HELFFERICH : *D. christl. Mystik*, etc., 2 parts, Gotha,
    1842. — R. A. VAUGHAN : *Hours with the Mystics*, Lond., 1856, 4th ed.,
    no date, with preface by Wycliffe Vaughan. — LUDWIG NOACK : *D.
    christl. Mystik nach ihrem geschichtl. Entwickelungsgang*, 2 parts,
    Königsb., 1863. — J. HAMBERGER : *Stimmen der Mystik*, etc., 2 parts,
    Stuttg., 1857. — W. PREGER : *Gesch. der deutschen Mystik im Mittelalter*,

of his life at Clairvaux and wrote a *Life* of St. Bernard. Migne, 185.
470-523. See Deutsch, Alanus, Herzog, I. 283 sqq. Hergenröther-Kirsch
frequently quotes Alanus.

[1] *Regulæ de sacra theologia*, Migne, 210. 621-684 ; and *de arte sive de
articulis catholicæ fidei*, Migne, 593-617.

[2] *Congregatio fidelium confitentium Christum, et sacramentorum subsidium*, Migne, p. 613. Under the title *liber sententiarum*, Migne, 229-264,
he wrote also on the Lord's birth, John the Baptist, and Mary.

[3] Walter speaks of the four labyrinths as "treating with scholastic levity
the mysteries of the Trinity and the incarnation and vomiting out many
heresies." Planck gave an analysis of Walter's work in *Studien und Kritiken*,
1844, pp. 823 sqq. Bulæus, in *Hist. universitatum*, vol. II. 402, 629, gives extracts, which are reprinted in Migne, 199, pp. 1127 sqq. Denifle also gives
quotations, *Archiv*, etc., 1885, pp. 404 sqq.

3 vols. Leip., 1874–1893. The Mysticism of the twelfth and thirteenth cents. is given, vol. I. 1–309. — CARL DU PREL : *D. Philosophie der Mystik*, Leip., 1885. — W. R. INGE : *Christ. Mysticism*, Lond., 1899. — The *Lives* of Bernard, Hugo of St. Victor, etc. — The *Histories of Doctrine* of SCHWANE, HARNACK, etc.

Side by side with the scholastic element in mediæval theology was developed the mystical element.   Mysticism aims at the immediate personal communion of the soul with the Infinite Spirit, through inward devotions and spiritual aspirations, by abstraction rather than by logical analysis, by adoration rather than by argument, with the heart rather than with the head, through the spiritual feelings rather than through intellectual prowess, through the immediate contact of the soul with God rather than through rites and ceremonies.   The characteristic word to designate the activity of the mystic is devotion; of the scholastic, speculation.   Mysticism looks less for God without and more for God within the breast.   It relies upon experience rather than upon definitions.[1]   Mysticism is equally opposed to rationalism and to ritual formalism.

In the Apostle John and also in Paul we have the mystical element embodied.   The centre of John's theology is that God is love.   The goal of the believer is to abide in Christ and to have Christ abide in him.   The true mystic has *felt*. He is no visionary nor a dabbler in occultism.   Nor is he a recluse.   Neither the mystics of this period nor Eckart and Tauler of a later period seclude themselves from the course of human events and human society.   Bernard and the theologians of St. Victor did not lose themselves in the absorption of ecstatic exercises, though they sought after

[1] Harnack, *Dogmengesch.*, III. 314 sqq., 373 sqq., turns to ridicule the alleged difference between scholasticism and mysticism. With the emotional or quietistic type of religion, *die Pektoraltheologie*, the cardiac theology, as the Germans call it, he has little sympathy. Piety, he says, is the starting-point of both and full knowledge their goal. He makes the brusque statement, p. 378, that "a mystic who does not become a Roman Catholic, is a dilettante." Ritschl had said before that there is "no normal mysticism except in connection with the hermit life. The love for it, widely prevalent among evangelical Christians, is dilettanteism." *Pietismus*, II. 12. Harnack, however, is willing to allow a distinction in the terms and to speak of scholasticism when the relation of God to the universe is thought of and of mysticism when we have in mind the union of the soul with God.

complete and placid composure of soul under the influence
of love for Christ and the pure contemplation of spiritual
things. "God," said St. Bernard, "is more easily sought
and found by prayer than by disputation." "God is
known," said both Bernard and Hugo of St. Victor, "so
far as He is loved." Dante placed Bernard still higher
than Thomas Aquinas, the master of scholastic thought,
and was led by him through prayer to the beatific vision of
the Holy Trinity with which his Divine Comedy closes.[1]

Augustine furnished the chief materials for the mystics of
the Middle Ages as he did for the scholastics. It was he
who said, "Thou hast made us for thyself and the heart is
restless till it rests in Thee." For Aristotle, the mystics
substituted Dionysius the Areopagite, the Christian Neo-
Platonist, whose works were made accessible in Latin by
Scotus Erigena.[2] The mystical element was strong in the
greatest of the Schoolmen, Anselm, Thomas Aquinas, and
Bonaventura.

The Middle Ages took Rachel and Leah, Mary and Martha
as the representatives of the contemplative and the active
life, the conventual and the secular life, and also of the
mystic and scholastic methods. Through the entire two
periods of seven years, says Peter Damiani,[3] Jacob was serving for Rachel. Every convert must endure the fight of
temptation, but all look forward to repose and rest in the
joy of supreme contemplation; that is, as it were, the embraces of the beautiful Rachel. These two periods stand
for the Old and New Testament, the law and the grace of
the Gospel. He who keeps the commandments of both at
last comes into the embraces of Rachel long desired.

Richard of St. Victor devotes a whole treatise to the comparison between Rachel and Leah. Leah was the more

---

[1] *Paradiso*, XXXI. 130, XXXIII. 49, etc.   Dr. Philip Schaff said, *Lit. and
Poetry*, p. 232, "Bernard defended orthodox mysticism and the theology of
the heart against speculative rationalism and the theology of the intellect in
contrast with Peter Abælard."

[2] "The mediæval mystics were steeped in Dionysius." Inge, p. 110.

[3] *De perf. monachi*, VIII. ; Migne, 145. 303.

fertile, Rachel the more comely. Leah represented the discipline of virtue, Rachel the doctrine of truth. Rachel stands for meditation, contemplation, spiritual apprehension, and insight; Leah for weeping, lamentation, repining, and grief. Rachel died in giving birth to Benjamin. So reason, after the pangs of ratiocination, dies in giving birth to religious devotion and ardor.[1]

This comparison was taken from Augustine, who said that Rachel stands for the joyous apprehension of the truth and, for that reason, was said to have a good face and beautiful form.[2] St. Bernard spoke of the fellowship of the active and contemplative life as two members of the same family, dwelling together as did Mary and Martha.[3]

The scholastic theology was developed in connection with the school and the university, the mystic in connection with the convent. Clairvaux and St. Victor near Paris were the hearth-stones of mysticism. Within cloistral precincts were written the passionate hymns of the Middle Ages, and the eucharistic hymns of Thomas Aquinas are the utterances of the mystic and not of the Schoolman.

The leading mystical divines of this period were Bernard, Hugo and Richard of St. Victor, and Rupert of Deutz. Mystical in their whole tendency were also Joachim of Flore, Hildegard and Elizabeth of Schönau, who belong in a class by themselves.

§ 104. *St. Bernard as a Mystic.*

For literature, see § 65, also, RITSCHL: *Lesefrüchte aus d. hl. Bernard*, in *Studien u. Kritiken*, 1879, pp. 317–335. — J. RIES (Rom. Cath.) : *D. geistliche Leben nach der Lehre d. hl. Bernard*, Freib., 1906, p. 327.

The works of Bernard which present his mystical theology are the *Degrees of Humility and Pride*, a sermon addressed to the clergy, entitled *Conversion*, the treatise on *Loving God*, his *Sermons on the Canticles*, and his hymns. The author's intimate acquaintance with the Scriptures is shown

---

[1] *De preparat. ad contemplationem sive Benjamin minor*, I. 73 ; Migne, 196. 52.

[2] *C. Faus. Man.*, XXII. 52.   [3] *Sermo in Cant.*, 51, 2.   See *De consid.*, I. 1.

on almost every page.   He has all the books at his command
and quotation follows quotation with great rapidity.   Bernard
enjoyed the highest reputation among his contemporaries as
an expounder of the inner life, as his letters written in answer to questions show.   Harnack calls him the religious
genius of the twelfth century, the leader of his age, the
greatest preacher Germany had ever heard.   In matters of
religious contemplation he called him a new Augustine,
Augustinus redivivus.[1]

The practical instinct excluded the speculative element
from Bernard as wordly ambition excluded the mystical
element from Abælard.   Bernard had the warmest respect for
the Apostle Paul and greatly admired Augustine as "the
mightiest hammer of the heretics " and " the pillar of the
Church."[2]   Far more attractive is he as a devotional theologian, descanting on the excellencies of love and repeating
Paul's words, " Let all your things be done in love," 1 Cor.
16 : 14, than as a champion of orthodoxy and writing, "It
is better that one perish than that unity perish."[3]

Prayer and personal sanctity, according to Bernard, are
the ways to the knowledge of God, and not disputation.   The
saint, not the disputant, comprehends God.[4]   Humility and
love are the fundamental ethical principles of theology.   The
conventual life, with its vigils and fastings, is not an end
but a means to develop these two fundamental Christian
virtues.[5]   Every convent he regarded as a company of the
perfect, *collegium perfectorum*, but not in the sense that all
the monks were perfect.[6]

The treatise on Loving God asserts that God will be
known in the measure in which He is loved.   Writing to

---

[1] *Dogmengesch.*, III. 301, 305. For Bernard's acquaintance with Scripture,
see Ries, pp. 11 sq.   [2] Ries, pp. 9, 15.

[3] *Omnia vestra in caritate fiant, Ep.*, 221.   *Melius est ut unus pereat quam
unitas, Ep.*, 102 ; Migne, 182. 257.

[4] *Non ea disputatio comprehendit sed sanctitas*, quoting *Eph.*, III., 18.
Sancti comprehendunt.   De consid., V. 14 ; Migne, 182. 804.

[5] *Ep.*, 142, 2 ; Migne, 182, 297.   Dr. Philip Schaff said that "love and
humility were the crowning traits of Bernard's character." *Lit. and Poetry*,
p. 232.   [6] Ries, pp. 35, sqq.

Cardinal Haimeric, who had inquired "why and how God is
to be loved," Bernard replied, "The exciting cause of love
to God, is God Himself. The measure of love to God is to
love God without measure.[1] The gifts of nature and the
soul are adapted to awaken love. But the gifts involved in
the soul's relation to the Father, Son, and Holy Spirit, whom
the unbeliever does not know, are inexpressibly more precious and call upon man to exercise an infinite and measureless love, for God is infinite and measureless. The soul is
great in the proportion in which it loves God."[2]

Love grows with our apprehension of God's love. As the
soul contemplates the cross it is itself pierced with the sword
of love, as when it is said in the *Canticles*, II. 5, "I am sick
from love." Love towards God has its reward, but love
loves without reference to reward. True love is sufficient
unto itself. To be fully absorbed by love is to be deified.[3]
As the drop of water dropped into wine seems to lose its
color, and taste, and as the iron held in the glowing flame
loses its previous shape and becomes like the flame, and as
the air, transfused by the light of the sun, becomes itself like
the light, and seems to be as the sun itself, even so all feeling
in the saint is wholly transfused by God's will, and God becomes all and in all.

In Bernard's eighty-six Sermons on the Song of Solomon,
we have a continuous apostrophe to love, the love of God and
the soul's love to God. As sermons they stand out like the
Petite Carême of Massillon among the great collections of
the French pulpit. Bernard reached only the first verse of
the third chapter. His exposition, which is written in Latin,
revels in the tropical imagery of this favorite book of the
Middle Ages. Everything is allegorized. The very words
are exuberant allegories. And yet there is not a single

---

[1] *Causa diligendi Deum Deus est, modus sine modo diligere.   De dilig.
Deo.* 1.   Migne, 182. 974.

[2] *In Cant.*, p. 919, as quoted by Ries, p. 212.

[3] *Sic affici deificari est.*   Bernard does not shrink from the use of this word
as also Origen and Gregory of Nyssa did not, and other Fathers who used it
or its Greek equivalent.

2 T

sensual or unchaste suggestion in all the extended treatment. As for the historical and literal meaning, Bernard rejects all suggestion of it as unworthy of Holy Scripture and worthy only of the Jews, who have this veil before their faces.[1] The love of the Shulamite and her spouse is a figure of the love between the Church and Christ, though some- times the soul, and even the Virgin Mary, is put in the place of the Shulamite.   The kiss of chapter 1:2 is the Holy Spirit whom the second person of the Trinity reveals.[2] The breasts of the bride, 4:5, are the goodness and long- suffering which Christ feels and dispenses, Rom. 2:4.   The Canticles are a song commemorating the grace of holy affec- tion and the sacrament of eternal matrimony.[3]   It is an epithalamial hymn; no one can hear who does not love, for the language of love is a barbarous tongue to him who does not love, even as Greek is to one who is not a Greek.[4]   Love needs no other stimulus but itself.   Love loves only to be loved again.

Rhapsodic expressions like these welled up in exuberant abundance as Bernard spoke to his audiences at different hours of the day in the convent of Clairvaux.   They are marked by no progress of thought.   Aphoristic statement takes the place of logic.   The same spiritual experiences find expression over and over again.   But the treatment is always devout and full of unction, and proves the justice of the title, "the honey-flowing doctor," — *doctor mellifluus* — given to the fervid preacher.

The mysticism of St. Bernard centres in Christ.   It is by contemplation of Him that the soul is filled with knowledge and ecstasy.   The goal which the soul aspires to is that Christ may live in us, and our love to God become the all- controlling affection.   Christ is the pure lily of the valley whose brightness illuminates the mind.   As the yellow pol-

---

[1] *Serm.*, LXXV. 2 ; LXIII. 1; LXXIII. 1, 2.

[2] *Serm.*, VIII. Migne, p. 810.

[3] *Divinitus inspiratus Christi et ecclesiæ laudes, et sacri amoris gratiam et æterni connubii cecinit sacramenta,* etc.   *Serm.*, I. 8. ; Migne, p. 788.

[4] *Serm.*, LXXIX. 1 ; Migne, p. 1163.

len of the lily shines through the white petals, so the gold of
his divinity shines through his humanity. Bethlehem and
Calvary, the birth and passion of Christ, controlled the
preacher's thought. Christ crucified was the sum of his
philosophy.[1] The name of Jesus is like oil which enlightens,
nourishes, and soothes. It is light, food, and medicine. Jesus
is honey in the mouth, melody in the ear, and in the heart, joy.[2]

Bernard was removed from the pantheistic self-deletion of
Eckart and the imaginative extravagance of St. Theresa.
From Madame Guyon and the Quietists of the seventeenth
century, he differed in not believing in a state of pure love
in the present life. Complete obedience to the law of love
is impossible here unless it be in the cases of some of the
martyrs.[3] His practical tendencies and his common sense
kept him from yielding himself to a life of self-satisfied contemplation and commending it. The union with God and
Christ is like the fellowship of the disciples in the primitive
Church who were together with one heart and one soul, Acts
4:32. The union is not by a confusion of natures, but by
a concurrence of wills.[4]

§ 105. *Hugo and Richard of St. Victor.*

LITERATURE FOR HUGO. — *Works*, first publ. Paris, 1518, 1525, etc. Migne,
vols. 175–177. — *Lives* by A. HUGONIN, in Migne, 175. XV–CXXV. In
Hist. Lit. de France, reprinted in Migne, 175. CXXVI. sqq. — * A.
LIEBNER: *Hugo von St. V. und d. theol. Richtungen s. Zeit.*, Leip.,
1832. — B. HAUREAU: *Hugues de S. V. avec deux opuscules inédits*, Paris,
1859, new ed. 1886. — A. MIGNON: *Les origines de la scholastique et*

---

[1] *Haec mea philosophia scire Jesum Christum et hunc crucifixum.* Serm.,
XLIII. 4 ; Migne, p. 995.

[2] *Jesus mel in ore, in aure melos, in corde jubilus.* Serm., XV. 6; Migne,
p. 847.

[3] See Vacandard, *Vie de S. Bernard*, II. 497, and Ries, pp. 198 sq.

[4] *Unitas quam facit non confusio naturarum, sed voluntatum consensio.*
Serm. in Cant., LXXI. 7 ; Migne, 183. 1124. Harnack, whose treatment of
St. Bernard is one of the most stirring chapters in his Hist. of Doctrine, never-
theless says unjustly, III. 304, that Bernard's mysticism naturally led to
Pantheism. In Bernard himself there is no trace of Pantheism. See Ries,
pp. 190 sq.

Hugues de St. V., 2 vols. Paris, 1896. — Kilgenstein : *D. Gotteslehre d. Hugo von St. V.*, Würzb., 1897. — Denifle : *D. Sentenzen H. von St. Victor*, in *Archiv*, etc., for 1887, pp. 644 sqq. — Stöckl, pp. 352–381. For Richard. — *Works*, first publ. Venice, 1506. Migne, vol. 196. — J. G. V. Engelhardt : *Rich. von St. V.*, Erlangen, 1838. — Liebner : *Rich. à S. Victore de contemp. doctrina*, Gött., 1837–1839, 2 parts. — Kaulich : *D. Lehren des H. und Rich. von St. Victor*, Prag., 1864. — Art. in *Dict. of Natl. Biogr.*, Preger, Vaughan, Stöckl, Schwane, etc.

In Hugo of St. Victor, d. 1141, and more fully in his pupil, Richard of St. Victor, d. 1173, the mystical element is modified by a strong scholastic current. With Bernard mysticism is a highly developed personal experience. With the Victorines it is brought within the limits of careful definition and becomes a scientific system. Hugo and Richard confined their activity to the convent, taking no part in the public controversies of the age.[1]

Hugo, the first of the great German theologians, was born about 1097 in Saxony.[2] About 1115 he went to Paris in the company of an uncle and became an inmate of St. Victor. He was a friend of St. Bernard. Hugo left behind him voluminous writings. He was an independent and judicious thinker, and influenced contemporary writers by whom he is quoted. His most important works are on Learning, the Sacraments, a *Summa*,[3] and a Commentary on the Cœlestial Hierarchy of Dionysius the Areopagite. He wrote commentaries on Romans, Ecclesiastes, and other books of the Bible, and also a treatise on what would now be called Biblical Introduction.[4]

[1] St. Victor, the convent which William of Champeaux, Hugo, and Richard made famous, had its filial houses not only in France but also in Ireland. With the French Revolution the convent and its grounds disappeared. Two streets of Paris, the Rue Guy de la Brosse and the Rue de Jussieu, were driven through them. See Wetzer-Welte, *St. Victor*, XII. 914 sqq.

[2] The argument in favor of Saxony is well stated by Preger, *Deutsche Mystik*, I. 227 sqq. So Zöckler in Herzog, and the art. on *Hugo*, in Wetzer-Welte.

[3] *Summa Sententiarum*, Migne, 176. 42–172. This work has been denied to Hugo by Denifle on insufficient grounds. Hugo opens the work with a treatment of the three cardinal virtues, faith, hope, and love, and proceeds to the discussion of the Trinity, creation, the five sacraments, and marriage.

[4] He discusses the senses of Scripture, the number of the books, the apocrypha, the translation, the historical difficulties of Scripture, etc. See Migne, 175. 9–28. The same topics are treated in his treatise on Learning. Migne, 176. 778–811.

He recognized a triple sense of Scripture, historical, allegorical, and anagogical, and was inclined to lay more stress than was usual in that period upon the historical sense. An illustration of these three senses is given in the case of Job. Job belonged to the land of Uz, was rich, was overtaken by misfortune, and sat upon the dunghill scraping his body. This is the historical sense. Job, whose name means the suffering one, *dolens*, signifies Christ who left his divine glory, entered into our misery, and sat upon the dunghill of this world, sharing our weaknesses and sorrows. This is the allegorical sense. Job signifies the penitent soul who makes in his memory a dunghill of all his sins and does not cease to sit upon it, meditate, and weep. This is the anagogical sense.

From Hugo dates the careful treatment of the doctrine of the sacraments upon the basis of Augustine's definition of a sacrament as a visible sign of an invisible grace. His views are given in the chapter on the Sacramental System.

The mystical element is prominent in all of Hugo's writings.[1] The soul has a threefold power of apprehension and vision, the eye of the flesh, the eye of reason, and the eye of contemplation. The faculty of contemplation is concerned with divine things, but was lost in the fall when also the eye of reason suffered injury, but the eye of the flesh remained unimpaired. Redemptive grace restores the eye of contemplation. This faculty is capable of three stages of activity: *cogitatio*, or the apprehension of objects in their external forms; *meditatio*, the study of their inner meaning and essence; and *contemplatio*, or the clear, unimpeded insight into the truth and the vision of God. These three stages are likened unto a fire of green fagots. When it is started and the flame and smoke are intermingled so that the flame only now and then bursts out, we have *cogitatio*. The fire burning into a

---

[1] Among his mystical writings are *de arca Noe morali*, Migne, 176. 619–680; *de arca mystica*, Migne, 176. 681–703; *de vanitate mundi*. Noah's ark is symbolical of the spiritual house and Christ is the "Captain, the supreme Noah." The wood, windows, and other parts of the ark are all spiritualized. In the second treatise the ark represents the cross.

flame, the smoke still ascending, represents *meditatio.* The bright glowing flame, unmixed with smoke, represents *contemplatio.* The carnal heart is the green wood from which the passion of concupiscence has not yet been dried out.[1]

In another place Hugo compares the spirit, inflamed with desire and ascending to God, to a column of smoke losing its denseness as it rises. Ascending above the vapors of concupiscence, it is transfused with light from the face of the Lord and comes to behold Him.[2] When the heart is fully changed into the fire of love, we know that God is all in all. Love possesses God and knows God. Love and vision are simultaneous.

The five parts of the religious life, according to Hugo, are reading, reflection, prayer, conduct, and contemplation.[3] The word "love" was not so frequently on Hugo's pen as it was on St. Bernard's. The words he most often uses to carry his thought are contemplation and vision, and he has much to say of the soul's rapture, *excessus* or *raptus.* The beatitude, "The pure in heart shall see God," is his favorite passage, which he quotes again and again to indicate the future beatific vision and the vision to which even now the soul may arise. The first man in the state of innocence lived in unbroken vision of God.

They who have the spirit of God, have God. They see God. Because the eye has been illuminated, they see God as He is, separate from all else and by Himself. It is the intellectual man that partakes of God's bliss, and the more God is understood the more do we possess Him. God made man a rational creature that he might understand and that by understanding he might love, by loving possess, and by possessing enjoy.[4]

More given to the dialectical method and more allegorical

---

[1] *Carnale cor quasi lignum viride necdum ab humore carnalis concupiscentiæ exsiccatum,* etc. See Liebner, p. 315.

[2] *De arca morali,* III. 7 ; Migne, 176. 654.

[3] *de erud. didasc.,* Migne, 176. 797.

[4] *Quia non potest dei beatitudo participari nisi per intellectum,* etc. *Summa,* II. 1 ; Migne, 176. 79.

in his treatment of Scripture than Hugo, was Richard of St. Victor. Richard is fanciful where Hugo is judicious, extravagant where Hugo is self-restrained, turgid where Hugo is calm.[1] But he is always stimulating. Of his writings many are extant, but of his life little is known. He was a Scotchman, became subprior of St. Victor, 1162, and then prior. While he was at St. Victor, the convent was visited by Alexander III, and Thomas à Becket. In his exegetical works on the Canticles, the Apocalypse, and Ezekiel, Richard's exuberant fancy revels in allegorical interpretations. As for the Canticles, they set forth the contemplative life as Ecclesiastes sets forth the natural and Proverbs the moral life. Jacob corresponds to the Canticles, for he saw the angels ascending and descending. Abraham corresponds to the Proverbs and Isaac to Ecclesiastes.[2] The Canticles set forth the contemplative life, because in that book the advent and sight of the Lord are desired.

In the department of dogmatics Richard wrote *Emmanuel*, a treatise directed to the Jews,[3] and a work on the Incarnation, addressed to St. Bernard,[4] in which, following Augustine, he praised sin as a happy misdemeanor, — *felix culpa*, — inasmuch as it brought about the incarnation of the Redeemer.[5] His chief theological work was on the Trinity. Here he starts out by deriving all knowledge from experience, ratiocination, and faith. Dialectics are allowed full sweep in the attempt to join knowledge and faith. Richard condemned the pseudo-philosophers who leaned more on Aristotle than on Christ, and thought more of being regarded discoverers of new things than of asserting established truths.[6] Faith is set forth as the essential prerequisite of Christian knowledge. It is its starting-point and founda-

---

[1] See Liebner, *Hugo von St. Victor*, pp. 81 sq.

[2] Migne, 196. 409.   [3] *De Emmanuele*, Migne, 196. 601–665.

[4] Migne, 196. 995–1011. Richard calls Bernard, *divus Bernardus*, and "my Bernard," V ; Migne, 195. 999. He also addressed other works to St. Bernard.

[5] *O felix culpa quæ talem ac tantum meruit habere redemptorem*, Migne, 196. 1003.   [6] See Engelhardt, pp. 14 sqq.

tion.[1] The author proves the Trinity in the godhead from
the idea of love, which demands different persons and just
three because two persons, loving one another, will desire a
third whom they shall love in common.

Richard's distinctively mystical writings won for him
the name of the great contemplator, *magnus contemplator*.
In the *Preparation of the Mind for Contemplation* or *Benjamin the Less*, the prolonged comparison is made between Leah
and Rachel to which reference has already been made.   The
spiritual significance of their two nurses and their children
is brought down to Benjamin.   Richard even uses the bold
language that Benjamin killed his mother that he might rise
above natural reason.[2]

In *Benjamin the Greater*, or the *Grace of Contemplation*, we
have a discussion of the soul's processes, as the soul rises
" through self and above self " to the supernal vision of God.
Richard insists upon the soul's purification of itself from all
sin as the condition of knowing God.   The heart must be imbued with virtues, which Richard sets forth, before it can rise
to the highest things, and he who would attempt to ascend
to the height of knowledge must make it his first and chief
study to know himself perfectly.[3]

Richard repeats Hugo's classification of *cogitatio, meditatio*,
and *contemplatio*. Contemplation is the mind's free, clear, and
admiring vision of the wonders of divine wisdom.[4]   It
includes six stages, the last of them being " contemplation
above and aside from reason," whereby the mysteries of the
Trinity are apprehended.   In transgressing the limits of
itself, the soul may pass into a state of ecstasy, seeing visions,
enjoying sublimated worship and inexpressible sweetness of
experience.   This is immediate communion with God.   The

---

[1] *Fides totius boni initium est atque fundamentum*, Migne, 196. 889.

[2] *Interficit matrem ubi omnem supergreditur rationem.   De prep.*, 86 ;
Migne, 196. 62, etc.

[3] *Animus qui ad scientiæ altitudinem nititur ascendere, primum et principale sit ei studium se ipsum cognoscere.   De prep.*, 75 ; Migne, 196. 54.

[4] *Contemplatio est libera mentis perspicacia in sapientiæ spectacula cum
admiratione suspensa.   De gratia*, I. 5 ; Migne, 196. 67.   Here, as in other
places, Richard quotes his teacher Hugo.

third heaven, into which Paul was rapt, is above reason and to
be reached only by a rapturous transport of the mind — *per
mentis excessum.* It is " above reason and aside from reason." [1]
Love is the impelling motive in the entire process of contemplation and "contemplation is a mountain which rises above
all worldly philosophy."   Aristotle did not find out any
such thing, nor did Plato, nor did any of the company of the
philosophers. [2]

Richard magnifies the Scriptures and makes them the test
of spiritual states.   Everything is to be looked upon with
suspicion which does not conform to the letter of Scripture. [3]

The leading ideas of these two stimulating teachers are
that we must believe and love and sanctify ourselves in order
that the soul may reach the ecstasy and composure of contemplation or the knowledge of God.   The Scriptures are
the supreme guide and the soul by contemplation reaches a
spiritual state which the intellect and argumentation could
never bring it to.

Rupert of Deutz. — Among the mystics of the twelfth century no
mean place belongs to Rupert of Deutz. [4]   A German by nationality, he
was made abbot of the Benedictine convent of Deutz near Cologne
about 1120 and died 1135.   He came into conflict with Anselm of Laon
and William of Champeaux through a report which represented them as
teaching that God had decreed evil, and that, in sinning, Adam had followed God's will.   Rupert answered the errors in two works on the *Will
of God* and the *Omnipotence of God.*   He even went to France to contend with these two renowned teachers. [5]   Anselm of Laon he found on
his death-bed.   With William he held an open disputation.

Rupert's chief merit is in the department of exegesis.   He was the most
voluminous biblical commentator of his time.   He magnified the Scrip-

---

[1] *Supra rationem et præter rationem.   De prep.,* 86 ; Migne, 196. 61.

[2] *De prep.,* 74 ; Migne, p. 54.

[3] *Suspecta mihi est omnis veritas, quam non confirmat scripturarum
auctoritas.   De prep.,* 81 ; Migne, 196. 57.

[4] A full edition of his works is given by Migne, vols. 167–170.   See Bach
and Schwane.   Also Rocholl, *Rupert von Deutz.   Beitrag zur Gesch. der
Kirche im 12ten Jahrh.,* Gütersloh, 1886.

[5] Rupert gives an account of his journey to France to meet William and
Anselm in disputation in his *De regula Benedicti,* I. 1 ; Migne, 170. 482 sq.

tures. In one consecutive volume he commented on the books of the Old Testament from Genesis to Chronicles, on the four Major Prophets, and the four evangelists.[1] The commentary on Genesis alone occupies nearly four hundred columns in Migne's edition. Among his other exegetical works were commentaries on the Gospel and Revelation of St. John, the Minor Prophets, Ecclesiastes, and especially the Canticles and Matthew. In these works he follows the text conscientiously and laboriously, verse by verse. The Canticles Rupert regarded as a song in honor of the Virgin Mary, but he set himself against the doctrine that she was conceived without sin. The commentary opens with an interpretation of the second verse of chap. 1, thus : " ' Let him kiss me with the kiss of his mouth.' What is this exclamation so great, so sudden? O blessed Mary, the inundation of joy, the force of love, the torrent of pleasure have filled thee full and wholly intoxicated thee and thou hast felt what eye has not seen nor ear heard nor has entered into the heart of man, and thou hast said, ' Let him kiss me with the kiss of his mouth ' for thou didst say to the angel ' Behold the handmaid of the Lord, let it be unto me according to thy word.' What was that word? What did he say to thee? ' Thou hast found grace,' he said, ' with the Lord. Behold thou shalt conceive and bare a son.' . . . Was not this the word of the angel, the word and promise of the kiss of the Lord's mouth ready to be given?" etc.[2]

Rupert also has a place in the history of the doctrine of the Lord's Supper, and it is an open question whether or not he substituted the doctrine of impanation for the doctrine of transubstantiation.[3]

[1] The name of the work is *De operibus sanctœ trinitatis*. Migne, 167. 199-1827. The first two parts represent the work of the Father and the Son and the third the work of the Holy Spirit, pp. 1571-1827.

[2] Migne, 168. 841.

[3] *De operibus S. trinitatis*, II. 10. Bellarmin pronounced Rupert a heretic because of his views on the Lord's Supper. Schwane, *Dogmengesch.*, p. 641, denies the charge.

CHAPTER XIII.

SCHOLASTICISM AT ITS HEIGHT.

§ 106. *Alexander of Hales.*

LITERATURE: For general works on Scholasticism see § 95. ALEX. OF
HALES: *Summa universæ theologiæ*, Venice, 1475, Nürnberg, 1482,
Basel, 1502, Cologne, 1611, 4 vols. — WADDING: *Annal. Min.*, III. —
STÖCKL: *Phil. des Mittelalters*, II. 313–326. — K. MÜLLER: *Der Um-
schwung in der Lehre von der Busse*, etc., Freib., 1892. — The Doctrinal
Histories of SCHWANE, HARNACK, SEEBERG, etc., *Dict. of Natl. Biogr.*,
I. 272 sq.

THE culmination of Scholasticism falls in the thirteenth
century. It is no longer as confident in the ability of reason
to prove all theological questions as it was in the days of
Anselm and Abælard a hundred years before. The ethical
element comes into prominence. A modified realism prevails.
The syllogism is elaborated. The question is discussed
whether theology is a science or not. The authority of Aristotle becomes, if possible, more binding. All his writings
have become available through translations. The teachings
of Averrhoes, Avicenna, and other Arabic philosophers are
made known. The chief Schoolmen belong to one of the two
great mendicant orders. To the Franciscan order belonged
Alexander of Hales, Bonaventura, Duns Scotus, Roger Bacon,
and Raymundus Lullus. Albertus Magnus and Thomas
Aquinas were Dominicans. All these men had to do with
the universities.

Alexander of Hales (Halesius or Halensis), called by his
pupils the Irrefragable Doctor — *doctor irrefragabilis* — and
the king of theologians — *monarcha theologorum* — was born at
Hales, Gloucestershire, England, and died in Paris, 1245.
After reaching the dignity of archdeacon, he went to Paris
to prosecute his studies. He entered the order of St. Francis,
1222, and was the first Franciscan to obtain the degree of

doctor and to teach in the University of Paris, which he continued to do till 1238.

Alexander was the first Schoolman to whom all the writings
of Aristotle were accessible. His chief work, the *System of
Universal Theology*, was completed by one of his pupils, 1252.[1]
His method was to state the affirmative and negative of a
question [2] and then to give the solution. In worldly things,
knowledge proceeds from rational conviction; in spiritual
things, faith precedes knowledge. Theology is, therefore,
rather a body of wisdom — *sapientia* — than a science — *scientia;* not so much knowledge drawn from study as knowledge
drawn from experience.[3] Alexander had a most important
part in the definition of some of the characteristic mediæval
dogmas, which passed into the doctrinal system of the Roman
Catholic Church. He declared for the indelible character of
baptism and ordination. By elaborate argument he justified
the withdrawal of the cup from the laity and stated the new
doctrine of penance. He is especially famous for having
defined the fund of merit — *thesaurus meritorum* — the vicious
doctrine upon which the practice of distributing and selling indulgences was based. He was one of the first to make
the distinction between *attritio* or imperfect repentance, due
to fear, *timor servilis,* and *contritio* or perfect repentance
based upon higher motives. In all these matters he had a
controlling influence over the later Schoolmen.[4]

§ 107. *Albertus Magnus.*

LITERATURE : *Works.* Complete ed. by Jammy, Lyons, 1651, 21 vols. ; revised by Augusti Borgnet, 38 vols. Paris, 1890. Dedicated to Leo XIII., containing a *Life* and valuable indexes. The *De vegetabilibus*, ed. by Meyer and
Jessen, Berl., 1867. — *Com. on Job*, ed. by M. Weiss, Freib., 1904. — Fullest

[1] Roger Bacon contemptuously said of it that it was heavier than a horse
in weight. *Natl. Dict. of Biogr.*, I. 273. Other MSS. ascribed to Alexander are found in Oxford, etc. The *summa de virtutibus*, Paris, 1509, a
Com. on the Apocalypse, Paris, 1647, published under his name, are of
doubtful authenticity.

[2] *Videtur quod sic, et videtur quod non.*

[3] *Cognitio secundum visum, cognitio secundum gustum.*

[4] See Chapter on the Sacramental System.

monograph J. SIGHART: *Alb. Mag., sein Leben und seine Wissenschaft*, Regensb., 1857, based upon the compilation of PETER DE PRUSSIA: *Vita B. Alb., doctoris magni ex ordine Prædicatorum*, etc., Col., 1486.— Sighart gives a list of the biogr. notices from Thomas of Chantimpré, 1261. — D'ASSAILY: *Alb. le Grand*, Paris, 1870.—G. VON HERTLING: *Alb. Mag., Beiträge zu s. Würdigung*, Col., 1880 ; *Alb. Mag. in Gesch und Sage*, Col., 1880, and his art. in Wetzer-Welte, I. 414–419. — Ueberweg-Heinze. — STÖCKL, II. 353–421. — SCHWANE, pp. 46 sqq. etc.— PREGER: *Deutsche Mystik*, I. 263–268.— HARNACK, SEEBERG.

The most learned and widely read man of the thirteenth century was Albertus Magnus, Albert the Great. His encyclopædic attainments were unmatched in the Middle Ages, and won for him the title, Universal Doctor — *doctor universalis*. He was far and away the greatest of German scholars and speculators of this era.

Albert (1193–1280) was born at Lauingen in Bavaria, studied in Padua, and, about 1223, entered the order of the Dominicans, influenced thereto by a sermon preached by its second general, Jordanus. He taught in Freiburg, Hildesheim, Strassburg, Regensburg, and other cities. At Cologne, which was his chief headquarters,[1] he had among his pupils Thomas Aquinas.[2] He seems to have spent three years in teaching at Paris about 1245. In 1254 he was chosen provincial of his order in Germany. Two years later we find him in Rome, called by Alexander IV. for counsel in the conflict over the mendicant orders with William of St. Amour.

He was made bishop of Regensburg, an office he laid down in 1262.[3] His presence at the council of Lyons, 1274,

[1] He speaks in his will of spending most of his life in the convent at Cologne. He appointed a brother by birth, Henry, one of his executors. Sighart, p 247.

[2] Leo XIII., in his letter allowing Borgnet to dedicate his edition of Albert's works to him, said: " Especially am I glad to grant this permission because our old love for the angelic doctor is not disjoined from love for his teacher." Borgnet's ed., I. p. vii. Labbé, the Jesuit editor of the acts of the councils, wrote a poem comparing Albert with his pupil, Thomas Aquinas, and greatly praising him for his eulogy of Mary. Borgnet, I. lxxii. sq.

[3] Sighart, pp. 148,152, ascribes his resignation to bitter opposition, and thinks Albert had this opposition in mind when he was writing the paraphrase to Aristotle's *Politics*. The slothful, Albert says, find fault with those who excel. They killed Socrates, drove out Plato from Athens, and banished Aristotle. These people have the same plan in the domain of letters and science

is doubtful.[1]   One of his last acts was to go to Paris and defend the teachings of Thomas Aquinas, after that theologian's death.   He died at the age of eighty-seven, in Cologne,
where he is buried in the St. Andreas Church.

Albert was small of stature and the story is told of his first
appearance in the presence of the pope; that the pope, thinking he was kneeling, bade him stand on his feet.   A few
years before his death he became childish, and the story runs
that the archbishop, Siegfried, knocking at the door of his
cell, exclaimed, "Albert, are you here?" and the reply came,
"Albert is not here.   He used to be here.   He is not here
any more."   In early life, Albert was called the dumb ox on
account of his slowness in learning, and the change of his intellectual power was indicated by the bon mot, "Albert was
turned from an ass to a philosopher and from a philosopher
to an ass."   In 1880, the six hundredth anniversary of his
death, a statue was erected to his memory at his birthplace.

Albertus Magnus was a philosopher, naturalist, and theologian; a student of God, nature, and man.   He knew no Greek,
but was widely read in the Latin classics as well as in the
Fathers.   He used the complete works of Aristotle, and was
familiar with the Arabic philosophers whom at points he con-
futed.[2]   He also used the works of the Hebrews, Isaac
Israeli, Maimonides, and Gabirol.[3]   His large indebtedness to
Aristotle won for him the title, Aristotle's ape, — *simia Aristotelis.* — but unjustly, for he often disagreed with his teacher.[4]

that the liver has in the body.   For everybody has gall which collects in the
liver and which dispenses itself and makes the whole body bitter.   Thus in
the domain of letters there are some bitter men filled with gall, who would
fain make all other men bitter, and will not allow them to seek after truth in
sweet company.

[1] So Von Hertling.   The records of the council do not mention his name.
Peter of Prussia affirms Albert was present, and is followed by Sighart, p. 225.

[2] Averrhoes, Avicenna, Algazel, etc.   The honor of first mastering all the
works of Aristotle and putting them into the service of Christian philosophy
belongs to Albertus, says Schwane, p. 40.

[3] This is brought out by J. Guttmann, in his *Die Scholastik des 13ten Jahrhunderts in ihren Beziehungen zum Judenthum und zur judischen Literatur,*
Breslau, 1902.

[4] He again and again says: "Aristotle erred," *e.g.* Borgnet's ed., III. 545,

He traversed the whole area of the physical sciences. No one for centuries had been such a student of nature. He wrote on the vegetable kingdom, geography, mineralogy, zoology, astronomy, and the digestive organs. The writings on these themes are full of curious items of knowledge and explanations of natural phenomena. His treatise on meteors, *De meteororibus*, for example, which in Borgnet's edition fills more than three hundred pages (IV. 477–808), takes up at length such subjects as the comets, the milky way, the cause of light in the lower strata of air, the origin of the rivers, the winds, lightning, thunder and cyclones, the rainbow, etc. In the course of his treatment of rivers, Albert speaks of great cavities in the earth and spongy regions under its flat surface. To the question, why the sun was made, if the prior light was sufficient to render it possible to speak of "morning and evening" on the first days of creation, he replied, "that as the earlier light amply illuminated the upper parts of the universe so the sun was fitted to illuminate the lower parts, or rather it was in order that the day might be made still more bright by the sun; and if it be asked what became of the prior light, the answer is that the body of the sun, *corpus solis*, was formed out of it, or at any rate that the prior light was in the same part of the heavens where the sun is located, not as though it were the sun but in the sense that it was so united with the sun as now no more to be specially distinguished from it." [1]

Albert saw into a new world. His knowledge is often at fault, but sometimes his statements are prophetic of modern discovery. For example, he said that the poles of the earth were too cold to be inhabited. He knew about the sleep of plants and many of the laws of the vegetable world. He was indefatigable in experimentation, the forerunner of the modern laboratory worker, and had much to do with arsenic, sulphur, and other chemical substances. He knew about

etc. He says: "He who believes Aristotle to have been a god, can believe he never erred. But if he was a man, then he could err like ourselves." Borgnet's ed., III. 553.

[1] *Sent.*, II. xiii., F. Borgnet's ed., XXVII. 249 sq.

gunpowder, but got his knowledge from others.[1] The succeeding age associated his name, as also the name of Roger
Bacon, with magic and the dark arts, but probably without
sufficient reason.

The world has had few such prolific writers as Albertus
Magnus. In Borgnet's edition of thirty-eight volumes, there
are, excluding the valuable indexes, no less than 27,014 pages
of two columns each. These writings may be said to take
up not only every topic of physical knowledge but to discuss
every imaginable subject in religion and philosophy. His
activity combined the travail of the original thinker with the
toil of the compiler. Twelve volumes in Borgnet's edition
are devoted to philosophy and the natural sciences, one to sermons, one to a commentary on Dionysius the Areopagite, ten
to commentaries on books of the Old and New Testaments,
and fourteen to theology. He freely used some of his predecessors among the Schoolmen as Anselm, Bernard, and
Hugo and Richard of St. Victor, as well as the Fathers and
the Greek and Arabic philosophers.

Albert's chief theological works are a Commentary on the
Sentences of the Lombard, a Study of Created Things [2] and
an independent *summa* of theology, which was left unfinished, and stopped with the discussion of sin. These
three works, in many subjects of which they treat, run parallel.
But each is fresh, elaborate, and has its own peculiar arrangement. The *Study of Created Things*, or *System of Nature* is
an attempt, whose boldness has never been exceeded, to
explain the great phenomena of the visible universe above
and below, eternity and time, the stars and the motion of the
heavens, angels and devils, man, his soul and body, the laws
of his nutrition, sleep, reason, intellect, and other parts of his
constitution, and events to which he is subject.

Albert's commentaries cover the Psalms in three volumes, the
Lamentations, Daniel, the Minor Prophets, Baruch, the Gospels, and the Apocalypse. His commentary on the Worthy

---

[1] An interesting survey of Albert's knowledge of nature is given by Sighart,
pp. 302–356 ; also Stöckl, II. 359 sqq.

[2] *Summa de creaturis*, vols. XXXIV., XXXV., in Borgnet's ed.

Woman of Proverbs 31 : 10–31 is drawn out to two hundred
pages of two columns each.

Theology, Albert defined to be a science in the truest sense,
and what is more, it is wisdom.[1] It is the practical science
of those things that pertain to salvation. The being of God
is not susceptible of positive *a priori* proof. It may be
proved in an indirect way from the impossible absurdities
which would follow from the denial of it.[2] The existence of
God is not, properly speaking, an article of theology, but an
antecedent of all articles. In his *Summa* he quotes Anselm's
definition, "God is greater than anything else that can be
conceived." The objection was made to it that what is
above what can be conceived we cannot grasp. He answers
the objection by showing that God can be known by positive
affirmation and by negation. The cosmological proof was
most to Albert's mind, and he argued at length the proposition that motion demands a prime mover. Matter cannot
start itself into motion.[3]

The Trinity is matter of revelation. Philosophy did not
find it out.[4] Albert, however, was not prevented from entering into an elaborate speculative treatment of the doctrine.

Following Augustine, Anselm, and Richard of St. Victor,
he argued for the procession of the Spirit from the Son as well
as from the Father as a necessity,[5] and laid stress upon love
as the chief principle within the sphere of the persons of the
godhead.

The usual scholastic list of questions about the angels,
good and bad, is treated by Albert with great exhaustiveness.
A number of angels, he decides, cannot be in one and the
same place at the same time, not because of the spatial inconvenience it might seem to imply, but on account of the possi-

[1] *Theologia verissima scientia est et, quod plus est, sapientia.* *Summa
theol.*, I. 1, 1 ; Borgnet's ed., XXXI. 9.

[2] *Summa*, I. 3, q. 17 ; Borgnet's ed., XXXI. 116.

[3] *Physic*, VII. ; Borgnet's ed., III. 483–502.

[4] *Philosophi pro propria ductu naturalis rationis non potuerunt cognoscere
trinitatem personarum.* Borgnet, XXXI. 60.

[5] *Summa*, I. 7, q. 31 ; Borgnet, XXXI. 326 sqq.

2 U

bility of the confusion of activity it might involve. He concludes it to be impossible for an angel to be in more than one
place at the same time. He discussed at length the language
and vocal organs of the angels.[1] Especially elaborate is his
treatment of the fall, and the activity and habitation of Lucifer
and the demons. In pruriency he is scarcely behind some of
the other Schoolmen. Every possible question that might
occur to the mind had to be answered. Here are some of the
questions. "Do the lost sin in hell?" "Do they wish any
good?" "Is a smoky atmosphere a congenial element for
the demons?" "What are the age and stature of those
who rise from the dead?" "Does the sight of the pains of
the lost diminish the glory of the beatified?" To this last
question he replied that such sight will increase the joy of the
angels by calling forth renewed thanks for their redemption.[2] The serious problem of what it was into which the
devil fell occupied Albert's careful and prolonged argumentation several times.[3] The views of the Universal doctor
on demonology will be taken up in another chapter. In another place also we shall speak of his answer to the question, what effect the eating of the host has upon a mouse.

The chief and ultimate cause of the creation of man is that
he might serve God in his acts, praise God with his mouth,
and enjoy God with his whole being. A second cause is
that he might fill up the gaps left by the defection of the angels.[4] In another place Albert explains the creation of man
and angels to be the product of God's goodness.[5]

Of all the panegyrists of the Virgin Mary before Alphonso

[1] *De locutione angelorum. Summa*, II. 9, q. 35 ; Borgnet, XXXII. 376–
387. He draws in his discussion from Augustine, St. Basil, and John of
Damascus.

[2] *Sent.*, IV. 50 ; Borgnet's ed., XXX. 699. Albert even goes so far as to
discuss whether unborn infants destroyed by abortion rise from the dead.

[3] *in quid cecidit diabolus. Summa de creaturis*, IX. 67 ; Borgnet's ed.,
XXXIV. 682 sqq. *Summa theol.*, II. 5, q. 23 sqq. ; Borgnet's ed., XXXII.
266–286.

[4] *Adjunctus autem finis est qui secutus est ex isto : et ille est reparatio
ruinæ angelicæ. Summa*, II. 12 sq., 74 ; Borgnet's ed., XXXIII. 57.

[5] *Quare est creatus homo vel angelus ? Brevi sermone, respondere potest.
Propter bonitatem ejus. Sent.*, II. 1, E.; Borgnet's ed., XXVII. 35.

da Liguori, none was so fulsome and elaborate as Albert. Of the contents of his famous treatise, *The Praises of Mary*, — *de laudibus B. Mariæ Virginis*,[1] — which fills eight hundred and forty-one pages in Borgnet's edition, a synopsis is given in the section on the Worship of Mary. In the course of this treatment no less than sixty different passages from the Canticles are applied to Mary. Albert leaves her crowned at her assumption in the heavens. One of the questions this indefatigable theologian pursued with consequential precision was Eve's conception before she sinned.

As for the ecclesiastical organization of the Middle Ages, the pope is to Albert God's viceregent, vested with plenary power.[2]

Albert astounds us by the industry and extent of his theological thought and labor and the versatility of his mind. Like all the Schoolmen he sought to exhaust the topics he discusses, and looks at them in every conceivable aspect. There is often something chaotic in his presentation of a theme, but he is nevertheless wonderfully stimulating. It remained for Albert's greater pupil, Thomas Aquinas, to bring a clearness and succinctness to the statement of theological problems, theretofore unreached. Albert treated them with the insatiable curiosity of the student, the profundity of the philosopher, and the attainments of a widely read scholar. Thomas added the skill of the dialectic artist and a pronounced practical and ethical purpose.

§ 108. *Thomas Aquinas.*

LITERATURE: I. *Works.* — U. CHEVALIER : Répertoire under Thomas Aq., pp. 1200–1206, and *Supplem.*, pp. 2823–2827. — *S. Thomæ Aquinatis Doctoris Angelici opera omnia*, jussu impensaque Leonis XIII., P. M., edita, Romæ ex typographia polyglotta S. C. de Propaganda Fide, vols. 1–11, 1882–1902, to be completed in 25 vols. For this edition, called from Leo's patronage *editio Leonina*, a papal appropriation has been made of 300,000 lire. See vol. I., p. xxv. — Older edd., Rome, 1570, 18 vols. by order of Pius V., and Venice, 1592–1594 ; Antwerp, by C. MORELLES,

---

[1] *Summa*, II. 14 ; Borgnet's ed., pp. 131 sq.

[2] *Habet potestatis plenitudinem quia est ordinarius omnium hominum et quia est vice Dei in terris. Summa*, II. q. 141, 3 ; Borgnet, XXXIII. 484.

1612 sqq., 18 vols. ; Paris, 1660, 23 vols. ; Venice, 1785-1790, 28 vols. ; with 30 dissertations by B. M. DE RUBEIS, Naples, 1846-1848, 19 vols.; Parma, 1852 sqq.; Paris, 1871-1880, 33 vols. by FRETTÉ and MARÉ. — The *Summa theologica* has been often separately published as by MIGNE, 4 vols. Paris, 1841, 1864 ; *DRIOUX, 15 vols. Paris, 1853-1856 ; with French trans., and 8 vols. Paris, 1885. Among the very numerous commentators of the *Summa* are Cajetan, d. 1534, given in the Leonine ed., Melchior Canus, d. 1560, Dominicus Soto, d. 1560, Medina, d. 1580, Bannez, d. 1604, Xantes Moriales, d. 1666, Mauritius de Gregorii, d. 1666, all Dominicans ; Vasquez, d. 1604, Suarez, d. 1617, Jesuits. The most prolix commentaries are by barefooted Carmelites of Spain, viz. the *cursus theologicus* of Salamanca, 19 vols. repub. at Venice, 1677 sqq., and the *Disputationes collegii complutensis* at Alcala in 4 vols. repub. at Lyons, 1667 sqq. — See WERNER : *D. hl. Thomas*, I. 885 sqq. — P. A. UCCELLI's ed. of the *contra Gentiles*, Rome, 1878, from autograph MSS. in the Vatican, contains a facsimile of Thomas' handwriting which is almost illegible. — Engl. trans. of the *Aurea Catena*, Oxford, 1865, 6 vols., and the *Ethics* by J. RICKABY, N.Y., 1896. — FR. SATOLLI, in *Summam theol. d. Th. Aq. prœlectiones*, Milan, 1884-1888. — L. JANSSEN : *Summa theol. ad modum commentarii in Aquinatis Summam prœsentis œvi studii aptatam*, Freib. im Br., 5 vols. 1902. — *La théol. affective ou St. Th. d' Aq. médité en vue de prédication*, by L. Bail, Paris, 12 vols.

II. LIVES, ETC. — The oldest Life is by WILLIAM DE THOCO, who knew Thomas personally, reprinted in the ed. Leonina, vol. I. Documents in *Chartularium parisiensis.* — F. B. DE RUBEIS : *De gestis et scriptis ac doctrina S. Th. Aq. dissertationes crit. et apolog.*, reprinted in the Leonina. — P. A. TOURON : Paris, 1737. — J. BAREILLE : 1846, 4th ed. 1862. — *KARL WERNER, Rom. Cath. Prof. at St. Pölten, Austria : *D. heilige Th. von Aquino*, 3 vols. 1858-1859, Regensb. Learned, exhaustive, but ill-digested. — R. B. VAUGHAN, Rom. Cath. abp. of Sydney : *Life and Labors of St. Th. of Aquino*, 2 vols. Lond., 1871-1872, based on Werner. — CICOGNANI : *Sulla vita de S. Tomasio*, Engl. trans., 1882. — P. CAVE-NAUGH : *Life of Th. Aq.*, *the Angelic Doctor.* N.Y., 1890. — DIDIOT : *Le docteur angélique S. Th. d' Aq.*, Bruges, 1894. — JOURDAIN : *Le Phil. de S. Th. d' Aq.*, 2 vols. Paris, 1861. — *F. X. LEITNER : *D. hl. Th. von Aq. über d. unfehlbare Lehramt d. Papstes*, Freib., 1872. — J. J. BAU-MANN : *D. Staatslehre des hl. Th. von Aq.*, Leip., 1873. — L. SCHÖTZ : *Thomas Lexicon* (explanation of technical terms), Paderb., 1881. — EICKEN : *D. Philos. d. Th. von Aq. und. d. Kultur d. Neuzeit*, Halle, 1886, 54 pp. ; also *Th. von Aq. und Kant, ein Kampf zweier Welten*, Berlin, 1901. — *F. H. REUSCH, Old-Cath. : *D. Fälschungen in dem Traktat des Th. von Aq. gegen die Griechen*, München, 1889. — F. TESSEN-WESIERSKY : *D. Grundlagen d. Wunderbegriffs n. Th. von Aq.* Paderb., 1899, p. 142. — J. GUTTMANN : *D. Verhältniss des Th. von Aq. zum Judenthum und zur jüdischen Literatur*, 1891. — WITTMANN : *D. Stellung d. hl. Th. von Aq. zu Avencebrol*, Münster, 1900. — DE GROOT : *Leo XIII. und der hl. Th. von Aq.*, Regensb., 1897.—M. GRABMANN : *D.*

Lehre d. hl. Th. v. Aq. v. d. Kirche als Gottcswerk, Regensb., 1903. — J. Göttler: *D. hl. Th. v. Aq. u. d. vortridentin. Thomisten üb. d. Wirkgn. d. Busssakramentes*, 1904. — Stöckl : *Philos. d. Mittelalters*, II. 421–728. The *Histt. of Doctr.* of Schwane, Harnack, III. 422–428, etc., and Loofs, pp. 284–304. — Lane-Poole : *Illustrations*, etc., pp. 226 sqq. — Baur : *D. Christl. Kirche des M. A.*, 312–354. — The art. in Wetzer-Welte, XI. 1626–1661. — T. O'Gorman: *Life and Works of St. Th. Aq.* in *Papers of Am. Soc. of Ch. Hist.*, 1893, pp. 81–97. — D. S. Schaff : *Th. Aq. and Leo XIII.* in *Princeton Rev.*, 1904, pp. 177–196. — Art. *Th. Aq. and Med. Thought*, in *Dubl. Rev.*, Jan., 1906.

In an altar piece by Traini, dating from 1341, in the church of St. Caterina, Pisa, Thomas Aquinas is represented as seated in the centre with a book open before him. At the top of the cloth the artist has placed Christ, on one side of him Matthew, Luke, and Paul and on the other, Moses, John, and Mark. Below Thomas Aquinas, and on the left side, Aristotle is represented standing and facing Thomas. Aristotle holds an open volume which is turned towards the central figure. On the right hand Plato is represented, also standing and facing Thomas with an open volume. At the foot of the cloth there are three groups. One at each corner consists of monks looking up admiringly at Thomas. Between them, Averrhoes is represented reclining and holding a closed book. This remarkable piece of art represents with accuracy the central place which has been accorded to Thomas Aquinas in the mediæval theology. Arabic philosophy closes its mission now that the great exponent of Christian theology has come. The two chief philosophers of the unaided reason offer to him the results of their speculations and do him homage. The body of monks admire him, and Christ, as it were, commends him.

Thomas Aquinas, called the Angelic doctor, — *doctor angelicus*, — 1225–1274, is the prince of the Schoolmen, and next to St. Augustine, the most eminent divine of the Latin Church. He was a man of rare genius, wisdom, and purity of life. He had an unrivalled power of orderly and vigorous statement. Under his hand the Scholastic doctrines were organized into a complete and final system. He expounded them with transparent clearness, and fortified them with powerful arguments derived from Scripture, tradition, and reason. Mystical piety and a sound intellect were united in him. As compared with many of the other Schoolmen, notably with Duns Scotus, Thomas was practical rather than speculative. Popes and councils have repeatedly acknowledged his authority as a teacher of Catholic theology. Thomas was canonized by John XXII., 1323, and raised to the dignity of "doctor of the church," 1567. In 1879, Leo XIII. commended him as the corypheus and prince of all the Schoolmen, and as the safest guide of Christian philosophy in the battle of faith and reason against the sceptical and revolutionary tendencies of the nineteenth century,[1] who "set to rest once for all the discord between faith and reason, exalting the dignity of each and yet keeping them in friendly alliance." In 1880 this pope pronounced him the patron of Catholic schools. In the teachings of Thomas Aquinas we have, with one or two exceptions, the doctrinal tenets of the Latin Church in their perfect exposition as we have them in the Decrees of the council of Trent in their final statement.

Thomas of Aquino was born about 1225 in the castle of Rocca Sicca — now in ruins — near Aquino in the territory of Naples. Through his father, the count of Aquino, he was descended from a princely house of Lombardy. His mother was of Norman blood and granddaughter of the famous Crusader Tancred. At five the boy was sent to the neighboring convent of Monte Cassino from which he passed to the University of Naples. In 1243 he entered the Dominican order, a step his family resented. His brothers who were serving in the army of Frederick II. took the novice by force and kept him under guard in the paternal castle for more than a year. Thomas employed the time of his

---

[1] *Encyclical*, Aug. 4, 1879. See text in Mirbt, pp. 391 sqq. Thomas is praised as "*inter scholasticos doctores omnium princeps et magister . . . ingenio docilis et acer, memoriæ facilis et tenax, vitæ integerrimus, veritatis, unice amator, divina humanaque scientia prædives.*" The preface to the papal edition attacks the *Lutheriana pestis* and the *Lutherianum virus*, which are to be counteracted by the works of Thomas *in cujus limpidissima et angelica mente veritas divinitus nobis patefacta.* See Schaff, *Thos. Aq. and Leo. XIII.*, p. 179.

confinement in studying the Bible, the *Sentences* of the Lombard, and the works of Aristotle.

We next find him in Cologne under Albertus Magnus. That great Schoolman, recognizing the genius of his pupil, is reported to have said, "He will make such a roaring in theology that he will be heard through all the earth."[1] He accompanied Albertus to Paris and in 1248 returned to Cologne as teacher. He again went to Paris and won the doctor's degree. William de St. Amour's attack upon the monastic orders drew from him a defence as it also did from Bonaventura. Thomas was called to Anagni to represent the case of the orders. His address called forth the commendation of Alexander IV., who, in a letter to the chancellor of the University of Paris, spoke of Thomas as a man conspicuous by his virtues and of encyclopædic learning. In 1261, Thomas left the teacher's chair in Paris and taught successively in Bologna, Rome, and other Italian cities. Urban IV. and Clement IV. honored him with their confidence. The years 1272–1274 he spent at Naples. He died on his way to the œcumenical council of Lyons, March 7, 1274, only forty-eight years of age, in the Cistercian convent of Fossa Nuova near Terracina. Dante and Villani report he was poisoned by order of Charles of Anjou, but the earliest accounts know nothing of this. The great teacher's body was taken to Toulouse, except the right arm which was sent to the Dominican house of Saint Jacques, Paris, whence, at a later date, it was removed to Rome.

The genuine writings of Thomas Aquinas number more than sixty, and fall into four classes. The philosophical works are commentaries on Aristotle's Ethics, Metaphysics, Politics, and other treatises. His exegetical works include commentaries on Job, the first fifty-one Psalms, Canticles, Isaiah, the Lamentations, the Gospels, and the Epistles of Paul. The exposition of the Gospels, known as the Golden Chain, — *aurea catena*,[2] — consists of excerpts from the

---

[1] William of Thoco, *ipse talem dabit in doctrina mugitum quod in toto mundo sonabit.*

[2] This title was given to the work after Thomas' death. Thomas, in his dedication to Urban IV., calls it *expositio continua.* The *Catena* is so con-

Fathers. A number of Thomas' sermons are also extant. The apologetic works are of more importance. The chief among them are works designed to convince the Mohammedans and other unbelievers,[1] and to promote the union of the Greeks and Latins, and a treatise against the disciples of Averrhoes.[2]

Thomas' works on dogmatic theology and ethics are the most important of his writings. The earliest was a commentary on the *Sentences* of Peter the Lombard. Here belong Expositions of the Apostles' Creed, the Lord's Prayer, the the decalogue, the Angelic salutation, and the sacraments. Thomas gave his first independent systematic treatment of the entire realm of theology in his *Compendium theologiœ.* The subject was presented under the heads of the three cardinal virtues, — faith, hope, and charity. His master-work is his *Summa theologica* which he did not live to finish and which is supplemented by compilations from the author's commentary on the Lombard. Thomas also made important contributions to the liturgy and to hymnology. In 1264, at the request of Urban IV., he prepared the office for the festival of *Corpus Christi*, in which were incorporated the *Pange lingua*, *Lauda Sion*, and other hymns.[3]

With Augustine and John Calvin, Thomas Aquinas shares the distinction of being one of the three master theological minds of the Western world. What John of Damascus did for the theology of the Greek Church, that Thomas did for the theology of the mediæval Church. He gave to it its most perfect form. His commanding eminence rests upon his clearness of method and his well-balanced judgment

trived that it reads like a running commentary, the several extracts being dovetailed together. The compiler introduced nothing of his own but connecting particles. See Preface to Oxford ed., p. iv.

[1] *Summa de veritate Catholicœ fidei contra Gentiles.* The first three books include the arguments from reason, the fourth the argument from revelation.

[2] *Contra errores Grœcorum* and *de unitate intellectus contra Averrhoistas.*

[3] See Koch, *Kirchenlied*, I. 137; Wackernagel, *Kirchenlied*, I. 143 sqq.; Werner, I. 791 sqq.

rather than upon his originality of thought.[1] He was not a great scholar and, like Augustine, he knew no Hebrew and little Greek. Abælard, Bonaventura, and Albertus Magnus seem to show a wider familiarity than he with the ancient authors, patristic and profane, but they differ widely. He leaned much upon Albertus Magnus.[2] Albertus had an eye more for the works of nature, Thomas for moral action. As was the case with the other Schoolmen, so Thomas had as his chief authorities Augustine and Aristotle, quoting the latter as "the philosopher." He was in full sympathy with the hierarchical system and the theology of the mediæval Church and at no point out of accord with them.

The *Summa theologica*, true to its author's promise, avoids many of the idle discussions of his predecessors and contemporaries.[3] The treasures of the school and Church are here gathered together, sifted, and reduced to an elaborate but inspiring and simple structure. The three books treat respectively of God, man, and the Redeemer, the sacraments being included under the last head. The matter is disposed of in 518 divisions, called *questions*, and these are divided into 2652 *articles*. Each article states the negative and positive sides of the proposition under discussion, the arguments for and against it, and then the author's solution. The same uniform threefold method of treatment is pursued throughout. This method would become insufferably monotonous but for the precision of Thomas' statement and the interest of the

---

[1] Eicken, *D. Philosophie d. Th. von Aq.*, p. 4, says, *er gehört nicht so wohl zu den schaffenden als zu den ordnenden Geistern.* "He belongs not so much to the originating as to the organizing minds." He repeats this judgment in his *Thomas von Aquino und Kant*, p. 27. He who would charge the Middle Ages with confused and abstruse deductions must look for examples elsewhere than in Thomas.

[2] Following Sighart, *Life of Albertus Magnus*, and Landerer, in art. *Albertus*, in Herzog, 2d ed. XV. 575, Stöckl says, II. 421, 734, that "Thomas stands wholly upon Albert's shoulders. Thomas finished what Albert began." Thomas received a strong impulse from Albert, but he went out especially in the departments of ethics and apologetics into regions not fully explored by his great teacher.

[3] *Multiplicatio inutilium quæstionum, articulorum et argumentorum.* Prologue.

materials.   Each article is a finished piece of literary art.
Here is an example on the simplicity of God.[1]   The question
is asked whether God is body, *utrum Deus sit corpus.*   In
favor of an affirmative reply is: 1. The consideration that God
seems to have a body, for a body has three demensions, and
the Scriptures ascribe to God, hight, depth, and length, Job
11: 8.   2. Whatever has a figure, has a body.   God seems
to have a figure, Gen. 1 : 26, for He said, "Let us make man
in our image." 3. Everything that has parts, has a body.
A hand, Job 40 : 4, and eyes, Ps. 24: 15, are ascribed to God.
4. God has a seat and throne, Isa. 6 : 1.   5. God has a local
termination which men may approach, Ps. 24 : 5.

But on the other hand must be noted what is said in John
4 : 24, "God is Spirit."   The absolute God, therefore, is not
a body.   1. No body moves that is not before moved and
God is the first mover.   2. God is the first entity, *primum
ens.* 3. God is the noblest among entities.

The answers to the objections are: 1. That the Scripture
passages, attributing to God bodily parts, are figurative.
2. The expression "image of God " is used simply to indicate God's superior excellency over man and man's excellence
over the beasts.   3. The ascription of corporeal senses, such
as the eye, is a way of expressing God's intelligence.

Theological speculation is, with Thomas, not an exhibition
of theological acumen, but a pious employment pursued with
the end of knowing and worshipping God.   It is in keeping
with this representation that, on his way to Paris, he is reported to have exclaimed, he would not give Chrysostom on
Matthew for all the city.   It is also related that during his
last years in Naples the Lord, appearing to him, asked what
reward he desired, for he had written well on theological
questions.   Thomas replied, " None other, Lord, but Thyself."

Thomas made a clearer distinction between philosophy and
religion, reason and revelation, than had been made before
by any of the Schoolmen.   The reason is not competent by

---

[1] *De Dei simplicitate*, I. q. 3 ;   Migne, I. 626 sqq.

its own powers to discover the higher truths pertaining to God, such as the doctrine of the Trinity.[1] The ideas which the natural mind can reach are the *præambula fidei*, that is, the ideas which pertain to the vestibule of faith. Theology utilizes the reason, not, it is true, to prove faith, for such a process would take away the merit of faith, but to throw light on doctrines which are furnished by revelation.[2] Theology is the higher science, both because of the certainty of its data and on account of the superior excellence of its subject-matter.[3] There is no contradiction between philosophy and theology. Both are fountains of knowledge. Both come from the same God.

As between the Scriptures and the Fathers, Thomas makes a clear distinction. The Church uses both to arrive at and expound the truth. The Scriptures are necessary and final. The testimony of the Fathers is probable. Thomas' controlling purpose is to properly present the theology of the Church as he found it and nothing more.[4]

Philosophy and theology pursue different methods in searching after truth.[5] In philosophy, knowledge based upon the visible creation goes before faith. In theology, or the *doctrina fidei*, faith looking to God as He is in Himself, precedes knowledge. The existence of God is not exclusively a matter of faith. It has been demonstrated by philosophers by irrefragable proofs. Anselm's ontological argument, Thomas rejected on the ground that a conception in the mind — *esse in intellectu* — is something different from real existence — *esse in re*. He adduced four cosmological arguments, and the argument from design.[6] The cosmological arguments are:

---

[1] *Summa*, I. 32, 1 ; Migne, I. 888, I. 1, 1 ; Migne, I. 607.

[2] *Summa*, I. 1, 8 ; Migne, I. 615.

[3] *Tum propter certitudinem tum propter dignitatem materiæ. Summa*, I. 1, 5 ; Migne, I. 610.

[4] *Seine Darstellung will gar nichts anders sein als das wissenschaftliche Bewusstsein der kirchlichen Lehre.* Baur, p. 354.

[5] *Non eodem ordine utraque doctrina procedit*, etc. See Werner, II. 151, and his quotation from the *contra Gentiles*.

[6] See Köstlin, *Beweise fürs Dasein Gottes*, in *Studien u. Kritiken*, 1876, pp. 10 sqq.

1. Motion presupposes an original mover. 2. An infinite series of causes, it is impossible to conceive. Therefore, there must be a First Cause. 3. The conditional demands that which is absolute, and 4. that which is imperfect implies that which is perfect as its standard. As for the teleological argument, objects and events have the appearance of being controlled by an overruling design as an arrow being shot by an archer.[1]

Creation was not a necessity for God on account of any deficiency within Himself. It was the expression of His love and goodness. With Aristotle, Thomas agrees that by the natural reason the world cannot be proved to have had a beginning.[2] The first four things to be created were the realm of spirits, the empyrean, time, and earthly matter. The garden of Eden was a real place. Geographers do not locate it. It is secluded by the barriers of mountains, seas, and a certain tempestuous region.[3]

In discussing the origin of evil, Thomas says that, in a perfect world, there will be all possible grades of being. The weal of the whole is more important than the well-being of any part. By the permission of evil, the good of the whole is promoted. Many good things would be wanting but for evil. As life is advanced by corruption in the natural world, so, for example, patience is developed by persecution.

The natural order cannot bind God. His will is free. He chooses not to work contrary to the natural order, but He works outside of it, *præter ordinem*.[4] The providence of God includes what to us seems to be accidental. The man digging finds a treasure. To him the discovery is an accident. But the master, who set him to work at a certain place, had this in view.

From the divine providence, as the starting-point, the decree of predestination is elaborated. Thomas represented

[1] *Sicut sagitta a sagittante. Summa*, I. 2, 3 ; Migne, I. 622 sqq.

[2] *Mundum incepisse est credibile, non autem demonstratibile vel scibile. Summa*, I. 46 ; Migne, I. 1008.

[3] *Ideo scriptores locorum de hoc loco mentionem non fecerunt. Summa*, I. 102, 1 ; Migne, I. 1433.

[4] *Summa*, I. 103, 7 ; Migne, I. 1446. Comp. Werner, II. 396 sqq., for the passages from *contra Gentiles*.

the semi-Pelagian standpoint. The elect are substituted for the angels who lost their first estate,[1] even as the Gentiles were substituted for the Jews. The number of the elect is unknown, but they are the minority of the race. Reprobation is not a positive act of God. God's decree is permissive. God loves all men. He leaves men to themselves, and those who are lost, are lost by their own guilt. God's decree of election includes the purpose to confer grace and glory.

In his treatment of the angels, Thomas practised a commendable self-restraint, as compared with Bonaventura and other Summists.

When he takes up man, the Angelic doctor is relatively most elaborate. In the discussion of man's original condition and his state after the Fall, many questions are proposed which dialectical dexterity must answer in view of the silence of Scripture. Here are examples. Could Adam in his state of innocence see the angels? Did he have the knowledge of all things? Did he need foods? Were the children born in his state of innocence confirmed in righteousness and had they knowledge of that which is perfect? Would original sin have passed down upon Adam's posterity, if Adam had refused to join Eve in sinning?[2]

Thomas rejected the traducian view as heretical, and was a creationist.[3] Following Peter the Lombard, he held that grace was a superadded gift to Adam, over and above the natural faculties and powers of the soul and body.[4] This gift disposed man to love God above all things.[5]

---

[1] *In locum angelorum cadentium substituti sunt homines.* *Summa*, I. 23, 6 ; Migne, I. 828.

[2] *Summa*, I. 2, q. 72, 5 ; Migne, II. 633 sq. Thomas replies that in this case original sin would not have passed down to Adam's posterity, for according to philosophers, the active principle in generation is the father. But if Adam had sinned and Eve had not sinned, original sin would have passed down to Adam's descendants.

[3] *Hæreticum est dicere quod anima intellectiva traducatur cum semine.* *Summa*, I. 118, 2 ; Migne, I. 1556.

[4] *Superadditio gratiæ.* *Summa*, I. 95, 1 ; Migne, I. 1405 sq. Comp. Loofs, *Dogmengesch.*, pp. 292–295.

[5] *Ad diligendum Deum naturaliter super omnia.* Migne, II. 909.

Man's original righteousness, but for the Fall, would have passed down upon Adam's posterity. The cause of sin was an inordinate love of self.[1] Original sin is a disorder of the moral constitution, and shows itself in concupiscence, that is irrational desire. It has become a fixed condition of the race, a corrupt disposition of the soul, — *habitus corruptus*, — just as sickness is a corrupt condition of the body. The corruption of nature, however, is partial, — a wound, not a total deadness of the moral nature.

Thomas approaches the subject of Christ and redemption by saying that "our Saviour, Jesus Christ, has shown us the way of truth in himself, the way by which we are able to attain through resurrection to the beatitude of immortal life." [2] Three main questions are taken up: the person of the Saviour, the sacraments, which are the channels of salvation, and the goal or immortal life. The Anselmic view of the atonement is adopted. The infinitude of human guilt makes it fitting that the Son of God should make atonement. God was not, however, shut up to this method. He can forgive sin as He pleases. Thomas takes up all the main data of Christ's life, from the conception to the crucifixion. Justification is not a progressive process, but a single instantaneous act.[3] Faith, working by love, lays hold of this grace.

Scarcely any teaching of Augustine and Thomas Aquinas arouses so much revolt in the Christian theology of this age as the teaching about the future estate of unbaptized children dying in infancy. These theologians agree in denying to them all hope of future bliss. They are detained in hell for the sin of Adam, being in no wise bound to Christ in His passion and death by the exercise of faith and love, as the baptized and the patriarchs of the Old Testament are. The sacrament of faith, that is, baptism, not being applied to

---

[1] Migne, II. 603.

[2] *Summa*, III. *Prologus;* Migne, IV. 10.

[3] *Justificatio impii non est successiva.* *Summa*, I. 2, q. 113, 7 sqq. Migne, II. 955. Justification is defined as "an infusion of grace whereby the freewill is moved and guilt is pardoned."

them, they are forever lost. Baptism liberates from original sin, and without baptism there is no salvation.[1]

The doctrine of the sacraments, as expounded by Thomas, is, in all particulars, the doctrine of the Catholic Church. Christ won grace. The Church imparts it. The sacraments are visible signs of invisible things, as Augustine defined them. The number is seven, corresponding to the seven cardinal virtues and the seven mortal sins. They are remedies for sin, and make for the perfecting of man in righteousness.[2] The efficacy lies in a virtue inherent in the sacrament itself, and is not conditioned by faith in the recipient. Three of the sacraments — baptism, confirmation, and ordination — have an indelible character. Every conceivable question pertaining to the sacraments is taken up by Thomas and solved. The treatment of baptism and the eucharist occupies no less than two hundred and fifty pages of Migne's edition, IV. 600–852.

Baptism, the original form of which was immersion, cleanses from original sin and incorporates into the body of Christ. Children of Jews and infidels are not to be baptized without the consent of their parents.[3] Ordination is indispensable to the existence of the Church. In the Lord's Supper the glorified body of the Redeemer is wholly present essentially, but not quantitatively. The words of Christ, "This is my body," are susceptible of only one interpretation — the change of the elements into the veritable body and blood of Christ. The substance of the bread undergoes change. The dimensions of the bread, and its other accidents, remain. The whole body is in the bread, as the whole body is also in the wine.[4]

Penance is efficacious to the removing of guilt incurred after baptism. Indulgences have efficacy for the dead as well as the living. Their dispensation belongs primarily

---

[1] *Per baptismum pueri liberantur a peccato originali et ab inferno.* *Summa*, III. 57, 7 ; Migne, IV. 485, 486.

[2] *Summa*, III. 65, 1 ; Migne, IV. 595. See Werner, II. 676–699.

[3] *Summa*, II. (2), 10, 12 ; Migne, III. 101 sqq.

[4] *Totus Christus sub utraque specie.* *Summa*, III. 76, 2; Migne, IV. 734.

to the pope, as the head of the Church. The fund of merit
is the product chiefly of the superabounding merit of Christ,
but also of the supererogatory works of the saints.[1]

In regard to the Last Things, the fire of hell will be physical. The blessed will be able to contemplate the woes of
the lost without sorrow, and are led, as Albertus had said,
by the sight of these woes to praise God supremely for their
own redemption. Their beatitude is not increased by this
vision. The body of the resurrection will be the same, even
to the bowels.[2]

In his consideration of ethics, Thomas Aquinas rises far
above the other mediæval writers, and marks an epoch in the
treatment of the subject. He devotes to it nearly two hundred questions, or one-third of his entire system of theology.
Here his references to the " philosopher " are very frequent.[3]
It is Thomas' merit that he proceeds into details in analyz-
ing the conduct of daily life.[4] To give an example, he
discusses the question of drunkenness, and, with Aristotle,
decides that it is no excuse for crime.[5] Thomas, however,
also allows himself to be led into useless discussions where
sophistry has free play, as when he answers the questions,
whether a " man should love his child more than his father,"
or " his mother more than his father."

Thomas opens his ethical treatment with a discussion of the
highest good, that is, blessedness, — *beatitudo*, — which does
not consist in riches, honor, fame, power, or pleasure.[6] Riches
only minister to the body, and the more we have of them,
the more are they despised, on account of their insufficiency
to meet human needs; as our Lord said of the waters of the
world, that whoever drinks of them shall thirst again,

[1] *Præcipue propter meritum Christi*, etc.   Supplem., XXV. 1 ; Migne, IV.
1014.

[2] *Summa*, III. 94 ; Migne, IV. 1343 sqq. See Werner, II. 712.

[3] Not infrequently are there two or three references to Aristotle on a
single page, *e.g.* I. (2), 2, 2 ; I. (2), 4, 2 ; Migne, II. 22, 46.

[4] Baur, pp. 429 sqq., pronounces Thomas' method descriptive rather than
consequential. The system is not developed from fundamental principles.

[5] *Summa*, II.(2), 150, 4 ; Migne, III. 1051.

[6] *Summa*, I. (2), 2, 1 sqq.; Migne, II. 19–37.

John 4 : 13.   Blessedness consists in nothing else than the
vision of God as He is in Himself.[1]   Satisfaction is a necessary concomitant of blessedness, as warmth is a concomitant
of fire.

The virtues are the three religious virtues infused by God,—
faith, hope, and love; and the four philosophical or cardinal
virtues,—prudence, righteousness, endurance, and continence.
These are treated at great length.[2]   The ethical sections
conclude with discussions bearing on the habits of the clerical profession.   In committing the same sins as laymen do,
clerics sin more grievously.   " Ought they to live of alms ? "
This and a multitude of other questions of the same kind
are handled with all gravity and metaphysical precision.
The essence of Christian perfection is love.[3]

In his theory of Church and State also Thomas did not rise
above his age.[4]   He fixed the theological statement concerning the supremacy of the spiritual realm, the primacy of the
pope, and the right to punish heretics with death.   His views
are laid down in his *Summa*, and in three other writings, on
the *Rule of Princes*,[5] the *Errors of the Greeks*, and the *contra
Gentes*.   Thomas' argument is that the State exists to secure
for man the highest end of his being, the salvation of his
soul, as well as for his material well-being in this life.   He
shows no concern for the separate European states and
nationalities.[6]   As the head of the mystical body of Christ,
the pope is supreme over the civil estate, even as the spiritual
nature is superior to man's physical nature.   Christian kings

---

[1] *In visione divinæ essentiæ.*   Migne, II. 43.

[2] No less than forty-six questions are devoted to the religious virtues,
Migne, III. 9-375; and one hundred and twenty-four to the philosophical,
Migne, III. 375-1194.

[3] *Per se et essentialiter consistit perfectio christianæ vitæ in charitate.*
Summa, II. (2), 84, 3; Migne, III. 1295.

[4] See Werner, I. 760 sqq., 794 sqq.   Köstlin, art. *Staat und Kirche*, Herzog Enc., 2d ed., XIV. 629 sqq.   Reusch, *Die Fälschungen*, etĊ.

[5] *De regimine principum ad regem Cypri.*   Two of the four books of this
famous work are certainly genuine.   The last two books are probably by
Thomas' disciple, Ptolemy of Lucca.   Poole has some judicious remarks on
this work, *Illustr. of Med. Thought*, pp. 240-266.

[6] Eicken, *D. Philosophie d. Thomas*, etc., p. 38.

2 x

owe him subjection, as they owe subjection to Christ himself,
for the pope is Peter's successor and the vicar of Christ.[1]
The *monarchia Christi* has taken the place of the old Roman
imperium.

As for the Church itself, Rome is the mistress and mother
of all churches. To obey her is to obey Christ. This is according to the decision of the holy councils and the holy
Fathers.[2] The unity of the Church presupposes a supreme
centre of authority.[3] To the pope, it belongs to determine
what is of faith. Yea, subjection to him is necessary to
salvation.[4] High churchmanship could no further go.

In his declarations about heresy and its treatment, Thomas
materially assisted in making the persecution of heretics unto

---

[1] *successor Petri, Christi vicarius Romanus Pontifex cui omnes reges populi Christiani oportet esse subdito sicut ipsi domino Jesu Christo.* De reg.
principum, I. 14.

[2] *Romanæ ecclesiæ magistræ et matris omnium ecclesiarum cui obediendum est tanquam Domino Deo Jesu, etc.* Contra errores Græcorum,
Reusch's ed., p. 9. Also Mirbt, *Quellen,* pp. 143 sq. This work contains a
discussion of four points : the Procession of the Holy Ghost, the primacy of
the pope, the use of unleavened bread in the eucharist, and purgatory. It was
written at the time when the reunion of the Greeks and Latins was the subject
of negotiations. In the preparation of this treatise, Thomas used a work put
into his hands by Urban IV., once patriarch of Jerusalem. Thomas refers to
it as *libellum ab excellentia vestra mihi exhibitum sanctissime Pater Urbane
Papa diligenter perlegi.* It is full of citations from Cyril of Jerusalem, Cyril
of Alexandria, Chrysostom, and other Fathers, as Reusch, following Launoy,
learnedly shows. Thomas accepts the quotations without a question as genuine. The tract has never been published in full. It was known to the abbot
Uccelli from a MS. in the Vatican, and parts of it bearing on the papacy were
issued by his hand, 1870. Reusch prints a portion of the Vatican MS., and
also a part of the unpublished MS., the *Thesaurus veritatis fidei* by the Dominican Bonacursius, who wrote later than Thomas, and drew from the same
source as Thomas did. The Dominicans were specially active in urging the
extravagant claims of the papacy as against the Greek patriarch.

[3] *Cum tota ecclesia sit unum corpus, oportet si ista unitas debet conservari,
quod sit aliqua potestas regitiva respectu totius ecclesiæ supra potestatem
episcopalem, qua uniquæque specialis ecclesia regitur, et hæc est potestas papæ.*
Summa, Supplem., 40, 7 ; Migne, IV. 1075.

[4] *Quod subesse Romano pontifici sit de necessitate salutis. contra errores
Græcorum.* Döllinger, in *Das Papstthum,* says that "Thomas was the first
theologian to discuss the theory of papal infallibility as an integral part of
systematic theology." Leitner, pp. 10–14, etc., denies this. See Chapter XV.

death the settled policy of the Church and the State. At any rate he cleared away all objections as far as it was possible to clear them away. Heresy, as has already been said, he taught, is a crime to be punished like coin-clipping. No one may be compelled to enter the Church, but once having entered it and turned heretic, he must, if necessary, be forced by violent measures to obey the faith — *hæretici sunt compellendi ut fidem teneant*. It will thus be seen from this survey, which is supplemented in the chapters on the sacraments, the future state and Mariology, that the theology of the Angelic doctor and the theology of the Roman Catholic Church are identical in all particulars except the immaculate conception. He who understands Thomas understands the mediæval theology at its best and will be in possession of the doctrinal system of the Roman Church.

Thomas Aquinas was elevated by the Dominican order to the position of authoritative teacher in 1286. His scholars were numerous, but his theology was not universally accepted.

Some of his statements were condemned by the University of Paris as early as 1277, and about 1285 William of Ware, [1] trained at Oxford, which was a citadel of the Franciscans, wrote against the eminent Dominican. Soon after the death of the Franciscan Duns Scotus, the differences between him and Thomas were emphasized, and involved the two orders in controversy for centuries. No less than eighty-six theological differences between these two teachers were tabulated. [2]

The theology of Thomas Aquinas controlled Dante. The first printed commentary on the *Summa* was written by Cardinal Cajetan, Venice, 1507–1522. The Thomists lost by the decree of the immaculate conception of Mary, 1854. That doctrine had been the chief bone of contention between them

---

[1] A number of MSS. left by Ware are preserved in Oxford.

[2] In the *controversiæ theol. inter Thomam et Scotum*, by De Rada, the Franciscan bishop of Trani, Cologne, 1620. Werner devotes the whole third volume of his *Life of Thomas*, filling 876 pages, to the posthumous influence of Thomas. It takes up the teaching of his pupils, the conflicts with the Franciscans and Jesuits, etc., and brings in the names of Des Cartes, Leibnitz, Malbranche, Schelling, etc. See also art. *Thomismus und Scotismus*, in Wetzer-Welte, XI. 1699–1710.

and the Franciscans. The decision of Leo XIII., making
Thomas' theology and philosophy the standard for all Catholic teaching, has again, as it were, equallized matters.

The Protestant Reformers, in their indignation against the
Scholastic theology, could not do justice to Thomas Aquinas.
Luther went so far as to call his *Summa* the quintessence of
all heresies, meaning papal doctrines. He spoke of him as
" the fountain and original soup of all heresy, error, and Gospel havoc, as his books bear witness." [1] " You are much to
be condemned," Luther said to Prierias, " for daring to
obtrude upon us, as articles of faith, the opinions of that
sainted man, Thomas, and his frequent false conclusions."
On one occasion, he compared Thomas to the star of the book
of Revelation which fell from heaven, the empty speculations
of Aristotle to the smoke of the bottomless pit, the universities to the locusts, and Aristotle himself to his master
Apollyon. [2]

Such polemic extravagances have long since yielded to a
more just, historical estimate of this extraordinary man.
Thomas merits our admiration by his candor and clearness as
a systematic theologian, and by his sincerity and purity as
an ethical thinker. In the great fundamentals of the Christian system he was scriptural and truly catholic. His errors
were the errors of his age above which he was not able to
rise, as three centuries later the clear and logical Protestant
theologian, John Calvin, was not able in some important particulars to rise above the beliefs current in his time, and that
in spite of his diligent study of the Scriptures and wide
acquaintance with their teachings.

The papal estimate, as given expression to in the encyclicals of Leo XIII., is a practical denial of any progress in
theology since the thirteenth century, and in effect ignores
the scientific discoveries of ages. From the standpoint of
an unalterable Catholic orthodoxy, Leo made no mistake
in fixing upon Thomas Aquinas as the model expounder of

---

[1] *Thomas war der Brunn und Grundsuppe aller Ketzerei, Irrthumb und
Vertilgung des Evangelium wie seine Bücher beweisen.* Erl. ed., 24. 240.

[2] Köstlin, *Leben M. Luthers*, I. 431.

Christian doctrine.   Protestants differ, regarding no theologian since the Apostles as infallible.   They have no ex-
pectation that the Schoolman's argumentation will settle the
theological and religious unrest of these modern days, which
grows out of biblical theories and scientific and religious
studies of which that great teacher never dreamed, and world-
wide problems which never entered into his mind.

The present age is not at all concerned with many of the
curious questions which Thomas and the other Schoolmen
proposed.   Each studious age has its own problems to settle
and its own phases of religious doubt to adjust its fundamental teaching to.   The mediæval systems can no more be
expected to meet the present demands of theological controversy than the artillery used on the battlefield of Crécy can
meet the demands of modern warfare.[1]   The rights of private
judgment are being asserted more and more, and, as there is
some reason to suppose, even within the pale of the Roman
communion.   In the broader communion of the whole Church,
we are glad to think that both Leo XIII., the wise pope,
and Thomas Aquinas, the clear-eyed Schoolman, occupy a
high place as members of the company of the eminent
Churchmen of all ages; but this is not because they were
free from mistakes to which our fallible human nature makes
us subject, but because in the essential matters of the Christian life they were expounders of the Gospel.

§ 109.   *Bonaventura.*

LITERATURE : WORKS. — edd. Strassburg, 1482; Nürnberg, 1499, 4 vols. ;
   Rome, 1588–1596, 8 vols.; Lyons, 1668, 7 vols. ; Venice, 1751, 13 vols.;
   Paris, A. C. PELTIER, ed., 1864–1871, 15 vols., and Quaracchi, 1882–
   1902, prepared by the Franciscans. — B. BONELLI : *Prodromus ad
   omnia opp. S. Bon.*, Bassani, 1767. — W. A. HOLLENBERG : *Studien zum
   Bon.*, Berlin, 1862. — A. M. DA VICENZA : *D. heil. Bon.*, Germ. trans.

---

[1] In the tract, *Thomas von Aquino und Kant*, Eicken contrasts Thomas
and Kant as the representatives of two antagonistic types of thinking and
study, the mediæval and modern, that which is mechanical and bound by external authority, and that in which the individual, the subjective, have their
proper place as the determining principles.   Kant is the creator of ideas, the
thinker ; Thomas, the compiler and systematizer of ideas previously announced.

from the Italian, Paderborn, 1874. — J. Richard : *Etude sur le mysti-cisme speculatif de S. Bon.*, Heidelberg, 1869. — A trans. of the *Medi-tations of Bon.* on the Life of Christ by W. H. Hutchings, London, 1881. — A. Margerie : *Essai sur la Phil. de S. Bon.*, Paris, 1855. — J. Krause : *Lehre d. heil. Bon. über die Natur der geistl. und körperl. Wesen*, Paderborn, 1888. — L. de Chérancé : *S. Bonaventure*, Paris, 1899. — Stöckl, II. 880–915. — The Doctrinal Histories of Schwane, etc. — Preger : *Deutsche Mystik*, I. 51–63. For other Lit. see Potthast, II. 1216.

Contemporary with Thomas Aquinas, even to dying the same year, was John Bonaventura. Thomas we think of only as theologian. Bonaventura was both a theologian and a distinguished administrator of the affairs of his order, the Franciscans. The one we think of as precise in his state-ments, the other as poetical in his imagery. Bonaventura 1221–1274, called the Seraphic doctor, — *doctor seraphicus*, — was born in Tuscany. The change from his original name, John Fidanza, was due to his recovery from a sickness at the age of four, in answer to the intercession of Francis d'Assisi. When the child began to show signs of recovery, his mother exclaimed, *O buon ventura*, good fortune! This is the saint's own story.[1]

The boy entered the Franciscan order, 1238. After having spent three years in Paris under Alexander of Hales, the teacher is reported to have said, "in brother Bonaventura Adam seems not to have sinned." He taught in Paris, fol-lowing John of Parma, on John's promotion to the office of general of the order of the Franciscans, 1247. He lived through the conflict between the university and the mendi-cant orders, and in answer to William de St. Amour's tract, *de periculis novissimorum temporum*, attacking the principle of mendicancy, Bonaventura wrote his tract on the Poverty of Christ.[2]

In 1257, he was chosen head of the Franciscan order in succession to John of Parma. He took a middle position

[1] Prologue to his *Life of St. Francis.*

[2] *De paupertate Christi.* Peltier's ed., XIV. 364–409. A few years later he presented the subject more at length in his *Apologia pauperum.* Peltier's ed., XIV. 410–520.

between the two parties which were contending in the Franciscan body and has been called the second founder of the order. By the instruction of the first Franciscan general council at Narbonne, 1260, he wrote the *Legenda S. Francisci*, the authoritative Franciscan Life of the saint.[1] It abounds in miracles, great and small. In his *Quæstiones circa regulam* and in letters he presents a picture of the decay of the Franciscans from the ideal of their founders. He narrowly escaped being closely identified with English Church history, by declining the see of York, 1265. In 1273 he was made cardinal-bishop of Albano. To him was committed a share in the preparations for the council of Lyons, but he died soon after the opening of the council, July 14, 1274. The sacrament of extreme unction was administered by the pope and the funeral took place in the presence of the solemn assembly of dignitaries gathered from all parts of Christendom. He was buried at Lyons.[2] He was canonized in 1482 and declared a " doctor of the church," 1587.

Gerson wrote a special panegyric of Bonaventura and said that he was the most profitable of the doctors, safe and reliable in teaching, pious and devout. He did not minister to curiosity nor mix up secular dialectics and physics with theological discussion.[3] Dante places him at the side of Thomas Aquinas,

" who with pure interest
Preferred each heavenly to each earthly aim."[4]

These two distinguished men will always be brought into companionship.[5] Stöckl, the historian of mediæval theology,

[1] Sabatier, *Vie de S. François*, lxxi.-lxxxviii., compares Bonaventura's life to the figures of saints exposed for sale on a dealer's shelves, all having a downcast, pious, but unreal look. The biography is given by Peltier, XIV. 293–363.

[2] His body, it seems, was burnt by the Calvinists in 1562. Only the head was saved. The right arm had before been removed to Bonaventura's birthplace. See Hergenröther. *Kirchengesch.*, II. 529 ; Wetzer-Welte, II. 1022.

[3] *Quæ veritatis sunt credenda de necessitate salutis.* Du Pin's ed. of Gerson's Works, 1728, I. 21. See also Gerson's *Epistola in laudem S. Bonaventuræ.* Du Pin's ed., I. 117.

[4] *Paradiso*, XII. 127.

[5] Sixtus V. in his encyclical admitting Bonaventura into the company of the Doctors of the Church places them side by side and brings out their dis-

calls them the illuminating stars on the horizon of the
thirteenth century.[1] Neither of them rose so high above
his contemporaries as did Bernard a hundred years before.
But both cast lustre upon their age and are the most
illustrious names of their respective orders, after Francis
and Dominic themselves. Thomas had the keener mind,
excelling in power of analysis. Bonaventura indulged the
habit of elaboration. The ethical element was conspicuous
in Thomas, the mystical in Bonaventura. Thomas was
the more authoritative teacher, Bonaventura the more ver-
satile writer. Both were equally champions of the theology
and organization of the mediæval Church.

Bonaventura enjoyed a wide fame as a preacher.[2] He was
also a poet, and has left the most glowing panegyrics of Mary
in the form of psalms as well as in prose.

Of his theological writings the most notable is his *Commentary on the Sentences of the Lombard*.[3] His *Breviloquium*
and *Centiloquium* are next in importance. The *Breviloquium*,[4] which Funk calls the best mediæval compend of
theology, takes up the seven chief questions : the Trinity,
creation, sin, the incarnation, the grace of the Holy Spirit, the
sacramental medium, and the final state. The Preface gives
a panegyric of the Scriptures and states the author's views
of Scriptural interpretation. Like all the Schoolmen, Bonaventura had a wide acquaintance with Scripture and shows

tinguishing characteristics. He calls them *potissimum gloriosi doctores* —
"those most illustrious teachers."

[1] *Sie sind die beiden leuchtenden Sterne am Horizont des 13ten Jahrhunderts.* Stöckl, II. 882.

[2] Peltier gives his sermons in vol. XIII. For his works on Mary, see
section 130.

[3] A number of the works once ascribed to Bonaventura are regarded as
ungenuine, e.g. *de six alis cherubim, de septem itineribus æternitatis,* etc.
The Venetian ed. of 1751 and Bonelli discuss the authorship of the many
writings associated with Bonaventura's name.

[4] Peltier's ed., VII. 240–343. Funk, *Kirchengesch.*, p. 354. An ed. was
published by Hefele, 3d ed., Tübingen, 1861, and also Vicenza, 2d ed. Freiburg, 1881. Sixtus V. said of Bonaventura's theology that "nothing more
fruitful for the Church of God" had appeared, Encyclical in Peltier's ed., I
p. viii.

an equipoise of judgment which usually keeps him from extravagance in doctrinal statement. However, he did not rise
above his age and he revelled in interrogations about the
angels, good and evil, which seem to us to be utterly trivial
and have no bearing on practical religion. He set himself
to answer more than one hundred of these, and in Peltier's
edition, his angelology and demonology occupy more than
two hundred pages of two columns each.[1] The questions
discussed are such as these : Could God have made a better
world? could He have made it sooner than He did ? can an
angel be in several places at the same time? can several
angels be at the same time in the same place ?[2] was Lucifer
at the moment of his creation corrupt of will? did he belong
to the order of angels? is there a hierarchy among the fallen
angels? have demons a foreknowledge of contingent events?[3]
Descending to man, Bonaventura discusses whether sexual
intercourse took place before the fall, whether the multiplication of men and women was intended to be equal, which of
the two sinned the more grievously, the man or the woman.

Bonaventura differs from Thomas in giving proof that the
world is not eternal. The mark of a foot, which represents
created matter, is not of the same duration as the foot itself,
for the mark was made at some time by the foot. And,
following Plato as against Aristotle, he declared that matter
not only in its present form but also in its essence is not
eternal. The world is not thinkable without man, for it has
all the marks of a habitation fitted up for a human being.
Christ would not have become incarnate without sin.

In the doctrine of the immaculate conception, Bonaven-

---

[1] II. 296–520.

[2] Peltier's ed., II. 298 sqq. The arguments given for an affirmative answer to
this question are that the angels are in a place not after a " bodily but spiritual
fashion." They are spiritual lights, as the Areopagite said, and consequently
are independent of space, etc. Bonaventura, however, answers the question
in the negative.

[3] Peltier's ed., II. 415 sqq. Bonaventura answers that foreknowledge belongs to God alone, but that by reason of their intellectual acuteness and long
experience the demons are sometimes able to accurately predict contingent
events.

tura agreed with Thomas in denying to Mary freedom from
original sin and disagreed with his fellow Franciscan, Duns
Scotus, whose teaching has become dogma in the Roman
Catholic communion.

It is as a mystic and as the author of the life of St.
Francis, rather than as a dogmatician that Bonaventura has
a characteristic place among the Schoolmen.[1] He evidently
drew from the mystics of St. Victor, used their terminology [2]
and did not advance beyond them. His mysticism has its
finest statement in his *Journey of the Mind to God*.[3] Upon
this pilgrimage of the soul to the highest divine mysteries,
no one can enter without grace from above. Nor can the
journey be continued without earnest prayer, pure meditation, and a holy life. Devout prayer is the mother and
beginning of the upward movement towards God. Contemplation leads us first outside ourselves to behold the
works of God in the visible world. It then brings us back
to consider God's image in ourselves and at last we rise
above ourselves to behold the divine being as He is in Himself.[4] Each of these activities is twofold, so that there are
six steps in the progress of the soul. In the final step, the
soul contemplates the Trinity and God's absolute goodness.

Beyond these six steps is the state of rapture, the ecstatic
vision, as the Sabbath day of rest followed the six days of
labor. The doorway to this mystical life is Christ. The
experience, which the soul shall have hereafter, is an ocean
of beatific ecstasy. No one can know it but the one who receives it; he only receive it who desires it; he only desire it

---

[1] Stöckl, II. 880, says, *Bonav. ist vorzugsweise Mystiker*, and expresses
the opinion that the mysticism of the Middle Ages reached its highest point
in him.

[2] e.g. *Cogitatio, meditatio, contemplatio, ascendere*, etc.

[3] *Itinerarium mentis in Deum.* Peltier's ed., XII. 1–22. His *Meditations
on the Life of Jesus*, his commentaries on Ecclesiastes, the Book of Wisdom,
and John and Luke belong to this class. The mystical element is also
strong in the *Breviloquium* and the *Centiloquium*. Other mystical writings
ascribed to Bonaventura, such as *Incendium amoris, de septem verbis domini*,
etc., are disputed.

[4] These three activities constitute the *theologia symbolica, theol. propria*,
and *theol. mystica*.

who is inflamed by the baptizing fire of the Holy Spirit. It is a grace not a doctrine, a desire not a concept, a habit of prayer not a studious task, a bride not a teacher. It is of God not of man, a flame of ardent love, transferring us into the presence and being of God.[1] As in the case of Bernard, so also in the case of Bonaventura, this mystical tendency found expression in devout hymns.

§ 110. *Duns Scotus.*

LITERATURE: WORKS.—Complete ed. by LUKE WADDING, 12 vols.,Lyons,1639, with a *Life* by WADDING, and the glosses of HUGH MacCAGHWELL (Hugo Cavellus, d. 1626), abp. of Armagh, MAURICE O'FIHELY, abp. of Tuam, etc. *New ed., 26 vols., Paris, 1891–1895, with some changes.—The *Opus Oxoniense,* Vienna, 1481, ed. by MACCAGHWELL together with the *Reportata Parisiensia* and *Quæstiones Quodlibetales* and a *Life,* Antwerp, 1620.—The *Quæstiones Quodlibet.,* Venice, 1474, 1505, Paris, 1513. —The *Logical Treatises* were publ. at Barcelona, 1475, Venice, 1491–1493, and ed. by O'FIHELY, 1504.—Duns' system was expounded by ANGELO VULPI in *Sacr. theol. Summa Joan. Scoti,* 12 vols., Naples, 1622–1640. For biogr. and analytic works publ. before 1800, see RIGG in *Dict. of Natl. Biog.* XVI. 216 sqq.—BAUMGARTEN-CRUSIUS: *De theol. Scoti,* Jena, 1826.—SCHNEID: *D. Körperlehre des J. Duns Sc. und ihr Verhältniss zum Thomismus und Atomismus,* Mainz, 1879.—*C. WERNER: *J. Duns Sc.,* Vienna, 1881, also *S. Thomas von Aquino,* III, 3–101.—KAHL: *D. Primat des Willens bei Augustinus, Duns Sc. und Des Cartes,* Strassb., 1886.— *R. SEEBERG: *D. Theologie des J. Duns Sc.,* Leip., 1900; also his art. in Herzog, 3d ed. and his *Dogmengesch.,* II. 129 sqq.—RENAN: art. *Scotus,* in *Hist. Lit. de France,* vol. XXV.—*DÖLLINGER: art. in Wetzer-Welte, X. 2123–2133.—J. M. RIGG: in *Dict. Natl. Biog.,* XVI. 216–220.— *SCHWANE: *Dogmengesch.,* pp. 74–76, etc.—HARNACK: *Dogmengesch.,* III. 459 sqq.—*A. RITSCHL: *Rechtfertigung und Versöhnung,* I. 58–86; *Gesch. des Pietismus,* I. 470.—P. MINGES: *Ist Duns Scotus Indeterminist?* Münster, 1905, p. 139.—The *Histt. of Philos.*

The last of the scholastic thinkers of the first rank and the most daring of mediæval logicians is John Duns Scotus. With his death the disintegration of scholastic theology begins. This remarkable man, one of the intellectual prodigies of the race, may have been under forty years of age when death overtook him. His dialectic genius and ingenuity won for him the title of the Subtle doctor, *doctor subtilis.* His intellectual independence is shown in the freedom with

[1] *Itin.,* 7.

which he subjected his predecessors to his searching and often sophistical criticisms. Anselm, the St. Victors, Albert the Great, Bonaventura, Thomas Aquinas, Henry of Ghent, and other Schoolmen he does not hesitate to mention by name and to assail their views. The discussions of Thomas Aquinas are frequently made the subject of his attack. Duns became the chief theological ornament of the Franciscan order and his theology was defended by a distinct school, which took his name, the Scotists. This school and the Thomists, who followed the teachings of Thomas Aquinas, are the leading schools of theology produced in the Middle Ages and came into violent controversy.

Duns' mind was critical rather than constructive. The abstruseness of his style offers difficulties almost insuperable to the comprehension of the modern student.[1] He developed no complete system.[2] It was his characteristic to disturb faith and to open again questions to which Thomas Aquinas and other Schoolmen were supposed to have given final statements. The sharp distinction he made between faith and knowledge, dogma and reason, and his use of the arguments from silence and probability, undermined confidence in the infallibility of the Church and opened the way for the disrepute into which scholasticism fell. Duns denied that the being of God and other dogmas can be proved by the reason, and he based their acceptance solely upon the authority of the Church. The analytic precision, as well as lucid statement of Thomas and Peter the Lombard, are wanting in the

---

[1] Döllinger, p. 2127, and Harnack, III. 429, agree in pronouncing Duns the "most acute thinker among the Schoolmen," *der scharfsinnigste scholastishe Denker*. Seeberg, *Theol. d. J. D. Scotus*, p. 2, speaks of "the enormous difficulty" — *ungeheure Schwierigkeit* — which the reading of Duns offers to one who is not thoroughly familiar with his mode of thinking and expression. Again, p. 6, he speaks of Duns' "sentences and arguments" as being "endlessly complicated." Schwane, p. 78, says that Duns' abstruseness of thought, lack of system in presenting his materials, and the thorny paths of his critical method have imparted to theology little glory. See also pp. 288, 292.

[2] *Die Hoffnung aus seinen Schriften ein System herzustellen ist vergeblich*, Seeberg, p. 644.

Subtle doctor, and the mystical element, so perceptible in the writings of Anselm, Thomas, and Bonaventura, gives way to a purely speculative interest.

What a contrast Duns presents to the founder of his order, Francis d'Assisi, the man of simple faith and creed, and popular speech and ministries! Of all the Schoolmen, Duns wandered most in the labyrinth of metaphysical subtleties, and none of them is so much responsible as he for the current opinion that mediæval theology and fanciful speculation are interchangeable terms. His reputation for specious ratiocination has given to the language the term "dunce." [1]

Of his personal history scarcely anything is known, and his extensive writings furnish not a single clew. Even the time and place of his entering the Franciscan order cannot be made out with certainty. The only fixed date in his career is the date which brought it to a close. He died at Cologne, Nov. 8, 1308. The date of his birth is placed between 1265–1274. [2]

England, Scotland, and Ireland have contended for the honor of being the Schoolman's native land, with the probability in favor of England. Irishmen since the fifteenth century have argued for Dun, or Down, in Ulster. Scotchmen plead for Dunse in Berwickshire, while writers, unaffected by patriotic considerations, for the most part agree upon Dunstane in Northumberland. [3] The uncertain tradition runs that he studied at Merton College, Oxford, and became teacher there on the transfer of William of Ware to Paris. In 1304, he

[1] "Remember ye not," said Tyndale, "how within this thirty years and far less, the old barking curs, Dunce's disciples, and like draff, called Scotists, the children of darkness, raged in every pulpit against Greek, Latin and Hebrew?" — Quoted by Trench : *The Study of Words*, p. 91.

[2] 1274 is the date accepted by Wadding, Cavellus, and Schwane. Döllinger, Rigg, and Seeberg adopt an earlier date. Seeberg, pp. 36 sqq., lays stress upon the refusal of the bishop of Lincoln, in 1300, to grant to Duns the privilege of hearing confession. A rule of the Franciscans, 1292, required that members of the order should be thirty before aspiring to this privilege. In this case Duns was born before 1270.

[3] Döllinger attaches much weight to a statement made in a MS. of one of Duns' works in Merton College, to the effect that he was born in Dunstane, England. O'Fihely, MacCaghwell, and Wadding, all Irishmen, are loyal to

was in the French capital, where he won the doctor's degree.
In 1308, he was transferred by the general of his order to
Cologne, where he died soon after. The story ran that he
was buried alive.[1] In 1707, the Franciscans tried in vain to
secure his canonization. A monument, reared to Duns in the
Franciscan church at Cologne, 1513, bore this inscription:—

> Scotia gave me birth, England nursed me,
> Gaul educated me, Cologne holds my ashes.[2]

Among the stories told of Duns Scotus is the following,
behind which more wisdom hides than is found in whole chapters of his labored discussions. On one occasion he stopped to
speak to an English farmer on the subject of religion. The
farmer, who was engaged in sowing, turned and said: "Why
do you speak to me? If God has foreknowledge that I will be
saved, I will be saved whether I do good or ill." Duns replied:
"Then, if God has foreknowledge that grain will grow out of
this soil, it will grow whether you sow or withhold your hand.
You may as well save yourself the labor you are at."

The works of Duns Scotus include commentaries on Aristotle, an extended commentary on the Sentences of the Lombard, called the *Opus oxoniense*, his theological lectures delivered at Paris, known as the *Reportata parisiensia*[3] and his
Quæstiones quodlibetales, being sundry discussions on theological and philosophical problems. A commentary on Genesis
and one on the Gospels, sermons and other writings of doubtful or denied authenticity are ascribed to Duns.[4]

In philosophy Duns was a moderate realist. The universals are not intellectual fictions, *fictiones intellectus*. Our ideas

the theory that he was of Irish nativity. Dempster gives twelve reasons to
prove Duns was a Scotchman. See *Dict. Natl. Biog.*, XVI. 216, and Seeberg,
p. 34.

[1] Seeberg, pp. 46 sqq. MacCaghwell in two tracts learnedly denied his
being buried alive.

> [2] *Scotia me genuit, Anglia me suscepit,*
> *Gallia me docuit, Colonia me tenit.*

[3] It fills 3 vols. in the Paris ed.; the *Opus Oxoniense*, 14 vols.; the *Quodlibetales*, vols. XXV., XXVI.

[4] Trithemius, 1495, distinctly speaks of two volumes of Duns' Sermons.
Seeberg, p. 63.

presuppose their reality.[1] The universal is gotten by abstraction and by noting points of agreement in individuals, and in
a certain sense it is a creation of the mind.   The individual
has its individuality, or *hæcceitas*, not by reason of its differ-
entiation from something else but by its own real essence, or
quidditas.   A stone is an individual by reason of something
positive, intrinsic within itself.   The individual is the final
form of being, *ultima realitas entis*.

Theology is a practical science and its chief value is in
furnishing to the will the materials of faith to lighten it on
the path of virtuous action.

The Scriptures contain what is to be believed, but the
authority of the Church establishes what these truths are.
Articles of faith are to be accepted, not because they are
demonstrable by reason.   Reason is unreliable or, at best,
obscure and many truths it cannot prove, such as the soul's
immortality, the unity of God, and transubstantiation.   A
doctrine such as the descent into hell, which is not found
in the Scriptures is, nevertheless, to be accepted because it is
found in the Apostles' Creed.   Other truths the Church
possesses which are not found in the Scriptures.   Our belief in
the Scriptures rests ultimately on the authority of the Church.[2]

The doctrines in which Duns differed most from his predecessors were the doctrines of God and transubstantiation.
In his treatment of God, Duns shows himself to be the most
positive of determinists.   The controlling element in the
divine nature is the will of God, and to submit to the will of
God is the highest goal the human will can reach.   Here he
differs widely from Thomas Aquinas, who places God's intelligence above His will.   The sufficient explanation of God's
action is His absolute will.[3]   God is good because God wills
to be so.   The will of God might have made what is now bad

---

[1] *Universali aliquid extra correspondet a quo movetur intellectus ad cau-
sandum talem intentionem.*   Seeberg, p. 69.

[2] *Libris canonici sacri non est credendum nisi quia primo credendum est
ecclesiæ approbanti et autorizanti libros istos et contenta in eis.*   Seeberg,
p. 120.

[3] *Quare voluntas voluit hoc, nulla est causa, nisi quia voluntas voluntas est,*
Seeberg, pp. 162 sqq., 660 sqq.

good, had God so chosen. He can do all things except what
is logically absurd.[1] He could have saved Judas after he was
condemned, but He cannot make a stone holy or change an
event which has already happened.

The will of God determines the salvation of men. The
predestination of the elect is an act purely of God's determination. The non-elect are reprobated in view of their foreseen
demerit. On the other hand, Duns seems to hold fast to
the doctrine that the elect merit the eternal reward by good
works. Without attempting to exhaust the apparent contradiction between divine foreordination and human responsibility, he confesses the mystery attaching to the subject.[2]

Sin is not infinite, for it is connected with finite beings.
Original righteousness was a superadded gift, forfeited
through the first sin. Eve's sin was greater than Adam's, for
Adam shrank from offending Eve — Eve sought to be equal
with God. Man's freedom consists in his ability to choose
the contrary. Original sin consists in the loss of original
righteousness which Adam owed to God.[3] Sin does not pass
down to Adam's descendants by way of infection. Duns
separated from Augustine in denying the doctrine of moral
inability, the *servum arbitrium*. It belongs to the very nature
of the will to be free. This freedom, however, the will can
lose by repeated volitions. Sin is inherent in the will alone,
and concupiscence is only an inclination of the will to desire
objects of pleasure immoderately.[4]

---

[1] Harnack, *Dogmengesch.*, III. 446, has chosen strong words to show the
unwillingness of Thomas Aquinas and Duns Scotus to pursue the narrow way
to the knowledge of God, that is, through the person of the historical Christ.
And Seeberg, p. 671, lays stress upon the failure of Duns to bring God near
to the soul. God remained a God afar off. According to both these modern
dogmaticians, it remained for the Reformation through the principles of a
living faith and God's love to bring God into nearness to the soul.

[2] Seeberg, *Dogmengesch.*, II. 135, *Theologie*, etc., 227 sq., 293 sqq.,
666 sq.; Schwane, p. 463.

[3] *Carentia justitiæ originalis.* Seeberg, 218 sq.; Loofs, *Dogmengesch.*,
p. 305. Harnack, III. 551, and Seeberg, p. 220, emphatically assert that
Duns abandoned the Augustinian conception of sin and moral corruption.

[4] *Pronitas in appetitu rationali*, i.e. *in voluntate ad concupiscendum delec-
tabilia immoderate.* Quoted by Stöckl, II. 362.

The ultimate questions why God permitted evil, and how He could foreknow evil would occur without also predetermining it, find their solution only in God's absolute will. God willed, and that must suffice for the reason.

The infinite value of the atonement likewise finds its explanation in the absolute will of God. Christ died as a man, and for that reason his merit of itself was not infinite. An angel, or a man, free from original sin, might have made efficient atonement if God had so willed. Nothing in the guilt of sin made it necessary for the Son of God to die. God determined to accept Christ's obedience and, in view of it, to impart grace to the sinner. Duns follows closely Anselm's theory, whose principles he carefully states.[1]

In his treatment of transubstantiation, Duns vigorously attacked the view of Thomas Aquinas as a transition of the body of Christ into the bread. He argued that if there were such transition, then at celebrations of the eucharist during the three days of Christ's burial the elements would have been changed into his dead body. To avoid this difficulty he enunciated the theory that the body of Christ, as of every man, has more than one form, that is, in addition to the rational soul, a *forma mixti sive corporeitatis*, which is joined to matter and constitutes it a human body. Into this corporal form of Christ, *corporeitas*, the elements are transmuted and this form remained with Christ's corpse in the grave. Duns declared that the doctrine of transubstantiation cannot be proved with certainty from the Scriptures, nor at all by the reason. He then argued that it is more probable than any other theory because the Church has accepted it, and the dogma is most in keeping with God's omnipotence. The dogma must be accepted on the authority of the Church.[2]

The doctrine upon whose development the Subtle doctor

---

[1] He concludes his account of Anselm's exposition by acknowledging his indebtedness to Anselm, in the words *hæc veraciter, ut potui, ex dictis ejus, collegi.* Seeberg, p. 283. Seeberg's full discussion of Duns' theory of the atonement, pp. 275-296.

[2] For quotations see Schwane, pp. 656 sqq. Seeberg finds in Duns' definition the doctrine of consubstantiation.

had altogether the most influence is the doctrine of the immaculate conception, which he taught in the form in which it was proclaimed a dogma, by Pius IX., 1854. Departing from the statements of Anselm, Bernard, Thomas Aquinas, and Bonaventura, Duns taught that Mary was conceived without sin. His theory is presented at length in the chapter on the Virgin Mary. The story ran that, in championing this theory, at a public disputation at Paris, he controverted Thomas' position with no less than two hundred arguments.[1] Duns' frequent attacks upon Thomas' statements were the sufficient cause of controversy between the followers of the two teachers, and this controversy belongs to the number of the more bitter controversies that have been carried on within the Roman Catholic communion. It was a contest, however, not between orthodoxy and heterodoxy, but between two eminent teachers equally in good standing, and between the two orders they represented.

Döllinger expressed the opinion that the controversy was turned into a blessing for theology by keeping it from "stagnation and petrifaction," and into a blessing for the Church, which took under its protection both systems and kept each from arrogating to itself the right of final authority.

The common view in regard to the place of Duns Scotus in the history of doctrine is that he was a disturber of the peace. Without adding any element of permanent value to theological thought, he shook to its base the scholastic structure upon which Anselm, Thomas Aquinas, and other theologians had wrought for nearly two centuries. The opinion will, no doubt, continue to prevail that Duns was a master in intellectual ingenuity, but that his judgment was unsound.[2] It is fair to say that Seeberg of Berlin, in his recent elaborate

[1] Döllinger regards the story as open to grave suspicion because, at the time at which the disputation is set, there was no conflict between the two orders. Wetzer-Welte, X. p. 2129.

[2] This is the view of such experts in the history of mediæval theology as Schwane, p. 78, etc., and Stöckl. Stöckl, II. 868, declines to compare Duns with Thomas as a trustworthy teacher, and says that Duns' only service to theology was through his polemics, which started an impulse to search for a firmer basis of certainty for doctrinal truth in reason and revelation.

and thorough monograph on the theology of Duns Scotus, takes an entirely different view. To him Duns was not a disturber of theological thought, but the head of a new period of development and worthy of equal honor with Thomas Aquinas. Yea, he ascribes to him a more profound and extensive influence upon theology than Thomas exerted. He broke a new path, and " was a historical figure of epoch-making importance." [1]

By his speculative piquancy, on the one hand, Duns strengthened the desire of certain groups in Europe for a saner method of theological discussion; and on the other hand stimulated pious minds along the Rhine to search along a better way after personal piety, as did Tauler and the German mystics. The succeeding generation of Schoolmen was brought by him as their leader into a disputatious attitude. What else could be expected when Duns, contrary to the fundamental principles of Thomas Aquinas, Albertus Magnus, and other divines, did not shrink from declaring a thing might at the same time be true in philosophy and false in theology? [2]

Ockam, who shared Duns' determinism, called him "the doctor of our order." In the dispute over the immaculate conception in the fifteenth century no divine was more quoted than he. A century later Archbishop MacCaghwell and other Irish theologians warmly expatiated upon his powers, wrote his biography, and edited his works.

One of the works of the Reformation was to dethrone Duns Scotus from his seat of authority as a teacher. Richard Layton wrote to Cromwell, 1535, " We have set Dunce in Bocardo and banished him from Oxford forever, and he is now made a common servant to every man fast nailed up upon posts in all houses of common easement." [3] Luther called

---

[1] pp. 33, 668, 672, 677. Ritschl was a student of Duns and praises his clearness of thought so long as he keeps free from syllogisms. He kept the Schoolman's Works constantly within reach. O. Ritschl, *A. Ritschl's Leben*, II. 483.

[2] See the reference to the *Reportata*, Schwane, p. 78.

[3] Quoted in *Dict. of Natl. Biog.* XVI. 219.

him the "most arrant of sophists," and he made him responsible for a revival of Pelagianism and exalting the consequent
value of good works by emphasizing the freedom of the will
and the natural powers.[1] Duns had no presentiment of any
other order than the papal and said nothing looking toward
a reformation in doctrine.

Among the contemporaries with whom Duns had theological affinity
were Henry of Ghent and the Englishman, Richard Middleton. HENRY
OF GHENT, named *doctor solemnis*, a celebrated teacher in Paris, was born
at Ghent and died, 1293, in Paris or Tournay. His *Quodlibeta* and *Summa*
were published in Paris, 1518 and 1520.[2] At points Henry combated
Thomas Aquinas and prepared the way for Duns Scotus, who adopts
some of Henry's views. Henry's discussions run far into the region of
abstruse metaphysics. He leaned to Platonism and was a realist.

RICHARD MIDDLETON was supposedly a predecessor of Duns at Oxford. Little is known of his life. He was a Franciscan, a scholar at
Paris, and was appointed by the general of his order to examine into the
doctrines of Peter Olivi, 1278-1288. He died about 1307. His commentary on the Sentences of the Lombard survived him.[3] Middleton was
known at Paris as *doctor solidus*. At the council of Constance he was
cited as an authority against Wyclif. His name is inscribed on the tomb
of Duns Scotus at Cologne, and the tradition runs that Duns was his pupil. In his teachings regarding the will, which he defined as the
noblest of the soul's faculties, he may have influenced Duns, as Seeberg
attempts to prove. Middleton compared the mind to a servant who carries a light in front of his master and does nothing more than to show
his master the way, while his master commands and directs as he pleases.

§ 111.   *Roger Bacon.*

LITERATURE: WORKS. — Among the early publications were *Speculum
alchymiœ*, Nurnb., 1541, Engl. trans. London, 1597 ; *De mirabili potestate
artis et naturæ*, Paris, 1542, Engl. trans. 1659 ; *De retardandis senectu-
tis accidentibus*, Oxford, 1590, Engl. trans. ; *The Cure of Old Age and
Preservation of Youth*, by the great mathematician and physician, Roger

---

[1] In spite of this, Seeberg, pp. 683-685, tries to make out that in his conception of God, Luther, howbeit " negatively," was influenced by Duns' view of
the divine will. Luther certainly did not acknowledge any such indebtedness.

[2] MSS. of other works are given by Ehrle, *Zur Biogr. Heinrichs von Ghent*,
in *Archiv für Lit. u. K. gesch.*, 1885, pp. 400 sq. See Schwane, pp. 71-76,
etc., and Wetzer-Welte, V. 1704 sqq.

[3] Publ. at Venice, 1489-1509, Brescia, 1591, etc. MSS. exist in Oxford and
elsewhere. See Little, *Grey Friars of Oxford;* Kingsford, in *Dict. of Nat.
Biog.*, XXXVII. 356 sq. ; Seeberg, pp. 16-33.

Bacon, ed. by R. Browne, London, 1683 ; *Opus majus* (six books only), by Samuel Jebb, London, 1733, reprinted Venice, 1750 ; *Opus minus* and *Opus tertium*, with valuable Preface by J. S. Brewer, London, 1859, Rolls Series ; *Opus majus*, with valuable Preface, by J. H. Bridges, all the seven books, 3 vols., London, 1900.

Biographical : Emile Charles : *R. Bacon, sa vie, ses ouvrages, ses doctrines*, Paris, 1861. — L. Schneider : *R. Bacon*, etc., Augsb., 1873 — the Prefaces of Brewer and Bridges as above. — Professor R. Adamson, in " Ency. Britt." III. 218–222, and *Dict. of Natl. Biog.*, II. 374–378. — White : *Warfare of Science and Theol.* I. 386–393.

Duns Scotus was a Schoolman and nothing more. Roger Bacon, his contemporary, belongs to a different order of men, though one of the greatest theological thinkers of his age. He did not take up the great questions of theology and seek to justify them by dialectical processes. The most he did was to lay down principles for the study of theology; but it is as the pioneer of modern science and the scientific method of experiment that he has his distinguished place in the mediæval galaxy of great minds. The fact that he had to suffer for his boldness of speech by imprisonment and enforced silence increases the interest felt in his teachings. His method of thought was out of accord with the prevailing method of his times. He was far ahead of his age, a seer of another era when the study of nature was to be assigned its proper place of dignity, and theology cease to be treated as a field for dialectical ingenuity.

Born in Somersetshire, England, Roger Bacon, called the Wonderful doctor, *mirabilis doctor*, 1214(?)–1294, studied in Oxford, where he came into close contact with Robert Grosseteste and Adam Marsh, whom he often mentions with admiration. He went to Paris about 1240, continued his studies, and entered the Franciscan order. He speaks in his *Opus tertium* of having been engaged more than twenty years in the study of the languages and science, and spending £2000 in these studies and the purchase of books and instruments, or £600 or £700 present value.[1] He went back to Oxford, but was recalled to Paris by his order, at the head of which Bonaventura then stood, and placed in

[1] Bridges' ed., p. xxiii.

more or less strict confinement, 1257. At first he was denied the privilege of writing, but was allowed to give instruction to young students in the languages.

Clement IV. who, before his elevation to the papal chair and as legate in England, had been his friend, requested copies of his writings. In about eighteen months, 1264–1266, Bacon prepared the *Opus majus* and then its two appendages, the *Opus minus* and the *Opus tertium*, and sent them to the pope. In 1268, he was again in Oxford. In 1278, he was relegated to closer confinement on account of " certain suspected novelties " about which we are not more particularly informed, adduced by the Franciscan general, Jerome of Ascoli, afterwards Nicolas IV. He was set free again in 1292, as we know. His body lies buried in the Franciscan church of Oxford. It was said that his books were nailed to the walls of the library at Oxford and left to perish. The story may be dismissed as untrue, but it indicates the estimate put upon the scholar's writings.

If we were to depend upon the influence he had upon his age, Roger Bacon would have no place here. At best he was thought of as a dabbler in the dark arts and a necromancer. He had no place of authority among his contemporaries, and the rarest notice of him is found for several centuries. D'Ailly, without quoting his name, copied a large paragraph from him about the propinquity of Spain and India which Columbus used in his letter to Ferdinand, 1498. It was not till the Renaissance that his name began to be used. Since the publication of his writings by Samuel Jebb, 1733, he has risen more and more into repute as one who set aside the fantastical subtleties of scholasticism for a rational treatment of the things we see and know, and as the scientific precursor of the modern laboratory and modern invention. Prophetic foresight of certain modern inventions is ascribed to him, but unjustly. He, however, expounded the theory of the rays of light, proved the universe to be spherical, and pronounced the smallest stars larger than the earth.[1]

---

[1] *Opus majus*, Bridges' ed., I. 152, 175.

With Anaxagoras, he ascribed the Nile to the melting of the snows in Ethiopia.[1] He was not the inventor of gunpowder of which the Arabs knew.

Bacon's works, so far as they are published, combine the study of theology, philosophy, and what may be called the physical sciences. His *Opus majus* in seven books, the *Opus minus*, and *Opus tertium* are measurably complete. Of his *Scriptum principale* or *Compendium studii philosophiæ*, often referred to in the writings just mentioned, only fragments were written, and of these only portions are left. The work was intended to be in four volumes and to include a treatment of grammar and logic, mathematics, physics, and last metaphysics and morals. The *Communio naturalium* and other treatises are still in manuscript.

The *Opus majus* in its list of subjects is the most encyclopædic work of the Middle Ages. It takes up as separate departments the connection of philosophy and theology, astronomy including geography, astrology, barology, alchemy, agriculture, optics or perspective, and moral philosophy, medicine and experimental science, *scientia experimentalis*.

By agriculture, he meant the study of the vegetable and animal worlds, and such questions as the adaptation of soil to different classes of plants. In the treatment of optics he presents the construction of the eye and the laws of vision. Mathematics are the foundation of all science and of great value for the Church. Alchemy deals with liquids, gases, and solids, and their generation. A child of his age, Bacon held that metals were compound bodies whose elements can be separated.[2] In the department of astrology, in accordance with the opinions prevailing in his day, he held that the stars and planets have an influence upon all terrestrial conditions and objects,

[1] I. 323.

[2] As an illustration of some of Bacon's chemical and medical advice the following receipt may be given. He says a combination of gold, pearl, flower of sea dew, spermaceti, aloes, bone of stag's heart, flesh of Tyrian snake, and Ethiopian dragon, properly prepared in due portions, might promote longevity to a length hitherto unimagined. *Op. maj.*, II. 206.

including man.   Climate, temperament, motion, all are more
or less dependent upon their potency.   As the moon affects
the tides, so the stars implant dispositions good and evil.
This potency influences but does not coerce man's free will.
The comet of 1264, due to Mars, was related to the wars of
England, Spain, and Italy.[1]   In the department of optics and
the teachings in regard to force, he was far ahead of his
age and taught that all objects were emitting force in all
directions.   Experimental science governs all the preceding
sciences.   Knowledge comes by reasoning and experience.
Doubts left by reasoning are tried by experience, which is
the ultimate test of truth.

The practical tendency of Bacon's mind is everywhere
apparent.   He was an apostle of common sense.   Speaking of
Peter of Maricourt of Paris, otherwise unknown, he praises
him for his achievements in the science of experimental
research and said: "Of discourses and battles of words
he takes no heed.   Through experiment he gains knowledge
of natural things, medical, chemical, indeed of everything in
the heavens and the earth.   He is ashamed that things should
be known to laymen, old women, soldiers, and ploughmen,
of which he is himself ignorant."   He also confessed he had
learned incomparably more from men unlettered and unknown
to the learned than he had learned from his most famous
teachers.[2]

Bacon attacked the pedantry of the scholastic method, the
frivolous and unprofitable logomachy over questions which
were above reason and untaught by revelation.   Again and
again he rebuked the conceit and metaphysical abstruseness
of the theological writers of his century, especially Alexander
of Hales and also Albertus Magnus and Thomas Aquinas.
He used, at length, Alfarabius, Avicenna, Algazel, and other
Arabic philosophers, as well as Aristotle.   Against the pride
and avarice and ignorance of the clergy he spoke with un-
measured severity and declared that the morals of Seneca and
his age were far higher than the morals of the thirteenth

---

[1] *Op. maj.*, I. 385 sqq.   [2] Bridges' ed., *Op. maj.*, I. pp. **xxv.**, 23.

century except that the ancient Romans did not know the
virtues of love, faith, and hope which were revealed by Christ.[1]
He quoted Seneca at great length. Such criticism sufficiently explains the treatment which the English Franciscan
received.

This thirteenth-century philosopher pronounced the discussion over universals and individuals foolish and meaning-
less. One individual is of more value than all the universals
in the world. A universal is nothing but the agreement
between several objects, *convenientia plurium individuorum
convenientia individui respectu alterius.* That which is common between two men and which an ass or a pig does not
possess, is their universal.

In the department of philology,[2] and in the interest of a
correction of the Vulgate and a new translation of Aristotle's
works, he urged the study of Arabic, Hebrew, and Greek.
He carried down the history of the translations of the Bible
to Jerome.

He recommended the study of comparative religions which
he arranges in six classes, — Pagan, Idolater, Tartar (Buddhist), Saracen, Jew, and Christian, — and concludes that
there can be only one revelation and one Church because there
is only one God.[3]   He finds in miracles especially the power
to forgive sins, the chief proof of Christ's divinity, and gives
six reasons for accepting the testimony of the Christian
writers; namely, sanctity, wisdom, miraculous powers, firmness under persecution, uniformity of faith, and their success
in spite of humble origin. It is characteristic of this philosopher that in this treatment he avails himself of the information brought to Europe by William Rubruquis whom he
quotes.[4]

He regarded philosophy as having been revealed to the
Jewish patriarchs, and the Greek philosophy as having been
under the guidance of providence, nay, as having been a divine
gift, as Augustine said of Socrates.[5]   Aristotle is the great

[1] *Op. maj.*, II. 303 sqq.   [2] Bridges' ed., I. 66–96.
[3] Bridges' ed., II. 366–404.   [4] I. 303, II. 367 sq.
[5] I. 41.

philosopher, and philosophy leads to the threshold of revealed truth, and it is the duty of Christians to avail themselves of it.[1] As Solomon, a type of Christ, employed Hiram and other outside workers at the temple, so the Church should utilize heathen philosophers.[2] He gives five reasons why the early Church did not make use of Greek philosophy except for the regulation of the calendar and its music,[3] a proposition which would seem very crude to the present advocates of the theory of the dependence of the Apostolic writers upon Hellenic modes of thought. Bacon magnified the supreme authority of the Scriptures in which all truth strikes its roots and which laymen should read. All sciences and knowledge are to be subordinated to the Catholic Church, which is the appointed guardian of human interests. Theology is the science which rules over all the others.[4] It seems almost incongruous that Bacon should have brought his *Opus majus* to a close by arguing for the "sacrament of the altar" as containing in itself the highest good, that is, the union of God with man. In the host the whole of the Deity is contained.

The admirable editor of Bacon's *Opus majus*, Dr. Bridges, has compared Bacon's procedure to a traveller in a new world, who brings back specimens of produce with the view of persuading the authorities of his country to undertake a more systematic exploration.[5] Without entering into the discussion of those great themes which the other Schoolmen so much delighted in, Bacon asserted the right principle of theological study which excludes from prolonged discussion subjects which have no immediate bearing upon the interests of daily life or personal faith, and pronounced as useless the weary systems which were more the product of human ingenuity in combining words than of a clear, spiritual purpose. To him Abælard is not to be compared. Abælard was chiefly a scholastic metaphysician; Bacon an observer of nature. Abælard gives the appearance of being a vain aspirant after

---

[1] I. 56–59.   [2] I. 37.   [3] I. 28–30.
[4] I. 33, *Una scientia dominatrix aliarum.*   [5] I. p. lxxxix.

scholastic honors; Bacon of being a patient and conscientious investigator.

Professor Adamson and Dr. Bridges, two eminent Baconian scholars, have placed Roger Bacon at the side of such thinkers as Albertus Magnus and Thomas Aquinas. A close student of the Middle Ages, Coulton, has recently gone so far as to pronounce him a greater intellect than Thomas Aquinas.[1] The honor accorded to him in these recent days in circles of scientific research is as genuine as the honor given to the Angelic doctor in the Catholic communion. There is, however, danger of ascribing to him too much. Nevertheless, this forerunner of modern investigation may by common verdict, though unhonored in his own age, come to be placed higher as a benefactor of mankind than the master of metaphysical subtlety, Duns Scotus, who spoke to his age and its immediate successors with authority.

[1] From *St. Francis to Dante*, p. 293.

CHAPTER XIV.

THE SACRAMENTAL SYSTEM.

§ 112. *Literature on the Sacraments.*

LITERATURE : — GENERAL WORKS : The Writings of Abælard, Hugo of St. Victor, Peter Lombard, Alb. Magnus, Th. Aquinas, Bonaventura, Duns Scotus, and other Schoolmen. — G. L. HAHN : *Lehre von d. Sakramenten*, Breslau, 1864. — *J. SCHWANE : *Dogmengesch. der mittleren Zeit*, 787–1517, Freib. 1882, pp. 579–693. — J. H. OSWALD : *D. dogmatische Lehre von d. hl. Sakramenten d. kathol. Kirche*, 5th ed., Munich, 1894. — The Histories of Christ. Doctr. of FISHER, pp. 254–263 ; HARNACK, II. 462–562 ; LOOFS, pp. 298–304 ; SEEBERG, II. 107 sqq. — HERGENRÖTHER-KIRSCH : *Kirchengesch.*, II. 682–701. The works on Canon Law of HINSCHIUS ; P. HERGENRÖTHER (Rom. Cath.), pp. 667–684 ; FRIEDBERG, pp. 374–495. — HEFELE-KNÖPFLER, V. VI. — The art. *Sakrament* in Wetzer-Welte and Herzog. — D. S. SCHAFF : *The Sacramental Theory of the Med. Ch.* in "Princeton Rev.," 1906, pp. 206–236.

ON THE EUCHARIST, §§ 115, 116 : DALGAIRNS : *The Holy Communion, its Philos., Theol., and Practice*, Dublin, 1861. — F. S. RENZ : *D. Gesch. d. Messopfer-Begriffs*, etc., 1st vol., *Alterthum und Mittelalter*, Munich, 1901. — J. SMEND : *Kelchversagung und Kelchspendung in d. abendländ. Kirche*, Götting., 1898. — A. FRANZ : *D. Messe im deutschen Mittelalter*, Freib., 1902. — Artt. *Communion, Messe, Transubstantiation* in Wetzer-Welte and *Abendmahl* and *Kindercommunion* in Herzog.

ON PENANCE AND INDULGENCES, §§ 117, 118 : JOAN MORINUS : *Comment. hist. de disciplina in administratione sacr. pœnitentiæ*, Paris, 1651. — F. BERINGER, S.J., transl. fr. the French by J. SCHNEIDER : *D. Ablässe, ihr Wesen und Gebrauch*, 12th ed., Paderb., 1900. — *K. MÜLLER : *D. Umschwung in der Lehre von d. Busse während d. 12ten Jahrhunderts*, Freib., 1892. — H. C. LEA : *A Formulary of the Papal Penitentiary in the 13th Century*, Phil., 1892 ; *A Hist. of Auricular Confession and Indulgences*, 3 vols. Phil., 1896. — *TH. BRIEGER : *D. Wesen des Ablasses am Ausgange des Mittelalters*, Leipzig., 1897. — A. KURTZ : *D. kathol. Lehre vom Ablass vor und nach dem Auftreten Luthers*, Paderb., 1900. — C. M. ROBERTS : *Hist. of Confession until it developed into, Auric. Conf. A.D. 1215*, London, 1901. — * W. KÖHLER : *Dokumente zum Ablassstreit vom 1517*, Tübing., 1902. Very convenient, containing thirty-two of the most important documents on the subject and including Jacob von Juterbocks, *Tract. de indulgentiis, c.* 1451, and excerpts from the *Cœlifodina*, 1502. — *A. GOTTLOB : *Kreuzablass u. Almosenablass*, Stuttg., 1906. — A. M. KOENIGER : *D. Beicht nach Cæsarius von Heisterbach*,

Mun., 1906. — Artt. *Ablass,* *Bussdisciplin by FUNK, II. 1562–1590, and
Busse, II. 1590–1614, in Wetzer-Welte and *Indulgenzen by TH. BRIEGER
in Herzog, IX. 76–94. For other lit. see Brieger's art. in Herzog.
ON EXTREME UNCTION, ETC., § 119 : See artt. *Oelung* and *Ordo* in Wetzer-
Welte, IX. 716 sqq., 1027 sqq., and *Oelung* by KATTENBUSCH and *Pries-
terweihe* in Herzog, XIV. 304 sqq., XVI. 47 sqq. For marriage, the
works on Christian Ethics. — VON EICKEN : *Gesch. u. System der mittel-
alterl. Weltanschauung,* pp. 437–487, Stuttg., 1887. — The artt. *Ehe* in
Herzog, V. 182 sqq. and Wetzer-Welte, IV. 142–231 (including a number
of subjects pertaining to marriage).
ON GRACE AND THE FUTURE STATE, §§ 120, 121 : ANSELM : *De conceptu vir-
ginali et originale peccato,* Migne, 158. 431–467. — P. LOMBARDUS : *Sent.,*
II.31, etc. — H. OF ST. VICTOR : *De sacramentis,* I. 7, Migne, 176. 287–306.
— ALB. MAGNUS : *In Sent.,* II. 31 sqq., etc., Borgnet's ed., XXVII. — BONA-
VENTURA : *In Sent.,* II., etc.; Peltier's ed., III. — TH. AQUINAS : *Summa,*
II. 71–90, III. 52 sqq.; *Supplem.,* LXIX. sqq., Migne, IV. 1215–1459. —
DUNS SCOTUS : *Reportata,* XXIV.-XXVI., etc. The Histories of Doc-
trine of SCHWANE, pp. 393–493, HARNACK, LOOFS, SEEBERG, SHELDON.

§ 113. *The Seven Sacraments.*

As the doctrines of the Trinity and the person of Christ
were wrought out in the Nicene and post-Nicene periods, so
the Schoolmen of the twelfth and thirteenth centuries
wrought out the Catholic doctrine of the sacraments. At no
point were the mediæval theologians more industrious or did
they put forth keener speculative force. For the Roman
Catholic communion, the results of this speculation continue
to be of binding authority. The theologians most prominent
in developing the sacramental system were Hugo of St. Victor, Peter the Lombard, Alexander of Hales, and Thomas
Aquinas. Hugo wrote the first treatise on the sacraments,
De sacramentis. Thomas Aquinas did little more than to
reformulate in clear statement the views propounded by Hugo,
Peter the Lombard, and especially by Alexander of Hales, and
with him the development comes to an end.[1] The substance

---

[1] Some idea of the importance attached to the subject of the sacraments
may be derived from the space given by the Schoolmen to their treatment.
Hugo of St. Victor gives 440 columns, Migne's ed., 176. 183–617, the Lombard
90 columns out of the 452 of his *Sentences,* Bonaventura 1003 pages out of
3875 of his *System of Theology,* Peltier's ed. and Thomas Aquinas 670 columns
out of 4854 of his *Summa,* Migne, IV. 543–1217. Dr. Charles Hodge's *System.
Theol.* devotes 207 pages out of its 2260 to the sacraments, Dr. Shedd's

of his statement was adopted by the councils of Ferrara, 1439, and Trent, 1560.

Through the influence of Peter the Lombard and Thomas Aquinas, the number of the sacraments was fixed at seven, — baptism, confirmation, the eucharist, penance, extreme unction, ordination, marriage.[1] Bernard had spoken of many sacraments and enumerated ten, including footwashing and the investiture of bishops and abbots. Abælard had named five, — baptism, confirmation, the eucharist, marriage, and extreme unction. Hugo de St. Victor in his *Summa* also seems to recognize only five, — baptism, confirmation, eucharist, penance, and extreme unction,[2] but in his work on the Sacraments, in which he brought together all he had said on the subjects in other writings, he enumerated thirty. Here, evidently, the word is taken in a wide meaning and is almost synonymous with a religious rite. Hugo divided the sacraments into three classes, — sacraments which are necessary to salvation, baptism and the eucharist, those which have a sanctifying effect such as holy water and the use of ashes on Ash Wednesday, and a third class which prepares for the other sacraments. He called the sprinkling with water a sacrament.[3] Thomas Aquinas also ascribed a quasi-sacramental character to such rites, *quædam sacramentalia.*[4]

The uncertainty concerning the number of the sacraments was a heritage from the Fathers. Augustine defined any sacred rite a sacrament. The Third Lateran, 1179, used the term in a wide sense and included the investiture of bishops

Dogm. Theol. 25 pages out of 1348, Dr. E. V. Gerhart's *Institutes* 84 pages out of 1666, and Dr. A. H. Strong's *Sys. Theol.* 30 out of 600 pages.

[1] Others about the time of Peter the Lombard had given the number as seven, as Rolandus (afterwards Alexander III.) in his *Sentences* and Otto of Bamberg in a sermon, 1158, reported by his biographer Herbord.

[2] Migne, 176. 127 sqq. Hugo follows up the treatment of the five sacraments with a treatment of marriage, but I do not see that he calls it a sacrament.

[3] *De sacr.*, II. 9, Migne, 176. 473. The *aqua aspersionis,* or water of sprinkling mixed with salt, Hugo derived from Alexander, fifth pope from Peter. The sprinkling of ashes on the head, *susceptio cineris,* he placed under "the minor sacraments," but in his definition calls it an "ecclesiastical rite," as he does also the use of palm branches on Palm Sunday, Migne, 176. 423.

[4] Migne, IV. 597, 1025.

and burial among the sacraments.   The Catholic Church to-day makes a distinction between certain sacred rites, called *sacramentalia*, and the seven sacraments.[1]   Thomas gave as the reason for this number seven—that three is the number of the Deity, four of creation, and seven represents the union of God and man.[2]

Ingenious and elaborate attempts were made to correlate the seven sacraments to all of man's spiritual maladies and to show their "congruity" or adaptation to meet all the requirements of fallen and redeemed human nature.[3]   Baptism corresponds to the defect of spiritual life, confirmation to mental weakness found in those recently born, the eucharist to the temptation to fall into sin, — *labilitas animi ad peccandum*, — penance to sins committed after baptism, extreme unction to the remainders of sin not cleared away by penance, ordination to the lost condition of mankind, matrimony to concupiscence, and the liability of mankind to become extinct by natural death.

The number seven also corresponds to the seven virtues, — baptism, extreme unction, and the eucharist to faith, hope, and love, ordination to enlightenment, penance to righteousness, marriage to continence, and confirmation to endurance. Bonaventura elaborates at length a stimulating comparison to a military career.   The sacraments furnish grace for the spiritual struggle and strengthen the warrior on the various stages of his conflict.   Baptism equips him on entering the conflict, confirmation encourages him in its progress, extreme unction helps him at the finish, the eucharist and penance renew his strength, orders introduce new recruits into the ranks, and marriage prepares men to be recruits.   Augustine had compared the sacraments to the badges and rank conferred upon the soldier, a comparison Thomas Aquinas took up.[4]

---

[1] Hergenröther, *Kathol. Kirchenrecht.*, pp. 667 sq.

[2] Alb. Magnus has a long treatment, *Cur sint sacr. septem*, *In IV. Sent.*, I. 2, vol. XXIX. 6–11.

[3] See Bonaventura, *Brevil.*, VI. 3, Peltier's ed., VII. 314; Thomas Aq., *Summa*, Migne's ed., IV. 594 sq.

[4] Bonaventura, *Brevil.*, VI. 3; Th. Aq., *Summa*, III. 63. 1, Migne's ed., IV. 571.

The sacraments were not needed in man's estate of innocence. Marriage which was then instituted was a "function
of nature " and nothing more. There were sacraments under the old covenant as well as under the new. The Schoolmen follow Augustine in declaring that the former prefigure
the grace to come and the sacraments of the New Testament
confer grace.[1]   With Albertus Magnus and other Schoolmen it was a favorite question why woman was not circumcised.[2]

In defining what a sacrament is — *quid est sacramentum* —
the Schoolmen started with Augustine's definition that a
sacrament is a visible sign of an invisible grace,[3] but went
beyond him in the degree of efficiency they ascribe to it.
Beginning with Hugo, they assert in unmistakable language
that the sacraments, or outward symbols, contain and confer
grace, — *continere et conferre gratiam*, — the language afterwards used by the council of Trent. They have a virtue
inherent in themselves. The favorite figure for describing
their operation is medicine. Hugo[4] said, God is the physician, man is the invalid, the priest is the minister or mes-
senger, grace is the antidote, the sacrament is the vase. The
physician gives, the minister dispenses, the vase contains, the
spiritual medicine which cures the invalid. If, therefore, the
sacraments are the vases of spiritual grace, they do not cure
of themselves. Not the bottle, but the medicine, cures the
sick. Bonaventura entitled his chapters on the sacraments
"Sacramental Medicine."[5]

The sacraments are remedies which the great Samaritan

---

[1] Th. Aq., *Summa*, III. 62. 6, Migne, IV. 569, *Sacramenta veteris legis non
habebant in se aliquam virtutem qua operarentur ad conferendam gratiam
justificantem*. See for quotations from the *Sentences* of Thomas, Loofs, p. 301.

[2] *In IV. Sent.*, I. 21, vol. XXIX. 37.

[3] Abælard, *Introd. ad Theol.*, Migne's ed., p. 984, had quoted this definition. Albertus Magnus and other Schoolmen subsequent to Hugo, after
quoting Augustine, usually quote Hugo, *e.g.* Peter the Lombard and Th. Aq.,
III. 66. 1.

[4] *De sacr.*, I. 9. 4, Migne, 176. 325.

[5] *Brevil.*, VI., Peltier's ed., VII. 311–330. The Lombard, Alb. Magnus, Th.
Aquinas, etc., also use the illustration of medicine.

brought for the wounds of original and actual sin.   They are
more than visible signs and channels of grace.   They do more
than signify.   They sanctify.   They are the efficient cause
of gracious operations in the recipient.   The interior effects,
Thomas Aquinas says, are due to Christ,[1] or, as he says in
another place, to the blessing of Christ and the administration of the priest conjoined.   The mode of this efficacy is *ex
opere operato*.   This expression, used by William of Auxerre
and Alexander of Hales, Thomas adopted and says again and
again that the sacraments make righteous and confer
grace, *ex opere operato*, that is by a virtue inherent in
themselves.[2]

By this, Thomas Aquinas does not mean that the religious
condition of the recipient is a matter of indifference, but that
the sacrament imparts its virtue, if need be, without the operation of an active faith.   The tendency of Protestant writers
has been to represent the Schoolmen as ascribing a magical
virtue to the visible sacramental symbol, if not irrespective
of the divine appointment, then certainly irrespective of the
attitude of the recipient.   Such is not the view of the Schoolmen.   Thomas Aquinas distinguishes between the original
cause of grace, which is God, and the instrumental cause,
which is the sacrament.   The virtue of the latter depends
upon God's appointment and operation.[3]   The benefits of
Christ's atonement pass over to the faithful through faith
and the sacraments.[4]   The Church, said Bonaventura, received
the sacraments from Christ and dispenses them to the salvation of the faithful.[5]   The sacraments are efficacious only to
those who are of a religious disposition.

[1] *Interiorem sacramentorum effectum operatur Christus*, III. 64. 3, Migne,
IV. 583.

[2] *Sacr. justificant et gratiam conferunt ex opere operato.*   See references in
Schwane, p. 581.

[3] *Summa*, III. 62. 1, Migne, IV. 562, *causa vero instrumentalis non agit per
virtutem suæ formæ sed solum per motum quo movetur a principali agente.*

[4] Migne, IV. 568 sq.   *Virtus passionis Christi copulatur nobis per fidem et
sacramenta.*

[5] *Ecclesia sicut sacramenta a Christo accepit sic ad fidelium salutem dispensat.   Breviloq.*, VI. 5, Peltier's ed., VII. 316.

2 z

Duns Scotus, whose opinions were set aside at the council of
Ferrara for those of Thomas Aquinas, insisted that God can
confer grace apart from the sacraments, and their efficacy is
dependent upon an action of the will.   They act indirectly,
not directly.   Duns controverted Thomas' view that the sacrament is a visible sign containing supernatural virtue in itself absolutely.[1]   The sacraments involve a psychological
process in the soul.   As symbols, they remind the soul of
God's grace and attract it.   A good state of the heart, however, is not a meritorious cause of their efficacy.   For their
reception, it is sufficient if there be no moral impediment,
obex, that is, no impeding indisposition.[2]   It is the
excellency of the sacraments of the new law, Duns says,
that the very reception of them is a sufficient disposition to
grace.[3]

The relation the priest sustains to the sacraments is a vital
one, and except in extraordinary cases his ministration is
essential.   Their efficacy does not depend upon the priest's
personal character, provided only he administer according to
the rite of the Church.[4]   An immoral priest may confer
sacramental grace.   To use the mediæval illustration, pure
water may be conveyed through a leaden pipe as truly as
through a silver pipe.   Even if the intention of conferring
grace is absent from the mind of the officiating priest, the efficacy of the sacrament is not destroyed.   The priest acts in the
name of the Church, and in uttering the words of sacramental appointment he gives voice to the intention of the
Church.   This intention is sufficient for the perfection of the
sacrament in any given case.   Ultimately, it is Christ who
works the effect of the sacrament and not the priest through

[1] See Seeberg, *Duns Scotus*, pp. 356–358.

[2] *Non requiritur bonus motus qui mereatur gratiam sed sufficit quod sus-
cipiens non ponat obicem.*   *In Sent.*, IV. 1. 6, quoted by Schwane, p. 581.
Nisi impediat indispositio, quoted by Seeberg, p. 343.

[3] *Susceptio est dispositio sufficiens ad gratiam.*   Seeberg, p. 349.   For the
differences between the Thomists and Scotists on the sacraments, see also
Harnack, II. 483.

[4] *Ministri ecclesiæ possunt sacramenta conferre etiamsi sint mali.*   Th. Aq.,
Migne's ed., IV. 586, 821, 824.

any virtue of his own.[1]   Here, too, Thomas followed Augustine.

On this point also, Duns differed from the great Dominican by declaring that "a virtual intention" on the part of the celebrant is essential to the efficacy of the sacrament. He illustrates his position by a pilgrim on the way to the shrine of St. James.   The pilgrim may not think of St. James during the whole progress of his journey, but he starts out with "a virtual intention" to go to his shrine and keeps on the way.   So a priest, during the progress of the sacramental celebration, may allow his mind to wander and forget what he is doing, but he has the virtual intention of performing the rite.[2]

The sacraments may be "useful," said Bonaventura, if performed outside of the Church, provided the recipient afterwards enter "holy mother Church."   This he illustrates by Augustine's comparison of the sacraments to the four rivers of paradise.   The rivers flowed into different lands.   But neither to Mesopotamia nor Egypt did they carry the felicity of life, though they were useful.[3]   So it is with the sacraments when administered outside of the pale of the true Church.

The sacraments are not all of equal necessity.   Baptism alone is indispensable to eternal life.   Baptism and the eucharist are the mightiest, but of all the most mighty — *potissimum* — is the eucharist, and for three reasons: 1. It contains Christ himself after a substantial manner.   2. The other sacraments are preparatory to it.   3. All the faithful partake of it—adults who are baptized, as well as those who are in orders.   Three sacraments have an indelible character,— baptism, ordination, and confirmation.   Their mark cannot be effaced nor may they be repeated.   They are related to salvation as food is related to life.   The other four

---

[1] *Ministri non gratiam conferunt sua virtute, sed hoc facit Christus sua potestate per eos sicut per quædam instrumenta.*   Th. Aq., III. 64. 5, Migne, IV. 586.

[2] Seeberg, p. 350.

[3] *Brevil.*, Peltier's ed., p. 317.   The illustration is carried out at length and is very interesting as an example of pious mediæval homiletics.

sacraments are necessary to salvation only in the way a horse is necessary to a journey.[1]

The Schoolmen were not fully agreed as to the author of some of the sacraments. Peter the Lombard expressly said that extreme unction was instituted by the Apostles. Alexander of Hales, Albertus Magnus, and Thomas Aquinas held they were all instituted by Christ.[2]

Hugo of St. Victor said, God might have saved man without the sacraments but no man can be saved who rejects them.[3] They were to the mediæval mind the essential food of the religious life, and, in building up the sacramental system, the mediæval theologian felt he was fortifying the very fabric of the Church. In the authority to administer them lay the power of the priesthood to open and shut the kingdom of heaven, to pass the judgment of bliss or woe for this life and for the life to come. This sacramental theory, based now upon a false now upon a one-sided interpretation of Scripture, and compactly knit by argumentation, substituted the mechanical efficiency of sacramental grace for the Saviour into whose immediate presence the soul has a right to approach through penitence of heart and prayer. The sacramental system became the Church's Babylonish captivity, as Luther called it in his famous tract, in which the rights and liberty of the Christian believer are fettered by the traditions of men.

§ 114. *Baptism and Confirmation.*

Baptism is the door to the other sacraments and to the kingdom of heaven.[4] It is essential to salvation, except for persons who desire to be baptized and have not the opportunity to receive the rite. The desire on their part to be

---

[1] Th. Aq., III. 65. 4, Migne, IV. 601.

[2] See also Duns Scotus, see Seeberg, p. 338.

[3] *De sacr.*, II. 9, 5, Migne, 176. 325. *potuit Deus hominem salvare si ista non instituisset, sed homo nullatenus salvari posset si ista contemneret.*

[4] *Janua omnium aliorum sacramentorum.* Bonavent., *Brevil.* VII., Peltier's ed., p. 318; Th. Aq., *Summa*, III. 62. 6, Migne, IV. 569; *Supplem.* XXXV. 1, Migne, IV. 1047.

regenerated by water and the Holy Spirit is certain evidence
that the heart is already regenerated. For the necessity of
baptism, Thomas Aquinas and the other Schoolmen rely upon
John 3 : 3, "Except a man be born of water and the Spirit,
he cannot see the kingdom of God." Of all the sacraments the
most necessary, baptism effects regeneration, nay, it is regeneration itself.[1] It removes the guilt and the punishment due
original sin and all sins actually committed.[2] The ablution
of water signifies the ablution from guilt, and the freezing of
water, to use the strange figure of Thomas Aquinas, the sub-
traction of all punishment. Baptism also has the positive
effect of conferring grace, an effect which is symbolized by
the clearness of water.

The validity of the sacrament requires the full use of the
threefold name of the Trinity. Hugo of St. Victor differs
from the later Schoolmen on this point, although in doubt
whether the use of the name of Christ alone or the name of
God alone be not sufficient. Bernard had allowed the use
of the formula "I baptize thee in the name of the Father
and of the true and holy cross." These men wrote before
the Fourth Lateran Council. Bonaventura and Thomas
acknowledged that, in early times, the Church had often been
satisfied with baptism into the name of Christ, the Trinity
being, in such cases, understood. But since the deliverance of the Fourth Lateran, the omission of a single syllable from the trine formula invalidated baptism.[3] Exorcism,
unction with oil, and the giving of salt were prescribed to be
used in the solemnization of the rite. Exorcism expelled
demons and prevented them from impeding the recipient's
salvation. Salt, put into the ears, signified the reception of
the new doctrine, into the nostrils, its approbation, and into

---

[1] *Baptismus qui est regeneratio hominis in vitam spiritualem.* Th. Aq., III.
66. 9; 67. 3; 68. 9; 72. 1, Migne, IV. 617, 626, 646, 678.

[2] *Omne peccatum per baptismum tollitur.* Th. Aq., 69. 1, Migne, p. 652.
Baptismus institutus est contra vulnus originalis peccati. Alanus ab Insulis, *cont. hær.*, I. 39, 43, Migne, 210. 345, 347.

[3] *Brevil.* VI., Peltier's ed., p. 318 ; Th. Aq., III. 66. 6, Migne, p. 611, *quicquid desit ad plenam invocationem trinitatis tollit integritatem baptismi.*

the mouth, confession. Oil signified the fitting of the recipient to fight demons.

The proper administrator of baptism is the priest, but, in cases of necessity, laymen may baptize, male or female, and parents may baptize their own children.[1] For in the kingdom of heaven there is neither male nor female. But a woman must administer the rite privately, even as she is not allowed to speak in public. Yea, Thomas Aquinas went so far as to say that an unbaptized man may, in case of necessity, lawfully administer baptism, for Christ is free to use the agent he pleases, and it is he who baptizes inwardly, John 1: 33. The main reason for allowing such baptism is to extend the limits of salvation as far as possible.[2]

Children are proper subjects of baptism because they are under the curse of Adam. As the mother nourishes her offspring in the womb before it can nourish itself, so in the bosom of mother Church infants are nourished, and they receive salvation through the act of the Church.[3] A child cannot be baptized before it is born; it is of the essence of baptism that water be applied to the body.[4] It was the view of Thomas Aquinas and most of the Schoolmen that it is unlawful to baptize the children of Jews and pagans without the consent of the parents. Duns Scotus was an exception and permitted the forcible baptism of the children of Jews, yea of adult Jews.[5]

---

[1] They were allowed to use the vernacular in the ceremony. Synods of Treves, 1227, Mainz, 1233. And priests were instructed to teach laymen the baptismal ceremony in the vulgar tongue that they might use it if the exigency arose. Fritzlar, 1243, Hefele, V. 1099. A child taken from its mother after her death, and itself dead, was to be buried unbaptized in unconsecrated ground. Treves, 1310. [2] Th. Aq., III. 67. 4 sq., Migne, IV. 628 sq.

[3] *Pueri non se ipsos sed per actum eccl. salutem suscipiunt.* Th. Aq., III. 68. 9, Migne, 646; Bonavent., *Brevil.* VII. Peltier's ed., VII. 320; Duns Scotus, see Seeberg, p. 360.

[4] P. Lomb., IV. 6. 2, Migne, II. 853. Th. Aq., Migne, IV. 649, and Duns Scotus (Seeberg, p. 360) agree that if the head of the infant protrude from the womb, it may be baptized, for the head is the seat of the immortal agent.

[5] Th. Aq., Migne, IV. 648. One reason Duns gives is that the children of such Jews, if they are well educated, turn out to be good Christians (*vere fideles*) in the third and fourth generations. Seeberg, p. 364.

The definition of baptism excludes all unbaptized children, dying in infancy, from heaven. The question is discussed by that mystic and lovable divine, Hugo of St. Victor, whether the children of Christian parents may be saved who happen to be put to death in a city besieged by pagans and die unbaptized. He leaves it unanswered, remarking that there is "no authority for saying what will become of them."[1] Duns Scotus makes it plain that children yet unborn are under the law of sin, not because they are connected with the bodies of their mothers, but because of their own bodies. He mercifully excepts from the law of perdition unborn infants whose mothers suffer martyrdom or blood baptism.[2] The Reformers, Zwingli excepted, shared the views of the mediæval theology that unbaptized children dying in infancy are lost. At a later date, about 1740, Isaac Watts and other Protestant theologians, as a relief from the agonizing thought that the children of non-Christian parents dying in infancy are lost and suffer conscious torment, elaborated the view that they are annihilated. It remained for a still later Protestant period to pronounce in favor of the salvation of all such children in view of the superabounding fulness of the atonement and our Lord's words, "for of such is the kingdom of heaven."

Water is essential to baptism. The Schoolmen agreed that wine, oil, or other liquid will not do. Duns Scotus said in regard to baptism in beer that its validity would depend upon a scientific test whether the beer continued to be a species of water or not.[3] The Lombard declared without qualification for immersion as the proper mode. Thomas Aquinas refers to it as the more general practice of his day

---

[1] *Summa*, V. 6, Migne, 176. 132.

[2] *In Sent.*, IV. 4, 3. 3, Paris ed., XVI. 406, 410.

[3] Seeberg, p. 359, *Summa*, III. 66. 7, Migne, IV. 613 sq. ; P. Lomb., IV. 3, 8, Migne, II. 845 ; Bonav., *Brevil.* VII., Peltier's ed., p. 319, Duns Scotus. *In IV. Sent.*, vol. XVI. 272. Gregory IX., on being asked by the archbishop of Drontheim whether a certain baptism administered with beer was valid, water not being at hand, replied in the negative. Potthast, 11,048. The synod of Aurillac, 1278, pronounced sweet, salt, or melted snow water proper material.

and prefers it as the safer mode, as did also Bonaventura and Duns Scotus.[1] At any rate, the water must be applied to the head, for this is the most important part of man, standing as it does for the immortal agent. Both trine immersion, the custom of the Greek Church, and single immersion are valid. Trine immersion symbolizes the three persons of the Trinity and the three days of the Lord's burial; single immersion the unity of the Deity and the uniqueness of Christ's death. Synods, as late as the synod of Tarragona, 1391, spoke of the submersion of children in baptism.

The sacrament of *confirmation* corresponds to the adult period as baptism does to the child period (1 Cor. 13 : 11). It completes, as it were, the earlier ordinance and confers the graces of strength and hardihood. The baptized thus become full Christians.[2] The Schoolmen differed as to whether the sacrament was instituted immediately by Christ or by the Apostles or by the councils of the Church. Thomas Aquinas took the view that it was founded by Christ, being implied in the promise of the Holy Spirit (John 16: 7).

The rite is performed by the bishop, who is the successor of the Apostles, who uses the words, "I sign thee with the sign of the cross, I confirm thee with the chrism of salvation, in the name of the Father, and of the Son, and of the Holy Ghost." Chrism, or sacred oil, which is the symbol of the Spirit, is applied, and the cross is signed upon the forehead, the most prominent part of the body.[3] It is there shame shows itself when young Christians lack the courage to acknowledge their profession.

---

[1] *Quamvis tutius sit baptizare per modum immersionis, potest tamen fieri baptismus per modum aspersionis vel etiam per modum effusionis.*

[2] *Confirmatio est quasi ultima consummatio baptismi.* Th. Aq., III. 72. 11, Migne, IV. 693.

[3] Th. Aq., III. 73. 9, quotes Ezek. 3 : 8, "I have made thy forehead hard against their foreheads." He commends the custom whereby the candidate for confirmation is supported by another, for "though he be an adult in body he is not yet an adult spiritually."

§ 115.   *The Eucharist.*

The eucharist, called by the Schoolmen the crown of the sacraments and the sacrament of the altar, was pronounced both a sacrament and a sacrifice.   In the elaboration of the doctrine, scholastic theology reached the highest point of its speculation.   Albertus Magnus devoted to it a distinct treatise and Thomas Aquinas nearly four hundred columns of his *Summa.*   In practice, the celebration of this sacrament became the chief religious function of the Church.[1]   The festival of *Corpus Christi,* commemorating it, was celebrated with great solemnity.   The theory of the transmutation of the elements and the withdrawal of the cup from the laity were among the chief objects of the attacks of the Reformers.

The fullest and clearest presentation of the eucharist was made by Thomas Aquinas.   He discussed it in every possible aspect.   Where Scripture is silent and Augustine uncertain, the Schoolman's speculative ability, though often put to a severe test, is never at a loss.   The Church accepted the doctrines of transubstantiation and the sacrificial meaning of the sacrament, and it fell to the Schoolmen to confirm these doctrines by all the metaphysical weapons at their command.   And even where we are forced by the silence or clear meaning of Scripture to regard their discussion as a vain display of intellectual ingenuity, we may still recognize the solemn religious purpose by which they were moved.   Who would venture to deny this who has read the devotional hymn of Thomas Aquinas which presents the outgoings of his soul to the sacrificial oblation of the altar?

> *Pange lingua gloriosi corporis mysterium.*
> Sing my tongue the mystery telling.[2]

---

[1] *Quasi omnis devotio in ecclesia est in ordine ad illud sacramentum.* Duns Scotus as quoted by Seeberg, *Dogmengesch.*, II. 113.

[2] See Schaff's *Christ in Song*, pp. 465 sqq.   The verse, depicting the doctrine of transubstantiation, runs : —

> *Verbum caro, panem verum verbo carnem efficit*
> *Fitque sanguis Christi merum ; etsi sensus deficit*
> *Ad firmandum cor sincerum sola fides sufficit.*

The culminating point in the history of the mediæval doctrine of the eucharist was the dogmatic definition of transubstantiation by the Fourth Lateran Council, 1215. Thenceforth it was heresy to believe anything else. The definition ran that " the body and blood of Christ are truly contained in the sacrament of the altar under the forms of bread and wine, the bread being transubstantiated into the body and the wine into the blood by divine power." [1] The council did not foist upon the Church a new doctrine. It simply formulated the prevailing belief.

The word "transubstantiation" is not used by Hugo of St. Victor and the earlier Schoolmen. They used " transition " and " conversion," the latter being the favorite term. The word "transubstantiation" seems to have been first used by Hildebert of Tours, d. 1134. [2] According to Duns Scotus, the doctrine cannot be proved with certainty from the Scriptures and must be accepted upon the basis of the decision of the Church. [3] The passages, chiefly relied upon for proving the doctrine, are John 6 and the words of institution, " this is my body," in which the verb is taken in its literal sense. Rupert of Deutz is the only Schoolman of the twelfth and thirteenth centuries who dissented from it. He seems to have taught the theory of impanation. [4]

Three names, applied to the eucharist, had special significance. [5] It is a *sacrifice* because it repeats Christ's oblation on the cross. It is a *communion* because it presents the unity of the Church. It is a *viaticum* because it is heavenly manna for pilgrims on their way to heaven. Thomas Aquinas also uses the term of John of Damascus, *assumption*, because the sacrament lifts us up into the Deity of Christ, and calls it *hostia*, or the host, because it contains Christ himself, who

---

[1] *Corpus et sanguis in sacramento altaris sub speciebus panis et vini veraciter continentur, transubstantiatis pane in corpore et vino in sanguinem potestate divina.*   [2] Migne, 171. 776.   [3] See Schwane, p. 656.

[4] Schwane, p. 641, and Rocholl under *Rupert* in Herzog, XV. 229 sqq.

[5] Th. Aq., III. 73. 4, Migne, IV. 701 ; Bonaventura, *Brev.* VI. 9, Peltier's ed., 322, *eucharistiæ dedit in sacrificium oblationis, et sacramentum communionis et viaticum refectionis.*

is the oblation of our salvation.[1] It was also called the mass.

The elements to be used are wheaten bread, either leavened or unleavened. Water is to be mixed with the wine as Christ probably mixed them, following the custom in Palestine. Water symbolizes the people, and the wine symbolizes Christ, and their combination the union of the people with Christ. The mixture likewise represents the scene of the passion. Thomas Aquinas also finds in the water flowing in the desert, 1 Cor. 10: 4, a type of this custom. He relied much, as did Albertus Magnus[2] before him, upon the words of Prov. 9 : 5, Come eat of my bread and drink of the wine which I have *mingled* for you. But the admixture of the two elements is not essential. The synods of Cologne, 1279, Lambeth, 1281, etc., prescribed two or three drops of water as sufficient.

At the moment of priestly consecration, the elements of bread and wine are converted into the very body and blood of Christ. The substance of the bread and wine disappears. The " accidents " — *species sensibiles* — remain, such as taste, color, dimensions, and weight. What becomes of the substance of the two elements ? asks Peter the Lombard. There are three possible answers. First, the substance passes into the four original elements or into the body and blood of Christ. Second, it is annihilated. Third, it remains in part or in whole. Duns Scotus adopted the second explanation, the substance is annihilated.[3] The Lombard, Bonaventura, and Thomas Aquinas adopted the view that the substance is converted into the body and blood of Christ. Against the theory of annihilation Thomas used the illustration that it does not follow because air, from which fire is generated, is

---

[1] *Hostia salutaris.* Eph. 5 : 2, is quoted where the word *hostia* is used in the Vulgate for Christ's sacrifice.

[2] *De euchar.* vol. XIII. 668. Th. Aquinas, III. 74. 1, Migne, IV. 705, speaks of the Cataphrygæ and Pepuziani as mixing with the dough of the sacramental bread the blood of children gotten by pricking their bodies, and also of the Aquarii who, from considerations of temperance, used only water.

[3] He defined transubstantiation as *transitus totalis substantiæ in substantiam.* Seeberg, p. 378.

not here nor there, that it has been annihilated. The
change on the altar is altogether supernatural. The body
of Christ is in the sacrament not quantitatively, *per modum
quantitatis*, but in substance; not in its *dimensions*, but by a
sacramental virtue, *ex vi sacramenti*, in a way peculiar to this
sacrament. It is on the altar and is apprehended by faith
only.[1]

Upon the basis of the separate existence of substance and
" accidents " the Schoolmen proceeded to perfect their theory.
What the substance of bread is, if it is not its nutritive
power, and how it is possible to think of bread without those
qualities which make it bread to us, the practical mind cannot understand. Scholastic dialectics professed to understand it, but the statements are nothing more than a fabric
of mystifying terms and gratuitous assumptions. Wyclif
thoroughly exposed the fallacious reasoning.

Thomas Aquinas went so far as to declare that, though the
substance of bread and wine disappears, these elements continue to preserve the *virtue* of their substance.[2] Luther said
the Schoolmen might as well have set up a theory of *trans-
accidentation* as of transubstantiation. Thomas Aquinas anticipated his objection and argued that by a providential arrangement this was not so for three reasons: 1. It is not the
custom for men to eat human flesh and drink human blood,
and we would revolt from eating Christ's blood and flesh under the form of bread and wine. 2. The sacrament would
become a laughing stock to infidels if Christ were eaten in
his own form. 3. Faith is called forth by the enveilment of
the Lord within the forms of bread and wine. The body
of Christ is not broken or divided by the teeth except in a
sacramental way.[3] Creation, said this great Schoolman, is

---

[1] Th. Aq., III. 75. 1, Migne, IV. 716, *neque sensu, neque intellectu depre-
hendi potest sed sola fide.* Bonaventura says, *Brevil.* VI. 9, *in specierum
utraque continetur totaliter, non circumscriptibiliter, nec localiter sed sacramentaliter totus Christus.*

[2] *Quamvis non sint substantia, habent virtutem substantiæ.* Th. Aq., III.
77. 6, Migne, IV. 755.

[3] Th. Aq., III. 77. 7, Migne, IV. 756; Bonaventura, *Brevil.*, 322.

easier to understand than transubstantiation, for creation is out of nothing, but in the sacrament the substance of bread and wine disappear while the accidents remain.

A second statement elaborated by the Schoolmen is that the whole Christ is in the sacrament, divinity and humanity, — flesh, bones, nerves, and other constituents, — and yet the body of Christ is not there locally or in its dimensions.[1]

This is the so-called doctrine of concomitance, elaborated by Alexander of Hales, Thomas Aquinas, and other Schoolmen with great subtilty. According to this doctrine the divinity of Christ and his body are never separated. Wherever the body is, there is also the divinity, whether it be in heaven or on the altar. The determination of this point was of importance because the words of institution mention only Christ's body.

A third integral part of the scholastic treatment of the eucharist was the assertion that the whole Christ is in each of the elements,[2] a view which offered full justification for the withdrawal of the cup from the laity. Anselm had taken this view, that the entire Christ is in each element, but he was having no reference to the withdrawal of the cup.[3]

Two serious questions grew out of this definition; namely, whether the elements which our Lord blessed on the night of

---

[1] *Non solum caro sed totum corpus Christi, scilicet ossa, nervi et alia hujusmodi.* Th. Aq., 76. 1, Migne, IV. 732. He lays stress upon the word "body," which is made up of constituent parts, and the "flesh" of John 6 : 56, he explains as standing for the body. Following the Aristotelian distinction of substance and form, Thomas Aquinas, Migne, IV. 726, and the other Schoolmen (see Schwane, p. 648) declared that the *form* of the bread and wine is also changed into the body and blood of Christ. The words *forma* and *species* are distinguished. The *species* of bread and wine remain, the *forma* disappears. Duns Scotus devoted much space to proving that a substance may have a variety of forms.

[2] *Sub utraque specie sacramenti totus est Christus.* Th. Aq., 76. 2, Migne, 733. *Sub utraque specie est unus Christus et totus et indivisus, scilicet corpus, et anima, et Deus.* Bonaventura, *Brevil.* VI. 9, Peltier's ed., VII. 322.

[3] *In acceptatione sanguinis totum Christum, Deum et hominem, et in acceptatione corporis similiter totum accipimus.* Ep. 4 : 107, Migne, vol. 159, p. 255. Anselm was making a distinction between the body and spirit of Christ, the spirit being represented by the blood and wine, and the body by the bread and flesh.

his betrayal were his own body and blood and what it was the disciples ate when they partook of the eucharist during the time of our Lord's burial.   To the second question the reply was given that, if the disciples partook of the eucharist in that period, they partook of the real body.   Here Duns Scotus brought to bear his theory that a thing may have a number of forms and that God can do what to us seems to be most unreasonable. As for the first question, Hugo of St. Victor shrank from discussing it on the sensible ground that such divine mysteries were to be venerated rather than discussed.[1]   The other Schoolmen boldly affirmed that Christ partook of his own body and blood and gave them to the disciples.   " He had them in His hands and in His mouth." This body, according to Thomas, was " immortal and not subject to pain."[2]   Thomas quoted with approval the lines : [3] —

> The King, seated with the twelve at the table,
> Holds Himself in His hands. He, the Food, feeds upon Himself.

This monstrous conception involved a further question. Did Judas partake of the true body and blood of the Lord? This the Schoolmen answered in the negative.   The traitor took only natural and unblessed bread.   Leaning upon St. Augustine, they make the assertion, upon a manipulation of Luke 22 and John 13 according to which Christ distributed the bread and the wine before Judas took the sop, that the sop, or immersed morsel, was delusive.   Judas was deceived.[4]

Another curious but far-reaching question occupied the

[1] *Summa*, II. VIII., Migne, 176. 462, *ego in ejusmodi divina secreta magis venerenda quam discutienda cerneo.*

[2] *Summa*, 81. 3, Migne, IV. 810–813.   Anselm used the same words. Migne, 159. 255.   Schwane agrees that this conception, that Christ ate His own body, was general among the Schoolmen, p. 645.

[3] *Rex sedet in cœna turba, cinctus duodena*
Se tenet in manibus et cibat ipse cibus.

[4] So Hugo, II, 8. 4; the Lombard, XI. 8; Thomas Aquinas, 81. 2, Migne. pp. 811 sq.   The delusion is called a *fictio*, and also '' Judas' communion.'' Synod of London, 1175.   The argument is in clear contradiction to the meaning of the Gospel narratives on their face.

minds of Albertus Magnus, Bonaventura, Thomas Aquinas, and other Schoolmen. Does a mouse, in eating the consecrated host, actually partake of its consecrated substance? Thomas argued in this way: the body and blood of Christ would not be withdrawn, if the consecrated host should be cast into the mire, for God allowed Christ's body even to be crucified. As for mice, they were not created to use the bread as a sacrament, and so they cannot eat Christ's body after a sacramental manner, *sacramentaliter*, but only the accidents of the elements, *per accidens*, just as a man would eat who took the consecrated host but did not know it was consecrated.[1] Bonaventura, quoting Innocent III., took the more reasonable view that the body of Christ is withdrawn under such circumstances. Peter the Lombard had said that an animal does not take the body of Christ in eating the bread. But what it does take and eat, God alone knows. Duns Scotus took up the similar question, what occurs to an ass drinking the water consecrated for baptism and sensibly called it a *subtilitas asinina*, an asinine refinement, for the virtue of ablution inhering in such water an ass could not drink.[2] To the theory of transubstantiation, Rupert of Deutz has been referred to as an exception. John of Paris was deprived of his chair at the University of Paris for likening the union of Christ's body and the bread to the coexistence of the divine and human natures in Christ's person. He died, 1306, while his case was being tried at Rome. Ockam tentatively developed the theory of impanation whereby Christ's body and the bread are united in one substance, but he expressed his readiness to yield to the dogma of the Church.

[1] For this theological and metaphysical curiosity, see Th. Aq., 80. 3, Migne, 789, *non tangit mus ipsum corpus Christi, secundum propriam speciem sed solum secundum species sacramentales . . . nec tamen animal brutum sacramentaliter corpus Christi manducat quia non est natum uti eo ut sacramento, unde non sacramentaliter sed per accidens corpus Christi manducat*, etc. Alb. Magnus, *In Sent.*, IV. 13. 38. Borgnet's ed., XXIX. 397, Bonaventura, *Sent.*, IV. 13. 2. 1, Peltier's ed., V. 550.

[2] Seeberg, p. 360.

The sacrificial aspect of the eucharist was no less fully developed. In Hugo of St. Victor we hear nothing of a repetition of the sacrifice on the cross. He speaks of the mass as being a transmission of our prayers, vows, and offerings — *oblationes* — to God.[1] Peter the Lombard said the sacrifice on the altar is of a different nature from the sacrifice on the cross, nevertheless it is a true sacrifice. The later Schoolmen, following Alexander of Hales, laid stress on the sacrificial element. The eucharist is an unbloody but "real immolation" performed by the priest.

The altar represents the cross, the priest represents Christ in whose person and power he pronounces the words of consecration,[2] and the celebration represents the passion on the cross. The priest's chief function is to consecrate the body and blood of Christ.[3]

The sacrifice may be offered daily, just as we stand daily in need of the fruits of Christ's death and as we pray for daily food. And because Christ was on the cross from nine till three o'clock, it is proper that it should be offered between those hours, at any rate during the daytime and not in the night, for Christ said, "I must work the works of him that sent me, while it is day: for the night cometh, when no man can work," John 9 : 4.

To the discussion of the twofold effect of the eucharist as a sacrament and as a sacrifice, the Schoolmen also give much attention. Like the other sacraments, the eucharist has the virtue of conferring grace of itself.[4] As a sacrament it inures to our nourishment and perfection in Christ; as a sacrifice to the removal of sins venial and mortal. As a sacrament it benefits those who partake; as a sacrifice its benefits accrue also to persons who do not partake, living and dead.[5] For

---

[1] The priest being the mediator. *Summa*, Migne, 176. 472.

[2] *Sacerdos gerit imaginem Christi*, Th. Aq., III. 83. 1, Migne, IV. 830.

[3] Th. Aq., *Supplem.* 37. 5, Migne, IV. 1062.

[4] *Ex seipso virtutem habet gratiam conferendi.* Th. Aq., III. 79. 1, Migne, IV. 774.

[5] Th. Aq., 79. 7, *Supplem.* III. 71. 10, Migne, IV. 782, 1246 sq.; Al. Magnus, I. 4, extended the benefits of the mass also to the glorified *pro salute vivorum, pro requie defunctorum, pro gloria beatorum.*

this position Thomas Aquinas quotes side by side the words of our Lord, Luke 22 and Matt. 26, "which is shed for *you*" and "which is shed for *many* for the remission of sins," the latter passage being taken to include parties not present in the benefits of the sacrifice on the altar.

§ 116.   *Eucharistic Practice and Superstition.*

The celebration of the eucharist is the central part of the service of the Latin Church.   Thomas Aquinas said it is to be celebrated with greater solemnity than the other sacraments because it contains the whole mystery of our salvation. He gives the meaning of the various ceremonies,[1] such as the signing with the cross, the priest's turning his face to the people a certain number of times with reference to Christ's appearances after the resurrection, the use of incense, the stretching forth of the priest's arms, the breaking of the bread, and the rinsing of the mouth after the wine has been taken.   How important the prescriptions were considered to be, may be inferred from the careful attention this great Schoolman gives to them.   If a fly, he says, or a spider, be found in the wine after consecration, the insect must be taken out, carefully washed and burnt, and then the water, mingled with ashes, must be thrown into the sacrary.   If poison be found in the consecrated wine, the contents of the cup are to be poured out and kept in a vessel among the relics.[2]

The priest's fitness to consecrate the elements lies in the sacerdotal power conferred upon him at his ordination.   He consecrates the elements not in his own name but as the minister of Christ, and he does not cease to be a minister by being bad, *malus*.[3]   He alone is the mediator between God and the people, so that it lies not within the power of a layman to administer the eucharist.   The Angelic doctor de-

---

[1] *Summa*, III. 83. 5 sq., Migne, IV. 844–853.

[2] Th. Aq., III. 83. 5, Migne, IV. 850.

[3] *Non ex hoc desinit aliquis minister esse Christi quod est malus*, Th. Aq., 82. 5, 7, Migne, IV. 821, 824; Anselm, ep. IV. 107, Migne, 159. 257, had said the same thing, *nec a bono sacerdote majus*, etc.

clares that, while in the other sacraments the benefits accrue
through the use of the elements, in the eucharist the benefit
consists in the consecration of the elements by the priest and
not in their use by the people.[1]

Ecclesiastical analysis and definition could go no farther
in divesting the simple memorial meal instituted by our Lord
of the element of immediate communion between the believer
and the Saviour, and changing it as it were into a magical
talisman.   It would be disingenuous to ignore that with
the Schoolmen the devotional element has a most prominent
place in their treatment of the eucharist.   Especially
when they are treating it as a sacrifice is emphasis
laid upon devotion on the part of the participants.[2]   But,
after this is said, the Protestant Christian still feels that they
did not appreciate in any adequate degree, the place of faith
as the necessary organ of receiving the divine grace extended
through this sacred ordinance.   The definition which the
mediæval theologians gave to the Church and the mediatorial
power they associated with the priesthood precluded them
from estimating faith at its true worth.[3]

The theory of the sacrificial efficacy of the mass encouraged superstition.   It exalted the sacerdotal prerogative of
the priest[4] who had it in his power to withhold or give this
viaticum, the spiritual food for pilgrims looking forward to
heaven.   The people came to look to him rather than to
Christ, for could he not by the utterance of his voice effect
the repetition of the awful sacrifice of the cross!   The frequent repetition of the mass became a matter of complaint.

[1] Th. Aq., III. 80. 12, Migne, IV. 809. *Perfectio hujus sacramenti non
est in usu fidelium sed in consecratione materiæ.*

[2] *Requiritur ut cum magna devotione et reverentia ad hoc sacramentum
accedat. . . . Eucharistia exigit actualem devotionem in suscipiente,* Th.
Aq., III. 80. 10, *Supplem.* III, 32. 4, Migne, IV. 805, 1038.

[3] We cannot help feeling strongly with Harnack when he exclaims, " In its
doctrine of the eucharist, the Church gave expression to all that she held
dear, — her theology, her mystical relation to Christ, the communion of
believers, the priesthood, sacrifice, etc., — only not to that faith which seeks
assurance and to which assurance is given," *Dogmengesch.,* II. 489 sq.

[4] *Populus indiget medio ad Deum qui per seipsum accedere ad deum non
potest.,* Th. Aq., III. 22. 4, Migne, IV. 219.

Albertus Magnus speaks of women attending mass every day from levity and not in a spirit of devotion who deserved rebuke.[1] Councils again and again forbade its being celebrated more than once a day by the same priest, except on Christmas and Easter, and in case of burial. Masses had their price and priests there were who knew how to sell them and to frighten people into making provision for them in their wills.[2]

The elevation and adoration of the host were practised in the Latin Church as early as the twelfth century. Honorius III., 1217, made obligatory the ringing of a bell at the moment the words of institution were uttered that the worshippers might fall on their knees and adore the host. The Lambeth synod of 1281 ordered the church bells to be rung at the moment of consecration so that the laboring man on the field and the woman engaged in her domestic work might bow down and worship. Synods prescribed that the pyx, the receptacle for the host, be made of gold, silver, ivory, or, at least, of polished copper. A light was kept burning before it perpetually. In case a crumb of the bread or a drop of the wine fell upon the cloth or the priest's garments, the part was to be cut out and burnt and the ashes thrown into the sacrary. And if the *corporale*, the linen cover prescribed for the altar, should be wet in the blood, it was to be washed out three times and the water drunk by a priest. If a drop happened to fall on a stone or a piece of wood or hard earth, the priest or some pious person was to lick it up.

The festival of the eucharist, Corpus Christi, celebrated the first Thursday after Trinity Sunday, had its origin in the vision of Juliana, a nun of Liège, who saw the full moon, representing the church year, with one spot on its surface. This spot indicated the Church's neglect to properly honor the real presence. She made her vision known to the bishop of Liège and the archdeacon, James Pantaleon. A celebration was appointed for the diocese, and when James became pope, under the name of Urban IV., he prescribed,

[1] *De euchar.* VI. 3.
[2] Councils of Würzburg, 1287, Paris, 1212, etc. See Hefele, V. 866.

in 1264, the general observance of the festival. John XXII. inaugurated the procession wherein, on Corpus Christi day, the host was carried about the streets with great solemnities.[1] The liturgical service used on Corpus Christi was prepared by Thomas Aquinas at the appointment of Urban IV. Two important changes occurred in this period in the distribution of the elements, — the abandonment of the communion of children and the withdrawal of the cup from the laity.

The communion of children practised in the early Church, and attested by Augustine and still practised in the Greek Church, seems to have been general as late as the reign of Pascal II. Writing in 1118, Pascal said it was sufficient to give the wine to children and the very sick, as they are not able to assimilate the bread. In their case the bread was to be dipped into the wine.[2] Just how the change took place is unknown. Odo, bishop of Paris, 1175, forbade the communion of children. The synod of Treves, 1227, denied to them the bread, and the synod of Bordeaux, 1255, the wine as well as the bread. The greater Schoolmen do not treat the subject. The *Supplement* of Thomas Aquinas' *Theology* says that the extreme unction and the eucharist were not administered to children because both sacraments required real devotion in the recipients.[3]

The denial of the cup to the laity, the present custom of the the Roman Catholic Church, became common in the thirteenth century. It was at first due to the fear of profanation by spilling the consecrated blood of Christ. At the same time the restriction to the bread was regarded as a wholesome way of teaching the people that the whole Christ is present in each of the elements. Among other witnesses in the twelfth cen-

---

[1] See artt. *Fronleichnamsfest* in Wetzer-Welte, IV. 2061 sqq., and Herzog, VI. 297 sqq. It was one of the first observances to call forth Luther's protest. Köstlin, *Leben Luthers*, I. 560.

[2] *Ep.*, 535, Migne, 163. 442, *qui panem absorbere non possunt*, etc., quoted in Herzog under *Kinderkommunion*, X. 289.

[3] *Suppl.*, XXXII. 4, Migne, IV. 1038. The council of Trent anathematized those who hold the communion of children to be necessary.

tury to the distribution of both the bread and the wine to the
laity are Rupert of Deutz and pope Pascal II. Pascal urged
that this custom be forever preserved.[1] But it is evident
that there was already at that time divergence of practice.
The Englishman, Robert Pullen, d. ab. 1150, refers to it and
condemned the dipping of the host into the wine as a Judas
communion, with reference to John 13 : 26.[2]

By the middle of the thirteenth century the feeling had
grown strong enough for a great authority, Alexander of
Hales, to condemn the giving of the cup to the laity and on the
doctrinal ground that the whole Christ is in each of the elements. As a means of instructing the people in this doctrine
he urged that the cup be denied. But Albertus Magnus, his
contemporary, has no hint justifying the practice.[3] Thomas
Aquinas followed Alexander, giving as his chief reason the
danger of profanation by spilling the sacred contents of the
chalice. It is sufficient, he said, for the priest to partake of
the cup, for the full benefit accrues by the participation of a
single element, *communio sub una specie*.[4] Christ distributed
bread only and not drink to the five thousand.

The usage gradually spread. The chapter of the Cistercians in 1261 forbade monks, nuns, and lay brethren of the
order to take the cup. The few councils which expressed
themselves on the subject were divided.[5]

The council of Constance threatened with excommunica-

---

[1] Migne, 163. 142. See Smend, p. 7, for other witnesses. Smend's book
is a most thorough piece of work and is indispensable in the study of the
subject. With the exception of some quotations, I depend upon him for the
contents of these paragraphs.

[2] Called *intinctio*. Hugo of St. Victor and Peter the Lombard were among
the first to condemn the practice. Also the synod of London, 1175, Hefele,
V. 688. See also V. 224 for the action of the synod of Clermont, 1095.

[3] Albertus makes no mention of the matter in his *De eucharistia* and *Com.*
on the *Sentences*. Peter Rokyzana, at the council of Basel in the fifteenth
century, appealed to him in his argument for giving the cup to the laity.

[4] Th. Aq., III. 80. 12, Migne, IV. 808 sq., *nihil derogat perfectioni hujus
sacr., si populus sumat corpus sine sanguine dummodo sacerdos consecrans
sumat utrumque.* So also Bonaventura, *Sent.*, IV. 11. 2.

[5] The synod of Lambeth, 1281, seems to have forbidden the cup to the
laity; the synod of Exeter, 1287, to have positively enjoined it.

tion all who distributed the wine to the laity. It spoke of
many "perils and scandals" attending the distribution of the
wine. Gerson, who voted for the enactment, urged the danger
of spilling the wine, of defilement to the sacred vessels from
their contact with laymen's hands and lips, the long beards
of laymen, the possibility of the wine's turning to vinegar
while it was being carried to the sick, or being corrupted
by flies, or frozen by the cold, the difficulty of always pur-
chasing wine, and the impossibility of providing cups for
ten thousand or twenty thousand communicants on Easter.
The council of Trent reaffirmed the withdrawal of the
cup as an enactment the Church was justified in making.
Gregory II. had commanded the use of a single chalice at
communion.[1]

Some strange customs came into vogue in the distribution
of the wine, such as the use of a reed or straw, which were
due to veneration for the sacred element. Many names
were given to this instrument, such as *fistula, tuba, canna,
siphon, pipa, calamus.* The liturgical directions required the
pope to drink through a *fistula* on Maundy Thursday and
Good Friday. He still follows this custom at the public
mass. The practice maintained itself in some parts of the
Lutheran Church as in Hamburg and vicinity, and Brandenburg down to the eighteenth century.[2]

Another custom was the practice of cleaning the mouth
with a rinsing cup of unconsecrated wine, after one or
both the elements had been received, and called in German
the *Spülkelch.* A synod of Soissons of the twelfth century
enjoined all to rinse their mouths after partaking of the elements. Peckham, archbishop of Canterbury, 1281, enjoined
priests to instruct the people that in partaking of the bread
they were partaking of the whole Christ, and that what
was given them in the cup was only wine, given that they

---

[1] See Migne, 89. 525. For an interesting account of the different shapes
of the chalice, see *Enc. Brit.*, XIX. 185 sq. The earlier chalices had two
handles and a small base, those of the thirteenth and fourteenth centuries no
handles and a broad base. Some of the later chalices were very capacious.

[2] See the interesting details given by Smend, pp. 18 sqq.

might the more easily swallow the sacred body.[1]   The custom of taking a meal immediately after the sacrament, dating
back to the fifth century, is also found in this period.[2]

This treatment of the mediæval theory of the eucharist
would be incomplete without giving some of the marvellous
stories which bear witness to the excessive reverence for
the sacred host and blood.   One of the most famous, the
story of the monk, who was cured of doubts by seeing the
host exude blood, is told by Alexander of Hales, Bonaventura,[3] and others.   Cases when real blood was seen in the
chalice were not infrequent.   The host sometimes remained
uninjured amid the ashes of a burnt church.[4]   Cæsar of
Heisterbach relates several cases when a snow-white dove
was seen sitting near the chalice at the celebration of the
mass and a number of cases of the appearance of Christ in
visible form in the very hands of the consecrating priest.
Thus one of the monks, present when the mass was being
said by Herman, abbot of Himmelrode, saw after the consecration of the host the Christ as a child in the abbot's hands.
The child rose to the height of the cross and then was reduced
again in size to the dimensions of the host, which was eaten
by the abbot.[5]   The same writer narrates that a certain
monk, Adolf, of the Netherlands, after consecrating the
host, saw in his hands the virgin carrying the child, Christ,
in her arms.   Turning the host, he saw on the other side
a lamb.   Turning it back again, he saw Christ on the cross.
Then there was nothing left but the visible form of the
bread, which the pious monk ate.   The writer goes on to
say that Adolf did not feel full joy over this vision, for he
kept a concubine.[6]   A Fleming woman of the town of
Thorembais, who had been refused the sacrament by a priest,

[1] *Vinum purum . . . ut facilius sacrum corpus glutiat.*   Smend, who gives
elaborate details, pp. 43–75.

[2] The object was to prevent the loss of any of the sacred element by
expectoration or vomiting, *per sputum vel vomitum.*   Chrysostom made a
recommendation of this sort, Smend, 44.

[3] *Sent.*, IV. 11, 2, 2, Peltier's ed., V. 496.

[4] Cæsar of Heisterb., *Dial.*, IV. 16.

[5] *Dial.*, IX. 29, Strange's ed., II. 186.   [6] IX. 3.

was visited the same night by Christ himself, who gave her the host with his own hands.[1]

At a church dedication in Anrode, the invited priests engaged in conviviality and while they were dancing around the altar, the pyx was overthrown and the five hosts it contained scattered. The music was at once stopped and search was made but without result. The people were then put out of the building and every corner was searched till at last the hosts were found on a ledge in the wall where the angel had placed them.[2]

Perhaps the most remarkable case related by the chronicler of Heisterbach is that of the bloody host of St. Trond, Belgium. This he had himself seen, and he speaks of it as a miracle which should be recorded for the benefit of many after generations. In 1223 a woman in Harbais, in the diocese of Liège, kissed her lover with the host in her mouth, in the hope that it would inflame his love for her. She then found she could not swallow the host and carefully wrapped it up in a napkin. In her agony, she finally revealed her experience to a priest who called in the bishop of Livland who happened to be in the town. Together they went to the place where the host was concealed and lo! there were three drops of fresh blood on the cloth. The abbot of Trond was called in and it was then found that half of the host was flesh and half bread. The bishop thought so highly of the relic that he attempted to carry off two of the drops of blood, but sixty armed men interfered. The sacred blood was then put in a vase and deposited among the relics of the church of St. Trond.[3] This case was fully believed by Cæsar, and he expresses no doubt about the many other cases he reports.

Another case related by Etienne of Bourbon[4] is of a farmer who, wanting to be rich, followed the advice of a friend and placed the host in one of his beehives. The bees with great reverence made a miniature church, contain-

[1] IX. 35, Strange's ed., II. 191.   [2] *Dial.*, IX. 15.

[3] See Kaufmann, trans. of Cæsar, II. 208-210.

[4] De la Marche's ed., pp. 266 sq.

ing an altar, on which they placed the sacred morsel. All
the bees from the neighborhood were attracted and sang
beautiful melodies. The rustic went out, expecting to find
the hives overflowing with honey but, to his amazement,
found them all empty except the one in which the host
had been deposited. The bees attacked him fiercely. He
repaired to the priest, who, after consulting with the bishop,
went in procession to the hive and found the miniature
church with the altar and carried it back to the village
church while the bees, singing songs, flew away.

These stories, which might be greatly multiplied, attest
the profound veneration in which the host was held and
the crude superstitions which grew up around it in the
convent and among the people. The simple and edifying
communion meal of the New Testament was set aside by
mediæval theology and practice for an unreasonable ecclesiastical prodigy.

§ 117. *Penance and Indulgences.*

The sacrament of penance was placed in close connection
with baptism by the Schoolmen, as it was later by the council of Trent, which called it a "sort of laborious baptism."[1]
Baptism serves for the deletion of original sin; penance for
the deletion of mortal sins committed after baptism. Using
Tertullian's illustration, the Schoolmen designated penance
the second plank thrown out to the sinner after shipwreck
as baptism is the first.[2] In daily religious life, penance
became the chief concern of the people and also the chief
instrumentality of the priesthood in securing and strengthening its authority. The treatment given to it by the School-

---

[1] Duns Scotus had spoken of the "satisfaction which is the doing of a laborious work," *quæ est executio operis laboriosi.*   Report IV. 16. 1, quoted by
Schwane, p. 669.

[2] Tertullian, de Poen, XII. So also Jerome. See the Lombard, *Sent.,* XIV.
1, Migne, 868; Bonaventura, *Sent.,* XIV. 1, Peltier's ed., V. 553 ; *Brevil.,* VI.
10, VII. 323; Th. Aq., III. 84. 6, Migne, IV. 862 ; *Supplem.,* VI. 3. 936;
Alb. Magnus, *In Sent.,* Borgnet's ed., XXIX. 404 sq.

men is even more elaborate than the treatment they give to
the eucharist.[1]

One feature in which this sacrament differs from the
others is the amount of positive activity it requires from
those who seek the grace involved in it. Contrition, confession to the priest, and the performance of good works prescribed by the priest were the conditions of receiving this
grace. Everything depends upon God, and yet everything
depends upon the subjection of the penitent to the priest and
his act of absolution. It is in connection with this sacrament
that the doctrine of the keys comes to its full rights. Here
a man is absolved from sin and reunited with the Church,
and reconciled to Christ through the mediation of the sacerdotal key.[2]

Two perversions of Scripture were the largest factors
in developing the theory of meritorious penance. The
first was the false interpretation of John 20 : 23, " Whosoever sins ye forgive they are forgiven, and whosoever sins
ye retain they are retained." The passage was interpreted to
mean that Christ conferred upon the Apostles and the Church
judicial authority to forgive sins. The Protestant theory is
that this authority is declarative. The second factor was the
Vulgate's translation of the New Testament for the word " repent," *pœnitentiam agite*, " do penance," as if repentance were
a meritorious external exercise, and not a change of disposition, which is the plain meaning of the Greek word μετανοέω,
" to change your mind." [3]

[1] The Lombard devotes two and a half times the space to penance that he
does to the eucharist ; Migne's ed., pp. 868–899, as against pp. 856–868 on the
eucharist ; Hugo of St. Victor, Migne's ed., 550–578, as against 462–471 on the
eucharist ; Th. Aquinas, Migne's ed., 852–1023, as against 695–852 on the eucharist, and Bonaventura nearly four times as much space devoting to penance, Peltier's ed., vol. V. 533–709, vol. VI. 1–129, and to the eucharist, vol.
V. 415–533.

[2] *Absolvitur homo a peccato, et reunitur ecclesiæ et reconciliatur Christo,
mediante clavi sacerdotali*, Bonaventura, *Brevil.*, VI. 10, Peltier's ed., VII.
323.

[3] The Rheims Version translates the word " do penance," though not uniformly, thereby utterly confusing the English reader who involuntarily puts
into the New Testament word the Church's sacramental invention.

The confusion of the New Testament idea and the Church's doctrine is evident enough from the twofold meaning Peter the Lombard and Thomas Aquinas give to the thing called penance.   Baptism, they said, is a sacrament, but penance is both a sacrament and a virtuous state of the mind.   In the New Testament the latter is intended.   The theologians added all the mechanism of penance.[1]

At the close of the twelfth century a complete change was made in the doctrine of penance.   The theory of the early Church, elaborated by Tertullian and other Church fathers, was that penance is efficient to remove sins committed after baptism, and that it consisted in certain penitential exercises such as prayer and alms.   The first elements added by the mediæval system were that confession to the priest and absolution by the priest are necessary conditions of pardon.   Peter the Lombard did not make the mediation of the priest a requirement, but declared that confession to God was sufficient.   In his time, he says, there was no agreement on three aspects of penance: first, whether contrition for sin was not all that was necessary for its remission; second, whether confession to the priest was essential; and third, whether confession to a layman was insufficient.   The opinions handed down from the Fathers, he asserts, were diverse, if not antagonistic.[2]

Alexander of Hales marks a new era in the history of the doctrine.   He was the first of the Schoolmen to answer clearly all these questions, and to him more than to any other single

---

[1] *Pœnitentia dicitur et sacramentum et virtus mentis*, Lombard XIV. 1, p. 869; Th. Aq., Migne, IV. 850 sqq.   While we use two words, " repentance " and "penance," the Schoolmen use only the one word, *pœnitentia*, thus mystifying the mind as if repentance of heart, or μετανοία, did not include the entire meaning of the original word.

[2] *Sent.*, XVII. 1, Migne, p. 880.   The finished sacramental theory of penance owed not a little to the tract *de vera et falsa pœnitentia*, composed perhaps in the twelfth century and foisted upon Augustine.   Gratian inserted nearly all of it in his Decretals, as did Peter the Lombard.   According to Lea, I. 210, the work was still quoted as Augustine's as late as the seventeenth century.   Lea regards it as the composition of two authors of the fifth and twelfth centuries.

theologian does the Catholic Church owe its doctrine of
penance.   Thomas Aquinas confirmed what Alexander
taught.[1]

In distinction from baptism, which is a regeneration,
Thomas Aquinas declared penance to be a restoration to
health and he and Bonaventura agreed that it is the efficacious remedy for mortal sins.   Thomas traced its institution back to Christ, who left word that "*penance* and
remission of sins should be preached from Jerusalem," Luke
24:47.   James had this institution in mind when he
called upon Christians to confess their sins one to another.[2]
Penance may be repeated, for we may again and again lose
our love to God.

Penance consists of four elements: contrition of heart, confession with the mouth, satisfaction by works, and the priest's
absolution.   The first three are called the substance of penance and are the act of the offender.   The priest's absolution
is termed the form of penance.[3]

1. *Contrition* was defined as the sorrow of the soul for its
sins, an aversion from them, and a determination not to commit them again.   The Lombard and Gratian taught that
such contrition, being rooted in love, is adequate for the
divine pardon without confession to a priest or priestly
absolution.[4]

At the side of the doctrine of contrition the Schoolmen,
beginning with Alexander Hales, placed the novel doctrine
of attrition, which was most fully emphasized by Duns Scotus.
Attrition is the negative element in contrition, a sort of half
repentance, a dread of punishment, *Galgenreue,* "scaffold-

---

[1] This is shown by Müller's notable work, *Der Umschwung*, etc.   Abælard's
statement presenting the old view, and the statement of Thomas Aquinas
representing the new view, are given in Köhler, pp. 11–18.

[2] *Summa*, III. 84. 7 ; *Supplem.*, VIII. 1, Migne, IV. 864, 943.

[3] Lombard, XVI. 1, Migne, p. 877; Alb. Magnus, Borgnet's ed., XXIX. 536.
Th. Aq., 90. 1, 2, Migne, IV. 912 sq., and Bonaventura, *Brevil.*, VI. 10, Peltier's
ed., VII. 323, also call the first three "the integral parts" of penance.   So
also Abælard, *Ethica*, 17–24.

[4] See Schwane's strong condemnation of this opinion, which he declares to
be beyond a doubt the Lombard's, p. 662.

repentance," as the Germans call it.[1] This state of the heart the Schoolmen found represented in the experience of the prodigal at the moment when the father went out to meet him. According to this doctrine, a man may be forgiven and saved who is actuated simply by the fear of hell and punishment and has neither faith nor filial love in his heart. All he is required to do is to diligently go through the other steps of the process of penance, and the priest's pardon will be forthcoming.[2]

2. *Confession* to the priest, the second element in penance, is defined by Thomas Aquinas as the making-known of the hidden disease of sin in the hope of getting pardon.[3] Not even the pope has the right to grant a dispensation from it any more than he may offer salvation from original sin without baptism.[4] It covers mortal sins. For the remission of venial sins, confession is not necessary. The Church makes daily supplication for such offences and that is sufficient. They do not separate the soul either from God or the Church.[5] They are simply a sluggish movement of the affections toward God, not an aversion to Him. They are removed by holy water and other minor rites.

By the action of the Fourth Lateran, 1215, confession to

---

[1] *Timor servilis principium est attritionis*, Alex. of Hales quoted by Schwane, p. 664. Th. Aquinas, *Supplem.*, I. 2, Migne, IV. 919, is much more moderate than Alexander, Bonaventura, and Duns. Cæsar of Heisterbach calls "servile fear a gift of God," Koeniger, p. 31. At the close of the Middle Ages, Gabriel Biel took the position that attrition is changed by confession and absolution into contrition. See Seeberg, *Dogmengesch.*, II. 121.

[2] See Hahn, p. 413; Schwane, p. 666. The council of Trent, XIV. 4 (Schaff's Creeds, II. 145 sq.), adopted the word "attrition" and defined it as an imperfect contrition. The doctrine of *attritio* formed a centre of discussion in the warm debate over indulgences started by Janssen's work and participated in by Kolde, Kawerau, Dieckhoff, etc. Harnack is very severe upon the doctrine as the dry rot in the Catholic system, *Dogmengesch.*, II. 482, 504 sqq.

[3] Aquinas quotes Augustine's definition, *Supplem.*, VII. 1, IX. 3, Migne, IV. 940, 954. [4] Migne, IV. 939.

[5] Th. Aq., III. 87. 1, Migne, IV. 890; *Supplem.*, VI. 1, 3, VIII. 3, Migne, IV. 934, 936, 945. With characteristic exhaustiveness, Thomas goes into the question whether a man can confess sins he has never committed, Migne, IV. 936.

the priest at least once a year was made a test of orthodoxy. Beginning with Alexander of Hales, the Schoolmen vindicate the positions that confession, to be efficacious, must be made to the priest, and that absolution by the priest is an essential condition of the sinner's pardon. Bonaventura, after devoting much time to the question, "Whether it is sufficient to confess our sins to God," answered it in the negative. At greater length than Peter the Lombard had done, he quoted the Fathers to show that there was no unanimity among them on the question. But he declared that, since the decision of the Fourth Lateran, all are to be adjudged heretics who deny that confession to the priest is essential. Before that decision, such denial was not heresy.[1]

Confession must be made to the priest as Christ's vicar. In case of necessity, no priest being available, a layman may also hear confession.[2] By such confession the offender may be reconciled to God but not to the Church, and in order to be so reconciled and admitted to the other sacraments he must also, as opportunity offers, confess again to the priest.

Priests were forbidden to look at the face of a woman at the confessional, and severe punishments were prescribed for betraying its secrets, even to degradation from office and life-long confinement in a convent.[3] The mendicant monks were confirmed by Clement IV. and Martin IV. in their right to shrive everywhere. A contemporary declared that the whole of the Jordan ran into their mouths.[4]

3. *Satisfaction*, the third element in penance, is imposed by the priest as the minister of God and consists of prayer, pilgrimages, fastings, payments of money, and other good works. These penal acts are medicines for spiritual wounds

---

[1] *In Sent.*, IV. 17. 2, Peltier's ed., V. 674, *ante hanc determinationem hoc non erat heresis*, etc. Albertus Magnus also declared it was not sufficient to confess to God only, Borgnet's ed. XXIX. 603.

[2] Th. Aq., *Supplem.*, VII. 1, 2, Migne, IV. 943 sq.; Bonaventura, *Sent.*, XVII. 3. 1, Peltier's ed., V. 695. Cæsar of Heisterbach speaks of confession to an unbeliever as efficacious in the article of death, provided the unbeliever does not ridicule the sacrament, Koeniger, p. 73.

[3] Fourth Lat., can. 21, synods of Treves, 1227, Canterbury, 1236, etc.

[4] See Hefele, VI. 30.

and a compensation to God for offences against Him, as
Thomas Aquinas,[1] following Anselm, taught.   The priest is
the judge of what the act of satisfaction shall be.   Among
the more notable cases of public penance were those of
Henry II. after Becket's death, Philip I. of France, and
Raymund of Toulouse.

Satisfaction differs from contrition and confession in the
very important particular that one person can perform it
for another.   To prove this point, Thomas Aquinas used
the words of the Apostle when he said, "Bear ye one
another's burdens."   Gal. 6 : 2.

4. The fourth element in the sacrament of penance was
the formal sentence of *absolution* pronounced by the priest.
This function, which Schwane calls the main part of the
sacrament of penance,[2] or the power of the keys, *potestas
clavium*, belongs primarily and in its fulness to the pope and
then, by distribution, to bishops and priests.   Its use opens
and shuts the kingdom of heaven to immortal souls.

§ 118.   *Penance and Indulgences.*

The year 1200 marks the dividing line between opinions
differing most widely on the meaning of the priest's absolution.   Peter the Lombard represented the prevailing view
of the earlier period when he pronounced the absolution, a
declarative announcement.   Alexander of Hales represented
the later period, when he pronounced it a judicial sentence.
According to Peter, God alone remits sins.   It was the
Lord who restored the lepers to health, not the priests to
whom he sent them.   They did nothing more than bear
witness to the healthy condition of the lepers.   The priest's
prerogative is ended when he "shows or declares those who
are bound and those who are loosed."[3]   This view of the
Master of Sentences the later theology set aside.

---

[1] *Supplem.*, XV. 3, Migne, IV. 978.   Duns Scotus (quoted by Seeberg,
412) says, satisfaction is the voluntary return of an equivalent *redditio
voluntaria œquivalentis.*   [2] Schwane, p. 670.

[3] *Potestas solvendi et ligandi*, i.e. *ostendendi homines ligatos vel solutos*,
etc.   IV. 18, 6, Migne, p. 887.

Before the end of the thirteenth century, the petitional form of absolution was in general, though not exclusive, use and the priest made intercession for the grace of forgiveness upon the offender.[1] After that, the positive forensic form was substituted, " I absolve thee in the name of the Father and of the Son and of the Holy Ghost," the form which Thomas Aquinas vindicated against all others.[2] Hugo of St. Victor had advocated this form and pronounced the contrary form more laughable and frivolous than worthy of refutation. He was followed by Richard of St. Victor who emphasized the distinction between the priest's right to remit the punishment of sin and God's prerogative which is to forgive the guilt of sin.[3] The priest's absolution effects the deletion of sin. He acts towards the sinner as Christ did toward Lazarus when he said, " Loose him and let him go."

The absolution from certain offences was reserved to the bishops, such as murder, sacrilege in the use of the eucharist or the baptismal water, perjury, poisoning, and letting children die without being baptized.[4] Other offences came under the exclusive jurisdiction of the papal chair, such as the abuse of the person of a priest or monk, the burning of church buildings, and falsifying of papal documents.

In the article of death, the sacrament of absolution is in no case to be refused. At such times works of satisfaction cannot be required, even as they were not required of the thief on the cross.

The extent to which absolution is efficacious called forth careful discussion and statement. Does it cover guilt as well as punishment and does it extend to the punishments of purgatory? The answer to these questions also was positive

---

[1] See the form used by Honorius of Autun about 1130, *indulgentiam et absolutionem de omnibus peccatis . . . tribuat vobis Pater et Filius et Sp. Sanctus et custodiet vos a peccatis et ab omnibus malis et post hanc vitam perducat vos in consortium omnium sanctorum.* Lea, I. 206.

[2] *Summa*, III. 84, 3, Migne, IV. 857. It was not sufficient to say, " The omnipotent God absolve thee," or " God bestow on thee absolution," etc.

[3] *De sacr.*, II. 14, 8, Migne, 176. 568. . . . *De potestate ligandi et solvendi.*

[4] So the synods of Treves 1227, Canterbury 1236, London 1237, etc. The unchastity of nuns came under the bishop's jurisdiction.

and distinct from the time of Alexander of Hales. Peter the Lombard was the last of the prominent Schoolmen to declare that the priest did not give absolution for guilt. The later Schoolmen with one consent oppose him at this point and teach that the priest absolves both from the guilt and the punishments of sin in this world and in purgatory. Thomas Aquinas asserted that, "if the priest cannot remit these temporal punishments, — for the punishments of purgatory are temporal, — then he cannot remit at all and this is contrary to the words of the Gospel to Peter that whatsoever he should loose on earth should be loosed in heaven."[1]

The ultimate and, as it proved, a most vicious form of priestly absolution was the indulgence. An indulgence is a remission of the guilt and punishment of sin by a mitigation or complete setting aside of the works of satisfaction which would otherwise be required. A lighter penalty was substituted for a severer one.[2] Gottlob[3] has recently divided indulgences into three classes: (1) indulgences which are secured by going on a crusade; (2) such as are secured by the payment of money for some good church cause, and (3) such as are secured by the visiting of certain churches.

Towards the close of this period this substitution usually took the form of a money-payment. For a lump sum absolution for the worst offences might be secured. It became a tempting source of gain to churches and the Roman curia, which they were quick to take advantage of. The dogmatic justification of this method of remission found positive expression before the practice became general. Alexander of Hales here again has the distinction of being the first to give it careful definition and unequivocal emphasis.

[1] *Si non potest remittere quantum ad pœnam temporalem, nullo modo remittere potest quod omnino contrarium dictis evangelii.* *Supplem.*, VIII. 2, Migne, IV. 988 ; *Sent.*, IV. 20, 1, 1–5.

[2] Beringer-Schneider, the chief Rom. Cath. writer on Indulgences, p. 2, defines an indulgence "as an act of mercy and goodness, a salvation by the order of the Church, an act of grace and forgiveness."

[3] *Kreuzablass*, etc., pp. 10 sqq. Gottlob, p. xv, says indulgences occupy a central place in the political and religious life of the last three centuries of the Middle Ages.

3 B

Thomas Aquinas, Bonaventura, and the other Schoolmen follow him closely and add little. Thomas Aquinas declared
it impious to say the Church might not dispense indulgences.[1]

The first known case occurred about 1016 when the archbishop of Arles gave an indulgence of a year to those participating in the erection of a church building.[2] The Crusades
furnished the popes the occasion to issue indulgences on a
magnificent scale. Urban II.'s indulgence, 1095, granting
plenary absolution to all taking the journey to Jerusalem
was the first of a long series of such papal franchises. That
journey, Urban said, should be taken as a substitute for all
penance. Granted at first to warriors fighting against the
infidel in the Holy Land, they were extended so as to include
those who fought against the Slavs, as by Eugenius III.,
1147, against the Stedinger, Albigenses, and the Hussites,
1425, and against all enemies whatsoever of the papacy, such
as Frederick II. and Manfred. Innocent II., in 1135, promised full remission to those who fought the battle of the
papal chair against Roger of Sicily, and the anti-pope,
Anacletus II. In these cases such expressions are used as
"remission and indulgence of penances," "relaxation or
remission from the imposed penance," "the relaxation of
the imposed satisfaction," and also "a lightening or remission
of sins."[3]

The free-handed liberality with which these franchises were
dispensed by bishops became so much of a scandal that the
Lateran council of 1215 issued a sharp decree to check it.
More than half a century before, in 1140, Abælard had condemned the abuse of this prerogative by bishops and priests
who were governed in its lavish exercise by motives of
sordid cupidity.[4]

---

[1] *Supplem.*, xxv–xxvii, Migne, IV. 1013 sqq. Lea devotes the entire third
volume of his *Hist. of Confession* to a noteworthy discussion of indulgences.

[2] See for the text Köhler, pp. 5 sq.

[3] *relaxatio, remissio, indulgentia de injuncta pœnitentia*, etc. See Brieger
for these expressions, and Brieger and Lea for numerous examples of papal
indulgences of this sort.   [4] *Ethica*, XL. See Köhler, p. 8.

The construction of bridges over rivers, the building of churches, and the visiting of shrines were favorite and meritorious grounds for the gifts of indulgence. Innocent III., 1209, granted full remission for the building of a bridge over the Rhone ; Innocent IV. for rebuilding the cathedrals of Cologne, 1248, and Upsala, 1250, which had suffered from fire.[1] According to Matthew Paris, Gregory IX., in 1241, granted an indulgence of forty days to all worshipping the crown of thorns and the cross in the chapel at Paris and, in 1247, the bishop of Norwich, speaking for the English prelates, announced a remission of all penances for six years and one hundred and forty days to those who would worship the Holy Blood at Westminster.[2] Indulgences for building bridges and roads were common in England.[3]

To the next period belongs the first cases of indulgence granted in connection with the Jubilee Year by Boniface VIII., 1300. Among the more famous indulgences granted to private parties and localities was the Portiuncula indulgence giving remission to all visiting the famous Franciscan shrine at Assisi on a certain day of the year,[4] and the *Sabbatina*, granting to all entering the Carmelite order or wearing the scapulary deliverance from purgatory the Saturday after their death.[5]

The practice of dispensing indulgences grew enormously. Innocent III. dispensed five during his pontificate. Less than one hundred years later, Nicolas IV., in his reign of two years, 1288–1290, dispensed no less than four hundred. By that time they had become a regular item of the papal exchequer.

On what grounds did the Church claim the right to remit the works of penance due for sins or, as Alexander of Hales put it, grant abatement of the punishment due sin?[6]

---

[1] Potthast, 3799, 12938, 14122.   [2] Luard's ed., IV. 90, 643.

[3] See Jusseraud, *Engl. Wayfaring Life in the M. Ages*, London, 1890, pp. 41 sqq., for many cases of indulgence for building bridges.

[4] Sabatier, *F. Bartholi de Assisio tractatus de indulgentia S. Mariæ de Portiuncula*, 1900.

[5] See p. 366, Lea, III. 270 sqq., and Wetzer-Welte, *Sabbatina*.

[6] *Summa*, IV. 83. 1, *relaxatio pœnæ debitæ pro peccato*, quoted by Brieger.

The statement was this: Christ's passion is of infinite merit. Mary and the saints also by their works of patience laid up merit beyond what was required from them for heaven. These supererogatory works or merits of the saints and of Christ are so abundant that they would more than suffice to pay off the debts of all the living.[1] Together they constitute the *thesaurus meritorum*, or fund of merits; and this is at the disposal of the Church by virtue of her nuptial union with Christ, Col. 1:24. This fund is a sort of bank account, upon which the Church may draw at pleasure. Christ relaxed the punishment due the woman taken in adultery, not requiring her to do the works of satisfaction which her offences would, under ordinary circumstances, have called for. So, likewise, may the pope, who is Christ's vicegerent, release from sin by drawing upon the fund of merit. Thus the indulgence takes the place of the third element of penance, works of satisfaction.

These statements of the Schoolmen received explicit papal confirmation at the hands of Clement VI. in 1343. This pontiff not only declared that this "heap of treasure," — *cumulus thesauri*, — consisting of the merits of "the blessed mother of God and the saints," is at the disposal of the successors of Peter, but he made, if possible, the more astounding assertion that the more this storehouse is drawn upon, the more it grows.[2] Like the wood of the true cross, it has the power of infinite self-expansion. It is, however, fair to say that the papal briefs granting this saving grace almost invariably gave it on condition of contrition and confession of the recipient.[3]

Down to the latter part of the thirteenth century, the theory prevailed that an indulgence dispensed with the usual works of penance by substituting some other act. Before the

---

[1] Th. Aq., *Summa*, III. 83, 1. *quorum meritorum tanta est copia quod omnem pœnam debitam nunc viventibus excedunt.* See Gottlob, pp. 271 sqq.

[2] *Quanto plures ex ejus applicatione trahuntur ad justitiam, tanto magis accrescit ipsorum cumulus meritorum.* See Friedberg, *Corp. jur. can.*, II. 1304 sq.

[3] *Vere pœnitentibus et confessis* was the common formula.

fourteenth century, another step was taken, and the indulgence was regarded as directly absolving from the guilt and
punishment of sins, *culpa et pœna peccatorum.* It was no
longer a mitigation or abatement of imposed penance. It
immediately set aside or remitted that which acts of penance
had been designed to remove; namely, guilt and penalty. It
is sufficient for the Church to pronounce offences remitted.
Wyclif made a bold attack against the indulgence "from
guilt and punishment," *a culpa et pœna,* in his *Cruciata.*
Now that it is no longer possible to maintain the spuriousness of such papal indulgences, some Roman Catholic writers
construe the offensive phrase to mean "from the penalty
of guilt," *a pœna culpœ.*

Such was the general indulgence given by pope Cœlestin V., 1294, to all who should on a certain day of the year
enter the church of St. Mary de Collemayo in which he had
been consecrated.[1] This view had been stated almost thirty
years before by Thomas of Chantimpré.[2] And, about 1280,
Peter of Olivi declared the indulgence granted to the Portiuncula church to be an "indulgence for all sins and from all
guilt and penalty."[3] It is evident from these documents that,
at the close of the thirteenth century, the formula *a culpa et
pœna,* "from guilt and punishment," was quite familiar.

Boniface VIII. probably included the guilt of sin when he
announced "full pardon for all sins," and succeeding popes
used the form constantly.[4] John XXIII., at the beginning of
the fifteenth century, was especially prodigal in the distribu

---

[1] Dr. Lea, III. 63, has shown the significance of this document.

[2] Köhler, p. 27, *quæ securam et mundatam animam ab omni culpa et
pœna fecerunt.*

[3] See Sabatier, *Fr. F. Bartholi,* etc., in part reprinted by Köhler,
pp. 27 sqq.

[4] See a number of instances in Brieger and especially Lea, III. 55–80.
Lea quotes Piers the Ploughman's Crede to show that this expressed the
popular belief.

> The power of the Apostells they posen in speche
> For to sellen the synnes for silver other mede
> And pulyche *a pena* the purple assoileth
> And *a culpa* also, that they may catchen
> Money other money wothe and mede to fonge.

tion of this kind of indulgence and in vain did the council of
Constance attempt to put some check upon the practice.
Tetzel was following the custom of two centuries when he
offered "remission and indulgence of *guilt* and penalty."

As for the application of the sacrament of penance to
souls in purgatory, Alexander of Hales argued that, if the
sacrament did not avail for them, then the Church prays in
vain for the dead.   Such souls are still under the cogni-
zance of the Church, that is, subject to its tribunal, — *de foro
ecclesiæ*.[1]   Altars and chapels, called in England chantries,
were built and endowed by persons for the maintenance of a
priest, in whole or in part, to pray and offer up masses for
their souls after their departure from this life.   The further
treatment of the subject belongs properly to the period just
preceding the Reformation.   It is sufficient to say here,
that Sixtus IV., in 1476, definitely connected the payment of
money with indulgences, and legislated that, by fixed sums
paid to the papal collectors, persons on earth may redeem
their kindred in purgatory.   Thus for gold and silver
the most inveterate criminal might secure the deliverance of
a father or mother from purgatorial pain, and neither contrition nor confession were required in the transaction.[2]   Such
was the ultimate conclusion of the sacramental doctrine of
penance, the sacrament to whose treatment the Schoolmen
devoted most time and labor.   The council of Trent reasserted the Church's right to grant indulgences.[3]   But what
could seem to be more agreeable to the plain statements of

One of the most striking instances of this form of indulgence is the *abso-
lutio plenaria a pœna et culpa* issued by Alexander V. to the members of the
council of Pisa, Von der Hardt, *Conc. Const.*, III. 688.

[1] In contrast to *de fore dei*, God's tribunal.   See Lea, II. 296–371, and
Brieger.

[2] Lea, III. 595 sq., and the instructions of Albert, abp. of Mainz, quoted
by Brieger, *nec opus est, quod contribuentes pro animabus in capsam sint
corde contriti et ore confessi.*

[3] Schaff, *Creeds*, II. 205.   Harnack, *Hist. of Doctr.*, II. 511 sqq., expresses
his moral indignation over the mediæval theory of penance.   Of *attritio,
sacramentum pœnitentiæ*, and *indulgentia*, he exclaims, *das ist die katholische
Trias !*   "That is the Catholic triad !"

Scripture than that men have the right of immediate access to Christ, who said, " Him that cometh unto me, I will in no wise cast out," and what more repugnant to its plain teachings than to make confession to a priest and the priest's absolution conditions of receiving pardon !

The superstitious, practical extravagances, which grew out of this most unbiblical penitential theory of the Middle Ages, are reported in the pages of the popular writers of the age, such as Cæsar of Heisterbach and De Voragine, who express no dissent as they relate the morbid tales. Here are two of them as told by De Voragine which are to be taken as samples of a large body of similar literature. A bishop, by celebrating thirty masses, helped out of purgatory a poor soul who was frozen in a block of ice. In the second case, a woman who had neglected, before dying, to make a confession to the priest, was raised from her bier by the prayer of St. Francis d'Assisi. She went and confessed to the priest and then had the satisfaction of lying down in peace and dying over again.[1]

§ 119. *Extreme Unction, Ordination, and Marriage.*

EXTREME UNCTION, — *unctio infirmorum*, — the fifth in the list of the sacraments, is administered to those who are in peril of death, and is supposed to be referred to by James 5 : 14. "Is any among you sick ? let him call for the elders of the church ; and let them pray over him, anointing him with oil in the name of the Lord." The earlier view, represented by Hugo of St. Victor, Peter the Lombard, and also by Bonaventura, was that the sacrament is of Apostolic institution. Thomas Aquinas traced it directly to Christ. Many things, he said, were spoken by Christ to the Apostles which are not contained in the Gospels.[2] Thomas was followed by Duns Scotus and the council of Trent. The effect of the sacrament is to remit venial sins and the remainders of sin left after penance, and to heal the body. It may be repeated. Extreme unction as well as the eucharist is to be denied to

---

[1] *Legenda aurea,* under All Souls and Francis d'Assisi. Temple Classics ed., VI. 113, V. 231.   [2] *Supplem.,* XXIX. 3, Migne, IV. 1027.

children on the ground that their bodily diseases are not caused by sin.[1] Some councils restricted it to those over fourteen.[2] The element used is oil, consecrated by the bishop, and it is to be touched to the eyes, ears, nostrils, lips, hands, feet, and loins.

ORDINATION conveys sacramental grace to seven orders of the ministry : presbyters, deacons, subdeacons, acolytes, exorcists, lectors, and ostiarii or door-keepers. These seven correspond to the seven graces of the Spirit mentioned in 1 Cor. 12. The first three orders were instituted by Christ ; the last four by the Church.[3] The bishops do not constitute a distinct order, but are of the order of the priesthood. The episcopate is an office, a function ; and as Peter Lombardus and Thomas Aquinas say again and again, it is not an order. Consecration to it has no sacramental character. The Schoolmen do not fail to insist upon the superior dignity of the bishop, but sacramental grace is exhibited in its highest form in empowering the priest to celebrate the mass. For the sake of " fulness " there are placed above the priesthood, the episcopate, patriarchate, and papacy.[4]

---

[1] Th. Aq., *Supplem.*, XXXII. 4, Migne, IV. 1038; Bonaventura, *Brevil.*, VI. 11, Peltier's ed., VII. 326.   [2] Cologne, 1279 ; Lambeth, 1330, etc.

[3] P. Lombardus, *Sent.*, IV. XXIV. 9 ; Hugo of St. Victor, *De sacr.*, II. 2, 5 ; Th. Aq., *Supplem.*, XXXVII. 2, Migne, IV. 1056; Bonavent., *Brevil.*, VI. 12.

[4] *Per modum complementi superponitur episcopatus*, etc., Bonavent., *Brevil.*, VI. 12. P. Lombardus, *Sent.*, XXIV. 9, Migne, p. 904, speaks of a fourfold rank of bishops, viz. patriarchs, archbishops, metropolitans, and bishops. These, he says, are not orders but " the names of dignities and offices." The teaching of Duns Scotus is uncertain. In one place he asserts the episcopate must be a distinct order, the eighth, because the bishop alone can administer several of the sacraments. See Seeberg, p. 441. On the other hand, he quotes Jerome to show that the episcopate was instituted by the Church and is not a matter of divine law. See Schwane, p. 684. It is still unsettled by canon law whether the episcopate is a separate order or not. See Friedberg, *Kirchenrecht*, p. 150. The council of Trent did not formally decide the question, though it speaks of the hierarchy of bishops, priests, and deacons. See Schaff, *Creeds*, II. 186 sqq. Innocent III. placed the subdeacon among the major orders. Friedberg, p. 150. According to Philip Hergenröther, *Kathol. Kirchenrecht*, pp. 208 sq., the episcopate is at the present time universally regarded in the Rom. Cath. Church as a distinct clerical order.

The tonsure, a requirement for admittance to orders, is a sign of rule and perfection, for it is made in a circle. It also indicates that the mind is withdrawn from temporal things and fixed upon the contemplation of divine things.[1]

According to Thomas Aquinas, there is more reason for regarding ordination a sacrament than for ascribing a sacramental character to the other six sacred ordinances, for ordination confers the power of administering the others. Its efficacious potency resides chiefly with the person dispensing the sacrament.[2] From him grace is transmitted. The form or the symbols, used in the ceremony, are of subordinate or little importance. In fact, the symbols are scarcely referred to by councils or Schoolmen in this period.[3]

Ordination confers an indelible character upon those admitted to any of the orders. Its virtue is not affected by the character of the person ordained.[4]

As for the validity of the sacramental acts of heretic and schismatic clergymen, great difference of opinion existed. The problem was so difficult as to appear to Gratian and Peter the Lombard insoluble or almost so. The difficulty was increased by the acts of councils, condemning as invalid the ordinations of anti-popes and the ordinations performed by bishops whom anti-popes had appointed.[5] The statements of Thomas Aquinas are difficult to understand.

[1] Th. Aq., *Supplem.*, XL. 1, Migne, 1071; Bonaventura, *Brevil.*, VI. 12, Peltier's ed., 327. The synods of London 1102, Soissons 1078, Rouen 1190, Fourth Lateran 1215, etc., decreed the tonsure must not be concealed.

[2] Th. Aq., *Supplem.*, XXXIV. 4, 5,·Migne, 1045 sq., *efficacia principaliter residet penes eum qui sacramentum dispensat.*

[3] Schwane, p. 681, says there was no development in the ritual of ordination during the Middle Ages. Thomas Aquinas refers to the imposition of hands only incidentally in his chapters on penance. *Summa*, III. 84, 3, Migne, IV. 850. The council of Florence, 1438, enjoined that the chalice and paten should be given at the consecration to some of the orders.

[4] Th. Aq., *Supplem.*, XXXVI. I, Migne, IV. 1051, *si malus ordinatur nihilominus ordinationem habet.*

[5] For example the 9th (Hefele, V. 380) and 11th œcumenical councils pronounced such judgment, naming the anti-popes. So also the synod of Piacenza, 1095, which declared invalid the ordinations of Wibert and other bishops.

He made a distinction between the power — *potestas* — of ordination and the jurisdiction to perform the sacrament. Schismatic or heretic bishops retain the power; otherwise when such a bishop is reconciled to the Church, he would be ordained over again, which is not the case.[1] But they have not the jurisdiction. As the bishop by his promotion to the episcopate receives no sacramental grace, so, as bishop, he possesses no indelible character. He is ordained not directly for God but for the mystical body of Christ. And those whom a schismatic bishop ordains do not in reality receive ordination, for they are ordained in the face of the prohibition of the Church.

As far as we can understand the Angelic doctor's position it is: the Church may withdraw from a bishop his right to confer orders while at the same time he retains the episcopal power to confer them. He insisted most strenuously on the permanence of the "bishop's power" received at consecration. The solution of the problem is of far-reaching importance, for it has a bearing on the sacramental efficacy of the acts of many priests who have been cut off from the Latin Church and the ecclesiastical titles of schismatic bodies, such as the Old-Catholics and the Jansenist Church of Holland.

MARRIAGE has the last place among the sacraments because it has the least of spirituality connected with it.[2] At first, the bed was undefiled, conception was without passion, and parturition without pain. Since the fall, marriage has become a remedy against lust and a medicine for unholy desire.[3] At first it signified the union of the soul with God.

---

[1] Th. Aq., *Supplem.*, XXXIX. 2, Migne, 1065. *Episcopus in hæresim lapsus . . . non amisit protestatem quam habebat ordines conferendi.* Thomas is most emphatic on this question and goes on: *Omnis protestas quæ datur cum aliqua consecratione, nulla casu contingente tolli protest*, etc. . . . . *Unde cum episcopalis protestas cum quadam consecratione detur, oportet quod perpetuo maneat quantumcumque aliquis peccet, vel ab ecclesia præcidatur.*

[2] Th. Aq., *Summa*, III. 65, 2, Migne, IV. 598, *quia minimum habet de spiritualitate.*

[3] Abælard, *Theol Christ.*, 31, *conjugium non confert aliquod donum sicut cetera sacramenta faciunt sed tamen mali remedium est . . . datur propter incontinentiam refrænendai* ›. Hugo of St. Vict.. *De sacr.*, II. 11, 3, Migne,

Since it became a sacrament, it signifies, in addition, the union of Christ and the Church and the union of two natures in one person. The Vulgate's false translation of Ephes. 5: 31, "this is a great sacrament," confirmed the Schoolmen in placing matrimony among the sacraments. That which constitutes the sacramental element is the verbal consent of the parties, and also, as Thomas Aquinas thought, the priest's benediction.[1]

Thomas was inclined to permit marriage for boys after the age of fourteen and girls after the age of twelve.[2] According to the same authority, children are to follow the social condition of the mother.[3] The impediments to marriage were carefully catalogued and discussed. Their number was put at twelve, such as kinship, mistake, vows, and misrepresentation, and couched in the lines which Bonaventura and Thomas Aquinas quote: —

> error, conditio, votum, cognatio crimen,
> cultus disparitas,[4] vis, ordo, ligamen, honestas,
> si sis affinis, si forte coire nequibis
> hæc socianda vetant connubia, facta retractant.

The Fourth Lateran modified some of the more severe restrictions of marriage within the limits of consanguinity, but declared children illegitimate whose parents were within the forbidden limits, even though the ceremony were per-, formed in the church. The councils of the thirteenth and

---

p. 481, *conjugium ante peccatum ad officium, post peccatum ad remedium.* Alanus ab Insulis, *Reg. Theol.*, 114, Migne's ed., p. 681, *conjugium sacramentum remedii contra incontinentiam.* So also, Bonaventura, *Brevil.*, VI. 13 ; Th. Aq., *Supplem.*, XLII. 2, Migne, IV. 1084; *Summa*, LXI. 2, Migne, p. 558.

[1] Th. Aq., *Supplem.*, XLII. 1, Migne, IV. 1083, *benedictio sacerdotis quæ est quoddam sacramentale.*

[2] These were supposed to be the "years of discretion." *Supplem.*, LVIII. 5, Migne, IV. 1165. The synod of Nismes, 1096, forbade the marriage of girls under twelve. For cases of the marriage of princesses under twelve, see Eicken, pp. 448 sq.

[3] "Just as the offspring of animals follow the nature of the mother." Thomas instances the mule, *Supplem.*, LII. 4, Migne, 1127.

[4] This refers to a marriage in which one party is a Catholic and the other a heretic, Jew, or infidel.

fourteenth centuries give frequent rules for marriage. They were to be performed before the Church and only after public announcement. The children of parties marrying unbelievers and the offspring of clandestine marriages were made illegitimate.[1]

Death dissolves marriage and the surviving party has the right to marry again to the fourth time or even more often. Otherwise the marriage bond is perpetual — *vinculum matrimonii est perpetuum.* This follows from two considerations: marriage involves the training of the children and is a symbol of the union between Christ and the Church. Matrimony becomes absolutely binding only upon copulation. Before that has taken place, one party or the other may go into an order and in this case the other party has the right to marry again.

Divorce was allowed for one cause only, fornication. The Schoolmen supported this position from the words of Christ. Divorce, however, is a separation, not a release with license to marry again. Marriage can never be annulled by the act of man. What God hath joined together, no man can put asunder.[2] Only after the death of the offending party may the innocent party enter again into a marriage contract.[3] The second and subsequent marriages are a sacrament as the first marriage is.

---

[1] Synods of London 1102, 1125, 1200, Fourth Lateran 1215, Treves 1227, Magdeburg 1261, etc. The synod of London, 1200, forbade either man or wife taking a long journey without the other's consent. Thomas Aquinas took the position that marriages between a believer and an unbeliever are not to be allowed because they prevent the education and training of children in the worship of God, which is one of the chief objects of the sacrament. *Supplem.*, LIX. 1, Migne, IV. 1167.

[2] Th. Aq., *Supplem.*, LXI. 2, Migne, IV. 1177. Thomas asserts that, before the *carnalis copula* takes place, the bond is a spiritual one and it may be broken by either party becoming spiritually dead, dying to the world and living unto God in a convent. After copulation the bond between man and wife is a carnal tie — *vinculum carnale* — and can be broken only by the death of the body.

[3] Th. Aq., *Supplem.*, LXII. 5, Migne, IV. 1184, *non licet uni, altero vivente, ad aliam copulam transire.* Either party may, however, enter a convent without seeking the consent of the other.

§ 120. *Sin and Grace.*

SIN. — The Schoolmen are unanimous in affirming that
the infection of original sin has passed down upon all
Adam's descendants and involved them all in guilt and
eternal death. Following Augustine, Anselm called the
race a sinning mass — *peccatrix massa.* By the Fall, man's
body, or flesh, was made, like the beast, subject to carnal
appetites and the mind, in turn, became infected with these
appetites.[1] If man had not sinned, his nature would have
been propagated as it was originally created by God. In
condemning Abælard, the synod of Sens, 1141, condemned
the heresy that Adam's guilt does not pass down to his
posterity.

Man does not secure his sinful nature by imitation of
Adam, but by inheritance through generation from Adam.
The flesh is tainted, being conceived in concupiscence, and
concupiscence is both a taint and guilt. Nay, it is original
sin, as the Lombard says.[2] Before the first sin, the man and
the woman came together without the passion of concupiscence and the bed was undefiled; but, after the Fall, they
could not join in marital intercourse without libidinous lust.[3]
These are the views of all the Schoolmen, yet they agree in
rejecting the doctrine of traducianism.[4] The flesh only is
carried down from parent to child, not the spirit.

Original sin is defined by Alexander of Hales and by
Thomas Aquinas as the want or the " deficiency of original
righteousness."[5] It involves the loss of superadded grace
and a wounding of the natural powers.[6] This wound, or
original sin, is a lasting quality or condition of depravity —

[1] *Carnalibus appetitis infecta, de conceptu.* II. Migne, 158. 434.

[2] *vitium concupiscentiæ, quod est originale peccatum.*

[3] *Post peccatum non valet fieri carnalis copula absque libidinosa concupiscentia quæ semper vitium est et etiam culpa.* P. Lomb., *Sent.,* II. 31, 3.

[4] *Etsi anima non traducatur, quia virtus seminis non potest causare
animam rationalem.* Th. Aquinas, *Summa,* II. 81, 1, Migne, II. 629.

[5] *Carentia . . . defectus originalis justitiæ est originale peccatum.* Schwane,
p. 401 ; Th. Aq., *Summa,* II. 81, 5.

[6] *Spoliatio in gratuitis et vulneratio in naturalibus.*

a *habitus corruptionis* or *vitium* — like a bodily disease. It is not merely a defect.   It is a depraved tendency — *inordinata dispositio*.   In another place, Thomas defines original sin to be in substance concupiscence or lust and in form a defect of original righteousness.[1]   God cannot be the author of sin because sin is an offence against order.

Thomas taught that the taint of original sin is inherited not from the mother but from the father who is the active agent in generation.   If Eve only had sinned and not Adam, the children would not have inherited the taint.   On the other hand, if Adam had sinned and Eve remained innocent, their descendants would have inherited original sin.[2]   According to Peter the Lombard, Albertus Magnus, and others, pride was the original root of sin.[3]

At much length, the Schoolmen elaborate upon the sin against the Holy Ghost and the seven "capital or principal" offences,[4] the number of which they base on Proverbs 6: 16, "These six things doth the Lord hate, yea, seven are an abomination unto Him."   The question as to whether there would have been any admixture of the sexes if Adam had not sinned was answered in the affirmative, in view of the command to be fruitful and to replenish the earth.   Bonaventura also elaborately discussed the question whether the number of male and female descendants would have been equal had man not sinned.   This he also answered in the affirmative, partly on the ground that no woman would have been without a husband and no husband without a wife, for in paradise there would be neither polygamy or polyandry. He also based his conclusion upon Aristotle's reason for the

---

[1] *Summa*, II. 82, 3, *materialiter quidem est concupiscentia, formaliter vero est defectus orig. just.*   *Vitium* and *corruptio* are the words most frequently used for the moral character of sin.   Hugo of St. Victor, *De sacr.*, I. 28, Migne, 176. 299.

[2] *Peccatum orig. non contrahitur a matre sed a patre*, etc.   *Summa*, II. 81, 5.

[3] P. Lomb., II. 42, 9; Alb. Magnus, Borgnet's ed., XXVII. 663 sqq., etc.

[4] P. Lomb., II. 42, enumerates them as *inanis gloria, ira, invidia, acedia vel tristitia, avaritia, gastrimargia, luxuria*.   Albertus Magnus skilfully discusses whether there could be any more than seven.   *In Sent.*, II. 42, Borgnet's ed., XXVII. 662 sqq.

unequal conception of male and female children which is now due to some weakness or other peculiarity on the part of one of the parents.[1] The ultimate purpose in the birth of children, had our first parents remained innocent, was that they might fill up the number of the elect angels.

Another question which was discussed with much warmth was which of the two sinned the more grievously, Adam or Eve, a question Hugo of St. Victor, Peter the Lombard, Albertus Magnus, Bonaventura, and other great Schoolmen united in attempting to solve — a question which arose quite naturally from Paul's statement, 1 Tim. 2 : 14, that the woman was beguiled and not the man. The conclusion reached was that the preponderance of guilt was with Eve. The Lombard is inclined to be lenient with Adam and makes out that when he yielded to the persuasions of his wife, he was actuated by sympathy and was unwilling to give her pain by refusing her request. He was inexperienced in the divine severity and his sin was a venial, not a mortal fault. In fact this theologian distinctly gives it as his belief that Adam would not have given way to the temptation of the devil.[2] Eve sinned by pride, desiring to be equal with God. Adam was not seduced by the devil at all and had in mind the mercy of God and intended later to make confession of his sin, and secure absolution. Eve's sin was the more grievous for she sinned against herself, against God, and against her neighbor. Adam sinned against himself and God, but not against his neighbor. Hugo of St. Victor said that the woman believed that God was moved by envy in forbidding them to eat the fruit of the tree. Adam knew this to be false. His sin was in consenting to his wife and

[1] *Utrum æqualis fieret multiplicatio virorum et mulierum. In Sent.*, II. 20, 2, Peltier's ed., III. 85. The three reasons which Bonaventura adduces to account for the differences in sex will have to be read in the original. He enters into the subject with the precision of statement and detail which is a characteristic of scholastic discussion. It is fair to say that he pronounced the question a difficult one and one upon which the physicians and natural philosophers of his day were much divided.

[2] *Sed dolo illo serpentino quo mulier seducta est, nullo modo arbitror illum potuisse seduci.*

not correcting her.[1]   Albertus Magnus seems inclined to
draw a more even balance.   In that which pertained to the
essence of sin, he said, Eve was the greater offender, but if
we look at Adam's endowment and at other circumstances,
Adam was the greater offender.[2]   Bonaventura laid down
the proposition that the gravity of sin depends upon three
things: ingratitude, lust, and the corruption which follows
the sinful act.[3]   Applying these rules to the Fall, he declared
that, so far as ingratitude goes, Adam's sin was the greater
and, so far as lust goes, the woman's sin was the greater.
As for the evil consequences flowing from the sin, Adam
sinned the more grievously as the *cause* of damnation to his
posterity and Eve the more grievously as the *occasion* of such
damnation.   But as Eve was also the occasion of Adam's
sinning, her sin and guilt must be pronounced the greater.

GRACE. — In the doctrine of grace, the mediæval theology
used the terminology of Augustine but makes the impression of departing from him in the direction of semi-Pelagian-
ism.[4]   The treatment which Thomas Aquinas gave to two
elements he found in the African father, namely, freewill
which man preserves after the Fall, and the doctrine of merit,
has the appearance of a de-Augustinianizing tendency.   In
reality Thomas taught that all that is good in man is from
God and he can have no merit before God except by the pre-
arrangement of a divine decree.[5]   In no other sense is an act

---

[1] *De sacr.*, I. 7, Migne, 176. 290.

[2] *In Sent.*, II. 22, E, Borgnet's ed., XXVII. 377.

[3] *In Sent.*, II. 22, I. 3, Peltier's ed., III. 123.

[4] *Man hatte augustinische Formeln und gregorianische Gedanken.* Loofs,
p. 291. Schwane, p. 455, praises Thomas' clear treatment of the doctrines of
grace, and says he taught them as they are taught in the Catholic systems of
dogmatics to-day. Loofs, Harnack, and Seeberg seem to me to go too far in
ascribing to Thomas a de-Augustinianizing tendency. His plain statements
of the necessity of divine grace and human inability are Augustinian enough.
Passing from the study of Thomas' theory of the sacraments, it is easy to
put upon the statements about grace a Pelagian interpretation. The fairer
way is to interpret his theory of the sacraments in the light of his teachings
on the doctrine of grace.

[5] *meritum apud deum esse non potest, nisi secundum præsuppositionem divinæ ordinationis.* *Summa*, II. 114, I. Migne, II. 960.

of righteousness — that is, the doing of what we owe — to be called a meritorious act. Without the grace of the Holy Spirit it is not possible to merit eternal life. Man is not even able to make the preparation necessary to receive the light of grace. Prevenient grace is essential to beget in him the disposition to holiness, — *interior voluntas*. The number of the elect is fixed even to the persons of the saved, and persevering grace is given to those who remain steadfast to the end. Man cannot even know the truth without help from above.[1]

Thomas distinguished two kinds of merit or meritorious works : the merit which comes by the proper use of our natural gifts, — *meritum de congruo*, — and the merit which comes from the proper use of the gifts of grace, — *meritum de condigno*. In his original state, man was enabled by the superadded gift of grace to love God above all things. In the fallen state, grace is required to restore this ability, and no works of this second sort can be done without the assistance of the Holy Spirit. Such statements as these could be multiplied almost indefinitely. There is, however, notwithstanding these clear statements, à tone in Thomas' treatment which makes the impression that he modified strict Augustinianism and made a place for the real merit of works, and in this the Catholic Church follows him.

As for the satisfaction of Christ, Thomas Aquinas followed Anselm in holding that Christ's death was not a price paid to the devil.[2] He did not lay down a very exact definition of the mode in which the atonement was made efficacious ; but he laid stress upon the merit which Christ won by the assent of his own will to the will of God. He does not speak of the propitiation of Christ in the way Abælard and Peter the Lombard [3] did as an exercise of love draw-

---

[1] *Verum non potest cognoscere sine auxilio divino.* Summa, II. 109, 2, 6, 7, Migne, II. 907 sqq.

[2] *Sanguis qui est pretium nostræ redemptionis non dicitur obtulisse diabolo sed deo.* Summa, III. 48, 4, Migne, III. 44.

[3] *Mors Christi nos justificat, dum per eam charitas excitatur in cordibus nostris.* Sent., III. 19, 1.

3 c

ing man to God. The love and obedience of Christ are
efficient, through the sufferings he endured on the cross, in
reconciling man to God and redeeming man from the power
of the devil.

Thomas very clearly states the consequences of Christ's
atonement. The first is that thereby man comes to know
how great the love of God is, and is provoked to love God
in return.[1] By the cross Christ set an example of humility,
righteousness, and other virtues. He also taught men the
necessity of keeping free from sin, overcoming the devil, and
conquering death by dying to sin and the world. God
might have pardoned man without the satisfaction of the
cross, for all things are possible with Him. This was in
opposition to Anselm's position that God could have redeemed man in no other way than by the cross.

Bonaventura went further in opposition to Anselm and
distinctly asserted that God could have liberated and saved
the race otherwise than He did. He might have saved it by
the way of pity — *per viam misericordiæ* — in distinction from
the way of justice. And in choosing this way he would have
done no injury to the claims of justice.[2] His chapter on this
subject he closes with the words, "It would be dangerous
for me to put a limit on God's power to redeem, for He is
able to do above what we are able to think."

No distinction was made by the mediæval theologians
between the doctrine of *justification* and the doctrine of
sanctification, such as is made by Protestant theologians.
Justification was treated as a part of the process of making
the sinner righteous, and not as a judicial sentence by which
he was declared to be righteous. Sanctification was so
thoroughly involved in the sacramental system that we
must look for its treatment in the chapters on the seven
sacraments, the instrumentalities of sanctification; or under

---

[1] *Per passionem Christi homo cognoscit quantum deus hominem diligat et
per hoc provocatur ad eum diligendum. Summa*, III. 46, 3, Migne, III. 417.

[2] *In Sent.*, III. 20, Peltier's ed., IV. 439. He attempts to show that he
is not out of accord with Anselm, but he makes poor work of it. Anselm's
statement is absolute. *Cur deus homo*, II. 10.

the head of the Christian virtues, faith, hope, and love, as in Bonaventura's treatment.[1] Thomas Aquinas discusses it under the head of the atonement and in special chapters entitled "the division of grace,"[2] by which he means the distinction between prevenient, or preparatory, and coöperant grace,—*gratia gratis data*, or the grace which is given freely, and the *gratis gratum faciens*, or the grace which makes righteous.

Justification, says Thomas, is an infusion of grace.[3] Four things are required for the justification of the sinner: the infusion of grace, the movement of the freewill to God in faith, the act of the freewill against sin, and the remission of sins. As a person, turning his back upon one place and receding from it, reaches another place, so in justification the will made free at once hates sin and turns itself to God.

Setting aside the distinction between justification and sanctification, there seems to be complete religious accord between Thomas Aquinas, the prince of the Schoolmen, and our Protestant view of redeeming grace as being from beginning to end the gracious act of God in view of the death of Christ. His theory of the sacraments, it is true, seems to modify this position. But this is an appearance rather than a reality. For the sacraments have their efficacious virtue by reason of God's prior and gracious enactment attaching efficacy to them.

FAITH. — In its definition of faith, the mediæval theology came far short of the definition given by the Reformers. The Schoolmen[4] begin their discussion with the words of the Epistle to the Hebrews 11 : 1, that faith is the substance of things hoped for, and define faith as the grace by which things which are not seen are believed. And they scarcely

---

[1] Peltier's ed., IV. 474 sqq.

[2] *De divisione gratiæ. Summa*, Migne, II. 927–960.

[3] *Tota justificatio impii consistit in infusione gratiæ . . . justif. fit, deo movente hominem ad justitiam. Summa*, II. 113, 3, 7, Migne, II. 946. 952.

[4] Hugo of St. Victor, *De sacr.* I. 10, 9, Migne, 176. 341 sqq. ; P. Lombardus, *Sent.*, III. 23, 24, Migne, pp. 295 sqq. ; Bonavent., *In Sent.*, III. 23, 24, Peltier's ed., IV. 475 sqq. ; Th. Aquinas, IV. 1–5, Migne, IV. 12 sqq. ; Alb. Magnus, *In Sent.*, III. 23, 24, Borgnet's ed., XXVIII. 408 sqq.

get beyond this definition. Although several of Paul's statements in the Epistle to the Romans are quoted by Thomas Aquinas, neither he nor the other Schoolmen rise to the idea that it is upon the basis of faith that a man is justified. Faith is a virtue, not a justifying principle, and is treated at the side of hope and love. These are called the "theological virtues" because they relate immediately to God and are founded ultimately upon the testimony of His Word alone. Christian faith works by love and is not a grace unless it be conjoined with love. The devils have intellectual faith without love, for they believe and tremble.

Faith manifests itself in three ways, in believing God, trusting God, and believing in God.[1] To believe God is to believe that He is. To trust God is to accept what He says as true. These two kinds of faith the devils have. To believe *in* God is to love God in believing, to go to Him believing, to be devoted to Him in believing, and to be incorporated with His members. This knowledge of faith is more certain than other knowledge because it is based upon God's Word and is enlightened by the light which proceeds from the Word.

The Schoolmen insist that without faith it is impossible to please God, and preachers, like Honorius of Autun, declared that as a fish cannot live without water, so no one can be saved without faith.[2] And yet Thomas Aquinas scarcely gets beyond the definition that faith is an assent of the intellect, *assensus intellectus*.[3] However, love and faith, he says, are so closely conjoined that love may be called a form of faith, a mode of its expression,[4] and without love faith is dead. A sufficient faith in Christ demands four things, said the Lombard: assent to his nativity, his death, his resurrection, and his coming again for judgment.[5] Thomas requires an explicit acceptance of the doctrine of the Trinity even by the Old Testament saints, for the Trinity was revealed in the be-

---

[1] *Aliud credere deo, aliud credere deum, aliud credere in deum.* P. Lomb., III. 23, 4.   [2] *Spec. eccles.*, Migne, 172. 823.

[3] *Summa*, IV. 4, 2, Migne, IV. 14, quoting 1 Cor. 13 : 12.

[4] *Charitas dicitur forma fidei*, etc., IV. 4, 3. Such faith which is without love is called *fides informis*.   [5] P. Lomb., III. 25, 3, Migne, p. 300.

ginning when God said, " Let *us* make man in our own image." There can be no belief in the incarnation without
belief in the Trinity. Faith ceases when the mind disbelieves a single article of the faith.[1] He who disbelieves a
single one of the articles of the Apostles' Creed has no faith
at all.[2] After quoting Rom. 4 : 5, this great theologian
stops with saying, that, in justification, an act of faith is required to the extent that a man believe that God is the jus-
tifier of men through the atonement of Christ.[3]

The Schoolmen did not understand Paul. The Reformers
were obliged to re-proclaim the doctrine of justifying faith
as taught in the epistles to the Romans and the Galatians.
On the other hand, it is the merit of the Schoolmen that they
emphasize the principle, that true faith worketh by love and
that all other faith is vain, *inanis.* The failure of Protestant
theologians always to set this forth distinctly has exposed
the Protestant doctrine to the charge that faith is sufficient,
even if it be unaccompanied by good works, or works of love
towards God and man.[4] The fault of the Schoolmen lay
chiefly in their unscriptural and dangerous theory of sacramental grace which led to the substitution of a series of outward exercises, recommended by the priest, for simple trust
in Christ's free grace.

§ 121. *The Future State.*

The unseen world of spirits was divided by the mediæval
theology into five distinct regions or abodes,—*receptacula animarum,*—as Thomas Aquinas calls them — heaven, hell, purgatory, the *limbus patrum,* or the temporary abode of the Old

---

[1] *Fides non remanet in homine postquam discredit unum articulum fidei.*
Summa, IV. 5. 3, I. 7 sqq., Migne, III. 63 sq.

[2] *In heretico discredente unum articulum fidei, non manet fides neque
formata neque informis.* IV. 5, 3, Migne, p. 63.

[3] *Summa,* II. 113, 4, Migne, II. 948.

[4] This is one of the charges brought with great vehemence against Luther
and the Reformation by Denifle, *Luther und Lutherthum,* I. 374–456. He
misunderstood or wilfully misrepresented Luther, who never intended to de-
tach a life of good works from faith as its necessary consequence.

Testament saints, and the *limbus infantum*, or the abode of children who die without being baptized.

Hell, the place of punishment or eternal dolors,[1] is the lake of sulphur and fire in which lost men and demons suffer eternal torment. It is a region of jet darkness, a deep prison as compared with heaven, into which the demons are thrust down.[2] The longings and passions of those confined there go on continually burning and are never satisfied. Its fires burn but do not consume. No other heat can compare with its heat.[3] The Schoolmen are agreed that the passages of Scripture, bearing on the fire of hell, are not figurative. The fire is material fire which afflicts both the spirits and bodies of the lost.[4] The degree of torture is according to the desert.

The *limbus patrum* corresponds to Abraham's bosom in the parable of Dives and Lazarus, the place where the worthies of the Old Testament dwelt till Christ descended into hades and released them. Before that time they enjoyed exemption from pain. Since then they have enjoyed heavenly bliss. Circumcision released them from original sin. Hell and this locality are probably in the same region or, at any rate, contiguous.[5] The view, that the patriarchs remained in hades till Christ's death, goes back to Hermas and Clement of Alexandria.

The *limbus puerorum* or *infantum* is the abode of children

---

[1] Thomas Aquinas calls it *locus dolorum* and *infernum damnatorum*.

[2] *Profundus carcer respectu amœnitatis cœli et est aer iste caliginosus in quem detrusi sunt demones*, etc. Alb. Magnus, *In Sent.*, III. 22, C, 4, Borgnet's ed., XXVIII. 393.

[3] *Ignis est in fortissima calididate . . . cui nil est comparabile.* Alb. Magnus, Borgnet's ed., XXX. 597.

[4] *Gehenna illa quæ stagnum ignis et sulphuris dicta est, corporeus ignis erit et cruciabit damnatorum corpora vel hominum vel dæmonum.* P. Lomb., *Sent.*, IV. 44, 6. *Absque dubietate corporeus ignis cruciat*, etc. Alb. Mag., *In Sent.*, Borgnet's ed., XXX. 393. *Ignis corporalis qui concremabit et affliget spiritus et etiam corpora . . . sed semper affliget, alios plus alios minus, secundum exigentiam meritorum.* Bonavent., *Brev.*, VII. 6.

[5] *Probabile est, quod idem locus vel quasi continuus, sit infernus et limbus.* Th. Aq., Migne, IV. 1222. Thomas calls the infernal regions interchangeably *infernus* and *inferni*. Alb. Magnus uses the neuter plural *inferna*. *In Sent*, III, 25, C, 392.

dying in infancy without having been baptized. They are there for original sin which only baptism can wash away.[1] According to Thomas Aquinas, this region is probably a little lower than the *limbus patrum*. These children are free from pain, but are like the lost in being deprived of the vision of God and physical light. Theirs is the punishment of eternal death, — *supplicium mortis œternœ*, — but their damnation is the lightest of all — *omnium levissima*. They have no hope of beatitude. God, in His justice, provides that they never make any advance nor go back, that they neither have joy nor grief. They remain forever unchanged.[2] Such is the hopeless doom to which the great Dominican and the great Franciscan theologians of the Middle Ages consigned all children dying unbaptized. Strange that the Schoolmen, in the interest of a more merciful doctrine, did not use Christ's blessed words, "Suffer the little children to come unto me for of such is the kingdom of God." But they did not. The doctrine of original sin and the doctrine of the necessity of water baptism for salvation were carried to their extreme logical conclusions without regard for the superabounding grace of God. So also Augustine had taught and so most of the Reformers taught at a later time.

Christ's descent into hades was carefully discussed by the Schoolmen. It occurred as soon as his soul was separated from the body at his death. He was in the infernal regions during the three days of his burial, but did not assume their pains. The reason for this visit was twofold, says Bonaventura, — to release the Old Testament saints and to confound the adversaries of the Gospel, the demons.[3] Thomas Aquinas tried to show that, when Job said, 17 : 16,

---

[1] Th. Aq., *Summa*, III. 69, 6, *originali peccato debebatur pœna œterna in limbo puerorum. Limbus* means edge or border. Alb. Magnus also calls it *limbus parvulorum*, the region of the little ones. Borgnet's ed., XXVIII. 392.

[2] *Pueris non adest spes beatœ vitœ*, etc. Th. Aq., *Supplem.*, p. 1223. *divinœ justitiœ œquitas perpetualiter eos consolidat, ut nec proficiant, nec deficiant, nec lœtentur, nec tristentur; sed semper per sic uniformiter maneant*, etc. Bonavent., *In Sent.*, II. 33, 2, 3, Peltier's ed., III. 419.

[3] *In Sent.*, III. 22, I. 4 sqq., Peltier's ed., IV. 467.

" my hope shall go down to the bars of Sheol," or into the
" deepest hell," as the Vulgate puts it, he meant that he
went no farther than the *limbus patrum* and not to the abode
of the lost.[1] Christ descended into hades, according to
Thomas,[2] for a threefold purpose, to deliver us from the necessity of going there ourselves; to release the Hebrew saints
by breaking the bars of hell—*vectes inferni,*—that is, by
" spoiling principalities and powers," Col. 2:15; and third,
to make show of his divinity—*manifestatio divinitatis*—to
the demons by preaching, 1 Pet. 3:19, and by enlightening
those dark spaces with his presence, as it is said, Ps. 24 : 7,
" Lift up your doors, O ye princes, and the king of glory
shall come in."   Here again the Vulgate is responsible for a
mistake, the word "gates" being translated "princes."[3]
Christ's descent into hades did not help the unbaptized children.   After this life it is too late to acquire grace.[4]

Purgatory is a sort of reformatory school for baptized
Catholics who are not good enough at death to go directly to
heaven.   They are there in that intermediate region for
actual transgressions,[5] whose guilt the sacrament of penance
and extreme unction had not fully removed.   The existence
of purgatory is based mainly upon 2 Mac. 12:40 and the
universal teaching of the Church.[6]   Its inhabitants belong
to the communion of saints and are within the reach of
human intercession.   Masses for the dead are instituted to
meet their case.   For infants in the *limbus puerorum*, such intercessory works are of no avail.   But one who has been
baptized in infancy or manhood, no matter how flagitious or
criminal his career may have been, for him there is hope, nay
there is certainty, that in time he will pass out of purgatory
into the company of the blessed.

[1] *Suppl.*, Migne, III. 1222.   The deepest hell —*profundissimus infernus*
—is the place of the lost. Bonavent., *Brevil.*, VII. 6, Peltier's ed., VII. 339.

[2] *Summa*, III. 52, 1, Migne, IV. 476.   [3] *Attolite portas, principes, vestras.*

[4] *Post hanc vitam non est tempus gratiam acquirendi.* Th. Aq., *Summa*,
III. 52, 7 ; *Suppl.*, Migne, IV. 1244.

[5] *Pœna purgatorii est in supplementum satisfactionis quæ non fuerat plene
in corpore consummata.*   Th. Aq., *Suppl.*, 71, 6, Migne, IV. 1242.

[6] Th. Aq., Migne, IV. 1239.

Heaven includes three kinds of rewards, said Bonaventura: the *substantial* reward or the vision of God; the *consubstantial* or the glorification of the body to which belong the qualities of transpicuity, lightness, agility, and impassibility which are granted in the degree we exercise love here on earth ;[1] and the *accidental* reward or the ornament of the aureole given for preaching and leading others to salvation, for virginal purity and martyrdom.

The bliss of heaven, said Thomas Aquinas, consists in the immediate vision of God.[2] It is a state from which there will be no lapse. The beatified know what is occurring on earth, hear the prayers that ascend to them, and by their merits intercede for their brethren here. St. Bernard, in his homilies on the Canticles,[3] and Anselm[4] give us lofty descriptions of the blessedness of the heavenly estate. And the satisfaction and glory of the soul in heaven has never been quite so well portrayed as in the poem of Bernard of Cluny : —

> O sweet and blessed country, the home of God's elect,
> O sweet and blessed country, that eager hearts expect ;
> Jesus in mercy bring us to that sweet land of rest,
> To be with God the Father and Spirit ever blest.

It remained for Dante to give to the chilling scholastic doctrines of purgatory and the lower regions a terrible reality in poetical form and imagery and also to describe the beatific vision of paradise.

The remarkable vision which a certain Englishman, Turchill, had of the future world, as related at length by Roger of Wendover [5] and others, reveals the crass popular ideas of the future state. St Julian appeared to this honest laborer, and took him off to "the middle of the world," where they entered a church which, as Turchill was told, received the souls of all those who had recently died. Mary, through her intercession, had brought it about that all souls born again should, as soon as they left the body, be taken to this church and so be freed from the attacks of

---

[1] *Claritas, subtilitas, agilitas, et impassibilitas quæ . . . secundum majoritatem et minoritatem prius habitæ charitatis.*   *Brevil.*, VII. 7, Peltier's ed., VII. 340.

[2] *Deum per essentiam videre in quo consistit perfecta hominis beatitudo.* *Summa*, III. 52, 5, Migne, IV. 482.   [3] *Serm.*, XI.

[4] *Proslog.*, XXIV. sqq.   [5] *An.* 1206, Luard's ed. of M. Paris, II. 497-512.

demons. Near one of the church walls was the entrance to hell through which came a most foul stench. Stretching from another wall was the great lake of purgatorial fire in which souls were immersed, some to their knees, some to their necks. And above the lake was a bridge, paved with thorns and stakes, over which all had to pass before they could arrive at the mount of joy. Those who were not assisted by special masses walked over the bridge very slowly and with excruciating pain. On the mount was a great and most wonderful church which seemed to be large enough to contain all the inhabitants of the world. St. Nicolas, St. James, and other saints had charge of the church of Mary and the purgatorial lake and bridge. Turchill also saw St. Peter in the church of Mary and before him the souls were brought to receive sentence. The devil and his angels were there to hurry off to the infernal regions those whose evil deeds tipped the balances. Turchill was also taken by a certain St. Domninus to behold the sports the devils indulge in. Coming to the infernal realm, they found iron seats, heated to a white heat and with nails driven in them, on which an innumerable multitude was sitting. Devils were sitting around against the walls poking fun at the unfortunate beings for the evils they had been guilty of in this life. Men of different occupations and criminal practices, the soldier, tradesman, priest, the adulterer, thief, and usurer, were then brought forth and made to enact over again their wicked deeds, after which their flesh was fiercely torn by the demons and burnt, but again restored. Such are the popular pictures which form the vestibule of Dante's Inferno.

Of all the gruesome religious tales of the Middle Ages, the tales representing the devil as torturing the naked soul were among the most gruesome. The common belief was that the soul, an entity with form as the Schoolmen defined it, is at death separated from the body. Cæsar of Heisterbach tells of an abbot of Morimond with whose soul the demons played ball, rolling it from hill to hill, across the valley between, until God allowed the soul to enter the body again. This was before the abbot became a monk.

Another of these stories, told by Cæsar of Heisterbach,[1] concerned a student to whom the devil gave a stone. As long as the student held it in his hand, he had supernatural knowledge. When he died, his body was taken to the church, and while his fellow-students stood around it singing, the devil carried his soul to hell. There the demons played ball with it. Their sharp claws stuck deep into it and gave it unspeakable pain. But, at the intercession of the saints, the Lord rescued the soul and reunited it with the body and the young man suddenly arose from his bier. In telling his experience he related that his soul had been like a round piece of glass through which he could see on every side. Fortunately, the fellow was scared badly enough to go to a convent and do sound

---

[1] *Dial*, I. 32, Strange's ed., I. 36–39.

penance.   Bernard of Thiron bore witness that he saw the devils carry an unfaithful monk's soul out of the window.[1]

The severity of the purgatorial pains is vouched for in this story by Thomas of Chantimpré,[2] for which he quotes Albertus Magnus.   A good man, after suffering from a severe sickness for a year, had this alternative offered him by an angel: to go to purgatory and suffer for three days or endure for a year longer his sickness and then go directly to glory.   He chose the first.   So his soul took its departure, but the purgatorial agony of a day seemed like the pains of ages and the sufferer was glad to have the opportunity of returning to his body, which was still unburied, and endure his sickness for another year.

Such stories are numerous and reveal the coarse theology which was current in convent and among the people.

---

[1] See Walter, *Die ersten Wanderprediger*, etc., p. 49.
[2] See Kaufmann, *Thos. von Chantimpré*, pp. 117 sq.

CHAPTER XV.

POPE AND CLERGY.

§ 122. *The Canon Law.*

LITERATURE : *Decretum Gratiani emendatum et notationibus illustratum. Una cum glossis, Gregorii XIII. Pont. Max. jussu editum,* 5 vols. Rome, 1582. — *Corpus juris canonici,* ed. J. H. BOEHMER, 2 vols. Halle, 1747, with Introductions by BOEHMER on Gratian's *Decretum,* I. 1–42, and the later collections of decretals, II. 1–34. — Best critical ed. by A. L. RICHTER, 2 vols. Leip., 1839, revised ed. by E. FRIEDBERG, Leip., 1879–1881, 2 vols. (vol. I., *Decret. Gratiani,* vol. II., *Decretalium collectiones*). — J. FR. VON SCHULTE (Old-Cath. Prof. in Bonn): *D. Gesch. der Quellen und Lit. des kanonischen Rechts von Gratian bis auf die Gegenwart,* 3 vols. Stuttg., 1875–1880. — DODD : *Hist. of Canon Law,* Oxf., 1884. — T. HINSCHIUS : *D. Kirchenrecht d. Katholiken und Protestanten,* etc., 6 vols. Berl., 1869–1897. — E. FRIEDBERG : *Lehrbuch des kath. und evangel. Kirchenrechts,* 5th ed., Leip., 1903. — A. VON KIRCHENHEIM : *Kirchenrecht,* Bonn, 1900. — P. HERGENRÖTHER (Rom. Cath.) : *Lehrbuch d. kathol. Rechts,* 2d. ed., Freib., 1905. — Other works by WALTER, 14th ed., 1871. — RICHTER-DOVE, 8th ed., Leip., 1877. — PHILLIMORE : *The Eccles. Law of the Ch. of Engl.,* 2 vols. London, 1873, *Supplem.,* 1876. — F. W. MAITLAND : *Rom. Can. Law in the Ch. of Engl.,* Lond., 1898. — The artt. in Herzog, vol. X. *Kanonen-Sammlungen, Kanonisches Rechtsbuch, Kirchenrecht.* — STUBBS : *Const. Hist. of Engl.,* II. 170 sqq., III. 295–388. — For extensive list of works on Canon Law, see FRIEDBERG : *Kirchenrecht,* pp. 3–11, and HERGENRÖTHER : *Kirchenrecht,* pp. 15 sqq.

NOT the least of the characteristic and imposing products of the mediæval Church was the gigantic fabric of the canon law.[1] It is embodied in a series of collections containing enactments of councils and papal decretals, beginning with the collection of Gratian in the twelfth century and ending with the decretals of John XXII. in the four-

---

[1] *Jus canonicum* or *ecclesiastica constitutio,* in distinction from the civil code, *jus civile.* See *Decr. Grat. Dist.,* III. Friedberg's ed., I. 5. The term "*canones*" was the prevailing term till the 12th century when the expression *jus canonicum* came into general use.

teenth century. The canon law became the legal buttress of the papal theocracy and remained the ruling code till the Reformation.

The science of canon law looks back to Gratian as its father, and Bologna was the chief centre for its study. Although works on the subject were produced in other lands, Italy, through her universities, was far in the lead in their production till late in the fifteenth century.[1]

Under the Roman state, the religious laws — the *jus sacrum, jus pontificium* — were not a distinct body of legislation. In the Christian Church the conception of a distinct and superior divine law existed from the beginning. The formulation of a written code followed the meeting of Christian synods and their regulations. As the jurisdiction of the hierarchy and the institution of the mediæval papacy were developed, this legislation came to include civil obligations and all civil penalties except the death penalty.[2] The Church encroached more and more upon the jurisdiction of the civil court. Conflict was inevitable. Not only was the independence of civil law as a distinct branch of procedure threatened, but even its very existence. It was not till the fourteenth century that the secular governments were able successfully to resist such encroachments and to regain some of the just prerogatives of which the civil courts had been robbed. "Oh, that the canon law might be purged from the superfluities of the civil law and be ordered by theology," exclaimed Roger Bacon, writing in the thirteenth century. "Then would the government of the Church be carried on honorably and suitably to its high position."[3]

Gratian's work was preceded by the Penitential Books and a number of imperfect collections of ecclesiastical deci-

[1] See Schulte, I. 2 sq.

[2] Döllinger-Friedrich, *Papstthum*, p. 403, says, "Leaving out the execution of the death penalty, I do not know a single function of the state which the Church did not assume. Is it, therefore, strange that the thought should arise, that the state is really superfluous or that its only significance is to act as a dumb executioner of the will of the Church?"

[3] Bridges's ed., I. p. lxxxiii.

sions, the chief of which were, two books of synodal cases
by Regino d. 915, the collections of Burchard, bishop of
Worms d. 1025, Anselm of Lucca d. 1086, Cardinal Deusdedit about 1087, and Ivo of Chartres d. 1117.[1] The pseudo-
Isidorian decretals also belong to this class and they were
much used, especially by Burchard.

The work of Gratian superseded these earlier compilations,
and it enjoys the honor of being the monumental work on
canon law. Gratian, a Camaldulensian monk, and an Italian
by birth, taught at the convent of St. Felix, Bologna, at the
same time that Irnerius was teaching civil law in the same
city. No details of his life have been handed down. His
biography is his great compilation which was made about
1140-1150. Its original title, A Concordance of Differing
Canons, *concordantia canonum discordantium*, has given way to
the simple title, *Decretum*, the Book of Decrees. The work
was a legal encyclopædia, and at once became the manual in
its department, as the *Sentences* of the Lombard, Gratian's
contemporary, became the manual of theology.[2] This recognition was not due to formal, papal, or synodal sanction, for
it never received any. It was issued again and again by
learned commentators, the first being one of Gratian's pupils,
Paucapalea. These editors and commentators were called
Summists or Glossarists. The official Roman edition was
prepared by a papal commission of thirty-five members and
issued by Gregory XIII. in 1582. Gregory declared the text
to be forever authoritative, but he did not pronounce upon
the contents of Gratian's work.[3]

Gratian's aim was to produce a work in which all real or
apparent contradictions between customs and regulations
in vogue in the Church should be removed or explained.

---

[1] For full list see Friedberg, p. 126 ; Schulte, I. 43 sqq.; Hergenröther,
p. 179.

[2] Peter the Lombard drew heavily from Gratian, especially in the fourth
book of his *Sentences*, where he reproduced many of Gratian's *distinctiones* entire. See Baltzer, *D. Sentenzen des P. Lombardus*, pp. 10 sq., etc.

[3] *Perpetuo integrum et incorruptum conservetur.* See Schulte's remarks
on Gratian's influence. I. 69-71.

This he secured by exclusion and by comments, called the *dicta Gratiani*, sayings of Gratian. The work is divided into three parts. The first, in one hundred and one sections or *distinctiones*, treats of the sources of canon law, councils and the mode of their convention, the authority of decretals, the election of the Roman pontiff, the election and consecration of bishops, the papal prerogative, papal legates, the ordination of the clergy, clerical celibacy, and kindred topics. The second, in thirty-six sections or *causæ*, discusses different questions of procedure, such as the ordination and trial of bishops and the lower clergy, excommunication, simony, clerical and church property, marriage, heresy, magic, and penance. The third part is devoted to the sacraments of the eucharist and baptism and the consecration of churches. The scholastic method is pursued. A statement is made and objections, if any, are then formally refuted by citation of synodal acts and the testimony of the Fathers, popes, and other churchmen. The first *distinction* opens with the statement that the human race is governed by two principles, natural law and customs. Then a number of questions are propounded such as what is law, what are customs, what kinds of law there are, what is natural law, civil law, and the law of nations?

Gratian's volume was soon found to require supplement. The two centuries following its appearance were most fruitful in papal decrees, especially in the pontificates of Alexander III., Innocent III., and Gregory IX. These centuries also witnessed the Lateran and other important councils. The deliverances of popes and synods, made subsequently to the age of Gratian, were called *extravagantes* or fugitives.[1] Five compilations, called "the old compilations," were made from 1191 to 1226.[2] The third of these, issued by authority of Innocent III. and containing his decretals,

---

[1] *Quia extra Decretum Gratiani vagabantur.*

[2] Friedberg's ed., *Quinque compilationes antiquæ*, Leip., 1882. The first, made by Bernard of Pavia, 1191 in his *Breviarium extravagantium*, distributes the materials under five heads, — judge, sentence, clergy, marriage, crime.

was sent by that pontiff to the university of Bologna to be included in its course of instruction. This compilation was the first book of canon law having papal sanction.

The demand for a complete collection of these materials induced Gregory IX. to commit the task of gathering them into a single volume to his chaplain Raymund de Pennaforte.[1] The work, usually called *Decretales Gregorii IX.*, was finished and sent to Paris and Bologna in 1234 with the direction that it be used for purposes of instruction, and in the trial of cases. The preparation of other compilations was strictly forbidden. Gregory's collection comprises 185 titles and 1871 decretals and follows the fivefold division of Bernard of Pavia's work.[2]

A new collection, called the Sixth Book, *liber sextus* — or, as by English writers, the *Sext*, — was issued by the authority of Boniface VIII., 1298, and carried the collections of Gratian and Gregory IX. into Boniface's reign. In 1314, Clement V. issued another collection, which included his own decretals and the decrees of the council of Vienne and was called the Seventh Book, *liber septimus*, or the *Clementines*. In 1317, John XXII. officially sent Clement's collection to the universities of Bologna and Paris. Subsequent to the publication of the Clementines, twenty of John's own decretals were added. In 1500 John Chappuis, in an edition of the *liber sextus* and the Clementines, added the decretals of John and seventy-one of other popes. This series of collections, namely, Gratian's *Decretum*, Gregory IX.'s *Decretales*, the *Sext*, the *Clementines*, and the *Extravagantes* of John XXII., constitutes the official body of canon law — *corpus juris canonici* — and was published in the edition of Gregory XIII.

The canon law attempted the task of legislating in detail for all phases of human life — clerical, ecclesiastical, social, domestic — from the cradle to the grave by the sacramental decisions of the priesthood. It invaded the realm of the

---

[1] Gregory's bull is given in Wetzer-Welte, III. 1446–1450.

[2] Friedberg gives the text, II. 6–927, and also Gregory IX.'s letter transmitting the decretals to the university of Bologna.

common law and threatened to completely set it aside. The Church had not only its own code and its specifically religious penalties, but also its own prisons.

This body of law was an improvement upon the arbitrary and barbaric severity of princes. It, at least, started out from the principles of justice and humanity. But it degenerated into an attempt to do for the individual action of the Christian world what the Pharisees attempted to do for Jewish life. It made the huge mistake of substituting an endless number of enactments, often the inventions of casuistry, for inclusive, comprehensive moral principles. It put a crushing restraint upon the progress of thought and bound weights, heavy to be borne, upon the necks of men. It had the virtues and all the vices of the papal system. It protected the clergy in the commission of crimes by demanding that they be tried in ecclesiastical courts for all offences whatsoever. It became a mighty support for the papal claims. It confirmed and perpetuated the fiction of the pseudo-Isidorian decretals and perpetrated new forgeries. It taught that the decisions of Rome are final.[1] As Christ is above the law, even so is the pope.[2] Döllinger closes his examination of the *Decretum*, by pronouncing it "filled through and through with forgery and error" and says "it entered like a mighty wedge into the older structural organization of the Church and split it apart."

The canon law also gave its sanction to the devilish principle of ecclesiastical compulsion, declaring that physical force is to be used to coerce ecclesiastical dissidents. It

---

[1] *Dist.*, XIX. 3, Friedberg, I. 61. *Romana ecclesia, cui nos Christus preesse voluit, posita est, omnibus, quicquid statuit, quicquid ordinat, perpetuo, irrefragabiliter observandum est.*

[2] *Causa*, XXV. I. 16; Döllinger, *Papstthum*, pp. 55 sqq. Gratian misquoted the 36th canon of the Sixth Œcumenical council which, giving to the patriarch of Constantinople equal rights with the patriarch of Rome, made it say the very opposite. Misquoting the synod of Carthage of 418, which forbade appeals across the sea, Gratian made the synod say the very opposite. *Causa*, II. 6, 37. Leaning upon pseudo-Isidore, Gratian allows the transfer of bishops from one see to the other with the assent of the pope. *Causa*, VII. I. 34.

justified wars against the enemies of religion and the persecution of heretics, even as Sarah, the type of the heavenly Jerusalem, persecuted her handmaid Hagar. And it declared, with Urban II., that he who kills one who is under the sentence of excommunication is not to be dealt with as a murderer.[1] These principles, set forth in clear statements, were advocated by Thomas Aquinas and the other Schoolmen and asserted by the greatest of the popes.

At last the legalistic tyranny became too heavy for the enlightened conscience of Europe to bear, as was the case with the ceremonial law in the days of the Apostles, against which Peter protested at the council of Jerusalem and Paul in his Epistles. The Reformers raised their voices in protest against it. Into the same flames which consumed the papal bull at Wittenberg, 1520, Luther threw a copy of the canon law, the one representing the effrontery of an infallible pope, the other the intolerable arrogance of a human lawgiver in matters of religion, and both destructive of the liberty of the individual. In his *Address to the Christian Nobles*, Luther declared that it did not contain two lines adapted to instruct a religious man and that it includes so many dangerous regulations that the best disposition of it is to make of it a dung heap.

Even in the Catholic world its enactments have been largely superseded by the canons of the council of Trent, the papal decretals issued since, and the concordats between Catholic princes and the papal see. By virtue of his official infallibility, the pope may at any time supersede them by decisions and dispensations of his own.

The words of Goethe may be applied to the canon law: —

Es erben sich Gesetz und Rechte
Wie eine ewige Krankheit fort
Sie schleppen von Geschlecht sich zum Geschlechte
Und schleichen sich von Ort zu Ort
Vernunft wird Unsinn, Wohlthat Plage.

[1] See·*Causa*, XXIII. 4, 5, 6, Friedberg's ed., I. 899-950.

§ 123. *The Papal Supremacy in Church and State.*

LITERATURE: See the chapp. on Gregory VII. and Innocent III., and the works there cited. — BERNARD: *de consideratione*, Migne, 182. 727–808. — TH. AQUINAS: *de regimine principum*, and *contra errores Græcorum*. The latter ed. by *F. H. REUSCH, d. 1900 : *D. Fälschungen in d. Tractat. d. Th. v. Aq. gegen die Griechen*, Munich, 1889. — The writings of Gregory VII., Alexander III., Innocent III., Gregory IX., etc. *Corpus juris canonum*, Friedberg's ed. — *MIRBT: *Quellen des Papstthums.* — C. LUX: *Constitutionum Apostolicarum de generali beneficiorum reservatione, 1265–1378*, . . . *collectio et interpr.*, Wratislav, 1904. — MAASSEN: *Primat des Bischofs von Rom*, Bonn, 1853. — SCHULTE: *D. Macht des röm. Papstthums*, Prag, 2d ed., 1871. — *DÖLLINGER-FRIEDRICH: *D. Papstthum*, Munich, 1892. — *F. X. LEITNER: *D. hl. Th. von Aquino über d. unfehlbare Lehramt d. Papstes*, Franf., 1872. Leitner wrote in opposition to Döllinger, and his work is of much importance. — *BRYCE: *Holy Rom. Emp.*, VI.–XI. — G. B. ADAMS: *Civilizat. during the M.A.*, chap. X. — W. BARRY: *The Papal Monarchy*, 590–1303, N.Y., 1902. — *J. HALLER: *Papsttum und Kirchenreform*, Berlin, 1903. — *A. HAUCK: *D. Gedanke der päpstl. Weltherrschaft bis auf Bonifaz VIII.*, Leip., 1904. — RANKE: *Weltgesch.*, vol. VI. — HARNACK: *Dogmengesch.*, II. 392–419. The manuals on Canon Law by FRIEDBERG, HINSCHIUS, HERGENRÖTHER.

The papal assumptions of Gregory VII. and Innocent III. have already been presented (pp. 27 sqq., 152 sqq.). A large part of the history of this period is occupied by popes in the effort to realize the papal theocracy, from the opening struggle of Gregory VII. with Henry IV. to the death of Conradin, the Hohenstaufen. Their most vigorous utterances, so far as they are known, were not to summon men and nations to acts of Christian charity, but to enforce the papal jurisdiction. It is not the purpose here to repeat what has already been said, *but* to set forth the institution of the papacy as a realized fact and the estimate put upon it by Schoolmen and by the popular judgment.

Among the forty-one popes who occupied the chair of St. Peter from Gregory VII. to Boniface VIII., some, as has become evident, were men of rare ability, and occupy a place of first prominence as rulers. There were no scandals in the papal household such as there had been during the preceding period. No emperors from the North were required to

descend upon Rome and remove pontiffs incompetent by reason of youth or profligacy.   On the other hand, Rome had
no reputation as a centre either of piety or of letters.
Convents became noted for religious warmth, and Bologna,
Paris, and other localities acquired a fame for intellectual
culture, but Rome's reputation was based solely upon her
authority as a seat of ecclesiastical prerogative.

The sin of the popes was hierarchical pride, and yet we
cannot help but be attracted by those imposing figures whose
ideals of universal dominion equalled in ambition the boldest
projects of the greater Roman emperors, but differed widely
from theirs in the moral element which entered into them.[1]

In this period the loftiest claims ever made for the papacy
were realized in Western Europe.   The pope was recognized
as supreme in the Church over all bishops, and with some
exceptions as the supreme ruler in temporal affairs.   Protest
there was against the application of both prerogatives, but
the general sentiment of Europe supported the claims.   To
him belonged fulness of authority in both realms — *plenitudo potestatis.*

The Pope and the Church. — A favorite illustration used
by Innocent III. to support the claim of supremacy in the
Church was drawn from the relation the head sustains to the
body.   As the head contains the plenitude of the forces of
the body, and has dominion over it, so Peter's successor,
as the head of the Church, possesses the fulness of her prerogatives and the right of rule over her.   The pope calls
others to share in the care of the Church, but in such a way
that there is no loss of authority to the head.[2]   Innocent II.,
in opening the second Lateran Council, had used the same
figure, and declared that no ecclesiastical dignity was lawfully
held except by permission of the Roman pontiff.   According

---

[1] Ranke wrote, *Weltgesch.*, VIII. 410, that at Rome the authorities put him
on the Index because he did not regard the papacy as a divine institution.
Nevertheless, he said, " I hold the papacy to be one of the mightiest of all
institutions that have appeared in history, and one that is most worthy of inspiring us with wonder and admiration."

[2] See Innocent's letter in *Decr. Greg.*, III. 8, 5, Friedberg's ed., II. 489.

to Gregory VII., he can depose and appoint bishops as he wills. The principle that the Apostolic see is subject to no human jurisdiction, stated by Gelasius, 493, was accepted by Bernard, though Bernard protested against the pope's making his arbitrary will the law of the Church.[1] The Roman church, said Lanfranc, 1072, is, as it were, the sum of all churches, and all other churches are, as it were, parts of it. The arrangement of all church matters is only authoritative when approved by Peter's successors.[2]

The Fourth Lateran formally pronounced the Roman Church the mother and teacher of all believers, and declared its bishop to be above the patriarchs of Constantinople, Jerusalem, Antioch, and Alexandria in rank and authority. Leo IX., d. 1054, asserted this pretension against Cærularius, the patriarch of Constantinople.[3] Innocent III. vindicated it by substituting a Latin patriarch for the Greek patriarch in that venerable see. The second council of Lyons, 1274, demanded that the Greeks should sign a document acknowledging the "full primacy" of the Roman pontiff and his right to rule over the universal Church.

This theory of papal absolutism found full theological and canonical recognition from Thomas Aquinas and Gratian. Gratian declared that to disobey the pope is to disobey God.[4] Thomas reasoned that, as the bishop is head of a diocese, so there must of necessity be a supreme head uniting all dioceses and guaranteeing pure morals and teaching within the Church. The Church triumphant has one ruler, so also must the Church militant have one ruler, the pope. To the pope is committed the plenitude of power and the prelacy over the whole Church. To him belongs the right of determining what are matters of faith.[5]

[1] *Sedes apost. a nemine judicatur.* For Bernard, see *Ep.*, 213; *de consid.*, III. 4. [2] See Gee and Hardy, *Doc. of Engl. Ch. Hist.*, p. 53.

[3] See Schwane, p. 531.

[4] *Causa*, XXV. 1, 11, Friedberg's ed., I. 1009. *Anathema apud deum, qui censuram Rom. pontificum violat.*

[5] *Christi vicarius in totam eccles. univ. prælationem obtinet. . . . Pontificem pertinet quæ fidei sunt determinare. C. errores Græc.*, II. 32, 36. Also Th. Aq., *Summa*, II. 2, q. I. 10.

Bonaventura took the same ground.   The pope is supreme in all matters pertaining to the Church.   He is the source of authority in all that belongs to prelatic administration, yea his authority extends from the highest to the humblest member of the Church.[1]   Great bishops might have their disputes with the Apostolic see, but, in the end, they yielded to its claim of supreme jurisdiction.   So it was with Robert Grosseteste, bishop of Lincoln.   He declared, "I know and know full well, that our lord, the pope, has authority to freely act concerning all ecclesiastical benefices."[2]

Clement IV. was simply expressing the general opinion of Latin Christendom, when he claimed for the Roman pontiff the "full right to dispose of all churches, ecclesiastical dignities, positions, and benefices."[3]

Theoretically it is a disputed point whether an œcumenical council or the pope was regarded as supreme.   But, in fact, popes controlled the legislation of the general councils in this period as though they were supreme, and they fixed the legislation of the Church, as was the case with Gregory IX.   The relative authority of pope and council did not become an urgent question till the thirteenth century.

The pope also claimed the right to levy taxes at will on all portions of the Church.   This claim, definitely made by the popes of the second half of the thirteenth century, led to the scandalous abuses of the fourteenth century which shocked the moral sense of Christendom and finally called forth the Reformatory councils of Pisa, Constance, and Basel.

Beginning with Innocent III., it became the fixed custom for the pope to speak of himself as the vicar of Christ and the vicar of God.   He was henceforth exclusively addressed as "holiness" or "most holy " — *sanctitas* or *sanctissimus*.[4]

---

[1] *Brevil.*, VI. 12, Peltier's ed., VII. 327. *Christi vicarius fons, origo, et regula omnium principatuum eccles.*, etc.

[2] *Ep.*, 49.   See Luard's ed., p. x.

[3] *Ad quem plenaria de omnibus totius orbis beneficiis eccles. dispositio pertinet*, etc. *Lib. Sext.*, Friedberg, II. 102.

[4] So Thomas Aquinas in his *c. errores Græc.* Bernard, *Epp.*, 187. 341, 356, 396, etc.

The Pope and the Individual. — For Cyprian's motto, " there is no salvation outside of the Church," was substituted, there is no salvation outside of the Roman Church.   It was distinctly stated that all who refuse subjection to the pope are heretics.[1]   From the pope's authority to loose and bind no human being is exempted.   Nothing is exempted from his jurisdiction.[2]

The Pope and the State. — England, Poland, Norway, and Sweden, Portugal, Aragon, Naples, Sardinia, Corsica, and Sicily, not to speak of portions of Central Italy, were in this period, for a longer or shorter time, fiefs of the Apostolic see.   In 1299, the same claim was made over Scotland. The nations from Edessa to Scotland and from Castile to Riga were reminded that Rome was the throbbing centre of divinely bequeathed authority.   The islands of the West were its to bestow.   To Peter was given, so Innocent wrote, not only the universal Church, but the whole earth that he might rule it.[3]   His practice, as we have seen, followed his pen.   There was a time when the pope recognized the superior authority of the emperor, as did Gregory the Great in 593.[4]   Peter Damiani, writing in the age of Gregory VII., recognized the distinction and coördination of the two swords and the two realms.[5]   But another conception took its place, the subordination of all civil authority under the pope.   To depose princes, to absolve subjects from allegiance, to actively foment rebellion as against Frederick II., to divert lands as in Southern France, to give away crowns, to extort by threat of the severest ecclesiastical penalties the payment of tribute, to punish religious dissenters with perpetual imprisonment or turn them over to the secular authorities, knowing death would be the punishment, to send and consecrate crusading armies, and to invade the realm of the civil court, usurp its authority, and annul a nation's

[1] The *Dictatus papæ* of Deusdedit. Mirbt, p. 113.

[2] *Deus nullum excepit, nihil ab ejus potestate subtraxit.   Reg.*, IV. 2.

[3] *Petro non solum universam eccles. sed totum reliquit seculum gubernandum. Ep.* I. 401, Mirbt, p. 130.

[4] Hauck, p. 1.   [5] Mirbt, *Quellen*, pp. 99 sq.

code, as in the case of Magna Charta, — these were the high
prerogatives actually exercised by the papacy.   The decision
rendered on the field of Roncaglia by the jurists of Bologna,
asserting the independent rights of the empire, was only an
episode, and popes snapped their fingers at the academic im-
pertinence.   Now and then the wearers of the tiara were defeated, but they never ceased to insist upon the divine
claims of their office.   In vain did emperors, like Frederick
II., appeal to the Scriptures as giving no countenance to the
principle that popes have the right to punish kings and deprive them of their kingdoms.

The declarations of the popes were clear and positive.
The figures employed by Gregory VII., comparing the two
realms to gold and lead, sun and moon, soul and body, Innocent elaborated and pressed.   Gregory asserted that it
rested upon him to give account for all the kingdoms of
God.[1]   To him had been committed universal dominion —
regimen universale.[2]   Innocent III. found in Melchizedek,
the priest-king, the full type of the pope combining in himself the sacerdotal and regal functions.

Men of less originality and moral power could do no
more than reaffirm the claims of these two master rulers and
repeat their metaphors.   Of these no one had more self-
assurance than Gregory IX., who, at an age when most men
are decrepit, bravely opposed to Frederick II.'s plans the
fiction of the Donation of Constantine.   Was not the Roman
sceptre committed to the Apostolic see by the first Christian
emperor, and did not the Apostolic see transfer the empire
from the Greeks to the Germans, Charlemagne and Frederick
himself being the successors of Arcadius, Valentinian, Theodosius, and the other Christian emperors of Rome.[3]   But Innocent IV., 1254, returned to the position assumed by Hildebrand, that the papacy does not depend upon Constantine
for secular dominion, as Peter received it directly from God.[4]

---

[1] *Reg.*, I. 63, Migne, 148. 569.   [2] *Reg.*, II. 51.   [3] Bréholles, IV. 914–923.
[4] See Döllinger, *Papstthum*, pp. 67, 404.   Leo X.'s bull against Luther
reaffirmed this fiction of the transfer of the empire from the Greeks to the
Germans by the pope.   See copy of the bull in this *Hist.*, VI. 233.

When the struggle with the Hohenstaufen had been brought to a close, and peace established by the elevation of Rudolf of Hapsburg to the imperial throne, Gregory X. wrote to Rudolf: "If the sacred chair is vacant, the empire lacks the dispenser of salvation; if the throne is empty, the Church is defenceless before her persecutors. It is the duty of the Church's ruler to maintain kings in their office, and of kings to protect the rights of the Church." This was a mild statement of the supremacy of the Apostolic see. It remained for Boniface VIII., in his famous bull, *unam sanctam*, 1302, to state exactly, though somewhat brusquely, what his predecessors from Hildebrand, and indeed from Nicolas I., had claimed — supreme right to both swords, the spiritual and the temporal, with the one ruling the souls of men and with the other their temporal concerns.

These claims were advocated in special treatises by Bernard and Thomas Aquinas, two of the foremost churchmen of all the Christian centuries. Bernard was the friend of popes and the ruling spirit of Europe during the pontificates of Innocent II. and Eugenius III. the mightiest moral force of his age. Thomas Aquinas wrote as a theologian and with him began the separate treatment of the papacy in systems of theology. In his *Rule of Princes* and against the *Errors of the Greeks*, Thomas unequivocally sets forth the supremacy of the Apostolic see over the State as well as in the universal Church. As for Bernard, both Ultramontane and Gallican claim his authority, but there are expressions in his work addressed to Eugenius III., *De consideratione*, which admit of no other fair interpretation than that the pope is supreme in both realms.

Bernard's treatise, filling eighty compact columns in the edition of Migne, summons Eugenius, whom he addresses as his spiritual son, to reflect in four directions: upon himself, upon that which is beneath him, upon that which is around about him, and upon that which is above him. Such a voice of warning and admonition has seldom been heard by the occupant of a throne. The author was writing, probably, in the very last year of his life.

Meditating upon himself, it became the pope to remember that he was raised to his office not for the sake of ruling but of being a prophet, not to make show of power but to have care of the churches. The pope is greatest only as he shows himself to be a servant. As pontiff, he is heir of the Apostles, the prince of bishops. He is in the line of the primacy of Abel, Abraham, Melchizedek, Moses, Aaron, Samuel, and Peter. To him belong the keys. Others are intrusted with single flocks, he is pastor of all the sheep and the pastor of pastors. Even bishops he may depose and exclude from the kingdom of heaven. And yet Eugenius is a man. Pope though he is, he is vile as the vilest ashes. Change of position effected no change of person. Even the king, David, became a fool.

The things beneath the pope are the Church and all men to whom the Gospel should be preached.

The things around about the pope are the cardinals and the entire papal household. Here, greed and ambition are to be rebuked, the noise of appealed judicial cases is to be hushed, worthy officials are to be chosen. The Romans are a bad set, flattering the pontiff for what they can make out of his administration. A man who strives after godliness they look upon as a hypocrite.

The faithful counsellor waxed eloquent in describing the ideal pope. He is one of the bishops, not their lord. He is the brother of all, loving God. He is set to be a pattern of righteousness, a defender of the truth, the advocate of the poor, the refuge of the oppressed. He is the priest of the Highest, the vicar of Christ, the anointed of the Lord, the God of Pharaoh; that is, he has authority over disobedient princes.

Bernard distinctly grants the two swords to the pope, who himself draws the spiritual sword and by his wink commands the worldly sword to be unsheathed.[1] It is true he lays stress upon Peter's Apostolic simplicity and poverty. Peter

---

[1] *De consid.*, IV. 3, Migne, 82, 776. *Uterque Ecclesiæ et spiritualis gladius et materialis ; sed is quidem pro Ecclesia, ille vero et ab Ecclesia exserendus : ille sacerdotis, is militis manu, sed sane ad nutum sacerdotis, et jussum imperatoris.*

wore no gems, was attended by no bodyguard, and sat on no white horse. In adopting such outward show "the popes had followed Constantine, not the Apostle." It is also true that Bernard follows his generation in making the pope the vicegerent of God on earth.[1]

The views of Thomas Aquinas have already received notice (p. 673). His statements are so positive as to admit of no doubt as to their meaning. In the pope resides the plenitude of power. To the Roman Church obedience is due as to Christ.[2] These are assertions made in his treatise against the errors of the Greeks written at a time when the second council of Lyons was impending and measures were being taken to heal the schism between the East and the West. The pope is both king and priest, and the temporal realm gets its authority from Peter and his successors.[3]

Thomas went further still. He declared for the infallibility of the pope. In confirmation of this view he quoted spurious writings of Cyril, but also genuine passages from the Fathers.[4]

The popular opinion current among priests and monks was no doubt accurately expressed by Cæsar of Heisterbach at the beginning of the thirteenth century when he compared the Church to the firmament, the pope to the sun, the emperor to the moon, the bishops to the stars, the clergy to the day, and the laity to the night.

---

[1] Bishop Reinkens, of the old Catholic Church, in his annotated translation of Bernard's treatise, *de consideratione*, argues for the other view ; namely, that Bernard does not present the theory of the " Cæsar-pope." He also argues, pp. vi sq., that Bernard regarded the bishops as receiving their authority not from the pope but directly from God. His edition was issued at the time of the Vatican council of 1870 and as a protest against the dogma of papal infallibility. The position taken above is the position of most writers, both Protestant and Catholic.

[2] *Rom. ecclesiæ obediendum est tanquam domino J. Christo.* Reusch's ed., p. 9.

[3] *Rom. episcopus dici potest rex et sacerdos. . . . Sicut corpus per animam habet virtutem et operationem ita et temporalis jurisdictio principum per spiritualem Petri et successorum eius. De regim.*, II. 10.

[4] See Werner, *D. hl. Thomas*, I. 760 sqq., 794 sqq. ; and especially Reusch and Leitner.

We stand amazed at the vastness of such claims, but there can be no doubt that they were sincerely believed by popes who asserted them and by theologians and people. The supremacy of the Roman pontiff in the Church and over the State was a fixed conviction. The passage, Render unto Cæsar the things that are Cæsar's and unto God the things that are God's, quoted to-day for the separation of the two realms, was quoted then but with another interpretation. The Church was defined, as it had been defined by Augustine, as the university of believers by Hugo of St. Victor,[1] — *universitas fidelium,* — or as the congregation of the faithful confessing Christ and the arsenal of the sacraments by Alanus de Insulis.[2] But the idea of the individual liberty of the Christian and his immediate responsibility to Christ, as revealed through the New Testament, had no hold. As a temporary expedient, the fiction of papal sovereignty had some advantage in binding together the disturbed and warring parts of European society. The dread of the decisions of the supreme pontiff held wild and lawless temporal rulers in check. But the theory, as a principle of divine appointment and permanent application, is untenable and pernicious. The states of Europe have long since outgrown it and the Protestant communions of Christendom can never be expected to yield obedience to one who claims to be the vicar of Christ, however willing they may be to show respect to any Roman bishop who exhibits the spirit of Christ as they did to Leo XIII.

§ 124. *The Pope and the Curia.*

LITERATURE: For the election of a pope. — The text of the laws of Nicolas II. and Gregory X. is given in MIRBT : *Quellen,* 57 sqq., 146, Friedberg's ed. of Gratian, I. 78 sq. — W. C. CARTWRIGHT : *The Papal Conclave,* Edinb., 1868. — ZÖPFFEL : *D. Papstwahlen etc. vom 11.–15. Jahrh.,* Götting., 1871. — T. A. TROLLOPE : *The Papal Conclaves as they were and as they are,* Lond., 1876. — L. LECTOR : *Le conclave,* etc., Paris, 1894. — HEFELE-KNÖPFLER, IV. 800–826 ; VI. 146 sqq. — SCHWANE: *Dogmengesch.,* pp. 522–589. — FRIEDBERG : *Kirchenrecht,* pp. 165 sqq. — HERGENRÖTHER : *Kirchenrecht,* pp. 267–302. — Artt. *Papstwahl.,* in Herzog, XI. 213–217, by HINSCHIUS and WETZER-WELTE, IX. 1442–1461. For the financial policy of the curia. — B. P. WOKER : *D. kirchl. Finanz-*

---

[1] *De sacr.,* II. 1, 2, Migne, 176. 141, etc.   [2] Migne, 210. 613.

wesen d. Päpste, Nördl., 1878. — FABRE : *Le libre censuum de l'église Romaine*, Paris, 1892. — *M. TANGL : *D. Taxenwesen der päpstl. Kanzlei vom 13. bis zur Mitte des 15. Jahrh.*, Innsbr., 1892. — *J. P. KIRSCH : *Die Finanzverwaltung des Kardinalkollegiums im XIII. und XIV. Jahrh.*, Munster, 1895. — *P. M. BAUMGARTEN : *Untersuchungen und Urkunden über die Camera Collegii Cardinalium, 1295–1437*, Leip., 1898. — *A. GOTTLOB : *D. päpstl. Kreuzzugssteuern des 13. Jahrh.*, Heiligens., 1892 ; *D. Servitientaxe im 13. Jahrh.*, Stuttg., 1903. — *O. JENSEN : *D. englische Peterspfennig*, Heidelb., 1903. — HALLER : *Papsttum u. Kirchenreform*, Berlin, 1903. — HURTER : *Inn. III.*, IV. 151 sqq. — For add'l lit. bearing on the financial policy of the popes, especially in the 14th century, see Part II. of this vol. under John XXII.

The curia is the designation given to the cardinals and minor officials of the papal household. Its importance increased greatly in this period through the centralization of authority in Rome. The pope was forced to employ an army of notaries, advocates, procurators, and other officials to share with him the burdens of the vast amount of business brought to his attention.

In a restricted sense, the word " curia " is applied to the college of cardinals. This body came to sustain to the pope a relation similar to the relation sustained by the chapter to the bishop and a cabinet to a prince. At the œcumenical councils of Lyons, 1245 and 1274, its members were given precedence over all other ecclesiastical dignitaries.

The legislation fixing the mode of choosing the pope originated in this period with Nicolas II., speaking through the council of Rome 1059, and Gregory X., speaking through the second council of Lyons, 1274. From the ninth century, the emperor had claimed the right to confirm or veto papal elections, a right set aside under the influence of Gregory VII. The law of Nicolas, conforming to Gregory's views, confined the right of election to the cardinals, and this became their primary function. It marks an important step in the complete independence of the papacy, though it was not strictly enforced till after its confirmation by Alexander III. at the Third Lateran, 1179. A majority of two-thirds of the cardinals was made necessary for an election. An important provision made papal elections conducted outside the city of Rome valid.

More precise regulations were shown to be necessary by the long pontifical vacancy of nearly three years following the death of Clement IV. (d. 1268). The law, as perfected under Gregory X., is, with slight modifications, still in force. It provides that, within ten days of a pope's decease and in the same building where he expired, the cardinals shall assemble to choose a successor. The conclave,—from *clavis*, meaning key,—or room of meeting, has given its name to the assembly itself. During the progress of the vote, the assembled ecclesiastics are kept secluded from the outside world and receive food through a window. If after three days no conclusion has been reached, the fare is reduced to a single dish for supper and a single dish for dinner. Should eight days pass without a choice, the fare is reduced to bread and wine. The secular authorities are intrusted with the duty of guarding the conclave against interruption and violence.

The committees, or congregations, into which the cardinals are now grouped is of late origin. The oldest, the Holy Office or Congregation of the Inquisition, was established 1542. The red hat was conferred upon them, as a sign of their office, by Innocent IV., 1245; the purple mantle, two hundred years later, by Paul II., 1464. They wear a sapphire ring and by the enactment of Urban VIII., 1630, are addressed as " Eminence." In 1586 their number was limited by Sixtus V. to seventy. The exact membership within this limit is dependent upon the pleasure of the reigning pontiff. The largest number at any time was under Pius IV., 1559, when there were seventy-six. In the latter half of the thirteenth century the number often ran very low and at one time was reduced to seven. Since Urban VI., 1378–1382, none but a cardinal has been elevated to the papal dignity. The pope's right to abdicate is based upon the precedents of Gregory VI., 1046, Cœlestin V., 1294, and Gregory XII., 1415.

The pope's coronation and enthronement were an occasion of increasing pomp and ostentation and were usually celebrated with a procession through the city from St. Peter's to the Lateran in which the nobility and civil authorities as well as the pope and the higher and lower clergy took part. The tiara, or triple crown, seems not to have been used till the reign of Urban V., 1362–1372. This crown is regarded as symbolical of the pope's rule over heaven, earth, and the lower world; or of his earthly power and his power to loose for time and eternity; or of Rome, the Western patriarchate and the whole earth.

To this period belongs the development of the system of papal legates which proved to be an important instrumentality in the extention of the pope's jurisdiction. These officials are constantly met with from the pontificate of Gregory VII. Clement IV. likened them to the Roman proconsuls. They were appointed to represent the Apostolic see on special occasions, and took precedence of the bishops in the regions to which they were sent, presided at synods, and claimed for themselves the respect due to the pope himself.

Gregory VII., in commending a legate, quoted Luke 10: 16, "whosoever heareth you, heareth me also."[1] He was represented by Cardinal Hugo in Spain and by other legates in Sardinia, France, Denmark, Poland, and England.[2] Hildebrand himself had represented the popes on special missions, and Adrian IV. won distinction by his successful administration of the legatine office in Northern Europe. Papal legates were present at the coronation of William the Conqueror, 1070.

Legates had the reputation of living like princes and depended for their support upon the countries to which they were despatched. Their encroachment upon the prerogatives of the episcopate and their demands for money called forth bitter complaint from one end of Europe to the other. Barbarossa wrote Adrian IV., refusing to receive the papal legates because they came to him as plunderers and not as priests.[3] John of Salisbury and Matthew Paris joined St.

---

[1] *Reg.*, II. 44, Migne, 148. 392.

[2] *Reg.*, I. 7; I. 29, VIII. 10; II. 32; II. 51; II. 73; I. 70, Migne, 148. 290, 312, 387, 405, 423, 345.

[3] Hefele, V. 565. The permanent nuntiatures at Catholic courts were first established in the 16th century. Such are now maintained at Munich, Vienna, Lisbon, Madrid, and Brussels.

Bernard in condemning their assumption and rapacity. Bernard succeeded in finding only two cases of incorruptible legates.   One, Martin, who had been sent to Dacia, returned to Italy so poor that he could with difficulty get to Florence and would have had to foot it from there to Rome but for the loan of a horse.   Bernard felt his description would be regarded as an idle tale, a legate coming back from the land of gold without gold and traversing the land of silver without possessing silver!   The other case was the legate Gaufrid of Aquitaine who would not accept even fish and vegetables without paying for them so that no one might be able to say, " we have made Abraham rich," Gen. 14 : 23.[1]

Salimbene, the genial Franciscan chronicler, also gives us a dark picture of papal legates of Northern Italy, some of whom he had known personally.   He gives the names of twelve, four of whom he specially accuses of unchastity, including Ugolino, afterwards Gregory IX., and mentioning some of their children by name.   Two of them were hard drinkers.   He makes the general charge that legates " rob the churches and carry off whatsoever they can."[2]

As the ultimate legal tribunal of Western Europe, the papal court assumed an importance never dreamed of before. Innumerable cases of appeal were brought before it.   If the contestants had money or time, no dispute was too trivial to be contested at Rome.   Appeals poured in from princes and kings, chapters and bishops, convents and abbots. Burchard of Ursperg says[3] that there was not a diocese or parish which did not have a case pending at Rome, and all parties who went had their hands full of gold and silver. There was a constant procession of litigants to the Eternal City, so that it once more became literally true that all roads led to Rome.   The hours of daylight, as Bernard lamented, were not long enough for these disputes, and the hearings were continued into the night.[4]   Appeals were encouraged

---

[1] *De consid.*, IV. 5.   [2] Coulton, *From St. Francis to Dante*, pp. 252 sqq.
[3] See Döllinger, *Papstthum*, p. 76.
[4] *Quale est istud de mane ad vesperam litigare, aut litigantes audire ? Utinam sufficeret diei malitia sua ! non sunt liberae noctes.*

by the curia, who found in them an inexhaustible source of revenue. Bernard, writing to Eugenius, lamented the time the chief bishop of Christendom took from his proper duties, and consumed upon the hearing of common lawsuits and personal complaints. The halls of the papal palace rang with the laws of Justinian rather than the precepts of the Lord. Bernard himself recognized the right of appeal as an incontestable privilege, but would have limited it to the complaints of widows and the poor, and excluded disputes over property.[1]

The expression *ad calendas Græcas* became proverbial in Rome for delays of justice till one party or the other was dead or, worn out by waiting, gave what was demanded. The following example, given by Bernard, will indicate the extent to which the right of appeal was carried. A marriage ceremony in Paris was suddenly checked by a complainant appearing at the altar and making appeal to Rome against the marriage on the ground that the bride had been promised to him. The priest could not proceed, and bride and bridegroom had to live apart until the case was argued before the curia. So great did the curia's power become that its decision was regarded as determining what was sound doctrine and what was heresy.[2]

In the thirteenth century, the papal exchequer gained an offensive notoriety through the exactions of the curia, but it was not till the fourteenth century, during the period of the Avignon exile, that they aroused a clamorous protest throughout Europe. The increased expenses of the papal household called for large sums, and had to be met. The supreme pontiff has a claim upon the entire communion over which he presides, and the churches recognized its justice. It was expressed by Pascal II. when he wrote to Anselm of Canterbury, 1101 : " You know well our daily necessities and our want of means. The work of the Roman church inures to the benefit of all the churches, and every

[1] *De consid.*, I. 4–6 ; III. 2.
[2] John of Salisbury, *Polycrat.*, VI. 64, *qui a doctrina vestra dissentit aut hereticus aut schismaticus est.*

church which sends her gifts thereby recognizes not only
that they are in debt to her but to the whole of Christendom
as well.[1]" It was the scandalous abuse of this just claim
that called forth bitter complaint.

As bearing on the papal revenues early in the thirteenth century, a ledger account of the income of Innocent III. has come
down to us, prepared by his chamberlain, Cencius, afterwards
made a cardinal.[2] Of the 633 bishoprics therein listed, 330
paid tribute of one kind or another to Rome. In addition
to gifts of money, all sorts of articles are catalogued — vegetables, wine, grain, fish, wood, wax, linen, yokes of oxen,
horses. Convents, churches, and hospitals made contributions to the pope's wants. The abbot of Reichenau, at his
induction, sent two white horses, a breviary, and a book of
the Gospels. A hospital in the see of Terouanne sent 100
herrings, St. Basil's, in Rome, two loads of fish.

In the latter half of the thirteenth century, the administration of the papal finances was reduced to a system, and
definite rules were adopted for the division of the revenues
between the pope and the college of cardinals. We are restricted to a single tax list[3] for this period, while for the
first half of the fourteenth century we have a number of detailed and highly interesting ledger accounts which give the
exact prices levied for papal privileges of all sorts. There,
we have fiscal contracts drawn up between prelates and
papal officials and receipts such as would be expected in a
careful banking system. These lists and other sources of
information enable us to conclude what methods were practised from 1250–1300.

The sources from which the papal treasury drew its revenues were the annual tributes of feudal states, called *census;*

[1] Quoted by Jensen, p. 42.

[2] See Hurter, *Innocent III.*, III. 121–149. One is amazed at the extent
and variety of the articles and at the curious names of the coins derived
from different countries.

[3] Tangl, pp. 7 sqq. The full treatment of the subject of the papal finances
belongs to the period of the Avignon exile. It has called forth a distinct
body of literature, beginning with the work of Woker and including the
careful works of Tangl, Kirsch, Goeller, Gottlob, Baumgarten, and others.

payments made by prelates and other holders of church benefices called *servitia*, *visitationes*, and *annates;* and the occasional taxes levied upon the Church at large, or sections of
it, for crusades and other special movements. To these
usual sources of revenue are to be added assessments for all
sorts of specific papal concessions and indulgences.[1]

The *servitia*,[2] *visitationes*, and *annates*, originally freewill
offerings of the clergy, had come by the end of the thirteenth
century to be recognized as obligatory assessments. The
annates were payments made by papal appointees of a
portion of a year's income of benefices which the pope
reserved to himself the right of filling, such as prebends, can-
onries, and other livings. The portion was usually one-half.
The *visitationes* were payments made by prelates; that is,
archbishops, bishops, and abbots on their visits in Rome.[3]
These visits were made at fixed periods, the time being
settled by law. The prelates, on taking their oath of office,
obligated themselves to make them.

The *servitia*[4] were gifts of money paid by archbishops,
bishops, and abbots at their confirmation in office. They

---

[1] Monies from these sources were called "monies of the college," *pe-
cuniæ collegii*, and were often entered into the books of the college of cardinals under the head of *servitia, census, visitationes*, and *proventus*. Kirsch,
Finanzverw., p. 5, Baumgarten, p. xcvi.

[2] The terms *servitia* and *annatæ* were used more or less interchangeably,
but the former was usually applied to the gifts of prelates, the latter to the
payments of the lower clerics. Gottlob, *Servitientaxe*, p. 1.

[3] Such a visit was called a *visitatio ad limina apostolorum*, and was not
limited to the city of Rome. The visits upon which a tax was paid were
called *visitationes reales* in distinction from other visits called *visitationes
verbales*. Kirsch, pp. 22 sq.

[4] For the meaning and history of the word, see Gottlob, *Servitientaxe*, pp.
14–17. They were called *servitia communia* in distinction from the *servitia
pro familia* or *servitia minuta*, which were smaller fees given to the officials
of the papal household and officials of the body of cardinals, called *famili-
ares*. These lesser fees were also matter of exact regulation, and usually
amounted to one-fourteenth or one-twentieth of the *servitium commune*. Up
to 1298 we hear of only two distinct fees for the members of the papal household. In 1299 we hear of three, and in the fourteenth century the number
of the *servitia minuta* was increased to five. Gottlob, *Servitientaxe*, pp.
101 sqq. ; Kirsch, pp. 12 sqq.

constituted a large source of revenue. The amounts to be paid in each case were computed upon the basis of a year's income. Once fixed they remained fixed and obligatory until new valuations were made.[1] The levy was usually, though not uniformly, one-third of a year's income.[2] The exact origin of this form of tribute is not known, but it was recognized as custom, having the force of law before the reign of Nicolas III. (1277–1280), and probably as early as the middle of the thirteenth century.[3] The tax was usually paid by the prelates on their visit in Rome, when the appointment was confirmed. Sometimes the obligation of payment was made through a commercial house.[4]

The *census* included the taxes paid by the State of the Church, the assessments paid by convents and churches under the special protection of the Apostolic see, the tributes of the vassal states, Naples, Sicily, Corsica and Sardinia, and England, and the income of Peter's Pence. The tribute of 1000 marks, promised by John for England and Ireland, was over and above the amounts due from Peter's Pence. The tribute of Sicily in 1272, amounting to 8000 oz. of gold, was divided into two equal parts by Gregory X., one part going to the cardinals. In 1307, a demand was made upon Charles II. of Naples for back payments on this account amounting to the enormous sum of 93,340 oz. of gold. In 1350, the amount due was 88,852 oz.[5]

The custom of paying Peter's Pence, or a stipulated amount for every household, was in vogue in England,

---

[1] Kirsch, p. 12, gives the documents in which appeals were made for a reduction of the tribute by the archbishops of Narbonne, 1341, and Cashel, 1332, and the abbot of Amiens, 1344. In the case of the abbot, the amount was reduced from 4000 to 2500 gold florins.

[2] See the cases from which Kirsch deduces the rule, p. 9.

[3] The case of the abbot of St. Edmundsbury seems to belong here. In 1248 he paid to the Roman see 800 marks. M. Paris, Luard's ed., V. 40 ; Tangl, p. 6.

[4] The promises to pay were called *obligationes*. Receipts, *quitationes*, were given by the papal treasurer, or the treasurer of the college of cardinals, or by both. Kirsch gives original documents. He was the first to clear up the subject of the *servitia*.   [5] Kirsch, p. 32.

Sweden, Denmark, Norway, Northern Germany, and Poland, but was never introduced into France though Gregory VII. attempted to collect it there but failed.[1]   Robert
Guiscard, in 1059, pledged for Sicily twelve denarii for every
yoke of oxen to be paid for all time.[2]   Far-off Greenland
also added its contributions to this tax and it was paid under
Olaf, bishop of Gardar, 1246.[3]

During the second half of the thirteenth century, the custom
was developed of dividing the revenues from *visitationes, servitia,* and *census* between the pope and the college of cardinals.[4]
Up to that time the cardinals had depended upon benefices held
in their own names and the tributes of castles and towns in the
papal territory set aside for them by popes.   To these sources
of revenue were added during the thirteenth century livings
in foreign lands which they administered, if administered
at all, through vicars.   A number of benefices were often
held by a member of the curia, but the abuse of pluralities did
not reach its largest proportions till the latter half of the fifteenth century.   In 1291, Benedict Gætani (Boniface VIII.)
cardinal of S. Nicolas in Carcere, held, in addition to that
living, two archdeaneries and two churches in France, three
churches in Rome and prebend stalls in Langres, Chartres,
Lyons, Paris, Anagni, Todi, Terouanne, and St. Peter's in
Rome.

The half portion, accruing to the cardinals, was divided
equally between those dignitaries.   In case a cardinal was
suspended his portion was divided equally between the papal
treasury and the other cardinals.   It became customary at
the close of the thirteenth century, in appointing a cardinal,
to announce that he was entitled to a share of the *servitia.*[5]

---

[1] Hurter, III. 136.   [2] Jensen, p. 36.

[3] See O'Gorman, *Hist. of the Cath. Ch. in the U.S.,* p. 6. Nicolas Breakspear, Adrian IV., as cardinal legate, secured the promise of Peter's Pence
from Norway and Sweden at the synod of Linkoping, 1152.   Jensen, p. 12.

[4] Kirsch, pp. 22, 23, 25.   Nicolas IV., 1288, was the first to establish an
equal division of the census in the bull *cœlestis altitudo.*

[5] Such a formula dating from 1296 is given by Kirsch, p. 58.   The number
of the cardinals is distinctly stated in the ledger-books and also the names
of cardinals who had forfeited their rights by deposition.

During the absence of a cardinal on legatine business or for other reasons, he ceased to participate in the fund.

These revenues were handled by two treasurers: a papal treasurer, or chamberlain, and a treasurer for the college of cardinals.[1] The latter held his office for life. The two offices were never vested in the same person. Each treasurer, at least from the time of Benedict XII. in the fourteenth century, kept his own set of books and at times copies of the papal ledgers were made and turned over to the cardinals. To such a system had the finances been reduced that, as early as the reign of Boniface VIII., the *Registers* of preceding pontiffs were consulted.[2] In the period 1295-1298, the college of cardinals received as their share, coin amounting to 85,431 gold florins, a sum equal in face value to $200,000.[3]

To the pope's own exchequer went the additional sums accruing from *annates* as defined above, the special taxes imposed by the pope at will, and the gifts for special papal favors. The crusades against the Saracens and Frederick II. were an inviting pretext for special taxation. They were the cause of endless friction especially in France and England, where the papal mulcts were most frequent and most bitterly complained of. The first papal levy for revenue in France seems to have been in 1188. As early as 1247 such a levy upon church property was met by a firm protest. In 1269, Louis IX. issued the pragmatic sanction which forbade papal taxes being put on church property in France without the sovereign's consent. One of the most famous levies of mediæval England was the Saladin tax, for a crusade against the Saracens.

---

[1] *camerarius collegii dominorum cardinalium.* The first treasurer whose name is known was William de Bray, cardinal-priest of St. Marks, 1272-1282. For a list of his successors to 1401, see Kirsch, pp. 44–46, and Baumgarten, pp. xliii sqq.

[2] Kirsch, p. 66. Baumgarten, p. xxiii, is of a different opinion and puts the first systematically kept ledgers in 1295.

[3] For a list of the strange coins paid into this fund and a computation of their value in gold florins, see Kirsch, pp. 56 sq. Kirsch estimates the gold florin as equivalent in face value to 10 marks or $2.50 and the mark in the 14th century as having four times the purchasing power of a mark to-day.

The curia was already, in the time of St. Bernard, notorious for its rapacity. No sums could satisfy its greed, and
upon it was heaped the blame for the incessant demands
which went out from Rome. Bernard presents a vivid, if
perhaps overcolored, picture of this hungry horde of officials
and exclaims: " When has Rome refused gold? Rome has
been turned from a shrine into a place of traffic. The
Germans travel to Rome with their pack animals laden with
treasure. Silver has become as plentiful as hay. It is to
Eugenius' credit that he has turned his face against such
gifts. The curia is responsible. They have made Rome a
place of buying and selling. The ' Romans,' for this was the
distinctive name given to this body of officials, are a pack of
shameless beggars and know not how to decline silver and
gold. They are dragons and scorpions, not sheep." [1]

The English chronicler, Matthew Paris, writing a century later, has on almost every other page of his chronicle a
complaint against the exactions of the papal tax gatherers.
One might easily get the impression from his annals, that
the English Church and people existed chiefly to fill the
Roman treasury. The curia, he said, was like a gulf swallow-
ing up the resources of all classes and the revenues of bishops
and abbots. [2] The contemporary Italian chronicler Salimbene
has biting words for the luxury and idleness of the cardinals
and reports the invectives of Hugh de Digne delivered at
the council of Lyons, 1245. [3]

Bernard of Cluny and other poets of the time lashed the
curia for its simony. [4] Everything at Rome had its price.

---

[1] *De consid.*, III. 1, 3. Bernard returns again and again (in his *de consid.*,
I. 11; IV. 4, etc., and his Letters) to the venality of the curia. He even
suggested that Eugenius might have to leave Rome to get away from its corruption, *De consid.*, IV. 3.

[2] Luard's ed., V. 96.   [3] Coulton's ed., pp. 261 sq.

[4] Bernard of Cluny in his *de contemptu mundi* has the following lines:—

> *Roma dat omnibus omnia, dantibus omnia Romœ*
> *Cum pretio : quia jure ibi via, jus perit omne*
> *Ut rota labitur, ergo vocabitur hinc rota a Roma*
> *Roma nocens nocet, atque viam docet ipsa nocendi*
> *Jura relinquere, lucra requirere, pallia vendi*

Poems, ascribed to Walter Map, abound in bitter invective against the wide-open mouths of the cardinals which only money could fill.   In one of them, the *Ruin of Rome*, the city is compared to the waters between Scylla and Charybdis, " more capacious of gold than of ships."

" The meeting place of our pirates, the cardinals"

> *Ibi latrat Scylla rapax et Charybdis auri capax*
> *Potius quam navium, ibi cursus galearum*
> *Et concursus piratarum, id est cardinalium.*

There, at that deep gulf, are the Syrtes and Sirens who threaten the whole world with shipwreck, the gulf which has the mouth of a man but the heart of a devil.   There the cardinals sell the patrimony, wearing the aspect of Peter and having the heart of Nero, looking like lambs and having the nature of wolves.[1]   In a conversation, purporting to have occurred between Thomas Aquinas and the pope, the pope said, as he showed the theologian the papal treasure-room, " Thomas, Peter could now no longer say as he once said to the lame man 'silver and gold have I none.'"   "Nor," was Thomas' reply, "has his successor the power now to lay his hand on the lame man and heal him."

§ 125.   *Bishops.*

Although the episcopate lost some of its ancient prestige through the centralization of power in the papacy, the incumbents of the great sees were fully as powerful as the greater secular princes.   The old theory, that all bishops are the successors of Peter, had a waning number of open advocates. Bernard said[2] that, like the pope, they were pastors and porters of the kingdom of heaven and fountains of authority, but, in power and rank, they were inferior to the pope who

---

[1] The *Latin Poems of Walter Mapes*, ed. by T. Wright, London, 1841, p. 218.

[2] *De consid.*, II. 8 ; III. 4 ; IV. 8.   After the resurrection, Peter went to Jesus on the lake.   The lake signified the world and Peter has charge over the world, and each Apostle charge over his own little boat.   James was satisfied with jurisdiction over Jerusalem and acknowledged Peter's authority over the entire Church.

is the immediate successor of the prince of the Apostles. A hundred years later Grosseteste still held to the equal dignity of all bishops as being successors of Peter.[1]

By the law of Gregory IX., archbishops took an oath of allegiance to the pope, and Martin V. (1417–1431) extended it so as to include all bishops. Gregory IX. and other popes made this oath the ground of demands for military service. Long before this, in 1139, Innocent II. had addressed the bishops as occupying a relation to the papal see such as vassals occupy to their prince. They were to be known as " bishops by the grace of God and the Apostolic see." [2] Innocent III. distinctly stated that bishops receive their authority by the grace of the pope in whom resides the fulness of authority.[3] The confirmation of bishops by the pope was made a fixed rule by Nicolas III. (1277–1280) [4] And the ancient right which bishops had exercised of resigning their sees was now denied and the privilege made dependent upon the pope's dispensation.

After the Concordat of Worms, 1122, the appointment of bishops by princes and other lay patrons, in theory, ceased. Pope after pope declared the right of election belonged to the cathedral chapters. But, in fact, the elections were not free.   Princes ignored the rights of the chapters and dictated the nominees, or had unsatisfactory elections set aside by appealing to Rome.   In France and Spain, a royal writ was required before an election could be had and the royal acceptance of the candidate was interposed as a condition of consecration.   In England, in spite of the settlement between Anselm and Henry I., the rights of the chapters were constantly set aside, and disputed elections were

[1] Letter 23, Luard's ed., *principes ecclesiastici qui vicem Petri tenent.*

[2] In a vigorous letter to Innocent, Bernard complained that bishops were deprived by the curia of the power to right wrongs in their own dioceses and to exercise the function of the keys. *Ep.*, 178, Migne, 182. 310.

[3] See Döllinger, *Papstthum*, pp. 73, 409 sq. Innocent referred back to Leo I., who had written to a bishop of Thessalonica, *vices enim nostras ita tuæ credidimus charitati, ut in partem sis vocatus sollicitudinis, non in plenitudinem potestatis. Ep.*, VI. Migne, LIV. 671.

[4] *Lib. Sextus*, I. 6, 16, Friedberg's ed., II. 954 sqq.

a constant recurrence. By John's charter, the election
took place in the chapter house of the cathedral, and the
king might exercise the right of nomination and confirmation.[1] In the case of disputed elections, the pope acted as
umpire and might set aside all candidates and order a new
election, as did Innocent III., in the case of Stephen Langton. The Fourth Lateran established the rule that a chapter,
failing to reach a conclusion in three months, forfeited the
right of election.

The law requiring a bishop to be at least thirty years old[2]
and of legitimate birth was often set aside. Geoffrey, natural son of Henry II., was appointed bishop of Lincoln before
he was twenty and for six years he enjoyed the revenues of
the see without being ordained priest. He was afterwards
made archbishop of York. Gerlach of Nassau was made
archbishop at twenty. We have in this period no case quite
so flagrant as that of Hugh of Vermandois, about 930, who,
after poisoning the archbishop of Rheims, put his own son, a
child of five, into the office. Disregard of the age-limit
reached its height in the latter half of the fifteenth century.
The larger sees were a tempting prize to noblemen, and
Innocent III. felt it necessary to emphasize merit as a qualification for the episcopal office as against noble birth.

The important right of canonization was withdrawn from
the bishops by Alexander III., 1181, and its exercise thenceforth restricted to the pope. Bishops were not popular
material for sainthood. Otto of Bamberg is a shining exception.

From the time of Otto the Great, German bishops had the
rank of princes.[3] In France, England, and other countries,
they were raised to the dignity of the peerage. The three
German sees of Treves, Mainz, and Cologne probably enjoyed
larger revenues and authority than any other sees in Western Christendom. They gave to the territory along the
Rhine the name of the " priests' alley." Their three prel-

---

[1] Stubbs, *Const. Hist.*, III. 303 sq., refers to "the shadowy freedom
of election."   [2] Third Lat., *can.* 3.   [3] Hauck, III. 28 sqq.

ates were among the seven electors of the empire. In
Northern Germany, the see of Bremen retained its relative
importance. Lund was the metropolitan see of Denmark
and Scandinavia. In France, the ancient archbishoprics of
Lyons and Rheims perpetuated the rank and influence of an
earlier period. In England, after the see of Canterbury,
Lincoln was the most influential diocese.

The cathedral and collegiate chapters grew in importance.
In the earlier part of this period, it was still the custom for
the canons belonging to a chapter to live under the same
roof and eat at the same table. In the thirteenth century a
great change took place. With the increasing wealth of the
churches, the chapters threatened to assert the rights of
distinct corporations, and to become virtually independent of
the bishops.[1] Prebends or stalls — *stallum in choro* — were
furnished with endowments of their own. The sons of
nobles coveted and secured these places which brought
emolument and influence without work. The canons lived
apart by themselves, supported by the revenues of their
stalls and their portion of the cathedral income. No places
were more often filled by papal appointment in the way of
reservation and expectance.[2]

The archdeacon, still called as of old "the bishop's eye,"
assisted the bishop in matters of diocesan administration,
visited churches, made investigation of the sacred robes and
vessels, adjudicated disputes, presided over synods, and,
as provided for by the English Constitutions of Otho, instructed the clergy on the sacraments and other subjects.
This official threatened to assume the rank of bishop-coadju-
tor, or even to become independent of the bishop.[3] His

---

[1] *capitula clausa.* Hurter, III. 355, pronounced the change a sign of decay.

[2] The prospective occupants of stalls were called *canonici in herbis*, canons
on the commons ; the actual incumbents, *canonici in floribus et fructibus.*
The Third Lateran forbade the appointment of canons to stalls not yet
vacant, but Alexander IV., 1254, sanctioned the appointment of as many as
four such expectants. See Art. *Kapitel*, Herzog, X. 38.

[3] Third Lat., *can.* 6, Friedberg, pp. 188 sqq. Innocent III. recognized the
archdeacon as the bishop's representative. Hurter, III. 362 sq.

duties are frequently dwelt upon by English, German, and French synods. The large dioceses employed a plurality of them. As early as the eleventh century, the see of Treves had five, Cologne six, and Halberstadt thirty.[1] After the Norman Conquest, the English dioceses adopted the system. Lincoln included the archdeaconries of Lincoln, Leicester, Stow, Buckingham, Huntingdon, Northampton, Oxford, and Bedford. Archdeacons were often appointed at an early age, and it became the custom for them to go abroad to pursue the study of canon law before entering upon the duties of their office. They were inclined to allow themselves more liberties than other ecclesiastics, and John of Salisbury propounded the question whether an archdeacon could be saved. Among the better known of the English archdeacons were Thomas à Becket, Walter Map, archdeacon of Oxford, and Peter of Blois, archdeacon of London. Peter complained to Innocent III. that he received no financial support from the 120 churches of London.

A hard struggle was carried on to remove the hand of the secular power from church funds. Synods, local and œcumenical, threatened severest penalties upon any interference of this kind. In 1209, Otto IV. renounced the old right of spoliation — *jus spolii* or *jus exuviarum*, — whereby the secular prince might seize the revenues of vacant sees and livings, and appropriate them to himself. The Church was exempted by Innocent III. from all civil taxation at the hands of laymen, except as it was sanctioned by pope or bishop, and lay patrons were enjoined against withholding or seizing for their own use church livings to which they had the right of appointment.[2] The goods, laid aside by clerics from their livings, were the property of the Church,[3] and in case a priest died intestate, it was, in some parts, the privilege of the bishop to administer his estate. Priests were

---

[1] Hauck, IV. 10 sqq.   Metz, Toul, Mainz, etc., also employed a number of archdeacons.

[2] Third Lat., *can.* 19, Fourth Lat., *can.* 46.   This principle was recognized by Frederick II., 1220.   Also Narbonne, 1127, *can.* 12 ; Toulouse, 1229, *can.* 20 sq., etc.   [3] Third Lat., *can.* 15.

exempt from personal taxation. For prescribed taxes, free gifts so called, were substituted. Peter of Blois commended the piety of certain princes who declined to levy taxes upon churches and other ecclesiastical institutions, even for necessary expenditures, such as the repair of city walls; but met them, if not from their own resources, from booty taken from enemies.[1]

Besides the usual income accruing from landed endowments and tithes, the bishop had other sources of revenue. He might at pleasure levy taxes for the spiritual needs of his see,[2] and appropriate the first year's income of newly appointed priests. Other additions, from the eleventh century on, came in the way of fees and collections for indulgences and gifts at the dedication of churches and altars, and the benediction of cemeteries. Abælard speaks of the throngs which assembled on such festal occasions, and the large offerings which were, in part, payments for the relaxation of penances.[3]

As for the pastoral fidelity and morals of the bishops, there was much ground for complaint, and there are also records of exemplary prelates. As a whole, the prelates were a militant class. No pope of this age wore armor as did John XII., and, at a later time, Julius II., though there were few if any pontiffs, who did not encourage war under the name of religion. Bishops and abbots were often among the bravest warriors and led their troops into the thickest of the fight both on European soil and under Syrian suns. Monks and priests wore armor and went into battle. When the pope asked for the release of the fighting bishop of Beauvais, whom Richard Cœur de Lion had seized, Richard sent him the bishop's coat of mail clotted with blood and the words taken from the story of Joseph, " We found this. Is it not thy son's coat ? " Archbishop Christian of Mainz (d. 1183) is said to have felled, with his own hand, nine antagonists in the Lombard war, and to have struck out the teeth

---

[1] *Epp.*, 112, 121.   [2] *Subsidium charitativum.*   Third Lateran.
[3] *Ethica*, 25, Migne, 178. 672 sq.

of thirty others. Absalom and Andrew of Lund were famous warriors.[1] So were Odo of Bayeux, Roger of York, and
Geoffrey, his successor, and many other English prelates.
The abbot Henry, afterwards archbishop of Narbonne, went
at the head of the armies sent against the Albigenses, and
did more, wearing the monk's garb, to encourage bloodshed
than he could have done in military dress.

The chastity of the bishops was often open to just suspicion. The Christian, already referred to, a loyal supporter
of Barbarossa, kept a harem.[2] When the confirmation of
Geoffrey Riddel to the see of Ely was being prosecuted at
the papal court, and Geoffrey was absent, the bishop of Orleans facetiously explained his absence by saying, " He hath
married a wife, and therefore he cannot come."[3] The case
of Henry of Liége, prince-bishop of Liége, is perhaps the
most notorious case. He was cited before Gregory X. at
the second council of Lyons, and forced to resign. He was
an illiterate, and could not read the book presented to him.
For thirty years he had led a shameless life. Two abbesses
and a nun were among his concubines and he boasted of having had fourteen children in twenty-two months. The worst
seems to have occurred before he was made priest. Innocent
IV. had been his strong friend. Salimbene tells the popular
tale of his day that the saintly Cistercian, Geoffroi de Pé-
ronne, came back from the other world and announced that
if he had accepted the bishopric of Tournai, as the pope
urged him to do, he would have been burning in hell. From
the pages of this chronicler we have the pictures of many
unworthy prelates given to wine and pleasure, but also of
some who were model pastors.[4]

The prelates of Germany had no better reputation than
those of Italy, and Cæsar of Heisterbach[5] reports the conversation of a Paris clerk, who declared that he " could
believe all things, but it was not possible for him to believe
that any German bishop could be saved." When asked the

---

[1] See Hurter, III. 292 sqq., for a list of warrior prelates.
[2] Gregorovius, IV. 610.   [3] Stubbs' ed. of *Hoveden*, II. 58.
[4] Coulton's ed., p. 264 sqq.   [5] *Dial.*, II. 27, Strange's ed., I. 99.

reason for such a judgment, he replied, that the German prelates carried both swords, waged wars, and were more concerned about the pay of soldiers than the salvation of the souls committed to them.

The other side to this picture is not so apt to be presented. Chroniclers are more addicted to point out the scandalous lives of priests than to dwell upon clerical fidelity. There were faithful and good bishops and abbots. The names of Anselm of Canterbury and Hugh of Lincoln, Bernard and Peter the Venerable only need to be mentioned to put us on our guard against accepting the cases of unworthy and profligate prelates which have been handed down as indicating a universal rule.

§ 126.   *The Lower Clergy.*

The cure of souls — *regimen animarum* — was pronounced by the Fourth Lateran, following Gregory the Great, to be the art of arts, and bishops were admonished to see to it that men capable in knowledge and of fit morals be appointed to benefices. The people were taught to respect the priest for the sake of his holy office and the fifth commandment was adduced as divine authority for submission to him.[1]

The old rule was repeated, making the canonical age for consecration to the priesthood twenty-five. Councils and popes laid constant stress upon the priest's moral obligations, such as integrity, temperance in the use of strong drink,[2] simplicity in diet and dress, abstinence from the practice of usury.[3] He was forbidden to frequent taverns, to play at dice, to attend theatrical and mimic performances, and to allow dances in church buildings and church yards.

[1] Innocent III. *Ep.*, II. 142. "Hundreds of times," says Hurter, III. 388, does this pope insist upon obedience from the priest to his superior and says ' the evil of disobedience is the crime of idolatry,' *inobedientiæ malum est scelus idolatriæ.*

[2] Fourth Lateran, *can.* 15.

[3] The practice of usury so frequently forbidden to priests was also forbidden to the laity, *laicis usura dampnabilis est.   Gratiani Decr.* causa, XIV. 4, 9, Friedberg's ed., I. 737.

The old rules were renewed, debarring from the sacerdotal office persons afflicted with bodily defects, and Innocent III. complained of the bishop of Angoulême for ordaining a priest who had lost a thumb.[1]

Beginning with the twelfth century, the number of parishes increased with great rapidity both in the rural districts and in the towns. In German cities the division of the old parishes was encouraged by the citizens, as in Freiburg, Mainz, Worms, and Lübeck, and they insisted upon the right of choosing their pastor.[2] On the other hand, the convents were busy establishing churches and, in Germany, there were thousands under their control.[3] The eleventh and twelfth centuries were a busy time of church building.

What occurred in Germany occurred also in England. But here the endowment of churches and chapels by devout and wealthy laymen was more frequent. Such parishes, it is true, often fell to the charge of the orders, but also a large share of them to the charge of the cathedral chapters and bishops.

Clerical incomes varied fully as much in those days as they do now, if not more. The poorer German priests received from one-tenth to one-twentieth of the incomes of more fortunate rectors and canons.[4] The Fourth Lateran made small salaries responsible for a poorly trained ministry.

The clergy depended for their maintenance chiefly upon the income from lands and the tithe. The theory was that the tenth belonged to the Church, "for the earth is the Lord's and the fulness thereof." The principle was extended to include the tithe of the fish-catch, the product of the chase, and the product of commerce.[5] The clergy also received fees for special sacerdotal services from bap-

---

[1] *Ep.*, I. 231.   [2] Hauck, IV. 29 sqq.

[3] The Gregorian *Decretals* discuss chapels controlled by monks. Friedberg's ed., II. 607 sqq.

[4] Hauck, IV. 47 sq. In some dioceses priests were said to receive only one-sixteenth of the tithes due them, the rest being appropriated by the lay patron or bishop. So the synod of Mainz, Hefele, VI. 75.

[5] The last claim, made by the archbishop of Bergen, was rejected by Innocent III. *Ep.*, I. 217.

tism to burial and rites pertaining to the soul after death. Such fees became general after the twelfth century, but not without vigorous protests against them.   The Second Lateran and other synods [1] forbade priests making charges for the administration of baptism, marriage, extreme unction, and other rites, and for sepulture.   The ground was taken by Innocent III. that, while gifts for such services were proper, they should be spontaneous and not forced.   The Fourth Lateran bade laymen see they were not overlooked.

Priests receiving their benefices from laymen were likened to thieves who came not in by the door but climbed in some other way.   The lay patron had the right of nomination — *presentatio*.   To the bishop belonged the right of confirmation — *concessio*.   Laymen venturing to confer a living without the consent of the ecclesiastical authority exposed themselves to the sentence of excommunication.[2] Stories were current of clerics who had bought their way to ordination and to benefices, who afterwards gnawed through their tongues in remorse.[3]   The system of pluralities was practised in spite of the decrees of œcumenical and local synods.[4]

The ideal of a faithful priest was not a preacher but one who administered the sacraments and other solemn rites upon the living and the dead.   Restricted as the education of the priest was, it greatly surpassed that of his lay brother, and it was not so meagre as it has often been represented. There were writers who held up the ignorance of the clergy to scorn, but it is dangerous to base wide generalizations on

---

[1] Piacenza, 1095; London, 1138, 1175; Oxford, 1222 ; Treves, 1227, etc. Cæsar of Heisterbach, *Dial.*, II. 7, tells of priests who for bribes gave burial to unchurched persons.

[2] First Lat., *can.* 9; Second Lat., *can.* 10; Third Lat., *can.* 17; synods of Nismes, 1096, Troyes, 1107, Rheims, 1119, etc.   The Gregorian Decretals are full on the subject of patrons and their rights.   Friedberg's ed., II. 609–622.   Innocent III. laid down the rule, *quod beneficia non possint conferri per sœculares.   Ep.*, I. 64, IX. 234, quoted by Hurter, III. 381.

[3] Hurter, III. 395.

[4] Third Lat., *can.* 13 ; Fourth Lat., *can.* 29 ; Paris, 1212, etc.

3 F

such statements. Statements of another kind can be adduced to show that a class of priests had literary interests as wide as the age was familiar with. The schools that existed were for the training of the clergy. Synods assumed that clerics could read and prescribed that they should read their breviaries even while travelling on journeys. Peter of Blois urged them to read the Scriptures, which he called David's harp, a plough working up the fallow field of the heart, and which he compared to drink, medicine, balsam, and a weapon. He also warned priests against allowing themselves "to be enticed away by the puerilities of heathen literature and the inventions of philosophers." When the universities arose, a large opportunity was offered for culture and the students who attended them were clerics or men who were looking forward to holy orders. The synod of Cologne, 1260, probably struck the medium in regard to the culture of the clergy, when it declared that it did not demand eminent learning of clerics but that they know how to read and properly sing the church service.

The function of parish-preaching was not altogether neglected. Bishops were enjoined by the Fourth Lateran to appoint men capable of preaching in all cathedral and conventual churches. In the eleventh century there was scarcely a German parish in which there was not some preaching during the year, and subsequent to that time, sermons were delivered regularly.[1] The sermons were sometimes in Latin and sometimes in German. Those which are preserved abound in stories and practical lessons and show more dependence upon the Fathers than upon the Scriptures. In England and other parts of Europe sermonizing was a less common practice. English priests were required to give expositions of the Creed, the Ten Commandments, the evangelical precepts, the seven works of mercy, the seven car-

[1] Hauck, IV. 40. Cruel, *Deutsche Predigt*, etc., expresses a less favorable judgment and estimates that one-half of the German clergy in the 13th century were uneducated and unable to preach. Coulton, p. 277, referring more especially to Italy, speaks "of the abyss of ignorance among the clergy at which we may well stagger."

dinal virtues, and the seven sacraments, and to cover these subjects once a quarter. Grosseteste called upon them to be diligent in visiting the sick night and day, to preach, and to carefully read the Scriptures that they might be able to give a reason for the hope that was in them.[1] In the regions infected with the Albigensian heresy, instruction was ordered given to children in the articles of the Catholic faith. The mendicant monks started out as preachers and supplied a popular demand. The ignorance of the priesthood at times called for inhibitions of preaching, as by the synod of Oxford, 1281.

Not the least important among the priest's functions was the supervision of wills that the Church might come in for seemly remembrance. State laws in conflict with this custom were set aside. Abuses were recognized by synods, and the synod of Paris, 1212, ordered that laymen should not be compelled to make provision in their wills for the payment of thirty mortuary masses. The priest's signature insured the validity of a will, and some synods made the failure to call in a priest to attest the last testament a ground of excommunication.[2]

Turning to the priest as a member of society, the Church, with unwavering emphasis, insisted upon his independence of the secular tribunal. In the seventh century, Heraclius had granted to the clergy, even in the case of criminal offences, the right of trial in ecclesiastical courts. The Isidorian fiction fully stated this theory. These and other privileges led many to enter the minor clerical orders who had no intention of performing ecclesiastical functions. Council after council pronounced the priest's person inviolate and upon no other matter was Innocent III. more insistent.[3] Violence offered to a priest was punished with the anathema, and civil au-

---

[1] The Constitutions of Otho, 1237. Grosseteste, *Letters*, LII., Luard's ed., p. 154 sqq.

[2] So the synods of Cashel, 1171, Narbonne, 1127, Rouen, 1231, etc.

[3] *Ep.*, VI. 199, etc. Writing to the abp. of Pisa, he expressed amazement that the abp. should have declared a cleric, receiving injury from a layman, might submit his case to a lay tribunal. *Ep.*, IX. 63.

thorities venturing to cite clerics to appear before them incurred the same penalty.[1] Such legislation did not, however, bring complete immunity from injury or exempt church
property from spoliation. In England, Thomas à Becket is
the most noteworthy example. A bishop of Caithness had
his tongue cut out. A Spanish bishop received the same
treatment at the hands of a king of Aragon. In Germany,
Bishop Dietrich of Naumburg, a learned man, was murdered,
1123; as were also Conrad, bishop of Utrecht, 1099; Arnold,
bishop of Merseburg, 1126, and other bishops. Lawrence,
archdeacon of York, was murdered in the vestibule of his
church by a knight. The life of Norbert of Magdeburg was
attempted twice.[2] The principle which the Church recognized in the punishment of clerical crimes was laid down by
Cœlestin III., 1192. Theft, homicide, perjury, or other
"mortal crimes" were punished with deposition. If the
priest persisted in committing offences, he was excommunicated and, at last, turned over to the state for punishment.[3]

There was no little complaint against the application of
the canon law. Roger Bacon complained bitterly against
the time given to its study in Bologna. He declared its
study was obliterating the distinction between the clerical
and lay professions. The doctors of law called themselves
clerks though they had not the tonsure and took to themselves wives. He demanded that, if clergymen and laymen
were to be subjected to the same law, it should be the law of
England for Englishmen, and of France for Frenchmen and
not the law of Lombardy.

Clerical manners were a constant subject of conciliar action.
Ordination afforded no immunity from vanity and love of
ostentation. The extravagance of bishops and other clergy
in dress and ornaments gave rise to much scandal. The

---

[1] Clermont, 1095, 1130; Rheims, 1131, 1148; Second Lat., Third Lat.,
can. 12, etc.

[2] Innocent III. *Ep.*, V. 79; M. Paris, IV. 578; Hauck, IV. 83 sqq.;
M. Paris, IV. 496; *vita Norberti*, 18. Salembene reports the murder of a
bishop of Mantua in a political quarrel. Coulton's ed., p. 35.

[3] Greg., *Decret.*, II. 1, 10, Friedberg's ed., II. 242.

Third Lateran sought to check vain display by forbidding a
retinue of more than 40 or 50 horse to archbishops, 25 to
cardinals, and 20 or 30 to bishops.   Archdeacons were reduced to the paltry number of 5 or 7 and deans to 2.   There
was some excuse for retinues in an age of violence with no
provision for public police.   The chase had its peculiar fascination and bishops were forbidden to take hounds or falcons
with them on their journeys of visitation.   Dogs and hunting
were in localities denied to clergymen altogether.[1]

The fondness of the clergy for gay apparel was often rebuked.   In Southern France, clergymen ventured to wear
red and green colors and to substitute for the close-fitting
garment the graceful and flowing open robe.   They followed
the fashions of the times in ornamenting themselves with
buckles and belts of gold and silver and hid the tonsure by
wearing their hair long.   They affected the latest styles of
shoes and paraded about in silk gloves and gilded spurs, with
gilded breastbands on their horses and on gilded saddles.[2]

Full as the atmosphere of the age was of war-clamor, and
many warring prelates as there were, the legislation of
the Church was against a fighting clergy.   The wearing of
swords and dirks and of a military dress was repeatedly forbidden to them.   Wars for the extermination of heresy were
in a different category from feuds among Catholic Christians.
It was in regard to the former that Peter des Roches, bishop
of Winchester, said, " As for the enemies of Christ, we shall
slay them and purify the face of the earth, that the whole
world may be subject to one Catholic Church and become one
fold and one shepherd."[3]   Priests were prohibited from attending executions, and also tournaments and duels, on the ground
that these contests presented the possibility of untimely death
to the contestants.   In case a combatant received a mortal
wound he was entitled to the sacrament but was denied

[1] Third Lat., etc.

[2] Fourth Lat., *can.* 16 ; Soissons, 1079, London, 1102, 1175 ; Rheims,
1171 ; Paris, 1212 ; Montpellier, 1215, etc.   Innocent III.'s letters also make
reference to the worldly garb of the priests.   See Hurter, III. 391.

[3] M. Paris, *an.* 1238.

ecclesiastical burial.[1]   The Fourth Lateran solemnly enjoined
ecclesiastics against pronouncing the death sentence or executing it, and the same council forbade surgery also, so far
as it involved cutting and burning, to deacons and sub-
deacons as well as to priests.

The period opens with the dark picture of clerical morals
by Peter Damiani who likened them to the morals of the
Cities of the Plain.   Bernard, a hundred years later, in
condemning clergymen for the use of military dress, declared
they had neither the courage of the soldier nor the virtues
of the clergyman.[2]   A hundred years later still Grosseteste,
in describing the low moral and religious state of the English
people, made the immoral lives of the clergy responsible
for it.

Dice were played even on the altars of Notre Dame, Paris,[3]
and dice-playing is often forbidden to priests in the acts
of synods.   Wine-drinking to excess was also a fault of the
clergy, and Salimbene knew Italian clerics who sold wine and
kept taverns.[4]   According to Cæsar of Heisterbach, wine
often flowed at the dedication of churches.   A Devonshire
priest was accustomed to brew his beer in the church-
building.

The most famous passage of all is the passage in which
Jacob de Vitry describes conditions in Paris.   Fornication
among clergymen, he says, was considered no sin.   Loose
women paraded the streets and, as it were by force, drew
them to their lodgings.   And if they refused, the women
pointed the finger at them, crying " Sodomites."   Things
were so bad and the leprosy so incurable that it was considered honorable to have one or more concubines.   In the
same building, school was held upstairs and prostitutes lived
below.   In the upper story masters read and in the lower
story loose women plied their trade.   In one part of the

---

[1] Rouen, 1083 ; Soissons, 1079 ; Clermont, 1095 ; Fourth Lateran ; Treves,
1227 ; Rouen, 1231.   The Constitutions of Otho, 1237, etc.

[2] *De consid.*, III. 5.   *habitu milites, quæstu clericos, actu neutrum exhibent.*

[3] *Chart. univ. Paris*, I. No. 470.

[4] Coulton's ed., 272 sqq.

building women and their procurors disputed and in another part the clergy held forth in their disputations.[1]

The Fourth Lateran arraigned bishops for spending the nights in revelry and wantonness.   The archbishopric of Rouen was occupied for 113 years by three prelates of scandalous fame.   Two of them were bastards of the ducal house and all rivalled or excelled the barons round about in turbulence and license.   A notorious case in high places was that of the papal legate, Cardinal John of Crema.   He held a council which forbade priests and the lower clergy to have wives or concubines; but, sent to the bishop of Durham to remonstrate with him over the debauchery which ruled in his palace, the cardinal himself yielded to a woman whom the bishop provided.   The bishop regarded it as a jest when he pointed out the cardinal in the act of fornication.

Marriage and concubinage continued to be practised by the clergy in spite of the Hildebrandian legislation.   Innocent III. agreed with Hildebrand that a priest with a family is divided in his affections and cannot give to God and the Church his full allegiance in time and thought.[2]   Writers, like Salimbene and Cæsar of Heisterbach, were severe on married priests.   According to the Fourth Lateran, bishops not only violated the canons of the Church themselves by committing the "crime of the flesh," as Gregory VII. called it, but winked at their violation by priests for a money-compensation.   A common saying among priests was, *si non caste, caute;* that is, "if not chaste, at least cautious."   In this way Paul's words were misinterpreted when he said, "If they cannot contain, let them marry."   Bonaventura, who knew the facts, declared "that very many of the clergy are notoriously unchaste, keeping concubines in their houses and elsewhere or notoriously sinning here and there with many persons."[3]

Conditions must have been bad indeed, if they equalled the priestly customs of the fourteenth century and the example set by the popes in the latter half of the fifteenth.   Who will

---

[1] See text; Rashdall, *Universities*, II. 690.

[2] *Ep.*, I. 469, VI. 103, etc., Migne, 214. 436; 215. 110.

[3] *Libellus apologet.* and *Quare fratres Minores prædicant.*

forget the example and mistresses of the first and only Scotch cardinal, Archbishop Beaton, who condemned Patrick Hamilton and Wishart to death! Were not the Swiss Reformers Bullinger and Leo Jud sons of priests, and was not Zwingli, in spite of his offence against the law of continence, in good standing so long as he remained in the papal communion!

The violation of the ecclesiastical law of celibacy was, however, by no means in all cases a violation of the moral law. Without the ceremony of marriage, many a priest lived honorably with the woman he had chosen, and cared for and protected his family. The Roman pontiff's ordinance, setting aside an appointment of the Almighty, was one of the most offensive pieces of papal legislation and did unspeakable injury to the Church.

§ 127.   *The Councils.*

The legislation of the œcumenical and local synods of this age gives the most impressive evidence of the moral ideals of the Church and its effort to introduce moral reforms. The large number of councils, as compared with the period just before 1050, was a healthy sign.[1] Their time was largely taken up with disciplinary and moral subjects. They legislated upon the relation of the Church to the empire, and the election of the pope, against simony and clerical marriage, upon heresy and measures for its repression, upon the crusades and the truce of God, on the details of clerical conduct and dress, and upon the rites of worship. The doctrine of transubstantiation, defined at the Fourth Lateran, was the only doctrine which was added by œcumenical authority to the list of the great dogmas handed down from the early Church.

At one period one subject, and at another, another subject, was prominent. The character of the legislation also differed with the locality. The synods in Rome, during the

---

[1] Hergenröther, *Kathol. Kirchenrecht,* p. 342, speaks of the rarity of synods from 900–1050 as a sign of the laxity of Catholic discipline.

latter half of the eleventh century, discussed clerical celibacy,
simony, and investiture by laymen. The synods of Southern
France and Spain, from the year 1200, abound in decrees
upon the subject of heresy. The synods of England and
Germany were more concerned about customs of worship
and clerical conduct.

A notable feature is the attendance of popes on synods
held outside of Rome. Leo IX. attended synods in France
and Germany, as well as in Italy. Urban II. presided at
the great synod of Clermont, 1095. Innocent II. attended a
number of synods outside of Rome. Alexander III. was
present at the important synod of Tours, where Thomas à
Becket sat at his right. Lucius III. presided at the council
of Verona, 1184. Innocent IV. and Gregory X. were present at the first and second councils of Lyons. Such synods
had double weight from the presence of the supreme head
of Christendom. The synods may be divided into three
classes: —

I. *Local Synods*, 1050–1122. — The synods held in this,
the Hildebrandian period, were a symptom of a new era
in Church history. The chief synods were held in Rome
and, beginning with 1049, they carried through the reformatory legislation, enforcing clerical celibacy and forbidding
simony. The legislation against lay-investiture culminated
in the Lenten synods at Rome, 1074 and 1075, presided over
by Gregory VII. Local synods, especially in France and
England, repeated this legislation. The method of electing a pope was settled by the Roman synod held by Nicolas,
and confirmed by the Third Lateran, 1179. The doctrine
of the Lord's Supper, as advocated by Berengar, d. 1088,
called forth action at Rome and Vercelli, 1050, and again at
Rome, 1059 and 1079. The legislation bearing on the conquest of the Holy Places was inaugurated at Piacenza and
more seriously at the synod of Clermont, both held in 1095.

II. *The Œcumenical Councils.* — Six general councils were
held within a period of one hundred and fifty years, 1123–
1274, as against eight held between 325–869, or a period of
five hundred years. The first four go by the name of the

Lateran Councils, from the Lateran in Rome, where they assembled. The last two were held in Lyons. They were called by the popes, and temporal sovereigns had nothing to do in summoning them.[1] They were presided over by popes, and the dockets of business were prepared by papal direction. The pope ratified their decrees. The first canon of the First Lateran ran, " by the authority of the Apostolic see, we forbid," etc., — *auctoritate sedis apostol. prohibemus*. It is true that the assent of the assembled prelates was assumed or, if expressly mentioned, the formula ran, " with the assent of the holy synod," or " the holy synod being in session," — *sacro approbante concilio*, or *sacro præsente concilio*. So it was with the Fourth Lateran. The six œcumenical councils are: —

1. The First Lateran, 1123, called by Calixtus II., is listed by the Latins as the Ninth œcumenical council. Its chief business was to ratify the Concordat of Worms. It was the first œcumenical council to forbid the marriage of priests. It renewed Urban II.'s legislation granting indulgences to the Crusaders.

2. The Second Lateran, 1139, opened with an address by Innocent II., consummated the close of the recent papal schism and pronounced against the errors of Arnold of Brescia.

3. The Third Lateran, 1179, under the presidency of Alexander III., celebrated the restoration of peace between the Church and the empire and, falling back on the canon of the Second Lateran, legislated against the Cathari and Patarenes. It ordered separate churches and burial-grounds for lepers. Two hundred and eighty-seven, or, according to other reports, three hundred or three hundred and ninety-six bishops attended.

4. The Fourth Lateran or Twelfth œcumenical, 1215, marks an epoch in the Middle Ages. It established the Inquisition and formulated the doctrine of transubstantiation, the two most far-reaching decrees of the mediæval

---

[1] Döllinger-Friedrich, *D. Papstthum*, p. 88 sqq.

Church.   Innocent III. dominated the council, and its disciplinary and moral canons are on a high plane and would
of themselves have made the assemblage notable.   It was
here that the matter of Raymund of Toulouse was adjudicated, and here the crusade was appointed for 1217 which
afterwards gave Frederick II. and Innocent's two immediate
successors so much trouble.   A novel feature was the
attendance of a number of Latin patriarchs from the East,
possessing meagre authority, but venerable titles.   The decisions of the council were quoted as authoritative by Bonaventura and Thomas Aquinas.[1]

5. The First council of Lyons, 1245, presided over by
Innocent IV., has its fame from the prosecution and deposition of the emperor Frederick II.   It also took up the distressed condition of Jerusalem and the menace of the Tartars
to Eastern Europe.

6. The Second council of Lyons or the Fourteenth œcumenical, 1274, was summoned by Gregory X., and attended
by five hundred bishops and one thousand other ecclesiastics.
Gregory opened the sessions with an address as Innocent III.
had opened the Fourth Lateran and Innocent IV. the First
council of Lyons.   The first of its thirty-one canons reaffirmed the doctrine of the procession of the Holy Spirit
from the Son.   It repeated the legislation of the Fourth Lateran, prohibiting the institution of new monastic orders.   The
council's chief significance was the attempt to reunite the
churches of the West and the East, the latter being represented by an imposing delegation.

These œcumenical assemblages have their importance
from the questions they discussed and the personalities they
brought together.   They had an important influence in uniting all parts of Western Christendom and in developing the
attachment to the Apostolic see, as the norm of Church unity.

III. *Local Synods*, 1122–1294. — Some of the local
synods of the twelfth and thirteenth centuries are of even
more importance than some of the œcumenical councils of the

---

[1] *Summa, supplem.*, VIII. 4, Migne, IV. 946, etc.

same period. If they were to be characterized for a single subject of legislation, it would be the repression of heresy. Some of them had far more than a local significance, as, for example, the synod of Tours, 1163, when Spain, Sicily, Italy, England, Scotland, and Ireland were represented as well as France. Alexander III. and seventeen cardinals were present. The synod legislated against heresy.

The synod of Verona, 1184, passed a lengthy and notable decree concerning the trial and punishment of heretics. It heard the plea of the Waldenses, but declined to grant it.

The synod of Treves, 1227, passed important canons bearing on the administration of the sacraments.

The synod of Toulouse, 1229, presided over by the papal legate, celebrated the close of the Albigensian crusades and perfected the code of the Inquisition. It has an unenviable distinction among the great synods on account of its decree forbidding laymen to have the Bible in their possession.

These synods were great events, enlightening the age and stirring up thought. Unwholesome as were their measures against ecclesiastical dissent and on certain other subjects, their legislation was, upon the whole, in the right direction of purity of morals and the rights of the people.

§ 128. *Church and Clergy in England.*

LITERATURE : I. The works of William of Malmesbury, William of Newburgh, Henry of Huntingdon, Roger of Wendover, M. Paris, Richard of Hoveden, John of Salisbury, Walter Map, Giraldus Cambrensis, Ordericus Vitalis, Peter of Blois, Grosseteste, etc.

II. PHILLIMORE: *The Eccles. Law of Engl.*, 2 vols. Lond., 1873, *Supplem.*, 1876. — STUBBS: *Select Charters of Engl. Const. Hist.*, 8th ed., Oxf., 1895 ; *Constit. Hist. of Engl.*, 6th ed., 1897, 3 vols. — GEE AND HARDY: *Documents Illustr. of Engl. Ch. Hist.*, Lond., 1896. — F. W. MAITLAND: *Rom. Canon Law in the Ch. of Engl.*, Lond., 1898. — JESSOPP: *The Coming of the Friars.* — H. D. TRAILL : *Social England, a Record of the Progress of the People*, etc., 2 vols. Lond., 2d ed., 1894. — W. R. W. STEPHENS: *A Hist. of the Engl. Church, 1066–1272*, Lond., 1901.— FREEMAN: *The Norman Conquest* and *William Rufus.* — Histt. of England and the Ch. of England, etc. — *Dict. of Nat. Biogr.*

With the Norman Conquest the Roman curia began to manifest anxious concern for the English Church and to reach out for her revenues. Reverent as the Saxon kings had been towards the pope, as was shown in their visits to Rome and the payment of Peter's Pence, the wild condition of the country during the invasions of the Danes offered little attraction to the Church rulers of the South. Henry of Huntingdon called the England of his day — the twelfth century — "Merrie England"[1] and said that Englishmen were a free people, free in spirit and free in tongue, with even more freedom in giving, having abundance for themselves and something to spare for their neighbors across the sea. The Romans were quick to find this out and treated the English Church as a rich mine to be worked. It is probable that in no other part of Christendom were such constant and unblushing demands made upon church patronage and goods.[2] On the other hand, in no country was so persistent a struggle maintained for popular rights in Church and state against the impositions both of pope and crown.

Among the first distinct papal encroachments upon the liberties of the English Church were the appointment of legates and the demand that the archbishop go to Rome to receive the pallium. The first legates to England seem to have been sent at the invitation of William the Conqueror, 1070, to take up the case of Stigand, the Saxon archbishop of Canterbury, who had espoused the cause of the antipope. It was not long before the appointment of foreign legates was resisted and the pope, after the refusal to receive several of his representatives, was forced to yield and made it a rule to associate the legatine authority with the archbishops of Canterbury and York, — a rule, however, which had many exceptions. The legates of English birth were called *legati nati* in distinction from the foreign appointees, called *legati a latere*.

The pope's right to interfere in the appointment of bishops and to fill benefices was asserted soon after the Conqueror's

---

[1] *Anglia plena jocis*. William Fitzstephen (quoted by Traill, I. 377 sq.) dwells upon the Englishman's love of sports ᴀᴜ that day, — football, boating, archery, etc.

[2] Haller, *Papsttum*, p. 27.

death. In such matters, the king showed an almost equally strong hand. Again and again the pope quashed the elections of chapters either upon his own motion or at the king's appeal. Eugenius III. set aside William, canonically chosen archbishop of York. Stephen Langton 1207, Edmund Rich 1234, the Franciscan Kilwardby 1273, Peckham 1279, and Reynolds 1313, all archbishops of Canterbury, were substituted for the candidates canonically elected. Bonaventura was substituted for William Langton, elected archbishop of York, 1264. Such cases were constantly recurring. Bishops, already consecrated, were set aside by the pope in virtue of his "fulness of power," as was the case when Richard de Bury, d. 1345, was substituted for Robert Graystanes in the see of Durham.

This violence, done to the rights of the chapters, led to a vast amount of litigation. Almost every bishop had to fight a battle at Rome before he obtained his see. Between 1215–1264 not fewer than thirty cases of contested episcopal elections were carried to Rome. It was a bad day when the pope or the king could not find a dissident minority in a chapter and, through appeals, secure a hearing at Rome and finally a reversal of the chapter's decision. Of the four hundred and seventy decretals of Alexander III., accepted by Gregory IX., about one hundred and eighty were directed to England.[1]

The regular appointment to benefices was also invalidated by the pernicious custom of papal reservations which threatened even in this period to include every high office in the English Church. A little later, in 1317, the supreme pontiff reserved for his own appointment the sees of Worcester, Hereford, Durham, and Rochester; in 1320 Lincoln and Winchester; in 1322, 1323 Lichfield and Winchester; 1325 Carlisle and Norwich; 1327 Worcester, Exeter, and Hereford.[2]

Another way by which the pope asserted his overlordship

[1] Maitland, p. 123 ; Jessopp gives many cases of these appeals.
[2] Stubbs, III. 322 sq.

in the English Church was the translation of a bishop from one see to another. This, said Matthew Paris (V. 228), " became custom so that one church seemed to be the paramour of the other."

The English clergy and the barons looked upon these practices with disfavor, and, as at the Mad Parliament, 1258, demanded the freedom of capitular elections. The Constitutions of Clarendon, 1164, clearly expressed the national opposition, but the pope continued to go his own way.

The convents, for the most part, escaped papal interference in the election of their abbots. The reason is to be sought in the support which the orders gave to the pope in his struggle to reduce the episcopate to subjection. Nor did the crown venture to interfere, repelled, no doubt, by the compact organization of the monastic orders, the order rising to the defence of an attacked abbey.

The participation of the English bishops in the House of Lords was based originally upon the tax of scutage. From this followed their equal right to deliberate upon public affairs with the barons. At a time when this body contained less than forty lay peers, it included twenty bishops and twenty-six abbots. Most of the bishops and abbots, it would seem, had houses in London, which had taken the place of Winchester as the centre of national life.[1] As the emoluments of the higher ecclesiastical dignities increased, they were sought and secured by noblemen for their sons and by members of the royal house. Odo, bishop of Bayeux, d. 1097, was the brother of William the Conqueror. Two of Stephen's nephews were made respectively bishop of Durham and archbishop of York. Ethelmar, brother of Henry III., received the see of Winchester, 1250,[2] and the archbishopric of Canterbury was provided for Henry's uncle, Boniface. Geoffrey, son of Henry II., was made bishop

---

[1] Fitzstephen, as quoted by Traill, I. 383.

[2] The king entered the chapter and forced the election. The pope yielded, but to prove " he had not sown on a barren coast without reaping benefit of harvest, at once made a demand of 5000 marks for a favorite." M. Paris, V. 179 sqq.

of Lincoln when a lad, and afterwards transferred to York. Among the men of humble birth who rose to highest ecclesiastical rank were Edmund Rich and Robert Kilwardby.

The honors of canonization were reached by Hugh of Lincoln, Rich of Canterbury, and Richard of Wyche, bishop of Chichester, not to speak of Anselm and Thomas à Becket. The cases of proud and warring prelates were numerous, and the custom whereby bishops held the chief offices at the court was not adapted to develope the religious virtues. Richard Flambard, bishop of Durham under William Rufus, Hugh, bishop of Lichfield, 1188–1195, and Peter des Roches of Winchester, 1205–1238, supporter of John, are among the more flagrant examples of prelates who brought no virtues to their office and learned none. William Longchamp, bishop of Ely and favorite of Richard I., was followed by a retinue of 1000 men.[1]   The council of London, 1237, presided over by the cardinal legate, Otho, reminded the bishops of their duty to "sow the word of life in the field of the Lord." And, lest they should forget their responsibilities, they were to listen twice a year to the reading of their oath of consecration.

The English chapters were divided almost equally between the two classes of clergy, monks and seculars. To the former class belonged Canterbury, Winchester, Durham, Norwich, Coventry, Rochester, Worcester, Ely, and Bath. The chapters of York, London, Exeter, Lichfield, Wells, Hereford, Lincoln, Salisbury, Llandaff, St. Asaph, St. David's, and Chichester were made up of secular clergy. As the chapters asserted the rights of distinct corporations, their estates were treated as distinct from those of the bishop. It not infrequently happened that the bishop lost all influence in his chapter. The dean, in case the canons were seculars, and the prior, in case they were monks, actu-

---

[1] Hurter, III. 331 sqq., speaks of the English bishops in the time of Innocent III. as most corrupt.   Stubbs, III. 327 sq., finds it to the credit of the bishops that there were so few instances of "removal from their sees for any penal reason."

ally supplanted the bishop in the control of the cathedral
when the bishop and canons were hostile to each other.
The Fourth Lateran, however, recognized the superior right
of the bishop to enter the church and conduct the service.
The Third Lateran ordered questions in the chapter settled
by a majority vote, no matter what the traditional customs
had been.

The pope and the English sovereign vied with one another
in appropriating the revenues of the English Church, though
it is probable the pope outdid the king.   In William Rufus'
reign, a high ecclesiastic was no sooner dead than a royal
clerk took inventory of his goods and rents, and appropriated them for the crown.   The evil was so great in Stephen's reign that the saying ran that "Christ and his saints
slept." Sees were kept vacant that the crown might se-
quester their revenues. The principle of taxing ecclesiastical property cannot awaken just criticism.   Levies for
military equipment on the basis of scutage go back into the
Saxon period. In the latter half of the twelfth century a
new system came into vogue, and a sum of money was substituted.   The first levy on the moveables of the clergy including tithes and offerings, called the *spiritualia*, seems to
have been made in 1188 by Henry II.   This was the famous
Saladin tax intended for use against the Turks.[1] For the
ransom of Richard I. even the sacred vessels and books of
the clergy were taxed.   Under John the taxation was on an
elaborate scale, but it became even more exacting under
Henry III., 1216–1272.   In 1294 Edward I. threatened to
outlaw the clergy if they refused to grant him a half of their
revenues for his war with France.   The dean of St. Paul's
remonstrated with the king for this unheard-of demand,
and fell dead from the shock which the exhibition of the
king's wrath made upon him.   Unwilling as the clergy may
have been to pay these levies, it is said they seldom refused
a tenth when parliament voted its just share. The taxes
for crusades were made directly by the popes, and also

---

[1] Stubbs, II. 180.

3G

through the sovereign.   As late as 1288, Nicolas IV. granted Edward I. a tenth for six years for a crusade.[1]

The papal receipts from England came from three sources — Peter's Pence, the tribute of John, and special taxations. Peter's Pence, which seems to have started with Offa II., king of Mercia, in the eighth century and was the first monetary tribute of the English people to Rome, was originally a free gift but subsequently was treated as a debt.[2]   The failure to promptly meet the payment became a frequent subject of papal complaint to king and bishops.   In letters to Henry I., 1115, and to the archbishop of Canterbury, Pascal reminded them that not one half of the "gift" had been paid to St. Peter.   Innocent III. gave his legate sharp orders to collect it and complained that the bishops kept back part of the tax for their own use.   The tax of a penny for each household was compounded for £201. 7s.; but, in 1306, William de Testa, the papal legate, was commanded to ignore the change and to revert to the original levy.   Beginning with the thirteenth century, the matter of collection was taken out of the hands of the bishops and placed in the hands of the papal legate.   By the law of Gregory X. two subcollectors were assigned to each see with wages of 3 soldi a day, the wages being afterwards increased to 5 and 8 soldi. Peter's Pence, with other tributes to Rome, was abolished by Henry VIII.'s law of 1534.

The tribute of one thousand marks, promised by John, was paid with great unwillingness by the nation or not paid at all.   In 1275, as John XXI. reminded the English king, the payments were behind seven years.   By 1301 the arrearage amounted to twelve thousand marks.   It would seem as if the tax was discontinued after 1334 and, in 1366, parliament

[1] Upon the valuation of 1291, the clerical tax should have amounted to £20,000.   Stubbs, III. 350.

[2] Jensen, *D. englische Peterspfennig*, Heidelb., 1903, and Liebermann, *The Peter's Pence and the Population of Engl. about 1164*, in Engl. Hist. Rev., 1896.   The Saxon designations of Peter's Pence were *romfeoh* and *heordpfennig*.   The Normans called it *romascot*, and the popes usually referred to it as *denarius, census,* or *res beati Petri,* and "gift," *eleemosyna.*

forbade its further payment and struck off all arrearages since 1334.[1] The popes, however, continued to make the claim, and the tax was paid in part or in whole.

The special taxes levied by popes were for the crusades in the East and against Frederick II. and for the expenses of the papal household. Gregory IX., 1229, with the king's sanction, levied a tax of a tenth for himself. The extraordinary demand, made by Innocent IV., 1246, of a third of all clerical revenues for three years and a half, was refused by a notable gathering of bishops and abbots at Reading and appeal was made to a general council.[2]

The most fruitful method which Rome employed for draining the revenues of the English Church was by requisition upon her benefices and special taxation of bishops and other dignitaries for their offices. The rapacity of the Roman proconsuls seemed to be revived. The first formal demand was made by Honorius III., 1226, and required that two prebends in each cathedral and two positions in each monastery be placed at the pope's disposal. Italians were already in possession of English livings.

In 1231, Gregory IX. forbade the English bishops conferring any more prebends until positions were provided for five Romans. In 1240, the same pontiff made the cool requisition upon the archbishop of Canterbury and the bishops of Lincoln and Salisbury of places for three hundred Italians.[3] It was a constant complaint that Italian succeeded Italian. And the bitter indignation was expressed in words such as Shakespeare used in his *King John* (Act III., Sc. 1):

> " that no Italian priest
> Shall tithe or toil in our dominions."

Innocent IV. was the most unblushing offender. He appointed boys to prebends, as at Salisbury, and Grosseteste spoke of some of his appointees as children, *parvuli*. A

---

[1] Jensen, pp. 60–64, with elaborate list of authorities.

[2] M. Paris, IV. 580.

[3] M. Paris, IV. 32. This chronicler says that Edmund, archbishop of Canterbury, was so harassed by these demands that in despair he exiled himself from the kingdom.

protest, directed to him, complained that " an endless number of Italians " held appointments in England and that they
took out of the kingdom 60,000 marks yearly or more than
half the amount realized by the king from the realm.[1]

As early as 1256, the pope claimed the first-fruits of
bishoprics, the claim to be in force for five years. Later
they were made a fixed rule.[2] The papal legates could not
be expected to fall behind their unscrupulous or complaisant
masters. When Martin arrived in 1244, he asked for 30,000
marks and seized benefices worth more than 3000 marks a
year. These officials were freely denominated indefatigable
extortioners, bloodsuckers, and " wolves, whose bloody jaws
were consuming the English clergy." [3] Money-getting was
also esteemed the chief business of the papal representatives
in Scotland.[4] Matthew Paris compared the " bloodsucking
extortion " to the work of a harlot, vulgar and shameless,
venally offering herself to all, and bent upon staining the
purity of the English Church. The people, he says, were es-
tranged in body, though not in heart, from the pope who acted
in the spirit of a stepfather and from the Roman Church who
treated England like a stepmother.[5] The popular indignation at times found vent in something more significant than
words. Martin, after receiving textures, vases, furniture,
and horses, as well as gold and silver, was given short shrift
by the barons to get out of the kingdom. When he applied
to the king for safe conduct, the king replied, " The devil
give you safe conduct to hell and all the way through it."

The Norman Conquest exerted a wholesome influence upon
the Church in England, and introduced a new era of church
building and the erection of monasteries and the regular and
canonical observance of the church's ritual. The thirteenth
century was a notable period of church extension. The
system of endowed vicarages was developed.

---

[1] M. Paris, IV. 285, 443.   [2] Stubbs, III. 348.

[3] M. Paris, II. 229, IV. 60, 100, 136, 160, 284, 626, etc.

[4] M. Paris, II. 210, IV. 610, says of Geoffrey, bishop of Bethlehem, legate
to Scotland, that it was hoped that as " adamant attracts iron, so he would
draw to himself the much coveted monies of Scotland."   [5] V. 233.

Hugh de Wells created several hundred vicarages and Grosseteste continued the policy and provided for their maintenance out of the revenues of the older churches. Chantries were endowed where mass was said for the repose of the souls of the dead, and in time these were often united to constitute independent vicarages or parishes. The synod of Westminster, 1102, provided for a more just treatment of the ill-paid vicars. The Constitutions of Otho forbade the tearing down of old historic buildings and the erection of new ones without the consent of the bishop.

The Normans also introduced a new era of clerical education. Before their arrival, so William of Malmesbury says,[1] the clergy were content with a slight degree of learning and could scarcely stammer the words of the sacraments. A satisfactory idea of the extent and dispersion of learning among the clergy it is difficult, if not impossible, to obtain. A high authority, Dr. Stubbs,[2] makes the doubtful statement that every one admitted even to minor orders must have been able to read and write. It happened, however, that bishops were rejected for failing in their examinations and others were admitted to their sees though they were unable to read.[3] As for preaching, a sermon from an English parochial priest in the Middle Ages was probably a rare thing. There were at all times some men of literary ability among the English clergy as is attested by the chronicles that have come down to us, by such writers as John of Salisbury, Walter Map, and Peter of Blois (who was imported from France), and by the Schoolmen who filled the chairs at Oxford in its early history.

In spite of the measures of Anselm and other prelates, clerical marriage and concubinage continued in England. Writing to Anselm, Pascal II. spoke of the majority of the English priests as married. Laws were enacted forbidding the people to attend mass said by an offending priest ; and women who did not quit priestly houses were to be treated as adulteresses and denied burial in sacred ground. An

---

[1] III. 245.   [2] III. 283.
[3] M. Paris, III. 170.   See Stubbs, III. 383, note.

English priest in the time of Adrian IV. named his daughter
Hadriana, a reminder to the pope that he himself was the
son of a priest.[1] Some relief was attempted by the introduction of the Augustinian rule, requiring priests to live together; but it was adopted in the single English cathedral
of Carlisle and in a few Scotch cathedrals. The records of
the courts leave no doubt of the coarse vice which prevailed
in clerical groups. Even after the twelfth century, many of
the bishops were married or had semi-legitimated families.
According to Matthew Paris, Grosseteste was on the point of
resigning his see on account of the low morals of his clergy.

The attempt to introduce the law of Gratian into England 'was never wholly successful. Archbishop Arundel
might declare that "in all cases the canons and laws were
authoritative which proceeded from the porter of eternal
life and death, who sits in the seat of God Himself, and to
whom God has committed the laws of the divine realm."[2]
But the barons, as at the parliament of Merton, 1236, resisted
the foreign claim. William the Conqueror provided for ecclesiastical courts, under the charge of bishops and archdeacons,
which took the place of the hundred court.

Suits, however, touching the temporalities of the clergy
were tried in the secular courts,[3] as were also offences
against the forestry laws and the laws of hunting. But all
matters pertaining to wills and to marriage were reserved
for the clerical court. These provisions gave the Church
vast power. It was inevitable, however, that there should
be a clash of jurisdiction, and, in fact, endless disputes arose
in the settlement of matters pertaining to advowsons, tithes,
and other such cases. The relative leniency of the penalties meted out to clerics led many to enter at least the lower
orders, and enroll themselves as clerks who never had any
idea of performing clerical functions.

The more important acts pertaining to the Church in
England in this period were, in addition to William's man-

---

[1] John of Salisbury, *Ep.* 27, Migne, 199. 18.   [2] See Maitland, p. 18.
[3] Stubbs, I. 306 sq., III. 353 sqq.

dates for dividing the civil and church courts, the canons of the council of London, 1108, the Clarendon Constitutions, 1164, John's brief surrendering his kingdom, 1213, the Constitutions of Otho, 1237, and the Mortmain Act of 1279. The Mortmain Act, which was one of the most important English parliamentary acts of the Middle Ages, forbade the alienation of lands to the Church so as to exempt them from the payment of taxation to the state.

§ 129.   *Two English Bishops.*

For HUGH OF LINCOLN : *The magna vita*, by his chaplain, ADAM, ed. by Dimock, Lond., 1864 ; — a metrical *Life*, ed. by Dimock, Lond., 1860. — G. G. PERRY : *St. Hugh of Avalon*, Lond., 1879. — H. THURSTON (Rom. Cath.) : *St. Hugh of Lincoln*, Lond., 1898, transl. from the French, with copious additions. — J. A. FROUDE : *A Bishop of the Twelfth Century*, in *Short Studies on Great Subjects*, 2d series, pp. 54–86.

For GROSSETESTE : His *Epistolæ*, ed. by Luard, Lond., 1861 ; *Monumenta Franc.*, ed. by Brewer. — M. PARIS, Luard's ed. — Lives of Grosseteste, by PEGGE, Lond., 1793. — LECHLER, in his *Life of Wiclif*, transl. by Lorimer, pp. 20–40. — G. G. PERRY, Lond., 1871. — FELTEN, Freib., 1887. — F. S. STEVENSON, Lond., 1899. — M. CREIGHTON : in *Hist. Lectt. and Addresses*, Lond., 1903. — C. BIGG, in *Wayside Sketches in Eccles. Hist.*, Lond., 1906. — *Dict. of Nat'l Biog.*

Most prominent among the English ecclesiastics of the period, as faithful administrators of their sees, are Hugh and Robert Grosseteste, both bishops of Lincoln.[1]

Hugh of Lincoln, or Hugh of Avalon, as he is also called, 1140–1200, was pronounced by Ruskin the most attractive sacerdotal figure known to him in history ;[2] and Froude passed upon him the eulogy that he " was one of the most beautiful spirits ever incarnated in human clay, whose story should be familiar to every English boy."

Born near Grenoble, France, he was taken in his ninth year, on his mother's death, to a convent ; afterwards he entered the Grande Chartreuse, and followed an invitation

---

[1] Stubbs, *Const. Hist.*, II. 313, in pronouncing the thirteenth century " the golden age of English churchmanship," has reference more particularly to the influence the bishops had upon the formation of the English constitution.

[2] *Præterita*, III. 1.

from Henry II., about 1180, to take charge of the Carthusian monastery of St. Witham, which the king had founded a few years before.   In 1186 he was chosen bishop of Lincoln, the most extensive diocese in England.[1]

Hugh's friendship with Henry did not prevent him from resisting the king's interference in the affairs of his diocese. When the king attempted to force a courtier into one of the prebends of Lincoln, the bishop sent the reply, "Tell the king that hereafter ecclesiastical benefices are to be bestowed not upon courtiers but upon ecclesiastics."   He excommunicated the grand forester for encroaching upon the rights of the people.   The king was enraged, but the bishop remained firm.   The forests were strictly guarded so as to protect the game, and also, as is probable, to prevent Saxons from taking refuge in their recesses.   The foresters and rangers were hated officials.   The loss of the eyes and other brutal mutilations were the penalties for encroachment.

Towards Richard and John, Hugh showed the same independent spirit as towards Henry.   At the council of Oxford, 1197, he dared to refuse consent to Richard's demands for money, an almost unheard-of thing.[2]   The king's wrath was allayed by a visit the prelate paid him at his castle on the rock of Andely.   This was the famous castle built in a single year, of which Philip said, "I would take it if it were iron."   To which Richard replied, "I would hold it if it were butter."   Upon Hugh's departure, Richard is reported to have said, "If all prelates were like the bishop of Lincoln, not a prince among us could lift his head against them."

Hugh's enlightened treatment of the Jews has already been referred to.   He showed his interest in the lepers, built them a house, cared for them with his own hands, and called them "the flowers of Paradise, and jewels in the

---

[1] Cencio's register gave the number of households owing Peter's Pence, as 10,080-for Lincoln, 4160 for Winchester, 3960 for London, and 1896 for Canterbury.

[2] Stubbs, ed. of Hoveden, IV. p. xcii, calls this a "landmark of English constitutional history, the first clear case of a refusal of a money grant demanded directly by the crown."

crown of heaven." The Third Lateran had ordered separate churches and burial grounds for lepers. His treatment
of the tomb of Fair Rosamonde was more in consonance with
the canons of that age than agreeable to the spirit of our
own. When, on a visit to Gadstow, he found her buried in
the convent church, with lamps kept constantly burning
over her body, he ordered the body removed, saying that her
life was scandalous, and that such treatment would be a les-
son to others to lead chaste lives. In his last moments
Hugh was laid on a cross of ashes. John, who was holding
a council at Lincoln, helped to carry the body to its resting-
place. The archbishop of Canterbury and many bishops
took part in the burial ceremonies. The Jews shed tears.
Hugh was canonized in 1220, and his shrine became a place
of pilgrimage.

One of the striking stories told of Hugh, the story of
the swan, is attested by his chaplain and by Giraldus
Cambrensis, who witnessed the swan's movements. The
swan, which had its nest at Stow, one of the bishop's
manors, was savage and unmanageable till Hugh first saw
it. The bird at once became docile, and learned to follow
the bishop's voice, eat from his hand, and to put his bill up
his sleeve. It seemed to know instinctively when the bishop
was coming on a visit, and for several days before would fly
up and down the lake flapping its wings. It kept guard
over him when he slept.

Robert Grosseteste, 1175–1253, had a wider range of influence than Hugh, and was probably the most noteworthy
Englishman of his generation.[1] No prelate of his century
was so bold in telling the pope his duty. To his other qualities he added the tastes and acquisitions of the scholar.
He was a reformer of abuses, and a forerunner of Wyclif in

[1] His name is spelt Grossetete, Grosthead, Greathead, etc. The Latin
forms, *Grossum Caput* and *Capito*, were also used. Fuller, with more
quaintness than authority, says he got his name from the bigness of his head,
"having large stowage to receive and store of brains to fill it." Stevenson,
p. 337, adduces three lines along which Grosseteste did conspicuous service;
namely, as an ecclesiastical reformer, a friend of learning, and a statesman.

his use of the Scriptures.   Roger Bacon, his ardent admirer,
said that no one really knew the sciences but Robert of
Lincoln.[1]   His great influence is attested by the fact that
for generations he was referred to as *Lincolniensis*, " he of
Lincoln."

Born in England, and of humble origin, a fact which was
made by the monks of Lincoln an occasion of derision, he
pursued his studies in Oxford and Paris, and subsequently
became chancellor of Oxford.   He was acquainted with
Greek, and knew some Hebrew.   He was a prolific writer,
and was closely associated with Adam Marsh.[2]

No one welcomed the advent of the Mendicant Friars to
England with more enthusiasm than did Grosseteste.   He
regarded their coming as the dawn of a new era, and delivered the first lectures in their school at Oxford, and left
them his library, though he never took the gray cowl himself, as did Adam Marsh.

On being raised to the see of Lincoln, 1235, Grosseteste
set out in the work of reforming monastic and clerical
abuses, which brought him uninterrupted trouble till the
close of his career.   He set himself against drinking bouts,
games in the churches and churchyards, and parish parades
at episcopal visitations.   The thoroughness of his episcopal oversight was a novelty.   He came down like a hammer upon the monks, reports Matthew Paris, and the first
year he removed seven abbots and four priors.   At Ramsey
he examined the very beds, and broke open the monks'
coffers like " a burglar," destroying their silver utensils and
ornaments.[3]   To the monks, who were about to choose an
abbot, he wrote : "When you choose one to look after your
swine, you make diligent search for a person possessing
proper qualifications.   And you ask the questions, Is he
physically capable ?   Has he the requisite experience ?   Is

---

[1] *Solus . . novit scientias.* Bridges' ed., I. 67. Gower, in his *confessio
amantis*, praises the "grete clerke Grosteste."

[2] The *Mon. Francisc.* gives sixty of Marsh's letters to Grosseteste.

[3] M. Paris, V. 226. The methods the bishop resorted to for determining
the fidelity of the nuns to their vows is also recorded by M. Paris.

he willing to take them into fitting pastures in the morning, to defend them against thieves and wild beasts, to watch over them at night ?   And are not your souls of more value than many swine?"

The most protracted contest of his life was with his dean and chapter over the right of episcopal visitation.[1] The canons preached against him in his cathedral. But Grosseteste cited the cases of Samuel, who visited Bethel, Gilgal, and Mizpeh, and David, who defended his father's flocks. He was finally sustained by the pope.

In no way did the great bishop win a more sure place in history than by his vigorous resistance to the appointment of unworthy Italians to English livings and to other papal measures. In 1252, he opposed the collection of a tenth for a crusade which had the pope's sanction. He declined to execute the king's mandate legitimatizing children born before wedlock. His most famous refusal to instal an Italian, was the case of the pope's nephew, Frederick of Lavagna. The pope issued a letter threatening with excommunication any one who might venture to oppose the young man's induction. Grosseteste, then seventy-five years old, replied, declaring, "I disobey, resist, and rebel."[2] Matthew Paris (III. 393), professing to describe the scene in the papal household when the letter was received, relates that Innocent IV. "raved away at the deaf and foolish dotard who had so audaciously dared to sit in judgment upon his actions." Notwithstanding this attitude to the appointment of unworthy Italians, the bishop recognized the principle that to the pope belongs the right of appointing to all the benefices of the church.[3]

---

[1] Letter 127.   See Luard's *Introd.*, p. 114.

[2] *Ep.* 128.   Adam Marsh referred to the letter "as that fearless answer written with so much prudence, eloquence, and vigor, which will, with God's aid, benefit all ages to come."   See Stevenson, p. 312. M. Paris, V. 257, states that Grosseteste declared he would be acting like the devil if he were to deliver the cure of souls over to the Romans, "whom he hated like poison."

[3] *De omnibus beneficiis eccles. libere potest ordinare.*   *Ep.*, 49, Luard's ed., p. 145.

On his visit to Lyons, 1250, Grosseteste's memorandum against the abuses of the clergy was read in the pope's presence. "Not in dispensing the mass but in teaching the living truth" does the work of the pastor consist, so it declared. " The lives of the clergy are the book of the laity." Adam Marsh, who was standing by, compared the arraignment to the arraignments of Elijah, John the Baptist, Paul, Athanasius, and Augustine of Hippo.

According to Matthew Paris, on the night of Grosseteste's death strange bells were heard. Miracles were reported performed at his tomb, and the rumor ran that, when Innocent was proposing to have the bishop's body removed from its resting-place in the cathedral, Grosseteste appeared to the pope in a dream, gave him a sound reprimand, and left him half dead. The popular veneration was shown in the legend that on the night of Innocent IV's death the bishop appeared to him with the words, "Aryse, wretch, and come to thy dome."

In the earlier part of his life, Grosseteste preached in Latin ; in the latter he often used the vernacular. He was the greatest English preacher of his age. He was not above the superstitions of his time, and one of his famous sermons was preached before Henry III. at the reception of the reputed blood of Christ.[1] His writings are full of Scriptural quotations, and he urged the importance of the study of the Scriptures at the university, and the dedication of the morning hours to it, and emphasized their authority.[2] Wyclif quoted his protest against the practices of Rome,[3] and he has been regarded as a forerunner of the English Reformation.

Of Grosseteste's writings the best known was probably his *de cessatione legalium*, the End of the Law, a book intended to convince the Jews. With the aid of John of Basingstoke,

[1] M. Paris, IV. 643 sqq., VI. 138-144.

[2] *Ep.* 2. *auctoritas irrefragabilis scripturæ.*

[3] Bishop Hall quoted Grosseteste for his scriptural views, and Field, *Of the Church*, IV. 384 sqq., quoted him against the pope's claim to supreme authority, but wrongly.

he translated the Testament of the Twelve Patriarchs, which Basingstoke had found in Constantinople.[1] He seems to have been a man of sterling common sense, as the following counsels indicate. To a friar he said : "Three things are necessary for earthly well-being, food, sleep, and a merry heart." To another friar addicted to melancholy, he prescribed, as penance, a cupfull of the best wine. After the medicine had been taken, Grosseteste said, "Dear brother, if you would frequently do such penance, you would have a better ordered conscience."[2]

Matthew Paris (V. 407) summed up the bishop's career in these words : —

"He was an open confuter of both popes and kings, the corrector of monks, the director of priests, the instructor of clerks, the supporter of scholars, a preacher to the people, a persecutor of the incontinent, the unwearied student of the Scriptures, a crusher and despiser of the Romans. At the table of bodily meat, he was hospitable, eloquent, courteous, and affable ; at the spiritual table, devout, tearful, and contrite. In the episcopal office he was sedulous, dignified, and indefatigable."

[1] Pegge devotes twenty-five closely filled pages with the list of the bishop's books.

[2] *Mon. Franc.*, p. 64.

CHAPTER XVI.

POPULAR WORSHIP AND SUPERSTITION.

§ 130. *The Worship of Mary.*

LITERATURE : The Works of the Schoolmen, especially, DAMIANI: *de bono suffragiorum et variis miraculis, præsertim B. Virginis*, Migne, 145. 559 sqq., 586 sqq., etc. — ANSELM : *Orationes et meditationes, de conceptu virginis*, Migne, vol. 158. — GUIBERT OF NOGENT : *de laudibus S. Mariæ*, Migne, 156. 537–579. — HONORIUS OF AUTUN : *Sigillum b. Mariæ*, Migne, 172. 495–518. — BERNARD : *de laudibus virginis matris*, Migne, 183. 55 sqq., 70 sqq., 415 sqq., etc. — P. LOMBARDUS : *Sent.*, III. 3 sqq. — HUGO DE ST. VICTOR : *de Mariæ virginitate*, Migne, 176. 857–875, etc. — ALB. MAGNUS : *de laudibus b. Mariæ virginis*, Borgnet's ed., 36. 1–841. — BONAVENTURA : *In Sent.*, III. 3, Peltier's ed., IV. 53 sqq., 105 sqq., 202 sqq., etc. ; *de corona b. Mariæ V., Speculum b. M. V., Laus b. M. V., Psalterium minus et majus b. M. V.*, etc., all in Peltier's ed., XIV. 179–293. — TH. AQUINAS : *Summa*, III. 27–35, Migne, IV. 245–319. — *Analecta Hymnica medii aevi*, ed. by G. M. DREVES, 49 Parts, Leipz., 1886–1906. — Popular writers as CAESAR OF HEISTERBACH, DE BOURBON, THOMAS À CHANTIMPRÉ, and DE VORAGINE : *Legenda aurea*, Englished by William Caxton, Kelmscott Press ed., 1892 ; Temple classics ed., 7 vols.

F. MARGOTT : *D. Mariologie d. hl. Th. v. Aquino*, Freiburg, 1878. — B. HÄUSLER : *de Mariæ plenitudine gratiæ secundum S. Bernardum*, Freiburg, 1901. — H. VON EICKEN : *Gesch. und System d. mittelalt. Weltanschauung*, Stuttg., 1887, p. 476 sqq. — K. BENRATH : *Zur Gesch. der Marienverehrung*, Gotha, 1886. — The Histt. of Doctr. of SCHWANE, pp. 413–428, HARNACK, II. 558–562, SEEBERG, SHELDON, etc. — SCHAFF : *Creeds of Christendom*, I. 108–128. The artt. in Wetzer-Welte, *Empfängniss*, IV. 454–474, *Maria, Marienlegenden, Marienfeste*, vol. VIII., *Ave Maria, Rosenkranz*, and the art. *Maria*, by ZÖCKLER in Herzog. — Mrs. JAMIESON : *Legends of the Monastic Orders.* — BARING-GOULD : *Lives of the Saints, Curious Myths of the M. Ages.* — BUTLER : *Legends of the Saints.*

Ave cœleste lilium, Ave rosa speciosa
Ave mater humilium, Superis imperiosa,

Deitatis triclinium ; hac in valle lacrymarum
Da robur, fer auxilium, O excusatrix culparum.
> BONAVENTURA, *Laus Beatæ Virginis Mariæ.*[1]

THE worship of the Virgin Mary entered into the very
soul of mediæval piety and reached its height in the doctrine
of her immaculate conception.   Solemn theologians in their
dogmatic treatises, ardent hymn-writers and minnesingers,
zealous preachers and popular prose-writers unite in dilat-
ing upon her purity and graces on earth and her beauty and
intercessory power in heaven.   In her devotion, chivalry and
religion united.   A pious gallantry invested her with all the
charms of womanhood and the highest beatitude of the
heavenly estate.   The austerities of the convent were softened by the recollection of her advocacy and tender guard-
ianship, and monks, who otherwise shrank from the company
of women, dwelt upon the marital tie which bound them
to her.   To them her miraculous help was being continually
extended to counteract the ills brought by Satan.   The
Schoolmen, in their treatment of the immaculate conception,
used over and over again delicate terms[2] which in conversation the pure to-day do not employ.

Monastic orders were dedicated to Mary, such as the Carthusian, Cistercian, and Carmelite, as were also some of
the most imposing churches of Christendom, as the cathedrals
at Milan and Notre Dame, in Paris.

The titles given to Mary were far more numerous than the
titles given to Christ and every one of them is extra-biblical
except the word " virgin."   An exuberant fancy allegorized
references to her out of all sorts of texts, never dreamed of
by their writers.   She was found referred to in almost every
figurative expression of the Old Testament which could be
applied to a pure, human being.   To all the Schoolmen, Mary
is the mother of God, the queen of heaven, the clement queen,

---

[1] Peltier's ed., XIV. 181.   A free translation runs, " Hail, heavenly lily,
Hail most graceful rose, Hail mother of the lowly, Reigning on high, Couch
of deity ; Give to us in this valley of tears strength, Lend aid O thou palliator
of sins. "

[2] *sinus*, bosom ; *pectus*, breast ; *viscera*, bowels ; *ubera*, breasts ; *uterus*, etc.

the queen of the world, the empress of the world, the medi-
atrix, the queen of the ages, the queen of angels, men and
demons,[1] the model of all virtues, and Damiani even calls her
"the mother of the eternal emperor."[2]

Monks, theologians, and poets strain the Latin language to
express their admiration of her beauty and benignity, her
chastity and heavenly glory.   Her motherhood and virginity
are alike subjects of eulogy.   The conception of physical
grace, as expressed when the older Notker of St. Gall called
her "the most beautiful of all virgins," filled the thought of
the Schoolmen and the peasant.   Albertus Magnus devotes
a whole chapter of more than thirty pages of two columns
each to the praise of her corporal beauty.   In his exposition
of Canticles 1:15, "Behold thou art fair, my love," he comments upon the beauty of her hair, her shoulders, her lips,
her nose, her feet, and other parts of her body.   Bonaventura's hymns in her praise abound in tropical expressions,
such as "she is more ruddy than the rose and whiter than
the lily."   Wernher of Tegernsee about 1173 sang:[3] —

> Her face was so virtuous, her eyes so bright,
> Her manner so pure, that, among all women,
> None could with her compare.

In a remarkable passage, Bernard represents her in the
celestial places drawing attention to herself by her form and
beauty so that she attracted the King himself to desire her.[4]
Dante, a century and more later, enjoying paradise in the
company of Bernard, thus represented the vision of Mary: —

> I saw the virgin smile, whose rapture shot
> Joy through the eyes of all that blessed throng:
> And even did the words that I possess
> Equal imagination, I should not
> Dare, the attempt her faintest charms to express.
>
> *Paradiso*, Canto **XXXI.**

---

[1] Bonaventura, *Speculum*, III. Peltier's ed., XIV. 240.

[2] Migne, 145. 566.

[3] *Ir antlutze war so tugentliche, Ir ougen also kunchliche, Ir gebaerde
also reine, Das sich ze ir glichte deheine, Under allen den frouen*, quoted by
von Eicken, p. 477.

[4] The word used is *concupiscentia*, the usual word for lust. Migne, 183. 62.

The Canticles was regarded as an inspired anthology of Mary's excellences of body and soul.   Damiani represents God as inflamed with love for her and singing its lines in her praise.   She was the golden bed on which God, weary in His labor for men and angels, lay down for repose.   The later interpretation was that the book is a bridal song for the nuptials between the Holy Spirit and the Virgin.   Bernard's homilies on this portion of Scripture are the most famous collection of the Middle Ages.   Alanus ab Insulis, who calls Mary the "tabernacle of God, the palace of the celestial King," says that it refers to the Church, but in an especial and most spiritual way to the glorious virgin.[1]   Writer after writer, preacher after preacher, took up this favorite portion of the Old Testament.   An abbess represented the Virgin as singing to the Spirit:[2] "My beloved is mine and I am his. He will tarry between my breasts."   The Holy Spirit responded, "Thy breasts are sweeter than honey."

To Mary was given a place of dignity equal or superior to Christ as the friend of the sinful and unfortunate and the guide of souls to heaven.   Damiani called her "the door of heaven," the window of paradise.   Anselm spoke of her as "the vestibule of universal propitiation, the cause of universal reconciliation, the vase and temple of life and salvation for the world."[3]   A favorite expression was "the tree of life" — *lignum vitæ* — based upon Prov. iii: 8.   Albertus Magnus, in the large volume he devotes to Mary's virtues, gives no less than forty reasons why she should be worshipped, authority being found for each one in a text of Scripture.   The first reason was that the Son of God honors Mary.   This accords with the fifth commandment, and

[1] *Specialissime et spiritualissime.*   Migne, 210. 53.
[2] See von Eicken, p. 481.   In a song to Mary written by the Dominican, Eberhard of Saxony, in the thirteenth century, occur the lines: —

> *Got in sinem hohen trone hat begehret diner schone*
> *Da er wil, o wiber Krone mit gelüste dich ansehen.*

"God on His throne desired thy beauty and wanted, O crown of womanhood, to look on thee with passion."
[3] *Orationes*, LII., Migne, 158. 954.

Christ himself said of his mother, " I will glorify the house
of my glory," Isa. lx : 7 ; house, according to the Schoolman, being intended to mean Mary.   The Bible teems with
open and concealed references to her.   Albertus ascribed to
her thirty-five virtues, on all of which he elaborates at length,
such as humility, sincerity, benignity, omnipotence, and
modesty.   He finds eighty-one biblical names indicative of
her functions and graces.   Twelve of these are taken from
things in the heavens.   She is a sun, a moon, a light, a
cloud, a horizon, an aurora.   Eight are taken from things
terrestrial.   Mary is a field, a mountain, a hill, a stone.
Twenty-one are represented by things pertaining to water.
She is a river, a fountain, a lake, a fish-pond, a cistern, a
torrent, a shell.   Thirty-one are taken from biblical figures.
Mary is an ark, a chair, a house, a bed, a nest, a furnace, a
library.   Nine are taken from military and married life.
Mary is a castle, a tower, a wall.   It may be interesting to
know how Mary fulfilled the office of a library.   In her,
said the ingenious Schoolman, were found all the books of
the Old Testament, of all of which she had plenary knowledge as is shown in the words of her song which run, "as
was spoken by our fathers."   She also had plenary knowledge of the Gospels as is evident from Luke ii : 19: " Mary
kept all these sayings in her heart."   But especially do
Mary's qualities lie concealed under the figure of the garden
employed so frequently in the Song of Solomon.   To the
elaboration of this comparison Albertus devotes two hundred and forty pages, introducing it with the words, " a
garden shut up is my sister, my bride," Cant. iv : 12.[1]

Bonaventura equals Albertus in ransacking the heavens
and the earth and the waters for figures to express Mary's
glories and there is a tender chord of mysticism running
through his expositions which is adapted to move all hearts
and to carry the reader, not on his guard, away from the
simple biblical statements.   The devout Franciscan frequently returns to this theme and makes Mary the subject

---

[1] *De laud. Mariæ*, Borgnet's ed., XXXVI. 600-840.

of his verse and sermons.[1] He exhausts the vocabulary for
words in her praise. She is prefigured in Jacob's ladder,
Noah's ark, the brazen serpent, Aaron's rod, the star of
Balaam, the pot of manna, Gideon's horn, and other objects
of Hebrew history. To each of these his *Praise of the
Blessed Virgin Mary* devotes poetic treatment extending in
cases to more than one hundred lines and carrying the reader
away by their affluence of imagination and the sweetness
of the rhythm.

Imitating the Book of Psalms, Bonaventura wrote two
psalteries, each consisting of one hundred and fifty parts.
Each part of the Minor Psaltery consists of four lines, its
opening lines being " Hail Virgin, tree of life; Hail Virgin, door of liberty; Hail Virgin, dear to God; Hail Virgin,
light of the world; Hail Virgin, harbor of life; Hail Virgin,
most beautiful." In the Greater Psaltery, Bonaventura
paraphrases the one hundred and fifty psalms and introduces
into each one Mary's name and her attributes, revelling
in ascriptions of her preëminence over men and angels.
Here are several selections, but no selection can give any
adequate idea of the liberty taken with Scripture. The first
Psalm is made to run, " Blessed is the man who loves thee,
O Virgin Mary. Thy grace will comfort his soul." The
Twenty-third runs, "The Lord directs me, O Virgin mother
of God — *genetrix dei* — because thou hast turned towards
me His loving countenance." The first verse of Psalm 121
reads, " I have lifted up my eyes to thee, O Mother of Christ,
from whom solace comes to all flesh."

Tender as are Bernard's descriptions of Christ and his
work, he nevertheless assigns to Mary the place of mediator
between the soul and the Saviour. In Mary there is nothing
severe, nothing to be dreaded. She is tender to all, offering
milk and wool. If you are terrified at the thunders of the
Father, go to Jesus, and if you fear to go to Jesus, then run
to Mary. Besought by the sinner, she shows her breasts and

---

[1] These works may not all be genuine. They belong, at least, to Bonaventura's age.

bosom to the Son, as the Son showed his wounds to the Father. Let her not depart from thine heart. Following her, you will not go astray; beseeching her, you will not despair; thinking of her, you will not err.[1]

So also Bonaventura pronounces Mary the mediator between us and Christ.[2] As God is the lord of revenge — *dominus ultionum,* — he says in his Greater Psaltery, so Mary is the mother of compassion. She presents the requests of mortals to the Second Person of the Trinity, softening his wrath and winning favors which otherwise would not be secured.

Anselm, whom we are inclined to think of as a sober theologian above his fellows, was no less firm as an advocate of Mary's mediatorial powers. Prayer after prayer does he offer to her, all aflame with devotion. "Help me by thy death and by thine assumption into heaven," he prays. "Come to my aid," he cries, "and intercede for me, O mother of God, to thy sweet Son, for me a sinner."[3]

The veneration for Mary found a no less remarkable expression in the poetry of the Middle Ages. The vast collection, *Analecta hymnica,* published by Dreves and up to this time filling fifteen volumes, gives hundreds and thousands of sacred songs dwelling upon the merits and glories of the Virgin. The plaintive and tender key in which they are written is adapted to move the hardest heart, even though they are full of descriptions which have nothing in the Scriptures to justify them. Here are two verses taken at random from the thousands: —

> *Ave Maria, Angelorum dia   Cœli rectrix, Virgo Maria*
> *Ave maris stella, Lucens miseris   Deitatis cella, Porta principis.*[4]

Hail, Mary, Mother of God, Ruler of heaven, O Virgin Mary . . . Hail, Star of the Sea, Lighting the wretched Cell of the Deity, Gate of the king.

Where the thinkers and singers of the age were so ardent in their worship of Mary, what could be expected from the

---

[1] *De assump.,* Migne, 183. 430 ; *De nativ. Mariœ,* Migne, 183. 441 ; *Super missus,* III., Migne, 183. 70.   [2] *In Sent.,* III. 1, 2, Peltier's ed., IV. 63.   [3] *Orat.,* LVIII, LX. Migne, 158. 964, 966. [4] Dreves, *Analecta,* I. 48 sqq.

mass of monks and from the people!   A few citations will
suffice to show the implicit faith placed in Mary's intercession and her power to work miracles.

Peter Damiani tells of a woman who, after being dead a
year, appeared in one of the churches of Rome and related
how she and many others had been delivered from purgatory
by Mary in answer to their prayers.   He also tells how she
had a good beating given a bishop for deposing a cleric who
had been careful never to pass her image without saluting it.[1]

Cæsar of Heisterbach abounds in stories of the gracious
offices Mary performed inside the convent and outside of it.
She frequently was seen going about the monastic spaces,
even while the monks were in bed.   On such occasions her
beauty was always noted.   Now and then she turned and
gave a severe look to a careless monk, not lying in bed in the
approved way.   Of one such case the narrator says he did
not know whether the severity was due to the offender's
having laid aside his girdle or having taken off his sandals.
Mary stood by to receive the souls of dying monks, gave
them seats at her feet in heaven, sometimes helped sleepy
friars out by taking up their prayers when they began to
doze, sometimes in her journeys through the choir aroused
the drowsy, sometimes stretched out her arm from her altar
and boxed the ears of dull worshippers, and sometimes gave
the staff to favored monks before they were chosen abbots.
She sometimes undid a former act, as when she saw to it that
Dietrich was deposed whom she had aided in being elected
to the archbishopric of Cologne.[2]

To pious knights, according to Cæsar of Heisterbach,
Mary was scarcely less gracious than she was to the inmates
of the convent.   She even took the place of contestants in
the tournament.   Thus it was in the case of Walter of
Birbach who was listed and failed to get to the tournament
field at the appointed hour for tarrying in a chapel in the
worship of Mary.   But the spectators were not aware of his

---

[1] *De variis mirac.*, Migne, 145. 586 sq. ; *De bono suffr.*, Migne, 145. 564.
[2] *Dial.*, VII. 13, 19, XI. 12, VII. 12, 39, 40, 51, etc.

absence. The tournament began, was contested to a close, and, as it was thought, Walter gained the day. But as it happened, Mary herself had taken the knight's place and fought in his stead, and, when the knight arrived, he was amazed to find every one speaking in praise of the victory he had won.[1] Thomas of Chantimpré[2] tells of a robber whose head was cut off and rolled down the valley. He called out to the Virgin to be allowed to confess. A priest, passing by, ordered the head joined to the body. Then the robber confessed to the priest and told him that, as a young man, he had fasted in honor of the Virgin every Wednesday and Saturday under the promise that she would give him opportunity to make confession before passing into the next world.

All these collections of tales set forth how Mary often met the devil and took upon herself to soundly rebuke and punish him. According to Jacob of Voragine[3] a husband, in return for riches, promised the devil his wife. On their way to the spot, where she was to be delivered up, the wife, suspecting some dark deed, turned aside to a chapel and implored Mary's aid. Mary put the worshipper to sleep and herself mercifully took the wife's place at the husband's side and rode with him, he not noticing the change. When they met the devil, the "mother of God" after some sound words of reprimand sent him back howling to hell.

Mary's compassion and her ability to move her austere Son are brought out in the Miracle Plays. In the play of the Wise and Foolish Virgins, the foolish virgins, after having in vain besought God for mercy, turned to the Virgin with these words : —

> Since God our suit hath now denied
> We Mary pray, the gentle maid,
> The Mother of Compassion,
> To pity our great agony
> And for us, sinners poor, to pray
> Mercy from her beloved Son.[4]

[1] *Dial.*, VII. 38.   [2] II. 264.
[3] The Assumption of Mary.   Temple Classics, IV. 249.
[4] Hase, *Miracle Plays*, 31.

The Church never officially put its stamp of commendation upon the popular belief that the Son is austere.   Nevertheless, even down to the very eve of the Reformation, the belief prevailed that Christ's austerity had to be appeased by Mary's compassion.

THE VIRGIN BIRTH OF CHRIST. — The literary criticism of the Bible of recent years was as much undreamed of in this period of the Middle Ages as were steamboats or telephones.   Schoolman and priest seem never to have doubted when they repeated the article of the Creed, " Conceived by the Holy Ghost, born of the Virgin Mary."   Homily and theological treatise lingered over the words of Isa. vii: 14: " Behold a virgin shall conceive," and over the words of the angelic annunciation: " Hail, thou that art highly favored.   The Lord is with thee.   Blessed art thou among women . . .   The Holy Ghost shall come upon thee and the power of the Highest shall overshadow thee."   They discussed the conception and virginal birth in every possible aspect, as to the part the Holy Spirit had in the event and the part of Mary herself.   Here are some of the questions propounded by Thomas Aquinas: Was there true matrimony between Joseph and Mary ?   Was it necessary that the angel should appear in bodily form ?   Was Christ's flesh taken from Adam or from David ?   Was it formed from the purest bloods of Mary ?   Was the Holy Spirit the primary agent in the conception of Christ ?   Was Christ's body animated with a soul at the instant of conception ?

None of the Schoolmen goes more thoroughly than Hugo of St. Victor into the question of the part played by the Holy Spirit in the conception of Jesus.   He was at pains to show that, while the Spirit influenced the Virgin in conception, he was not the father of Jesus.   The Spirit did not impart to Mary seed from his own substance, but by his power and love developed substance in her through the agency of her own flesh.[1]

---

[1] *De Mariæ virg.*, Migne, 176. 872.   Bernard even uses the word " impregnate," *impregnare*, to indicate the Spirit's influence.   Migne, 183. 59.

According to Anselm, God can make a human being in four ways, by the co-operation of a man and woman ; without either as in the case of Adam ; with the sole co-operation of the man as in the case of Eve; or from a woman without a man.   Having produced men in the first three ways, it was most fitting God should resort to the fourth method in the case of Jesus.   In another work he compares God's creation of the first man from clay and the second man from a woman without the co-operation of a man.[1]

Thomas Aquinas is very elaborate in his treatment of Mary's virginity.   " As a virgin she conceived, as a virgin gave birth, and she remains a virgin forevermore."   The assumption that she had other children derogates from her sanctity, for, as the mother of God, she would have been most ungrateful if she had not been content with such a Son. And it would have been highest presumption for Joseph to have polluted her who had received the annunciation of the angel.   He taught that, in the conception of Christ's body, the whole Trinity was active and Mary is to be called " rightly, truly, and piously, *genetrix Dei*," the mother of God.[2]

The mediæval estimate of Mary found its loftiest expression in the doctrine of the immaculate conception, the doctrine that Mary herself was conceived without sin.   The Schoolmen were agreed that she was exempt from all actual transgression.   They separated on the question whether she was conceived without sin and so was immaculate from the instant of conception or whether she was also tainted with original sin from which, however, she was delivered while she was yet in her mother's womb.   The latter view was taken by Anselm, Hugo of St. Victor, Albertus Magnus, Thomas Aquinas, and even Bonaventura.[3]   The view that she was conceived without sin and thus was never tainted with original sin was advocated by Duns Scotus, who, however, did not go further than to assert for it probability.   Bernard, writing to

[1] *Cur Deus homo*, II. 8 ; *De concept. virg.*, Migne, 158. 445.
[2] *Summa*, III. 28, 1, etc., Migne, IV. 258, 262, 294, 298, etc.
[3] *In Sent.*, III. 5, IV. 3, 1, Peltier's ed., IV. 53 sqq., V. 59.

the church of Lyons, condemned it for having introduced the
festival of the immaculate conception, which he said lacked
the approval of the Church, of reason and tradition.   If
Mary was conceived without sin, then why might not sinless
conception be affirmed of Mary's parents and grandparents
and her ancestors to remotest antiquity.   However, Bernard
expressed his willingness to yield if the Church should
appoint a festival of the immaculate conception.[1]

Bonaventura gave three reasons against the doctrine exempting Mary from original sin; namely, from common consent, from reason, and from prudence.[2]   According to the
first she suffered with the rest of mankind sorrows, which
must have been the punishment of her own guilt inherited
from Adam.   According to the second, the conception of the
body precedes its animation, the word "animation" being
used by the Schoolmen for the first association of the soul
with the body.   In the conception of the body there is always concupiscence.   The third argument relied upon the
Fathers who agreed that Christ was the only being on earth
exempt from sin.   Bonaventura did not fix the time when
Mary was made immaculate except to say, that it probably
occurred soon after her conception and at that moment passion or flame of sin — *fomes peccati* — was extinguished.

Thomas Aquinas emphatically took this position and declared it was sufficient to confess that the blessed virgin committed no actual sin, either mortal or venial.   "Thou art all
fair, my love, and no spot is in thee," Cant. iv : 7.[3]

Nowhere else is Duns Scotus more subtle and sophistical
than in his argument for ·Mary's spotless conception whereby
she was untainted by hereditary sin, and no doctrine has
become more closely attached with his name.   This argument is a chain of conjectures.   Mary's sinless conception,
he said, was only a matter of probability, but at the same
time seeming and congruous.   The threefold argument is as
follows: 1. God's grace would be enhanced by releasing

---

[1] *Ep.*, 174, Migne, 332–336.

[2] *Sententia communior, rationabilior et securior*.   Peltier's ed., IV. 67.

[3] *Summa*, III.. 27, 4, Migne, IV. 252.

one individual from all taint of original sin from the very beginning. 2. By conferring this benefit Christ would bind Mary to himself by the strongest ties. 3. The vacancy left in heaven by the fallen angels could be best filled by her, if she were preserved immaculate from the beginning. As the second Adam was preserved immaculate, so it was fitting the second Eve should be. Duns' conclusion was expressed in these words: "If the thing does not contradict the Church and the Scriptures, its reality seems probable, because it is more excellent to affirm of Mary that she was not conceived in sin."[1]

The warm controversy between the Thomists and Scotists over the immaculate conception has been referred to in another place. Saints also joined in it. St. Brigitta of Sweden learned through a vision that Mary was conceived immaculate. On the other hand the Dominican, St. Catherine of Siena, prophesied Mary had not been sanctified till the third hour after her conception. The synod of Paris, 1387, decided in favor of the Scotist position, but Sixtus IV., 1483, threatened with excommunication either party denouncing the other. Finally, Duns Scotus triumphed, and in 1854, Pius IX. made it a dogma of the Church that Mary in the very instant of her conception was kept immune from all stain of original sin.[2]

The festival of the immaculate conception, observed Dec. 8, was taken up by the Franciscans at their general chapter, held in Pisa, 1263, and its celebration made obligatory in their churches.

One more possible glorification of Mary, the humble mother of our Lord, has not yet been turned into dogma by the Roman Church, her·assumption into heaven, her body not having seen corruption. This is held as a pious opinion and preachers like St. Bernard, Honorius of Autun, Gottfried of Admont, and Werner of St. Blasius preached sermon after

---

[1] *Si auctoritati eccles. vel scripturæ non repugnet videtur probabile quod excellentius est attribuere Mariæ videlicet quod non sit in originali peccato concepta.* *Sent.*, III. 3, Paris ed., XIV. 165. See Seeberg, p. 247 sq., and Schwane, p. 424 sqq.   [2] Schaff, *Creeds of Christendom*, II. 211.

sermon on Mary's assumption. The belief is based upon the story, told by Juvenal of Jerusalem to the emperor Marcian at the council of Chalcedon, 451, that three days after Mary's burial in Jerusalem, her coffin but not her body was found by the Apostles. Juvenal afterwards sent the coffin to the emperor.[1] Even Augustine had shunned to believe that the body of the mother of our Lord saw corruption. The festival of the Assumption was celebrated in Rome as early as the middle of the eleventh century.[2] The synod of Toulouse, 1229, included the festival among the other church festivals at the side of Christmas and Easter. Thomas Aquinas spoke of it as being tolerated by the Church, not commanded.

The *Ave Maria*, "Hail Mary, thou that art highly favored, the Lord is with thee. Blessed art thou among women and blessed is the fruit of thy womb" made up of the words of the angelic salutation and the words of Elizabeth, Luke i : 28, 42, was used as a prayer in the time of Peter Damiani,[3] and was specially expounded by Bonaventura and Thomas Aquinas. The petitionary clause, "Holy Mary, Mother of God, pray for us sinners, now and in the hour of death" appears in the sixteenth century and was introduced into the Roman breviary 1568.[4] The so-called Ave, or Angelus, bell was ordered rung by John XXII. (d. 1334) three times a day. When it peals, the woman in the home and the workman in the field are expected to bow their heads in prayer to Mary.

In few respects are the worship and teaching of the Middle Ages so different from those of the Protestant Churches as in the claims made for Mary and the regard paid to her. If

---

[1] Addis and Arnold, *Cath. Dict.*, 6th ed., commend the tradition as inherently probable as no relics of Mary's body have ever been found.

[2] Damiani, *De Mirac.*, Migne, 145. 586.

[3] *De bono suffr.*, Migne, 145. 564.

[4] According to Cæsar of Heisterbach, the *Ave Maria* took the place of sugar and honey in the mouths of nuns who repeated it on their knees daily fifty times and it tasted like honey. A priest who tried it found, after six weeks, that his spittle had turned to honey. *Sermons*, as quoted by Cruel, *Gesch. d. deutschen Predigt*, p. 284.

we are to judge by the utterances and example of Pius IX. and Leo XIII., the mediæval cult still goes on unchanged in the Roman communion. And more recently Pius X. shows that he follows his predecessors closely. In his encyclical of Jan. 15, 1907, addressed to the French bishops, he says, " In full confidence that the Virgin Immaculate, daughter of our Father, mother of the Word, spouse of the Holy Ghost, will obtain for you from the most holy and adorable Trinity better days, we give you our Apostolic benediction." It was the misfortune of the mediæval theologians to fall heir to the eulogies passed upon Mary by Jerome and other early Fathers of the early Church and the veneration in which she was held. They blindly followed, having inherited also the allegorical mode of interpretation from the past. In part they were actuated by a sincere purpose to exalt the glory and divinity of Christ when they ascribed to Mary exemption from sin. On the other hand it was a Pagan, though chivalric, superstition to exalt her to a position of a goddess who stands between Christ and the sinner and mitigates by her intercession the austerity which marks his attitude towards them. This was the response the mediæval Church gave to the exclamation of St. Bernard, " Who is this virgin so worthy of honor as to be saluted by the angel and so lowly as to have been espoused to a carpenter ? " [1] The tenderest piety of the Middle Ages went out to her and is expressed in such hymns as the *Mater dolorosa* and the companion piece, *Mater speciosa*. But this piety, while it no doubt contributed to the exaltation of womanhood, also involved a relaxation of penitence, for in the worship of Mary tears of sympathy are substituted for resolutions of repentance.

§ 131.   *The Worship of Relics.*

LITERATURE : See Lit., p. 268 sq. GUIBERT OF NOGENT, d 1124: *de pignoribus sanctorum*, Migne, vol. 156, 607-679. — GUNTHERUS : *Hist. Constantinopol.*, Migne, vol. 212. — PETER THE VENERABLE : *de miraculis*, Migne, vol. 189. — CÆSAR OF HEISTERBACH, JACOB OF VORAGINE, SALIMBENE, etc. — P. VIGNON : *The Shroud of Christ*, Engl. trans., N.Y., 1903.

[1] *De laude virginis.*   Migne, 183. 58.

The worship of relics was based by Thomas Aquinas upon the regard nature prompts us to pay to the bodies of our deceased friends and the things they held most sacred. The bodies of the saints are to be reverenced because they were in a special manner the temples of the Holy Ghost. The worship to be paid to them is the lowest form of worship, *dulia*. *Hyperdulia*, a higher form of worship, is to be rendered to the true cross on which Christ hung. In this case the worship is rendered not to the wood but to him who hung upon the cross. *Latreia*, the highest form of worship, belongs to God alone.[1] Following the seventh œcumenical council, the Schoolmen denied that when adoration is paid to images, say the image of Peter, worship is given to the image itself. It is rendered to the prototype, or that for which the image stands.[2]

In the earlier years of the Middle Ages, Italy was the most prolific source of relics. With the opening of the Crusades the eyes of the Church were turned to the East, and the search of relic-hunters was abundantly rewarded. With open-mouthed credulity the West received the holy objects which Crusaders allowed to be imposed upon them. The rich mine opened up at the sack of Constantinople has already been referred to. Theft was sanctified which recovered a fragment from a saint's body or belongings. The monk, Gunther, does not hesitate to enumerate the articles which the abbot, Martin, and his accomplices stole from the reliquary in one of the churches of the Byzantine city. Salimbene[3] mentions a present made to him from one of the churches of Ravenna of the bones of Elisha, all except the head, which had been stolen by the Austin friars.

The Holy Lance was disclosed at a critical moment in the siege of Antioch. The Holy Grail was found in Cæsarea in 1101. The bones of the three kings, Caspar, Melchior, and Belthazar, reputed to have been the magi who presented

---

[1] Th. Aq., *Summa*, III. 25, 6, Migne, IV. 240 sq. ; Bonavent., Peltier's ed., IV. 206 sq., VIII. 196. Thomas accords a single brief chapter to relics and quotes Augustine but not Scripture in favor of their worship.

[2] Bonavent., III. 27, 2, Peltier's ed., IV. 619.   [3] Coulton's ed., p 253.

their gifts at the manger, were removed from Milan to Cologne, where they still repose. In the same city of Cologne were found, in 1156, the remains of Ursula and the virgin martyrs, put to death by the Huns, the genuineness of the discovery being attested by a vision to Elizabeth of Schönau. Among the endless number of objects transmitted to Western Europe from the East were Noah's beard, the horns of Moses, the stone on which Jacob slept at Bethel, the branch from which Absalom hung, our Lord's foreskin, his navel cord, his coat, tears he shed at the grave of Lazarus, milk from Mary's breasts, the table on which the Last Supper was eaten, the stone of Christ's sepulchre, Paul's stake in the flesh, a tooth belonging to St. Lawrence. Christ's tooth, which the monks of St. Medard professed to have in their possession, was attacked by Guibert of Nogent on the ground that when Christ rose from the dead he was in possession of all the parts of his body. He also attacked the genuineness of the umbilical cord.[1] The prioress of Fretelsheim claimed to be in possession of two relics of the ass which bore Christ to Jerusalem.

The holy coat, the blood of Christ, and his cross have perhaps played the largest part in the literature of relics. Christ's holy coat is claimed by Treves and Argenteuil as well as other localities. It was the seamless garment — *tunica inconsutilis* — woven by Mary, which grew as Christ grew and was worn on the cross.[2] A notice in the *Gesta Trevirorum* (1105–1124) carries it back to the empress Helena who is said to have taken it to Treves. In the time of Frederick Barbarossa it was one of the glories of the city. On the eve of the Reformation it was solemnly shown to Maximilian I. and assembled German princes. At different dates, vast bodies of pilgrims have gone to look at it;

[1] *De pignoribus*, Migne, 156. 649 sqq.

[2] Among the legends of its discovery is the following: Herod gave the coat to a Jew because the drops of blood would not come out. The Jew threw it into the sea. A whale swallowed it. Orendel, son of the king of Treves, on his way to Jerusalem caught the fish and rescued the garment. It is described as five feet one inch long, and of the color of a sponge.

the largest number in 1891, when 1,925,130 people passed through the cathedral for this purpose. Many miracles were believed to have been performed.[1]

The arrival of some of Christ's blood in England, Oct. 13, 1247, was solemnized by royalty and furnishes one of the strange and picturesque religious scenes of English mediæval history. The detailed description of Matthew Paris speaks of it as "a holy benefit from heaven."[2] Its genuineness was vouched for by the Masters of the Templars and the Hospitallers, and by the seals of the patriarch of Jerusalem, and the archbishops and other prelates of the Holy Land. After fasting and keeping watch the night before, the king, Henry III., accompanied by the priests of London in full canonicals and with tapers burning, carried the vase containing the holy liquid from St. Paul's to Westminster, and made a circuit of the church, the palace, and the king's own apartments. The king proceeded on foot, holding the sacred vessel above his head. The bishop of Norwich preached a sermon on the occasion and, at a later date, Robert Grosseteste preached another in which he defended the genuineness of the relic, giving a memorable exhibition of scholastic ingenuity.[3]

The true cross was found more than once and fragments of it were numerous, so numerous that the fiction had to be invented that the true cross had the singular property of multiplying itself indefinitely. A choice must be made between the stories. The first Crusaders beheld the cross in Jerusalem. Richard I., during the Third Crusade, was directed to a piece of it by an aged man, the abbot of St. Elie, who had buried it in the ground and refused to deliver it up to Saladin, even though that prince put him in bonds to force him to do so. Richard and the army kissed it with pious devotion.[4] Among the objects which the abbot, Martin, secured in Constantinople were a piece of the true cross and a drop of the Lord's blood. The true cross, how-

---

[1] See Wetzer-Welte, *Der hl. Rock*, X. 1229 sqq.

[2] Luard's ed., IV. 641–643.

[3] Luard, VI. 138–144. See Stevenson's *Grosseteste*, p. 263.

[4] De Vinsauf, *Chronicle of Richard's Crusade*, LIV.

ever, was still entire, and in 1241 it reached Paris.   It
had originally been bought by the Venetians from the king
of Jerusalem for £20,000, and was purchased from the
Emperor Baldwin by Louis IX.   The relic was received with
great ceremony and carried into the French capital by the
king, with feet and head bare, and accompanied by his
mother, Blanche, the queen, the king's brothers, and a great
concourse of nobles and clergy.[1]   The crown of thorns was
carried in the same procession.   At a later time these relics
were placed in the new and beautiful chapel which Louis built,
a supposed holy coat of Christ, the iron head of the lance
which pierced his side, and the sponge offered to him on
the cross, together with other relics.

The English chronicler's enthusiasm for this event seems
not to have been in the least dampened by the fact that the
English abbey of Bromholm also possessed the true cross.
It reached England in 1247, through a monk who had found
it among the effects of the Emperor Baldwin, after he had
fallen in battle.   The monk appeared at the convent door
with his two children, and carrying the sacred relic under
his cloak.   Heed was given to his story and he was taken in.
Miracles at once began to be performed, even to the cleansing of lepers and the raising of the dead.[2]

Some idea of the popular estimate of the value of relics
may be had from the story which Cæsar of Heisterbach relates of a certain Bernard who belonged to Cæsar's convent.[3]
Bernard was in the habit of carrying about with him a box
containing the relics of St. Peter and St. Paul.   Happening
to give way to sensual thoughts, the two saints gave him a
punch in the side.   On Bernard's assuming a proper mental
state, the thumping stopped, but as soon as he renewed the
unseemly thoughts the thumping began again.   Bernard
took the hint and finally desisted altogether.   Cæsar had
the satisfaction of knowing that when Bernard had these
experiences, he was not yet a monk.

---

[1] Luard's *M. Paris*, IV. 90 sq.; De Voragine, VII. 210.
[2] Luard's ed., III. 30 sq.   [3] *Dial.*, VIII. 67, Strange's ed., II. 138.

The resentment of relics at being mistreated frequently came within the range of Cæsar's experience.   One of St. Nicolas' teeth, kept at Brauweiler, on one occasion jumped out of the glass box which contained it, to show the saint's disgust at the irreverence of the people who were looking at it.   Another case was of the relics of two virgins which had been hid in time of war and were left behind when other relics were restored to the reliquary.   They were not willing to be neglected and struck so hard against the chest which held them that the noise was heard all through the convent, and continued to be heard till they were released.[1]

An organized traffic in relics was carried on by unscrupulous venders who imposed them upon the credulity of the pious.   The Fourth Lateran sought to put a stop to it by forbidding the veneration of novelties without the papal sanction.   According to Guibert of Nogent,[2] the worshipper who made the mistake of associating spurious relics with a saint whom he wished to worship, did not thereby lose any benefit that might accrue from such worship.   All the saints, he said, are one body in Christ (John 17:22), and in worshipping one reverence is done to the whole corporation.

The devil, on occasion, had a hand in attesting the genuineness of relics.   By his courtesy a nail in the reliquiary of Cologne, of whose origin no one knew anything, was discovered to be nothing less than one of the nails of the cross.[3] Such kind services, no doubt, were rare.   The court-preacher of Weimar, Irenæus, 1566–1570, visiting Treves in company with the duchess of Weimar, found one of the devil's claws in one of the churches.   The story ran, that at the erection of a new altar, the devil was more than usually enraged, and kicked so hard against the altar that he left a claw sticking in the wood.[4]

[1] *Dial.*, VIII. 68, 85.   [2] Migne, 156. 627.   [3] Hauck, IV. 74.

[4] Treves, Cologne, and Aachen were distinguished by the number of their reliquary possessions.   Gelenius, a Cologne priest, in his *de admiranda sacra et civili magnitudine Coloniæ*, 1645, enumerated a great number of relics to be found in Cologne, such as pieces of the true cross, the manger, some of the earth on which Mary stood when she received the angelic

The attitude of the Protestant churches to relics was expressed by Luther in his Larger Catechism when he said, "*es ist alles tot Ding das niemand heiligen kann.*" They are lifeless, dead things, that can make no man holy.

§ 132. *The Sermon.*

LITERATURE : A. NEBE : *Charakterbilder d. bedeutendsten Kanzelredner,* Vol. I. Origen to Tauler, 1879. — J. M. NEALE : *Med. Preachers,* Lond., 1853, new ed., 1873. — J. A. BROADUS : *The Hist. of Preaching,* N.Y., 1876. A bare sketch. — *H. HERING : *Gesch. d. Predigt.* (pp. 55–68), Berlin, 1905. — E. C. DARGAN : *Hist. of Preaching, from 70 to 1570,* N.Y., 1905.

For the French Pulpit : *LECOY DE LA MARCHE : *La chaire franc. au moyen âge speciallement au XIIIe siècle,* Paris, 1868, new ed., 1886. — L. BOURGAIN : *La chaire franc. au XIIme siècle d'après les Mss.,* Paris, 1879. — J. VON WALTER : *D. ersten Wanderprediger Frankreichs,* 2 parts, Leip., 1903, 1906.

For the German Pulpit: W. WACKERNAGEL : *Altdeutsche Predigten und Gebete,* Basel, 1876. — *R CRUEL : *Gesch. d. deutschen Predigt im MtA.,* Detmold, 1879. — *A. LINSENMAYER (Rom. Cath.) : *Gesch. der Predigt in Deutschland von Karl dem Grossen bis zum Ausgange d. 14ten Jahrhunderts,* Munich, 1886. — HAUCK : *Kirchengesch.* —Collections of med. Ger. sermons. — H. LEYSER : *Deutsche Predigten d. 13ten und 14ten Jahrhunderts,* 1838. — K. ROTH : *Deutsche Predigten des XII. und XIII. Jahrhunderts,* 1839. — F. K. GRIESHABER : *Deutsche Predigt. d. XIII. Jahrhunderts,* 2 vols. Stuttg., 1844. — *A. E. SCHÖNBACH : *Altdeutsche Predigten,* 3 vols. Graz, 1886–1891 ; *Studien zur Gesch. d. altdeutschen Predigt.* (on Berthold of Regensburg), 3 parts, Vienna, 1904–1906. — A. FRANZ : *Drei Minoritenprediger aus d. XIII. u. XIV. Jahrh.,* Freib., 1907.

For the English Pulpit : R. MORRIS : *Old Engl. Homilies of the Twelfth and Thirteenth Centuries,* 2 vols. Lond., 1868–1873. — See T. F. CRANE : *Introd. to the Exempla of Jacob de Vitry,* Folklore Soc., Lond., 1890. — RICHARDSON: *Voragine as a Preacher,* Presb. Rev., July, 1904.

Although the office of the preacher in the Middle Ages was overshadowed by the function of the priest, the art of preaching was not altogether neglected. The twelfth and

announcement, one of John the Baptist's teeth, a piece of his garment, hairs from the head of Bartholomew, and remains of the children of Bethlehem. As recently as Nov. 30, 1898, the archbishop of Cologne announced that one of St. Andrew's arms would be shown after having lain in repose for one hundred years. It was found in a chest with other relics which had been packed away during the French Revolution.

the thirteenth centuries have each contributed at least one
pulpit orator of the first magnitude: St. Bernard, whom we
think of as the preacher in the convent and the preacher of
the Crusades, and Berthold of Regensburg, the Whitefield
of his age, who moved vast popular assemblies with practical
discourses.

Two movements aroused the dormant energies of the pulpit: the Crusades, in the twelfth century, and the rise of the
Mendicant orders in the thirteenth century.   The example of the heretical sects preaching on the street and the
roadside also acted as a powerful spur upon the established
Church.

Ambrose had pronounced the bishop's chief function to be
preaching.   The nearest approach made to that definition by
a formal pronouncement of these centuries is found in the
tenth canon of the Fourth Lateran.   After emphasizing the
paramount necessity of knowing the Word of God, the council commended the practice whereby bishops, in case of their
incapacity, appointed apt men to take their place in preaching.   Pope Innocent III. himself preached, and fifty-eight
of his sermons are preserved.[1]   The references to preaching
in the acts of councils are rare.   Now and then we hear an
admonition from a writer on homiletics or a preacher in
favor of frequent preaching.   So Honorius of Autun, in an
address to priests, declared that, if they lived a good life and
did not publicly teach or preach, they were like the "watch-
men without knowledge" and as dumb dogs (Isa. 56 : 9).
and, if they preached and lived ill, they were as blind leaders
of the blind.[2]   Etienne de Bourbon speaks with commendation of a novice of the Dominican order who, on being urged
to go into another order, replied: "I do not read that Jesus
Christ was either a black or a white monk, but that he was
a poor preacher.   I will follow in his steps."

It is impossible to determine with precision the frequency
with which sermons were preached in parishes.   Probably

---

[1] See Hurter's judgment of Innocent as a preacher, II. 729 sqq.
[2] *Spec. eccles.*, Migne, 172. 862.

one-half of the priests in Germany in the twelfth century did not preach.[1] The synod of Treves, 1227, forbade illiterate priests preaching. A sermon in England was a rarity before the arrival of the friars. A parson might have held a benefice fifty years without ever having preached a sermon. There were few pulpits in those days in English churches.[2]

In the thirteenth century a notable change took place, through the example of the friars. They were preachers and went among the people. Vast audiences gathered in the fields and streets to listen to an occasional popular orator, like Anthony of Padua and Berthold of Regensburg. At the beginning of the fourteenth century, the Franciscans received formal permission from Clement V., "to preach on the streets the Word of God."

Nor was the preaching confined to men in orders. Laymen among the heretics and also among the orthodox groups and the Flagellants exercised their gifts.[3] Innocent III., in his letter to the bishop of Metz, 1199, and Gregory IX., 1235, condemned the unauthorized preaching of laymen. There were also boy preachers in those days.[4]

The vernacular was used at the side of the Latin.[5] Samson, abbot of Bury St. Edmunds, preached in English, and Grosseteste in the later years of his life followed his example. Bishop Hermann of Prague, d. 1122, preached in Bohemian.[6] Of Berthold's sermons which are preserved, five hundred are in Latin and seventy-one in German.

Congregations were affected much as congregations are to-day. Cæsar of Heisterbach, who himself was a preacher, tells of a congregation that went to sleep and snored during a sermon. The preacher, suddenly turning from the line of his discourse, exclaimed: "Hear, my brethren, I will tell you something new and strange. There was once a king called Artus." The sleepers awoke and the preacher continued, "See, brethren, when I spoke about God, you slept, but

---

[1] Cruel, pp. 210, 262.   [2] Jessopp, *Coming of the Friars*, p. 86.
[3] Linsenmayer, p. 125 sqq.   [4] Salimbene, Coulton's ed., p. 305.
[5] Hurter, IV. 507 ; Cruel, p. 217.
[6] His *homiliarium* was ed. by Hecht, 1863.

when I began to tell a trivial story, you pricked up your ears
to hear."[1] Cæsar was himself present on this occasion.

The accounts of contemporaries leave no room to doubt
that extraordinary impressions were made upon great audiences.[2] The sermons that have come down to us are almost
invariably based upon a text or paragraph of Scripture and
are full of biblical instruction, doctrinal inference, and moral
application. It was well understood that the personality of
the preacher has much to do with the effectiveness of a
discourse. Although the people along the Rhine did not
understand the language of St. Bernard, they were moved
to the very depths by his sermons. When his language was
interpreted, they lost their power.

Four treatises have come down to us from this period on
homiletics and the pulpit, by Guibert of Nogent, Alanus ab
Insulis, Humbert de Romanis, and Hugo de St. Cher.[3] Their
counsels do not vary much from the counsels given by writers
on these subjects to-day. Guibert, in his What Order a
Sermon should Follow,[4] insists upon the priest keeping up
his studies, preparing his sermons with prayer, and cultivating the habit of turning everything he sees into a symbol of
religious truth. He sets forth the different motives by
which preachers were actuated, from a desire of display by
ventriloquism to an honest purpose to instruct and make
plain the Scriptures.

In his Art of Preaching,[5] Alanus counsels preachers to
court the good-will of their audiences by cultivating humility of manner and by setting forth useful instruction. He
must so impress them that they will think not of who is
talking, but of what is being talked about. He advises the
use of quotations from Gentile authors, following Paul's
example. After giving other counsels, Alanus in forty-

---

[1] *Dial.*, IV. 36.

[2] Dargan, p. 229, says that " probably the largest audiences ever gathered
to hear preaching" were gathered in the thirteenth century.

[3] *Speculum ecclesiæ*, Lyons, 1554.

[4] *Quo ordine sermo fieri debeat*, Migne, 157. 20–34.

[5] *Summa de arte prædicatoria*, Migne, 210. 111–198.

seven chapters presents illustrations of the treatment of
different themes, such as the contempt of the world, luxury,
gluttony, godly sorrow, joy, patience, faith.   He then
furnishes specimens of exhortations to different classes of
hearers: princes, lawyers, monks, the married, widows, virgins, the somnolent.

Humbert de Romanis, general of the order of the Dominicans, d. 1277, in a much more elaborate work,[1] pronounced
preaching the most excellent of a monk's occupations and set
it above the liturgical service which, being in Latin, the
people did not understand.   Preaching is even better than
the mass, for Christ celebrated the mass only once, but was
constantly engaged in preaching.   He urged the necessity
of study, and counselled high thought rather than graceful
and well-turned sentences, comparing the former to food
and the latter to the dishes on which it is served.

To these homiletical rules and hints must be added the
notices scattered through the sermons of preachers like
Honorius of Autun and Cæsar of Heisterbach.   Cæsar said,[2]
a sermon should be like a net, made up of texts of Scripture ;
and like an arrow, sharp to pierce the hearts of the hearers ;
straight, that is, without any false doctrine ; and feathered,
that is, easy to be understood.   The bow is the Word of
God.

Among the prominent preachers from 1050 to 1200, whose
sermons have been preserved, were Peter Damiani, d. 1072,
Ivo of Chartres, d. 1116, Hildebert of Tours, d. 1133, Abælard, d. 1142, St. Bernard, d. 1153, and Maurice, archbishop
of Paris, d. 1196.   Of the eloquence of Arnold of Brescia,
Norbert, the founder of the Premonstrant order, and Fulke of
Neuilly, the fiery preacher of the Fourth Crusade, no specimens are preserved.   Another class of preachers were the
itinerant preachers, some of whom were commissioned by
popes, as were Robert of Abrissel and Bernard of Thiron who
went about clad in coarse garments and with flowing beards,
preaching to large concourses of people.   They preached

---

[1] *De eruditione prædicatorum.*   [2] Quoted by Cruel, p. 249.

repentance and sharply rebuked the clergy for their worldliness, themselves wept and brought their hearers to tears.

Bernard enjoys the reputation of being, up to his time, the
most brilliant luminary of the pulpit after the days of
Gregory the Great.   Luther held his sermons in high regard
and called him "the golden preacher"— *der güldene Prediger.*
Among the preachers of France he is placed at the side of
Bourdaloue and Bossuet.   He has left more than two hundred and fifty discourses on special texts and themes in
addition to the eighty-six homilies on the Song of Solomon.[1]
The subjects of the former range from the five pebbles which
David picked up from the brook to the most solemn mysteries of Christ's life and work.   The sermons were not written
out, but delivered from notes or improvised after meditation
in the convent garden.   For moral earnestness, flights of
imagination, pious soliloquy, and passionate devotion to religious themes, they have a place in the first rank of pulpit
productions.   " The constant shadow of things eternal is over
them all," said Dr. Storrs, himself one of the loftiest figures
in the American pulpit of the last century.   One of the
leading authorities on his life, Deutsch, has said that Bernard combined in himself all the qualities of a great preacher,
a vivid apprehension of the grace of God, a profound desire
to help his hearers, a thorough knowledge of the human
heart, familiarity with the Scriptures, opulence of thought,
and a faculty of magnetic description.[2]

Fulke of Neuilly, pastor in Neuilly near Paris, was a man
of different mould from Bernard, but, like him, his eloquence
is associated with the Crusades.[3]   He was a born orator.
His sermons on repentance in Notre Dame and on the streets
of Paris were accompanied with remarkable demonstrations,
the people throwing themselves on the ground, weeping and
scourging themselves.   Usurers " whom the devil alone was

---

[1] *See* Vacandard, *S. Bernard*, I. 474 sqq., and Storrs, *St. Bernard*, pp.
355–427, Migne, 183. 73–747, 784–1105.

[2] Art. *Bernard*, in Herzog, II. 634.

[3] A. Charasson, *Un curé plébéien au XIIe siècle Foulques, curé de Veuilly*,
Paris, 1905.

able to make," fallen women, and other offenders turned from their evil ways.   Called forth by Innocent III. to proclaim the Fourth Crusade, Fulke influenced, as he himself estimated, no less than two million to take the cross.   He did not live to hear of the capture of Constantinople, to which event unintentionally he made so large a contribution.

The great preachers of the thirteenth century were the product of the mendicant orders or, like Grosseteste, sympathized with their aims and methods.   The Schoolmen who belonged to these orders seem all to have been preachers, and their sermons, or *collations*, delivered in the convents, many of which are preserved, received the highest praise from contemporaries, but partook of the scholastic method.   Albertus Magnus, Thomas Aquinas, and Bonaventura were preachers, Bonaventura[1] being a great preacher.   Albertus' thirty-two sermons on the eucharist, based upon Proverbs 9 : 5, constitute one of the first series of discourses of the Middle Ages.

To the mendicant orders belonged also the eminent popular preachers, Anthony of Padua, John of Vicenza, and Berthold of Regensburg.   Anthony of Padua, 1195–1231, born at Lisbon, entered the Franciscan order and made Northern Italy the scene of his labors.   He differed from Francis in being a well-schooled man.   He joined himself to the Conventual party, at whose head stood Elias of Cortona. Like Francis he was a lover of nature and preached to the fishes.   He preached in the fields and the open squares. As many as thirty thousand are reported to have flocked to hear him.   He denied having the power of working miracles, but legend has associated miracles with his touch and his tomb.   The fragments of his sermons, which are preserved, are mere sketches and, like Whitefield's printed discourses, give no clew to the power of the preacher.   Anthony was canonized the year after his death by Gregory IX.   His remains were deposited, in 1263, in the church in Padua reared

---

[1] Peltier's ed., XIII. 1–636, etc.   For Thomas' sermons, see Bourin, *La prédication en France et les sermons de Thomas*, Paris, 1882.   Vaughan is fulsome in praise of Thomas as a preacher.   *Life*, etc., I. 459 sq., II. 104 sqq., 112–117.

to his memory. Bonaventura was present. The body was found to have wholly dissolved except the tongue.[1]

Berthold of Regensburg, d. 1272, had for his teacher David of Augsburg, d. 1271, also a preacher of renown. A member of the Franciscan order, Berthold itinerated from Thuringia to Bohemia, and from Spires to the upper Rhine regions as far as the Swiss canton of the Grisons. He was familiarly known as *rusticanus*, "the field preacher." According to contemporaries, he was listened to by sixty thousand at a time. His sermons were taken down by others and, to correct mistakes, he was obliged to edit an edition with his own hand.[2]

This celebrated preacher's style is exceedingly pictorial. He drew illustrations from the stars and the fields, the forests and the waters. The most secret motives of the heart seemed to lie open before him. Cruel, the historian of the mediæval German pulpit, gives as the three elements of his power: his popular speech easily understood by the laity, his personality which he never hid behind a quoted authority, and his burning love for God and man. He preached unsparingly against the vices of his age: usury, avarice, unchastity, drunkenness, the dance, and the tournament, and everything adapted to destroy the sanctity of the home.

He urged as motives the fatherhood of God and the brotherhood of man. But especially did he appeal to the fear of perdition and its torments. If your whole body, he said, was glowing iron and the whole world on fire, yet are the pains of the lost many times greater, and when the soul is reunited with the body in hell, then it will be as passing from dew to a burning mountain. The sermons are enlivened by vivacious dialogues in which the devil is a

[1] The writer in Wetzer-Welte, I. 995, declares that the tongue remains whole to this day. See Lempp, *Leben d. hl. Antonius v. Padua.*

[2] The works and collections of Berthold's sermons are numerous. Cruel, pp. 307–322 ; Linsenmayer, pp. 333–354 ; E. Bernhardt, *Bruder Berthold von Regensb.*, etc., Erf., 1905. Ed. of his sermons by Kling, Berlin, 1824; Pfeiffer, Vienna, 1862 ; J. Strobel, 2 vols. Vienna, 1880 ; Gobel, 2 vols. Schaffh., 1850 ; 4th ed., Regensb., 1905 ; also *Predigten a. d. Sonn und Festtagen*, 2 vols. 1884 ; G. Jacob, *D. latein. Reden d. Berthold*, etc., Regensb., 1880.

leading figure.   Berthold demanded penitence as well as works of penance.   But he was a child of his time, was hard on heretics, and did not oppose any of the accepted dogmas.

A considerable number of sermons, many of them anonymous, are preserved from the mediæval pulpit of Germany, where preaching seemed to be most in vogue.[1] Among the preachers were Gottfried, abbot of Admont, d. 1165, Honorius of Autun, d. 1152, and Werner of St. Blasius in the Black Forest, d. 1126.   Gottfried's sermons, of which about two hundred are preserved, occupy more than a thousand columns in Migne (174. 21-1133), and are as full of exegetical and edifying material as any other discourses of the Middle Ages.

Honorius and Werner both prepared *homiliaria*, or collections of sermons which were meant to be a homiletical arsenal for preachers.   Honorius' collection, the Mirror of the Church — *Speculum ecclesiæ*[2] — is made up of his own discourses, most of the texts being taken from the Psalms. The sermons are arranged under thirty-six Sundays or festival days, with as many as three or four sermons under a single head.   In one of them he addresses himself to one class after another, calling them by name.   One of the interesting things about these model discourses is the homiletical hints that are thrown in here and there.   The following two show that it was necessary, even in those good old times, to adapt the length of the sermon to the patience of the hearers.   " You may finish here if you choose, or if time permits, you may add the following things."   " For the sake of brevity you must sometimes shorten this sermon and at other times you may prolong it."

Werner's collection, the *Deflorationes sanctorum patrum*, or Flowers from the Fathers, fills more than five hundred columns in Migne (151. 734-1294), and joins, with discourses from patristic times, other sermons, some of them probably by Werner himself.   Thirteen are taken from Honorius of

[1] See Cruel, 146-208 ; Linsenmayer, 191-320.
[2] Migne, vol. 172. See Rocholl, in Herzog, VIII. 327-331; Endres, *Honor. August.*, Leip., 1903. Honorius called himself Augustoduniensis, but it is doubtful whether Autun or Strassburg is meant.

Autun.   It would be interesting, if there were space, to give specimens of the sermonic literature contained in these collections.

Of the pulpit in England there is not much to be said. It had no preachers equal in fame to the preachers of Germany and Italy.   The chief source of our information are the two volumes of Old English Homilies by Morris, which contain an English translation at the side of the Saxon original.   The names of the preachers are lost.   The sermons are brief expositions of texts of Scripture, the Creed, the Lord's Prayer, and on Mary and the Apostles, and are adapted to the wants and temptations of everyday life.   In a sermon on the Creed [1] the general statement of the introduction is such as might be made by a wise preacher to-day : " Three things there are that each man must have who will lead a Christian life, a right belief, baptism, and a fair life, for he is not fully a Christian who is wanting in any of these."   One of the sermons quaintly treats of the traps set by the devil in four pits : play, and the trap idleness; drink, and the trap wrong-doing; the market, and the trap cheating; and the Church, and the trap pride.   In the last trap the clergy are ensnared as when the priest neglects to perform the service or to speak what he ought to, or sings so as to catch the ears of women. [2]

A general conclusion to be drawn from the sermons of this period of the Middle Ages is that human passions and the tendency to shirk religious duties or to substitute the appearance for the reality were about the same as they are to-day.   Another conclusion is that the modes of appeal employed were about the same as the earnest preacher employs in this age, except that in those days much more emphasis was laid upon the pains of future punishment.

§ 133.   *Hymns and Sacred Poetry.*

LATIN HYMNS : H. A. DANIEL : *Thesaurus Hymnol.*, 5 vols. Halle and Leipzig, 1855–1856. — F. J. MONE : *Latein. Hymnen d. Mittelalters*, 3 vols. Freib., 1853–1855. — R. C. TRENCH : *Sacr. Lat. Poetry with Notes*, Lond., 1849, 3d ed., 1874. — G. A. KÖNIGSFELD : *Latein. Hymnen und*

---

[1] *Old Engl. Hom.*, II. 14.   [2] II. 209 sqq.

Gesänge d. MtA., 2 vols. Bonn, 1847-1863 with transll. — J. M. NEALE : *Med. Hymns and Sequences*, Lond., 1851, 3d ed., 1867 ; *Hymns chiefly Med. on the Joys and Glories of Paradise*, Lond., 1862, 4th ed., by S. G. HATHERLEY, 1882. — W. J. LOFTIE : *Lat. Hymns*, 3 vols. Lond., 1873-1877. — F. W. E. ROTH : *Lat. Hymnen d. MtA.*, Augsb., 1888. — * G. M. DREVES and C. BLUME : *Analecta hymnica medii œvi*, Leipz., 1886-1906, 49 parts in 16 vols. — U. CHEVALIER : *Repertorium hymnol. Cat. des chants, hymnes, proses, sequences, tropes*, etc., 2 vols. Louvaine, 1892-1897 ; *Poésie liturg. du moyen âge*, Paris, 1893. — S. G. PIRMONT : *Les hymnes du Bréviare rom.*, 3 vols. Paris, 1874-1884. — ED. CASWALL: *Lyra Catholica* (197 transll.), Lond., 1849. — R. MANT : *Anc. Hymns from the Rom. Brev.*, new ed., Lond., 1871. — F. A. MARCH : *Lat. Hymns with Engl. Notes*, N.Y., 1874. — D. T. MORGAN : *Hymns and other Poems of the Lat. Ch.*, Oxf., 1880. — W. H. FRERE : *The Winchester Tropar from MSS. of the 10th and 11th centt.*, Lond., 1894. — H. MILLS : *The Hymn of Hildebert and the Ode of Xavier*, with Engl. transll., Auburn, 1844. — W. C. PRIME : *The Seven Great Hymns of the Med. Ch.*, N.Y., 1865. — E. C. BENEDICT: *The Hymn of Hildebert and other Med. Hymns*, with transll., N.Y., 1867, 2d ed., 1869. — A. COLES : *Dies Iræ and other Lat. Poems*, N.Y., 1868. — D. S. WRANGHAM : *The Liturg. Poetry of Adam de St. Victor*, with Engl. transll., 3 vols. Lond., 1881. — OZANAM : *Les Poètes Franciscains en Italie au XIIIe siècle*, Paris, 1852, 3d ed. 1859. — L. GAUTIER : *Œuvres poet. d'Adam de St. Victor*, Paris, 1858, 2d ed., 1887 ; *Hist. de la poésie liturg. au moyen âge*, Paris, 1886. — P. SCHAFF: *Christ in Song, a Collection of Hymns*, Engl. and trans. with notes, N.Y. and Lond., 1869. — SCHAFF and GILMAN : *Libr. of Rel. Poetry*, N.Y., 1881. — SCHAFF: *Lit. and Poetry*, N.Y., 1890. Contains essays of St. Bernard as a Hymnist, the *Dies iræ, Stabat mater*, etc. — S. W. DUFFIELD : *Lat. Hymn Writers and their Hymns*, N.Y., 1889.

FOR GERMAN HYMNS, etc. : C. E. P. WACKERNAGEL: *D. deutsche Kirchenlied von d. ältesten Zeit bis zum 1600*, 5 vols. Leip., 1864-1877. — Ed. E. KOCH : *Gesch. des Kirchenlieds und Kirchengesangs*, 2 vols. 1847, 3d ed., by LAUXMANN, 8 vols. 1866-1876. — Artt., *Hymnus and Kirchenlied* in Wetzer-Welte, VI. 519-551, VII. 600-606; *Kirchenlied*, in Herzog, by DREWS, X. 409-419, and *Lat. and Ger. Hymnody in Julian's Dicty. of Hymnology*.

NOTE. — The collection of Latin hymns by Dreves and Blume, members of the Society of Jesus, is a monument of persevering industry and scholarship. It is with few exceptions made up of hitherto unpublished poems. The collection is meant to be exhaustive and one is fairly amazed at the extent of mediæval sacred poetry. There are about seven hundred pages and an average of eleven hundred poems to each volume. Monasteries and breviaries of every locality in Western Europe were searched for hymnological treasures. In cases, an entire number, or *Heft* (for the volumes have appeared in numbers), is given up to the poems of a single convent, as No. VII., pp. 282, to the proses of St. Martial

in Limoges. No. XL. contains *sequences* taken from English MSS., such
as the missals of Salisbury, York, Canterbury, and Winchester, and is
edited by H. M. Bannister, 1902. Among the more curious parts is No.
XXVII., pp. 287, containing the religious poems of the Mozarabic, or
Gothic liturgy. If Dreves adds a printed edition of the mediæval Latin
poetry found in Mone, Daniel, and other standard collections, his collection will supersede all the collections of his predecessors.

The mediæval sermon is, at best, the object of curious
search by an occasional student. It is otherwise with some
of the mediæval hymns. They shine in the cluster of the
great hymns of all the ages. They have entered into the
worship of all the churches of the West and continue to
exercise a sanctifying mission. They are not adapted to the
adherents of one confession or age alone, but to Christian
believers of every age.

The Latin sacred poems of the Middle Ages, of which
thousands have been preserved, were written, for the most
part, in the shadow of cloistral walls, notably St. Gall, St.
Martial in Limoges, Cluny, Clairvaux, and St. Victor near
Paris. Few of them passed into public use in the church
service, or were rendered by the voice. They served the purpose of devotional reading. The rhyme is universal after 1150.

These poems include liturgical proses, hymns, sequences,
tropes, psalteries, and rhymed prayers to the rosary, called
rosaria. The psalteries, *psalteria rhythmica*, in imitation of
the Psalms, are divided into one hundred and fifty parts,
and are addressed to the Trinity, to Jesus and to Mary, the
larger number of them to Mary.[1] Sequence, a word first
applied to a melody, came also to be used for a sacred poem.
Notker of St. Gall was the first to adapt such poems to
sequences or melodies.[2] The tropes were verses interpolated
into the offices of the liturgy, and were joined on to the
Gloria, the *Hosanna*, and other parts. They started in
France and were most popular there and in England.[3]

[1] In No. XXXV., 254–270, Dreves gives two psalteries, ascribed to Anselm.

[2] *Anal. Hymn.*, XLVII. 11 sq.

[3] Blume has collected hundreds of tropes in *Anal. Hymn.* They extended from two or three to as many as fifty lines. Gautier was the first to
call the attention of modern students to this forgotten form of med. poetry.

The authorship of the Latin mediæval poetry belongs
chiefly to France and Germany. England produced only a
limited number of religious poems, and no one of the first
rank. The best is Archbishop Peckham's (d. 1292) rhymed
office to the Trinity, from which three hymns were taken.[1]
One verse of the poem runs: —

Adesto, sancta trinitas	Come near, O holy Trinity,
Par splendor, una deitas,	In splender equal, in deity one;
Qui exstas rerum omnium	Of all things that exist
Sine fine principium.	The beginning, and without end.

The number of mediæval hymns in German is also large.
The custom of blending German and Latin lines in the same
hymn was also very common, especially in the next period.
The number of Saxon hymns, that is hymns produced in
England, was very limited.[2]

Although the liturgical service was chanted by the priests,
singing was also in vogue among the people, especially in
Northern Italy and in Germany. The Flagellants sang.
Gerhoh of Reichersberg (d. 1169) said that all the people
poured forth praises to the Saviour in hymns.[3] At the battle
of Tusculum, 1168, the army sang,

Christ der du geboren bist.

St. Bernard, when he left Germany, spoke of missing the
German songs of his companions. At popular religious
services the people also to some extent joined in song.
The songs were called *Leisen* and Berthold of Regensburg
was accustomed, at the close of his sermons, to call upon the
congregation to sing.[4] He complained of heretics drawing
away children by their songs. Honorius of Autun gives
directions for the people to join in the singing, such as the

[1] They are found in prose renderings in the Primer of Sarum of about
1400 (ed. by Maskell, *Mon. ritualia*, Vol. III.). Daniel gives all three, I. 276,
etc. Dreves gives the *adesto* and the *festi laudes*, No. IV., 14, and calls
the former, " a hymn in the strict sense of the word." See No. XXIII.,
5, 6, where Dreves pronounces Peckham as, beyond dispute, their author.

[2] Two addressed to Mary and one to God are given by Morris, *Old Engl.
Hom.*, II. 255 sqq.

[3] Hauck, IV. 60.   [4] Linsenmayer, *Deutsche Predigt*, pp. 70, 132.

following: "Now lift high your voices," or "Lift up your song, Let us praise the Son of God."

As compared with the hymns of the Ambrosian group and of Prudentius, the mediæval sacred poems are lacking in their strong and triumphant tone. They are written in the minor key, and give expression to the softer feelings of the heart, and its fears and forebodings. They linger at the cross and over the mystery of the Lord's Supper, passionately supplicate the intercession of Mary or dwell on her perfections, and also depict the awful solemnities of the judgment and the entrancing glories of paradise. Where we are unable to follow the poet in his theology, we cannot help but be moved by his soft cadences and the tenderness of his devotion.

Among the poets of the earlier part of the period are Peter Damiani, some of whose hymns were received into the Breviaries,[1] Anselm of Canterbury, and Hildebert, archbishop of Tours (d. 1134). Some of Hildebert's lines were used by Longfellow in his "Golden Legend." Abælard also wrote hymns, one of which, on the creation, was translated by Trench.[2]

Bernard of Clairvaux, according to Abælard's pupil, Berengar, cultivated poetic composition from his youth.[3] Five longer religious poems are ascribed to him.[4] From the Rhythmic Song on the name of Christ — *Jubilus rhythmicus de nomine Jesu* — the Roman Breviary has drawn three hymns, which are used on the festival of the name of Christ. They are: —

---

[1] Migne, 145. 930 sqq. See *Libr. of Rel. Poetry*, pp. 897, 980.

[2] Cousin gave 97 of these poems in his ed. of Abælard, 1849.

[3] *Apol. pro Abælardo*, Migne, 178. 1857.

[4] See Herold, *Bernhard's Hymnen*, in Herzog, II. 649. The text of the hymns is found in Migne, 184. 1307 sqq., and in part in Schaff, *Lit. and Poetry*, etc. Mabillon, whose edition Migne reproduced, casts doubt upon the genuineness of all but two of these poems, and Vacandard (*Vie de S. Bern.*, II. 103) and Haureau (*Les poèms attribués à S. Bern.*, Paris, 1890) upon all of them. But they are ascribed to Bernard by the oldest tradition and no one can be found so likely to be their author as Bernard. Herold advocates the Bernardian authorship.

Jesus, the very thought of thee.   *Jesu, dulcis memoria.*
Jesus, King most wonderful.   *Jesu, rex admirabilis.*
O Jesus, thou the beauty art.   *Jesu, decus angelicum.*

The first of these hymns has been called by Dr. Philip Schaff, "the sweetest and most evangelical hymn of the Middle Ages."

The free version of some of the verses by Ray Palmer is the most popular form of Bernard's poem as used in the American churches.

> Jesus, thou Joy of loving hearts,
>   Thou Fount of life, thou Light of men,
> From the best bliss that earth imparts
>   We turn unfilled to thee again.

The poem to the Members of Christ's body on the Cross — *Rhythmica oratio ad unum quodlibet membrorum Christi patientis* — is a series of devotional poems addressed to the crucified Saviour's feet, knees, hands, side, breast, heart, and face. From the poem addressed to our Lord's face — *Salve caput cruentatum* — John Gerhardt, 1656, took his

> *O Haupt voll Blut und Wunden.*
> O sacred head, now wounded,
>   With grief and shame weighed down.

Much as Bernard influenced his own age in other ways, he continues to influence our own effectively and chiefly by his hymns.

Bernard of Cluny, d. about 1150, has an enduring name as the author of the most beautiful and widely sung hymn on heaven, "Jerusalem the Golden." He was an inmate of the convent of Cluny when Peter the Venerable was its abbot, 1122–1156. From his probable place of birth, Morlaix, Brittany, he is sometimes called Bernard of Morlaix. Of his career nothing is known. He lives in his poem, "The Contempt of the World" — *de contemptu mundi* — from which the hymns are taken which go by his name.[1] It

[1] Ninety-six lines of the original were made known to English readers by Trench. Neale's transl. is given in the *Libr. of Rel. Poetry*, pp. 981–985; a prose transl. of the whole poem by Dr. S. M. Jackson, in *Am. Journ. of Theol.*, 1906. See note in Schaff's *Christ in Song*, Lond. ed., pp. 511 sq.

contains nearly three thousand lines, and was dedicated to Peter the Venerable. At the side of its glowing descriptions of heaven, which are repetitions, it contains a satire on the follies of the age and the greed of the Roman court.[1] It is written in dactylic hexameters, with leonine and tailed rhyme, and is difficult of translation.

The most prolific of the mediæval Latin poets is Adam of St. Victor, d. about 1180. He was one of the men who made the convent of St. Victor famous. He wrote in the departments of exegesis and psychology, but it is as a poet he has enduring fame. Gautier, Neale, and Trench have agreed in pronouncing him the "foremost among the sacred Latin poets of the Middle Ages"; but none of his hymns are equal to Bernard's hymns,[2] the *Stabat mater*, or *Dies iræ*. Many of Adam's poems are addressed to Mary and the saints, including Thomas à Becket. A deep vein of piety runs through them all.[3]

Hymns of a high order and full of devotion we owe to the two eminent theologians, Bonaventura and Thomas Aquinas. Of Bonaventura's sacred poems the one which has gone into many collections of hymns begins, —

> *Recordare sanctæ crucis*
> *qui perfectam viam ducis.*
> Jesus, holy Cross, and dying.

Three of Thomas Aquinas' hymns have found a place in the Roman Breviary. For six hundred years two of these have formed a part of the ritual of Corpus Christi : namely,—

[1] For this reason Flacius Illyricus printed the poem entire in his collection of poems on the corruption of the Church, — *Varia doctorum piorumque virorum de corrupto ecclesi statu poemata*, Basel, 1557. I have a copy of this rare volume.

[2] Deutsch, art. *Adam de S. Victor*, Herzog, I. 164, Migne, vol. 196, gives 36 of Adam's poems. Gautier, in 1858, found 106 in the Louvre library, whither they had been removed at the destruction of St. Victor during the Revolution. He regards 45 as genuine.

[3] Wrangham has given translations of all of Adam's hymns. March gives eight poems in the original. Some of these have gone into English Hymnals. See Julian, p. 15.

> *Pange, lingua, gloriosi corporis mysterium,*
> Sing, my tongue, the mystery telling,

and

> *Lauda, Zion, salvatorem.*
> Zion, to thy Saviour singing.[1]

In both of these fine poems, the doctrine of transubstantiation finds full expression.

No other two hymns of ancient or mediæval times have received so much attention as the *Dies iræ* and the *Stabat
mater*. They were the product of the extraordinary religious fervor which marked the Franciscan order in its earlier period, and have never been excelled, the one by its
solemn grandeur, and the other by its tender and moving
pathos.

Thomas of Celano, the author of *Dies iræ*,[2] was born about
1200, at Celano, near Naples, and became one of the earliest
companions of Francis d'Assisi. In 1221 he accompanied
Cæsar of Spires to Germany, and a few years later was made
guardian, *custos*, of the Franciscan convents of Worms,
Spires, Mainz, and Cologne. Returning to Assisi, he wrote,
by commission of Gregory IX., his first *Life of St. Francis*,
and later, by command of the general of his order, he wrote
the second *Life*.

The *Dies iræ* opens with the lines, —

> *Dies iræ, dies illa*
> *solvet sæclum in favilla,*
> *teste David cum sibylla.*

In the most familiar of the versions, Sir Walter Scott freely
reproduced the first lines thus : —

> That day of wrath, that dreadful day,
> When heaven and earth shall pass away,
> What power shall be the sinner's stay ?
> How shall he meet that dreadful day ?

---

[1] Julian, pp. 662 sqq., 878 sqq. Also *Christ in Song*, Engl. ed., pp. 467
sqq. Daniel gives five of Thomas' hymns, I. 251–256, II. 97.

[2] The first mention of his authorship is in the *liber conformitatum*, about
1380. The oldest MS. is a Dominican missal in the Bodleian of the same
date.

This solemn poem depicts the dissolution of the world and the trembling fear of the sinner as he looks forward to the awful scene of the last day and appeals for mercy. It has been characterized by Dr. Philip Schaff,[1] "as the acknowledged masterpiece of Latin Church poetry and the greatest judgment hymn of all ages." The poet is the single actor. He realizes the coming judgment of the world, he hears the trumpet of the archangel through the open sepulchre, he expresses this sense of guilt and dismay, and ends with a prayer for the same mercy which the Saviour showed to Mary Magdalene and to the thief on the cross. The stanzas sound like the peals of an organ; now crashing like a clap of thunder, now stealing softly and tremulously like a whisper through the vacant cathedral spaces. The first words are taken from Zephaniah 1: 15. Like the Fathers and Michael Angelo and the painters of the Renaissance, the author unites the prediction of the heathen Sibyl with the prophecies of the Old Testament.

The hymn is used on All Souls Day, Nov. 2. Mozart introduced it into his requiem mass. It has been translated more frequently than any other Latin poem.[2] Walter Scott introduced it into the Lay of the Last Minstrel, and Goethe made Gretchen tremble in dismay on hearing it in the cathedral.

The most tender hymn of the Middle Ages is the *Stabat mater dolorosa.* The first verse runs: —

Stabat mater dolorosa	At the cross her station keeping,
juxta crucem lachrymosa	Stood the mournful mother weeping,
dum pendebat filius;	Close to Jesus to the last ;
cujus animam gementem	Through her heart, His sorrow sharing,
contristatam ac dolentem	All His bitter anguish bearing,
pertransivit gladius.	Now at length the sword had passed.[3]

[1] *Lit. and Poetry*, pp. 135–186.

[2] Julian, pp. 299 sqq., gives a list of 133 versions, 19 of which are used in hymn books. The *London Athenæum*, July 26, 1890, gave a still larger list of 87 British and 92 American translations. The first English version is that of Joshua Sylvester, 1621, and one of the best, that of W. J. Irons, 1848.

[3] Caswall's transl. Dr. Schaff gives a number of versions. *Lit. and Poetry*, pp. 187–218.

This hymn occupies the leading place among the many mediæval hymns devoted to Mary and, in spite of its mariolatry, it appeals to the deepest emotions of the human heart. Its passion has been transfused into the compositions of Palestrina, Astorga, Pergolesi, Haydn, Bellini, Rossini, and other musical composers.

The poem depicts the agony of Mary at the sight of her dying Son. The first line is taken from John 19 : 25. The poet prays to Mary to be joined with her in her sorrow and to be defended by her on the day of judgment and taken into glory. The hymn passed into all the missals and was sung by the Flagellants in Italy at the close of the fourteenth century.[1]

Jacopone da Todi, the author of these hymns, called also Jacobus de Benedictis (d. 1306), was converted from a wild career by the sudden death of his wife through the falling of a gallery in a theatre. He gave up the law, both degrees of which he had received from Bologna, and was admitted to the Franciscan order.[2] He abandoned himself to the extreme of ascetic austerity, appearing at one time in the public square walking on all fours and harnessed like a horse. He wrote a number of poems in the vulgar tongue, exposing the vices of his age and arraigning Boniface VIII. for avarice. He espoused the cause of the Colonna against that pope. Boniface had him thrown into prison and the story went that when the pope asked him, when he expected to get out, Jacopone replied, " when you get in." Not until Boniface's death, in 1303, was the poet released. He spent his last years in the convent of Collazone. His comfort in his last hours was his own hymn, *Giesu nostra fidanza* — Jesus our trust and confidence.

---

[1] The companion hymn, *Stabat mater speciosa*, "Stands the fair mother," ascribed to the same author, was discovered in 1852. See *Lit. and Poetry*, pp. 219–230.

[2] See Julian, pp. 1080–1084, the art. *Jacopone*, by Lauxmann-Lempp, in Herzog, VIII. 516–519, and the references to Wadding there given. The Florentine ed. of his works, 1490, contains 100 Italian poems ; the Venetian ed. of 1614, 211.

§ 134. *The Religious Drama.*

LITERATURE: W. HONE: *Anc. Mysteries*, Lond., 1823. — W. MARRIOTT: *Col. of Engl. Miracle Plays*, Basel, 1838. — J. P. COLLIER: *Hist. of Engl. Dram. Poetry*, 2 vols. Lond. 1831; new ed., 1879. — TH. WRIGHT: *Engl. Mysteries*, Lond., 1838. — F. J. MONE: *Altdeutsche Schauspiele*, Quedlinb., 1841; *D. Schauspiel d. MtA.*, 2 vols., Karlsr., 1846. — *KARL HASE: *D. geistliche Schauspiel*, Leip. 1858, Engl. transl. by A. W. Jackson, Lond. 1880. — E. DE COUSSEMAKER: *Drames liturg. du moyen âge*, Paris, 1861. — E. WILKEN: *Gesch. d. geistl. Spiele in Deutschland*, Götting., 2d ed., 1879. — A. W. WARD: *Hist. of Engl. Dram. Lit.*, Lond., 1875. — G. MILCHSACK: *D. Oster und Passionsspiele*, Wolfenbüttel, 1880. — *A. W. POLLARD: *Engl. Miracle Plays, Moralities and Interludes* with Introd. and Notes, Lond., 1890, 4th ed., 1904. — C. DAVIDSON: *Studies in the Engl. Mystery Plays*, 1892, printed for Yale Univ. — W. CREIZENACH: *Gesch. des neueren Dramas*, 3 vols. Halle, 1893–1903. — HEINZEL: *Beschreibung des geistl. Schauspiels im deutschen MtA.*, Leip., 1898. — O'CONNOR: *Sacred Scenes and Mysteries*, Lond., 1899. — *E. K. CHAMBERS: *The Mediæval Stage*, 2 vols. Oxf., 1903. — Art. in *Nineteenth Century*, June, 1905, *Festum stultorum* by Mrs. V. HEMMING. — J. S. TUNISON: *Dram. Traditions of the Dark Ages*, Cincinnati, 1907. See the large list of works in Chambers, I. xiii–xlii.

An important aid to popular religion was furnished by the sacred drama which was fostered by the clergy and at first performed in churches, or the church precincts. It was in some measure a mediæval substitute for the sermon and the Sunday-school. The old Roman drama received hard blows from the Christian Fathers, beginning with Tertullian, and from synods which condemned the vocation of the actor as inconsistent with a Christian profession. In part as a result of this opposition, and in part on account of the realistic obscenity to which it degenerated, the Roman stage was abandoned. According to the two codes of German law, the Sachsenspiegel and the Schwabenspiegel, actors had no legal rights.[1] But the dramatic instinct was not dead and after a lapse of time it showed itself again in Western Europe.

The mediæval drama was an independent growth, a product of the convent and priesthood, and was closely associated with the public religious services. Its history includes two

---

[1] Eicken, p. 674.

periods, roughly divided by the latter half of the thirteenth
century. In the earlier period, the representations were
largely under the control of the clergy. Priests were the
actors and the intent was exclusively religious. In the later
period, the elements of pantomime and burlesque were freely
introduced and priests ceased to be the controlling factors.
The modern drama begins in the sixteenth century, the age
of Shakespeare.

The names given to the mediæval representations were
ludi, plays, mysteries, miracle-plays, and moralities. The
term " morality " is used for plays which introduced the virtues and vices, personified, and carrying on dialogues teaching wholesome lessons of daily prudence and religion. The
term "mystery" comes from the word *ministerium*, meaning a sacred office.[1] The earlier period of religious dramati-
zation was also the age of itinerant singers and jesters who
went about on their mission of entertainment and instruction.
Such were the troubadours of Provence and Northern Italy,
and the joculatores and jougleurs of France who sang descriptive songs — *chansons de geste*. The minnesingers of
Germany and the English minstrels belong to the same
general group. How far these two movements influenced
each other, it is difficult to say, — the one starting from
the convent and having a strictly religious intent, the
other from the people and having for its purpose amusement.

The mediæval drama had its first literary expression in
the six short plays of Hroswitha, a nun belonging to the
Saxon convent of Gandersheim, who died about 980. They
were written in imitation of Terence and glorify martyrdom
and celibate chastity. One of them represents a Roman
governor making approaches to Christian virgins whom he
had shut up in the scullery of his palace. Happily he was
struck with madness and embraced the pots and kettles and,
covered with soot and dirt, was unceremoniously hustled

---

[1] Not from *mysterium*. The early French word was *misterre*. The term
" mystery " was not used in England. The terms in use were plays, miracles, and miracle-plays.

about by the devil. It is not known whether these plays
were acted out or not.[1]

Hroswitha was an isolated personality and the mediæval
play had its origin not with her, but in the liturgical ritual
for the festivals of Easter, Good Friday, and Christmas. To
make the impression of the service more vivid than the reading or chanting of the text could do, dramatic features were
introduced which were at first little more than the simplest
tableaux vivants. They can be traced beyond the eleventh
century and have their ancestry in the tropes or poetical
interpolations inserted into the liturgy for popular effect.[2]

The first dramatic action was associated with the services on
Good Friday and Easter. On Good Friday the cross was hid
in a cloth or in a recess in the walls, or in a wooden enclosure,
specially put together. Such recesses in the walls, called
"sepulchres," are still found in Northwold, Navenby, and other
English churches. On Easter day the crucifix was taken out
from its place of concealment with solemn ritual. In Davis'
Ancient Rites of Durham is the following description : [3] —

"Within the church of Durham upon Good Friday there was a marvellous solemn service in which two of the ancient monks took a goodly
large crucifix all of gold of the picture of our Saviour Christ, nailed upon
the cross. . . . The service being ended, the said two monks carried the
cross to the *Sepulchre* with great reverence (which *Sepulchre* was set up
that morning on the north side of the quire, nigh unto the high altar
before the service time) and there did lay it within the said *Sepulchre*
with great devotion."

To this simple ceremony, adapted to impress the popular
imagination, were soon added other realistic elements, such
as the appearance of the angels and the women at the
sepulchre, the race between Peter and John, and the conversation between Mary and the gardener. Dialogues made up
of biblical language were introduced, one of the earliest of

---

[1] The text is given by Migne, 137. 975–1062, together with some poems
attributed to Hroswitha, one of which, "The Fall and Conversion of St.
Theophilus," has often been regarded as the original of the tale of Faust.

[2] See Blume, *Tropen d. Missale in Analecta hymn.*, XLVII. 7.

[3] Chambers II. 310.

which is the conversation between the women and the
angels : —

> Whom seek ye in the sepulchre, worshippers of Christ ?
> Jesus of Nazareth, the crucified, O heavenly denizens.
>
> *Quam quæritis in sepulchro, Christocolæ ?*
> *Jesum Nazarenum, crucifixum, O cœlicolæ.*

On Christmas the dramatic action included the angels,
the Magi, and other actors, and a real cradle or manger.
Priests in the garb of shepherds, as they approached the
stable, were met with the question, —

> Whom seek ye in the stable, O shepherds, say ?
> *Quem quæritis in præsepe, pastores, dicite ?*

To which they replied,

> The Saviour, Christ the Lord, the infant wound in swaddling clothes.

From such beginnings, the field was easily extended so as
to include all Scriptural subjects, from Adam's fall to the
last judgment.

The first notice of a miracle play in England is the play
of St. Katherine, presented by the schoolboys of Dunstable
abbey, soon after the year 1100.[1]   William Fitz-Stephen,
writing about 1180, contrasted the religious plays performed
in his day in London with the stage of pagan Rome.

An ambitious German play of the thirteenth century
represents Augustine seated in front of a church, Isaiah,
Daniel, and other prophets at his right hand, and at his left
the High Priest and Jews.   Isaiah uttered his prophecy of
the Messiah.   The Sibyl pointed to the star.   Aaron entered
with the budding rod.   Balaam and the ass then take their
turn.   An angel blocks the way.   The ass speaks.   Balaam
recites his prediction of the star of Jacob.   The prophetic
announcements being made, the high priest appeared with
much circumstance, and a discussion followed between him
on the one side and the prophets and Augustine on the
other.   Another act followed and the angel announced the

---

[1] Pollard, p. xix.   M. Paris calls it a "miracle," — *quem miracula vulgari-
ter appellamus.*

Saviour's birth. The child was born. The three kings and the shepherds come on the scene. The journey to Egypt followed and Egypt's king met the holy family. Herod is eaten by worms. And so the play went on till anti-Christ made his appearance. Here we have a long advance upon the simple dramatic ceremonies of the century before, and at the same time the germ of the elaborate drama which was to follow. The materials, however, are all religious.

The dramatic instinct was not satisfied with a serious treatment of biblical themes. It demanded the introduction of the burlesque and farcical. These elements were furnished by Judas, the Jews, and the devil, who were made the butts of ridicule. Judas was paid in bad coin. The devil acted a double part. He tempts Eve by his flatteries, he holds the glass before Mary Magdalene while she makes her toilet before going out to dance with every comer, wheels the unfortunate into hell on a wheelbarrow, and receives the lost with mock ceremony into his realm. But he is as frequently represented as the stupid bungler. He was the mediæval clown, the dupe of devices excelling his own in shrewdness. He sallied out from the stage, frightening little boys and followed with laughter and jibes by the older onlookers. His mishaps were the subject of infinite merriment.

The association of plays with the church was not received with universal approbation. Gerhoh of Reichersperg opposed them as a desecration. Innocent III. in 1210, if he did not condemn them altogether, condemned their abuse.[1] The synod of Treves, 1227, and other synods forbade priests holding "theatrical plays" in the church buildings. Cæsar of Heisterbach represents the rigoristic feeling when, hearing from a priest of a stage that was struck by lightning and twenty men burned to death, declared the burning was a proper punishment for the friends of frivolity and that it was a wonder the priest, who was present, escaped.[2]

---

[1] The meaning of Innocent's brief is disputed. It may have reference only to the Feast of Fools. The text is in the *Decretals*, III. 1, 12, Friedberg's ed., II. 452.   [2] *Dial.*, X. 28, Strange's ed., II. 238.

By the end of the thirteenth century, the plays were no longer acted in the churches, but were transferred to the public squares and other open spaces. Gilds and companies of actors took them up and acting again began to be a recognized vocation. The religious element, however, was retained, and religious and moral subjects continued to be the basis of all the plays. Even after they began to be acted on the public squares, the plays, like a modern political gathering, were introduced with prayers and the *Veni creator spiritus* was chanted. Among the earlier societies, which made it their business to present them, was the confraternity of the Gonfalone. In its chapel, St. Maria della Pieta in the Colosseum, plays were given perhaps as early as 1250. In Passion week the roof of the chapel was turned into a stage and the passion was acted.[1] The first company of play actors in Paris was called *confrèrie de la passion*, the " brotherhood of the passion."

The Feasts of the Fools and the Ass.—In these strange festivals, which go back to the eleventh century, full vent was given by the clergy to the love of the burlesque. At first, they were intended to give relief to the otherwise serious occupation of the clergyman and, while they parodied religious institutions, they were not intended to be sacrilegious, but to afford innocent amusement. Later, the observance took on extravagant forms and received universal condemnation. But, already in this period, the celebration in the churches and cathedrals was accompanied with revels which called forth the severe rebuke of Bishop Grosseteste[2] and two centuries later of John Huss. Both festivals were celebrated at Christmas tide and the early days of January. The descriptions are confusing, and it is difficult to get a perfectly clear conception of either festival.

On the Feast of the Fools, — *festum stultorum*,[3] — the deacons and sub-deacons elected a boy as bishop or pope and in drollery allowed him episcopal functions. Prescriptions for the boy-bishop's dress are found in the annals of St. Paul and York and Lincoln cathedrals, and included a white mitre and a staff. The ceremony was observed at Eton. The festival, however, was most popular in France. The boy-prelate rode on an ass at the head of a procession to the church amid the ringing of bells

---

[1] Gregorovius, *Hist. of the City of Rome*, VI. 712.

[2] Luard's ed., pp. 118, 161. On these festivals, see *Eselsfest*, in Herzog, V. 497 sq., and *Feste*, in Wetzer-Welte, IV. 1398–1407; Chambers, I. 274–372.   [3] Called also *jestum hypodiaconorum*, feast of the deacons, etc.

and the jangle of musical instruments. There he dismounted, was clad in bishop's vestments, and seated on a platform. A banquet and religious services followed, and in turn dancing and other merriment. The ceremonies differed in localities and a number of rituals have come down to us.

In the feast of the Ass, — *festum asinorum*, — the beast that Balaam rode was the chief *dramatis persona*. The skin of the original animal formed a valuable possession of a convent in Verona. The aim was to give dramatic representation to biblical truth and perhaps to do honor to the venerable and long-suffering beast which from time immemorial has carried man and other burdens. At Rouen the celebration took place on Christmas day. Moses, Aaron, ·John the Baptist, the Sibyl, Virgil, the children who were thrown into the furnace, and other ancient characters appeared. Balaam, wearing spurs and seated on an ass, was the centre of attraction. A fire was started in the middle of the church around which stood six Jews and Gentiles. The prophets, one by one, made addresses attempting to convert them. The ass spoke when his way was barred by the angel, and Balaam uttered his prophecy of the star. The ass was then placed near the altar and a cope thrown over him. High mass followed.

At Beauvais the festival was celebrated on the anniversary of the Flight of the Holy Family to Egypt, Jan. 14. The ass, bearing "a most beautiful maiden" with a child in her arms, was led into the church and stood before the altar during the performance of mass. At the close of the ritual, the priest instead of repeating the customary formula of dismissal, *ite, missa est,* made three sounds like the braying of an ass, — *sacerdos tres hinhannabit,* — and the people responded three times, *hinham.*

The improprieties and revels which became connected with these celebrations were adapted to bring religion into disrepute and called forth the rebukes of Innocent III. and Innocent IV., the latter mentioning a boy-bishop by name and condemning the travesty upon serious subjects. In 1444 the theological faculty of Paris spoke of grave and damnable scandals connected with the celebrations, such as the singing of comic songs, the men being dressed in women's attire and the eating of fat cakes at the altar. Councils, as late as 1584, joined in condemning them. At the close of Henry VIII.'s reign and at Cranmer's suggestion the festivals were forbidden in England.

§ 135. *The Flagellants.*

LITERATURE : The Chronicles of SALIMBENE, VILLANI, etc. : GERSON : *Contra sectam flagellantium,* 1417, Du Pin's ed., Antwerp, 1706. Gerson's letter to Ferrer and his address to the council of Constance concerning the Flagellants are given by VAN DER HARDT : *Constant. concilium,* Frankf., 1700, III. 92–104. — J. BOILEAU : *Hist. Flagel.,* Paris,

1700, new ed., 1700. — *E. G. Förstemann : *D. christl. Geisslergesell-schaften*, Halle, 1828. — W. M. Cooper: *Flagellation and the Flagel-lants, A Hist. of the Rod in All Countries*, Lond., 1877 ; new ed., 1896. — Fredericq, in *Corpus doc. inquis.*, etc. gives reports of their trials in Holland, I. 190 sqq., etc. — *F. Neukirch : *D. Leben d. P. Damiani*, Gött., 1875. — Lea : *Hist. of Inq.*, I. 72 sqq., II. 381 sqq. — Artt. *Geissler* and *Geisselung* in Wetzer-Welte by Knöpfler, IV. 1532 sqq. and in Herzog by Haupt, VI. 432 sqq. For the older lit., see Förste-mann, pp. 291-325.

A genuine indication of .popular interest in religion within orthodox circles was the strange movement represented by the Flagellants. Gregorovius has gone so far as to pro-nounce their appearance "one of the most striking phe-nomena of the Middle Ages."[1] Although they started within the Church and are not to be classed with the mediæ-val sectaries, the Flagellants in a later age came to be re-garded with suspicion, were formally condemned by the council of Constance, and were even the object of ecclesias-tical prosecution. They appeared first in 1259, then in 1333, 1349, 1399, and last at the time the council of Constance was sitting. The most notable appearance was in 1349, at the time the Black Death was raging in Europe.

The movement had no compact organization, as is shown from its spasmodic character. It grew out of discontent with the Church and a longing for true penitence and amend-ment of life. The prophecies of Joachim, who set 1260 as the time for the appearance of anti-christ, probably had something to do with stirring up unrest ; perhaps also the famine in Italy, of 1258, which was followed by a strange physical malady, characterized by numbness of the bodily organs. Salimbene reports that the bells were left untolled for funerals, lest the sick should be terrified. The enthusiasm took the form of processions, scourgings, and some novel and strange ceremonies. It was a species of evangelism, and attempted a campaign against physical and other sins, as the Crusades did against the Saracens of the East. It sought

---

[1] *Hist. of City of Rome*, V. 333. They were called *flagellarii, flagellantes, crucifratres, verberantes, cruciferi, acephali*, or independents, from the charge that they had broken with the heretics.

to make popular the discipline of flagellation, which was practised in the convent, and to secure penitential results, such as the monk was supposed to reach.

The most notable adept of this conventual flagellation was Dominicus Loricatus (d. 1060), who got his name from the iron coat he wore next to his skin. He accompanied the repetition of every psalm with a hundred strokes with a lash on his naked back. Three thousand strokes were equivalent to a year's penance. But Loricatus beat all records and accomplished the exercise of the entire Psalter no less than twenty times in six days, the equivalent of a hundred years of penance. Peter Damiani, to whom we are indebted for our account, relates that the zealous ascetic, after saying nine Psalters in a single day, accompanying them with the required number of lashes, went to his cell to make sure the count was right. Then removing his iron jacket and taking a scourge in each hand, he kept on repeating the Psalter the whole night through till he had finished it the twelfth time and was well into the thirteenth when he stopped.

What is your body, exclaimed Damiani, who contented himself with prescribing forty psalms a day for his monks, — " what is your body ? Is it not carrion, a mass of corruption, dust, and ashes, and what thanks will the worms give for taking good care of it ? " [1]

Under the appeals of preachers like Fulke of Neuilly and Anthony of Padua, there were abnormal physical manifestations, and hearers set to work flagellating themselves.

The Flagellant outbreak of 1259 started at Perugia and spread like an epidemic. All classes, young and old, were seized. With bodies bared to the waist, carrying crosses and banners and singing hymns, newly composed and old, they marched to and fro in the streets, scourging themselves. Priests and monks joined the ranks of the penitents. Remarkable scenes of moral reform took place. Usurers gave up their ill-gotten gains; murderers confessed, and, with

---

[1] Migne, 144. 1017. Damiani says of Loricatus, *lorica ferrea vestitur ad carnem*, Migne, 145. 747. He compared the body to a timbrel which is to be struck in praise to God.

swords pointed to their throats, offered themselves up to
justice; enemies were reconciled.   And as the chatty chronicler, Salimbene, goes on to say, if any would not scourge
himself, he was held to be a limb of Satan.   And what is
more, such persons were soon overtaken with sickness or
premature death.[1] Twenty thousand marched from Modena
to Bologna.   At Reggio, Parma, and other cities, the chief
officials joined them.   But all were not so favorable, and the
Cremona authorities and Manfred forbade their entering
their territories.

The ardor cooled off quickly in Italy, but it spread beyond
the Alps.   Twelve hundred Flagellants appeared in Strassburg and the impulse was felt as far as Poland and Bohemia.
The German penitents continued their penance thirty-three
days in memory of the number of the years of Christ's life.
They chastised themselves and also sang hymns.   Here also
the enthusiasm subsided as suddenly as it was enkindled.
The repetitions of the movement belong to the next period.

§ 136.   *Demonology and the Dark Arts.*

LITERATURE: ANSELM: *de casu diaboli*, Migne, 158. 326–362. — P. LOMBAR-
DUS: *Sent.*, II. 7 sqq. — ALB. MAGNUS: *In Sent.*, Borgnet's ed., XXVII.
etc. — TH. AQUINAS: *Summa*, I. 51 sqq., II. 94–96, Migne, I. 893 sqq.,
II. 718 sqq., etc. Popular statements, *e.g.* P. DAMIANI, Migne, 144, 145. —
PETER THE VENERABLE: *de mirac.*, Migne, 189. 850–954. — JOHN OF
SALISBURY: *Polycraticus*, Migne, 199. 405 sqq. — Walter Map — CÆSAR
OF HEISTERBACH: *Dial. mirac.* Strange's ed., 2 vols. Bonn, 1851, espe-
cially Bk. V. — THOS. A CHANTIMPRÉ: *Bonum universale de apibus*,
Germ. Reprod. by A. KAUFMANN, Col. 1899. — JAC. DE VORAGINE:
Golden Legend, Temple Class. ed. — ETIENNE DE BOURBON, especially
Part IV. — * T. WRIGHT: *Narrative of Sorcery and Magic*, 2 vols. Lond.,
1851. — *G. ROSKOFF: *Gesch. des Teufels*, 2 vols. Leipzig, 1869. —
* W. G. SOLDAU: *Gesch. der Hexenprocesse*, Stuttg., 1843; new ed., by
HEPPE, 2 vols. Stuttg., 1880. — * LEA: *Hist. of the Inquis.*, III. 379–550.
— LECKY: *Hist. of the Rise and Influence of the Spirit of Rationalism
in Europe*, chap. I. — DÖLLINGER-FRIEDRICH: *D. Papstthum*, Munich,
1892. — A. D. WHITE: *Hist. of the Warfare of Science and Theol. in
Christendom*, 2 vols. N.Y., 1898. — *JOSEPH HANSEN: *Zauberwahn,
Inquisition und Hexenprocess im Mittelalter und die Entstehung der
grossen Hexenverfolgung*, Munich, 1900; * *Quellen und Untersuchun-*

---

[1] Coulton, *From St. Francis to Dante*, pp. 192 sq.

gen zur Gesch. des Hexenwahns und der Hexenverfolgung im MtA., Leip., 1901. — GRAF VON HOENSBROECH : D. Papstthum in seiner sozial-kulturellen Wirksamkeit, Leipzig, 2 vols. 1900; 4th ed., 1901, vol. I. 207–380. For special lit. on Witchcraft, 1300–1500, see next volume.

At no point do the belief and experience of our own age differ so widely from the Middle Ages as in the activity of the devil and the realm of evil spirits. The subject has already been touched upon under monasticism and the future state, but no history of the period would be complete which did not give it separate treatment. For the belief that the satanic kingdom is let loose upon mankind was more influential than the spirit of monasticism, or than the spirit which carried on the Crusades.

The credulity of monk and people and the theology of the Schoolmen peopled the earth and air with evil spirits. The writings of popular authors teem with tales of their personal appearances and malignant agency, and the scholastic definitions are nowhere more precise and careful than in the department of satanology. After centuries of Christian culture, a panic seized upon Europe in the first half of the thirteenth century about the fell agency of such spirits, a panic which continued powerfully to influence opinion far beyond the time of the Reformation. The persecution to which it led, was one of the most merciless forms of cruelty ever practised. The pursuit and execution of witches constitute a special chapter in the history, but it is not fully opened till the fifteenth century. Here belong the popular and scholastic conceptions of the devil and his agency before the witch-craze set in.

The sources from which the Middle Ages derived their ideas of the demonic world were the systems of classical antiquity, the Norse mythology, and the Bible as interpreted by Augustine and Gregory the Great. In its wildest fancies on the subject, the mediæval theology was only following these two greater authorities.

The general term for the dark arts, that is, the arts which were supposed to be under the control of satanic agency, was *maleficium*, a term inherited from the Romans.

The special names were magic, sorcery, necromancy, divina-
tion, and witchcraft.   Astrology, after some hesitation, was
included in the same list.[1]

I. *The Popular Belief.* — The popular belief is set forth
by such writers as Peter Damiani, Peter the Venerable,
Cæsar of Heisterbach, Jacob of Voragine, Thomas of Chantimpré, Etienne de Bourbon, and the French writers of
poetry.   Even the English writers, Walter Map and John
of Salisbury, both travelled men and, as we would say, men
of the world from whom we might have expected other
things, accepted, with slight modification, the popular views.
Map treats Ceres, Bacchus, Pan, the satyr, the dryads, and
the fauns as demons, and John discusses in six chapters the
pestiferous familiarity of demons and men — *pestifera famil-
iaritas dœmonum et hominum.*[2]

Peter Damiani, the contemporary of Hildebrand, could
tell of troops of devils he had seen in the air with his own
eyes, and in all sorts of shapes.

Cæsar of Heisterbach furnishes a storehouse of tales which
to him were as much realities as reports of the Dark Continent by Stanley or Speke would be to us.   This genial
writer represents an old monk setting at rest the doubts of
a novice by assuring him that he himself had seen the devil
in the forms of a Moor, an ox, a dog, a toad, an ape, a pig,
and even in the garbs of a nun and a prior.   Peter the Venerable likewise speaks of Satan as taking on the form of a
bear.[3]   He also assumed the forms of a black horse, rooks,
and other creatures.   French poetry and the popular imagination invested him with horns, claws, and tail.[4]

The devil made his appearance at all hours of the day and
night, in the time of health, and at the hour of death.   The
monk was no more exempt from his personal solicitations

---

[1] Alex. of Hales distinguished eight sorts of demonic agency through
human instrumentalities, mantic, sortilegium, maleficium, augurium, pres-
tigium, mathesis or astrology, ariolatio, and the interpretation of dreams.

[2] *De nug. curalium*, Wright's ed., II. 14 ; *Polycrat.*, Bk. I. VIII.–XIII.
Migne, 199. 404 sqq.   [3] *De mir.*, Migne, 189. 883.

[4] The *Roman de la Rose*, 1280, is an exception and makes light of tail and
horns, and the belief that women are transported through the air at night.

while engaged at his devotions than at other times. One of the places where the evil spirits took particular delight in playing tricks was in the choir when the monastics were met for matins and other services. Here they would vex the devout by blowing out the lights, turning to a wrong leaf, or confusing the tune.[1]

On one occasion Herman of Marienstadt saw three who passed so near to him that he might easily have touched them, had he so desired. He noted that they did not touch the floor and that one of them had the face of a woman, veiled. Sometimes a troop appeared and threw one part of the choir into discord, and when the other part took up the chant, the demons hastened over to its side and threw it into the same confusion, so that the two wings of the choir shouted hoarsely and discordantly one to the other.[2]

On another occasion Herman, then become abbot, a monastic whom Cæsar calls a man of marked piety, saw the devil in the form of a Moor sitting on one of the windows of the church. He looked as if he had just emerged from hell-fire, but soon took his flight. When Herman was praying to be delivered from such visions, the devil seizing his last opportunity appeared to the abbot as a bright eye as big as a fist, and as if to say, " Look straight at me once more for this is the last time." Nevertheless, the abbot saw the devil again and this time at the sepulture of Countess Aleidis of Freusberg. While the lady's body was lying in its shroud, the devil appeared, peering into all corners as if he was looking for something he had lost.

It was a bad symptom of the monkish imagination that when the devil was seen in convents, it was often in the form of a woman and a naked woman at that. Sometimes monks got sick from seeing him and could neither eat, drink, nor sleep for days. Sometimes they lost their minds from the same cause and died insane. At times, however, vigilant nuns were able to box his ears.[3] A demon entered the ear

---

[1] *Dial.*, V. 53, etc., Strange's ed., I. 336.

[2] *Dial.*, V. 5, Strange's ed., I. 287 sqq.

[3] *Dial.*, III. 11, V. 28, 45, Strange's ed., I. 123, 311, 330.

of a woman when her husband said to her, " Go to the devil."
Children were known to drink the devil in their milk as did
one child of four who remained possessed for thirty years.
The devil, as might have been expected, was fond of dice
and, as in the case of a certain knight, Thieme, after playing
with him all night carried him through the roof so that, according to the testimony of the man's son, he was never seen
again.[1] Bernard, by his own statement, cast out demons,
as did Norbert and most of the other mediæval saints. Norbert's biographer reports that the devil struck some of the
Premonstrants with his tail. At other times he imparted
to would-be monks an unusual gift to preach and explain the
Bible, and the Premonstrants were about to receive some of
this class into their order when the trick was revealed. On
one occasion, when Norbert was about to cast out a demon
from a boy, the demon took the shape of a pea and sat upon
the boy's tongue and then impudently set to work asserting
that he would not evacuate his dwelling-place. " You are a
liar," said the ecclesiastic, "and have been a liar from the
beginning." That truth the devil could not gainsay and so
he came out and disappeared but not without leaving ill
odors behind and the child sick.[2]

The devil, however, to the discomfiture of the wicked often
told the truth. Thus it happened in Norbert's experience
at Mæstricht, that when he was about to heal a man possessed and a great crowd was gathered, the demon started
to tell on bystanders tales of their adultery and other sins,
which had not been covered by confession. No wonder the
crowd quickly broke up and took to its heels.[3] The devil
prayed the Lord's Prayer but with mistakes so that he was
easily detected.[4] Once his identity was discovered, it was
no difficult thing to get rid of him. The sign of the cross,
spitting, and saying the *Ave Maria* were sufficient to drive
him away.[5] Peter the Venerable gives many cases showing
how the crucifix, the host, and holy water protected monks,
insidiously attacked by " the children of malediction " and

[1] *Dial.*, V. 11, 26, 34.   [2] *Vita Norb.*, XIII.   [3] *Vita Norb.*, XIV.
[4] *Dial.*, III. 6.   [5] *Dial.*, III. 6, 7, 13, 14, VII, 25, etc.

" the old enemy of souls" — *antiquus hostis*. Sometimes resort was had to sprinkling the room and all its furniture with holy water, — a sort of disinfecting process — and the imps would disappear.

De Voragine tells how St. Lupe, as he was praying one night, felt great thirst.   He knew it was due to the devil and asked for water.   When it was brought, he clapped a lid on the vessel, " shutting the devil up quick."   The prisoner howled all night, unable to get out.[1]

Salimbene gives a droll case of a peasant into whom the devil entered, making him talk Latin.   But the peasant tripped in his Latin so that " our lector laughed at his mistakes."   The demon spoke up, " I can speak Latin well enough, but the tongue of this boor is so thick that I make sorry work wielding it." [2]   Luther's easy explanation of mice, fleas, and other pests as the devil's creations, is called up by the following statement : A certain Cistercian, Richalmus, of the thirteenth century, in a book on the devil's wiles, said, " It seems incredible but it is true, it is not fleas and lice which bite us but what we think is their bites are the pricks of demons.   For those little insects do not live off our blood, but from perspiration, and we often feel such pricks when there are no fleas." [3]

These incidents may be brought to a close by the following interesting conversation reported by Cæsar of Heisterbach as having been carried on by two evil spirits who had possessed two women who got into a quarrel.   " Oh, if we had only not gone over to Lucifer," said one, " and been cast out of heaven ! "   The other replied, " Hold your peace, your repentance comes too late, you couldn't get back if you would." " If there were only a column of iron," answered the first, " though it were furnished with the sharpest knives and saws, I would be willing to climb up and down it till the last judgment day, if I could only thereby make my way back to glory."

---

[1] Temple ed., V. 88.

[2] Coulton, *From St. Francis*, etc., p. 298.

[3] *Lib. revelationum de insidiis et versutiis dæmonum*, quoted by Cruel, *Deutsche Predigt*, p. 268.

These stories are records of what were believed to be real occurrences. The denizens of the lower world were everywhere present in visible and invisible form to vex and torment saint and sinner in body and soul. No voice is heard protesting against the belief. It is refreshing, however, to have at least one case of scepticism. Thus Vincent de Beauvais tells of a woman who assured her priest that she and other women were under the influence of witchcraft and had one night succeeded in getting into the priest's bedchamber through the keyhole. After in vain trying to persuade her that she was laboring under a delusion, the priest locked the door and putting the key into his pocket, gave her a good drubbing with a stick, exclaiming, " Get out through the keyhole now, if you can."

II. *The Theological Statement.* — The wildest popular conceptions of the agency of evil spirits are confirmed by the theological definitions of Peter the Lombard, Albertus Magnus, Bonaventura, Thomas Aquinas, and other Schoolmen. According to the mediæval theology, the devil is at the head of a realm of demons who are divided into prelacies and hierarchies like the good angels.

The region into which the devil and his angels were cast down was the tenebrous air. There, in the pits of darkness, he and his followers are preserved until the day of final judgment. Their full degree of torment will not be meted out to them till then. In the meantime, they are permitted to trouble and torment men.[1] For this view such passages as Matt. 8 : 29 and Luke 8 : 31 are quoted.

Albertus Magnus, who, of all the Schoolmen, might speak on such a subject with precision, fixed the exact location of the aery realm. Following the philosophers, as he said, he defined three zones in the superterrestrial spaces : the higher, lower, and the middle zone.[2] The higher zone is light and tranquil, constituted of thin air and very hot. Its light is great in proportion to the propinquity of that sphere to the

---

[1] *Dæmones in hoc aere caliginoso sunt ad nostrum exercitium.* Th. Aq., *Summa,* I. 64, 4. So also P. Lomb., II. 7, 6.

[2] *Zonas, interstitia. In sent.,* II. 6, 5, Borgnet's ed., XXVII. 132.

stars and because the rays of the sun permeate it for a longer time. The lower zone, enveloping and touching the solid earth, is made bright by the powerful reflection of the sun's rays. The intermediate zone is exceedingly cold and dark. Here the tempests are bred and the hail and snows generated. This is the habitation of the evil spirits, and there they move the clouds, start the thunders, and set a-going other natural terrors to frighten and hurt men. The exact distance of that sphere from the earth the philosophers measure, but Albertus does not choose to determine the measurement.

In defining the mental power and the influence of evil spirits, Thomas Aquinas and the other Schoolmen follow Augustine closely, although in elaboration they go beyond him. The demons did not lose their intellectual keenness by their fall.[1] This keenness and long experience give them power to foretell the future. If astronomers, said Albertus Magnus, foresee future events by the natal constellations, much more may demons through their shrewdness in observation and watching the stars. Their predictions, however, differ from the predictions of the prophets by being the product of the light of nature. The prophets received a divine revelation.

The miracles which the evil spirits perform are, for the most part, juggleries.[2] Thomas Aquinas, however, asserts for these works a genuine supernatural quality. They are at times real works, as when the magicians, by the help of the devil, made frogs in Egypt; or as in the case of Job's children upon whom fire came down from heaven. They are not able to create out of nothing, but they have the power to accelerate the development of germs and hidden potencies, to destroy harvests, influence the weather, and produce sickness and death.

The special influence which they exercise over human beings in sorcery and witchcraft they exercise by virtue of a compact entered into between them and men and women,

---

[1] Aquinas' treatment is found in his *Summa*, I. 51 sqq., II. 94–96, Migne, I. 893 sqq., II. 718 sqq. ; P. Lombard, *Sent.*, II. 7 sqq.

[2] *Præstigia* is the word used by Alb. Magnus, John of Salisbury, etc.

Isa. 28 : 18 : " We have made a covenant with death, and with sheol are we in agreement." The most fiendish and frequent of these operations is to disturb the harmony of the married relation. Men they make impotent; women sterile. The earlier fiction of the *succubus* and the *incubus*, inherited from Pagan mythology and adopted by Augustine, was fully accepted in the Middle Ages. This was the shocking belief that demons cohabit with men, the *succubus*, and lie with women, the *incubus*. The Schoolmen go so far as to affirm that, though the demons have no direct offspring, yet after lying with men they suddenly transform themselves and communicate the seed they have received to women.[1]

This view which the Schoolmen formulated was common belief. The story of Merlin, the son of an incubus and a nun, was a popular one in the Middle Ages.[2] Guibert of Nogent states that his father and mother for three years were prevented from exercising the rights of wedlock until the incubus was driven off by a good angel. Matthew Paris reports the case of a child which went for the offspring of an incubus.[3] The Huns were popularly believed to be the offspring of demons and offcast Gothic women.[4] Eleanor, wife of Louis VII. and then of Henry II. of England, so report went, was likewise the child of a demon.[5] Cæsar of

---

[1] This is stated at length by Thomas Aquinas, *Summa*, I. 51, 3, *idem dæmon qui est succubus ad virum fit incubus ad mulierem*. For other quotations to the same effect from Bonaventura, Duns Scotus, etc., see Hansen, p. 186. Albertus Magnus, Borgnet's ed., XXVII. 175, speaks of immense cats appearing at these assignations, but the passage is too foul to be repeated. This Schoolman went so far as to say that demons preserved human seed in vessels. As an instance of ultramontane honesty, Hoensbroech, *D. Papstthum*, I. 222, cites the Dominican Schneider who, in his German translation of Thomas Aquinas, omits altogether the passage, part of which has just been quoted, though he makes the introductory assertion that the translation contains the " entire text."

[2] Merlin, the " prophet of Britain " as Cæsar of Heisterbach calls him, *Dial.*, III. 12, Strange's ed., 1. 124. The nun was seduced on a night when she happened to retire without making the sign of the cross. It was thought by some that anti-christ would be engendered in this way.

[3] *an.*, 1249. The child in six months had a full set of teeth and was of the stature of a boy of 17, the mother wasted away and died.   [4] *Dial.*, V. 12.

[5] See quotation in Kaufmann's *Cæsar of Heisterbach*, II. 80.

Heisterbach gives many stories of the cohabitation of demons with priests and women.[1]

This malign activity upon the marital relation was made by Thomas Aquinas a proper ground of divorce.[2] The transport of men and women through the air is also vouched for by this theologian, and as far back as the twelfth century the Patarenes were accused of practices, as by Walter Map, which were at a later period associated with witches. They held their meetings or synagogues behind closed doors and after the lights were put out the devil descended in the shape of a cat, holding on to a rope. Scenes of indiscriminate lust followed. Map was even willing to believe that the heretics kissed the cat under the tail.[3]

The mind of Europe did not become seriously exercised on the subject of demonic possession until after heresy made its appearance and the measures to blot it out were in an advanced stage. The Fourth Lateran did not mention the dark arts, and its failure to do so can only be explained on the ground that the mind of Christendom was not yet aroused. It was not long, however, before violent incursions of the powers of darkness, as they were supposed to be, rudely awakened the Church, and from the time of Gregory IX. the agency of evil spirits and heresy were closely associated. In one of his deliverances against the Stedinger, this pope vouched for the belief that heretics consulted witches, held communion with demons, and indulged in orgies with them and the devil who, as he said, met with them in the forms of a great toad and black cat. Were the stars in heaven and the elements to combine for the destruction of such people without reference to their age or sex, it would be an inadequate punishment.[4]

---

[1] Sometimes demons took the place of loose women with whom priests had made assignations, *Dial.*, III. 10. Cæsar tells of a woman who had committed whoredom with a demon for seven years and, while confessing her sin to the priest, fell dead.

[2] He gives a full chapter to the subject. *In Sent.*, IV. 34, 1.

[3] Wright's ed., p. 61. *plurimi sub cauda, plerique pudenda.*

[4] A translation of the bull dated June, 1233, Potthast, I. no. 9230, is given by Hoensbroech, I. 215 sqq.

After 1250 the persecution of heretics for doctrinal error diminishes and the trials for sorcery, witchcraft, and other demonic iniquity become frequent.[1] In his bull, *ad exstirpanda*, 1252, Innocent IV. called upon princes to treat heretics as though they were sorcerers, and in 1258 Alexander IV. spoke of sorcerers as savoring of heresy.[2] Before this, magic and sorcery had come exclusively under the jurisdiction of the state.

At this juncture came the indorsement of Thomas Aquinas and his great theological contemporaries.   There was nothing left for the ecclesiastical and civil authorities to do but to ferret out sorcerers, witches, and all who had habitual secret dealings with the devil. A craze seized upon the Church to clear the Christian world of imaginary armies of evil spirits, demonizing men and especially women. Pope after pope issued orders not to spare those who were in league with the devil, but to put them to torture and cast them into the flames.[3] The earliest trials for sorcery by the Inquisition were held in Southern France about 1250, and the oldest Interrogatories of the Inquisition on the subject date twenty-five years later.[4] These prosecutions reached their height in the fifteenth century, and the papal fulminations found their ultimate expression in the bull of Innocent VIII. against witches, 1484.

Men like Albertus Magnus and Roger Bacon were popularly charged with being wizards. Bacon, enlightened beyond his age, pronounced some of the popular beliefs delusions, but, far from denying the reality of sorcery and magic, he tried to explain the efficacy of spells and charms by their being made at seasons when the heavens were propitious.

---

[1] Hansen dates the new treatment of sorcery by the Church with 1230 and carries the period on to 1430, when he dates the period of witchcraft and its punishment by the Church.   [2] Hansen, *Quellen*, p. 1.

[3] Hansen gives a number of such bulls and quotes an author who speaks of 103 papal bulls directed against sorcery, a number Hansen doubts. *Quellen*, p. 1.

[4] Hansen, *Quellen*, pp. 43 sqq., gives it under the title *forma et modus interrogandi augures et ydolatras*, and assigns it to 1270, *Gesch.*, p. 243. Douais places it a little earlier. A portion of Bernard Gui's *Practica inquisitionis* (1320) is an interrogatory of practisers of the occult arts, *interrog. ad sortileges et divinos ei invocatores dæmonum.* See Douais' ed., Paris, 1886.

§ 137. *The Age passing Judgment upon Itself.*

The preceding pages have shown the remarkable character of the events and movements, the men and ideas which
fill the centuries from Hildebrand's entrance into Rome
with Leo IX., 1049, to the abdication of the simple-minded
Cœlestin, 1294. The present generation regards the events
of the last half-century as most extraordinary. The same
judgment was passed by Matthew Paris upon the half-century
of which he was a spectator, 1200–1250. Useful inventions and
discoveries, such as we associate with the second half of the
nineteenth century, there were few or none in the thirteenth
century, and yet those times were full of occurrences and
measures which excited the deepest interest and the speculation of men. The retrospect of the fifty years, which the clear-
headed English monk sums up in his Chronicles, furnishes
one of the most instructive pieces of mediæval literature.

Here is what Matthew Paris says : There occurred in
this time extraordinary and strange events, the like of which
had never been seen before nor were found in any of the
writings of the Fathers. The Tartars ravaged countries inhabited by Christians. Damietta was twice taken and retaken,
Jerusalem twice desolated by the Infidel. St. Louis was
captured with his brothers in the East. Wales passed under
the domination of England. Frederick, the Wonder of the
World, had lived his career. The Crusades had given to a
great host a glorious death. As for natural wonders, an
eclipse of the sun had occurred twice in three years, earth-
quakes had shaken England several times, and there had
been a destructive rise of the sea such as had never been seen
before. One night immense numbers of stars fell from the
heavens, a reason for which could not be found in the Book
of Meteors, except that Christ's threat was impending when
he said, "There shall be signs in the heavens."

Among things distinctively religious, the chronicler notes
that an English cardinal was suffocated in his palace, as
was supposed, for having his eye on the tiara. The figure

of Christ appeared in the sky in Germany and was plainly
seen by every one.   Elizabeth of Hungary and St. Hildegard
flourished.   The ordeal of fire and water was abolished.
Seville, Cordova, and other parts of Spain were rescued from
the Moors.   The orders of the Minorites and the Preachers
arose, startling the world by their devotion and disgusting it
by their sudden decline.   Some of the blood of Christ and a
stone, bearing his footprints, arrived in England.

Such are some of the occurrences which seemed wonderful
to the racy English historian.   If he had read over the
leaves of his Chronicles as we do, how many other events he
might have singled out, — from the appearance of the
elephant, a gift of the king of France to the king of England,
which, as he says, was the first ever seen in England and the
appearance of the sea-monster thrown up in Norwich,[1] to his
instructive accounts of the doings of popes and emperors,
and the chafings of the English people under papal injustice.

Life was by no means a humdrum, monotonous existence
to the people who lived in the age of the Crusades and Innocent III.   On the contrary it was full of surprises and attractive movements, from every turn of the papacy and empire,
to the expeditions of the Crusaders and the travels of Marco
Polo and Rubruquis.

A historical period is measured by the judgment passed
upon it by its contemporaries and by the judgment of succeeding generations.   What did the period from 1050 to
1294 offer that seemed notable to those who were living
then and what contribution did it make to the progress and
well-being of mankind ?   The first of these questions can be
answered by the generation which then lived; the second, best
by the generations which have come since.

It is the persuasion of a school of mediæval enthusiasts
that this period was a golden age of faith and morals and
tenable systems of belief, an age when the laws of God were
obeyed as they have not been since, an age when proper attention was given to the things of religion, an age of high ideals

---

[1] Luard's ed., V. 448 sq.

and spiritual repose.   Is this judgment justified or is the
older Protestant view the right one that the Middle Ages
handed down nothing distinctive which has been of permanent value; but, on the contrary, many of the superstitions
and false doctrines now prevailing in the Church are an
inheritance from the Middle Ages, and it would have been
better if the Church had passed directly from the patristic
age and skipped the mediæval.[1]

Neither judgment is right.   A more just opinion is beginning to prevail, and upon a modification of the extreme views
of Protestants and Roman Catholics on the subject depends
to a considerable extent the closer fellowship between the
ecclesiastical communions of the West.   Much chaff will be
found there mixed with the wheat.   On the other hand, in this
mediæval period were also sown the seeds of religious ideas
and institutions which are now in their period of bloom or
awaiting the time of full fruitage.

The achievement of absolute power by the papacy, magnificent as it was, represents an ideal utterly at fault, whether
we consider the teaching of Scripture or the prevailing judgment of the present time.   Ambition, pride, avarice, were
mingled in popes with a sincere belief that the Roman see
inherited from the Apostle plenitude of authority in all realms.
Europe, more enlightened, cannot accept such a claim and
the moral degeneracy and spiritual incompetency of the popes,
in the period following this, were an experimental proof that
the theory was wrong.

As for the priesthood and hierarchy, evidence enough has
been adduced to show that ordination did not insure devotion
to office and personal purity.   Dante's hell contains more
than one pontiff of this period.   The nearer we approach
Rome, the more numerous the scandals are.   The term "the
Romans" was synonymous with unscrupulous greed.   Gregory X. in 1274 declared that "the prelates were the ruin of
Christendom."   Frederick II., though pronounced a poor

---

[1] For a terse description of the social, religious, and moral condition of
mediæval England and the prevalence of disease, see Jessopp, *Coming of the
Friars*, p. 111, etc.

churchman, was a keen observer and no doubt indicated a widespread discontent with the lives the clergy were leading when he declared that, if they would change their mode of living, the world might again see miracles as in the days of old.[1]

The distinctively mediæval ideal of a religious life has little attraction to-day. The seclusion of the monastery presents a striking contrast to the active career demanded of a Christian profession in this age. The example of St. Bernard and his praise of monasticism, as the praise of other writers, are so weighty that one cannot deny that the best men saw in monastic solitude the highest advantage. Monastic institutions had a most useful part to play as a leavening force in the wild and unsettled society of that time. But the discipline and ardor of monastic orders quickly passed away, in spite of the devotion of Francis d'Assisi and other monastic founders. Simplicity yielded to luxury, and spiritual devotion to sloth and pride. It was the ardent Franciscan, Bonaventura, who instances the vices which had crept into his order and Jacques de Vitry, cardinal-bishop, d. 1240, who said that a girl's virtue was safe under no Rule except the Cistercian. What can be said of the ideal of human life as it is set forth in the tale of St. Brandon, not to speak of innumerable similar tales told by Jacob de Voragine, archbishop of Genoa, d. 1298 ! What shall be thought of the example of the Blessed St. Angela of Foligno, admired and praised by so many Franciscan writers, who on her " conversion " prayed to be relieved of the impediments of obedience to husband, respect to mother and the care of children and rejoiced to have her request granted by their deaths !

If we desire priestly rule, there was enough of it to satisfy any one. But with the rule of the priesthood came the loss of individual freedom and the right of the soul to determine its own destiny in the sight of the Creator. De Voragine[2] speaks of Thomas à Becket, by great abstinence

---

[1] M. Paris, Luard's ed., IV. 538 sq.
[2] *Legenda*, Temple Classics ed., II. 189.

making his body lean and his soul fat. He had a right to do as he pleased. But it was the same prelate who expressed the hierarchical pride of the age when he exclaimed to an English king that priests are the fathers and masters of kings. The laity, according to Cæsar of Heisterbach, as already quoted, were compared to the night, the clergy to the day. The preacher Werner of St. Blasius called the peasants the feet whose toil was appointed to maintain the more worthy parts of the body, — bishops, priests, and monks.[1] The thinkers of this period had no vision of the Reformation.

The Middle Ages have been praised as a period of religious contentment and freedom from sectarian strife. The very contrary was the case. The strife between the friars and the secular clergy and, in cases, within the monastic orders themselves equals in bitterness any strife that has been maintained between branches of the Protestant Church. It was a question not whether there was religious unrest but, from the days of Arnold of Brescia on, how the established Church might crush out heretical revolt. There was also religious doubt among the monks, and there were women who denied that Eve had been tempted by an apple, as Cæsar of Heisterbach assures us.

The superstitions which prevailed were largely inherited from preceding ages. The worship of Mary clouded the merits of Christ. What can be said when Thomas of Chantimpré, d. about 1263, relates in all seriousness that a robber, whose head had been cut off, kept calling upon the Virgin, as the body rolled down a hill, until the parts were put together by a priest. The criminal then told how, as a boy, he had devoted Saturdays and Wednesdays to Mary and she had promised he should not die till opportunity was given him to make confession. So he made confession and died again, and, as the reader is left to believe, went into the other world rejoicing.

The gruesome tales of demoniacal presence and influence indicate a condition of mind from which we do well to be

---

[1] Migne, 157. 1047.

thankful we are delivered.   John of St. Giles, the admirable
English Dominican, used to say, as he retired to his cell in
the evening, " Now I await my martyrdom," meaning the
buffetings of the devil.   The awful story of how Ludwig
the Iron, 1100-1172, was welcomed to hell and shown all its
compartments and then pitched mercilessly into quenchless
flames is no worse than the visions of Dante, but too revolting in the apparent callousness of it to the suffering of
others not to call forth a shudder to-day.[1]

Such representations, however, do not warrant the conclusion that human charity was dead.   St. Francis and Hugh
of Lincoln kissed the hands of lepers.   The Knights of St.
Lazarus were intrusted by Louis IX. with the care of this
class of sufferers.   Houses for lepers were established in
England by Lanfranc, Mathilda, queen of Henry, King
Stephen at Burton, and others.   Mathilda washed their feet,
believing that, in so doing, she was washing the feet of Christ.[2]
The oldest of the military orders and the Teutonic knights,
as well as other orders, were organized to care for the sick
and distressed.

On the other hand the period sets, in some respects, an
example of great devotion, and has handed down to us the
universities and the cathedrals, some of the most tender
hymns and imposing theological systems which, if they cannot be accepted in important particulars, are yet remarkable
constructions of thought and piety.   And, above all, it has
handed down to us a group of notable men who may well
serve as a stimulus to all generations which are interested
in the extension of Christ's kingdom.

But in the judgment of these very men, the period was
not an ideal one either in morals or faith.   If we go to
preachers, like Berthold of Regensburg, we find evidence
of the prevalence of vice and irreligion among all classes.
If we go to popes and Schoolmen, we hear bitter complaints
of the evils of the age and of human lot which would fit in

---

[1] Heisterbach, *Dial.*, XII. 2, Strange's ed., II. 316.

[2] See Creighton in Traill, I. 368 sq., and Geo. Pernet, *Leprosy*, in *Quart.
Rev.*, 1903, pp. 384 sqq.

with the most pessimistic philosophy of our times. Innocent
III., in his Disdain of the World, — *De contemptu mundi*, —
poured out a lamentation, lugubrious enough for the most
desolate and forsaken. Anselm dilates under the same title,
and Hugo of St. Victor [1] carries on the plaint in his Vanity
of the World —*De vanitate mundi*. Walter Map wrote on
the world's misery — *de mundi miseria*, declaring that the
world was near its destruction, that justice was exiled from
society and the worship of Christ was coming to an end.

> *Exulat justitia, cessat Christi cultus.*

The most famous of the longer poems of the period repeats
Innocent's title, and its author, Bernard of Cluny, is most
severe upon the corruption in church and society. The poem
starts in the minor key.

> The last times, the worst times are here, watch.
> Behold the Judge, supreme, is at hand with His wrath.
> He is here, He is here. He will terminate the evils. He will
>   reward the just.
>
> *Hora novissima, tempora pessima sunt, vigilemus*
> *Ecce minaciter, imminet arbiter ille supremus.*
> *Imminet, imminet, et mala terminet, æqua coronet.*

The greater Bernard of Clairvaux exclaimed, "Oh! that I
might, before dying, see the Church of God led back to the
ideal of her early days. Then the nets were cast, not to catch
gold and silver, but to save souls. The perilous times are not
impending. They are here. Violence prevails on the earth." [2]
The Englishman, Adam Marsh, writing to Grosseteste, spoke
of "these most damnable times," *his diebus damnatissimis*.[3]
Edmund of Abingdon, archbishop of Canterbury, dying in
exile at Potigny, exclaimed, " I have lived too long, for I see all
things going to ruin; Lord God receive my soul." [4] Roger
Bacon found rottenness and decay everywhere, and he agreed
with other moralists of his day, in making the clergy chiefly
responsible for the prevailing corruption. The whole clergy,

---

[1] Migne, 158. 705 sqq., 176. 703–739.
[2] *Ep.*, 238, to Eugenius, Migne, 182. 430. *De consid.* I. 10.
[3] *Mon. Franc.*, *Ep.* XXVI. p. 116.   [4] Creighton, *Hist. Lectures*, p. 132.

he says, "is given to pride, avarice, and self-indulgence. Where clergymen are gathered together, as at Paris and Oxford, their quarrels and strife, and their vices are a scandal to laymen."[1]

With a similar lament Hildebrand, at the opening of the period, took up the duties of the papacy.

The prophet Joachim looked for a new dispensation as the only relief.

The real greatness of this period lies not in its relative moral and religious perfection, as compared with our own, but in a certain imposing grandeur of conception and of faith, as shown in the Crusades, the cathedrals, the Scholastic systems, and even the mistaken ideal of papal supremacy. Its institutions were not in a settled condition, and its religious life was not characterized by repose. A tremendous struggle was going on. The surface was troubled, and there was a mighty undercurrent of restlessness. It would be an ungracious and a foolish thing for this generation, the heir of twice as many centuries of Christian schooling as were the twelfth and thirteenth centuries, to boast as though Christian charity and morality and devotion to high aims had waited until now to manifest themselves. The Middle Ages, from 1050 to 1300, offer a spectacle of stirring devotion to religious aims in thought and conduct.

[1] Brewer's ed., pp. 399 sqq.

INDEX OF NAMES AND TOPICS

[The authors of the more important works mentioned in the lists of literature are included in this table. In the body of this volume Konrad is sometimes spelled Conrad; Matilda, Mathilda, and Eugenius III., Eugene III.]

Aaron of Lincoln, 451.
Abælard, 98, 99; on miracles, 354; Pet. de Bruys, 482; schools, 538, 588, 590, 609 sqq.; studies, 610; cathedral schools, 611; personal traits, 611; and Héloise, 612 sqq.; letters, 615; at Genevieve, 616; the Trinity, 616 sqq.; tried at Sens, 617; and Bernard, 617 sqq.; condemned, 618; death, 619; Pet. Ven. on, 620; theol., 620; philos., 622; source of authority, 622 sq.; atonement, 625; sin, 626; a "Pagan," 626, 644 sqq.; the sacraments, 702; on marriage, 748.
Abbott, 122, 142, 145.
Abrahams, 442.
Absalom of Lund, 798.
Absolution, 730, 734; a pæna et culpa, 736, 741.
Accidents, 716.
Acre, 204; evacuated, 207; residence of patr. of Jerus., 247; fell, 249; distance to Marseilles, 258; besieged by Richd., 261, 265; St. Louis there, 284; lost, 286 sq., 300; St. Francis in, 433.
Adam of St. Victor, 861.
Adams, G. B., 290.
Adamson, 693.
Ad exstirpanda, 523, 888.
Adhemar, 229; Gibbon on, 234; death, 237, 240.
Adrian IV., 106 sqq.; Gregorovius on, 109.
Adrian V., 205.
Alanus of Auxerre, 342.
Alanus ab Insulis, 459, 494, 502, 635 sq.; on Mary, 833; on preaching, 853, etc.
Albanenses, 474.
Albers, 330, 337.
Albert of Aachen, 213, 226, 231, 233, 242.
Albertus Magnus, 653 sqq.; Leo XIII. on, 653, 654; acquaintance with nature, 555; writings, 656; on demons, 658; Mary, 659 sq., 832 sq.; the pope, 659, 713; sin, 751; the devil, 884, 886.

Albigenses, crusades against, 507 sqq.; Cæsar of Heisterb. on cruelty of, 511; 4th Lat. on, 513; end of, 514.
Aldinger, 190.
Alençon, 389.
Alexander II., 21, 24, 40, 86, 536.
Alexander III., 110 sqq., in France, 112; returns to Rome, 117; and Becket, 130, 136.
Alexander IV., 200; and August. Rule, 359; against Gerardo, 378; and the Mendicants, 387; on Paris Univ., 569.
Alexander of Hales, 588, 651 sqq.; on penance, 731; withdrawal of the cup, 717; indulgences, 739; fund of merit, 740; purgatory, 742; the dark arts, 880.
Alexis, St., 494.
Alexius Comnenus, 224.
Alphandéry, 458, etc.
Amalric, kg. of Jerus., 250.
Amalric, of Bema, 176, 486.
Anacletus II., 94 sqq.
Anagni, 117, 185.
Anastasius IV., 106.
Anathema of Henry IV., 50; Otto IV., 163; Phil. Aug., 164; Fredk. II., 184, 185, 191, 194, 196; Hospitallers exempt, 299; Pontius of Cluny, 333.
Ancient Observance, 367.
Angels, 657 sq.; Th. Aq. on, 669; Bonavent. on, 681.
Angelus bell, 843.
Anna Comnena, 213, 233, 243.
Annates, 787 sq.
Anonymous of Passau, 459, 469, 502.
Ansbert, 256.
Anselm of Baggio (Alex. II.), 12.
Anselm of Canterbury on celibacy, 43, 84; and Wm. Rufus, 87 sqq.; leaves Engl., 90; on monasticism, 315, 318; school discipline, 542 sq., 598 sqq.; at Bec, 599; abp. of Cant., 599; writings, 600; philos. principle, 600; God's existence, 601 sqq.; the atonement, 604 sqq.; mysticism, 607; withdrawal of the cup, 717; sin, 753, 863.

Anselm of Laon, 538.
Anthony of Padua, 415, 852, 856.
Anthony's Fire, 367.
Antioch and 1st Crus., 237; 2d Crus., 255; Fredk. I. buried there, 259; falls, 285.
Anti-popes, Cadalus, 22, 59; Wibert, 61, 77; Sylvester IV., 73; Victor IV., 111; Pascal III., 113; ordination of, 745.
Antonites, 367.
Apparallamentum, 478.
Arabic philos., 654, 661, 696.
Archdeacons, 795 sq.
Archer and Kingsford, 212; on Peter the Hermit, 242; Crusades, 292.
Aristotle, 591; condemned by Greg. IX., 592, 651; Luther on, 676.
Arnold, Matthew, 408.
Arnoldists, 106, 521.
Arnold of Brescia, 98 sqq.; expelled fr. France, 100; ideals, 100; ban'd. fr. Rome, 101; Hefele and Gregorovius on, 101; poverty, 382; and Abælard, 618.
Arnold of Citeaux, 511, 513.
Asceticism, see Monasticism, Flagellants.
Ashes, sprinkling with, 702.
Assizes of Jerus., 247.
Assumption of Mary, 842 sq.
Astralabius, 612.
Atonement, Anselm on, 604; Abælard, 625; Th. Aq., 670; D. Scotus, 689; not a price to the devil, 753.
Attritio, 652, 732.
Augustine, 28; and scholasticism, 589, 591, etc.; mysticism, 639; sacraments, 707; eucharist, 718; demons, 879.
Augustinians, 358 sqq.
Ave Maria, 843, 882.

Bacon, Roger, on the trsll. of Aristotle, 591; Alex. of Hales, 652, 693 sqq.; op. majus, 694; experimental philos., 695; scholasticism, 696; compar. relig. and philology, 697; eucharist, 698; canon law, 765; Grosseteste, 826.
Baldric of Dol, 211, 219, 228.
Baldwin I. of Jerus., 235, 237, 248.
Baldwin II., 250.
Baldwin III., IV., V., 250, 255.
Baldwin II., III. of Constant., 192, 276, 301.
Baldwin, abp. of Cant., 258, 261.
Baltic Provinces, 306, 428 sqq.
Baltzer, 631.
Baluze, 151.
Balzani, 102.
Bannister, H. M., 860.
Baptism, 478; Th. Aq. on, 671, 710; and regeneration, 709; formulá, 709; mode, subjects, element, 710 sq.; and salvation, 711.
Baptism, Infant, among the sects,

485; Waldenses, 504; of Jews, 711.
Barefoot monks, 367.
Barine, 390.
Baring-Gould, 8, 830.
Baronius on Arnold of Brescia, 98.
Barry, 7.
Basnage, 442.
Baumgarten, 683, 781.
Baur, 2, 598.
Bec, 536.
Becket, Thomas à, 120 sqq.; archdeacon, 124; chancellor, 126; personal habits, 126; in France, 127; abp., 128 sqq.; bef. Alex. III., 130; struggle with Henry II., 130; rejects Clar. Constt., 135; flees to Continent, 136; meets Alex. III., 136; excommunicates bpp., 137; returns to Engl., 139; murdered, 140 sqq.; canonized, 146; performs miracles, 148.
Beghards, 487, 491.
Beguines, 487 sq.
Behringer, 700.
Benedict IX., 38.
Benedict X., 16.
Beneficium, 108 sq.
Benrath, K., 370, 830.
Berengar of Tours, 14; condemned, 17.
Berengar on miracles, 354, 609.
Berengaria, 260.
Bernard Guy, 458, 467, 517, 528.
Bernard of Caux, 528.
Bernard of Chartres, 538.
Bernard of Clairvaux, 94; supports Inn. II., 95; on Arnold of Brescia, 98; Crusades, 218; 2d Crus., 253 sq.; its failure, 256, 349; the Templars, 301; writings, 308; monasticism, 315, 316, 340; Cluny, 334 sq., 349; and Pet. Ven., 335; the Cistercians, 338, 342 sqq.; canonized, 344; parentage, 345; on the papacy, 351, 771, 777 sqq.; realism, 351; Luther on, 344, 351; mirac. power, 352; Map on, 353; Morison on his miracles, 354; and Abælard, 355, 616 sqq., 626; practical tendency, 355; praised by Joachim, 356; on Malachy, 356; personal unworthiness, 357; Deutsch on, 357; on the Carthusians, 364; Hildegard, 371 sq.; Jews, 448; and Dante, 638; mysticism, 640; papal legates, 784; papal exactions, 791; Mary, 830, 832 sq.; as a preacher, 855; hymnwriter, 863, 882, 895.
Bernard of Cluny, 336, 761; on corruption at Rome, 791, 864, 895.
Bernard of Fontis Calidi, 459, 503.
Bernard the Cistercian, 430.
Berthold of Calabria, 365.
Berthold of Regensburg, 851, 857 sq., 862, 894.
Besant and Palmer, 212.

Bigg, C., 823.
Bishops, subject to state, 46; not an order, 774, 792 sqq.; unworthy, 794 sq.; warlike, 797; German, 799; good, 799; murdered, 804; morals of, 807; trsll. of, 815; forced upon sees, 815 sq.; canonized, 816.
Black Friars, 383.
Blood of Christ, 847.
Boehmer, 2, 389, 764.
Bogomili, 471.
Bohemund, 234, 250.
Bologna jurists at Roncaglia, 108; Becket at, 124; Univ., 564 sqq.; Fredk. I. and, 564; government, 565; salaries, 566; women proff., 566; civil and canon law, 567; text-books, 567; centenary, 568; Bacon on study of law at, 765.
Bompiani, Sofia, 460.
Bonacursus, 658.
Bonaventura, 389; Life of St. Francis, 414; and Wm. of St. Amour, 573, 678 sq.; cardinal, 678; death, 679; Gerson on, 679; mysticism, 680 sq.; works of, 680; on angels, 681; imm. concept., 681, 840 sq.; sacraments, 705, 707; baptismal formula, 709; penance, 732; sin, 751; the atonement, 754; heaven, 761; Mary, 831, 834.
Bongars, 211.
Boniface VIII., 5, 209 sq., 777, 789.
Bonizo, 7.
Bononia docet, 565.
Books, borrowed, 364; St. Francis on, 384, 415; text-books, 540, 544 sq.; in convents, 544; catalogues, 545; gifts of, 546; loaned, 547, 548; bookroom, 548; copying, 548; price, 550; Abælard's, 611.
Borgnet, 652.
Bourbon, Etienne de, 458; on eucharist, 728; preaching, 851.
Bourgain, L., 850.
Bouvines, battle of, 163.
Bramhall, E. C., 217.
Brandon, St., 319.
Brewer, 391, 693.
Bridges, 693, 698, etc.
Brieger, 700.
Brigitta, St., 842.
Broderick, 575.
Brothers of the Sword, 432.
Bruno of Col., 362.
Bryce, 2; on Fredk. II., 199, etc.
Bugres, 471.
Bulæus, 551.
Bulgari, 471.
Bursa, 560.
Butler, A., 308.

Cadalus, 22.
Cæsar of Heisterbach, 219, 309; on monasticism, 311; religion, 324; eucharist, 727; penance, 743; purgatory, 762 sq., 779 morals of

German bpp., 798; Mary, 827; relics, 848; preaching, 852 sq.; the devil, 880, 883, etc.
Cæsar of Spires, 416.
Calixtus II., 94; and Hospitallers, 199, 331, 333.
Calixtus III., 113, 115.
Cambridge Univ., 576 sq.
Canonici puri, 535.
Canon law, 564, 764 sqq.; Decretum, 767; aim, 768 sq.; Döllinger on, 769; justif. force in relig., 769; Luther, 770; R. Bacon, 804; in Engl., 822.
Canons regular, 359.
Canossa, 54, 56; Bismarck on, 59; Gregorovius on, 68.
Canticle to the Sun, 402, 407 sq.
Canticles, 352, 650, 833.
Carcassonne, 511.
Cardinals, elect pope, 17 sq., 118, 204; French, 209, 781 sqq.; revenues, 789 sq.
Carmelites, 365 sqq.
Carpentarius, 247.
Carta charitatis, 339.
Carthusians, 362 sqq.; Pet. Ven. on, 363.
Cartwright, 780.
Cassani, 563.
Cassino, Mønte, 70, 331.
Caswall, Ed., 860.
Cataphrygæ, 715.
Catena aurea, 663.
Cathari, 470–482; no., 473; sects, 474; doctt., 476; rites, 477, sq.; marriage, 479; capital punishment, 479; oaths, 481; organization, 481; steadfastness, 480; and Protestantism, 482; Rupert on 650, 833.
Cathedrals, 581 sqq.; Norman, 583 sq.; Gothic in Italy, etc., 586 sqq.
Catherine of Siena on Mary, 842.
Cavellus, 683.
Cavenaugh, 660.
Celano, Thomas à, 389, 866.
Celibacy, clerical, 14, 36, 39; in Engl., 42, 821; Spain, 43; France, 44; triumph of, 44, 807 sq.
Cencius, 49, 786, 824.
Census, 787.
Cernay, 460.
Cessations, 556, 571 sq.
Chalandon, 212.
Chambers, E. K., 869.
Chappuis, 768.
Charlemagne on schools, 535; and Paris Univ., 569.
Charles, E., 693.
Charles II., 208.
Charles of Anjou, 201; and East. Emp., 206; death, 207.
Chartreuse, 569.
Chartularium, 551.
Chaucer, 148, 325, 388.
Check Greek, 262.
Chevalier, 3, 659, 860.

Children's Crusades, 266 sq.
Chrism, 712, 714.
Christian of Mainz, 797.
Chrodegang, 359.
Church, R. W., 597.
Church and State, theory, 27, 28, 31; Greg. VII. on, 36, 45; Leo XIII. on, 67; in Engl., 82, 123 sqq.; in conflict, 107, 110 sq.; Becket on, 128 sqq., 134 sqq.; Inn. III. on, 156 sqq.; Th. Aq., 673, 775 sqq.
Church Courts, 86, 135, 803 sq. ; Church funds and taxation, 796.
Circumcisi, 488, 521.
Cistercians, 337 sq.; Engl. houses, 341; war agt. the Albigenses, 509.
Clairvaux, 314, 346 sq.
Clara Sciffi, 399.
Clarendon Constt., 132, 815.
Clarisses, 410.
Clary, Robt. de, 269.
Class. studies, 346, 540.
Clement III., see Wibert.
Clement IV., 201, 204, 774.
Clementines, 768.
Clergy, legislation in favor of, 172; cond. of, 464; education, 560, 799 sqq.; bodily defects, 800; salaries, 800; Inn. III. on, 801; lity. interests and preaching, 802; wills, 803; show in dress, etc., 804; not to attend executions, 805; of Paris, 806 Bonavent. on, 807; in Engl., 815 sqq.; culture in Engl., 821; see Celibacy.
Clermont, syn. of, 1095, 73, 227.
Cluny, 321, 330 sqq.; teacher of popes, 331; rule, 331; in Engl., 332; decline, 333; and Pet. Ven., 333, 336; and schools, 542.
Cœlestin IV., 190.
Cœlestin V., 208 sq., 210, 415.
Cola di Rienzi, 102.
Coleridge quoted, 289.
Coles, A., 860.
Colleges, 560, 579.
Cologne cathedral, 585.
Columbus and Crusades, 214, 409.
Comba, 460, 494.
Compayré, 552.
Conclave, 204, 782; see Cardinals.
Concomitance, 717.
Concorrezzi, 474.
Concupiscentia, 634, 840.
Conder, 246.
Confirmation, 712.
Conrad III., 254.
Conrad IV., 200.
Conradin, 200 sqq.
Conrad of Eberbach, 337.
Conrad of Montferrat, 252, 262, 279.
Consolamentum, 477 sq.
Constance, see Henry VI., Fredk. II.
Constantine, donation of, 109.
Constantinople, Lat. conq., 159, 164; empire, 223, 274 sqq.; Lat. patr., 277.

Contrition, 730, 732.
Convent and hymns, 861.
Conventuals, 412, 414.
Conversi, 315.
Cooper, C. H., 575.
Cooper, W. M., 876.
Corpus Christi, 713, 723.
Coulton, 370, etc.
Councils, 808 sqq.; œcumen., 809; local, 809, 811 sq.
Cousin, 609.
Crawford, Marion, 252.
Creationist, 669.
Credentes, 477.
Creighton, 385, 392, 460, 823.
Cross, the true, 241, 250, 276; enemies of, 289, 802, 846 sq., 850, 857.
Crown of thorns, 276, 848.
Croyland, abbey of, 545.
Cruel, 850, etc.
Crusades, Greg. VII. and, 30, 34, 211 sqq.; causes, 214 sq.; leading Crusaders, 215; titles, 216; began in France, 219; aim, 220; mistake of, 220; Hegel on, 220; routes, 224; decided on at Clermont, 229; the 1st, 230 sqq.; sufferings of Crusaders, 238 sq.; 2d, 252 sqq.; 3d, 257; results, 265 sq.; Children's, 266; 4th, 268 sq.; 5th, 278; St. Louis and the last Crusade, 281 sq.; losses, 285 sq.; judged, 289; failure, 290 sq.; good effects, 291; on lit. of, 292 sq.; agt. Poland, 432; the Jews, 448, 450, 452; heretics, 468; the Albigenses, 507 sqq.; Stedinger, 514.
Cumulus thesauri, 740.
Cup, withdrawal of, 717, 725 sq.
Cur deus homo, 604 sq.
Curia, 781 sq.; see Cardinals.
Curzon, 296.

Dagobert, 246.
Dalgairns, 700.
Damian, order of, 208; chapel of, 395; sisters of, 410.
Damiani, 12, 15; on Greg. VII., 16; legate to Milan, 21; cler. marriage, 37; cler. morals, 38; heresy, 466, 470; two swords, 775; Mary, 833, 837, 877, 880.
Damietta, 183, 279; taken by Louis IX., 283.
Dandolo, 269, 271.
Dante, 4, 154; on Cœlestin V., 210; and Mendicants, 379 sq., 394; on Bonavent., 679, 761; Bernard, 638; Mary, 832.
Dargan, E. C., 850.
David of Augsburg, 459.
David of Dinant, 487.
Davidson C., 869.
De consideratione, 351, 777 sqq.
De contemptu mundi, 153, 864.
Decretum Gratiani, 111, 766.
Delacroix, 459.

De militia Christi, 252.
Demonology, 879 sqq.; pop. belief, 880 sq.; theol. belief, 884; treatment by the popes, 887, 893 sq.
Denifle, 1, 309; on Luther and Bernard, 344, 370, 391, 419, 551, 563, 631, 644; on faith, 757.
Determinism, 687, 690.
Deutsch, 151, 337, 342; on Bernard, 337, 609.
Deutz, Rupert of, 455, 649 sq.
Devil, Anselm on, 606, 617; burlesqued, 873, 879 sqq., 881 sqq.; abode of, 885.
Dictatus papæ, 30.
Dice-playing, 799, 806.
Dieckhoff, 460, 507.
Dies irae, 154, 866 sq.
Divorce, 748, 887; see Marriage.
Doctors of the Church, 344, 679; doctor mellifluus, 344; irrefragabilis, 651; universalis, 653; angelicus, 661; seraphicus, 678; subtilis, 683; mirabilis, 559, 693; Bologna doctors lectured everywhere, 597.
Döllinger, 2, 56, 199, 296, 370; on Joachim, 375, 442; the Jews, 448, 458; Henry of Lausanne, 485, 551; papal inquis., 674; D. Scotus, 684, 690; canon law, 769, etc.
Dominic, 310; estimate of 380, 419 sqq.; and heretics, 420, 424; and Inn. III., 420; preaching, 423; papal favors, 422; preachers, 440; lit., 442.
Dominicans, 383; spread, 421 sq.; inquisitors, 522 sqq.
Dominicus Loricatus, 877.
Dorylæum, 236.
Douais, 459.
Drama, 869 sqq.
Drane, Miss, 419, 534.
Dreves, 860, 862.
Drioux, 660.
Dugdale, 308.
Duns Scotus on monasticism, 327, 683 sqq.; subtlety, 683 sqq.; and Th. Aq., 684; obscure, 684; Franciscan, 685; birthplace, 685; writings, 686; theol., 687; and scripture, 687; determinism, 687; on sin, 688; atonement, 689; transubstantiation, 689; imm. concept., 690, 841 sq.; sacraments, 706 sq.; bapt. of Jews and infants, 710 sq.; eucharist, 716 sq.

Eadmer, on celibacy, 43, 81, 89, 597.
Eastern Church, 26, 28, 205, 290, 772 sq.
Eccleston, 391.
Edessa, taken by Baldwin, 237, 249; fall of, 252, 256.
Ehrle, 1.
Eicken, von, 309, 660, 665, 677, 701.
Ekkehardus, 213, 223.
Eleanor, 125; at Antioch, 225.

Elias of Cortona, 403, 405, 409, 413.
Elizabeth of Hungary, 531.
Elizabeth of Schönau, 323, 373.
Endura, 480.
Engelhardt, 644.
England, Ch. in, under the Saxons, 82; the Normans, 83, 123 sqq., 133, 812 sqq.
England, interdict, 168; given to France, 169; fief of Rome, 170; Augustinians, 359; Premonstrants, 361; Carthusians, 364; Carmelites, 366; Franciscans, 416 sq.; Jews, 451; heresy, 473, 533; architecture, 583 sq.; papal abuses in, 814; bpp. in, 815; revenues of, 817; Italians in, 819; preaching in, 859.
Erasmus, on the Crusades, 289.
Erigena Scotus, 486, 596.
Ermengaudus, 458.
Eternal Gospel, 375, 378.
Ethics, 589; of Abælard, 622; Th. Aq., 672.
Eubel, 391.
Eucharist, 671; Bacon on, 698, 713 sqq.; elements, 715; Judas' communion, 718; as sacrifice, 720; effect of, 720 sq.; celebration, 721; priest's fitness, 721; frequency of celebration, 723; withdrawal of cup, 725; customs, 726 sq.
Eudo, 482.
Eugenius III., 97, 100; 2d Crus., 333; at Clairvaux, 351; on Hildegard, 372.
Extravagantes, 767.
Extr. Unction, 743 sq.
Eymericus, 460, 529.

Fair Rosamonde, 825.
Faith, 755 sq.
Felder, 391, 568.
Felten, 823.
Ferree, 581.
Feudalism, 45; in Palestine, 247; decadence of, 290.
Ficker, 461.
Finke, 204.
Fisher, Geo. P., 3, etc.
Fisher, H., 151, 197 sqq., 202, 346.
Flade, 461.
Flagellants, 862, 876 sqq.
Font Evraud, 368.
Foot-washing, 355.
Förstemann, 876.
France, and the Jews, 450; heresy in, 473; enlarged, 514; Inquis. in, 528 sq.; architecture in, 585.
Francis, St., 310; and Dominic, 380; Harnack on, 380; and learning, 385; biogg. of, 389 sq., 394–418; Dante on, 394; studies, 395; and lepers, 395; in Rome, 397; Syria, 339; will, 401; last sickness, 402; Canticle to the Sun, 402; love of nature, 402; death, 403; stigmata, 404; estimates, of 407; 1st Rule, 409;

Life by Bonavent., 414; and Bonavent., 679.
Franciscans, guardians of the Holy Places, 248; characterized, 383; papal favors, 384, 386; Inn. III. and, 385; ban'd by Fredk. II., 386; Lit. on, 392 sq.; 1st Rule, 396, 400; spread of, 408 sq.; 2d, 3d Rules, 409; and learning, 415; preaching, 852.
Fratres di pœnitentia, 383.
Frederick Barbarossa puts Arnold to death, 101, 103, 107; and Alex. III., 112 sqq.; crowned in Rome, 113; death and estimate of, 120; and 3d Crus., 259; and Bologna Univ., 562, 564.
Frederick II., 103, 160; Inn. III. his guardian, 161; crowned kg., 163; renounces imper. rights, 163; prominence, 181 sq.; crowned emperor, 182; takes cross, 183; and Greg. IX., 185; appeals to Christendom, 185; 5th Crus., 185 sq., 279; marriage to Isabella of Engl., 186; quotes Scripture, 188; deposed, 189, 193; charges against, 193; death, 196; M. Paris, Ranke, etc., on, 197, 199; Freeman on, 280; and Jews, 445; on Inquis., 521; papacy, 775.
Frederick of Swabia, 305.
Fredericq, 458, 532, etc.
Freeman, 7, 81, 85, 92, 110, 121, 128, 129; on Fredk. II., 199, 280.
Friedberg, 764, etc.
Froude, J. A., 122, 196, 823.
Froude, R. H., 121.
Fulcher of Chartres, 211, 249, etc.
Fulke of Neuilly, 270 sq., 855.
Fulke the Black, 222.
Fuller, Thos., 173, 195; and the Jews, 452, 575.
Fund of merit, 652.
Funk, 2; on med. morals, 38, 181, 246; on Fredk. II., 279, 296, 701.

Gasquet, 332, 418, 453, etc.
Gaufrid of Clairvaux, 342; on Bernard, 353 sq.
Gaunilo, 603.
Gee and Hardy, 82, etc.
Geoffrey of Vinsauf, 256, etc.
Gerardus of Borgo, 337.
Gerhoh of Reichersberg, 96, 873.
Germany, celibacy in, 41; Inn. III. in, 161; civil war, 162 sq.; missions, 429–433; and the Jews, 451; the Inquis., 530; architecture, 585; preaching in, 852, 857.
Gerson, on Bonavent., 679; on withdrawal of the cup, 726, 875.
Gervaise of Cant., 81, 609, etc.
Gesta Franc., 213.
Gesta Rom., 354.
Gfrörer, 8.
Gibbon, 2; on Crusades, 214; Tancred, 236; Prester-John, 439.

Giesebrecht, 297, etc.
Gieseler, 459, 596.
Gilbertines, 366.
Gilbert of Poictiers, 618, 628 sq.
Giles, 121.
Giotto, 397.
Giraldus Cambrensis, 256, 577.
God, argtt. for existence of, by Anselm, 601 sqq., 657; Th. Aq., 668.
Godfrey of Bouillon, 234; kg. of Jerus., 246; death, 247, 298.
Godfrey of St. Omer, 301.
Goetz, 391.
Gottfried of St. Victor, 592.
Gottlob, 212; on indulgences, 732, 781, 787.
Gottschalk, Crusader, 233.
Grabmann, 660.
Graetz, 442, 456, etc.
Grammont, 369.
Gratian, 124, 564, 765, 767: on papacy, 773.
Gray, 266.
Gray Friars, 383.
Greenland, 789.
Greenwood, 7.
Gregorovious, 2; on Greg. VII., 68; Arnold of Brescia, 101; Fredk. II., 199; Inn. III., 178; Crusades, 220; Urban II.'s speech, 227; the Flagellants, 876, etc.
Gregory VII., 9 sqq.; characterized, 10; parentage, 10; education, 11; enters Rome with Leo IX., 12; pope, 24; on the state of society, 26; theory of papacy, 29 sq.; treatment of the kingdoms, 33; Crusade, 30, 34, 225; moral reformer, 36 sqq.; investiture, 46 sq.; strife with Henry IV., 49 sqq.; excommunicated Henry, 52, 63; deposed him the 2d time, 61; flees from Rome, 64; death, 65; estimate of, 66 sq.; Crusades, 776; legates, 783.
Gregory VIII., 258.
Gregory IX. and Fredk. II., 184 sqq.; calls council at Rome 1241, 189; death, 190; Decretals, 190; Child. Crus., 268; on mendicant friars, 386; Franciscans, 399, 404; heresy, 466; Stedinger, 514; Inquis., 522 sq.; on Paris Univ., 571; baptism, 711; canon law, 711.
Gregory X., 204; in Palestine, 287; on the empire, 777.
Gross, 568.
Grosseteste, 171, 195, 379, 417; and the Jews, 448, 693; on papacy, 774; papal appointments, 819, 821, 823 sqq.; writings, 828; M. Paris on, 829, 847.
Guibert of Nogent, 213; and the Crusades, 216, 230, 534; at school, 542, 830, 853.
Guiscard Robt., 19, 63.
Guizot, 3, 281.

Guizot, Madame, 609.
Gunther Ligurinus, 102.
Guntherus, 844.

Hades, Christ's descent into, 759 sq.
Hadriana, 822.
Hagenmeyer, 213, 214, 226, 233, 237, 242, etc.
Hahn, 212, 290, 427, 459, 700.
Hale, E. E., 461.
Hallam, 3; on Francis, 394.
Haller, 771.
Hampden, 587.
Hansen, J., 878, 884.
Harding, 338.
Harnack, 3, 309; on monasticism, 310; Francis, 394, 407; Anselm, 606 sq.; Bernard, 639; mysticism, 637; D. Scotus, 688; eucharist, 722, etc.
Hase, Karl, 390, 405, 869.
Haskins, 461.
Hasse, 81, etc.
Hauck, 2, 160, 328, 459, 800, etc.
Hauréau, 587, 643.
Hausrath, 97; on stigmata, 406; on Abælard, 627.
Haussleiter, 560.
Heaven, 761.
Heeren, 289, 534.
Hefele-Knöpfler, 2; on med. morals, 38, 55, 56, etc.
Hegel, on Crusades, 230, 231.
Hell, 758, 894.
Héloise, 613 sqq.
Helyot, 295.
Henry I., 90 sqq.
Henry II., 109 sqq., 122 sqq., 131, 139, 146, 170.
Henry IV., 16, 32, 41, 47, 53 sqq., 64, 47, 225.
Henry V., 74, 75.
Henry VI., 103, 160, 265.
Henry VIII., 149.
Henry of Ghent, 692 sq.
Henry of Huntingdon, 81, 813, etc.
Henry of Lausanne, 483 sq.
Henry of Liége, 798 sq.
Heppe, 534, 878.
Heresy, Arnold of Brescia, 98; 4th Lat., 176, 461 sqq.; records of, 462, 465; cause of outbreak, 462; Hildegard on, 464; likened to poison, etc., 464; Bernard and Th. Aq. on, 467, 518, 775; outbreak of, 472; Albigensian, 507 sqq.; Fredk. II. on, 519; state legislation, 521; in Rome, 522; c. of Constance on, 524, 893.
Heretic, defined, 465; likened to foxes, etc., 466; Fredk. II. on, 468; number of, 468; groups, 469; burnt, 472; 527, 529, etc.
Hergenröther, Ph., 764, etc.
Hergenröther-Kirsch, 3, 337, 362, 383, etc.
Hering, H., 850.

Hermann of Metz, 30, 32, 52, 62, 68.
Hermann of Salza, 306, 432.
Herzog, 1, 461, 507.
Hildebert of Tours, on transubstantiation, 714, 863.
Hildegard, 371; study of nature, 372; on heretics, 464.
Hodgson, 269, 337, 341.
Hoensbroech, 879, 886.
Höfler, 7, 180.
Hohenstaufen, 103; Gregorovius on, 104, 110; doomed, 199 sqq.
Holy Lance, 845.
Holy Office, 525.
Holy Sepulchre, 294; see Crusades.
Holzapfel, 419.
Honorius II., 22, 94.
Honorius III., character, 182; on Crusades, 278; on Dominic, 421, 432.
Honorius of Autun, 308, 316, 851, 858, 862.
Hospital, 298, 306.
Hospitallers, 285; Lit. on, 295, 298; privileges, 299; organization, 299; officials and extension, 300; move to Rhodes, 300; to Malta, 301.
Host, adoration of, 723 sq., 727 sq.
Hoveden, 81, 293, etc.
Howorth, 428.
Hroswitha, 870.
Hugh, Little, 448.
Hugh de Wells, 821.
Hugh of Lincoln, 823 sqq.
Hugh of Vermandois, 234, 250.
Hugo de Payens, 301.
Hugo of Cluny, 26, 331 sq.
Hugo of St. Victor, 644 sqq.; mysticism, 645; sacraments, 702; name of the Trinity, 709; on absolution, 736; sin, 751.
Huillard-Bréholles, 180; on Fredk. II., 198, 286, etc.
Humbert de Romanis, 288, 291, 384, 424, 854.
Humblina, 348.
Humiliati, 382, 411, 496 sqq.
Hurter, 151, 274, and often.
Hymns on Mary, 836, 860 sqq.

Iceland, 164.
Imm. Conception, Bernard on, 355; Franciscans and, 387; Bonavent. on, 681, 840; D. Scotus on, 690, Th. Aq. on, 840, 840 sq.
Impanation, 719.
Imposters, three, 188, 197.
Incubus, 886.
Indulgences, Urban II. and, 216; Eugenius and Inn. III., 217; Crusades and, 291; Albigenses, 509; Stedinger, 515, 737 sqq.; Th. Aq. on, 738; a pœna et culpa, 741 sq.; and purgatory, 742; stories of, 743.
Inge, 637.
Innocent II., 94 sqq.; at Clairvaux, 350; supported by Norbert, 361;

on Abælard, 617, 772; on indulgences, 738.
Innocent III., 152 sqq.; family, 153; writings, 153; election of, 154; papal theory, 156 sq.; a persecutor, 159; policy towards the state, 161; John of Engl., 166 sq.; Magna Charta, 172; death, 173; Gregorovius, Ranke, etc., on, 178; Child. Crus., 268; 4th Crus. 269 sqq.; on capt. of Const., 274; 5th Crus., 278; Hospitallers, 299; monastic orders, 326; Franciscans, 385, 397 sq.; Dominicans, 420; heresy, 466; Albig. wars, 508, 510; Inquis., 518 sqq.; indulgences, 739; canon law, 768; papacy, 776; on clerical fees, 801; cath. chapp., 803; on preaching, 851.
Innocent IV., 190 sqq., 200; mendicant friars, 387; on papacy, 777; and Grosseteste, 828; demonology, 888.
Innocent V., 205.
Inquisition and Dominicans, 424, 507; origin of, 515–525; a papal institution, 516; its advocates, 517; defended by Th. Aq., 517 sq.; Inn. III. on, 518, 520; and Mohammedans, 519; councils on, 519; Fredk. II. on, 519; Council of Toulouse, 520; state legislation, 521; in Rome, 522; Canon Law, 523; inquisitor murdered, 524; rights, 524 sq.; c. of Constance on, 524; procedure, 525–542; war against the dead, 528; in S. France, 528; Italy, 530; Germany, 530; Holland, 532; Engl., 533.
Intemperance, clerical, 799, 806.
Interdict, over Rome, 101; Scotland, 119; France, 164; Engl., 168; Sicily and Aragon, 207; Jerus., 280; Toulouse, 509; Parma, 523; Oxford, 578.
Investiture, 45, 75; Engl., 85, 89 sq., 92.
Iolanthe, 183, 252, 279.
Ireland, 109.
Irish students, 579.
Isaac Angelus, 259, 271, 273.

Jacobs, 442, 445, 451.
Jacopone da Todi, 399, 868.
Jacques, St., 384, 421.
Jacques de Vitry, 458; on heresy, 462; Paris clergy, 806, 892.
Jaffé, 7, 94.
Janssen, 442, 660.
Janauschek, 337.
Jeafferson, 575.
Jensen, 781.
Jerome on classics, 535, 540.
Jessopp, 309, 312, 328, 364, 891.
Jerusalem, pilgrimages to, 222, in hands of Moslems, 223; taken in 1st Crus., 239; under interdict, 280; lost to Chorasmians, 281.

Jerus. kingd. of, 186, 246 sqq., 280.
Jews and Inn. III., 155; of Bristol, 169; distinct dress, 177, 446, 443–457; and the popes, 444; their lit., 445; 4th Lat., 447; Pet. Ven. and Bernard on, 443, 448; Grosseteste on, 449; in France, 450; in Germany, 451; in Engl., 451; the Crusades, 448, 450; in Spain, 453 sqq.; putting children to death, 454; tracts against, 455; attempts to convert, 456; Richd. of St. Victor on, 647; see Baptism.
Joachim of Flore, 4th Lat. on, 175; and Crusades, 288, 370 sqq.; 3 periods of history, 375; prophecies fulfilled, 380, 414; on heresy, 464, 473; and P. Lombard, 635; and Hugh of Lincoln, 825.
John VIII., 216.
John XXI., 205.
John XXII., 366.
John XXIII., 742.
John de Crema, 807.
John of Brienne, 183.
John of England, 159, 166 sqq.; Lingard on, 166; deposed, 169; morals, 169; feudatory of Rome, 170; death, 174; tribute in arrears, 818 sq.
John of Giles, 573, 894.
John of Gray, 167.
John of Matha, 368.
John of Monte Corvino, 440.
John of Paris, 719.
John of Parma, 378, 678.
John of Roncho, 497.
John of Salisbury, 96; and Becket, 141, 534; on classical study, 537; archdeacons, 796, 880, etc.
Joinville, de, 264, 281, etc.
Joppa, 239, 262; taken by Richd. I., 264.
Jordanus da Giano, 391.
Josephini, 489.
Jubilee Year, 739.
Judas' communion, 718.
Julian of Spires, 390.
Jundt, 458.
Jusseraud, 739.
Justification, 754.

Kaiser, 370, 609.
Kaufmann, 308.
Kaulich, 587, 644.
Kerboga, 237.
Keys, power of, 735.
Kilwarby, 418.
Kings deposed, Henry IV., 62; Otto, 163; John, 169; Fredk. II., 193.
Kington, 180.
Kirsch, 781, 788, etc.
Knox-Little, 390.
Koch, E. E., 860.
Koeniger, 700, etc.
Köhler, 701.
Kolde, 358.

Königsfeld, 859.
Konrad III., 100, 103, 254 sq.
Konrad of Marburg, 531.
Köstlin, 344, 604, etc.
Krabbo, 180.
Kublai Khan, 440.
Kugler, 212, 252.
Kunibert of Turin, 39.
Kurtz, 700.
Kutter, 330, 343.

Labbæus, 1.
Lacordaire, 419.
Lambert le Bègue, 490.
Lambert of Hersfeld, 40; on Greg. VII., 56.
Lambeth, synod of 1281, 723.
Lane-Poole, Stanley, 246, 251; on Saladin, 263, 281.
Lanfranc, on celibacy, 42, 84, 135, 773.
Langen, 7.
Langton, 166 sqq.; and Magna Charta, 171, 173.
Languedoc, heresy in, 462; desolated, 509, 514.
Lateran Council of 1059, 20.
Lateran I., 79, 220, 810.
Lateran II., 96, 99, 801, 810.
Lateran III., 117, 450; on Waldenses, 495; on sacraments, 703, 807, 811.
Lateran IV., 174 sqq.; forbids orders, 314, 327; on Jews, 447; heresy, 466; Raymund of Toulouse, 513; transubstantiation, 714; penance, 733; marriage, 747 sq.; the papacy, 773; preaching, 811, 851; relics, 849.
Laurie, 552.
Lay patronage, 801.
Lea, 39, 212, 299; on Francis, 394; the Franciscans, 404, 442; on the Cathari, 481; on Inquis., 528, 700.
Lecky, 3.
Lecoy de la Marche, 458, 850.
Legates, papal, 782 sq., 807; to Engl., 813.
Legati nati, 813, 820.
Leisen, 862.
Leitner, 660, 771.
Lempp, 390, 391, 463.
Leo I., 29.
Leo IX., 13; prisoner to the Normans, 14; death, 15.
Leo XIII., 28, 59, 67; on scapulary, 366; rosary, 425; on Th. Aq., 528, 590, 662, 677; and intolerance, 525; on Alb. Magnus, 653.
Lepers, St. Louis, 282; Francis, 395; Hugh and, 825, 894.
Le Roulx, 295.
Letold of Tournay, 239.
Libraries, 544 sqq.; at Croyland, 545; tax for, 547; librarians, 547.
Liebner, 643 sq.
Limborch, 460.
Limbus infantum, 760.
Limbus patrum, 758 sq.
Lincoln, archdeaconries, 796, 824 sqq.

Lingard, 165.
Linsenmayer, 850.
Little, 391.
Littledale, 309.
Lombard, Peter the, 631 sq.; Sentences, 632 sq.; on God's existence, 634; atonement, 634; accused of heresy, 635; immersion, 711; penance, 731; ordin. of bpp., 744.
Lombard League, 113; defeats Fredk. I., 114; Fredk. II.'s claims, 183, 186 sq.; Fredk. abandons, 195.
Lombardy, iron crown of, 107.
Louis VII., 253, 369, 509.
Louis VIII., 513.
Louis IX., and the Crusades, 215, 281, 284; 2d Crus., 285 sqq.; and the Mend. Friars, 379; the Jews, 450; Albigenses, 513.
Love, Bernard on, 640 sqq., 647.
Luard, 165, etc.
Luchaire, 568.
Luciferans, 489.
Lucius III., 119.
Ludwig, the Iron, 894.
Lupe, St., and the devil, 883.
Luther quoted, 307, 344; Augustinian friar, 360; on Paris Univ., 569; on Th. Aq. and Aristotle, 676; Bab. captivity, 708; on the "accidents," 716; can. law, 770.
Lyons, councils of, 192 sq., 205 sqq., 811.

Macaulay, G. C., 189.
Madonnet, 391.
Magna Charta, 71 sq., 82.
Maitland, Prof., 122, 132, 308, 534, 764.
Maitland, S. R., 534, etc.
Malachy, 356.
Malagola, 563.
Malik-al-Kameel, 278.
Manfred, 200.
Mangu Khan, 441.
Mansi, 1.
Map, 97; enemies of the cross, 289; on Crusades, 290; Bernard, 353; Waldenses, 495; education, 537, 650; the curia, 792, 880, 887, 895.
Marienburg, 306.
Maronites, 38.
Marriage, see Celibacy, and the Maronites, 38; the Cathari on, 479, 746, 807, 887.
Marsh, Adam, 417, 693, 826 sqq., 895.
Martène-Durand, 460.
Martens, 8.
Martin IV., 206 sq.
Martin, the abbot, 270, 845.
Martin, legate in Engl., 820.
Mary, and Cistercians, 338; Carmelites, 365 sq.; abbess of St. Evraud, 368; seen by Eliz. of Schönau, 373, 425; Anselm on, 608; Alb. Mag., 658; worship of, 831 sqq.; titles, 831 sq.; reasons for worship, 833;

and Christ, 836; mediator, 836; prayers and hymns to, 836; stories of her aid, 839 sq.; in miracle plays, 878; virgin birth, 839 sq.; imm. concept., 840; assumption of, 843; Pius X. on, 844, 893.
Mathews, Shailer, 1.
Matilda, 49, 51, 54, 57, 64, 76, 162, 171.
Matthew Paris, 168, 169, 173; on Fredk. II., 191, 196; on Inn. IV., 200; Crusades, 219; crown of thorns, 276, 418; Jews, 452; on papal extortion, 791, 820; Grosseteste, 827 sqq.; on the Middle Ages, 889 sq.
Maturines, 368.
Maud, Queen, 91.
M'Cabe, 609, etc.
Medicine and Surgery, 555, 564; women practise, 567.
Meinhard, 432.
Mendicancy, Carmelites, 367; absolute, 382; modified, 413.
Mendicant orders, 379 sqq.; characterized, 383; Wm. of St. Amour on, 388; Gerson on, 389; at Paris, 573 sqq.; confession, 734; see Franciscans and Dominicans.
Merlin, 886.
Metalogicus, 538, 541, 629, etc.
Michaud, 212, 534.
Michelet, 296.
Middle Ages, characterized, 3 sq.; personalities of, 6, 891 sqq.
Middleton, R., 692.
Migne, 1.
Mignon, 643.
Milan, celibacy at, 20, 112; Bernard on, 354; centre of heresy, 462.
Military orders, no aid to Fredk. II., 186, 293, 295 sqq.; rivalry, 297.
Milman, 2, 442; on scholasticism, 589.
Milton, 441.
Minocchi, 390.
Minorites, 408; see Franciscans.
Miracle Plays, 869 sq.
Miracles, at Becket's tomb, 145 sq., 188; in convents, 317; Pet. Ven. on, 334; Bernard's, 350, 352 sq.; Morison and Abælard on, 354; Neander and Storrs on, 355; Hildegard's, 372; of the devil, 885.
Mirbt, 2, 8, 58, 73, 94, etc.
Mission Institutes, 435.
Missions, in N. Germany, 427 sqq.; am. the Moham., 433 sqq.; the Mongols, 437 sqq.
Mohammedans, missions am., 433 sqq.; effect of Crusades on, 433.
Molinier, 461.
Monasticism, 4, 308 sqq.; famous monks, 310; 5 periods, 310; motto of, 313; ideal life, 314, 322; princes and, 316; the devil and, 317 sqq.; names of convents, 320; convent buildings, 322; and the poor, 322; services of, 324 sq.; and papacy, 325; Inn. III. on, 326; D. Scotus on,

327; papal favors, 327; and heret. sects, 329; manual labor, 339; idealism, 347; Bernard on, 348 sq., 881, 892.
Monastic prophets, 320.
Moneta Crem., 458.
Mone, 859, 869.
Mongols, 192, 203, 206, 437 sqq.
Monologium, 600 sq.
Montalembert, 308, 313.
Montfort, and 4th Crus., 271, 273.
Morals, clerical, 797 sq.; see Clergy.
Morison, 342; on Bernard's miracles, 354.
Morris, R., 850.
Mouse, and the host, 716.
Müller, K., 2, 391, 460; on Humiliati, 497; Inquis., 515, 651, 700; penance and indulgences, 732 sq.
Mullinger, 534, 575.
Munro, 212, 214; on Pet. the Hermit, 242.
Muratori, 1.
Mystery Plays, 870.
Mysticism, Anselm, 607 sq., 637 sqq.; nature of, 637; comparison to Rachel, 638; Augustine, 639; of Bernard, 639 sq.; Richd. and Hugo of St. Victor, 638, 646 sqq.; Bonavent., 682.

Nature, love of, 346, 402.
Neale, J. M., 850, 860.
Neander, 342; on med. miracles, 355.
Nestorians, 438.
Neukirch, 7.
Newman, A. H., 458.
Newman, J. H., 2, 337; on med. education, 537, 551.
Nicæa, taken by Crusaders, 233, 235, 236.
Nicolaitanism, 20, 36.
Nicolas, boy-crusader, 267.
Nicolas I., 29.
Nicolas II., 16, 40.
Nicolas III., 206.
Nicolas IV., 207, 287; and Franciscans, 411 sq.
Nicolas Breakspear, 106; see Adrian IV.
Norbert, 310; miracles, 355; founder of Premonstrants, 360; Bernard on, 361; in Holland, 482; and the devil, 882.
Normans, and Leo IX., 15, 17, 19; conquests in Italy, 19; in Engl., 19, 23, 26; called by Greg. VII., 63; support Anacletus II., 95; and Ch. in Engl., 820 sq.
Notker of St. Gall, 861.
Nureddin, 250.

Oaths, 480, 504.
Observants, 412; see Spirituals.
Ockam, 691, 719.
Odo of Clugny, 330.
Odo of Deuil, 252.

O'Fihely, 683.
O'Gorman, 661.
Oliphant, Mrs., 390.
Olivi, 378, 415, 496.
Oman, 269.
Omnibene, 627, 632.
Ordericus Vitalis, 94, 636, etc.
Ordination, 744 sqq.
Ortlieb, 488.
Ortroy, 390.
Otho, Constt. of, 820.
Otto IV., 161, 163, 796.
Otto of Bamberg, 430.
Otto of Frising, on Henry IV.'s deposition, 52, 97 sqq., 102, 252; on monasticism, 315, 438, 596, etc.
Otto of Wittelsbach, 162.
Oxford, 571; origin, 575; colleges, 579; teachers, 580.
Ozanam, 121, 860.

Pandulf, 170.
Papacy, necessity of, 4; lowest stage, 9; and empire, 107, 110 sqq.; at peace, 115 sq., 202 sq.; golden age of, 152, 157 sq.; and John, 159; the Hohenstaufen, 199; taken by the French, 201; and monasticism, 325; and Mend. orders, 386 sqq.; Alb. Mag. on, 659; absolute power of, 891.
Papal fiefs, 33, 775; crown, 155, 783; interregna, 204, 207, 208; exchequer, 785 sq.; taxation, 785 sq., 790 sq.; revenues from Engl., 818.
Paraclete, convent of, 614, 620.
Paris, Univ. of, 568 sqq.; Luther on, 569; origin, 569; statutes, 569 sqq.; nations, 570; Greg. IX.'s charter, 571; rector, 571; cessations, 572; influence, 574.
Passagii, 488.
Pascal II., 44, 73, 75, 76, 91.
Pascal III., 113.
Patarenes, 22, 41, 462, 521.
Pataria, 21.
Paucapalea, 766.
Pauperes Christi, 383.
Pears, 269, 273, 277.
Peckham, abp., 726, 862.
Pegge, 823.
Penance, Th. Aq. on, 671, 732, 729 sqq.; D. Scotus on, 729; Vulgate trsl., 730; change of doctr., 731, 735; Alex. of Hales on, 731, 797.
Perfecti, 477, 640.
Perry, F., 281.
Perry, G. G., 823.
Peter Barthélemy, 237.
Peter de Bruys, 483 sq.
Peter de Vinea, 195.
Peter Lombard; see Lombard.
Peter of Blois, and Jews, 456; on classics, 541, 796 sq.
Peter of Castelnau, 509.
Peter of Catana, 400, 410.
Peter of Murrhone, 208.

Peter of Pisa, 350.
Peter of Poictiers, 636.
Peter of Roya, 540.
Peter Tudebodus, 211.
Peter's Pence, 34, 788 sq., 813, 818.
Peter the Hermit, 220, 225, 229; appearance, 230 sq.; at Antioch, 237; Mt. of Olives, 239; death, 241; note on, 241 sqq.
Peter the Venerable, 308; on monasticism, 317, 323, 333 sq.; and Bernard, 335; on Carthusians, 363; the Jews, 443, 447, 459; the devil, 883.
Petrobrusians, 483 sq.
Pflugk-Harttung, 2, 295.
Philip Augustus, excommunicated, 164; England given to, 169; Crusader, 258 sq.
Philip I., 33, 71.
Philip of Swabia, 161 sq., 164, 273.
Philosophy and scholasticism, 589, 697.
Piacenza, syn. of 1076, 49; 1095, 227.
Pius II., on clerical marriage, 38.
Pius IX., 118, 523.
Pius X., 844.
Plenitudo potestatis, 158, 772.
Poland, 33, 430 sqq.
Pollard, A. W., 869.
Polycraticus, 630.
Poole, R. L., 534, 609, 627, 630, etc.
Poor Men of Christ, 494.
Poor Men of Lombardy, 382.
Poor Men of Lyons, 382, 411, 497; see Waldenses.
Pope, election of, 18, 25, 118; see Conclave; in exile, 95, 109, 111, 118, 119; French, 201–206; and Jews, 440; and heresy, 467; and synods, 774, 809; supremacy, 771 sqq.; Th. Aq. and Gratian on, 773.
Portiuncula, 381, 396, 741.
Potthast, 3.
Poverty, St. Francis and, 398, 415; Waldenses, 506.
Preaching, 1st Crus., 230; Dominic, 424; Waldenses, 502; in Engl., 821, 852; Grosseteste's, 828, 834, 850 sq.; lay, 852; in vernacular, 852; Cæsar of Heisterb. on, 852, 854; Bernard, 853, 855; great preachers, 854, 856; subjects, 857; books on, 858.
Preger, 370, 460.
Premonstrants, 360 sqq.
Prester-John, 437.
Priests, chief function, 720, 799 sqq., 892 sq.; see Celibacy.
Proslogium, 600.
Prussia, 306, 430 sqq.
Prutz, 102, 212, 290, 296.
Psalteries, 835, 861.
Ptolemais, see Acre.
Pullani, 248.
Pullen, 628, 632.
Purgatory, 742, 760.

Quadrivium, 539.
Quétif-Echard, 419.

Rachel and Leah, 638 sq.
Radulph, 448.
Rahewin, 102.
Rainerius Sacch., 458.
Ralph of Escures, 92.
Ranke, 2, 58; on Greg. VII., 67, 160;
 on Fredk. Barb., 259; papacy,
 772, etc.
Rashdall, 552, 561, 564, etc.
Raspe, 195.
Raymund of Aguilers, 211.
Raymund of Pennaforte, 768.
Raymund of Puy, 298.
Raymund of Toulouse, 229, 234, 510,
 etc.
Raymundus Lullus, 288, 427, 434 sqq.;
 and Jews, 456.
Realism, 594 sq.; Abælard on, 619;
 D. Scotus on, 686.
Red Rose, 119.
Reinkens, 343, 779.
Relics, 4th Lat. on, 177; Const., 275,
 451, 844 sqq.
Religion, Compar., 697.
Rémusat, 81, 609.
Renan, 370, 683.
Reusch, 660, 771.
Reuter, 102.
Riant, 211, 269.
Richard I., 126; itinerary of, 215,
 256; on Crusade, 258; valor, 264;
 seized, 265; on Templars, 304, 797.
Richard of Cornwall, 202.
Richard of Devizes, 256; and Jews,
 448.
Richard of St. German, 180.
Richard of St Victor, 647, 648.
Ries, 639.
Rigg, 81, 683.
Ritschl, 598, 683.
Robert of Abrissel, 368, 382, 463, 854.
Robert of Courçon, 569.
Roberts, C. M., 700.
Robertson, 120, 309.
Robert the Monk, 211, 226, 228, 237,
 240, etc.
Robinson Paschal, 389, 400.
Roger of Sicily, 95 sq., 350.
Roger of York, 130, 134 sq., 138.
Röhricht, 212, 246.
Rolls Series, 1, 81.
Roman Church, Th. Aq. on, 676,
 773.
Roman Law, 765.
Roman Synods, 39, 40, 47.
Rome described by Hildebert, 63;
 and Inquis., 530; govt. of, 160 sq.
Roncaglia, 108, 564.
Rosary, 425.
Roscellinus, 592, 600, 613.
Rosedale, 389.
Rubruquis, 440, 697.
Rudolf of Hapsburg, 204.
Rudolf of Swabia, 60 sq.

Rule, M., 597.
Runcarii, 497.
Rupert of Deutz, 714, 719.

Sabatier, 390, 394.
Sabbatina, 366, 739.
Sacerdotium et imperium, 31, 158;
 see Papacy, Pope.
Sack, Brothers of, 369.
Sacraments, Hugo on, 645, 702;
 Th. Aq., 671, 702; sacred, 703;
 congruity of, 703; definition, 704;
 number, 704; effects 705 sqq.; rel-
 ative value, 707; author of, 708; con-
 tempt of, 708.
Saladin, 250 sq.; 3d Crus., 257, 261;
 gifts to Hospitallers, 264; death, 265.
Saladin tax, 258, 817.
Salimbene, 180; on new orders, 369,
 784, 798; on relics, 845; the Flag-
 ellants, 876, 878; the devil, 883.
Salve Burce, 497, 501, etc.
Sandolati, 494.
Sandys, 534.
Saracens, 4th Lat. and, 177.
Savigny, 551, 563.
Scapulary, 367.
Schaarschmidt, 534.
Schaff, D. S., 442, 661, 700.
Schaff Ph., 212; on Bernard, 343,
 368; Waldenses, 506, 552, 563;
 Bologna, 568, 598; Th. Aq., 713;
 on med. hymns, 860, 864, 867.
Scheffer-Boichorst, 102, 110.
Schiller, quoted, 205.
Schmidt, C., 459, 470, 474, etc.
Schneider, 693, 700.
Schnürer, 296, 390.
Scholasticism, 587 sqq.; character-
 istics, 588; aims, 588; and philos.,
 589, 666; piety, 589; ethics, 589;
 Augustine and, 589, 591, etc.;
 periods, 592 sq.; vocabulary, 593;
 curious questions, 593, 658; cul-
 mination, 651; Th. Aq. and, 661;
 Bacon on, 696 sq.
Schönbach, A. E., 850.
Schoolmen, and the Fathers, 588;
 classified, 592.
Schools, Gerson on, 218, 417, 435;
 Roman, 534; early med., 535;
 Charlem. and, 535; cathedral,
 535; in France, 536; teachers,
 537 sq.; curriculum, 539; text-
 books, 540; classics in, 540; dis-
 cipline, 541; Guibert's experience,
 542; at Cluny, 542; Anselm on, 543.
Schottmüller, 296.
Schubert, von, 2.
Schulte, von, 764, 771.
Schwane, 587, etc.
Scotland, under interdict, 119, 258;
 cathedrals of, 586.
Scott, quoted, 212, 214, 866.
Scriptures, Bernard and, 351, 642;
 Joachim, 374 sq.; St. Francis, 396;
 trsl. into Tartar, 442; Cathari, 463;

quoted agt. the sects, 475; Beghards, 491; Waldenses, 495, 500; copied, 547; Schoolmen, 588; Abælard, 623; senses of, 645, 656; the St. Victors, 647; emphasized, 649; commentaries on, 650; Th. Aq., 663, 667; Bonavent., 680; D. Scotus, 686 sq.; Bacon, 698; Pet. of Blois and Grosseteste, 802 sq.; and Mary, 834.

Sects, 461 sqq.

Seeberg, 683, 684, 688, 690, etc.

Seppelt, 384, 391, 568.

Sequences, 861.

Sermons, Inn. IV.'s, 193; on Canticles, 641; in Germany and Engl., 802 sq., 850 sqq.

Servitia, 787.

Sext, 768.

Shakespeare, 165, 174, 221, 819.

Sheldon, 2.

Sic et Non, 623.

Sicilian Constt., 521, 525.

Sicilian vespers, 207.

Sicily sides with Alex. III., 112; and Fredk. II., 193; rebellion in, 195; count of Anjou, 201; Richd. I. in, 266.

Siegfried of Mainz, 41, 49, 56, 60, 223, 654.

Sighart, 653.

Simon of Montfort, 4th Crus., 271; Albig. Crus., 510 sqq.; killed, 513.

Simony, 13, 20, 22, 36, 86, 801.

Sin, Abælard on, 626; Th. Aq., 668, 670; D. Scotus, 688, 749 sqq., 840 sq.

Singing, 862.

Smend, 700.

Soissons, syn. of, 596, 726.

Spain, 33, 164; and heresy, 521.

Specht, 534.

Speculm perfectionis, 389, 396, 405, 413, etc.

Speronistæ, 489, 521.

Spirituals, 412, 414.

Spülkelch, 726.

Stabat mater, 867.

State product of violence, 32; and investiture, 46; in Engl., 85; see Papacy.

Stedinger, 514, 887.

Stephen, Leslie, 2.

Stephen IX., 15; of Blois, 234; of Chartres, 235; Child Crusader, 266.

Stephens, W. R. W., 82.

Stevenson, F. S., 392, 825.

Stigand, 86.

Stigmata, 404.

Stirrup, holding the, 107, 112.

Stock, Simon, 366.

Stöckl, 587, etc.

Storrs, 342; on Bernard's preaching, 855.

Stubbs, 82, 328, 627; on educ. of Engl. clergy, 821; on 13th cent., 823.

Student life, 561 sqq.; cost of, 562, 578.

Studium generale, 554.

Succubus, 886.

Swestriones, 492.

Sybel von, 213; on Pet. the Hermit, 243.

Tagliacozzo, 202.

Tanchelm, 482.

Tancred, 235, 240.

Tangl, 781.

Tannenberg, 306, 433.

Tarleton, 105.

Tasso, 212.

Taunton, 308.

Templars, at Tiberias, 251; Acre, 261, 285; lit., 295; fame, 301; Bernard on, 301, 349; spread, 302; organization, 303; services, 304; suppression, 305.

Tennyson, 125, 128, 132, 150.

Tertiaries, 383, 410, 411, 425.

Tesserants and Textores, 471.

Teutonic Knights, 296, 305, 432.

Thaddeus of Suessa, 192, 195.

Thatcher, 105, 242.

Theology, queen of studies, 555; at Paris, 572; systems of, 588; Anselm's, 600 sq., 652, 656; Th. Aq., 664; D. Scotus, 687; experimental, 698, 701.

Theresa, St., 367.

Thesaurus meritorum, 652, 740 sq.

Thibaut d'Estampes, 576.

Thomas Aquinas, 218, 426; on heresy, 517, 674 sq.; at Paris, 573, 661 sqq.; services to theology, 661, 664; canonized, 662; Leo XIII., on 662; in Paris, 663; Writings, 663; hymns, 664, 713; philos., 667; argtt. for God's existence, 668; on sin, 668, 670, 749; free will, 668; angels, 669; anthropology, 669; a creationist, 669; the atonement, 670; salvation of infants, 670; sacraments, 671; eucharist, 671; penance, 671; future state, 672, 757; ethics, 672; Ch. and state, 673; Rome's supremacy, 674; the theologian of the Rom. Cath. Ch., 675; contributes to Dante, 675; and D. Scotus, 675; the Prot. Reformers, 676; on baptism, 710; the eucharist, 713, 715 sq., 721; penance, 733; indulgences, 738; ext. unction, 743; orders, 745 sq.; marriage, 747; the atonement, 754; justification, 755; faith, 756; papacy, 771, 773, 777, 792; on Mary, 840 sq.; on relics, 845; 865; the devil, 885, 887.

Thomas of Chantimpré, 308, 763, 838, 878.

Thurston, H., 823.

Tilemann, 391.

Tocco, 458.

Tonsure, 745.
Toulouse, syn. of 1229, 520, 812; centre of heresy, 507, 514; university of, 514.
Tours, syn. of, 113, 130, 812.
Traill, H. D., 812.
Transubstantiation, 687, 689, 713, 715 sq., 808, 810.
Trench, R. C., 2, 859.
Trent, c. of, 151, 726, 729, 744.
Trevelyan, 383.
Treves, syn. of, 710, 812.
Trinitarians, 368.
Trinity, Joachim on, 376 sqq.; 4th Lat. on, 377 sq.; Anselm on, 600; Abælard on, 613, 616, 618, 624; Gilbert on, 628; Pet. Lomb., 631; Alanus, 636, 657, 701, 709; name in baptism, 709.
Trivium, 539, 597.
Trond, St., 728.
Tropes, 861.
Tschackert, 427.
Two Swords, 775, 777 sq.

Ubertino of Casale, 378, 415.
Ugolino, see Gregory IX.
Uhlhorn, 295, 296.
Unam Sanctam, 777.
Universities, 552–581; a med. institution, 552; origin, 552; the literary guild, 553; first, 554; faculties, 555; model, 556 sqq.; nations, 557 sq.; rector and chancellor, 558; degrees, 558; teachers, 559; and clergy, 566; attendance, 561; influence, 563; list, 580 sq.; see Schools.
Urban II., pope, 70; wars with Henry IV., 71; 1st Crus., 225; syn. of Clermont, 227 sq.; Gregorovius on his speech, 227; death, 241; and indulgences, 738.
Urban III., d. of grief, 257.
Urban IV., 201; and Corpus Christi feast, 723.
Usury forbidden, 450.

Vacandard, 342, 347, 351, 461, 609, etc.
Vacarius, 577.
Vedder, 460.
Venice, Peace of, 115.
Verona, syn. of, 468, 496, 519, 812.
Vicar of God, 152, 157, 774.
Vicelinus, 431.
Victor II., 15.
Victor III., 65, 70.
Victor IV., 111.
Villehardouin, 216, 269, 271, 272, etc.
Vincent, M. R., 8.
Vincent de Beauvais, 884.
Virtues, relig. and theol., 673, 756.
Visitationes, 787.
Vivetus, 498.
Vogelweide, von der, 464.
Voragine, de, 308, 319, 743, 838, etc.
Vulgate, mistakes of, 730, 760.

Wadding, 391, 615.
Waldenses, 469, 493–507; names of, 494; Crusades against, 498; tolerated, 498; in Italy, 499; Inn. VIII., 499; in Austria, 499; doctrines, 501; and Prot. Reform., 502; inf. bapt., 504; oaths, 504; lit. on, 507.
Walter, von, 366, 369, 629, 637.
Walter of Coventry, 165.
Walter of St. Victor, 636.
Walter the Penniless, 232.
War, 805; warlike prelates, 797 sq.
Warini, 489.
Wattenbach, 3, 543, etc.
Weingarten, 3.
Welch, 81, 598.
Wends, 429.
Werner, 587, 660, 683.
Werner of St. Blasius, on heresy, 465; on preaching, 858.
Wernher of Tegernsee, 832.
Wetzer-Welte, 2, etc.
White, A. D., 878.
White Canons, 360 sq.
Whittier, 231, 493, 500.
Wibert, 41, 61 sq., 65, 73, 75.
Wilcke, F., 295.
Wilken, F., 212.
William of Aquitaine, 331.
William of Auxerre, 705.
William of Champeaux, 537, 611.
William of Conches, 537 sq.
William of Hirschau, 310, 331.
William of Malmesbury, 81; on Crusades, 232; on monks, 324, 338, 821.
William of Newburgh, 81.
William of St. Amour, 308, 324, 388, 573, 663, 678.
William of Thierry, 342, 347, 356, 616.
William of Tyre, 213, 217, 226, 240, 241, 246, 255.
William of Ware, 675, 685.
William the Conqueror, 19, 23, 26, 34, 42, 44, 84.
Wills, 194, 803.
Witham, St., 364, 824.
Woker, 783.
Woman and the Crusades, 215; the convent, 348; at St. Evraud, 369; preach, 503; lecture, 566; low idea of, 567; practise medicine, 567; age of marriage, 747; her sin, 750 sq.
Woodhouse, 295.
Wordsworth, 224.
Worms, Concordat of, 47, 78, 80, 793.
Wright, Th., 869, 878.
Wyclif, 171, 528, 533, 561, 716, 741.

Zenos, 3.
Zwemer, 427.
Zwingli, 28, 711.